D0328724

MIDDLE EAST CONTEMPORARY SURVEY

Volume XV: 1991

MIDDLE EAST CONTEMPORARY SURVEY
Published for
The Moshe Dayan Center
for Middle Eastern and African Studies
The Shiloah Institute
Tel Aviv University

HAIM SHAKED, Founding Editor

MIDDLE EAST
CONTEMPORARY SURVEY

Volume XV
1991

AMI AYALON
Editor

Barbara Newson, Executive Editor

**The Moshe Dayan Center
for Middle Eastern and African Studies
The Shiloah Institute
Tel Aviv University**

Westview Press
BOULDER, SAN FRANCISCO, & OXFORD

Ref
DS
628
M53
V.15

Other volumes in this series:

Volume I, 1976–77
Volume II, 1977–78
Volume III, 1978–79
Volume IV, 1979–80
Volume V, 1980–81
Volume VI, 1981–82
Volume VII, 1982–83
Volume VIII, 1983–84
Volume IX, 1984–85
Volume X, 1986
Volume XI, 1987
Volume XII, 1988
Volume XIII, 1989
Volume XIV, 1990

Middle East Contemporary Survey

Copyright © 1993 by Tel Aviv University

Published in 1993 in the United States of America by Westview Press, Inc., 5500 Central Avenue, Boulder, Colorado 80301-2877, and in the United Kingdom by Westview Press, 36 Lonsdale Road, Summertown, Oxford OX2 7EW

Typeset in Israel, Graph-Chen Ltd., Jerusalem

Library of Congress Catalog Card Number: 78-648245
ISBN: 0-8133-1869-6
ISSN: 0163-5476

Printed and bound in the United States of America

The paper used in this publication meets the requirements of the American National Standard for Permanence of Paper for Printed Library Materials Z39.48-1984.

10   9   8   7   6   5   4   3   2   1

About the Series and Editor

Established in 1977, the *Middle East Contemporary Survey* (*MECS*), is acknowledged as the standard reference work on events and trends in the region. Designed to be a continuing, up-to-date reference for scholars, researchers and analysts, policymakers, students and journalists, it examines in detail the rapidly changing Middle Eastern scene in all its complexity.

In each volume, the material is arranged in two parts. The first contains a series of essays on broad regional issues and on the overall relations of the region with other parts of the world. Subjects explored in detail include Arab-Israeli and inter-Arab relations, Islamic affairs, Palestinian issues, economic developments, and the relations between major world powers and the Middle East. The second part consists of country-by-country surveys of the Arab states, as well as Iran, Israel, and Turkey. The North African states of Tunisia, Algeria, and Morocco are not covered separately. Regional aspects of foreign policies and internal developments that have wider implications are discussed in the chapters on inter-Arab relations and Islamic affairs, respectively. The emphasis in the second part is on elucidating the inner dynamics of each country's policy and society.

Ami Ayalon is Chairman of the Department of Middle Eastern and African History and Senior Research Fellow at the Moshe Dayan Center at Tel Aviv University.

Preface

The present volume of *Middle East Contemporary Survey* is the fifteenth in a series which provides a continuing up-to-date reference work recording the rapidly changing events in an exceptionally complex part of the world. Every effort has again been made to use the widest range of source material and maintain the highest possible academic standards.

Most of the essays in this volume have been researched and written by the members of the Shiloah Institute of the Moshe Dayan Center for Middle Eastern and African Studies at Tel Aviv University. Other contributions have been made by academics and experts from other institutions in Israel and abroad. An international committee of renowned scholars has assisted the editor with counsel and advice.

The fellows of the Center were deeply grieved by the sudden passing of Prof. Elie Kedourie, who was also a member of this international committee. Prof. Kedourie and his contribution to our field of scholarship will surely be missed.

The volume covers the year 1991, a watershed period in the Middle East in more ways than one, although in the annals of the region's history it will probably be remembered, above all, as the year of the Gulf War. The war, in January-February, pitted regional and international forces of unprecedented might against each other in fierce confrontation. Political developments during the rest of the year revolved mainly around the search for a "new order" in the area, inspired by the US-led victory over Iraq, the disintegration of the Soviet Union and other global changes. Yet again, the relevance of Western political modes to Middle Eastern societies was raised for reexamination, only to highlight the formidable complexities of such options. One form of local response to these changes was a surge of Islamic sentiment, sometimes militant in nature, manifested primarily in Sudan, Algeria, Jordan, Egypt and amongst the Palestinians. In another development, likewise US-inspired and spearheaded, the Middle East peace process entered a more dynamic phase, as a multilateral peace conference in Madrid, in October-November, ushered in a new era of direct Arab-Israeli negotiations. In contradistinction, the Arab system was slow to recover from the painful impact of the Gulf War, and inter-Arab relations continued to be characterized more by mutual vindictiveness than by reconciliation. On the whole, this was a year of considerable flux and uncertainty with some events equally promising the inauguration of a new course of development for the region — or simply passing without a sequel or longtime impact.

The period surveyed in this volume, unless otherwise indicated, is from January to December 1991. In order to avoid excessive repetition while achieving a comprehensive survey of the affairs of each country individually, extensive cross-references have been used.

The Editor

Acknowledgments

While *MECS*, like all collective works, has an editor responsible for its merits and shortcomings, it is — perhaps more than most such publications — a team project. We are grateful to a large number of contributors who have made this volume possible. First and foremost, we recognize the work of the staff of the Moshe Dayan Center and its Shiloah Institute for Middle Eastern and African Studies at Tel Aviv University, whose individual contributions are acknowledged separately.

In the process of preparing this volume, Judy Krausz played a central role, both as a master of style and as a critical reader of the text. Barbara Newson's help as executive editor has been indispensable. Much help in matters of style was also given by Susan Menashe. The exacting work of indexing has been carried out by Ronald Watson. Ruth Beit-Or prepared the maps for publication, and David Levinson proofread large parts of the volume.

At the Dayan Center, Edna Liftman and Amira Margalith, assistants to the Head of the Center, were responsible for the complicated coordination of the production of the volume, and fulfilled a variety of other executive tasks with accuracy, skill, and unflagging care. Others at the Center who must be singled out for special thanks are Lydia Gareh, whose skillful and devoted work has been an indispensable pillar of the production of *MECS*, Ilana Greenberg, Sarit Azar, and the Moshe Dayan Documentation System team, headed by Yigal Sheffy. Finally, we would like to express our sincere thanks to Barbara Ellington, Susan L. McEachern, and the staff of Westview Press for their help in the production and distribution of this volume of *MECS*.

Haim Shaked gave form and purpose to the series as founding editor and has guided its publication for over a decade. The contribution made by the late Max Holmes and by Colin Legum to the launching of this project and to setting its standards, and by Frederick A. Praeger to the shaping of its present format, remains invaluable and much appreciated.

The Editor

Table of Contents

PART ONE: CURRENT ISSUES

THE MIDDLE EAST IN PERSPECTIVE

THE MIDDLE EAST AND WORLD AFFAIRS

REGIONAL AFFAIRS

List of Maps

Transliteration

The **Arabic** language has been transliterated as follows:

b	for	ب	q	for	ق
d	for	د ، ض	r	for	ر
dh	for	ذ	s	for	ص ، س
f	for	ف	sh	for	ش
gh	for	غ	t	for	ت ، ط
h	for	ه، ح	th	for	ث
j	for	ج	w (or u)	for	و
k	for	ك	y (or i)	for	ي
kh	for	خ	z	for	ز ، ظ
l	for	ل	'	for	ا ، ء
m	for	م	'	for	ع
n	for	ن			

In addition, the following should be noted:

Long vowels are not marked for distinction from short ones. Thus ناظر = *nazir*, but also نظير = *nazir*.

The *hamza* is used only in the middle of a word.

The *shadda* is rendered by doubling the consonant containing it.

The *ta marbuta* is not shown, except in construct phrases. Thus *madina, madinat Nasr*.

The definite article is always shown as "al-", regardless of the kind of letter following it.

Exceptions to the above are names of Lebanese and North African personalities who have adopted a French spelling for their names.

In transcribing **Persian**, frequent allowance is made for pronunciation; thus Khomeyni (not Khumayni). Names appearing in both Arabic and Persian texts are transcribed according to the language of the relevant text. Thus Hizballah (Arabic) or Hizbollah (Persian).

Recommended Method for Citation from *MECS*

In the interest of accuracy, consistency, and simplicity, the editors of *MECS* recommend the following method of citation. Based on the classification of *MECS* as a periodical, published annually, the method conforms to the *Chicago Manual of Style*.

In a footnote: Asher Susser, "Jordan," *Middle East Contemporary Survey*, Vol. X (1986), p. 445.

In a bibliography: Susser, Asher. "Jordan," *Middle East Contemporary Survey*. Vol. X (1986), pp. 425–64.

The accepted abbreviation of the periodical's title is *MECS*. The year is that covered by the volume as indicated on the volume binding and title page, not the year of publication. No mention need be made of editors or publishers, who have changed several times since the establishment of *MECS*. Some styles may require mention of place of publication, usually in parentheses following the title of the periodical. For Volumes I through VII, the place of publication was New York; for Volumes VIII and IX, Tel Aviv; since Volume X, Boulder, Colorado.

List of Initials and Acronyms

ADP	Arab Democratic Party (Israel)
Aids	Acquired Immune Deficiency Syndrome
ALCM	air-launched cruise missile
ALF	Arab Liberation Front
AMU	Arab Maghrib Union
ANC	African National Congress
APC	armored personnel carrier
AUB	American University of Beirut
Awacs	airborne warning and control system (radar)
BBC(E)	Bank of Credit and Commerce Emirates
BCCI	Bank of Credit and Commerce International
b/d	barrels per day
bn.	billion
BoE	Bank of England
Brig. Gen.	Brigadier General
c.	*circa* (about)
CBS	Central Bureau of Statistics (Jerusalem)
CC	(Palestine) Central Council
Centcom	US Central Command
Chevron	Standard Oil of California
CIA	Central Intelligence Agency (US)
CIS	Commonwealth of Independent States
Col.	Colonel
CP	Communist Party
CRM	Citizens' Rights Movement (Israel)
DFLP	Democratic Front for the Liberation of Palestine
DLP	Democratic Left Party (*Demokratık Sol Partisi*; Turkey)
DOD	Department of Defense (US)
DSP	Defense Support Program
DUP	Democratic Unionist Party (Sudan)
EC	European Community
EMIS	electromagnetic isotope separation
EPRDF	Ethiopian People's Revolutionary Democratic Front
FIS	Front Islamique du Salut (Islamic Salvation Front; Algeria)
FLN	Front de Libération Nationale (Algeria)
FRC	Fath Revolutionary Council
GCC	Gulf Cooperation Council
GDP	gross domestic product
Gen.	General
GHQ	General Headquarters
GNP	gross national product
GPC	General People's Congress (Yemen)
G7	the seven great industrial countries
Hamas	*Harakat al-muqawama al-Islamiyya* (Islamic Resistance Movement)
IAEA	International Atomic Energy Agency
ICO	Islamic Conference Organization
ICP	Israeli Communist Party
IDF	Israel Defense Forces

IEA	International Energy Agency
ILO	International Labor Organization
IMF	International Monetary Fund
in.	inch
IRA	Irish Republican Army
IRP	Islamic Revival Party (Yemen)
JANDA	Jordanian Arab Nationalist Democratic Alliance
JFC-E	Joint Forces Command-East
JFC-N	Joint Forces Command-North
KGB	Committee of State Security (Russian Secret Police)
km.	kilometer
KTO	"Kuwait Theater of Operations"
LF	Lebanese Forces
LNG	liquefied natural gas
Lt. Gen.	Lieutenant General
m.	million
Maj. Gen.	Major General
ME	Middle East(ern)
MERIP	Middle East Research and Information Project (Washington)
Minurso	Mission for the Referendum in the Western Sahara
MK	Member of Knesset
MMC	Ministerial Monitoring Committee (of Opec)
MP	Member of Parliament
MTCR	Missile Technology Control Regime
MWL	Muslim World League (*Rabitat al-'alam al-Islami*)
Nato	North Atlantic Treaty Organization
NBC	nuclear, biological and chemical
NCHALC	Nationwide Committee of Heads of Arab Local Councils (Israel)
NCO	noncommissioned officer
NDP	National Democratic Party (Egypt)
NEP	Nationalist Endeavor Party (*Milliyetçi Çalışma Partisi*; Turkey)
NFSL	National Front for the Salvation of Libya
NGL	natural gas liquid
NIF	National Islamic Front (Sudan)
NPUG	National Progressive Unionist Grouping (Egypt)
NRP	National Religious Party (Israel)
NSC	National Security Council (US)
O.C.	Officer Commanding
OECD	Organization for Economic Cooperation and Development
OLF	Oromo Liberation Front
Opec	Organization of Petroleum Exporting Countries
OPROD	Centcom Operations Order
p.a.	per annum
PCC	Palestinian Central Council
PCP	Palestine Communist Party
PDF	Popular Defense Forces (Sudan)
PDP	Popular Democratic Party (Jordan)
PDRY	People's Democratic Republic of Yemen
PDUP	Popular Democratic Unionist Party (Jordan)
PFLP	Popular Front for the Liberation of Palestine
PFLP-GC	Popular Front for the Liberation of Palestine — General Command

PKK	*Parti Kerkeren Kurdistan* (Kurdistan Workers' Party)
PLF	Palestine Liberation Front
PLO	Palestine Liberation Organization
PLP	People's Labor Party (*Halkın Emek Partisi*; Turkey)
	Progressive List for Peace (Israel)
p.m.	post meridiem
PNC	Palestine National Council
PNSF	Palestinian National Salvation Front
Polisario	Front for the Liberation of Al-Saqiyya al-Hamra and Rio de Oro
POWs	prisoners of war
PPSF	Palestine Popular Struggle Front
PSP	Progressive Socialist Party (Lebanon)
RAF	Royal Air Force (UK)
RCC	Revolutionary Command Council (Iraq)
RCCNS	Revolutionary Command Council for National Salvation (Sudan)
Res.	Reserve
ret.	retired
RGFC	Republican Guard Forces Corps
RSFSR	Russian Soviet Federative Socialist Republic
SAM	surface-to-air missile(s)
SCC	State Consultative Council (Oman)
SDPP	Social Democrat Populist Party (*Sosyaldemokrat Halkçı Parti*; Turkey)
SEEs	State Economic Enterprises (Turkey)
SLA	South Lebanese Army
SLP	Socialist Labor Party (Egypt)
SOF	special operation forces
SPLA	Sudanese People's Liberation Army
SPR	Strategic Petroleum Reserve
SSM	surface-to-surface missile(s)
SUNY	State University of New York
TPP	True Path Party (*Doğru Yol Partisi*; Turkey)
UAE	United Arab Emirates
UK	United Kingdom
UN	United Nations
UNC	Unified National Command
Unesco	United Nations Educational, Scientific, and Cultural Organization
Unicef	United Nations (International) Children's (Emergency) Fund
Unifil	United Nations Interim Force in Lebanon
UNRWA	UN Relief and Works Agency for Palestine Refugees in the Near East
UP	Umma Party (Sudan)
US	United States
USSR	Union of Soviet Socialist Republics
UTA	Union des Transports Aériens (France)
VAT	value added tax
WP	Welfare Party (*Refah Partisi*; Turkey)
WTI	West Texas Intermediate
YAR	Yemeni Arab Republic
YRG	Yemen Reform Group
YSP	Yemeni Socialist Party
YUP	Yemeni Unionist Party

List of Sources

Newspapers, Periodicals, Irregular and Single Publications

Name (Place, Frequency of Publication)	Abbreviation	Comments
Abrar (Tehran, daily)		Appeared before the revolution under the name *Ayandegan*; expresses radical views
Al-Afkar (Beirut, weekly)		
Africa Confidential (London, biweekly)	*AC*	
Africa Report (New York, monthly)	*AR*	
Al-Ahali (Cairo, weekly)		Organ of the National Progressive Unionist Grouping
Al-Ahali (Nicosia, weekly)		
Al-Ahram (Cairo, daily)		
Al-Ahram al-Duwali (London, daily)		
Al-Ahram International (London, daily)		
Al-Ahram al-Iqtisadi (Cairo, weekly)		
Al-Ahram al-Masa'i (Cairo, daily)		
Al-Ahram Weekly (Cairo, weekly)		
Al-Ahrar (Cairo, weekly)		Organ of the Liberal Party
Air Force Magazine (Arlington, VA, monthly)		
Al-Akhbar (Cairo, daily)		
Akhbar al-'Alam al-Islami (Mecca, weekly)	*AAI*	Published by the Muslim World League
Akhbar al-Khalij (Bahrain, daily)		
Akhbar al-Sudan (Athens, weekly)		
Akhbar al-Usbu' (Amman, weekly)		
Akhbar al-Yawm (Cairo, weekly)		
Akhir Khabar (Nicosia, weekly)		
Akhir Sa'a (Cairo, weekly)		
Al-'Alam (London, weekly)		

Al-'Alam
(Rabat, daily)
'Al-Hamishmar　　　　　　　　　　　　Organ of the United Workers' Party
(Tel Aviv, daily)　　　　　　　　　　　　(Mapam)
Alif Ba
(Baghdad, weekly)
Al-Anba
(Cairo, weekly)
Al-Anwar
(Beirut, daily)
Al-'Arab
(Qatar, daily)
Arab Oil and Gas　　　　　　　*AOG*　　Published by the Arab Petroleum
(Paris and Beirut, fortnightly)　　　　　Research Center
Armed Forces Journal
(Washington, DC, monthly)
Armor
(Fort Knox, KY, monthly)
Army
(Arlington, VA, monthly)
Atlanta Constitution
(Atlanta, GA, daily)
Atlanta Journal
(Atlanta, GA, twice weekly)
Aviation Week and Space Technology
(Washington, DC, weekly)
Al-Ayyam
(Khartoum, daily)
Babil
(Baghdad, daily)
Baghdad Observer
(Baghdad, daily)
Al-Balagh
(Kuwait, weekly)
Al-Ba'th
(Damascus, daily)
Al-Bayadir al-Siyasi
(East Jerusalem, biweekly)
Al-Bayan
(Dubai, daily)
Bayan　　　　　　　　　　　　　　　Edited by and close to Mohtashami;
(Tehran, monthly)　　　　　　　　　　　radical
Al-Bayraq
(Beirut, daily)
Berliner Zeitung
(Berlin, daily)
Al-Bilad
(Jidda, daily)
Bild
(Hamburg, daily)
Briefing
(Ankara, weekly)
Christian Science Monitor　　　*CSM*
(Boston, daily)
Commentary
(New York, monthly)
Comparative Politics
(New York, quarterly)

Country Profile (London, annually)		Published by Economist Publications
Country Reports (London, quarterly)	*CR*	Published by Economist Publications. Formerly *Quarterly Economic Review*
Cumhuriyet (Istanbul, daily)		
Daily Telegraph (London, daily)	*DT*	
Davar (Tel Aviv, daily)		Organ of the Israeli Trade Union Federation (Histadrut)
Al-Da'wa al-Islamiyya (Tripoli, Libya, bimonthly)		
Al-Dawliyya (Paris, weekly)		
Dawn (Karachi, daily)		
Defense News (Springfield, VA, weekly)		
Al-Difa' (Cairo, monthly)		
Al-Diyar (Beirut, daily)		
Al-Dunya (Beirut, weekly)		Supplement of the Lebanese paper, *al-Haqiqa*
Al-Dustur (Amman, daily)		
Al-Dustur (London, weekly)		Published in English
Al-Duwaliyya (Paris, weekly)		
Echo of Iran (Tehran and London, monthly)		
The Economist (London, weekly)		
Egypt Focus (Wiederweg, Meckenheim, Germany, monthly)		
Emirates News (Abu Dhabi, daily)		
Ettela'at (Tehran, daily)		
L'Express (Paris, weekly)		
Facts on File (New York, weekly)		
Al-Fajr (East Jerusalem, daily)		
Al-Fajr (East Jerusalem, weekly)		English- and Hebrew-language editions of the daily *al-Fajr*
Al-Fajr al-Jadid (Tripoli, daily)		
Al-Fallah al-Misri (Cairo, monthly)		
Le Figaro (Paris, daily)		
Filastin al-Muslima (Manchester, monthly)		

Filastin al-Thawra		Organ of the PLO
(Nicosia, weekly)		
The Financial Times	*FT*	
(London, daily)		
Flight International		
(Sutton, Surrey, weekly)		
Foreign Affairs		
(New York, five per year)		
Foreign Report	*FR*	Published by Economist
(London, weekly)		Publications
Government and Opposition		
(London, quarterly)		
The Guardian		
(London, daily)		
Gulf Daily News		
(Manama, daily)		
Gulf News		
(Dubai, daily)		
The Gulf States		
(West Sussex, biweekly)		
Ha'aretz		
(Tel Aviv, daily)		
Al-Hadaf		Organ of the PFLP
(Damascus, weekly)		
Hadashot		
(Tel Aviv, daily)		
Al-Haqiqa		
(Beirut, daily)		
Al-Haqiqa		
(Cairo, weekly)		
Al-Haras al-Watani		
(Riyadh, monthly)		
Ha-Umma		
(Tel Aviv, quarterly)		
Al-Hawadith		
(London, weekly)		
Al-Hayat		
(Beirut, daily)		
Al-Hayat		
(Cairo, weekly)		
Al-Hayat		From 1991 onwards, published in
(London, daily)		Beirut
Al-Hilal al-Duwali		
(London, bimonthly)		
Hürriyet		
(Istanbul, daily)		
Al-Hurriyya		Organ of the DFLP
(Nicosia, weekly)		
The Independent		
(London, daily)		
Al-Inqadh al-Watani		
(Khartoum, daily)		
International Defense Review		
(Coulsdon, Surrey, monthly)		
International Herald Tribune	*IHT*	
(Paris and Zurich, daily)		
International Security		
(Cambridge, MA, quarterly)		

Iran Focus
(Bonn, monthly)
Al-'Iraq
(Baghdad, daily)
Al-Iraq al-Hurr
(London, biweekly)
Al-Islam wa-Filastin
(Nicosia, irregular)
Israel Air Force Magazine
(Zahal, bimonthly)
Al-Ittihad
(Abu Dhabi, daily)
Al-Ittihad
(Haifa, daily)
Al-Ittihad al-Ishtiraki
(Rabat, daily)
Izvestiia   Organ of the Government of the
(Moscow, daily)   USSR
Jahan-e Islam   Published since 1991. Radical; edited
(Tehran, daily)   by Hadi Khamene'i
Al-Jamahiriyya
(Tripoli, Libya, weekly)
Jane's Defence Weekly
(London, weekly)
Jane's Soviet Intelligence Review
(Coulsdon, Surrey, monthly)
Al-Jarida al-Rasmiyya
(Damascus, monthly)
Al-Jazira
(Riyadh, daily)
Al-Jazira al-'Arabiyya   Published by Shi'i opposition to
(London, monthly)   Saudi monarchy
The Jerusalem Post   *JP*
(Jerusalem, daily)
Jerusalem Report
(Jerusalem, weekly)
Jordan Times   *JT*
(Amman, daily)
Journal of Palestine Studies
(Berkeley, CA, quarterly)
Journal of Strategic Studies
(London, quarterly)
Judea, Samaria and Gaza Area   *JSGAS*   Published by Israel Central Bureau
   Statistics   of Statistics
(Jerusalem, irregular)
Al-Jumhuriyya
(Baghdad, daily)
Al-Jumhuriyya
(Cairo, daily)
Jomhuri-ye Islami   *JI*   Organ of the Islamic Republican Party
(Tehran, daily)
Kayhan   Reflects views of exiled opposition
(London, weekly)   groupings
Kayhan
(Tehran, daily)
Kayhan al-'Arabi
(Tehran, daily)

Kayhan International (Tehran, daily)	*KI*	English-language paper published by *Kayhan*; often expresses radical views, mainly on foreign relations
Al-Khalij (Sharja, daily)		
Komsomolskaia Pravda (Moscow, daily)		
Krasnaia Zvezda (Moscow, daily)		
Kull al-'Arab (Paris, weekly)		
Kull al-Nas (London, weekly)		
Kurier (Vienna, daily)		
The Lebanon Report (Beirut, monthly)		Published by the Lebanese Center for Policy Studies
Le Liban du Citoyen (Paris, monthly)		Published by the Lebanon citizens' movement
Al-Liwa (Beirut, daily)		
Liwa al-Islam (Cairo, monthly)		
Al-Liwa al-Islami (Cairo, weekly)		Islamic publication of the ruling National Democratic Party
Liwa al-Sadr (Tehran, weekly)		
London Gazette (London, five per week)		
Los Angeles Times (Los Angeles, daily)	*LAT*	
Ma'ariv (Tel Aviv, daily)		
Al-Madina (Jidda, daily)		
Al-Majalla (London, weekly)		
Al-Masa (Cairo, daily)		
Al-Mawqif al-'Arabi (Nicosia, weekly)		
May (Cairo, weekly)		Organ of the National Democratic Party
Medina, Mimshal ve-Yahasim *Beynleumiyim* (Jerusalem, three to four per year)		
Memo (Limassol, biweekly)		
MERIP Middle East Report (Washington, DC, bimonthly)		
The Middle East (London, monthly)	*ME*	
Middle East Defense News (Paris, biweekly)	*MedNews*	
Middle East Economic Digest (London, weekly)	*MEED*	

Middle East Economic Survey (Nicosia, weekly)	*MEES*	Published by the Middle East Research and Publishing Center, Beirut
Middle Eastern Studies (London, quarterly)	*MES*	
Middle East Insight (Washington, DC, quarterly)		
Middle East International (London, monthly)	*MEI*	
Middle East Journal (Washington DC, quarterly)	*MEJ*	Published by the Middle East Institute, Washington
Middle East Mirror (London, daily)		
Middle East Report (New York, six per year)		
Mideast Markets (London, biweekly)	*MM*	Published by *FT* Business Information
Mideast Mirror (Beirut, weekly)		
Military Intelligence (Fort Huachuka, AL, bimonthly)		
Milliyet (Istanbul, daily)		
Misr al-Fatat (Jiza, weekly)		Organ of Young Egypt Party
Monday Morning (Beirut, weekly)		
Le Monde (Paris, daily)		
Monthly Bulletin of Statistics (Jerusalem, monthly)	*MBS*	Published by Israel Central Bureau of Statistics
Monthly Oil Market Report (Paris, monthly)	*OMR*	Published by International Energy Agency
Der Morgen (Berlin, daily)		
Al-Muharrir (Paris, weekly)		
Al-Mukhtar al-Islami (Cairo, monthly)		
Al-Musawwar (Cairo, weekly)		
Al-Nahar (Beirut, daily)		
Al-Nahar (Jerusalem, daily)		
National Journal (Washington, DC, weekly)		
Neues Deutschland (Berlin, daily)		
New African (London, monthly)		
New Horizons (Khartoum, weekly)		
New Republic (Washington, DC, weekly)		
Newsreport (London)		

Newsweek
(New York, weekly)
New Times
(Moscow, weekly)
The New York Review of Books
(New York, fortnightly)
The New York Times   *NYT*
(New York, daily)
The New York Times Magazine   *NYT*   Weekly supplement to *The New*
(New York, weekly)   *Magazine*   *York Times*
Nezavismaiai Gazeta
(Moscow, daily)
Al-Nur   Islamic publication of the Liberal
(Cairo, weekly)   Party
The Observer
(London, weekly)
October
(Cairo, weekly)
Oil and Gas Journal
(Tulsa, weekly)
Oman
(Muscat, daily)
Oman Daily Observer
(Ruwi, daily)
Orbis
(Philadelphia, PA, quarterly)
Orient
(Hamburg, quarterly)
L'Orient le Jour
(Beirut, daily)
Petroleum Economist   *PE*
(London, monthly)
Le Point
(Paris, weekly)
Policy Papers   Occasional papers published by the
(Washington, DC, irregular)   Washington Institute for Near East
                                                  Policy
Pravda   Organ of the Central Committee of the
(Moscow, daily)   CPSU
Profil
(Vienna, weekly)
Publius   Published by the Center for the Study
(Denton, TX, quarterly)   of Federalism (Department of Political
                                                  Science), University of North Texas

Al-Qadisiyya
(Baghdad, daily)
Qarun al-Mu'arada
(Cairo, weekly)
Al-Quds al-'Arabi
(London, daily)
Al-Quwat al-Musallaha
(Khartoum, weekly)
Al-Rabita
(Mecca, monthly)
Al-Ra'y
(Amman, daily)
Al-Raya
(Doha, daily)

Ray'at al-Istiqlal
(Nicosia, monthly)
La Repubblica
(Rome, daily)
Resalat
(Tehran, daily)
Resmi Gazete
(Ankara, irregular)
Al-Ribat
(Athens, weekly)
Risalat al-Jihad
(Tripoli, monthly)
Al-Riyad
(Riyadh, daily)
RUSI Journal
(London, quarterly)
Ruz al-Yusuf
(Cairo, weekly)
Sabah al-Khayr
(Cairo, weekly)
Al-Sabil
(Oslo, Norway, monthly)
Al-Safir
(Beirut, daily)
SAIS Review
(Washington, twice yearly)

Salam
(Tehran, daily)
Sawt al-Haqq wal-Hurriya
(Umm al-Fahm, weekly)
Sawt al-Ittihad
(Ferndale, MI, frequency unknown)
Sawt al-Kuwait al-Duwali
(London, daily)
Sawt al-Sha'b
(Amman, daily)
Sawt al-Watan
(Nicosia, monthly)
The Seattle Times
(Seattle, daily)
Security Studies
(London, quarterly)
Al-Sha'b
(Cairo, weekly)
Al-Sha'b
(East Jerusalem, daily)
Al-Sharq
(Beirut, daily)
Al-Sharq al-Awsat
(London, Jidda, and Riyadh, daily)
Al-Sharq al-Jadid
(London, monthly)
Al-Shihan
(Amman, weekly)
Al-Shira'
(Beirut, weekly)

Pragmatist, close to Rafsanjani and to
Tehran's bazaar circles
Official gazette

Publication of the Jordanian Muslim
Brotherhood
Published by the World Islamic Call
Society

Published by the Royal United
Services Institute

Published by the School of Advanced
International Studies, Johns Hopkins
University, Washington
First published in 1991, edited by
and close to Kho'iniha; radical

Organ of the Socialist Labor Party

Shu'un al-'Arabiyya
(Cairo, quarterly)

Publication of the Arab League

Shu'un Filastiniyya
(Nicosia, monthly)

Published by the PLO
Research Center

Al-Sinara
(Nazareth, weekly)
Al-Siyasa
(Kuwait, daily)
Al-Siyasa al-Duwaliya
(Cairo, quarterly)
Al-Siyasi
(Cairo, weekly)
Skirot
(Giv'at Haviva; irregular)

Occasional paper published by the
Institute of Arab Studies

Sourakia
(London, weekly)
Sovetskaia Rossiya
(Moscow, daily)
The Soviet Union and the Middle East
(Jerusalem, monthly)

Published by the Marjorie Mayrock
Center for Soviet and East European
Research, Hebrew University of
Jerusalem

Der Spiegel
(Hamburg, weekly)
The Star
(Amman, weekly)
Statistical Abstract of Israel   *SA*
(Jerusalem, annually)

Published by Keterpress for the
Israel Central Bureau of Statistics

Der Stern
(Hamburg, weekly)
Al-Sudan al-Hadith
(Khartoum, daily)
Sudanow
(Khartoum, monthly)
Sunday Times   *ST*
(London, weekly)
Survival
(London, bimonthly)

Published by the International
Institute for Strategic Studies

Svenska Dagbladet
(Stockholm, daily)
Al-Tadamun
(London, weekly)
Al-Tadamun al-Islami
(Mecca, monthly)
Al-Tali'a
(Jerusalem, weekly)
Al-Tasawwuf al-Islami
(Cairo, monthly)

Published by the national forum
of Sufi orders

Tehran Times   *TT*
(Tehran, daily)

Reflects government's views; close
to Rafsanjani

Al-Thawra
(Baghdad, daily)

Organ of the Iraqi Ba'th Party

Al-Thawra
(Damascus, daily)
Al-Thawra
(San'a, daily)
Time
(New York, weekly)

The Times
  (London, daily)
Tishrin
  (Damascus, daily)
Trud
  (Moscow, daily)
Truppendienst
  (Vienna, bimonthly)
Turkey Confidential
  (London, 10 per year)
'Ukaz
  (Jidda, daily)
Al-Umma al-Islamiyya
  (Jidda, weekly)
Union
  (San Diego, daily)
Al-Usbu' al-'Arabi
  (Beirut, weekly)
Al-Usbu' al-Jadid
  (Jerusalem, biweekly)
US News and World Report
  (Washington, DC, weekly)
Vanity Fair
  (London, monthly)
Verejnost
  (Bratislava, daily)
Al-Wafd   Organ of the New Wafd Party
  (Cairo, daily)
The Wall Street Journal   WSJ
  (New York, daily)
The Washington Post   WP
  (Washington, DC, daily)
Washington Quarterly
  (Washington, quarterly)
The Washington Times   WT
  (Washington, DC, daily)
Al-Watan
  (Nazareth, weekly)
Al-Watan al-'Arabi
  (Paris, weekly)
Al-Watani
  (Cairo, weekly)
World Policy Journal
  (New York, quarterly)
Al-Yasar
  (Cairo, monthly)
Al-Yawm al-Sabi'   Affiliated to the PLO
  (Paris, weekly)
Yedi'ot Aharonot
  (Tel Aviv, daily)
Al-Zahira
  (London, daily)
Die Zeit
  (Hamburg, weekly)
Zo Haderech
  (Tel Aviv, weekly)

News Agencies

Full Name	*Abbreviation*
Agence France Presse (Paris)	AFP
Algérie Presse Service (Algiers)	APS
Allgemeiner Deutscher Nachrichtendienst (Berlin)	ADN
Associated Press (New York)	AP
Deutsche Presse-Agentur (Hamburg)	DPA
Gulf News Agency (Manama)	GNA
Interfax (Moscow)	
Iraqi News Agency (Baghdad)	INA
Islamic Revolution News Agency (Tehran)	IRNA
Jamahiriyya Arab News Agency (Tripoli)	JANA
Jordanian News Agency (PETRA; Amman)	JNA
Kuwaiti News Agency (Kuwait)	KUNA
Kyodo Tsushin (Kyodo News Service; Tokyo)	Kyodo
Maghreb Arabe Presse (Rabat)	MAP
Middle East News Agency (Cairo)	MENA
Novinska Agencija Tanjug (Belgrade)	TANJUG
Novosti Press Agency (Moscow)	
Oman News Agency (Muscat)	
Opec News Agency (Vienna)	OPEC NA
Pan-African News Agency (Dakar)	PANA
The Press Association (London)	
Reuters (London)	
Saudi Press Agency (Riyadh)	SPA
Sudanese News Agency (Khartoum)	SUNA
Syrian Arab News Agency (Damascus)	SANA
Telegrafnoe Agentstvo Sovetskovo Soiuza (Moscow)	TASS
United Press International (New York)	UPI
Wakalat al-Anba al-Filastiniyya (Palestinian News Agency; Damascus)	WAFA

Radio and Television Stations, and Monitoring Services

(Radio stations known by the location of their principal transmitter are not listed — their names being self-explanatory.)

Name	*Abbreviation*	*Notes*
American Broadcasting Company	ABC	Headquarters in New York City
Antenne 2 (Télévision)	Antenne 2 (TV)	Paris
British Broadcasting Corporation	BBC	
British Broadcasting Corporation, Summary of World Broadcasting: The ME and Africa	SWB	Monitoring reports published in English translation
Cable News Network Inc.	CNN	Atlanta, GA
Daily Report: Middle East and Africa	DR	Monitoring reports published in English translation by the US Foreign Broadcasting Information Service
Daily Report: Soviet Union	DR:SU	
Egyptian Space Channel		Daily broadcasts from Cairo
Independent Television	ITV	London
Islamic Republic of Iran Broadcasting	IRIB TV	Tehran

Israel Defense Forces Radio	R.IDF	
Joint Publication Research Services:	JPRS	English-language translation from
Near East and North Africa		foreign press. Occasionally includes
Soviet Union		monitoring reports as well
Sub-Saharan Africa		
West Europe		
Middle East Broadcasting	MBC TV	Saudi-backed, news television
Corporation Television		by satellite from London
National Broadcasting Company	NBC	New York
Al-Quds — Palestine Arab Radio	R. al-Quds	PFLP-GC radio,
		broadcasting from Syria
Radiodiffusion Télévision	RTM TV	Rabat
Marocaine		
Radio France Internationale	RFI	Paris
R. Peace and Progress		Official USSR station transmitting
		from Moscow to the ME
R. SPLA		Voice of the Sudanese People's
		Liberation Army
Türkiye Radyo Televizyon	TRT TV	Turkish Radio-Television
Kumuru		Corporation, Ankara
United States Information Agency	USIA	Washington, DC
United States Information Service	USIS	Washington, DC
Voice of Free Iraq	VoFI	
Voice of Free Lebanon		Military station of the Lebanese
		Phalanges
Voice of the Great Arab Homeland	R. Tripoli,	Libyan transmitter to Arab
	VoGAH	audiences outside Libya, previously
		known as Voice of the Arab Homeland
		(VoAH)
Voice of Iraqi Kurdistan	VoIK	
Voice of the Iraqi People	VoIP	
Voice of the Iraqi Opposition	VoIO	
Voice of the Islamic Republic of Iran		Iran's national radio network
Voice of Israel	VoI	Israeli national radio
Voice of Lebanon	VoL	Radio station operated by the
		Kata'ib
Voice of the Masses	R. Baghdad,	A series of special programs in Arabic,
	VoM	Kurdish, and Farsi broadcast over R.
		Baghdad for a few hours each day
Voice of the Mountain		Radio station of the Progressive
		Socialist Party, operating from the
		Shuf mountains
Voice of the Oppressed		A clandestine Hizballah mouthpiece,
		Lebanon
Voice of Palestine (Algiers)	VoP	PLO daily program over
	(Algiers)	R. Algiers
Voice of Palestine (Baghdad)	VoP	PLO main radio station
	(Baghdad)	
Voice of Palestine (San'a)	VoP	PLO daily program over R. San'a
	(San'a)	
Voice of the People		Communist Party clandestine radio
		station, based in Lebanon
Voice of the People of Kurdistan	VoPK	
Wireless File	WF	Published by the USIA Library,
		Washington

Note: Radio and news agency material not otherwise attributed is available in Hebrew translation at the Moshe Dayan Center archives.

Notes on Contributors

AMI AYALON, PhD (Princeton University, 1980). Senior Research Fellow at the Moshe Dayan Center and Chairman of the Department of Middle Eastern and African History, Tel Aviv University. Author of *Language and Change in the Arab Middle East* (1987), *Press and Journalism in the Arab World* (forthcoming) and numerous articles on modern Middle Eastern political and cultural history. Editor of *Regime and Opposition in Egypt under Sadat* (1983, in Hebrew).

GAD BARZILAI, LLB, MA, PhD (Hebrew University, Jerusalem, 1987). Lecturer, Department of Political Science, Tel Aviv University. Fields of specialization: politics and governments in democratic regimes; Israeli politics; law, social order, war studies, political behavior, and politics. Published articles on Israeli politics, national security crises and democracies, voting behavior, military force and politics. Author of *A Democracy in Wartime: Conflict and Consensus in Israel* (1992; in Hebrew); *The Impact of Intercommunal Conflict: The Intifada and Israeli Public Opinion* (1991; in Hebrew); coeditor: *The Gulf War and its Global Aftermath* (forthcoming); and coeditor of *Society and Law: Israeli Public Opinion and the Supreme Court* (forthcoming, 1993; in Hebrew).

MORDECHAI GAZIT, MA (Hebrew University). Senior Research Fellow at the Moshe Dayan Center, Tel Aviv University and the Leonard Davis Institute for International Relations, Hebrew University. Formerly Director-General, Office of the Prime Minister of Israel (1973–75); Director-General, Israel Ministry for Foreign Affairs (1972–73); Ambassador to France (1975–79); Minister, Embassy of Israel, Washington, DC (1960–65); Fellow, Center for International Affairs, Harvard University (1980–81).

GIDEON GERA, PhD (Tel Aviv University, 1978). Senior Research Fellow at the Moshe Dayan Center. Fields of specialization: political and strategic problems of the Middle East, on which he has published several articles. Author of *Libya under Qadhdhafi* (1983; in Hebrew).

GAD G. GILBAR, PhD (School of Oriental and African Studies, University of London, 1974). Professor, Department of Middle Eastern History, University of Haifa, and Senior Research Fellow at the Moshe Dayan Center. Fields of specialization: economic and demographic history of the modern Middle East, with special reference to Iran, Egypt and the Palestinians. Author of *The Economic Development of the Middle East in Modern Times* (1990; in Hebrew), and *The Palestinians: Studies in Demographic and Economic History, 1870–1990* (1993). Editor of *Ottoman Palestine 1800–1914: Studies in Economic Social History* (1990), and coeditor of *At the Core of the Conflict: The Intifada* (1992; in Hebrew), and *The Muslim Waqf: Social and Economic Aspects* (1993).

GALIA GOLAN, PhD (Hebrew University, 1970). Director of the Mayrock Soviet and East European Research Center and Darwin Professor of Soviet and East

European Studies in the Department of Political Science at the Hebrew University of Jerusalem. Author of eight books on the Soviet Union and on Eastern Europe, the most recent of which are *Soviet Policies in the Middle East from World War Two to Gorbachev* (Cambridge University Press), and *Moscow's Policy in the Middle East: New Thinking on Regional Conflict* (Royal Institute for International Relations).

WILLIAM M. HALE, MA (Oxon.), PhD (Australian National University). Senior Lecturer in Politics, School of Oriental and African Studies, England. Author of *The Economic and Political Development of Modern Turkey* (1981, 1983). Coauthor of *Aspects of Modern Turkey* (1976) and *Four Centuries of Turco-British Relations* (1984). Published numerous articles on Turkish politics and economic development.

WILLIAM W. HARRIS, PhD (University of Durham, 1979). Lecturer in Geography, University of Otago, New Zealand. Fields of specialization: Middle East politics and political geography. Frequent visits and periods of residence in Lebanon from 1983 to the present. Published papers on Lebanese political developments, especially on Syrian interventions. Author of *Taking Root: Israeli Settlement in the West Bank, the Golan, and Gaza-Sinai 1967-1980.*

JOSEPH KOSTINER, PhD (London School of Economics and Political Science, University of London, 1982). Senior Research Fellow at the Moshe Dayan Center; Senior Lecturer in the Department of Middle Eastern and African History at Tel Aviv University. Fields of specialization: history and current affairs of the Arabian Peninsula states. Published several papers on this subject. Author of *The Struggle for South Yemen* (1984), *South Yemen's Revolutionary Strategy* (1990), and *From Chieftaincy to Monarchical State: The Making of Saudi Arabia 1916-1936* (1992). Coeditor (with P.S. Khoury) of *Tribes and State Formation in the Middle East* (1991).

MARTIN KRAMER, PhD (Princeton University, 1982). Associate Director and Senior Research Fellow at the Moshe Dayan Center. Fields of specialization: Islamic and pan-Islamic activism. Author of *Islam Assembled: The Advent of the Muslim Congresses* (1986), and published articles on the modern history of the Middle East; editor of: *Protest and Revolution in Shi'i Islam* (1985; in Hebrew); *Shi'ism, Resistance and Revolution* (1987); and *Middle Eastern Lives* (1991).

URI M. KUPFERSCHMIDT, PhD (The Hebrew University, 1979). Senior Lecturer in the Department of Middle Eastern History, University of Haifa. Author of *The Supreme Muslim Council, Islam under the British Mandate for Palestine* (Leiden, 1987) and articles on Islamic institutions and society in Palestine and Egypt. Coedited with Gabriel R. Warburg the volume *Islam, Nationalism, and Radicalism in Egypt and the Sudan* (New York, 1983).

ANAT LAPIDOT, BA (Tel Aviv University, 1986). Instructor in the Department of Middle Eastern and African History, Tel Aviv University. PhD candidate at Durham University (England). Title of dissertation: "Islam and Nationalism: A Study of Contemporary Thought in Turkey (1980-1990)."

MEIR LITVAK, PhD (Harvard University, 1991). Research Fellow at the Moshe Dayan Center, and Instructor in the Department of Middle Eastern and African History, Tel Aviv University. Fields of specialization: Modern Shiʻi history and Palestinian politics.

BRUCE MADDY-WEITZMAN, PhD (Tel Aviv University, 1988). Research Fellow at the Moshe Dayan Center, and Lecturer at the Overseas Students Unit, Tel Aviv University. Fields of specialization: contemporary Middle Eastern history, inter-Arab relations, and the Arab-Israeli conflict. Published articles on Arab politics, the Iraqi-Iranian conflict, and Maghrib affairs. Forthcoming book entitled *The Crystallization of the Arab State System* (Syracuse University Press).

DAVID MENASHRI, PhD (Tel Aviv University, 1982). Senior Research Fellow at the Moshe Dayan Center and Associate Professor in the Department of Middle Eastern and African History, Tel Aviv University. Field of specialization: the history and politics of Iran. Author of: *Education and the Making of Modern Iran* (1992), *Iran: A Decade of War and Revolution* (1990), and *Iran in Revolution* (1988; in Hebrew). Editor of *The Iranian Revolution and the Muslim World* (1990), and published papers on Iranian politics.

UZI RABI, BA (Tel Aviv University, 1986). Researcher at the Moshe Dayan Center and Instructor in the Department of Middle Eastern and African History and in the Preparatory Program, Tel Aviv University. Field of specialization: Persian Gulf states.

DAVID RACHOVICH, PhD (Tel Aviv University, 1990). Instructor in the Department of Middle Eastern History, University of Haifa. Fields of specialization: Industrialization in the Middle East and Middle Eastern oil.

ELIE REKHESS, PhD (Tel Aviv University, 1987). Senior Research Fellow at the Moshe Dayan Center. Fields of specialization: the Israeli Arabs and the Arabs on the West Bank and Gaza Strip. Published papers and studies on the Arab intelligentsia in Israel and the West Bank; political trends and socioeconomic changes within the Arab population in Israel, the West Bank and Gaza; and on the Communist movement in Israel and the Arab world.

YEHUDIT RONEN, MA (Tel Aviv University, 1991). Research Fellow at the Moshe Dayan Center. Fields of specialization: Sudan and Libya. Published articles and book reviews on the modern political history of Arab countries.

BARRY RUBIN, PhD (Georgetown University, 1978), is a fellow of Johns Hopkins University's Foreign Policy Institute. He is author of *Paved with Good Intentions, Secrets of State, Modern Dictators, Istanbul Intrigues, The Arab States and the Palestine Conflict*, and *The Great Powers in the Middle East*. He is coeditor of *The Israel-Arab Reader* and *The Human Rights Reader*. His most recent book is *Cauldron of Turmoil: America in the Middle East*.

YIGAL SHEFFY, MA (Tel Aviv University, 1988). Director of the Documentation System, Moshe Dayan Center. Field of specialization: military history of the Middle East. Researching PhD dissertation on "The Intelligence Dimension of the Palestine Campaign, 1914–1918."

ASHER SUSSER, PhD (Tel Aviv University, 1986). Senior Research Fellow at the Moshe Dayan Center and Head of the Center. Fields of specialization: history and politics of Jordan and the Palestinians. Author of *Between Jordan and Palestine: A Political Biography of Wasfi al-Tall* (1983, in Hebrew); *The PLO after the War in Lebanon* (1985; in Hebrew); and *On Both Banks of the Jordan* (forthcoming 1993); coeditor of *At the Core of the Conflict: The Intifada* (1992; in Hebrew).

JOSHUA TEITELBAUM, MA (Tel Aviv University, 1988). Research Fellow at the Moshe Dayan Center and Instructor in the Overseas Students Program, Tel Aviv University. Fields of specialization: Palestinian history and politics, modern Islamic movements, and the history of the Arabian Peninsula. Researching PhD dissertation on "State and Society in the Hashimite Kingdom of the Hijaz, 1916–1925."

ONN WINCKLER, MA (Haifa University, 1992). Instructor in the Department of Middle Eastern History, University of Haifa. Field of specialization: demographic trends in the Middle East.

EYAL ZISSER, PhD (Tel Aviv University). Researcher at the Moshe Dayan Center, and Instructor in the Department of Middle Eastern and African History, Tel Aviv University. Fields of specialization: the history and politics of Syria and Lebanon. Title of thesis: "The Challenge of Independence — Lebanon under Bishara al-Khuri, 1943–1952."

PART ONE:
CURRENT ISSUES

THE MIDDLE EAST
IN PERSPECTIVE

The Middle East in 1991: A Year of Promises Unfulfilled

GIDEON GERA

The dramatic events that had shaken the Middle East during the latter part of 1990 continued into 1991, reflecting, in many ways, the fundamental power shift that was taking place in world politics. This "new world order" had been ushered in by the collapse of the Soviet empire in Eastern Europe in 1989, and was attested to by the end of the Cold War in 1990 and the disintegration of the Soviet Union in late 1991.[1] With Soviet influence rapidly fading away, this was the moment of the US in the ME (see chapter on the US and the ME). Indeed, the Gulf War of January-February 1991, which ended with the military defeat of Iraq by a US-led coalition, was the first case of major post-Cold War conflict, a conflict which might not have occurred in the previous era: with the USSR as Iraq's ally and posing a constant threat to Europe, the West might have acted less resolutely.[2]

The principal focus of events during the remainder of the year was on American attempts to establish a "new order" in the region. A major problem was the continued rule of Saddam Husayn in Iraq. Militarily defeated but unvanquished and unrepentant, he ruthlessly repressed Kurdish and Shi'i rebellions in his country, revealed Iraq's surprising nuclear-weapons program, only under duress, rebuilt the country's ruins, and nourished his ambitions. No traditional Arab reconciliation took place between Iraq and its Arab adversaries; rather, mutual vindictiveness was the rule. Moreover, the shaken Gulf states, led by liberated Kuwait, soon made it clear that they preferred security arrangements with the US to Arab (i.e., Egyptian-Syrian) ones. However, the pro-US axis comprising Saudi Arabia, Egypt and Syria remained intact and enabled Washington to initiate direct talks between the Arabs and Israel in the fall. The realities of the postwar situation also led Jordan to resume its pro-Western policies and join the peace process, and, even more importantly, convinced the Palestinians that this process was their only practical option. While there was little domestic instability in the ME during 1991, and no regime was overturned, the gains of the Islamic Salvation Front in Algeria's elections at year's end evoked widespread apprehension of radical Muslim fundamentalism throughout the region. Iran, one of the major beneficiaries of the war, devoted itself to fence-mending with its Gulf neighbors and with Western Europe, while continuing to pursue its militant aims in Sudan, Algeria and the newly independent and increasingly important central Asian republics of the defunct Soviet Union. By the outset of 1992, then, the viability of long-entrenched, intricate ME patterns and relationships appeared to curtail many of the hopes for a "new order" in the region.

THE GULF WAR AND ITS OUTCOME

THE WAR

Saddam, obdurately misreading US resolve to evict him from Kuwait and ignoring explicit warnings of the grave consequences of war by Secretary of State James Baker in a meeting with Iraqi Foreign Minister Tariq 'Aziz on 9 January 1991, rejected all the diplomatic opportunities to avoid war proffered to him by the USSR and France among others, even at the last moment.[3]

The Gulf War was a military rarity, taking place at a moment when the US could bring to bear the full weight of its richly equipped forces against an enemy that did not yet possess nuclear weapons and modern missiles and was maladroit, or strangely passive, in the face of its menacing build-up. Time was available for the US to plan and to prepare its forces; a supportive infrastructure was also in place.[4] Moreover, the US used the time to forge a vast international coalition against Iraq comprising 34 countries, including the Gulf states, Egypt, Syria and Morocco (for a list of participants see *MECS* 1990, p. 89. See also chapter on the Gulf War in this volume). The war began on the night of 16–17 January with an air offensive that lasted over five weeks, followed by a four-day ground offensive launched on 24 February, during which Kuwait was liberated and coalition troops advanced into southern Iraq up to the Euphrates near Nasiriyya. On 28 February, after 100 hours of fighting on the ground, President Bush abruptly ordered a cease-fire. (For details of the campaign, see chapter on the Gulf War.)

Saddam consistently attempted to draw Israel into the confrontation, indeed making Israel a major issue of the crisis (see *MECS* 1990, chapter on Iraq) and, once the war began, labeling it a "Zionist war" fought "with American blood." The bombardment of Israel with missiles (c. 40 improved *Scuds*), therefore, came as no surprise, yet its duration and impact were painful. Saddam later praised the missile units which "made Israel cry" and which thereby enhanced "the image of the Arab nations."[5] The US, anxious to dissuade Israel from retaliating, lest such a move antagonize its Arab allies, deployed antitactical ballistic missile (*Patriot*) batteries in Israel for protection against the *Scuds*.

While the coalition's military losses were astonishingly low, the financial cost of the campaign was high, and the US, unable to carry it by itself without severe economic difficulty, received c. $53 bn. in international contributions. No reliable data on Iraq's military losses were available, although casualty estimates ranged from 10,000 dead (probably too low) to 100,000. An official US estimate of Iraqis killed during the air war alone was c. 9,000, mainly in frontline infantry divisions that were composed primarily of Shi'i and Kurdish draftees.[6] Iraqi Deputy Prime Minister Tariq 'Aziz stated that no official statistics were available due to "confused" data. The Iraqis may have found it difficult or undesirable to separate war casualties from casualties suffered during the subsequent rebellions, which according to Saddam's son 'Uday, "were many times" those caused by the air and ground war.[7]

The coalition air campaign caused enormous damage to Iraq's industrial facilities, particularly those suspected of manufacturing weapons of mass destruction, and to its infrastructure, including communications facilities, power plants, roads and bridges. The Pentagon stated after the war that heavier damage than intended was inflicted on Iraq's civilian infrastructure because of faulty communications. An official Iraqi estimate of material losses to the "industrial sector," including power plants, was $4bn.[8]

END GAME

The timing of President Bush's much-criticized decision to halt the ground war after 100 hours (144 hours were planned) may have been influenced by the "fog of war" — by difficulties in assessing Iraq's military and political position accurately. The bulk of the elite Republican Guard (four divisions) escaped entrapment by the coalition forces near Basra, and their move toward Baghdad was not impeded. Moreover, Iraq salvaged considerably more heavy equipment, especially T-72 battle tanks, than estimated by the US during and immediately after the campaign.[9] These forces and weapons served as the cornerstone of Saddam's recovery.

American domestic and military considerations involved in the decision to halt the fighting, such as the fear of a protracted campaign and a large number of casualties, are of less concern to this survey than regional ones. What seemed to have weighed most were the US wish to preserve the established territorial order in the region, its fear of Iraq's disintegration and "Lebanonization" and the immediate impact on the balance of power in the region, and its animosity toward Iran. This thinking may have been reinforced by misgivings on the part of some of the US allies (reportedly Saudi Arabia, Egypt, France and Turkey). The Administration seemed to prefer an Iraq united under a weakened Saddam to an Iraq embroiled in a civil war that would have left it prey to its neighbors.

Whatever the American reasoning, the consequences of the cease-fire decision were momentous. The US adopted a policy of nonintervention in Saddam's domestic affairs, which was reflected in the terms of the cease-fire dictated to the Iraqis, especially the 26 March decision permitting them to fly helicopters for "administrative" purposes. Although during the war President Bush called on the Iraqi people and the military to force Saddam out, once the cease-fire was declared he refrained from aiding the incipient rebellions in southern and northern Iraq. According to *The New York Times,* "a bizarre convergence of interests with Saddam" emerged; while the *New Republic* reasoned that "a [military] coup would never take place while Saddam was fighting off the Kurds and Shi'ites,"[10] whom his loyal supporters perceived as traitorous rebels.

The Shi'i rebels, who took control of major cities in the south and held them for two weeks, were the first to be brutally repressed, with some 1m. rebels fleeing to Iran in early March.[11] The Kurds in the north were then driven out of Kirkuk on 28 March, with 500,000–700,000 Kurds escaping to the mountains on the Turkish border. The chairman of the Supreme Assembly of the Islamic Revolution (the main Shi'i opposition group), Muhammad Baqir al-Hakim, estimated that over half a million died in both rebellions.[12] While very little was done to alleviate the hardships suffered by the Shi'is (with the exception of aid by Iran), by early April pressure by Turkey and West European countries, as well as by domestic public opinion, forced the US to intervene militarily, along with several Nato allies, on 7–8 April. Sanctioned by UN Security Council Resolution 688 of 6 April 1991, a "safe haven" for the Kurds of c. 4,000 sq. km. was established in Iraq north of the 36th parallel, with Allied protection and supplies enabling them to maintain this autonomous region and defy Saddam throughout the rest of the year.[13]

MILITARY IMPLICATIONS

The lessons of the Gulf War were still under study by strategic and military experts everywhere. One of the most significant lessons, with fateful consequences for the region, was that high-tech worked. During both the air and the ground phases of the campaign, high-tech American arms and equipment, such as the F-117A stealth fighter, the *Tomahawk* cruise missile and the Global Positioning System, which proved essential for orientation and movement in the desert, were used successfully, many of them combat-tested for the first time,[14] while shortcomings and breakdowns that developed were analyzed.[15]

However, American technology was not the only one to work. A persistent technological and tactical problem was Iraq's ability to launch *Scud* missiles against targets in Saudi Arabia and Israel unimpeded throughout most of the war.[16] The US and Israel attempted to intercept the *Scuds* with *Patriot* missiles, but the 159 *Patriot* missiles fired succeeded in destroying only c. 24 and (possibly as few as 10) of the c. 40 missiles launched against Israel and a similar number against Saudi Arabia. Moreover, in deflecting or breaking up some of the *Scuds*, the *Patriots* probably increased damage to urban areas in Israel.[17]

Indeed, the inability to detect the *Scuds* during the fighting was seen as one of four US failures that had serious consequences for the region. The others were miscalculating Saddam personally, overrating the Iraqi army and ignoring the scope of Iraq's nuclear effort.[18]

AFTERMATH

The most salient feature of the ME in the months following the Gulf War was the unprecedented political and strategic domination of the region by the US. Kuwait was liberated and Iraq was militarily defeated as a result of US efforts. The UN Security Council, urged by the US, regulated and supervised the disarmament of Iraq's nonconventional weapons, the imposition of sanctions against it, and the establishment of a safe area for the Kurds (with possible long-range consequences), through the passage of numerous resolutions. The Arab state system was saved from domination by a single local power. The Gulf states openly concluded bilateral security arrangements with the US. The US also set in motion an Arab-Israeli peace process (see below). At the end of the year, US pressure applied against Libya resulted in Security Council Resolution 731 of January 1992 forcing the trial of two suspected Libyan terrorists responsible for the explosion of Pan Am flight 103 over Lockerbie, Scotland.

The other side of this coin was that Saddam still ruled Iraq — defiant, resilient and eager for revenge.[19] Fighting for survival by every means, Saddam first quelled the rebellions in his country and later contained them: the Shi'is were pursued in the southern marshes unabatedly, and the Kurdish enclave was blockaded for all intents and purposes. Concurrently, he consolidated his grip on the regime, relying chiefly on his family and clan.[20] Saddam also purged the ineffective ranks within the Ba'th Party and the Administration, including the prime minister he had appointed after the defeat, and rewarded loyalty. He initiated reconstruction of the destroyed infrastructure soon after the cease-fire, and progress was rapid, so that by February 1992, 75% of damaged industrial "projects and installations" were said to have been rebuilt.[21] Another way that Saddam consolidated his power was by using scarce food and medical supplies to reward loyal or pivotal regions (such as the capital), regulating and even halting the distribution of supplies by international agencies in order to pressure the outside world to lift the sanctions.[22] Part of his strategy for generating popular support was to call for Iraqi steadfastness under foreign pressure and in the face of the UN sanctions. Moreover, he firmly resisted UN efforts to uncover and destroy Iraq's arsenal of weapons of mass destruction, relenting only when punitive steps became unavoidable. The forcible unveiling of Iraq's long-term, multibillion dollar covert nuclear weapons program, including the possibility that Iraq could have produced a nuclear weapon in 1992 had the Gulf War not occurred, was a rude shock to the US, which had provided considerable scientific and technological assistance to Iraq for almost a decade in many ways.[23] By January 1992, Saddam, no longer satisfied with calling the war an achievement, termed it a victory: "If anyone viewed the battle from a conventional and material viewpoint, then he would conclude...that the gathering of the faithful had been defeated...[But] now that the victory of the believers has been proven to be in accordance with their constant faith...everyone asks...: Who triumphed after one-half year of blockade and after fighting against the gathering of infidelity?"[24]

Pan-Arabism and its advocates suffered a severe setback while state interests triumphed. Some observers concluded that the Arab world "reached the limits of its own contradictions" in 1991. Others perceived "the end of Arab nationalism."[25] By denying the legitimacy of the Kuwaiti borders (drawn by the British in 1922) and the existence of Kuwait, Saddam had implicitly questioned the legitimacy of virtually all the Arab states. His eventual forced acceptance of the UN Security Council ruling on the Kuwaiti borders reaffirmed that legitimacy. At the first Arab League meeting after the war, the Arab coalition states (the six Gulf states, Egypt and Syria) wasted no time in emphasizing that "each state has sovereignty over its natural and economic resources."[26]

The Iraqi invasion of Kuwait had upset traditional norms, patterns, and modalities of inter-Arab political and security relations, causing the emergence of a new alignment in the Arab state system. The split in Arab ranks, accompanied by unrelenting vindictiveness, endured throughout 1991, with supporters of Iraq suffering severe repercussions. The Gulf countries halted their financial assistance to Jordan and the PLO. Later they snubbed them at the Islamic summit in Dakar in December. Moreover, a decade-long trend in labor migration was reversed with the expulsion from Kuwait of c. 400,000 Palestinians (most of them fled to Jordan, aggravating that country's economic crisis), and the expulsion of several hundreds of thousands of Yemeni workers from Saudi Arabia.

Yet Iraq's defeat was traumatic for all Arabs, victors included, and was compared by some to the great schism (*fitna*) in Islam during the seventh century. It was perceived as painfully demonstrating Arab dependence on the West after three generations of Arab nationalist striving to evict the West from the region. It was also perceived as embarrassing: for the first time, major Arab states fought each other, with both governments and masses openly pitted against one another, unmaking years of effort to achieve Arab cooperation. Moreover, it was seen as humiliating in that foreign armies crushed an Arab force recently depicted as defenders of the Eastern gates of the Arab world, while its soldiers were filmed kissing the hands and boots of US troops.[27]

Another development in the region under the impact of the war was the strengthening of radical Islam. After two years in power, Sudan's National Islamic Front regime tightened its hold on the country and continued turning it into an Islamic state. Despite severe economic difficulties and even famine, the regime kept up the war against the rebellious south. Supporting Islamic radicals abroad, Sudan developed close relations with both Iraq and, increasingly, Iran, although its radical policy harmed its neighborly relations with Egypt.[28] In Algeria, an anticipated victory of the Islamic Salvation Front in parliamentary elections (based on its gaining 188 seats out of 231 in the first round of elections on 26 December) was prevented at the last minute by the forced resignation of President Chedli Benjedid on 11 January 1991 and the annulment of the second round of elections scheduled for January 1992, which was followed by a military takeover. The near-victory of fundamentalists in Algeria, however, sent a shudder of fear throughout the region, from Rabat to Riyadh, via Cairo and Amman.[29]

The war did not cause an oil crisis (despite the brief jump in prices in the fall of 1990), as the disappearance of both Iraqi and Kuwaiti oil from the market was offset by increased Saudi and Iranian production and slack demand. During 1991 the price of a barrel of oil barely rose above $21, and at year's end fell to $17, that is, to $4 below the June 1990 reference minimum.[30]

Iran gained considerably from the Gulf War. The stabilization of President Hashemi Rafsanjani's rule led to the adaptation of more pragmatic policies, including normalizing many foreign ties. Among other developments, Iran was instrumental in bringing about the release of Western hostages in Lebanon held by Hizballah and its clandestine offshoots. It accelerated the reconstruction of its economy and its military forces, benefiting from windfall oil profits and from the buyers' market in weapons in the former USSR, as well as from the appropriation of many of the Iraqi military aircraft that had sought asylum during the war. Iran also seemed to be making progress in developing a nuclear option.[31] Reemerging as a regional power, it strove to reassert its role in the Gulf and extended its influence into Africa, in Sudan and Algeria (although the military takeover there in January 1992 was considered a reverse) and south of the Sahara, as well as in central Asia, where it aimed, according to its foreign minister, 'Ali Akbar Velayati, at creating "a new strategic balance."[32] Within the ME proper it maintained its relationship with Syria, managing somehow to forgive it for participating in the peace process, and its position in Lebanon through the Hizballah. It demonstrated its unchanged militant stand against Israel by sponsoring the "International Conference to Support the Islamic Revolution of the Palestinian People" (Tehran, 19–22 November 1991), which called for the destruction of Israel.

The war reaffirmed Turkey's role as a ME power. It played a role in the Gulf War, in the regional aspects of the peace process (the water aspect of the multilateral talks) and in the emerging contest over central Asia between itself, as representing the West, and Iran.

THE US "NEW WORLD ORDER" IN THE REGION

The "four key challenges" in building a "framework for peace" in the ME, outlined by President Bush in his victory speech to the US Congress on 6 March 1991, may serve as a convenient guide to the unfolding of the "new order" in the region. The perceived challenges were: (1) the creation of regional security arrangements, since "our vital national interests depend on a stable and secure Gulf"; (2) control of the proliferation of weapons of mass destruction and the missiles to deliver them, with "special vigilance" required for Iraq, as a new arms race in the region "would be tragic"; (3) the creation of "new opportunities for peace and stability in the region," especially regarding the Arab-Israeli conflict; and (4) fostering regional economic development "for the sake of peace and progress." The Arab-Israeli peace process became a central US effort during 1991. Plans for regional arms control and economic development were to be taken up by its multilateral forum, which met for the first time in Moscow in January 1992.

One additional challenge went unmentioned as such — although it was implied — the elimination of Saddam Husayn, "the villain" who was "accountable" to his own people, to Kuwait "and to the entire world."[33] In the months following the war, the US Administration increasingly felt that the victory over Iraq was incomplete so long as Saddam remained in power and refused to "play the chastened...foe ready to preserve a Pax Americana in the Gulf," in the words of one observer.[34] By the fall, election year concerns, as well as increased Saudi anxiety, intensified the Administration's uneasiness with Saddam. A covert plan of action to topple him was devised, endorsed by President Bush in November and conveyed to Congress. The existence of the plan was widely publicized in early 1992, possibly to harry Saddam, with US sources describing Saddam's control of Iraq and support for him by key elements there as "eroding."[35]

REGIONAL ECONOMIC DEVELOPMENT
Although no regional economic development per se took place during 1991, there was a reallocation of economic aid, partly to offset war-related expenditures. The oil states had cut off aid and subsidies to Iraq and its Arab supporters in 1990, and benefited their two Arab supporters, Egypt and Syria, in 1991.

REGIONAL ARMS CONTROL
The regional proliferation of weapons of mass destruction and the destabilizing impact of ballistic missiles on the region (which had become active since the Iraqi-Iranian War) worried the US increasingly in 1991. According to one observer, this constituted "the greatest single threat to world security for the rest of our lives, [making] a new international order...a matter of the sheerest prudence." Prewar Iraq was depicted as the prototype of this threat.[36] Moreover, proliferation was expected to accelerate: gone were both the protective and dampening effects of the Cold War on regional "clients," while more technology (and expert manpower) was available, adding to the growing military capabilities of the Arab countries.[37]

When he urged the necessity of special vigilance regarding Iraq, Bush was probably unaware of the real extent of Iraq's clandestine nonconventional weapons programs (see above). Even if all materials, equipment and facilities were discovered and destroyed (which was unlikely, since some of them were probably hidden intact), through the dogged efforts of the UN Special Commission, Iraq would not have had to restart from scratch, for the potential inherent in the cadre of up to 15,000 nuclear scientists and technicians (not to mention those employed in the development of chemical and biological weapons and missiles), and the bulk of the technical documentation, were still there.[38] Clearly, the incentive persisted as well. For Saddam, a nuclear bomb and other weapons of mass destruction were essential for him to assume the leadership of the Arab world and to establish Iraq as the regional superpower. They would be even more essential for his "resurrection," and for his revenge on Saudi Arabia. One analyst concluded that "as long as Saddam or a similarly militaristic leader remains in power in Baghdad, secret efforts to rebuild Iraq's nuclear program will surely continue."[39]

Nevertheless, a new arms race began in the region right after the war, and, although called "tragic" by President Bush, it was, in fact, led by the US. Deciding not to limit sales of "sophisticated conventional weapons" to its allies in the ME, the US sold them $8.6bn. worth in 1991.[40] Other weapons suppliers followed suit, among them Western and Eastern Europe. With much of the arsenal of the former USSR up for sale, and at bargain prices, the successor republics sold arms to the region (worth unknown), allegedly including some nuclear materials.[41] China continued to supply arms to the region, including nuclear materials to Iraq, Iran and Algeria.[42] North Korea supplied improved *Scuds* to Syria and possibly to other states.

This renewed arms race was attributable to three main factors:

(1) Political: One lesson of the Gulf War, obvious to would-be Saddams, was not to repeat the latter's mistake of acting before possessing actual nuclear capability. The military success of the US with conventional arms combined with the disappearance of USSR protection, may have created a paradox: radical regimes might consider proliferation an attractive security option, with nuclear arms constraining and/or offsetting US moves against them and in defense of its local allies.[43] An additional political motive was the shaken self-confidence of the rich Gulf states as a result of their obvious military weakness.

(2) Technological: The achievements of US high-tech weaponry, as well as the Iraqi nonconventional weapons programs, elicited enormous interest in sophisticated technologies such as stealth and counterstealth, thermal imaging, precision-guided munitions, electronic warfare, and especially technologies making missiles less interceptable and more effective and accurate.

(3) Economic: Competitive pressures in the international arms market were intensified by the US recession and by the dire financial need of the former Soviet states.

REGIONAL SECURITY
Although no regional security agreements were concluded in 1991, foundations for "a secure Gulf" were laid. The Arab coalition partners, under the impact of the war, at first wanted to apply the idea of collective security for the Gulf region, and the US, eager to withdraw the bulk of its forces from the peninsula, concurred. As announced in the Damascus declaration by Egypt, Syria, Saudi Arabia, the United Arab Emirates, Kuwait, Qatar, Bahrain and Oman on 6 March 1991, and endorsed by Secretary of State James Baker after meeting with the foreign ministers of those countries a few days later, an Arab peacekeeping force was to be set up with the Egyptian and Syrian contingents as its nucleus. At the same time, the US would maintain an enhanced naval presence in the Gulf and conduct regular exercises with the Arab force.[44] But the idea of Egyptian and Syrian troops in Saudi Arabia guaranteeing "the security and safety of Arab Gulf states," as envisaged in the declaration was soon discarded,

possibly because of exaggerated financial demands by Egypt and Syria, whose contingents left the Gulf by late spring. An argument continued among the "Damascus states," however, as to the possible role of Egyptian and Syrian troops. It was agreed, in August, that they could be "employed" by any of the Gulf states so desiring; but in November the eight foreign ministers abandoned the idea of an Arab force in the Gulf, entirely because "it stirred up sensitivities" in the Gulf countries and in Iran.[45]

Kuwait, shocked by its war experience, decided on the previously unthinkable — a bilateral security arrangement with the US — and concluded a 10-year "Defense Cooperation Agreement" in Washington on 19 September. The US committed itself to defending Kuwait, while Kuwait was to provide the major part of the costs and the essential facilities and agreed to preposition US equipment.[46] Kuwait signed a similar "Memorandum on Security Understanding" with Britain in early 1992.[47] Saudi Arabia decided to double its forces and to procure more modern weapons, while quietly expanding its arrangements for prepositioning US equipment and for holding joint exercises.[48] It is probable that Saddam's vindictiveness, and the revelations about his arsenal, strengthened the resolve of the Gulf states to rely increasingly on the US for their security. At year's end, the US military presence in the Gulf amounted to 25,000 personnel, 200 combat aircraft and 35 ships.[49]

THE ARAB-ISRAELI PEACE PROCESS

The most conspicuous achievement among the challenges outlined by President Bush was creating "new opportunities" for settling the Arab-Israeli conflict. Through the sustained involvement of Secretary of State Baker, who made eight visits to the region in seven months, and helped by the responsive mood of its Arab partners, the US put in motion a triple-tiered peace process between Israel and the Arabs. The Madrid conference at the end of October — a meeting of all parties involved, in the presence of the presidents of the US and the USSR — constituted the symbolic opening. It was followed by separate bilateral talks between Israel and a Syrian, a Lebanese and a Jordanian-Palestinian delegation, where problems were thrashed out face-to-face beginning in December. Finally, a multilateral conference, which convened in Moscow at the end of January 1992, was to deal with regional issues in five subconferences.

One of the major difficulties during the seven-months-long negotiations involved in convening the Madrid conference was the parties' differing levels of readiness for participation in it.[50] Once the ground rules were established, Israeli participation was assured, though friction continued between the Israeli and US governments on the issue of settlements in the territories. Among the Palestinians, there was a growing realization by those under Israeli rule (the "inside") that the Intifada, despite much hardship and many losses, and despite its obvious political impact, had been unable to rid them of Israel (their outburst of popular adoration for Saddam Husayn practically admitted that). Moreover, they were aware that the political gains of the Intifada were almost completely nullified by the disastrous pro-Iraqi policies of the PLO leadership during the Gulf crisis.[51] This awareness, along with US and Egyptian prodding and obvious Saudi impatience, led the PLO to join the peace process, however reluctantly and indirectly. But the Palestinians may have expected too much: by year's end, grass-roots pressure on the delegation for tangible results mounted in the territories.

For Jordan, which had endured great economic hardship as a result of the war and the ensuing influx of over 300,000 refugees, joining the process was a convenient way to modify its pro-Iraqi stand and rebuild its relations with the US. To that end, King Husayn excluded the Muslim Brothers from the government in early October and agreed to a joint Jordanian-Palestinian delegation to the talks, thereby easing an important procedural obstacle for the US. The king was frank in telling his people that "every state has limits regarding the freedom of its actions," that "this world is led and organized in accordance with the balance of power," and that "each Arab state has its own national priorities."[52] Still, without Syria's President Asad dropping his previous insistence on a UN-sponsored conference (a demand included in the Damascus declaration of March 1991) and agreeing to participate, in July, the peace talks would not have taken place. This did not necessarily indicate any perceptible change in Syria's attitude toward Israel. A consequence of US acquiescence in Syria's domination over Lebanon in 1990 was that the Syrians controlled Lebanese conduct in the peace talks, including its nonparticipation in the multilateral meetings. Indeed, earlier, on 22 May, a "treaty of brotherhood, cooperation and coordination" was concluded between the two countries.[53]

The USSR (later, Russia), although a cosponsor of the process, played a minor role, described by one journalist as "Waiters at the Table."[54] Then-president Gorbachev mainly pleaded for help for his country at the Madrid conference.

The great expectations engendered during the war and by the Madrid conference had clearly not been realized by the end of 1991. The talks did not take on a life of their own, the Arab-Israeli chasm was not bridged, and skeptics could say that the process was mostly theater and little substance, with each participant playing to his audience (President Bush, for example, began his campaign for reelection immediately after the Madrid conference). Still, a major achievement was the continuation of the process and a halting but palpable moderation in positions. While not ceding very much, none of the regional parties wanted to endanger its relations with the US by walking away.[55]

CONCLUSION AND OBSERVATIONS

At year's end, neither the dire predictions of the outcome of the Gulf War nor the bright hopes raised by it had materialized, eliciting considerable criticism and what was termed "postvictory blues."[56] The main event of 1991 was the undisputed establishment of US preponderance in the ME as a result of a largely successful show of military power in the first post-Cold War conflict. The conflict did not cause an oil crisis, as had been feared, and free access to Arab oil was maintained. Another result of the war was that pro-Western regimes were buttressed. Moreover, a US-initiated Arab-Israeli peace process got under way, however haltingly.

The war institutionalized changes in the Arab world. Not only were the pro-Western regimes (the "Arab coalition members") not swept out of power by the "Arab masses" as predicted by Saddam, but after the war they claimed the fruits of victory. Dictating the new order in inter-Arab affairs, they reaffirmed the legitimacy and sovereignty of individual states, and neither forgot nor forgave their adversaries, including the PLO. One aspect of this development was a reversal (at least temporarily) of the "new Arab order," predicted a decade previously under the impact of oil wealth and the subsequent migration of Arab labor. Not only were hundreds of thousands of expatriate workers unceremoniously sent back to their pro-Iraqi home countries in 1990–91, but Saddam's oft repeated appeal for a redistribution of oil riches appeared to have had the opposite effect. Some riches were indeed redistributed (e.g., Gulf subsidies to Egypt and Syria), but this was aimed at the political consolidation of friendly regimes rather than at alleviating social pressures. Thus, one unintended effect of the Gulf War was to reinforce the Arab status quo.[57]

At the same time, threats to both regional and domestic stability persisted as a result of the following factors:

(1) Saddam continued to constitute the uppermost threat for many. Unyielding and vengeful, he was able to conserve a significant portion of his weaponry.[58] If let alone, it was thought, he could rebuild his nuclear capability in five to 10 years.[59] His survival in power spurred his neighbors to better protect themselves, be it politically, by security arrangements with the US, or militarily, by building up their armed forces.

(2) Two other, related sources of potential regional turmoil were the possible emergence of a Kurdish political entity, and the reassertion of Iran as a regional power.

(3) There appeared to be growing Arab resentment of US dominance, which could have domestic repercussions in Egypt, Syria and among the Palestinians. This resentment was nourished, for instance, by the US-inspired Security Council resolutions against Libya in December and was fanned by Iraq, on the one hand, and by Islamic militancy, on the other.[60]

(4) As the Gulf War receded into history and US priorities changed, the slow pace of the peace process was thought to generate the possibility of bitterness and backpedaling, with new tensions possibly developing in Israeli-Palestinian relations or in the context of the ongoing arms race.

(5) There was an incipient regional competition between Turkey (backed by the US), Iran and, to a lesser extent, Saudi Arabia over the future orientation of the newly independent, militarily well equipped but needy Muslim republics of central Asia.

No decisive turning point occurred in the ME in 1991. But, as in other parts of the world, a "new order" had begun to emerge. As in all historical processes, both persistence and change were interwoven in these developments. There was legitimate doubt as to whether an enduring change in Arab outlook and attitudes, in political culture, had taken place. A lucid observer warned early in the year: "We will find, sooner than we expect, yesterday's evasions and complexities, old friends who can't deliver, and old foes who will patch up their grievances." Another observer stated: "Appearances in the Middle East are almost always deceiving....Any expectations that the victory of arms would reverse historical trends, shatter traditional alliances, and bring gains for peace and stability in the region seemed...to have been very premature."[61] Nevertheless, processes initiated or accelerated by the Gulf War could be expected to mature. Both promises and risks abounded in the ME in 1991, but their realization or abandonment would be determined in the future.

NOTES

For the place and frequency of publications cited here, and for the full name of the publication, news agency, radio station or monitoring service where an abbreviation is used, please see "List of Sources." Only in the case of more than one publication bearing the same name is the place of publication noted here.

1.   Cf. Joseph S. Nye, Jr., "What New World Order?" *Foreign Affairs,* 71, No. 2 (Spring 1992), pp. 83–96.

2. On this, cf. Robert Jervis, "The Future of World Politics: Will It Resemble the Past?" *International Security*, 16, No. 3 (Winter 1991/92), p. 60.
3. Cf. Thomas Friedman and Patrick Tyler, "From the First, US Resolved to Fight," *NYT*, 3 March 1991. For the Iraqi version of the Baker-'Aziz meeting, INA, 11, 12, 13 January — DR 13 January 1992.
4. Bobby R. Inman, Joseph S. Nye, Jr., William J. Perry and Roger K. Smith, "Lessons from the Gulf War," *Washington Quarterly*, 15, No. 1 (Winter 1992), pp. 57, 69.
5. INA, 25 March — DR, 26 March 1992; *NYT*, 30 January 1991. Israel's great dread was *Scuds* armed with chemical warheads, but these were not used by the Iraqis, who were probably deterred by Israeli threats of reprisals and/or by technical uncertainties. Iraq's stock of chemical warheads, unverified before the war, was later discovered to have been substantial. Cf. *Svenska Dagbladet*, 20 March — DR, 27 March 1992.
6. *NYT*, 3 June 1991, 24 April 1992.
7. *Akhir Khabar*, 2 December — DR, 4 December 1991; *al-Dustur* (Amman), 22 February — DR, 28 February 1992.
8. *NYT*, 23 February; INA, 27 February — DR, 3 March 1992.
9. *NYT*, 10 March 1991, 24 April 1992; *US News and World Report*, 20 January, pp. 40–44, 16 March 1992, pp. 36–37.
10. Elaine Sciolino, "Iraq is Left to the Mercy of Saddam Hussein," *NYT*, 7 April 1991; Laurie Mylroie, "Still Standing," *New Republic*, 13 April 1992.
11. Speeches by Saddam, R. Baghdad, 16 March, and 'Ali Khameneh'i, R. Tehran, 5 April — DR, 18 March, 8 April 1991.
12. *Al-Hayat* (London), 23 February — DR, 26 February 1992.
13. Eric Schmitt, "US Forces Find Work as Angels of Mercy," *NYT*, 12 January 1992. For a critical comment on US policy during this episode, see Strobe Talbott, "Post-Victory Blues," *Foreign Affairs*, 71, No. 1 (Winter 1992), pp. 53–69, esp. 62–65.
14. *NYT*, 10 March; Inman et al. (see Note 4), p. 58; Eliot A. Cohen, "After the Battle," *New Republic*, 1 April; William J. Perry, "Desert Storm and Deterrence," *Foreign Affairs*, No. 70 (Fall, 1991), pp. 66–82; Gregg Easterbrook, "Operation Desert Shill," *New Republic*, 30 September 1991, p. 32. A spate of books and articles on lessons of the Gulf War, some edited by the above authors, were in the process of being published in the US. A lengthy Defense Department report on the war, and a briefer congressional report, were published in April 1992.
15. Barton Gellman, "A Lower Grade for 2 Weapons Used in the Gulf," *IHT*, 11–12 April; Michael R. Gordon, "Pentagon Study Cites Problems With Gulf Effort," *NYT*, 23 February; Eric Schmitt, "A Tally of Iraqis in War is Doubted," ibid., 24 April. For a summary of the effectiveness of the high-tech weaponry in the war, see *The Economist*, 2 May 1992, p. 53.
16. Cf. Saddam's comments, INA, 25 March — DR, 26 March 1992.
17. "Patriot Games" (editorial), *NYT*, 9 April 1992. On the controversy about the effectiveness of the *Patriots*, see Theodore A. Postol, "Lessons of the Gulf War Experience with the Patriots," *International Security*, 16, No. 3 (Winter 91/92), pp. 119–71; Robert M. Stein, "Patriot ATBM Experience in the Gulf War" — article distributed by Raytheon Co. to all *International Security* subscribers.
18. Public address by Samuel Lewis, President of the US Institute of Peace and former ambassador to Israel, at University of Toronto, 6 February 1992.
19. Cf. Uriel Dann, "Getting Even," *New Republic*, 3 June 1991, p. 18.
20. A revealing public display of Saddam's family hold on the regime was afforded by the decoration of his two brothers, Watban Ibrahim al-Hasan, minister of interior, and Sab'awi Ibrahim al-Hasan, director of public security, and his two sons Qusay Saddam Husayn, chief of the "Special Security Body" and 'Uday Saddam Husayn, president of the Iraqi National Olympic Committee, a cousin, and Col. 'Abd al-Hasan Majid, assistant director of intelligence. Another cousin, 'Ali Hasan al-Majid, the minister of defense, was in attendance. R. Baghdad, 11 January — DR, 13 January 1992.
21. Statement by Minister of Industry and Minerals 'Amir Hamidi al-Sa'di, INA, 27 February — DR, 3 March 1992.
22. Patrick Tyler, *NYT*, 10 November, 1 December; *The Economist*, 30 November 1991, p. 39; Talbott, p. 67.

23. Gary Milhollin, "Building Saddam Hussein's Bomb," *NYT Magazine*, 8 March; Leonard S. Spector, "Nuclear Proliferation in the Middle East," *Orbis*, 36, No. 2 (Spring 1992), pp. 181–86; William J. Broad, "Warning on Iraq and Bomb Bid Silenced in '89," *NYT*, 20 April 1992. For an earlier view, see Avner Cohen and Marvin Miller, "Nuclear Shadows in the Middle East," *Security Studies*, 1, No. 1 (Autumn 1991), p. 62.

24. R. Baghdad, 17 January — DR, 17 January 1992. Cf. INA, 29 October — DR, 1 November 1991.

25. Youssef M. Ibrahim, "The Arab World Comes to the End of Illusions," *NYT*, 29 December 1991; Fouad Ajami, "The End of Arab Nationalism," *New Republic*, 12 August 1991. Cf "Out of Focus: A Survey of the Middle East," *The Economist*, 28 September 1991, pp. 4–5; cf. Note 62.

26. Summation by then-Egyptian foreign minister 'Ismat 'Abd al-Majid, MENA, 30 March — DR, 1 April. This point was included in the earlier Damascus declaration of these states, R. Damascus, 6 March — DR, 7 March 1991.

27. Cf. Shimon Shamir, "New Ideas After the War," *Ha'aretz*, 4 April 1991.

28. Cf. Jane Perlez, "Sudan is Seen as Safe Base for Mideast Terror Groups," *NYT*, 26 January 1992.

29. Cf. *The Economist*, 4 January, pp. 34–35, 15 February 1992, p. 45; Ihsan A. Hijazi, "Results Bring Joy to Region's Muslims," and Youssef M. Ibrahim, "Tunis Chief Calls for Arab Repression of Militants," *NYT*, 29 December 1991, 5 January 1992.

30. *The Economist*, 25 April; Opec NA, 15 February — DR, 18 February 1992.

31. Spector, pp. 186–89; *The Economist*, 18 January, p. 18, 16 February 1992, p. 20.

32. R. Tehran, 21 February — DR, 21 February 1992.

33. *NYT*, 7 March 1991.

34. Thomas L. Friedman, "A Rising Sense That Iraq's Hussein Must Go," *NYT*, 7 July 1991.

35. Patrick Tyler, "Saudis Press US for Help in Ouster of Iraq's Leader," *NYT*, 19 January; idem, "Plan on Iraq Coup Told to Congress," 9 February; *The Economist*, 25 January, p. 37; *Statement by the director of Central Intelligence before the Foreign Affairs Committee, US House of Representatives*, 25 February 1992 (roneotyped; hereinafter CIA, 1992).

36. Charles Krauthammer, "The Unipolar Moment" in Graham Allison and Gregory F. Treverton (eds.) *Rethinking America's Security* (New York: Norton, 1992), p. 303; cf. idem, "The Unipolar Moment," *Foreign Affairs*, 70, No. 1 (Winter 1991), pp. 30–31.

37. Jed C. Snyder, "Weapons Proliferation and the New Security Agenda" in Andrew W. Marshall, J. J. Martin and Henry S. Rowen (eds.), *On Not Confusing Ourselves* (Boulder: Westview Press, 1991), p. 275; Paul D. Wolfowitz, "The New Defense Strategy" in Allison and Treverton, p. 179; John J. Mearsheimer, "Disorder Restored," ibid., p. 234.

38. CIA, 1992; Spector, p. 185; Martin Indyk, "Watershed in the Middle East," *Foreign Affairs*, 71, No. 1 (Spring 1992), pp. 74–75.

39. Spector, p. 186; Thomas L. Friedman, "Explaining Saddam: Hard Gambling," *NYT*, 28 September 1991.

40. Patrick Tyler, "Cheney Wants No Limits on Arms for Gulf Allies," *NYT*, 20 March 1991; "F-15 Sale: Wrong New World Order" (editorial), ibid., 8 March, 1992.

41. CIA, 1992; cf., e.g., Patrick Tyler, "Days of Nuclear Anxiety and Moments of Hope," *NYT*, 15 December; William J. Broad, "US Moves to Bar Americans Buying Soviet Technology," ibid., 1 March; "Khazakhstan's Nuclear Deal," ibid., 8 March, 1992.

42. Spector, pp. 183, 188–92; *The Economist*, 26 October, 9 November 1991; CIA, 1992.

43. Snyder, p. 280; Wolfowitz, p. 179; cf. Patrick L. Garrity, "The Depreciation of Nuclear Weapons in International Politics: Possibilities, Limits, Uncertainties," *Journal of Strategic Studies*, 14, No. 4 (December 1991), pp. 473–74.

44. Text of the declaration, R. Damascus, 6 March — DR, 7 March; *NYT*, 11 March 1991.

45. IRNA, 29 June, MENA, 6 August, 13 November, R. Tehran, 28 September — DR, 1 July, 7 August, 14 November, 30 September; *The Economist*, 7 September 1991.

46. KUNA, 24 August, 17, 20 September, 25 November — DR, 26 August, 18, 23 September, 26 November 1991.

47. *Sawt al-Kuwait al-Duwali*, 6 February; R. Kuwait, KUNA, 8 February — DR, 12 February 1992.

48. Indyk, p. 76.

49. Chairman, Joint Chiefs of Staff, Gen. Colin Powell, "US is Reshaping Military, Reducing its Size," US Embassy, Ottawa, *Text*, 92–13, 27 February 1992.
50. Cf. Richard N. Haas, "Ripeness and the Settlement of International Disputes," *Survival*, 30 (1988), pp. 232–51.
51. According to a June 1991 survey, only 37.5% of Kuwaitis agreed that the Palestine question was "the central cause of the Arab nation," while 42.5% disagreed. However, only 39% were prepared to recognize Israel. *Al-Hayat* (London), 30 June, reprinted in *Journal of Palestine Studies*, 21, No. 1 (Autumn 1991), pp. 167–68. I am indebted to Prof. Rex Brynen for this reference.
52. R. Amman, 22 May — DR, 23 May 1991; on the economic difficulties of Jordan — *The Economist*, 5 October 1991.
53. R. Damascus, 22 May — DR, 23 May 1991. This treaty was augmented by a "defense and security" agreement, ratified on 17 August; *al-Nahar* (Beirut), 7 September — DR, 10 September 1991.
54. Thomas L. Friedman, *NYT*, 30 October 1991.
55. Cf. Clyde Haberman, "Why Sounds of Gunfire Haven't Drowned Out Peace Talks," *NYT*, 23 February 1992.
56. Cf. Talbott, op. cit.
57. Abby Harrison, "The Haves and Have-Nots of the Middle East Revisited," *SAIS Review*, 11, No. 2 (Summer/Fall 1991), p. 164; cf. Sa'd El-Din Ibrahim, *The New Arab Social Order: A Study of the Social Impact of Oil Wealth* (London: Croom Helm, 1982).
58. Cf. his speeches, R. Baghdad, 6 January, INA, 5 April — DR, 8 January, 6 April 1992.
59. CIA, 1992.
60. "Survey," *The Economist*, 28 September 1991, pp. 4–9, 22; Alan Cowell, "Why It's Proven Difficult to Make Qaddafi Give In," *NYT*, 26 April; cf. Youssef M. Ibrahim, "The Arabs Find a World in Which They Count Less," ibid., 5 April 1992; As'ad Khalil, "A New Arab Ideology? The Rejuvenation of Arab Nationalism." *MEJ*, 46, No. 1 (Winter 1992), pp. 22–36.
61. Fouad Ajami, quoted in Thomas Friedman, "Clashing Visions for the Middle East," *NYT*, 10 February; Judith Miller, "Old Habits Ensnare the Middle East Again," ibid., 21 April 1991.

THE MIDDLE EAST
AND WORLD AFFAIRS

The United States and the Middle East*

BARRY RUBIN

Nineteen ninety-one was one of the most momentous years in the eventful history of relations between the United States and the Middle East. The year began with the US-led coalition expelling Iraq from Kuwait in the January-February Gulf War (see chapter on the Gulf War). When the war ended, the US Government decided neither to overthrow the regime of Saddam Husayn nor to help antigovernment Kurdish and Shi'i revolts. Although there was some effort to build a security structure in the Gulf and maintain pressure on Iraq, the focus of US attention turned to Arab-Israeli diplomacy (see chapter on the ME peace process), culminating in the October-November Madrid peace conference and direct negotiations in Washington which started in December.

The US role in the region had been important for many decades, and 1991 marked an unprecedented peak in this role. Since the mid-1950s, the US had been engaged in a Cold War with the USSR, with significant consequences for regional politics. In 1991, with the decline of the Soviet Union and the end of the Cold War, the US became the world's only superpower. Its wealth, military might, range of alliances, technological superiority, diplomatic indispensability and strategic assets also made it the most powerful force in the region. The US was the sole potential mediator for the Arab-Israeli conflict and the only likely guarantor of security in the Gulf.

Much of US involvement in the ME had developed as a result of the Cold War. Nevertheless, the collapse of the Soviet Union did not put an end to conflict between the US and local extremist countries. The US opposed Iranian and Iraqi aggression in the Gulf; bombed Libya; and sent Marines to Lebanon to block a Syrian takeover. Yet none of these specific issues directly involved the Soviet Union and the local regimes were not acting as Moscow's client in these cases.

Washington's power was further enhanced by its willpower and ability to respond to Iraq's aggression, assembling and preserving such a disparate anti-Iraq alignment, and decisively winning the Gulf War (see *MECS* 1990, chapters on US policy and on the Gulf crisis). Even if overall US involvement in world affairs was declining, the ME remained a relatively high priority.

The highest levels of the Bush Administration were engaged in ME policy-making. Key decisions on these matters were made by President Bush, Secretary of State James Baker, Secretary of Defense Richard Cheney, and National Security Adviser Brent Scowcroft. The National Security Council (NSC), whose chief ME staffer was Richard Haas, worked more closely with White House Chief of Staff John Sununu and was particularly concerned with Arab demands in the peace process.

Within the State Department, Baker worked with a small, trusted group of "outsiders" to the bureaucracy, especially Policy Planning staff director, Ambassador Dennis Ross, and deputy assistant secretary of state Dan Kurtzer. The assistant

21

secretary of state for Near East and South Asian affairs, John Kelly, and his bureau's staff handled more routine matters and had less influence. Compared with most US administrations, there was a relatively low level of internal conflict in the Bush Administration. Both Bush and Baker took a keen interest in the region. It was mainly because of these two men's personal views that such particular emphasis was placed on identifying Israeli settlements in the West Bank as a chief barrier to peace and putting a high priority on opposing them[1] (see below).

US priorities for the postwar period were named by Bush in his 6 March victory speech to a joint session of Congress. These were a mutual security arrangement in the Gulf; controlling proliferation of unconventional weapons; an end to the Arab-Israeli conflict; and regional economic cooperation and development. The US agreed to help build this regional security network but was not prepared to maintain ground troops there on a permanent basis. Although there was some public and academic debate over the idea of US support for democracy in the ME, there was little or no such sentiment in the Administration.[2]

Some observers felt that little changed during the year because of US errors. The Washington correspondent of the British *Financial Times* newspaper summarized the case against Bush, and US policy, in June 1991 as follows: "The ME looks as confused and chaotic as ever." There was no peace conference, much less a solution, for the Arab-Israeli conflict. "Plans for a new security system in the Gulf appear to be in disarray." There were "widespread reports of human rights violations" instead of elections in Kuwait. The White House had to concede that much of Iraq's arsenal remained intact, and it was clear that US military claims of destruction had been greatly exaggerated. Furthermore, Washington was obliged to admit that Baghdad was continuing to build missiles. The Administration could only offer wishful thinking that Saddam would fall without being pushed too hard.[3]

US assistant secretary of state John Kelly responded by citing the Administration's achievements, "The assembling of an international coalition that included 28 nations, the passage by the UN of more than a dozen critical resolutions...and the brilliant prosecution of the war itself by American military forces all add up to a resounding success." To this he added breakthroughs in advancing the Arab-Israeli peace process.[4]

US POLICY AND THE GULF WAR

On 29 November 1990, the UN Security Council passed Resolution 678 demanding that Iraq withdraw from Kuwait or face war by 15 January 1991. As a last-ditch effort to avoid war, Bush offered Iraq one more chance: a meeting between Secretary of State James Baker and Iraqi Foreign Minister Tariq 'Aziz on 7 January. In that seven-hour meeting at the Intercontinental Hotel in Geneva, Baker tried to warn Iraq but failed to convince Saddam that the US was intent on war if Iraq did not pull out of Kuwait. The US had retreated from Vietnam and Lebanon, and deserted the Shah, and Iraqi officials claimed that this policy would remain consistent.

Although the Administration was intent on fulfilling its threat, the US's own past record and domestic dissent over the policy undermined its credibility. "Within six months," said Senator Ernest Hollings, a Democrat from South Carolina, "every fundamentalist mullah, every Arab nationalist, will say, 'the US came here and invaded this Third World country for oil.'...And, face it, they will be speaking the truth!" Former undersecretary of state George Ball, a veteran "observer of Arab affairs," commented, "There will be bitter talk of the Crusades and Western colonialism, and all the occasions in history where the Western world has appeared to intervene in what the Arabs regard as [their] own affairs."[5]

New York Times columnist Tom Wicker proclaimed, "Bush stands warned — Congress is unlikely to support a war." Opposition continued during the last-minute congressional debate in January. Senate Democratic leader George Mitchell cautioned, "There has been no clear rationale, no convincing explanation for shifting American policy from one of sanctions to one of war." The risks included high casualties, "billions of dollars spent, a greatly disrupted oil supply and oil price increases, a war widened to Israel, Turkey or other allies, long-term American occupation of Iraq, increased instability in the Persian Gulf region, long-lasting Arab enmity against the US, a possible return to isolationism at home."[6]

In the same vein, Judith Kipper, a Brookings Institution fellow and the ME expert most often appearing on American television predicted: "We will be seen as the big bullies, no matter how many Arabs we have around us." Prof. Michael Hudson of Georgetown University observed that Saddam was "going over the heads of the Arab leaders and appealing directly to the people. And he seems to be having some success." Prof. L. Carl Brown of Princeton, who had earlier opined that Europe was replacing the US as the area's chief power, warned, "A crushing military defeat of Saddam Husayn will convert the bully of Baghdad into a martyr."[7]

Like Arab support for Saddam, the terrorist factor was also overestimated. Representative Lee Hamilton, a Democrat from Indiana, considered to be the most knowledgeable member of Congress on the ME, said, "If war comes, it will be difficult to imagine where Americans will be safe in the Middle East for some time to come." Senator John Kerry, a Democrat from Massachusetts, former Defense Secretary James Schlesinger, the columnists Evans and Novak and many others agreed that terrorism would be widespread and effective.[8]

Many American politicians and experts still doubted that the coalition would be able to sustain itself in battle as it had in peace. Hamilton said a few days before the war began that "Support for the US from coalition partners will be questionable in the case of hostilities." War, he added, would "split the coalition; estrange us from our closest allies; make us the object of Arab hostility; endanger friendly governments in the region; and not be easy to end, once started." Ball claimed, "The coalition would almost fall apart overnight" and the US would be left "with not a single friend except Israel" in the region.[9]

Iraq's biggest American advocates from the 1980s became the most ardent pessimists on America's chances. The columnists Evans and Novak claimed that almost all Arab leaders agreed that if one Iraqi soldier were killed, they would all leave the coalition. They insisted that Iraq's conquest of Kuwait "cannot now be undone from outside" and, further, that Syria and Iran would not act against Saddam. They also claimed that Bush's policy was losing support at home and abroad.[10]

Former national security adviser Zbigniew Brzezinski, who was the originator of the idea that the US could make Iraq an ally in the 1970s, warned that an attack on Iraq would lead to a split with European allies, Arab anti-American hostility, financial disaster and the loss of any gains from the US victory in the Cold War. He forecast "a global wave of sympathy for Iraq." He also claimed that Israel might "take advantage of an expanded war to effect the expulsion of all Palestinians from the West Bank," a notion that reflected the most extreme Arab propaganda.[11]

But many political leaders and observers supported the necessity of a tough stand to force Iraq's retreat from Kuwait. The Administration refused to back down after sending over 500,000 soldiers to the Gulf and Saddam failed to provide a peaceful alternative. Five days after Baker and 'Aziz met in Geneva on 7 January, Congress passed a joint resolution authorizing Bush to use force. This resolution was only passed after a sharp debate: in the Senate, 52 for and 47 against; and in the House, 250 for and 183 against.

After Bush obtained congressional support to attack, Senator Joseph Biden, Democrat from Delaware, warned the president on the Senate floor, "The Senate and the nation are divided on this issue. You have no mandate for war." Senator Edward Kennedy, Democrat from Massachusetts, added in his speech, "There is still time to save the president from himself — and save thousands of American soldiers in the Persian Gulf from dying in the desert in a war whose cruelty will be exceeded only by the lack of any rational necessity for waging it." These powerful Americans were so firmly against war that it was natural that Saddam did not expect the US to fight.

There were already many stories in the US media about low morale among the soldiers, frictions in the coalition, the problems of repairing equipment and the troops' longing for alcohol. If Bush had retreated, he would have faced the next election as an apparent fool and an appeaser; if he had procrastinated, he would have had to face the rising costs and domestic complaints entailed in keeping several hundred thousand soldiers marooned in the Saudi desert. Bush was so eager to end the crisis that he wanted to attack Iraq sooner rather than wait longer. In the days up to 15 January, this congenital American impatience operated against Iraq.

The US commander, Gen. Norman Schwarzkopf, commented on the war's first day, "The Iraqis have no concept of what they were getting involved in." Yet this lack of comprehension was partly due to a failure on the part of US policy to show them better the consequences of their intransigence.[12]

In one sense, however, Saddam was correct. The US eagerness to bring its troops home and end its foreign responsibility had made it spoil the diplomatic outcome after winning military victories in two world wars. The Vietnam War and Iran hostage crisis had turned into political disasters because, regardless of their outcome, they could not be concluded fast enough. Saddam understood that the US could not fight a war if it could not secure a swift victory, keep casualties low, and get out quickly. His mistake was that he did not think that Bush could defeat Iraq and fulfill these conditions. Nevertheless, this same need to keep the war short, losses to a minimum, and bring the troops home as soon as possible also meant that the US did not have the willpower and staying power to bring down the Iraqi ruler.

Under Secretary of State Lawrence Eagleburger came to Israel just before war broke out to urge patience and promise that the US air force would knock out the missile launchers. At the end of December 1990, the US had offered two batteries of *Patriot* defensive missiles, but Israeli crews were still training at Fort Bliss, Texas. The US then rushed batteries manned by American crews to defend Israeli cities, requesting that Israel wait for the coalition's bombing and secret commando raids to knock out the *Scud* launchers rather than attack them itself. It argued that any Israeli action might make Arab members drop out of the coalition (see chapter on the Gulf War).

THE AFTERMATH OF THE WAR

On 27 February, Bush announced the ceasefire and ordered a suspension of attacks on Iraqi forces, on condition that Iraq comply with all UN resolutions and release prisoners of war and detained Kuwaitis. As the war came to an end, Bush's policy was highly praised in the US. His approval rating in an April poll stood at a phenomenal 80%. Shortly thereafter, however, both Bush's domestic popularity and an expectation for a "New Order" in the ME began to decline.[13]

The key element in this growing criticism was the fact that the US had not tried harder to topple Saddam or to help the Shi'ite and Kurdish revolts which ensued after the end of the fighting (see chapter on Iraq). Secretary of State James Baker held out an olive branch to Iraq even before the shooting stopped. "The time of reconstruction and recovery should not be the occasion for vengeful actions against a nation forced to war by a dictator's ambition. The secure and prosperous future everyone hopes to see in the Gulf must include Iraq."[14]

Within the White House and State Department, a number of arguments were marshaled to justify Bush's decision to stop short of overthrowing the Iraqi leader either directly or indirectly. First, it was asserted that to bring down Saddam would necessitate a US occupation of Baghdad and a commitment to keep troops in the country for an extended period of time. The US would become bogged down in Iraq, Administration officials argued, suffering casualties and becoming increasingly unpopular there. This clearly reflected the bitter lessons learned in Vietnam and Lebanon.

Second, it was suggested by Administration officials that the US destruction of Iraq's government would stir a dangerous anti-American backlash because many in the Arab and Muslim world would be convinced that the US was motivated by aggressive and imperialistic considerations. Third, officials argued that the overthrow of Saddam would lead to a disintegration of Iraq itself, leaving a vacuum which would then be filled by Iran or Syria, so that one of these states would then become the dominant, threatening power in the Gulf.

Fourth, the Bush Administration assessed that such a step would be opposed by US allies, such as Turkey, which feared that a successful Kurdish insurgency would spill over into its own territory, and Saudi Arabia. Finally, it was hoped that the defeat and continued sanctions would bring about Saddam's downfall without any US military or covert action being necessary. It will be recalled that Bush had never considered Saddam's removal from power as an official war aim, although he had indicated that this was what he hoped would happen. "Our policy," said a member of the White House's NSC staff, "is to get rid of Saddam Husayn, not his regime."[15] Bush, however, overestimated the likelihood that Saddam would be thrown out by his colleagues and generals.

Officials backed the president's decision not to try to remove Saddam. Overthrowing him, claimed one official, "would have meant deploying troops throughout the country, occupying Baghdad, going after helicopters, airplanes, tanks, artillery." Another official said, "We achieved a military victory, from which a political victory would ensue and for us to redefine our mission would have been trouble with American voters and the armed forces, who had been told for several months, 'You win this and you're out of there.'"[16] Former State Department official, James Akins, wrote that the US did not need to eliminate Saddam since he would "soon be dead at the hands of his own countrymen" or in exile. The US would be seen as the "destroyers" not "the saviors of Arabs or Islam." There would be growing anti-American demonstrations and terrorism; US allies in Egypt, Syria and Morocco "will be shaken and could be overthrown"; and the Saudi regime would last only a few years longer.[17]

Even without such extremely pessimistic scenarios, the Administration did not want to intervene further militarily in the area. Once a truce with Iraq was signed, the US was not firm in insisting that Iraq should fulfill its conditions. Schwarzkopf told interviewer David Frost that Iraq fooled him by breaking promises it had made at the truce talks. When Iraq's delegates asked to be trusted, Schwarzkopf recalled, "You almost feel like coming back and saying 'Why?'" If Iraq's rulers "broke the rules," he asserted, "they would pay for it."[18]

But the US did not retaliate when Iraq failed to fulfill its promises. Bush said that Iraq's use of combat helicopters violated the truce and Schwarzkopf warned that Iraqi aircraft flights did the same. The White House then publicly announced in April 1991 that it would not involve itself in Iraq's internal strife. In early April, US troops began withdrawing from southern Iraq.[19]

When Kurdish and Shi'i Iraqis revolted against the regime in March (see chapter on Iraq), Bush denied that the US had any commitment to help them. This was technically true, but Iraq's Kurds and Shi'is interpreted Bush's clear, oft-voiced wish that Saddam be deposed as a call to action and an offer of help. Bush disclaimed all responsibility for the upheaval and made it clear that he had no intention of helping out. The US let Saddam survive and, consequently, its plan for a postwar new world order was badly subverted though not altogether ruined.

Nevertheless, humanitarian action was taken to help the Kurdish refugees. US troops were sent into northern Iraq to establish a safe haven for them. On 5 April, Operation Provide Comfort (a name indicating its nonpolitical intent) began to transport emergency supplies and food. This was the largest such US relief effort in modern history. In June, US forces were withdrawn from northern Iraq but a 2,500-member multinational contingency force, including US troops, was stationed in southeastern Turkey to protect the refugees from any Iraqi attack.[20]

"In about two weeks," wrote a *New York Times* reporter, "Mr. Bush moved from refusing to become involved in Iraq's internal problems, to a small-scale food drop, to a major direct intervention. He went from threatening Mr. Husayn with a war-crimes trial to wondering, almost wistfully, if there were some broker who might arrange for the Iraqi leader to take shelter in another country."[21]

Similarly, the US criticized Saddam's refusal to cooperate completely with UN inspectors and destroy his unconventional weapons. Yet, other than maintaining the trade embargo, no action was taken. In May, the US ended its air patrols in southern Iraq and began withdrawing its troops from Kuwait.[22]

From then on, US policy was tough but largely passive toward Iraq. As summarized by Baker, "We respect Iraq's territorial integrity and sovereignty and do not wish to see Iraq fragmented as a state. We have no quarrel with the people of Iraq....We intend to continue to act with others to isolate Saddam Husayn's regime. That means we will never normalize relations with Iraq so long as Saddam Husayn remains in power." Sanctions would also continue until Saddam was no longer ruling Iraq. Bush affirmed that the US opposed lifting the trade embargo completely while Saddam remained in power. The US wanted 50% of any Iraqi oil revenue permitted by a partial lifting of the embargo to go to Kuwait and other victims of Iraq's actions as reparations.[23]

As part of its effort to reward coalition allies and to strengthen its position in the Gulf region, the US gave Turkey $200m. in supplementary aid immediately after the termination of fighting. Bush paid a brief visit to Turkey in July.[24]

US POLICY AND THE GULF SECURITY SYSTEM

Paradoxically, the overwhelming US strategic advantage rendered all the more unnecessary the formal Gulf security structure advocated by Washington, secured by treaties and guarded by the permanent presence of outside troops. The Saudis wanted to keep the arrangement informal since their recent invitation to US troops made them want to show their independence by not having them stay. The Saudis were also not interested in hosting more politically acceptable Egyptian or other Arab troops. After all, the Saudis felt that the US army, which was the best in the world, was on retainer as a guard to be summoned when needed. The new reality in the region was that the US had become the guarantor of Gulf stability and security, even without having troops on the scene or formal defense treaties with the local states. This situation was quite sufficient for US purposes since it did not involve a constant or large-scale American presence.

The US favored an "Arab solution" to Gulf security to the greatest possible extent. Even before the fighting ended, Baker stressed his expectation that the Gulf Cooperation Council (GCC) would take the lead in "building a reinforcing network of new and strengthened security ties."[25] In March, Baker met with eight Arab foreign ministers from the anti-Iraq coalition — the GCC states, Egypt and Syria. In Damascus, an agreement was reached to station Egyptian and Syrian troops in the Gulf. Secretary of Defense Richard Cheney took a trip to the Gulf in early May to discuss pre-positioning and joint exercises. "Responsibility for security in the Gulf ultimately rests with those nations most directly involved — the Gulf states themselves," said assistant secretary of state Kelly, "We therefore are encouraging close defense cooperation among the states of the region."[26]

The Saudis themselves rejected the idea of accommodating foreign Arab units, which might prove subversive. Saudi Arabia paid the US about $19.8bn. as reimbursement for the cost of the war. It also wanted to buy large amounts of arms from the US to build up its own armed forces. The Saudis insisted that all US equipment be withdrawn, rather than pre-positioning supplies for a division. The Kuwaitis also preferred US to Arab protection, while, at the same time, keeping the Americans at arm's length. They did, however, allow some pre-positioning of US equipment in Kuwait, maintained by civilian US contractors.[27]

ARMS CONTROL

In a speech on 29 May, at the US Air Force Academy, Bush made his main statement on arms control. He announced an initiative aimed at, "Halting the proliferation of conventional and unconventional weapons in the Middle East...while supporting the legitimate need of every state to defend itself." Specific proposals included a verifiable ban on the production or acquisition of weapons-grade nuclear material by ME countries; that the region's states join the Non-Proliferation Treaty and Chemical

Weapons Convention; the strengthening of the Biological Weapons Convention; and a freeze, and eventually destruction, of surface-to-surface missiles. This plan would have no effect on conventional arms.[28]

US leaders believed that the war showed the need for greater arms control, especially with regard to unconventional weapons, and demonstrated a change in the strategic situation. Scowcroft and others claimed, for example, that the Gulf War had showed that territory was not important, and hence that Israel should be more willing to give it up. Baker commented, "It does not appear to me that the occupied territories played any part in mitigating the *Scud* attacks. Some could argue just the reverse — that in this day of weapons of that nature — that ground, the occupied territories as such, does not afford the kind of security that it might have in the past."[29]

US policy found arms control to be a tougher issue than Gulf security or the Arab-Israeli peace process. After all, explained the British magazine, *The Economist,* the lessons of the Kuwait crisis

> point in the other direction. Iraq's neighbors have learnt that it was a mistake to let their own power fall so far behind Saddam Husayn's. Israelis will conclude that, but for their country's undeclared nuclear deterrent, Iraq would already have doused them in toxic chemicals. And Mr. Husayn has been taught to acquire nuclear arms, if he has the chance, before next pouncing on a weaker neighbor.[30]

Nevertheless, there was little progress on any of these fronts. Just as the region preferred American protection to mutual agreements, it had a similar attitude toward arms limitations. In fact, the US victory in the Gulf eased the pressure on the arms race by lessening the risk of local war. Moreover, the Administration's interest in selling more conventional arms to Saudi Arabia and other ME states, so they could better defend themselves, also undermined attempts at limitations.

The one case where there was an effective consensus and controls on proliferation was in Iraq. In June, a defecting Iraqi scientist gave the US information about how Iraq had hidden its nuclear research installations and equipment. He also warned that the US military had greatly exaggerated its success in destroying Iraq's unconventional weapons during the war and pointed out that much of these arms and materials remained intact.[31]

Assistant secretary of state Kelly said that the US would continue vigorously to press for implementation of UN Resolution 687, calling for international supervision and elimination of Iraq's remaining weapons of mass destruction and its missiles with ranges of over 150 km., and for a continuing embargo on military equipment to Iraq. In his September speech to the UN, Bush warned, "Saddam continues to rebuild his weapons of mass destruction...[and] continues his contempt for UN resolutions....We must keep sanctions in place as long as he remains in power. We cannot compromise for a moment."[32]

The only way to counter a threat of proliferating missiles and nuclear arms was by US-led international efforts to limit an influx of them. Since there were enough ambitious companies and indigenous scientists to ensure that such arms could be smuggled or locally produced, US deterrence would have to block their use. US policy did not intend to apply pressure equally: the US sold arms to Egypt, Israel and Saudi Arabia while trying to block the spread of nuclear arms to Syria, Libya and Iraq, and tacitly accepting Israel's possession of them.

THE ARAB-ISRAELI PEACE PROCESS

In the aftermath of the Gulf War, many of the circumstances previously hindering progress on the Arab-Israeli peace process seemed to have altered. Formerly, the Arab states had appeased the most radical forces among them. After the war, however, the Arab countries needed to have good relations with Washington and, therefore, had to show some interest in making peace. This gave the US an opportunity to use its power as leverage. For the Bush Administration and Baker this issue had a high priority. Consequently, it could arguably be considered the most important effort in US foreign policy during the rest of the year. (For further discussion of these and other aspects of Arab-Israeli diplomacy after the war, see chapter on the ME peace process.)

As soon as the war ended, Bush and Baker began working on the peace process. "We have got to find a way for the Arab states and Israel to make peace," said Baker in early March. "And we have got to find a way for Israel and the Palestinians to begin a dialogue. That, therefore, suggests a two-track approach to this problem." Baker seemed firm: "We cannot let this historic opportunity pass," he said, "the time is now" to move forward.[33]

The Administration did not intend to reestablish the US-PLO dialogue, suspended in June 1990 (see *MECS* 1990, chapter on the US and the ME). The PLO leaders, Baker said, had "damaged themselves significantly" by siding with Saddam in the Kuwait crisis. In the projected peace process, "It was not contemplated that the Palestinians would be represented by the PLO." Baker added that "the PLO knows what is required if there is to be a reopening of the dialogue." But negotiating with the PLO would be "very difficult with its present leadership." In his own victory speech to Congress on 6 March, Bush said that any diplomatic settlement must be based on trading "territory for peace" and respecting "legitimate Palestinian rights."[34] Baker said he had "no illusions" about the difficulty of the task "but I also had a strong sense that the Gulf War might have created some new possibilities for peacemaking in the region and that the US has a unique obligation to help explore the possibilities. It would be very sad, of course, if it turns out that the old obstacles are more formidable than new opportunities. But I think it would be sadder still if the US failed to energetically pursue a chance for peace, because such chances don't come along very often in the Middle East."[35]

The effort was based on an attempt to start direct negotiations. The Gulf War, Baker said, was a "grim reminder" of the dangers of conflict and escalating military competition. It was also a reminder that the state-to-state dimension of the Arab-Israeli issue remained important, and that Israel and the Arab states "sometimes find common ground between them." Baker stressed five points: agreement on the need for a comprehensive settlement based on UN resolutions 242 and 338; a two-track process involving simultaneous negotiations between Israel and Arab states and between Israel and the Palestinians; the Camp David formula of an interim arrangement to be followed by an agreement on the permanent status of the territories; Palestinian representation by residents of the territories; and cosponsorship of the conference by the US and USSR as a "launching pad" for direct talks. The US would not try to impose a settlement. Baker argued that the agreement of the GCC to attend regional talks was an important breakthrough.[36]

In his endeavors to promote negotiations, Baker made eight trips to the ME between March and October, each of which included meetings with the leaders of Egypt, Israel, Jordan, Saudi Arabia and Syria, along with talks with a Palestinian delegation in Jerusalem. In his trips in March, April (twice), May, June and July, he tried to remove barriers to initiating talks. Baker also met with Israeli Foreign Minister David Levy in Washington on 13 June.[37]

During these months, Bush successfully maintained a high level of secrecy about the details of the negotiations. The prospects for achieving success often looked poor. Baker particularly criticized the construction of new Jewish settlements on the West Bank, to which he referred by saying, "It is easier to obstruct peace than to promote it." While on a visit to the Soviet Caucasus, in April, Baker was asked if he could see his way to peace in the ME. "About as clearly as I can see Mount Elbrus," he replied, gesturing at a fog-shrouded peak in the distance.[38]

Baker and the Administration believed that the US could not impose a settlement, and that to attain it the local forces had to be willing. "It goes without saying," said Baker on one of his trips, "that you're not going to have a conference until the countries that are the participants...make a firm decision that this is what they want." Both sides often acted as if the US was the party that most needed peace. Syria's government newspaper *Tishrin* greeted Baker's visit in May 1991 by claiming that diplomatic failure damaged the countries directly engaged in the conflict less than "it jeopardized American credibility."[39]

Consequently, the Administration was willing to make concessions to Arab states — as it had done earlier in order to hold together the anti-Iraq coalition — in exchange for their agreement to enter the peace process. Therefore, Bush quickly forgave King Husayn for Jordan's pro-Iraqi behavior during the Kuwait crisis. Congress voted in 1990 to freeze $55m. aid to Jordan and make it available on condition that Amman helped advance the peace process. Bush released the aid to Jordan in March 1991 in exchange for Amman's agreement to attend an Arab-Israel peace conference. The Administration gave Syria a free hand in Lebanon and raised no objections when Syria spent $2bn., which had been given by the Saudis as aid, on new military equipment.[40]

Baker said, "In the Gulf War, the US happened to share a common goal with Syria" which fought "alongside US forces." Moreover, he claimed there had been a "clear reduction in terrorist activity" by groups based in Syria, although not enough to warrant removing it from the US State Department list of countries sponsoring terrorism. He argued that the agreement enhancing Syrian influence in Lebanon was also in line with US policy. Kelly reiterated the US policy of supporting the "independence, sovereignty and territorial integrity of Lebanon, the withdrawal of all non-Lebanese forces, and the disbanding of all militias."[41]

Nevertheless, while more open toward the idea of peace, both Israel and the Arabs were aware that building a good image in Washington might be done without making real concessions. The Arabs hoped that the US would force Israel to hand them the West Bank, Gaza, and Golan without their giving up anything directly. The US accepted the Saudi and Kuwaiti decision not to participate in bilateral negotiations, though they agreed to join regional talks. Saudi authorities, though, refused to let US Senator Frank Lautenberg (Democrat-New Jersey) enter the country because he had an Israeli stamp on his passport. Rather than protest, the US State Department issued him with a second, unmarked, passport. An angry *Washington Post* editorial called this "an offense against the US [that the Saudis] and not the US Government will determine the validity of an American passport."[42]

To encourage Israel to participate in talks, the US also took some steps to improve bilateral relations. In March, Congress agreed to give Israel $650m. to offset costs incurred during the war. In his speech to the UN in September, Bush urged the repeal of the UN "Zionism as racism" resolution. "This body cannot claim to seek peace and at the same time challenge Israel's right to exist," he said. The US spearheaded a successful effort to annul the resolution in late 1991.[43]

At the same time, the Administration also made clear its strong opposition to continued Israeli settlements in the West Bank. When the Israeli housing minister, Ariel Sharon, visited Washington in May, US Secretary of Housing and Urban Development Jack Kemp was ordered not to receive his counterpart officially, in order to punish Sharon for his active role in building settlements. Instead, the two men met at Israel's embassy.[44]

What seemed to be a key breakthrough in the Arab-Israeli peace process came in June and was confirmed directly during Baker's sixth trip in July: Syria accepted the US proposal for direct talks at a peace conference. That step, Baker commented, "gives us something to work with." He then pressed Israel, Jordan and the Palestinians for their agreement to attend. "In our view," he said, "the Palestinians have the more to gain from a viable and active peace process than do almost anyone else." Baker also said to Israel, "This is a moment of historic opportunity [since] Israel now has Arab partners willing to engage in direct negotiations."[45]

The problems in structuring negotiations were gradually resolved. In October, Baker met in Washington with a delegation of West Bank and Gaza Strip residents and then made his eighth trip to the region. On 18 October, the US and USSR issued a formal invitation to the ME conference, starting on 30 October to be held in Madrid. "The road to peace," said Baker, "will be extremely difficult, with many problems, many hitches and probably many interruptions along the way." Nevertheless, the peace conference and the ensuing bilateral meetings were genuine achievements for US diplomacy. The Bush Administration's thinking, summarized *The New York Times*, was that "only on the basis of 'real peace' and Arab respect for Israel's 'reasonable' security needs does Mr. Bush expect Israel to make concessions. But, he made clear, he does expect concessions, specifically including territorial concessions as well as 'fairness' to Palestinians."[46]

Bush, in his speech at the Madrid meeting, stressed that the US would be a "catalyst," but the parties must make their own decisions. "Our objective...is not simply to end the state of war in the Middle East" in exchange for nonbelligerency, but rather to achieve "real peace....Treaties, security, diplomatic relations, trade, investment, cultural exchange, even tourism. What we seek is a Middle East where vast resources are no longer devoted to armaments" and war. "We aim to reach agreement within one year." Any agreement must be acceptable to all sides and give the "Palestinian people meaningful control over their own lives and fate and provides for the acceptance and security of Israel....And now is the ideal moment for the Arab world to demonstrate that attitudes have changed, that the Arab world is willing to live in peace with Israel and make allowances for Israel's reasonable security needs."[47]

The Administration wanted the peace process to succeed but was also aware that it could not impose a settlement. The object was to move the parties as close as possible, then try to bridge the remaining gaps. Pressure from the US could move each of the parties marginally, but would not drastically change their stands. The US had no blueprint of its own, but, in line with its traditional policy, opposed both Israeli annexation of the territories and an independent Palestinian state.

The one exception to this general approach was the Administration's tough line in opposing Israeli settlement in the territories. This was largely due to the personal views of Bush and Baker that such activity was the major stumbling block in the way of peace and a central concern of the Arabs. On 22 May, Baker told Congress that the settlements were the biggest obstacle to peace in region. He had been particularly angered by the establishment of small new settlements, timed to coincide with his visits to Israel.[48]

The question became the most contentious issue in US-Israel relations when Israel requested a US guarantee of $10bn. in loans that Israel wanted to borrow to build housing for Soviet Jewish immigrants. Apart from US policy's traditional opposition to Jewish settlements and Bush's own position, the White House's hostility to the proposal was heightened by a post-Cold War domestic mood in favor of reducing foreign aid, the US economic recession, and some criticisms of Israel's economic policy.

In July, Bush said that there "ought to be a quid pro quo" between freezing settlements and receiving the guarantees. On 25 July, Vice President Dan Quayle warned Israeli Defense Minister Moshe Arens, during a Washington visit, that linkage between the two was possible. Baker asked Israeli Prime Minister Shamir to delay the request for guarantees. Meanwhile, a joint letter was signed by 71 senators urging going ahead with the guarantees.[49]

In September, Bush met with Senate supporters of Israel and asked them to accept a four-month delay in the consideration of guarantees in order to head off congressional approval of the plan. Bush claimed that immediate action on the issue would threaten prospects for the ME peace conference. "If Congress chooses to press forward now, we stand a very real chance of losing the participation of either our Arab or Israel's negotiating partners." He promised not to seek any further delay after January 1992.[50]

As part of its campaign on the question, the Administration leaked critical reports on the Israeli economy. When pro-Israel citizens came to Washington to urge congressional support for the proposal, Bush spoke at a press conference of "a thousand lobbyists descending on Capitol Hill." Bush, wrote *The New York Times* columnist Leslie Gelb, "stepped in front of the cameras...and declared political war on Israel." He threatened to veto the loan guarantees measure if it was passed by Congress. Congress accepted the requested delay as it did not want a confrontation and wanted to avoid seeming responsible for damaging the peace process. It also lacked the necessary votes to override a veto. Moreover, there was an economic recession in the US and a general public interest in cutting foreign commitments.[51]

THE END OF THE US HOSTAGE ISSUE

The postwar power of the US was acknowledged even by Iran, which tried to settle old quarrels and economic disputes. All the remaining US hostages held in Lebanon were released unconditionally during 1991.

The US Government reminded Iran that releasing the hostages was a precondition for normalizing bilateral relations. It also urged Syria to help in this effort. "Since the war," said this message, "it has become clear that we're the ones you have to do business with in the Middle East and we've made it clear that for some players — especially Iran — there will be no business while there are American hostages still being held."[52]

A UN official, Giandomenico Picco, handled the actual negotiations, which also included trying to free British and Israeli hostages. Official US policy opposed making deals with hostage-holders. Consequently, the Administration did not want to ask Israel to release Lebanese prisoners as Hizballah demanded. It did, however, make clear its wish on this matter, and Israel complied. Edward Tracy, a book salesman (kidnapped in November 1986), was released on 11 August. Bush called for an end to hostage-holding in his September UN speech.[53]

Other releases quickly followed: Jesse Turner, a teacher at Beirut University (kidnapped in January 1987), was released on 21 October; Thomas Sutherland, dean at the American University of Beirut (kidnapped in June 1985), was freed from captivity on 18 November; and a week later, the US and Iran settled their last bilateral financial conflict from the prerevolutionary era. The US paid Iran $278m. in compensation for military equipment ordered by the Shah but never delivered.[54]

The last three US hostages were set free shortly thereafter: Joseph Cicippio (seized in September 1986), deputy comptroller of the American University of Beirut, was released on 1 December; Alan Steen, a teacher at Beirut University (taken in January 1987), was freed on 3 December; and Terry Anderson, the Associated Press's chief ME correspondent (kidnapped in March 1985), was set free on 4 December. Bush praised Iran and Syria for their assistance.[55]

Although US policy was in the midst of its effort to implement its postwar policies at the end of 1991, a new series of challenges had clearly begun for the country's role in the region.

NOTES

For the place and frequency of publications cited here, and for the full name of the publication, news agency, radio station or monitoring service where an abbreviation is used, please see "List of Sources." Only in the case of more than one publication bearing the same name is the place of publication noted here.

*   The research on US policy has been assisted by a grant from the US Institute for Peace.
1. Morton Kondracke, "Baker's Half Dozen," *New Republic,* 24 February 1992; Christopher Madison, "Scrambling Vicar," *National Journal,* 20 April 1991, pp. 924–28.
2. Ibid.; *IHT,* 8 March 1991.
3. Lionel Barber, *FT,* 17 June 1991.
4. Testimony to the House of Representatives Foreign Affairs Committee, 17 June 1991.
5. Morton Kondracke, "Party Pooper," p. 10 and Jacob Weisberg, "Gulfballs," p. 19, *New Republic,* 25 March 1991.
6. *NYT,* 2 December 1990; *WP,* 11 January 1991.
7. 11 October, 13 December 1990, cited in *WT,* 22 March; Weisberg, op. cit.
8. 11 January 1991, cited in *WT,* 20, 21 March 1991; 27 November 1990 and 7 January 1991, cited in *WT,* 11, 12 March 1991.
9. 11, 12 January 1991, cited in *WT,* 21 March 1991.

10. Columns of 13, 29, 30 and 31 August, 21 September, 22 October, 7, 12, 16 and 30 November, and 28 December 1990, and 7 January 1991.
11. *WT*, 22 March 1991; Weisberg, op. cit.
12. *Middle East Mirror, NYT*, Reuters, 18 January 1991.
13. *NYT*, 21 April 1991.
14. Baker testimony, House Foreign Affairs Committee, 6 February 1991.
15. Senate Foreign Relations Committee, *Civil War in Iraq* (Washington, 1991), p. 15.
16. *NYT*, 21 April, 1991.
17. James Akins, *IHT*, 4 March, 1991.
18. *NYT*, 28 February 1991; televised interview with David Frost.
19. *NYT*, 14, 16 March, 9 April; *WP*, 16, 27 March 1991.
20. *NYT*, 12, 13 April, 22 June, 13 July 1991.
21. Andrew Rosenthal in *NYT*, 21 April 1991.
22. *NYT*, 20 April, 7, 8 May 1991.
23. Baker testimony to House Foreign Affairs Committee, 22 May; Bush speeches of 29 April and 20 May; *NYT*, 21 May; *WP*, 4 June 1991.
24. *NYT*, 23 March; *WP*, 24 March 1991.
25. Baker testimony, House Foreign Affairs Committee, 6 February 1991.
26. *NYT*, 7, 8, May 1991. See, for example, assistant secretary of state John Kelly's testimony to the House of Representatives Foreign Affairs Committee, 20 March and 17 June 1991.
27. *NYT*, 10 March; WP, 20 October 1991.
28. *NYT, WP*, 30 May 1991.
29. *IHT*, 8 March 1991.
30. *The Economist*, 6 October 1990.
31. *WP*, 14 June; *NYT*, 15 June 1991.
32. Testimony to House of Representatives Foreign Affairs Committee, 17 June, 1991; *NYT* and *WP*, 25 September 1991.
33. "Meet the Press" and "This Week with David Brinkley," 3 March; *JP*, 12 March 1991.
34. Ibid.; *JP*, 18 February; Madison, op. cit.; *IHT*, 8 March 1991.
35. Testimony to House of Representatives Foreign Operations Subcommittee, 22 May 1991.
36. Ibid.
37. *NYT*, 14, 19 June 1991.
38. *IHT*, 25, 29 April 1991.
39. *LAT*, 17 May 1991.
40. *NYT*, 23 March; *WP*, 24 March 1991.
41. Testimony to House of Representatives Foreign Operations Subcommittee, 22 May, 17 June 1991.
42. *WP*, 16 April 1991.
43. *NYT*, 6 March; *IHT*, 24 September 1991.
44. *NYT*, 2 May 1991.
45. *IHT*, 19 July, 3–4 August; *The Economist*, 20 July; text of Baker's remarks in Jerusalem, 22 July 1991.
46. *NYT*, 31 October; *WP*, 18, 19, 27 October 1991.
47. *The Economist*, 2 November; text, *WP*, 31 October 1991.
48. *NYT*, 23 May; *JP*, 24 May 1991.
49. *IHT*, 6 September 1991.
50. *NYT*, 10 September 1991.
51. *IHT*, 19 June, 13 September 1991.
52. *NYT*, 18 August 1991.
53. *IHT*, 24 September 1991.
54. *NYT*, 28 November; *WP*, 19 November 1991.
55. *WP*, 5 December 1991, 19 January 1992.

The Soviet Union and the Middle East

GALIA GOLAN

THE IMPACT OF THE GULF CRISIS ON SOVIET MIDDLE EASTERN RELATIONS

THE SOVIET UNION AND ISRAEL

In the era before Soviet leader Mikhail Gorbachev came to power, a major crisis in the Middle East might have been expected to interfere in, or at least slow down, the growing Soviet-Israeli relationship. Even if the Soviet Union did not blame Israel in some way, or find a connection between the Arab-Israeli conflict and the crisis in the Gulf, a temporary, more cautious approach toward Israel would have been expected, given the sensitivity to Arab or Muslim reaction to Soviet opposition to an Arab-Muslim state. However, during the Gulf crisis this did not occur, and consequently, this strongly suggested that the change in policy toward Israel was the result of a firm decision taken early in the Gorbachev era and pursued virtually regardless of other events, either in Moscow or in the region itself. A further and most surprising asset of this situation was the fact that even after the resignation of Foreign Minister Eduard Shevardnadze on 20 December, and Gorbachev's temporary retreat from many elements of *perestroika* in his struggle with conservative opponents, there was no change in the new policy toward Israel.

With the outbreak of the crisis, there were indeed those who likened Iraq's invasion of Kuwait to Israel's occupation of the West Bank and Gaza. Opponents to the new Soviet policy toward Israel drew a parallel between the two situations, claiming that American military moves against Iraq were designed purely to preserve Israel's position in the region, while others demanded that the same vigorous standard of implementation of UN resolutions against Iraq should also be applied to the resolutions regarding Israel. Furthermore, some argued that, at the very least, the crisis should not be permitted to divert attention from the more serious or deeper Arab-Israeli conflict.[1]

Much of the discussion about the Gulf crisis and renewed ties with Israel was, in fact, symbolic of the broader questions of *perestroika* and new thinking. Consequently, in addition to conservative Arabists and nationalists, the negative attitude toward Israel was taken up by military and conservative party elements who had launched a full-scale attack on *perestroika* and what was called "new thinking" in Soviet foreign policy. The cumulative opposition of these conservative party elements was, among other things, to Shevardnadze's foreign policies, and specifically, to the arms agreements with the West and the "loss" of Eastern Europe. To the opposition, Moscow's support of the US in the Gulf crisis was one more intolerable example of the Soviet Union's loss of standing and power (and potential arms buyers). Indeed, for some in the military, such as Warsaw Pact Commander in Chief Gen. Vladimir

35

Lobov, such support was actually aiding the US in its heinous plans to transplant Nato to the ME, and from there to influence events negatively in the troubled republics of the southern Soviet Union.[2]

Not all conservative criticism of Gorbachev's Gulf policy focused on Israel. For many, especially in the military, American intervention in Guatemala and Panama were more appropriate analogies than Israeli occupation. Nevertheless, Iraqi leader Saddam Husayn's effort to link the withdrawal from Kuwait to a resolution of the Arab-Israeli (and Lebanese) conflicts was echoed by many of these critics.[3] Some even went so far as to use this to justify the *Scud* attacks on Israel. The conservative *Sovetskaia Rossiya* suggested that Saddam was provoked by daily raids of over 1,000 enemy planes, and consequently, "hardly had any other recourse than to play the Israel card and try to stop the allies...as for limited missile strikes at Israel, it would be strange if the main guilty party for complications in the region — Israel — sat in peace during time of war."[4] Such critics portrayed Israel as urging the US to war and being desperate to join in the fighting. The conservative press forewarned of dire scenarios of escalation and conflagration in the event that Israel had its way.[5] The more conservative papers, such as *Pravda, Sovetskaia Rossiya,* and *Krasnaia Zvezda,* reported various claims that Israel was actually participating in the fighting although they did not make such claims themselves.[6]

Despite the various reports and criticisms, official Soviet policy and most of the media did not support linkage. When Saddam first raised the idea, Nikolai Shishlin, then central committee adviser (and close to both Gorbachev and Gorbachev's adviser Alexander Yakovlev), told an Arab interviewer that Saddam Husayn's offer to withdraw from Kuwait on condition that Israel withdraw from the occupied territories, was not a "serious initiative," but rather designed "to split the Arab world" and spread "erroneous ideas."[7] As clarified by the Foreign Ministry and Shishlin, the Soviet Government did not accept Saddam's idea of "linkage" for Iraqi withdrawal, nor agree that the Arab-Israeli conflict constituted a source of the Gulf crisis.[8] Foreign Ministry spokesman Gennady Gerasimov explicitly ruled out linkage, explaining that although the Security Council resolutions on the Arab-Israeli conflict should be implemented, according to TASS, he "was not sure the two situations should be linked. The annexation of Kuwait is now on the agenda and to link the matter with Israeli aggression against occupied territories means putting off the solution of the conflict indefinitely."[9] Similarly, Shevardnadze's report to the Supreme Soviet in December ruled out linkage, as did the comments of the new Foreign Ministry's information chief, Vitali Churkin, made around the same time. Both of these were in response to criticism of Soviet support for US positions in the crisis.[10]

The only type of linkage advocated was sequential linkage, which would be accepted by the US as well. In other words, the Arab-Israeli conflict would be tackled once the Gulf crisis was settled. This was alluded to in the communiqué issued at the close of the summit between Gorbachev and US President Bush in September 1990, which spoke of settling the present crisis and then making subsequent security arrangements, adding that all "remaining conflicts in the Middle East and Gulf" should be resolved.[11] It was repeated in the communiqué between US Secretary of State Baker and Shevardnadze's replacement, Alexander Bessmertnykh, at the close of their talks in January 1991.[12]

Furthermore, the Soviet Government did not accept the anti-Israel sentiments of the conservative opposition. Although the government paper, like many others, expressed concern over possible Israeli participation in the war in response to the *Scud* attacks, it also reported Israeli restraint. In fact, the Soviet Foreign Ministry issued the following statement immediately after the first Iraqi missile attack on Israel:

> On the night of 17 January, Iraq staged missile attacks on the suburbs of Tel Aviv, Haifa and some other populated localities of Israel.
>
> Obviously, the purpose of that action was to transform the Kuwaiti problem into a regional conflict and to kindle military conflagration throughout the Middle East.
>
> The Soviet Union has firmly opposed this development of events and expressed this view during contacts with the Iraqi leadership. We believe that it is not desirable to resolve one problem by creating another.
>
> The Soviet Union hopes that the Israeli Government will also display the needed restraint and will not take the path leading to further heightening of tension in the Middle East.[13]

Foreign Minister Bessmertnykh subsequently expressed his support for Israel's policy of restraint when he told the Supreme Soviet in February that: "We are satisfied that, despite systematic missile firing, Israel has refrained from involvement in military actions against Iraq."[14] This comment further testified to the extraordinary transformation that had taken place in the Soviet attitude toward Israel in the Gorbachev era.

The new attitude was apparent not only in words, but also in deeds, even during the Gulf crisis. Disregarding Arab dissatisfaction, which was augmented in some circles as a result of the Soviet position on the Gulf, Moscow continued to improve relations with Israel. In the fall, two Israeli government ministers, Finance Minister Yitzhak Moda'i and Science and Energy Minister Yuval Ne'eman, were received by Gorbachev in Moscow, marking the first such high-level talks since the severing of relations in 1967. In October, Shevardnadze met with Israeli Foreign Minister David Levy.[15] Although it was nothing out of the ordinary for the two foreign ministers, their talks marked the announcement of the creation of permanent consular missions between the two countries, the first formal step toward resumption of full diplomatic relations.[16] Indeed, on 25 December 1990, Aryeh Levin presented his credentials as consul general to Shevardnadze and the consulate was officially reopened at the beginning of January, in Israel's former chancellery. Shevardnadze also held an equally significant meeting with Israeli Prime Minister Yitzhak Shamir in Washington in December, when rumors abounded over Soviet agreement finally to implement direct flights between Israel and the Soviet Union, and in March 1991, Shamir met with Soviet Prime Minister Valentin Pavlov in London. In fact, regular direct flights were quietly inaugurated between Tel Aviv and Moscow (followed by Riga, Baku and other Soviet cities), although initially on a charter basis, in other words, round-trip only, so as to exclude their use by emigrants.

At the same time, lower-level ties were established, including commercial and scientific agreements.[17] Although Moscow gradually assumed an economic interest in these relations, particularly in the area of Israeli agricultural products, machinery and know-how, as well as the high-tech and diamond industries, trade was slow to develop.[18] Soviet imports from Israel in 1990 totaled roughly $5m. and exports to Israel some $18m. The figures for the first quarter of 1991 showed a significant increase, with $5m. in Soviet imports and $15m. in exports from January to March 1991 alone.[19] Contacts were developed between Israel and various republics, most notably during the visit to Azerbaijan by Israeli Science Minister Yuval Ne'eman in May 1991. Israel did not make clear that it was officially interested in such relations, presumably following the American example of refraining from undermining Gorbachev's efforts to keep the Union together. This may have been the explanation for the refusal by the Knesset Foreign and Security Affairs Committee to agree to a visit from its counterpart in the Supreme Soviet of the Russian Republic. Nevertheless, commercial, cultural, scientific and other ties were developed with Estonia, Latvia, Moldavia and other republics.

During the visit to Azerbaijan, Ne'eman held a meeting with the President of the Azerbaijan Republic, Ayaz Mutalibov. Ne'eman claimed that "there is a lot of readiness in the Muslim republics of the Soviet Union to deal with Israel."[20] This announcement was something of a surprise, since these republics had been developing active bilateral relations with the Muslim countries, including Pakistan, and particularly with Iran. Their commercial and cultural-religious ties with these countries raised the question of the influence of Soviet Muslims over Soviet policy toward the ME and the possibility of their opposing the growing Soviet-Israeli relationship. Indeed, Muslim slogans in a number of the republics, as well as at the opening of a center for Islam in Moscow in June 1991, included a call for the "liberation of Jerusalem" and occupied Palestinian lands. Moreover, the press reported receiving numerous letters from people wishing to volunteer to fight for Saddam.[21] There were many, particularly in the Russian Federation, who feared the growing Islamic sentiment of the Muslim population in Russia (in Moscow alone, there were some 800,000 Muslims). Ne'eman's trip seemed to suggest that this would not, in fact, influence policies toward Israel. However, the future impact of Islamic identification and ties with ME Muslims remained a potentially important and complex question.

Emigration from the Soviet Union to Israel not only continued but increased significantly, even during the Gulf crisis. The crisis, and the obvious danger of war awaiting Soviet immigrants in Israel, did not outweigh the concerns of Soviet Jews over their safety and future well-being in the USSR, particularly in view of the influence of conservatives in Moscow, which had risen over the winter. In fact, there was a record-breaking influx of Soviet immigrants to Israel just prior to the outbreak of the war in the Gulf due to the increased anti-Semitism and the growing role of the military. This emigration, which eventually brought the total number of emigrants to 265,000 between January 1990 and June 1991, led to the American suspension of the 1974 Jackson-Vanik amendment (which had linked US-Soviet trade to freedom of emigration). This suspension was urged by Shamir during his trip to Washington (and talks with Shevardnadze) in December 1990.[22]

Despite the progress made in bilateral relations, even during the Gulf crisis, there was concern by the end of the war on the part of Israel that the rise in influence of conservatives in Moscow would have a negative effect on postwar policy. Israeli deputy foreign minister Binyamin Netanyahu said that he hoped that the Soviet Union was not showing signs of returning to the days when it "automatically lined up with the most predatory and most radical Arab states, armed them and gave them the benefit of diplomatic cover."[23] Netanyahu was responding to Soviet efforts to prevent the ground war through an early cease-fire with Iraq, negotiated primarily by Gorbachev's adviser Evgenii Primakov. It is most likely that Gorbachev condoned the Primakov initiative in February because of the pressures on him from the Soviet military and party conservatives, who were concerned about preserving Soviet positions in the ME. The move was designed to dissociate the USSR from the Americans, in order to preserve some semblance of an independent policy in the region, without, as far as Gorbachev was concerned, actually challenging the anti-Iraq coalition. Gorbachev was treading a fine line between pleasing domestic critics, so as to continue his own plans for *perestroika,* on the one hand, and maintaining the relationship with the West, so essentially a part of *perestroika,* on the other.

Gorbachev's intentions notwithstanding, the last minute moves to prevent the ground war increased the skepticism in various quarters, both in Washington and Jerusalem, as to how reliable the Soviet new thinking on the ME was. Moreover, the resignation of Shevardnadze in December 1990, and his replacement with the forward-thinking but nonauthoritative Bessmertnykh, left unanswered questions regarding the direction and personalities to be involved in future Soviet policy in the ME. Primakov appeared to be the most senior official dealing with this region, by virtue of his background as an Arabist, his role during the war, and his membership in the newly created National Security Council of the Soviet Union. Primakov was obviously a new thinker, and indeed was credited with shaping some aspects of new thinking. His efforts during the war, together with the apparent rise of the military and conservatives, added some ambiguity to Soviet policy.[24]

In time, it became apparent that nothing had really changed with regard to Soviet policies, either toward Israel or the Arab-Israeli conflict. The pressures of the conservatives and Primakov's own efforts had each contributed to the complex domestic power struggles. These had been much more concerned with *perestroika* and the Soviet relationship to (and independence from) the US and preservation of the Soviet Union's status as a great power than with the relationship with Israel or even the Arabs. Indeed, after the war, Gorbachev's conservative opponents appeared to back down even on the Soviet-American question, which was more relevant to the military and party conservatives than the ME issue. It was possible that Gorbachev's warning, at the end of February, about the "fragility" of the Soviet-American relationship may have influenced their change of heart, since the military and military-industrial complex maintained an interest in Western economic assistance, despite their dissatisfaction with Gorbachev's policies. Moreover, by the spring, Gorbachev had managed to reach an accord with Russian President Boris Yeltsin and nine of the republics, which was a most important development toward preserving the Union, thereby greatly strengthening his position domestically, and consequently presumably freeing his hand in foreign policy.

Moscow's announcement, in April, that Bessmertnykh intended to visit Israel, in his May tour of the ME, was another clear indication that Moscow was continuing its pursuit of improved relations with Israel. This announcement came at a time of widespread speculation that shortly full diplomatic relations would finally be resumed. In April, the Soviets may, in fact, have been anticipating a renewal of full diplomatic relations, in view of the fact that a great deal of progress seemed to have been made regarding the convening of a conference on the Arab-Israeli conflict. An Israeli agreement to negotiations was still a Soviet condition, but it appeared that such an agreement might well be secured by Baker in his shuttle visits to the region. However, by the time Bessmertnykh's trip actually took place, the chances of an Israeli agreement to negotiations appeared to be much slimmer. Consequently, Moscow did not have a pretext that might justify resuming diplomatic relations. Yet the continued absence of full diplomatic relations was an anomaly, as pointed out by Soviet officials and commentators alike, including Bessmertnykh himself. Indeed, once again there was the appearance of a new, more favorable definition of Zionism in the government press.[25] The Soviets even permitted the convocation of a National Zionist Conference in Moscow, and domestic Zionist as well as Jewish activities flourished as never before in the history of Russia or the Soviet Union.[26] Nevertheless, full diplomatic relations, which, at this point, were of symbolic rather than practical importance, were still not resumed, presumably because of Soviet domestic considerations.

One of the major results of the Gulf War for the Soviets, however, was that the US agreed to bring the Soviet Union into the peace process as a joint venture with the US (for further discussion of the process leading to the peace conference, see chapter on the ME peace process). This was agreed at the September summit and reaffirmed during Bessmertnykh's talks in Washington in January. Although Israel continued to push for the resumption of full diplomatic relations as a condition for Soviet participation, the raising of relations to permanent consular level, just after the summit, may well have been a quid pro quo for the American concession. During Baker's trips to the region following the war, Soviet commentators, in particular those from the conservative *Pravda*, were to argue that the Soviet Union was in fact vitally necessary to any settlement in the region.[27] The *Pravda* correspondent in Washington claimed that the US viewed Soviet cooperation as a key element in the stabilization of the region and hoped that the Soviet Union would use its influence in the Arab world.[28] This was Moscow's endeavor to show that the Soviet Union was still a great power. According to Bessmertnykh, the two countries had decided to work jointly, with all the different countries, as distinct from the times when the Soviet Union and the US each had its own camp, with which it dealt exclusively.[29]

The Israeli response to a Soviet role in the peace process was ambivalent: Foreign Minister Levy welcomed the expanded role of the Soviets whereas Shamir appeared to be concerned that Soviet participation would mean an international conference, which Jerusalem continued to oppose.[30] The Soviets themselves altered their position about an international conference after the war when the US was seeking a new framework for negotiations. In March 1991, the Soviet foreign minister was asked if Moscow still linked renewal of relations with an Israeli agreement to an international conference. He responded that such a conference was still part of "our vision" of a solution, "but you know we also think of various approaches to that problem. So a conference is part of that many-sided process. It should not rule out other approaches."[31] The other approach turned out to be what Bessmertnykh termed as a compromise: on a lesser scale than an international conference but more than a regional conference. It was to be a "peace conference."[32] The distinction was that not "all the points" would be on the agenda, but the talks would also not be limited to discussing merely bilateral problems. As explained by Bessmertnykh, in addition to "direct talks between the immediate participants," the conference would include a group working on regional problems such as water resources, security, ecology, and the economy, all of which necessitated more than bilateral talks.[33]

This interpretation raised two issues — that of outside participants and the issue of stages, which was a critical element in the composition of a conference. The Soviet Union and the US were to cochair a conference, but the UN and Europeans were also to have some role, according to Bessmertnykh, although it had not yet been agreed upon what that role would be.[34] One Soviet account of Bessmertnykh's position explained that the cochairmen and the "world community" could act as a catalyst for getting the process started and possibly also play an important role at "subsequent stages."[35] This interpretation suggested the idea of stages, which the Soviets were apparently willing to accept. Following a meeting with Baker in Kislovodsk, when the term "peace conference" was apparently agreed upon, and just prior to his trip to the ME, Bessmertnykh said that "already before the conference begins, we must all know exactly in which stages the settlement is supposed to take place. It will surely stretch over several years. A comprehensive international conference...could then be the culmination of this process."[36] This also appeared to be Primakov's view; he told an interviewer that he preferred bilateral negotiations between the sides to the conflict first, and then a "permanent peace conference."[37] Bessmertnykh confirmed that the reference was to substantive as well as procedural stages when he explained that a "preliminary variant of the Palestinian problem will have to be worked out and, gradually, a final solution will be found, leading to a general settlement in the region. This means that the solution will be found step by step."[38] That this was viewed by some, including the Arabs, as a Soviet retreat from the idea of a comprehensive settlement was indicated by *Pravda* commentator, Pavel Demchenko. He said that the tactics of settling the conflict by stages did not represent a "retreat or passiveness" from the Soviets' strategic goal of a comprehensive settlement.[39]

No details were offered as to the parameters of a settlement, neither in the interim nor final agreement. Bessmertnykh, like Baker, said only that Resolutions 242 and 338 were the agreed upon "internationally legal basis" for a settlement.[40] While there were admittedly very different interpretations of these resolutions, certainly in the ME, the Soviet foreign minister claimed that there was Soviet-American agreement on the various issues connected with the peace process. It was not clear if this referred to substantive or only procedural issues.[41] However, from the Soviet point of view it was repeatedly stated that Moscow would accept any agreement reached by the parties concerned, although it refused to offer any blueprint for an accord, beyond the principle of taking into account the interests of all sides involved in the conflict.[42] The only time greater detail could be heard, regarding, for example, Israeli withdrawal or even a Palestinian state (which were characteristic of pre-Gorbachev Soviet positions), was in statements by conservative elements such as those expressed occasionally in *Pravda* or *Sovetskaia Rossiya.*

If these conservative elements were opposed to the role assumed by Moscow in the peace efforts of the spring of 1991, they did not make this clear. Since conservative objections had been raised over the fact that the Soviet Union had forfeited the international arena in general, and during the Gulf crisis, the ME in particular to the US, Gorbachev could now point to the active Soviet stand. Nevertheless, Bessmertnykh's trip to the region and substantive positions did not completely meet the demand for an independent policy, which was being pressed by many of the Arabists and conservatives at home and in the Arab world. Indeed, one commentator concluded that Bessmertnykh's trip could not dispel sentiments amongst the Arabs that the Soviets were "weak" and "not opposing the Americans."[43] Yet, the trip was described by the conservative army daily as a "turning point" in Soviet ME policy because it marked an active role being played by Moscow, along with the US, in the regional peace process.[44] Bessmertnykh also described his trip as the Soviet Union's entering into an "active phase," which he claimed was welcomed by all parties concerned, including Israel.[45] He revealed that a special unit had been set up in the Foreign Ministry to tackle all issues connected with this peace process and he favored continued attention to this region of the world.

Despite these comments, there was neither priority given nor independence gained in the Soviet foreign policy with regard to the conflict, as a result of the Soviet Union's active role. Bessmertnykh's historic trip was, in fact, accorded little attention within the Soviet Union, presumably because of the enormous problems and political maneuvering which preoccupied the Soviet leadership, in addition to the issues connected with Western aid and the need to resolve Soviet-US strategic issues prior to a summit. In fact, it was not the conservatives' demands for an independent policy that were being met, but those of outspoken "new thinkers," who had demanded a Soviet ME policy based on Soviet national interests, rather than the interests of their Arab friends in the region.[46] Moreover, this interest appeared to include a new, direct relationship with Israel.[47]

There was an apparent need to explain the first-ever trip by a Soviet foreign minister to Israel, both to domestic and Arab critics. Soviet officials explained that the brief meetings were being held in Jerusalem only because that had been decided as the location by the host country. It did not indicate a change in Moscow's continued refusal to recognize Jerusalem as the capital of Israel.[48] The importance of the visit itself was similarly played down by Foreign Ministry spokesman Churkin, at least to Arab reporters. He said that the trip was part of the overall effort to achieve a settlement in the region. The Soviet dialogue with Israel — which he said was not new — played a role in this effort. Therefore, he said, there was no element of surprise in the trip.[49] However, the official communiqué on the visit acknowledged the unprecedented significance of Bessmertnykh's "brief working visit" to Israel, saying:

> The Soviet Foreign Minister's visit is the first such event in the history of relations between the Soviet Union and Israel. It is apparently an important milestone in the natural development of Soviet-Israeli relations, which will become full-scale diplomatic relations with the passage of time.

From the Soviet point of view, the importance of the visit was more psychological than political; Bessmertnykh repeatedly referred to the outcome as the breaking down of stereotypes and the understanding of each other's positions and viewpoints, which could be achieved only through personal contact. He hailed this achievement as the direct result of new thinking, and predicted not only the development of bilateral Soviet-Israeli relations as the outcome, but also the achievement of a peace accord. Although his optimism on the peace issue was not shared by all Soviet observers, many of whom continued to depict Israel as the main obstacle to peace talks, open interest in and sympathy for Israel increased in the wake of the Gulf War. Moreover, official Soviet treatment of Israel was increasingly "normal" in every aspect, from political to commercial and scientific domains, despite the absence of full diplomatic ties. Israel could and did point to Moscow's continued arming of Arab states, as a contradiction of its nascent even-handedness, but it was no longer fantasy to conceive of Israeli purchases of military items from the Soviet Union. Rumors of such offers by Moscow, in June 1991, were subsequently denied. Yet, this was a sign of just how far Soviet-Israeli relations had progressed and the extraordinary transformation occurring in Moscow's perception of the Jewish State. So long as Gorbachev remained in power, this aspect of new thinking appeared to be consistent and secure.

THE GULF CRISIS AND SOVIET-PLO RELATIONS

As a result of the Gulf crisis, there was a definite cooling, and even distancing in Soviet-PLO relations. This trend had already begun under Gorbachev with relations becoming less close, as well as far less important to Soviet ME policy. This cooling off was mutual: the Soviets criticized the PLO's support for Saddam Husayn, and what they viewed as an unwise Palestinian policy; and the PLO resented Moscow's support for the anti-Iraq coalition, and what it viewed as lack of Soviet understanding for the Palestinian position. The relationship was further affected by Saddam Husayn's symbolic use of the Palestinian-Arab-Israeli question and by domestic Soviet opponents to Gorbachev's (and Shevardnadze's) policy during the crisis.

Soviet officials were actually in close contact with the Palestinians throughout the crisis. PLO leaders, such as Abu Mazin and Yasir 'Abd Rabbuh, followed by Na'if Hawatima and George Habash, paid frequent visits to Moscow. Contact was also maintained in the course of ME trips by deputy foreign minister Alexander Belonogov and Gorbachev's envoy Primakov. The highest level contact was, apparently, a meeting between Yasir 'Abd Rabbuh and Abu Mazin with Foreign Minister Bessmertnykh a few weeks after the latter replaced Shevardnadze. Thus, on the surface, normal relations were maintained, and official Soviet responses to Intifada-related events in Israel continued to be supportive. For example, the Foreign Ministry issued a statement condemning the October 1990 killings of Palestinians by Israeli police and Border Guard units on the Temple Mount-al-Aqsa area in Jerusalem (see *MECS* 1990, chapter on Israel), and supported the Palestinian move to have a UN mission investigate the incident. (The US also joined the UN condemnation of Israel.)[50]

Yet, underneath the surface Soviet officials had misgivings, and were reportedly even angry, about PLO Chairman Yasir 'Arafat's demonstrative support for Saddam Husayn. Their differences were often evident from what was not said. For example, press reports issued after various meetings, such as the talks between PLO Political Department Chief Faruq Qaddumi and Shevardnadze in October, the meeting in Tunis of deputy foreign minister Vladimir Petrovsky with 'Arafat, and the 'Abd Rabbuh-Abu Mazin meeting with Bessmertnykh, referred mainly to opinions expressed by the Soviets and the "exchange of views" rather than joint statements or agreement.[51] In his meeting with the PLO officials, Bessmertnykh called for all parties concerned to exercise maximum restraint and caution to prevent "implementation of plans aimed at an even greater exacerbation of the Arab-Israeli conflict" and the continuation of the war. This comment was interpreted as a warning to the PLO not to engage in terrorist acts, in conjunction with Saddam's war effort, as advocated, for example, by George Habash and Abu al-'Abbas.[52]

The Soviet media accorded the PLO little attention in its coverage of the crisis, often reporting actions or statements by 'Arafat, without making any comment, for example, on those made in support of Saddam. A few commentators even referred to "extremists" or, as one journalist put it, "bellicose Palestinians led by 'Arafat," while others warned that the PLO's support for Saddam would only hurt the movement.[53] Former PLO representative in Moscow, Rami Sha'ir, for example, warned that if the Palestinians participated in Saddam's forces, it would undermine world sympathy for the movement and constitute "political suicide."[54] On a more official level, Foreign Ministry information chief, Churkin, in response to domestic criticism of Moscow's Gulf policy, explained that Iraq's move had harmed the Palestinian cause by diverting world attention away from the Arab-Israeli conflict "and doing so at a time when encouraging signs [presumably the possibility of Israeli-Palestinian talks in Cairo] had appeared on the diplomatic horizon."[55] Churkin rejected the idea of "linkage" between the solution of the two problems, thus reflecting official policy.

The Soviet rejection of linkage was not essentially motivated by problems or dissatisfaction with the Palestinians. It was dictated by Moscow's anti-Iraq position and Soviet support for the anti-Iraq coalition. However, it was a clear sign of the change that had taken place in Soviet policy. In pre-Gorbachev days, as pointed out by various Soviet commentators, Moscow could have been expected to have championed the battle for linkage, attributing virtually all ME crises to the continued Israeli occupation of Palestinian lands, and so forth. The Soviets had come to reject linkage, explicitly exposing it as Saddam's futile ploy to avoid withdrawal from Kuwait, and a ploy which could actually harm the Palestinians. The Soviets were willing to speak only of sequential linkage, as agreed upon between Bush and Gorbachev at their summit in September and reiterated in subsequent joint pronouncements. This sequential linkage promised Soviet-American efforts to settle the Arab-Israeli conflict, including the Palestinian issue, once the Gulf crisis was resolved.[56]

Shevardnadze actually took a defensive stand on the issue, responding to what he called reproaches for taking Kuwait's side, with tough measures, while "doing nothing for the Palestinians."[57] He argued that it would hardly help the Palestinians "if we were to 'forgive' Iraq's aggression....For that undermines the basic principle of a settlement of the Palestinian question enshrined in the well-known Security Council Resolution 242 — the principle of the impermissibility of acquiring territory by force. That point is the main hope of the Palestinians." These comments were part of a document on Shevardnadze's policy in the Gulf crisis, which he circulated to the members of the Supreme Soviet. This document was in answer to the criticisms of Shevardnadze's policy, which, shortly thereafter, prompted his resignation.

The main criticism of Gorbachev's Gulf policy was not, in fact, directly related to the Palestinian question. The criticism focused more on Moscow's cooperation with Washington. In fact, the Gulf issue became part and parcel of the domestic power struggle and disputes over new thinking and *perestroika*. As a result, support for the Palestinian issue, and for linkage, were often invoked for purposes which were not concerned with an interest in Soviet ME policy or the Palestinians. Thus, the criticism expressed by journalists and academics, which we have already noted with regard to Soviet ME policy, was expanded by party and military elements, who exploited these issues in their broader campaign against *perestroika*. As these forces grew stronger in the domestic struggle, in the winter of 1990–91, support for linkage and defending the Palestinians increased somewhat.

There were those who sought to explain away the Palestinian position, even claiming that popular enthusiasm for Iraq from Palestinians under Israeli occupation was not supported by the PLO leadership. One Arabic-language broadcast quoted Abu Mazin as claiming that Iraq had deceived the Palestinians, and furthermore, its invasion of Kuwait merely harmed the "Arab nation, primarily the Palestinians."[58] The commentator maintained that the Palestinians gradually understood this, and quoted 'Abd Rabbuh on the harm done to the Palestinian cause by the Iraqi move, mainly because it gave Israel additional propaganda cards and a basis for demanding additional US arms, as well as a cover for "escalating anti-Palestinian measures."

Such statements were typical of articles in the conservative *Sovetskaia Rossiya*, the army's *Krasnaia Zvezda*, and the party's *Pravda*, which sought to justify the Palestinian position, usually by focusing on Palestinian support for a peaceful solution to the crisis or PLO opposition to American involvement in the crisis, in other words, the view that American motivation was based on the strengthening of its ally, Israel.[59] The call for linkage was most common, not only with regard to a solution of the crisis, but in the sense of drawing an analogy between Iraq and Israel in their occupation of land, and in the demand to apply the same standards and responses to Israel as was being done toward Iraq.[60] In drawing comparisons, one article went so far as to suggest that Iraq and Israel, as like-minded aggressors, might even strike a deal to set up a Palestinian state in Jordan.[61] Others also employed the theme of Palestinians as victims, rather than supporters of Iraq's moves, apparently in efforts to dissociate the PLO from the stigma of Saddam Husayn.[62] By February, there were even Soviet reports that Iraq was dissatisfied with 'Arafat and the PLO's inaction during the war.[63]

Shevardnadze claimed that there was no ill feeling between Moscow and the PLO, over the differences in their positions in the crisis. He said that 'Arafat and the PLO understood the Soviet position and had raised no questions.[64] Palestinian comments suggested otherwise. The Palestinian Ambassador in Moscow, Nabil 'Amr, was particularly critical of Soviet press coverage of the Gulf crisis and what he considered the misrepresentation of the PLO's position.[65] Responding to what he called criticism by the Soviet press of the PLO's stance, 'Amr accused the media of merely repeating American and other Western press accounts.[66] He said, "I have noticed that the Soviet press has recently carried many articles containing unfavorable statements about Palestinians. However, few journalists try to understand the motives of their actions. In this way the press carries one-sided and biased information about us."

The PLO's complaints went beyond the media. PLO Executive member 'Abdallah Hawrani characterized Soviet policy during the crisis as "an attempt to please the Zionist movement and obtain American money."[67] According to a Soviet journalist who visited the PLO in Tunis, some of the PLO members (although not, according to the journalist, 'Arafat or Abu Iyyad) felt abandoned by the Soviet Union, which because of its economic situation was trading with its principles.[68] Hawrani concluded that: "It is no longer possible to regard Moscow as a friend and ally of world forces of liberation, including the Arab world and the Palestinian people and cause."[69] This statement probably reflected the sentiments of others as well. Hawrani repeated this response just after Shevardnadze's resignation, commenting that Shevardnadze's policy had not served either the Soviet Union or the Arab people.[70] This evaluation would explain what a Soviet journalist described as the Palestinians' "restrained rejoicing" over the resignation of Shevardnadze.[71] In December, 'Arafat refused to meet with Shevardnadze in Turkey. This was clearly an expression of this same appraisal of the foreign minister's position and PLO dissatisfaction with Soviet policy in the crisis. Such dissatisfaction continued, even after Shevardnadze's resignation, as was indicated by 'Arafat's comments following the war, when he slighted the Soviet Union by referring to the US as "the only superpower left."[72]

Thus, the general trend in Soviet-PLO relations remained unchanged by current events, as did the Soviet-Israeli relationship. The decline in Soviet-PLO relations continued, even with the replacement of Shevardnadze, and despite crisis events, such as Primakov's efforts during the war to dissociate Moscow, to some extent, from Washington's policies, in the hope of improving the Soviet image in various ME circles. In fact, if anything, various groups in the Soviet Union appeared to be subjecting the relationship to more critical scrutiny. These critics undoubtedly included persons who had previously condemned Soviet preferences for the Palestinians. They were now joined by many, especially intellectuals, who were simply reacting to the PLO's ostentatious support for Saddam Husayn, in contrast to Israel's restrained behavior during the war.[73] It was presumably this critical reaction which prompted Nabil 'Amr's angry comment over the "fashion" of pro-Israeli sentiment in the USSR following the war.

The most radical and surprising comments not only directly challenged 'Arafat's leadership, but even went so far as to question the PLO's leadership of the Palestinians altogether. Analysts raised doubts as to 'Arafat's ability to remain in office following his miscalculations during the war. There were reports of various Arab criticisms of 'Arafat and of efforts to unseat him, for example, by the Saudis, as well as reports of differences within the organization.[74] Even the more conservative *Pravda* published a call by ex-Palestine National Council chairman, Khalid al-Fahum, for elections for a new leadership of the PLO, on the grounds that 'Arafat's stance during the war had harmed the PLO.[75] Alexander Bovin, who was *Izvestiia*'s senior commentator, stated "There has been an appreciable fall in the political stock of Y. 'Arafat, who supported S. Hussayn unconditionally, even encouraging the use of *Scud* missiles against Israel."[76] Furthermore, influential political commentator Nikolai Shishlin said on his central television program that the clouds were thickening over the PLO and its leader, 'Arafat, for "there is a penalty to be paid for assisting the aggressor in its aggression against Kuwait, and the penalty may turn out to be very high, even the highest possible."[77]

In a commentary by Bovin, it was hinted that the question might be more than just that of 'Arafat's position. Bovin spoke of the hope emerging in "some quarters" that the PLO would be deprived of its status as the Palestinians' sole representative. He went on to criticize Palestinians who lived hundreds of miles away from the occupied territories and who called from so far away, for recalcitrance, while continuing with "petty intrigue and squabbling, and seeking and replacing benefactors."[78] *Izvestiia*'s ME editor, Vladimir Skosyrev, eventually presented the most open version of the issue. After a trip to the region in March, he concluded that the PLO still had the support of the people in the occupied territories, but he published an article in May, that directly challenged the PLO's claim to represent the Palestinians. Admitting that the Palestinians would be essential to a peace conference, he wrote:

The question is, who will represent them there? Whereas we used to ritually repeat the formula that the PLO is the sole legitimate representative of the Palestinian people, today this formula is unsuitable. To paraphrase Napoleon, it can be said that the PLO leadership during the Gulf crisis committed something worse than a crime — it made a mistake by supporting Saddam Husayn. As a result, the PLO's international reputation has been undermined and the position of the Palestinians on the West Bank and Gaza Strip has become simply desperate.

Under such circumstances, it would be shortsighted for us to rely exclusively on the PLO, as we have in the past. Of course, neither Israel, the great powers, nor the Arab states are entitled to decide who will represent the Palestinians. This can only be decided by the Palestinian people themselves, but the PLO leadership has received no such mandate from them.[79]

In the era of *glasnost,* the importance of opinions expressed by one journalist should not be exaggerated. Nevertheless, Skosyrev was a ME authority for the official government newspaper, and the expression of this view was indicative of the thinking of some authorities in Moscow. The ideas expressed by Skosyrev (and also Bovin and Shishlin), combined with increasing references to the importance and legitimacy of Palestinian leaders in the occupied territories, suggested the possibility of a shift in Soviet emphasis along the lines of the American position — away from reliance solely on the PLO in Tunis and toward more variegated ties with local Palestinians.

There were still those who defended 'Arafat and the PLO position, warning that the organization was still a force to be reckoned with. The conservative *Pravda* argued that claims that the PLO had discredited itself with its pro-Iraqi position were mere excuses to ignore the Palestinian problem. Moreover, the *Pravda* correspondent in Cairo argued that the Palestinians, both in the territories and outside, still regarded the PLO as their "only legitimate defender."[80] *Sovetskaia Rossiya,* which was even more conservative, defended 'Arafat and the PLO for their positions during the crisis, in an article quoting and agreeing with a comment by American lawyer, Rita Hauser, that "'Reports of the PLO's death are premature.'"[81] The *Sovetskaia Rossiya* article by Novosti correspondent in Tunis, Ivan Men'shikov, reported that despite the efforts to discredit the organization, "calm and good sense reign at PLO headquarters."

The Palestinians also contributed to this Soviet discussion, expressing their dismay over what appeared to be, at the very least, Soviet neglect of the Palestinian issue. For example, *Pravda* commentator Demchenko quoted Abu Mazin as saying that he understood but regretted that he termed Soviet preoccupation with domestic problems being the reason for Soviet inactivity on the issue.[82] 'Arafat told an interviewer that, with regard to the Soviet attitude toward the Palestinian question, one must "understand that there are international changes that must be taken into consideration."[83] The Palestinians were particularly concerned about two issues. The first was the possibility of the resumption of Soviet-Israeli diplomatic relations. The second issue was Soviet Jewish emigration to Israel, a problem which had been bothering them, but had been eclipsed during the Gulf crisis. Regarding the first issue, Palestinian Ambassador 'Amr argued that the improvement of Soviet-Israeli relations, reflected by Bessmertnykh's trip to Israel in May, was exploited by Israel to gain a unilateral advantage.[84] According to Hawatima, the renewal of relations should be dependent on the beginning of a peace conference.[85] He maintained that this was an important card for Moscow to play in relations with Israel. Both Hawatima and

Bassam Abu Sharif, a spokesman for 'Arafat, raised the second issue of concern to them when they proposed similar "linkage" of Jewish emigration with Israeli cooperation regarding a peace conference. Abu Sharif argued that, since the Soviet Union was a major source of refugees to Israel, Moscow had a good deal of leverage over Israel's policies.[86]

This issue was a serious Palestinian grievance, which Hawatima and Bassam Abu Sharif had expressed diplomatically. A pamphlet published by the Intifada leadership in the territories was less subtle. Call No. 71, issued in the name of the PLO, said that:

> in light of...Bessmertnykh's visit to Israel, our people affirm the gravity of the Soviet stand of allowing emigration to Israel, a matter which is incompatible with the declared peace policy of the Soviet Union. This emigration encourages the extremist Likud government to increase settlement in the occupied territories and whets its appetite for establishing Greater Israel. This, in itself, is a blatant violation of the national rights of another people and the national sovereignty of our Palestinian State. We repeat our requests to the Soviet Union to reconsider this policy.[87]

But it was Skosyrev's article with its challenge to the PLO's right to represent the Palestinians, which drew the sharpest response from the PLO. Palestinian Ambassador 'Amr told an interviewer that the Skosyrev article had "embarrassed" him, and that he doubted whether such publications "could help ease the quest for a ME settlement."[88] Aside from the fact that the UN and "the whole world, except Israel" recognized the PLO, 'Amr said that there were no other groups or organizations that could represent the interests of the Palestinian people. 'Amr also denied that the article represented a change in Soviet policy toward the PLO. He claimed that at their Geneva meeting, in May, 'Arafat had presented Bessmertnykh with material that would help the Soviet Union "to speak on behalf of the Palestinians in discussing or solving certain issues." While he refused to elaborate "yet," 'Amr clearly sought to emphasize that the Soviet-PLO relationship was a close one, and that Moscow was actually willing to represent the interests of the PLO.

It was difficult to determine just how close the relationship actually was and to what extent the critical comments by Soviet analysts did indeed represent official Soviet thinking. Following 'Amr's claims, a senior Soviet Foreign Ministry source was quoted as denying that the 'Arafat-Bessmertnykh meeting had been anything but a symbolic gesture, presumably necessitated by Bessmertnykh's presence in the region. The Soviet foreign minister had made special efforts to meet with 'Arafat in Geneva, after it had not been possible to obtain a meeting in the region.[89] The TASS report on the meeting hardly indicated Soviet enthusiasm. Although 'Arafat was effusive about the "warm and positive as always" nature of the talks, which he claimed demonstrated the "strength of the tried and tested Soviet-Palestinian relations [sic]," Bessmertnykh's only comment was that the talks had focused on ways "to find the most productive means to ensure the national interests of the Palestinian people" at a time of "increasing opportunities." In contrast to 'Arafat's enthusiasm, Bessmertnykh offered only that the talks were "very much to the point and extremely useful."[90]

The Soviet foreign minister declined to meet with Palestinians from the territories during his brief stay in Israel, although it was not clear whether this was actually a matter of policy. The leading local Palestinian, Faysal al-Husayni, was in London at the time and, in fact, it was the Palestinians who hesitated to set up a meeting. They presumably first requested permission from Tunis, and only then decided to be fitted into Bessmertnykh's packed five-hour schedule in Israel, by which time it was too late. A subsequent comment by the Soviet Consul General in Israel, to the effect that Moscow had opened contacts with local Palestinians, suggested that the Soviets were interested in additional channels.[91] The PLO had, after some debate, approved of such contacts for the Americans (viz., the meetings Baker held with Faysal al-Husayni and a group of local Palestinians, both in Jerusalem and Washington), so, theoretically at least, similar channels should have been open to Moscow. It may have been of significance, despite PLO claims to the contrary,[92] that Bessmertnykh did not refer to the PLO as the "sole legitimate representative of the Palestinians" during his trip. On the eve of his departure, he said that the PLO was "an organization representing the interests of the Palestinian people" and therefore should play "its part in the process of seeking solutions to the Near East conflict, at the center of which lies the Palestinian problem."[93]

The issue of Palestinian representation at the planned peace conference was, in fact, a central topic of Bessmertnykh's tour. The Soviets consistently maintained that this was a matter to be worked out by the Palestinians themselves. However, repeated references to the three possibilities under consideration suggested that Moscow was once again urging the PLO to be flexible especially about demands for open or exclusive PLO participation. The idea of an independent delegation was one of the options presented by the Soviets, along with the idea of an all-Arab or joint Palestinian-Jordanian delegation. A report in Interfax, as well as informal comments in Moscow, indicated that a joint Jordanian-Palestinian delegation idea was the most likely option.[94]

The Jordanian-Palestinian option was not necessarily a Soviet idea. It was suggested by local Palestinians, as well as others, and deemed acceptable to the Israelis. Bessmertnykh included Jordan in his trip, and talks there were very warm. Consequently, it may also have been the case that Moscow was giving some thought to the "Jordanian option."[95] However, this was not the same idea as that of the Israeli Labor Party, for whom the Jordanian option meant returning (some of) the occupied territories to Jordan; nor was it the same as the "Jordan is Palestine" idea of the Israeli right. (Although, in a strange comment, Shishlin quoted an American source which had said during the war that if the king of Jordan "cared so much about the Palestinian question, it would be enough for King Husayn to resign and go away, leave the throne and that will be the Palestinian state, especially as a good half, if not more, of the population there are Palestinians.")[96] However, Bessmertnykh's agreement to a joint Palestinian-Jordanian delegation may have been an indication of growing Soviet support for the idea of a Jordanian-Palestinian federation. Primakov, who became the central figure in Soviet ME policy in the course of the Gulf crisis, was an Arabist who was rumored to prefer dealing with states and was particularly interested in Jordan. Although unwilling to give a specific answer on this matter, Primakov did tell an interviewer that, according to some Palestinians, so long as they had formal independence even "for half an hour" they might form a federation with Jordan.[97]

On this matter, as on virtually all specifics of an eventual settlement, the Soviets did not in fact express an opinion or advocate a particular position. While this was viewed by some as a lack of policy, Soviet officials preferred to define this as flexibility, by virtue of which any solution reached by the parties concerned to any question would be acceptable to Moscow. As we have seen, this even went so far as accepting the idea of an interim settlement, rather than a comprehensive agreement, which clearly accounted for Palestinian independence. Defending this position, *Pravda's* Pavel Demchenko explained that tactics changed according to changing conditions but "in fact, the tactics are aimed at the adoption of the shortest route to the achievement of strategic goals. Hence, there is no reason whatsoever to be afraid or to describe the changes in Soviet-Israeli relations or the approval of the solution of the ME question by stages, as Baker has proposed, as retreat or passiveness."[98] What was not said publicly, but was apparently the case, was that the Palestinians were going to have to be satisfied with Soviet and American guarantees that an interim settlement would eventually be followed by a permanent solution of the Palestinian question.

Demchenko's comments were made in response to what he himself described as concern and misunderstanding of the growing Soviet-American cooperation on the Arab-Israeli conflict, symbolized perhaps by the May meetings in Cairo between Baker and Bessmertnykh. The Palestinians were most concerned about the unity between the two superpowers' positions, proudly proclaimed by the Soviet officials. This unity not only signified the loss of the Soviet Union as a champion and powerful defender — and counterweight to America's support for Israel — but also the dominance of ideas and solutions produced in Washington. In this sense, 'Arafat's remark that the US was the only superpower left, was not only a sign of PLO dissatisfaction, but also acknowledgment of a new reality that was to have a good deal of significance for the Palestinians.

It was not a foregone conclusion that this new reality would be detrimental to Palestinian interests, depending upon exactly how these interests were defined. It could be that Soviet-American cooperation stood a better chance of producing some sort of settlement than the previous competition between the two powers. Consequently, the Palestinians might find themselves at least farther along the road to the resolution of their situation than they were previously. At the very least, the joint perception of both superpowers that the Arab-Israeli conflict had to be resolved and that the Palestinian issue was an integral, if not central, part of this conflict, promised to bring some progress. It is conceivable that, had it not been for 'Arafat's open support for Saddam and for Moscow's preoccupation with internal problems, the Soviets might have demanded something closer to the PLO demands, which were for an overall settlement providing for Palestinian statehood. Nevertheless, it seems likely that, in any case, the general policies, introduced by new thinking and favored by Gorbachev (as well as by the democratic forces in the USSR), would have brought Moscow closer to the more modest — and possibly more realistic — step-by-step approach of the Americans. One could certainly argue that this approach, advanced by Soviet-American efforts, had a better chance of moving Israel toward a settlement with the Palestinians than earlier maximalist positions. If this were indeed to prove to be the case, and Soviet-American guarantees materialized, Gorbachev's policies would prove to have been more promising for the Palestinians than they were inclined to believe at the time.

SOVIET-SYRIAN RELATIONS

There was much in the new Soviet policy to arouse Syrian concern and criticism, from the Soviet rapprochement with Israel and the emigration of Soviet Jews to the internal Soviet debate over arms sales. These came in addition to the many issues that had long been a source of disagreement between the two, such as Syria's presence in Lebanon, its quest for "strategic parity" with Israel, and control of the PLO. The primary Syrian concern was over what appeared to be Soviet disengagement from the Arab-Israeli conflict, that is, the increasing unwillingness, indeed, inability of the Soviets to provide Damascus with the kind of political and military support required for the pursuit of its strategy in the conflict. Moreover, the crumbling of the Soviet empire in Eastern Europe and the disintegration of the Soviet economy had done little to encourage Moscow's allies in Damascus, placing doubt not only on the Soviet will to stand by its clients but also on the continuation of trade and aid to which Syria had become accustomed from the Soviet bloc as a whole.

While many of the signs of a new Soviet attitude toward Syria did lead to a deterioration in Soviet-Syrian relations, they were not necessarily an indication of a willingness entirely to abandon the Soviet relationship with Damascus. Syria was still Moscow's only state ally in the context of the Arab-Israeli conflict and an important element in whatever negotiations or accord Moscow hoped to bring about. Moreover, there were strong forces in Moscow that wished to see the maintenance of Soviet military interests in the region in competition with the US there. Thus, despite the differences over arms supplies, the Soviets did continue deliveries, meeting many of Syria's requests, albeit at a diminishing rate, insisting upon cash payment. They maintained close political contact and sought to reassure the Syrians that Moscow would not neglect Syrian interests, particularly with regard to defense. Following a brief period, in 1989 and 1990, of criticism of Syria's presence in Lebanon, Moscow also supported the May 1991 Lebanese-Syrian agreement which virtually sealed Syrian influence over Lebanon. Yet this was a position which accorded with that of the US and, following the Ta'if Accord, most of the Western and Arab world.

Gorbachev clearly placed the continued relationship with Damascus on a new basis, virtually oblivious to Syria's complaints and dissatisfaction. Moreover, he appeared undaunted, possibly even satisfied that Asad responded to the difficulties with what appeared to be the beginning of a reorientation in Syrian foreign policy, particularly a warming of relations with the US. With the end of the zero-sum game approach, Gorbachev seemed to have little concern over such developments and even praised the Arab decisions that brought US-Syrian cooperation in the Gulf crisis.

The strengthening of conservative forces inside the USSR may have precipitated a slight alteration of this position. As the forces favoring greater Soviet concern for the maintenance of power and influence in the Arab world became stronger in Moscow, the Soviets sought to assure Damascus that their alliance with Syria and support for its positions remained unchanged. This was basically the message Bessmertnykh sought to convey to Asad in Damascus in May 1991, but it did not appear to be backed up by concrete deeds. The Soviets continued to press for payment of the c. $16.5bn. debt, initiating what appeared to be a cutback in arms deliveries. There continued to be serious difficulties in negotiating a new arms deal, the still elusive 1990–95 agreement. Moscow did agree to reduce the debt by $5bn., but it refused to offer new credits for arms, and it adhered to the principle, adopted two years earlier, of providing arms in keeping with the principle of "reasonable defensive sufficiency."[99] As a result, the $2bn. Syria received from Saudi Arabia during the Gulf crisis was used, apparently, for the purchase of missiles and tanks from North Korea, China and Czechoslovakia.[100] Moreover, Moscow exerted pressure on Syria with regard to negotiations with Israel. Following talks with Baker in Cairo, Bessmertnykh agreed to return to Damascus a second time during his May 1991 tour of the region, in an attempt to press Syria to reach a compromise with Israel regarding the opening of peace talks. Thus, the Soviets did not appear to have abandoned any of the positions that had been the source of some of the strain in their relationship with Damascus.

IMPACT ON THE SOVIET POSITION IN THE GULF

At the regional level, the Gulf crisis had a mixed impact on Soviet relations with the ME states and peoples. Support for the anti-Iraqi coalition brought Moscow dividends in the form of improved relations with Egypt (with whom relations had already been improving) and, far more significantly, the opening of diplomatic relations with Saudi Arabia. This had been sought for some time by Moscow, expected after the withdrawal from Afghanistan, and finally accorded by Riyadh as a token of appreciation for Soviet cooperation in the crisis. The Saudi move brought a boost to the Soviet standing in the Gulf region itself, including the opening of relations with Bahrain, and a $4bn. credit from the Kuwaiti Government, Saudi Arabia and the United Arab Emirates.[101] Political gains were also registered in Soviet-Iranian relations, as Moscow engaged Tehran in its peacemaking trips back and forth to the region. A degree of dissociation from the Americans during the war, as urged by conservatives in Moscow, was of particular importance for the benefits that accrued to the Soviets in their dealings with Iran. Following the war, the Soviets negotiated a deal to sell Soviet aircraft to Iran, apparently in addition to previously agreed arms deals. On the whole, the warming of Soviet-Iranian and Soviet relations with the other Gulf states was perceived in Moscow as a major achievement, with a good deal of potential for the sagging Soviet economy.

The Soviet military, however, was concerned over the possibility of an expanded, permanent American military presence in the Gulf as a result of the war. This, along with American arms sales to various ME states, was in fact the focus of many of their anti-American diatribes following the war. Acknowledgment of these concerns was apparent in Moscow's March proposals for post-Gulf War arrangements, which called for a reduction of the foreign military presence in the area to the 1 August levels, with security to be ensured by the regional actors themselves and the UN.[102] These proposals actually suggested the creation of a UN naval force (originally proposed by the Soviets in the Iraqi-Iranian War primarily to remove the expanded US naval presence at that time), as part of a regional security system. Such a system would convert the Gulf into a zone free of weapons of mass destruction; it would be accompanied by balanced cuts in supplies of weapons to the region, beginning with offensive weapons and especially missiles. How this would jibe with the Soviets arms sales to the Gulf states was not explained, except by comments in the military press that indirectly justified such deals by reference to new American arms sales to the region. Officially, the Soviets were willing to limit such supplies to conventional, defensive weapons only, based on the principle of "reasonable defensive sufficiency." This was unlikely to be unilateral, however. In the event of international agreement to such arms controls, Soviet compliance would most likely be dependent, as so many other features of new thinking, on the relative power of conservatives versus new thinkers, with the former reinforced by economic expediencies on this particular issue. For this reason, there seemed to be greater likelihood of progress in the area of nonconventional weapons supplies and technology transfer, including missiles, inasmuch as Soviet missile sales fell within the range permitted, for example, by the Missile Technology Control Regime (MTCR) accords with which Moscow had agreed to comply as of February 1990.

While Soviet relations with Iran and with the Arab states of the anti-Iraqi coalition improved with the Gulf crisis, Moscow's prestige in the region was not significantly enhanced. Although the Arab coalition states undoubtedly appreciated the Soviet cooperation that facilitated (some might say even enabled) the coalition to form and function, they were also aware of the clearly subordinate role and importance of the Soviet Union as a power able or willing to act on their behalf. The lessons already being learned prior to the crisis, with regard to the reduced value of Soviet support in view of Moscow's new policies and problems, was now more clearly driven home. While these states appeared to follow the American lead in overlooking the Gorbachev-Primakov lapses, the potentially problematic moves by Primakov, for example, did not have the desired effect on Iraq and the Arab states supporting it. It is possible that there was some gratitude to the Soviets for trying to prevent or limit hostilities, but reportedly there were also those in Iraq and elsewhere who dismissed these efforts as merely futile gestures designed to cover up or compensate for what was in fact Soviet cooperation with the anti-Iraqi coalition. At the very least, the failure of Primakov's efforts further demonstrated to these elements, as well as to those opposing Iraq, the relative unimportance and ineffectiveness of the Soviet Union in its present situation.

THE AFTERMATH OF THE ATTEMPTED COUP IN THE SOVIET UNION AND THE BREAKUP OF THE USSR

The abortive coup attempt of 19–21 August precipitated a virtual revolution. These factors were of particular importance: the defeat of the conservatives, particularly in Russia, and the accompanying demise of the Communist Party, apparat, and nomenclature; the dissolution of the KGB; and the massive restructuring and personnel changes in the military and interior ministry forces, parallel to personnel changes throughout the system; the strengthening of Russian nationalism as a dominant force accompanying the near eclipse of Gorbachev by the hero of the anticoup resistance, Boris Yeltsin, and the emergence of Russia (and Yeltsin) as equal with the central organs of power in authority and strength; and ultimately the breakup of the Union, with the declarations of independence of nearly all the 15 republics, the dissolution of the Congress of People's Deputies and reconstitution of the Supreme Soviet, and the attempt to forge a new system to be based on political, economic, military, and scientific accords. To these accords the republics (or states) might adhere, in whatever form they chose, creating certain all-Union bodies which would apparently be subjected to strong control and direction by the member republics.

The defeat of the conservatives cleared the way for new thinking to be fully implemented in all its aspects, regarding the ME as well as other issues. Theoretically, this meant unfettered pursuit of cooperation with the West, particularly the US, with an overriding interest in obtaining economic aid and economic ties, in exchange for a willingness to introduce the kinds of economic and military reforms demanded by the West, including massive cuts in defense spending. The first concrete signs of this cooperative approach were the agreements for a ban on Soviet and American arms supplies to Afghanistan and for the withdrawal of Soviet forces from Cuba. Personnel changes were expected to reflect this opportunity to implement fully the cooperative approach. Indeed, several important proponents of this approach, such as Shevardnadze and Yakovlev, now found their way back into Gorbachev's advisory bodies, their public authority enhanced by their active role in the resistance to the coup. In November, Shevardnadze returned to his former position as Soviet foreign minister, although by that time, it was unclear just how much authority any central office would have. In the interim, following the coup, Bessmertnykh had been replaced by Boris Pankin, promising continuation of the implementation of the policies that had been decided at higher levels. Pankin was as much a supporter of new thinking as his predecessor, but no more of an authoritative figure than Bessmertnykh. In fact, Pankin had far less experience or knowledge of ME affairs, and thus it was possible that he might rely more on the ministry's professionals, including Arabists, with regard to ME policy. Nevertheless, personnel changes were expected to weed conservatives out of the Foreign Ministry and the Defense Ministry. The appointment of Evgenii Primakov to head the new foreign intelligence agency greatly enhanced Primakov's influence. By virtue of Primakov's own expertise, it was likely that the ME would receive more than usual attention in intelligence. However, it was less certain to what extent the experienced Arabist would assume a dominant decision-making role regarding this region.

The decision on arms supplies to Afghanistan might serve as a model for relating to the Arab-Israeli conflict, in the future, or even the region as a whole, that is, cessation of arms supplies at the source. However, Gorbachev's postcoup policy called for even greater cooperation with the US than previously, and the US was pursuing an Arab-Israeli peace conference rather than an arms control or regional approach at the time. Consequently, the only change that might have been expected, at least with regard to the Arab-Israeli conflict, would have been immediate renewal of full diplomatic relations with Israel, without the preconditions set before the attempted coup.[103] However, Moscow was to maintain those conditions; Foreign Minister Pankin announced that relations would be fully renewed only on the eve of the conference. And indeed, they were only finally renewed, in October, when Pankin and Baker issued, in Israel, the formal invitations to the conference, just two weeks before its opening in Madrid.[104]

The continued influence of Primakov may have had an effect on the persistent, albeit short-lived, reluctance to renew relations with Israel immediately, despite the weakening, if not disappearance, of the conservative advocates of such a policy. However, this reluctance may also have been due to the second phenomenon which emerged from the events of August: the rise of Russian nationalism. Yeltsin's power was derived, to a large extent, from Russian nationalism, and there were strong Russian nationalists in his entourage. These nationalists were by no means necessarily anti-Semitic, but some of them clearly were, and some of them were also Arabists by training and profession. Having already opposed the rapprochement with Israel, and pressed for continued loyalty to the Arabs, these elements could have some influence on Yeltsin's own positions. With the breakup of the Soviet Union, the Russian Parliament became increasingly important, and this was known to contain people of conflicting views on ME issues. For example, discussion on resuming Russian diplomatic relations with Israel had been avoided by the Russian Supreme Soviet International Affairs Committee in the past, because of differences of opinion. To some degree, these differences were the result of concern over the Muslims of the Russian Republic, of whom there were close to 10m.

However, countervailing pressures were to be expected from foreign policy experts, such as Russian Foreign Minister Andrei Kosyrev, who was a staunch advocate of withdrawal from regional conflict, or even more influential Vladimir Lukin, head of the Russian Parliament's Committee on International Affairs, who visited Israel in early September. Indeed, Lukin and others in the Russian Parliament were apparently pressing for independent Russian relations with Israel even before the final collapse of the Union. While this did not come to fruition, partly because of Israel's own reluctance to take such a step while Gorbachev and the central government were still in power, it was apparently Russian pressure that led Moscow to demonstrate its good intentions in two significant ways. In November, Moscow cooperated with the US in bringing about the abrogation of the 1975 "Zionism is racism" resolution in the UN General Assembly. This move had been long demanded by Jerusalem and clearly opposed by the Palestinians and many Arab states. At approximately the same time, journalist Alexander Bovin was chosen to be Soviet ambassador to Israel; he presented his credentials in December 1991, as the first Russian ambassador to Israel. Bovin had been an outspoken advocate of renewing relations with Israel as an integral part of and sign of new thinking. As early as 1989 he had urged renewed relations with Israel, arguing that the continued absence of relations demonstrated a failure to apply new thinking to the ME. Even during the years when he had been a speech writer for Leonid Brezhnev and an adviser to Politburo member Yuri Andropov, Bovin had consistently exhibited candor, originality, independence and insight in his writings about the ME as well as other foreign policy issues. Moreover, his appointment clearly ignored the Foreign Ministry diplomatic establishment that was generally dominated by Arabists whose attitude toward Israel had been ambivalent at best.

There may also have been those among the Russian nationalists who supported further rapprochement with Israel as a symbol of new thinking, a rejection of past Communist policies, or out of an interest in the economic benefits to be derived from extensive relations with Israel. In connection with possible economic benefits, the new phenomenon of hundreds of thousands of their former countrymen now living in Israel was considered as an added potential for economic relations, and encouraged an interest in good official ties with Israel. Many Russians, as well as officials of other republics, viewed Israel not only as a potential partner for commercial relations, but as a stepping-stone to ventures with Western companies and Western investment.

Economic motivation also included the matter of arms sales, and in that connection, wealthy Arab states and Iran were economically more promising partners. Yet, if such an economic (or other) interest was permitted to affect political positions dictated by cooperation with the US, the broader, more important economic interests with the West might be negatively affected. Therefore, a key to the role of Russian nationalism, and the matter of arms sales, as well as to the Muslim factor, was going to be the relationship between the republics and the degree of their coordination within the structure replacing the former Union, in the areas of foreign policy and foreign trade.

The Commonwealth of Independent States (CIS), which replaced the USSR in December 1991, envisaged its 11 or 12 member states as full and equal members of the international community. They would, therefore, have the right to establish direct diplomatic, consular, trade and other relations with foreign countries; exchange representatives with them; conclude international treaties; and participate in the activity of international organizations. It was not clear as to whether there would be any limitations on these rights with regard to mutual interests, or the interests and commitments of the various member states. For example, some coordination of foreign policy was planned, but it was not clear how extensive or detailed this was to be, nor how it would be employed.

There were bound to be clashes of interests between the various member states, particularly as military and economic considerations overlapped onto foreign policy decisions. An important problem, which had already appeared, revolved around natural resources. Russian control over its reserves of oil and natural gas, control assumed by Russia (RSFSR) after the coup, gave the RSFSR jurisdiction over what had been the former Union's main export item and source of hard currency. The Russian republic produced over 90% of Soviet oil and 76% of its natural gas. By freeing Russian (or Uzbek or Kazakh) oil production from central Soviet control, and thereby permitting the conclusion of individual deals of the type negotiated by Chevron with the Kazakhstan, for example, production capacity could be improved and the structure of production and marketing as well as prices could be changed. A similar result might be expected in other industries such as fisheries and timber, particularly in Russia. Together with competition within and between the newly independent states, depending upon the degree to which the market system and privatization were introduced, these changes could be expected to have an effect on foreign business arrangements and possibly foreign affairs in general, in Russia as well as in the other republics.

There could be an effort to subject the military industries to central coordination or even controls, but like natural resources, the military industries were already being expropriated by the republics in which they were located. The autonomous regions and districts, in Russia for example, were also interested in sharing in, if not totally controlling, the profits from these industries. Regularization from a central coordinating body appeared to be only a distant goal. It was more likely that a good deal of competition would emerge between enterprises in different states and between states, which could affect foreign contracts, conditions and prices in the area of military deliveries — with potentially serious foreign policy ramifications, for the ME as well as elsewhere.

The military itself promised to be a far less significant arm of foreign policy than previously. It appeared that there would be only a limited, if any, joint force for all the states in the Commonwealth, while the Ukraine and other republics began to form their own armies. Thus, both the size of the emerging military forces, as well as the ability to deploy beyond state Commonwealth borders, would be greatly reduced by the reforms and constitutional changes being introduced. Not only would it be necessary to gain parliamentary approval for the deployment of troops outside state borders, it seemed likely that some Commonwealth force or command would even be required to negotiate with the local governments in the border areas, for example, in order to station or transport troops through their territory. At the same time, it was at least theoretically possible that states bordering on the ME, for example, Azerbaijan, might one day seek to use their own forces independently abroad.

The "Muslim factor" assumed a somewhat different meaning with the breakup of the Soviet Union. It became possible to conceive of a "Muslim" foreign policy, in other words, a policy by the Muslim republics oriented toward and possibly determined by interests in links with the Muslim countries of the ME and Asia. Even before the attempted coup, the five Central Asian republics had joined together in a mainly economic cooperative union. Their Central Asian identification seemed likely to guide them in matters of foreign policy as well, in pursuit of expansion of already established cultural and economic links with Muslim countries. Moreover, as they combat what may be perceived as Russian domination or influence, from the millions of Russians living in the Muslim republics (particularly Kazakhstan), as well as from the center, the identification with Islam could become stronger. With the exception of Khirghistan, the Muslim republics continued to be ruled by autocratic communists, and the unrest caused by this in the period after the attempted coup saw a rallying of religious as well as democratic forces against these Communist rulers. Many of the same communists had been espousing nationalism, as they had previously espoused communism, as an instrument of power.

However, as already pointed out, the Muslim factor was an extremely complicated one. Even if the Muslim republics were to progress beyond their preoccupation with domestic issues and internal problems, it was not certain that their foreign policy efforts would be directed any more toward the Arab or Islamic countries than, for example, Turkey, which was Muslim but secular, with a strong appeal for the mainly Turkic populations of Central Asia and Azerbaijan. With the exception of Tadzhikistan, Islamic fundamentalism might hold little attraction for the many ethnic groups concerned. Indeed, the predominance of Sunni Muslims in Central Asia, rather than Shi'ites, could limit the influence of Iran and its fundamentalism, while the Turkish origin of even some Soviet Shi'ites could have the same effect. Turkey, and even China (with its nearly 10m. Muslims in neighboring Sinkiang) might hold greater interest due to its ethnic ties.

Moreover, economic interests rather than nationalist or religious inclinations were already dictating many of the contacts between the Muslim republics and the outside world. Such contacts could be expected to include expansion of the already emerging commercial relations with non-Muslim countries, such as South Korea, Japan and even Israel. Israel was regarded not only as a stepping-stone to American business, but as a potentially useful partner for trade and cooperation in the areas of agricultural goods and technology, high-tech industry and diamonds. Azerbaijan had already concluded some contracts with Israel and discussed cooperation in nuclear research with Israel's Science Minister Yuval Ne'eman. The oil-rich but economically backward Kazakhstan might find it more beneficial to deal extensively with countries such as Japan and South Korea, rather than the spiritually closer countries of the ME. Indeed, republics such as Kazakhstan would now be free to develop thriving economic relations with Japan, unburdened by the political problems between Russia, the Soviet Union and Japan over the Kuriles. For example, the Japanese indicated that they were interested in making Kirghistan a model for economic relations with Japan.

While investment from Muslim countries might be preferred, for example in the banking sphere, these republics and their component parts might well look elsewhere when seeking technology and manufactured goods. It was, therefore, not a foregone conclusion that the Muslim republics would necessarily become allies of the Arab states and/or Iran, or even play an important, independent role in the region. Complex cultural, social, and economic factors, as well as the still undetermined domestic political arrangements, could produce foreign policies of a far more ambiguous nature.

If the ME interests of the Muslim republics remained unclear, those of the newly independent Ukraine and powerful Russian Republic were almost totally unformed. Their orientation and concentration would presumably be directed toward Europe and the US, while economic interests would direct some of their efforts to Asia as well. Natural markets for their goods might be found in the region, but the economic assistance and investment, as well as trade needed from Europe and the West in general, promised to tie these two states (and the Commonwealth as a whole) more closely to the European than the ME economies. Politically, it was clear that the interest and role of the former Soviet Union in the ME was marginal. Moscow had virtually ceased to be a player in the ME arena in any but a purely symbolic way. This was due to the fact that it had become indistinguishable from the US in its policies. Furthermore, even before the breakup of the Soviet Union, Moscow was weakened and had become preoccupied with internal problems. This was abundantly clear at the opening of the Arab-Israeli peace talks in Madrid in November, when Pankin, who was still Soviet foreign minister was virtually an addendum to the US, seeking and receiving almost no attention whatsoever. The US later granted Russia certain status, acknowledging it as the successor to the Union, and relating to it as if it still constituted a world power. However, Russia evinced little interest in the region. Thus, while traditional geopolitical interests of those states bordering on the ME would presumably remain in force, the ethnic, religious and also economic interests could lead in various directions. Regional stability, however, may well remain the preferred condition for the pursuit of these, as well as international and domestic interests, for the new states emerging from the former USSR.

NOTES

For the place and frequency of publications cited here, and for the full name of the publication, news agency, radio station or monitoring service where an abbreviation is used, please see "List of Sources." Only in the case of more than one publication bearing the same name is the place of publication noted here.

1. See, e.g., Foreign Ministry spokesman Churkin, *Sovetskaia Rossiya,* 13 December 1990.
2. R. Moscow, "Observers Roundtable," 2 September 1990.
3. See, e.g., *Pravda,* 25 August, 19 October; *Sovetskaia Rossiya,* 19 September 1990.
4. *Sovetskaia Rossiya,* 2 February 1991.
5. See, e.g., *Krasnaia Zvezda,,* 8 December; *Pravda,* 31 December; *Sovetskaia Rossiya,* 28 December 1990.
6. See *The Soviet Union and the Middle East,* XVI, 1, 1991, p. 22.
7. *Al-Sharq al-Awsat,* 19 August, 1990.
8. *Pravda's* ME specialist Yuri Glukhov, in *Pravda,* 18 September 1990, ridiculed linkage as "absurd logic." A domestic broadcast even termed "unconvincing" Saddam's anti-

imperialist "historical" explanation for his annexation of Kuwait; R. Moscow, 23 August 1990.
9. TASS, 6 September 1990.
10. *Pravda, Sovetskaia Rossiya,* 13 December 1990.
11. Text of statement and transcript of press conference, *WP,* 10 September 1990.
12. *Izvestiia,* 31 January 1991.
13. *Izvestiia, Pravda,* 19 January 1991, quoting TASS.
14. *Pravda,* 21 February 1991.
15. The two ministers were invited by the Soviet Chamber of Commerce and Industry.
16. *Izvestiia,* 1 October 1990. It was also agreed to launch regular official exchanges of Foreign Ministry experts. These exchanges had, in fact, begun with a trip to Moscow in September of high-level Israeli Foreign Ministry officials, to be followed by a Soviet delegation the following summer.
17. Israel opened a branch of its Chamber of Commerce in Moscow in November and, in the same month, an agreement was signed between the Soviet Academy of Sciences and the Israeli Ministry of Science; *Izvestiia, Komsomolskaia Pravda,* 23 November 1990.
18. Judith Perera, "Israel and the USSR-Reconciliation," *MEI,* 12 October 1990 said that Israel, the Soviet Union and the US were working on a joint project to refit Soviet Tu-204s and Il-96s with US Pratt and Whitney engines and with US and Israeli avionics for a US-Soviet commercial airliner to compete with the European Airbus. There were other rumors of a joint Soviet-Israeli aircraft venture dating from the days of Shimon Peres as finance minister; Finance Minister Moda'i later referred to this and a possible energy deal, as well as irrigation projects, following his talks with Gorbachev in September; *JP,* 17 September 1990.
19. *Ha'aretz,* 11 June 1991. The Soviet export figures of goods to Israel includes the shipments of belongings imported by the new emigrants.
20. *JP,* 23 May 1991.
21. R. Moscow, 22 February 1991 — DR:SU, 25 February 1991, also reported this phenomenon.
22. *JP,* 13 December 1990. It was suspended on 2 December for six months and, on 2 June, for one year; TASS, 4 June 1991. The passage of the Soviet law freeing emigration (thus relieving some of the pressures on Jews to accelerate their departure) together with reports of the difficulties faced by Soviet immigrants in Israel, led to a decline in the immigration anticipated by Jerusalem for the second half of 1991; *NYT,* 7 July 1991.
23. Leslie Susser, "Shamir's Soviet Card," *Jerusalem Report,* 7 March 1991, p.11.
24. Primakov was probably less influenced by the pressures of the conservatives than he was convinced that, because of his personal relationship with Saddam, he could be the person to bring about a solution to the crisis and an end to the war, in a way designed to please most, if not all, elements in Moscow (and possibly the Arab world) and at the same time, achieve Iraqi withdrawal from Kuwait.
25. TASS, 24 September 1990, 24 March 1991; *JP,* 17 March; *Izvestiia,* 27 May 1991. Many pointed to the large number of former Soviet citizens living in Israel as an additional reason for diplomatic relations. Shishlin argued for renewed diplomatic relations to serve Soviet economic interests in dealing with Israel; R. Moscow, 24 March — DR:SU, 25 March 1991. Shevardnadze told an interviewer he was "sorry" that he had not succeeded in having full diplomatic relations restored, commenting that "regrettably we are divided in our country on this score, as the world is," Interfax, 21 May 1991. Reporter Lev Aleinik defined Zionism as the "way of thinking and operating, directed at repatriation to Israel, the historic homeland of their [the Jews'] ancestors." Aleinik's article, a report on the Zionist conference in Moscow, went on to explain that "only recently the Zionist movement was ruthlessly persecuted in the USSR. Thousands of destinies were destroyed because of a desire to carry out their right, written in the International Declaration of Human Rights, the freedom to choose their place of residence."
26. They were not yet willing to support abrogation of the UN resolution branding Zionism as racism, although they said that they would not interfere in a US move to change the UN ruling.
27. Demchenko, R. Moscow (in Arabic), 1 May 1991.

28. *Pravda*, 12 May 1991. *Izvestiia* also reported that it was believed in the ME that Moscow's active participation in the peace process enhanced the chances of a settlement because of the Soviet Union's traditional ties with the Arab states; *Izvestiia*, 13 May 1991.
29. Moscow TV, first program, 18 May 1991 — DR:SU, 21 May 1991.
30. *NYT*, 13 September 1990.
31. *JP*, 17 March 1991.
32. Interview with *Berliner Zeitung*, reported by ADN, 13 May — DR:SU, 14 May 1991.
33. TASS, 12 May 1991.
34. *Neues Deutschland*, 29 April; ADN (interview to *Berliner Zeitung*), 13 May 1991. Bessmertnykh said the conferences should be under UN auspices with a very active role for Europe. However, references to the UN and Europe were generally absent from Soviet pronouncements.
35. Pavel Vasilyev, TASS, 16 May 1991.
36. *Neues Deutschland*, 29 April 1991. See also *Izvestiia*, 27 April, report on the Kislovodsk talks, and Foreign Ministry spokesman Churkin, TASS, 26 April 1991.
37. *La Repubblica*, 10 May — DR:SU, 14 May 1991.
38. Interview with *Verejnost*, 2 May 1991.
39. R. Moscow (in Arabic), 1 May — DR:SU, 3 May 1991.
40. TASS, 15 May 1991.
41. TASS, 11 May 1991.
42. E.g., *Izvestiia*, 16 May 1991. While there were numerous Soviet references in general to the need for regional security arrangements and arms limitation, Shevardnadze's security proposals were not formally raised nor mentioned during Bessmertnykh's trip to the region (see Soviet proposals for Gulf security, *Izvestiia*, 19 March 1991).
43. Skosyrev in *Izvestiia*, 16 May 1991.
44. *Krasnaia Zvezda*, 16 May 1991.
45. TASS, 15 May; Moscow TV, first program, 18 May 1991.
46. Bovin and Shishlin, R. Moscow, first program, 24 March — DR:SU, 25 March; Bovin, *Izvestiia*, 20 March 1991.
47. Vladimir Nosenko, "Ever Wiser Thanks to Saddam Hussein," *New Times*, 39, 1990, p.15.
48. Interfax, 17 May 1991.
49. *Al-Sharq al-Awsat*, 8 May 1991. A Soviet broadcast in Arabic said the visit had been historic for the normalization of Soviet-Israeli relations, but that such a normalization "cannot be at the expense of Soviet-Arab relations"; R. Peace and Progress (in Arabic), 13 May — DR:SU, 17 May 1991.
50. TASS, 9 October 1990.
51. E.g., *Izvestiia*, 3 October, 17 November 1990, 26 January 1991.
52. *Izvestiia*, 26 January; Israeli TV, 31 January 1991; *Krasnaia Zvezda*, 19 December 1990 and 24 January 1991 (Abu al-'Abbas and Habash, respectively, declared their willingness to hit US targets all over the world). *Krasnaia Zvezda* had covered, without comment, non-Soviet press reports of PLO intentions to aid Saddam through terrorism; *Krasnaia Zvezda*, 3, 27 October 1990.
53. Leonid Vasilyev, "What is Saddam Husayn Banking On?," *New Times*, 12–18 February 1991, p.14; R. Peace and Progress (in Hebrew), 27 August — DR:SU, 28 August; R. Moscow (in Arabic), 28 September — DR:SU, 1 October 1990.
54. *Izvestiia*, 1 January 1991.
55. *Sovetskaia Rossiya*, 13 December 1990.
56. Shevardnadze told a press conference that the Palestinian issue had been thoroughly discussed at the Helsinki summit and again in his talks with Baker in Moscow; TASS, 12 September 1990.
57. *Pravda*, 13 December 1990.
58. R. Moscow (in Arabic), 28 September — DR:SU, 1 October 1990.
59. E.g., journalist Karen Geivandov, after a trip to Tunis, spoke of radicals and moderates in the PLO, concluding that 'Arafat and the leadership sought a peaceful solution of the Gulf crisis; *Izvestiia*, 10 October 1990. See also *Sovetskaia Rossiya*, 14 November and *Pravda*, 28 August 1990 for favorable references to the PLO and Jordan's peaceful position, echoed by R. Moscow (in Arabic), 19 September 1990, in which commentator Vladimir Kavalev

said, "There is no doubt that the PLO is contributing its share in the search for a peaceful formula in the Gulf region"; DR:SU, 27 September 1990.

60. E.g., *Pravda*'s correspondent in Cairo Vladimir Beliakov in *Pravda*, 25 August and 19 October; *Krasnaia Zvezda*, 23 September; *Sovetskaia Rossiya*, 19 September; Alexei Vasiliev in *Pravda*, 23 August; Yuri Glukhov in *Pravda*, 18 September; A. Shal'nev in *Izvestiia*, 16 September; Karen Geivandov in *Izvestiia*, 17 August, 10 October; Albert Balebanov for TASS, 28 August 1990.
61. *Pravda*, 23 August 1990.
62. *Pravda*, 13 November; *Sovetskaia Rossiya*, 4 November 1990.
63. *Komsomolskaia Pravda*, 12 February; *Trud*, 6 February 1991.
64. *Pravda*, 13 December 1990.
65. Letter from the Palestinian Embassy to the Soviet radio, R. Peace and Progress, 26 September — DR:SU, 27 September 1990.
66. Dimitry Zgersky's interview with Nabil 'Amr, *New Times*, 38, 1990, pp. 6–7.
67. Reuters, 27 September 1990.
68. V. Kedrov, *Sovetskaia Rossiya*, 4 December 1990.
69. Reuters, 27 September 1990.
70. Men'shikov, *Sovetskaia Rossiya*, 26 December 1990.
71. Ibid.
72. *IHT*, 15 March 1991.
73. A comment by journalist Leonid Vasiliev in the democratically oriented new daily *Nezavismaia Gazeta*, 18 April 1991, attested to this when criticizing the US for abandoning the Kurds following the war, the author said, "The problem of the Kurds is, after all, far more serious than the Palestinian problem, of which the whole world is sick and tired. More serious because there are several times more Kurds than Palestinians and because they do not have their own state, although there is a very great and natural desire to create one."
74. *Izvestiia*, 4 March 1991.
75. *Pravda*, 15 March 1991.
76. *Izvestiia*, 20 March 1991.
77. Moscow TV, 23 March — DR:SU, 25 March 1991.
78. *Izvestiia*, 20 March 1991.
79. *Izvestiia*, 16 May 1991.
80. *Pravda*, 16 March 1991. In the same paper, journalist and ME specialist Yuri Glukhov defended 'Arafat and the PLO, admitting that their support for Saddam had been a miscalculation, but one that was understandable and probably inevitable, given the Palestinians' feelings of despair; *Pravda*, 8 March 1991.
81. *Sovetskaia Rossiya*, 19 March 1991.
82. R. Moscow (in Arabic), 1 May — DR:SU, 3 May 1991.
83. *Sawt al-Sha'b*, 2 June — DR, 3 June 1991.
84. Interfax, 27 May 1991.
85. R. Moscow (in Arabic), 21 June — DR:SU, 24 June 1991.
86. Interview reported on R. Moscow (in Arabic), 3 May — DR:SU, 6 May 1991.
87. VoP (Algiers), 2 June — DR, 3 June 1991, 'Arafat was careful not to criticize the Soviets (at least publicly) on this issue, limiting his criticism to American "insistence on continuing to send Jewish immigrants from Eastern Europe and Ethiopia"; *Sawt al-Sha'b*, 2 June — DR, 3 June 1991.
88. Interfax, 27 May 1991.
89. *Izvestiia*, 9 May 1991, said that none of Bessmertnykh's local hosts was willing to hold the meeting, and the PLO was not willing to have 'Arafat go to Jordan at that time.
90. TASS, 15 May 1991. At the close of his talks with King Husayn, Bessmertnykh was actually more forthcoming saying that the dialogue in Jordan had been useful from every point of view and had confirmed that the sides' positions coincided on the main issues under discussion.
91. VoI, 11 June 1991. Aleksei Chistyakov said "We have found that there is room and possibilities for cooperation between us and the Palestinians in the occupied territories. We have just started this cooperation now and we intend to pursue it."

92. Hawatima to *al-Sharq al-Awsat,* 3 April and R. Moscow (in Arabic), 21 June — DR:SU, 24 June; 'Arafat to *Sawt al-Sha'b,* 2 June — DR, 3 June 1991.
93. TASS, 8 May 1991. Foreign Ministry spokesman Vitali Churkin was more forthcoming, saying that the PLO would remain the Palestinians' legitimate representative and emphasizing that the Palestinians' interests were dear to the Soviet Union, which was bound to them by old and staunch relations, according to an interview with *al-Sharq al-Awsat,* 8 May 1991.
94. Interfax, 17 May 1991.
95. Bessmertnykh spoke of the "key role" to be played by Jordan in a settlement since it "occupies a particular place at the crossroads of interests of the various sides"; TASS, 9 May 1991.
96. R. Moscow, 1, 24 March — DR:SU, 25 March 1991.
97. *La Repubblica,* 10 May — DR:SU, 14 May; *Ruz al-Yusuf,* 16 June 1991, claimed that Abu Mazin had told the Soviets that the PLO was willing to agree to link the West Bank and Gaza with Jordan in a confederal or federal union. Other elements of the PLO's proposals, reportedly conveyed to the Soviets, were demilitarization of the territories for a limited period; postponement of resolution of the status of Jerusalem until the final stages of a settlement; and security assurances to Israel for the postsettlement period. There were disagreements within the PLO over the degree of cooperation with Jordan; this was apparently one of the disputed issues in the split which occurred in the DFLP, between 'Abd Rabbuh and Hawatima. Interview with Hawatima, *al-Sharq al-Awsat,* 3 April, and Zaki Shihab, *al-Sharq al-Awsat,* 5 April 1991.
98. R. Moscow (in Arabic), 1 May 1991.
99. *FT,* 20 November 1989.
100. From February through July 1991 there were repeated reports that a deal had been struck for anywhere between $2bn. and $8bn. The most frequently cited figure was $2bn., said to include the latest Soviet tanks, aircraft and air-defense systems, without indicating if the overall figure were for one year (a reversion to pre-1985 high levels of $2bn. a year average) or a five-year period as customary (which would be a severe reduction of even the 1985–89 $1bn. yearly average). With regard to the Czechoslovak-made tanks, President Vaclav Havel decided in the summer of 1991 to cancel the deal with Syria.
101. *Izvestiia,* 24 December 1990.
102. *Izvestiia,* 19 March 1991.
103. Direct flights, including for Jewish emigrants, were finally inaugurated in the fall of 1991, but this was actually agreed upon during an exchange of visits by delegations of the Transportation Ministries of the two countries just prior to and following the attempted coup.
104. Pankin's trip to Israel in October was of far less significance than the earlier one by Bessmertnykh, both because it no longer represented a precedent, and because the imminent collapse of the Soviet Union, combined with Pankin's own lack of stature, led to an almost total eclipse of the Soviet foreign minister by US Secretary of State Baker. Unlike his predecessor, Pankin met with the local Palestinians, who pressed him to resist the conditions being set by Jerusalem regarding the composition of the Palestinian delegation to the peace talks. At this point, however, Pankin had neither the power nor the authority, and possibly not even the inclination to deviate, in any way, from the position taken by Washington.

The Military Dimension of the Gulf War

YIGAL SHEFFY

On 2 August 1990, in the space of seven hours, the Iraqi army invaded and overran Kuwait, leaving the international community to face an unexpected *fait accompli.* The first international reaction was an effort to stop Iraq from further aggression, specifically against Saudi Arabia, a move which seemed highly probable at the time.[1] International efforts then focused on forcing the Iraqi army to withdraw from occupied Kuwait. The extensive diplomatic activity during this period, along with the formation of the US-led multinational military coalition and the massive buildup of forces in the Gulf between 2 August 1990 and 16 January 1991 — the date the crisis turned into a full-scale war — was dealt with in *MECS* 1990. In summary, the largest American and Allied military expedition since World War II, with contingents from 36 countries, had been built up in the Saudi desert and the Gulf waters under UN auspices, with the Security Council setting 15 January as the deadline for Iraq's withdrawal from Kuwait or risk the prospect of "all necessary means" being used to force it out. By the middle of January, the multinational coalition had grown into an army of 760,000 troops (532,000 American), 3,250 tanks, 1,820 combat aircraft and c. 300 men-of-war and auxiliary ships (see Table 1).[2]

As early as 8 August, six days after the invasion, President George Bush outlined US objectives and conditions for ending the crisis, which were to remain intact to the last day of hostilities:

(1) Immediate, complete and unconditional withdrawal of all Iraqi forces from Kuwait.
(2) Restoration of Kuwait's legitimate government.
(3) Security and stability of Saudi Arabia and the Persian Gulf.
(4) Safety and protection of the lives of American citizens abroad.[3]

Based on these goals, which complied fully with UN resolutions, US military objectives were then defined:

(1) Neutralization of the Iraqi national command authority's ability to direct military operations.
(2) Ejection of Iraqi forces from Kuwait and destruction of Iraq's offensive threat to the region, including the Republican Guard in the Kuwait Theater of Operations.
(3) Destruction of known nuclear, biological and chemical weapons production and delivery capabilities, to include Iraq's known ballistic missile program.
(4) Assistance in the restoration of the legitimate government of Kuwait.[4]

Although explicitly denied by Washington, the widely held assumption that the physical elimination of the Iraqi president was also a US objective could not be ruled

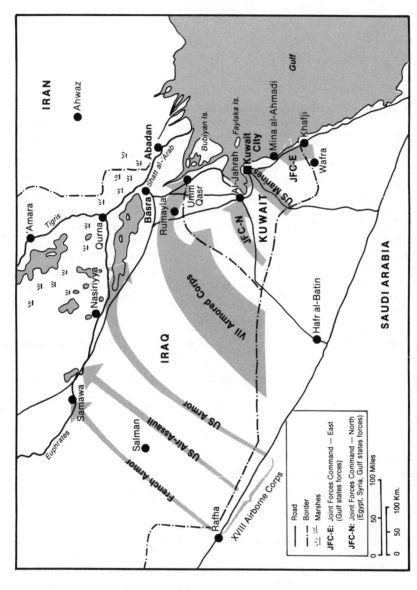

The Gulf War — Operation "Desert Saber"

out. Indeed, it was supported by such evidence as the bombing of the Iraqi presidential palace on the first night of the air attack, and the crash development and eventual launching, on the last day of war, of two "bunker-buster" bombs to destroy a bunker identified as Saddam Husayn's command post in al-Taji air base.[5] Another unofficial aim, this one barely concealed, was to keep Israel out of the conflict, for fear that any military involvement on its part would alienate the Arab members of the coalition and jeopardize its stability and even its legitimacy.

"WE WILL MAKE THEM SWIM IN THEIR BLOOD": IRAQ'S MISPERCEPTION

Analysts have pointed out that, both prior to the invasion and soon afterward, the Iraqi president, while partially aware of the risks of a full-scale war with a superpower, believed that events would not reach that stage.[6] Realizing that the international community was resolved to keep the Kuwaiti issue on its agenda, he rechanneled his efforts to creating a political atmosphere strong enough to stop the US from initiating armed retaliation, and emotional enough to discourage the Arab states from taking part in a coalition against him.

Judging from official Iraqi statements, Baghdad based this strategy on two foundations that it regarded as certain: the "ghost of Vietnam," and the Israeli connection. The former — presumably a deterrent to the US against waging a war that would result in heavy American casualties — was reflected in Saddam's blunt remark to US Ambassador April Glaspie just before the invasion: "Yours is a society which cannot accept 10,000 dead in one battle."[7] The latter involved closing Arab ranks behind a sister state and preventing foreign intervention in an "inter-Arab" issue by linking the Gulf crisis to the Arab-Israeli conflict, particularly the Palestinian question. Iraq probably reckoned that these trump cards would make the international community reluctant to use force and would lead to a diplomatic compromise, which would thus enable Baghdad to keep its prey without being forced into an armed conflict at all — a classic case of eating one's cake and having it too.[8]

Upon realizing that war was unavoidable after all, Baghdad "upgraded" these two trump cards, from mere threats and propaganda themes to actual cornerstones of its defense policy. The recent war with Iran convinced the Iraqi high command that strong linear infantry cum obstacle defense, secured by millions of mines and supported by massive artillery fire, would block the enemy's thrust and, even more significantly, cause heavy enemy casualties.[9] Hence, a fortified line built along Kuwait's eastern coast and its southern border with Saudi Arabia was to be the basis for the Iraqi strategy in the "mother of all battles": it would dictate the pace of the battle, wear down the attackers, take a heavy toll in their ranks, and force the coalition into a military deadlock. Extensive discussion in the American press on the estimated human toll of such a war, with as many as 20,000 casualties predicted,[10] might have helped reinforce this line of thought. "If the Americans are involved," Saddam Husayn assured his listeners, "you will see how we will make them swim in their blood."[11]

The second theme — an Iraqi offensive act against Israel — would, according to Iraq's calculations, provoke an Israeli counterstrike besides fulfilling Iraq's deep-rooted desire to settle the score for Israel's destruction of the Tammuz nuclear reactor in 1981 (see *MECS* 1980–81, pp. 182–213). This would evoke favorable public opinion and supportive mass demonstrations in the Arab states, putting pressure on the Arab coalition partners to abandon the battlefield. Iraqi Foreign Minister Tariq 'Aziz told US Secretary of State James Baker at their meeting on 9 January 1991: "Your Arab allies will desert you. They will not kill other Arabs. Your alliance will crumble and you will be lost in the desert."[12] This combination of inflicting insufferable casualties on the coalition, on the one hand, and weakening its political cohesiveness, on the other hand, underlay Iraq's strategy to force the US to compromise.

With a million soldiers, Iraq had the fourth largest armed force to implement its defense strategy. After eight years of war with Iran, many of its 66 divisions were considered combat-tested and capable of conducting successful multicorps defensive and offensive operations, with an advanced armor corps and artillery support.[13] Iraq had also demonstrated its absence of compunction about using chemical weapons and surface-to-surface missiles (SSMs). Its air defense was impressive, based on a modern and redundant early-warning system, 17,000 surface-to-air missiles and 10,000 antiaircraft guns, while the Iraqi air force and the army air arm supported military operations with 550–750 combat fixed-wing and 160 armed rotary-wing aircraft respectively.[14]

However, its numerical strength notwithstanding, the Iraqi army had basic faults, which had been exposed during the war with Iran: a rigid, overcentralized command-and-control system, which hampered fighting echelons from responding effectively to enemy moves or exploiting combat opportunities; a defensive approach in planning and in conducting operations; overextended and inflexible logistic support; inadequate technical and operational control of advanced weapons systems; vulnerability to air strikes; and ineffective intelligence.[15] The Iraqi air force also had several weaknesses, first and foremost the Iraqi regime's near obsession with preserving it intact as a strategic force. It also suffered from poor leadership, lack of initiative, unimaginative planning, insufficient aggressiveness and inability to provide adequate support to the ground forces. Moreover, only 175 of its aircraft were considered advanced.[16]

Judging from the Iraqi deployment, the high command prepared for attacks on the Kuwaiti front alone, and did not seriously consider the possibility of an enemy ground offensive against Iraqi territory. This Iraqi assessment, besides being based on pure military considerations, such as difficult trafficability in the western desert *vis-à-vis* the convenient roads and the short distances to Kuwait City and Basra from the east, was, however, rooted in misinterpretation of the coalition's main objective — liberating Kuwait. Apparently taking this objective literally, the Iraqis assumed that the coalition forces would not advance beyond the territory of Kuwait into Iraq. The Iraqi ground defense, therefore, was based on a forward line along the Kuwaiti-Saudi border manned by infantry troops of two army corps in the south and west, and a third army corps along the coast. The corps' armored reserves were deployed to the rear of the infantry divisions. A second echelon, consisting of an armored corps, was deployed further north, while several divisions of the elite Republican Guard Forces Corps (RGFC) were concentrated as theater reserve near the Iraqi-Kuwaiti border. Southeastern Kuwait became the center of the entire defense with the best regular troops on the forward front line dug in there. Altogether, the Iraqi order of battle in what the US Army defined as the "Kuwait Theater of Operations" (KTO) was 43 divisions including seven armored and four mechanized divisions.[17] Between 300,000 and 500,000 soldiers were concentrated there, equipped with 2,500 armored personnel carriers (APCs) and 3,500–4,000 of the 6,000 tanks that Iraq was believed to have.[18] Mired in Iraq's basic misconception, which was reinforced by the coalition's deceptiveness (see below), these forces anticipated an amphibious assault in tandem with a ground attack along the coastal road (see map on p. 64).

NO MORE VIETNAM: THE COALITION STRATEGY

Military commanders, who generally function under political constraints, can only envy the almost totally free hand given to US Chairman of the Joint Chiefs of Staff Gen. Colin Powell, and to the commander in chief of the US Central Command (Centcom) and the coalition forces, Gen. Norman Schwarzkopf.[19] Not only were they given a clear objective, which facilitated their mission, but they were not burdened by repeated political interference from Washington. Moreover, widespread popular support exempted them, almost to the end, from diplomatic pressure for an early cease-fire. At the same time, the Vietnam syndrome, which so influenced Saddam, had the opposite effect on the American high command: it was determined to strike suddenly, decisively and with sufficient force to end the war quickly and with minimum loss of life.[20]

The 15 January 1991 deadline set by UN Security Council Resolution No. 678, on 29 November 1990, after which "all necessary means to drive Iraq from Kuwait" could be used, allowed the coalition a sufficient period for military buildup so as to gain superiority over the Iraqi forces in Kuwait. However, from the US point of view, the longer this period was, the greater the risk of Saddam accomplishing what the American Administration, according to several sources, viewed as "a nightmare": complying with UN resolutions by effecting a minimal withdrawal, thereby putting the entire coalition military operation in question while keeping Iraq's offensive power intact.[21] In this context, indecisive views expressed by American politicians and the media seeking peaceful solutions probably bolstered Iraq's self-confidence and reinforced its resolve not to surrender an inch of Kuwait.

Having launched the air offensive, Gen. Powell, slightly oversimplifying, summarized the campaign strategy adopted by the coalition: "Our strategy for dealing with this army is very simple. First we're going to cut it off, and then we're going to kill it. It is sitting there waiting to be attacked, and attacked it will be."[22] The Centcom operational plan originated in the Air-Land Battle Doctrine, US Army's basic fighting credo, based on the concept of the inherently three-dimensional nature of modern warfare and the need for unified air, ground and sea operations throughout the theater.[23] Implementing the doctrine's basic tenets — initiative, agility, depth and synchronization — the Centcom plan was to neutralize Iraq's strong points, such as chemical-warfare capability, dense obstacles, heavy artillery support and large masses of troops, and exploit its above-mentioned weakness, while simultaneously maximizing the coalition's air superiority as well as superiority in technology, intelligence, maneuverability and firepower.

The war plan called for two phases: an air campaign, followed by a ground offensive. The air campaign was designed to prepare the battlefield for the ground offensive by maximal weakening of the forces defending Kuwait, while simultaneously paralyzing Iraq's strategic military capability. The ground offensive, conceptualized as early as October,[24] was designed to make maximum use of the armored, mechanized and heliborne troops to surprise and envelop the enemy. Mobile elements were to be transferred secretly from the Kuwaiti-Saudi border westward in order to launch a rapid deep major envelopment via the western desert. At the same time, a secondary offensive would penetrate the Iraqi defense line in southern Kuwait, resulting in annihilation or surrender of all forces in the KTO, including the RGFC formations south of Basra, once they were encircled. The element of surprise would be achieved by concealing the coalition's intentions and actions, preventing intelligence reaching the Iraqis and initiating deception that was aimed at reinforcing Iraqi's faulty assessment of the main coalition effort, ostensibly directed against Kuwait itself from the east and the south (see map on p. 78).[25]

LAST-MOMENT DIPLOMACY

Last-moment efforts were made to stop the wheels of war from rolling on. On 6 January, French President François Mitterrand, consistent with his previous political line, proposed a UN Security Council resolution linking an Iraqi pullout to the Arab-Israeli conflict.[26] This was opposed by the US, and on 9 January James Baker met with Tariq 'Aziz in Geneva, with a personal message from President Bush to the Iraqi president: immediate and unconditional withdrawal from Kuwait or facing the terrible consequences.[27] The meeting, described by Bush as "perhaps the final chance" to resolve the conflict peacefully, failed to achieve any agreement and ended in a deadlock.[28] On 13 January, UN Secretary-General Pérez de Cuellar met with the Iraqi president in Baghdad, offering to send a neutral peacekeeping force to Kuwait, if Saddam agreed to withdraw, an offer that remained unanswered. The day before, the US Congress had passed a resolution giving President Bush full authority to use the US armed forced to drive Iraq out of Kuwait, which elicited a vote by Iraq's National Assembly to go to war rather than bow to the UN demands. Another French peace initiative, on 14 January, calling for Iraq to withdraw with guarantees that it would not be attacked afterward, was summarily rejected by the US. The UN Secretary-General's final appeal to Baghdad "to turn the course of events away from catastrophe" was simply ignored.[29]

THE CURTAIN GOES UP: THE AIR CAMPAIGN

The air campaign, begun on the night of 16–17 January, was the coalition's principal military vehicle for the first 38 days of the operation. During the final four days, air power operated closely with fast-moving ground forces. A total of 112,000 combat missions were flown against Iraq by 1,370 American and 450 Allied fixed-wing combat aircraft involving all aspects of air warfare from offensive counterair to close air support and bombing and delivering 95,000 tons of munitions.[30] The air campaign was planned as a four-phase step-by-step operation: establishment of air superiority, strategic bombing, preparation of the battlefield and support for ground forces during the battle. Achieving immediate air-dominance, the 11-nation air armada could carry out the first three phases simultaneously. The air campaign was unified and well-orchestrated, launched from Saudi air bases in the south, Turkish airfields in the north (which coalition planes were permitted to use from 20 January), and six aircraft carriers in the southeast. About 40 different types of military aircraft took part in the campaign, from long-range B-52 bombers which took off from Europe, Diego Garcia Island in the Indian Ocean and directly from the US, to tactical A-64 *Apache* attack helicopters.

The air offensive was characterized by extensive utilization of modern technology. It marked the first combat appearance of advanced F-117 stealth fighters — 42 in all — which successfully exploited their low-observable technology and precision delivery capability against 40% of all strategic targets, although they flew only 2% of the total attack sorties.[31] It was also the first combat precision bombing of fixed sites and multiple targets by *Tomahawk* cruise missiles, launched from warships and nuclear submarines stationed in the Gulf, the Red Sea and the Mediterranean, as well as by cruise missiles (ALCMs) launched from B-52G bombers.[32] Additional innovations were the substantial utilization of precision guidance munitions against highly rated targets and highly defended installations with a near-100% hit rate; extensive air refueling, which granted operational range to tactical aircraft and enabled operational aircraft to fly strategic missions; wide utilization of advanced night-vision technology; and efficient use of airborne electronic warfare, control, guidance and intelligence systems.

The goal of establishing air superiority and suppressing the Iraqi air defense was necessary in order to implement strategic bombing and aerial ground preparation in the KTO. The first coalition sorties aimed at early-warning and aviation command and control installations, caught the Iraqis by surprise and guaranteed safe corridors for the attack aircraft which followed to strike airfields, air defense systems and strategic sites. However, the coalition euphoria, prompted by overoptimistic assessments of the first-night success, i.e., that the Iraqi air force had been completely wiped out, was quickly dispelled by subsequent reports that only 16 Iraqi planes had been destroyed and that Iraq's damaged runways were being repaired. Nevertheless, a state of paralysis did overtake Iraq's air defense, which facilitated repeated coalition attacks on air bases, the use of concrete-penetration bombs to damage aircraft hidden in special hardened shelters, and the destruction of command and control systems. From the start, the Iraqi air force was unable to coordinate any major air response and, besides sporadic efforts to interdict coalition aircraft, only once did Iraqi planes attack ground targets in Saudi territory, on 24 January, resulting in two Iraqi escorts being shot down by a Saudi pilot.[33] The coalition gained absolute air superiority in just one week,[34] prompting US Maj. Gen. Robert Johnston of Centcom to assure reporters at the beginning of February that "for all practical purposes, his [Saddam's] air force is no longer involved in the battle. It is totally ineffective".[35]

The Iraqi air force, in an admission of defeat, began smuggling its best aircraft to Iran on 25 January to save them from coalition bombing. Within the course of several days, 148 high-quality planes were taken out of the country, among them all 25 of Iraq's Sukhoi-24 all-weather night fighters.[36] There was no evidence of a preliminary understanding with Tehran, regarding these planes, as had been suspected at the time. Once the war was over, Iran was in no hurry to send them back, and even considered refitting them for its own needs.[37] It was estimated that nearly 270 Iraqi fixed-wing aircraft and 70 helicopters were destroyed, while the coalition lost 62 aircraft for all causes including accidents.[38]

Strategic bombing was directed at 12 sets of target in Iraq and Kuwait, ranging from leadership command facilities to military storage sites. By the end of January, 26 strategical command facilities were attacked, with 60% of them destroyed or heavily damaged, including the presidential palace, the Ministry of Defense, telephone switchboards and international, civilian and military communications centers. The aim of cutting off logistic support to the huge army in Kuwait involved numerous attacks on industrial and production facilities, storage sites, railroads and bridges. The 123 bridges that were destroyed or damaged included most of the 36 major bridges designated as vital for the Iraqi war effort, including all the Tigris river bridges in Baghdad.[39] By 30 January, the flow of supplies to Iraqi forces in the KTO was reduced by 90% to only 2,000 tons a day, and all communications from Basra southward were under constant attack.[40] Civilian infrastructure facilities raided from the air included all 25 electrical power sites, which were badly damaged, resulting in a drop of over 50% of the supply of electricity, while most oil refining and distribution sites were damaged or shut down.[41]

The Iraqi navy, although small, had 10 missile boats and several fast patrol boats and minelayers that were considered a threat to the coalition naval armada. These craft were attacked in their Umm Qasr base, and several of them, trying to leave the port, possibly to find sanctuary in Iran, were destroyed later outside the harbor. Coalition naval aircraft attacked the last boats in mid-February, thereby reinforcing the amphibian element of the deception by drawing Iraqi attention to the naval dimension of the war. The Iraqi navy practically ceased to exist at that point.[42]

Iraq's proven capability to deliver chemical agents by bombs and artillery shells, as well as the universal assessment that it possessed biological munitions and chemical warheads for its SSMs, were a source of grave concern for the coalition. This concern was heightened by reports of chemical ammunition being delivered to Iraqi forces in Kuwait at the end of 1990 and by Baghdad's open threats to use it against the coalition forces and against Israel (albeit only in a retaliation for attack by unconventional weapons on Iraq or Iraqi troops.)[43] Not surprisingly, Iraqi facilities for research, production, storage and delivery of mass destruction weapons headed the coalition target list. Aircraft and cruise missiles attacked 31 known nuclear, biological and chemical (NBC) sites and, according to Centcom spokesman, completely destroyed four nuclear-research laboratories in Tuwaytha and Taji, three biological and chemical production sites and 11 storages, and caused heavy damage to the two nuclear reactors, the Tammuz-2 and IRT 5000, in Tuwaytha.[44] However, announcements that Iraq's NBC capability was "almost destroyed"[45] were extremely overoptimistic. Intelligence on Iraq's NBC effort was grossly deficient and exposed only the tip of the iceberg. The immense progress Iraq had made in research and development of nuclear weapons, its stockpile of at least 64,000 chemical projectiles (including 30+ *Scud* SSM warheads) and its network of installations, many of them hitherto unknown and therefore left intact, were partially revealed only close to a year after the war, with the aid of Western intelligence agencies, four defecting Iraqi nuclear scientists and engineers and several UN inspection teams.[46]

The first few days of the air offensive sufficed to establish the superiority of precision-guided munitions over ordinary steel bombs for surgical strikes, prompting the coalition air force to make more use of them.[47] This also helped to reduce the extent of collateral damage and civilian casualties in attacks on strategic targets situated in populated areas. Nevertheless, the unrealistic US goal of a "sterile war" proved to be a contradiction in terms. Setting aside unconfirmed reports, or purely

Iraqi propaganda to the effect that there was extensive civilian damage (such as in the bombing of a biological-weapons plant in Baghdad on 21 January, portrayed by Iraq as an infants milk-powder factory),[48] there were more than just isolated confirmed cases of collateral damage, sometimes because a bomb missed the mark, at other times, ironically, because it precisely hit the target. From 2 February onward, casualties among Jordanian and Iraqi civilian truck drivers were reported on the Amman-Baghdad desert highway as a result of the coalition effort to destroy *Scud* missile vehicles on the road.[49] Mounting reports of civilian casualties elicited angry accusations by coalition spokesmen that the Iraqis were using schools, religious sites and residential areas to shield military installations.[50] The most serious incident was recorded on 13 February, when a laser-guided missile was fired by an F-117 at a bunker which had been identified as a military communications center, in the Baghdad suburb of Amiriyya. Hitting the bull's-eye, according to an Iraqi account, the missile killed and injured c. 300 civilians, who, unknown to coalition intelligence, had crowded into the bunker, seeking shelter during the air raids.[51] This tragic event, which clearly demonstrated the difficulties of acquiring pinpointed real-time intelligence, elicited a vociferous emotional reaction not only in the Arab countries, but in Europe and the US as well, particularly when the grim consequences were projected by CNN on television. Yet its actual effect on the ongoing air offensive was negligible, amounting to Washington becoming the ultimate clearing house for strategic targeting lists instead of Centcom in Riyadh — an exceptional step in a war distinguished by minimal political interference in operational decision-making.[52]

Air preparation of the battlefield prior to the ground offensive was aimed at reducing the fighting capability of the Iraqi forces in the KTO by half, demoralizing them, and depriving them of ongoing intelligence on the westward movement of the vast assault force. Special attention was paid to artillery positions on the front line, logistic depots and routes at the rear and RGFC formations, which were targeted for about 20% of the 35,000 sorties flown over the KTO during the preparatory phase alone.[53] Shortly before the commencement of the ground offensive ("G-Day"), intensified strikes were directed at the minefields protecting the defense line, using special fuel air explosives ("Daisy Cutter") that created shockwaves to detonate mines over a wide area.[54] The enormous destructive capability of the B-52s, focused on tactical targets, virtually obliterated whole sections of the front line.

By the end of five weeks of continuous aerial bombardment, Iraq's combat efficiency in the KTO was seriously reduced: entire formations became noneffective; command and control systems were disrupted and headquarters lost touch with subordinate units; heavily damaged transport, water and communications systems contributed to isolating the battlefield; and weapons, vehicles, ammunition, food, water and equipment, once destroyed, were not replaced. Most significant was the psychological effect on the stranded troops in Kuwait, who had no means to retaliate against the attacks. Their frustration and fear, exacerbated by psychological pressure through leaflets, broadcasts and, from 15 February, by repeated exposure of Saddam Husayn's acceptance of the demand to withdraw from Kuwait, broke their already reduced morale, as neither soldiers nor officers were prepared to be sacrificed for a lost cause.[55] When the coalition forces finally launched the ground offensive, they confronted an enemy which had lost its morale and its physical combat capability and was unable to maintain its defensive position, much less to initiate coordinated counterattacks.

The aerial offensive contributed considerably to accomplishing the coalition's war objectives: it seriously damaged the Iraqi leadership's capability to command and control its forces in the KTO; it destroyed major components of Iraq's conventional as well as unconventional offensive infrastructure; and it substantially reduced the Iraqi army's capability to carry out military operations. Above all, it broke the will of the Iraqi forces in Kuwait.[56] The combination of this collapse, on the one hand, and Baghdad's apparently belated fear of the approaching ground attack, on the other, led to the Iraqi decision to pull its forces out of the "19th District" — Kuwait — which was the coalition's primary objective. In order to achieve the remaining objectives, "Desert Saber," the code name for the ground offensive, was launched at dawn on 24 February.

KHAFJI AND *SCUD*S: THE IRAQI RESPONSE

Iraq's response to the air offensive was twofold: passive defense and active retaliation. Tanks and missile launchers were camouflaged, aircraft were dispersed and hidden in shelters and airfields, and command and control installations were repaired. At the same time, the Iraqis simulated damage to undamaged runways and buildings, while sophisticated decoys of aircraft and missile launchers, emitting the correct amount of radiation, were also used for deceiving the electronic sensor as well as the human eye. Although these measures did indeed divert a small proportion of coalition air sorties, improvised "seek and destroy" tactics subsequently limited their effect and forced the Iraqis to send their best planes to Iran.[57]

Besides scattered artillery shelling, Iraq initiated an offensive ground operation only once: an entire army corps of three to four armored and mechanized divisions was to temporarily or permanently occupy the Saudi coastal area around the small border town of Khafji, the only junction on the coastal road leading to Kuwait City. Coalition troops drawn into the area were to be hit by an armored force coming from the west, and cut off by troops landing from the sea. The attack by the first-wave division began on the night of 29–30 January, when three brigade-size prongs, strung out between the coast and Wafra, 65 miles to the west, crossed the border. After the penetration, the plan was for the western armored columns to turn east and link up with the eastern column that would advance parallel to the coast.[58] The strategic objective of this operation remained unclear. Possibly it was undertaken to show some military achievement for morale purposes, which might explain Iraq's premature bragging about a forthcoming military surprise on its part.[59] Operationally, the Iraqis might have been aiming at depriving the coalition of its assembly area for what they believed to be its main coalition attack. Or, they may have been trying to provoke the coalition to begin the anticipated ground assault, still convinced they could inflict heavy casualties on it.[60] Apart from an initial success by a battalion-size Iraqi combat group in occupying the deserted town of Khafji on the first night, all the other aspects of the plan failed. Detected while still forming up on the Iraqi side of the border, and surprised to encounter US forces so close to the border — which was part of the American tactical deception[61] — the Iraqis were pinned down by ground action and air strikes. The seaborne force, launched in 17 small boats, was also detected quickly, well offshore, and was destroyed by British and US naval air units. Every effort made by the Iraqis to reinforce their forward assault forces with additional armored and mechanized forces was disrupted the following day (30 January) by air raids, which destroyed as many as 80 tanks before they even crossed the border. During the night of 30–31 January, Saudi and Qatari forces, supported by US Marine ground and heliborne artillery, counterattacked at Khafji and regained the town, killing and imprisoning most of the Iraqi troops. No clearer evidence was required regarding Iraqi limitations in coordinating attacks and operating under round-the-clock aerial harassment.[62]

On 18 January, seven *Scud* SSMs launched from western Iraq landed in populated areas in Israel. By 26 February, between 86 and 92 missiles had been fired by Iraq, approximately half at Israel and the rest at Saudi Arabia, mainly Dhahran.[63] The US, dealing with probable Israeli retaliation, which, it believed, would threaten coalition harmony, acted to restrain Israel on three levels. Politically, American leaders put heavy pressure on Israeli decision-makers to refrain from a military response, speaking to their counterparts in Jerusalem daily.[64] Militarily and on the defensive-psychological level, the US sent four American-manned *Patriot* air defense missile batteries to Israel and assisted in activating an additional two Israeli-manned batteries. It also sent a special military mission to Tel Aviv and established a real-time early warning link with the Israel Defense Forces (IDF), based on Defense Support Program (DSP) satellites used to detect and locate missile launchings by means of heat sensors. This measure gave the Israeli air defense authorities two minutes initially, and later five to seven minutes, to sound air-raid sirens as well as alert the *Patriot* batteries.[65] Offensively, the US diverted air resources and special forces from the KTO to western Iraq to destroy the launchers and thwart the actual launching.

Long before the hostilities had begun, US planners had given the *Scud* launchers, estimated then to be located at 30 fixed sites and on 20 mobile vehicles,[66] high priority on the strategic target list. However, striking at the fixed platforms proved to be inadequate, inasmuch as the Iraqis mainly used mobile launchers, and estimates as to the quantity of the launchers proved to be pure guesswork. The launchers remained hidden by day, emerging at night to quickly execute the launchings from previously surveyed positions and then rushing back to their hiding places. Missiles were fired at Israel every one to three nights at a rate of one to four missiles per night, approximately half of them hitting populated areas. A similar number of missiles fired at Saudi Arabia caused almost no damage, since most of them fell in unpopulated open areas.

Coalition preventive operations focused on western Iraq, and involved such improvised tactics for combating the evasive launchers as daily air raids on probable hiding places and missile dumps and nightly air patrols by attack aircraft over roads and other suspected areas in order to destroy the mobile launchers after identifying movements and preparatory activity. The only two experimental E-8 *Jstars* surveillance and targeting aircraft in the theater, with radar systems that identified nighttime ground movement, were diverted from the KTO in order to assist in hunting the launchers. US and British special operation forces (SOF) also penetrated western Iraq in order to locate the launchers and destroy them directly or provide terminal guidance for precision-guided air munitions.[67]

However insensitive Gen. Schwarzkopf's statement was that he "would be more afraid standing in a lightning storm in southern Georgia than standing out in the streets of Riyadh when the *Scud*s are coming down,"[68] he was correct in dismissing the SSMs as "militarily insignificant to the ongoing war."[69] Overall, *Scud* attacks claimed the lives of 20 Israelis, of whom only two were killed directly, and the rest died of protection-equipment accidents;[70] one Saudi; and 29 US servicemen who perished when a missile scored a direct hit on their barracks in Dhahran, on 25 February. However, the commander in chief misjudged the effects of the missiles politically, psychologically and in terms of morale, with almost 12,000 Israeli apartments in hundreds of buildings destroyed or damaged. Of all Iraqi military activities from 16 January onward, none had such a powerful impact in the short run: Israel was afraid of a chemical-warheads attack, and, moreover, for the first time ever endured repeated attacks on civilian areas without retaliating (see chapter on Israel), while the US, endeavoring to restrain Israel, was still uncertain about Israel's reaction and how this might bear upon the war. The plentiful resources allocated to suppress the *Scud* threat, later estimated by the US air force as equivalent to a week's air activity,[71] clearly demonstrated the importance that the US Government attached to restraining Israel. According to Israeli sources, SOF operations in western Iraq were indeed planned and IDF pilots were positioned in their cockpits ready to take off and attack Iraqi targets, only to cut off their engines because of last-moment pressure from the US.[72] Washington did not deny reports that as the missile attacks dragged on, it considered consenting to an Israeli aerial strike to "let off steam," and even planned to open a corridor for Israeli planes by temporarily pulling out coalition aircraft from western Iraq airspace.[73] Despite Schwarzkopf's premature assurance that allied pilots "had destroyed a rather considerable percentage of the Iraqi mobile launchers"[74] no reliable estimate of destroyed launchers (nor, for that matter, of how many there were altogether) became available.[75] Further study would also be required to determine whether more extensive employment of larger SOF would have achieved better results. Nevertheless, it is clear that the coalition's efforts greatly restricted the Iraqi SSM units' freedom of action. Between 4–9 February, no *Scud* launching against Israel was detected, and from then until the cease-fire 18 days later, only 11 missiles were fired on five nights, while no fewer then 21 missiles hit Saudi Arabia at the same time.

In the long run, the *Scud* episode combined with the grim revelation of the dimensions of Iraq's NBC arsenal, may have influenced the US and other Western governments to take a firmer stand on the question of Third World countries seeking unconventional arms capability. In the Middle East, where this new dimension in warfare is considered primarily within the context of the Arab-Israeli conflict, it may well have effected changes in national perceptions of defense policy, deterrence, proliferation of unconventional weapons and arms control.

SURPRISE AND DECEPTION: THE KEY TO VICTORY

A cornerstone of the coalition strategy and operational planning was surprising the Iraqi leadership and its army. To achieve this, three related and coordinated deception operations were initiated. The first, during the early phases of the buildup, was aimed at deterring Iraq from attacking the coalition forces, which were then still weak, by projecting a picture of a strong and battle-ready army already deployed in Saudi Arabia.[76] The second operation aimed at concealing the starting date of hostilities, despite UN Resolution 678 which implicitly linked it with the 15 January deadline for Iraqi withdrawal. Statements by US military officials published in the press that troops would not be fully prepared to take the offensive until sometime in February reinforced this line, with or without intention.[77] Training flights similar to those planned for the first-wave air assault were carried out during the preceding weeks, so as to render Iraq's air defense accustomed, and thus oblivious to them on the night of the real attack. Indeed, on that night "they were seeing a situation that we had been showing them since August," said US Air Force Chief of Staff Gen. Merrill McPeak in an interview.[78] Taha Yasin Ramadan, Iraq's first deputy premier, admitted to Japan's ambassador to Baghdad that his government had been taken by surprise, which he ascribed to Iraq's assessment that the Soviet Union and China would not countenance a coalition attack without further deliberations in the UN Security Council.[79] Iraqis claimed that they were surprised because "officials had announced fighting would start later."[80]

The third and most important deception, which was integral to the ground offensive operational plan, had been conceived in mid-October and deemed crucial to the execution of the offensive. It aimed to convince the Iraqis that coalition efforts were focused on Kuwait alone. Kuwait, according to the deception story, would be attacked in a combined multipronged operation involving a large-scale amphibious Marine landing on the Kuwaiti coast and assault by two army corps on the fortified front line in the south, east of Hafr al-Batin — the dry ravine separating Kuwait from Iraq and Saudi Arabia.[81] The initial deployment of coalition forces along the Saudi-Kuwaiti border from August 1990 onward to block possible Iraqi movement southward, accompanied by ample press coverage, formed the basis for conveying the message across the border that all attention was turned toward the Kuwaiti border alone. This was later augmented by real and fictional moves, most prominently the deployment of all forces east of Hafr al-Batin, toward Kuwait. A large Marine force of four brigades was held on amphibious ships in the Gulf and in the northern Arabian Sea, engaged in several widely publicized amphibious exercises and naval commando raids along the Kuwaiti shore.[82]

Once hostilities began, the deception was given even greater credibility by actual combat operations mostly carried out for the sole purpose of reinforcing it: the Iraqi navy was attacked and destroyed; nine maritime oil rigs off Kuwait, held by the Iraqis, were attacked by aircraft and special forces; *Silkworm* shore-to-sea missile batteries were bombed; paths were cleared in the minefields protecting Kuwait's shore so that warships — including the spectacular 16-in. guns USS *Missouri* and *Wisconsin* — could approach and shell targets along the coast; and SOFs landed on the beach and carried out patrols, ambushes and raids. Bona fide press coverage, which was then strictly censored, played a key role in supporting the deception story by reporting extensively on amphibious training; referring to the parallels with the tradition of Normandy, Anzio, Okinawa and Inchon; and speculating about the impact of thousands of heliborne troops assaulting Kuwait City, and dozens of amphibious assault ships landing their troops ashore, on the outcome of the fighting.[83] Vast activity was also carried out near the western border of Kuwait to strengthen Iraq's faulty assessment that the Hafr al-Batin area was to be the extreme western flank of the main coalition offensive, and to provide a plausible explanation for the westward movement of troops should it be exposed by Iraqi intelligence.[84] Iraq indeed attached great importance to the area, and even launched several missiles against the "massed aggressors" there.[85]

The enormous movement westward began three weeks before "G-Day" and involved shifting 250,000 troops, 11,000 tracked vehicles and 53,000 wheeled vehicles a distance of 220–570 km. in complete radio silence without being detected by the Iraqis. Besides being a formidable logistic achievement (beyond the scope of this paper),[86] it was a tribute to coalition operational security and to its success in suppressing Iraqi air and field intelligence collection assets, principally by achieving air superiority. The press played a role in the deception by publishing both innocent and probably several "doctored" reports that downgraded the volume of the westward traffic while emphasizing the role of northbound convoys and the "aggressive patrolling which has been carried out into Iraq's frontline obstacle belt, designed to find the 'soft spots' in the line of defenses guarding southern Kuwait."[87] The air campaign reinforced the deception plan by focusing initially on strategic sites, on the isolation of Kuwait, and on the destruction of defenses in the east. Targets to the west had lower priority until the week before the ground offensive began.[88] Conflicting press reports about the date of the ground offensive probably contributed to the ambiguity as well.[89]

Iraq's basic perception of the coalition's operational plan was a heaven-sent opportunity for the deception-planners, who, in time-honored tradition, coordinated their scenario with the enemy's a priori convictions. The coalition planners were apparently well aware that the Iraqis had accepted the deception story, as they received information from deserters, visual intelligence and probably from signal intelligence as well. The Iraqi command, convinced that the main attack would be launched from the sea and the coastal region, devoted considerable resources and effort to securing and fortifying the coast and the southeastern region of Kuwait and massed six to seven divisions along the coastline in anticipation of an amphibious assault.[90] Shortly after the beginning of the air offensive, they spilled c. 11m. barrels of crude oil into the Gulf, probably to clog the suction filters of the Marine's landing craft or to deter the coalition from landing at all. The spill from five tankers and from the Sea Island oil terminal apparently started on 19 January and continued for eight days until it was stopped by accurate US bombing of the manifolds of the pipelines linking the oil fields to the offshore terminal. The oil slick caused an ecological disaster that endangered Gulf plant and bird life.[91]

Pinning down a considerable part of the Iraqi forces in a secondary sector of the theater of operations, for the duration of the campaign, contributed directly and substantially to the quick success of the ground offensive. The surprise element that had been achieved on "G-Day" certainly accelerated the weakening of morale and the combat efficiency of the Iraqi units that found themselves under unexpected attack by powerful forces emerging from an unanticipated direction. Yet even if the Iraqis had revealed the westward movement of the offensive forces prior to "G-Day" and grasped its implications, it is by no means certain that they could have utilized this intelligence to redeploy their forces, in view of the total superiority of the coalition air power.

FUTILE DIPLOMACY

On 11 February, with the air offensive over Iraq intensified in preparation for the land assault, Soviet envoy Evgenii Primakov visited Baghdad to pursue a Soviet initiative to end the war and persuade Iraq to withdraw from Kuwait. As a result of this visit, the Iraqi Revolutionary Command Council (RCC), which had apparently rejected an Iranian proposal for a cease-fire just a day previously,[92] tentatively agreed on 15 February to "deal with Security Council Resolution No. 660 of 1990 with the aim of reaching a...political solution including withdrawal," but under several conditions: an immediate cease-fire; the rescinding of all UN resolutions; an end to all sanctions; the withdrawal of all foreign troops from the region; Israel's withdrawal from the occupied territories; and an Iraqi role in the future government of Kuwait. In comparison with the tone thath Iraq used to present its conditions in its "initiative" of 12 August 1990, there was less stridency and an implicit unlinking of the Iraqi pullout and actual Israeli withdrawal, indicating, perhaps, that Saddam was finally contemplating evacuating Kuwait in order to frustrate the impending ground offensive and halt the war.[93] However, the US had not come that far, only to be stripped of the fruits of its victory by Saddam remaining in power and retaining a substantial part of his offensive potential intact. US President Bush, whether aware of the new nuance or not, promptly termed the Iraqi response a "cruel hoax" and made his most explicit call yet for the overthrow of the Iraqi leader, declaring that the Iraqi people and the military could end the war by "taking matters into their own hands to force Saddam Husayn, the dictator, to step aside."[94]

Iraqi Foreign Minister Tariq 'Aziz flew to Moscow on 17 February, probably to seek a quick and "honorable" way out. Soon afterward, Soviet President Gorbachev informed the US of a new Soviet peace proposal calling for an Iraqi withdrawal on the one hand and for allowing it to keep its sovereignty on the other, only to receive Bush's immediate response that the proposal "falls well short" of US demands for an unconditional Iraqi withdrawal from Kuwait.[95] On 21 February, Moscow announced that Iraq accepted the Soviet proposal and agreed to "a full and unconditional withdrawal" from Kuwait,[96] but the US responded on the following day that it had "serious concerns" about this proposal and set noon of 23 February — an intentionally unrealistic short timetable — for Iraq to begin a one-week-long total pullout, or face a ground offensive.[97] Realizing that nothing would stop the offensive, Iraq ignored the deadline and launched a scorched-earth policy by setting fire to 700 of Kuwait's 950 oil wells, thereby paving the way for the start of "Desert Saber."

THRUSTING THE SABER

The ground offensive began at dawn on 24 February with three separate thrusts involving a total of 14 divisions and 12 independent brigades.[98] It faced a demoralized Iraqi army, with most of its 43 KTO divisions disorganized and deflated by casualties and desertions.[99] To the east, a secondary effort involving three pincers — portrayed as the main offensive — attacked along the 190 km.-long Saudi-Kuwaiti border. Its mission was to pin down as many Iraqi formations as it could in Kuwait, keeping alive the impression that the main offensive was from the south and the east. The eastern prong of the secondary effort comprised the Joint Forces Command — East (JFC-E), an inter-Arab force of Saudi, Kuwaiti and Gulf states units, which was to engage and pin down Iraqi forces along the coast of Kuwait. Two US Marine divisions to the west were to advance toward Kuwait City, fixing enemy mobile forces in the east. On the western flank of this effort, Joint Forces Command - North (JFC-N), consisting of two armored/mechanized Egyptian divisions and a Syrian division at the rear,

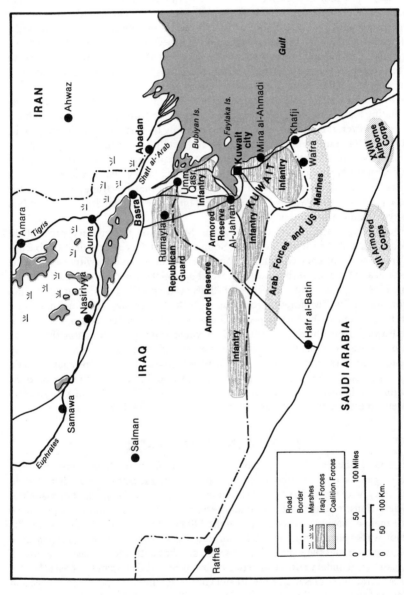

The Gulf War — Disposition of Forces on the Eve of the War

were to attack and pin down mobile forces in southwest Kuwait. Assigning the Arab forces to the liberation of Kuwait only, freed the coalition's ME partners from the political embarrassment of violating Iraqi territory, while militarily keeping the agile formations in the main effort homogeneous, sparing them cumbersome coordination.

To flash out the desired picture, a special deception unit which was attached to JFC-E simulated an additional army corps in the eastern sector by means of electromagnetic and communications emissions. Moreover, the Marines, deployed near the coast before moving westward, left behind deception teams to give the impression that they were still there. Several demonstrations by naval and Marine units off al-Shu'ayba area and off Bubiyan and Faylaka Islands, and the fact that the eastern force was the first to engage the enemy on "G-Day," long before the Iraqis even identified the movements of the main force, also helped to maintain the deception and keep Iraqi forces pinned down.[100] Supported by massive air, naval and ground artillery, the Marines broke through the obstacle belt along the border, overpowered uncoordinated resistance and easily defeated a lone armored counterattack. The Marines' unexpected rapid advance facilitated the Egyptian thrust, which was directed at Kuwait City and which was to cut off the two Iraqis army corps defending southeast Kuwait from the army strategic reserve to the north. The Egyptians penetrated the forward defense line toward evening, but, fearing an Iraqi counterattack, stopped for the night.[101] The Syrian division did not join the operation, since Damascus banned it from participating in offensive operations. On the coastal sector, Saudi units crossed the border and fighting advanced northward.[102] Reinforcing Iraq's erroneous perception, Centcom reserve division was assigned to continue feinting in the Hafr al-Batin area east of the main arena of operations.

To the west, the US Seventh Armored Corps of three divisions along with a British division involving a total of 1,300 tanks, heading toward the Saudi-Iraqi border, launched its main attack. The Corps aimed to maneuver around the western Iraqi flank by advancing northward and then turning east, making a wide hook in the direction of Basra in order to achieve its objective: destroying the main Iraqi armored forces of six divisions, including RGFC, positioned in northern Kuwait and southern Iraq. Rapid successes along the forward line, combined with intensive air and artillery preparatory bombardment, that eliminated all effective resistance by the Iraqi infantry forces defending the front line, enabled the main attack to begin earlier than planned. By nightfall, the obstacle belt had been relatively easily penetrated and three armored divisions crossed over into Iraqi territory, destroying Iraqi infantry and armored units along the way.

In the far west, a flank-protecting secondary effort was begun by the Eighteenth Airborne Corps, which consisted of two airborne/air assault US divisions, one mechanized division, a French light-armored division and a British tank brigade. This corps was to move north rapidly toward the Euphrates River valley in western Iraq and isolate the Iraqi forces in the KTO by cutting off the roads leading northward near Nasiriyya, 300 km. within Iraqi territory, as well as assist eventually in the destruction of the RGFC. The light, mobile corps advanced much faster then anticipated, maximizing its maneuverability and firepower, without encountering much opposition. An airborne division was brought in by 400 helicopters to establish a bridgehead at the north of the desert, while other air-lifted forces erected a forward logistic area 80 km. inside Iraq, that enabled armored formations, which reached it during the following days, to resupply and move on rapidly.

The general advance continued the second day, again leaving behind the simulated combat activity on the coast and the feints around Hafr al-Batin to contribute to the Iraqi turmoil and confusion. Iraq's RCC and GHQ, realizing that saving the army was preferable to sacrificing it, yet apparently still not fully aware of the true state of their forces, had issued orders during the day for an organized withdrawal of the Iraqi army from Kuwait.[103] The unrelenting coalition pressure, however, turned the retreat into a rout. In the desert, the main armored force continued to penetrate deep into the northeast uninterruptedly, while the Iraqi forces in that sector were still focused on Hafr al-Batin, where the US and British forces were fighting on its west bank. On the western flank, an airborne brigade was flown into Nasiriyya valley to cut off the highway to Baghdad, while the rest of the Eighteenth Corps units rushed forward ahead of the original timetable.

The three days that followed witnessed the final disintegration of the Iraqi army in Kuwait. On 26 February, the Marine divisions surrounded Kuwait City, waiting for the coalition Arab forces, which lagged behind to enter the capital and liberate it officially. The next day, after one of the Marine divisions completely annihilated an Iraqi armored division in the vicinity of the town, the resulting clear avenue of approach enabled a Kuwaiti brigade to lead a victorious coalition into the city. A second Marine division reached the two major roads from Kuwait to Basra north of the city, crowded with thousands of vehicles trying to escape, and tightened their hold on the newly formed Kuwaiti pocket, while constant air attacks turned the main north-south highway into what became known as the "highway of death." In the Samawa zone further west, airborne and ground troops of the Eighteenth Airborne Corps reached the road network connecting south and central Iraq, and on 26 February took control of the Basra-Baghdad highway, cutting off the main escape route northward. The Seventh Corps continued its advance deep into Iraq and, after attacking rear armored and mechanized units, turned right and headed east along the Kuwaiti-Iraqi border, encountering and destroying units of the Republican Guard.

That same day, in another last-moment effort to save the army, Saddam Husayn personally announced his decision to withdraw from Kuwait, with his spokesmen supplying the interpretation that this was an unconditional acceptance of the original UN Resolution 660 of 2 August.[104] US Ambassador to the UN Thomas Pickering, anticipating an imminent military victory, persuaded his Soviet colleague that no special Security Council session was needed following this announcement.[105] The following dawn, on 27 February, three-and-a-half US armored and mechanized divisions of the Seventh Corps attacked an equal number of Iraqi armored divisions, mostly of the RGFC. Bad weather prevented the Iraqis from detecting the approaching American tanks, which, due to their sophisticated technological capacity for positioning, target acquisition and fire control, were able to strike well behind the effective range of the Iraqi guns. Two US divisions destroyed c. 600 armored vehicles and struck thousands of enemy troops with US casualties amounting to only several soldiers and armored vehicles. Another RGFC armored division from Basra which counterattacked units of the advancing Eighteen Corps in the Nasiriyya area was put out of action. Medina RGFC armored division tried to ambush American tank columns near Safwan the next morning, in what became the largest tank battle of the war — "The Battle of Medina Ridge." Superior performance by US M-1A1 tanks and crews alike resulted in the destruction of 100 Iraqi T-72 tanks and 30 BMP APCs in the space of 45 minutes.[106]

The Iraqi army in the KTO had collapsed completely with all surviving units in retreat, saved from total annihilation by an unexpected cease-fire declared by the US president, which was to take effect at midnight, 27–28 February (28 February, 7 a.m. local time), 100 hours after the ground offensive had begun and 44 hours before it was scheduled to end.[107] The reasons for this decision — which may well have saved Saddam's regime — have not been given officially, although several possible explanations emerged, none of them militarily persuasive: an overestimation of Iraqi losses and an inflated battle damage assessment; the desire to end the campaign with a minimal number of American casualties; mounting pressure by coalition Arab participants especially Egypt; and the impact of the aerial photographs showing what appeared to be carnage along the "highway of death."[108] Yet, the political echelon was not solely responsible for the decision. Despite Gen. Schwarzkopf's optimistic conclusion that "the gate is closed" and that southern Iraq was hermetically sealed,[109] it turned out that gaps in the ground cordon, along with weather constraints that hampered air activity north of the Euphrates River, facilitated the retreat of entire Iraqi regular and elite units, which soon took part in suppressing the rebellion in southern Iraq against the Ba'thi regime (see chapter on Iraq).[110]

On 3 March, military talks between coalition and Iraqi officers were begun in Safwan to conclude the cease-fire arrangements and the second Gulf War came to an end.

CONCLUSIONS

During the 43 days war, the coalition forces liberated Kuwait, occupied about 20% of Iraq's territory, put 29 of the 43 divisions in the KTO out of action, killed an unknown number of Iraqi soldiers,[111] and destroyed or damaged an estimated 3,800 tanks, 1,400 APCs and 2,900 artillery guns.[112] The US-led coalition achieved most of its official military and political objectives, with minimal casualties of 478 dead from all causes,[113] and negligible material losses. In the short run, the extensive damage to the Iraqi war machine, combined with instilling the evil image of Saddam Husayn and the Ba'th regime in the collective consciousness of the international community, ended the Iraqi threat to the Gulf and ME states. It was assumed that as long as Saddam remained in power, any sign of aggression on his part against another sovereign state, would be met with some sort of international or multinational counteraction. However, the coalition stopped short of eliminating two important elements of Iraq's strategic offensive capability, which, although considerably weakened, still posed a potential threat in the long run. The elite Republican Guard Forces, as well as other first-line regular formations, remained as a potential nucleus for a new army; and, even more significantly, Iraq's mass-destruction capability was far from eliminated. As a result of Iraq's extensive efforts to conceal this capability and the failure of all the intelligence services to uncover it, the full range of Iraq's potential in this area remained unknown, while its scientific and technological knowledge was intact. Even the UN inspection teams operating inside Iraq from March 1991 found it difficult to shed light on this subject.[114]

The moment the US Government resolved to adopt all the necessary means to achieve its objectives, the military outcome of the war had been determined, even though this was not clear at the time. "Considering the advantages possessed by Schwarzkopf's force," one commentator wrote, "it would have been amazing had the outcome not been what it was."[115] In addition to favorable political circumstances, such as the international isolation of Iraq, the marginal role of the USSR, and worldwide support for the US policy, without which the military challenge would have been much more difficult, the following factors proved to be integral in the military triumph achieved by the coalition:

(1) Political freedom of action, with minimal interference by the political echelon in military affairs, enabled the Pentagon and Centcom to plan and act according to operational dictates only. Gen. Schwarzkopf's assertion that he "feels no hot breath down his neck"[116] was proven when, because of operational requirements, and despite political judgment to the reverse, he prolonged the war by continuing the air offensive beyond the original timetable before commencing the ground assault. The one time that a political decision interfered with military operations, imposing the cease-fire prematurely, it prevented the completion of the military mission. In contrast with the coalition's flexibility, the Iraqi field forces' operational decisions were highly restricted by constant interference from the political leadership and the military high command, and the field commanders, therefore, had difficulty in responding to changing battlefield situations in time.

(2) There was a successful adjustment to the coalition-type war. Potential time bombs in the form of conflicting national political interests, which frequently undermine coalition forces, were defused by the a priori definition of limited, specific and internationally accepted war objectives, by achieving harmony between political objectives and military implementation and by establishing a unified command. The US military leadership was sensitive to potential nationally inspired discords and nipped them in the bud, e.g., by assigning the Arab forces to the Kuwaiti front only, or regrouping the British units before the start of "Desert Saber" and giving them a special sector under their own command.[117]

(3) The coalition forces had absolute technological superiority in all systems in every field. This superiority is attributable to main weapons systems such as the F-117 stealth fighter, the A-64 *Apache* attack helicopter, sea- and air-launched cruise missiles and the M-1A1 tank; to advance capability in passive and active electronic warfare; to precision-guided and stand-off munitions; to aerial, naval and ground systems for combat management, target acquisition and fire control; and to satellites for communications, intelligence, navigation and positioning. The Iraqi army did not fully understand the meaning and implications of a modern technological war, let alone approach the coalition's capability.

(4) A suitable combat doctrine was drawn up. The Gulf War could be considered as a textbook implementation of the US AirLand doctrine. The unified command of all arms and all contingents facilitated operational flexibility, such as advancing the timetable for all forces as a result of the unexpectedly rapid success of one segment. Decentralized control encouraged commanders to act on their own initiative in dealing with changing situations. Thorough preparation of the battlefield successfully reduced the combat efficiency of the enemy. Nonlinear air and ground battles in the entire battlefield were carried out in simultaneous close, deep and rear operations.

Offensiveness, maneuverability, speed and ground and vertical indirect approach were the ground rules, with strategic, operational and tactical deception integrated into operational planning. Iraq, on the other hand, prepared its forces for a different kind of warfare: a static war of attrition dominated by obstacles and artillery against an Iran-like enemy whose air power was practically nil.[118] In a nutshell, the Iraqi army could not match the AirLand approach, which completely unbalanced it.

(5) The coalition had better intelligence. In fact, US Intelligence failed on several levels. Strategically, it failed to anticipate the invasion of Kuwait and it underestimated the progress of Iraq's nuclear program.[119] Operationally, it had great difficulty in assessing the damage caused by aerial bombing, causing uncertainty about the combat effectiveness of Iraqi units in the KTO. This probably led to the postponement of the ground attack until intelligence was convinced that the frontline formations had been reduced to only 50% of their effectiveness. At the same time, it tended to overestimate the total damage done to the Iraqi armed forces and to its defense network.[120] Tactically, it failed to locate the *Scud* mobile launchers. Nevertheless, it is clear that in the intelligence war between the two adversaries — a crucial variable in this campaign — the coalition clearly had the upper hand. Iraq remained totally ignorant of the coalition's real intentions, and was taken in by the deception schemes. In addition, satellites and aerial intelligence systems provided the coalition troops with tactical intelligence, partially on a real-time basis, day and night, with an emphasis on target acquisition for air and ground weapons systems. While some criticism was directed at the imperfect functioning of the tactical intelligence system, mostly in relation to an inadequate dissemination process and a slow time factor,[121] the total asymmetry between the belligerents prevented this shortcoming from seriously affecting the final outcome.

The second Gulf War ended in a military triumph for the coalition but left the implicit American political goal unfulfilled: Saddam Husayn remained in power. Whether this triumph would turn into complete victory was yet to be seen.

TABLE 1: COALITION FORCES

Country	Indirect Support[a]	Ground Forces	Troops	Tanks	Aircraft	Helicopters	Ships
Afghanistan							
Argentina			300				2
Australia			450		2(NC)	2	3
Bahrain[b]						2-4	
Bangladesh		1 infantry brigade	3,500	24[c]			
Belgium	{ financial, 1 fighter squadron to Turkey	1 infantry brigade	2,000		4(NC)		4
Canada			1,700		30	5	3
Czechoslovakia	{ medical team, NBC defense team						
Denmark	financial						1
Egypt		{ 1 armored division, 1 mechanized division, 1 SF regiment	40,000	358			
France		1 armored division	20,000	110	60	130	
Germany	{ financial, 1 fighter squadron + air defense to Turkey[e]						18/7[d]
Greece	medical team						1
Hungary	medical team						
Honduras			(150)[e]				
Italy	{ 1 fighter squadron to Turkey				8		8
Kuwait		{ 2 infantry brigades, 1 mechanized brigade	7,000	30	35		2

Country	Indirect Support[a]	Ground Forces	Troops	Tanks	Aircraft	Helicopters	Ships
Morocco		1 infantry battalion	2,000				2
Netherlands	financial; 1 fighter squadron to Turkey[e]						
New Zealand						2(NC)	
Niger		1 infantry battalion	480				
Norway							2
Oman[b]		1 infantry brigade	2,500	25			12
Pakistan		1 armored brigade / 1 infantry battalion	10,000		50[c]		
Poland	medical team						
Portugal							2
Qatar[b]		1 mechanized battalion	?	24	19[c]		1
Republic of Korea	financial / medical team						9
Saudi Arabia[b]	financial	4 mechanized brigades / 1 armored brigade / various units	60,600	267	216[c]		15
Senegal	medical team						
Sierra Leone		1 infantry battalion	500				
Singapore	medical team						
Spain	financial				4(NC)		3
Sweden	medical team						
Syria		1 armored division / 1 SF regiment	14,300	250?			
Turkey	financial		(120,000)[f]				
UAE[b]		1 mechanized brigade	4,000	14	50–78[c]		2

Country	Indirect Support[a]	Ground Forces	Troops	Tanks	Aircraft	Helicopters	Ships
UK		1 armored division	45,000	180	118	83–105	22
USA		2 airborne divisions 3 mechanized divisions 2 armored divisions 2 Marine divisions 2 armored regiments 1 SF group	532,000	2,070	1,376 +500(NC)	1,900[g]	180

SOURCES:

Norman Friedman, *Desert Victory: The War for Kuwait* (Annapolis: Naval Institute Press, 1991); US Department of Defense, *Conduct of the Persian Gulf Conflict: An Interim Report to Congress* (Washington, DC: July 1991), Appendix A; Bruce Watson et al., *Military Lessons of the Gulf War* (London: Greenhill Books, 1991); House of Commons, Defence Committee, *Preliminary Lessons of Operation "Granby": Tenth Report* (London: HMSO, July 1991).

NOTES

NC — noncombatant
SF — special forces
a — Finland, Japan and Luxembourg also assisted with financial contributions.
b — All the armed forces of these were put under coalition command. This figure represents the ground forces that took part in the offensive.
c — Figure representing the total strength of the air force. There is no information as to how many aircraft actually participated.
d — Located in the eastern Mediterranean, for defense only.
e — Offered but not accepted.
f — Troops deployed on the Iraqi border with a defense commitment only. US squadrons were also stationed at Incirlik.
g — Approximate figures.

NOTES

For the place and frequency of publications cited here, and for the full name of the publication, news agency, radio station or monitoring service where an abbreviation is used, please see "List of Sources." Only in the case of more than one publication bearing the same name is the place of publication noted here.

1. US Department of Defense, *Conduct of the Persian Gulf Conflict: An Interim Report to Congress* (Washington, DC: July 1991, hereafter: *Interim Report*), Appendix A, p. A-1; Bruce Watson et al., *Military Lessons of the Gulf War* (London: Greenhill Books, 1991, hereafter: Watson, *Military Lessons*), pp. 226–60.
2. No reliable evidence has been published to show that Iraq actually intended to advance beyond Kuwait. Claims to that effect were not substantiated, apart from descriptions of Iraqi low-level military planning to cross the Saudi border, which would be standard procedure for any army in a state of readiness. See, for example, statement by US Secretary of Defense Richard Cheney before the Senate Armed Services Committee, 3 December 1990 — DR, 3 December 1990; Norman Friedman, *Desert Victory: The War for Kuwait* (Annapolis: Naval Institute Press, 1991, hereafter: Friedman, *Desert Victory*), pp. 40–41; Gary Melton, "XVIII Airborne Corp: Desert Deception," *Military Intelligence*, October/December 1991, (hereafter: Melton, "Desert Deception"), p. 43.
3. *WP*, 9 August 1990.
4. *Interim Report*, p. 1–1.
5. *US News and World Report*, 20 January 1992.
6. For a detailed discussion of Iraq's motives and objectives in invading Kuwait, see chapter on Iraq, *MECS* 1990, pp. 379–423; Lawrence Freedman and Efraim Karsh, "How Kuwait Was Won: Strategy in the Gulf War," *International Security*, Fall 1991 (hereafter: Freedman-Karsh, "How Kuwait Was Won"), pp. 5–15.
7. *NYT*, 23 September 1990.
8. INA, 7 January — DR, 8 January 1991.
9. US Army Intelligence and Threat Analysis Center, *How They Fight: "Desert Shield" Order of Battle Handbook* (September 1990), pp. 60ff.; Richard Philipps, "Tactical Defensive Doctrine of the Iraqi Ground Forces," *Jane's Soviet Intelligence Review*, March 1991, pp. 116–19.
10. E.g., *IHT*, 7, 8, 14 January 1991.
11. R. Baghdad, 9 January — DR, 10 January 1991. For similar statements, see R. Baghdad, 26 September — DR, 28 September 1990; Saddam Husayn's address to the American people, INA, 26 September — DR, 26 September 1990.
12. *NYT*, 3 March 1991.
13. John Antall, "The Sword of Saddam. An Overview of the Iraqi Armed Forces," *Armor*, November/December 1990, pp. 8–12; Aaron Danis, "A Military Analysis of the Iraqi Army Operations," ibid., pp. 13–18.
14. No definitive data on the strength of the Iraqi air force was available. The lowest number of combat aircraft — 550 — was mentioned in *Interim Report*, p. 2–4. The highest number — 750 — is cited in the Second Supplement to the *London Gazette*, 28 June 1991, attached to House of Commons Defence Committee, *Preliminary Lessons of Operation "Granby". Tenth Report* (London: HMSO, July 1991). See also Joseph Alpher (ed.), *The Middle East Military Balance 1989–90* (Tel Aviv: Jaffee Center for Strategic Studies, Tel Aviv University, 1990), pp. 229–35; Friedman, *Desert Victory*, p. 308; Watson, *Military Lessons*, p. 228.
15. Anthony Cordesman and Abraham Wagner, *The Lessons of Modern War* (Boulder: Westview Press, 1990), Vol. II: *The Iran-Iraq War*, pp. 412 ff.; Aaron Danis, "Iraq Army, Operations and Doctrine," *Military Intelligence*, April/June 1991, pp. 8 ff.
16. For a detailed discussion on the Iraqi air force, see R. A. Marson, "The Air War in the Gulf," *Survival*, May/June 1991, pp. 211–14.
17. *Interim Report*, p. 4–13
18. Reliable data concerning the Iraqi military strength is yet to be published. The pre-15 January official US intelligence estimate of the number of troops in KTO — 540,000 — was

later deemed too high, the maximum number assessed at 300,000–400,000. Jeffrey Smith, *IHT*, 19 March 1991; Friedman, *Desert Victory*, p. 119.

19. Technically, the coalition armies operated under two commanders in chief, who coordinated their operations via the Coalition Coordination, Communication and Integration Center: Gen. Schwarzkopf, who commanded the non-Arab forces, and Lt. Gen. Khalid Ibn Sultan Ibn 'Abd al 'Aziz, chief of staff of the Saudi armed forces, who commanded the Arab forces.

20. Statement by Gen. Colin Powell before the Senate Armed Services Committee, 3 December — USIA, 3 December 1990.

21. For a list of these sources, see Friedman-Karsh, "How Kuwait Was Won," p. 16.

22. Pentagon briefing, 23 January — WF, 23 January 1991.

23. US Department of the Army, FM 100-5, *Operations* (Washington, DC: 1986).

24. *Interim Report*, p. 2–3

25. Objectives defined in Centcom Operations Order (OPROD) 91-001, dated 17 January 1991, cited in ibid.

26. *NYT*, 7 January 1991.

27. "Gulf crisis: Chronology for Jan. 1–15, 1991" — USIS, 16 January 1991.

28. INA, 12 January — DR, 15 January; *NYT*, 11 January 1991.

29. INA, 14 January — DR, 15 January; *JP*, 16 January 1991.

30. For the coalition air order of battle, see Watson, *Military Lessons*, pp. 226–27 and *Interim Report*, Appendix A. *Flight International*, 6–12 March 1991, gave the total number of the fixed-wing aircraft as 2,100, of which 1,700 were US combat and transport aircraft.

31. *Interim Report*, p. 6–2.

32. Ibid. p. 6–8; US Defense Department briefing, 16 January — WF, 16 January 1991.

33. *Al-Madina*, 25 January 1991.

34. Gen. Powell, Pentagon briefing, 23 January — WF, 23 January 1991.

35. Maj. Gen. Johnston, Riyadh briefing, 3 February — WF, 3 February 1991.

36. The planes that reached Iran consisted of 114 combat aircraft and 33 military/civilian transports, six of them expropriated from Kuwait Airways. Friedman, *Desert Victory*, p. 360; Watson, *Military Lessons*, p. 230.

37. *Jane's Defence Weekly*, 1 February 1992, p. 158.

38. Only 127 of the 270 aircraft were confirmed destroyed. Friedman, *Desert Victory*, pp. 353–56; Watson, *Military Lessons*, pp. 229–30.

39. *Ha'aretz*, 21 January 1992.

40. Gen. Schwarzkopf, Riyadh briefing, 30 January — WF, 30 January; *WP*, 31 January 1991.

41. Reuters (Baghdad), 21 January 1992.

42. For details on Iraqi naval strength and a list of destroyed naval units, see *The Middle East Military Balance 1989–1990*, p. 236; Friedman, *Desert Victory*, pp. 361–64.

43. Interview with Nizar Hamdun, state secretary in the Iraqi Foreign Ministry, Vienna TV, 3 July — DR, 5 July; interview with Saddam Husayn, *Le Figaro*, 9 July — DR, 13 July 1990; interview with Saddam Husayn, CNN TV, 30 January 1991. Only a small amount of chemical stock was found in Kuwait following the Iraqi pullout. Friedman, *Desert Victory*, p. 351.

44. *NYT*, 21 January; Gen. Powell, Pentagon briefing, 23 January — WF, 23 January 1991.

45. E.g., R. Riyadh, 18 January — DR, 22 January 1991.

46. *MedNews*, 23 December 1991, 6 January 1992; *US News and World Report*, 20 January 1992. Of the 30 *Scud* warheads adjusted to carry chemical payloads, 14–16 were discovered filled with nerve agents. *Jane's Defence Weekly*, 23 November 1991.

47. *NYT*, 11 March 1991.

48. INA, 21 January — DR, 22 January; US Secretary of Defense Richard Cheney, Pentagon briefing, 23 January — WF, 23 January 1991.

49. Statement by Jordanian Prime Minister Mudar Badran, R. Amman, 4 February — DR, 4 February 1991.

50. *FT*, 5 February. Unattributed claims to this effect were published earlier in London: *al-Zahira*, 24 January — DR, 28 January. See also statement by Lt. Gen. Charles Horner, Central Command Air Force commander, *Air Force Magazine*, June 1991.

51. The exact number of casualties reported by the Iraqi authorities was 293; R. Baghdad, 15 February — DR, 16 February. For details of the incident and the US official version, see Riyadh briefing, 13 February — WF, 14 February; *Newsweek,* 25 February 1991.
52. Rod Alonso, "The Air War," (hereafter: Alonso, "Air War"), in Watson, *Military Lessons,* p. 74.
53. *Interim Report,* p. 4–5.
54. *Truppendienst,* April, pp. 171–72; *Armed Forces Journal,* July 1991, p. 6.
55. *Interim Report,* p. 5–3.
56. For a discussion on the role of the coalition air power, see, e.g., Edward Luttwak, "Victory Through Air Power," *Commentary,* August 1991, pp. 27–30.
57. *Interim Report,* p. 24–1; Alonso, "Air War," p. 74; *al-Hayat* (Cairo), 27 January 1991.
58. Friedman, *Desert Victory,* p. 198.
59. INA, 29 January — DR, 29 January 1991.
60. INA, 3 March 1992. As late as the beginning of February, Baghdad, apparently still convinced that a ground battle would work in its favor, "reproached" President Bush for evading a land battle. R. Baghdad, 3 February — DR, 4 February 1991.
61. Melton, "Desert Deception," p. 43
62. Riyadh briefing, 31 January — WF, 31 January; Joint Arab Command briefing, 2 February — WF, 2 February; *al-Majalla,* 6–12 February 1991; R. Kuwait, 29 January 1992.
63. The sources disagree as to the total number of *Scuds* that were fired: Watson, *Military Lessons,* pp. 224–25; *JP,* 1 March 1991; *Hadashot,* 10 January 1992. Friedman, *Desert Victory,* p. 365, claimed that three of the missiles were launched against Bahrain.
64. *Yedi'ot Aharonot,* 10 January; Richard Cheney's interview, *Ma'ariv,* 19 June 1991.
65. *AWST,* 28 January; *Time,* 4 February 1991; *Yedi'ot Aharonot,* 10 January 1992.
66. Maj. Gen. Robert Johnston, Riyadh briefing — *NYT,* 19 January 1991.
67. *Newsweek,* 17 June; Gen. Sir Peter de la Billière, Commander of the British Forces, Middle East during the war, "The Gulf Conflict: Planning and Execution," *RUSI Journal,* Winter 1991, p. 11.
68. Schwarzkopf to Britain's Independent TV News, 23 January — *WT,* 24 January 1991.
69. Riyadh briefing, 30 January — WF, 30 January 1991.
70. *Yedi'ot Aharonot,* 10 January 1992.
71. Friedman, *Desert Victory,* p. 194
72. Interview with Israeli Defense Minister Moshe Arens, *Ha'aretz,* 21 March; interview with Israeli Air Force Commander Maj. Gen. Avihu Ben Nun, *Israel Air Force Magazine,* December 1991; *Yedi'ot Aharonot,* 10 January 1992.
73. Maj. Gen. Avihu Ben Nun, ibid.
74. *NYT,* 22 January 1991.
75. Israeli chief of air intelligence at the time, Brig. Gen. Y., stated that there was no evidence that any mobile launcher had actually been destroyed. *Israel Air Force Magazine,* December 1991.
76. Gen. Schwarzkopf, Riyadh briefing, 27 February — WF, 27 February; *Union,* 21 July 1991.
77. *WP,* 2 January; *NYT,* 13, 15 January 1991.
78. *Air Force Magazine,* May 1991; *Interim Report,* p. 24–2.
79. *NYT,* 18 January 1991.
80. R. Tokyo, 25 January — DR, 28 January 1991.
81. Melton, "Desert Deception," p. 44; Lt. Gen. John Yeosock, "H+100: An Army Comes of Age in the Persian Gulf," *Army,* October 1991 (hereafter: Yeosock, "H+100"), p. 52. Yeosock was commanding general of the Third US Army (the Army segment in Centcom) during the war.
82. B. L. Cyr et al., "Naval Operations" in Watson, *Military Lessons,* pp. 131–32; Gen. Schwarzkopf, Riyadh briefing, 27 February — WF, 27 February 1991.
83. *IHT,* 9 January; *JP,* 28 January; *Ha'aretz,* 17 February; *NYT,* 18 February 1991.
84. Yeosock, "H+100," p. 52.
85. INA, 14 February — DR, 14 February 1991.
86. Yeosock, "H+100," p. 56. For a detailed presentation of "Desert Storm" logistics, see Lt.

Gen. Jimmy Ross (US deputy chief of staff for logistics), "Victory: The Logistics Story," *Army*, October 1991, pp. 128–38.
87. *IHT*, 4 February; *NYT*, *Time*, 18 February 1991.
88. Yeosock, "H+100," p. 54.
89. *Ha'aretz*, 11 February; *NYT*, 12 February 1991.
90. Watson, *Military Lessons*, pp. 131–32; *Interim Report*, p. 24–2.
91. *IHT*, 28 January; Riyadh briefing, 27 January — *NYT*, 28 January; interview with Dr. Farouk al-Baz, director of Boston University's Center for Remote Sensing — WF, 3 December 1991.
92. AFP (Baghdad), 10 February — DR, 11 February 1991.
93. Text of Saddam Husayn's initiative, R. Baghdad, 12 August — DR, 13 August 1990; statement by the Iraqi RCC, 15 February — DR, 15 February 1991.
94. Bush statement, *NYT*, 16 February 1991.
95. *NYT*, 21 January 1991.
96. *IHT*, 23 February 1991.
97. Transcripts of statements by Bush and Fitzwater, *NYT*, 23 February 1991.
98. The following discussion is based mainly on Yeosock, "H+100"; *Interim Report*; William Taylor and James Blackwell, "The Ground War in the Gulf," *Survival*, May/June 1991, pp. 230–39; Peter Tsouras and Elmo Wright, "The Ground War" in Watson, *Military Lessons*, pp. 81–120.
99. Several reports put the number of Iraqi troops left in the KTO on the eve of the ground attack at no more than 200,000, but no authoritative data on this were published. *IHT*, 19 March 1991.
100. *Interim Report*, p. 24–2; Melton, "Desert Deception," p. 45. The success of the naval demonstrations is reflected in Iraqi communiqués about the "heroic" resistance of the islands. Armed Forces Communiqué No. 63, R. Baghdad, 25 February — DR, 26 February 1991.
101. For a detailed account of the Egyptian contingent, see interview with Lt. Gen. Muhammad 'Atiyya Halabi, commander of Egyptian forces in the Gulf, *al-Jumhuriyya* (Cairo), 18 April 1991. For an account of the passive role of the Syrians, see testimony of Edward Djerejian, US assistant secretary of state for Near East and South Asian Affairs before the House Foreign Affairs Subcommittee on the Middle East, 20 November — WF, 21 December 1991.
102. *'Ukaz*, 26 February; *al-Riyad*, 27 February 1991.
103. R. Baghdad, 25 February — DR, 26 February 1991.
104. R. Baghdad, 26 February — DR, 26 February 1991.
105. *Ma'ariv*, 10 January 1992.
106. *US News and World Report*, 20 January 1992; *Interim Report*, p. 6–5.
107. President Bush address, *NYT*, 28 February 1991.
108. *IHT*, 28 March 1991; *US News and World Report*, 20 January 1992; Freedman-Karsh, "How Kuwait Was Won," p. 36.
109. Gen. Schwarzkopf, Riyadh briefing, 27 February — WF, 27 February 1991.
110. *US News and World Report*, 20 January 1992.
111. The US Defense Intelligence Agency estimate of Iraqi casualties just after the war was 100,000 soldiers. The US DOD *Interim Report* declined to estimate either military or civilian Iraqi casualties, claiming that "very limited information is available on which to base an assessment....Iraq probably cannot accurately account for its casualties." (p. 27–1). This gave rise to highly polarized unofficial estimates, ranging from 200,000 to 8,000. Freedman-Karsh, "How Kuwait was Won," p. 37; *US News and World Report*, 20 January 1992.
112. Yeosock, "H+100," p. 58. These updated figures were higher than those presented by Gen. Schwarzkopf in his briefing in Riyadh on 27 February 1991.
113. Killed in action: US - 148 (35 from friendly fire), non-US coalition — 192. *Interim Report*, p. 27–1.
114. *WP*, 20 April; President Bush letter to Congress, 15 November — USIA, 18 November; *WP*, 3 November — WF, 3 November 1991.
115. Gregg Easterbrook, "Operation Desert Shill," *New Republic*, 30 September 1991.

116. *NYT,* 5 February 1991.
117. De la Billière, "The Gulf Conflict," pp. 9ff.; *NYT,* 24 March 1991.
118. For a description of typical fortifications, see Murray Hammick, "Iraqi Obstacles and Defensive Positions," *International Defense Review,* September 1991, pp. 989–91; Muhammad Ridda Foda, "The War for the Liberation of Kuwait" (in Arabic), *al-Haras al-Watani,* April 1991, pp. 47ff.
119. For a detailed discussion, see *NYT,* 20 October 1991; *The NYT Magazine,* 8 March 1992, p. 30; Gerald Hopple, "Indications and Warning (I&W) and Intelligence Lessons," in Watson, *Military Lessons,* pp. 147ff.
120. *Jane's Defence Weekly,* 20 April 1991.
121. *Interim Report,* pp. 14–1ff. For an overview of US field intelligence in the war, see Brig. Gen. John Stewart, "Desert Storm: A 3d US Army Perspective," *Military Intelligence,* October/December 1991, pp. 22–31; *NYT,* 13 June 1991.

REGIONAL AFFAIRS

The Middle East Peace Process

MORDECHAI GAZIT

It could be predicted that with the Gulf War over the Middle East peace process would resume. However, what was not predictable was whether the US would go on promoting the peace process in the same way as it had before, or would adopt new ways. It soon became obvious that, in 1991, US diplomacy was to be radically different from that in 1989–90. American Secretary of State James Baker paid four visits to the region in the space of two months (March-May) and a total of eight visits in seven months, whereas he had not been in the region at all during the earlier round. It may be concluded from this that US President George Bush had instructed his secretary of state to apply once again the important lesson learned from all past successful mediation efforts in the ME — that the mediator must be involved at the highest level in order to stand a chance of persuading the parties concerned to seriously consider the ideas presented to them.

Baker had clearly reached the conclusion that there was a new mood among a group of Arab countries, otherwise he would not have acted as vigorously and relentlessly as he did. Meeting with eight Arab foreign ministers (10 March), he found them more ready than before to accept Israel as part of the region. Furthermore, it was clear to the secretary of state that Israel would cooperate with the new American peace effort, since he had tailored the program to fit the Israeli peace initiative of 14 May 1989, which had not been the case in 1989–90. The US was now ready to try to move the process forward along two tracks — one aimed at peace between Israel and the Arab countries, and the other between the Israelis and the Palestinians. In the case of the latter, the immediate goal would be a five-year self-rule (autonomy) arrangement. Israel would be expected to negotiate with Palestinian residents of the West Bank and Gaza, but not with representatives of the PLO. Israel would not be asked to include Palestinians from East Jerusalem in the negotiations. It had proved impossible to achieve agreement on these points in the former round. They now became the ground rules for the 1991 efforts.

Egypt could certainly be counted upon to be cooperative, if for no other reason than because of its desire to end its isolation as the only Arab country at peace with Israel.

Jordan, as it frequently avowed, had at least two good reasons for seeking peace. It needed peace because of its long border with Israel and also because a comprehensive peace settlement would settle the problem of the West Bank Palestinians and thus relieve Jordan of the deep-rooted fear that it would again become the land of refuge, if another wave of Palestinians were to cross the Jordan River. Moreover, Jordan urgently needed to turn over a new leaf in its relations with the US. Jordan's policy of support for Iraqi leader Saddam Husayn in the Gulf War had gravely harmed that relationship.

Saudi Arabia, too, seemed to have reached the conclusion that the Arab-Israeli conflict had to be resolved. The Saudis felt that the ME must be pacified in order to ensure stability in the region, and thus enhance Saudi Arabia's chances of survival. The Saudis were even more inclined to support the American peace effort after having been so reliant on the US for the defense of the kingdom in the year under review, as the massive military operation carried out by the Americans proved. In line with this reasoning, in an unusual gesture, King Fahd publicly declared that the "doors to peace were open."

Syria's willingness to join the process and its readiness to enter into bilateral negotiations with Israel caused surprise in many quarters, which ought not to have been the case. There was no reason to question President Hafiz al-Asad's affirmation that Syria had not changed its position since 1973, when it adopted Resolutions 242 and 338. At that time, Syria had boycotted the opening session of the Geneva conference, but, according to Henry Kissinger, the US secretary of state at the time, it agreed to the concept of negotiations with Israel under "appropriate auspices"[1] as stated in Resolution 338. Former US President Jimmy Carter had more recently also attested to the fact that this continued to be Syria's position.[2] Months before the 1991 peace efforts, Asad told President Mubarak that he would negotiate directly with Israel. Therefore, the real issue was not the question of bilateral negotiations or Syria's participation in the Madrid conference, but whether Syria had abandoned its "rejectionist" policies and was ready for "real peace," as Asad had said on a few occasions. At the end of the year under review, it was debatable whether it would be possible to make any headway with Syria judging by the cold, formal attitude of the Syrian delegation toward the Israelis in Madrid and Washington, as well as Syria's decision not to participate in the multilateral conference.

Lebanon fully coordinated its policies with Syria and announced that it would boycott the multilateral talks. In the bilateral meetings, Lebanon focused on its demand for Israel's withdrawal from the south of Lebanon. Furthermore, it avoided making any explicit reference as to its readiness to make peace with Israel.

The Palestinians accepted the American proposals, at least formally, and seemed willing to cooperate. They were prepared, so it appeared at first, to negotiate with Israel a five-year interim arrangement for Palestinian self-government in the West Bank and Gaza. However, it soon emerged that they viewed the transitional phase as a stage in the process that would lead to statehood, a goal not supported by the US and strongly opposed by Israel. At the end of the year under review, it remained unclear as to whether they would cooperate with the plan developed by Baker in his eight visits to the region.

Israel made several concessions. It allowed the PLO to have a more conspicuous role in the process than it would have liked; it accepted a more pronounced separate role for the Palestinians; it agreed to the presence of a UN observer at the conference; and it conceded the beginning of a substantive role to the Europeans. However, on two issues Israel did not give way: on its settlement activity in the West Bank and Gaza and on the demand that it accept the "territory for peace" formula. Although these issues did not cause the negotiating process to break down in 1991, when it had barely started, they remained nevertheless the ones on which Israel's negotiating partners seemed determined not to give way.

The Soviet Union acted as cosponsor of the Madrid conference, but this was no more than a formality. President Mikhail Gorbachev addressed the assembled delegates, devoting most of his remarks to the grave problems of his country. With the dissolution of the Soviet Union, the Russian Republic took over the Soviet role. It showed even less interest in the peace process than the Soviet Union had done in the last year of its existence.

The US, for its part, succeeded in carrying out a complex triple approach for the promotion of peace between the Arabs and Israel. Madrid provided the symbolic beginning, mobilizing world opinion in favor of the peace effort. The bilateral negotiations provided the opportunity for face-to-face talks. The multilateral conference enabled many more countries to be directly involved in the process, including countries that had a great deal to contribute. These three approaches were complementary and intended to create a system of incentives to help surmount the enormous difficulties on the road ahead.

ISRAEL

During the Gulf crisis, the US reassured Israel that the crisis and the Arab-Israeli conflict would not be linked.[3] Secretary of State Baker noted that linkage would "tend to be read [everywhere] as a reward for aggressors and it would jeopardize future peace in the region."[4] As a result of the American attitude, Israeli leaders confidently looked forward to renewed US efforts to resolve the Arab-Israeli and Israeli-Palestinian conflict, once the Gulf crisis was resolved.

When Foreign Minister David Levy, one of the strongest critics of the 1989–90 peace efforts (see MECS 1990, chapter on the ME peace process), assumed his post in the new Israeli Government (June 1990), he stated that a different and less risky process for Israel was possible. In January 1991, he was ready not only to support such an effort, but also to promote it. He was encouraged by the change which had taken place in US thinking toward the end of 1990, in the wake of Iraq's invasion of Kuwait. When Israel presented its peace initiative in May 1989 (see MECS 1989, chapter on the ME peace process), the US had no inclination to make an effort to promote all the objectives Israel had defined (in particular, peaceful relations with all Arab states; improvement of the living conditions and rehabilitation of the inhabitants of the refugee camps in the West Bank and Gaza; and free elections in the territories). The US focused almost exclusively on the Palestinian issue.

However, as the US began to show that it was ready to address the issue of terminating the state of war between Israel and the Arab states, Levy was willing to cooperate. Prime Minister Shamir, too, was greatly relieved that the US no longer accepted the Arab position that the issue of relations between Israel and the Arab countries could not be tackled until after the Palestinian problem was resolved.[5] Since the US was considering various ideas concerning the "New Order in the Middle East," Israel estimated that a sound basis existed for an understanding with the US on how to advance the peace process. Furthermore, the US had recognized that the PLO could no longer play a role in advancing peace.[6]

For the first time, there were good prospects of reducing the dangers and threats to Israel from the Arab countries. It also looked likely that attempts would be made to resolve the Palestinian question. Shamir informed the US that Israel would cooperate when the peace process was resumed.[7]

However, Israel's willingness to cooperate was not unqualified. Israel expected the US to assist in persuading the Arab countries to agree to bilateral face-to-face negotiations. It saw no need for an international conference, as insisted on by the Arabs. It hoped that the Gulf War would make the Arabs realize how dependent they were on the US and make them more accommodating in the matter of moving toward peace with Israel, without the obstacles of bothersome procedures and modalities.

The Shamir government (a coalition of the Likud Party, three small right-wing parties and four religious parties) was realistic enough to know that substantial problems would still remain, even if Israel and the US agreed on most of the problems concerning the form and manner of proceeding. The Likud was ideologically opposed to ceding territory ("parts of the land of Israel") even in order to achieve peace.[8]

One consequence of Israel's commitment not to give up territory was the government's intensive settlement activity in the West Bank and Gaza. In 1991, the Jewish population of these areas exceeded the 100,000 figure.[9] The settlement issue continued to be a major point of contention with the Bush Administration throughout the year. The Palestinians and other Arabs viewed these activities as proof of Israel's "expansionism" and claimed that Israel had no intention of reaching a settlement which involved withdrawal. The Israeli Government countered such claims by asserting that Jewish settlement activity was compatible with negotiations. It continually rejected calls for a freeze on settlements, and would not even consider a temporary halt. Israel maintained that it was not an issue to be discussed in the context of talks for an interim agreement on the establishment of Palestinian self-rule. The government further claimed that the settlement issue could be raised only in the third year, when negotiations on permanent status for the West Bank and Gaza began.

Although seemingly procedural, another question concerning the Palestinians was of considerable significance. The 1989 Israeli peace initiative called for Palestinian elections in the territories, the details of which would be discussed with a Palestinian delegation formed for this purpose. Consequently, the US secretary of state's efforts in 1989–90 were centered on the formation of such a delegation. Early in the year under review, it became clear that Israel was having second thoughts about this issue. Levy said that Israel's call for direct negotiations with the Arab countries was also addressed to the Palestinians in the territories. He further stated that a group of local leaders would be acceptable to Israel, if they had reached the conclusion that the PLO had led them to disaster, and therefore came forward to negotiate on the basis of the Israeli peace initiative, without insisting on holding elections first.[10] This approach also included Jordan in any arrangement with the Palestinians. Israel was anxious to involve Jordan, so that "an Arab living in Samaria [West Bank] or on the other side of the Jordan River would feel that he is at home...and Israel too would have the feeling of living normally with Arabs on both sides of the Jordan River border."[11]

At the end of February 1991, Secretary of State Baker announced that he intended to visit the ME soon and explore "prospects for constructing a new Arab-Israeli peace process"[12] that would encompass both the Arab states and the Palestinians. "This suggested," said Baker, "a two-track approach." As far as the Palestinians were concerned, the US officials admitted that it would be "very difficult" for the US to negotiate with the PLO. Alternatives would have to be sought.[13]

Israel welcomed the secretary of state's visit somewhat cautiously. The US had stood by Israel since its inception and there was no doubt about US friendship. Nevertheless, there were serious differences over the terms of a settlement of the Arab-Israeli conflict. President Bush's address to a joint session of the US Congress (6 March), on the eve of Baker's trip, referred to the *"principle* of territory for peace." This caused concern in Israel, even though Bush further qualified his reference by saying, "this principle must be elaborated to provide for Israel's security, and at the same time for legitimate Palestinian political rights."[14]

On 11 March, Baker arrived in Israel, on what was to be the first of eight trips to the region. He conveyed to Shamir his impression from his meetings held with eight Arab foreign ministers in Riyadh (10 March) that there was a new mood among the Arabs and that there existed a better chance than ever before — he called it a "historic opportunity" — of settling the dispute. He reassured the Israelis that the US would act as a "catalyst," but could not impose a settlement. He claimed that he did not have a blueprint, only ideas that he would discuss.[15] Israel immediately agreed to one of his ideas — that efforts should be made along the Arab and Palestinian tracks concurrently. This coincided with one of the ideas expounded in Israel's 1989 peace initiative. The Arabs had not yet endorsed the idea, but the Israelis were convinced that it was a very realistic approach. The secretary of state also raised the idea of a regional meeting, under joint US-Soviet sponsorship (the UN was not mentioned). Since Shamir had already accepted a similar suggestion in 1987, he had no reason to object. The idea proposed in 1987 was for a purely formal, ceremonial and onetime event. The negotiations that would develop would have to be bilateral and not in an "international setting."[16] Israel was prepared to agree that the Soviet Union cosponsor this onetime event, only after the reestablishment of full diplomatic relations with Israel and after the Soviets had committed themselves to accepting the objectives of the peace process, as it was being elaborated with the US.

The Israelis were relieved that the secretary of state did not raise the "territory for peace" issue, particularly since he told them that President Asad had said that he would not meet with them unless he was assured that they would return the Golan.[17] During his stay in Jerusalem, Baker met a large group of Palestinian personalities headed by Faysal al-Husayni. The meeting had been approved by the PLO in Tunis (see below). Shamir and Levy did not protest to Baker about the meeting. Nevertheless they claimed that it was futile; Faysal al-Husayni and his group rejected Israel's approach, based on the Camp David accords. It was, therefore, pointless to talk to them. There were, they said, other Palestinians who accepted the offer of autonomy.

On 8 April, Baker paid his second visit to Israel. He explored the circumstances under which the Israelis would be prepared to embark on this two-track process and what US assurances they required in order to do it. Since there were four other parties involved (Syria, Lebanon, Jordan, the Palestinians), any understanding between the US and Israel would have to be compatible with the understandings the US reached with the Arab countries concerned.

The Israelis presented their interpretation of Resolution 242, which was the agreed basis for any settlement. They posited that the resolution was open to various interpretations. If one accepted the Arab view that 242 called for total Israeli withdrawal from the occupied territories, then, Israel claimed, there was nothing left to negotiate. Israel proposed that it be understood that each side should come to the talks with its own interpretation.[18] To bolster the Israeli case, Israel's minister of justice recalled that 242 had been based on there being two sovereign countries with conflicting claims. However, in the case of the West Bank, Jordan had given up its claims and this had therefore created a new situation.[19]

There were many other points raised by the Israelis, apart from the interpretation of 242. According to leaks in the Israeli press, Levy told the Israeli cabinet (11 April) that agreements had been reached on many other points. It was more likely that these other points were still being discussed, but that they did not seem to pose any special problems. The main points were:[20]

(1) A two-track approach would be pursued: between Israel and the Arab countries, and between Israel and a Palestinian delegation.

(2) A Palestinian state was not to be the final outcome of the process.

(3) The Palestinian representation would be composed of persons agreed upon and who would come from the territories only. There would be no demand to include in the delegation Palestinians from abroad or East Jerusalem.

(4) Israel was not being asked to hold talks with the PLO, nor was the US holding talks with it.

(5) The negotiations with the Palestinian delegation from the territories would be based on the lines set forth by the Israeli peace initiative of May 1989; in the first stage, negotiations for self-government, in the second stage, at the end of three years, negotiations would start on a final settlement.

(6) The Soviet Union would upgrade the level of its relations with Israel to full diplomatic relations. It would accept the principles agreed upon between the US and Israel concerning the political process.

When asked about these understandings, a US spokesperson merely said that Levy had "overly simplified" the matter.[21]

The US secretary of state paid his third visit to Israel on 18 April. After three days, he interrupted his stay to meet the Soviet foreign minister in the Caucasus. He offered the Soviets cosponsorship of the conference, but told them that Israel expected them to establish full diplomatic relations, an expectation shared by the US. Baker reported to the Israelis that the Arabs wanted the UN and Europe to participate in the conference, which ought to have a permanent mechanism to accompany the negotiations throughout. As far as the Palestinians were concerned, little progress seemed to have been made. They were still adhering to all the PLO terms, including that East Jerusalem be represented in the Palestinian delegation.

According to one news report, the secretary of state asked the Israelis whether they insisted on having a final say (i.e., a quasi-veto), on the composition of the Palestinian representation.[22] This was a clear indication that this condition was most likely to be rejected by the Palestinians.

This round of talks was not exactly a case of plain sailing. This was because Baker was angered by the news that another Jewish settlement had been established while he was in the region.[23] Shamir continued to demand that the peace conference be strictly a one- or two-day event. However, before this and other procedural issues could be thrashed out, the secretary of state was forced to cut short his visit, because of the death of his mother.[24]

By the conclusion of this visit, progress seemed to have been made on two points. Baker was ready to accept Israel's demand to be free to argue in favor of its own interpretation of 242. Furthermore, the matter of European Community (EC) participation seemed to be nearing a solution. From a leak in the Israeli media concerning the issue of the conference's meeting more than once, it was possible to surmise that Israel would be ready to have the conference reconvene from time to time, solely for the purpose of keeping it briefed on progress in the bilateral negotiations. However, Israel would have to agree to such a meeting.[25]

The two most obvious points of contention were the role of the the UN and East Jerusalem. On the first point, Shamir claimed that matters were being held up by Syria's insistence that the conference be "indeed an international one under UN auspices."[26]

Baker's fourth visit to Israel took place a month later (15–16 May). As expected, a week before his arrival, Shamir indicated flexibility on the issue of European participation, but unwillingness to compromise on the UN role or the issue of withdrawal. He saw the last question as inextricably linked to that of the settlements.[27] Nevertheless, the secretary of state declared himself satisfied with the result of his talks on this visit. As he departed, he said that there were "many more areas of agreement with respect to [the peace process] on the part of Israel than there are areas of disagreement."[28] Apart from East Jerusalem and the Palestinian representation, the unresolved issues seemed to be the role of the UN and the reconvening of the conference. Baker proposed a compromise on the issue of reconvening, which Israel was likely to accept: namely, that this conference would reconvene merely to hear reports, provided both sides agreed. Asad had apparently rejected the compromise, and Shamir was not yet ready to accept it. As far as the role of the UN was concerned, Baker suggested that the UN be represented by an observer with no functional role. This suggestion did not go far enough for Asad and was too much for Shamir.[29] Nevertheless, Israeli and US teams began to draft a document containing the points agreed upon. Work on this memorandum was to continue intermittently until close to the opening of the conference.

On 11 May, Baker announced that the Gulf Cooperation Council (GCC) had agreed to send an observer to the conference to represent all its members (Saudi Arabia, Kuwait, Oman, Bahrain, Qatar and the United Arab Emirates). This announcement was greeted with cautious apprehension by some in Israel. However, in time, it came to be regarded in a positive light.[30]

Although the issue of Israel's settlement activity did not feature prominently in the talks with Baker, it was looming large in the background. In reply to a question in a session of a congressional committee, the secretary of state complained that, on each of his four trips, he had been met with the announcement of new settlement activity. There was, in his view, "no bigger obstacle to peace than the settlements."[31] The Israeli reaction to this statement was that the US and Israel had been in disagreement over this issue for many years, and even if the Bush Administration chose to spotlight this difference, Israel would not halt this activity.[32]

Two months later, on 21 July, Baker returned to Israel on his fifth visit. This visit immediately followed Asad's reply to a letter from Bush (see below). Shamir was pleased with Asad's move, and even went so far as to say that Asad was undergoing a process similar to that which had ultimately led to negotiations with Egyptian President Anwar al-Sadat, and to peace.[33] Shamir reported to his cabinet that the US secretary of state believed that there had been a revolutionary change in Syria's position. Syria had agreed to direct talks with Israel and to restrict the role of the UN.[34]

The secretary of state was satisfied with his talks in Israel: Shamir promised he would respond to what Baker called the "American Proposals," which had already been accepted by several Arab governments. Baker once more claimed that this was a "moment of historic opportunity." He revealed that the US had made sure that the Arabs understood that there were differing interpretations of the requirements of Resolution 242. As far as reconvening the conference was concerned, Baker said that the US was of the opinion that all parties would have to consent before such a reconvening could take place. Furthermore, the UN would send an observer and the US and the Soviet Union would keep the secretary-general of the UN notified on what transpired in the negotiations.[35] These were considered solid achievements for Israel, and enabled Levy to say that most obstacles to convening the conference had been removed.[36]

However, the issue of the Palestinian representation was still unresolved. Baker was unable to reassure Israel that none of the Palestinian delegates to the conference would be PLO members or residents of East Jerusalem. Nevertheless, in response to Baker's appeals,[37] Shamir informed him that Israel would go to the conference, subject to a US memorandum of understanding containing assurances that would allay Israel's concerns.[38] Shamir's message reached Baker in Moscow, in time for Bush and Gorbachev to announce on 31 July: "The US and the Soviet Union, acting as cosponsors, will work to convene in October a peace conference designed to launch bilateral and multilateral negotiations."[39] Bush also announced that Baker was returning to the ME to "obtain Israel's answer to our proposals for peace."[40]

On 1 August, the secretary of state arrived in Israel on his sixth visit. He was clearly ready to give Shamir the assurances the latter demanded. Despite the fact that the US-Israel memorandum was still being discussed, in a joint news conference with Baker on 1 August, Shamir announced that Israel was ready "to enter peace negotiations in accordance with the US proposals subject to a satisfactory solution of the issue of Palestinian Arab representation in the Jordanian-Palestinian delegation." If this happened, Shamir said, "I will recommend to our cabinet to approve the proposal." Baker was pleased and described the announcement as "extraordinarily positive and significant."[41] He was clearly aware that if he failed with the Palestinians, his understanding with Shamir would no longer apply.[42]

The drafting of the memorandum of understanding, which was begun in May, proved to be considerably more difficult a task than was originally thought. The US insisted that the memorandum should reflect its own positions and not merely those of Israel. Consequently, if Israel expressed its opposition to withdrawal, the US would state its support for "territory for peace." Furthermore, if Israel objected to a Palestinian state, the US would merely declare its "nonsupport" for it. In September, the full Israeli draft of the memorandum was leaked to the Israeli press. This indicated that Israel no longer seriously counted on reaching an agreement with the US on the memorandum.[43]

Before Baker's next visit to Israel, the disagreement over Israel's settlement activities in the territories came to a head. The US had asked Israel not to submit an application for a housing-loan guarantee before September (on the issue of loan guarantees, see chapter on the US and the ME). As September approached, the US asked Israel to agree to a further postponement, of four months, which Shamir refused to do. He explained that the guarantee was vitally important in order to obtain loans, which were crucial for the building of homes for the many Jewish immigrants who had arrived in Israel from the Soviet Union (360,000 since mid-1989). Bush and Baker asked Congress to defer the matter until the peace conference. Israel suspected, and not without reason, that the US was delaying because it wanted Israel to commit itself to halt settlement activity.[44] Bush wrote to Congress: "If Congress chooses to press forward [on the loan guarantees] now, we stand a very real chance of losing the participation of either our Arab or Israeli negotiating partner."[45] In a televised press conference, Bush subsequently attacked the American Jewish community for supporting the Israeli request. He said that he was "up against some powerful political forces" and he took a stand against these "very strong and effective groups" although he was just "one lonely little guy."[46]

Against the backdrop of this crisis, Secretary of State Baker arrived in Israel on 15 September, on his seventh visit. This time, he and Shamir focused almost entirely on the peace conference and the written US assurance, making considerable progress. They discussed a unilateral "Letter of Assurance," which the US would give to Israel and they abandoned the format of the memorandum of understanding.[47] However, they made no progress on the housing-loan guarantee issue. Shamir was not so concerned about the 120-day delay, which the US had requested, as he was about the US Administration's refusal to say what it would do after this delay.[48]

On 16 October, Baker began his eighth and final visit before the conference. In the intervening four weeks since his previous visit, efforts had centered on the preparation of the letter of assurance and on resolving the issue of Palestinian representation. The secretary of state arrived in Israel after talks in Damascus and Amman. He had failed to persuade Asad to make the commitment that Syria would attend the multilateral talks.[49] Moreover, in Amman, he had discovered that the Palestinian representatives had not yet prepared a list of names (see section on the Palestinians and the PLO in this chapter). With Israel, he had reached a preliminary agreement on the US assurances, although Israel wanted various changes.

At the end of Baker's visit these issues had either been settled or satisfactorily dealt with, to the extent that the convening of the conference would no longer be obstructed. This was, indeed, no mean achievement. Although not completely satisfied with the letter of assurance, Shamir concluded that its shortcomings did not justify a "negative attitude toward the whole process."[50] Moscow finally restored full diplomatic relations with Israel, during the visit to Israel of the Soviet foreign minister, Boris Pankin, which coincided with Baker's visit. Israel and the Soviet Union signed a compact restoring relations between the two countries.[51]

The issue of Palestinian representation was the last item to be settled. Although they did not admit it, the Israelis made several concessions. They accepted a certain measure of behind-the-scenes PLO involvement. Moreover, they agreed to a more pronouncedly independent role for the Palestinians than they would have in a joint Palestinian-Jordanian delegation. Shamir said of the PLO: "To my regret we cannot banish this organization from the face of the earth, so it will be somewhere."[52] Immediately after his appointment, the head of the Palestinian delegation, Dr. Haydar 'Abd al-Shafi, told an Israeli paper: "We are not going to refrain from affirming that we are supporters of the PLO."[53]

The Israeli cabinet approved Shamir's recommendation to attend the conference by a majority of 16 to three. The venue of the conference was to be Madrid.[54] Shamir decided to lead the Israeli delegation to the conference himself. This decision was a disappointment to Levy, who consequently did not to go to Madrid.[55]

In general terms, the text of the invitation to the conference (see Appendix I) was acceptable to Israel. Israel prevailed upon the US to make up for the shortcomings of the invitation by inserting more explicit language in the letter of assurance where necessary (see Appendix II). One example of this was the specific reference to "peace treaties with full diplomatic relations between Israel and its Arab neighbors" as the declared objective of the process. The invitation had used the vague terminology favored by the Syrians ("lasting and comprehensive settlement"). Another example was the clarification that no negotiations were to take place at the conference itself. This highlighted the strictly circumscribed and essentially ceremonial role of the conference, as insisted on by Israel.

As an additional precaution, Shamir sent a letter to Baker (28 October), in which he made the following points: Israel would not be a party to negotiations on Jerusalem at any stage; Israel would sign an agreement on self-government for the Palestinians only with a joint Jordanian-Palestinian delegation (Israel wanted Jordan to be associated with the agreement); and it would uncompromisingly oppose the establishment of a Palestinian state in the territories.[56] All three points dealt with questions on which the US and Israel had not fully agreed and had therefore been avoided by the US in its letter of assurance.

Shamir addressed the Madrid conference (30 October-2 November) twice, as did all the heads of delegations. In his first address, on 30 October, he dwelt on the importance of direct bilateral negotiations as signifying the parties' mutual acceptance of each other. He emphasized that the objective of the negotiations was the signing of peace treaties and interim self-government arrangements with the Palestinian Arabs. He made known that he was aware that the Arabs would make territorial demands on Israel, but said that it would be regrettable if the talks focused primarily and exclusively on territory — this would lead to an impasse.[57]

In his second address, on 1 November, he declared that Israel had no designs on Lebanese territory and assured the Palestinians of the importance Israel attached to reaching accommodation with them.[58]

The Arabs were disappointed that Shamir had not referred to Resolutions 242 and 338 in his two speeches and had not been forthcoming on the territorial issue. Syria's foreign minister reacted angrily to references made by Shamir to Syria's involvement in terrorism, and to the treatment of its small Syrian Jewish community.[59] Consequently, the opening sessions were marred by speeches that were not very different from those that the two sides had been exchanging for decades at the UN.

There were no substantive issues discussed in the bilateral meetings between the Israelis and the three Arab delegations (the Jordanian-Palestinian, the Syrian and the Lebanese), which took place after the conclusion of the opening sessions. However, the very fact that face-to-face meetings had been held constituted the high point of the conference and, it was to be hoped, the beginning of the more substantive bilateral phase of the process. The next round of talks was held five weeks later (10–18 December) in Washington DC. Israel had argued in favor of the talks being held in the ME, but without success. Israel suspected that the Arabs were not really interested in direct talks, but preferred talking to the Americans and, as an official statement said, "through them to try and exert pressure on Israel." The statement also said that the Israeli inner cabinet decided to accept the US invitation to come to Washington but would limit the time span of the talks.[60]

Once in Washington, the Israelis found that their fears that the Arabs would try to go around them and talk to the Americans instead were without foundation. Although the venue for the talks was the State Department building, the US kept a discreet distance. The talks between Israel and all three delegations started slowly. Israel could not meet in formal session with the joint Jordanian-Palestinian delegation even once. The three delegation heads (Israeli, Jordanian, and Palestinian) met in the lounge outside the assigned meeting room for many hours. They were attempting to find a solution to the problem that arose when the Palestinians insisted on meeting with the Israelis as if they were a quasi-separate delegation. However, the invitation to Madrid, which set the ground rules, stated that the Palestinians would be "part of the joint Jordanian-Palestinian delegation" (see Appendix I). The three delegation heads failed to resolve this problem by the time the Washington round of talks ended, but were hopeful that the matter would be settled at their next meeting in 1992. (For details, see sections on the Palestinians and the PLO, and on Jordan.)

THE PALESTINIANS AND THE PLO

The Palestinians and their leadership, the PLO, reaffirmed their support for Saddam Husayn on the eve of the Gulf War.[61] They condemned the war as a "treacherous and aggressive war" launched by the US "against Iraq and the Arab nation."[62] 'Arafat viewed the war as a military operation seeking to "destroy the Iraqi force because it represents real Arab power." The battle was therefore also the "battle of Palestine, the battle of Arab and Islamic nations."[63] After the war, 'Arafat tried to rationalize his pro-Iraqi stance by arguing that it was incorrect to say that he had supported Saddam. In actual fact, it was the other way round: Saddam had been the first to establish a link between the Arab and the Palestinian cause and had therefore given 'Arafat full support. The Palestinians would never forget Saddam's attitude.[64]

'Arafat was clearly aware that his pro-Saddam policy had seriously weakened his standing in Washington. Nevertheless, he was convinced that no peace process would be possible without Palestinians, and furthermore that no Palestinians would come forward to negotiate with the US or Israel without PLO approbation. He therefore wasted no time in welcoming Bush's address of 6 March and stated that the PLO responded favorably to the positive elements it contained. 'Arafat claimed that Bush had rejected Saddam's linking Iraq's withdrawal from Kuwait to Israel's withdrawal from the occupied territories (see *MECS* 1990, chapter on the ME peace process, section on Iraq). However, since Bush had given assurances that "he would deal with the Palestinian issue immediately after the war, it was now up to Bush, said 'Arafat, to keep his word.[65]

The PLO was weakened internationally and also among the Arab states that had been aligned against Saddam Husayn. Consequently, it considered that its best option was to cooperate with the US in the peace process. After it had welcomed Bush's address, it could authorize meetings between Palestinians and Baker, in line with its previous policy of approving meetings with high-ranking personalities. Until then, the

PLO had excluded Americans. Accordingly, on 9 March, the eve of the secretary of state's arrival in the ME, an official spokesman of the PLO announced its decision "to approve a meeting between a national group of Palestinian personalities inside the occupied homeland and Baker." The spokesman also emphasized that this decision had been taken at a meeting of the Palestinian leadership "chaired by President Yasir 'Arafat."[66] Although announced as a onetime decision, it set a precedent for PLO cooperation, albeit indirect, with the US-led peace process throughout 1991.

The PLO was eager to make known that it was playing a key role in the actions and decisions of the Palestinians. Therefore, in order to avoid giving the unwanted impression that the Palestinian personalities inside the territories acted on their own, before every meeting between the Palestinian personalities and Baker, the PLO in Tunis took great pains to announce giving its go-ahead, and after each meeting it always published details. Moreover, the Palestinian leaders in the territories affirmed time after time that they had been appointed by the PLO, were acting under its instructions, and that the PLO was the Palestinians' recognized leadership. Before the first meeting, the head of the Palestinian team, Faysal al-Husayni, director of the Arab Studies Center in Jerusalem, explained publicly, and also told the secretary of state that he and his team were acting under instructions from the PLO leadership.[67] Even such modalities as the number of Palestinians who would attend the meetings with Baker were decided by the PLO. At the first meeting, 12 were present, at the second, six, and thereafter only three.[68]

After the first meeting, an official PLO spokesman praised "the performance of the Palestinian nationalist personalities." They had dwelt on the "indivisible unity between the Palestinian masses inside and outside the occupied homeland and the Palestinian people and its leadership."[69] When 'Arafat was asked whether he was not concerned that the US might be looking for negotiating partners other than the PLO, he always replied that all Palestinians represented the PLO and would not act without its approval. He also said that the Palestinians were not only those who lived in the occupied territories, but also the millions who lived in other countries.[70]

The Palestinians considered the first meeting with Baker as positive. However, they were disappointed that the secretary of state urged them to sidestep the PLO, while they asked him, in vain, whether the US would resume its dialogue with the PLO. They were also displeased that Baker had not promised that the US would exert pressure on Israel if the latter did not implement the Security Council resolutions, in other words, withdraw from the territories.[71]

The second meeting with Baker was held on 9 April. The Palestinians were disappointed with its outcome. The US continued to oppose PLO participation and did not promise to stop Israeli settlement activities in the territories. The US would apply political persuasion but not sanctions.[72] Baker asked the Palestinians whether they would accept a regional conference instead of an international one. He proposed the idea of a "self-governing authority," by which, he said, he meant something "more than autonomy but also less than a state."[73] The Palestinians retorted that they had no authority to discuss this proposal. They were not empowered to discuss anything short of self-determination.

On 20 April, the Palestinians met with Baker for the third time, only 11 days after the second meeting. On this occasion, the three Palestinians, Faysal al-Husayni, Dr. Hanan 'Ashrawi and Dr. Zakariyya al-Agha, who was from Gaza,[74] were more satisfied with the meeting. The three personalities were to conduct the talks with the secretary of state throughout his visits. Dr. 'Ashrawi said Baker's approach showed flexibility and "greater sympathy toward the Palestinians in the territories and Kuwait."[75] Baker was also receptive to the participation of the EC and the UN in a conference. Those were both long-standing Palestinian demands. With these concessions, the US had, in effect, agreed to let the regional conference assume an international character.[76]

A positive Palestinian attitude soon emerged toward these developments in the American position. In an interview with a London weekly in Arabic, only two days after the third meeting, Faysal al-Husayni said that the Palestinians no longer rejected autonomy if it "constituted a stage in a plan leading toward comprehensive agreement under international guarantees based on Resolutions 242 and 338." The US had explained to the Palestinians, so Faysal Husayni said, that it would continue to adhere to its policy of not supporting the establishment of a Palestinian state, but would not oppose it if the parties to the conflict agreed on its establishment. This explanation caused the important change in the Palestinian position. Another obstacle to autonomy was removed when Baker said if the Palestinians accepted a joint Jordanian-Palestinian delegation, it would be possible to appoint Palestinians from outside the territories and from Jerusalem (they would be members of the Jordanian delegation).[77] The PLO had not yet accepted this proposal.

It also appeared that the US had modified its policy of ignoring the PLO. It seemed to be searching for ways of dealing with the PLO without provoking a confrontation with Israel. Husayni felt that he and his colleagues had succeeded in conveying to the Americans that there was no alternative to the PLO and, thus, no alternative to an independent Palestinian delegation, which would represent all Palestinians and not just those living in the territories.[78]

The Palestinians' fourth meeting with Baker on 14 May did not run smoothly. Faysal al-Husayni used the word "confrontation" to describe the atmosphere. He complained that the US still had no "definite positions," and that this consequently obliged the Palestinians to try, by means of difficult and protracted discussions, to understand what the Americans had in mind.[79]

The fifth meeting between the Palestinians and the secretary of state took place on 21 July. On this occasion, as on all the others, a Palestinian source in Tunis announced that the PLO authorized the Palestinians inside the territories to meet Baker. In a news conference following the meeting, Husayni said that the secretary of state had provided replies to some, but by no means all, of the questions which they had put to him. No progress had been made on the issue of the UN representative at the peace conference. This was apparently because the Palestinians were surprised when informed as to the Syrian position on this issue. Husayni continued to demand that the "UN come to the conference endowed with authority to ensure the implementation of its resolutions."[80]

Another unresolved issue was Palestinian representation at the conference. Although the PLO had not rejected the idea of a joint Jordanian-Palestinian delegation, it had still not decided in its favor. The PLO seemed to think that an independent Palestinian delegation would better serve its interests. Dr. 'Ashrawi explained that the option of a joint Jordanian-Palestinian delegation depended on whether there was a long-term political agreement with Jordan "based on equality and respect for each side's sovereignty."[81]

The other question that had not yet been settled was that of American assurances, particularly those concerning Jerusalem. This question was seen by the Palestinians as dealing with substance and content and not with procedure. The Israelis had demanded that no member of the Palestinian delegation be a Palestinian resident of East Jerusalem in order to prevent negotiations on the future of that section of the city. The Israeli demand was unacceptable to the Palestinians.

The Palestinians met Baker for the sixth time on 2 August, two days after Bush and Gorbachev announced the decision to convene a peace conference in October. The PLO welcomed this announcement,[82] although the Palestinians still had to reach an understanding with the secretary of state. Syria and Israel assented to the conference — the latter subject to a satisfactory solution of the issue of Palestinian representation in the Jordanian-Palestinian delegation. The Palestinians were now the only ones still not to have agreed to the conference. Baker urged them to give their assent, emphasizing that they had "most to gain from a viable and active peace process...and most to lose if there is no process."[83] However, the negotiating team of three presented Baker with a statement issued by the PLO. This statement listed five points on which assurances would have to be made to the Palestinians.[84] The secretary of state assigned some of his aides to work on the matter in an attempt to accommodate the Palestinians' demands.

Six weeks later, a PLO official spokesman announced that the organization had approved yet another meeting with Baker in Jerusalem. This meeting was held on 16 September. The Palestinians were ready to inform Baker of the PLO's "official position on the guarantees required from the US," and, after detailed discussion, Dr. 'Ashrawi admitted that some progress had been made.[85] However, the US assurances were still not completely to the Palestinians' satisfaction and required further working out. Husayni left for London to consult with PLO experts.[86] The talks had moved into high gear.

The next meeting with Baker, the last before the conference convened, was held on 16 October. A few days earlier, on 12 October, Husayni and his colleagues met with the secretary of state in Washington, for what was, no doubt, a last-minute attempt to improve the terms under which the Palestinians would go to the conference. One well-informed correspondent reported that they had told Baker that, as things stood, on the eve of the conference, they were being asked "to go into a negotiation stripped of all their symbols and without any promises on the outcome as well."[87] However, the letter of assurance that the Palestinians received from the US, six days later, contained several important concessions. Some of those must have been made at the last moment to make them acceptable to the Palestinians (see Appendix III). To the extent that Husayni felt that he had not gotten all he wanted, he could console himself with the thought that the Palestinians could as a last resort have recourse to the UN Security Council, and the US would not oppose such a move, if taken after the conference had collapsed.[88] Such a move was clearly not excluded by the letter.

Baker must have been disappointed when, on his arrival in Amman on 14 October, he did not find the Palestinian team he had talked to four days earlier. He had hoped they would be waiting for him, ready to hand him a list of the names of the Palestinians from the territories who would represent the Palestinians in the Jordanian-Palestinian delegation. Instead, Baker found a high-level PLO delegation that had been sent to Amman to negotiate the matter of the Palestinian representation with Jordan. This was a way for the PLO to assert its exclusive and preeminent role. Difficulties between the Jordanians and the PLO had arisen over the precise terms of the partnership in the joint delegation. The PLO insisted on stressing the separate character of the Palestinian delegation. Only after these problems had been settled, did the Palestinians from the territories arrive in Amman, once again declaring that only the PLO, and not they, had the authority to conclude the agreement with Jordan.[89] On 16 October, the visiting PLO delegation made an unofficial announcement that agreement had been reached, adding that the agreement would have to be approved by the Palestinian Central Council (PCC), before it became official.[90] The PCC soon gave its approval and it also approved Palestinian participation in the conference.[91]

The Jordanian-PLO agreement proved to be satisfactory to the PLO (see Appendix IV). It stated that, at the conference, there would be "two equal and independent Jordanian and Palestinian delegations. Each delegation would deal with the issues which concerned it. There would be two chairpersons, one Jordanian and one Palestinian." The PLO had thus achieved its goal of equal status with Jordan, even if the Palestinian delegates were not to be officially members of the PLO.

This was definitely a considerable achievement for the organization, taking into account the fact that when it had joined the peace process seven months previously, it was laboring under the serious handicap of its pro-Saddam and anti-American stance. Since then, it had succeeded in normalizing its relations with Egypt and Syria, relations which were at a low ebb because of the Gulf War. This was accomplished despite opposition from within the organization and also from the outside. Even the US had accepted the behind-the-scene role that the PLO was playing in the peace process, a role that was becoming increasingly conspicuous. The Palestinians were quite satisfied with the letter of assurance given to them by the US, considering the careful balance that the US had to maintain between the Palestinians and Israel. In some cases, the US had had to tread a very fine line in order not to upset this balance. One case in point was the explicit statement that the US did "not recognize Israel's annexation of East Jerusalem or the extension of its municipal boundaries." Another was the US promise to accept any outcome agreed between the parties, including a confederation. In this context, it is worthy of note that Jordan's prime minister recalled that, since Jordan was an independent sovereign country, it could only unite with another country, in this case Palestine, when there was Palestinian sovereignty. This was, according to him, the meaning of confederation.[92]

In the letter of assurance to the Palestinians the US did not reiterate its policy of not supporting an independent Palestinian state. This omission was a US concession to the Palestinians as was the promise not to "support a competing or parallel process in the UN Security Council" while the peace process was "actively going on." This promise seemed to carry a hidden message: it hinted that the US was willing not to veto moves to censure Israel in the Security Council, if and when the peace efforts collapsed. The Palestinians actually assumed that in such a case they could count on European support. As they saw it, the Security Council had set a precedent in the way it had dealt with Iraq, and this should also be applied to Israel. On the negative side, from a Palestinian point of view, the most crucial flaw was the absence of a clear US assurance to support their demand for self-determination.

The final decision could no longer be delayed. Immediately after approval of the

Jordanian-PLO agreement by the PCC, the PLO Executive Committee was asked to decide the final composition of the Palestinian delegation.[93] The Executive Committee acted quickly and appointed 14 personalities from the territories. The list was headed by Dr. Haydar 'Abd al-Shafi from Gaza. However, it was Faysal al-Husayni who made the announcement of the final composition of the Palestinian delegation.[94] 'Arafat again declared that all the Palestinians at the peace conference would be representing the PLO.[95] In a bid to further stress the PLO role, he appointed a seven-member advisory committee, headed by his political adviser, Nabil Sha'th, to be in Madrid for the duration of the conference. Four of its members were originally from Jerusalem and three were from outside the occupied territories.[96]

In order to further safeguard its position, the PLO addressed a letter to Baker and the Soviet foreign minister. It stated, inter alia, "Acceptance of unfair and unjustified restrictions on the form of our participation [in Madrid]...does not constitute in any way whatsoever a precedent for or acceptance of the essence of the Israeli negotiation stance."[97]

The Madrid conference offered the Palestinians an opportunity which they utilized to project an image of moderation and reasonableness. Shafi's speech contained an appeal to the Israeli people. He told the Israelis that the Palestinians were willing "to live side by side [with them] on the lands and [share] the promise of the future."[98] The speech was praised by the PLO for satisfactorily expressing the Palestinian problem, the PLO demands, and the "oneness of Palestinian representation" in the territories as well as in the Palestinian diaspora.[99] The Palestinians felt that the inroads they had made in Madrid in international public opinion would "pave the way for subsequent steps and help mobilize public opinion for the next phase...to bring pressure to bear on Israel" to oblige it to carry out the UN resolutions.[100]

In his speech, Shafi addressed his Jordanian partners telling them that together they "would strive to achieve peace...[and] our [Palestinian] sovereignty, while proceeding...to prepare the grounds for a confederation between the two states of Palestine and Jordan." He did, however, express willingness to accept the "proposal for a transitional stage, provided interim arrangements are not transformed into permanent status" and he asked for international protection and/or trusteeship during this stage. He also said that, at this stage, the refugees who had fled in 1967 would be repatriated. This implied that the problem of all the other refugees would be dealt with later during the permanent status negotiations.

As agreed beforehand, the Jordanian-Palestinian delegation met with the Israeli delegation, on 3 November, after the conclusion of the official part of the conference. The meeting dealt with procedure and marked the beginning of the bilateral phase of the negotiations. The two delegations met again a month later in Washington on 10–18 December. However, formal bilateral talks did not materialize and only informal "corridor" meetings took place between the three delegation heads (see section on Jordan in this chapter). The Palestinians insisted on negotiating with the Israelis separately, in order to emphasize their independent identity. The letter of invitation, sent by the sponsors, said: "Palestinians will be invited to attend as part of a joint Jordanian-Palestinian delegation." The Palestinians interpreted this as not expressly forbidding separate negotiations between them and the Israelis. Buoyed by their public relations successes, and by the Jordanians supporting them in their demand to go it alone, the Palestinians did not give way. Various compromise formulas were put forward, but without success. In these circumstances, the parties did not heed the American suggestions made in a letter, at the end of November, to the effect that both the Israelis and the Palestinians:

> provide a detailed plan of how and in what sequence Israel might cede some of the self-rule authority to the Palestinians. The objective should be to define as many areas of overlap as possible. Once they have each demonstrated that they can agree on most of the basic functions that Palestinian self-rule should contain, then they can try to tackle the biggest issue of controlling land and water."[101]

JORDAN

Jordan's relations with the US were damaged by its policy of support for Saddam Husayn during the Gulf crisis. Consequently, US Secretary of State Baker missed out Jordan when he began his peacemaking efforts in March. It was only during his second visit, in April, that he met with the Jordanian foreign minister, Tahir al-Masri, and even then, Baker did not go to Jordan: they met in Geneva on 12 April. Before the meeting took place, there had been some concern in Jordan that it might be left out of the peace process altogether. Jordan had enjoyed close cooperation with the US in the past and now found it embarrassing to have to admit that it did not know what proposals the Americans were about to put forward.[102] Masri was, therefore, relieved to find that the secretary of state did not, in fact, have any new proposals. Masri no doubt repeated to Baker that although Jordan did not seek to represent the Palestinians, it was ready to form a joint Jordanian-Palestinian delegation to negotiate with Israel in an international conference, if the Palestinians asked it to do so.[103] King Husayn had just reiterated this traditional Jordanian policy, that Jordan would act so as to be of assistance to the Palestinians but would not negotiate in their place: it was for the Palestinians to choose their policies and priorities.[104]

This attitude did not mean that Jordan had changed its basic assessment, which was that it had a vital interest in working for a settlement with Israel. Jordan reasoned that a settlement between the Palestinians and Israel would inevitably also lead to an agreement between it and Israel. Most Jordanians believed that there was no serious direct conflict between Jordan and Israel and that the real issue concerned the Palestinians.[105] The Palestinian issue affected Jordan so crucially that it could not remain passive. Husayn explained this clearly when he said that Jordan was affected by everything that happened to the Palestinians and "was living through all the difficulties...all the dangers."[106] It was this sense of urgency which prompted Husayn to welcome all three parts of the American proposal: the conference, the direct negotiations with Israel, and the multilateral meetings.[107] Jordan believed that peace with Israel would prove to be extremely beneficial to all concerned. Crown Prince Hasan stated unequivocally that Jordan would not hesitate to recognize Israel and establish diplomatic relations with it.[108] King Husayn further stated that the old taboos, prohibiting contact and discussion with Israel, were never taken too seriously by Jordan, as the "open bridges" across the River Jordan testified.[109]

In a widely publicized interview with a French magazine, Husayn said: "I firmly believe that taboos and clichés have to be put aside...we should not be concerned or worried to talk to anybody at any time...it is early to speak of this but I believe it will have to come soon."[110] This created the impression that Husayn was about to initiate talks with Israeli leaders. The Jordanians promptly denied any such intention.[111] However, since Husayn had never been reluctant to meet Israeli leaders (see *MECS* 1987, chapter on the ME peace process), the denial referred more to the timing than to the principle.

During the course of his eight visits to the region for the purpose of convening a peace conference between March and October, the US secretary of state visited Jordan six times (20 April, 14 May, 21 July, 2 August, 19 September and 14 October). Jordan, throughout, was not opposed to the formation of a joint Jordanian-Palestinian delegation. In May, during a news conference, which Baker and Husayn held jointly, Husayn said that Jordan viewed this idea "very favorably." However, he also noted that the Palestinians, for their part, had yet to ask Jordan to set up such a delegation.[112]

Two months later, the Palestinians had still not approached Husayn with the request for what he called the "umbrella" of a joint delegation. The umbrella seemed to him a fitting device, because it could also solve the issue of the representation of the Palestinians from outside the occupied territories. Since there were many Palestinians in Jordan from outside the territories, they could represent the Palestinians from the diaspora.[113] Jordan was in constant contact with the PLO, but the Palestinians were slow in making their decision (see section on the PLO in this chapter). Husayn and other Jordanian leaders constantly repeated their offer to the Palestinians, always stating that only the "Palestinian element" in such a joint delegation, and no one else would deal with the "Palestinian-Israeli" component of the problem.[114] It was not until October, just two weeks before the Madrid conference, that Husayn could say that he would soon announce the results of his long dialogue with the Palestinians. He said that he had been in touch with Palestinians from the occupied territories, and he noted further that, unlike the Americans, he was "in a position to be in touch with Palestinians in the diaspora [this referred to the PLO] in addition to those in the occupied territories."[115]

In July, Husayn declared in Baker's presence that Jordan would be among the first to attend the conference.[116] However, Jordan's Foreign Minister 'Abdallah al-Nasur explained that Jordan had not decided that it would go to the conference without the PLO — the PLO would have to announce its decision first.[117] This was probably in order to allay PLO fears. Since the Palestinians were involved in hard bargaining with the secretary of state throughout this period, it seemed most likely that they would come to the conference, once their demands were met.

Husayn coordinated Jordan's position with Syrian President Hafiz al-Asad. When Asad gave his positive reply to the US on 14 July, there remained only one matter on which the two leaders did not see eye to eye. Unlike Husayn, Asad refused to attend the multilateral meetings. Husayn felt that those meetings could serve a useful purpose, not only because they added the long-standing Jordanian requirement of an international component to the conference (over a dozen countries would be represented), but they would also make it possible for Jordan to raise important and pressing issues, such as water.[118]

In June, Masri was chosen by Husayn to take over the premiership from the more conservative Mudar Badran. Masri removed the five Muslim Brotherhood ministers who had been in Badran's cabinet (see chapter on Jordan), and so during most of the period leading up to the peace conference, Husayn was not hindered by their presence in Jordan's administration. As expected, the Muslim Brotherhood continued to voice its absolute rejection, not only of peace with Israel, but also of Israel's very presence in the region. They declared the day of the opening of the Madrid conference a day of mourning. However, they did not resort to violence. In fact, their spokesman stated: "We do not want any confrontation with the government...any conflict will only be harmful to the cause."[119]

Jordan's ideas on how to settle the conflict with Israel remained unchanged. Husayn's "Letter of Designation" to Zayd Ibn Shakir, appointing him prime minister after Masri's resignation on 21 November, enumerated the following objectives: pursuance and participation in the peace process so as to contribute to its success — comprehensive peace on the basis of the "territory for peace" formula; implementation of Resolutions 242 and 338, which applied to all occupied Arab territories, including Arab Jerusalem; and resolving the Palestine question, in all its dimensions, on the basis of UN resolutions, so that the Palestinians would acquire their national rights, including self-determination.[120]

Jordan considered the issues of Jerusalem and the Israeli settlement activities in the West Bank and Gaza as crucial. Husayn addressed himself to two distinct issues concerning Jerusalem. First, there was the issue of "Arab Jerusalem," by which he meant those sections of the city which had been controlled by Jordan prior to 1967. There was no question in his mind that those parts of Jerusalem would revert to Arab control. Second, there was the question of the future status of the city, emanating from its sacredness. Husayn was willing to find a solution to this question. He noted the need to make the "city a symbol of peace for the followers of three divine religions." However, he also took pains to explain that he was referring to those parts of Jerusalem where there were holy places. He appeared to accept the fact that a future status of Jerusalem, which he advocated, would not extend over the western part of the city, where there were no Islamic holy sites and which was, he noted, the capital of Israel.

As to the settlement issue, Jordan's view was that it was pointless to discuss the status of the occupied territories while Israel's building activities continued. They ought to be halted at the start of the negotiations.[121]

In the year under review, Husayn alluded to the question of the future border between Jordan and Israel, to the effect that he did not reject some modification of the old (1949) cease-fire (armistice line).[122] This was an issue about which he did not frequently make statements.

Husayn did not change his favorable attitude toward an eventual confederal link between Jordan and the Palestinian entity, when it came into being. He was resigned to a solution that he did not consider to be the "ideal model." He would have preferred a proper union, in other words, a federation rather than a confederation. However, the latter being the *formula that exists now,* with the Palestinians preserving their special identity and the Jordanians theirs, he would go along with the looser arrangement. The scenario he envisioned was the same as that envisioned by the PLO. When the territories were returned to the Palestinians, they would first exercise their right to self-determination. Then, they would decide about the link with Jordan.[123] Clearly, Husayn was not prepared to reconsider Jordan's decision to disengage from the West Bank (see *MECS* 1988, chapter on Jordan).

In Madrid, Jordan's new foreign minister, Kamil Abu Jabir, made a most significant statement. He said: "Let me speak plainly, Jordan has never been Palestine and will not be so."[124] The Jordanian delegation to the conference estimated that they had been able "to affirm the clarity of the Jordanian identity." The head of the Jordanian delegation, 'Abd al-Salam al-Majali, said: "the clear [Jordanian] identity stands alongside the Palestinian identity....The conference made it clear to the entire world that there are two identities, despite the work of two delegations within the framework of one delegation."[125] The Palestinians in the joint delegation had their own reasons for making the most of the success of projecting two identities. It strengthened their claim to represent a separate entity — one with political demands of its own. It was for this reason that the joint delegation, that came to Washington in December, insisted on seating arrangements that would highlight their separateness. This created a crisis with the Israeli delegation, the result being that the joint Jordanian-Palestinian delegation did not meet with the Israeli delegation in formal session.

Majali explained in interviews why such a Jordanian-Palestinian stance was justified. Referring to the rejectionist forces in the Arab world, he said that any move that appeared to subsume the Palestinians threatened the peace process and the lives of any Jordanians appearing to negate Palestinian national identity. He listed the Jordanians who had been killed for seeming to have been making this attempt, among them his own cousin, Hazz'a al-Majali, the Jordanian prime minister, who was assassinated in August 1960.[126]

The official invitation to the Madrid conference sent out by Bush and Gorbachev (see Appendix I), stated: "Palestinians will be invited and attend as part of a joint Jordanian-Palestinian delegation." The phrase "as part of" was deemed as sufficiently unambiguous, by a ranking US official, for him to be able to say that the terms of reference were clear in this regard. However, the obvious importance that the Jordanians and Palestinians attached to a looser interpretation obliged him to add: "How the parties organized themselves within this framework was up to the parties themselves to work out."[127]

Upon inviting the delegation at the end of November to the Washington round, the US suggested to Jordan and Israel that they begin considering how to solve problems together, "by settling some old, rather minor disputes over where exactly the border between them runs in the northern Negev desert region known as the Arava."[128] However, due to the procedural impasse over the seating arrangements, the Jordanians and Israelis did not, in fact, reach the stage where they had to decide whether to start their bilateral substantive discussions with this particular, not very pressing issue.

SYRIA

Syria's relations with the US underwent a significant change when Syria joined the US-led coalition against Saddam Husayn's occupation of Kuwait in 1990. President Hafiz al-Asad and President George Bush had a successful meeting in Geneva on 23 November 1990[129] and this led to a rapprochement between the two leaders.

Asad was impressed by Bush's readiness to consider the convening of an international peace conference on the ME, at an appropriate time, on the basis of UN Security Council Resolutions 242 and 338. When US Secretary of State James Baker came to Damascus, on the eve of the concerted military offensive against Iraq, the

Americans were more specific as to the timing of such a conference. Baker promised that the peace efforts would be resumed "after the conclusion of the Gulf crisis."[130] The Syrian foreign minister, Faruq al-Shar', considered this a serious pledge, which the US would have to live up to, if it "wished to maintain its credibility with the Arabs."[131]

Asad and other Arab leaders viewed President Bush's address to a joint session of the US Congress on 6 March 1991, as proof that when the peace process was resumed, it would be conducted by the US along lines which the Arabs considered balanced. Bush made certain points which appealed to them in particular. These were:

(1) Comprehensive peace must be grounded in the two Security Council resolutions and in the principle of "territory for peace" (they noted the use of the word "principle").

(2) Legitimate Palestinian political rights must be provided for.

(3) In the modern age, geography cannot guarantee security (this observation weakened Israel's argument that territory was vital for its security).[132]

Following Bush's address, Secretary of State Baker opened his efforts in the ME. After his meetings with Asad in Damascus, in a joint press conference with Shar', he noted that Syria was ready to "pursue an active peace process."[133] Baker sensed a change of attitude in the region, as a result of the Gulf War, with all the countries concerned wishing to take advantage of this opportunity to make progress.

The secretary of state explained that the purpose of the peace process was to achieve real peace and reconciliation between Israel and the Arabs. However, the US could do nothing if the parties did not wish to attain these objectives, since no outside party could impose peace on the ME. For his part, Shar' said that he detected an American determination to implement the Security Council resolutions, thereby attaining a "just and comprehensive settlement of the Arab-Israeli conflict and the Palestinian issue."[134]

Baker paid a second visit to Damascus a month later. This was seen by the Syrian media as evidence that the US had made a real commitment to promote a settlement. On this visit, the secretary of state discussed the structure and composition of the peace conference. The Syrians preferred a conference with the participation of the permanent members of the Security Council, although Baker proposed a different kind of conference, limited mainly to the regional countries and the two sponsors, the US and the Soviet Union. The Syrians also envisaged the participation of the EC. While not rejecting Baker's proposal out of hand, they nevertheless insisted that the UN be accorded an important role and that the conference's objective should clearly be the implementation of the two Security Council resolutions.[135] This attitude was not in accordance with Baker's view that the conference should not impose solutions. As he saw it, the Security Council resolutions provided a framework for the parties to meet directly in order to accommodate their differences. Despite these disagreements between the US and Syria, Baker discerned "a real desire to move ahead."[136]

Eleven days later, the secretary of state returned on his third visit. Among the more important problems still to be resolved were the permanency of the conference and the role of the UN. Syria wanted the conference to accompany the negotiations in continuous session. They did not accept the idea of a mere ceremonial opening session, as agreed on by Israel. Syria also continued to argue in favor of a significant role for the UN.

At the conclusion of the talks, both Baker and Shar' agreed that they had made some progress. Baker pointed out that Syria and Israel had agreed that the objective of convening a conference was to achieve a comprehensive settlement on the basis of Resolutions 242 and 338. Since Syria and Israel had different interpretations of what was required, they would hold direct bilateral talks so as to reach agreement.[137] Secretary of State Baker again made it clear that the US "rejected solutions based on imposition from outside." Significantly, the idea of imposing a settlement was also rejected by the Soviet foreign minister, Alexander Bessmertnykh, when he came to Damascus two weeks later. He said: "I do not believe that pressure should be put on any party to talk it into accepting any plan that runs counter to its national interest."[138]

Baker returned to Syria, for the fourth time, two days after Bessmertnykh's visit. No news conference was held at the conclusion of his talks.[139] Syria and Israel still remained as far apart as ever on whether the UN should attend the peace conference and whether the conference should be a onetime event or reconvene from time to time.[140] Shar' stated explicitly: "We believe that the UN should be in the conference and that the conference remain in session." Asad blamed Israel for placing "hundreds of noes in the face of the peace process. No to the return of territories to their owner, no to the UN, no to Europe's participation in the peace conference, no to the rights of the Palestinians, and many more noes...."[141] However, he did not shut the door to further efforts. In his last talk with Baker, he had expressed readiness to cooperate further with the US secretary of state to reach an acceptable formula.[142]

Over two months passed before Baker came again to Damascus on his fifth visit (18 July). However, during this unusually long interval, the American efforts had not come to a complete standstill. At the end of May, Bush had sent letters to Asad and to Prime Minister Shamir of Israel. On 1 June, Shar' met with Baker in Lisbon and indicated a willingness to come closer to the American proposals.[143] The fact that Syria viewed Bush's letter as "fair and balanced to a large extent" had encouraged Syria to make a compromise.[144] Shar' told Secretary of State Baker that Syria agreed to restrict the UN role to that of an observer and to have the conference reconvene merely to receive updates on the negotiations.[145] As a result of this Syrian shift, the US was able to conclude that it could resume its efforts after Asad replied to Bush's letter and included the new Syrian position in his reply. Asad's reply was handed over to the US ambassador in Damascus on 14 July. It was welcomed by the Americans. Baker described Asad's reply as a very positive one that pushed the peace "efforts forward more than any previous efforts I know."[146] In the letter, Asad told Bush that he considered his (Bush's) proposals, and the subsequent clarifications, positive and balanced, constituting an acceptable basis for achieving a comprehensive solution and a peace process in the region. He (Asad) also expressed satisfaction because Bush's proposals were based on the principle of international legitimacy, gave special attention to the UN role in the peace conference, and stressed European participation. He highly assessed Bush's pledge that the US and the USSR would be catalysts for peace and would assume a special responsibility to make the conference succeed in its objectives as defined by the relevant UN resolution.[147]

Asad's letter served to remove most of the remaining obstacles. Moreover, the US secretary of state knew that he would find the Syrian president businesslike because of his statements in a news conference held jointly with President Mubarak on 17 July.[148] On the issue of the UN role, Asad reaffirmed that the UN would have only observer status. This role would be significant by virtue of the fact that the conference was convened on the basis of UN resolutions. Asad said that it was not important that the UN would not be a full participant, since no votes would be taken at the conference. For all practical purposes, the UN would be equal with the other participants. It was worthy of note that Asad also said that if Syria had not obtained all it wanted, it was because it had acted according to the the Arab proverb: "Do you want to have the grapes or to fight the watchman?" Syria preferred the grapes.[149]

After his meeting with Asad on 18 July, Baker was able to announce that Syria had agreed to the US proposals. He consoled the Syrians over the diminished role of the UN by saying that the UN would be a "point of reference." Shar' indicated that this took care of Syria's concerns because if Israel's "obstructionism" brought about the breakdown of the conference, the problem would be referred to the UN Security Council by the European countries. Then, if the UN Security Council found Israel guilty, there would be a unified international rallying against it, reminiscent of that against Iraq after it had invaded Kuwait.[150] Baker said that the conference could be reconvened with the consent of all the main parties. The secretary of state also noted that the US position of not recognizing Israel's 1981 effective annexation of the Golan Heights remained unchanged.[151] At the end of July, Asad gave an interview to a US correspondent. The Syrian president made, inter alia, the following observations, which revealed more details about Syria's position on the peace process:

(1) It was obvious that Syria, like any other country, when it decided to go to a conference was doing so in order to negotiate. However, negotiations were merely discussions based on the UN resolutions held in bilateral committees, set up by the conference. In the last resort, it was the conference which would establish the program leading to the implementation of the resolutions and to comprehensive peace.

(2) Negotiations should not be seen as distinct from the conference, nor should they lead to partial, separate and noncomprehensive agreements with one or the other Arab states. Separate negotiations were possible, but the conference would remain "standing" until peace was established.

(3) Syria wanted real peace and had been proclaiming this for 20 years. Its adherence to the UN resolutions meant that it would carry out everything stipulated by them, thereby responding to the peace requirements.

(4) The question of Palestinian representation could be solved either through elections or by a delegation that would include all the Palestinian factions and not merely some of them. However, if the Palestinians came up with another solution concerning their representation, Syria would support it too.[152]

As expected, Syria gave a positive reply to the joint US-Soviet invitation to the conference announced on 31 July. Syrian commentators expressed the hope that it augured the "return of international law to the region."[153] Accordingly, Baker's visit to Damascus, on 19 September, dealt with the issues that still had to be resolved before the convening of the conference that was set for October. One such issue was that of the US letter of assurance to Syria which had previously been discussed. The exchanges of letters between Asad and Bush and talks between officials from both countries had to be consolidated in final letter form. Secretary of State Baker brought a draft with him and the Syrians promised to study it. Shar' stated in a press conference, in Baker's presence, that in the Syrian view, Resolutions 242 and 338 meant that in the final settlement Israel must withdraw from *all* occupied Arab territories, including the Golan Heights. The secretary of state's statement was, by implication, less categorical. He thought that 242 "must be applied on all points" and that the US was "prepared to declare once again the US policy in regard to the nonrecognition of the application of Israel's laws on the Golan." Baker had to take into account President Ford's letter to Israel, in 1975, which promised, inter alia, "to give great weight to Israel's position that any peace agreement with Syria must be predicated on Israel remaining on the Golan Heights."[154] Baker revealed that this promise had also been discussed in Damascus.[155]

Baker's eighth visit took place a month later, on October 16, and was his last before the conference. One issue still remained unresolved: Syria's refusal to attend the multilateral negotiations, which the letter of invitation to the conference set for two weeks after the opening of the conference.

Shar' declared that Syria would not attend the multilateral negotiations, which was intended to deal with regional problems. He posited that it was impossible to deal effectively with those issues before achieving results at the peace conference and in the bilateral negotiations. Asad affirmed that to participate in multilateral talks was "putting the cart before the horse" and would be a waste of time. In principle, Syria was not opposed to the adoption of measures that would give momentum to the peace process, but only after discussing how to implement the UN resolutions.[156]

The US letter of assurance to Syria was not officially published, but a text that appeared in an Arab daily in London seemed to provide the complete text (see Appendix V). Certain explicit references were of special importance to the Syrians, namely the allusion to the "land for peace principle as applicable to all fronts, including the Golan Heights" as well as the reaffirmation that the US "does not intend to recognize or accept unilateral actions by Israel with regard to imposing its laws, rule or administration on the Golan Heights." The expression of willingness by the US to guarantee the border, when agreed upon, between Israel and Syria was of similar significance to Syria.

The peace conference opened in Madrid on 30 October and lasted three days. Shar' said in his speech that, in the Syrian view, the implementation of Resolutions 242 and 338 should not be the subject of bargaining during the bilateral negotiations, but must simply be implemented. Syria had come to the conference ready to reach a settlement despite the many reservations concerning the format and terms of reference of the conference. Throughout his speech, he stressed Syria's demand that the settlement be comprehensive, that Israel withdraw "from every inch of the occupied Syrian Golan, the West Bank, Jerusalem, the Gaza Strip and the south of Lebanon." He criticized the proposal to hold multilateral talks, since they did "not fall within the framework of Resolution 242" and ought not to begin "until substantive and concrete achievement has been made in bilateral negotiations."[157]

Syria viewed the opening session in Madrid as the first part of an ongoing conference. Consequently, when the chairman, the Soviet foreign minister, declared the session concluded, Shar' intervened to say that Syria considered the conference merely adjourned.[158]

The Syrians were disappointed with the bilateral meeting between Syrian and Israeli officials (3–4 November). The head of the Syrian delegation complained that he had tried, in vain, to see if there was any readiness on the part of the Israelis to withdraw from occupied Arab territory and carry out the Security Council resolutions.[159] Nevertheless, Shar' noted one positive outcome of the conference — it had demonstrated the importance the world attached to the achievement of peace in the ME. He promised that Syria would persist in its peace efforts.[160]

The next round of talks was held in Washington DC a month later (10–18 December). Two weeks prior to the meetings, the Americans sent letters to Syria and Israel containing proposals on how, in the US view, the two delegations could start a normal dialogue. They suggested to the Syrians that they ask the Israelis what Israel would give them by way of withdrawal from the Golan Heights, if Syria were prepared to give a peace treaty.[161] (For the suggestion made to Israel, see section on Israel in this chapter.) The two delegations ignored the US suggestions. They met for a total of 16 hours. Although the atmosphere of the meetings was cold and formal, the talks continued. US assistant secretary of state Edward Djerejian summed up his impressions in a prepared statement to Arab and Israeli reporters. He said that the US was encouraged by the attitudes of the parties. He characterized the exchanges as "intensive and substantive."[162]

LEBANON

In 1989 and 1990, Lebanon was totally preoccupied with its own internal problems, caused by the civil war, and therefore did not take part in the peace efforts. Its relations with Israel remained tense. In 1984, Lebanon canceled the agreement it had signed with Israel in May 1983. If ratified by the Lebanese parliament, this agreement would have established a de facto peace. However, since the agreement was not ratified, Israel decided not to withdraw completely from Lebanon, in 1985, and to maintain a military presence in South Lebanon, in what it called a "security zone." On the basis of UN Security Council Resolution 425 of 19 March 1978, Lebanon demanded the withdrawal of Israel from its territory, asserting that its army was capable of maintaining quiet along the Israeli border. Israel refused to withdraw. It was obvious that, unless a new agreement was signed between the two countries, this issue would not be resolved.

In mid-1991, as the Lebanese army moved south to reestablish the state's authority over these areas, Lebanese leaders made statements indicating that the Lebanese army was ready to take over the Israeli-held zone. Lebanese President Ilyas Hirawi went so far as to declare: "We have to guarantee Israel's demand for security in its northern region."[163] At a meeting with President Bush, Hirawi told him that as soon as "Israel withdrew or committed itself irrevocably to withdraw, not one single gunshot will be fired from Lebanese territory."[164]

In the year under review, Lebanon signed two treaties with Syria:

(1) The Treaty of Brotherhood, Cooperation and Coordination, 22 May 1991.
(2) Defense and Security agreement, 17 August 1991 (see chapter on Lebanon).

The two treaties provided for close links between Lebanon and Syria. Consequently, after consultation with Syria, Lebanon decided that in the talks with Israel, it would demand Israel's withdrawal from the strip in South Lebanon as the first item to be discussed at the peace conference. The Lebanese delegation would deal with the issue of peace with Israel at a later stage, only after Israel had withdrawn. Lebanese leaders, therefore, said virtually nothing about peace with Israel at the Madrid conference. This was a decision which Hirawi and Asad had made when they met, on 27 July, to coordinate their policies, in accordance with Article 1 of the Treaty of Cooperation between them.

Like the other parties who were invited to the conference in October, Lebanon also received a letter of assurance from the US. The full text of the letter was not published, but its essential points were reportedly revealed by Lebanon's Foreign Minister Faris Buwayz. The letter contained assurances that the implementation of Security Council Resolution 425, dealing with Israeli withdrawal from South Lebanon, would be separated from Resolutions 242 and 338 and "would be implemented." The Israeli withdrawal would be dealt with as a separate issue from the Syrian withdrawal from Lebanon, on the ground that Resolution 425 called for an Israeli withdrawal, while a Syrian withdrawal was laid down by the Ta'if agreement. The letter also contained a reminder that the Ta'if accord stipulated the withdrawal of all non-Lebanese forces from Lebanon.[165]

Buwayz also said that Lebanon would not participate in the multilateral negotiations until "concrete progress is made [at the conference] and guarantees are provided that the Arab states will regain their territories and the brother Palestinians regain their legitimate rights."[166] This Lebanese policy closely resembled that of Syria. Buwayz articulated these policies at the conference in Madrid. As to Resolution 425, he demanded "immediate, complete and unconditional withdrawal of Israel from all Lebanese territories." He repeated the promises made by Hirawi, to the effect that, once the resolution was implemented, Lebanon would not allow any security violations across its border.[167] Regarding peace with Israel, there was no explicit expression of readiness to discuss the issue.

Israeli Prime Minister Shamir said in his speech at the Madrid conference (1 November): "We have no designs on Lebanese territory, and in the context of a peace treaty and the removal of the Syrian presence, we can restore stability and security on the borders between our two countries."[168] In his reaction to this statement, Buwayz said that Lebanon "noted" this Israeli commitment but "wondered" about Israel's reason for occupying the Lebanese south. He also said that "Lebanon's relations with Syria ought not to be a matter of concern for Israel....Israel ought not to try to link its occupation to the Syrian presence." The Syrian presence, he said, "is regulated by the Ta'if arrangement, which has the endorsement of the international community led by the US."[169]

The Lebanese-Israeli bilateral talks, which began with the session in Madrid, and continued with nearly 20 hours of meetings in the Washington round (10–18 December), were conducted in a "frank" atmosphere.[170] The Israelis described it as "good and pleasant."[171] Before the Washington round, the US suggested that the two delegations should consider discussing security arrangements in Southern Lebanon.[172] The two delegations did not strictly follow this advice, but they did not completely ignore it either. One Lebanese weekly reported that an agreement was reached that Lebanese and Israeli military experts would meet to discuss the issues connected with a Lebanese takeover of the security zone, ensuring that Israel's security concerns would be taken care of.[173] Moreover, Buwayz declared that there was no truth in the often-heard charges that Israel was siphoning water from the south. Lebanon had thoroughly checked this and found no evidence.[174] This showed that some progress had indeed been made. The head of the Lebanese delegation to the talks in Washington said that the fact that Israel entered the negotiations with assurances that "they have no claims or designs on Lebanese territory, not even one centimeter" or "one drop of Lebanese water" was a "good base" for negotiations.[175]

EGYPT

In the year under review, Egypt remained actively involved in the peace process. It enjoyed the privileged position of a country which maintained contacts with all sides, including Syria (with which relations were normalized in December 1989). Egyptian leaders made it clear that although Egypt was not acting as a mediator between the Arabs and Israel, it was doing all it could to persuade the parties concerned to start negotiations as quickly as possible. President Mubarak explained that time was of the essence, since the US would be preoccupied with presidential elections by the end of 1991.[176] The Egyptians believed that it was important to include most Arab countries in the process, certainly key countries such as Syria, Saudi Arabia and Jordan.[177]

Egypt's standing among the Arab states was fully restored in 1989, when it was readmitted to the Arab League. Its standing was further enhanced when 'Ismat 'Abd al-Majid, Egypt's deputy prime minister and foreign minister, was elected to be the secretary-general of the Arab League. Egypt felt confident enough to give advice to Israel and the Palestinians, not only through diplomatic channels, but also publicly, when it even often admonished them.[178]

Egypt had a great deal to offer, in particular to the Palestinians. The Palestinians needed Egyptian diplomatic support as well as expert guidance, which Egypt was in a position to give, having negotiated the autonomy agreements with Israel for several years (1979–82). One Palestinian spokesperson mentioned the many documents that these negotiations had produced, documents that could assist the Palestinians in their talks with Israel.[179]

At the Madrid peace conference, Egypt's foreign minister, 'Amr Musa, promised that his country would do everything possible to promote peace by virtue of its "unique role on the level of the entire region." He promised that Egypt would address regional questions in the multilateral talks, such as arms limitation, prevention of the proliferation of weapons of mass destruction, and nuclear weapons in particular.[180]

Although Egypt continued to support the Arab positions on the conflict with Israel, it also displayed a certain degree of pragmatism on matters of procedure. In fact, it acted as a catalyst in helping to overcome several obstacles that blocked the convening of the peace conference. The Egyptians explained to the Arabs that they ought not to insist on any particular name for the conference. It was not important whether the conference was called "international" or "regional"; what really mattered was that agreement should be reached on holding the conference, so that it convened with US, Soviet, EC and UN participation. This would constitute the point of departure for the bilateral negotiations. This line was consistently pursued by Egypt.[181]

Egypt had a similar attitude to the question of the UN role at the conference. It believed that there was no need to insist that the UN be accorded a special role there; it was enough to ensure that it would be present. There was no getting away from the fact that the conference would meet on the basis of UN resolutions, thus making the

UN "a point of reference" with regard to the "principles defined and established by the UN."[182] Furthermore, since the conference would not be the forum for the actual negotiations, Egypt insisted that it was imperative that they stop arguing over these essentially procedural points and move the process forward.[183] The Egyptians also adopted a pragmatic attitude on the issue of the permanency of the conference. Since it was likely that the parties would need international support during the negotiations, the Egyptians believed that there was bound to be some kind of follow-up by the conference. This issue should not be allowed to hold up agreement on convening the conference either.[184]

Despite the disagreement between Egypt and the PLO over the latter's support for Saddam Husayn (see *MECS* 1990), the official Egyptian attitude remained one of declared readiness to "cooperate with any leader the Palestinians will choose," including 'Arafat. However, Mubarak's trust in 'Arafat was now seriously shaken.[185] One influential Egyptian journalist noted that, since Israel rejected the PLO, other Palestinians would have to be found, "but must of course have some connection with the PLO."[186] Butrus Butrus-Ghali, deputy prime minister for foreign relations, explained that although Egypt did not "always agree" with the PLO, a role ought to be reserved for it in a compromise that would make it possible "to include Palestinians in the negotiations with a mandate from the PLO."[187] Mubarak admitted that relations with 'Arafat were not good, but said that he would nevertheless meet with him.[188] He first met with him outside Egypt, in Benghazi, on 28 August, and eventually in Cairo on 30 October.

Nevertheless, meetings at the working level continued throughout. Mubarak was of the opinion that the Palestinian representation would have to be jointly with Jordan. His close adviser, 'Usama al-Baz, the Egyptian foreign ministry's first under secretary and the director of the president's office for political affairs, was quite specific that the Palestinian inhabitants of the occupied territories should be considered first, because they were the ones "who have suffered the most from the occupation." However, he did not exclude Palestinians from outside these territories.[189] Two months later, Baz noticed that the "Palestinian leadership," a circumlocution for the PLO, had "accepted what has been demanded from it [and] this has facilitated Arab support for Palestinian demands."[190] In his speech at the Madrid conference, Foreign Minister 'Amr Musa refrained from mentioning the PLO specifically. When asked about this, he explained that his speech had been prepared for the conference where the Palestinian people were represented by a Palestinian delegation."[191] With PLO acquiescence, Egyptian pragmatism made this reply possible.

The Egyptians had learnt from past experience that Palestinian flexibility could not be taken for granted. Palestinian behavior had been completely inflexible for many decades. Mubarak referred to this in several of his speeches and interviews, criticizing the Palestinians for having missed opportunities in the past[192] and for "heaping invective" on Egypt for suggesting compromises.[193]

Egypt's efforts to promote the peace process naturally did not exclude Israel, but were low key in that respect. The Egyptians were critical, often publicly, of the Israeli Government's attitude toward the peace process. They doubted Shamir's intentions, and Mubarak, as in past years, refused to meet with him. He saw no point in a meeting unless assured in advance of its "success," by which he meant a substantive shift in the Israeli position.[194] On several occasions, he described Shamir as a man who would say "no" to everything.[195] On the eve of a visit to Egypt by Israel's foreign minister, David Levy (29–31 July), Mubarak told the BBC that he doubted whether Shamir would let the peace conference succeed. "He will play the game of elections... so as to delay the whole process."[196] Apart from Levy's visit, there were no other high-level official visits between the two countries.

Egypt's substantive views on Arab terms for a settlement remained essentially unchanged. When, at Israel's insistence, the US accepted that Resolution 242 lent itself to various interpretations besides "territories for peace," the Egyptians countered that the preambular provision of that resolution emphasized the "inadmissibility of the acquisition of territory by war." This was a nonnegotiable principle of the resolution, its interpretation agreed on long before by the international community. Only the modalities of its implementation were open to discussion.[197] However, on two occasions, a more lenient Egyptian attitude could be discerned. The Egyptian ambassador in Israel published an article in an Israeli paper in which he said that Resolution 242 "meant territories for peace and this applied, ladies and gentlemen, to 'territories' and not '*the* territories' — a significant difference."[198] In an interview, Egyptian Foreign Minister Musa also stated that the main interpretation of Resolution 242 was that any "territorial changes should not reflect the weight of conquest."[199] The very mention of territorial changes by an Egyptian foreign minister and an Egyptian diplomat was worthy of note.

On the issue of East Jerusalem, Egypt's position remained unaltered. Israel was called upon "to understand that the status of Jerusalem concerns the entire Islamic world as much as it concerns Jews and Christians."[200] Nevertheless, the Egyptians helped to persuade the Palestinians not to insist that their delegation to the peace conference include a resident of East Jerusalem. The Egyptians were pragmatic, even on this sensitive issue, and they argued that the Palestinians ought not to fear that, by accepting this compromise now, they would lose their right to participate in the negotiations on the final status of Jerusalem, set for a date three years after the transitional arrangements were put into effect.[201]

The Egyptian idea for a long-term solution for Jerusalem was revealed by Mubarak's adviser, 'Usama al-Baz: the city need not be partitioned again; the historical, legal and cultural rights of the Arabs would be restored; the city's administration could be united; and sovereignty over the city would be divided, with part of it coming under Arab control.[202]

APPENDIX I: TEXT OF INVITATION TO THE MADRID PEACE CONFERENCE (30 OCTOBER 1991)

The following invitation was issued jointly by the US and the Soviet Union on Friday, 18 October, to Israel, Syria, Jordan, Lebanon and the Palestinians:

After extensive consultations with Arab states, Israel and the Palestinians, the US and the Soviet Union believe that an historic opportunity exists to advance the prospects of genuine peace throughout the region. The US and the Soviet Union are prepared to assist the parties to achieve a just, lasting and comprehensive peace settlement, through direct negotiations along two tracks, between Israel and the Arab states, and between Israel and the Palestinians, based on UN Security Resolutions 242 and 338. The objective of this process is real peace.

Toward that end, the president of the US and the president of the USSR invite you to a peace conference, which their countries will cosponsor, followed immediately by direct negotiations. The conference will be convened in Madrid on 30 October 1991.

President Bush and President Gorbachev request your acceptance of this invitation no later than 6 p.m. Washington time, 23 October 1991, in order to ensure proper organization and preparation of the conference.

Direct bilateral negotiations will begin four days after the opening of the conference. Those parties who wish to attend multilateral negotiations should focus on region-wide issues, such as arms control and regional security, water, refugee issues, environment, economic development, and other subjects of mutual interest.

The cosponsors will chair the conference, which will be held at ministerial level. Governments to be invited include Israel, Syria, Lebanon and Jordan. Palestinians will be invited and attend as part of a joint Jordanian-Palestinian delegation. Egypt will be invited to the conference as a participant. The EC will be a participant in the conference, alongside the US and the Soviet Union and will be represented by its presidency. The GCC will be invited to send its secretary-general to the conference as an observer, and GCC member states will be invited to participate in organizing the negotiations of multilateral issues. The UN will be invited to send an observer, representing the secretary-general.

The conference will have no power to impose solutions on the parties or veto agreements reached by them. It will have no authority to make decisions for the parties and no ability to vote on issues or results. The conference can reconvene only with the consent of all the parties.

With respect to negotiations between Israel and Palestinians who are part of the joint Jordanian-Palestinian delegation, negotiations will be conducted in phases, beginning with talks on interim self-government arrangements. These talks will be conducted with the objective of reaching agreement within one year. Once agreed, the interim self-government arrangements will last for a period of five years. Beginning the third year of the period of interim self-government arrangements, negotiations will take place on permanent status. These permanent status negotiations, and the negotiations between Israel and the Arab states, will take place on the basis of Resolutions 242 and 338.

It is understood that the cosponsors are committed to making this process succeed. It is their intention to convene the conference and negotiations with those parties who agree to attend.

The cosponsors believe that this process offers the promise of ending decades of confrontation and conflict and the hope of a lasting peace. Thus, the cosponsors hope that the parties will approach these negotiations in a spirit of goodwill and mutual respect. In this way, the peace process can begin to break down the mutual suspicions and mistrust that perpetuate the conflict, and allow the parties to begin to resolve their differences. Indeed, only through such a process can real peace and reconciliation among the Arab states, Israel and the Palestinians be achieved. And, only though this process, can the peoples of the Middle East attain the peace and security they richly deserve.

SOURCE: *JP*, 21 October 1991.

APPENDIX II: US LETTER OF ASSURANCE TO ISRAEL (18 OCTOBER 1991)

Israel's decision to attend a Middle East peace conference to launch direct bilateral and multilateral peace negotiations is an important step, bringing Israel closer to the peace and security it so richly deserves. Now is the time for decisions by all sides so that we can move quickly to a conference and to negotiations. Indeed, only through direct negotiations, can real peace and security be achieved.

In the context of the process on which we are embarking, we want to respond to your request for certain assurances related to this process. These assurances constitute US understandings and intentions concerning the conference and ensuing negotiations.

From the beginning, we made clear that the US would be prepared to provide assurances that were consistent with our policy and that did not weaken or contradict the framework we have created for convening the peace conference. We have also said that there will be no assurances to one party that are not known to all the others.

This process of negotiations is based upon the special relationship that exists between our two countries. It is based on shared values, common interests, and mutual respect for democracy. Since the establishment of the State of Israel, the US has understood that the challenges Israel has confronted involve its very existence. For too long, Israel has lived in a region where its neighbors have refused to acknowledge its existence and have tried to destroy it. That is why the key element in our efforts to promote peace has always been a recognition of Israel's security requirements and the need for close cooperation between our two countries to meet those requirements.

Let us assure you that our commitment to Israel's security remains unshakable. Anyone who seeks to drive a wedge between us, in an effort to compromise that commitment, fails to understand the deep bonds that link our two countries and the enduring nature of our commitment to Israel's security, including our commitment to maintain Israel's qualitative edge. We want to reiterate our position that Israel is entitled to secure and defensible borders, which should be directly negotiated and agreed with its neighbors.

The US believes that the objective of this process is a just and lasting peace settlement, achieved through direct negotiations based on UN Security Council Resolutions 242 and 338, and including the conclusion of peace treaties with full diplomatic relations between Israel and its Arab neighbors.

You and other parties have informed us that there are different interpretations of UN Security Council Resolution 242, and that these will be presented during the negotiations.

With regard to the conference, it will have no power to impose solutions on the parties, or veto agreements reached by them. It will have no authority to make decisions and no ability to vote on issues or results. The conference can reconvene only with the consent of all the parties.

Direct bilateral negotiations will begin four days after the opening of the conference. Those parties who wish to attend multilateral negotiations will convene two weeks after the opening of the conference to organize those negotiations. The US supports participation in and organization of these multilateral negotiations. We believe those negotiations should focus on regional issues such as water, environment, arms control and regional security, economic development, refugee issues and other subjects.

The US is committed to achieving a comprehensive settlement of the Arab-Israeli conflict and will do its utmost to ensure that the process moves forward along both tracks toward that end. The US hopes to broaden the orbit of peace to include other regional states that continue to maintain a state of belligerency with Israel.

The US does not support linkage between the various negotiations; in pursuit of a comprehensive settlement, all the negotiations should proceed as quickly as possible toward agreement.

The US position is that no party in the process will have to sit with anyone it does not want to sit with. There should be no surprises regarding the nature of representation at the conference or in the negotiations. The US believes that Palestinians will be represented in a joint Jordanian-Palestinian delegation. Palestinians who are residents of the West Bank and Gaza, who accept a two-track approach and negotiations in phases, and who are willing to live in peace with Israel, will participate in the delegation and in the negotiations on interim self-government arrangements.

Furthermore, it is not the aim of the US to bring the PLO into this process or to bring Israel into dialogue or negotiations with the PLO.

The US will act as an honest broker in trying to resolve the Arab-Israeli conflict.

Because the issues at stake are so complex and the emotions so deep, the US has long maintained that a transitional period is required to break down the walls of suspicion and mistrust, and lay the basis for sustainable negotiations. With respect to negotiations between Israel and Palestinians, negotiations will be conducted in phases, beginning with talks on interim self-government arrangements. These talks will be conducted with the objective of reaching agreement within one year. Once agreed, the interim self-government arrangements will last for a period of five years. Beginning the third year of the period of interim self-government arrangements, negotiations will take place on permanent status.

In light of our special relationship with Israel, the US agrees to consult closely with Israel and take Israel's position on peace process issues into account. At the same time, the US reserves the right to maintain its long-standing positions and state them when appropriate.

You have expressed particular security concerns about the Golan Heights. In this regard, the US continues to stand by the assurance from President Ford to Prime Minister Rabin of 1 September 1975 that the US will support the position that an overall settlement with Syria, in the framework of a peace agreement, must assure Israel's security from attack from the Golan Heights.

The US further supports the position that a just and lasting peace must be acceptable to both sides. The US has not developed a final position on the borders. Should it do so, it will give great weight to Israel's position that any peace agreement with Syria must be predicated on Israel remaining on the Golan Heights. In this connection, the US is prepared to offer a US guarantee of the border security arrangements which are agreed upon between Israel and Syria, subject to our constitutional processes.

With regard to Lebanon, and consistent with long-standing US policy, the US believes that Israel has a right to security along its entire northern border. Furthermore, the US remains committed to the withdrawal of all non-Lebanese forces from Lebanon and the disarming of all militias.

We continue to see the Egyptian-Israeli peace treaty and relationship as a cornerstone of our policy in the region and support the full implementation of the Egyptian-Israeli peace treaty and implementing agreements.

These are the assurances that the US is providing concerning the implementation of the initiative we have discussed. Working together, on the basis of the mutual trust and confidence that have always characterized our relationship, Israel and the US can move toward the peace that Israel has so long been denied.

SOURCE: *Ma'ariv*, 21 October 1991 (author's translation from the Hebrew).

APPENDIX III: US LETTER OF ASSURANCE TO THE PALESTINIANS

The Palestinian decision to attend a peace conference to launch direct negotiations with Israel represents an important step in the search for a comprehensive, just and lasting peace in the region. The US has long believed that Palestinian participation is critical to the success of our efforts.

In the context of the process on which we are embarking, we want to respond to your request for certain assurances related to this process. These assurances constitute US understandings and intentions concerning the conference and ensuing negotiations.

These assurances are consistent with US policy and do not undermine or contradict UN Security Council Resolutions 242 and 338. Moreover, there will be no assurances provided to one party that are not known to all the others. By this, we can foster a sense of confidence and minimize chances of misunderstandings.

As President Bush stated in his 6 March 1991 address to Congress, the US continues to believe firmly that a comprehensive peace must be grounded in UN Security Council Resolutions 242 and 338 and the principle for security and recognition for all states in the region, including Israel, and for legitimate political rights of the Palestinian people. Anything else, the president noted, would fail the twin tests of fairness and security.

The process we are trying to create offers Palestinians a way to achieve these objectives. The US believes that there should be an end to the Israeli occupation, which can occur only through genuine and meaningful negotiations. The US also believes that this process should create a new relationship of mutuality, where Palestinians and Israelis can respect one another's security, identity and political rights. We believe Palestinians should gain control over political, economic, and other decisions that affect their lives and fate.

Direct bilateral negotiations will begin four days after the opening of the conference. Those parties who wish to attend multilateral negotiations will convene two weeks after the opening of the conference to organize those negotiations. In this regard, the US will support Palestinian involvement in any bilateral or multilateral negotiations on refugees and in all multilateral negotiations. The conference and the negotiations that follow will be based on UN Security Council Resolutions 242 and 338. The process will proceed along two tracks through direct negotiations between Israel and Arab states, and Israel and Palestinians. The US is determined to achieve a comprehensive settlement of the Arab-Israeli conflict and will do its utmost to ensure that the process moves forward along both tracks toward this end.

In pursuit of a comprehensive settlement, all the negotiations should proceed as quickly as possible toward agreement. For its part, the US will work for serious negotiations and will also seek to avoid prolongation and stalling by any party.

The conference will be cosponsored by the US and the Soviet Union. The EC will be a participant in the conference alongside the US and the Soviet Union and be represented by its presidency. The conference can reconvene only with the consent of all the parties.

With regard to the role of the United Nations, the UN secretary-general will send a representative to the conference as an observer. The cosponsors will keep the secretary-general apprised of the progress of the negotiations. Agreements reached between the parties will seek the council's endorsement of such agreements. Since it is in the interest of all parties for this process to succeed, while this process is actively ongoing, the US will not support a competing or parallel process in the UN Security Council.

The US does not seek to determine who speaks for Palestinians in this process. We are seeking to launch a political negotiating process that directly involves Palestinians and offers a pathway for achieving the legitimate political rights of the Palestinian people and for participation in the determination of their future. We believe that a joint Jordanian-Palestinian delegation offers the most promising path toward this end.

Only Palestinians can choose their delegation members, who are not subject to veto from anyone. The US understands that members of the delegation will be Palestinians from the territories who agree to negotiations on two tracks, in phases, and who are willing to live in peace with Israel. No party can be forced to sit with anyone it does not want to sit with.

Palestinians will be free to announce their component of the joint delegation and to make a statement during the opening of the conference. They may also raise any issue pertaining to the substance of the negotiations during the negotiations.

The US understands how much importance Palestinians attach to the question of East Jerusalem. Thus, we want to assure you that nothing Palestinians do in choosing their delegation members in this phase of the process will affect their claim to East Jerusalem, or be prejudicial or precedential to the outcome of negotiations. It remains the firm position of the US that Jerusalem must never again be a divided city and that its final status should be decided by negotiations. Thus, we do not recognize Israel's annexation of East Jerusalem or the extension of its municipal boundaries, and we encourage all sides to avoid unilateral acts that would exacerbate local tensions to make negotiations more difficult or preempt their final outcome. It is also the US position that a Palestinian resident in Jordan with ties to a prominent Jerusalem family would be eligible to join the Jordanian side of the delegation.

Furthermore, it is also the US position that Palestinians of East Jerusalem should be able to participate by voting in the elections for an interim self-governing authority. The US further believes that Palestinians from East Jerusalem and Palestinians outside the occupied territories who meet the three criteria should be able to participate in the negotiations on final status. And, the US supports the right of Palestinians to bring any issue, including East Jerusalem, to the table.

Because the issues at stake are so complex and the emotions so deep, the US has long maintained that a transitional period is required to break down the walls of suspicion and mistrust, and lay the basis for sustainable negotiations on the final status of the occupied territories. The purpose of negotiations on transitional arrangements is to effect the peaceful and orderly transfer of authority from Israel to Palestinians. Palestinians need to achieve rapid control over political, economic and other decisions that affect their lives and to adjust to a new situation in which Palestinians exercise authority in the West Bank and Gaza. For its part, the US will strive from the outset and encourage all parties to adopt steps that can create an environment of confidence and mutual trust, including respect for human rights.

As you are aware, with respect to negotiations between Israelis and Palestinians, negotiations will be conducted in phases, beginning with talks on interim self-government arrangements. These talks will be conducted with the objective of reaching agreement within one year. Once agreed, the interim self-government arrangements will last for a period of five years. Beginning the third year of the period of interim self-government, negotiations will take place on permanent status. It is the aim of the US that permanent status negotiations will be concluded by the end of the transitional period.

It has long been our position that only direct negotiations based on UN Security Council Resolutions 242 and 338 can produce a real peace. No one can dictate the outcome in advance. The US understands that Palestinians must be free, in opening statements at the conference and in the negotiations that follow, to raise any issue of importance to them. Thus, Palestinians are free to argue for whatever outcome they believe best meets their requirements. The US will accept any outcome agreed by the parties. In this regard and consistent with long-standing US policies, confederation is not excluded as a possible outcome of negotiations on final status.

The US has long believed that no party should take unilateral actions that seek to predetermine issues that can only be resolved through negotiations. In this regard, the US has opposed, and will continue to oppose, settlement activity in the territories occupied in 1967, which remains an obstacle to peace.

The US will act as an honest broker in trying to resolve the Arab-Israeli conflict. It is our intention, together with the Soviet Union, to play the role of a driving force in this process to help the parties move forward toward a comprehensive peace. Any party will have access to the cosponsors at any time. The US is prepared to participate in all stages of the negotiations, with the consent of the parties to each negotiation.

These are the assurances that the US is providing concerning the implementation of the initiative we have discussed. We are persuaded that we have a real opportunity to accomplish something very important in the peace process. And we are prepared to work hard together with you in the period ahead, to build on the progress we have made. There will be difficult challenges for all parties. But with the Palestinians' continued commitment and creativity, we have a real chance of moving to a peace conference and to negotiations and then on toward the broader peace that we all seek.

SOURCE: *JP*, 31 October 1991 (the letter was given to the Palestinians on 18 October).

APPENDIX IV: JORDANIAN-PLO AGREEMENT ON JOINT DELEGATION

General Objectives
The agreement seeks to:
* Ensure Israel's withdrawal from Palestinian territories and the other Arab territories occupied in 1967, including holy Jerusalem, implementing Security Council Resolution 242 and the relevant UN resolutions.
* Solve the refugee issue in accordance with the UN resolutions, especially Resolution 194.
* Enable the Palestinian people to exercise their right of self-determination, in order to establish a confederal Jordanian-Palestinian union.
* Ensure the Arabism of holy Jerusalem and reaffirm its status as an indivisible part of the Palestinian territories occupied in 1967, and an area which, in accordance with Security Council and UN resolutions, is subject to that which is applicable to the other occupied territories.

Working Plan
The agreement defines the working plan for implementing the agreement. Through movement with all the parties concerned, the two sides will seek to ensure the bases necessary for the convocation and success of the peace conference and for securing the Arab and Palestinian rights.

The agreement calls for a joint effort to bolster cooperation and coordination among the Arab parties directly concerned with the peace process, so as to underline Arab commitment to a comprehensive solution to the Palestinian issue and to the Arab-Israeli conflict. It further calls for a joint effort to secure comprehensive and sustained Arab support, at the various levels, for the Arab parties participating in the peace conference.

The agreement also calls for efforts to apply Security Council Resolution 242 to all phases of the solution, so as to ensure that they are interconnected and so that the comprehensive solution will achieve Palestinian sovereignty over the land, natural resources, political and economic affairs and so forth.

Likewise, the agreement calls for efforts to secure international protection for the Palestinian people and the occupied territories throughout all phases of the settlement. The Jordanian-Palestinian agreement also sets forth the tasks of the joint Jordanian-Palestinian delegation to the peace conference as follows:

(a) The Palestinian delegation will be responsible for discussing the various aspects connected with the Palestinian issue in the committees designated for the purpose. The Jordanian delegation will have the same responsibility in matters pertaining to Jordan.

(b) One or more coordinating members from the Jordanian side will participate in the Palestinian-Israeli committee. One or more coordinating members from the Palestinian side will also participate in the Jordanian-Israeli committee.

(c) Through the joint political committee, agreement will be developed on the subjects and issues that both sides in the joint delegation can discuss within the conference committees, such as the issues of borders, security, water and so forth.

(d) Following the pattern of the opening session, both sides in the joint Jordanian-Palestinian delegation will take part in the multilateral negotiations.

The Jordanian-Palestinian agreement defines how the Jordanian-Palestinian delegation to the peace conference will be formed. The delegation will consist of two equal and independent Jordanian and Palestinian delegations and each delegation will refer to its political leadership for authority. The agreement also provides for forming a higher political authority, including King Husayn and Yasir 'Arafat, to coordinate and direct the joint delegation's activities. The two Jordanian and Palestinian sides have further agreed to form a joint political committee that will be considered a direct authority for the Jordanian and Palestinian delegations, and that will organize their activities periodically.

The Jordanian-Palestinian delegation chairmanship consists of two chairpersons, a Jordanian and a Palestinian.

It should be noted that the Jordanian-Palestinian agreement on the peaceful solution process has been approved by the Jordanian Council of Ministers and the PLO Executive Committee.

SOURCE: *Al-Sharq al-Awsat*, 27 October — DR, 5 November 1991.

APPENDIX V: US LETTER OF ASSURANCE TO SYRIA

The peace conference and subsequent talks must be based on Security Council Resolutions 242 and 338.

The conference's task is to secure the holding of direct talks within two days after the opening of the conference and multilateral talks on regional issues within two weeks. The process will be conducted within the framework of a two-track approach: the first represented by direct talks between Israel and the neighboring Arab states, and the second by direct talks between Israel and the Palestinians.

The US intends to make every endeavor to arrive at a comprehensive settlement of the Arab-Israeli dispute, and will do its utmost to continue the process in that direction along the two tracks mentioned. The US does not support linkage between the various negotiations. In the interests of a comprehensive settlement, all negotiations must be conducted as quickly as possible in order to reach agreement.

The conference will be held under US and Soviet sponsorship, and can only be reconvened with the approval of all the parties.

The role of the UN will be that of an observer sent by the secretary-general. The US and the Soviet Union will keep the secretary-general apprised of the progress of negotiations. Agreements reached between the parties will be registered with the UN Secretariat and the Security Council will be informed of them. The participating parties will seek Security Council endorsement of such agreements.

Since the US is aware of the interests of all the parties in the success of this process, it does not intend to support any counter or parallel process in the UN Security Council, while the process is actively proceeding.

A final settlement can be attained only in accordance with mutual concessions during the course of the talks. During the talks, the US will continue to insist that Security Council Resolution 242 and the "land for peace" principle are applicable to all fronts, including the Golan Heights.

The US does not intend to recognize or accept unilateral actions by Israel with regard to imposing its laws, rule, or administration on the Golan Heights.

The US will continue to oppose Israel's activity regarding building settlements in the territories occupied in 1967, which remain an obstacle to peace.

The US expresses its willingness to guarantee the border to be agreed between Israel and Syria.

The US will continue to act as an honest broker, working sincerely to resolve the Arab-Israeli dispute on the basis of understanding all the parties' needs and requirements. It will remain, together with the Soviet Union, the driving force in the process to help the parties to make progress toward a comprehensive peaceful settlement.

The US and the Soviet Union express their willingness to be in constant contact with any party to the peace process at any time. The US is also willing to participate in the talks at any stage, with the approval of the parties involved in the talks concerned.

SOURCE: *Al-Sharq al-Awsat,* 15 October — DR, 18 October 1991. (The English is as provided by DR with minor changes made by the author on the basis of the English text of the letter of assurance to the Palestinians, Appendix III).

NOTES

For the place and frequency of publications cited here, and for the full name of the publication, news agency, radio station or monitoring service where an abbreviation is used, please see "List of Sources." Only in the case of more than one publication bearing the same name is the place of publication noted here.

1. Henry Kissinger, *Years of Upheaval* (Boston: Little-Brown, 1982), pp. 767–88.
2. Jimmy Carter, *The Blood of Abraham* (Boston: Houghton Mifflin, 1985), pp. 69, 72, 73, 200.
3. White House spokesman, Marlin Fitzwater, 8 January, as reported by *JP,* 9 January 1991. (For earlier US statements, see *MECS* 1990, chapter on ME peace process, section on Israel.)
4. *JP,* 10 January 1991.
5. Shamir, Knesset address, VoI, 4 February — DR, 5 February 1991.
6. Levy, Knesset address, Israel TV, 20 February — DR, 21 February 1991.
7. Note 1 above, and Yossi Ben-Aharon, Shamir's adviser, on VoI, 8 January — DR, 8 January 1991.
8. Shamir's interview, R. IDF, 26 February — DR, 27 February 1991.
9. *Ha'aretz,* 17 April — DR, 19 April 1991.
10. Levy, interview with VoI, 27 February — DR, 27 February; *JP,* 11 March 1991.
11. Ben-Aharon, interview with VoI, 28 February — DR, 28 February 1991.
12. *JP,* 1 March 1991.
13. National Security Adviser Brent Scowcroft on ABC TV as reported in *JP,* 4 March 1991.
14. *Facts on File,* Vol. 51, 7 March 1991, p. 156.
15. Baker's press conference, Jerusalem, 11 March, *Ha'aretz,* 12 March; *JP,* 12, 15 March; *IHT,* 13 March 1991.
16. Ibid.; also, Shamir's interview, VoI, 27 April — DR, 29 April 1991.
17. *JP,* 18 March 1991.

18. Shamir's interview, Israel TV, 10 April — DR, 11 April 1991.
19. Dan Meridor's interview, VoI, 10 April — DR, 11 April 1991.
20. *Ha'aretz,* 28 April; *JP,* 14 April 1991.
21. *JP,* 12 April 1991.
22. *Davar,* 21 April 1991.
23. *NYT,* 21 April 1991.
24. *JP,* 28 April 1991.
25. *JP,* 30 April and VoI, 26 April — DR, 29 April 1991.
26. Shamir's interview, VoI, 28 April — DR, 29 April 1991.
27. Shamir's interview, *Der Spiegel,* 6 May — DR, 7 May 1991.
28. *IHT,* 17 May; *JP,* 17 May 1991.
29. *NYT,* 16 May 1991.
30. *JP,* 12 May 1991.
31. Statement before the US House Subcommittee on Foreign Operations, 22 May 1991.
32. Ben-Aharon's press statement, 24 May — DR, 28 May; Shamir's speech, *JP,* 19 June 1991.
33. *JP,* 24 July 1991.
34. VoI, 22 July — DR, 22 July; Levy's interview on Israel TV, 21 July — DR, 22 July 1991.
35. Baker's Jerusalem press conference, WF, 22, 23 July 1991.
36. *Ha'aretz,* 23 July 1991.
37. VoI, 30, 31 July — DR, 31 July 1991.
38. *Ha'aretz,* 1 August — DR, 1 August 1991.
39. *JP,* 1 August 1991.
40. Bush's Moscow conference, WF, 1 August 1991.
41. *JP,* 2 August 1991.
42. Shamir-Baker joint press conference, *NYT,* 2 August 1991.
43. *Davar,* 16 September 1991.
44. *NYT,* 5 September 1991.
45. *NYT,* 11 September 1991.
46. *JP,* 13 September; *WP,* 16 September 1991.
47. Shoval, Israel's ambassador to the US, interviews, R. IDF, 17 September; VoI, 26 September — DR, 26 September 1991.
48. Ibid., *NYT,* 16 September 1991.
49. Levy's interview, Israel TV, 16 October — DR, 17 October 1991.
50. *Ha'aretz,* 18 October 1991.
51. *JP,* 20 October 1991.
52. Shamir's news conference, 18 October — DR, 21 October 1991.
53. Interview, *Yedi'ot Aharonot,* 21 October — DR, 21 October 1991.
54. *JP,* 2 October 1991.
55. Israel TV, 23 October — DR, 24 October 1991.
56. *Yedi'ot Aharonot,* 30 October — DR, 30 October 1991.
57. Complete text in *JP,* 1 November 1991.
58. Full text in *JP,* 3 November 1991.
59. Shar''s second address, R. Damascus, 1 November — DR, 1 November 1991.
60. Israel's Prime Minister's Office statement after an inner cabinet meeting, *JP,* 28 November 1991.
61. 'Arafat's interview with Spanish TV, VoP (Baghdad), 8 January — DR, 10 January 1991.
62. PLO Executive Committee statement of 17 January, VoP (Algiers) — DR, 18 January 1991.
63. 'Arafat's interview with *Sawt al-Sha'b* (Amman), 17 February — DR, 20 February 1991.
64. 'Arafat's interviews with *Le Figaro,* 18 March — DR, 20 March; and *Der Spiegel,* 11 March — DR, 13 March 1991; Turkish TV, 6 May — DR, 7 May 1991.
65. 'Arafat's interview with *Der Spiegel,* 11 March — DR, 13 March 1991.
66. VoP (Algiers), 11 March — DR, 12 March 1991.
67. VoP (Algiers), 14 March — DR, 15 March 1991.
68. Sa'id Kamal, PLO representative in Cairo, interview with *al-Sharq al-Awsat,* 14 April — DR, 19 April; *JP,* 21 April; Husayn's interview, VoI, 22 July — DR, 23 July 1991.
69. VoP (Algiers), 13 March — DR, 14 March 1991.

70. Interviews with ITV, 9 March — DR, 13 March; *La Repubblica,* 12 March — DR, 14 March 1991.
71. Faysal al-Husayni's interview with *al-Sharq al-Awsat,* 29 March — DR, 5 April 1991.
72. *JP,* 10 April 1991.
73. Faysal al-Husayni's interview, *Sawt al-Kuwait al-Duwali,* 12 April — DR, 17 April 1991.
74. VoI, 20 April — DR, 22 April 1991.
75. Interview with R. Algiers, 20 April — DR, 22 April 1991.
76. *JP,* 21 April 1991.
77. Interview with *al-Majalla,* 1-7 May — DR, 6 May 1991.
78. Ibid.
79. R. Monte Carlo, 15 May — DR, 16 May 1991.
80. R. Tunis, 20 July — DR, 23 July 1991.
81. 'Ashrawi's interview with *al-Fajr,* 29 July — DR, 1 August 1991.
82. MENA, 1 August — DR, 2 August 1991.
83. *IHT,* 2-4 August 1991.
84. *IHT,* 3-4 August; *JP,* 4 August 1991.
85. Arab sources reported the contents of the US draft that was discussed. It was reproduced in *Davar,* 19 September 1991.
86. VoI, 17 September — DR, 17 September 1991.
87. Thomas L. Friedman, *NYT,* 14 October 1991.
88. Husayni's interview with *al-Jumhuriyya* (Cairo), 13 October — DR, 16 October 1991.
89. R. Amman, 15 October — DR, 16 October; *JP,* 15, 16 October; *NYT,* 15 October; *JT,* 16 October — DR, 16 October 1991.
90. AFP, 16 October — DR, 16 October 1991.
91. *Al-Nahar* (Jerusalem), 17 October — DR, 18 October; R. Monte Carlo, 18 October — DR, 18 October 1991.
92. Tahir al-Masri on Algerian TV, 4 October — DR, 4 October 1991.
93. R. Tunis, 18 October — DR, 18 October 1991.
94. AFP, 22 October — DR, 23 October 1991.
95. R. Paris, 22 October — DR, 23 October 1991.
96. *Al-Dustur* (Amman), 24 October — DR, 24 October 1991.
97. *Al-Dustur* (Amman), 26 October — DR, 28 October 1991.
98. Shafi's two speeches, *JPS,* Vol. XXI, No. 2, (Winter 1992), pp. 133–37, 144–46.
99. PLO Executive Committee member Mahmud 'Abbas (Abu Mazin) to *al-Quds al-'Arabi,* 2-3 November — DR, 6 November 1991.
100. PLO Executive Committee member Sulayman al-Najjab, quoted in *al-Sharq al-Awsat,* 4 November — DR, 6 November 1991.
101. This paragraph appeared in Thomas L. Friedman's article in *NYT,* 20 November 1991.
102. Masri, quoted in *Sawt al-Sha'b* (Amman), 10 April — DR, 10 April 1991.
103. Masri to Jordan TV, 13 April — DR, 17 April 1991.
104. Husayn's interview with *NYT,* 13 March; interview with NBC, 21 March — DR, 23 March; interview with *al-Ra'y,* quoted by *Ha'aretz,* 7 April 1991.
105. Masri's interview with *JT,* 21-22 March — DR, 21 March 1991.
106. Husayn's press conference, R. Amman, 9 May — DR, 10 May 1991.
107. Address to the Royal Jordanian War College, R. Amman, 22 May — DR, 23 May 1991.
108. Interview with ABC, 12 March — DR, 15 March 1991.
109. Husayn's press conference, R. Amman, 20 April — DR, 22 April 1991.
110. Husayn's interview with *Le Point* (Paris), quoted by *JT,* 4 June — DR, 4 June 1991.
111. Masri to R. Monte Carlo, 3 June — DR, 4 June 1991.
112. Husayn to Jordan TV, 14 May — DR, 15 May 1991.
113. Husayn in a joint news conference with Baker, Jordan TV, 21 July — DR, 22 July 1991.
114. Husayn in a joint news conference with Baker, R. Amman, 19 September — DR, 20 September 1991.
115. Husayn in a joint news conference with Baker, Jordan TV, 14 October — DR, 15 October 1991.
116. Husayn's news conference, Jordan TV, 21 July — DR, 22 July 1991.
117. Foreign Minister 'Abdallah al-Nusur, *al-Dustur* (Amman), 16 August — DR, 16 August;

interview with *Akhbar al-Usbu'* (Amman), 22 August — DR, 23 August 1991.
118. Masri to R. Monte Carlo, 9 November — DR, 12 November 1991.
119. *JT*, 30 October — DR, 5 November 1991.
120. R. Amman, 21 November — DR, 22 November 1991.
121. Husayn interview with *al-Quds al-'Arabi*, 29 October — DR, 8 November 1991.
122. Ibid.
123. Ibid.
124. R. Amman, 30 October — DR, 31 October; *JP*, 1 November 1991.
125. Majali's interview with *al-Fajr*, 11 November — DR, 14 November 1991.
126. *JP*, 15 December 1991. Majali also mentioned King 'Abdallah (assassinated in 1951) and Prime Minister Wasfi al-Tall (assassinated in 1971).
127. *Ha'aretz*, 19 December 1991. The remark was made by US assistant secretary of state Edward Djerejian.
128. *NYT*, 26 November 1991.
129. Asad called the meeting a positive one. Asad's interview, *Ruz al-Yusuf*, 10 December 1990 — DR, 11 January 1991.
130. Baker's Damascus news conference, SANA, 12 January — DR, 14 January 1991.
131. Interview with *Le Monde*, 8 February — DR, 11 February 1991.
132. Full text in *Facts on File*, 7 August 1991, pp. 155–56.
133. News conference, R. Damascus, 14 March — DR, 14 March 1991.
134. Baker-Shar' joint press conference, SANA, 14 March — DR, 15 March 1991.
135. As reported in *JP*, 9 April 1991.
136. Baker-Shar' joint press conference R. Damascus, 12 April — DR, 12 April 1991.
137. R. Damascus, 24 April — DR, 24, 25 April 1991.
138. R. Damascus, 9 May — DR, 10 May 1991.
139. R. Damascus, 11 May; SANA, R. Monte Carlo, 12 May — DR, 13 May 1991.
140. News agencies, as reported in *JP*, 13 May 1991.
141. Asad in a joint news conference with Mubarak, R. Damascus, 19 May — DR, 20 May 1991.
142. R. Monte Carlo, 12 May — DR, 13 May 1991.
143. *JP*, 7 June 1991.
144. Shar''s interview, *Newsweek*, R. Damascus, 26 June — DR, 27 June 1991.
145. *JP*, 11 June 1991.
146. R. Damascus, 15 July — DR, 15 July 1991.
147. Syrian TV, 14 July — DR, 15 July 1991.
148. Syrian TV, 17 July — DR, 18 July 1991.
149. Press conference, Syrian TV, 17 July — DR, 18 July 1991.
150. R. Damascus, 25 July — DR, 26 July 1991.
151. Baker-Shar' press conference, R. Damascus, 19 July — DR, 19 July 1991.
152. Interviews with *WP* and *Newsweek*, SANA, 29 July — DR, 29 July 1991.
153. R. Damascus, 7 August — DR, 8 August 1991.
154. *Can Israel Survive a Palestinian State?* (Jerusalem: Institute for Advanced Strategic and Political Studies, 1990). See also *MECS* 1990, chapter on the ME peace process, section on Syria.
155. Joint press conference, R. Damascus, 19 September — DR, 19 September 1991.
156. Baker-Shar' press conference, R. Damascus, 16 October — DR, 18 October 1991; Asad's interview with CNN, SANA, 27 October 1991.
157. Jordan TV, 31 October — DR, 1 November 1991.
158. Head of the Syrian negotiating team's interview with Syrian TV, 8 November — DR, 20 November 1991.
159. Interview with Muwaffaq al-'Allaf, R. Amman, 4 November — DR, 5 November 1991.
160. Madrid news conference, R. Damascus, 5 November — DR, 5 November 1991.
161. *NYT*, 26 November 1991.
162. *Ha'aretz*, 22 December 1991.
163. Interview with *al-Bayraq*, Voice of the Mountain, 28 June — DR, 28 June 1991.
164. Interview with *Le Monde*, 22 October — DR, 25 October 1991.
165. *Al-Hayat* (London), 16 October — DR, 17 October 1991.

166. Buwayz to correspondents, R. Beirut, 20 October — DR, 21 October 1991.
167. R. Beirut, 1 November — DR, 1 November 1991.
168. *JP,* 3 November 1991.
169. Buwayz's speech, R. Beirut, 1 November — DR, 1 November 1991.
170. Lebanese chief delegate to R. Amman, 1 November — DR, 5 November 1991.
171. A member of the Israeli delegation to R. IDF, 3 November — DR, 4 November 1991.
172. *NYT,* 26 November 1991.
173. *Al-Watan al-'Arabi* as reported in *Ha'aretz,* 24 December 1991.
174. Voice of Free Lebanon, 11 November — DR, 12 November 1991.
175. Suhayl Shammas, *JP,* 22 December 1991.
176. Musa, quoted by MENA, 5 June — DR, 6 June; Mubarak's interview with BBC, MENA, 11 July; also Musa, MENA, 21 October — DR, 22 October 1991.
177. 'Ismat 'Abd al-Majid, MENA, 21 April — DR, 22 April; Musa quoted by MENA, 5 June — DR, 6 June 1991.
178. Mubarak's speech, R. Cairo, 6 October — DR, 8 October 1991.
179. Dr. Hanan 'Ashrawi, MENA, 28 October — DR, 28 October 1991.
180. Musa's Madrid address, Egyptian TV, 30 October — DR, 31 October; Musa's second speech, Jordan TV, 1 November 1991.
181. Mubarak's Rome news conference, MENA, 19 May — DR, 20 May 1991.
182. Musa's interview with *al-Ittihad* (Abu Dhabi), MENA, 31 May 1991.
183. Mubarak's interview with *al-Jumhuriyya* (Cairo), MENA, 18 July — DR, 28 July 1991.
184. Musa, quoted by MENA, 6 June — DR, 7 June 1991.
185. Interview with *WSJ,* quoted by *Ha'aretz,* 24 March 1991.
186. Article by Anis Mansur, *al-Ahram,* 6 April — DR, 10 April 1991.
187. Interview with *Davar,* 15 May — DR, 17 May 1991.
188. Mubarak to Italian TV, MENA, 19 May — DR, 20 May 1991.
189. Baz's interview, *al-Sharq al-Awsat,* MENA, 26 July — DR, 5 August 1991.
190. Baz's speech to Pugwash seminar, MENA, 7 October — DR, 9 October 1991.
191. Musa's Madrid press conference, 1 November — DR, 4 November 1991.
192. Interview with *al-Hayat* (London), 16 July — DR, 18 July 1991.
193. Interview with *Ma'ariv,* MENA, 7 November — DR, 8 November 1991.
194. Interview, *Der Spiegel,* 14 July — DR, 15 July 1991.
195. See, e.g., interview with Israeli TV, 13 November — DR, 14 November 1991.
196. BBC interview, quoted by *JP,* 29 July 1991.
197. Musa's statement to the press, MENA, 30 July — DR, 31 July 1991.
198. Ambassador Muhammad Basyuni, article in *Yedi'ot Aharonot,* 11 March 1991.
199. Musa's interview with *al-Sharq al-Awsat,* 24 September — DR, 27 September 1991.
200. Mubarak, MENA, 7 August — DR, 8 August; Musa's interview with *al-Liwa,* MENA, 27 August — DR, 28 August 1991.
201. Musa's interview, *JP,* 31 July 1991.
202. Baz's interview with *al-Sharq al-Awsat,* 26 July — DR, 5 August 1991.

Inter-Arab Relations

BRUCE MADDY-WEITZMAN

Iraq's forcible incorporation of Kuwait on 2 August 1990 had triggered the worst inter-Arab crisis in the conflict-ridden 45-year history of the Arab state system. Only 18 months earlier, Egypt and Iraq had institutionalized their wartime anti-Iranian alliance through the formation, together with Jordan and the Yemeni Arab Republic, of the Arab Cooperation Council. But in response to Iraq's brazen challenge to the regional status quo, Egypt joined Saudi Arabia in mobilizing a bare majority of the 21 Arab League members, to condemn the Iraqis and support the American-led multinational coalition formed to force Iraq out of Kuwait. Particularly noteworthy was the participation in the coalition of Syria, whose long-standing antipathy toward its geopolitical rival and ideological Ba'thi twin, and its concurrent need to "come in from the cold" in both the inter-Arab and international contexts, outweighed its uneasiness at sanctioning Western intervention in Arab affairs. Of the states that refused to line up behind the anti-Saddam coalition, most, if not all, were less than enthusiastic about Iraq's swallowing up of Kuwait. However, a combination of internal pressures, existing relations with Iraq, barely concealed antipathy toward the oil-rich Gulf states, and genuine unhappiness with the massive injection of Western military forces (the exact mix varied from country to country) led them to stake out more ambiguous positions in the crisis and incessantly seek to broker an "Arab solution" to the crisis.

Iraq's invasion of Kuwait, however, had badly polarized inter-Arab affairs. The anti-Saddam coalition was convinced from the outset of the crisis that as long as Iraq was unwilling to reverse its move and unconditionally withdraw from Kuwait, mediation attempts would be perceived by Saddam as a sign of weakness and thus embolden him further. For his part, Saddam steadfastly refused to indicate to numerous Arab and international interlocutors that he was indeed willing to relinquish control of Kuwait. Thus, there was little or no room for would-be rebuilders of the shattered vessel of inter-Arab cooperation. In addition, Saudi Arabia and its Gulf Cooperation Council (GCC) partners, in particular, imposed a heavy economic and diplomatic penalty on at least two of the self-styled mediators, Jordan and Yemen. Relations between the Arab members of the anti-Saddam coalition, on the one hand, and the PLO and Sudan, on the other, both of which were also perceived as being totally supportive of Iraq, also sharply deteriorated. As for the members of the Arab Maghrib Union (AMU) members, Morocco actively joined the anti-Iraqi coalition and dispatched a small contingent of troops to Saudi Arabia; Libya and Algeria managed to largely insulate their bilateral relations with the states opposed to Saddam from the larger crisis; Tunisia adopted a profile as low as possible; while Mauritania's remoteness meant that it could adopt a pro-Iraqi stance with comparatively little consequence.

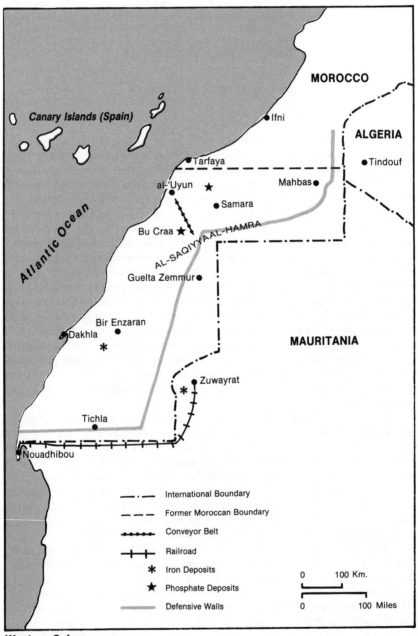

Western Sahara

By the end of 1990, the Arab world, along with the international community as a whole, was holding its collective breath in anticipation of the UN Security Council's 15 January 1991 deadline for an unconditional Iraqi withdrawal. The imminence of war weighed heavily on both the anti-Saddam countries and those more sympathetic to him, on the elites as well as the broader sectors of Arab societies. It was clear to all that the future course of inter-Arab relations — indeed, of Middle Eastern political, social and economic developments as a whole — would be profoundly influenced by the outcome of the impending war.

THE GULF WAR

THE FINAL COUNTDOWN

The key members of the anti-Saddam coalition devoted the two weeks before the 15 January deadline to shoring up their regional and domestic positions. Top officials engaged in continuous consultation and repeatedly justified in public their support for the impending military encounter. In addition, lines of communication were kept open at least to some of the Arab states that had not joined the coalition.

Two important sets of high-level multilateral meetings were held during the first week of January. The first was a four-way summit meeting on 3 January hosted by Libya's Mu'ammar al-Qadhdhafi at the Misurata airfield, with the participation of Egypt's President Husni Mubarak, Syria's Hafiz al-Asad and Sudan's 'Umar al-Bashir. Two rounds of talks between the Egyptian, Syrian and Libyan foreign ministers in Cairo a day previously had paved the way for the summit. Egyptian-Libyan relations had improved significantly in 1990 (see *MECS* 1990, pp. 567–68) and Mubarak and Qadhdhafi had taken care during the early stages of the Gulf crisis to insulate their bilateral rapprochement from wider developments, the differences between them notwithstanding. The summit meeting provided an additional indication to that effect, even though Qadhdhafi had surprised Mubarak by inviting Sudan's Bashir to the meeting without Mubarak's prior knowledge.[1] Despite the absence of a concluding joint statement, and despite Qadhdhafi's endorsement of further Arab mediation efforts,[2] Mubarak returned home reasonably certain that his mercurial neighbor to the West would avoid adopting a blatantly anti-Egyptian stand as the Gulf crisis unfolded. Whereas Libyan-Egyptian relations were on the upswing, Sudanese-Egyptian relations had sharply deteriorated during the previous year, owing to Sudan's adoption of a more pronounced Islamic fundamentalist orientation and its concomitant support for Iraq after 2 August (see *MECS* 1990, pp. 642–43). The Bashir-Mubarak encounter at the summit, although apparently civil, did not lead to any easing of the tension between their two countries.

Two days later, on 5 January, the foreign ministers of Egypt, Syria and Saudi Arabia met in Riyadh for two days of consultations. The joint statement issued at the close of the gathering reiterated their essential positions: (1) welcoming international efforts toward a "complete and unconditional implementation" of UN and Arab resolutions on the crisis, and regarding the upcoming meeting on 9 January between US Secretary of State James Baker and Iraqi Foreign Minister Tariq 'Aziz as the "one last chance" to do so peaceably; (2) "rejecting any settlement based on a partial withdrawal from Kuwait or on rewarding the aggressor"; (3) affirming that Iraq would bear "full responsibility" if war were to break out; (4) denouncing Iraq's attempt to "exploit the question of Palestine to justify its invasion of Kuwait," while expressing desire to intensify the quest, once the Gulf crisis was resolved, for a settlement to the Arab-Israeli conflict based on Israeli withdrawal from the occupied territories and the establishment of an independent Palestinian state; and (5) welcoming a December 1990 GCC summit statement regarding its desire to deepen coordination between the GCC states, on the one hand, and Egypt and Syria, on the other.[3]

In the meantime, the various would-be Arab mediators renewed their desperate efforts, in tandem with European parties and the UN secretary-general or independently, in the hope of achieving an eleventh-hour breakthrough. Algeria was particularly active, with Foreign Minister Sid Ahmad Ghozali meeting Tariq 'Aziz in Geneva on 9 January, in an attempt to promote a dialogue between Iraq and the EC. Algeria's President Chedli Benjedid himself also attempted a last-minute effort, but his proposed visits to Baghdad and Washington were canceled. An Algiers radio commentary placed the onus on Washington's inflexibility, while the political bureau of the ruling *Front de Libération Nationale* (FLN) called for the peoples of the region to prepare to resist the now-imminent war.[4]

On 14 January, Libya's second-in-command, 'Abd al-Salam Jalud, traveled to Baghdad to meet with Saddam Husayn, joining PLO leader Yasir 'Arafat, who was already conferring with Saddam. Later that day, a high-level Yemeni delegation, headed by Prime Minister Haydar al-'Attas, arrived as well. The focus of the Baghdad discussions was a six-point proposal, sponsored jointly by Algeria, Libya and Yemen, calling for an Iraqi pledge to withdraw from Kuwait in return for a promise that it would not be attacked, that economic sanctions would be lifted, and that the Security Council would commit itself to resolving the Palestinian issue. The proposal paralleled concurrent French suggestions,[5] and was also similar to Syria's position, expressed two days earlier in a message from Asad to Saddam broadcast over Radio Damascus (and endorsed by Qadhdhafi).[6]

However, the die had been cast: the US and Britain were sharply opposed to anything that appeared to them to smack of a dilution of the relevant Security Council resolutions, while Saddam, despite Yemeni and Algerian insistence on Iraq's desire to resolve the crisis peacefully,[7] remained unwilling to disgorge Kuwait. All that was left for the Arab governments to do was to watch and wait, in the hope that the imminent war would not generate unmanageable shock waves among their own populations, while making preparations for just such a contingency. Morocco's King Hasan, for example, delivered a nationally televised address on 15 January in which he warned that "if there is the slightest hint of disorder, we will declare a state of siege." Throughout the crisis, Hasan had trod a fine line between his traditional Arab and Western allies, on the one hand, and considerable pro-Saddam sentiment at home on the other. Hasan thus reiterated in his speech that Morocco's small contingent of troops (1,000–1,200) in Saudi Arabia were deployed in defensive lines only, "far from the Kuwaiti-Saudi borders." Still, he commented soberly, "the waves of death may reach them." The war itself, he warned, would be "destructive and merciless," and he beseeched "God Almighty" to "put out this fire" and "spare us this war."[8] Just over 24 hours later, the anti-Saddam coalition launched operation Desert Storm.

THE INTER-ARAB ARENA DURING THE WAR
(17 JANUARY–28 FEBRUARY)

Speculation in the West that the anti-Saddam Arab coalition would not prove durable once war commenced centered on two possible scenarios. One was that Israel would be drawn into the war by Iraq, thereby forcing the anti-Saddam states to reconsider, lest they expose themselves to the charge of fighting alongside Israel against a fellow Arab state. The other was that the longer the war dragged on, the more untenable their position would be vis-à-vis public opinion in their own countries. As it happened, however, neither of these hypotheses were put to the test. Israel refrained from responding to Iraq's missile attacks, and the war itself, particularly the final, ground phase, was swift. Consequently, existing inter-Arab alignments were unaltered. The anti-Saddam coalition members continued to stand together in support of the military campaign to force Iraq to disgorge Kuwait, with the partial exception of Morocco, which was the weakest link in the anti-Saddam grouping. Moreover, on the eve of the final phase of the war, Egypt, Syria and the GCC states collectively expressed their determination to translate their military and political successes into more lasting preeminence and fashion the postwar regional order according to their own predilections. As for the Arab minority grouping, it sought an immediate end to hostilities and a negotiated solution to the conflict. As the American-led air campaign progressed into February and the efforts of the "neutrals" came to naught, the leaders of this camp sharpened their condemnations of the "pro-war" Arab and Western governments, while public support for Iraq within these countries, expressed in mass demonstrations, the mass media and fund-raising campaigns, reached feverish proportions. Inevitably, bilateral tensions between various members of the two Arab groupings worsened.

Initial diplomatic efforts by both Jordan and the Maghrib states were directed toward seeking a UN Security Council cease-fire resolution. These culminated in a call by the five AMU foreign ministers on 23 January, meeting in Tripoli, for an emergency meeting of the Security Council, which would be addressed by concerned Arab heads of state.[9] This proposal, however, was swiftly rejected by the US and Britain. Other, individual efforts included a cease-fire initiative by Libya (which, to Qadhdhafi's displeasure, drew no response from Iraq)[10] and a Moroccan appeal on 19 January to "brother Saddam" to agree to replacing Iraqi forces in Kuwait with units from the "greater Arab Maghrib."[11] While the degree of likemindedness among AMU countries had its limitations and contributed to the postponement of a previously scheduled summit, on the whole AMU members continued to insulate their relations with one another successfully (see below), as they had from the outset of the Gulf crisis.

The Algerian authorities and mass media were particularly vocal in condemning the war, no doubt a reflection of the government's need to compete with the powerful *Front Islamique du Salut* (FIS) during the campaign for parliamentary election scheduled for June. At the same time, Benjedid resisted calls from FIS activists to open military training camps for volunteers who wanted to join Iraq in the fight. King Hasan, too, was alert to the efforts of opposition parties and Islamic fundamentalist groups to make political capital out of the crisis. Following a number of unauthorized demonstrations, a one-day general strike sponsored by opposition elements and numerous arrests, Hasan sanctioned the holding of a mass antiwar demonstration in

Rabat on 3 February. He responded to pressure by the opposition to remove Morocco's small military contingent from Saudi Arabia by repeatedly justifying its presence, insisting that it had been dispatched for defensive purposes only, and that the decision had been made prior to the Arab League Cairo summit sanctioning collective action. His reward came in the form of a $700m. grant from Saudi Arabia toward the end of 1990 and a further $1bn. in April 1991.[12]

Jordan's King Husayn walked a tightrope throughout the war. His prime concern was to avoid being dragged into hostilities, a distinct prospect if Israel were to decide to retaliate against Iraq following repeated missile attacks against it. The king's numerous public condemnations of the war, the harshest of which was delivered on 6 February, were geared primarily toward the home front, where public opinion among both East Bank Jordanians and Palestinians was solidly and vociferously behind Iraq. The king also steadfastly refrained from public criticism of Iraq, while the Jordanian media tilted heavily toward Iraq's version of events. One Western journalist reported that Iraq's foreign ministry satellite communications system had been transferred to Amman, that Iraq was using Jordanian radio systems to retransmit military communiqués to its troops after its own system had been disabled by American bombings, and that Iraqi soldiers had been trained by Jordanian instructors in the use of US-made *Hawk* antiaircraft missiles confiscated in Kuwait.[13] At the same time, King Husayn sought to project himself as a man of peace and to alter the image, widely held both in the West and among Iraq's Arab opponents, that he was merely acting as Saddam's shill. Jordan, he declared at a 19 January press conference, was concerned with halting these "tragic events" as soon as possible. However, despite its limited means, it would "try to prevent *any party* [author's emphasis] from using our airspace and territory."[14] The king maintained at the same press conference that he had not been in contact with Iraq since the war's outbreak, and denied in another interview that he had any influence at all on Saddam, stating that while he had been "very close to him...during a certain phase [the Iraqi-Iranian War]," Saddam had never revealed any of his intentions to him in advance.[15] In a further attempt to distance the kingdom from Iraq, and at the same time ease Jordan's regional isolation, Foreign Minister Tahir al-Masri traveled to Tehran on 27 January for meetings with his Iranian counterpart, 'Ali Akbar Velayati (Jordan had restored diplomatic relations with Iran earlier in the month). Subsequently, Jordan endorsed a five-point Iranian peace initiative (see chapter on Iran).

Overall, however, Jordan continued to pay a price for its perceived tilt toward Iraq. Its formerly close relations with Saudi Arabia and Egypt deteriorated further, with the media and the leaders of both countries trading increasingly acrimonious insults and accusations with Jordan. Jordanian newspapers, declared a Saudi official source to the Saudi Press Agency, were publishing "open lies" in their attempts to "foment divisions" among GCC member states, "spread intrigues," and "mislead...Arab public opinion"; Egyptian journalists, stated a Jordanian newspaper editorial, are supporters of the "art of instigation, propagation of hatred [and] distortion of facts."[16] Relations with Syria also soured, with the Syrians imposing temporary restrictions on border crossings in retaliation, apparently, for anti-Syrian broadcasts in the Jordanian media.

Relations between the other Arab "neutrals" and the anti-Saddam Arab states were polarized as well. The Algerian and Saudi media, for example, engaged in a welter of vitriolics and mutual vituperation. On 18 February, Egypt suspended flights by the Algerian national airline into Cairo airport. Egyptian-Sudanese relations also deteriorated further, and Husni Mubarak issued a sharp warning that Sudan would "pay a very high price" were it to assist the Iraqis in carrying out a reported threat to strike at the Aswan High Dam, or even if Saddam managed to deploy anything in Sudan. "For me," Mubarak declared, "this is absolutely no joking matter."[17]

On 6 February, Iraq formally broke diplomatic relations with Egypt and Saudi Arabia, as well as with the US, Britain, France and Italy.(By contrast, Iraq and Iran had maintained their formal diplomatic relations during most of the eight-year war between them.) Three days later, Egypt's minister of interior, Maj. Gen. Muhammad 'Abd al-Halim Musa, announced that an Iraqi plan to launch a terror campaign within Egypt had been uncovered. The scheme, he charged, was supervised directly by Saddam Husayn and his intelligence agencies, and was to be carried out by the Abu Nidal and Islamic Jihad groups. Seventeen suspected terrorists of various nationalities had been arrested while trying to infiltrate into Egypt, with 10 more arrests made in mid-February.[18]

On the other side of the inter-Arab abyss, key members of the anti-Saddam coalition held a number of bilateral and multilateral meetings during the war. Egypt's Foreign Minister 'Ismat 'Abd al-Majid and presidential adviser 'Usama al-Baz flew to Damascus on 20 January for talks with the Syrian leadership; the GCC Ministerial Council met in Riyadh on 26 January and issued a ringing endorsement of the military campaign to restore independence to its member; and Egypt's Husni Mubarak journeyed to Riyadh on 30 January for consultations with King Fahd. The culmination of these wartime deliberations came on 15-16 February in Cairo, with a gathering of the foreign ministers of Egypt, Syria and the six GCC states. The statement issued at the close of these meetings rejected Iraq's conditional acceptance of Security Council Resolution 660 (see below) and called for its unconditional withdrawal from Kuwait and the implementation of all related Security Council resolutions. In a rebuke to the PLO and Yasir 'Arafat, the traditional Arab endorsement of self-determination for the Palestinian people failed to include a reference to the PLO as the Palestinians' "sole, legitimate representative." More generally, the statement provided a rough outline of the anti-Saddam coalition's vision of a postwar "new Arab order." On the one hand, its guiding principles were not at all new: they were derived from the founding charter of the Arab League and the 1950 Joint Defense and Economic Cooperation Agreement, which stipulated good neighborliness, the inviolability of interstate boundaries, the resolution of regional conflicts by peaceful means, and the promotion of economic cooperation. However, the underlying message of what was termed the "six-plus-two" group was that its members would be more assertive in defending their particular interests and less bound than in the past by the nebulous, elusive norms of all-Arab solidarity. GCC Secretary-General 'Abdallah Bishara was particularly vocal in this regard stating:

> We in the Gulf and the people of Kuwait have paid the price of fixed emotional positions and of basing our policy on so-called solidarity....My view of the Arab future is based on a concept which destroys the myth of Arab fraternity, the myth of Arab security, and the myth of the one homeland. Future Arab links should be based on the Arab dimension of civilized interests, not on futile emotional theories.[19]

Reflecting this hard-nosed view, the final statement of the Cairo meeting took special note of the need to "respect the principle of every Arab country's sovereignty over its natural and economic resources," a rejection of Saddam Husayn's insistence that Arab oil wealth belonged to the whole Arab nation.[20] A further meeting of the group was scheduled for 5 March in Damascus to work out more concrete and institutionalized aspects of the alliance, including, according to press reports, the establishment of an Arab security force for the Gulf, comprising Egyptian, Syrian and GCC units, and the implementation of the GCC's December 1990 summit decision to establish a development fund of $10bn. or $15bn. with Egypt presumably to be a prime beneficiary.[21]

At the same time, on 15 February, Iraq's Revolutionary Command Council (RCC) declared Iraq's "readiness to deal with Security Council Resolution No. 660...with the aim of reaching an honorable and acceptable political solution, including withdrawal." It was the first time that "withdrawal" had been explicitly mentioned by Baghdad. However, its implementation was linked by Iraq to a host of conditions deemed completely unacceptable by its adversaries. They included abolition of the 11 other Security Council resolutions pertaining to the crisis, removal of the international embargo against Iraq, withdrawal of all foreign forces from the region, Israel's withdrawal from all occupied Arab territories, prevention of the Al Sabah family from resuming power in Kuwait, payment for wartime damages to Iraq and cancellation of all Iraqi debts to the countries that attacked it.[22] Iraq's Arab and Western adversaries promptly rejected the RCC statement, while the "neutrals" rushed to endorse it as the basis for a negotiated end to hostilities. Morocco also expressed its approval. Concurrently, Iraq's deputy prime minister Sa'dun Hammadi visited North African capitals to lobby for support of the proposal. However, his public call for the withdrawal of Moroccan troops from Saudi Arabia, while he was in Rabat, drew a stern rebuke from the Moroccan Royal Palace.[23]

A week later, virtually on the eve of the ground war, Iraq offered a less equivocal indication that it would withdraw from Kuwait if a cease-fire were to be effected, eliciting similar responses as previously. In the event, the ground assault commenced on schedule.

Throughout the war, the American-led round-the-clock bombing campaign gave rise increasingly to accusations from its Arab opponents that the real purpose of the war was to destroy Iraq, not to liberate Kuwait. This, for example, was the thrust of a speech by King Husayn on 6 February. Saddam's Arab adversaries repeatedly denied that this was so, or that they were seeking to oust Saddam from power. Nonetheless, the concept of fighting alongside Western forces against a fellow Arab state remained a sensitive topic. Egypt's forces, and even more so Syria's, were reportedly reluctant to engage in military operations (see chapter on the Gulf War). The swiftness and decisiveness of the ground war thus came as a relief to them. Most, although not all, Arab officials seem to have supported Bush's decision to end the war when he did.[24]

At the same time, Arab leaders in the anti-Saddam group were clearly hoping that the destruction of Iraq's military might would not only reduce Iraq's threat to manageable proportions but also lead to Saddam's overthrow by forces within the ruling Sunni Arab elite. Kuwait had been liberated, public opinion contained, and the Iraqi armed forces severely punished. Hopefully, the military was ready to take revenge on Saddam. The initial mood in Cairo and Riyadh was one of near euphoria over Iraq's swift defeat at such a low price, and optimistic about the chances of translating their anti-Saddam wartime alliance into an unchallengeable bloc which would decisively shape the postwar era in their own image. However, the postwar upheaval in Iraq would pose new dilemmas for the anti-Saddam group. Moreover, establishing a durable postwar regional order would prove to be a more daunting task than it had first seemed.

THE AFTERMATH: A NEW ARAB ORDER?

THE DAMASCUS EIGHT AND GULF SECURITY

On the morrow of the cease-fire, widespread unrest broke out in Iraq in the predominantly Shi'i south and within the predominantly Kurdish area in the north (see chapter on Iraq). For Iraq's Arab rivals, this presented a new specter: the possible dismemberment of Iraq as a state, and a radical alteration of the regional order (e.g., the creation of an Iranian-backed Shi'i entity in southern Iraq, a Kurdish entity in the north, and/or intervention by Iran or Turkey or both). This prospect was anathema to all of them, for the preservation of existing territorial boundaries in the Arab world was a cardinal value. "We must say it loud and clear," declared Egypt's Mubarak. "No to the dismemberment of Iraq. The territorial integrity of Iraq is sacred."[25] Thus, Saddam's move in subsequent weeks to crush his Kurdish and Shi'i opponents evoked little comment. As the prospect of a rebellion within the Sunni ruling elite diminished, the anti-Saddam Arabs resigned themselves, at least for the time being, to Saddam's remaining in power, clearly preferring that to the possibility of a geopolitical reshuffle.

In the meantime, the "six-plus-two" group met as scheduled in Damascus on 5–6 March and at the close of the meetings issued the Damascus declaration, which spelled out the members' vision of the postwar Arab and regional order in greater detail than at the preparatory Cairo meeting. As previously stated in Cairo, it was to be based on strict adherence to the Arab League and UN charters, with particular emphasis on respecting the unity and territorial integrity of each state, "the inadmissability of seizing territories by force, nonintervention in domestic affairs, and a commitment to settle disputes by peaceful means." Each state's control over its natural resources was to be respected. Economic cooperation was to be bolstered, with the objective of establishing an "Arab economic grouping" that would be able "to keep pace" with developments resulting from the establishment of regional economic groupings elsewhere in the world. Western press reports stated that the GCC states had committed themselves to providing $5bn. in aid to help Egypt and Syria restructure their economies along free-market lines, a sum that was reported to be the first installment of a $10bn.–$15bn. package.[26]

The declaration addressed a number of other matters as well, including advocating the convening of an international peace conference "to end the Israeli occupation of Arab territories and to guarantee the Palestinian people's national rights based on the pertinent UN resolutions"; having the Middle East declared a "zone free of all weapons of mass destruction, especially nuclear weapons"; encouraging the private sector in Arab states in the development process; supporting scientific research centers and facilitating contacts between them; and introducing a mechanism for settling disputes in the Arab League charter. (For the text of the declaration, see Appendix I.)

Of greatest immediate interest was the question of a postwar defense system in the Gulf. Egyptian and Syrian forces were defined as constituting "a nucleus for an Arab peace force" that would safeguard the security of the Arab states in the Gulf, as well as serve as "an example that would guarantee the effectiveness of the comprehensive Arab defense order." GCC Secretary-General Bishara praised the "strategic linkage" that was being established between the GCC states and the two Arab military powers.[27] Measures taken in this regard, declared the signatories, "will not be directed against any other party," but rather would be the basis for "opening [a] dialogue with the Islamic and international parties who respect the higher interests of the Arab nation and abide by the principles of international legitimacy." Like so many newly formed inter-Arab coalitions in the past, the signatories to the Damascus declaration also proclaimed their intention to formalize their alliance, first through periodic meetings of foreign ministers and then to institutionalize them through a "contractual formula." The new grouping was open to all Arab states that subscribed to the declaration's principles, a traditional formula designed to defend the parties against charges of forming an "axis" or divisive bloc within the Arab system. However, the failure of the Damascus declaration to spell out the details of the proposed defense system indicated, in fact, that institutionalizing the alliance would be no simple matter (see below).

Four days later, on 10 March, the foreign ministers of the "six-plus-two" group met in Riyadh with US Secretary of State James Baker. For the US, the meeting signified its desire to see the wartime US-Arab coalition serve as a basis for the postwar regional order. For the Arab parties, it was an acknowledgment that their interests dovetailed closely with those of the West. The statement that they issued at the end of the meeting expressed their appreciation for the US stand during the Gulf crisis and their resolve to work with the US in promoting regional security as well as a resolution to the Palestinian question. The principles of the Damascus declaration were reiterated in full, and were thus implicitly endorsed by the US.[28] Apart from the content of the meeting, the very fact that it took place marked another inter-Arab watershed precipitated by the Gulf crisis. Never before had a high-level inter-Arab meeting been attended by a Western, let alone American, official. The willingness of the anti-Saddam states to declare openly, and in this case even advertise, their pro-American tilt was unprecedented in the Arab world.

Reaction to the Damascus declaration among the Arab "neutrals" was generally muted. Only the Libyans were quick to criticize it as an "entrenchment of the unnecessary division of the Arab nation and the creation of two Arab leagues." What was needed, declared a Libyan news agency commentator, was the abandonment of the "futile axis policy" in favor of a return to the Arab League, which should then be upgraded to the level of an Arab federation (Qadhdhafi's long-standing proposal).[29]

Iran also reacted promptly. Foreign Minister Velayati and Vice President Hasan Habibi hurried to Damascus for clarification from their Syrian ally, while an Iranian radio commentary argued that the question of Gulf security should be addressed only by the Gulf littorals themselves, not by other Arab states or Western powers.[30]

The GCC states, sensitive to Iran's unhappiness, made efforts to reassure Tehran. For example, Saudi Arabia resumed diplomatic relations with Iran in late March, after having broken them in the fall of 1987 following the chaotic clashes between Iranian pilgrims and Saudi security forces at the Hajj that year (see *MECS* 1987, pp.

172–74). In acting to placate Iran, the GCC states resumed their traditional balancing act between their more powerful neighbors, but by taking cognizance of Iran's concerns, they rendered it more difficult to satisfy Egypt, and the prospect for an inter-Arab Egyptian-dominated force for the Gulf, the linchpin of the Damascus declaration, began to founder.

As the weeks passed without any progress in actualizing the declaration, the Egyptians became increasingly restless. They were especially annoyed by the Kuwaitis for what Egypt viewed as a lack of gratitude for its role in liberating Kuwait. Compensation for losses suffered by Egyptian workers in Kuwait remained in dispute, reports were received that Kuwaiti vigilante groups had allegedly tortured and killed Egyptians suspected of collaborating with the Iraqis during Iraq's occupation, and Kuwaiti pledges to give Egypt a share of up to 13% of its reconstruction contracts[31] seemed to be in doubt.

In late April, the GCC economic and finance ministers announced more detailed plans for a $10bn. Arab economic development fund first decided upon at the GCC's December 1990 summit in Doha, Qatar (see MECS 1990, pp. 164–65). Especially noteworthy was the Council's decision to link the program to plans already approved by such Western financial institutions as the International Monetary Fund (IMF) and the World Bank, as well as an increased emphasis to be placed on private-sector projects. For the GCC states, the plan was another indication of their desire to avoid returning to the old style of inter-Arab relations in which aid was doled out according to political, and not developmental criteria, and as often as not to radical Arab regimes as "protection money." However, the Egyptians, whose relationship with the IMF over the years was frequently troubled, viewed the GCC's move as another indication that the hoped-for financial windfall from their wartime coalition would not be forthcoming.[32] Egypt's pique with Kuwait in particular was manifested throughout the year, climaxing in an angry rejection by the Egyptian People's Assembly of a $250m. Kuwaiti loan offer to assist Egyptians returning from the Gulf to set up their own businesses, because of what were perceived as onerous terms.[33]

On 8 May, Husni Mubarak announced suddenly that he had ordered the Egyptian forces in Kuwait and Saudi Arabia to begin returning home immediately. The Syrians followed suit in June. Mubarak's move was reminiscent of his predecessor Anwar al-Sadat's foreign policy "shock tactics," although on a far smaller scale. His explanation for the move was terse: Egyptian troops had been sent for a specific purpose upon the request of Saudi Arabia, and their mission had been completed. He had already decided upon the withdrawal a month earlier, he told journalists, and some troops had already arrived home. The withdrawal was to be completed within three months.[34] An Egyptian spokesman denied that the Damascus declaration had become moribund, but did stress that it was up to the Gulf states themselves to define their security requirements in detail, which he stated had not yet been done.[35] Both Mubarak, who visited Kuwait on 18 June, and other Egyptian officials, denied any friction in Kuwaiti-Egyptian relations, reiterating consistently that military cooperation did not entail the permanent presence of Egyptian and Syrian troops.[36] However, the editor of a pro-government Egyptian daily was more candid: if the Damascus declaration had been touted as the basis for maintaining Gulf security, he asked, why did the GCC states link Gulf security with Iran and other foreign parties? "What is the fate of the document signed by eight foreign ministers of their own free will without coercion or pressure," he argued, "a document whose ink has not yet dried?"[37]

The answer, at least with regard to the issue of regional defense, was not long in coming. On 17 June, "Damascus eight" officials held a preparatory meeting in Doha, devising, according to Western press reports, a draft agreement to station a combined Saudi-GCC-Egyptian-Syrian "tripwire" force of 26,000 along the Iraqi-Kuwaiti border to back up behind what would be a reconstituted Kuwaiti army. The Egyptian and Syrian contributions would be mainly symbolic, 6,000 men in total.[38] However, even this scaled-down presence proved to be problematic. Soon afterward, Bahrain's Crown Prince Shaykh Hamid Ibn 'Isa Al Khalifa gave the first public indication of continuing differences among the group of eight, the result, he said, of hastily developed ideas in the wake of Kuwait's liberation. He himself favored the creation of a regional rapid deployment force, and not standing concentrations of forces that would have "many negative aspects."[39]

On 15–16 July, the "six-plus-two" foreign ministers met again in Kuwait and issued a revised, "final version" of the Damascus declaration. The revised text was nearly identical with the previous one, save for the fact that Egyptian and Syrian forces were no longer described as "constituting a nucleus for an Arab peace force" that would guarantee Gulf security. Instead, Egypt's and Syria's assistance were praised in general terms as a "perfect example" of how to implement the 1950 Arab League's joint defense agreement and as "a basis for effective security cooperation." Any GCC country, it declared, had the right to utilize Egyptian and Syrian forces on its territory. As for the future, the "group of eight" expressed the intention to formulate a "comprehensive protocol" for common defense and security, which would serve as a model for a future all-Arab defense and security system. This protocol, they pledged, would be deposited with the Arab League.[40] Clearly, however, the prospects for stationing an inter-Arab non-GCC military force in the Gulf were receding, owing to a combination of the GCC states' desire to placate Iran, and their wariness of a permanent Egyptian and Syrian military presence on their soil. This last concern was, no doubt, the result of their unpleasant experience during the previous decades as targets of Egyptian- and Ba'thi-inspired radical Arab nationalism. The meeting of the "six-plus-two" foreign ministers in Cairo on 11 November provided additional evidence to this effect. Apparently, the "Damascus eight" would henceforth be a political grouping with economic features but without the military/security aspect so highly touted at the beginning of the year.[41]

IRAN AND GULF SECURITY

A report published on 18 November by a pro-Syrian Lebanese publication stated that Egypt had rejected a GCC request that Iran, a non-Arab country, should be allowed to adhere to the Damascus declaration.[42] Although the report was not confirmed elsewhere, it was consistent with the GCC's balancing act between Iran and Egypt as well as with Syria's desire to nurture its 12-year alliance with post-Pahlavi Iran. Another pro-Syrian Lebanese publication had reported some months earlier that Syria's President Hafiz al-Asad had suggested to Mubarak on 5 June, during a visit by the Syrian leader to Cairo, that their two countries should establish a joint military committee with Iran that would address matters relating to the Gulf and to the ME as a whole.[43] In addition to Syria, Lebanon and Oman also reportedly tried their hand at mediating between Egypt and Iran.[44]

GCC sensitivity to Iranian concerns was reflected by a desire for closer ties with Tehran, which was mentioned repeatedly in GCC ministerial communiqués. At the December 1990 GCC summit in Doha, Oman's Sultan Qabus had been charged with promoting a dialogue with Iran as part of his responsibilities as head of a "security committee" designed to formulate the GCC's future security requirements. The role was an apt one for Qabus: throughout the Iraqi-Iranian War, while Kuwait and Saudi Arabia had tilted progressively toward Iraq, Oman had consistently favored maintaining links with Tehran. (Geopolitical considerations had, in fact, dictated a close relationship with Iran during the 1970s as well.) As the prospects of an Egyptian-Syrian-GCC force receded, Iranian-GCC contacts expanded. In late September, Iran's Foreign Minister Velayati and the six GCC foreign ministers met in New York while the UN General Assembly was in session. At the end of their discussions, they announced plans for another meeting during the first quarter of 1992 that would establish a framework to bolster cooperation in all fields.[45] Velayati also spoke confidently about the possibility of establishing a "six-plus-one" grouping (Iran and the GCC states), more significant than the "six-plus-two" in terms of the likely degree of "comprehensive cooperation...political, economic, commercial, technical and cultural" between them.[46] On the bilateral level, Saudi Arabia and Iran exchanged high-level visits following restored diplomatic relations between them; Iran avoided confrontations with Saudi Arabia on oil-pricing matters (see chapter on oil developments); and 150,000 Iranians made the pilgrimage to Mecca for the first time since the violent clashes at the 1987 pilgrimage (see chapter on Islamic affairs). Relations between Riyadh and Tehran were thus, in the words of Iran's deputy foreign minister Muhammad 'Ali Besharati, better than at any time in recent years.[47] Also in November, Qatar's Crown Prince Shaykh Hamad Ibn Khalifa Al Thani paid a state visit to Tehran and signed five agreements to further cooperation in various fields (see chapter on Qatar). Economically, Iranian-GCC trade exceeded $2bn. and was expected to continue to rise.[48]

Despite official Egyptian denials, differences between Egypt and Iran over the shape of postwar security arrangements in the Gulf resulted in considerable tension between Tehran and Cairo, expressed mainly in periodic media broadsides in which each side accused the other of harboring hegemonic designs. The GCC states were clearly uncomfortable with this state of affairs, and in September, Oman's Foreign Minister Yusuf Ibn 'Alawi visited Tehran and Cairo to mediate the differences between them. Cairo-Tehran tensions also spilled over into the Egyptian-GCC sphere periodically, although officials on all sides steadfastly maintained otherwise. The concurrent warming of relations between Tehran and the GCC added fuel to the fire. One indicator was a harsh blast at GCC leaders in general, and Qatar's leaders in particular, by al-Akhbar's editor Ibrahim Sa'da, who frequently reflected official thinking in Egypt. Reacting to an interview with Iran's Vice President Hasan Habibi in a Qatari paper, in which Habibi rejected any Egyptian role in maintaining Gulf security, and to the concurrent state visit to Tehran by Qatar's crown prince, Sa'da addressed Qatar's rulers:

> Why would you publish insolent remarks against Egypt by Iranians, big and small alike, in a fraternal paper? If you approve of the Iranian viewpoint on

excluding Egypt from the Gulf security order, why do you not declare it openly and directly, without resorting to a Persian Iranian tongue to say it on your behalf?![149]

Gulf states' sensitivity to Tehran's concerns did not extend to Iranian disapproval of the GCC's pursuit of closer security ties with the West. By the end of the year, Kuwait had openly placed itself under the Western defense umbrella, signing pacts with the US, Britain and France, and Bahrain had expanded its defense links with the US. While the Saudis did not see eye-to-eye completely with the US on defense issues, and still preferred a relatively low American profile in the region, nonetheless the Saudi-led GCC had become more than ever a pro-American, pro-Western club.

In addition to their arrangements with the West, the GCC states continued to hold discussions on forming an expanded GCC security force to replace the prewar "Peninsula Shield" force of 10,000 that had proven totally inadequate in the face of the Iraqi challenge. GCC chiefs of staff met in late October for discussions, which centered around Oman's proposal to establish an army of 100,000 under a command that would be rotated among the member states. The proposal was the centerpiece of the Qabus committee's "comprehensive strategic report," which was submitted to GCC heads of state at the December summit in Kuwait (see below).

THE GCC: CONTINUITY AND CHANGE
The Iraqi threat had created an unprecedented sense of solidarity and common destiny among member states of the GCC, by far the most coherent and like-minded of all inter-Arab groupings with regard to regional issues. GCC foreign ministers' meetings repeatedly issued sharp condemnations of Iraq and calls for continued UN and international pressure on Baghdad to force it to comply with Security Council resolutions relating to the war. The GCC's willingness to participate in an Arab-Israeli peace conference (see below) further illustrated the degree of like-mindedness among its members. So did their strong desire to prevent a return to the kind of inter-Arab patterns that had existed prior to Iraq's invasion of Kuwait. Nowhere was this more in evidence than in the continued antipathy displayed toward the PLO and Jordan. Examples were diverse: Kuwait's policy of drastically reducing the size of its Palestinian community, cutting off its funding to the PLO, and continuing to maintain downgraded diplomatic links with Jordan; Saudi Arabia's cessation of financial aid to Jordan and sharp curtailing of funds to the PLO, its reluctance to restore full air and land links with Amman, giving the diplomatic cold shoulder to King Husayn; and periodic media broadsides by both Saudi Arabia and Kuwait against the PLO and Jordan (see also the relevant country chapters). There was also close coordination in the realm of oil pricing and production (see chapter on oil developments).

However, the GCC members were not eager to increase substantially political, military or economic integration. In fact, each remained jealously protective of its own domain, as exemplified by the renewal of a border dispute between Bahrain and Qatar during the summer months (see chapters on Bahrain and Qatar; for background, see *MECS* 1986, pp. 294–96). At issue were the Hawara, Fash al-Dibal and al-Jarada islets under Bahrain's control but contested by Qatar: their dispute stemmed from a number of factors, but was now aggravated over Qatar's fear of possible encroachment on its adjoining rich natural gas field. A unilateral appeal by Qatar to the International Court of Justice at the Hague incensed Bahrain, which had wanted to make a joint appeal.[50] A number of subsequent GCC ministerial and committee meetings were either postponed or disrupted because of the dispute, and, although Saudi Arabia energetically sought to mediate the matter, as it had done in the past, it met with no success, as Bahrain was reportedly opposed to Saudi involvement.[51]

The end of the year witnessed a renewed flurry of GCC meetings: an interior ministers' meeting in Doha on 10 December, a joint meeting of foreign, economy and finance ministers in Kuwait on 22 December, at which they reportedly approved the much-heralded $10bn. program for Arab economic development,[52] and finally, the annual GCC summit conference, held in Kuwait on 23–25 December.

The convening of the summit in Kuwait City was especially meaningful for the restored Kuwaiti monarchy. With the trauma of Iraqi occupation and GCC impotence still fresh in his mind, Kuwait's emir, Shaykh Jabr al-Ahmad al-Jabr Al Sabah, called upon GCC leaders in his opening speech to draw the appropriate conclusions, declaring that the GCC was facing a "completely new situation" that demanded closer unity and realistic and practical cooperation.[53]

Two documents were issued at the conclusion of the summit. In one, entitled "the Kuwait declaration," GCC members reiterated the broad policy themes that had crystallized during the previous 18 months: support for the Damascus declaration principles, for the GCC's program to promote regional economic development, and for a united stand against Iraq and those that "collaborated with it in its spiteful aggression," until Baghdad implemented all pertinent UN Security Council resolutions.[54] The second document was a more detailed final communiqué (for the texts of both documents, see Appendix II). Relations among GCC states, the statement declared, were governed by the "unique destiny" of its members. The summiteers had reviewed the "GCC march" — a decade of joint activity along the road to "coordination, integration and unification" — and pledged to redouble their efforts in all fields. Regarding the all-important security dimension, the statement emphasized the members' willingness to continue promoting military and security cooperation within the framework of a "unified strategic concept" and thanked Sultan Qabus for his efforts as head of the security committee. However, it was clear that the parties had failed to agree on essential details, such as the size, structure and command of the proposed 100,000-man force.[55] This lack of agreement was matched by a lack of urgency: Secretary-General Bishara told an interviewer that there would surely be a "Gulf deterrent force" within five years.[56]

In the economic sphere, the statement reiterated the members' determination, expressed in past years as well, to implement gradually the provisions of their "unified economic agreement" of 1981 (see *MECS* 1980–81, pp. 462–63), designed to remove obstacles in the way of free movement of persons, goods and capital. The statement's treatment of wider regional issues was similarly characterized by high-minded platitudes that tended to mask differences and unresolved issues. GCC heads of state expressed their "extreme satisfaction" with the results of cooperative efforts with Syria and Egypt, and termed the Damascus declaration framework a "nucleus of joint Arab action" and a proper basis for inter-Arab relations. They also expressed their eagerness to intensify the improvement of ties with Iran, in line with the 1990 Doha summit statement, with Qatar's emir continuing to be charged with responsibility in this area.

Overall, 1991 was a momentous year for the GCC states. The independence and sovereignty of one of them had been restored, their perpetually precarious security had been immeasurably enhanced by Iraq's defeat, and their collective legitimacy was reinforced vis-à-vis the challenges of powerful forces in the region that jealously eyed their oil wealth. But their collective capacity to move toward greater substantive integration remained in doubt.

The impact of the Gulf crisis on long-term domestic political trends within the GCC states could not yet be measured. However, a gathering of Gulf intellectuals in Kuwait on the eve of the December summit showed that increased like-mindedness was not limited to the ruling elites. The conference produced a sharp critique of the Gulf regimes for their monopolization of power and their failure to broaden the basis of political participation.[57] The issue was particularly pressing for the Kuwaitis, owing to the well-articulated demands within Kuwait for democratization. Future developments there were likely to reverberate throughout the other GCC member states.

THE ARAB LEAGUE

Although the functioning of the Arab League had been severely damaged by the Gulf crisis, the Egyptian-led majority grouping had overruled the opposition of Iraq and its supporters, and implemented the precrisis decision to transfer the League headquarters back to Cairo 12 years after it was removed from there to Tunis (see *MECS* 1990, pp. 158–59). By the beginning of 1991, the move had been completed. Compensation terms for employees not relocating to Cairo had been worked out; a decision had been made that three subsidiary League organizations were to remain headquartered in Tunis (the Union of Arab Radios, the Arab Interior Ministers' Council and the Arab Organization for Education, Culture and Science); and Kuwait had pledged funds to help complete the long-unfinished headquarters building in Tunis that would house the organizations. Yet, the Iraqis kept up a rearguard action against the Egyptian-dominated League, with one of its nationals, Salah al-Mukhtar, resigning in protest from his post as assistant secretary-general on 2 January. In February, a Saudi-financed newspaper reported that Iraq and other states were attempting to undermine the move back to Cairo by funneling their membership dues to the former headquarters in Tunis and attempting to block the transfer of League documentation from Tunis to Cairo.[58]

Once the war was over, however, both the Iraqis and the "neutrals" deemed it advisable to resume participation in routine League activities in order to begin a process of "normalizing" relations with the victorious "six-plus-two" group. Thus, the League's regular semiannual meeting opened as scheduled in Cairo on 30 March with all states, including Iraq, attending (for subsequent Iraqi activity vis-à-vis the League, see below). But letting bygones be bygones was not a simple matter. A substantive healing of inter-Arab divisions was not yet possible, so the meeting itself could only be brief — 90 minutes — followed by an adjournment till mid-May. The Iraqi representative maintained silence throughout the session, much of which was taken up by a speech of Egypt's Foreign Minister 'Abd al-Majid. After praising the liberation of Kuwait and the restoration of its sovereignty and legitimate government, 'Abd al-Majid emphasized the need to learn the lessons of the crisis so as to "prevent such a thing from recurring." He then expanded on the principles embodied in the Damascus declaration regarding pan-Arab security, good neighborliness and solidarity, joint action in the field of economic development and a resolution of the Arab-Israeli conflict.[59] There was no discussion on the Gulf crisis itself, a fact that considerably irked the Kuwaiti delegate to the League, who warned against continuing "with our old ways" and proposed putting an end to "embracing and kissing each other when our hearts harbor something different." Only through "frankness and realism," he declared, could the Arabs hope to address their current problems.[60]

The League resumed its discussions on 15 May, officially at the foreign ministerial level. Noteworthy was the unanimous election of Egypt's Foreign Minister 'Abd al-Majid to the post of secretary-general, which had been vacated by Chedli Klibi of Tunisia in September 1990 (see *MECS* 1990, pp. 158–59). Symbolically, 'Abd al-Majid's election marked the final step of Egypt's return to centrality in the Arab arena, as well as the renewal of a tradition: prior to Klibi, the League secretaries-general had all been veterans of Egypt's foreign ministry. In his acceptance speech and in subsequent interviews, 'Abd al-Majid emphasized that "clearing the Arab atmosphere" and healing the unprecedented rifts that had opened up over the Gulf crisis were central to his mandate. More generally, he declared, a revitalized League was essential for overcoming past inter-Arab differences and addressing new regional and international challenges, not only in the political area but also in the economic, social, environmental and human rights spheres. Structurally, there was a need to develop ties between the League and Arab regional groupings, to devise appropriate conflict-resolution mechanisms for dealing with disputes as they arose, and to create a system of regular consultations. The long-delayed process of amending the Arab League charter also needed to be completed forthwith, he stated, in order to cope properly with these new exigencies.[61]

But the May League meeting itself showed that these were not easy tasks, for heated accusations were exchanged between the heads of the Kuwaiti and Iraqi delegations. Kuwait's Foreign Minister Salim al-Sabah al-Salim reminded the other delegates of Iraq's "crimes, violation of sanctities...murders...and burning of oil installations" while also bitterly castigating those who had "contributed to the breaking of Arab ranks" by supporting Iraq, for which they should bear "historic responsibility." In turn, Iraqi Minister of State for Foreign Affairs Muhammad Sa'id al-Sahaf declared his readiness to "reopen files" that would show Kuwait's responsibility for the crisis. However, he said, Iraq preferred to follow the path outlined by 'Abd al-Majid in his acceptance speech, namely to close ranks and deal with issues facing all Arabs with "reason and objectivity."[62] (For subsequent Iraqi-Kuwaiti tensions and the role of the League, see below.)

Other meetings took place on the sideline of the Cairo discussions. The foreign ministers of the "six-plus-two" group exchanged views on the implementation of the Damascus declaration; the five AMU foreign ministers met to exchange views in advance of the League's plenary session; and the Saudi and Lebanese foreign ministers discussed efforts being made to implement the 1989 Ta'if Accords for the stabilization of Lebanon. According to Saudi Foreign Minister Sa'ud al-Faysal, sufficient progress was being made in Lebanon, so that there was no need to convene the Algerian-Moroccan-Saudi Arabian tripartite committee that had been formed in May 1989 to help broker a solution to Lebanon's impasse (see *MECS* 1989, pp. 138–43). Faysal explained that the failure of the committee to convene thus far during 1991 resulted not from lack of interest but from the overwhelming Arab preoccupation with the

Gulf crisis and its aftermath, and from Algeria's and Morocco's concern with internal affairs. Contact between them was going on nonetheless, he emphasized,[63] a statement borne out by a meeting between Morocco's King Hasan and the committee's three foreign ministers in New York in October.

Apart from the unresolved aspects of the Gulf War and the Arab-Israeli conflict (traditionally the League's premier subject of discussion), a number of other issues were dealt with by the League at different junctures during the year. In late June and early July, it became involved in hurried efforts to contain fighting in Southern Lebanon between PLO forces loyal to Yasir 'Arafat and Lebanese army units seeking to extend the Lebanese central government's authority there. This effort was made in response to urgent appeals by 'Arafat, and followed the failure of an earlier mediation attempt by Algeria[64] (see chapters on the PLO and Lebanon). Overall, however, the Lebanese issue had been downgraded on the collective Arab agenda and handed over to Syrian patronage.[65] 'Abd al-Majid also sought during the latter half of the year to involve the League in bringing about a cessation of the vicious bloodletting in Somalia, which was formally a League member. However, its capabilities of influencing events there were quite limited. Toward the end of the year, renewed tension between Libya and the US, Britain and France resulted in considerable concern in the Arab world, especially in Egypt, which sought to mediate a solution under the auspices of the League (see below).

IRAQ AFTER THE WAR

Iraq's postwar inter-Arab policies were geared toward normalizing relations with its adversaries and maintaining links with its friends. Only thus could it hope to "come in from the cold," that is, ease its regional isolation and apply more effective pressure for the removal of the Security Council sanctions. Regarding its rivals, Iraqi officials repeatedly expressed a desire to renew diplomatic relations with Egypt and Saudi Arabia and establish cooperative ties with all states based on the principles embodied in the Arab League charter, although they steadfastly refrained from any admission of error regarding the Gulf crisis and continued to insist that "Kuwait is Iraq" just as "Palestine is Arab."[66] Iraqi diplomats continued to pay regular visits to Baghdad's sometime allies and sympathizers in North Africa, Sudan, Jordan and Yemen.

The Iraqi strategy also included paying renewed attention to the Arab League, beginning with attending the League meetings in Cairo, however uncomfortable this was (see above). For the remainder of the year, Iraq actively sought to use the League as a forum to mobilize support for its policies, while at the same time opposing attempts to amend the League charter which, it feared, would strengthen its adversaries.[67] In mid-July, Baghdad proposed that the League set up a committee to acquaint itself with Iraq's "peaceful nuclear program." Concurrently, it called for an emergency meeting of Arab foreign ministers, to demonstrate how Iraq was fulfilling its obligations to cooperate with UN inspection teams, thereby mustering support against what it termed US and Western "blackmail" in preparation for a "comprehensive new military aggression against Iraq." The issue, wrote Foreign Minister Ahmad Husayn to League Secretary-General 'Abd al-Majid, "is not a political one among the Arab states, as the situation was during the Kuwait problem, but...[one] of sovereignty, safety and security of an Arab state, the fate of its people, and their right to live a decent life."[68] The anti-Iraqi Arab majority, however, refused to countenance a special session requested by Baghdad, and Egypt warned Iraq not to repeat its miscalculation of six months earlier and to cooperate with UN efforts to inspect its nuclear facilities lest it suffer another military attack.[69] At the same time, unlike the situation during the countdown to the Gulf War, the Egyptian media publicly expressed opposition to the possibility of renewed Western attacks against Iraq.[70] Iraq also scored some success in the inter-Arab arena regarding the issue of trade sanctions, as evidenced by 'Abd al-Majid's urging UN Secretary-General Javier Pérez de Cuellar to lift the blockade in order to alleviate the "sufferings of the people...especially the children and the poor."[71]

Baghdad also found the League a useful forum for countering Kuwait's charges of Iraqi perfidy in the months following the war's end and for promoting its own version of events. It expressed willingness to cooperate with 'Abd al-Majid's inquiry into Kuwaiti charges that Iraq still held thousands of Kuwaiti prisoners taken mainly during the last days of Iraq's occupation (which Iraq vehemently denied).[72] It rejected Kuwaiti charges of aggression following incidents at the end of August on Kuwait's Bubiyan Island, and submitted a memo to the League's secretariat calling for Kuwait's expulsion from the organization following its signing of a defense pact with the US in September.[73] Iraq also welcomed a League fact-finding mission on Kuwaiti-Iraqi relations in late September.[74] In late August, it called on the League to pressure Turkey to withdraw its troops from Iraqi territory, where they were temporarily engaged in operations against anti-Turkish Kurdish guerrillas, and welcomed a condemnation of Turkey's action by the League's assistant secretary-general 'Adnan 'Umran.[75] On 3 September, Iraq lodged an official protest with 'Abd al-Majid over "repeated violations of Iraqi airspace by US spy planes coming from Saudi airspace."[76] Two weeks later, it demanded that the League condemn the US for burying alive hundreds of Iraqi soldiers during the Gulf War.[77] In December, the Iraqis strongly supported Libya at an emergency Arab League meeting called to discuss the brewing crisis between Libya and the US, Britain and France (see below). For Baghdad, the possibility of an American military strike against Libya was seized on as further confirmation of American hegemonic designs in the region and as further justification for Iraq's resistance, no matter what the cost. At best, however, the Iraqis were conducting a rearguard operation. The League continued to be dominated by the anti-Saddam states, and thus provided little potential for mobilizing support.

THE INTER-ARAB ARENA: THE VIEW FROM CAIRO
The outcome of the Gulf crisis was a vindication of Husni Mubarak's decision in August 1990 to take the lead, with all the risk that it entailed, in mobilizing the anti-Saddam coalition. Cairo's hopes for a transformed Arab world were expressed in Mubarak's "pan-Arab appeal" for a new era in inter-Arab relations, to be based on the promotion of peace, security, development and the gradual widening of political participation, delivered to a joint session of Egypt's two houses of parliament on 3 March.[78]

More prosaically, the favorable outcome of the latest round in the age-old conflict between the Nile- and Mesopotamian-based power centers bolstered Mubarak's status internally and also gave the Egyptian authorities ample reason to believe that the postwar Arab order was to be led, unchallenged, by Cairo, backed by generous GCC financial support and Western approval. The ascension of Egypt's Foreign

Minister 'Abd al-Majid to the leadership of the Cairo-based Arab League seemed to confirm this view. So did, if indirectly, the selection of another senior Egyptian diplomat, Butrus Butrus-Ghali, to the post of UN secretary-general toward the end of the year — the first Arab to hold this position.

Overall, however, Egyptian expectations were, at best, only partially borne out. To be sure, Iraq's crushing defeat and continued quarantine ensured Egypt's preeminent and unchallenged status as primus inter pares among Arab countries, not only demographically and culturally but politically as well. Renewed momentum in the Arab-Israeli peace process following the war (see below) provided further confirmation of the changes wrought by the war and justified Egypt's long-standing advocacy of a diplomatic solution to the conflict. But the difficult point was translating the principles of the Damascus declaration into a lasting basis for a new inter-Arab order. Nothing illustrated the limitations of Egypt's regional position more aptly than the failure to establish a joint security force for the Gulf.

Only time would tell whether Egypt's other expectations from the GCC states (in terms of aid, trade, labor migration and business contracts) would be realized and thus decisively influence future inter-Arab trends. Cairo could at least point to a measure of improvement in relations with Kuwait, after a rocky initial postwar period. At the end of the year, an agreement was reportedly being negotiated between the Egyptian Investment Authority and its Kuwaiti counterpart to set up a joint stockholding company with an initial capital of $500m. for the purpose of encouraging investment in Egypt, in the areas of agricultural projects, land reclamation, construction, petroleum-related services and transport. Concurrently, oil ministers of both countries met to discuss efforts by Egyptian companies seeking contracts to repair damaged oil installations and drill new ones. A new joint airline company was established which would specialize in freight traffic between the two countries. By the end of the year, 110,000 Egyptians were working in Kuwait, a figure still below the prewar total of 180,000 but one which promised to rise as the process of reconstruction and normalization of life in Kuwait gathered momentum.[79] The labor situation in Saudi Arabia was even better: the number of Egyptians working there was c. 1.25m., constituting the single largest foreign community in the kingdom.

Egyptian-Libyan relations warmed considerably during the year, as both states found it useful to insulate the practical bilateral aspects of their relations from divergences over larger regional issues. Despite their differences, Qadhdhafi and Mubarak maintained lines of communication throughout the Gulf crisis. The acceleration of the Arab-Israeli peace process during the latter half of the year, a process championed by Egypt but rejected foursquare by Libya, likewise did not interfere with their blossoming ties. Qadhdhafi and Mubarak met on seven different occasions during the year and numerous official delegations exchanged visits as well. The movement of goods and people across their common border was brisk, and a number of joint economic projects were initiated. On a number of occasions, Mubarak spoke approvingly of Qadhdhafi's more tempered behavior in international relations, viewing the continued strengthening of mutual ties as contributing further to this trend. Libya depicted its improved ties with Egypt as a model for building a lasting basis for true Arab unity, and Qadhdhafi expressed his hope that the Arab League under 'Abd al-Majid would adopt his long-standing proposal for an all-Arab confederation.[80]

Apart from the concrete economic benefits stemming from improved relations with Libya, it was clear that Mubarak was counting on regional political dividends, namely that Qadhdhafi would moderate his formerly subversive behavior, thus further strengthening Mubarak's policies of promoting sober-minded regional cooperation and the resolution of disputes by peaceful means. That Libya was deriving diplomatic benefits from its closer relationship with Egypt, and by extension with the Arab League as a whole, became apparent in November-December with the growing tension between Libya and the US, Britain and France. At issue was America's insistence on the extradition of two Libyan intelligence officers for their alleged involvement in the February 1988 midair explosion of Pan American Airways Flight No. 103 over Lockerbie, Scotland. On 17 November, the Arab League secretariat voiced its "deep concern" over Western threats against Libya, confirmed Libya's commitment to international law, and called on all sides to exercise restraint.[81] Concurrently, Mubarak reportedly urged US President George Bush not to use force against Libya, saying that it would undermine the peace process.[82] On 5 December, an Arab League Council emergency session praised Libya's willingness to help reveal the facts of the case and called for the formation of a joint Arab League-UN committee to examine the issue.[83] League Secretary-General 'Abd al-Majid, serving as the point man for Arab diplomatic efforts, met with both British and Libyan officials during December and suggested that the two suspects be sent to a neutral capital under UN custody for interrogation by an international judicial panel.[84] Although the Libyans were not keen on the idea, they could take some comfort in the public praise for their willingness to cooperate by the League and by Egyptian ministrations to Western capitals to prevent a repetition of the 1986 American bombing of Tripoli.[85] Having risked the wrath of the Arab "street" for supporting the war against Iraq, Egypt, not to mention Syria — Libya's long-standing ally in the radical, anti-American camp — were in no mood to witness the use of force by Western governments against another Arab state. The issue was unresolved at the end of the year.

Qadhdhafi also continued his efforts to mediate between Mubarak and Sudan's President 'Umar al-Bashir, first manifested by their meeting in early January on the eve of the Gulf War (see above). However, Mubarak rejected further suggestions by both Libya and Sudan that Bashir should come to Cairo.[86] The problem, he told an interviewer, was not Bashir personally but the inordinate influence of Islamic extremists in Sudan led by Hasan al-Turabi who sought to propagate his "destructive principles" through acts of terror all over the world.[87] Consequently, Sudanese-Egyptian relations remained tense throughout 1991, although in September Libya reportedly hosted a meeting of Egyptian and Sudanese officials.[88] Toward the end of the year, an additional complication emerged when Sudan strengthened its ties with Iran, as demonstrated by an official visit by Iran's President Rafsanjani to Khartoum in mid-December. Thereafter, an office of Iran's Revolutionary Guards was reportedly established in Khartoum and Sudan reportedly provided training camps for Islamic militants with Iran's assistance.[89]

Jordanian-Egyptian relations remained cool throughout the year. Mubarak and King Husayn did not meet, although they did hold a number of telephone conversations.[90] Husayn was particularly disappointed by the failure of most Arab leaders (including Mubarak, King Fahd and Asad) to personally attend the December Islamic Conference Organization (ICO) summit in Dakar, Senegal, where he had planned to press for a return to inter-Arab normalcy.

Although Egypt and Jordan held similar views on the need to move the Arab-Israeli peace process forward (see below), the legacy of the Gulf War continued to sour mutual relations. A new round of accusations and vituperations was evoked by Jordan's publication in late August of a white book documenting and justifying its activity during the Gulf crisis. The book included a heretofore undisclosed letter from King Husayn to Saddam Husayn on 22 September 1990 in which the king beseeched Saddam to withdraw his forces from Kuwait. Both Egyptian officials and the Cairo press reacted sharply to the white book's reiteration that Egypt and Saudi Arabia were to blame for the failure to achieve an "Arab solution" to the conflict during the first week of the Gulf crisis. Mubarak personally expressed disappointment that despite indications that King Husayn was correcting his past errors, he had issued a document which contained statements that had been "turned around 180 degrees."[91]

The Saudis were also critical, with Foreign Minister Sa'ud al-Faysal declaring that the responsibility for improved Saudi-Jordanian ties rested with Amman, which should stop trying to justify its hostile positions by blaming them on the GCC.[92] Saudi Crown Prince 'Abdallah and King Husayn reportedly had a sharp exchange on this issue at the ICO summit.[93] At the end of the year, King Husayn was resigned to the situation for the time being, expressing hope, in an interview, that eventually the other Arabs would come to understand Jordan's position on the Gulf crisis, but stating that Jordan could not do much more on behalf of easing inter-Arab fragmentation, and its own isolation, than it had already.[94]

INTER-ARAB RELATIONS AND THE ARAB-ISRAELI PEACE PROCESS

Throughout the Gulf crisis, the anti-Saddam coalition had rejected Iraq's insistence on linking a solution in the Gulf to parallel efforts in the Israeli-Palestinian sphere. However, broad sectors of public opinion in the Arab world were convinced that a double standard existed in the West, and that while UN Security Council resolutions against Iraq were being firmly implemented, no parallel pressure had ever been exerted on Israel to comply with UN directives. With the end of the Gulf War, therefore, most Arab leaders were especially desirous of seeing a speedy renewal of American diplomatic efforts to recharge the Arab-Israeli peace process, stalled since the spring of 1990 (see *MECS* 1990, chapter on the ME peace process). The US Administration, for its part, believed that the results of the Gulf War, combined with the collapse of Soviet power, provided it with a unique opportunity to break the Arab-Israeli status quo. Thus it launched an intensive and sustained diplomatic effort which was to culminate in the convening of the Madrid conference on 30 October (for details, see chapter on the ME peace process).

In inter-Arab terms, the path toward diplomatic progress in the Arab-Israeli sphere had rarely, if ever, been so free of obstacles: never before in the history of the conflict had there been such a broad consensus on the need to cooperate with American-led diplomatic efforts. The GCC's willingness to delegate an observer to the proposed peace conference, expressed publicly for the first time on 11 May, provided a concrete indication of the Gulf states' belief in the necessity of lining up with the US, as well as further confirmation of their newfound confidence and assertiveness in regional affairs. So did Saudi willingness to countenance a proposal floated by Mubarak and the US during the summer to suspend the long-standing Arab boycott of Israel in return for Israel's cessation of settlement activity in the West Bank and Gaza. On 12 September, the Arab League Council called upon the four countries bordering Israel and upon the PLO to seek a common position. On the eve of the Madrid conference, an extraordinary meeting of the GCC ministerial council reiterated its commitment to dispatching an observer and also announced that member countries would participate in the projected multilateral meetings designed to address a variety of regional issues.[95] The AMU adopted a similar position: observer status at Madrid for the organization's secretary-general and for the foreign ministers of Morocco, Algeria, Tunisia and Mauritania, and individual participation in the multilateral talks. Libya expressed its reservations but did not stand in the way of the AMU secretary-general's participation.

Neatly juxtaposed with the broad Arab consensus favoring Arab-Israeli diplomacy was the fact that the prospects of mobilizing a hard-line opposition coalition to the process had never been so remote. Iraq, which had taken the lead in this area during the previous year, was completely neutralized. Libya's ties with Egypt, its AMU affiliation and its overall limited capabilities effectively silenced Qadhdhafi. The PLO recognized that there was little alternative to cooperation with American efforts, lest it compound both the international and inter-Arab damage it had suffered during the Gulf crisis and marginalize itself irrevocably. As for Syria, whose opposition to American-sponsored diplomacy dated back to the Sinai II Egyptian-Israeli disengagement agreement of September 1975, it too was persuaded that the Gulf crisis, the collapse of its Soviet patron, and its ongoing need to maintain lines of communication (and credit) with the GCC states and with Egypt necessitated greater diplomatic flexibility than in the past. By the spring, it too gave cautious approval to US Secretary of State James Baker's efforts.

Ever since the Kissinger-led American diplomatic efforts had been launched in the aftermath of the 1973 war, Syria had been especially concerned about the prospect of being left alone to face Israel while the other Arab parties negotiated their own, separate agreements. Thus, it opposed the Sinai II Agreement of September 1975, the Camp David Accords of 1978, and the 17 May 1983 Israeli-Lebanese Agreement, and applied as much pressure as possible to block their implementation. Predictably, as the Madrid conference became a closer possibility, Syria stepped up efforts to coordinate Arab positions in order to bring them into line with its own thinking. As far as it was concerned, attending the conference was as far as the Arabs should go, and they should not hold bilateral or multilateral discussions with Israel on matters dealing with the normalization of relations until Israel first committed itself to the principle of withdrawing from the territories conquered during the June 1967 war.

Jordan was especially sensitive to the concerns of its more powerful neighbor to the north, and mindful of past bouts of tension and conflict with it over just this issue. Jordan thus took pains to reassure Syria that it too favored a comprehensive settlement of the conflict. At the same time, however, its need to restore itself in the West's good graces dovetailed with King Husayn's long-standing advocacy of full peace between Israel and the Arabs, so that the Jordanians were careful to avoid Syria's embrace. The PLO, for its part, was also in a weak position[96] and had to juggle various concerns. Having reluctantly accepted the principle of a joint Jordanian-Palestinian delegation to negotiate an interim settlement for the West Bank and Gaza Strip, it deemed coordination with Jordan essential to preserve the PLO's standing and advance its interests. At the same time, 'Arafat sought to ease Asad's long-standing hostility toward him, with success or failure having important ramifications for 'Arafat's leadership in general and the position of his loyalists in Lebanon in particular. As it happened, both Asad and 'Arafat were interested in convening a summit conference of the five states bordering Israel: Syria hoped to impose its peace-conference strategy on Jordan, the PLO and Lebanon, and 'Arafat needed renewed Arab endorsement of the PLO's preeminence in any political process. This dovetailing of interests resulted in Asad inviting 'Arafat for a meeting in Damascus in late October, the first since 'Arafat's expulsion eight years earlier (another meeting was to be held after the Madrid conference), and in the reopening of the PLO office in the Syrian capital, also after an eight-year hiatus.

King Husayn favored a five-way summit as well, in order to bolster his standing both in the region and at home. Egypt, on the other hand, was not enthusiastic, fearing that a summit would project an image of Arab inflexibility and thus sabotage the American-sponsored process. What resulted was a compromise: a five-way meeting not of heads of state but of foreign ministers. The two-day meeting was held in Damascus on 23–24 October, a week prior to the Madrid conference, and was also attended by Saudi Foreign Minister Sa'ud al-Faysal, on behalf of the GCC, and Morocco's Foreign Minister 'Abd al-Latif al-Filali, on behalf of the AMU. The parties issued a statement announcing that they had agreed on "full coordination" of positions at the conference in order to assure a "united Arab stand" throughout the various stages of the negotiations, and that the conferees would periodically meet to review and evaluate the course of the negotiations with any of the parties.[97]

But the Syrians did not achieve the level of coordination to which they had aspired. Only the Lebanese delegation conducted itself at Madrid in accordance with Syria's wishes, whereas the Jordanians and Palestinians refused to make the start of their own bilateral talks with Israel conditional on Syria's approval. Israeli Television reported that Saudi Arabia's ambassador to the US, Prince Bandar Ibn Sultan, was especially active behind the scenes in Madrid in countering Syria's efforts and encouraging the Jordanians and Palestinians not to throw a wrench into the carefully orchestrated process. For the remainder of the year, the peace process took on an almost routine character and had little impact in the inter-Arab sphere. Egyptian and Jordanian officials both minimized differences with Syria over the question of participation in the multilateral talks.[98] Although 'Arafat called for another five-way meeting in December to assess the negotiations, none was held.

MAGHRIB AFFAIRS

The progress of Algeria's democratic experiment was the single most important feature of Maghrib affairs during 1991. In fact, rarely if ever, had domestic developments within a Maghrib state appeared to serve as such a bellwether in the Arab world as a whole, and thus attract so much official and media attention. The crisis in Algeria had been produced by a combination of factors familiar throughout the Arab world: "state exhaustion" (the government's congenital inability to promote sustained economic growth, social justice and a sense of personal well-being); widespread disillusionment with a bankrupt political and economic order by an increasing politically conscious (and cynical) public; and an active and expanding Islamic opposition movement. The exact blend of political, socioeconomic, religious, ethnic and historical components differed considerably from country to country. However, there was little doubt that the outcome of the democratic experiment in Algiers, whatever it would be, would have major implications throughout the Maghrib and beyond.

In both Morocco and Tunisia, the ruling elites watched anxiously to see whether the veritable explosion of democratic politics, which had occurred during the previous two years, would produce (1) a new social and political contract enabling the Algerian authorities to begin addressing the massive socioeconomic crises that had developed during a quarter century of single-party heavily centralized rule; (2) the coming to power of a dynamic fundamentalist Islamic movement whose commitment to democratic processes was suspect; or (3) the cessation of the democratic process entirely and the reimposition of rule by elements of the military and the ruling FLN, with or without the cooperation of President Chedli Benjedid. In the face of somewhat similar challenges, the governments of both Morocco and Tunisia were engaged in their own cautious attempts to widen political participation and were particularly concerned with the implications of the growing success of the Algerian fundamentalists.

The similarities between Moroccan, Algerian and Tunisian circumstances were highlighted at the beginning of the year by the Gulf War (see above). Support for Iraq in all of these countries was vociferous and nearly universal, characterized by massive street demonstrations, sympathy strikes and the formation of popular committees to raise funds and gather supplies for the Iraqi civilian population. Their genuine sympathy for Iraq notwithstanding, opposition political movements seized on the Gulf crisis to bolster their public standing, forcing the ruling regimes to breathlessly follow their lead. Thus, both Tunisia's President Zayn al-'Abidin Ben 'Ali and Algeria's Benjedid were quick to call for a cease-fire and vehemently condemn what Ben 'Ali called the "intolerable...destruction and devastation" being rained on Iraq, threatening its very existence.[99] At the same time, Benjedid firmly resisted calls by FIS leaders to establish training camps for volunteers wishing to join the battle on Iraq's behalf. The Moroccan Government had somewhat greater difficulty than its neighbors in competing with opposition groups on the Gulf War issue because of its dispatch of troops to help defend Saudi Arabia. Eventually, the Rabat authorities felt compelled to reverse a ban on demonstrations and sanction a mass march of solidarity with Iraq on 3 February.

AMU foreign ministers met twice during the war to exchange views and coordinate positions, but their efforts first to promote a cease-fire and then to stave off the ground war came to naught. The swift end of the Gulf War came as a relief to the Maghrib governments, but the passions that had been aroused would not be easily forgotten, with the real test in Algeria yet to take place. The regimes were given additional breathing space some months later when the Algerian authorities decided in June to postpone the imminent parliamentary elections and to crack down on the FIS. This move, which was accompanied by the appointment of a new Algerian prime minister, was greeted with quiet satisfaction in both Rabat and Tunis.[100] For the time being, there was little that the leaders of the regimes there could do besides watch and wait, while managing their own domestic arenas with caution.[101]

Unlike Algeria, neither Tunisia nor Morocco permitted Islamic fundamentalists to organize themselves as political parties. In Tunisia, however, the Islamic Renaissance Movement (*Harakat al-nahda al-islamiyya*) posed a growing challenge to the Ben 'Ali regime. In the spring, the government claimed to have discovered evidence of a plot by al-Nahda to seize power violently, and arrested hundreds of members, driving the movement further underground. Al-Nahda's exiled leader, Rashid Ghannushi, rejected the charges, telling an interviewer that the movement strongly opposed "physical and moral violence as a means of settling intellectual and political disputes" and favored "dialogue, *shura* [consultation], pluralism and the arbitration of the people's will through the ballot box under international supervision." The question was, he said, whether or not Tunisia's "minority regime" had "the courage to engage in a democratic experiment like Algeria, Yemen, Jordan or even Morocco."[102] However, President Ben 'Ali viewed matters differently, describing al-Nahda's leaders as "intolerant and antidemocratic." Moreover, they were part of a "fundamentalist international," coordinated from Sudan, whose activities focused primarily on Algeria, which they believed offered the most promising possibilities and could form the future "cornerstone" of an Islamic regional system.[103]

Links between al-Nahda and Algeria's FIS[104] were becoming more disturbing than ever to the Tunisian Government. On 4 October, following the exposure of an alleged al-Nahda plot to assassinate Ben 'Ali, Tunisia's Interior Minister 'Abdallah al-Kilal hurried to Algeria and strongly remonstrated with his interlocutors for the shelter and facilities that the movement was receiving there, insisting on the implementation of a 1983 bilateral treaty of friendship and concord that prohibited the harboring of opposition movements dedicated to violent change. Algeria's Prime Minister Sid Ahmad Ghozali met with Ben 'Ali in Tunis a few days later to discuss the same topic. Concurrent with the Tunisian interior minister's visit, the Algerian press reported that Tunisia had moved troops toward their common border, a report which the Tunisians denied.[105] The Algerian authorities were reportedly receptive to the Tunisian demands,[106] and by early December there were numerous press reports on the expulsion by Algeria of dozens of al-Nahda's leaders, including Ghannushi, although he denied that he had left Algeria under duress.[107]

The moment of truth for Algeria came at the end of 1991. The first round of general elections, held on 26 December, produced an overwhelming victory for the FIS. The second round, scheduled for early January 1992, was expected to provide the FIS with an absolute majority in parliament and, at the very least, lead to a constitutional clash with President Benjedid and strengthen FIS demands for immediate presidential elections as well. The FIS triumph evoked profound unease in Tunis and Rabat, although officials generally refrained from making attributable statements on the issue.[108] Before the elections could take place, however, the Algerian military intervened, compelling Benjedid to resign, nullifying the results of the first round, banning the FIS and arresting its leaders and activists, and imposing martial law. What would happen next was anybody's guess.

THE ARAB MAGHRIB UNION

Markedly contrasting with the drama unfolding in Algeria was the routinization of activities in the Maghrib states' collective organizational apparatus, the AMU. This routine reflected two contrasting trends: the limited capabilities of the individual governments as well as of the collective regional framework, and the ongoing common interests of the ruling elites in Algeria, Tunisia and Morocco.

The AMU had been founded in February 1989 in response to the desire of North African leaders to achieve greater political and economic coordination in the face of challenges posed both at home (rapid population growth, stagnant economies and growing Islamic-based opposition movements) and abroad (particularly the move toward European economic union, which threatened to close off the North African littorals from both European markets and European labor outlets). In addition, the AMU framework was useful in helping repair Moroccan-Algerian relations, which had been poisoned for nearly 15 years by the Western Sahara issue. The AMU's activities in the economic and development spheres had been promoted during its first two years with much fanfare. However, its achievements were mostly limited to increased political coordination among the members and to an agreement to insulate their subregional relations from wider inter-Arab issues in the event of differences. These tendencies were demonstrated repeatedly during 1991 in regard to both the Gulf crisis and the Arab-Israeli peace process. In late November, King Hasan, in his capacity as current chairman of the AMU's presidential council, was mandated by Libya to pursue a "peaceful solution" to the brewing confrontation between Libya and the US, Britain and France over alleged Libyan involvement in the bombings of American and French civilian aircraft[109] (for parallel Arab League efforts, see above).

Two AMU summit conferences, a number of foreign ministers' meetings, and various specialized ministerial gatherings were held during the year. The first summit, held on 10–11 March in the Tripoli suburb of Ra's Lanuf, was noteworthy mainly because of the absence of King Hasan, who had sought a postponement in order to hold further consultations regarding the consequences of the Gulf War, and was openly annoyed when the meeting went ahead as scheduled.[110] Qadhdhafi followed suit and absented himself from the second summit, hosted by Hasan in Casablanca on 15–16 September. In each case, the absent leader was represented by a lower-ranking official; together, the absences indicated that neither Hasan nor Qadhdhafi believed that the AMU summits had any particular significance. The Ra's Lanuf meeting was marked mainly by a number of Libyan proposals to strengthen the AMU's presidency, to allow complete freedom of movement between them for their citizens (none of which was adopted), and to study further proposals for monetary unification.[111] The summit's final statement called for the immediate lifting of the UN-imposed embargo on Iraq and warned against any attempt to interfere in Iraq's internal affairs or undermine Iraq's territorial integrity. It was also decided that another extraordinary meeting would be held later on in the spring, after Ramadan[112] (as it happened, the meeting was never held). The Casablanca meeting resolved a number of outstanding organizational matters that had previously been the subject of disagreement. Each member would serve as the host country for a different AMU body, with the most important, that of the AMU's general secretariat, to be established in Morocco. Algeria would host the "Consultative Council"; Mauritania, the "Judicial Body"; Tunisia, the "Maghribian Bank for Investment and External Trade"; and Libya, the "Maghribian University and Academy of Sciences" (the latter three existed mainly on paper). To compensate Tunisia, which had been extremely anxious to host the general secretariat, it was agreed that the AMU's first secretary-general would be a Tunisian.

A month later, Muhammad Amamou, a Tunisian diplomat, assumed the post in time to attend the Arab-Israeli peace conference in Madrid as an observer.

Concern over future relations with Europe was high on the AMU's agenda. In late October, AMU foreign ministers and officials conferred in Algiers with their counterparts from the northwestern Mediterranean — France, Italy, Spain and Portugal, with Malta as an associated participant — to discuss economic and political issues as well as the sensitive matter of North African migration to Europe (an important safety valve for Morocco and Algeria) and the treatment of the migrants. A summit meeting of the heads of state of the 10 countries was scheduled for January 1992, to be hosted by Tunisia.[113]

A rare acknowledgment of the gap between the AMU's aspirations and the sober realities standing in the way of implementation was made by Morocco's Foreign Minister 'Abd al-Latif al-Filali at the end of a ministerial council meeting in July. He and his colleagues, he said, had conducted an "intense and frank" dialogue, but had been unable to make substantive progress toward realizing the goal of creating a free trade zone, a common market and several joint economic projects. They had decided, therefore, to pause and reflect on the AMU's achievements, which would then allow the members to establish a "new working strategy" for the short, medium and long terms.[114]

THE WESTERN SAHARA ISSUE

For a decade and a half, the struggle between Morocco and the Algerian-backed Polisario movement for control over the Western Sahara (formerly Spanish Sahara) had served as a focal point for a bitter and potentially explosive geopolitical struggle between Rabat and Algiers for regional hegemony. However, the late 1980s had witnessed an Algerian-Moroccan rapprochement that included a gradual exclusion of the issue from their overall relationship. This had been made possible by a number of factors: the stalemate between Moroccan preeminence in the territory and Polisario's diplomatic successes internationally, the waning of Algerian interest in seeing the conflict continue, particularly in light of the regime's increasing preoccupation with internal affairs, and the dynamic and sustained efforts of the UN secretary-general to organize a referendum to decide the future of the territory. After a hiatus during the Gulf crisis, the UN effort gathered renewed momentum during the spring of 1991.

On 19 April, UN Secretary-General Javier Pérez de Cuellar issued his long-delayed implementation plan for a UN-sponsored referendum. The plan's main features included: the effecting of a general cease-fire (subsequently set to begin on 6 September); reducing the Moroccan troop presence by approximately half and deploying the troops in defensive, static positions only; deploying a similar proportion of Polisario units in designated areas; drawing up voter-registration rolls for participation in the referendum; and facilitating the return of eligible Sahrawis to the territory. If all went according to plan, the referendum would take place in January 1992, with the voters choosing between integration in Morocco and independence. The entire process would be overseen by the UN Mission for the Referendum in the Western Sahara (Minurso), a projected multinational, c. 3,000-man combined military and civilian body to be established for that purpose.[115]

From King Hasan's viewpoint, as well as that of Morocco's secular opposition, the successful resolution of the issue — namely, the international legitimation of

Morocco's incorporation of the territory into the kingdom — constituted a top priority on their respective agendas. With the announcement of the UN plan, they again focused their energies on the issue. The opposition parties, particularly the Istiqlal, had consistently presented themselves as the true guardians of Morocco's historical rights and territorial integrity. By their definition, a referendum on the fate of the Western Sahara was, at best, completely unnecessary and, at worst, an insulting challenge to Morocco's national sovereignty. Consequently, they spared no criticism of the referendum idea, although they refrained from blatant confrontation with the authorities. King Hasan, on the other hand, surprised many observers both in Morocco and abroad by agreeing to the UN plan, with all the attendant risks it contained, particularly since Morocco had already established unshakable de facto control over c. 80% of the territory. Since a defeat in the referendum would most certainly generate severe shock waves within both the military and civilian spheres, and even possibly cost Hasan his throne, Hasan's task, from his point of view, was to do everything he could to ensure a Moroccan victory in the referendum.

His initial steps to curry favor with the Sahrawi electorate included a high-profile four-day visit in mid-May to various towns in the Western Sahara, where he promised that a host of development projects would be implemented,[116] and that all Sahrawis who had been captured in military operations or who had gone "astray" and were living abroad would be pardoned.[117] Polisario was sharply critical of both moves, calling his visit "inopportune" and suggesting that the two parties conduct a prisoner exchange (which would equalize Polisario's status as well as enable it to present its own list of prisoners of war) and that Morocco release the hundreds of Sahrawi civilian detainees it was allegedly holding.[118] But Hasan was not about to cooperate with Polisario in implementing the UN plan.

As the date of the referendum process approached, Hasan stepped up pressure. In early August, he decided to flex Morocco's military muscles, dispatching the Moroccan air force on bombing raids of Polisario concentrations in the northeastern area of Western Sahara between Morocco's network of defensive walls and the Mauritanian border, followed by sweeps of the area by ground forces. Operations continued throughout the month. Polisario protested sharply, stating that the attacks violated the unofficial truce between them and claiming that civilians were being specifically targeted. It called for "urgent intervention" by Pérez de Cuellar,[119] who met with Morocco's Foreign Minister Filali several days later on 13 August, and with Polisario officials two weeks thereafter.

On 20 August, Hasan served notice to the UN that his cooperation in implementing the referendum should not be taken for granted. Up to that point, UN officials had refused to expand the list of voters eligible to participate so as to include the 120,000 persons Morocco claimed had been made refugees from the area in 1958. These "aggregate lists," UN special representative Johannes Manz told Le Monde on 3 August, "have nothing to do with the UN's plan."[120] With the resident population included in the 1974 Spanish census — the basis for the electoral list being prepared — evenly divided between the two sides (and presumably favoring their respective Moroccan or Polisario authorities), expanding the voter rolls was absolutely essential to insure a Moroccan victory. Moreover, the king was sensitive to his political opposition's criticism that Morocco was abdicating its sovereignty in the territory to Minurso. He had already refused to allow two ships flying UN colors to dock in

Layoune, the capital of the region, and had also refused to permit Manz to enter the territory in order to start his work.[121] Under increased pressure, he complained that the UN should have worked out a "written accord" with Morocco regarding its prerogatives and he declared that, all in all, conditions for preparing the referendum had not been fulfilled and that the process should therefore be postponed.[122]

In the event, Hasan's declaration did not turn out to be an ultimatum. Even though Morocco and Polisario continued to accuse each other of encroachments and violations of the cease-fire, advance UN units began moving into the territory, and the general cease-fire came into force on schedule on 6 September. However, the scheduled timetable for implementing the referendum process remained stalled, with delays occurring in the full deployment of Minurso, the paring down of the Moroccan military presence, Minurso's assumption of authority, the return of Sahrawi refugees, and, most importantly, determining the final electoral list. As long as this last point was not resolved to Morocco's satisfaction, Rabat apparently intended to hinder Minurso's activities.

Polisario was especially unhappy with the course of events, accusing UN officials of passing on computer disks containing information pertinent to the electoral lists and sensitive military information to Morocco.[123] Even more disturbing to them were reports that Morocco had begun a large-scale transfer of civilians into the territory in an apparent repeat of its 1975 "Green March" in order to flood the territory with Moroccans and thus make it impossible to distinguish them from genuinely eligible voters. Estimates placed the number of new arrivals at c. 35,000.[124] The Moroccans, for their part, were active both diplomatically and militarily, calling for the expulsion of "terrorists" if they interfered with the UN mission (a reference to alleged Polisario infiltrations into the territory) and continuing reconaissance flights.[125]

Hasan projected confidence that the referendum would confirm Morocco's control over the Western Sahara. Most of the elements for success were now in place, he declared in a speech marking the anniversary of the Green March, and only the final touches on the list of eligible voters were needed.[126] In late December, two developments indicated that this confidence was not misplaced: the UN's formal postponement of the referendum on 19 December, accompanied by the resignation of Johannes Manz from his post of UN special representative, and, even more important, Pérez de Cuellar's decision to partially accommodate Morocco's demands to expand the electoral rolls to include those who could prove to have resided in the territory for six consecutive years or 12 years intermittently prior to 1974, as well as members of their immediate family. It was expected that this would add c. 30,000 persons to the lists.[127] Whether or not the change would be sufficient for Hasan to allow the referendum to go forward, or, alternatively, whether or not Polisario would seek to make an eleventh-hour deal with Morocco that would provide for an autonomous Sahara region within Morocco but fall short of their goal of independence, remained to be seen.

CONCLUSION

From one perspective, inter-Arab affairs were calmer at the end of 1991 than at any time in recent memory. The crushing military defeat of Iraq and the subsequent UN-imposed quarantine, as well as the efforts by Iraq's erstwhile supporters to repair the ruptures in their relations with the anti-Saddam coalition, meant that no rival Arab challenge to the Egyptian-GCC grouping could be seen to be emerging. Moreover, the attraction of Saddam's "Robin Hood" appeal to the Arab masses over the heads of their governments had proven to be transitory and containable. But neither was a "new Arab order" on the horizon. The failure to translate the anti-Iraqi wartime coalition into an effective defense and political structure provided renewed evidence of both the mutual suspicions and the jealously guarded sovereign prerogatives which have always characterized inter-Arab politics. It also served as another painful reminder of the collective Arab weakness vis-à-vis both its immediate non-Arab neighbors and the West. This failure, when combined with the acute chronic domestic challenges confronting nearly every Arab state, resulted in a depressing reality for ruling Arab elites and Arab intellectuals alike, not to mention for wider segments of Arab societies. Stocktaking and analysis of the Gulf crisis and its aftermath was widespread. Husni Mubarak was particularly blunt:

> The Arab role as it is now is very bad. All the Arabs are losers. The Arabs are devouring one another. Foreign states from outside the Arab region will have ambitions in the Arab world. The Arabs must wake up and reassess their position in order to be able to discern their future.[128]

Suggested formulas for altering the grim realities included calls for closer government-to-government cooperation and the strengthening of Arab League institutions,[129] and specific proposals to facilitate conflict resolution such as the establishment of an early-warning monitoring system, and an Arab rapid-deployment force to be attached to the office of the Arab League secretary-general.[130] Others called for the democratization of Arab political life,[131] a complete renaissance of Arab life in order to complete what was begun 200 years earlier,[132] or Islamic revival. The escape from backwardness and the salvation of the Arab nation, wrote Kamil Abu Jabr just prior to being appointed Jordan's foreign minister, can only come from its own endeavors and efforts.[133] The challenge for Arab governments was how to maneuver between the pitfalls and minefields of domestic and regional politics, on the one hand, and the far-reaching changes in the international system, on the other, in order both to preserve their positions and achieve a modicum of progress for their populations.

APPENDIX I: DAMASCUS DECLARATION
Issued by the Foreign Ministers of Egypt, Syria, Saudi Arabia, Kuwait, the United Arab Emirates, Bahrain, Qatar and Oman: 6 March 1991

In the name of God, the compassionate, the merciful: the Damascus declaration for coordination and cooperation among the Arab states:

The Gulf Cooperation Council Arab member states, the Arab Republic of Egypt, and the Syrian Arab Republic which participated in the meetings in Damascus on 19 and 20 Sha'ban 1411 Hegira, corresponding to 5 and 6 March 1991, proceeding from the feelings of fraternity and solidarity linking them, which are the product of a genuine heritage of dedication, cohesiveness, common struggle, and a deep awareness of the unity of hopes and challenges, the identity of aims, and the unity of destiny;

In order to further their capabilities for assuming their pan-Arab responsibilities in upgrading the standing of the Arab nation serving its causes, safeguarding its security, and achieving its common interests;

Within a framework of strict adherence to the objectives and principles established by the charters and resolutions of the Arab League, the Islamic Conference Organization, and the United Nations; out of awareness of the deep changes taking place in the international arena and the serious challenges they place before the Arab nation and because the confrontation of these challenges requires the maximum degree of coordination and cooperation among the Arab states; while they once again reiterate their position in rejecting and refusing to side with the policy of aggression, as was the case during the aggression by the Iraqi regime's troops and their occupation of the State of Kuwait, with this occupation constituting a flagrant violation of all Arab, Islamic, and international norms and rules and sweeping away many of the concepts and achievements of the common Arab action at a time when the Arab nation was, more than any time before, in need of closing its ranks and mobilizing its resources to confront several unprecedented dangers;

They declare their welcome of the liberation of the State of Kuwait and the restoration of legitimacy there, express their deep pain and extreme sorrow for what the fraternal Kuwaiti people have suffered as a result of the aggression of the Iraqi regime, and express their deep regret for what the Iraqi people are being subjected to in terms of the most abominable forms of suffering as a result of the Iraqi leadership's disregard for their interests. In this respect, they affirm that they stand alongside the Iraqi people in their ordeal and stress their full eagerness to preserve the Iraqi lands' unity and territorial integrity.

The participants emphasize their determination to try to instill a new spirit in the common Arab action and to establish fraternal cooperation among the members of the Arab family on solid bases that rest on the following principles:

First: The Principles of Coordination and Cooperation
Coordination and cooperation will be on the following bases:
(1) Working in accordance with the charter of the Arab League, the United Nations, and the other Arab and international charters; respecting and promoting the historical and fraternal ties and the relations of neighborliness; and commitment to respect the unity and territorial integrity, the equality of sovereignty, the inadmissibility of seizing territories by force, nonintervention in domestic affairs, and commitment to settle disputes by peaceful means.
(2) To build a new Arab order to bolster joint Arab action. The agreed-upon arrangements among the parties concerned shall be considered a basis for achieving this. The door will be left open before the other Arab states to contribute to this declaration considering the agreement of interests and objectives.
(3) To enable the Arab nation to direct all its resources to confront the challenges threatening security and stability in the region, and to achieve a just and comprehensive solution to the Arab-Israeli conflict and the Palestine question based on the UN charter and its pertinent resolutions.
(4) To bolster economic cooperation among the parties concerned in order to establish an economic group among them with the objective of achieving economic and social development.
(5) To respect the principle of each Arab state's sovereignty over its natural and economic resources.

Second: The Objectives of Coordination and Cooperation
(1) In the political and security fields:
    (a) The parties concerned consider the current stage that followed the liberation of Kuwait from the occupation of the Iraqi regime's forces to provide the best circumstances to confront the other challenges and threats the region is being exposed to, in the forefront of which are the challenges resulting from the continued Israeli occupation of the Arab territories and the settlement of Jews in them. The parties concerned believe that holding an international conference for peace under UN auspices is an appropriate framework to end the Israeli occupation of Arab territories and to guarantee the Palestinian people's national rights based on the pertinent UN resolutions.
    (b) The parties concerned stress their respect for the principles of the Arab League charter, their commitment to the collective Arab defense pact and economic cooperation among the Arab League member states, as well as their determination to act jointly to guarantee the security and safety of the Arab states. While referring in particular to Article 9 of the Arab League charter, they consider the presence of the Egyptian and Syrian forces in the territory of the Kingdom of Saudi Arabia and other Arab states in the Gulf region to be in response to the desire of these states' governments and to have the objective of defending their territories and as constituting a nucleus for an Arab peace force to be prepared to guarantee the security and safety of the Arab states in the Gulf region, and an example that would guarantee the effectiveness of the comprehensive Arab defense order. The parties concerned also stress the coordination and cooperation among them will not be directed against any other party, but that it can be an introduction for opening dialogue with the Islamic and international parties who respect the higher interests of the Arab nation and abide by the principles of international legitimacy, particularly those related to respecting the states' sovereignty, noninterference in domestic affairs, and settling conflicts through peaceful means.
    (c) The participating parties will seek to declare the Middle East a zone free of all weapons of mass destruction, especially nuclear weapons, and will work to achieve this through the concerned international departments.
(2) In the economic and cultural fields: in harmony with the Arab League charter, the joint defense and economic cooperation pact between the Arab League states, and other agreements on joint Arab action, the participating parties will seek to:
    (a) Define the rules of economic cooperation among the founding parties as a first step which can be built upon with the other Arab states with the aim of expanding the scopes of cooperation.
    (b) Adopt economic policies whose purpose is to achieve balanced economic and social development as a prelude to the establishment of an Arab economic grouping to confront the challenges and to keep pace with the developments resulting from the establishment of major economic groupings in the world.
    (c) Encourage the private sector in the Arab states to participate in the economic and social development processes, including supporting the ties between the Arab chambers of commerce, industry, and agriculture and opening the doors for small and mid-sized establishments to benefit from the fruits of joint cooperation in an easy and tangible way.
    (d) Support the role of scientific research centers and facilitate contacts among them to enable them to prepare joint research to achieve integration in various fields.

(e) Benefit from skills and human resources in the field of cultural and information exchange while respecting the ideals of the participating states and their traditions and not interfering in their internal affairs.

(3) In the field of the joint Arab action establishments: supporting the Arab League confronting all the attempts to weaken or disintegrate it, and reaffirming adherence and commitment to the goals and principles incorporated in the Arab League charter. This charter can be developed by adding appendices to it and by benefiting from the results of the work of the committee charged with amending the charter, including the introduction of a mechanism for settling disputes.

Third: The Organizational Framework for Coordination and Cooperation
Coordination and cooperation among the founding states occurs to achieve the referent objectives through meetings hosted in turn by each of the participating states at the foreign ministerial level. The assistance of experts and specialists will be sought to study the aspects of cooperation to arrive at a new contractual formula for Arab cooperation among the participating states. This formula will be open for all Arab states.

Fourth: General Rules
This declaration has been initialed in Damascus in eight original copies in Arabic, each of them with the same validity, on 2 Sha'ban 1411 Hegira, corresponding to 6 March 1991. This declaration shall become effective after its official ratification, and the ratification documents shall be deposited at the Ministry of Foreign Affairs of the Syrian Arab Republic.

SOURCE: R. Damascus, 6 March — DR, 7 March 1991.

APPENDIX II:
KUWAIT DECLARATION
Issued by the 12th GCC Summit: 25 December 1991

Proceeding from the sentiments of brotherhood and solidarity that bind them and in order to embody common objectives, fate and the higher interests of their people; to enhance their abilities to shoulder their responsibilities with regard to providing security, stability and prosperity to their sons; to epitomize the most splendid forms of cohesion as represented by a mixture of the chaste Gulf blood on Kuwaiti territory that forged the most sublime manifestations of sacrifice; out of concern for realizing the principles and objectives contained in the GCC basic law; out of a desire to attain unity in the political, security, military, economic, and social fields; in accordance with the sublime directives of their majesties and highnesses — the GCC leaders — with regard to enhancing the cohesive ties among the citizens of the GCC countries; out of an awareness of the regional and international changes and developments and the grave challenges they pose — challenges that require serious and persistent efforts to achieve the highest degree of coordination and cooperation; to affirm their position, which rejects the aggressive course and support for it — the course represented by the blatant aggression against the State of Kuwait and its brutal occupation by Iraq — and the threat that this posed to all GCC states, given that aggression launched against any GCC member state is tantamount to aggression against all member states and given that the security of GCC members is an indivisible whole, not to mention that this aggression reflected a departure from proper Arab, Islamic, and international rules of conduct, norms, and values, and was an infringement against a host of concepts and accomplishments of joint Arab action; to express their appreciation and gratitude for the Arab, Islamic, and friendly states which supported right, denounced aggression, and moved to eliminate it; and within the framework of their adherence to the principles and objectives embodied in the charters and resolutions of the Arab League, the Damascus declaration, the Islamic Conference Organization, and the United Nations, the GCC member states declare:

(1) In their international dealings, the GCC member states respect the principle of good-neighborliness and adhere to the principles of respecting the sovereignty of states, the inadmissibility of the acquisition of land by force, noninterference in domestic affairs, the settling of conflicts through peaceful means, and respecting each state's sovereignty over its resources.

(2) The GCC member states affirm the unity of their position in confronting the Iraqi regime and the other regimes that collaborated with it in its spiteful aggression against Kuwait, and in not allowing these regimes to penetrate this position. The GCC member states also affirm their determination to pursue this position until the Iraqi regime implements all the UN Security Council resolutions related to its aggression against the State of Kuwait.

(3) The GCC member states express their support for the Arab action within the framework of the Arab League, consider the principles and objectives included in the Damascus declaration as a basis for establishing a new Arab order, and also consider the GCC program on supporting economic development efforts in the Arab states the basis for any efforts aimed at achieving economic development in the Arab world.

(4) The GCC member states express their support for the peace efforts that are aimed at achieving a just and lasting solution to the Palestine question, and ending the Arab-Israeli conflict on the basis of the internationally legitimate resolutions, particularly Resolutions 242 and 338, which are based on the principle of land for peace, and Resolution 425 regarding Israel's unconditional withdrawal from Southern Lebanon. The GCC member states also stress their participation in the third phase [of the Middle East peace talks], proceeding from the fact that achieving a just and comprehensive peace and reaching an agreement to tackle the issues to be discussed at this phase is in harmony with the higher interests of the GCC member states.

(5) The GCC member states congratulate fraternal Lebanon on the positive steps the Lebanese Government has made within the framework of its efforts to achieve security, stability and prosperity for its sons. They also express the GCC's readiness to support these efforts.

(6) The GCC member states welcome the current changes in the international arena, particularly the changes related to the emergence of the dawn of the new world order, taking into consideration that the liberation of Kuwait is one of the fruits of this order, and especially since this order will guarantee both big and small states' right to live in peace and security and to control their natural and economic resources. They also welcome these changes out of their belief that they will contribute to providing the requirements of the GCC member states' security and stability in a way safeguarding their higher interests.

SOURCE: GNA, 25 December — DR, 26 December 1991.

FINAL STATEMENT OF THE 12TH GCC SUMMIT
Issued in Kuwait: 25 December 1991

At the invitation of His Highness Shaykh Jabir al-Ahmad al-Jabir Al Sabah, emir of the State of Kuwait, the Higher Council held its 12th session in Kuwait during the period 17 to 19 Jamada al-Thani 1412, corresponding to 23 to 25 December 1991, in the presence of their majesties and highnesses: His Highness Shaykh Zayid Ibn Sultan Al Nuhayan, president of the United Arab Emirates; His Highness Shaykh 'Isa Ibn Salman Al Khalifa, emir of the State of Bahrain; King Fahd Ibn 'Abd-al-'Aziz Al Sa'ud, custodian of the two holy mosques and king of the Kingdom of Saudi Arabia; His Majesty Qabus Ibn Sa'id, sultan of the Sultanate of Oman; His Highness Shaykh Khalifa Ibn Hamad Al Thani, emir of the State of Qatar; and His Highness Shaykh Jabir al-Ahmad al-Jabir Al Sabah, emir of the State of Kuwait.

The Higher Council has studied developments in the Gulf region in light of Kuwait's liberation and its regaining freedom, independence, and sovereignty, praising God Almighty for making successful the resistance to aggression and the aggressors. It also congratulates the Kuwaiti leadership and people for recovering legitimacy under the leadership of His Highness Shaykh Jabir al-Ahmad Al Sabah, emir of the State of Kuwait.

The Higher Council expresses its pride in the spirit of fraternal solidarity and principled support among its member states, and notes with admiration the stance of the citizens of the Council member states which affirms the depth of affiliation and interlinkage, and the unique destiny among the members of the Gulf community, and shows the sincere cohesion between the citizens and their leadership. The Council valued the sacrifices made by the citizens during the ordeal and hard times.

The Higher Council praises the support of the fraternal and friendly states that adopted a stand on the side of justice, right and the principles of international law, which had an effective role in expressing international will and the implementation of the resolutions of international legitimacy.

The Higher Council expresses its respect and gratitude to those historic contributions in the defense of the sovereignty of the law, in supporting justice, and consolidating firm foundations for security and stability in the region made in the service of worldwide peace. The Council affirms the stance of its member states toward the Iraqi regime by refusing to deal with it as long as it does not commit itself to implementing all the UN Security Council's resolutions related to its aggression against the State of Kuwait.

The Higher Council addresses prayers to God Almighty to accept into his paradise the martyrs of justice and duty, and to bestow mercy on them.

The Higher Council notes with great concern the fact that the Iraqi regime is still obstructing and delaying the implementation of a number of articles of the UN Security Council related to its aggression against the State of Kuwait.

While it condemns the policies of settlement, the Council affirms that it will resist attempts to bypass the resolutions of international legitimacy. It also asks Iraq to speed up the implementation of all the relevant UN Security Council resolutions. It particularly stresses the necessity to implement fully and quickly all the articles of Resolution 687 and the cease-fire conditions, particularly those related to the immediate release of Kuwaiti and other states' nationals who are prisoners and are being detained, the demarcation of borders between the State of Kuwait and Iraq, in accordance with UN Security Council Resolution 687, and the payment of compensation for the human and material losses caused by Iraq's aggression.

The Higher Council urges the international community, and the UN Security Council in particular, to put more pressure on the Iraqi regime to secure the full and immediate implementation of the resolutions of international legality and to prevent the Baghdad regime from ridding itself of its international commitment.

The Higher Council notes with great regret the continued suffering of the Iraqi people, who are still paying the price of bad policy of the Iraqi regime, its persistent intransigence, its playing down of the rules of international behavior and legality, its persistence in practicing the policy of humiliating the Iraqi people, its insistence on continuing the ordeal and human tragedy experienced by the Iraqi people which will be alleviated or removed only by the Iraqi regime's meeting its international obligations and fully carrying out the resolutions of the UN Security Council, including Resolutions 706 and 712, which permit the securing of humanitarian needs as well as the Iraqi people's needs for food and medicine. The Higher Council reaffirms its sympathy with the Iraqi people and its full eagerness concerning Iraqi territorial integrity and regional safety.

[KUNA in Arabic at 1145 GMT on 25 December transmitted a service message advising that the previous sentence should be deleted.]

The GCC March

The Higher Council reviewed the results of a full decade of common action in the political, security, military, economic, and social fields, and expresses its satisfaction over the achievements of the march of good, growth and construction realized on the road to coordination, integration and unification in order to realize the aspirations of the citizens of the GCC member states.

Proceeding from a firm conviction of the importance of strengthening security and military cooperation among member states, and the reinforcing of their defense capabilities in light of the lessons learned from the aggression of the Iraqi regime, the Higher Council affirms its determination to continue coordination and cooperation in the military and security fields, and to promote defense capabilities within the framework of a unified strategic concept that meets the requirements of security, faces up to the challenges of the situation, achieves stability, and guarantees the nonrecurrence of such aggression.

Their majesties and highnesses express their great appreciation and deep gratitude to His Majesty Sultan Qabus Ibn Sa'id of Oman for the effort he exerted in assuming the responsibility of the Higher Security Committee, for his generous help in the committee's work and his patronage of its activities, and for putting his expertise and experience in the comprehensive strategic report that was prepared for the summit. This was an expression of the faith of his majesty in the march of the Council, and his eagerness that the work of the Council be marked by scientific and objective preparation.

The Higher Council affirms its resolve to continue the process of joint action with rapid steps for the sake of entrenching the building of cooperation and continuous conformity with the aspirations of the citizens and strengthening this blessed march toward achieving the desired objectives. It also affirms its determination to realize more qualitative achievements through the planned program compiled by the ministerial committees for gradual implementation of the provisions of the unified economic agreement in a way that ensures strengthening the interlinking of interests among the citizens and builds more joint projects and removes all obstacles in the way of movement of citizens, trade and the flow of investment. It stresses to the specialized ministerial committees the need to speed up the taking of steps and of necessary and essential measures to complete the implementation of what is left of the provisions of the unified economic agreement.

Proceeding from its belief and conviction in the role of the GCC states in taking part in a comprehensive Arab development, and proceeding from its conviction and belief in the importance of concerting local and international resources toward realizing this in accordance with the concepts of free economy, the Council approved the agreement on setting up a program ....

The Current Arab Situation

The Higher Council studied the peace efforts in the Middle East, and praised the rapid and sincere efforts that have been shown by the international community, particularly by the United States.

In this connection, while the Higher Council would like to express its satisfaction with the results of the Madrid peace conference, in which the Council took part as an observer, it would like to express its utmost regret regarding the faltering of bilateral negotiations that began in Washington on 10 December 1991, despite the readiness of Arab delegations to enter into serious and committed negotiations, and were met by continuous Israeli obstinacy and attempts to sabotage the peace process.

While the Council looks forward to the resumption of the next round of bilateral negotiations next January without any further Israeli obstacles and without raising procedural issues, it hopes that these negotiations will achieve tangible progress to reach the desired goals.

The Higher Council stresses its support for the peace efforts and the firm determination of its states to take part in the multilateral meetings out of their desire to enhance regional security through fundamental solutions to all the conflicts of the region in the shadow of a new world order that perpetuates the will of peace and bolsters international stability, and out of their contribution to the advancement of the peace process and the achievement of a just and comprehensive settlement to the Arab-Israeli conflict and the Palestinian issue which would guarantee the legitimate rights of the Palestinian people and recover the occupied Arab territories, holy Jerusalem first of all, on the basis of UN Security Council Resolutions 242 and 338, resolutions of international legitimacy, and on the principle of land for peace.

The Higher Council emphasizes the need to clear the whole Middle East region of all kinds of weapons of mass destruction, including nuclear, chemical and biological weapons.

The Council expresses its strong concern over the displeasure with the continuation of the policies of the Israeli occupation authorities aimed at entrenching and expanding the illegal settlements in occupied Arab areas, the continuation of attacks on the sacred shrines in holy Jerusalem, the high-handed measures against the Palestinian people, and the increase in the number of victims of occupation: martyrs, wounded, detainees, homeless and deportees. The Council condemns the policies of imposing the status quo by force and the acts of oppression that are not in harmony with the current peace efforts. It reaffirms its stand alongside and its complete support for the steadfastness of the Palestinian people in the occupied Arab areas.

The Council welcomes the positive developments in fraternal Lebanon and the steps taken by the Lebanese Government to safeguard Lebanon's independence and the integrity of its territory and sovereignty, and to realize national agreement. It calls for the unconditional implementation of UN Security Council Resolution 425 and the withdrawal of Israeli forces from Southern Lebanon without any delay or postponement. It reaffirms its support for the international construction and development fund in Lebanon.

In reviewing Arab relations in light of the results of the Iraqi aggression against the State of Kuwait, the Council expresses its extreme satisfaction with the results of cooperation between the GCC states and both the Arab Republic of Egypt and the Syrian Arab Republic within the framework of the Damascus declaration. It reaffirmed that it looks forward to the realization of the principles and objectives that were agreed on by the eight states, and that the declaration will open new and wide horizons in Arab affairs and cooperation because it is considered to be the nucleus of joint Arab action within the framework of the Arab League and a basic contribution to laying down firm and clear foundations based on commitment in word and deed to the Arab and international charters for the sake of realizing joint Arab interests.

The Council stresses that its dealings within the framework of inter-Arab relations will be on the basis of the principles of the Damascus declaration, and it calls on the Arab states to support this position and to be committed to these principles.

The Council expresses its great concern and regret over the deterioration of the security situation and the continuation of the state of division between brothers in Somalia, stressing its standing on the side of the Somali people in their painful ordeal. It urges all Somali nationalist forces to remove the causes of differences between them, to consider national interests before any self-interest, and to work to preserve the unity and safety of Somalia, which is their greatest and first responsibility.

The council hails the good reconciliation efforts exerted by King Fahd Ibn 'Abd-al-'Aziz, custodian of the two holy mosques, and it is looking forward to the return of security and stability to fraternal Somalia, given the importance of this to peace and stability throughout the Horn of Africa.

Relations with Iran

Having heard a presentation by His Highness Shaykh Khalifa Ibn Hamad Al Thani, emir of Qatar and chairman of the preceding session of the Higher Council, on the chairmanship's contacts with the Islamic Republic of Iran regarding relations between the GCC member states and Iran, and bringing to mind its decision at the Doha summit affirming the wish to improve relations with that country, the Council expresses its satisfaction over the positive and tangible development in relations between the two sides. The Council affirms its eagerness to lend momentum to bilateral relations with the Islamic Republic of Iran in the service of common interests in accordance with Islamic and international principles and conventions, and as a reflection of the depth of the ties of religion and neighborliness between them.

The International Situation

The Higher Council followed the positive international developments, the end of the Cold War, the retreat of ideological and traditional conflict, and the disappearance of political barriers. It followed the efforts aimed at reducing the arms race and proceeding toward constructive international cooperation in finding basic solutions to the hotbeds of regional tension by peaceful means in accordance with practical and rational means and sponsoring the policy of international openness, free economy, working for bolstering development, and employing resources for the good of the peoples and their well-being. The Council expresses its extreme satisfaction with these developments and affirms the resolve of the member states to be involved in effective participation in entrenching the pillars of the new world order on the basis of justice, fair play, and with whatever is in harmony with the higher interests of the member states.

The Higher Council followed with extreme concern the current events and developments in the Soviet Union and expresses the satisfaction of the member states with the emergence of the Commonwealth and their readiness to recognize its members in the shadow of these states' being committed to international agreements and treaties. The GCC states also hope that the political leaderships in these independent states will accomplish whatever strengthens world stability, peace and security.

The Higher Council expresses highest appreciation and gratitude to his Highness Shaykh Jabir al-Ahmad al-Jabir Al Sabah, emir of the State of Kuwait, and to his government and people for the welcome, hospitality and genuine fraternal sentiments accorded to the leaders of the GCC states. It praises the excellent preparations and the great efforts that were made in order to provide comfort for the delegations and to ensure the success of the meeting and the realization of the positive results achieved by the meeting. The Higher Council prays to Almighty God to provide His Highness continuing health and happiness, and to ward off all bad things from Kuwait and its people.

The Council looks forward to its 13th session in the United Arab Emirates in December 1992 in response to a noble invitation by His Highness Shaykh Zayid Ibn Sultan Al Nuhayan, president of the United Arab Emirates.

Issued in Kuwait on 19 Jamada al-Thani 1412, corresponding to 25 December 1991.

SOURCE: KUNA, 25 December — DR, 26 December 1991.

NOTES

For the place and frequence of publications cited here, and for the full name of the publication, news agency, radio station or monitoring service where an abbreviation is used, please see "List of Sources." Only in the case of more than one publication bearing the same name is the place of publication noted here. In this chapter, however, all references to *al-Hayat* refer to the London daily.

1. Mahfuz al-Ansari, in *al-Jumhuriyya* (Cairo), 5 January 1991.
2. R. Monte Carlo, 3 January — DR, 4 January 1991.
3. SPA, 6 January — DR, 7 January 1991.
4. R. Algiers, 15 January — DR, 15 January; APS, 13 January — DR, 17 January 1991. Benjedid later elaborated on his efforts, indicating that he had tried to obtain a secret understanding with US President George Bush that an international conference on the Arab-Israeli issue would be held if the Iraqis agreed to withdraw from Kuwait, an agreement which he then would have conveyed to Iraq. Speech to National Assembly, R. Algiers, 23 January — DR, 24 January 1991.
5. *NYT,* 15 January 1991.
6. R. Damascus, 12 January, JANA, 13 January — DR, 14 January 1991.
7. R. Amman, 14 January — DR, 16 January 1991.
8. RTM TV, 15 January — DR, 16 January 1991.

9. JANA, 22 January — DR, 24 January 1991.
10. R. Monte Carlo, 20 February — DR, 22 February 1991.
11. R. Rabat, 19 January — DR, 23 January 1991.
12. *FT,* 27 March 1991.
13. John Wallach, foreign editor of Hearst newspapers, cited in *JP,* 30 January 1991.
14. R. Amman, 19 January — DR, 22 January 1991.
15. MBC TV, 28 January — DR, 29 January 1991.
16. SPA, 13 September, *al-Dustur* (Amman), 3 September — DR, 17, 4 September 1991.
17. Mubarak's interview with Egyptian Space Channel, 22 January — DR, 23 January 1991.
18. *Al-Ahram,* 9 February; *Akhir Sa'a,* 13 February; *JP,* 19 February 1991.
19. *Al-Sharq al-Awsat,* 6 February — DR, 8 February 1991.
20. Text of the final statement in MENA, 16 February — DR, 19 February 1991.
21. *Al-Jumhuriyya* (Cairo), 12 February 1991.
22. R. Baghdad, 15 February — DR, 15 February 1991.
23. Rabat TV, 13 February — DR, 14 February 1991.
24. According to congressional testimony by US assistant secretary of state for Near Eastern and South Asian affairs John Kelly, there was "a great deal of support, public and private," among the Arab members of the anti-Saddam coalition, for President Bush's decision to halt the hostilities when he did. WF, 18 June 1991, p. 64. On the other hand, reports in both *NYT* (10 March 1991) and *Newsweek* (20 January 1992) indicated that the Saudis and Egyptians recommended that Saddam's forces, and even Saddam himself, be pursued further.
25. R. Cairo, 16 March — DR, 18 March 1991.
26. *IHT,* 6 April 1991.
27. Ibid.
28. Text of the statement in *NYT,* 12 March 1991.
29. JANA Arab affairs editor, cited by Tripoli TV, 2 March — DR, 7 March 1991.
30. R. Tehran, 6 March — DR, 7 March 1991.
31. *Al-Ahram,* 20 February 1991.
32. *IHT,* 24 April; SPA, 24 April — DR, 25 April; *al-Ahram,* 27 April; Mamoun Fandy, *NYT,* 16 May 1991.
33. *CR,* Egypt, No. 4, 1991, p. 20.
34. MENA, 8 May — DR, 8 May 1991.
35. Interview with Dr. Mamduh al-Biltaji, head of the Egyptian General Information Authority, R. Monte Carlo, 8 May — DR, 9 May 1991.
36. Mubarak's interview in *al-Hayat,* 16 July — DR, 18 July; Foreign Minister 'Amr Musa's interview in *al-Musawwar,* 7 June — DR, 11 June 1991.
37. Mahfuz al-Ansari, *al-Jumhuriyya* (Cairo), 10 May, quoted by MENA, 10 May — DR, 10 May 1991.
38. *FT,* 16 June; *NYT,* 8 July 1991.
39. Interview in *al-Sharq al-Awsat* and *al-Ayyam,* quoted by *Ha'aretz,* 27 June 1991.
40. MENA, 6 August — DR, 7 August 1991.
41. *Al-Musawwar,* 15 November 1991.
42. *Al-Shira',* 18 November 1991.
43. *Al-Safir,* 7 June 1991.
44. *Ruz al-Yusuf,* 16 September; MENA, 30 September — DR, 1 October 1991.
45. Riyadh TV, 28 September — DR, 30 September 1991.
46. *JI,* 25 August — DR, 6 September 1991.
47. *Al-Sharq al-Awsat,* 26 September 1991.
48. Wm. Scott Harrop, "Iran's Emerging World Order," *Middle East Insight,* Vol. 8, No. 2, September-October 1991.
49. *Al-Akhbar,* 19 November — DR, 26 November 1991.
50. *Al-Hayat,* 29 July — DR, 2 August; *al-Hayat,* 9 October 1991.
51. *Al-Sharq al-Jadid,* November 1991.
52. *MEI,* 10 January 1992.
53. MBC, 23 December — DR, 24 December 1991.
54. GNA, 25 December — DR, 26 December 1991.

55. *MEI,* 10 January 1992.
56. *Al-Ittihad* (Abu Dhabi), 7 September, cited by AFP, 7 September — DR, 9 September 1991.
57. *MEI,* 10 January 1992.
58. *Al-Sharq al-Awsat,* 11 February 1991.
59. MENA, 30 March — DR, 1 April 1991.
60. *Sawt al-Kuwait al-Duwali,* 17 April, quoted by KUNA, 17 April — DR, 24 April 1991.
61. MENA, 16 May — DR, 16 May; *al-Musawwar,* 17 June; *al-Sharq al-Awsat,* 2 June; *al-Ahram,* 6 June — DR, 12 June 1991.
62. MENA, 15 May — DR, 16 May; *IHT,* 16 May 1991.
63. MENA, 14 May — DR, 15 May 1991.
64. *Al-Sharq al-Awsat,* 16 April 1991.
65. *Al-Hayat,* 24 July 1991.
66. Prime Minister Sa'dun Hammadi, in *Alif Ba,* 16 April; Hammadi's news conference, INA, 25 April — DR, 26 April; first deputy prime minister Taha Yasin Ramadan's interviews in *Sawt al-Sha'b* (Amman), 27 May, and *al-Sha'b* (Cairo), 28 May 1991.
67. INA, 18 September — DR, 19 September 1991.
68. R. Baghdad, 13 July — DR, 15 July; INA, 17 July — DR, 18 July 1991.
69. Statement by presidential spokesman Muhammad 'Abd al-Mun'im, reported in *JP,* 14 July 1991.
70. *Al-Wafd,* 15 July; *al-Jumhuriyya* (Cairo), 18 July 1991.
71. INA, 18 September — DR, 19 September 1991.
72. For Iraq's denial, see interview with Taha Yasin Ramadan, *Misr al-Fatat* (Cairo), 9 September — DR, 12 September; for Iraq's willingness to cooperate with Majid, see MENA, 28 July — DR, 29 July 1991.
73. The Iraqi memo described the Kuwait-US pact as a gross violation of Article 10 of the League charter stipulating that members would not conclude international treaties which stood in contradiction to the objectives of the charter. Kuwait, the memo charged, was "opening the doors for the return of colonization" to the region, and expediting America's hegemonic objectives. INA, 24 September — DR, 25 September 1991.
74. Arab League envoy 'Abdallah 'Adam's mission resulted in the release of 14 Egyptian detainees in Iraq and optimistic statements that the Kuwaiti detainees, numbering c. 3,500, would be released shortly. (MENA, 18 October — DR, 18 October 1991.)
75. INA, 20 August — DR, 22 August 1991.
76. R. Baghdad, 4 September — DR, 5 September 1991.
77. INA, 17 September — DR, 18 September 1991.
78. R. Cairo, 3 March — DR, 4 March 1991.
79. *Egypt Focus,* Vol. 1, No. 2, December 1991.
80. R. Monte Carlo, 20 May — DR, 20 May 1991.
81. MENA, 17 November — DR, 18 November 1991.
82. R. Monte Carlo, 17 November — DR, 18 November 1991.
83. Text of the statement in JANA, 6 December — DR, 9 December 1991.
84. *October,* 8 December 1991.
85. For Libyan praise of the Arab League's expression of "total solidarity" with Libya, see interview with Dr. 'Ali al-Turayki, R. Tripoli, VoGAH, 7 December — DR, 9 December 1991.
86. *Al-Wafd,* 26 June — DR, 28 June 1991.
87. *Al-Hayat,* 16 July 1991.
88. *Al-Hayat,* 19 October 1991.
89. *FT,* 17 December 1991.
90. Mubarak's interview in *al-Hayat,* 16 July 1991.
91. *Sabah al-Khayr* (Cairo), 19 September 1991.
92. *Sawt al-Kuwait al-Duwali,* 1 October 1991.
93. R. Cairo, 11 December — DR, 12 December 1991.
94. Amman TV, 17 December — DR, 18 December 1991.
95. SPA, 27 October — DR, 29 October 1991.
96. One sign of this weakness was reported opposition, apparently from GCC members, to the

Arab League Council's reiteration of the standard Rabat Arab summit formula of 1974 declaring the PLO to be the "sole legitimate representative" of the Palestinians. (*Al-Hayat*, 13 September 1991.)

97. R. Damascus, 24 October — DR, 25 October; *IHT*, 25 October 1991.

98. Egypt's foreign minister 'Amr Musa to *al-Hayat*, 2 November; Jordan's Prime Minister Tahir al-Masri to *JT*, 5 November — DR, 6 November 1991.

99. Ben 'Ali's address to the nation, R. Tunis, 26 January — DR, 28 January 1991.

100. Report of meeting between the Tunisian and Moroccan prime ministers, R. Rabat, 19 June — DR, 24 June 1991. "The events have been a little bit tragic," said Morocco's Prime Minister 'Izz al-Din al-Laraki, "but I trust, we trust the Algerian leaders, we trust President Chedli, we trust Algerian patriotism and we're certain that the Algerians will triumph over the current difficulties they are encountering." Regarding the possibility of the fundamentalist threat spreading to Morocco, he acknowledged that "ideas, be they Islamic or other ideologies, move with ease" but felt that "we in Morocco are protected against certain forms of Islamicism." R. France International, 7 June — DR, 10 June 1991.

101. *Al-Siyasa al-Duwaliya*, October 1991, pp. 115–21.

102. *Al-Hayat*, 15 December — DR, 18 December 1991.

103. *Le Monde*, 12 July 1991.

104. *Al-Hawadith*, 31 May 1991.

105. *Al-Hayat*, 5 October 1991.

106. *Al-Sharq al-Awsat*, 6 October 1991.

107. Ghannushi's interview in *al-Hayat*, 15 December — DR, 18 December 1991.

108. *Le Monde*, 30 December 1991; *MEI*, 10 January 1992.

109. RTM TV, 25 November — DR, 26 November; *al-Sharq al-Awsat*, 27 December — DR, 30 December 1991. In late December, however, Morocco's Foreign Minister Filali stated that Morocco had no special role to play in resolving the crisis. (*Al-Hayat*, 20 December — DR, 24 December 1991.)

110. R. Rabat, 10 March — DR, 12 March 1991.

111. Ibrahim Bishari, secretary of the Libyan General People's Committee for External Liaison and International Cooperation, to *al-Hayat*, 13 July — DR, 17 July 1991.

112. R. Tripoli, 11 March — DR, 12 March 1991.

113. *Al-Ittihad al-Ishtiraki*, 29 October 1991.

114. MAP, 24 July — DR, 25 July; *FT*, 25 July 1991.

115. For details of the UN's efforts, see Bruce Maddy-Weitzman,"Conflict and Conflict-Management in the Western Sahara: Is the Endgame Near?," *MEJ*, Vol. 45, No. 4, Autumn 1991.

116. MAP, 20 May — DR, 22 May 1991.

117. MAP, 13 June — DR, 14 June 1991.

118. R. Algiers, 21 May — DR, 22 May; Algiers TV, 14 June — DR, 24 June 1991.

119. R. Algiers, 8 August — DR, 9 August 1991.

120. *Le Monde*, 3 August — DR, 21 August 1991.

121. *AC*, 13 September 1991.

122. *JP*, 21 August 1991.

123. *MEI*, 22 November 1991.

124. *Al-Hayat*, 19 October 1991.

125. *Al-Hayat*, 5 October, 6 November 1991.

126. *Al-Hayat*, 8 November 1991.

127. *MEI*, 10 January 1992.

128. *Sawt al-Kuwait al-Duwali*, 19 September — DR, 23 September 1991.

129. 'Isa Darwish, Syria's ambassador to Cairo, *Ruz al-Yusuf*, 22 April; statement by Asad al-Asad, acting secretary-general of the Arab League, *Shu'un al-'Arabiyya*, June 1991.

130. Clovis Maksoud, "The Arab World's Quandary," *World Policy Journal*, Vol VIII, No. 3, Summer 1991; Yusif al-Hasan al-Ta'qib, *al-Siyasa al-Duwaliya*, October 1991.

131. 'Ali al-Din Hilal, *al-Hayat*, 29 October 1991.

132. Qustantin Zurayq, *al-Hayat*, 18 October 1991.

133. Kamil Abu Jabr, *al-Hayat*, 25 July 1991.

Islam in the New World Order

MARTIN KRAMER

The year 1991 was also year one of the "new world order." Following the collapse of the Soviet Union, the US became the sole great power — a power bent on translating its Cold War victory into a global regime of stability. The world of Islam watched these events with apprehension. The Soviet breakup promised hitherto unimagined opportunities, including the expansion of the Muslim world northward into the newly independent Muslim republics of the former Soviet empire. But in the here and now, the US seemed determined to impose a strict regime of American-style order, whether by persuasion or by force. In 1991, Washington decided both to wage war and make peace in the Middle East in order to consolidate its triumph. In both instances, there were Muslims who issued clarion calls to Jihad, in the name of another truth: the divinely promised primacy of Islam.

THE JIHAD THAT FAILED

The year began under the storm cloud of the Iraqi occupation of Kuwait, dating from the Iraqi invasion of 2 August 1990. This first crisis of the post-Cold War era had sorely divided the Muslim world, as rival camps coalesced around Iraq and Saudi Arabia. Both sides in the looming confrontation employed the idiom of Islam to justify their actions. Iraq claimed to have seized Kuwait in the collective interest of Islam's downtrodden masses, and Saudi Arabia claimed to have invited in foreign forces to restore the freedom of the oppressed Muslim people of Kuwait. Some Muslims chose sides in this struggle for Islamic legitimation; others maintained a confused or calculated neutrality. (For the issue of Islam in the debate over the Iraqi invasion of Kuwait, see *MECS* 1990, pp. 194–203.)[1]

THE CLASH OF THE CONFERENCES

As the 15 January deadline set by the UN for Iraqi withdrawal approached, Iraq and Saudi Arabia made final efforts to persuade the Muslim world of the Islamic virtue of their irreconcilable stands. During the week before the deadline, two conferences purporting to represent the same organization met in Baghdad and Mecca, and passed completely contradictory resolutions on the Gulf crisis. This was not a case of double vision: the organization, known as the Popular Islamic Conference, had been split asunder by the crisis.

The Popular Islamic Conference, headquartered in Baghdad, had been founded by Iraq and Saudi Arabia early in the Iraqi-Iranian War. The Saudi purpose was to lend some of its international Islamic prestige to Iraq at a time when the two states were allied against Iran. Dr. Ma'ruf al-Dawalibi, a veteran Muslim activist in Saudi pay, headed the organization. (On the Popular Islamic Conference, see *MECS* 1982–83, pp. 243–45; 1984–85, p. 151; 1987, p. 438; 1990, pp. 194–95.)

As the crisis peaked, Iraq decided to turn the Popular Islamic Conference against Saudi Arabia. Iraq sought to convene the organization's members in Baghdad in order to frighten Iraq's adversaries with the specter of Islamic terror. The gathering, held from 9-11 January, drew a mixed bag of participants, including Shaykh 'Abd al-Hamid al-Sa'ih, chairman of the Palestine National Council (PNC); Ibrahim Shukri, leader of Egypt's Labor Socialist Party; and Jordan's minister of religious affairs. Sa'ih set the menacing tone of the gathering: "The world will become the theater of operations targeting American interests."[2] Saddam Husayn also addressed the conference, but left it to his guests to issue the more vivid threats.[3] At its conclusion, the conference called on all Muslims to rise up in Jihad should Iraq be attacked.[4]

Saudi Arabia, for its part, invited the executive council of the same Popular Islamic Conference to Mecca on precisely the same dates, for exactly the opposite purpose of condemning Iraq's violence against Kuwait's Muslims. The executive council met in Mecca from 9-11 January, with Saudi Arabia's most faithful Muslim clients, led by Dawalibi himself, attending. Saudi Arabia's ally, Egypt, sent Shaykh al-Azhar Jad al-Haqq 'Ali Jad al-Haqq and Shaykh Muhammad al-Ghazali. Not surprisingly, the conferees declared that Iraq's invasion of Kuwait "violated the very principles of Islam," and that those 'ulama who had approved Saddam's actions "are committing a sinful act, particularly after it has become clear to them that he is using Islam as a tool and is not at all committed to its teachings and principles." The rival conference in Baghdad was called "illegal," inasmuch as most of the members of the organization's executive committee had stayed away.[5]

Who spoke for the Popular Islamic Conference? The organizers of the Baghdad conference called the Mecca conference "null and void."[6] The organizers of the Mecca conference called the Baghdad conference "inappropriate procedurally and legally."[7] Ultimately, it did not much matter who stood on higher ground. In the international cacophony of resolutions and threats that preceded the war, the verdicts of two gatherings in Baghdad and Mecca counted for little. But the splitting of the Popular Islamic Conference did demonstrate the depth of the division in Sunni Islam on the brink of war.

THE IRRESOLVE OF ISLAM

Some inkling of what might have happened had the crisis been left to Islam's own powers of conflict-resolution could be deduced from the posture of the Islamic Conference Organization (ICO), the Jidda-based organization of Islamic states. The invasion of one member state by another had occurred in the very midst of the ICO's annual conference of foreign ministers, underlining once again the division within Islam that had dogged the ICO from its inception. In the subsequent crisis, the ICO ceased to function. (On the ICO's past performance, see *MECS* 1981–82, pp. 283–84, 298–301; 1982–83, pp. 235–37; 1983–84, pp. 158–65; 1984–85, pp. 146–48; 1986, pp. 127–30; 1987, pp. 153–58; 1988, pp. 180–83; 1989, pp. 178–81; 1990, pp. 192–94.)

As an organization supported largely by Saudi and Arab Gulf money, the ICO quickly condemned the Iraqi invasion. However, it did little more thereafter. The ICO secretariat indefinitely postponed the triennial Islamic summit scheduled for January in Dakar, Senegal, and postponed all activities scheduled for February as well.[8] Plainly, the organization was overwhelmed by events, and by the role of the organized international community, which leapt to the challenge while the ICO shrank back. One member, Iran, tried to prod the ICO to independent action, issuing an official call on 6 January for an emergency Islamic summit conference,[9] but nothing came of the initiative. As Hamid Algabid, ICO secretary-general, apologetically explained, the ICO had no security council of its own. Even its long-standing plan for an international Islamic court of justice — to be headquartered, ironically, in Kuwait — remained a paper project.[10]

The ICO twice emerged from hiding to claim the Gulf War as a war of Islamic consensus. On both occasions, Algabid convened the bureau of the previous foreign ministers' and summit conferences, in what amounted to small-scale gatherings of foreign ministers. The first of these gatherings met in Jidda on 8 January, just before the air war began; the second met in Cairo on 21 February, just before the land war started. These ICO meetings "strongly condemned" the Iraqi invasion of Kuwait and Iraq's "attempts to take advantage of the Palestine question to justify its invasion of Kuwait."[11]

But in the midst of crisis and war, few took notice of the meetings, which merely reiterated past resolutions. Indeed, the ICO could scarcely have been more irrelevant. After the "liberation" of Kuwait, Algabid scrambled to repair the damage by conducting a congratulatory tour of the Arab Gulf states. There he promoted the foreign ministers' conference scheduled for August in Istanbul and the delayed Islamic summit conference, rescheduled for December in Dakar[12] (see below). But the paralysis of the ICO during the crisis left little doubt that member states did not command the resolve or resources to deal effectively with conflict among themselves.

THE ELUSIVE MUSLIM "STREET"

On the popular level, the war produced a swell of conflicting emotions in the Muslim world. Muslims were bombarded by the manipulated images of war and by contradictory appeals made in the name of Islam. While Saudi Arabia had the support of most states in the region, Saddam claimed a following in the so-called "street," among the anonymous masses of the Muslim world, who were urged to rise up against their governments. The Popular Islamic Conference (Baghdad branch) called Muslims to Jihad on 18 January:

> Jihad has become the duty of every Muslim east and west of the universe. Topple the coward traitor Husni [Mubarak, president of Egypt], remove the slave of the infidels, the accursed traitor [King] Fahd [of Saudi Arabia]. Oh *mujahidin* everywhere, disperse the ranks of enemies and shake the ground under their feet. Kill them wherever you find them. Urge your governments to declare Jihad against the infidels and apostates. Unseat the miserable rulers who have no dignity, sense of honor, or faith.[13]

Various Islamists echoed this threat. Jordan's *Mufti* declared that "this is a golden opportunity for Muslims to wage Jihad against the forces of the Crusader-Zionist infidels to win the strength of this world and paradise in the hereafter. Is not the current war the hour of Jihad that Muslims have been longing for?"[14] A similar threat issued from Shaykh As'ad Bayyud al-Tamimi, the Hebron-born leader of the

Amman-based Islamic Jihad Bayt al-Maqdis, who had attended the Baghdad conference. He promised, in January, that "fatal attacks" in support of Iraq would begin "within the next few days" against targets both in the West and in the ME, namely in Egypt, Saudi Arabia, Syria, and the West Bank and Gaza.[15]

But the Jihad appeal failed to progress from sentiment to deed, from word to action. While the anger against the war among many Muslim activists was undoubtedly sincere, overflowing in angry demonstrations that filled the streets of Algiers, Rabat, Khartoum, Amman, San'a and Lahore, this rage remained diffuse. The world of Islam was too saturated in the counterpropaganda of the anti-Iraq coalition to ignite spontaneously. A commentary in a Jordanian paper the week after the war showed the disappointment of Islamists:

> All these calls for Jihad have, at best, continued to be shouts in the air, ink on paper, or hopes welling up in breasts. Of course, the reason is clear: namely, that every committee, thinker, or leader was content with issuing a statement calling for Jihad. This means that the call for Jihad has continued to lack a mechanism to implement it. Enthusiastic individuals do not know how to translate their enthusiasm into action.[16]

But while the Jihad appeal proved ineffective, it did sharpen domestic debate. Islamic opposition movements in the Muslim Brethren mold sought to translate rage against the war into leverage against entrenched regimes. It is impossible to survey the full range of responses to the war by Muslim movements and individual activists. Still, it is possible to examine the pattern of responses through four representative examples. (For more information, see chapters on individual countries.)

Algeria and Jordan

In Algeria and Jordan, two states that had moved hesitantly toward political pluralism and whose regimes were challenged by strong Islamic opposition parties, Islamists sought to use the war to domestic advantage. In particular, the Islamists demanded that the authorities train "volunteers," i.e., that they forfeit their monopoly on means of coercion by arming the Islamists.

When the war started, 'Ali Belhadj, second-in-command of Algeria's Islamic Salvation Front (usually known by its French acronym, FIS) demanded that barracks be opened and "the people" be armed for an "Islamic militia." The authorities denied this request, arguing that there were already 1m. reservists (some of whom were indeed mobilized — to defend foreign embassies and government buildings from demonstrators). The FIS threatened that if the government did not act to arm and train volunteers, it would do so itself, through the hundreds of local councils and provinces under its control.[17] Algeria's Islamists saw the war as a chance to break the monopoly on guns held by the Algerian army (the same army which in 1992 used that monopoly in a coup to deny power to the Islamists). In the end, however, the Islamists did little more than vent their anger in marches and slogans. A contingent of 300 Islamist volunteers from Algeria reached Jordan only after the cease-fire.[18]

The same demand arose in Jordan: the Muslim Brethren, along with several Islamist members of the Chamber of Deputies urged that the entire population be armed for the Jihad with government armory supplies. The regime responded by claiming that this was unnecessary, since many citizens were already members of the

People's Army or served in the military. Jordan's Islamists had the same aim as those in Algeria: to use the war to undermine the standing of the army and break the regime's monopoly on coercive force. The Islamists claimed that they needed the arms to help defend the country against external aggression by Islam's enemies, should the war spread; their real objective, however, was to shift the domestic balance decisively in their favor. Although this failed, Islamist deputies in parliament did succeed in translating popular support into five cabinet positions during a government reshuffle in January.[19]

Significantly, in neither country did Muslim activists answer the Iraqi call to Jihad by committing acts of violence, although they issued many threats against the anti-Iraq coalition. While they condemned the war as an example of the West's callous contempt for Muslim lives, they did not hold up Saddam as a model of Islamic rectitude. The spokesman for Jordan's Muslim Brethren even noted that the Brethren in Iraq were "banned and persecuted," and urged that "Islamic parties be given the freedom to operate in Iraq."[20] Lingering doubts about Saddam meant that while Islamists in Jordan and Algeria were prepared to fill the streets, they did nothing to put themselves at risk. This pattern was repeated in other countries as well, most notably in Morocco and Pakistan.

Egypt and the Palestinians

Elsewhere, Saddam's call for Jihad echoed through empty streets. Such was the case in Egypt and in the West Bank and Gaza, where the Islamic movements displayed rather more ambivalence toward the Iraqi cause, while the authorities showed more resolve in blocking manifestations of support for Saddam.

Egypt, as a full partner of the US in the anti-Iraq coalition deploying fighting forces in Saudi Arabia, took the precaution of extending the semester break at its universities, as well as putting problematic mosques under surveillance. The regime also mobilized the religious establishment in a massive campaign to justify Egypt's participation in the war against Iraq. "Does Saddam at all represent Islam?" asked Shaykh Muhammad Mutawalli al-Sha'rawi, a popular television preacher. "How is it that he sends Tariq 'Aziz [Iraq's foreign minister and a Christian] to speak for the Muslims in their conferences?! Does Islam assent to the crushing of a weak state like Kuwait? The West found one Muslim standing against another, and said it would take the side of the weak, to assure its rights. How could we refuse it?"[21] The regime felt confident that the great majority of Egyptians supported this decision, and that they understood the calculation of national interest that put Egypt in the coalition.

The Islamic opposition apparently reached the same conclusion. It was true that they opposed Egyptian policy: the general guide of the Muslim Brethren, Muhammad Hamid Abu al-Nasr, urged Mubarak to withdraw Egypt's troops from Saudi Arabia. Even if Saddam were a tyrant, said Abu al-Nasr, this did not alter the fact that the millions of Iraqis were "an important part of our Islamic and Arab nation."[22] Brethren leader Ma'mun al-Hudaybi declared it "better that we struggle for 20 years to free Kuwait, than for America to intervene or for a foreign foot to be set on Arab soil." Saddam was a Ba'thist dictator, he admitted, but now was not the time to criticize him.[23] The Muslim Brethren reserved their criticism for the US, Israel and Saudi Arabia. But, with the exception of a few protests by students and professionals organized by the Muslim Brethren, antiwar activism remained confined to the columns of opposition newspapers. Most notably, the Islamists refrained from calls for mass demonstrations.[24]

The streets were empty in the West Bank and Gaza as well, but for a different reason: when the war began and Iraqi *Scuds* began to fall on Tel Aviv, the Israeli military government imposed a rigid curfew on Palestinians in the West Bank and Gaza (see chapter on Israel). Although Palestinian Islamists had violated curfews as a matter of course during the Intifada, when the call of Jihad summoned them to strike against Israel from within while Iraq struck from without, they did nothing of the sort.

The Palestinian Islamists of the mainstream Hamas did celebrate the *Scud* attacks. A Hamas statement lambasted US President George Bush as "the head of the infidel alliance of the world evildoers, trying once again to humiliate the Muslims, to plunder their wealth, and to pave the way for the establishment of greater Israel in accordance with the distorted prophecy of the Talmud if, God forbid, the new Crusaders succeed."[25] Still, Hamas remained ambivalent about the war, largely because its principal rival, the PLO, had so closely identified itself with Saddam's cause. Hamas responded by nuancing its position in such a way as to distinguish it from the PLO's. Some of its leaders went so far as to question Saddam's sincerity. The linkage of Palestine and the Gulf had been made only after Iraq invaded Kuwait, said Khalil al-Quqa, an exiled Hamas leader. Such linkage had not been Iraq's prior intention, and if Iraq had wanted to champion the Palestinian cause, it could have done so directly, without oppressing the Kuwaiti people.[26] After the war, when the restored Kuwaiti regime began to force resident Palestinians out of the country, Hamas reminded Kuwaitis of the sympathy shown by Palestinian Islamists for Kuwait.[27]

In sum, for Egyptian and Palestinian Islamists there was little to gain at home by close identification with the cause of Saddam. They were prepared to issue statements against the anti-Iraq coalition, and to denounce the war as a "new Crusade" against Islam launched in large measure to benefit the Jews,[28] but they did not take their protest to the streets, and to the extent that they supported the Jihad, they appeared to believe that the obligation to act fell upon others. This pattern was also repeated elsewhere, most notably in Turkey and Tunisia.

As the ground war quickly turned into an Iraqi rout, the Jihad bubble burst. While the response of Muslim activists to the war had not been monolithic, and was conditioned by local circumstances everywhere — demonstrating yet again the difficulty of formulating a single Islamic position — still, there had been a collective desire among Islamists to see the West's nose bloodied just once. Iraq's last-minute decision to back down and withdraw, and its rapid collapse, surprised and disappointed many Islamists. Their embarrassment deepened as rumors of Iraqi atrocities in Kuwait were confirmed. Moreover, although Sunni Islamists remained largely indifferent to Saddam's crushing of the subsequent Shi'i rebellion in the south of Iraq, they were appalled by Baghdad's suppression of the Kurds in the north. The general guide of the Egyptian Muslim Brethren, Abu al-Nasr, issued a statement that condemned the "barbaric measures" taken against the Kurds by "the Ba'thist ruler" Saddam Husayn, and called for the creation of an Islamic government in Iraq to replace the Ba'thist regime.[29] Muslim Brethren spokesman Hudaybi, who had refrained from criticizing Saddam during the crisis, later spoke out: "Our position is that his regime will never change. Our principle is that acceptance of the Ba'th regime is impossible, because the Ba'th creed clearly opposes Islam."[30] An Egyptian Brethren spokesman summarized the war in this way: "The crazy man known as Saddam Husayn fell into the clutches of American intelligence," by providing the US with a pretext to deploy in Arabia.[31]

Thus ended the improbable romance of fundamentalist Islam with Ba'thist Iraq. In August, the Iraqi authorities indicated their intention to reconvene the Popular Islamic Conference in Baghdad, in order "to draw up a joint strategy to confront international plans against the Middle East."[32] But in October, Iraq announced that the gathering would not be convened, because preparations "have not been completed."[33] The real reason must have been Iraq's inability to assure a turnout for an Islamic gathering under its flag. It was an official admission that the Jihad of Saddam Husayn, the man who would be Saladin, had failed.

It had failed not because of the rallying of Islam against him. He had successfully confused and paralyzed a large segment of Muslim opinion, so that even in this greatest of emergencies, it had been impossible to fashion an Islamic consensus. The US, however, neither confused nor paralyzed, provided the backbone of the war coalition. US resolve made it the guarantor of international law and civil order in the domain of Islam.

COALITION ISLAM

Saudi Arabia and Egypt were quick to hold up the outcome of the Gulf War as a confirmation not only of their strategy, but also of their Islamic virtue. The moment had come to reward those Muslim organizations and associations that had stood by them in the battle, and to punish the others. For this purpose, they employed two instruments: Saudi money and Egyptian prestige. Each of these tools alone was imperfect, but in combination they created an impression that the victory over Iraq was somehow also a victory of true Islam.

SAUDI VINDICATION

During the course of the crisis and war, the Saudi decision to rely on foreign arms to defend the kingdom was criticized even by Muslims who had supported Saudi positions in the past, including many who had received Saudi funds. Islamic demonstrations of support for Saddam angered and offended the Saudi royal house, and even raised concerns about the spread of such criticism to Saudi Arabia itself (see chapter on Saudi Arabia). Once Saddam's Jihad had fallen flat, the Saudis set out to settle scores, moving swiftly to slash support for Muslim clients who had wavered when the fate of the monarchy hung in the balance. Prince Sultan, the minister of defense, announced that Saudi Arabia would continue supporting Islamic institutions and societies throughout the world,[34] but the criteria for receiving official or semiofficial support stiffened, and many former recipients could no longer meet them. Many of these subsequently denied they had ever received funds from Saudi Arabia. 'Abbas Madani, leader of the Algerian FIS, announced that "we never need, God willing, any state, and if we need money, you [the people] are ready and you will never disappoint us."[35] Rashid al-Ghannushi, an exiled leader of the Tunisian al-Nahda Party, declared that "we have not suffered financially from this as we are self-financing — not even the government, our greatest critics, have accused us of getting aid either from Iran or Saudi Arabia."[36]

But no Islamist completely denied receiving *private* donations from rich Saudis. In the past, representatives of Islamic movements visited Saudi Arabia during the pilgrimage to tug at the heartstrings and purse strings of Saudi millionaires. After the war, the government sought to dissuade Saudi donors from giving to the politically ungrateful. The effectiveness of the campaign, however, could not be monitored, since there were no currency exchange controls in Saudi Arabia, and many wealthy Saudis made their donations from private deposits abroad.[37]

The Saudis also became selective in their support of Afghan Mujahidin groups, which they had backed almost indiscriminately throughout nearly 14 years of war in Afghanistan. Not all of these groups offered Saudi Arabia support during the war. A small contingent of Mujahidin who joined the anti-Iraq coalition were denounced by leading Mujahidin, for example by Mujahidin leader Gulbuddin Hikmatyar, who stated that "there are a few individuals who have been sent by some people to appease the US. Perhaps they are people who have never participated in the Afghan Jihad."[38] The Saudi Government was also disturbed to learn that some of its own fundamentalist opponents had been trained and sheltered in Afghan Mujahidin bases in Pakistan. The authorities began to shut down the Saudi bank accounts of groups they regarded as extreme.[39] Yet as the Afghan resistance approached victory, Saudi Arabia continued to utilize diplomacy, money and intelligence to assure that its chosen Mujahidin gained power — a goal the Saudis were to achieve in 1992.

The Mecca-based Muslim World League (MWL: *Rabitat al-'alam al-Islami*), the missionary body devoted to the dissemination of Saudi Islam, circulated its agents throughout the Muslim world to line up Muslim support for Saudi Arabia during the prelude to the war, issuing dozens of statements and organizing conferences and meetings which were funded almost exclusively by the Saudi Government. (On the MWL's activities during the crisis, see *MECS* 1990, pp. 201–2.) The aftermath of the Gulf War, however, offered the MWL an opportunity to secure significant private funding, something which had always eluded it, for the organization could assure private Saudi donors that their funds would go to charitable causes that had been proven loyal, and not to the war chests of unapproved political movements. MWL Secretary-General 'Abdallah 'Umar al-Nasif launched a campaign to raise money from private sources based on specific themes, such as aid for Muslims of the former Soviet Union, and saving mosques slated for destruction in China.[40] It was not clear whether these campaigns brought any significant shift in the MWL's resource base, although the organization did approve a new postwar budget of SR38m. for the building of mosques, schools and hospitals abroad.[41] Nasif himself was awarded the coveted Faysal Prize for service to Islam.

EGYPT VICTORIOUS

Egypt's broad Islamic influence had never rested on money. It was based on the prestige of its religious institutions, above all the millennium-old mosque-university of al-Azhar. In the crucible of war, it became clear that the Islamic legitimacy of the anti-Iraq coalition derived largely from articulation by Egypt's religious establishment. Egyptian rhetoric, not Saudi riyals, created a credible Islamic justification for the deployment of foreign and Egyptian forces in Saudi Arabia. With the war over, Egypt decided to consolidate its achievement in the form of an Islamic conference.

The task was entrusted to the Supreme Council for Islamic Affairs, a subsidiary of the Ministry of Religious Endowments. Created by Nasser in 1960 in order to promote his brand of Arab-Islamic socialism, the Supreme Council subsequently declined in importance, but in recent years the Egyptian regime revived it as part of an effort to strengthen official Islam. The Supreme Council had convened annual Islamic conferences on various themes since 1988. As recently as 1989, it had held a conference in Baghdad, in cooperation with Iraq, to support Iraq's position in peace negotiations with Iran.[42] In 1991, Egypt called upon the Supreme Council to mark the victory over Iraq. The fourth conference of the Supreme Council met in Cairo on 25 April, presided over by Muhammad 'Ali Mahjub, Egypt's minister of religious endowments.[43]

Although the organizers chose the theme of Islamic unity and the future of the Islamic and Arab nation in the aftermath of the Gulf War, they did not invite any Iraqis. The event was a gathering of the victors: 450 moderate Muslim activists (280 of them Egyptians), largely from the religious establishments of the coalition states. They included Shaykh 'Abd al-Wahhab 'Abd al-Wasi', Saudi minister of pilgrimage; Hamid Algabid, secretary-general of the ICO; government officials from Kuwait and the Gulf states; 'Abdallah 'Umar al-Nasif of the MWL; and dignitaries from Egypt's traditional zones of Islamic influence in Black Africa and the Balkans. As a gesture of reconciliation, the conference also invited the Jordanian minister of religious endowments, who attended.

The need to denounce Iraq had diminished, and the conferees instead suggested various ways to heal the wounds of war through (Egyptian-led) cooperation. The resolutions, reflecting Egypt's postwar preoccupations, called for the creation of an Islamic security force (which Egypt would obviously dominate) and an Islamic development fund (with Egypt the greatest beneficiary).[44] The conference thus worked to confer Islamic legitimacy on Egypt's claims to the gratitude and money of the Gulf states it had defended — claims that would largely be disappointed during the course of the year (see chapter on inter-Arab affairs).

MUSLIM FOREIGN MINISTERS IN ISTANBUL

An ICO foreign ministers' conference placed the final seal of official Islamic approval on the outcome of the war. Iraq had invaded Kuwait in the very midst of the previous foreign ministers' conference, held in Cairo (see *MECS* 1990, pp. 192–94). The ICO had taken an unequivocal stand against the Iraqi move, but the organization had practically suspended its activities during the crisis (see above). Now that the war had ended, the time had come to affirm the consensus of Muslim states, accomplished at the 20th ICO foreign ministers' conference in Istanbul from 4–8 August.

The Istanbul conference quickly turned into an event of collective score-settling against Iraq. Resolutions not only reiterated past condemnations of the invasion, but called on Iraq to pay compensation. The conference also refused to accept Iraq's proposal that the ICO call for the sanctions to be lifted, and determined that the suffering of Iraq's people was "due to the noncompliance of the Iraqi regime with UN resolutions."[45] Indeed, an official Iraqi spokesman later claimed that Saudi Arabia "and some mercenaries had deliberately sought to peddle an odious draft resolution calling for maintaining the unjust, immoral economic blockade on Iraq and its Muslim people."[46] Summarizing the climate in Istanbul, Jordanian Foreign Minister 'Abdallah al-Nusur said: "The overall atmosphere in the conference was negative. I cannot claim that it was positive or that it reflected understanding... the aftermath of the Gulf War still overshadowed the meetings."[47]

While the ICO could celebrate consensus — achieved the more easily for the fact that Iraq had been soundly defeated — still, not all of Islam had been heard at Istanbul. Other more strident voices were not silenced by the war.

OPPOSITION ISLAM

In the aftermath of the war, conventional wisdom assumed that Islamic movements, by recklessly linking their fortunes to Saddam, had misread history, and that Islamic fundamentalism had entered into decline. In the new era of *pax Americana,* so the argument went, political Islam had become an anachronism.

The *Foreign Report,* published by *The Economist,* gave fullest expression to this view in a lead article in April entitled "The Islamic Wave Recedes." The article noted that over the past decade, "a wave of militant Islam began to threaten secular governments throughout the Arab world and to alarm the West." However, "it is now starting to recede," for a variety of reasons. First, there was the "failure" of Islamic fundamentalist parties. Once they had entered parliaments and municipalities, they had failed to "perform economic miracles," a failure that was costing them popular support. Second, Iran had lost interest in "exporting the revolution" to Arab lands, and Saudi Arabia had cut off money to Islamic fundamentalist movements that had backed Iraq in the war. Finally, the disillusionment with Saddam that followed his defeat had carried over to disillusionment with the Islamists who supported him. While the region would continue to see "political ferment" because of failing economies and growing unemployment, according to this view, "the Islamic fundamentalists have lost an opportunity to reap the advantage."[48]

The decline of political Islam was also predicted for individual countries where it had experienced a sudden ascent over the past few years. According to a former Jordanian cabinet minister, "the war in the Gulf was portrayed as one between good and evil by the Islamists, as mainly represented by the Muslim Brethren. When Iraq lost, people were disenchanted with propagators of this line. Mythology had lost to technology, and this is how support for the Brethren declined."[49] *L'Express* wrote in March: "Saddam's defeat has turned the Algerian political situation upside down," leaving the FIS in the worst position of all."[50] The FIS, according to *Foreign Report,* was "no longer expected to win power in the parliamentary election scheduled for June... the FIS will be lucky to win a third of the vote in June. It will be kept out of power by a coalition of secular parties."[51]

This analysis rested on flawed foundations in every particular. First, the masses of Muslims did not blame Islamic parties for failing to perform economic or other miracles. These were not ruling parties; they did not command national resources. In a few countries, they had controlled municipal budgets for a short time, and in Jordan they had briefly held some ministerial portfolios. But they had not failed, because they had never had the opportunity to succeed or fail. Islam still remained an untried solution, especially for those disillusioned with the record of regimes that had enjoyed absolute control of national resources for a generation.

Second, the revival of Islam was not a product of Iranian subversion or Saudi support. It emerged from deep-seated social and economic grievances that fed a populist groundswell. Iran and Saudi Arabia sensed this groundswell and tried to capitalize on it, continuing their support of Islamist movements in a more discriminating way after the war. But even if they had ended all such support, this would not have crippled the broad-based movements that drew upon deep sources of popular resentment. These movements felt increasingly self-sufficient, and their dependence on foreign infusions diminished as they shifted increasingly to reliance on a broad populist appeal at home. Even where Iran and Saudi Arabia did cut back on their support of Islamic movements, the populist domestic appeal of those movements was undiminished.

Finally, the defeat of Saddam did not discredit Islam as a solution, nor did it discredit Islam's fundamentalist proponents. Hardly anyone in the region mistook Saddam for a paragon of Islam, and no Islamist regarded Iraq's defeat as the defeat of a true Islamic state. There was disappointment that Saddam had not bloodied the nose of the West, but no disillusionment with Islam, on which Saddam himself had never truly relied. Nor were threatened regimes always in a position to wag their fingers at Islamic movements for choosing to support Saddam. In several countries, the regimes themselves had competed with Islamist movements in professing support for Iraq. Neither King Husayn of Jordan nor the ruling party in Algeria could claim they had shown better judgment than their Islamic oppositions.

In sum, the political dramas of 1991 did not alter the trajectory of Islam in the region — a trajectory which, for deep-seated social and economic reasons, was still generally ascending. The old order had been propped up by the champion of a "new order" — precisely the order that fed the rage, precisely the order which the Islamic revival rose to overturn. This was hardly a formula for disillusionment with Islam. The outcome of the war was too ambiguous in too many ways to purge the region of the passions that stirred fundamentalism.[52] The events of the second half of the year, which culminated in an overwhelming electoral triumph for the FIS in Algeria that electrified the region, confirmed this assessment. One year after dismissing the fortunes of political Islam, *The Economist* ran this headline: "Islam Resumes its March."[53] But had the march ever stopped, had the wave ever receded? The cycle of Islamic revival (if it were indeed a cycle) now seemed much longer: not a decade, but a generation, and possibly more.

THE KHARTOUM CONFERENCE

As Iraq's defeat in war grew inevitable, the many Islamic movements of the Muslim Brethren variety closed ranks to withstand the expected backlash.[54] A who's who of Sunni fundamentalism met in Khartoum, at an Islamic Arab Popular Conference organized by the authorities from 25–28 April. The event, initiated by Hasan al-Turabi, the fundamentalist Tom Thumb who sat squarely in the ear of Sudan's ruling military junta, reportedly drew over 200 participants from 55 countries.[55]

The Khartoum conference represented a counterforce to the Cairo conference (see above), which convened on precisely the same day. Participants included 'Abdallah Fadil, Iraq's minister of religious endowments; 'Abd al-Latif 'Arabiyyat, the Islamist speaker of Jordan's parliament; 'Abd al-Rahman Khalifa, leader of the Jordanian Muslim Brethren; 'Adnan Sa'd al-Din, leader of a major faction of the Syrian Muslim Brethren; Rashid al-Ghannushi of the Tunisian Nahda Party; Ibrahim Ghawsha, spokesman of the Palestinian Hamas; Gulbuddin Hikmatyar, leader of the Afghan

Mujahidin faction, Hizbe Islami; Muhammad Ahmad al-Sharif, secretary-general of Libya's World Islamic Call Society; Qazi Husayn Ahmad, leader of Pakistan's Jama'ate Islami; Ma'mun al-Hudaybi and Mustafa Mashhur, representatives of the Egyptian Muslim Brethren; and Fathi al-Shiqaqi, leader of the (pro-Iranian) branch of the Palestinian Islamic Jihad.

But the conference did more than bring together the connected world of Islamic fundamentalism. It sought to link the Islamists with their secular soul mates who had tilted (or toppled) toward Iraq during the war. And so, mingling among the Islamists at Khartoum, were Yasir 'Arafat, George Habash and Na'if Hawatima. Even a representative of Egypt's Nasserists attended — this, despite the well-known history of animosity between Nasserists and the Muslim Brethren. The conference clearly sought to reconcile Islam and Arabism on the basis of their shared repudiation of Western hegemony.

The conferees passed familiar resolutions calling for support of the Palestinian and Afghan causes. More notable was their demand that the West leave Iraq alone, a position taken as an act of defiance in the face of defeat. They called for a lifting of economic sanctions against Iraq, and rejected the demand for the unilateral destruction of Iraq's weapons. Resolutions denounced foreign intervention in Iraq's internal affairs, called for the preservation of Iraq's territorial integrity, and declared 17 January to be an annual day of solidarity with Iraq. Lastly, the conference resolved to establish a general secretariat composed of 15 persons, and an assembly composed of 50 persons which would meet every three years.[56] Turabi was named secretary-general. In subsequent appearances abroad, Turabi introduced himself with this title, and claimed that the new organization represented an alternative to the ICO.[57]

The Khartoum conference would later be cited by opponents of the Islamists as evidence of the existence of a global Islamic conspiracy. President Zayn al-'Abidin Ben 'Ali of Tunisia, referring to the Khartoum conference, declared that "there is absolutely no doubt that there is a fundamentalist 'international.' The fundamentalist movements stem from the same source and have the same way of exploiting religion....We know that they are in close contact with one another. Their activities are coordinated from Sudan."[58] Hudaybi, of the Egyptian Muslim Brethren, put a more benign face on the conference: "In these conferences we meet many Islamic and non-Islamic leaders... the [Khartoum] conference attempted to shed light on the postwar phase, and leaders of various schools participated, including Arab nationalists and non-Islamic movements."[59] Was there more to the Khartoum conference than met the eye? For example, were Iranians and Algerians active behind the scenes, extending and soliciting support for Islamic revolution? The Khartoum conference raised the question of Sudan's role in the wider world of Islamic fundamentalism, now that Sudan had been recast as an Islamic state. (For the domestic context of the country's Islamic transformation, see chapter on Sudan.)

SUDAN: NET EXPORTER OF REVOLUTION?

As the year progressed, diplomatic and intelligence sources in the West and the ME began to fuel public speculation about Sudan as a regional base of Islamist activism. Turabi himself revealed a plainly pan-Islamic perspective. He spoke of the development of a global trend resting on "the experiences of Iran in the heart of Asia, Sudan in the heart of Africa, and Algeria which is very near to the European continent."[60] His favorite lecture subject abroad was "Islam as a Pan-National Movement."[61] Speculation about Sudan's role was also evoked by Sudan's offer of refuge to Islamists exiled from their own countries, as well as by its developing relationship with Iran.[62]

Specifically, certain rumors asserted that Sudan actively promoted revolution in other states, especially Tunisia and Algeria. Allegedly, Sudan plotted with the exiled Rashid al-Ghannushi, a leader of the Tunisian Islamic opposition, in order to foment a coup in Tunisia. (During 1991, the Tunisian authorities arrested hundreds of Islamists on suspicion of conspiracy.) It also reputedly worked with 'Abbas Madani, leader of the Algerian FIS, to cause disturbances or at least to plan election strategy in Algeria. (Madani was reportedly in Khartoum at the time of the April conference.)[63] The reliability of these reports could not be measured. It was known, however, that the Sudanese Government granted passports, including diplomatic passports, to foreign Islamists who lacked travel documents. Ghannushi entered France on such a passport, leading Tunisia to lodge an official protest with Sudan.[64]

Turabi also angered Saudi Arabia, both by his support of Saddam and his criticism of the Saudi monarchy. In the immediate afterglow of the electoral success of the FIS in Algeria, Turabi asked: "If the [Algerian] FLN with all its glorious anti-colonial record was unable to withstand the wave of Islamic revivalism, then what about these regimes in Arabia which neither have an impressive record in patriotic struggle or Jihad, nor have they employed their wealth to the benefit of their people?"[65]

Sudan's relations with Iran also gave rise to speculation. Originally, Sudanese strongman 'Umar Hasan al-Bashir had close ties with Saudi Arabia, but after a visit to Tehran in 1990 he gradually began to move Sudan to the opposite pole of Islam. Iranian President 'Ali Akbar Hashemi-Rafsanjani, visiting Khartoum from 12–16 December to promote cooperation, stated that "we are determined to establish military and security relations in the future, but for the time being our cooperation concentrates on economic and commercial matters."[66] But other reports spoke of secret military understandings, and the provision of arms and training by Iran to Sudan. A US official even visited Turabi on the eve of Rafsanjani's visit and warned him of the consequences if any terrorist act were to be traced to Sudan.[67] Sudan seemed to be playing both sides of its Iranian relationship — intensifying it sufficiently to evoke the concern and attention of the West, but limiting it sufficiently to preclude any Western justification for isolating Sudan.

Had Khartoum really become an axis of worldwide Muslim Brethren activism, based on ties cultivated over decades by Sudan's Islamists? Or was the importance of these ties exaggerated by threatened regimes, always eager to cast their own Islamists as pawns of "foreign paymasters"? Information emanating from Sudan formed an incomplete picture, and Turabi denied that he stood at the center of an international conspiracy of revolution.[68] Yet the course chosen by Sudan attracted increasing attention from Islamists elsewhere. Palestinian Hamas spokesman Mahmud al-Zahhar, asked whether his movement looked toward the model of Iran, replied: "No, we are not Shi'is. The only country run today in the way we envisage is Sudan. Sudan is very different from what is reported about it in [the] international media. For the first time, it has managed to supply its own needs in grain. Corruption has always played an important part in starvation in various countries."[69] Not since the Mahdist state of the previous century had Sudan purported to provide a model for wider Islam.

Whether it could attain this achievement again, in the midst of poverty and civil war, remained to be seen.

IRAN AND THE POWER OF ISLAM

The events of 1991 made it impossible for Islamic Iran to be anything but pragmatic. Iran could not afford another war. It stood aside not only when the US-led coalition vanquished Iraq, but also when Saddam Husayn crushed the Shi'i rebellion in southern Iraq. Iranians were distressed by the images of massed American forces on their frontiers and the shell-torn Shi'i holy shrines in Iraq, but Iran's leadership, under President 'Ali Akbar Hashemi-Rafsanjani, decided that this would not be Iran's fight. (For more on this decision, the internal debate surrounding it, and Iranian foreign policy, see chapter on Iran.)[70]

Iran's neutrality served its national interest, although it did little to enhance Iran's reputation as standard-bearer of Islam in the eyes of Islamists. A few of the Sunni Islamists who tilted far toward Iraq even voiced open disapproval. "Masses of believers, from Indonesia to Morocco, were aligned with Iraq," declared Layth Shubaylat, a prominent Islamist deputy in Jordan's parliament. "Now, of all times, Iran decides to become friends with Saudi Arabia."[71] But Iranian press commentary dismissed such criticism: "The cadre of the Muslim Brethren in Jordan would do well to criticize the US domination over the Middle East and especially over the country in which they live before they choose to pass a judgment on Islamic Iran's policy of neutrality in the recent war."[72]

Iran's neutrality also disappointed Iraq's Shi'i opposition. After Iraqi forces were expelled from Kuwait and Iraq's Shi'is rose in revolt against Saddam, some looked to Iran for logistical support. After all, Islamic Iran once had waged a lengthy war against Iraq, partly in the hope that Iraq's Shi'is would launch just such an uprising. But that war had ended, and Iran now offered only limited assistance to its Shi'i brethren. "We do not want to intervene in the internal affairs of Iraq," Rafsanjani explained. "Our support only extends to the granting of refuge to Iraqis fleeing their country.... Our export of the revolution is not accomplished through war or the toppling of regimes. We export the revolution only by disseminating the thought of the Imam Khomeyni."[73] The Shi'i revolt needed guns, however, not thought, and while Iran did allow Iraqi Shi'i exiles in Iran to provide some tangible assistance to the rebellion, this did not suffice, and Iraq's Republican Guard ultimately crushed the Shi'i uprising (see chapter on Iraq).[74]

In both instances — Iran's neutrality toward the war and the rebellion — it seemed as though Iran under Rafsanjani had given up on its Islamic mission, and now pursued only narrow national interests. But was this the case? In 1991, the full extent of Iran's Islamic vision became clear following the breakup of the Soviet Union. What the West interpreted as a victory for democracy, Iran interpreted as a triumph for Islam. "We heard the sound of the rotten bones of communism and socialism being crushed because Islam revealed their true natures," declared the leader of the Iranian-backed Hizballah during a visit to Tehran.[75] The collapse of communism as an ideological system left Islam as the only viable alternative to Western materialist capitalism. Under the right guidance, the solution of Islam might be transformed into political and military might.

In the opinion of the Tehran newspaper *Jumhuriyye Islami,* Islam could now be transformed into "a single, effective world power.... Muslim nations should rise up to take their appropriate place in the new global power structure."[76] On another occasion, the newspaper asked:

> Why should the Islamic world, which has one fifth of the world's population, not play a suitable role in decisions on the contemporary world? Why are our part and our role being intentionally ignored in the system that rules the world? Why should the Islamic world not play a part in key decisions on the future of the world and on a world order which is fit for the future world?[77]

The only way to stake a claim to such status was through unity. Only a united Islam could deter Western aggression, argued the newspaper *Abrar,* and that required "a military, political, and economic pact....For this to succeed, all minor differences over ideological issues and systems of government should be set aside in view of the great danger threatening Islamic countries' national interests and territorial integrity."[78]

Iran's Islamic policy had taken a new tack. For a decade, Islamic Iran had advocated Islamic revolution and appealed to the downtrodden Muslim masses over the heads of their misguided regimes. In practice, however, none of these regimes fell before the masses. Now Iran was prepared to overlook the failings of the regimes — once-fatal flaws were downgraded to "minor differences" — and work with them in order to unite Muslim states into one bloc. Individually, no Muslim state could acquire great power status. Collectively, they could fill the vacuum left by the collapse of the Soviet Union.

Actually, this state-oriented variety of Islamic solidarity had been the policy of Saudi Arabia for nearly 30 years, and had been institutionalized in the ICO. How then did Rafsanjani's vision differ? In fact, he saw Iran supplanting Saudi Arabia as the hub of Muslim solidarity. In his view, the Arab states had stumbled badly in the fratricide that followed Iraq's invasion of Kuwait. The Gulf War had undermined their legitimacy and divided them against one another. Saudi Arabia was forced to rely on unbelievers for its defense, and the Arabs had grown so weak that they had accepted the inadmissible: the State of Israel. Perhaps the Arab moment of primacy in Islam might be ending; perhaps the moment of Iran had arrived. Furthermore, now that central Asia and the Caucasus had escaped the grip of the Soviet bear, the geopolitical center of Islam was shifting eastward and northward — in the direction of Iran. In this scenario, Iran would relieve the Arabs of the banner of Islamic primacy and succeed, where they had failed, in transforming Muslim states into a global power bloc. This partly explained Rafsanjani's decision to reach an agreement with Saudi Arabia over the pilgrimage — an agreement which assured that Iran's contingent to the pilgrimage would be the largest. It also explained Rafsanjani's decision to be the first head of Islamic Iran to attend an Islamic summit, and Iran's demand that an upcoming summit be held in Tehran (see further below).

This did not mean that Iran abandoned its support of popular Muslim movements, although it did withdraw its backing for Shi'i revolutionaries who wished to overthrow the monarchies and emirates across the Gulf. But those groups that gave Iran leverage in the Arab-Israeli arena won expanded support, especially Lebanon's Hizballah and the pro-Iranian branch of the Palestinian Islamic Jihad. Moreover, the list of movements befriended by Iran no longer remained limited to Shi'i revolutionary groups and small Jihad cells. In recent years, Iran had blazed a trail to the major Islamic movements of the Muslim Brethren variety in Sunni lands, gaining special appreciation from them by standing alone among ME states against the American initiative for Arab-Israeli peace. Iran now rested its Islamic reputation not on its promotion of Islamic revolution, but on its support for Islamic Jihad against Israel, and for the rejectionist groups that waged it. Iran acquired enough credibility on this score to draw many leading Sunni and Shi'i Islamists to an October conference in Tehran, held in opposition to the Madrid peace conference (see below).

Iran, then, had not yet become a state like all other states. In the breadth of its vision, it still deserved to be called Islamic Iran, combining a pursuit of Iranian national interest with Khomeyni's vision of a united Islam. While differences remained within Iran's clerical elite over the balance between Iranian interest and Islamic vision, especially when they pulled in opposite directions, these differences were over the choice of the road, not over the destination.

RUSHDIE IN LIMBO

As if to emphasize the tenacity of Khomeyni's vision, Iran was unwilling to resolve the case of the Indian-born British author, Salman Rushdie. *The Satanic Verses,* Rushdie's postmodernist novel, had evoked a premodernist *fatwa* (religious edict) from Khomeyni in February 1989 calling upon believers to put Rushdie to death for having committed apostasy by blaspheming the Prophet Muhammad in his book. Following Khomeyni's own death, no one in Iran had the authority or will to free the novelist from the grip of this capital sentence. Rushdie's subsequent attempt to void the *fatwa* by professing Islam met with mixed results. Egypt's religious establishment accepted his statements of contrition, but prominent figures in the Muslim world continued to demand that the book be withdrawn, that Rushdie be abducted for trial in Iran, or that he be "executed." (For the genesis of the Rushdie affair, see *MECS* 1989, pp. 173–80; 1990, pp. 177–80.)

Under close guard by Scotland Yard, Rushdie made a growing number of public and media appearances in Britain in order to keep his case alive. In December 1991, he even appeared in New York before a university audience, his first public appearance outside Britain since the *fatwa*.[79] But his enemies did not relent. The private foundation in Iran which led the campaign against him held a seminar in Tehran on the "dynamism" of the *fatwa* against Rushdie, from 1–3 March. The seminar resolved that the *fatwa* was "irrevocable," and the foundation, which had initially offered $1m. to anyone who succeeded in taking Rushdie's life, doubled the reward to $2m.[80] Rushdie received two grim reminders of the seriousness of the threat in July 1991, when the Italian translator of *The Satanic Verses* was seriously wounded in a knife attack in Milan, and the book's Japanese translator was stabbed to death in Tokyo.[81]

Ultimately, the only resolution lay in a diplomatic deal with Iran that might produce a new *fatwa,* possibly in exchange for improved ties. But which Western government would bear the responsibility for securing Rushdie's freedom as its price for expanded trade and ties? The US held that the Rushdie affair was "primarily a British matter because he is a British citizen."[82] The British, however, had already joined the rush to normalize ties, a haste that took the bite out of its demarches on Rushdie's behalf. As one of Rushdie's fellow authors wrote, "most countries, including his own, Britain, are [already] doing business with Iran, buying its oil and cashew nuts, and selling the Iranians new cars and wristwatches, and sending them paper and ink so they can print their fatuous laws."[83] The freeing of British hostages in Lebanon during the year (see below) did offer some hope to Rushdie. Moreover, the actual propaganda for the *fatwa* was conducted outside the Iranian Government. Still, Islamic Iran had not reached the point where it could or would undermine Khomeyni's *fatwa,* which the West saw as a standing incitement to murder in the name of Islam.

THE REVIVAL OF HIZBALLAH

The pride of Islamic Iran's export of revolution remained Hizballah, the Lebanese Shi'i movement of protest that had been created in Khomeyni's image in 1982. Nowhere had Iran's message been assimilated so thoroughly, and with such direct benefit to Tehran, as in Lebanon.

But from 1988 through 1990, Hizballah had been locked in battle with its Lebanese Shi'i rival, the Amal movement, in a ruthless struggle that pitted Shi'i against Shi'i.[84] Only in 1991, after that struggle ended, could Hizballah return to the agenda set by Islamic Iran. During the year, Hizballah freed its long-held American and British hostages, winning Iran the gratitude of the West. It also renewed the Jihad against Israel in South Lebanon, earning Iran the respect of all opponents of the peace process.[85] (For background on Iran's role in Hizballah, see *MECS* 1983–84, pp. 171–73; 1984–85, pp. 155–59; 1986, pp. 139–44; 1987, pp. 165–69; 1988, pp. 191–94; 1990, pp. 182–84. For more on Hizballah's Lebanese context, see chapter on Lebanon.)

Hostage Clearance

For most of the 1980s, Hizballah was involved in the taking of Western hostages in Lebanon, for two principal reasons. First, an embargoed Iran sought money and weapons from Western governments, and regarded hostage-holding as an efficient form of leverage. Hizballah carried out the abducting as a service to Iran. Second, Hizballah sought to free its own members in Western and ME prisons, and took foreign hostages to acquire cards for its own hand. Following the Iranian-Iraqi cease-fire in 1988, the international embargo of Iran loosened and Tehran adopted more acceptable ways of securing finance and weapons. Hostage-holding had become a political burden, and Rafsanjani began to close the hostage file by arranging the release of all French hostages in 1988. These efforts were greatly aided by the escape in 1990 of Hizballah militants held in Kuwait, whose release had been demanded by the holders of American and British hostages in Lebanon. (For background and more details, see *MECS* 1990, pp. 183–84.)

By 1991, there was no longer anything to gain by keeping the remaining American and British hostages, and between August and December they all went free. The last six American and three British hostages included journalists Terry Anderson and John McCarthy, and Anglican Church envoy Terry Waite. Islamic Jihad and the Revolutionary Justice Organization, which held the hostages on Hizballah's behalf, enjoyed one last chance to bask in the limelight and to boast that "we shall always remain in the vanguard of the defenders of the causes of Islam and the Muslims,"[86] while the publicity surrounding the release of the longest-held hostages did much to enhance the images of Iran and Syria.[87]

Israel still held several hundred Hizballah fighters and the abducted cleric Shaykh

'Abd al-Karim 'Ubayd, whom it had seized to get back its own missing soldiers from Hizballah's hands. For its part, Hizballah admitted to having possession of two Israeli soldiers or their bodies, and was assumed to have control of an Israeli airman. For a while, it seemed as though a larger deal involving Israel was in the works, mediated by Giandomenico Picco, special envoy of UN Secretary-General Javier Pérez de Cuéllar. Hizballah even provided proof that one Israeli soldier was dead, in exchange for the release of several of the more than 300 Shi'i detainees held by Israel. But there it ended. Iran's organization of political opposition to Arab-Israeli talks, and Hizballah's escalation of its military campaign against Israel's security zone (see below), precluded any overall deal. By the year's close, hope of an exchange of prisoners between Israel and Hizballah had vanished, much to Israel's consternation.

Two German hostages also remained in the hands of Hizballah's affiliates at the end of the year. Both were held to secure freedom for a convicted Hizballah hijacker imprisoned in Germany. The hijacker, Muhammad 'Ali Hamada, had killed an American passenger in the 1985 hijacking of an American airliner to Beirut, which made his release difficult if not impossible. (The two Germans were released in June 1992; Hamada remained in prison.)

In retrospect, the hostage decade cemented the partnership between Islamic Iran and Hizballah. Hizballah's actions followed the example set by Iran in the seizure of the US Embassy in Tehran at the outset of the revolution. Not only did keeping hostages in Lebanon bring concessions and publicity, but it also bought the time needed by Hizballah to consolidate its position. Hizballah's verdict was that "hostage-taking, as a message, succeeded in sending certain signals to those concerned and made them call off many of their conspiratorial designs against our people."[88] As for Iran's rulers, the hostage decade created a bond of obligation toward their Lebanese clients, which assured that even the "moderates" in Tehran would not abandon Hizballah.

The Islamic Resistance

With the freeing of the American and British hostages, attention turned to the future role of Hizballah in Lebanon. In the years when Hizballah had been locked in battle with Amal, Arab mediators had engineered the Ta'if Accords for internal reconciliation in Lebanon. The 1989 agreement, based on a reformed confessionalism, left no avenue for the possible transformation of Lebanon into an Islamic state. It enjoyed the support of Syria and the endorsement of the US, while Hizballah became its most vocal Lebanese critic. "The fact is that the Ta'if decision is an American decision wearing an Arab headdress," declared Sayyid Muhammad Husayn Fadlallah, the spiritual mentor of Hizballah.[89] No amount of persuasion could induce Hizballah to accept the accord, even the offer of a cabinet portfolio, which it rejected.[90] Hizballah continued to demand a referendum on the creation of an Islamic state. According to Shaykh Subhi al-Tufayli, the movement's secretary-general, "we believe that everyone has the right to choose, through a general referendum, following which the Lebanese would be committed to abiding by the will of the majority (as expressed in such a referendum). It goes without saying that we ourselves would be committed to whatever the majority decides."[91] Muslims constituted a clear majority in Lebanon, and Hizballah believed it could do as well as any fundamentalist party in turning discontent into ballots for Islam.

But for Hizballah, the more immediate problem posed by the Ta'if Accords was its provision for the disarming of all militias, which were to be incorporated wherever possible into the Lebanese army. In March, the Lebanese cabinet ordered the implementation of this decision, and the Lebanese army deployed southward, where it absorbed part of the Amal militia. Hizballah, however, claimed a general exemption from the disarming. "We will not hand over our weapons," declared movement leader 'Abbas al-Musawi. "Lives depend on these weapons."[92] To justify this refusal, Hizballah emphasized that its weapons were aimed only against Israel. Fadlallah supported the general disarming of militias, but argued that the Islamic Resistance — Hizballah's guerrilla arm in Southern Lebanon — prosecuted the struggle against Israel that the Lebanese army was unable or unwilling to conduct. Hizballah also claimed an exemption for Iran's Revolutionary Guards from the Ta'if provision for the evacuation of all foreign forces from Lebanon. "The Revolutionary Guards are neither a militia nor a paramilitary organization in Lebanon," announced Tufayli. "They are here as experts who came to share their knowledge and experience in a number of spheres with the Lebanese people. They also train Resistance fighters.... When the Islamic Republic [of Iran] decides to withdraw them, they will leave. This matter is not linked to weapons, gunmen, militias, or anything of that kind."[93]

In fact, for the better part of two years, Hizballah's guns had been turned on Amal, not Israel. Tufayli was asked in April about lack of operations against Israel. "The Resistance was affected by the fighting between the Amal movement and Hizballah over the last two years," he admitted. "Now, following resolution of the problems between ourselves and Amal, I believe the Resistance will be operating more effectively than it has before."[94] Tufayli was right. As the US-initiative for an Arab-Israeli peace process progressed, Islamic Iran called on Hizballah to mount an offensive against Israel's "security zone" in Southern Lebanon, which was patrolled by the Israel-backed South Lebanese Army (SLA). Fadlallah explained the rationale behind the offensive: "It is not impossible to suppose that the Resistance could inflict such losses on the enemy as to force him to pull out of the strip, just as the Israelis withdrew from the rest of the south between 1983 and 1985 as a result of Resistance operations."[95] The thinking was that this would spare Lebanon the need to negotiate an Israeli withdrawal in return for peace — a peace which Islamic Iran and Hizballah adamantly opposed. "We do not accept any peace as long as Israel is in existence," declared Hizballah commander Husayn al-Musawi, "and Israel must be obliterated. This means that our struggle has to be continued against Israel."[96]

Hizballah had no intention of accepting any settlement that would emerge from the negotiations. As 'Abbas al-Musawi stated:

> In the same way as the May 17th agreement concluded by the Lebanese regime and parliament [with Israel in 1983] was not binding on us, whatever commitments the Arabs and the Palestinians may conclude concerning the issue of Palestine and the sacred sites will not be binding on us as well, and we will seek to confront and abort them at all levels.[97]

Even the Lebanese Government would be confronted, if necessary. According to Tufayli, "we defend the principle of resistance, and we will oppose any attempt to hamper the activities of the resistance fighters, even if such an attempt is made by the Lebanese authorities."[98]

The opening of Hizballah's offensive was signaled by the "election" of 'Abbas al-Musawi as secretary-general of the movement in May 1991 to replace Subhi al-Tufayli, an appointment which marked the shift in Hizballah's priorities. 'Abbas al-Musawi, a cleric schooled in Najaf, had more military acumen than any of Hizballah's other clerics. He had been trained by the Revolutionary Guards, had commanded the Islamic Resistance, and had proven himself a master of operational planning. The chief accomplishments of his tenure included the planning of two "self-martyrdom" (or suicide) bombings: one that killed 12 Israeli soldiers in March 1985, and another that killed eight soldiers in October 1988. Yet he was less identified, at least publicly, with the holding of Western hostages, which therefore won him the ubiquitous tag of "moderate" by the Western press. 'Abbas al-Musawi perfectly personified the decision to free the hostages while escalating the Jihad against Israel.[99]

After Musawi's appointment, Hizballah launched a successful drive to reestablish itself in the south, whence it had been expelled by Amal. Clerics and fighters who had been driven out by Amal in earlier fighting came flooding back into the south. The number and boldness of armed operations against the SLA and Israeli forces increased, while Israeli retaliatory strikes also increased in quantity and extent.[100]

Hizballah continued to escape the closing vise of the new order in Lebanon and the world during 1991. It filled the no-man's land between Israel and Syria in Lebanon, maneuvered in the political zone between factions in Iran, and bought time by carefully discarding its American and British hostage cards. But a cloud loomed on the horizon: "When Israel withdraws its forces," said Syrian Defense Minister Mustafa Talas, "we'll disarm Hizballah, and that's a promise."[101] The beginning of direct Israeli-Lebanese negotiations in October seemed to bring that day of reckoning a step closer.

THE PILGRIMAGE OF 1991

For a decade, the Muslim pilgrimage to Mecca and Medina had been buffeted by the storm of Iran's Islamic revolution. Iranian pilgrims and Saudi police had clashed bloodily during the decade, and Iran had boycotted the pilgrimage since 1987. But as Iran's priorities shifted, the climate surrounding the pilgrimage began to improve, allowing Saudi-Iranian negotiations for a return of Iran's pilgrims. In late 1990, a sudden cloud appeared on the horizon, as foreign troops massed in Saudi Arabia to wage war against Iraq. But this brief, "Desert Storm" would pass quickly, leaving few marks on the pilgrimage.[102] (For past pilgrimage conflict, see *MECS* 1981–82, pp. 284–88, 301–3; 1982–83, pp. 238, 249–51; 1983–84, pp. 175–77; 1984–85, pp. 161–64; 1986, pp. 149–51; 1987, pp. 172–76; 1988, pp. 177–85; 1989, pp. 182–84; 1990, pp. 189–91.)

Although Iraq and Saudi Arabia waged a bitter propaganda campaign before the war, Iraq did not call for a boycott of the pilgrimage until well after the air war began. On 11 February, Iraq finally announced a boycott in protest against the presence of foreign forces on the "sacred soil" of Arabia. Iraq also sought to persuade other Muslim states to follow its lead, but without success.[103] Even the Muslim Brethren movement in Jordan, which sided with Saddam in the confrontation, determined that the pilgrimage remained obligatory for all who could perform it, regardless of the nature of the regime that controlled the holy places.[104]

The start of the air war over Iraq raised a host of questions about the pilgrimage, which was to take place in June 1991. Could the pilgrimage, with its complicated logistics and thousands of incoming flights, be conducted in the midst of a war? Would there be a danger of violence, this time by pilgrims supportive of Saddam Husayn's call for Jihad? Saudi and American officials agreed that Saudi Arabia could not wage war and conduct the pilgrimage at the same time, a conclusion that argued for an early and swift land war against Iraq.[105] In the event, Iraq was defeated three months before the pilgrimage season began, in ample time for governments and pilgrims to make their arrangements.

A more familiar question then dominated the politics of pilgrimage: would Iran's pilgrims appear? Since the violent confrontation of 1987, which claimed the lives of several hundred Iranian pilgrims, Iran's pilgrims had absented themselves. Iran's leaders refused to accept the drastic reduction in the quota of Iranian pilgrims imposed by the Saudi authorities, while also rejecting the stringent limits on their political activities which the Saudis sought to enforce. But following Iran's decision to improve relations with Gulf Arab states, a compromise took shape. From the autumn of 1990, direct Saudi-Iranian talks took place on the highest diplomatic level, involving five meetings between Saudi Foreign Minister Sa'ud al-Faysal and Iranian Foreign Minister 'Ali Akbar Velayati. Omani mediation helped to produce a written agreement, signed by the two foreign ministers in Muscat in March, setting the parameters for the return of Iran's pilgrims. (The agreement also provided for restored diplomatic relations, which had been severed in April 1988 over the pilgrimage dispute.)

The agreement resolved the two outstanding issues that had divided Saudi Arabia and Iran. First, it set the number of Iranian pilgrims at 110,000, a figure later raised to 115,000. This was significantly more than the annual quota of 45,000 that Saudi Arabia had imposed for a three-year period after 1987, a measure that had produced a total Iranian boycott. Yet it was also less than the 150,000 Iranian pilgrims who had arrived annually through 1987. Second, Iran would be permitted to conduct one rally in a fixed place in Mecca, where a message from Khamene'i could be read to assembled pilgrims, as Khomeyni's message had been read in the past. This rally had turned into a violent march toward the Great Mosque in 1987; the new agreement included an Iranian commitment to prevent any flow of demonstrating pilgrims from the rallying point.

Two complications briefly endangered this understanding. In April, Khamene'i appointed Khomeyni's son, Ahmad, as his representative to the pilgrimage.[106] It is the task of this representative to set the tone for Iran's pilgrims, and Ahmad Khomeyni had a reputation as a firebrand. He immediately announced that he saw the pilgrimage as an opportunity for "confrontation," not just with America and Israel but with "regional reactionaries."[107] Saudi Arabia, alarmed by the appointment, informed Iran that it put their agreement in jeopardy. The message got through: eight days later, Ahmad Khomeyni resigned (he was needed at home by his mother, he claimed),[108] and a Rafsanjani stalwart, Muhammad Muhammadi-Reyshahri, was appointed in his stead.[109]

The second complication, which emerged after the pilgrimage was under way, involved the choice of a site for Iran's rally. The Saudis proposed a number of sites, all of them remote from the heart of Mecca and not easily accessible. The Saudis clearly wished to put as much distance as possible between the rallying pilgrims and the center of the city. Iran rejected these sites, arguing that their location made it impossible for the rally to draw pilgrims from other countries. At the last minute, the Saudi authorities relented and allowed the rally to gather in a square near the headquarters of Iran's pilgrimage representative, a site which was still a good distance away from the Great Mosque.[110]

On the eve of the pilgrimage, Rafsanjani and Reyshahri made several statements that set a conciliatory tone for the pilgrimage.[111] Iran's pilgrims then arrived, and the planned rally took place as scheduled on 18 June. Khamene'i's message, warning against "American Islam" and compromise with Israel, was read without incident.[112] At the last minute, Velayati himself arrived as a pilgrim, and during his stay had two audiences with Saudi King Fahd and three meetings with his Saudi counterpart, Sa'ud al-Faysal. "Saudi Arabia's conduct has been proper," he announced, "and we hope that in view of good understanding between Iran and Saudi Arabia we will see the pilgrimage rituals performed more splendidly than ever before in coming years."[113] After the pilgrimage, the two countries raised their diplomatic ties to the ambassadorial level. In addition, Saudi Arabia agreed to receive some 3,000 Iranians a week over a seven-month period to perform the minor (out-of-season) pilgrimage ('umra). There were 300,000 Iranians on the waiting list for this pilgrimage.[114]

Thus ended yet another cycle of Saudi-Iranian confrontation over the pilgrimage — the third such cycle since the Saudis established their rule over Mecca in 1924.[115] For some time, Islamic Iran had been moving away from a strategy of revolution in the Gulf to a strategy of persuasion. The past promotion of revolution had only driven the Arab Gulf regimes to seek safety in American arms. The present campaign of persuasion reassured the Arab Gulf regimes, and above all Saudi Arabia, that they faced no threat from Iran, and indeed faced greater dangers from their ostensible protectors — Iraq, most recently, and the US in the future. Iran's revised approach found symbolic expression in the pilgrimage reconciliation. The old pilgrimage prejudices on both sides lapsed into a latent state, from which they could be summoned if and when politics demanded it.

The new animosity between Saudi Arabia and Iraq did not make itself felt in this pilgrimage. Few pilgrims came from Jordan and Yemen, whose governments had tilted toward Iraq, yet neither government boycotted the pilgrimage, and small numbers of pilgrims did arrive from both countries. Even vanquished Iraq finally sent a token delegation of 400 pilgrims at the last minute.[116] At the same time, change elsewhere in the world resulted in increased demand for the pilgrimage. The Saudis played host to 4,700 pilgrims from the Soviet Union in the last year of its existence, the largest number ever. In Dagestan, police had to fire over the heads of demonstrators demanding the hard currency necessary for the journey to Mecca.[117] Albania, once sealed to the world, was represented by 180 pilgrims. The Saudis clearly derived satisfaction from the smooth operation of the pilgrimage, given the criticism they had endured in recent years. The only event to mar the occasion was the crash near Jidda of an airliner carrying 247 Nigerian pilgrims and a crew of 14, all of whom perished.

ISLAM AND THE PEACE PROCESS

Even before the dust settled in the Gulf, the US launched a major initiative to advance the Arab-Israeli peace process. The defeat of Iraq and the breakup of the Soviet

Union strengthened the hand of American diplomacy, which achieved a breakthrough with the convening of an Arab-Israeli peace conference in Madrid on 30 October. The months that followed witnessed several rounds of bilateral talks in Washington between Israel and Syria, Lebanon, Jordan and a Palestinian delegation. (For the development of the initiative, see chapter on the ME peace process.)

Islam figured prominently in the debate over the admissibility of these talks and over the ultimate prospect of recognizing Israel as part of a peace settlement. Rival interpreters of the faith condemned or condoned the peace talks in the name of Islam, just as they had differed over the foreign deployment in Arabia. Representatives of establishment Islam in the countries that had formed the war coalition generally sanctioned the talks and spoke of the Islamic imperative for peace. The leaders of opposition Islam, joined by Islamic Iran, generally reviled the talks and cited the Islamic duty of Jihad.

ISLAMIC OPPOSITION TO MADRID

The fundamentalist view of the Arab-Israeli conflict remained uncompromisingly theological. Palestine was a land sacred to Islam, a land which had been stolen by the Jews. Not an inch could be alienated. Israel was a cancer in the Islamic world, implanted by imperialism and nurtured by the US. Israel had to be fought, passively through nonrecognition, actively through Jihad. This view was shared by Islamists of all stripes, especially by the many Sunni movements in the Muslim Brethren tradition and by Shiʻi movements that adhered to Iran's line.

The approaching Madrid conference evoked dozens of statements and declarations by them rejecting both the conference and Israel's existence. "We view the recognition of the Jewish state as a breach of the pledge to God and His messenger," announced the Muslim Brethren deputies in the lower house of Jordan's parliament.[118] "We are the major nation in this region," said Hizballah leader ʻAbbas al-Musawi on the eve of the Madrid conference, "whereas the Jews are an alien and temporary entity. It is our judgment that the Jews should leave the region. The state of Palestine will be established over the entire land of Palestine."[119] Hamas spokesman Ibrahim Ghawsha affirmed that "no one, whoever he may be, has the right to cede even a single inch of Palestinian territory." Ghawsha also articulated the Islamic view of the historical nature of the conflict — a conflict that would outlive the "new world order":

> We think the conflict between the Arabs and Jews, between the Muslims and the Jews, is a cultural conflict that will continue to rage throughout all time.... Algeria fought for 130 years. Even the Baltic states, which were occupied by the Soviets, have had their independence recognized by world states 45 years after they were occupied. The Palestine question is only 40 years old [sic], considering that it came into being in 1948. We are at the beginning of the road. Our adversary needs to be dealt with through a protracted and continuous confrontation.[120]

But if the Muslims lost faith, he warned, their loss of Palestine would become permanent. Islamists saw an irony in the Madrid setting of the conference, for Spain was a land that had once been part of Islam and then had been remade by conquest into a part of Christendom. As the same Hamas spokesman put it, Spain would yet witness the Arabs handing over of the keys of Jerusalem to Israeli Prime Minister

Yitzhak Shamir, just as Spain saw Muhammad Abu 'Abdallah (Boabdil) surrender the keys of Granada to the Christians in 1492.[121]

But what of the possibility that negotiations might produce an Israeli withdrawal from occupied Arab lands? Islamists prophesied that Israel would never budge. Hizballah's mentor, Fadlallah, declared the negotiations a ploy by which Israel would buy five years in order to absorb masses of new immigrants. "The maximum conceivable Israeli concession would be in regard to the Gaza Strip. I cannot imagine any concession being offered in regard to the West Bank."[122] Other Islamists went further, arguing that Israel actually had further plans for expansion. "More than ever before," claimed 'Abbas al-Musawi, "Israel is now stating most insolently and frankly that it wants the whole region from the Nile to the Euphrates."[123] According to a Palestinian Hamas statement, "America strives to convene a peace conference whose main objective is to liquidate the Palestine question and entrench the false existence of the Zionist entity by establishing the state of Greater Israel from the Nile to the Euphrates."[124]

Islamists appealed for unity to defeat this conspiracy. But it was unclear just how they would unite, and who would unite them.

THE TEHRAN CONFERENCE

In anticipation of the Madrid conference, a new call to Jihad was issued, this time from Tehran, not Baghdad. Islamic Iran set out to become the capital of Islamic steadfastness, mobilizing Muslim movements against the "sale" of sacred Palestine to the Jews. To this end, the Iranian Majlis convened an International Conference to Support the Islamic Revolution of the People of Palestine, which met in Tehran from 19–22 October. The event, timed to precede the Madrid conference by a week, drew over 400 participants from 45 countries. A similar conference for Palestine had been held in Tehran the previous year (see *MECS* 1990, p. 185). However, this new gathering drew far more attention, for it emerged as a counterconference to Madrid.

Iran's leaders clearly regarded the gathering as an event of the utmost importance. Majlis Speaker Mehdi Karrubi presided. The conference was addressed by Ayatollah Khamene'i, President Rafsanjani, Foreign Minister Velayati, Supreme Court President Ayatollah Muhammad Yazdi, Revolutionary Guard Commander in Chief Mohsen Reza'i, and the late Khomeyni's son Ahmad. Reports said that the Majlis appropriated $20m. for the conference, and that costs eventually reached $100m.[125]

The credibility of the conference depended on the extent of participation by Muslims from outside Iran, who fell into three categories. The first category included Iran's long-standing clients, most of them Shi'is. Arriving from Lebanon were Fadlallah; 'Abbas al-Musawi; Shaykh Sa'id Sha'ban, "emir" of the Iranian-backed Islamic Unification Movement in Tripoli; and Fathi al-Shiqaqi, leader of the branch of the Palestinian Islamic Jihad supported by Iran and based in Lebanon. Sayyid Muhammad Baqir al-Hakim, Tehran-based leader of the Iraqi Shi'i opposition, also attended, as did Kalim Siddiqui, the Pakistani director of the Muslim Institute in London, who had led the campaign against Rushdie in the UK. Participants in this first category added little to the weight of the conference, since they were already frequent fliers to Tehran.

The second category consisted of Islamists usually not in Iran's camp, whom Iran had persuaded to come to Tehran as an act of protest against Madrid. The most important of these protestors were representatives of the Muslim Brethren in Arab countries. Islamic Iran and the Muslim Brethren had drawn closer in 1990 against the background of the foreign deployment in Saudi Arabia. Leading Muslim Brethren from the Arab world had joined a delegation to Tehran and had participated in a previous Tehran conference on Palestine (see *MECS* 1990, p. 185). The advance of the peace process after the Gulf War brought them still closer together. Jordanian delegates were 'Abd al-Rahman Khalifa, general supervisor of the Muslim Brethren, and 'Abd al-Latif 'Arabiyyat, the Islamic speaker of the Jordanian parliament. Lesser representatives of the Egyptian Muslim Brethren, and its parliamentary ally, the Socialist Labor Party, as well as of the Palestinian Hamas, also attended. Burhan al-Din Rabbani, leader of the Afghan *Jami'at-e Islami* (the Sunni Afghan Mujahidin faction that overran Kabul in April 1992), also participated. Also present was the Sudanese government minister charged with Islamizing his country's culture, 'Abdallah Muhammad Ahmad. The presence of participants in this second category added Islamic credibility to the conference, since they could not be portrayed as clients of Iran.

The third category consisted of representatives of the PLO, Syria and Algeria which had joined the American peace initiative but which sent delegations to Tehran in order to deflect the heat of the conference resolutions. The PLO was represented by Shaykh 'Abd al-Hamid al-Sa'ih, chairman of the PNC, whose task was to defend the PLO decision to sanction a Palestinian delegation at Madrid and prevent any challenge by Hamas to the PLO's representative standing. 'Abd al-'Aziz Belkhadem, speaker of the Algerian parliament and a leader of the ruling party, represented official Algeria and was there to prevent a shift of Iranian support away from the Algerian regime and toward its Islamic opposition. Syria sent an official delegation whose mission was to assure that the conference resolutions did not denounce the states participating in the Madrid conference by name and, in particular, that no criticism be leveled at Syria. In order to accommodate these delegations, Iran convened the conference with the formal purpose of supporting the Intifada, not of denouncing Madrid. Algeria's Belkhadem was thus able to state: "The Tehran conference is not related to the Middle East peace conference. I came here to express support for the Palestinian Intifada."[126]

The rest of the conferees comprised a grab bag: in an effort to pack the conference, Iran welcomed all. Oddities included Walid Junblat, chief of Lebanon's Druze community, who, although hardly an Islamic zealot, had drawn closer to Hizballah and its Iranian sponsors for tactical reasons. Also in attendance was Shaykh As'ad Bayyud al-Tamimi, the octogenarian leader of the Bayt al-Maqdis faction of the Palestinian Islamic Jihad, who had hailed Saddam Husayn as caliph earlier in the year, but was veering to another extreme in his search for a hero who would liberate some part of Palestine.

In one respect, the proceedings of the Tehran conference were wholly predictable. Speaker after speaker rejected the very existence of Israel and condemned the US for its attempts to impose the Jewish state upon Islam. Velayati called Madrid "a ridiculous show." To his mind, the only solution lay in the "elimination" of the "Zionist regime" and the return of Palestine to the Muslims.[127] 'Ali Akbar Mohtashemi, former Iranian ambassador to Syria and godfather of Hizballah, went so far as to declare that the Madrid participants "may be killed with impunity."[128]

Yet the Tehran conference could not conceal the differences among its own participants over Madrid. This produced some acrimonious exchanges. "Hasn't the PLO ganged up with Zionists today?" asked Ahmad Khomeyni in the presence of the PLO delegation under Shaykh al-Sa'ih. "Hasn't 'Arafat joined hands with Bush today?"[129] A Hamas representative informed the conference that the PLO did not represent all the Palestinian people, and that those Palestinians slated to appear at Madrid were "merchants, seeking cheap publicity."[130] In a heated exchange, Shaykh Husayn Ghabris, a Lebanese cleric, demanded that Shaykh al-Sa'ih resign from the presidency of the PNC in protest against the decision to go to Madrid.[131] Sa'ih countered by pointing out that the Palestinian people themselves, through the PNC, had opted for participation in the Madrid conference.[132]

Syria's decision to participate in the Madrid conference also struck a discordant note, although the discord was confined to the media. According to the Syrian media, Iranian Foreign Minister Velayati met with members of the Syrian delegation to the Tehran conference and expressed his "appreciation" for Syria's position on Madrid (a position in favor of participation),[133] but according to Iran's media, Veyalati told the Syrians that Madrid "serves solely the interests of the Zionist regime."[134] Whatever the truth, however, no one took Syria to task in the conference itself, even though its decision did not differ in essence from the PLO's.

The final 28-point declaration of the conference called "the Zionist regime" a "fictitious and illegitimate entity" which would have to be "eliminated" through "all-out Jihad." The declaration called for the creation of an Islamic fund to support the Intifada and an Islamic army to liberate Palestine, and urged Islamists in parliaments everywhere to form parliamentary committees for the same purpose.[135] Yet the declaration did not specifically denounce any state for its participation in the Madrid conference, or the PLO for allowing the participation of West Bank and Gazan Palestinians. Despite its strident tone, the final declaration represented a compromise, demonstrating the obstacles to the formation of any alliance against the US initiative. Nevertheless, the conference did initiate Iran's effort to bring opponents and skeptics of the peace process into some alignment — and into Tehran's own orbit.

The next step involved the transformation of the Tehran conference into a permanent organization. The participants urged the creation of a permanent secretariat that would work to implement the resolutions of the conference.[136] At the end of the deliberations, Majlis deputy 'Abd al-Vahid Musavi Lari was elected to head this secretariat, which was to have its headquarters in Tehran and branches throughout the world.[137] Mohtashemi, in his customarily strident tone, declared that the creation of an Islamic army would also be implemented. "This is not mere talk," he announced. "This enormous potential exists and the Iranians are prepared for sacrifice and Jihad, whether in an organized war and a regular army or through qualitative suicide operations all over the world, not just in Palestine, but against the Zionists throughout the world."[138]

The Tehran conference demonstrated the double nature of Iran's policy. Iran professed neutrality during the Gulf War, worked to improve its relations with the Arab clients of the US, and secured the release of the last American and British hostages — policies that served the national interest. Yet Iran also raised the slogan of Islam as a world power, bolstered Hizballah in Lebanon, and appealed to a wide spectrum of radical groups to assault the US-brokered peace process — policies that asserted the primacy of Islam. By raising dualism to an art, Iran was able to win world praise for its moderation even as it preached Jihad.

ISLAMIC SUMMIT IN DAKAR

By the end of the year, the new world order in the ME looked suspiciously like the old one. No one had paid the ultimate price of political error. Saddam Husayn remained secure behind his praetorian guards, and the emir of Kuwait returned to his palaces. No new borders were drawn, no territory changed hands. Political scientists launched massive projects to scour the ME for seeds of democracy, without any notable success. The ME remained bound up in the old contest between authoritarian states and authoritarian oppositions — a contest conducted largely in the political language of Islam.

The states had long since forged a collective instrument for this purpose: the ICO's triennial summit conferences. These were rituals of solidarity meant to persuade Muslim peoples and the world that Islam was moving toward unity. The summits were intended to show Muslim heads of state bent over one planning table and shoulder-to-shoulder in prayer. But in the divided state of Islam, even this ritual became difficult to carry off. The ICO convened its sixth summit conference in Dakar, Senegal, from 9–12 December, but half the players never appeared.

THE ABSENT ARABS

The first ICO summit ever set in Africa had been scheduled for the fateful month of January 1991, which meant that it had to be postponed. But ICO Secretary-General Hamid Algabid was not willing to postpone it indefinitely, even if the Gulf War wounds had not healed. The ICO's charter called for triennial summit conferences. It was preferable to risk the embarrassment of a divided conference than the ridicule of repeated postponement. Furthermore, the African Muslim states put great store in the selection of Dakar. Even if the Arab states could not agree, could they not set aside their differences to demonstrate Afro-Arab solidarity in Islam? Saudi Arabia had already assisted Senegalese President Abdou Diouf with more than $130m. for the construction of an appropriate summit facility and adjoining hotel named after Saudi King Fahd.

But King Fahd did not come. Neither did Husni Mubarak of Egypt, Hafiz al-Asad of Syria, Mu'ammar al-Qadhdhafi of Libya, Zayn al-'Abidin Ben 'Ali of Tunisia or Hasan II of Morocco. Only six of the 21 Arab heads of state attended. The absences arose from the lingering resentments of the Gulf War, and in particular from the presence at the summit of PLO Chairman Yasir 'Arafat. The absent Arab heads of state had not yet forgiven him for romancing Saddam Husayn, and especially did not wish to be trapped by 'Arafat in an unwanted bear hug before cameras. So they sent their foreign ministers to the Dakar summit in their stead. Senegalese host Abdou Diouf pronounced himself "very disappointed" at the absence of Arab heads of state, since African members of the ICO would see this as "concerted policy by Arab states, no matter what good or bad reasons they gave for their absence." According to Abdou Diouf, "we respect the Arabs more than they respect us, and this sixth summit of the ICO is an example."[139]

Without the full battery of heads of state, the summit could not fulfill its ritual function as a display of unity. Nevertheless, the absent leaders had no intention of turning over the proceedings to the likes of 'Arafat, and their foreign ministers worked to assure the constancy of the ICO position on war against Iraq and peace with Israel. It was a foregone conclusion that Saudi Arabia would push through a resolution for continued sanctions against Iraq, and that Iraq would boycott the summit. The Saudis in particular bore their grudge openly. The Saudi Crown Prince 'Abdallah Ibn 'Abd al-'Aziz pointedly shook 'Arafat's hand instead of embracing him, a gesture intended as a rebuke,[140] and exchanged sharp words with King Husayn over Jordan's stand in the Gulf crisis.[141]

ZIONISM AND JIHAD

The settling of Gulf scores notwithstanding, the conference quickly moved on to the Arab-Israeli peace process, which was restored to the top of the Islamic agenda. Nothing the summit could decide would have the least effect on the outcome of that process, but the debates indicated just how divided the ICO's membership remained. Two issues figured prominently in the deliberations. First, should the summit endorse or repudiate the initiative for the repeal of the 1975 UN General Assembly resolution equating Zionism with racism?[142] Second, should the Dakar summit reiterate or repudiate the declaration and resolutions of the 1981 Mecca summit, which first pledged Jihad for the liberation of Jerusalem? (On the ICO and Jihad, see *MECS* 1980–81, pp. 124, 128–29.)

On the issue of "Zionism is racism," Syria, Iran and the PLO joined together to denounce the attempt to repeal the 1975 resolution, while Egypt and Jordan took a contrary position. In the end, the summit decided to oppose attempts to annul the resolution "until the reasons for its adoption disappear." According to Bangladesh's foreign minister, this decision would not harm the Arab-Israeli peace process: "We would like to see peace first and then anything can be withdrawn. Now the timing is not right. It could come later."[143] In the event, the reaffirmation of the UN resolution did not prevent 10 ICO members from abstaining from the vote of repeal in the UN General Assembly in New York a few days later.

However, 'Arafat pushed too hard when he asked the Dakar summit to reiterate the pledge of the 1981 Mecca summit, calling for Jihad for the liberation of Jerusalem. Apparently, he had decided to make an issue of the Jihad pledge in order to outflank his own Islamic opposition at home. But a great deal had changed over the previous decade. During those years, Jihad had been invoked too often as a justification for assassination and abduction of both Muslims and Westerners by a wide array of Muslim extremists. Spin control of a Jihad pledge would be more difficult than it once had been. Furthermore, in a world moving toward the dream of global peace, a Jihad pledge would strike Western public opinion as anachronistic, even primitive. Lastly, most members of the ICO supported the Arab-Israeli peace process, a point that would be difficult to reconcile with a Jihad appeal.

The Senegalese successfully carried the flag against 'Arafat's proposal. "The political situation has changed," declared Senegal's Foreign Minister Djibo Ka. "The ICO summit encourages the current Middle East peace process on the basis of the exchange of land for peace."[144] Turkish Foreign Minister Hikmet Çetin believed it would be "inconsistent to talk about a Jihad to resolve the Middle East problem when the

Middle East peace process has already started."[145] 'Arafat expressed indignation. He could do without money or weapons, so he claimed, "but don't take away the Jihad. Leave us the word." He reminded the summit that "you publicly committed yourselves at the Mecca summit in 1981 to continuing the Jihad for liberating holy Jerusalem and the occupied territories. I am astonished now that you have abandoned this commitment."[146] When Abdou Diouf kept him off the floor during the last debate on the subject, 'Arafat stormed out of the conference. But this was all smoke and mirrors in order to indulge the Palestinian audience at home. In his summit speech, 'Arafat called the negotiations with Israel "an historic and important occasion which should not be countered by complications or provocations."[147] In the end, the conference statement did not mention Jihad. Instead it hailed the Arab-Israeli peace process and called for a "just and global peace on the basis of UN Security Council Resolutions 242 and 338 and the land-for-peace formula."[148]

In the absence of so many Arab heads of state, many of those who did attend decided to quit early, including King Husayn, who was disappointed that he could not meet with leaders he had wanted to see, and Algeria's Chedli Benjedid, who did not even deliver his speech but had it handed out after his premature departure. Reviewing the summit, *The Economist* opined that "the ICO may be ready to join the non-aligned movement and the Group of 77 in the junkyard of history."[149]

IRAN'S SUMMIT BLITZ

Still, the ICO made a striking new convert at Dakar: the Islamic Republic of Iran. Neither the Shah nor Khomeyni had put much store in the ICO, which they had both regarded as a pliant tool of their Saudi rivals. No Iranian delegation at any level had attended any of the previous three ICO summit conferences held since Iran's revolution. But President Rafsanjani thought it possible to use ICO summitry to promote his vision of Islam as an emerging world power.

Rafsanjani therefore took the bold step of attending the Dakar summit as head of state. In the absence of many Arab leaders, he cut the largest figure on the scene, conducting a dizzying series of bilateral meetings, including one with Saudi Crown Prince 'Abdallah, the highest-level contact between Iran and Saudi Arabia since 1979. The Iranian media gave extensive and positive coverage to his doings, portraying him as a wise statesman in the midst of quarreling and petty Arabs. Iran's attitude to ICO summitry now swung to the other extreme, and Foreign Minister Velayati announced Tehran's desire to host the seventh summit of the ICO, scheduled for 1994. Indeed, argued Velayati, this was Iran's "right," since it had never hosted either a foreign ministers' or a summit conference of the ICO.[150] The Saudis, however, perhaps not quite convinced that Iran could be trusted, claimed the right to host the next summit: Rafsanjani would first have to pray in Mecca as the guest of King Fahd. But it was agreed that Iran would host the eighth summit, scheduled for 1997.[151]

Regarding the Arab-Israeli peace process, there could be no doubt about Iran's preference. Rafsanjani favored a pledge of Jihad for Jerusalem, and Iran expressed "strong reservations" concerning the summit resolution endorsing the peace process.[152] But these reservations were not accompanied by attacks on the ICO itself. Iran even sponsored a new ICO member: Rafsanjani flew into Dakar with an official delegation from newly independent Azerbaijan, which promptly applied for membership. Rafsanjani had executed a remarkable turnabout on the ICO, comparable to the swing in Iran's pilgrimage policy. The ultimate objective was to share in the control of the ICO and ultimately to turn it around.

In the meantime, however, Saudi Arabia still set the agenda of the ICO's secretariat. At the Dakar summit, Saudi Arabia announced a donation of $10m. toward the activities of the secretariat,[153] which was enough to keep Secretary-General Algabid flying, although the organization's membership arrears totaled $59m.[154] Saudi Arabia also tried to soothe the hurt pride of the African Muslim members, waiving $310m. in debts owed by eight African members of the ICO.[155] The summit also passed a resolution calling for (Western) compensation to African countries that were stripped of their assets by (Western) colonialism. (A similar resolution had been passed at an Organization of African Unity summit in Nigeria, but it had also asked compensation for the slave trade. The ICO resolution omitted all reference to compensation for slave trading, presumably because this could have been read as obligating Arab Muslims to bear a share of such compensation as well.)[156]

It was far too early to tell whether the Dakar summit signaled a subtle shift in the internal balance of Islam. However, Iran's bid did suggest that the ICO — "a pallid creature," in the words of *The Economist,* "without much sense of purpose"[157] — stood to become hotly contested ground, and that Saudi Arabia would need to strive still harder to keep the consensus of Muslim states in its orbit.

In fact, all the Muslim states would have to strive still harder to retain their control of Islam. Away from the conference halls, Islam had become more vital than at any time in recent history. The Islamists increasingly challenged the establishment Islam of governments and put forward a rival vision of a solution to the ills that afflicted Muslim peoples. It was a very different vision of a world order, predicated on perpetual struggle. Ahmad Khomeyni, son of the man who had started it all, encapsulated the vision in one sentence: "After the fall of Marxism, Islam replaced it, and as long as Islam exists, US hostility exists, and as long as US hostility exists, the struggle exists."[158]

On 26 December, the FIS in Algeria shocked the world and thrilled Islamists by scoring an overwhelming electoral victory against the ruling party. Although the victory was to be nullified two weeks later by a military coup, the electoral results signaled the daunting breadth of Muslim resentment born on a wave of poverty and youth. Many more Muslim voices now shouted the slogans of unity — but not in unison.

NOTES

For the place and frequency of publications cited here, and for the full name of the publication, news agency, radio station or monitoring service where an abbreviation is used, please see "List of Sources." Only in the case of more than one publication bearing the same name is the place of publication noted here.

1. See also James Piscatori (ed.), *Islamic Fundamentalisms and the Gulf Crisis* (Chicago: American Academy of Arts and Sciences, 1991), and especially Piscatori's introductory essay, "Religion and Realpolitik: Islamic Responses to the Gulf War," pp. 1–27.
2. AFP, 10 January — DR, 11 January 1991.
3. Saddam's speech, R. Baghdad, VoM, 11 January — DR, 14 January 1991.
4. R. Baghdad, 11 January — DR, 14 January 1991.

5. SPA, 11 January — DR, 14 January; *AAI,* 14 January; al-Tadamun al-Islami, Sha'ban 1411 (February 1991); *al-Rabita,* March 1991.
6. INA, 8 January — DR, 8 January 1991.
7. SPA, 11 January — DR, 11 January 1991.
8. *AAI,* 4 February 1991.
9. IRNA, 9 January — DR, 10 January; *MEI,* 11 January 1991.
10. Interview with Algabid, *al-'Alam,* 22 June 1991.
11. Text of final statement of the Cairo meeting, Egyptian Space Channel, 21 February — DR, 22 February 1991.
12. KUNA, 3 April — DR, 5 April 1991.
13. SWB, 21 January 1991.
14. *Al-Ra'y* (Amman), 23 January — DR, 25 January 1991.
15. AFP, 21 January — DR, 22 January; cf. *The Star,* 24–30 January; Tamimi's interview, *Kull al-'Arab,* 21 January 1991.
16. *Al-Ra'y* (Amman), 22 January 1991.
17. *Al-Afkar,* 1 April 1991.
18. See also Hugh Roberts, "A Trial of Strength: Algerian Islamism," in Piscatori, pp. 131–54.
19. See also Beverly Milton-Edwards, "A Temporary Alliance With the Crown: The Islamic Response in Jordan," ibid., pp. 88–108.
20. *JT,* 13 March 1991.
21. Ramadan address by Sha'rawi, *Kull al-Nas,* April 1991.
22. *Al-'Alam* (London), 26 January 1991.
23. Interview with Hudaybi, *al-Musawwar,* 1 February 1991.
24. See also Gehad Auda, "An Uncertain Response: The Islamic Movement in Egypt," in Piscatori, pp. 109–30.
25. Hamas communiqué, 22 January, *Filastin al-Muslima,* February 1991.
26. Interview with Quqa, *al-'Alam* (London), 26 January 1991.
27. *Sawt al-Sha'b* (Amman), 7 March — DR, 19 March; *al-Dustur* (Amman), 26 March — DR, 27 March 1991. See also Jean-François Legrain, "A Defining Moment: Palestinian Islamic Fundamentalism," in Piscatori, pp. 70–87.
28. E.g., interview with Ibrahim Ghawsha of Hamas, *Filastin al-Muslima,* May 1991.
29. Statement by Abu al-Nasr, *al-Mukhtar al-Islami,* June 1991.
30. Interview with Hudaybi, ibid., August 1991.
31. Interview with Dr. Ahmad al-Mallat, *al-Hilal al-Duwali,* 1 September 1991.
32. *Al-Qadisiyya,* 25 August — DR, 29 August 1991.
33. *Al-Jumhuriyya* (Baghdad), 28 October 1991.
34. R. Riyadh, 26 March — DR, 27 March 1991.
35. R. Algiers, 30 March — DR, 9 April 1991.
36. *ME,* September 1991.
37. *NYT,* 1 March 1992.
38. *Dawn,* 19 February — DR, 21 February 1991.
39. *Al-Jazira al-'Arabiyya,* November 1991.
40. Interview with Nasif, *al-Liwa al-Islami,* 29 August 1991.
41. *Al-Liwa al-Islami,* 25 April 1991.
42. The first conference met in Cairo in 1988 and dealt with the problems of youth. The second conference met in Baghdad in 1989 to discuss the question of peace in Islam. The third conference met in Cairo in 1990 to consider ways to promote cooperation among Muslims.
43. Accounts of the conference, *al-Liwa al-Islami,* 25 April; *Akhir Sa'a,* 1 May; *al-Tasawwuf al-Islami,* June 1991.
44. Text of the resolutions, MENA, 27 April — DR, 29 April; *al-Umma al-Islamiyya,* June; *al-Rabita,* June 1991.
45. *MEI,* 16 August 1991.
46. INA, 4 December — DR, 4 December 1991.
47. JNA, 8 August — DR, 9 August 1991.
48. *FR,* 11 April 1991.
49. *JT,* 4–5 April 1991.
50. *L'Express,* 22 March 1991.

51. *FR,* 11 April 1991.
52. See Martin Kramer, "The Prospects of Islamic Revival," *The Middle East in the Aftermath of the Gulf War: Précis of a Colloquium* (Tel Aviv: Tel Aviv University, 1992), p. 26.
53. *The Economist,* 4–10 April 1992.
54. According to one source, representatives of the major Islamist movements met in Lahore, Pakistan, in mid-February, following Iraq's announcement that it would withdraw from Kuwait. The gathering, convened by Qazi Husayn Ahmad, president of Pakistan's Jama'ate Islami, included representatives from the Egyptian, Jordanian, and Syrian Muslim Brethren, the National Islamic Front in Sudan, al-Nahda Party in Tunisia, the Palestinian Hamas, and the Afghan Mujahidin factions led by Gulbuddin Hikmatyar, Burhanuddin Rabbani, and 'Abd Rabb al-Rasul Sayyaf. They pledged themselves to the "complete liberation" of Palestine, victory for the Afghan Mujahidin, and support for Kashmiri self-determination. They also denounced the existing borders between states as legacies of imperialism. *Al-Mukhtar al-Islami,* April 1991.
55. Turabi's speech, *al-Islam wa-Filastin,* 28 June 1991.
56. Summaries of resolutions, *al-Inqadh al-Watani,* 29 April; *al-Da'wa al-Islamiyya,* 8 May 1991.
57. *MEI,* 1 May 1992.
58. *Le Monde,* 12 July 1991.
59. Interview with Hudaybi, *al-Mukhtar al-Islami,* August 1991.
60. *MEI,* 20 March 1992, quoting Turabi's interview in *al-Quds al-'Arabi.*
61. Report of Turabi's lecture in London, *MEI,* 1 May 1992.
62. For the background of that relationship, see John O. Voll, "Islamization in the Sudan and the Iranian Revolution," in John L. Esposito (ed.), *The Iranian Revolution: Its Global Impact* (Miami: Florida International University Press, 1990), pp. 283–301.
63. *Al-Wafd,* 2 June 1991; *MEI,* 20 March 1992.
64. R. SPLA, 11 April — DR, 16 April 1991. Ghannushi later announced he had returned his Sudanese passport; the Tunisian authorities then claimed he had begun to travel on an Iranian diplomatic passport.
65. *MEI,* 20 March 1992, quoting Turabi's interview in *al-Quds al-'Arabi.*
66. *MEI,* 7 February 1992.
67. *NYT,* 26 January 1992.
68. Ibid.
69. Interview with Zahhar, *Ha'aretz,* 23 August — DR, 27 August 1991.
70. See also Said Amir Arjomand, "A Victory for the Pragmatists: The Islamic Fundamentalist Reaction in Iran," in Piscatori, pp. 52–69.
71. *Jerusalem Report,* 6 June 1991.
72. *Kayhan* (Tehran), 3 March — DR, 13 March; IRNA, 3 March — DR, 4 March 1991.
73. Rafsanjani's interview, *Der Speigel,* translated in *Ha'aretz,* 1 April 1991.
74. See also Amatzia Baram, "From Radicalism to Radical Pragmatism: The Shi'ite Fundamentalist Opposition Movements of Iraq," in Piscatori, pp. 28–51.
75. Interview with 'Abbas al-Musawi, *Kayhan* (Tehran), 18 December 1990 — DR, 2 January 1991.
76. *JI,* 3 July 1991.
77. Ibid., 9 December — DR, 16 December 1991.
78. *Abrar,* 25 April — DR, 17 May 1991.
79. *IHT,* 13 December 1991.
80. IRNA, 5 March — DR, 14 March; *al-Hilal al-Duwali,* 4 April 1991. The sponsor was the 15th of Khordad Foundation.
81. *IHT,* 13 July 1991.
82. Official quoted by Leslie Gelb, *NYT,* 29 December 1991.
83. Paul Theroux in *NYT,* 13 February 1992.
84. For the dynamics of this intra-Shi'i struggle, see Martin Kramer, "Sacrifice and Fratricide in Shiite Lebanon," in M. Juergensmeyer (ed.), *Violence and the Sacred in the Modern World* (London: Cass, 1992).
85. See Martin Kramer, "Hizbullah: The Calculus of Jihad," in M. Marty and R. S. Appleby (eds.), *Fundamentalisms and the State: Remaking Polities, Militance, and Economies*

(Chicago: Chicago University Press, 1992), The Fundamentalism Project, Vol. 3, pp. 539–56.

86. Text of Islamic Jihad letter, *NYT,* 13 August 1991.
87. Background articles on the releases in *FR,* 13 June, 22 August; *NYT,* 9, 18 August, 13 September, 21 October; *Ha'aretz,* 9 August; *Monday Morning,* 9 December; *ME,* September, November 1991, January 1992. See also Jim Muir's reportage in *MEI* during this period.
88. Voice of the Oppressed, 16 August — DR, 16 August 1991.
89. Interview with Fadlallah, *Monday Morning,* 13 May 1991.
90. Interview with Hizballah Secretary-General Subhi al-Tufayli, ibid., 22 April 1991.
91. Ibid.
92. Interview with 'Abbas al-Musawi, *al-Hayat* (London), 18 July — DR, 23 July 1991.
93. Interview with Tufayli, op. cit. Later in the year there were reports that Iran had informed the Lebanese Government of its intention to withdraw the contingent in stages; *MEI,* 25 October 1991.
94. Interview with Tufayli, op. cit.
95. Interview with Fadlallah, op. cit.
96. Interview with Husayn al-Musawi, *KI,* 22 December 1990 — DR, 4 January 1991.
97. Voice of the Oppressed, 12 December — DR, 12 December 1991.
98. Interview with Tufayli, op. cit.
99. On Musawi's career, see Martin Kramer, "Musawi's Game," *New Republic,* 23 March 1992.
100. For comprehensive accounts of Hizballah's offensive, see *JP,* 2 August; *FR,* 5 December 1991.
101. *NYT Magazine,* 26 January 1992.
102. For general assessments of the 1991 pilgrimage, see *ME,* May; *al-'Alam* (London), 8 June; *Le Monde,* 22 June; *MEI,* 28 June; *Iran Focus,* July–August 1991.
103. AFP, 11 February — DR, 12 February 1991.
104. *Al-'Alam* (London), 11 May 1991.
105. *NYT,* 10 February 1991.
106. Letter of appointment, R. Tehran, 6 April — DR, 8 April. He replaced Mehdi Karrubi, who had been Khomeyni's representative to the 1987 pilgrimage; *al-'Alam* (London), 20 April 1991.
107. R. Tehran, 8 April — DR, 9 April 1991.
108. Letter of resignation, R. Tehran, 14 April — DR, 16 April; *MEI,* 19 April 1991.
109. Letter of appointment, R. Tehran, 26 April — DR, 29 April 1991.
110. Velayati and Reyshahri gave an account of these negotiations on Tehran TV, 20 July — DR, 24 July 1991.
111. *Al-'Alam* (London), 8 June 1991.
112. Text of Khamene'i message, R. Tehran, 19, 20 June — DR, 20, 21 June 1991.
113. IRNA, 29 June — DR, 1 July 1991.
114. IRNA, 9 May — DR, 10 May; R. Tehran, 9 July — DR, 10 July 1991.
115. Iran boycotted the pilgrimage in 1927 and in 1944–47 in light of Saudi treatment of Shi'i holy sites and Iranian pilgrims. For the previous cycles and their contexts, see Martin Kramer, "Khomeini's Messengers: The Disputed Pilgrimage of Islam," in E. Sivan and M. Friedman (eds.), *Religious Radicalism and Politics in the Middle East* (Albany: SUNY Press, 1990), pp. 174–97.
116. INA, 10 June — DR, 10 June 1991.
117. *NYT,* 14 June 1991.
118. *Al-Ribat,* 30 April 1991.
119. Voice of the Oppressed, 31 October — DR, 31 October 1991. Peace could only be achieved, said a Hizballah statement on the eve of the Madrid conference, "by eliminating Israel from existence and liberating all the territories of usurped Palestine." Voice of the Oppressed, 29 October — DR, 29 October 1991.
120. Ghawsha's interview, R. Monte Carlo, 31 October — DR, 1 November 1991.
121. Ibrahim Ghawsha, quoted in *Filastin al-Muslima,* November 1991.
122. Interview with Fadlallah, *Monday Morning,* 19 August 1991.

123. Interview with 'Abbas al-Musawi, *al-Hayat* (Cairo), 18 July — DR, 23 July 1991.
124 Hamas statement of 23 September, *al-Ra'y* (Amman), 24 September — DR, 25 September 1991.
125. *MEI*, 25 October, 8 November 1991. Both accounts suggested that Rafsanjani disapproved of the initiative to hold the conference.
126. Belkhadem's interview, *Ettela'at*, 23 October — DR, 8 November 1991.
127. IRNA, 21 October — DR, 23 October 1991.
128. Ibid., 30 October — DR, 31 October 1991. The remarks were not made during the Tehran conference, but immediately afterward.
129. Ibid., 20 October — DR, 21 October 1991.
130. Ibid., 21 October — DR, 23 October 1991.
131. *Al-Ahram al-Duwali*, 21 October 1991.
132. Sa'ih's remarks, ibid., *al-Ra'y* (Amman), *al-Dustur* (Amman), 22 October 1991.
133. R. Damascus, 22 October — DR, 23 October 1991.
134. IRNA, 22 October — DR, 23 October 1991.
135. Conference declaration, Voice of the Islamic Republic of Iran, 22 October — DR, 23 October; *JI*, 23 October; *al-Hilal al-Duwali*, 16 November; *Filastin al-Muslima*, November 1991.
136. Conference declaration, R. Tehran in English, 22 October — DR, 23 October 1991.
137. IRNA, 23 October — DR, 24 October 1991.
138. Interview with Mohtashemi, *al-Diyar*, 28 October — DR, 19 November 1991.
139. Interview with Abdou Diouf, *Le Monde*, 10 December 1991.
140. AFP, 12 December — DR, 12 December 1991.
141. R. Cairo, 11 December — DR, 11 December 1991.
142. See Bernard Lewis, "The Anti-Zionist Resolution," *Foreign Affairs*, Vol. 55 (October 1976), pp. 54–64.
143. AFP, 8 December — DR, 9 December 1991.
144. Ibid., 12 December — DR, 12 December 1991.
145. Interview with Çetin, TRT TV, Ankara, 12 December — DR, 13 December 1991.
146. Algiers TV, 12 December — SWB, 14 December 1991.
147. 'Arafat's speech, VoP (Algiers), 11 December — DR, 12 December; AFP, 10 December — DR, 11 December 1991.
148. MAP, 12 December — DR, 12 December 1991.
149. *The Economist*, 3 January 1992.
150. IRNA, 6 December — DR, 9 December 1991.
151. SPA, 6 January 1992.
152. IRIB TV, 12 December — DR, 13 December; interview with Velayati, R. Tehran, 12 December — SWB, 14 December 1991.
153. Speech by Prince 'Abdallah Ibn 'Abd al-'Aziz, SPA, 10 December — DR, 13 December 1991.
154. AFP, 10 December — DR, 11 December 1991.
155. SPA, 11 December — DR, 13 December 1991.
156. BBC World Service, 11 December — DR, 13 December 1991. For the origins of Arab apprehension on this score, see Bernard Lewis, *Race and Slavery in the Middle East* (New York: Oxford University Press, 1990).
157. *The Economist*, 3 January 1992.
158. Khomeyni's speech, 20 October — DR, 21 October 1991.

PALESTINIAN ISSUES

The Palestine Liberation Organization

JOSHUA TEITELBAUM

The PLO went through difficult times in 1991, as it tried to recover from the political and financial isolation it encountered as a result of its support for Iraq in the Gulf War. After the war, it endeavored to recover its considerable influence on the Palestinian component of the peace process, even as the US and the Gulf countries tried to limit it. With the PLO weakened, the leadership in the West Bank and Gaza Strip insisted on going ahead with the peace talks, even though the PLO was not directly represented. The political setbacks suffered by the PLO, combined with unhampered Jewish immigration to Israel, may have convinced the organization's leadership to conclude that time was no longer working in its favor. It had lost the veto over Palestinian action, even if temporarily, and the only realistic course of action, however painful, was to go along. The organization therefore gave its reluctant consent for participation in the Madrid peace talks, based on a decision of the 20th session of the 'Arafat-dominated Palestine National Council (PNC), which convened in Algiers in September.

'Arafat's support of Iraq during the war produced some serious disagreements in Fath, but no serious challenge. After several years of internal dissent, the Democratic Front for the Liberation of Palestine (DFLP) finally split into two factions, one headed by Na'if Hawatima and the other by Nasir 'Abd Rabbuh. In Lebanon, the deployment of the PLO was significantly constricted to refugee camps around Sidon and Tyre, following the Lebanese Army's Syrian-backed deployment in the south. Finally, as if these were not enough, the PLO leadership made the tactical error of practically endorsing the abortive coup in the Soviet Union in August,[1] a step which raised serious doubts in the West concerning the organization's support for the emerging post-Cold War alignments.

RIDING OUT THE STORM: THE PLO AND THE GULF WAR

As the year opened, the biggest challenge facing the PLO was the impending war between the US-led coalition and Iraq. The organization had firmly established itself on the side of Iraq after the invasion of August 1990 (see *MECS* 1990, pp. 222–26), and continued frantically until the last minute to use diplomacy to prevent a war, believing that conflict in the Arab world rarely served the Palestinian cause. As the dust settled after the war, the PLO and the Palestinians paid a high price for the organization's stance. Isolated politically, there was internal dissent over the PLO's position, and Fath Central Committee member Salah Khalaf (Abu Iyyad), who opposed Iraq, was assassinated; the Palestinians in Kuwait suffered the revenge of the returning Kuwaitis; and the PLO suffered financially due to severe limitations on funding by the wealthy Gulf states which had opposed Iraq.

PLO Chairman Yasir 'Arafat engaged in last-minute diplomacy to head off a war between the US and Iraq, visiting Baghdad in early January. He continued to insist that the UN Security Council link a solution to the conflict with Iraq to the Palestine issue.[2] By linking the two, 'Arafat hoped to stifle internal criticism that his position undermined the Palestinians' own claim to support withdrawal from the occupied territories (see below). While it had no hope of succeeding, the linkage strategy, aimed at convening an "international conference of peace in the Gulf and Palestine"[3] gave the political cover deemed necessary for a position that was essentially based on visceral support for a militant Arab country, a sworn enemy of the PLO's enemy, Israel. He supported Iraqi President Saddam Husayn's initiative of 15 February to end the war, saying that its purpose was to "tell the allies that if they want to have O-I-L, then they have to also take P-L-O."[4] On 7 January, 'Arafat addressed a rally in Baghdad and challenged the US that if it wanted war, "then I say welcome, welcome, welcome to war....Iraq and Palestine" would be "together, side by side," he added.[5]

On the day hostilities broke out, the PLO Executive Committee condemned the "aggressive US war," and repeated the theme of the double standard (see *MECS* 1990, p. 225), that the US supported UN resolutions against Iraq, but not against Israel. In view of the danger to the Arabs, the statement added, "we and the Arab nation — armies, masses, and regimes — have no option but to exercise our right to self-defense. We...are being subjected to aggression, and an Arab capital — the capital of [Harun] al-Rashid...is being attacked...."[6] The war was "the mother of all battles for the sake of the mother of causes: our beloved Palestine."[7]

Responding to popular opinion in the Palestinian street, the PLO began plans to attack Israel from Lebanon. Iraq would not be alone in its attacks on Israel. On 16 January, it called a general mobilization.[8] The PLO Executive Committee issued a statement on 29 January which called on "all the peoples of our nation and its dynamic forces to participate in the battle of confronting American and allied aggression...."[9] Rockets were fired on Israel on the same day, in what was described by reporters as the biggest barrage in eight years. A PLO spokesman in Sidon said that the rocket attack was in "defense of Iraq and its people."[10] However, the PLO issued a denial of responsibility for the attack, and 'Arafat was reported to have reprimanded his representative in Lebanon, Zayd Wahba, for his warlike pronouncements.[11] Wahba had said that "we now have an open-war border with Israel. This is Saddam Husayn's northern front."[12] Despite the PLO denial, its 29 January call to arms, the statement's proximity to the attacks, and the assumption that Wahba would not have acted and spoken without authorization from 'Arafat, all led to the conclusion that the PLO was responsible. Israel retaliated immediately against the PLO in Lebanon. The PLO's attack on Israel from Lebanon during the war was to be one of the last straws in Lebanese and Syrian efforts to severely curtail Palestinian activity in the south (see below).

To further justify support of Iraq, and perhaps also to put cracks in the allied coalition, the PLO leadership was reduced to contending that Israel was directly involved in the fighting. The Executive Committee member from the DFLP, Yasir 'Abd Rabbuh, claimed that Israeli planes were taking off from Turkey to attack Iraq; 'Arafat repeated this claim, and added that he had "information" that Israel had fired missiles from the Negev at western Iraq.[13]

Muhammad Jihad, Fath Central Committee member, tried to justify the PLO's support of Saddam's *Scud* attacks on Israel by saying that they were aimed at military targets. "For example," he maintained, "one *Scud* hit the Israel Defense Ministry in Tel Aviv. A *Scud* was also aimed at a technical institute that belongs to the Defense Ministry in Haifa. Another *Scud* was fired at a military plant near Tel Aviv."[14]

There was no doubt that the PLO's position during the war damaged the PLO and the Palestinian cause, at least in the short term. Yet 'Arafat knew where the real source of his strength lay, and he was not repentant. "Among our masses we are at a peak, with the Arab masses, at a peak; with the Muslim nation we're at a peak, and throughout the Third World," he told *The New York Times*. On another occasion he said: "I have gained credibility among my people and the entire Arab nation. Have you seen all the demonstrations...? My picture is being brandished everywhere."[15] These statements were self-explanatory and made clear his real reasons for supporting Iraq during the war: he had to maintain the loyalty of the Palestinian rank and file. Their sentiments were with Saddam, and without them he had nothing. He would ride out the storm of criticism, and once the war was over, his policy would shift to damage control and rebuilding influence among the Gulf states and in the West.

Other major PLO factions were just as supportive of Saddam. George Habash's Popular Front for the Liberation of Palestine (PFLP) instructed its "fighters, secret cells, and friends in Arab and international organizations to open fire at US, Atlantic, Zionist, and reactionary interests at whatever cost."[16] For the PFLP, the war was an "imperialist-Zionist conspiracy against the Arab nation." Iraq was not responsible for the war; it had broken out, rather, because of US concerns and the decision of Jewish and Zionist circles, wrote the PFLP organ, *al-Hadaf*.[17]

Na'if Hawatima's DFLP hailed the Iraqi missile attacks on Israel, adding that this action called for celebration by the Palestinians and the Arab peoples.[18] *Al-Hurriyya*, the DFLP weekly, called for the Arab masses to further jeopardize US interests by boycotting cars and other products, and encouraged the "Islamic resistance movement" to broaden its activities against American imperialism.[19]

INTERNAL DISSENT IN FATH AND AMONG ITS SUPPORTERS DURING THE GULF WAR, AND THE ASSASSINATION OF SALAH KHALAF

It was well known among journalists and those close to PLO leaders that Salah Khalaf was vehemently opposed to 'Arafat's policy on the invasion (see *MECS* 1990, p. 226). His view had been that it was wrong to support Iraq's invasion, since Kuwait had done so much for the Palestinians and their movement.[20] Khalaf may have felt just a few weeks before his assassination that it was worth his while to dispel some of the rumors concerning his opposition to 'Arafat's policy, particularly after the Palestinian street supported it so dramatically. He told a rally in Amman that "it is an honor for the Palestinian revolution to stand at Iraq's side in case war breaks out....Defending Iraq is like defending Palestine."[21]

Khalaf was killed on 14 January in Tunis, along with Ha'il 'Abd al-Hamid (Abu al-Hawl), head of Fath's "western sector" operations apparatus, and Abu Muhammad Fakhri al-'Umari, an aide to Khalaf. The assassin was one Hamza Abu Zayid, a former member of Sabri al-Banna's (Abu Nidal) Fath Revolutionary Council (FRC), who had defected to Fath. There were three primary theories propounded in the press as to the party behind the assassination: Israel, Iraq, or Abu Nidal acting on his own. The only certain common denominator in all of the theories was that the assassination was carried out by the FRC, but the question was whether he was operating on behalf of Iraq, Israel, or al-Banna himself.[22] The truth may never be known. In April, it was reported that the assassin would be transported from Tunis to Yemen for execution, since Tunisian law did not allow the death penalty.[23] (For the effect of the death of the Fath officials on internal politics in the movement, see below.)

Leading the opposition in the PLO to 'Arafat's policy on the Iraqi invasion of Kuwait were the Hasan brothers, Khalid and Hani, both of whom were Fath Central Committee members. Khalid took the lead between the two, and led opposition to 'Arafat even after the war (see below). During the war, however, they kept a fairly low profile (Hani was apparently in Riyadh), not willing to buck the massive Palestinian sentiment in favor of Saddam.[24] Reports, mostly in the anti-'Arafat Gulf press, carried stories of Palestinian figures who were planning to replace 'Arafat.[25] Following the Palestine Central Council's (CC) meetings of 21–23 April, Khalid al-Hasan, referring to 'Arafat's policy on Iraq, said that the CC's resolutions were not acceptable since they did not deal with the period between the "council's recent session...and the previous session."[26]

Edward Said, a prominent spokesmen for the Palestinian cause in the US and a member of the PNC at the time, described 'Arafat's alliance with Saddam as a "blunder, a terrible mistake"; although the PLO leader may have had no choice, it was a short-sighted move, he said.[27] Said left the PNC before its September 1991 session, claiming that he and Ibrahim Abu Lughod, also a Palestinian-American academic, had resigned in order to "see new blood in the Palestinian legislative body."[28] Another source said that Said had resigned for health and personal reasons.[29] This may have been so, but Said may also have been motivated to resign by his disappointment with the PLO's failure to publish a "white paper" dealing with its position on the war, as it had promised to do following the April CC meetings.[30] Walid Khalidi, a leading Palestinian-American intellectual, wrote that the principles violated by Saddam in his invasion of Kuwait were the very principles from which the Palestinian cause drew its moral strength. Furthermore, wrote Khalidi, the "PLO's failure to come out publicly, repeatedly and forcefully against the invasion of Kuwait and in favor of Iraqi withdrawal in accordance with the UN resolutions has gravely damaged its political credibility and international standing."[31]

RELATIONS WITH THE GULF STATES
The Fate of the Palestinians in Kuwait
Some of the Palestinians in Kuwait, as well as Palestinians brought in by Iraq, cooperated with the occupying Iraqis. Others, however, were part of the Kuwaiti armed opposition. In any case, Palestinians in Kuwait suffered a great deal as a direct result of the PLO's stance on the invasion. Palestinian officials did not escape the wrath of the armed Kuwaitis. In early January, two guards outside the PLO headquarters were shot by Kuwaitis.[32] On 29 January, Rafiq Shafiq Qiblawi (Abu Ziyad) was slain in Kuwait. He was an aide to Fath Central Committee member Salim Za'nun (Abu al-Adib), the deputy speaker of the PNC.[33] 'Arafat said that he was killed by the "so-called Kuwaiti resistance."[34] The first secretary of the Palestinian Embassy in Qatar was expelled, as were several other Palestinians from Qatar.[35]

About 350,000 Palestinians lived in Kuwait prior to the Iraqi invasion; by July the

Palestinian chargé d'affaires in Kuwait, Muhammad Abu Jabir, reported that the community had shrunk to 90,000, and he projected a drop to between 30,000 and 40,000 by November.[36] This was due to the flight of Palestinians from Kuwait after the invasion, and a determined policy on the part of Kuwait to prevent them from returning and to force others to leave. After the Iraqis were forced out of Kuwait, the government began a large-scale harassment of Palestinians, rounding up suspected collaborators and torturing many in what was a deliberate campaign of intimidation.[37] A large number of Palestinians in Kuwait would not be "helpful to our security," remarked the Kuwaiti ambassador to the US, Sa'ud Nasir Al Sabah.[38] The PLO and the PFLP threatened retaliation against Kuwait.[39]

The Financial and Political Ramifications of the PLO's Pro-Iraqi Stance

One of the most readily apparent results of the PLO's support of Saddam was the financial and political damage to the organizations's relations with the Gulf states. 'Arafat said in March that since the beginning of the crisis the PLO had lost $6m. a month from Saudi Arabia, $2m. a month from Kuwait, and $4m. a month from Iraq. This, according to 'Arafat, was in addition to at least $11bn. lost by Palestinians in Kuwait and the c. $1.4bn. in income lost by those in the West Bank and Gaza working in Kuwait.[40] In September, Saudi Arabia reportedly renewed some of its funding of the PLO — it released $9m., which it collected via the 5% tax on Palestinians working in the kingdom.[41] The PLO announced initial spending cuts in April.[42] At the 20th PNC in September, Jawid al-Ghusayn, Executive Committee member and chairman of the Palestine National Fund, announced that the PLO's budget would have to be cut by more than one half, and that several austerity measures would be instituted, such as closing several PLO missions abroad, a ban on first-class travel and cocktail parties, and a freeze on hiring.[43]

The Gulf states isolated 'Arafat and dropped political support for the PLO in international forums. The Gulf media were merciless: "Was Kuwait not the homeland that gave Abu 'Ammar [Yasir 'Arafat] the opportunity to change from an engineer to a leader? Was it not on the land of Kuwait that the first signs of struggle occurred?"[44] The PLO's request, in March, to reopen its embassy in Kuwait was termed "insolent" by the Kuwaiti press.

> Did the PLO think that we did not know what its organs and agents were doing in Kuwait? Did it misconstrue Kuwaiti tolerance as foolishness and stupidity? Does the PLO want to control the Kuwaiti media once again by having its agents infiltrate the press, the news agency, and the radio newsdesk? They were the ones who led the enemy to the Kuwaiti transmitters and dismantled the news agency equipment and Kuwaiti press printing presses, and took them to Baghdad, and much more than that.[45]

Certain Arab Gulf states were quick to support the US peace initiative after Bush's speech in early March. In May, the Gulf Cooperation Council announced that it would send an observer to the peace conference without waiting for the PLO to clarify its position.[46] Although the Arab interlocutors in the peace process did not want to exclude the PLO from the peace talks — a testimony to the organization's staying power — they apparently did not raise the issue of PLO participation in talks with the US and dropped the traditional mention of the PLO from official statements.[47]

In October, Fath Central Committee member and Executive Committee member, Faruq Qaddumi, said that there had been no direct contacts between the Gulf states and the PLO, apart from a meeting of the Arab League Council in September.[48] In October and November, there was a spate of reports that ties would soon resume,[49] but by the end of the year, this did not seem to have taken place.

The Islamic Conference Organization (ICO) summit in December in Dakar, Senegal, was illustrative of the PLO's problems in the international arena. When 'Arafat reportedly moved to embrace Saudi Crown Prince 'Abdallah, the prince said angrily, "no kissing, please," and drew back, extending his right arm to avoid the PLO leader.[50] The PLO insisted that the summit's final communiqué should contain a call for Jihad to liberate Palestine, as had been done in the past. When the ICO refused, 'Arafat threatened to walk out, all to no avail.[51] The Gulf countries just stood by and let him stew in his own juice; they probably enjoyed seeing 'Arafat get his comeuppance.

UN General Assembly Resolution 3379, adopted in 1975, which proclaimed Zionism a form of racial discrimination, has often been seen as a high point in the organizational career of the PLO, coming as it did on the heels of the Rabat Arab summit resolution of 1974, which designated the PLO as the "sole legitimate representative of the Palestinian people." 'Arafat himself had addressed the UN in 1974. On 16 December 1991, the UN General Assembly repealed the resolution. It was only the second time in the UN's history that this had happened. The repeal showed that the PLO had lost its influence among former socialist and Third World countries as they struggled to find a place in the US-dominated "new world order."

MAINTAINING THE RELEVANCE OF THE ORGANIZATION: THE PLO, THE PEACE PROCESS, AND THE SHIFTING CENTER OF GRAVITY

Ever since the beginning of the Intifada in late 1987, the Palestinian political community had seen a growing shift in the balance of power between the residents of the territories and the PLO leadership based in Tunis, in favor of the former (see *MECS* 1988, pp. 230–35). Arguably, the entire turn in the PLO's political discourse from a hard line to a more conciliatory one was largely a result of this shift. The drastic decline in the influence of the PLO in the West and among the Gulf countries, following the war, led to a concomitant rise in the influence of West Bank and Gaza personalities, several of whom were chosen to represent the Palestinians, when peace talks began in Madrid in early November. After months of maneuvering, when all was said and done, Palestinian representation in Madrid was eventually based on the Israeli desiderata — to the total exclusion of an official PLO role. This notwithstanding, the PLO maintained a considerable influence on the Palestinian delegation, but was cautious not to give Israel an excuse to withdraw by overstating it. The Palestinians selected for the delegation were mainly moderates who engaged the PLO in a relationship of mutual dependence. They needed the organization to provide political cover and legitimacy for their actions, which were opposed, sometimes violently, by DFLP-Hawatima and PFLP activists in the territories who supported the more rejectionist policies of their counterparts outside the territories, as well as by Hamas. On the other hand, the PLO needed the West Bank and Gaza leaders, as they were the only vehicle left for maintaining the relevance of the PLO to the ongoing peace process.

THE PEACE PROCESS: THE VIEW FROM TUNIS

For the Palestinians, the progression of the peace process from the end of the Gulf War to the Madrid peace conference in October represented a constant eroding, a long string of concessions in the traditional PLO stance. In 1990, the PLO appeared ready to sanction a meeting with the Israelis in Cairo, but the Israeli Government collapsed over the issue before the PLO could be put to the test. The US had cut off relations with the PLO in June 1990, and the organization had returned to a more hard-line policy (see *MECS* 1990, pp. 219–21). Then came the Iraqi invasion of Kuwait, and the peace process appeared to be stymied. After the Gulf War, the US was supreme, the Soviet Union was disintegrating, and the Arab Gulf states had abandoned the PLO. The game run by the US was the only one in town, and the PLO had no choice but to play along, lest it be relegated to the sidelines of history. Its stance during the Gulf War made it even more imperative that the organization try to recoup its losses among Western public opinion, and particularly in the US.[52] Desperate to regain influence after the war, the PLO welcomed US President George Bush's 6 March speech on the Middle East, stating that it contained positive elements.[53] It was a case of looking at the glass as half-full, but the positive aspect in the speech for the PLO was that the despised UN Security Council Resolution 242 was coupled with the "land for peace" formula, making it slightly more palatable.[54]

The organization was hesitant about allowing prominent West Bank and Gaza personalities to meet with US Secretary of State James Baker when he came to the region in March (see chapter on the West Bank and the Gaza Strip), but it really had no choice if it wanted to remain a part of the process. Personalities from the territories wanted to go ahead, but they needed the blessing of the PLO, which the organization provided for this meeting as well as for all the other meetings throughout the year. The document submitted by the Palestinians to Baker made full reference to the PLO as the "sole legitimate representative of our Palestinian people inside and outside and wherever they exist,"[55] and also made clear that they were operating according to PLO instructions.[56] However, the irony for the organization was that the PLO itself was now being "represented" by people who could not publicly identify themselves as PLO members. While on the one hand this certainly pointed up the growing influence of those "inside," it also illustrated the complex nature of the PLO, which was more than an organization — it was the embodiment of a national identity that transcended geography. Statements by Palestinians that "we are all PLO" were therefore quite true in a sense, but just who would lead the organization, which Palestinians would dominate in this Palestinian polity was very much up for grabs, and the balance was tipping toward the residents of the territories.

As in the past, 'Arafat's adviser, Bassam Abu Sharif, was chosen to test the waters. In mid-March, Britain's Sky News reported that Abu Sharif had said that the PLO was dropping its demands for representation and would accept less than the entire West Bank and Gaza Strip. The remarks came in the context of what Abu Sharif was promoting as the PLO's new peace plan, which he was to announce in London.[57] Abu Sharif denied making the remarks attributed to him, but did confirm that the PLO, according to him, would be prepared to negotiate borders with Israel, since there would need to be a corridor between the Gaza Strip and the West Bank. This implied readiness not to insist at some stage on the total Israeli withdrawal from all the territories captured in 1967.[58] Abu Sharif began to retract immediately after making the statement, and Yasir 'Abd Rabbuh said that Abu Sharif's remarks "do not represent" and "are in total contradiction with" the position of the PLO.[59] It was also reported that Abu Sharif had offered to resign, but he denied this too.[60]

The traditional PLO constants (full and separate Palestinian representation by the PLO; recognition of Palestinian self-determination; the right of return to what is now Israel; an international conference under UN auspices leading to an Israeli withdrawal; and the establishment of a Palestinian state) were slowly whittled away as the peace process progressed. On the issue of representation, the PLO was clear on the principle, but decidedly pragmatic on its implementation. In principle, "our people have their leadership outside, and we cannot allow the Israelis to set conditions of this type for dialogue," 'Arafat stated.[61] On another occasion, he asked rhetorically, "Why are the Palestinian people regarded as just those in the occupied territories? There are only three million Palestinians in the occupied territories, but there are over six million of us."[62] Yet, the PLO's star was most certainly declining in the territories, and the PLO had to take this into consideration, as well as the fact that the US would have nothing to do with it. The organization's resignation to this was expressed by Sa'id Kamal, PLO representative in Egypt, who stated that the PLO would be represented at the peace talks, whether by its members or by Palestinians inside the occupied territories.[63]

Even during the Gulf War, Palestinians in the territories were confiding to Israeli officials that the weakening of 'Arafat in the international arena would strengthen the independence of Fath supporters in the West Bank and Gaza who would consequently feel freer to initiate political activity without direct instructions from the PLO in Tunis.[64] On 12 March, local Palestinians were reportedly "shocked," when Baker told them that none of the Arab leaders to whom he had spoken lately would talk with 'Arafat.[65]

The problem of representation was further complicated by the growing independence of the putative Palestinian leadership in the territories. The first public sign of this, after the war, was an article in the East Jerusalem al-Fajr, in which editor Hana Siniora demanded that the next session of the PNC contain an equal number of members from inside and outside the territories.[66] Radi al-Jara'i, a Fath activist who had spent 13 years in Israeli jails, wrote two articles in al-Fajr calling for the dissolution of the PNC and elections in the territories under UN supervision for a new PNC. Elections would also be held outside. Then a provisional government would be formed, including members from the West Bank and Gaza.[67] These articles ignited a debate in the territories, with Faysal al-Husayni supporting such proposals, and those to his left, Ghassan al-Khatib and Riyad al-Maliki, saying that the time was not right.[68] Another election proposal was floated by Talal 'Afif al-Safi, a journalist and lawyer from East Jerusalem; he, too, had "credentials," having served a total of over two years in administrative detention (for more details, see chapter on the West Bank and the Gaza Strip).[69]

An editorial in al-Fajr, in June, was scathing in its attack on the PLO leadership. It upbraided the organization for not doing enough to protect the Palestinians in Kuwait: "The memories of Sabra and Shatila are still fresh in our minds and it is therefore beyond anyone's comprehension how the Palestinian leadership could fail so miserably....The PLO needs some serious reassessment of itself and its modus operandi. Maybe it is time some new blood be introduced into the Palestinian leadership."[70] While this criticism was limited to the PLO's failure to act to protect Palestinians in Kuwait, it came in the context of all the various independent initiatives, and was therefore a direct and comprehensive challenge to the leadership. Moreover, an internal memorandum by Fath military leader Abu 'Ali Shahin was leaked to the press; Shahin accused the PLO of corruption and called for reforms.[71]

During the year the press carried reports of the establishment of three political parties based primarily in the West Bank. These were the Democratic Party of Palestine, the Palestinian National Party (sometimes called the Unified Palestinian National Party), and The Fourteenth of January Corrective Movement. (The name of the third party suggested that they identified with Salah Khalaf, who was assassinated on 14 January.)[72] While not significant in terms of numbers, or even staying power (these parties all gave indications of being flashes in the pan), the appearance of such groups signified a growing dissatisfaction with the PLO leadership.

While the PNC was meeting in Algiers in late September discussing whether or not to go to the peace conference, in the territories public meetings were held to discuss the same thing. Here the debate was practically a mirror image of the debate at the PNC. Fath, the Palestine Communist Party (PCP), and DFLP-'Abd Rabbuh supporters tended to think that the PNC should approve Palestinian participation in the peace conference, while PFLP and DFLP-Hawatima adherents opposed participation.[73]

The relationship between the Palestinians outside the territories and those inside was complex and convoluted. The older leadership in the West Bank and Gaza, symbolized by Faysal al-Husayni, tended to be more moderate and draw its counterpart outside the territories — 'Arafat and the Fath mainstream — toward more moderate positions. But many in the territories, not to mention Hamas, took issue with the Husayni-'Arafat axis and were decidedly more hard-line. Thus the PCP supporter Ghassan al-Khatib, who eventually went to Madrid, initially vehemently opposed some of the meetings with Secretary Baker, even though they had been sanctioned by the PLO in Tunis. The PCP in the territories was initially also opposed to these meetings, but eventually relented[74] (see chapter on the West Bank and Gaza). This showed that the debate was not solely over the path to be taken, but also over where decision-making would lie, regardless of the specific political issue at stake. Husayni stated that "in political action differences do occur between leaderships and between people and leadership. We respect others when they have disagreements but agree on the main objective. We want others to respect us equally. We have our own will, and we are capable of choosing our own leadership."[75] At times, the split was generational, with younger activists in the territories calling into question the positions of the leadership within and without the territories. As one activist in Dahaysha said, "We love 'Arafat and Faysal al-Husayni. They are our history, our historical leadership. But we are the real leadership of the Palestinian people now."[76]

This type of activity and debate was not a challenge to the PLO as an institution and embodiment of Palestinian nationalism. Rather, it reflected a growing frustration with the PLO leadership outside, a desire for more input on the part of the residents of the territories. 'Arafat maintained his role as the personification of Palestinian nationalism, but such debate and questioning of his leadership suggested that he might be heading for some kind of figurehead role, although it was still too early to tell.

Due to the lack of support from the US and the Arab states, the PLO became resigned to a premier role in the peace process for West Bank and Gaza personalities and to its own pro forma exclusion. However, there was still the issue of representation from East Jerusalem to settle. The issue of Palestinians from outside the territories had been solved in the context of a joint delegation with Jordan (see below), but the status of East Jerusalem representation remained open. By late July and early August, Baker had won over most of the parties to the conference while the Palestinians were still balking on this issue. Baker told the West Bank and Gaza leadership that the US had not promised the Israelis that East Jerusalemites would be excluded from the final stage of the negotiations,[77] but the PLO officially rejected "the exclusion of Jerusalem as an issue and representation during any stage of the peace process." The rejection was contained in a five-point document, a copy of which was handed to Baker by Palestinian negotiators in the territories. The PLO document also sought to have the US agree to Palestinian self-determination; that the PLO would decide the composition of the delegation; an immediate halt to Israeli settlement activities in the territories; and that the conference would assure Israeli withdrawal from all the occupied territories, including East Jerusalem.[78]

Nevertheless, the Palestinians were being worn down by a US administration that was convinced that the Palestinians had no choice but to go along, since they were the weakest party and had the most to lose by not joining the process. In September, the PLO instructed the local Palestinian interlocutors to obtain guarantees from the US concerning what they saw as their minimum demands. If the PLO was going to authorize other Palestinians to attend the peace conference, it wanted to be compensated in the realm of principles, such as a US guarantee of the Palestinians' right to self-determination. But talks on this issue were inconclusive, and Baker cautioned the Palestinians that "it is going to be a long, long time before the bus ever comes by again."[79] The US was prepared only to offer the Palestinians a memorandum which more or less simply restated standard US positions. On the issue of self-determination, the US was only willing to recognize Palestinian "legitimate political rights." As far as the East Jerusalem issue was concerned, the US was only prepared to state that selection of members for the first stage of the talks would not prejudice the results of the negotiations respecting East Jerusalem, that the US supported a united Jerusalem, and that the final status of the city should be determined in negotiations.[80] The PLO rejected the memorandum, but, at the last minute, authorized Hanan 'Ashrawi, an English professor at Bir Zayt University, to meet with Baker one more time in Amman on 20 September.[81] In what amounted to a last-minute plea, 'Ashrawi said that 'Arafat had told her to ask Baker for three assurances, which were very much scaled-down versions of traditional PLO demands: a halt to settlements; a US acknowledgment of the Palestinians' right to self-determination; and that East Jerusalem was occupied territory. The PLO had indeed been brought low, yet the US still did not concede. On the way back to Washington, officials traveling with Baker were talking about simply issuing invitations to the conference, without the prior consent of the parties.[82]

The PLO had been brought to this situation by a combination of the desire of the Palestinians in the territories to get to the conference, the negotiating skills of Baker, and Israeli obduracy in refusing the organization an official role. By the time the 20th session of the PNC convened in Algiers in late September, 'Arafat was ready to go to the peace conference, even though many traditional Palestinian demands and concerns had not been dealt with to his satisfaction. Over the objections of the PFLP and the DFLP-Hawatima faction, the PNC voted to give the PLO leadership the leeway to decide for itself how to proceed on the peace process (for further discussion of the PNC session and its resolutions, see below). It was then left to work out the details, and the PLO was still insistent on the issues of settlements and East Jerusalemites.[83] The US, however, did not budge. It rested, therefore, with the PLO to try to get these issues solved through the joint delegation with Jordan. On 15 October, Palestinian leaders from the territories meeting in Amman, with PLO officials in the background, announced that an agreement on a joint delegation had been reached.[84]

Among the other issues of crucial importance was the type of conference to be held. The PLO had traditionally held fast to the view that a conference had to be international and have coercive powers. This was to avoid direct bilateral talks with Israel and bring third-party pressure on it, as well as to prevent the Arab states from cutting a separate deal. But when the US began floating the idea of a so-called "regional conference," in what was a concession to Israel's objection to an international one, the PLO eventually gave in. Initially, the idea was rejected out of hand by the organization.[85] In an interview with Moroccan television, 'Arafat said that a regional conference would bring the Arab states to normalize relations with Israel at the expense of the Palestinian problem, and demanded a UN-sponsored conference that would have coercive powers.[86] However, Radwan Abu 'Ayyash, head of the Arab Journalists' Union in the West Bank, said that the idea was worth discussing.[87] At a meeting of the CC in late April, the regional conference idea was explicitly rejected.[88] But by June, PLO officials were saying that the conference should be held under international supervision or "under the supervision of a commission from the USSR, the United States, and Europe;"[89] in other words, a regional conference.

Another concern of the PLO was that the US and Israel envisaged a transitional stage before discussions on the final settlement. The PLO took some time coming around to this notion, but it eventually did so in mid-April.[90]

As for the issue of a joint delegation with Jordan, in late March it was first reported that the PLO was ready to consider such a delegation[91] in what seemed to be a return to the spirit of the Amman agreement of 1984 (see *MECS* 1983–84, pp. 195–200), a document which 'Arafat eventually abrogated in return for a reconciliation with the DFLP and PFLP. As late as the beginning of May the organization was still denying it, insisting on an independent delegation.[92] Apparently, the leadership knew that this was inevitable, but was still trying to get the best deal it could. By June, however, the joint delegation was being openly discussed by officials.[93] 'Arafat traveled to Amman in late August to discuss coordination with King Husayn. Following the meeting, a committee of Jordanians and Palestinians was announced "to follow up on developments concerning better conditions for Palestinian participation in the peace conference."[94] A meeting of this committee took place in Amman on 10 September. Later that month, 'Arafat got the PNC to approve a resolution which gave the Executive Committee the green light to form a delegation with Jordan (this was implicit, not explicit; see Appendix III for text). Within days, an Executive Committee delegation was in Amman to work out the details.[95] The PLO wanted to be sure that Jordan would conduct the joint delegation on PLO terms when Palestinian issues were under discussion. 'Arafat himself held talks with Husayn on 20 October.[96] A joint delegation was not only a default option for the PLO, allowing it to influence the talks; it had another advantage: by having Palestinians from Jerusalem included in the Jordanian part of the delegation, the PLO could have Jerusalemites present who could not participate otherwise, due to Israeli objections.[97] In a report based on what was purported to be the full text of the agreement on the joint delegation (see Appendix I), it was stated that the Palestinian part would take charge of Palestinian issues, and the Jordanian part of Jordanian issues, with a coordinating member from each part present during discussions. The agreement was approved by the Executive Committee and the Jordanian Council of Ministers. PLO leaders implied that there had been a qualitative change in the role of Jordan since it had disengaged from any interest in determining the future of the West Bank; now things were on a more equal footing.

On 17 October, the CC endorsed PLO participation,[98] and reports of a list of delegates began to filter out. The list was composed in consultation with the leaders attending the CC, but — according to leaders in the territories speaking off the record — was "not some arbitrary dictate from Tunis."[99] Although leaders in the territories were cooperating with the PLO in composing the list, the fact that the list was handed by Husayni to Baker in Jerusalem on 19 October and not announced in Tunis only showed how far the PLO had fallen. On 18 October, satisfied that the Palestinians would choose delegates acceptable to Israel, the US and the Soviet Union issued invitations to the conference.[100] The names were initially kept secret so as not to give the appearance that they were being vetted for Israeli approval,[101] but were announced officially on 22 October. 'Arafat reacted with typical aplomb: "No one can hide the sun with their fingers. Everyone knows that the Palestinians will represent the PLO. Every Palestinian is a member of the PLO, inside and outside the territories."[102]

On the issue of representation, Israel may have been outmaneuvered by the PLO, which arranged a delegation of "advisers." These advisers included people objectionable to Israel, such as Faysal al-Husayni and other Palestinians from abroad, such as University of Chicago Professor of Middle Eastern History, Rashid Khalidi. As far as the PLO was concerned, even though they would not be official participants, that they were going along emphasized the unity of all Palestinians, no matter where they lived, whether in Jerusalem or in the "Palestinian diaspora."

As soon as the invitations had been issued, 'Arafat flew to Damascus for a meeting with the Syrian leadership (for further discussion of developments in the PLO's relationship with Syria, see below), arriving on 19 October. The PLO had been searching for new regional allies ever since the end of the Gulf War and had sent out feelers to the Syrians. Now, with the peace conference in the offing, 'Arafat sought out Syria as a natural ally and counterbalance to the Jordanian-Palestinian delegation. Syrian pressure would be useful if the Palestinian negotiators decided to buck the line from Tunis. He also wanted to prevent the Syrians from striking any separate deals with Israel on the Golan Heights. It was reported that the two had agreed that the multilateral talks should not be held until Israel withdrew from the territories. In meetings of the Arab leaders concerned in Damascus, on 24 October, an attempt was made to coordinate positions, but the Arab leaders refused to support a Syrian demand that the Arabs boycott the multilaterals.[103]

The Jordanian component of the joint delegation was announced on 26 October. It also included East Jerusalem Palestinians, such as former PNC member Walid

Khalidi, born in Jerusalem but living in the US, and Anwar al-Khatib, one-time governor of the Jerusalem region.[104]

As Palestinians began arriving in Madrid at the end of October, the tension was palpable. It was an extremely important occasion; for the first time since the defeat of 1948 the Palestinians were to have (nearly) independent representation in peace talks on the issues that concerned them most directly. This being the case, they were extra cautious not to give Israel an excuse to walk out, and were consequently willing to continue the game of "hiding" the PLO. 'Arafat said that he would not seek a role in Madrid, and would not even communicate with the Palestinian delegation. "Any Palestinian anywhere is a representative of the PLO," he said.[105] This kind of caution was echoed by advisory committee member Sari Nusayba, who commented: "I think the principal goal of the conference is to mobilize the world to our side against Israel, which means we have to do whatever we can to avoid alienating or embarrassing those parties whose support we seek [i.e., the US]."[106] As PLO officials such as Bassam Abu Sharif and Nabil Sha'th arrived in town, their mission was to "monitor" the conference, according to the head of the PLO mission in Madrid, 'Issam Salim. Muhammad Shitayi, one of several Palestinian spokespeople in Madrid, was firm on avoiding any association with the PLO: "We have not talked to anybody on the phone from the PLO. We have no contact with the PLO delegation. This is a Palestinian delegation from the occupied territories."[107] A sharp-eyed photographer for the Associated Press did manage, however, to catch Sha'th standing just behind Haydar 'Abd al-Shafi, although an editor at *The New York Times* seemed to miss the scoop, since Sha'th was not identified.[108]

Amid the frenzied activity of the media in Madrid, the cameras were trained on Hanan 'Ashrawi, Faysal al-Husayni, and Haydar 'Abd al-Shafi. When the Palestinians finally had their day in the international limelight, the faces were not those of anyone on the PLO Executive Committee. Palestinians were at last represented in peace talks, but the faces were those of 'Abd al-Shafi, Husayni, and 'Ashrawi, and not Yasir 'Arafat and Faruq Qaddumi. Nevertheless, the PLO tried to put matters in the best light possible. An issue of the official PLO organ *Filastin al-Thawra* dedicated to the peace conference was headlined: "The Madrid Peace Conference: The Palestinians Represent the Palestine Liberation Organization."[109] The tables had surely turned. The PLO, the sole, legitimate representative of the Palestinians, was now being represented by Palestinians, and not the other way around.

'Abd al-Shafi's speech was an emotional, heartfelt presentation of the Palestinian case. The text was replete with references to the issue of representation, without an explicit mention of the PLO: "We come here wrenched from our sisters and brothers in exile to stand before you as the Palestinians under occupation, although we maintain that each of us represents the rights and interests of the whole. We have been denied the right to publicly acknowledge our loyalty to our leadership and system of government. But allegiance and loyalty cannot be censored or severed. Our acknowledged leadership is more than [the] justly democratically chosen leadership of all the Palestinian people. It is the symbol of our national unity and identity...." 'Abd al-Shafi did mention the PLO's peace initiative which followed the 19th PNC session of November 1988, and cited "Chairman 'Arafat" by name, quoting his speech to the UN General Assembly in 1974.[110] A member of the advisory committee, who requested anonymity, stated that the speech had been faxed to Tunis and approved by

'Arafat. In Tunis, 'Abd Rabbuh said that it reflected the position of the PLO.[111]

After the speeches, the order of business was bilateral meetings to determine the next stage, but the Syrians balked. When they tried to pressure the Jordanian-Palestinian delegation to go along with them, Husayni, 'Ashrawi, Zahira Kamal and Ghassan al-Khatib flew with Nabil Sha'th to Morocco to see 'Arafat, who gave them his support. According to reports, when Syrian President Hafiz al-Asad telephoned 'Arafat to protest, the PLO leader replied that his hands were tied by his people in Madrid.[112] 'Arafat had accepted the logic of the Palestinians from the territories, that putting up obstacles at this point served no useful purpose, since there was much to be gained and way too much to lose.

At the bilateral Jordanian/Palestinian-Israeli talks the atmosphere was good. The final statement said that the two delegations had met to "start direct negotiations on the basis of Security Council Resolutions 242 and 338."[113] Although this passed without notice by many, it showed how far the Palestinians had come toward the Israelis. There was no mention of the "land for peace" clause, not to speak of self-determination, which the Palestinians had always wanted to tack on to 242. Years back, it would have been hard to imagine the PLO ever giving its blessing to such a formulation, but since the Intifada, the growing political weight of the Palestinians in the territories had wrought many changes in the Tunis-based organization, and this was a major one.

Toward the end of the Madrid conference, with the Israelis fully committed, the Palestinian delegates were not as keen on keeping such a low profile for the PLO, and neither was the PLO. Nabil Sha'th spoke on 2 November at a reception organized by the local Palestinian community — no cameras or tape recorders were allowed. "Enough with this farce," he proclaimed. "The delegation before you is that of the PLO."[114]

For the Palestinians, the whole experience was a heady one. Everything was happening for the first time, it was historic, and they were enthused by it all. For the PLO, however, it must have been a bitter pill to swallow, notwithstanding the gratifying Palestinian representation. When the moment came, they were not there. "Most of the faxes went from here to Tunis. Not the other way around," said a Palestinian delegate.[115] This was also reflected in 'Arafat's rather muted reaction to the event: the Madrid conference constituted a "satisfactory start to the peace process," he said.[116]

After Madrid, the question remained over where and under what circumstances the talks would continue. The PLO was still insisting that Israel meet various demands first, such as a freeze on settlement activity in the territories.[117] The mutual interdependence between the PLO and the Palestinians in the territories was illustrated by the problem of venue. The US unilaterally announced on 21 November that the next round would be held in Washington on 4 December. For the Palestinians, the main objection was that they would not enjoy the same conditions as they had in Madrid, where top PLO officials could be present. For Washington, they would have to get special visas. This was a concern of the representatives of the territories, because the presence of PLO officials gave them cover for any outcome. For the PLO, it affirmed their representative status. The first step was to try to get the US-PLO dialogue — which was suspended in June 1990 (see *MECS* 1990, pp. 219–21) — started again. When this was not achieved, the PLO tried to get visas for several officials.[118] On 24 November, Haydar 'Abd al-Shafi announced that the Palestinian delegation would attend,[119] even though the visa question was still open. However, there was no announcement from Tunis. The task of the PLO was made easier when the Israelis balked, angered at the unilateral invitation. Realizing that there were significant gains to be made in the media battle if they could point to empty Israeli chairs, the PLO gave its approval. Again, years back this would not have happened, but the organization was no longer calling the shots. While the US at first firmly refused to grant any special visas to PLO officials,[120] it eventually did grant visas to two West Bank deportees: the former editor of the East Jerusalem *al-Sha'b*, Akram Haniyya, often described as an adviser to 'Arafat, and Taysir 'Aruri, a PCP member.[121] Nabil Sha'th, who had been in Madrid and had visited the US many times, was denied a visa. This was probably because he was a member of the Fath Central Committee. Also denied entrance, according to reports, were the PLO spokesman, Ahmad 'Abd al-Rahman; Mamduh Nawfal, former operations officer for the DFLP, now sympathetic to 'Abd Rabbuh; Samir Abu Ghazala, PLO representative in Cyprus; and Palestinian national poet Mahmud Darwish, an Executive Committee member. Applications for the visas were made by the delegates from the territories at the US consulate in East Jerusalem.[122]

When Palestinians arrived in Washington for the talks, the US denied them their media advantage, as the State Department had conceded to the Israelis that no photographers would be allowed in the negotiating room until all teams were present. The US was taken to task for this by Sha'th, speaking from Cairo.[123]

'Ashrawi had already set the tone and issues for the talks, at the end of November, when she averred that the Palestinians would negotiate separately with Israel in Washington.[124] This became the main issue of discussions between the Palestinians and the Israelis when they finally began to talk on 10 December. Executive Committee member, Sulayman al-Najjab, rejected the Israeli opposition to this step.[125] But in general, PLO officials stayed in the background as far as the media was concerned, not giving too many interviews. Media people were interested in what was happening in Washington, and the PLO was not there.

In Tunis, PLO officials were keeping a low profile when discussing their strategy for the continuation of talks, almost always insisting on anonymity. The goals of the Fath mainstream were essentially the same as the delegates from the territories: to give the transitional period of self-rule as much of the trappings of a state as possible, and use the time to build up the infrastructure of a state.[126] On this they were in agreement with the delegates, but the confluence of thought on this issue overshadowed possible difficulties which began to emerge in the territories. While all could agree what should be done, the battle would be over influence during the process.

Nevertheless, 'Arafat would sometimes assert a harder line, which seemed contradictory to what he said his delegates were pursuing in the peace talks. Thus, he said that he had never agreed to any kind of self-rule, not even transitionally. "These are Israeli ideas that we will not accept, even if the Americans do."[127] If he had, in fact, not agreed to this, then the delegates that he said spoke for him were following a different agenda indeed.

The talks adjourned on 18 December, with the issue still unresolved. Before the year ended, however, the PLO fired the next salvo: it would demand to be officially represented at the multilateral talks that were scheduled for January 1992 in Moscow.[128]

DEVELOPMENTS WITHIN THE VARIOUS PLO COMPONENTS

DEVELOPMENTS WITHIN FATH

The assassinations of Salah Khalaf and Ha'il 'Abd al-Hamid in January left two vacancies on the Fath Central Committee.[129] Both veterans of the Fath leadership, their deaths created the possibility of some new, younger blood coming into the organization. Indeed, with the death of Khalaf, coming on the heels of Khalil al-Wazir's assassination in 1988, it seemed as if Fath's leadership might shift in a more pragmatic direction, oriented in a greater way toward the new global realities and reconciliation with Israel and the West, at the expense of hard-line members such as Faruq Qaddumi (Abu Lutf) and Mahmud 'Abbas (Abu Mazin) who had good relations with the then Soviet Union, with Eastern Europe and radical Arab states such as Syria and Libya.

In the event, 'Arafat prevented a discussion of bringing in new people to fill the empty positions, most probably due to the political pressures of keeping pace with the peace process; discussion in Fath centered instead on which current Central Committee members would take over the portfolios formerly held by Khalaf (unified security) and 'Abd al-Hamid (western sector). Both were posts that dealt with operations. 'Arafat's choice to take over Khalaf's duties was Hakam Bal'awi, PLO ambassador to Tunis and Khalaf's deputy in charge of unified security. It was reported that 'Arafat had unilaterally handed over funds budgeted for security matters to Bal'awi.[130] According to Khalid al-Hasan, who opposed 'Arafat, most Central Committee members did not want Bal'awi.[131] Opposition to Bal'awi seems to have been led by the Hasan brothers, who held two seats on the Central Committee. By the end of the year, there was no indication that new members of the Central Committee had been chosen to replace Khalaf and 'Abd al-Hamid.

With the backing of the Gulf states, Central Committee member Khalid al-Hasan mounted a challenge to 'Arafat.[132] Hasan had lived in Kuwait for many years and had a financial base there. He was particularly incensed at 'Arafat for his position on the Iraqi invasion of Kuwait, which cost him and many other thousands of Palestinians both a home and untold fortunes. After the war, most of Hasan's opposition focused on instituting a provisional government for the Palestinians. In principle, the formation of such a government had been agreed upon at the 19th PNC in 1988, but like many such resolutions and "reforms," its actual implementation had been left to the Executive Committee, which was controlled by 'Arafat, who opposed a provisional government. Hasan now saw a provisional government as a way to advance the peace process, give residents of the territories more power, and limit 'Arafat's prerogatives.

At a PLO CC meeting at the end of April, Hasan made his proposal official. He envisaged that the provisional government would be formed after elections in the territories for membership in the PNC, which would in turn appoint a president, "acceptable on both the Arab and international levels." 'Arafat, of course, was already president. Hasan made clear that he favored a radical change in the PLO. The provisional government would not, like the current Executive Committee, represent the various guerrilla groups. Over 50% of the PNC members should be "real struggling independents — not organization members posing as independents as happened in the past." According to Hasan, the government should be comprised of technocrats with real experience in the issues that would face the Palestinians. "In other words, it is necessary now for the inside to participate with the outside, since it is no longer permissible that the outside issue orders to the inside. That stage ended with the eruption of the Intifada inside. Following the Gulf War, there must be a real partnership between the inside and outside."[133] Hasan railed against 'Arafat's leadership which, he said, had led to the political and financial isolation of the PLO. He proposed Walid Khalidi and Anis al-Qasim to head the government.[134]

Those opposed to the plan included the Fath leadership and the leadership of the DFLP and PFLP, all of whom saw the plan for what it was — a challenge to the old order. 'Abd Rabbuh said that the plan was to replace the PLO, and therefore only served those who cast doubt on the organization as the representative of the Palestinians. 'Arafat would only say that the "present situation is inappropriate for setting up a provisional government."[135]

Although his challenge to 'Arafat was personal, Hasan also seems to have been motivated by a change of heart. In previous years, he had been among those who had formulated the Fath mainstream view that time was on the side of the Palestinians, that eventually they would overwhelm the Israelis by sheer numbers and Israel, an unnatural entity, would eventually disappear; he had termed this the "auxiliary option."[136] But now, Hasan told the *Jordan Times*, one had to understand the current realities.

> As the son of Haifa, I should reject this whole thing [the peace process]. But what happens if I do? There is a colonial occupation. There were 50,000 Jews, then one million, and then 3.5 million Jews. There are two million Jews on the way from the Soviet Union, other than the Falashas [Ethiopian Jews], those from Yugoslavia and Albania. They're taking the land, farming it, and there are three generations of Jews born there.[137]

The Hasan brothers' challenge was unsuccessful. By placing themselves in opposition, they seem to have lost influence in the PLO and Fath. They were, however, the harbinger of growing discontent among many Palestinians, of various shades of opinion, inside and outside the territories. There were several examples of this discontent during the year. Edward Said and Walid Khalidi organized at least two meetings in London during the year (in August and September), which included official PLO members, Palestinians from the territories, the US and Europe. At the September meeting, one participant, who not surprisingly asked not be identified, said: "If there is any message that we are sending back to the PLO leadership now, it is that not a single obstacle should be placed in the face of the peace talks by the Palestinians."[138]

One aspect of discontent in Fath and the PLO which went virtually unnoticed in the press was the problem of Fath forces based in Tunisia. In what seems to have been a move brought about by Fath's increasingly precarious financial problems, 'Arafat ordered a reported 75% of Fath forces to Libya, where they would serve under Libyan command as guards in the Sara region, along the border with Chad. In exchange, Libya promised to provide food, medical care and salaries for the fighters. During the course of 1991 and in early 1992, hundreds of those who had been ordered to Libya or had already been posted there began turning up in Scandinavia and requesting political asylum. Some were interrogated by Israeli intelligence, at the request of the

Norwegian Government. Press inquiries into how they could afford to come to Scandinavia and settle resulted in reports that some of the funds for this had come from Gulf states, which were interested in undermining 'Arafat by increasing desertion among his followers.[139]

DEVELOPMENTS IN THE POSITION OF THE PFLP

Throughout the year, George Habash's PFLP continued to hold the hardest of lines, advocating maximalist demands. Habash seemed to hold fast to the idea that time was still on the side of the Palestinians. He maintained that all of Palestine had to be liberated; if the international conditions were not ripe and could not guarantee the right of return, self-determination and an independent state, then the Palestinians should boycott all peace efforts. If the PNC approved the "proposed capitulation process," he threatened to remove the PFLP from the Executive Committee.[140]

The PNC did agree to go to the peace conference (see below), and the PFLP protested. It coordinated its moves with the DFLP (Hawatima faction) and Hamas.[141] Riyad al-Maliki, the most visible PFLP activist in the territories, threatened to turn the lives of the Palestinian delegates to the peace conference "into a nightmare."[142] Such threats could not be taken lightly. All concerned no doubt remembered the assassination of Nablus mayor Zafir al-Masri and the torching of cars belonging to Hana Siniora's family (see *MECS* 1986, p. 46, and 1987, p. 232); responsibility for both was taken by the PFLP. On the eve of the Madrid talks, the PFLP turned its wrath on Jewish settlers, claiming responsibility for an attack on a bus in the West Bank, in which a mother of seven was killed and several others injured.[143] On 6 November, Habash held a press conference in Damascus and announced the suspension of the PFLP's participation in the Executive Committee. He cited the quick slide from the principles accepted at the 20th PNC (which he had rejected), to the CC decisions of 17 October, which were also abandoned when the leadership accepted the whole US plan.[144] In mid-November, he even threatened to leave the PLO entirely.[145] Efforts by Fath to get Habash to return were futile.[146] Coordination continued throughout the year between the PFLP, DFLP (Hawatima faction) and Hamas to oppose the peace talks.[147]

THE SPLIT IN THE DFLP IS MADE OFFICIAL

While for most of 1990 the two factions of the DFLP had tended to paper over differences and ascribe them to spirited debate in the democractic tradition of the organization, in 1991 the DFLP officially split, one faction headed by Hawatima and the other by 'Abd Rabbuh. At the 20th PNC, both factions were represented on the newly constituted Executive Committee.

In early April, the DFLP Central Committee ('Abd Rabbuh controlled the Central Committee's secretariat, while Hawatima controlled the political bureau) announced in Tunis that 'Abd Rabbuh had been chosen as secretary-general to replace Hawatima. The move was apparently prompted by a letter from Hawatima to 'Arafat saying that he wanted Taysir Khalid to be an observer on the Executive Committee, since 'Abd Rabbuh no longer represented the DFLP. In response to 'Abd Rabbuh's action, the political bureau issued a statement declaring 'Abd Rabbuh removed from his post as assistant secretary-general and representative of the DFLP on the PLO Executive Committee, and stating that Taysir Khalid had replaced him.[148]

In August and September, 'Abd Rabbuh convened what he called the DFLP Central Committee and the third General Congress in Amman, under his chairmanship. These meetings were held in Jordan, suggesting that Amman was supportive of 'Abd Rabbuh against Hawatima. Moreover, the Jordanian press gave much sympathetic and uncritical coverage to the events. At 'Abd Rabbuh's General Congress, a 16-member political bureau was elected, half of whom were unnamed and from the territories. Those named in addition to 'Abd Rabbuh were Salih Ra'fit, Jamil Hilal, 'Issam 'Abd al-Latif, Mamduh Nawfal, 'A'isha 'Awda, 'Azmi al-Shu'aybi, and Salim Dardana.[149]

The reasons for the split could be linked to 'Abd Rabbuh's aligning himself with 'Arafat when Hawatima opposed the resolutions of the 19th PNC in 1988. The issues of conflict were the peace process, ideological orientation and the participation of residents of the territories in the leadership of the DFLP. 'Abd Rabbuh's group wanted closer ties with Jordan and an enhanced role for the residents of the territories. According to 'Abd Rabbuh and a member of his new political bureau, Jamil Hilal, ever since the beginning of the Intifada, which shifted the struggle to the occupied territories, the DFLP had not come to grips with the new reality, and had not involved residents of the West Bank and Gaza in leadership positions — "the monopoly of the outside on the inside had to be broken," said Hilal. 'Abd Rabbuh and Hilal accused the Hawatima faction of concentrating too much on the armed struggle, to the exclusion of the new political realities. They claimed that Hawatima's people had turned the DFLP into a bureaucratic mess, comprising the unemployed and hangers-on, under a regime of "democratic centralism" which was a "hierarchical dictatorship of the elite." The breakaway group also rejected Marxism-Leninism and any class basis to their struggle, which they described as national, progressive, democratic and nonsectarian. For Hawatima and his supporters, charged Hilal, Marxism-Leninism and class theory were now "nothing more than a futile effort to keep the old guard in power and turn Marxism into an ideological fundamentalism which allows it to keep their places in the leadership."[150] These comments reflected the general decline worldwide in the influence of the Soviet Union, communist and leftist ideologies, and the fact that 'Abd Rabbuh was one with Fath in terms of political ideology and program.

The split came as a blow to Hawatima, who had founded the DFLP and had led it since its inception. He had opposed 'Arafat's political line — which 'Abd Rabbuh had supported — since 1988, and in 1991 spoke vehemently against Baker's efforts and 'Arafat's concessions. He opposed talks between Baker and West Bank and Gaza Palestinians and joined the PFLP in rejecting the Madrid peace talks, arguing that under the strict terms of Palestinian representation, the Palestinians should not have gone. The PLO had simply made too many concessions on that score and had not followed the resolutions of the 20th PNC and the CC decisions of mid-October.[151] Hawatima punctuated his opposition with his usual call for a "collective leadership" of the PLO which would help to control 'Arafat.[152]

Hawatima and his supporters stressed that 'Abd Rabbuh's group enjoyed the financial and moral support of "right-wing forces in the PLO" (i.e., Fath), and demanded that they refrain from using the DFLP name. Hawatima-faction-DFLP political bureau member, Qays al-Samara'i (Abu Lula), defended the DFLP's democratic centralism, stressing that communist parties in the West and the East suffered precisely because they abandoned it.[153]

At the 20th PNC, the split was made official, with each faction having a representative on the newly constituted Executive Committee (see below).

A NOTE ON THE PCP
In a move reflecting the fall of communism, the PCP changed its name late in the year to the Palestinian People's Party.[154] In 1990, the PCP had attempted to form an alliance of the left, led by the PCP, and had failed (see *MECS* 1990, pp. 233–34). At that time, it had insisted on keeping its name. But with communism down and out, the organization must have felt a need to change with the times.

THE 20TH SESSION OF THE PNC
The 20th session of the PNC convened in Algiers from 23–28 September, under the banner "Session of Jerusalem the Venerable — Session of the Three Martyrs" (*Dawrat al-Quds al-sharif — dawrat al-shuhada al-thulatha*). The slogan reflected the importance attached by the organization to the issue of Jerusalem being represented in the peace talks, and also honored the departed leaders assassinated on 14 January. The main topic on the agenda was the peace process. 'Arafat believed he needed a mandate before the next great step, similar to that which he had received at the 19th PNC in November 1988. The factions attending were Fath, the PFLP, the DFLP (both factions), the Palestine Liberation Front (PLF), the Palestine Popular Struggle Front (PPSF), the Arab Liberation Front (ALF), and the PCP. According to 'Arafat, there were a total of 669 PNC members, 186 of whom were from the territories and prevented from attending by Israel, leaving 483 eligible to attend; about 413 actually did.[155] As had often happened, PLO constituent organizations attempted terrorist attacks on Israel on the eve of the session. Fath tried to land six gunmen in Nahariyya (northern Israel), but the squad was stopped near Naqura, in Lebanon. A DFLP squad, most probably of Hawatima's branch, attempted to infiltrate Israel through Syria.[156] Preparations for the session involved negotiations with Hamas, a process which had begun in 1990, and, under Syrian pressure, with the Damascus-based faction of the Palestinian National Salvation Front (PNSF).

THE PNC: PREPARATORY NEGOTIATIONS
Negotiations with Hamas
Hamas presented a twofold challenge to the PLO: it represented a very popular group based in the territories (which did not recognize the PLO as the sole, legitimate representative of the Palestinian people); and it challenged the PLO's nonsectarian nature. In 1990, negotiations had been held with Hamas but were broken off after the Islamic group demanded an unheard-of 40%–50% share of the seats in the PNC (see *MECS* 1990, pp. 227–29). Fath officials were concerned that "fraternal Hamas," as they often called the organization, was not interested in working within the PLO framework, but rather wanted to substitute for it.[157] The threat of Hamas was perceived as a threat to the very essence of Palestinian institutional existence. In late August, talks were held between Hamas and the PLO in Amman. Chaired by PNC Speaker Shaykh 'Abd al-Hamid al-Sa'ih, the talks ended with no agreement. Hamas demanded either 40% of the PNC seats, or elections in the territories and outside. It

also insisted on the cancellation of the resolutions of the 19th PNC in 1988, which had been the basis of the PLO's peace strategy. The PLO, said Hamas representative to the talks, Ibrahim Ghawsha, had to commit itself to "the liberation of Palestine from the sea to the river."[158] In early September, Hamas announced that it would not attend the upcoming PNC, claiming that the PLO refused to hold elections and only offered Hamas 18 seats, or about 4% of the PNC.[159]

On the eve of the PNC session, Hamas issued a statement explaining its nonparticipation. The PNC was about to sell out parts of Palestine, and was "not qualified and not authorized to make a decision representing the Palestinian people."[160] As the peace conference was about to convene in Madrid, Ghawsha stated that the PLO-approved delegation did not represent the Palestinian people, "only itself."[161] For the PLO, the point was that Hamas had to accept the PLO's legitimacy by working within it; if they wanted to, they could press their case at the PNC.[162] 'Abd Rabbuh said, "We want the Hamas movement to be a part of the national coalition and not outside of it," and 'Arafat condemned the Gulf states for funding "these fundamentalists inside the occupied territories out of spite for the PLO."[163]

Both on the eve of the PNC and of the Madrid conference, Hamas clashed with Fath supporters in the territories and threatened the lives of two delegates. The organization also disrupted an appearance by Faysal al-Husayni in Tulkarm.[164]

The cumulative effect of the conflict between the PLO and Hamas was to strengthen the alliance between the Fath-dominated PLO leadership outside and the moderate West Bank and Gaza personalities, against Hamas, the DFLP and the PFLP, all of which threatened to derail the peace process.

Negotiations with the PNSF[165]

The Syrian-controlled PNSF exploited the PLO's stand on the Iraqi invasion of Kuwait during and immediately after the Gulf War to attack 'Arafat. His leadership was feeble, said PNSF Chairman Khalid al-Fahum, and had led to Palestinian suffering in the Gulf and the territories. He saw the weakening of the PLO as a chance to push for a new PNC, since, in his view, all sessions since 1984 (the first session after the Syrian-inspired revolt against 'Arafat in 1983) were illegitimate. What was needed, said Fahum, was for 'Arafat to relinquish the leadership.[166] On 8 April, the PNSF issued an official statement calling for a dialogue (with Fath) to form a "preparatory committee made up from all factions on an equal basis and some personalities in order to form a new Palestine National Council from which a new Palestinian leadership will emerge." Later, Fahum elaborated that all the PNSF organizations, as well as Hamas and Islamic Jihad, should be given seats on the PLO Executive Committee.[167]

At other times, such calls would have met with derision from Fath, which would hardly have given them another thought. Fath correctly saw the PNSF as totally subservient to Syria and completely lacking in any grass-roots legitimacy. But in 1991, the PLO was looking to coordinate with a Syrian harder line as the peace process developed, and so Qaddumi met quietly with the PNSF in late May in Damascus while he was there for talks with the Syrians.[168] However, the meeting with the PNSF was more a gesture to the Syrians than anything else. PLO officials made no statements which showed that they took Fahum's initiative seriously. For Fath, the best that it hoped for was to co-opt the PNSF back into the PNC, and then let it get lost in the shuffle. In June, PNC Speaker 'Abd al-Hamid al-Sa'ih invited several PNSF factions as well as Fahum and former Executive Committee members 'Abd al-Muhsin Abu Mayzar and Muhammad Zuhdi al-Nashashibi, to a preparatory meeting for the PNC.[169] This was as far as Fath was prepared to go. There was no indication that any of them attended, although Nashashibi was returned to the Executive Committee at the September PNC session.

In fact, no serious dialogue was held with the PNSF, because Fath was simply not interested. A perfunctory meeting with 'Arafat in Tunis in mid-July yielded nothing. The PNSF included groups such as Abu Musa's, which had revolted and taken up arms against 'Arafat in 1983. The PNSF wanted Abu Musa's group to take the name "Fath-Corrective Movement," an idea rejected out-of-hand by Fath. There were reports that Fahum even wanted to bring in the FRC, the sworn enemy of Fath, although he denied them.[170]

On the eve of the convening of the PNC, the PNSF issued a statement explaining its reasons for not attending. It blamed the PLO leadership for rejecting attempts to hold a dialogue in San' a or Tripoli, Libya. The PNSF rejected the PNC resolutions and later condemned the PLO's agreement to the peace talks.[171] Members of the PNSF, as well as George Habash and Speaker Sa'ih, attended the "International Conference to Support the Islamic Revolution of the People of Palestine" held in Tehran in October to oppose peace talks.[172]

THE PNC: PROCEEDINGS

The previous (19th) PNC had convened in November 1988 when the uprising in the West Bank was in its prime, and when the PLO was benefiting from the unprecedented sympathy won by the residents of the territories as they confronted the Israelis. In the heady atmosphere of that occasion, the State of Palestine was proclaimed. The resolutions of the session inaugurated a process, which, by the end of the year, led to the opening of a dialogue with the US. But almost three years had passed, and as the 20th PNC convened in Algiers in September, the PLO was under siege. The Intifada seemed to be waning, having greatly deteriorated into killing of Palestinians by Palestinians. Geopolitically, the deployment of the Lebanese army in Southern Lebanon had restricted the organization's freedom of movement in that country (see below), shrinking the PLO's area of influence. The PLO's stance in the Gulf War had crippled the group financially and diplomatically, so that when the peace process got under way again it was the residents of the territories, the US, Israel and the Gulf states who set the rules. Moreover, the Soviet Union was doing the bidding of the US and could no longer be relied on for support; worse still, its Jewish population was immigrating to Israel in massive numbers, threatening what many leaders had seen as the Palestinians trump card, demography. To top it off, Israel was building settlements in the territories at an unprecedented rate. There was a painful sense that the PLO might be losing the veto power over the Palestinian issue that it had enjoyed for so many years. As a result, at the PNC session, 'Arafat, who dominated the body and controlled PLO funds, found himself compelled to argue for a peace process in which the PLO was not allowed a visible role.

Although 'Arafat and his supporters dominated the PNC, the forum had always been one of open debate, and it was again this time. 'Arafat saw his task as obtaining a mandate from the PNC to carry on in the peace process, leaving him and the Executive Committee he controlled to decide what to do. His opening speech emphasized the Palestinian constants: the right to self-determination, the right of return, and the right to establish an independent state. At the same time, 'Arafat set a realistic and flexible tone. The traditional demand for an international conference was notably absent. He pointed out that the world was moving toward a new order, that the situation had changed, and that the Palestinians would deal with the opportunity for peace seriously and with an open mind. The speech concluded with the Palestinians' readiness to bring about the success of the peace conference and to overcome remaining obstacles, but this was balanced by a rejection of "the Israeli extortion and the Israeli conditions."[173]

Both Qaddumi and Khalid al-Hasan came out strongly in favor of attending the peace conference. In his political report to the PNC, Qaddumi matter-of-factly recalled the stages of negotiations between Baker and the West Bank and Gaza leaders, all of whom were authorized and directed (he maintained) by the PLO leadership. Like 'Arafat, he asserted the PLO constants and admitted that the situation had changed. The PLO was politically and financially isolated and new centers of power had emerged which the PLO could not ignore and with which it had to deal.[174]

The speech of Khalid al-Hasan expressed the mood of resignation among the PNC members toward the peace conference. Absolute ideals could not continue to be rehashed as the world was changing. If they were, the Palestinians would be left out. Hasan summarized the essence of the PLO's predicament. The US was in the catbird seat, and the PLO could do nothing about it. Time was working against the Palestinians, and if the PLO did not act, it would become just another "Arab Higher Committee." "It is not enough for us to say that our conscience rejects, and therefore we have to reject everything. We are dealing with politics, with the future of a people, and not with wedding arrangements." What Hasan appeared to be suggesting was a radically different "theory of stages." Whereas this strategy, originally enunciated in 1974, sought to liberate all of Palestine and eliminate Israel by initially accepting whatever land was possible, Hasan may now have been suggesting that a new theory of stages had to be invoked: first self-rule, and then a state, but all limited to the West Bank and Gaza (for excerpts from his important speech, see Appendix II).

George Habash and Na'if Hawatima both spoke out strongly against going to the peace conference. Habash chastised the members of the PNC for approving the "capitulationist" resolutions of the 19th PNC (which the PFLP had voted against), since they had not drawn the PLO any closer to a Palestinian state. "The establishment of the Palestinian state is a mission of struggle before it is a mission of diplomacy," cried Habash, "which can be achieved by not being content with the [leadership's] formula of continuation of the Intifada plus international support, but also by escalation of the Intifada and the infliction of human and economic losses on the Zionist enemy, with the affirmation of refraining from granting free concessions."[175] "We refuse to enter the [peace] conference of liquidation," Habash stressed, "and we reject the formula of yes, but. We must clearly say no."[176]

Hawatima also rejected the conference. The US, he said, does not recognize the Palestinians as a people, otherwise it would let them be represented by the PLO. "They're asking us to put our head under an axe," he exclaimed. All that was left was the armed struggle; the Arab states, while not supporting the PLO politically, were also preventing attacks on Israel by Palestinian groups.[177]

Three important organizational events also occurred at the 20th PNC: the removal of the PLF's secretary-general, Muhammad 'Abbas (Abu al-'Abbas), from the Executive Committee; the split in the DFLP (discussed above); and the choosing of a new Executive Committee. As early as March, 'Arafat had mooted the proposal that 'Abbas might be removed from the Executive Committee if the US would, in exchange, renew its dialogue with the PLO, suspended after 'Abbas's group had carried out an attack on Israel in May 1990.[178] By early September, the issue was already being characterized by the PLO as a proposal to be submitted to the PNC.[179] On the eve of the PNC, reading the writing on the wall, 'Abbas announced that he would not nominate himself to the Executive Committee again.[180] His organization, however, maintained its seat. 'Arafat stated later that now he expected the US to renew the dialogue.[181] In late November, the State Department refused to reopen the dialogue, saying that the time was not right. Moreover, stated the State Department spokeswoman, the PLO had not condemned the May 1990 attack, which was another condition for resuming the dialogue.[182]

The split in the DFLP (for background, see above) was formalized at the 20th PNC. Hawatima had threatened to boycott the PNC if the Fath-dominated PLO leadership did not recognize him as the leader of the DFLP and 'Abd Rabbuh's group as a new, different organization.[183] As the PNC was about to convene, differences were not resolved: 'Abd Rabbuh said that he was the candidate of the DFLP for the Executive Committee, while Hawatima stated that 'Abd Rabbuh's DFLP "dissidents" would be represented by an independent candidate.[184]

At the PNC the two factions clashed when 'Abd Rabbuh insisted on speaking in the name of the DFLP and demanded the PLO funds allocated to the DFLP. While Hawatima wanted to get rid of them, the 'Abd Rabbuh faction said it was interested in an alliance of the left.[185] In the event, representatives of both factions, 'Abd Rabbuh himself and Hawatima's representative, Taysir Khalid, were put on the Executive Committee.

The number of Executive Committee members was raised at the PNC from 15 to 18. The newly constituted Executive Committee was as follows (it should be noted that the independents support Fath; the asterisk indicates new members):

1. Yasir 'Arafat (Abu 'Ammar, Fath).
2. Faruq Qaddumi (Abu Lutf, Fath).
3. Mahmud 'Abbas (Abu Mazin, Fath).
4. Yasir 'Abd Rabbuh (DFLP, his faction).
5. Sulayman al-Najjab (PCP).
6. 'Abdalla Hawrani (independent).
7. Mahmud Darwish (independent).
8. Jamal al-Surani (independent).
9. Jawid al-Ghusayn (independent, chairman of the Palestine National Fund).
10. 'Abd al-Rahim Malluh* (PFLP, replaced Abu 'Ali Mustafa al-Zibri).
11. 'Ali Ishaq* (PLF, replaced Muhammad 'Abbas).
12. Mahmud Isma'il* (Abu Isma'il, ALF, replaced 'Abd al-Rahim Ahmad).
13. Taysir Khalid* (DFLP, Hawatima faction).
14. Samir Ghawsha* (PPSF, first time for organization on Executive Committee).
15. Shafiq al-Hut* (independent, PLO representative in Beirut).
16. Muhammad Zuhdi al-Nashashibi* (independent, a former Executive Committee member).

17. Yasir 'Amru (independent).

18. Archbishop Iliya Khuri (independent).

Muhammad Milhim and 'Abd al-Razzaq al-Yahya were not returned to the Executive Committee.

'Arafat was reelected president of the state of Palestine during the session. As *Filastin al-Thawra* reported it, no sooner had Executive Committee member Jamal al-Surani begun to read to the PNC plenary the CC's decision to reappoint 'Arafat (the PNC was supposed to vote on it) — than the assembled multitude burst into protracted applause, which was understood as unanimous consent.[186]

'Arafat's closing speech was a riveting appeal for support from the international community. He implored the Gulf states to put the past behind them, and spoke movingly about the predicament of the Palestinian:

> Without an identity and without a nationality! Our children — our children! A Palestinian is a problem from the day he is born until he dies. Where does one register his birth?...What is more, when a Palestinian dies, I cannot find a place where I can bury him....Does President Bush know this? Do the US people know? Is Europe aware that the Palestinian individual has no place where he can be buried?[187]

One interesting sidelight at the session was the reported presence of Husayni and 'Ashrawi. Journalists cited reliable sources which maintained that the two had been there, and had given well-received speeches. According to one source, they received a three-minute standing ovation, and some delegates wept openly when 'Ashrawi spoke. Husayni, 'Ashrawi, and 'Arafat denied that the event had taken place.[188] They were, of course, well aware of the Israeli law which declares contacts with the PLO illegal.

THE PNC: THE POLITICAL STATEMENT

The PNC issued its political statement (*al-bayan al-siyasi*; text in Appendix III) on 28 September. Two hundred and fifty-six voted in favor, 68 against, and 12 abstained.[189] The effect of the resolution was to give the 'Arafat-dominated Executive Committee and CC carte blanche to continue PLO involvement in the process. The leadership was to act on the basis of several enunciated goals, but these were not conditions for negotiations. When all was said and done, 'Arafat was in control, and could move ahead as he wanted. In effect, it was another in a long series of victories for the PLO leader.

The resolution stated that a peace settlement should be based on the following principles: UN Security Council Resolutions 242 and 338 and their implementation, land for peace, and the national and political rights of the Palestinians; Jerusalem as part of the occupied territories; a halt to settlements; the right of the PLO to form the Palestinian delegation from within and without the homeland, including Jerusalem, participating on an equitable basis; coordination of positions with the Arab countries; and connection between all stages of the settlement. These principles were to form the basis for the following goals which the PLO would try to accomplish: right to self-determination; full Israeli withdrawal from all territories occupied in 1967, including Jerusalem; solving the Palestinian refugee problem in accordance with UN resolutions, particularly General Assembly Resolution 194, which called for the return of Palestinian refugees to Israel or their compensation; provisional arrangements to include sovereignty over land, water, natural resources, and all political and economic affairs; international protection for the Palestinians before the implementation of self-determination; and guarantees that the settlements would be removed.

Although not explicit, on the basis of the text there appears to be a greater recognition of Israel. Previously, the concept of "self-determination" was left unexplained, in a manner that left it to be understood to include all of Palestine, since the partition of Palestine and the establishment of a Jewish state (Jewish self-determination) were seen, by definition, as a denial of the Palestinians' right to self-determination (see *MECS* 1988, pp. 251–54). In the political statement of the 20th PNC, the right of self-determination was more clearly linked and limited to the territory from which Israel would withdraw, not Israel itself. Moreover, in the goals with which the leadership was charged to carry out, the issue of the refugees was to be dealt with in accordance with Resolution 194, which also mentions compensation. In other words, there was no explicit insistence on the actual physical return of the refugees to Israel (the "right of return") although that right is mentioned in another section of the document. What this did was to bring the written record, the "constitutional" documents of the PLO, in line with some of what PLO leaders had been saying since 1988, namely, that compensation was an option for solving the refugee issue, and that Israel need not be threatened by a mass return of former residents.

The door was left open for the leadership to continue, and even to form a joint delegation with Jordan. Operationally, the Executive Committee was authorized to continue the peace process in accordance with PNC resolutions, but was obligated to bring the results of its efforts to the CC for a final decision. Since both the Executive Committee and the CC were controlled by 'Arafat, the statement also amounted to a blank check and gave a green light to the peace process.

On another issue, the political statement paid lip service to those who called for PLO reform, by calling for an increase in the role of the CC in implementing PNC resolutions "as a way of consolidating democracy and its practice."

STRATEGIC ATTITUDES

In interviews with the Israeli and Western-language press, 'Arafat was more conciliatory than ever with respect to recognizing Israel and living with it side-by-side. He told *Yedi'ot Aharonot* that the establishment of a state or confederation alongside Israel would constitute an end to the conflict. In correspondence with Israeli peace activist Abie Nathan, he reaffirmed remarks made at his press conference in Geneva in which he recognized Israel (see *MECS* 1988, p. 256). He told *Le Figaro* that he would continue to wear the PLO insignia, which showed Palestine from the sea to the river, until he reached a territorial agreement with Israel. "Then," he continued, "the badge I wear will only show the confines of the state on which we have reached agreement." Khalaf, however, set a far less conciliatory tone. Contrary to his positive statements toward the peace process and Israel in 1990 (see *MECS* 1990, p. 218), he resumed his militant tone at a rally in Amman in support of Saddam in early January: "We shall not abandon Palestine," he announced. "We renew the pledge to liberate all of Palestine from the sea to the river, inch by inch [*shibran shibran*]...Our conflict with the Zionists has not stopped and will not stop. It will continue with arms, knives, stones, and everything that is within our reach. The main thing is that we must continue to fight them, and the fire of our struggle must remain alive until we kick out the last Zionist from our homeland, Palestine."[190] Perhaps Khalaf let his guard down as he was carried away by the enthusiasm of the crowd. In any case, the conflicting statements reflected the continuing ideological uncertainty in the PLO over the historical concessions needed to reach a peace settlement.

TUNIS VIEWS THE INTIFADA

In 1991, the PLO leadership became increasingly disappointed with the direction that the Intifada was taking. Popular mobilization had dropped drastically, and the initiative had been taken up by masked youths, who killed more Palestinians during the year than did the Israelis (as also happened in 1990).[191] This, too, was another contributing factor which forced the PLO to move more quickly and be more flexible in the peace process, since, as the leadership came to believe, time was working against the Palestinians. The specter of the deadly infighting in the Arab rebellion of 1936–39 must have been in everyone's mind. The glory of the Intifada had turned ugly — masked youths with knives were taking the place of the well-organized merchants' strike. It was the moderate leadership in the territories that was the most frightened by these developments, and they turned to the PLO for help. The masked youths were from all factions, including Fath, but the leadership outside the territories was not always in complete control (see chapter on the West Bank and the Gaza Strip).

Articles in the local Palestinian press condemned the masked youths, and the leaflets of the Unified National Command (UNC), also broadcast on the PLO's Voice of Palestine, banned the wearing of masks under any pretext. The leaflets also prohibited the killing of suspected collaborators.[192] The same call was echoed by the PLO from Tunis, and 'Arafat himself.[193]

The killings led the leadership outside and inside to perceive that the Intifada was in crisis, moribund, a kind of malaise. There were calls for greater coordination between the inside and outside, for isolating what was termed "negative social phenomena," and for greater unity. But most of these ideas came from the inside; on the outside, they were mostly expressed by minor personalities.[194] No doubt the PLO was concerned about the direction that the Intifada had taken, but little was said about it publicly. The Intifada was the jewel in the crown of the Palestinian struggle, and to call negative attention to it was not deemed good politics.

LOSING LEBANON

In 1990, the PLO had made efforts to establish a place for itself and the Palestinians in Lebanon after the Ta'if agreement, and had strengthened its presence in the Tyre refugee camps (see *MECS* 1990, pp. 234–35). In 1991, the Lebanese army, backed by the Syrians, expanded its presence to the south, eliminating significant independent action for the PLO in the land of the cedars.

In a policy statement issued on 9 January, Lebanese Prime Minister 'Umar Karami announced that all "Lebanese and non-Lebanese militias" would be dissolved and would have to hand over their weapons.[195] The "non-Lebanese" referred to were primarily the Palestinians. As Israel and the PLO were battling in the south in late

January and early February (see above), the Lebanese Government announced that its troops would begin deploying there on 7 February.[196] The timing was not coincidental. Israeli attacks gave the PLO a raison d'être for being in the south, to protect Palestinian concentrations. But the attacks undermined the government, which was intent on extending its practical sovereignty. Moreover, if Israel was going to be convinced it should withdraw from its security zone in the south, removing the PLO would help greatly. It seems that the Israeli attacks then, and even more so later in the year, were aimed at reinforcing this impression. And lastly, the support of the PLO for Iraq gave Syria the extra leeway it needed to rid Lebanon of 'Arafat loyalists.

The Lebanese were intent first on deploying in the Tuffah region, where the 'Arafat loyalists, now numbering about 800, had interposed themselves between Amal and Hizballah in 1990, ostensibly to prevent fighting, but in reality to gain strategic depth in the region adjoining Sidon. Amal and Hizballah agreed to withdraw from the region, thus robbing the PLO of its pretext for being there.[197] As the 7 February deadline approached, local PLO officials announced that they would stop rocket attacks on Israel.[198] It was at this juncture that Israel stepped up its attacks in an attempt to encourage the Lebanese Government to deploy.[199] The Lebanese army did so in the Tuffah region beginning on 7 February, continuing until the middle of the month, although the PLO apparently still maintained a small presence in the Tuffah region, and kept its weapons.

As the move to disband and disarm all militias in Lebanon gathered momentum in April, the PLO dug in its heels. Lebanon was the last place on earth that the PLO could act with relative independence. As a guerrilla organization, it needed to maintain the armed struggle, and this could not be done from Tunis or Baghdad. Moreover, if its presence was limited, its influence over a major part of its constituency would be curtailed. Initially, the PLO refused to disarm or disband. Zayd Wahba announced that the Palestinians would not lay down their weapons, which were not, he maintained, for use in domestic conflicts, "but for regional considerations required for the struggle" against Israel.[200] 'Arafat said that the PLO should be allowed to keep the weapons in order to protect the camps, within the framework of an arrangement with the government.[201] However, because the PLO was becoming weaker on the international level, Lebanese leaders were encouraged and spoke of the organization in terms unheard of in earlier years. The minister of defense, Michel al-Murr, declared: "Palestinian guns have not liberated one inch of Palestine for the past 16 years. Under no circumstances will we allow the Palestinians to use their weapons to establish a state within our state."[202] Initially, however, Syria decided to exempt the Palestinians from disarming, most probably because they had agreed with Iran to exempt Hizballah.[203]

In mid-May, the Lebanese army deployed around the refugee camps near Tyre: Rashidiyya, Shabriha and Jall al-Bahr. While officially welcoming the deployment, Palestinian officials were waiting for the outcome of talks, which were supposed to reach an agreement with the government. Qaddumi, who headed the Palestinian side of the talks, said that no Palestinian would give up his arms. At this stage, the PLO did not.[204]

The Lebanese Government set 1 July as the deadline for its deployment in the Sidon area — in Sidon proper and particularly around the Palestinian camps of 'Ayn al-Hilwa and Miya wa-Miya, as well as extensions of those positions in several villages in the hills to the east of the city. The PLO was opposed. Talks in Cairo between the two sides were essentially a failure, as the Lebanese refused to agree to several Palestinian conditions, which included the establishment of a PLO embassy in Beirut, normalization of relations between the government and the PLO, guarantees of security, and political, social and civic rights for Palestinians living in Lebanon.[205] As the deadline approached, the PLO vowed that "Palestinians have decided to defend their guns in Southern Lebanon."[206]

Although the deployment in Sidon proper on 1 July went smoothly as the city was taken over from Mustafa Sa'd's Sunni militia, fighting broke out with the Palestinians. Battles continued for a few days; the PLO finally agreed to surrender and give up its arms, but the flushing out of resisters continued for several days more. Syrian troops were poised to back up the Lebanese should they need it. Wahba termed the offensive a "massacre." PLO forces evacuated several positions to the east of Sidon by 5 July, although they remained firmly entrenched in 'Ayn al-Hilwa and Miya wa-Miya. By 8 July, the PLO had turned over 97% of its heavy and medium weapons, according to Lebanese officials.[207] In Tyre, the army expanded its deployment to collect heavy arms from the Palestinians, encountering no resistance.[208]

At the end of the year, the PLO presence was confined to the refugee camps around Sidon and Tyre. PLO armed men maintained personal arms, but had given up most of their heavy and medium weapons. Although there were rumors that PLO men would be transferred out of the south, or out of Lebanon altogether, at the end of year there was no indication that this had taken place to any significant extent. Thus, while 1990 had seen a strengthening of Fath in Lebanon, 1991 saw the movement's wings severely clipped. The Palestinian movement "is not dead yet," proclaimed Wahba, "we will get back at the Israelis with other methods and from other front lines."[209]

As had often been the case, Lebanon was the arena for a series of battles between Palestinians. In Lebanon, Palestinian warlords had their own militias and were often free from direct control, although they owed some allegiance to one faction or another. Reasons for conflict were often personal, sometimes with a veneer of ideological justification.

In mid-February, clashes broke out in Palestinian positions east of Sidon between Fath-'Arafat members; one faction was led by the commander of Fath forces in South Lebanon, Col. 'Ala al-Afandi, and the other by the commander of the Sa'd Sa'il battalion of Fath, Lt. Col. Abu Muhammad Za'rura. Fighting later spread to Rashidiyya. The fighting was apparently the result of Za'rura's kidnapping and beating of Afandi, his superior officer. Za'rura's move was essentially a revolt against 'Arafat, who had agreed to withdraw Palestinian forces from east of Sidon; Za'rura did not want to leave. The conflict may also have been over money. Along with Afandi, Fath's treasurer was also abducted. 'Arafat had ordered Za'rura to cut expenses because of the financial drain on the PLO as a result of its stand on the Gulf War. After battles which left tens wounded, Za'rura was captured and executed, along with 20 others, by an "emergency tribunal" set up along lines ordered by the PLO from Tunis, according to local Palestinian sources.[210]

There were other, less serious, incidents during the year. For example, in late October 300 Fath men reportedly seized their headquarters in 'Ayn al-Hilwa as a protest against the PLO's agreement to participate in the peace conference[211] (see also chapter on Lebanon).

RELATIONS WITH JORDAN

The year 1991 saw a beginning of the turning of the tables in the Jordanian-PLO relationship. Whereas in 1988 Jordan had "disengaged" from the Palestinian issue, acknowledging the victory of the PLO in the ongoing struggle between the two, in 1991 it was the PLO which was knocking on Jordan's door. Many of the themes of the elaborate political dance of previous years began to replay themselves; the parties needed each other, but neither was happy about it.

The PLO found itself in the humiliating position of going back to the old formula of a joint Jordanian-Palestinian delegation, and of needing Jordan's help to have it include East Jerusalemites. King Husayn knew that his efforts to help the Palestinians out of their dilemma would be well received in the US, and he needed Washington's goodwill after he had chosen the opposing side during the Gulf War. When the PLO dragged its feet on the joint delegation issue, Husayn expressed himself in a manner that had not been heard for a long time, and in a way which attempted to widen the rift between the Palestinians in the territories and the PLO leadership. Referring to the PLO as being "by definition a temporary body," he stressed that the Palestinians living under occupation were "the ultranationalists who stood their ground and suffered....It is not for people outside of the suffering...to pontificate on what should or should not be done," Husayn remarked. It was, rather, "the people in the occupied territories [who] have the right for us to be concerned about their conditions and see what can be done."[212] On another occasion, he announced that "the time had come to take into account the needs of the Palestinian people, and I mean the people, not organizations, governments, or [public] personalities."[213]

RELATIONS WITH SYRIA

Syria released several thousand Palestinian prisoners loyal to 'Arafat in mid-March.[214] The gesture seemed to have two different but complementary goals: first, to strengthen the hand of PNSF Chairman Khalid al-Fahum, whom they were considering as a replacement for 'Arafat, or at least to get him back in the PNC to control the PLO leader;[215] and second, to make 'Arafat a bit beholden to Syria as the peace process got under way following the Gulf War. As noted above, the PLO also needed Syria to counter Jordan and, sometimes, the West Bank and Gaza leadership. Moreover, the organization feared a possible Syrian sell-out of the Palestinians, by making a separate deal with Israel for the Golan Heights. The PLO thanked the Syrians dryly for the release: "While expressing its appreciation of this positive step, the PLO hopes that it will lead to more measures and steps...."[216]

As noted above, in May Faruq Qaddumi led an Executive Committee delegation to Syria in order to see how much they could count on Syria for support during the peace process. They also discussed the issue of Lebanon, as the PLO sought Syrian support for institutionalizing the organization's presence there and allowing it freedom of movement. However, it received no consolation on that score (see above). At the end of the visit, PLO leaders tried to portray relations with Damascus in a positive light, but there was still little love lost between the parties.[217]

'Arafat visited Damascus in October, November and December to discuss the peace process with Syrian President Asad. Although the Arab participants in the peace talks and the PLO met in late October and agreed to bar separate deals with Israel,[218] which the PLO wanted very much, in Madrid the Palestinians stood up to the Syrians and began bilateral talks, leaving Damascus with no choice but to go along. According to reports, Asad was quite upset about this, telling 'Arafat that such moves only served Israel's interests.[219]

Despite these differences, after the PNC, during which the Syrians were not able to get Fahum and his supporters in, and after Madrid when they and the Palestinians-PLO were engaged in talks with Israel, Syria began to normalize relations by apparently telling the PLO in November that it would soon be allowed to reopen its offices in Damascus. PLO officials were quite ecstatic about this, stating that relations had returned to normal.[220] However, by the end of the year, there was no indication that the offices had actually been reopened.

APPENDIX I: REPORT ON DETAILS OF THE PLO-JORDAN AGREEMENT ON A JOINT DELEGATION TO THE PEACE CONFERENCE[221]

General Objectives
The agreement seeks to:
* Ensure Israel's withdrawal from Palestinian territories and the other Arab territories occupied in 1967, including the venerable Jerusalem, implementing Security Council Resolution 242 and the relevant UN resolutions.
* Solve the refugee issue in accordance with the UN resolutions, especially Resolution 194.
* Enable the Palestinian people to exercise their right of self-determination, in order to establish a confederal Jordanian-Palestinian union.
* Ensure the Arabism of venerable Jerusalem and reaffirm its status as an indivisible part of the Palestinian territories occupied in 1967, and a part which, in accordance with Security Council and UN resolutions, is subject to that which is applicable to the other occupied territories.

Working Plan
The agreement defines the working plan for implementing the agreement. Through movement with all the parties concerned, the two sides will seek to ensure the bases necessary for the convocation and success of the peace conference and for securing the Arab and Palestinian rights.

The agreement calls for a joint effort to bolster cooperation and coordination among the Arab parties directly concerned with the peace process, so as to underline Arab commitment to a comprehensive solution to the Palestinian issue and to the Arab-Israeli conflict. It further calls for a joint effort to secure comprehensive and ceaseless Arab support, at the various levels, for the Arab parties participating in the peace conference.

The agreement also calls for efforts to apply Security Council Resolution 242 to all phases of the solution, so as to ensure that they are interconnected and so that the comprehensive solution will achieve Palestinian sovereignty over the land, natural resources, political and economic affairs, and so forth.

Likewise, the agreement calls for efforts to secure international protection for the Palestinian people and the occupied territories throughout all phases of the settlement.

The Jordanian-Palestinian agreement also explains the tasks of the joint Jordanian-Palestinian delegation to the peace conference as follows:
* A. The Palestinian delegation will take charge of discussing the various aspects connected with the Palestinian issue in the committees designated for the purpose. The Jordanian delegation will have the same responsibility in matters pertaining to Jordan.
* B. One or more coordinating members from the Jordanian side will participate in the Palestinian-Israeli committee. One or more coordinating members from the Palestinian side will also participate in the Jordanian-Israeli committee.
* C. Through the joint political committee, agreement will be developed on the subjects and issues that both sides in the joint delegation can discuss within the conference committees, such as the issues of borders, security, water, and so forth.
* D. Following the pattern of the opening session, both sides in the joint Jordanian-Palestinian delegation will take part in the multilateral negotiations.

The Jordanian-Palestinian agreement defines how the Jordanian-Palestinian delegation to the peace conference will be formed. The delegation will consist of two equal and independent Jordanian and Palestinian delegations and each delegation will refer to its political leadership for authority. The agreement also provides for forming a higher political authority, including King Husayn and Yasir 'Arafat, to coordinate and direct the joint delegation's activities. The two Jordanian and Palestinian sides have further agreed to form a joint political committee that will be considered a direct authority for the Jordanian and Palestinian delegations, and that will organize their activities periodically.

The Jordanian-Palestinian delegation chairmanship consists of two chairpersons, a Jordanian and a Palestinian.

It should be noted that the Jordanian-Palestinian agreement on the peaceful solution process has been approved by the Jordanian Council of Ministers and the PLO Executive Committee.

APPENDIX II: EXCERPTS FROM KHALID AL-HASAN'S SPEECH TO THE PNC[222]

In the resolutions of the 1988 PNC, we talked about the right to self-determination. The American position says "no" to self-determination.

We demanded the right of return [to former Palestinian homes in Israel]. In the American memorandum there is no reference to the right of return.

We mentioned Jerusalem as the capital of the State of Palestine. The Americans say that Jerusalem is united and that the future is subject to negotiations.

We said the PLO is the legitimate representative of the Palestinian people. They say "no" to the PLO.

We proposed a peace initiative, including a comprehensive solution to the question of Palestine. They answered: a peace based on ending the occupation that took place during the 1967 war, but not the withdrawal of the Israeli forces.

We talked about an effective international conference. They answered by talking about bilateral negotiations and a ceremonial international conference.

We said an independent Palestinian state. They said "self-rule."

We said national rights for our people. They said "political rights only."

Will the PLO be able to pursue its effectiveness? Or will it merely become another "Arab Higher Committee"? Can the PLO revert and once again become an underground movement? Do we have to start from square one? Will the enemy wait for us until we rebuild our strength and change the balance of power, as some in this session have tried to imply? Or will he persist in his policy of settlement, deportation, and the implementation of the mass transfer of the Palestinian population? Does this serve the interests of the future of our people? It is not enough for us to say that our conscience rejects, and therefore we have to reject everything. We are dealing with politics, with the future of a people, and not with wedding arrangements.

APPENDIX III: POLITICAL STATEMENT, 20TH SESSION OF THE PNC, ALGIERS, 23–28 SEPTEMBER 1991[223]

In the name of God, the merciful, the compassionate. From the date of its beginning in 1965, the Palestinian revolution has embarked on a long, bitter and strenuous struggle during which our people have made huge sacrifices. This beginning came after years of excluding the Palestinian question and considering it a refugee question.

The long years of struggle in all forms, under the PLO leadership, the sole legitimate representative of our people, have again posed the question of Palestine to the international community on the grounds that it is the national cause of a people entitled to liberation, self-determination and independence.

The question of Palestine occupied a central position in the Arab-Israeli conflict. Peace, security, and stability in the ME cannot be secured unless this conflict is resolved.

Then came the blessed Intifada, with its popular and democratic depth, as a creative continuation of the Palestinian national struggle. It has constituted a distinct phase which has left its imprint on the whole world and reverberated around it. It has consolidated international recognition of our people's rights and of the PLO, which has always and immediately put such international support and polarization to use.

Thus, our National Council convened its 19th session and launched the Palestinian peace initiative, and the historic birth of the state of Palestine was proclaimed on 15 November 1988.

The world had welcomed our peace initiative through the resolutions of the UN General Assembly in its 43rd session, which was held in Geneva. Also, most countries recognized the state of Palestine and established diplomatic and political relations with it.

Despite the international welcome with which the Palestinian initiative and the historic speech by the President of the state of Palestine, brother Yasir 'Arafat, who demonstrated to the whole world our wish for a just peace, was met — for the first time the US announced the opening of an official dialogue with the PLO — the Israeli policy of stubbornness and pressure led to the failure of all initiatives and peaceful efforts, bringing them down a dead-end street.

Afterward, there came regional and international developments, most prominent of which was the Gulf War and the changes that occurred in the socialist bloc. This resulted in a substantial change in the balance of power. Thus, the Cold War came to an end, and the features of a new age in international relations began to develop, especially in the field of US-Soviet relations and cooperation between the two nations to resolve regional conflicts and problems peacefully.

The PLO has closely monitored the course of events in the world and their effect on the Palestinian question and the Arab-Israeli conflict. If the Palestinian people have had their homeland usurped as a result of the prejudices of the old world order, it is impermissible, according to any logic, that they be denied these rights in a phase witnessing the emergence of the new world order that raises slogans of democracy, human rights, and the sanctity of peoples' rights to self-determination. The current situation requires us to deal with it in the spirit of political responsibility and national realism and to examine the new regional and international developments. This situation also requires us to learn the lessons and experience from the popular Intifada that has turned the aim of Palestinian independence into a feasible program.

In harmony with the Palestinian initiative proposed in 1989 and with international and Arab legitimacy, the PLO has dealt positively and effectively with international and peaceful ideas, proposals and initiatives that relied on international legality. The PLO also welcomed the positive elements mentioned in the declaration of US President George Bush and the positions of the European Community (EC), the Soviet Union, the Nonaligned Movement states and other international quarters.

The PLO, which had welcomed the current peaceful efforts and initiatives and dealt with them positively, including the call launched by Presidents Bush and Gorbachev for convening a peace conference related to settling the conflict in the ME, believes that the success of the efforts aimed at holding the peace conference requires the continuation of work with the other sides so as to achieve the following foundations:

1. The peace conference should rely on international legitimacy and its resolutions, including UN Security Council Resolutions 242 and 338, and should undertake to implement them. These resolutions secure a full Israeli withdrawal from Arab and Palestinian occupied territories, including sacred Jerusalem; the realization of the land-for-peace exchange principle; and the national and political rights of the Palestinian people.

2. It must be stressed that Jerusalem is an indivisible part of occupied Palestine territory and that what applies to the rest of the occupied territories applies to it, as stipulated by the resolutions of the Security Council and the UN.

3. Halting settlement in the occupied territories, including holy Jerusalem, is an indispensable necessity to start the peace process, and international guarantees must be provided to achieve that.

4. The PLO, as the legitimate and sole representative of the Palestinian people, has the right to form the Palestinian delegation from within and outside the homeland, including Jerusalem, and to define the formula of their participation in the peace process on an equitable basis and in a way that stresses its authority.

5. Arab positions should be coordinated to ensure the realization of a comprehensive settlement, excluding unilateral solutions, in accordance with the resolutions of Arab summits.

6. The connection between the stages of the settlement toward reaching a comprehensive settlement should be ensured according to the resolutions of international legitimacy.

The PLO, which starts from these bases and premises on the peace efforts, aims to accomplish the following:

1. The right to self-determination must be secured for our Palestinian people in a way that guarantees the right to freedom and national independence.

2. There must be a full Israeli withdrawal from all Palestinian and Arab lands occupied in 1967, including holy Jerusalem.

3. The problem of Palestinian refugees driven out of their homeland by force and against their will must be resolved, in accordance with UN resolutions, especially Resolution 194, issued by the UN General Assembly.

4. Any provisional arrangement must include the right of our people to sovereignty of land, water, natural resources and all political and economic affairs.

5. International protection for the Palestinian people, in preparation for the exercise of the right to self-determination, must be provided.

6. Full guarantees must be provided for an effort to remove the existing settlements by declaring them illegal, in accordance with the resolutions of international law, including UN Security Council Resolution No. 465.

The National Council charges the Executive Committee to continue current efforts to provide the best conditions for guaranteeing the success of the peace process in accordance with the resolution of the PNC. However, the committee will submit the results to the CC to make a final decision in light of the supreme national interest of our people.

The PLO, which in the previous phase made all possible efforts to propel the peace process, hopes that the other parties, especially the US and the USSR, will also make efforts to help ease the obstacles placed by Israel before this ongoing political process and to leave the door open for a return to the UN Security Council so as to implement the resolutions of international legitimacy.

Working toward the achievement of our national objectives in the next phase and toward facing up to obstacles marring our struggle requires the consolidation and entrenchment of national unity in various fields. It requires developing the contribution of all national forces, bodies and personalities inside and outside the occupied homeland — along with the political leadership of the PLO — to all issues related to our people's future and the ongoing political process, and to finding the appropriate formula for achieving this purpose.

In this respect, the PNC calls for increasing the activities and role of the PLO CC in monitoring and implementing the resolutions of the National Council as a way of consolidating democracy and its practice. The Council considers promoting the Intifada and consolidating its popular and democratic character and the participation of our entire people in backing and supporting it to be the real guarantee for securing the political and national objectives in the next phase of our national struggle.

In this respect, the Council addresses its struggle greetings to the masses of the brave Intifada and stresses the consolidation of the role and prestige of the UNC of the Intifada, the development of its struggle wings, the continuation of the formation of cadres, and the setting up of supreme sectorial councils.

The Council reaffirms that the protection and support of the Intifada and the provision of all requirements for its development are at the forefront of Palestinian national action.

The Council extends greetings to our heroic prisoners in the detention centers of Zionist occupation and to our brave wounded who are watching over the path of the Intifada, which was built by our pure martyrs.

The National Council extends its struggle greetings to the masses of our steadfast people in Galilee, the Triangle, Negev and the coast, and reaffirms its appreciation of their struggle in defense of their rights against the policies of persecution and segregation and their active support for the brave Intifada.

The Council also affirms that guaranteeing the realization of the objectives of our people and Arab nation, through the peace process, in order to secure a full Israeli withdrawal from Arab and Palestinian lands, and to guarantee the right of return, the self-determination to our people, and the setting up of a Palestinian state with holy Jerusalem as its capital, require the restoration of inter-Arab solidarity in order to protect the Arab future in light of current international and regional changes.

In this respect, the Council invites the five Arab states concerned in the peace process to achieve the highest levels of political and diplomatic coordination between them, in order to face up to the requirements of the coming stage and to reinforce the Arab negotiating position, so as to guarantee the realization of a comprehensive solution at all levels and prevent any separate solutions at the expense of the national rights of our people and the rights of our Arab nation.

The National Council invites all the international community to promote its support and backing to the cause of the Palestinian people and its just struggle, and to enhance its resistance in the occupied homeland. The Council appreciates the role of the EC member states, and invites them to contribute effectively to providing conditions for success for the peace process on a balanced basis and in accordance with international law, in order to protect international security and stability in the ME and Mediterranean region.

The Council expresses its appreciation for, and tribute to, the positions of His Holiness the Pope and the Vatican in supporting the rights of our people. The National Council expresses its appreciation for the role of the Soviet Union, the People's Republic of China, the nonaligned states, the African states and the Islamic states' organization in backing the Palestinian cause, and their adherence to the bases of international law in resolving the conflict in the region.

The Council studied the relations of the PLO at the Arab level and made the following resolutions:

* The PNC salutes, at its 20th session, fraternal Algeria — the president, the government, and the people — for harboring the cause of Palestine, playing host to the PNC sessions, and continuously supporting the rights of our people since the flag of freedom and independence was hoisted in the Algeria of 1.5m. martyrs.

* The Council salutes, at its 20th session, fraternal Tunisia — the president, the government, and people — for their warm shelter to the leadership of the PLO, and for bearing a great deal of sacrifice that has reached the level of the mixing of Tunisian and Palestinian blood. Our eternal gratitude to Tunisia for its warm hospitality and fraternal solidarity.

* The Council thanks, in particular, His Majesty King Hasan II, chairman of the Jerusalem Committee, for his continuous efforts and endeavors in supporting the rights of the Palestinian people and the PLO, and for the support extended by the fraternal Kingdom of Morocco to the steadfastness of our people in the occupied homeland.

* The PNC expresses, at its 20th session, its appreciation for the continuous support given by the fraternal Libyan Jamahiriyya to the masses of the brave Palestinian Intifada.

* The PNC salutes the Arab Maghrib Union member states for their continuous support for the cause of Palestine and the PLO, and it appreciates the vital role played by these states on the road to recovering inter-Arab solidarity.

* The PNC expresses, at its 20th session, its deep solidarity with the fraternal Iraqi people in their suffering, and it asks the international community to immediately move to put an end to the economic boycott which endangers the lives of Iraqi children, women and men because of the lack of medicine and food. The PNC urges the masses of the Arab nation and the fraternal Arab states to extend a helping hand and support to fraternal Iraq. It also calls for an end to all forms of interference in its domestic affairs.

* The PNC also calls for serious and continuous action to retrieve inter-Arab solidarity between the sons of the Arab nation. The PNC salutes the Palestinian-Jordanian brotherhood and calls for its strengthening and deepening in all spheres. It confirms its previous resolutions on the special and distinguished relations linking the two fraternal Palestinian and Jordanian peoples. It calls for the continuation and reinforcement of coordination and cooperation between the PLO and sister Jordan in all fields.

* The PNC affirms its decisions on building future relations on the basis of a confederation between Jordan and Palestine.

* The PNC salutes sister Lebanon and hails the sacrifices of the Lebanese people in support of the Palestinian cause, and wishes success to the procession of the Lebanese national accord that aims to restore Lebanon's unity and sovereignty and ensures the authority of legitimacy on its territory. It also stresses full support in the battle of the liberation of the south from Israeli occupation toward the implementation of Resolution 425, which stipulates an Israeli withdrawal from all Lebanese territory.

* The Council calls for the entrenchment of fraternity between the peoples of Lebanon and Palestine through the organization of Lebanese-Palestinian relations on a solid basis that ensures political, struggle and social rights to the Palestinian people in Lebanon and provides security to the Palestinian camps in facing up to Israeli aggression and on the basis of close cooperation with the legitimate Lebanese authorities.

* The National Council stresses the necessity of completing the dialogue between the Lebanese Government and the PLO with a view to tackling Lebanese-Palestinian relations positively in all fields for the mutual interests of the two fraternal peoples.

* The National Council calls upon the five Arab countries directly involved in the Arab-Israeli conflict — Jordan, Egypt, Syria, Lebanon and Palestine — to achieve the highest level of political and diplomatic coordination to face up to the requirements of the coming political stage, and to strengthen the Arab negotiating position. The coordination between these fraternal countries should reach the summit level.

* The National Council refers with appreciation to the special significance of the holding of two sessions for the Arab foreign ministers within the framework of the Arab League on the land of sister Egypt, which continues to play an effective and fundamental role in reviving Arab solidarity and realizing a unified Arab position.

* The Council also alludes to the position of sister Egypt vis-à-vis the inalienable national rights of our people and her constant efforts to safeguard those rights.

* The Council calls for continuing the work toward the reinforcement of Syrian-Palestinian relations and the promotion of

coordination between sister Syria and the PLO toward serving the mutual national and pan-Arab interests and facing up to the challenges.

* The PNC appreciates the firm and continued support provided by the Kingdom of Saudi Arabia over long years for our Palestinian people and the PLO, and appreciates its continued hospitality and the facilitating of the employment and residence of the sons of our people on its territories. It hopes that the support will continue for the blessed Intifada, which is facing a war of starvation and attempts to destroy the economic structure waged by the Israeli occupation authorities against our people.

* The National Council salutes the peoples of fraternal Sudan and Yemen and their leaders and governments, and expresses its gratitude on behalf of the Palestinian people for the support to our people and hospitality to our forces being provided by our brothers in Sudan and Yemen despite their difficult circumstances.

* The PNC urges the international community to deal with the issue of Jewish colonizing emigration in a way that ensures that Israel does not use it to serve its objectives of expansion, colonization, and depriving our people of the right to decide their destiny in the territory of their homeland. The Council believes that the continuation of this emigration, in accordance with Israeli plans to intensify settlement in our occupied land, constitutes a direct obstacle, a danger threatening the future of peace in the region, and a violation of the Palestinian people's rights and international conventions.

* The PNC draws attention to the attempts and endeavors currently under way in some international circles to repeal the UN General Assembly's resolution on Zionism as a form of racism. The Council urges the Executive Committee to work with the friendly and fraternal states to face up to these attempts and to abort them.

* The Council salutes the struggle of all the peoples aspiring for equality, justice, spreading democracy and achieving equality in international relations. In this respect, the Council appreciates the struggle of the people of South Africa, under the leadership of the ANC [African National Congress] and the struggling leader Nelson Mandela, for equality and the removal of racism. The Council expresses its full solidarity with the people of South Africa in their just struggle in confronting racism and against the acts of sabotage perpetrated by the hostile instruments of racism. The PNC stresses the need to further give all forms of backing and support to the struggling and friendly people of South Africa.

* The Council also underlines its support and backing for and its solidarity with the African frontline states in the face of aggression and racism.

* The Council addresses greetings to the UN special committee to ensure the exercise of the Palestinian people's inalienable rights, to international nongovernmental fraternal and friendly institutions, and to the correspondents and news media that have stood and are standing on the side of the Intifada and struggle of our people.

* The PNC reiterates its commitment to the UN resolutions that affirm the right of peoples to resist foreign occupation, colonialism, and apartheid, and their right to struggle for their independence. The Council declares once again its rejection of terrorism in all its forms, including state terrorism.

* Finally, the PNC addresses greetings, compassion and love to our steadfast and patient Palestinian people, both inside our occupied land and in the diaspora, and to the masses of our Arab nation and its influential forces for their positions supporting and backing the Jihad of our Palestinian people and their national inalienable rights. The Council urges them to stand firmly in the face of the conspiracies hatched by the enemies of our Arab nation in order to preserve our Arab nation, its existence, pride, dignity and national security.

* The Council also addresses its greetings and appreciation to all the friends and the peace- and freedom-loving noble forces for their honorable positions on the side of the just causes of our people.

It is revolution until victory. Peace and the blessings of God be upon you.

NOTES

For the place and frequency of publications cited here, and for the full name of the publication, news agency, radio station or monitoring service where an abbreviation is used, please see "List of Sources." Only in the case of more than one publication bearing the same name is the place of publication noted here. The author wishes to thank Na'ama Gilad for her assistance in the preparation of this chapter.

1. AFP, 19 August — DR, 19 August; Reuters, 19 August; *Sawt al-Sha'b*, 20 August — DR, 20 August 1991.
2. *NYT*, 3 January 1991.
3. *Filastin al-Thawra*, 10 February 1991.
4. *JT*, 23 February 1991.
5. *NYT*, 21 January 1991.
6. VoP (Algiers), 17 January — DR, 18 January 1991.
7. VoP (Algiers), 10 February — DR, 10 February 1991.
8. AFP, 16 January — DR, 17 January; *Ha'aretz*, 17 January 1991.
9. VoP (Algiers), 29 January — DR, 30 January 1991.
10. *NYT*, 30 January 1991.

11. *NYT*, 31 January 1991.
12. *IHT*, 31 January 1991.
13. 'Abd Rabbuh, cited by TANJUG, 27 January — DR, 28 January; 'Arafat to Antenne 2 (TV), 29 January — DR, 30 January; see also 'Arafat to R. Monte Carlo, 30 January — DR, 31 January 1991. 'Abd Rabbuh held this office until the 20th PNC session in September when another DFLP representative was added, reflecting the split in the organization (see below).
14. Jihad to *Der Morgen*, 30 January — DR, 5 February 1991.
15. *NYT*, 15 March; *Le Figaro*, 11 February 1991.
16. R. Baghdad, 13 February — DR, 13 February 1991.
17. *Al-Hadaf* (Damascus), 27 January 1991.
18. R. Monte Carlo, 20 January — DR, 22 January 1991.
19. *Al-Hurriyya*, 3 February 1991.
20. *Izvestiia*, 18 October 1990. *Vanity Fair*, April 1991, carried an interview with ABC correspondent Pierre Salinger, who related: "He said he'd told Saddam to his face that what he'd done was disastrous for the Palestinian people. He told Saddam he was costing them lives and jobs. He told Saddam he was ruining the Palestinians' chances of ever getting a homeland of their own." "He told me he was never going back to Baghdad."
21. VoP (Baghdad), 3 January — DR, 3 January 1991.
22. It is beyond the scope of this chapter to go into the detail of the various theories on the assassination. PLO leaders tended to blame Israel, which they said they believed ran the FRC (see 'Arafat to *Le Figaro*, 11 February; 'Arafat, cited by MENA, 27 August — DR, 27 August; 'Arafat to *al-Ra'y* (Amman), 12 September 1991). In doing so they were voicing the theory most recently elaborated by Patrick Seale in his book *(Abu Nidal, a Gun for Hire: The Secret Life of the World's Most Notorious Arab Terrorist* [New York: Random House, 1992], pp. 312–17), that the FRC was controlled by Israeli intelligence. Seale seems to accept the PLO explanation. Even so, the initial statement issued by Fath after the assassination seemed to hint that they believed Iraq was behind it, as it maintained that the "killer is linked to an agent and a mercenary side" (VoP [Algiers], 15 January — DR, 16 January 1991). The theory that Khalaf may have been killed by the FRC operating on behalf of Saddam, because of Khalaf's opposition to the Iraqi annexation of Kuwait was the subject of much informed speculation by the press (see, for example, *NYT*, 17 January; *Bild*, 18 January — DR, 18 January 1991). As for the theory that Abu Nidal acted alone, this seemed to be the most likely. Before surrendering, Abu Zayid reportedly asked for 'Atif Abu Bakr, so that he could kill him. Abu Bakr was a former member of the FRC who had split from the organization in 1989 in a move organized by Fath, and most prominently, Abu Iyyad (on the Fath-engineered split in the FRC and fighting between Fath and the FRC in Lebanon, see *MECS* 1989, pp. 220–21). The most detailed articles on the assassination are in *MEI*, 25 January; and *Vanity Fair*, April 1991.
23. *Ha'aretz*, 8 April 1991.
24. *MEI*, 22 February 1991.
25. See, for example, *al-Sharq al-Awsat*, 18 February — DR, 25 February 1991.
26. *Sawt al-Kuwait al-Duwali* (London), 2 May — DR, 8 May 1991.
27. *JP*, 6 February, 1991, citing an interview with Said in the *LAT*.
28. *Al-Fajr* (English), 6 January 1992.
29. *Ha'aretz*, 13 December 1991.
30. On the white paper, see *Ha'aretz*, 5 May 1991.
31. *NYT*, 21 January 1991.
32. *IHT*, 2 January 1991.
33. *NYT*, 30 January; *Ha'aretz*, 18 March 1991, gave his name as 'Awni Batash, and it was reported that he was Fath's highest official in Kuwait, and that he was killed during allied bombing.
34. 'Arafat to *Le Figaro*, 11 February 1991.
35. *Ha'aretz*, 28 January 1991.
36. *JP*, 26 July 1991.
37. For reports on the Kuwaiti Government's treatment of its Palestinian residents, see *NYT*, 6, 14 March, 3 April, 6 May, 9 June 1991.
38. *IHT*, 5 July 1991.

39. *JP*, 24 February; VoP (Algiers), 3 March — DR, 5 March; *Sawt al-Sha'b* (Amman), 7 March — DR, 8 March 1991.
40. 'Arafat to *NYT*, 15 March 1991. Palestinian finances are notoriously difficult to follow, as they are not open to inspection. For a more comprehensive survey of the influence of the Gulf crisis on the financial state of the Palestinians and the PLO, see *al-Majalla*, 20 March 1991.
41. AFP, 26 September — DR, 27 September; *Ha'aretz*, 29 September 1991.
42. *JP*, 3 April 1991.
43. *Jerusalem Report*, 10 October 1991.
44. R. Riyadh, 6 February — DR, 7 February 1991.
45. *Sawt al-Kuwait al-Duwali*, 23 March — DR, 23 March 1991.
46. *NYT*, 11, 12 March, 12 May 1991.
47. Lamis Andoni, "The PLO at the Crossroads," *JPS*, Vol. 12, No. 1 (Autumn 1991), pp. 54–65.
48. Qaddumi to *al-Safir*, 11 October — DR, 16 October 1991.
49. R. Tunis, 25 October — DR, 25 October; *al-Dustur* (Amman), 11 November — DR, 12 November; *Shihan*, 16–22 November — DR, 15 November 1991.
50. *NYT*, 11 December 1991.
51. *MEI*, 20 December 1991.
52. In February, the European Community specifically ruled out meetings with 'Arafat (*JP*, 20, 27 February; *Ha'aretz*, 20 February), and in May Unesco again rejected the PLO's application for the "State of Palestine" to be admitted to the organization (*Ha'aretz*, 22 May 1991).
53. VoP (Algiers), 7 March — DR, 8 March 1991.
54. *JT*, 16 March 1991.
55. VoP (Algiers), 9 March — DR, 11 March; *al-Ra'y*, 12 March 1991.
56. Bethlehem mayor Ilias Freij to *al-Sharq al-Awsat*, 18 March — DR, 21 March; Faysal al-Husayni to *al-Sharq al-Awsat*, 29 March — DR, 5 April 1991.
57. *IHT*, 14 March 1991. That Abu Sharif was sending up another trial balloon seemed to be confirmed in late March when the PLO leader unveiled what was touted as a new peace plan that was said to offer Israel "substantial" territorial concessions, but actually differed little from previous initiatives (*FT*, 26 March 1991).
58. BBC World Service, R. Amman, 13 March — DR, 13, 14 March 1991.
59. AFP, 13 March — DR, 13 March 1991.
60. R Monte Carlo, MENA, 19 March — DR, 19 March; *NYT*, 21 March 1991.
61. 'Arafat to *Le Figaro*, 18 March 1991.
62. 'Arafat to *La Repubblica*, 12 March — DR, 14 March 1991.
63. MENA, 14 April — DR, 17 April 1991.
64. *Ha'aretz*, 1 January, citing a "Palestinian industrialist."
65. *JP*, 13 March 1991.
66. *Al-Fajr* (Arabic), 25 March — DR, 27 March 1991.
67. *Ha'aretz*, 25 March; *MEI*, 3 May 1991.
68. *Al-Fajr* (English), 1 April 1991.
69. *Ha'aretz*, 13 May; interview with Safi, *'Al-Hamishmar*, 13 May 1991.
70. *Al-Fajr* (English), 24 June 1991.
71. Andoni, op. cit.
72. *Al-Safir*, 4 March — DR, 8 March; R. IDF, 20 June — DR, 25 June; *NYT*, 23 June; *ST*, 14 July; *The Seattle Times*, 19 August 1991.
73. *Ha'aretz*, 25 September; *Ma'ariv*, 29 September 1991.
74. Ghassan al-Khatib to *al-Fajr* (Arabic), 29 July — DR, 2 August 1991.
75. Husayni to *Sawt al-Kuwait al-Duwali*, 12 April — DR 17 April 1991.
76. *MEI*. 10 January 1992.
77. *NYT*, 31 July, 3 August 1991.
78. R. Tunisia, citing WAFA, 2 August — DR, 2 August; *NYT*, 3 August; *Davar*, 4 August; see also Executive Committee statement, VoP (Algiers), 8 August — DR, 8 August 1991.
79. *JP*, 19 September; *NYT*, 20 September 1991.
80. For the purported text of the US memorandum to the Palestinians, see *al-Sharq al-Awsat*, 22 September — DR, 25 September 1991.

81. *Ha'aretz*, 20 September; *NYT*, 21 September 1991.
82. *NYT*, 21 September 1991.
83. *NYT*, 29 September, 7, 12, 13, 14, 15 October 1991.
84. *NYT*, 16 October 1991.
85. VoI, 8 April — DR, 9 April; *JP*, 15 April 1991.
86. *Davar*, 15 April 1991.
87. *JP*, 14 April 1991.
88. CC resolution of 23 April, VoP (Algiers), 25 April — DR, 26 April; *MEI*, 3 May 1991.
89. *Al-Dustur* (Amman), 11 June, citing WAFA — DR, 11 June 1991.
90. *Ha'aretz*, 19 April 1991.
91. *Al-Safir*, 29 March — DR, 2 April 1991.
92. 'Abd Rabbuh, *JP*, 5 May 1991.
93. See, e.g., Palestinian ambassador to Jordan, al-Tayyib 'Abd al-Rahim, to Jordan TV, 27 June — DR, 28 June 1991,
94. Yasir 'Abd Rabbuh, *NYT*, 26 August 1991.
95. Jordan TV, 2, 4 October — DR, 3, 4 October; *JT*, 5 October; R. Monte Carlo, 5 October — DR, 7 October 1991.
96. *JT*, 5 October; Jordan TV, 20 October — DR, 21 October 1991.
97. Nabil Sha'th, quoted in *JT*, 24–25 October; 'Arafat on VoP (Algiers), 23 November — DR, 25 November 1991.
98. R. Monte Carlo, 18 October — DR, 18 October 1991.
99. Israel TV, 17 October — DR, 18 October 1991.
100. *NYT*, 19 October 1991.
101. *NYT*, 20 October 1991. The Israeli press did get hold of an approximate list; see *Yedi'ot Aharonot*, 20 October 1991.
102. *NYT*, 23 October 1991.
103. On the meetings in Syria, see *NYT*, 20 October; *JP*, 21, 22 October; *NYT*, 25 October 1991. It was not clear if the PLO supported the Syrian position on the multilaterals at the Damascus meeting of Arab leaders on 24 October, but it seemed likely due to its previous agreement on the issue and the fact that it did not participate in the talks when they were actually held in early 1992.
104. *NYT*, *Ha'aretz*, 27 October 1991.
105. *NYT*, 27 October 1991. 'Arafat was speaking by satellite from Tunis on "Pozner and Donahue," a current events program broadcast from New York.
106. *NYT*, 28 October 1991.
107. *NYT*, 29 October 1991.
108. *NYT*, 3 November 1991.
109. *Filastin al-Thawra*, 27 October 1991.
110. Jordan TV, 31 October — DR, 1 November. 'Abd al-Shafi's speech was given in English.
111. *Ha'aretz*, 1 November 1991.
112. *NYT*, 3, 4 November 1991
113. *NYT*, 4 November 1991.
114. *Ha'aretz*, 4 November 1991.
115. VoP (Algiers), 5 November — DR, 6 November 1991.
116. *NYT*, 4 November 1991.
117. *Ha'aretz*, 15 November 1991.
118. *Ha'aretz*, 24 November 1991.
119. *Ha'aretz*, 25 November 1991.
120. *FT*, 27 November 1991.
121. *FT*, 3 December 1991.
122. *Ha'aretz*, 3 December 1991.
123. *NYT*, 4 December; MENA, 7 December — DR, 9 December 1991.
124. AFP, 25 November — DR, 26 November 1991.
125. Najjab to *al-Sharq al-Awsat*, 10 December — DR, 17 December 1991.
126. *NYT*, 2 December 1991.
127. 'Arafat to *al-Musawwar*, 15 November — DR, 20 November 1991.
128. *JP*, 16 December 1991.

129. There were actually a total of three vacancies on the Fath Central Committee, one of which had remained unfilled since the Fifth Fath Congress in 1989 (see *MECS* 1989, pp. 216–18, 230). There was no indication that this position was filled in 1991.
130. *Ha'aretz*, 12 May; *JP*, 23 July 1991.
131. Khalid al-Hasan to *Sawt al-Kuwait al-Duwali*, 2 May — DR, 8 May; *Ha'aretz*, 12 May 1991.
132. See, e.g., *al-Wafd*, 19 April — DR, 26 April 1991.
133. *MEI*, 3 May; Hasan to *al-Sharq al-Awsat*, 12 May — DR, 17 May; *al-Hawadith*, 5 July — DR, 9 July; GNA, 21 August — DR, 22 August 1991.
134. Hasan to *al-Hawadith*, 5 July — DR, 9 July; *al-Hayat* (London), 17 July — DR, 23 July; *Sawt al-Kuwait al-Duwali*, 13 August — DR, 15 August 1991.
135. *MEI*, 3 May; 'Abd Rabbuh to *Sawt al-Sha'b* (Amman), 6 May — DR, 8 May; 'Arafat, cited on VoP (San'a), 29 August — DR, 3 September 1991.
136. See A. Susser, "Double Jeopardy: PLO Policy towards Israel and Jordan," *Policy Papers*, No. 8, 1987.
137. *JT*, 3 August 1991.
138. *JP*, 18 August; *NYT*, 10 September 1991.
139. *Ha'aretz*, 19 April 1991, 16, 17 February 1992; on Fath forces in Lebanon, see also *Jerusalem Report*, 3 October 1991.
140. Habash to *al-Quwat al-Musallaha* (Amman), cited in *Ha'aretz*, 30 June; *JP*, 14 August; *JT*, 14 August; Habash to *Sawt al-Sha'b* (Amman), 21 September — DR, 23 September 1991.
141. *NYT*, 22 October 1991.
142. *NYT*, 23 October 1991.
143. Antenne 2 (TV), 31 October — DR, 1 November 1991.
144. R. al-Quds, 6 November — DR, 7 November 1991.
145. Habash to MBC TV (London), 16 November — DR, 18 November 1991.
146. *Ha'aretz*, 18 November 1991.
147. *Ha'aretz*, 4 December; *MEI*, 20 December 1991.
148. KUNA, *al-Dustur* (Amman), *al-Ra'y* (Amman), 5 April — DR, 8 April; *al-Sharq al-Awsat*, 5 April — DR, 9 April 1991.
149. *Sawt al-Sha'b* (Amman), 14 August, 16 September — DR, 14 August, 17 September; *al-Ra'y* (Amman), 13 September — DR, 17 September 1991.
150. 'Abd Rabbuh was speaking to *Sawt al-Sha'b* (Amman), 6 January — DR, 13 January; *al-Ra'y* (Amman), 13 September — DR, 17 September; Hilal spoke to *al-Hadaf* (Damascus), 10 November 1991.
151. *Al-Dustur* (Amman), 6 March — DR, 8 March; *NYT*, 22 October; Algiers TV, 22 October — DR, 23 October; *Le Figaro*, 31 October; *JT*, 6, 13 November 1991.
152. R. Monte Carlo, 30 March — DR, 1 April 1991.
153. Hawatima to *al-Hayat* (London), 7 August — DR, 9 August; Hawatima to R. Monte Carlo, 20 September — DR, 23 September; al-Samara'i to *al-Hadaf* (Damascus), 10 November 1991.
154. Taysir 'Aruri to MBC TV (London), 3 December — DR, 4 December; *Hadashot*, 3 December 1991.
155. *Davar*, 23 September; *The New York Review of Books*, 7 November 1991.
156. *NYT*, 23 September; *Jerusalem Report*, 3 October 1991. The PFLP tried to attack Kibbutz Malkiya or Yiftah on the Lebanese border in January, and there were three other attempted attacks by the DFLP in January, March, and December (*JP International*, 19 January; *al-Ra'y* (Amman), 3 February; *JP*, 7 March; *NYT*, 17 December 1991).
157. See, e.g., Fath Central Committee member, 'Abbas Zaki, to *al-Dustur* (Amman), 17 June — DR, 18 June 1991.
158. Ghawsha to *al-Dustur* (Amman), 4 September — DR, 5 September. On the Hamas-PLO talks, see *Sawt al-Sha'b* (Amman), 25 August — DR, 26 August; AFP, 26 August — DR, 27 August; *al-Ra'y*, 28 August — DR, 28 August; *JT*, 29–30 August — DR 30 August 1991.
159. MENA, 10 September — DR, 11 September; *JT*, 3–4 October, 1991.
160. *Al-Ra'y* (Amman), 24 September — DR, 25 September 1991.
161. Ghawsha to R. Monte Carlo, 31 October — DR, 1 November 1991. Ghawsha added that

"we know the Jews quite well. This knowledge was particularly granted to us by the Holy Koran. Behold, they give not a farthing to their fellowmen [part of a Koranic verse]."

Islamic fundamentalists were represented at the PNC in the person of Shaykh As'ad Bayud al-Tamimi, the "emir" of the Fath-supported Islamic Jihad-Bayt al-Maqdis. He addressed the PNC (see R. Algiers, 25 September — DR, 26 September 1991), and is pictured seated next to 'Arafat on the dais in the 6 October issue of the PLO organ, Filastin al-Thawra.

162. Sa'ih to Akhbar al-Usbu', 5 September — DR, 6 September 1991.
163. 'Abd Rabbuh to APS, 24 September — DR, 25 September; 'Arafat to al-Musawwar, 15 November 1991.
164. JP, 22 September, 31 October; VoI, 27 October — DR, 28 October; VoI, 30 October — DR, 30 October; VoI, 30 December — DR, 31 December 1991.
165. The PNSF comprised its chairman, Khalid al-Fahum, the former speaker of the PNC, Muhammad Khalifa's al-Sa'iqa, Ahmad Jibril's Popular Front for the Liberation of Palestine-General Command (PFLP-GC), Sa'id Musa Muragha's (Abu Musa) Fath-the Uprising and Samir Ghawsha'sPPSF; the latter, a minuscule faction with some terrorist attacks to its credit, had attended the 1988 PNC, despite its PNSF membership. Its attendance at the 1991 PNC was rewarded with a seat on the Executive Committee.
166. Al-Sharq al-Awsat, 9 February — DR, 12 February; R. Monte Carlo, 12 March — DR, 19 March; Ha'aretz, 15 March; al-Majalla, 20–26 March 1991.
167. Monte Carlo, 8 April — DR, 9 April; Fahum to al-Hawadith, 7 June — DR, 11 June 1991.
168. NYT, 30 May 1991.
169. Sawt al-Sha'b, 16 June — DR, 19 June 1991.
170. Andoni, op. cit.; Fahum to al-Sharq al-Awsat, 13 September — DR, 18 September 1991.
171. Al-Dustur (Amman), 19 September — DR, 20 September; MENA, 21 September — DR, 24 September; R. al-Quds, 23 September — DR, 24 September; R. al-Quds, 1 October, 10 December — DR, 2 October, 10 December 1991.
172. Ha'aretz, 18, 25 October; Ma'ariv, 21 October 1991.
173. 'Arafat's speech was carried on VoP (Algiers), 23 September — DR, 24 September 1991. An Arabic version is in Filastin al-Thawra, 29 September 1991.
174. Qaddumi's political report was broadcast on VoP (Algiers), 24 September — DR, 25 September; he commented on the report on VoP (Algiers), 26 September — DR, 27 September 1991. The Arabic text of the report may be found in Filastin al-Thawra, 6 October 1991.
175. R. Algiers, 24 September — DR, 25 September 1991.
176. R. Monte Carlo, 24 September — DR, 25 September 1991. The PFLP had also been calling throughout the year, as in years past, for reform in the PLO to make it more representative of the factions and to give 'Arafat less leeway. The PFLP's political bureau issued a detailed program in late April calling for organizational reforms, many of which echoed reforms agreed upon by 'Arafat at the 18th PNC in 1987, but which were never implemented (for the program, see al-Hadaf [Damascus], 28 April 1991). The PFLP's latest proposal was ignored.
177. R. Monte Carlo, 24 September — DR, 25 September; The Economist, 28 September 1991.
178. Ha'aretz, 31 March 1991. In February, Italy granted an early release to two PLF members convicted of helping the hijackers of the Achille Lauro cruise ship in October 1985 (NYT, 6 February 1991).
179. R. Monte Carlo, 10 September — DR, 11 September 1991.
180. 'Abbas to Sawt al-Sha'b, 20 September — DR, 23 September 1991.
181. AFP, 28 September — DR, 30 September; NYT, 29 September 1991.
182. JP, 1 October 1991.
183. JT, 22 September 1991.
184. 'Abd Rabbuh to al-Dustur (Amman), 24 September — DR, 24 September; Hawatima to R. Monte Carlo, 24 September — DR, 24 September 1991.
185. Qays al-Samara'i (Hawatima faction) and Jamil Hilal ('Abd Rabbuh faction) to al-Hadaf (Damascus), 10 November 1991.
186. Filastin al-Thawra, 6 October 1991.
187. VoP (Algiers), 30 September — DR, 1 October 1991.

188. *NYT*, 24, 25, 27 September; VoI, 27 September — DR, 27 September; *JP*, 3 October; *The New York Review of Books*, 7 November 1991.
189. R. Amman, 28 September — DR, 30 September 1991.
190. 'Arafat to *Le Figaro,* 11 February — DR, 13 February; Khalaf cited in *al-Ra'y* 2 January; see also PNC Speaker Sa'ih's similar remark in *Akhbar al-Usbu'*, 5 September — DR, 6 September 1991. Compare with the following statement by Faysal al-Husayni: "In the past, up to 1988, our struggle was for 'pure justice,' for our right to the whole of Palestine — from the Jordan River to the sea. This is no longer the case. We recognize that there cannot be any pure justice for us, that we must come to a compromise....[W]e must set down for once and all: Here is Israel with its borders, here is a Palestinian state with its borders." (*Kurier*, 19 April — DR, 22 April 1991.)
191. On the killings, see *NYT*, 12 June 1991.
192. *NYT*, 1 January; VoP (Baghdad), 2 January — DR, 15 January; VoP (San'a), 3 September — DR, 4 September 1991.
193. VoP (Algiers), 2 June — DR, 3 June; VoI, 10 June — DR, 10 June 1991.
194. See, e.g., *Ray'at al-Istiqlal*, July; *Sawt al-Watan*, July; *al-Hadaf* (Damascus), 22 September 1991.
195. *NYT*, 10 January 1991.
196. VoL, 2 February — DR, 2 February 1991.
197. *NYT*, 4 February 1991.
198. R. Free Lebanon, 4 February — DR, 5 February; *NYT*, 5 February 1991.
199. *NYT*, 6, 7, 8 February (citing Israeli Defense Ministry communiqué); AFP, 6 February — DR, 12 February; *JP*, 6 February 1991.
200. *NYT*, 2 April 1991.
201. VoL, 7 April — DR, 9 April 1991.
202. *NYT*, 4 April 1991.
203. *NYT*, 30 February, 7 May 1991.
204. *NYT*, 13, 18 May; R. Monte Carlo, 16 May — DR, 17 May 1991.
205. *NYT*, 13 June; *JP*, 27 June 1991.
206. VoP (Algiers), 1 July — DR, 2 July 1991.
207. *NYT*, 2, 3, 5, 6, 7, 9, 10 July 1991.
208. *Ha'aretz*, 10, 12 July; *NYT*, 11 July; *JP*, 12 July 1991.
209. *NYT*, 9 July 1991.
210. VoI, 15 February, AFP, 15 February — DR, 15 February; VoL, 15 February, AFP, 15 February — DR, 19 February; *NYT*, 16, 17 February; *Ha'aretz*, 22 February 1991.
211. *NYT*, 28 June, 25 October 1991.
212. Husayn to *NYT*, 30 July 1991.
213. *Ha'aretz*, 13 September 1991.
214. *NYT*, 14 March; *JP*, 15 March 1991.
215. VoP (Algiers), 15 March — DR, 17 March 1991.
216. On replacing 'Arafat by Fahum and a Syrian-dominated collective leadership, see APS, 18 April — DR, 18 April 1991.
217. *NYT*, 30 May; Executive Committee statement, VoP (Algiers), 31 May — DR, 3 June; 'Arafat to R. Monte Carlo, 2 June — DR, 6 June; Sulayman al-Najjab to *al-Dustur* (Amman), 9 June — DR, 10 June 1991.
218. *NYT*, 25 October 1991.
219. *Ha'aretz*, 8 November 1991.
220. *NYT*, 10 November; Qaddumi to *JT*, 10 November; AFP, 13 November — DR, 14 November; 'Arafat, quoted by SANA, 3 December — DR, 4 December 1991.
221. *Al-Sharq al-Awsat*, 27 October — DR, 5 October 1991.
222. Printed in Scott MacLeod, "Inside the PLO," *The New York Review of Books*, 7 November 1991.
223. Translation, with some minor changes from *al-Dustur* (Amman), 29 September — DR, 30 September; official Arabic version in *Filastin al-Thawra*, 6 October 1991.

The West Bank and the Gaza Strip

ELIE REKHESS

FROM THE WAR TO THE PEACE PROCESS

THE EFFECT OF THE GULF WAR

The reaction of the Palestinians in the territories to the eruption of the Gulf War in January 1991 was mixed. Initially, there was shock and surprise combined with anger and frustration, with feelings of outrage directed at the US. However, when the *Scud* missile attacks on the greater Tel Aviv area began, apprehension was replaced with a noticeable sense of jubilation. Saddam Husayn's acts were the first Arab attempt since the 1973 war to strike at Israel's densely populated areas. The Palestinians momentarily felt that their much-criticized support of Saddam Husayn, whom they saw as their potential liberator, was indeed justified. They saw in him a courageous underdog fighting alone against 28 countries, including the most powerful one — the US. His initial success in withstanding the allied attack was considered a miracle.

Many West Bank and Gaza residents were elated, therefore, when the first missiles fell on Israel. Some climbed onto the roofs of their homes to watch, chanting such slogans as: "the chemical [warhead] has arrived."[1] Similarly, Faysal al-Husayni, the most prominent Fath leader in the territories, was quoted as saying that "the launching of missiles toward Tel Aviv [was] a blessing," and that "the war [had] shown all the Israeli politicians and the military that there [were] no safe borders."[2] Following a public storm in Israel and calls for his deportation, Husayni retracted his statement and denied having praised the missile attacks. Instead, he maintained that he was "against bombing of any civilians, wherever they are";[3] but the point he was making was that the missile attacks and electronic warfare as demonstrated in the Gulf War proved that Israel's security did not depend on the continued occupation of the West Bank and Gaza.

The loud expression of sympathy for Saddam Husayn by the Palestinians was particularly condemned by the Israeli left. Most outspoken in his criticism was MK Yossi Sarid, hitherto a fervent supporter of dialogue with Palestinian leaders, who wrote that now that the Palestinians had identified with the Iraqi militant act against Israel, they would have "to woo him" rather than the other way around. "The Palestinians are a consistent people," he commented cynically. "They invariably adopt stupid policies."[4]

Risking a rift with the Israeli left, the Palestinian leadership in the territories continued, nevertheless, to back the PLO's official policy of support for Saddam Husayn. The only public figure to criticize the uncompromising Iraqi stand as the main factor leading to the outbreak of war, was the longtime mayor of Bethlehem, Elias Freij.[5]

With the outbreak of the war, the West Bank and the Gaza Strip were placed under a round-the-clock curfew, lifted only to enable the population to obtain food suplies. The purpose of the curfew, which lasted for the duration of the hostilities from 16 January-25 February, was to prevent any violent activity or disruption of public order. A report submitted by the UN secretary-general to the Security Council in April 1991 claimed that the curfew had curtailed access to medical facilities. While acknowledging that the measures taken by the Israeli authorities had led to a decline in clashes between Palestinians and Israeli troops, the report also said: "The practice of confining Palestinians throughout the West Bank and Gaza Strip to their homes for a period of weeks brought severe hardships to the population as a whole."[6]

The existing economic crisis in the territories was further aggravated by the curfew. Losses to Palestinian workers, both those employed in the territories and those employed in Israel, were estimated at $130.5m. Besides the losses in wages and production, some 60% of the grain harvest was destroyed during the curfew and field crops rotted.[7] Agricultural exports were also badly hit since farmers were unable to market their produce via the Jordan River bridges. West Bank and Gaza industry, already weak, lost contracts and customers, by failing to deliver manufactured products. Tourism, the third largest economic sector in the territories, also suffered serious losses.[8]

The end of the war elicited mixed feelings in the territories. Supporters of the Democratic Front for the Liberation of Palestine (DFLP), who had sided with Iraq, interpreted the outcome as a complete victory for Saddam Husayn. "It was the heroic Iraqi army which compelled fascist Bush to stop his aggressive war," stated a leaflet distributed in the West Bank and Gaza on 1 March.[9] Similarly, the Unified National Command (UNC) of the Intifada emphasized the positive results from an Arab perspective. Call No. 69, issued in March, highlighted "the achievement of Iraqi steadfastness in defeating the Zionist security theory" which relied on the use of the territories as "security shields."[10]

These viewpoints, however, were representative of a small minority. The more general reaction was that of confusion, disappointment and frustration. In private, prominent figures conceded that the Palestinians had made wrong judgments and that betting on the Iraqi horse had been a bitter mistake both politically and economically. Spokesmen for the Fath mainstream block refrained from blaming the PLO leadership and PLO Chairman 'Arafat personally, adopting an apologetic stand instead. The oft-repeated argument was that the Palestinians could not have followed any other line in view of Saddam's profound commitment to defend them and to fight for their cause.

MEETINGS WITH SECRETARY OF STATE BAKER (MARCH-JULY)
The situation became more complex when, immediately after the war, the US took concrete steps to implement its new peace initiative, an idea that had been developing throughout the Gulf crisis and war (see chapter on the Middle East peace process). Plans for US Secretary of State James Baker to visit Israel and meet with the Israeli and the Palestinian sides posed a dilemma for the mainstream pro-PLO local Palestinian leadership. American envoys had been boycotted by the West Bank-Gaza Palestinians since May 1990 when the US suspended its dialogue with the PLO following an abortive PLO-sponsored terrorist attack on Israel. Palestinian

spokesmen representing the Fath mainstream, nevertheless, did not rule out the possibility of responding positively to the American overtures in March 1991.

The willingness of Palestinians in the territories to confer with Baker so soon after the Gulf War, and against the background of strong anti-American sentiment, was unexpected. According to a knowledgeable Palestinian observer, a number of factors influenced the Palestinian stand:

> (a) The outcome of the war, which had a sobering effect on Palestinian attitudes, making clear once again the ongoing reality of occupation and the centrality of the US role in any possible change; (b) President Bush's speech on 6 March, confirming support for Palestinians' "legitimate political rights" and the principle of "territory for peace"; (c) A PLO-approved meeting in the occupied territories was seen as a way of keeping the PLO relevant and precluding Arab government attempts to create a PLO substitute.[11]

Supporters of the initiative, nevertheless, had to address themselves to challenging obstacles. From the outset, the projected meeting with Baker was fiercely opposed by secular nationalists, on the one hand, and representatives of militant Islam, on the other. (See discussion of the opposition, below.)

Another complicated dilemma which the mainstream pro-PLO leadership faced was how to respond to the American challenge without antagonizing the external PLO leadership. The local activists, in unofficial contacts with Tunis-based PLO representatives, attempted to convince their interlocutors that the meeting was important and that the Palestinians could benefit from its outcome. At the same time, Faysal al-Husayni made it clear to the Americans that participation in the meeting was entirely conditional upon prior approval by the Tunis-based PLO Executive Committee. Eventually, a compromise was found: an official State Department announcement of the meeting was followed by a PLO statement approving it.[12] The Palestinian delegates who later met with Secretary Baker were keenly aware of the risk of being accused of independently negotiating with the Americans and thus circumventing the external PLO leaders. They consequently made painstaking efforts to make it clear to Baker that they "were appointed by the PLO to listen, talk and to report," that only the PLO was authorized to sign any agreement, and that any negotiation was conditional upon preliminary recognition of the PLO's legitimacy.[13]

The Palestinian delegation, headed by Faysal al-Husayni, met with Baker in Jerusalem on 12 March. Participants included Mustafa al-Natsha, the pro-Fath, deposed mayor of Hebron; Elias Freij, mayor of Bethlehem; Dr. Hanan 'Ashrawi, a woman, Fath leading figure and an English professor at Bir Zayt University; Dr. Sa'ib 'Urayqat, a Fath activist and a political scientist at al-Najah National University in Nablus; Khalil Makhshi, an educator; Mahir al-Masri, a Nablus businessman; and Furaykh Abu Madyan, chairman of the Gaza Strip Bar Association. The Palestinian representatives stressed, in the one-hour meeting, that in no respect did they comprise an alternative leadership to the PLO. They presented Baker with an 11-point memorandum which highlighted the role of the PLO as the "sole legitimate leadership...embodying the national identity and expressing the will of the Palestinians everywhere,"[14] and raised specific problems pertaining to the occupation, while Baker repeated the formal US positions.

The major achievement of the first meeting with the secretary of state was that it set the stage for future talks. A second round of talks with Baker was held in Jerusalem on 9 April, although only after 'Arafat gave the go-ahead to the local leaders. The original delegation of 10 was reduced to six on orders from the PLO to lower the profile of the encounter because of mounting criticism both from within the territories and from outside[15] (see below). The Palestinian delegates presented Secretary Baker with a six-point memorandum addressing key issues in their view: (1) The need for the US to recognize PLO representation of the Palestinian people everywhere and to restore the US-PLO dialogue as "an essential ingredient for facilitating tangible achievements in the peace process"; (2) The necessity for substantive achievements and qualitative progress in concrete terms; (3) The need to address the "brutal Israeli measures carried out against the lives, rights, lands and resources of the Palestinian people under occupation," and to take immediate action against "Israel's frenzied intensification of the settlement policy [and] its stepped-up confiscation of land"; (4) The need to implement UN Resolutions 242 and 338, "as reiterated by President Bush"; (5) The preference for "a comprehensive and integrated approach" over the two-track approach combining progress on peace between Israel and the Arab states with progress on the Palestinian issue; (6) The designation of the peace process as an interim stage in an overall process leading to independence and statehood.[16]

Secretary Baker elaborated on the idea of a regional conference as a prelude to a permanent settlement of the Israeli-Palestinian conflict. An international conference, he told the delegates, was not viable because of Israeli opposition and the only alternative was a regional gathering sponsored by the two superpowers. The outcome of such a conference would be Palestinian self-government for a period of three years, after which Israelis and Palestinians would negotiate the implementation of Resolution 242. He explained that the permanent status of the territories, according to the American vision, would be more than the autonomy plan suggested by Israel and less than an independent state suggested by the Palestinians. He also raised the question of a Palestinian delegation to the regional conference, outlining the possibilities of a separate Palestinian delegation on condition that none of its members were from the PLO; a joint Palestinian-Jordanian delegation; or a Palestinian delegation incorporated into a larger Arab one. The secretary of state and his aides advised the Palestinians to accept whatever was offered to them by the Israelis in future negotiations, stressing that the American Administration was sympathetic to their plight and was willing to assist their cause.[17]

Palestinian reactions to the meeting varied from cautious optimism to pronounced pessimism. "We felt that the US [was] serious in its efforts to bring the parties to a negotiating table," said Mustafa al-Natsha, one of the participants.[18] Others were more restrained and critical. The results were not encouraging, stated Zakariyya al-Agha, a pro-Fath figure and head of the Gaza Medical Society, explaining that when he asked Baker if the US accepted the right of the Palestinians to self-determination, the reply was that if what was meant was the creation of an independent state, then the US remained opposed to the idea. Nor did Baker show any flexibility on the PLO, according to Mahir al-Masri, who also participated in the meeting. "The US was determined to keep the PLO out of any negotiations," he said. Palestinian expectations were also frustrated because of "the apparent refusal of the US to press Israel regarding human rights, settlements or deportation."[19]

By the time Secretary of State Baker returned to Jerusalem in mid-April for a third round of talks, the Palestinians had changed their strategy. Prior to the meeting, the delegation, on its own initiative, presented the American consul general in Jerusalem, Philip Wilcox, with a list of 11 questions which signaled a growing Palestinian willingness to discuss specific details regarding some form of self-government and the idea of an interim period. The questions dealt, inter alia, with the issues of: the nature of legislation to be enacted by the proposed self-government; the international guarantees for the interim period; the form which the Israeli presence in the territories would take during the transitional stage; the structure of the projected joint Palestinian-Jordanian delegation; and the American interpretation of the Palestinian people's legitimate political rights.

Partial answers were given by the American consulate, and the rest of the issues were discussed during the meeting with Baker, which took place on 20 April. The number of Palestinian delegates was reduced again, from six to three. This time, the Palestinian participants, Faysal al-Husayni, Hanan 'Ashrawi and Zakariyya al-Agha, came out of the meeting more optimistic. "Previously we talked about the obstacles, now about the measures to overcome them," stated Husayni, explaining that more substantive matters were raised and more concrete promises than before were made.[20] Secretary Baker was reportedly more forthcoming and receptive to the demands of the Palestinian side. For example, he was ready to consider European participation in a regional conference, a long-standing demand of the Palestinians who felt that the inclusion of the EC was mandatory due to its sympathetic viewpoint regarding the Palestinian cause.[21] According to Hanan 'Ashrawi, at the meeting, the US displayed strong opposition to Israeli measures in the West Bank and Gaza, particularly the establishment of settlements.[22]

Despite the apparently satisfactory outcome of the third meeting, the gaps between the American and Palestinian sides remained wide, with major points of contention still unresolved after the fourth and fifth meetings with Baker held on 14 May and 21 July respectively. These two meetings dealt with the question of the participation of an East Jerusalemite in the delegation to a future conference, to which Israel was vehemently opposed; the issue of a freeze on Israeli settlements; and the active involvement of the PLO in issues of procedure and substance pertaining to the negotiating process.[23]

LOCAL OPPOSITION
The Baker peace initiative and the series of meetings he held with Palestinian representatives between March and July were vehemently criticized by the left-wing organizations in the territories, namely, the Communist Party, the Popular Front for the Liberation of Palestine (PFLP) and the DFLP, as well as by the Islamic fundamentalist movements — the Islamic Resistance Movement (Hamas) and the Islamic Jihad. Prior to Baker's first postwar visit, the PFLP and DFLP issued warnings against anyone who intended to shake "Baker's bloodstained hands."[24] The two Palestinian factions, in a joint statement issued in April, criticized Baker's visit in light of ongoing US support for the Israeli occupation, accusing the Americans of "blackmailing" the PLO and offering a one-sided solution that reflected the Camp David accords and Shamir's initiative. The statement also reiterated the commitment of the PFLP and DFLP to boycott the meeting, and called on "all those invited not to accept the American invitation."[25]

In an article published in the daily *al-Fajr,* Dr. Riyad al-Maliki, a leading PFLP activist and one of the main protagonists in the local opposition, listed five reasons why, in his opinion, all contacts with the Americans should be severed immediately: the US suspension of the dialogue with the PLO; its refusal "to recognize all the inalienable and legitimate rights of the Palestinian people, first and foremost their right to repatriation, self-determination and the establishment of an independent Palestinian state whose capital is Jerusalem; its rejection of an international (as opposed to regional) conference with PLO participation on an equal footing with other parties; its attempt to create an alternative leadership [to the PLO]; and its insistence on holding a monopoly on settling the Palestinian problem."[26]

The Communist viewpoint was similar. While not categorically opposing any contact with American officials, the communists felt that in view of the American determination to ignore the PLO, there was no possibility of responding to the American initiative. Other spokesmen for the radical camp, such as Bassam al-Shak'a, the former mayor of Nablus, disqualified the US as a potential mediator because of what they termed its "anti-Palestinian activity."[27]

Hamas joined the anti-Baker campaign as well, depicting his visit as an attempt to "impose humiliating American-Zionist solutions." A Hamas leaflet issued on 8 April called for a boycott of the meeting, stating: "Any party or individual that departs from this position, regardless of where they stand or their history, [does] not represent our people and the Intifada." The leaflet also called for unity in action and "escalation of the glorious Intifada to foil the American-Zionist conspiracy."[28]

The American-Palestinian dialogue in Jerusalem sharpened the ideological and operational differences between the Islamic and the pro-PLO camps in the territories. Tensions reached boiling point in June when widespread clashes erupted between Hamas supporters and Fath activists in the West Bank and Gaza. On 1 June, Hamas published its 75th serialized leaflet which, condemning all efforts toward making peace with the "murderous occupiers," also accused Fath followers of terrorizing Nablus residents. The Fath-aligned UNC in Nablus responded by issuing a leaflet denouncing threats made by Hamas activists on the life of Dr. Shawkat al-Kaylani, president of the city's al-Najah National University, after he had refused to employ a group of their supporters. The debate deteriorated into fierce street fighting involving the use of submachine guns, pistols, knives, axes and fists and at least 15 Palestinians were injured.[29] With the local Hamas and Fath commanders seeming to have lost control, the Amman leadership of both organizations intervened. In an attempt to calm the situation, 'Abbas Zaki, a member of Fath's Central Committee, and Ibrahim Ghusha, a senior Hamas official, issued a joint call for national unity and for an awareness of "suspected attempts" to weaken the Intifada. They condemned the interfactional attacks and announced the formation of a coordinating committee to maintain Hamas-Fath peace.[30]

NEW THINKING
While the veteran PLO-aligned leadership followed Tunis directives to the letter, other pro-Fath groups adopted a more independent line. A group of young activists in the semiclandestine Fath network, all former security prisoners, emerged after the war and advocated a more pragmatic attitude, supporting local elections to the Palestine National Council (PNC) and an interim settlement based on an adjusted

version of autonomy. They also came out publicly in favor of a more outspoken line toward the "external" PLO, demanding parity and a greater role in shaping Palestinian policy. "For the first time," wrote Ehud Ya'ari, an Israeli expert in Arab affairs, "they allow themselves to express ideas not cleared in advance with PLO Tunis, even containing a degree of criticism of 'Arafat's policies."[31] This wave of "new thinking" was a genuine reflection of both the frustration and the process of sobering up following the war, based on a realistic assessment that Palestinians in the territories should take matters into their own hands in view of the weakening of the PLO, the severe economic crisis and the anticipated peace process.

The intra-PLO debate was initiated by Radi Jara'i, a 40-year-old journalist for *al-Fajr* and a leading Fath activist who had served long prison terms in the 1970s and 1980s. As a result of the war, he wrote in March 1991, there was "no longer a strategic pressure factor [Iraq or a joint Arab coalition] that forced Israel to give up the occupied territories." The war "tipped the balance of power in the region toward Israeli interests." The US, Jara'i further assessed, had became the only decisive power in the ME and the Gulf War proved that the Arab regimes preferred a favorable relationship with the US over supporting the Palestinian cause. The Palestinians, he went on, suffered a political blow because of Iraq's defeat and the PLO was significantly weakened.[32]

Jara'i offered an innovative alternative in light of this situation. Emphasizing the growing role of the Palestinians "inside," he explicitly called upon these Palestinians in the territories to take initiatives on their own. As a first step, he proposed dissolving the PNC and reconstructing it in such a way that the inhabitants of the West Bank and Gaza would be given appropriate representation. This goal could be achieved by holding elections to the PNC in the West Bank and Gaza Strip under UN supervision. While advocating the strengthening of the PNC, Jara'i was ambiguous regarding the future role of the PLO.[33] The second step, he suggested, would entail the establishment of a transitional government, or a government-in-exile, which would include the delegates from the territories and which would supervise all national institutions in the West Bank and Gaza. Lastly, he called upon the Palestinians to announce a willingness to negotiate a peace agreement based on UN resolutions, which would result in the establishment of a Palestinian state with a confederative link to Jordan.[34]

Jara'i's provocative article aroused minimal criticism. The fact that he came from within Fath ranks lent special weight to his critical remarks. One of the first to react was *al-Fajr*'s Editor in Chief Hana Siniora, who agreed that "the Palestinian national institutions [in the territories] should elect new members to represent the new generations." He proposed that the next PNC body include 200 representatives from each of the two major concentrations of Palestinians — in the territories and in the diaspora.[35] Siniora laid special emphasis on the need to adopt and internalize norms of democracy and to endorse a "democratic and critical spirit, free of emotionalism and fear," commenting that "Democracy [was] not the exclusive property of the Western world or the State of Israel."[36]

Interestingly, the new proposals aroused minimal criticism. The mainstream body of PLO loyalists in the territories supported the idea of elections, although they expressed reservations regarding the best timing for implementing it. One of the few public figures who did come out against Jara'i's views was the veteran mayor of Tulkarm, Hilmi Hanun, who questioned the benefit of holding elections when, in practice, the PLO enjoyed wide support. Elections should be held only after the establishment of a Palestinian state, he asserted, criticizing the election proposals as a device to circumvent the PLO leadership.[37]

Both Siniora and Jara'i responded defensively, explaining that the views they had expressed were only personal and that they had no intention of weakening the PLO. On the contrary, they had hoped to strengthen the organization by reinforcing the ties between the "inside" and the "outside." The proposal to elect a new PNC was not an end in itself, Jara'i maintained, but rather an appropriate response to Shamir's plan for elections intended to pave the way for an alternative Palestinian leadership.[38]

Talal Abu 'Afif al-Safi, a lawyer and former Shabiba [Fath youth organization in the territories] activist who had been imprisoned on security charges for two years, took Radi al-Jara'i's ideas a step further in mid-May outlining a peace proposal that advocated an interim settlement with Israel and the postponement of three major issues for three years: statehood, Jerusalem and Jewish settlement.[39] The innovative element in Safi's proposal was that it abandoned the traditional PLO demand for immediate implementation of the Palestinian rights of statehood and self-determination. Instead, it advocated a stage-by-stage negotiating process with interim agreements, ultimately leading to a Jordanian-Palestinian confederation. While Safi, too, maintained that the plan reflected his own personal viewpoint, his approach was indicative of the challenging new mood which emerged within the younger leadership stratum following the Gulf War.

The first stage of Safi's plan, which was to last three years, called for a series of Israeli confidence-building measures such as the cessation of settlement activity and land expropriations and the implementation of "local elections to choose 200 representatives to a new 500-member PNC. The local delegates would also form a separate Palestinian administrative council to run local affairs during [the] interim period."[40] The second stage envisaged the establishment of an interim Palestinian authority and extended self-rule in the West Bank and the Gaza Strip for another three-year transitional period. Internal civil affairs, including a local police force, would come under Palestinian responsibility, and Israeli forces would withdraw from Arab-populated areas. Within two years of this stage, the PLO and the PNC would complete the task of amending the Palestine National Charter. Stage three, envisioned as lasting two years, called for negotiations between an Israeli and a joint Palestinian-Jordanian delegation for a permanent settlement. Talks would take place within the framework of an international conference with UN participation. The permanent solution envisaged was the establishment of an independent demilitarized Palestinian state in the West Bank and Gaza Strip, to be confederated with Jordan.[41]

Safi's plan came under strong criticism. The Arab press argued that the proposal ignored the PLO's role in a final solution and that it was too close to the Camp David formula. Moreover, demilitarization, it claimed, could not apply only to the Palestinian side; Israel should also be demilitarized. The aspect most criticized was that relating to Jerusalem,[42] namely, Safi's suggestion that East Jerusalem be internationalized under UN rule, which was utterly rejected. Jerusalem, it was stated, was an Arab city, considered the future capital of a Palestinian state, and therefore was not subject to negotiation. In response, Safi claimed that he had been misunderstood, that his plan differed from the Camp David accords on 15 points, and that "from the beginning the PLO [was] involved."[43] Regarding Jerusalem, he asserted that the wording as published was not what he had intended, and was the result of a printer's error. All of Jerusalem was meant to be internationalized, he explained, and not only the Arab parts of the city.[44]

Although the ideas advocated by Jara'i and Safi were not incorporated into the Palestinians' meetings with Baker, the fact that they were put forward constituted encouragement for the delegates to continue the negotiations.

FURTHER MEETINGS WITH BAKER (AUGUST-OCTOBER)
The joint American-Soviet announcement on 31 July regarding the convening of the peace conference in October was welcomed cautiously by the pro-Fath mainstream in the territories.

Two days after the announcement, Secretary Baker met with the Palestinian delegation in Jerusalem for a sixth round of talks. Unlike past meetings, this one was seen by the Palestinians as having resulted in a major political breakthrough. "We moved from the question-and-answer stage to more practical grounds," explained Faysal al-Husayni, who again represented the Palestinians along with Hanan 'Ashrawi and Zakariyya al-Agha. He announced that in light of Baker's clarifications regarding several pending questions, the Palestinians agreed in principle to participate in the projected peace conference. The Palestinian delegation and the American side had also begun drafting a joint memorandum of understanding on the peace process, he said.[45]

The Palestinians during these meetings presented Baker with a document summarizing their positions on five controversial key issues.[46] The first point related to the goal of the proposed peace conference, with the Palestinians demanding concrete American assurances that the initiative was based on UN Resolutions 242 and 338 which, in their interpretation, aimed at ending Israeli occupation in all occupied Arab territories, including East Jerusalem. Baker's reply that he accepted the principle of "land for peace," seemed to have satisfied the Palestinians. The second point concerned the status of the PLO and the composition of the Palestinian delegation. The participants insisted that the PLO had the ultimate right to name the Palestinian representatives to the conference. Elaborating on this question in an interview held after the meeting, Dr. Sa'ib 'Urayqat stated that "the mere talk" of an Israeli veto over the choice of Palestinian delegates was "humiliating, ridiculous and absurd." He said: "There has never been a situation in the history of conflict resolutions in which two enemies [were] about to sit down to make peace and one side cho[se] his own representatives [as well as] those of his enemy."[47] The Americans replied that although it had been decided a priori that the PLO would not be invited to participate, the US acknowledged the right of the Palestinians in the territories to appoint their own delegates. Baker strongly recommended that the Palestinians be represented within a joint Palestinian-Jordanian delegation, and the participants seemed to have accepted his viewpoint.

The third point dealt with was the issue of the participation of a Palestinian from East Jerusalem. The Palestinians steadfastly rejected various proposals to bypass the problem by including a Jerusalem-born Palestinian residing either in Jordan or abroad, as any concession would be interpreted as Palestinian recognition of Israel's annexation of East Jerusalem. The matter remained unresolved.[48]

The fourth and fifth points were the transitional period and Israeli settlements. A basic Palestinian fear was that Israel would perpetuate the interim period of autonomy indefinitely, whereas the transitional period, the Palestinians argued, was supposed to lead to independence, including control over water, land, the economy, education and internal security, as well as immunity from arrest by the Israeli military.[49] The delegation reiterated its past demand for an immediate cessation of settlement activity "on all occupied lands, especially in Jerusalem."[50] While expressing sympathy to the Palestinian demands, the Americans were unable to persuade the Israeli side to accept them.

As the prospects for a peace process became brighter, the opposition from within mounted. The fiercest criticism came from the militant Islamic groups, which also threatened the lives of the Palestinian delegates. "Faysal al-Husayni and the handful of negotiators should comprehend," stated a leaflet issued by the Islamic Jihad organization in the territories on 1 August, "that their fate will be similar to that of King Abdallah [King Husayn's grandfather, who was assassinated in 1950 by a Palestinian] and other traitors."[51] A Hamas leaflet issued shortly thereafter warned those leaning toward participation in the conference that its purpose was to sell out Arab Jerusalem and the al-Aqsa mosque. In a rare joint statement, the PFLP and Hamas condemned diplomacy with the Americans, emphasizing that the Husayni delegation did not represent the Palestinians.[52] The PFLP, while not issuing personal death threats, did nevertheless call upon the population to "boycott and isolate those leadership elements" who conferred with Baker, since their ultimate objective was "to Judaize all of Palestine."[53]

Dr. Ghassan al-Khatib, whose name had been mentioned as a potential participant in a future delegation, explained in an interview that the oppositional trend did not reject the principle of a negotiated solution, but it did reject the features of the one prompted by the Americans. A process that was unilaterally controlled and supervised by the US could not be of any benefit to the Palestinians. Only a process based on "international legitimacy" and on all the UN resolutions pertaining to the Palestinian problem could be accepted, Khatib said.[54]

Interestingly, the broad-based UNC also shared this critical approach, probably because of the influence of PFLP and DFLP representatives. Its Call No. 73, issued on the eve of Baker's sixth meeting with the Palestinian delegation, sharply condemned the American efforts "to impose a United States submissive solution, the essence of which [was] based on autonomy instead of legitimate national right."[55] A month later, however, the UNC changed its tune. While still maintaining its basic opposition to the conference, it condemned the "threats directed to the nationalist Palestinian figures that met with Baker," advocating democratic dialogue, rather than the assassin's bullet as the appropriate method to voice opposition.[56]

In any event, Faysal al-Husayni and the other members of the Palestinian delegation were not deterred by local manifestations of opposition. Self-confident, backed by the PLO, Husayni even welcomed the criticism, describing it as solid proof that not only the Israelis, but the Palestinians as well, were divided. "It would have been a disaster if all Palestinians thought alike," he commented.[57]

The three-member Palestinian delegation met with Baker again in Jerusalem on 16 September seeking more concrete American assurances regarding the issues in dispute. Apparently, all that Secretary Baker would apparently offer were variations on existing American policy guidelines. He reasserted that Israeli settlements were an obstacle to peace, that the US had never recognized the Israeli annexation of East Jerusalem, and that his government acknowledged the Palestinians' "political rights," although not their right to self-determination because that implied statehood.[58]

Palestinian political activity gathered momentum during the latter part of September when the PNC convened in Algiers during 23–28 September to formulate the PLO position on the peace process. Hanan 'Ashrawi and Faysal al-Husayni, who had left Israel for a series of meetings in Europe, reportedly traveled to Algiers to attend the conference and to meet with Yasir 'Arafat secretly. The two Palestinian leaders denied having been present at the convention, since Israeli law prohibited citizens or residents from having any contact with PLO officials, and in any event Israel refrained from prosecuting them after the US cautioned that a hard-line attitude "could complicate Baker's efforts."[59] In resolutions adopted at the conference the PNC conditionally endorsed Palestinian participation in the peace process, a development that was warmly received in the territories. The Palestinian delegation that had met regularly with Secretary Baker interpreted the resolutions as providing the necessary basis for the final drafting of a memorandum of understanding with the Americans.[60]

This optimistic interpretation, however, was not shared by the oppositionist groups in the territories, namely the Islamic militants and the radical leftists, who urged the local population to boycott the PNC and questioned Washington's credibility as an honest broker, given its traditional support for Israel.[61] Their criticism focused mainly on an American "plot," or "conspiracy," that was aimed at "eradicating the Palestinian issue." However, although vociferous, the oppositionist camp failed to suggest a feasible alternative to the political path. One political observer accurately described their criticism as characterized by the "barrenness of the rejectionist's position."[62] As popular support for the PNC resolutions increased, criticism diminished significantly.

Encouraged by the PNC resolutions, the Palestinian representatives negotiating with Baker intensified their painstaking efforts. On 10 October, they met with the secretary of state in Washington to examine yet another draft of the proposed US positions regarding Palestinian-Israeli differences on the participation of East Jerusalemites and the authorization of delegates by the PLO.[63]

The three-member delegation, joined by Dr. Sari Nusayba, a leading Fath personality, met Secretary Baker once again on 16 October in Jerusalem to finalize the last details regarding the anticipated Palestinian participation in the peace conference. Two days later the American consul general in Jerusalem, Molly Williamson, handed Faysal al-Husayni the official letters of invitation to the conference, accompanied by a US letter of guarantees. This letter assured the Palestinians that the US stance interpreted UN Resolutions 242 and 338 as based on the principle of land for peace, a position that was seen by the Palestinians as a basis for future Israeli withdrawal from the occupied territories. The following day, Husayni announced that the Palestinians had accepted the invitation to attend the Madrid conference as part of a joint Jordanian-Palestinian delegation.

THE MADRID CONFERENCE

Husayni's immediate task was to assemble the delegation in the face of a series of contradictory pressures. On the one hand, the list had to conform with the Israeli preconditions that no East Jerusalemites be included. On the other, PLO approval of the delegation was necessary. In addition, various interest groups in the territories made their own demands. A preliminary list which Husayni reportedly submitted to PLO headquarters in Tunis was returned with a firm stipulation that three additional personalities be included: Elias Freij, Mustafa al-Natsha, the deposed mayor of Hebron, and Radwan Abu 'Ayyash, head of the West Bank Journalists' Association and a pro-Fath activist, who was released from administrative detention in September. While accepting the first two, who represented the older, more established stratum of West Bank leaders, Husayni firmly rejected the inclusion of Abu 'Ayyash, known to be a personal opponent. In the event, Abu 'Ayyash did eventually go to Madrid as a member of an advisory committee (see below) after Husayni was forced to bow to demands from the West Bank refugee population, Abu 'Ayyash's strongest constituency. He also had to concede to pressures within the territories to include representatives of various sectors: refugees, villagers, town dwellers, Christians and residents of the northern and the southern districts of the West Bank and the Gaza Strip. Observers noted that PLO officials were consulted daily regarding the composition of the list, which implied that the West Bank representatives followed the directions of the Tunis-based Palestinian leadership.

The final list drawn up in October constituted a compromise formula. Heading the delegation was Dr. Haydar 'Abd al-Shafi, a Gaza physician, head of the Red Crescent Association, a known left-wing nationalist, a founding member of the PNC and a member of the first PLO Executive Committee in 1964–65. Other members included Elias Freij; Dr. Zakariyya al-Agha; Furaykh Abu Madyan; Mustafa al-Natsha; Dr. Sa'ib 'Urayqat; Dr. Sami al-Kaylani; Dr. Nabil Qasis, deputy president of Bir Zayt University; Samih Kan'an, a former security prisoner; Dr. 'Abd al-Rahman Hamad, dean of the College of Engineering at Bir Zayt University; Dr. Mamduh al-'Akr, a pro-Fath figure and a Nablus surgeon; Dr. Nabil al-Ja'bari, an independent, a dentist and chairman of the board of trustees of Hebron University; Dr. Ghassan al-Khatib, a Communist activist; and Dr. Samir 'Abdallah, a lecturer in the Economics Department at Bir Zayt University and affiliated with the Communist Party. A striking feature of the delegation was that it was composed mostly of young, educated professionals who had gradually replaced an older generation of pro-PLO leaders.

The manner in which the delegation and the advisory committee were composed, however, came under criticism, as its members were selected not for their diplomatic experience or negotiating skills but out of regional, factional, family and clan considerations. There was a widespread feeling that many of the delegates were insufficiently qualified to stand up to the task of facing the professional Israeli diplomats. Criticism was also voiced about the unpreparedness of the delegation. Little work had been done to prepare position papers and policy proposals on conditions in the territories and possible future models for Palestinian political, economic, cultural and social institutions.[64]

According to the Israeli Government demand, no East Jerusalem residents could be included in the list. However, this condition was circumvented by the establishment of an "advisory committee" attached to the Palestinian delegation, which was approved by the Americans. The committee, which was given the task of coordinating the Palestinian position in Madrid, included leading representatives from East Jerusalem, the West Bank and abroad. Israeli protests against the entry of East Jerusalemites into the process through the "back door" were rejected by the Americans. The coordinator of the advisory committee was Faysal al-Husayni. Other members included: Dr. Hanan 'Ashrawi; Dr. Sari Nusayba, a professor of philosophy at Bir Zayt and a leading Fath activist; Radwan Abu 'Ayyash; Zahira Kamal, a West Bank DFLP leader identified with the relatively moderate Yasir 'Abd Rabbuh faction; Salah Abu Laban, a West Bank DFLP activist; Jamil Tarifi, a pro-PLO figure of refugee origins; Dr. Ahmad al-Yaziji, a Fath leader in the Gaza Strip; 'Abd al-Hadi Abu Husa, a refugee leader from the Gaza Strip; Prof. Rashid Khalidi, a Palestinian-American historian; Anis al-Qasim, a jurist residing in Jordan, and Kamil Mansur, a lawyer residing in Paris.

The Palestinian acceptance of the invitation to take part in the Madrid conference aroused lively public debate. In a rally held at the East Jerusalem Hakawati theater, Dr. 'Abd al-Shafi conceded that the Palestinians would be attending the conference "under Israeli conditions" and that they were forced to relinquish many of their fundamental demands including the freezing of settlements, recognition of their right to self-determination, and direct participation of the PLO as a separate and equal party in a UN-sponsored international conference. The Palestinians, he said, were "stripped of their [national] symbols and institutional representatives with no advance assurances that the conference would necessarily lead to their goals: full Israeli withdrawal and statehood."[65] However, despite these apparent disadvantages, he and other leaders of the delegation argued that the Palestinians had no alternative but to follow the American path. Failure to attend the conference, they asserted, would have had worse consequences for the Palestinians.

A variety of arguments were presented by public figures in favor of Madrid to substantiate their view despite the deficiencies in the American assurances of future self-determination. "The Palestinians had realized," explained Elias Freij, "that time was on Israel's side and that the only way out of the dilemma was face-to-face negotiations."[66] Dr. Sari Nusayba similarly assessed that the conference was the only way "to reshuffle the cards," reducing the pressure on the Palestinians and placing it on the Israelis. The conference itself, he said, could generate political change inside Israel in the direction of a peaceful solution.[67] Palestinian participation in Madrid, wrote ME commentator Daoud Kuttab, could be a significant step toward the establishment of a Palestinian state, with the self-governing measures promised in the interim period providing the economic and social infrastructure for the future state.[68]

Another argument frequently raised to justify participation in the conference was that the delegation was, in fact, representing the PLO. Indeed, to ensure the standing of the delegation with the Palestinian public, Husayni continuously emphasized that the Palestinians on the "inside" entrusted the Tunis-based PLO with all major decisions. Even more explicitly Dr. Sa'ib 'Urayqat, a member of the delegation, told a CNN correspondent that "the PLO asked me to take part in the delegation and appointed me as a member,"[69] a statement that drew a complaint from the Israelis and caused the Americans to suggest that delegates refrain from such provocative declarations. Husayni, disassociating himself from 'Urayqat's statement, said: "We were not selected by the PLO but by the residents [of the territories]."[70]

The opening ceremonies of the conference on 31 October, and in particular Dr. Haydar 'Abd al-Shafi's opening speech, precipitated a surge of euphoria in the territories. (For a further discussion of the speech, see chapter on the ME peace process.) West Bank and Gaza Strip residents took to the streets and waved olive branches, celebrating what they perceived as the international recognition of their cause. Newspapers as well as prominent members of the local community commented that 'Abd al-Shafi's speech conveyed the feelings and hopes of all Palestinians for "the dawn of a new era." The front page of the Palestinian daily al-Sha'b read: "'Abd al-Shafi's speech heals our sorrowful hearts."[71]

It was widely held that the Palestinian delegation had made great strides at Madrid. From the eloquent opening speech to their punctual appearances for talks with the Israeli team, wrote commentator Joel Greenberg, they demonstrated responsibility and restraint.[72] It was generally felt that by attending the conference, the Palestinian negotiators had demonstrated political maturity. Their readiness to accept limited achievements in the form of interim arrangements instead of clinging to unattainable demands was highly praised by Fath supporters. Had the Palestinians refused to attend, it was argued, they would have lost the invaluable chance to present their cause to the world to restore international sympathy "unfairly lost during and after the Gulf War."[73]

The Palestinians were heartened by their gains in terms of worldwide recognition and status. By sitting at the negotiating table opposite the Israeli delegation as equals and not as subjects, the Palestinian delegates were perceived to have succeeded in transforming the nature of the Palestinian-Israeli relationship. Again and again, Palestinian spokesmen highlighted the fact that their representatives received equal speaking time, traveled in motorcades, and were treated as an official state delegation.[74]

REPERCUSSIONS AT HOME: INTERNAL DEBATE

Upon their return home the delegates received a heroes' welcome. The international legitimacy gained by the Palestinians in Madrid, the symmetry established vis-à-vis the Israelis, and the unprecedented widespread media exposure converged to create a euphoric atmosphere. Within a very short time, however, the overall enthusiasm began to wane in the face of harsh reality.

The first obstacle was local opposition. A strange yet pragmatic alliance had developed between the secular pro-Syrian nationalists of the PFLP and Na'if Hawatima's faction of the DFLP nationalists, on the one hand, and the Islamic militants — Hamas and the Islamic Jihad organization — on the other. The major point of contention of this Islamic-left coalition was that the Madrid conference represented a complete sellout of Palestinian interests and a gratuitous capitulation to American imperialism and Zionist expansionism. Prominent speakers for the opposition, including Dr. Riyad al-Maliki, associated with the PFLP, and 'Ali Abu Hilal, a DFLP leader who was allowed to return to the West Bank in May 1991 after being expelled in 1986 (see below), repeatedly scorned the conditions under which the Palestinians had accepted the American invitation, claiming that the delegation had conceded too much both on issues of procedure and of substance. Hamas reportedly was guided by a religious opinion issued by the scholars of al-Aqsa mosque in Jerusalem, which warned Palestinians against betraying Islam by giving up Palestinian land.[75] Criticism gathered momentum toward the end of October when the opposition "vowed to thwart the negotiations" and threats were made to turn the lives of the members of the negotiating team into a "nightmare" by exposing them to daily demonstrations outside their homes and "a barrage of harassing telephone calls and letters."[76]

On 24 October, Hamas and the two radical factions jointly called for a general strike to last the length of the conference, which they subsequently modified to a call for a strike on the first two days of the conference only. The strike was observed in most areas, although fighting broke out when Fath activists attempted to break the strike in various towns, removing roadblocks and pulling down black mourning flags from roof tops. The worst incidents occurred in Gaza, where the two rival factions fought each other with knives, resulting in the hospitalization of four Hamas members. An estimated total of 50 Palestinians were injured in the interfactional fighting.[77]

Overall, however, the positive achievements in Madrid appeared to cause a temporary setback for the opposition. Results of elections to the Gaza Strip Chamber of Commerce held in early November, shortly after the Madrid conference, led observers to believe that Palestinians in the territories had begun to shift their support from hard-line Islamic militants to relative moderates in favor of the peace process.[78] For some time, the PLO had been seen as losing power to fundamentalist Islam in the territories. A victory by the Islamists in the Hebron Chamber of Commerce elections in mid-June 1991 was interpreted as a reflection of this trend. The outcome was the opposite, however, in the Gaza Chamber of Commerce elections, with 13 of the available 16 seats going to representatives of the "National Bloc," identified with mainstream Fath, while the "Islamic Bloc," representing Hamas, won only three seats. The landslide victory of the Fath faction in the Gaza Strip, known for its traditional pro-Islamic politics, was seen as a clear indication of popular support for the Palestinian delegation's political line at the expense of that of the rejectionist Islamic opposition.[79]

Leaders of the Madrid delegation and the advisory committee felt secure enough to allow their rivals to take part in public forums organized by the pro-Fath camp in November for the purpose of explaining the achievements of the conference and recruiting public support. Over 30 of these seminars throughout the territories involved the participation of members of the opposition. In Bir Zayt, for example, Hanan 'Ashrawi, Ghassan al-Khatib, Radwan Abu 'Ayyash and Zahira Kamal confronted hundreds of radical university students who criticized the Madrid team members for agreeing to consider an interim period of self-government. Hamas followers, shouting the traditional call allahu akbar ("God is Greatest"), blamed the Madrid participants for starting to commit treason. The delegates responded that this was "a landmark achievement of international recognition, a first step toward Palestinian goals and an implementation of PLO policy."[80]

Another central problem which the delegation faced upon its return was the internal cohesion of their supporters in light of divisions which emerged at that time within the Fath-oriented, pro-PLO camp. While the intellectual elites of Ramallah and Jerusalem praised Hanan 'Ashrawi's assertive performance and "the way she was able to project an appealing image of the Palestinians to Western audiences,"[81] the masses in the refugee camps and the fellahin in remote rural areas did not share this assessment. For them, 'Ashrawi was an academician who had not experienced the harsh realities of the Intifada. Moreover, in the predominantly Muslim environment of the territories, her Christian affiliation was a contributing factor to the sense of alienation from her.[82]

Internal tension had, in fact, surfaced in Madrid, where Faysal al-Husayni was bitterly criticized for dominating his counterparts, especially by Radwan Abu 'Ayyash, Elias Freij and Mustafa al-Natsha who were among the dissatisfied delegates reportedly pushed aside. Frustrated Fath activists who stayed behind in the territories, either willingly, as an act of protest, or because they were not selected for the delegation articulated their position following the return home of the delegation. At a homecoming rally at the Hakawati theater in Jerusalem on 10 November, the delegates first learned about "political action committees" which had been established in the territories during their absence by Dr. Sari Nusayba and Ziyad Abu Ziyad, both leading Fath personalities.[83]

The unexpected initiative reportedly took Husayni by surprise. Reacting swiftly, he called for the suspension and reformulation of the existing bodies and announced that "more general committees" representing "all political lines within the Palestinian community" would supplement them. Husayni's leadership position remained uncontested. Nusayba and Abu Ziyad accommodated themselves to the new line and later joined Husayni in his efforts to recruit public support for the peace process. Shortly thereafter, the committees were expanded to include dozens of Fath followers known to be personally supportive of Husayni — members of the Palestinian People's Party and activists from the 'Abd Rabbuh faction of the DFLP, totaling c. 150 committee members by mid-November.[84] This reestablished committee network became Fath's grass-roots stronghold in the territories. It consisted of middle-level activists, mostly in their thirties, who were "graduates" of Israeli prisons and who became actively involved in reassessing the results of the Intifada after the Gulf War [see below]. They were instrumental in creating an atmosphere in the West Bank and the Gaza Strip that enabled Husayni to press the PLO in Tunis to accept the idea of Palestinian participation in talks on the US and Israeli terms for the peace process.[85]

The Madrid peace conference had contradictory effects on the relationship between the "inside" Palestinians and the "outside" Tunis-based leadership. On the one hand, ties between them were significantly strengthened with the delegates maintaining daily contacts with PLO officials in Madrid, Tunis and elsewhere through the advisory committee. Spokesmen for the delegation took every opportunity to assert their allegiance to the PLO. "The truth is," wrote the editor of the East Jerusalem weekly al-Bayadir al-Siyasi, "that the delegation [was] a part of the PLO in its structure, in the way it was selected, in its personalities, [and] in its points of departure."[86] Yet, at the same time, the West Bank-Gaza Palestinians seemed to have made gains at the expense of the external PLO establishment as a result of their outstanding performance at the peace conference. Madrid led to the evolution of the leadership in the territories into "a growing counterweight to the PLO leaders in Tunis, steadily pushing them to adopt pragmatic positions."[87]

The official letter of invitation to the bilateral talks due to begin in Washington on 4 December was delivered to the Palestinian delegation in late November by the US consul general in East Jerusalem. Under the terms reaffirmed at the one-day bilateral round held in Madrid, during the peace conference, the Palestinians were to negotiate initially within the framework of a joint Jordanian-Palestinian delegation, which would then split into two groups — one primarily Jordanian, the other primarily Palestinian. The Palestinian delegation, led by Dr. Sari Nusayba who had temporarily replaced Faysal al-Husayni, arrived in Washington as scheduled. The talks, however, were delayed for a week due to Israel's protest over the venue, and once started, soon reached a deadlock over procedural matters. After more than a week of conversations in the hallways of the State Department, in what was named "corridor diplomacy," the talks were concluded with no decisive results.[88]

REASSESSING THE INTIFADA

The Palestinians made substantial gains during the first two years of the Intifada 1988–89. The popular uprising had a strong impact on Israeli public opinion, with a growing number of Israelis becoming convinced that holding on to the territories did not guarantee security, that there was no military solution to the conflict, and that the dispute should be resolved politically, while conversely the recurring hostility convinced other Israelis that the Arabs' primary objective was to eliminate Israel. For the inhabitants of the territories, the Intifada restored a sense of pride, dignity and self-confidence. It dispelled the myth of the invincibility of the Israel Defense Forces (IDF) and attracting extensive media coverage, it brought the plight of the Palestinians into every home in the West. The Intifada's most significant achievement in the intra-Palestinian political realm was the pressure it exerted on the external PLO leadership to put forward the relatively moderate November 1988 Palestinian political initiative, endorsed by the Algiers convention of the PNC.

Starting in 1989, however, the Intifada began to lose momentum, particularly in its confrontation with the Israeli army. This development was caused by several factors: the army's response to the demonstrations became more efficient; a sizable number of activists were arrested; the world's attention, and media interest, gradually waned; and a measure of fatigue began to set in. During the Gulf War, the Intifada almost faded out, with the comprehensive curfew imposed over all of the West Bank and the Gaza Strip significantly hampering the mobility of the Intifada activists. Still, the UNC in February 1991 called for continued struggle to be integrated with the fighting in the "Iraqi and Southern Lebanon fronts."[89] In a later announcement, which reflected the weakening position of the Iraqi army toward the end of the war, reference to the Iraqi and Lebanese fronts was omitted and instead the UNC called for working "in a way which [was] proportional to...Israeli repressive measures and the aggressive war against Iraq."[90]

After the war ended, Palestinian militants renewed their efforts to revive the Intifada but were unable to restore the fervor and the popular character of the uprising in its first years. The Palestinians in the territories, frustrated by the outcome of the war, the weakened position of the PLO, and the deepening economic crisis, were much less inclined to indulge in organized civil unrest, mass demonstrations, stone throwing and daily confrontations with Israeli troops.

However, while grass-roots activity against the Israeli occupation was losing ground there was a steep rise in the number of violent terrorist acts carried out by individuals belonging to radical organizations such as the PFLP, Islamic Jihad and Hamas starting in late February. Knife-attacks were particularly widespread. On 28 February, a yeshiva student was knifed and killed in the Muslim quarter of Jerusalem's old city. In early March, four Jerusalem women were stabbed to death by a Gaza youth. In late April, a French tourist was knifed to death in Bethlehem by an 18-year-old Palestinian. Islamic Jihad claimed responsibility for a stabbing in Jerusalem in May in which three Jews were injured.

Simultaneously, much of the energy that was once expended against the external enemy was turned inward against alleged collaborators with the Israeli authorities. Beginning in late 1988, with the first internecine killings of Palestinians by fellow Palestinians, internal executions became almost a daily event. In 1989, 139 residents were executed, and in 1990 the figure was 165. Following the Gulf War, the rate of assassinations reached new heights, with 26 killings recorded during April 1991, and a total of 183 during 1991 (IDF figures). By late 1991, the total number of Arabs killed for suspected collaboration since the beginning of the Intifada was 471, according to figures provided by human rights organizations (see below) and according to IDF figures.[91] Total casualty ratios in the territories had thus been reversed with the number of Palestinians murdered by local hit squads far exceeding the number of Arabs killed in shooting incidents with the IDF.

Most of the executions were carried out at the personal directives of local PLO and Islamic activists with no authorization by higher Intifada command echelons. Victims were not given any opportunity to present their case. Many of those killed had almost no previous contact with the Israeli authorities. Rather, they were assassinated for alleged moral deviations such as gambling, criminal offenses, drug-dealing and prostitution, or due to interfactional disputes and private feuds. In most cases, the killings were brutal. Suspected informers were axed to death, decapitated, hung from electric poles, burned or buried alive. Bodies were mutilated and ears were cut off. In March 1991 a Nablus woman in her eight month of pregnancy was found hanging from a tree; the "Wounding Hawk" (al-Saqr al-jarih) squad claimed responsibility. Earlier in the year, a schoolteacher employed by UNRWA in the Khan Yunis refugee camp was killed in front of his students. The uprising was cannibalizing itself, noted a commentator.[92] Attempts on the part of the UNC to stem the slaying were ignored.[93]

The prolonged wave of barbaric murders aroused unprecedented resentment and deep revulsion in the territories. Mounting criticism was articulated by Tulkarm journalist 'Adnan Damiri, a high-level Fath activist. In an incisive article published in al-Fajr on 5 June under the title "The Fear and the Ambiguity," he sharply denounced the masked vigilantes, mostly teenagers, who terrorized the local inhabitants, turning the Intifada upon itself. People had become more fearful of anonymous killers than of Israeli soldiers, he declared. He scorned those who presumed to act as judges and executioners, calling upon his fellow Palestinians to intervene immediately. "For too long we have been trying to find excuses for all these executions of people who work[ed] with the authorities," he said. Now, "the genie [has] escaped from the bottle."[94]

Damiri's message inspired an open debate. The fact that criticism came from a figure of nationalist standing, who had served long terms in Israeli prisons, encouraged other nationalist Palestinian leaders representing a wide spectrum of political views to follow suit. Sirhan Sulayma and Nabhan Khuraysha, two Fath activists who were former security prisoners publicly questioned the legitimacy of the executions, while others called for a proclamation that Palestinian blood was sacred and should not be spilled purposelessly.[95] Even 'Arafat, after a long silence on this issue, sent a letter confirming recent UNC instructions ordering an end to killing without trial.[96]

The condemnation of the killings prompted a wider discussion on the shortcomings of the Intifada in its fourth year. Newspapers were filled with critical essays. In Jerusalem, a symposium was held in June at the Hakawati theater on the topic "The

Intifada — between Reality and Anticipations." Leading figures of the East Jerusalem pro-PLO political elite, including Faysal al-Husayni, joined the general debate, expanding on Damiri's, Jara'i's and Safi's viewpoints (see above). "The two older generations of the Palestinian leadership," observed a political analyst in the *Jerusalem Post*, "the over-50s 'leading personalities' and the under-40s 'leading Fath activists' now appear ready to do something about the third-generation Shabiba [Fath youth organization] who were the children of the Intifada and fast becoming its dictators."[97]

The reassessment of the Intifada focused on the necessity of shifting the emphasis from violent confrontation to the rebuilding of the Palestinian economy. In May, alarmed by the deteriorating economy as a result of the war, Husayni stressed the need to "win the economic battle, as well as the battle for social and cultural reconstruction."[98] Public figures began to question the efficiency of the Intifada's frequent strikes, alluding to the cumulative economic damage. It was time, Husayni asserted, to find an alternative to the rigid rule of commercial strikes that forced stores to shut at 1 p.m. daily and for a full day several times a month, paralyzing local commerce.[99] In the same vein, the East Jerusalem daily *al-Quds* doubted whether the Palestinians profited from the daily afternoon commercial strike imposed by the Intifada command. It turned the population into people "who sleep in the afternoon," the paper cynically commented.[100]

Toward the end of the year, some Palestinians began to openly ignore the various strike calls. In December, shops and businesses remained open despite a call for a general strike made by the PFLP and the DFLP to protest about the opening of the bilateral talks in Washington; while Fath activists reportedly made it clear to the Islamic and the radical opposition groups that they would not tolerate attempts to enforce the strike.[101]

The Palestinian population also became growingly critical of the continued paralysis of the educational system in the territories. As a result of the Intifada, a whole generation was losing its chance for education, critics claimed. A public campaign to reopen schools closed by the Israeli authorities because of recurring riots was initiated by parents and public figures.

The mounting pressure to return to normal life, the inability of the UNC to mobilize the local population for mass anti-Israel demonstrations, the reassessment of the Intifada, and the upcoming peace process led certain Israeli commentators to conclude, during the year, that the Intifada had reached its end. However, such an interpretation was doubtlessly premature.[102] Commenting in December on the security situation in the territories, Maj. Gen. Danny Yatom, Commander in Chief of the IDF Central Command, noted that while there was an apparent decline in the number of mass demonstrations, stone-throwing incidents and widespread confrontations with the army, there had also been a significant increase in the Palestinians' use of firearms. "If the peace process stumble[d] or was seen as producing few gains," he cautioned, "the uprising could be easily ignited."[103]

ISRAELI SECURITY POLICY

Israel's overall security policy in the territories in 1991 was strongly affected by the Gulf War and the beginning of the peace process, with a tougher line adopted during the winter and spring, easing later on in the year. The noticeable rise in terrorist acts perpetrated against Israeli civilian and military targets both in the territories and in Israel itself led the government to impose periodic bans on the entry of Arabs from the territories into Israel and to deport militant leaders. In May, the military authorities barred thousands of Palestinian laborers with criminal or security records from entering Israel. Moreover, all Palestinians wishing to gain access to Israel or to the city of Jerusalem were required to obtain a new special permit issued by the civil administration.[104]

In January, Israel expelled four Gaza Strip Hamas activists for subversive and terrorist activity and in May, after an unsuccessful appeal to Israel's High Court, four Gazans alleged to be senior Fath leaders were deported to Lebanon. The four Fath activists were depicted for throwing hand grenades at Israeli soldiers, killing Arab residents, and committing other security offenses. The Israeli decision, made at the start of Secretary Baker's peace efforts, was sharply condemned by the Bush Administration, but was justified by Defense Minister Moshe Arens, who said he was convinced that expulsion was an effective and appropriate punishment for incitement to violence. Commenting on American pressure on Israel to reverse its decision, Arens said: "We know that the American Government takes issue with this punishment. We have studied all of their arguments and understand them, but the difference between us is that we must contend with problems of unrest, violence and murder here in the field."[105] The May deportations brought to 69 the number of Palestinians expelled from the territories since the beginning of the uprising in December 1987.[106]

As negotiations for the proposed peace conference progressed, Israel relaxed its security policy significantly. Reports published by the US Government, Israeli human rights groups and the IDF spokesman, while differing on figures, all indicated that Israel's treatment of Palestinians in the territories showed an overall improvement and that there was a considerable decline in the scope of human rights violations. A central finding was the decline in the number of Palestinian casualties attributed to the use of ammunition and force by the security forces. Estimates of figures varied, but according to the US State Department's annual report on human rights practices, almost all categories of violence decreased substantially during 1991. US figures indicated that a total of 97 Palestinians were killed by the security forces in 1991 (75 according to the IDF), compared to 140 (93 according to the IDF) in 1990, and that 4 Palestinians were killed by Israeli civilians in 1991 compared to 10 in 1990. The estimated number of Palestinians wounded by security forces, according to IDF data, was 1,475 in 1991, compared to 3,862 in 1990. Israeli Government sources also reported that Palestinians killed one soldier and six Israeli civilians and injured 685 soldiers and policemen and 230 civilians in 1991.[107]

The marked decline in the number of casualties in 1991 was attributed to fewer mass demonstrations organized by the UNC, more restrictive army regulations on opening fire, and a sharp reduction of IDF patrols in the territories in order to avoid incidental confrontations with the local population. However, a report released in December by the Betselem organization, Israel's human rights group, stressed that the army continued to widely violate various aspects of human rights regularly. The IDF spokesman insisted that the number of complaints of beatings and physical abuse had declined compared to the previous year. Army sources also reported that three soldiers were tried in military courts during 1991 for causing the death of Palestinians.

One was convicted, the indictment of another was rescinded and the trial of the third was still ongoing at the end of the year.[108]

A change in policy guidelines was palpable in other areas of security policy as well. Demolition of security offenders' homes decreased to 49 in 1991 from 90 the previous year and 286 during 1988–89. The number of houses that were sealed dropped to 46 in 1991 from 100 in 1990. There was a sharp decline in the number of administrative detentions, which peaked at c. 1,400 in February 1991 during the Gulf War, and decreased to less than 350 in December. IDF data also indicated that the total number of Palestinian prisoners declined in 1991. In December 1991 there were nearly 11,300 Palestinians in military detention centers and prisons, of whom c. 60% had been tried and were serving sentences.[109] A contributing factor to the decrease in the number of Palestinians in Israeli prisons was the Defense Ministry's decision in April to release 1,250 prisoners. The Israeli step was seen as a conciliatory gesture related to Secretary of State Baker's visit to Israel. The release was part of the ministry's twofold effort to apply an iron-fist policy against the hard core of Intifada activists involved in terror, on the one hand, and ease restrictions and show flexibility, on the other.

According to a *Jerusalem Post* analysis, advocates of this policy believed that "with support for the PLO in the Arab world at an unprecedented low, and with the seeming realization among some Palestinian leaders that violence got them nowhere, this [was] the time to take 'confidence-building measures.'"[110] The message transmitted to the inhabitants of the territories was clear: Israel's willingness to engage in a peaceful political dialogue was conditional upon a substantive decline in the level of violence.

Toward the latter part of 1991 the government indeed began to implement measures intended to ease some of the restrictions and lighten the burden of occupation. It allowed the return to the West Bank of 'Ali Abu Hilal (a DFLP activist deported in 1986) in exchange for the body of slain IDF soldier Samir As'ad, relaxed bridge-crossing formalities between Israel and the West Bank, and shifted responsibility for approving curfews of more than a few hours to higher-level Israeli officers.

Government efforts in the economic sphere concentrated on three areas: taxation, industrialization and elections to chambers of commerce. The general aim of the Israeli plan was to compensate the territories economically for cuts in foreign income caused by the war (the halt of aid from Saudi Arabia and the gulf states as well as the end to remittances from Palestinian workers there) and for restrictions imposed on the entry of laborers from the West Bank and Gaza Strip into Israel. The plan was aimed at cutting taxes and encouraging economic development and investment in the West Bank. The civil administration promised to lower the tax burden in the West Bank by 25% from January 1992, a measure that had been approved for Gazans earlier in the year. This new policy followed a previous decision to grant tax breaks to new or expanding factories with 10 or more employees and a capital investment of up to $50,000. The authorities also provided incentives for economic entrepreneurship by exempting new industrial ventures from income tax for the first three years. Simultaneously, the civil administration called for investment by Palestinian businessmen to create new jobs, in view of the relatively high rate of unemployment.[111] Efforts were also directed at holding elections to local chambers of commerce in order to stimulate commerce and thereby encourage financial investment and economic activity. The first such elections were held in Hebron on 18 June, followed by elections in the Gaza Strip in November.[112]

NOTES

For the place and frequency of publications cited here, and for the full name of the publication, news agency, radio station or monitoring service where an abbreviation is used, please see "List of Sources." Only in the case of more than one publication bearing the same name is the place of publication noted here.

1. *Shu'un Filastiniyya*, 215–16 (February-March 1991), p. 128.
2. *Ha'aretz*, 28 January 1991.
3. *JP*, 28 January 1991.
4. Ibid., 1 February 1991.
5. *Ha'aretz*, 19 February 1991.
6. *JP, Ha'aretz*, 14 November 1991.
7. Daoud Kuttab, "In the Aftermath of the War," *JPS*, 20, 4 (Summer 1991), pp. 115–16.
8. *Ha'aretz*, 1, 5 February; *JP*, 8 February 1991.
9. *Al-Hurriyya*, 10 March 1991.
10. *Filastin al-Thawra*, 7 April 1991.
11. Kuttab, op. cit.
12. "Palestinian Politics after the Gulf War, an Interview with Faisal Husseini," *JPS*, 20, 4 (Summer 1991), p. 102.
13. *JP, Ha'aretz*, 21 April 1991; "Palestinian Politics," p. 106.
14. *Al-Fajr* (English ed.), 18 March 1991.
15. *Ha'aretz*, 9 April; *JP*, 8 April 1991.
16. *Al-Fajr* (English ed.), 15 April; *JP*, 10 April 1991.
17. Maher Abu Khater, *Al-Fajr* (English ed.), 15 April 1991.
18. Ibid.
19. Ibid.; *JP*, 10 April 1991; Kuttab, op. cit., p. 121.
20. *Ha'aretz*, 21 April 1991.
21. *JP*, 21 April 1991.
22. Kuttab, op. cit., p. 122.
23. *Ha'aretz*, 21, 23, 26 July; *al-Sha'b* (Jerusalem), editorial, 23 July; *al-Fajr*, 29 July 1991.
24. *Ha'aretz*, 13 March 1991.
25. Ibid.; *al-Fajr* (English ed.), 15 April 1991.
26. *Al-Fajr*, 10 April 1991.
27. VoI (in Arabic), 2 March — DR, 10 March; *Ha'aretz*, 17 March 1991.
28. *Al-Fajr* (English ed.), 15 April 1991.
29. *JP*, 2 June 1991.
30. *JP*, 2, 3, 7 June; *Ha'aretz*, 4 June; *Filastin al-Thawra*, 9 June 1991.
31. *Jerusalem Report*, 20 June 1991.
32. *Al-Fajr*, 24 March 1991.
33. Ibid.; *JP*, 29 March; *al-Fajr* (English ed.), 1 April 1991.
34. *Al-Fajr*, 24 March 1991.
35. Ibid.; *al-Fajr* (English ed.), 1 April 1991.
36. *Al-Fajr* (English ed.), 8 April 1991.
37. *Al-Fajr*, 27 March; *al-Fajr* (English ed.), 1 April 1991.
38. *Al-Fajr*, 22 April 1991.
39. *JP*, 14 May 1991.
40. Ibid.; *Ha'aretz*, 13 May; *al-Fajr* (English ed.), 20 May 1991.
41. *Al-Fajr* (English ed.), 20 May 1991.
42. *Al-Fajr*, 21, 22 May 1991.
43. *JP*, 31 May 1991.
44. *Al-Fajr*, 31 May 1991.
45. Israel TV, 2 August — DR, 5 August; *al-Fajr* (English ed.), 5 August; *Ha'aretz*, 6 August 1991.
46. *Davar, Ha'aretz*, 4 August 1991.
47. *JP*, 9 August 1991.
48. *Ha'aretz*, 26 July, 2 August; *al-Fajr*, 5 August 1991.
49. *JP*, 9 August 1991.

50. *Davar,* 4 August 1991.
51. Cited in *Ha'aretz,* 12 August 1991.
52. Ibid.; *MEI,* 26 July 1991.
53. *Ha'aretz,* 26 July; interview with Riyad al-Maliki, *al-Fajr* (English ed.), 26 August 1991.
54. Interviewed in *al-Fajr* (English ed.), 5 August; cf. a similar article by Bassam al-Salihi in the Communist weekly, *al-Tali'a,* 15 August 1991.
55. VoP (Algiers), 2 August — DR, 5 August 1991.
56. VoP (San'a), 3 September — DR, 4 September 1991.
57. *Ha'aretz,* 23 July; *MEI,* 26 July 1991.
58. *NYT,* 21 September 1991.
59. *IHT,* 9 October 1991.
60. *JP,* 2 October 1991.
61. Ibid., 24 September; *Ha'aretz,* 27 September 1991.
62. Jon Immanuel, *JP,* 29 September 1991.
63. *Ha'aretz,* 11 October; *NYT,* 13 October 1991.
64. *JP,* 25 October; *Ha'aretz,* 20, 22, 24, 25 October; *Yedi'ot Aharonot,* 20 October 1991.
65. Joel Greenberg, *JP,* 25 October 1991.
66. *WP,* 24 October 1991.
67. *JP,* 25 October 1991.
68. *Al-Fajr* (English ed.), 30 September 1991.
69. *Ha'aretz,* 24 October 1991.
70. *JP, Ha'aretz,* 25 October 1991.
71. *JP, Ha'aretz, al-Sha'b* (Jerusalem), 1 November; *al-Fajr* (English ed.), 4 November 1991.
72. *JP,* 8 November 1991.
73. Khalil Tuma, *al-Fajr* (English ed.), 18 November 1991.
74. Ibid., 18 November; *al-Bayadir al-Siyasi,* 16 November 1991.
75. *Jerusalem Report,* 28 November 1991.
76. *Ha'aretz,* 24 October; *JP,* 25 October; DFLP leaflet, published in *al-Hurriyya,* 3 November 1991.
77. *Ha'aretz,* 24 October; *JP,* 31 October 1991.
78. *NYT,* 6 November 1991.
79. *Ha'aretz,* 5 November; *NYT,* 6 November; *al-Fajr* (English ed.), 11 November 1991.
80. *JP,* 15 November 1991.
81. *Jerusalem Report,* 28 November 1991.
82. Elie Rekhess, "Peace Takes Time and Patience," *JP,* 11 November 1991.
83. *Yedi'ot Aharonot,* 11 November; *JP,* 15 November 1991.
84. VoI, 13 November — DR, 14 November; *Jerusalem Report,* 20 November 1991.
85. *JP,* 29 November; *Jerusalem Report,* 28 November 1991.
86. *Al-Bayadir al-Siyasi,* 2 November 1991.
87. Joel Greenberg, *JP,* 8 November; *Ha'aretz,* 22 November 1991.
88. *Al-Fajr* (English ed.), 30 December 1991.
89. VoP (Algiers), 18 February 1991; *al-Hadaf* (Damascus), 24 February 1991.
90. *JP,* 18, 22 February 1991.
91. *'Al Hamishmar,* 6 December; *Ha'aretz, JP,* 9 December 1991.
92. Clyde Haberman, *NYT,* 9 December 1991.
93. See, for example, an appeal in UNC Call No. 71 "to stop covering one's face with headgear...stop kidnapping, interrogating and killing," VoP (Algiers), 2 June — DR, 3 June 1991.
94. *Al-Fajr,* 5 June; *JP,* 6 June; *Ha'aretz,* 7 June; *Jerusalem Report,* 20 June 1991.
95. Cited in *Ha'aretz,* 14 June 1991.
96. *JP,* 11 June 1991.
97. Jon Immanuel, ibid., 9 June. Also see Roni Shaked, *Yedi'ot Aharonot,* 14 June 1991.
98. "Palestinian Politics," p. 102.
99. *NYT,* 9 December 1991.
100. *JP,* 9 June; *Yedi'ot Aharonot,* 14 June; *Jerusalem Report,* 20 June 1991.
101. *Ha'aretz,* 4 December; *JP,* 5 December 1991.
102. Danny Rubinstein, *Ha'aretz,* 11 June, and reply by Zeev Schiff, ibid., 19 June 1991.

103. *NYT,* 9 December 1991.
104. *Ha'aretz,* 1 May 1991; US Department of State, "Country Report on Human Rights Practices for 1991: Israel and the Occupied Territories," *JPS,* 21, 3 (Spring 1992), p. 121.
105. *JP,* 26 March 1991.
106. *NYT,* 19 May. For an interview with the four deportees, see *al-Hadaf* (Damascus), 26 May 1991.
107. "Country Report," p. 119; *Ha'aretz,* 9 December 1991.
108. "Country Report," ibid.
109. Ibid., p. 118; *Ha'aretz,* 3 September; *JP,* 7 October; *'Al Hamishmar,* 6 December 1991.
110. *Ha'aretz,* 29 March; *JP,* 12 April, 20 June 1991.
111. *JP,* 9 May; *Ha'aretz,* 26 June 1991.
112. *Ha'aretz,* 18, 23 June; *JP,* 19 June; *NYT,* 20 June 1991.

MIDDLE EAST
ECONOMIC AND
DEMOGRAPHIC ISSUES

Middle East Oil Developments

DAVID RACHOVICH

The international community was highly apprehensive at the beginning of 1991 regarding the possible outcome of the Gulf crisis, as the area contained a quarter of the total world oil production (see Table 9), two thirds of the world's total proven reserves (see Table 10), and about half of the world's remaining conventionally recoverable crude oil resources. About 60% of the oil imported by Japan, over 30% imported by the US, and a similar percentage imported by Europe came from the Gulf. The share of oil from the Gulf in world oil exports approached 45%. All this made the Gulf area vital to the world economy. Moreover, world dependence on Gulf oil was rising, and it was clear that this trend would continue. It must be stressed that no amount of energy conservation, offshore drilling or synthetic fuels could constitute a full alternative for oil from the Gulf. Thus, a serious dislocation in the supply of oil from this region was liable to harm the world economy. This explained, at least in part, the formation of a broad coalition of states, headed by the US, with the aim of acting vigorously to ensure the free flow of Gulf oil to the world markets, alongside several other important goals. The world was not willing to permit Iraq to take control of such large oil reserves and to dictate price policy.

When all diplomatic efforts at solving the dispute peacefully failed and it seemed that war was inevitable, predictions were made that with the outbreak of hostilities oil prices would increase perhaps fivefold, leaping as high as $100 a barrel; but these predictions proved wrong. The oil market displayed rare maturity from the very first day of the fighting to the end. Oil continued to flow and the anticipated crisis was avoided. In the end, Iraq was militarily defeated and Kuwait was liberated.

The year 1991 was also marked by the considerable strengthening of Saudi Arabia's position in the Organization of Petroleum Exporting Countries (Opec). Saudi Arabia increased its production and in fact dictated the organization's policy. Although disputes in Opec continued as in the past, the organization no longer resembled what it had been before the war in the Gulf.

PRICE, SUPPLY AND DEMAND

THE GULF CRISIS AND THE GULF WAR

Oil prices opened the year at relatively high levels: Brent and West Texas Intermediate (WTI) were close to $27 a barrel, while Dubai fluctuated at around $22.50 a barrel (see Tables 1 and 2). Still, these levels were lower than the peak achieved in October 1990 at the height of the Gulf crisis (see *MECS* 1990, pp. 291–92, Tables 1 and 2). A trend toward a fall in oil prices began early in January (see Table 2), with the price of WTI falling to $24.90 a barrel on 4 January, its lowest level since Iraq's invasion of Kuwait on 2 August 1990. The spot price of Brent fell gradually and on 9 January reached

277

$22.45 a barrel, which was almost its level at the outbreak of the crisis ($22.28).[1] The spot price of Dubai lost $4 a barrel in the course of a week, and on 9 January reached $18.70 a barrel (see Table 1). The fall in oil prices reflected the glut of oil on the markets as well as widespread optimism regarding finding a peaceful solution to the crisis by means of the talks held in Geneva on 9 January between US Secretary of State James Baker and Iraqi Foreign Minister Tariq 'Aziz[2] (for this, and subsequent developments related to the war, see chapter on the Gulf War). However, following the failure of the Geneva talks, and the approach of the ultimatum deadline set by the UN for Iraqi withdrawal from Kuwait (15 January), the trend was reversed and oil prices began to climb again.

When it appeared that an Iraqi pullout from Kuwait would not take place, the analysts increasingly predicted that oil prices would jump and would reach anywhere from $40 a barrel to $60 or more once the war broke out.[3] However, this did not happen. Although oil spot prices gained strength following the news of the attack on Iraq on the night of 16–17 January, they then experienced their greatest drop in history in a single day a few hours after optimistic reports were received on the results of the first coalition air strikes against Iraqi targets. These reports had led to the market's conclusion that the war would not last long and that Saudi oil installations would not be damaged. The fall in oil prices was also due to the announcement by the International Energy Agency (IEA) on 17 January, regarding the implementation of its emergency plan of 11 January, whereby its members were obliged to add 2.5m. barrels per day (b/d) to oil supplies within 15 days, and primarily by the release of oil into the markets from emergency stocks in the Western countries.[4] As part of this plan US President Bush ordered the sale of 1.125m. b/d from the Strategic Petroleum Reserve (SPR) for a period of 30 days.

WTI for February delivery rose on the New York market from $32 a barrel at the close of 16 January to $38.50 during the first hours of the war and then plummeted to $20.30 in the middle of trading on 17 January, before rising slightly to close at $21.45 a barrel (see Table 2 and Figure 1)[5] — namely, a fall of $10.55 (or about 33%) in a single day. Significantly, there was a difference of $18.20 a barrel between the highest and lowest WTI rates that day. Similarly, the spot price of Brent on London's International Petroleum Exchange fell from $29.10 a barrel on 16 January to $20.80 on 17 January — that is, about $8 in a day, while the Dubai spot price lost $7.45 in value. The fall in oil prices continued on 18 January, too, as the euphoria surrounding the early military successes mounted, with the principal types of oil losing a further $2 on average, so that their level was lower than that recorded on 1 August 1990 (see Table 2). Thereafter, the market generally concentrated on the fundamental supply and demand situation, which was bearish despite fading hopes that the war would be short. At the same time, continuous reports on the Gulf situation were responsible for frequent fluctuations in oil prices (see Figure 1), a condition which had prevailed before the war broke out as well.[6]

By early January, oil stocks held on land by the member states of the Organization for Economic Cooperation and Development (OECD) reached 469.1m. tonnes (3,424m. barrels), the highest level since 1982,[7] equivalent to 96 days' consumption. Despite the fall in oil prices, the IEA decided to extend its emergency plan on 28 January (see above), although in fact this was not implemented entirely.[8] In addition, Saudi Arabia and Iran had huge floating stocks of at least 80m. barrels (Saudi Arabia, about 60m. barrels; Iran, 20m. barrels),[9] while production in these two countries picked up during February after a fall in January with the onset of hostilities (see Table 4, and cf. with Table 3 in *MECS* 1990, p. 293). Saudi production was over 8m. b/d, amounting to c. 35% of total Opec production. The Saudi increase largely compensated for the loss of Iraqi and Kuwaiti oil and served to moderate the price level.

On the demand side, moreover, the need for oil in the industrialized states declined, mainly owing to the economic slowdown. The dramatic reduction in air travel also lowered the demand for fuel.[10] On 14 February, the spot price of Brent fell to $18.90 a barrel, Dubai to $14.55 and WTI to $22.30 — a loss of $1.19 a barrel on average compared with their level on 17 January at the outbreak of the war. Political and psychological factors — Iraq's proposal to withdraw its troops from Kuwait, and the USSR's diplomatic initiative to find a solution to the crisis — served to weaken the oil prices for several days subsequently,[11] with the Brent spot price reaching what was considered its lowest level throughout 1991 — $16.70 a barrel — on 19 February and Dubai spot prices also reaching a nadir at $12.75 a barrel. A mild recovery took place after the ground attack against Iraq on the night of 23–24 February, and a further strengthening was registered on 28 February with President Bush's announcement of the cease-fire in the Gulf (see Table 2).

AFTER THE GULF WAR

There were two main trends in oil prices from the end of the war in the Gulf to the end of the year: an erratic, modest rise in prices until about the last week of October, and, by contrast, a distinct fall thereafter. The average price of the seven types of oil contained in the Opec basket rose from $17.19 a barrel in March (see Table 3) to $20.80 in the fourth week of October.[12] This price was only $0.20 a barrel off the reference price of $21 a barrel that Opec had fixed for itself. In November, the price of the Opec basket fell to $19.79 a barrel, and in December to $17.35 (see Table 3).

Oil prices rose after the termination of hostilities in the Gulf, continuing the trend that was observable in the last week of February as a result of the widely held supposition that Opec would decide to cut production at its Geneva meeting on 11–12 March.[13] The prices rose on 13 March as well, a day after Opec's decision to reduce production to a level of 22.3m. b/d for the second quarter of the year (see Table 5),[14] but when the markets reevaluated that the cut was actually undertaken on a voluntary basis, prices fell. For example, the Brent spot price, which had risen from $18.80 a barrel on 28 February to $20.05 on 13 March, fell to $18.15 on 27 March.[15]

In April, the trend changed again and oil prices continued to rise as well as to stabilize, the spot price of Brent at c. $19.50 a barrel and Dubai at c. $15.50 (see Table 1), while WTI reached a level of c. $21.[16] This strengthening of prices stemmed from the publication of IEA figures confirming Opec's intention to cut no less than 1m. b/d of its production. Opec Secretary-General Dr. Subroto stated in Dallas on 8 April that the organization's latest agreement was beginning to show favorable results.[17] Short-term prospects for the market also improved somewhat with the publication of American Petroleum Institute data on 9 April, indicating that the decline in crude and product stocks was larger than expected.[18]

A further tendency toward a rise in oil prices was evident in the first week of May (see Table 1), for two main reasons: first, various reports on Opec production in April showed that the organization was keeping to its commitments to cut production as required by the agreement reached on 12 March. A first estimate by the IEA indicated a reduction of Opec production in April to a level of 22.6m. b/d, rather more than its ceiling (22.3m. b/d) but significantly less than its actual production in March (23.1m. b/d).[19] Later reports showed that Opec had fulfilled its goal in April even more accurately, with most, if not all, of the reduction in production undertaken by Saudi Arabia (cf. Table 4 with Table 5). The second reason for the rise was optimistic forecasts regarding world demand for oil during the rest of the year.[20]

Prices slackened, however, from about the second week of May to the end of June, with the spot price of Brent falling from $19.85 a barrel on 8 May to $18.10 a barrel on 26 June, and Dubai from $16.10 a barrel to $15.27 a barrel in the same period (see Table 1). This fall in prices was due to a new combination of supply and demand forces. Demand for oil was on the decline owing both to the continued recession in the industrialized countries, primarily the US, and to the seasonal drop in demand for oil (see Table 6).[21] Supply, by contrast, was increasing, mainly on account of excess production by Opec members who exceeded their quotas, especially in June (cf. Table 4 with Table 5). The markets reacted unenthusiastically to the decision of the 4 June Opec conference in Vienna to roll the overall production ceiling of the organization onto the third quarter without setting obligatory quotas.[22] Similarly, oil production in the US rose in the first half of the year for the first time since 1985, and oil stocks in the OECD grew substantially in the second quarter compared with the first quarter.[23]

A general rise in oil prices was recorded in the third quarter of the year, with the spot price of Brent rising from $18.50 a barrel on 3 July to $20.70 on 25 September, and of Dubai from $15.75 a barrel to $17.75 during that period (see Table 1). Three new factors began to influence the oil markets: the resumption of Kuwaiti oil exports, the question of resumed exports of Iraqi oil, and the impact of the situation in the USSR on its oil production and export.

Kuwait resumed oil production on 11 June for the first time since the war ended, at a rate of 25,000 b/d,[24] evoking a temporal and uneven reaction by the market of a fall in prices, e.g., a fall was registered in the spot prices of Dubai after 19 July, too.[25] On 28 July, Kuwait resumed oil exports from al-Ahmadi port with a quantity of c. 2m. barrels.[26] This, however, did not give rise to any special concern, since the resumption of exports was perceived more as symbolic than real in view of the fact that Kuwait was still occupied with extinguishing the fires raging in its wells. A second consignment of Kuwaiti oil of a similar amount was shipped only on 5–7 August.[27] Significantly, both shipments had difficulty finding buyers owing to questions about the quality of the oil.

The issue of oil exports from Iraq began to interest the markets from the fourth week of July onward, with the prices of benchmark crudes falling by about $0.50 a barrel on 23 July in response to signs that the US would agree to limited export of Iraqi oil for humanitarian reasons. But the delay in a decision by the UN Security Council regarding Iraq's request to sell $1.5bn. worth of oil removed some of the fears of excess supply.[28] On 15 August, the Security Council adopted Resolution 706 allowing Iraq to export $1.6bn. worth of oil for six months under UN supervision, and Resolution 705 on payment of compensation by Iraq to the extent of 30% of the value of Iraqi exports.[29] But Iraq rejected these resolutions, regarding them as a humiliation and an infringement of its sovereignty. A month later, on 19 September, the Security

Council approved resolutions on the conditions under which Iraq could export oil, but the Iraqis rejected them as well for similar reasons.[30]

The markets began to focus more intensively on the situation in the USSR during the second half of the year. The continuing fall in Soviet production and export of oil to the West, together with fears of a complete halt in exports, obsessed the oil market, especially in light of the attempted coup in August[31] (see chapter on the Soviet Union and the Middle East). Even before this event, oil production in the USSR had fallen by 9% during the first half of the year, compared with the first half of 1990, and stood at 10.75m. b/d, of which c. 1.7m. b/d was earmarked for export.[32] The threat of a further fall in Soviet oil production had an impact on the markets, with the prices of benchmark Brent crude rising by almost $2 a barrel to $22.20 on 19 August, the day the attempted coup began. When the attempt failed, prices fell to below $20 on 21 August,[33] and fears of disruptions in Soviet oil production decreased thereafter, although they continued to exist. The prices of Brent steadied at c. $20 a barrel at the end of August, reflecting a certain degree of concern over political instability in the USSR and the anticipated rise in demand during the last quarter with the approach of winter and other factors.[34]

Saudi Arabia began to rebuild the oil stocks it kept in floating storage and in transit, a trend which was intensified in August after its stocks fell as a result of being heavily drawn down in the second quarter of 1991. The acceleration in stock accumulation was also due to fear of a fall in Soviet oil exports and the expectation of a harsh winter.[35] This expansion of stocks formed the background to an increase in production by Saudi Arabia (see below), which in August and September exceeded the previously committed level by c. 400,000 b/d (cf. Table 4 with Table 5). The other Opec members also exceeded the production quotas they had voluntarily undertaken. However, the increase in Opec production to the highest levels since the beginning of the year (see Table 4) did not generally weaken prices, both because of the rise in world demand for oil, particularly in the US, during the third quarter of the year, and the fall in oil production in the USSR and several non-Opec states.

Oil prices continued to rise until the start of the last week in October, reaching their highest levels since the end of the Gulf War on 22 October: the spot price of Brent reached $22.35 a barrel, Dubai $18.95 and WTI $23.55.[36] This was the highest nominal price level since the collapse of prices at the beginning of 1986, discounting the six exceptional months between the Iraqi invasion of Kuwait and the outbreak of the war in the Gulf. The causes for the upward movement in prices were the approach of winter in the northern hemisphere and the consequent replenishment of refinery stocks, concern over a fall in Soviet production, the lack of spare capacity by the members of Opec, and the market assessment that the renewal of Iraqi oil exports would come about later than expected.[37]

Prices began to fall on 23 October, a trend which continued until the end of the year. Between 22 October and 23 December, WTI lost $4.90, Brent $4.85 and Dubai $4.50.[38] The change in tendency in October reflected a reevaluation by the markets regarding future oil market supplies, i.e., an evaluation that Opec production would reach almost 24m. b/d; a less pessimistic assessment of the prospects for Soviet oil exports; and the anticipation of a mild winter.[39]

These evaluations did indeed prove correct. Opec's Ministerial Monitoring Committee (MMC) decided at a meeting in Geneva on 25 September to raise the organization's production ceiling from 22.30m. b/d to 23.65m. b/d for the last quarter, in accordance with anticipated demand for Opec oil by the IEA. However, in view of vociferous Saudi demands at the conference for production of 8.5m. b/d, all the members were in fact permitted to continue to produce as they wished, and individual quotas were not set (see Table 5). Opec production leaped, therefore, to 24.3m. b/d in November and 24.5m. b/d in December, the latter figure representing the organization's highest production rate in 11 years.[40]

In Kuwait, the last burning oil well was extinguished on 6 November, which was sooner than expected. Of Kuwait's 935 wells, 749 had been damaged during the Iraqi occupation, with 647 of them burning or gushing oil when the country was liberated.[41] However, the intensive reconstruction of Kuwait's oil industry resulted in a larger volume of production and exports than initially forecast. During the first week of November, Kuwaiti production reached 0.5m. b/d (including its share in the Neutral Zone), and crude exports reached 350,000 b/d.[42]

At the beginning of December, the fall in oil prices was also influenced to some extent by rumors that Iraq intended to reverse its decision not to accept the conditions for oil export imposed on it by the UN. A meeting of Iraqi and UN representatives on this question was due to take place at the beginning of January 1992.[43] (The meeting was duly held in Vienna on 8 January 1992.)

All in all, fears in the third quarter of the year that the supply of oil would constrict were not realized by the year's end. Soviet oil continued to flow into the world markets, though in diminished quantities, the weather in the US and in Japan was mild, oil stocks were very high, and refinery capacity was exploited to only about 82% — a low level for this period.[44]

Simultaneously, the demand for oil remained sluggish due to continued economic weakness in the West, particularly in the US where an economic upswing discerned in the third quarter of the year petered out by the year's end.[45] The US gross national product for 1991, according to initial estimates, fell by 0.5% (in 1982 dollars), following a rise of 0.9% in 1990.[46] This fall ended eight continuous years of economic growth and was responsible for the drop in demand for energy by the US. A rise in domestic oil production in 1991 (mainly owing to an increase in production in Alaska), together with the drop in local demand due to the economic slowdown, resulted in a reduction in petroleum imports. Most of the year-on-year decline was in petroleum product imports, although a fall was also recorded in the import of crude oil (see Table 7). Saudi Arabia, nevertheless, was able to expand its share of the American market considerably, increasing its crude export to the US from 1.20m. b/d in 1990 to 1.68m. b/d on average in 1991 — namely, a rise of 40% (see Table 8). With the growth of the Saudi share in the total import of crude oil to the US from about 20% to 29% in 1991, Saudi Arabia fortified its position in 1991 as chief oil supplier to the American market.

The rate of Saudi oil production was high during 1991, reaching a yearly average of 8.2m. b/d, as compared with 6.3m. b/d in 1990.[47] Undoubtedly, the increase in Saudi production (see Table 9) was one of the major causes of the relative stability of the markets during 1991, paralleling the situation that had prevailed during the Gulf crisis in 1990 (see *MECS* 1990, pp. 278–82).

OPEC'S POLITICS

OPEC'S MMC MEETING ON 11-12 MARCH IN GENEVA

Prior to the Opec MMC meeting in March, the Saudis let it be known that they would oppose the production cutback formulas that had been agreed upon in earlier consultations among six Opec countries — Algeria, Gabon, Indonesia, Libya, Nigeria and Venezuela — which took place in Vienna on 25-26 February.[48] These consultations had been held at the initiative of the Algerian minister of mines and industry, Sadiq Boussena, who was also the president of Opec then, in order to discuss anticipated developments in the world oil market. The invitation to these informal talks, which had been sent out by the Opec president, was declined by Saudi Arabia, the United Arab Emirates (UAE) and Kuwait, which preferred to adhere to the original date of the Opec gathering fixed at the last conference in December (namely, the meeting scheduled for 11 March). Iraq, Iran and Ecuador also decided to absent themselves from the February meeting.[49] The six Opec countries decided at that meeting that Saudi Arabia must cut back 1.2m.-1.5m. b/d to a level of 6.9m.-7.2m. b/d for the second quarter.

The MMC conference on 11-12 March showed that henceforth the Saudis would be setting the tone for the organization. The outcome of the two days of talks, which dealt mostly with production quotas, represented a victory for the Saudi proposal,[50] with production by the kingdom cut by only about 400,000 b/d for the second quarter, far less than proposed at the consultation in February. The Geneva meeting also accepted the Saudi argument that the crisis in the Gulf was not yet over, and therefore that the circumstances were extraordinary, so that the agreement reached in Geneva was to be interpreted as a voluntary production limitation rather than an imposition of formal quotas.

Assuming that Kuwait and Iraq were not yet ready to market their oil, the agreement provided for a voluntary cutback of 5% by 10 Opec members for the second quarter, based on their highest monthly production in the August 1990- February 1991 period (Algeria was not included in this cutback). It was determined that the organization's new ceiling would be 22.3m. b/d, in consequence of an overall reduction of more than 1m. b/d (see Table 5). Iran and Algeria had reservations about this ceiling, which they considered too high for the purpose of achieving the reference price of $21 a barrel, a price that had been fixed at the last Opec conference before the crisis in the Gulf, on 27 July 1990 (see *MECS* 1990, p. 285) and reaffirmed by Opec in Geneva. Algeria called for a ceiling closer to 21m. b/d, while Iran proposed 21.5m. b/d,[51] both of them insisting that their reservations be included in the official announcement scheduled for the end of the Opec meeting.

Not only did the 12 March arrangement at Geneva allow Saudi Arabia to produce at a rate of 8m. b/d, but it also increased the Saudi market share in Opec to 36%. The Saudi share in Opec had been on the decline in previous years: from 26.16% in 1987 to 23.92% in July 1990.[52] In the Geneva deal, most of the members accepted the Saudi estimate of anticipated demand for Opec oil in the second quarter — 22.45m. b/d — despite the consensus of c. 21m. b/d for that quarter that had prevailed at the informal talks held in February, and despite the fact that the Saudi estimate was higher than that of the IEA as well as other estimates.

On a practical level, Saudi Arabia tried to impart greater credibility to the organization by a sharp voluntary cutback in its production in April (and to a lesser extent in May) to below the level required by the Geneva arrangement (see Tables 4 and 5), which contributed to a firming of prices. Generally, the rest of the Opec members did not take the arrangement seriously. Iran, for example, interpreted its quota as higher than stated,[53] while the UAE looked more to the formal quota it was to be granted in the future, arguing that it was not satisfied with the quota of 1.5m. b/d it had been awarded in July 1990.[54] Once Saudi Arabia became aware of production deviations by these Opec members, it too began to increase production.

OPEC'S 89TH CONFERENCE ON 4 JUNE IN VIENNA

At a one-day conference, one of the shortest in its history, Opec decided to retain the second-quarter production ceiling of 22.3m. b/d for the third quarter, together with the minimum reference price of $21 a barrel.[55] This time, too, the Saudi position prevailed in a major quarrel that erupted over production and prices. A group of members headed by Algeria, Nigeria and Libya called for a production cutback in the third quarter in order to close the gap between oil prices and the Opec reference price as quickly as possible. Saudi Arabia, leading the predominant camp in opposing the reduction, made it clear, however, that it would not be prepared to lower its production below 8m. b/d. The hawkish faction (price hawks) argued that the term "minimum reference price" meant the "floor price," which had to be protected automatically by a production cutback whenever oil prices fell below the reference price. Saudi Minister of Oil Hisham Nazir, however, stated that he considered the minimum reference price merely as the desirable price, not necessarily requiring any automatic response such as cutting production. "We have always felt that we will support $21 but we never said that we will force that on the market by a deliberate creation of shortage," he said.[56]

The Saudis, pleased to see prices rise to $21 a barrel, nevertheless expressed reservations about a rise above this level, fearing to harm the demand for oil while the West was experiencing a recession. By contrast, the price hawks would have liked prices to rise significantly higher than $21 a barrel.

Although the June Opec meeting did not add to market confidence, and Opec produced far above its ceiling, prices rose during the third quarter of the year because of prevailing conditions (the fall in Soviet production, the increase in world demand, etc.). With demand anticipated to continue rising, the leading Opec members began indicating their positions on production quotas for the last quarter of the year (to be decided at the next conference in September) as early as July. Saudi Arabia spoke of the need to adopt a higher Opec ceiling and a larger quota for itself in order to satisfy the increased demand for oil.[57] Iran and Algeria, on the other hand, stated that they would oppose raising the ceiling so long as prices did not move significantly toward the Opec reference price, a position which Iran had stated at the June Opec conference.[58]

OPEC'S MMC MEETING ON 24–25 SEPTEMBER IN GENEVA

Opec agreed to raise its oil production ceiling by 1.35m. b/d to 23.65m. b/d for the last quarter of the year at this meeting, but the new ceiling had little practical significance because individual quotas were not set (see Table 5). The meeting focused on two subjects: the Saudi demand for higher production and the concern of the other members about prices.

The Saudi minister of oil surprised the conferees with a declaration that his kingdom required an increase of its quota from 8m. b/d to 8.5m. b/d. Even prior to the start of the conference he had told reporters: "Nobody has to approve what Saudi Arabia produces."[59] The eventual 6% raise in the Opec ceiling represented a victory for the Saudi position, although Saudi Arabia had wanted to raise the previous ceiling (22.3m. b/d) by c. 10% (to 24.5m. b/d).[60] Many Opec members had not favored a change in the ceiling before the conference. Even the UAE minister of oil, Yusuf Ibn 'Umayr Ibn Yusuf, stated on 23 September that it would not be wise to raise the ceiling before the reference price of $21 a barrel was achieved.[61] This idea had long been supported by Algeria and Iran. The Nigerian minister of oil, on the other hand, proposed a small rise in the organization's total production to 22.5m. b/d[62] in order to achieve the reference price. In the setting of these conflicting views Saudi Arabia went so far as to threaten to leave Opec in the midst of the conference, declaring that it would produce 8.5m. b/d with Opec's blessing or without it,[63] a move which might have turned the organization into a meaningless body. But consensus was reached at last, even with Iran, Algeria and Libya accepting the Saudi position that the increasing demand for oil would maintain stability of prices even if prices did not actually reach $21 a barrel, especially as oil production in the USSR was declining. Rising oil prices at the time the conference was held led Saudi Arabia to expect the actual demand for Opec oil to reach 24.5m. b/d and more in the last quarter of the year.

One of the results of the Geneva meeting was the formation of a new oil grouping within Opec whose members produced "sweet," light oil,[64] namely Algeria, Libya, Indonesia and Nigeria (and later Gabon). The group, which intended to protect its members' oil prices through restraints on production, held its first meeting after the organization's conference, eliciting some fear by the other Opec members that these states might quit the organization if it failed to advance their interests. When oil prices began to fall, the members of the new grouping stressed the need for a return to the quota system and wanted the matter to be raised for discussion as early as the next Opec conference in November.[65]

The September Opec meeting enabled its members to produce without restriction, and in October their production exceeded the new ceiling (cf. Table 4 with Table 5). Moreover, production by Kuwait was on the rise, with Kuwait announcing in November that after reaching its quota level before the crisis (1.5m. b/d), it would strive for still higher production if justified by demand.[66] Kuwait was thus restating its position at the beginning of 1990 (see *MECS* 1990, p. 282), identifying, as in the past, with the Saudi camp.

OPEC'S 90TH CONFERENCE ON 26–27 NOVEMBER IN VIENNA
A debate between the two main camps evolved at Opec's end-of-the-year conference over the quotas that the organization would adopt for the future. One camp consisted of the traditional price hard-liners (including Iran and Algeria), which supported an immediate return to the quota system in effect prior to the Gulf crisis, at least in terms of market-share percentages fixed by the agreement of 27 July 1990. This meant that the heaviest burden of the production cutback required to meet the fall in demand or rise in supply of Iraqi and Kuwaiti oil would be assumed by the members of Opec that had significantly increased their production during the Gulf crisis — primarily Saudi Arabia. The other camp was represented by the countries chiefly responsible for

compensating for the loss of Iraqi and Kuwaiti oil during the Gulf crisis (Saudi Arabia, the UAE and Venezuela). Deeming the quota numbers established by the 27 July 1990 agreement no longer relevant, this group indicated, nevertheless, that it would be prepared to support cutbacks on the basis of current production levels or on the basis of production capacity with individual reductions distributed among all Opec members proportionally.[67] Opposition to the Saudi camp also arose by the members of the newly formed group producing light, low-sulfur crudes (see above), which stressed the need for lowering the organization's ceiling.[68]

The upshot of all these disputes was the decision at the end of the Opec conference to retain the September production ceiling (23.65m. b/d) for the first quarter of 1992, without setting individual quotas as in the past. This, too, may be seen as a gain for the Saudi position. As previously, Saudi Minister of Oil Hisham Nazir argued that his country was not bound by any quota and that no state had the right to interfere in determining the kingdom's production level. He stated also that Opec was obliged to satisfy demand lest a shortage of oil push prices up and harm world economic growth.[69]

The Opec decision was facilitated by the continued absence of Iraqi oil from the markets, for although the UN Security Council had decided to allow Iraq to sell oil worth $1.6bn., Baghdad had rejected the conditions involved. The new Opec president, Jibril Aminu, who was the Nigerian minister of oil, justified the organization's decision not to raise its ceiling by the fact that oil prices had still not reached the reference price of $21 a barrel. On the other hand, he explained prices had not fallen so much as to justify lowering the ceiling, and considering the situation in the USSR, and the fact that Kuwait and Iraq had not yet returned to the markets, the decision to retain the September production ceiling was logical.[70] Contrary to his predictions, however, oil prices continued to fall steeply (see Table 1), prompting Algeria to call for an emergency meeting of Opec before its next scheduled conference of 12 February 1992.[71]

The most significant development in the context of the oil politics after the Gulf War was the strengthened Saudi position in Opec. Its market share in the organization rose substantially, as did its influence over other members. This situation contrasted markedly with that before the Gulf crisis when Iraq, Iran, Algeria, Libya and other Opec members tried to force prices up by restraining the organization's production at the expense of Saudi Arabia. While the traditional divisions between the supporters of high prices and the supporters of increased production and lower prices remained, the Saudi position ultimately tipped the scales in Opec's last decision. It seemed reasonable to suppose that even when Iraq resumed oil exports it would not regain the quota of 3.1m. b/d that it had before invading Kuwait on account of Saudi Arabia's determination to increase its own share of Opec production.

Furthermore, Iraq's absence from the market made it possible for Iran to assume the status of the second-largest producer in Opec. Tehran's neutral position in the Gulf War allowed Iranian Minister of Oil Gholam Reza Agazadeh to develop closer relations with his Saudi counterpart, Hisham Nazir, which were further enhanced in May 1991 when Nazir became the first Saudi oil minister in ten years to visit Iran.[72] Significantly, Iran had helped Saudi Arabia to stabilize oil prices by building up floating stocks and selling them in the first half of 1991. Both countries declared that they intended to expand their production capacity in the coming years to respond to the increasing demand for oil in the future.[73] According to the Iranian minister of oil, Iran planned to reach a production capacity of at least 4.5m. b/d by March 1993,[74] while the Saudis aspired to a production capacity of 10m. b/d by 1993.[75] Saudi Arabia had actually intended to reach this goal in the mid-1990s, but the Gulf crisis spurred the process. Moreover, Saudi Arabia aspired to become the leading producer in the world. However, the harmony between Iran and Saudi Arabia was not perfect, since Iran wanted to attain higher oil prices in order to solve its economic problems. There was also disagreement between the two countries over the quotas that Opec ought to adopt in the future.

SUMMARY

The conflict in the Gulf, the breakup of the USSR, and the continuing recession in the industrialized countries were the major factors affecting the oil markets in 1991. Frequent fluctuations in oil prices during the Gulf crisis and war reflected market nervousness because of the uncertainty of the situation. Nevertheless, contrary to pessimistic forecasts, the war in the Gulf did not cause another "oil shock," since market fundamentals played a central role in moderating prices.

In the second half of the year, the focus of the market shifted from the Opec states to the situation in the USSR. The continued fall of Soviet production, coupled with political developments in the country after the attempted coup exacerbated the apprehension of disruptions in production and export of Soviet oil. However, the drop in production turned out to be not as steep as anticipated. On average, oil production in the USSR dropped to 10.4m. b/d in 1991 from 11.5m. b/d in 1990, after a peak of 12.78m. b/d in 1987. Soviet oil exports, nevertheless, fell considerably: from 1.98m. b/d during 1990 to 1.078m. b/d during 1991 — namely a fall of 0.902m. b/d, or 46%.[76]

The economic slowdown in the industrialized world affected oil consumption. There was no change in average oil consumption in the OECD area from 1990 to 1991: it remained at 38m. b/d, principally on account of the fall in oil consumption in the US. Demand for oil in the whole of North America dropped from 18.9m. b/d in 1990 to 18.5m. b/d on average in 1991 (2.1%), while in the Pacific area (Japan, Australia and New Zealand) it rose from 6.0m. b/d to 6.1m. b/d (1.7%), and in Europe from 13.0m. b/d to 13.3m. b/d (2.3%) in the same period.[77]

It was estimated that oil prices in 1992 would depend on such variables affecting supply and demand as the economies of the Commonwealth of Independent States (CIS), the US and Europe, and the timing and speed of reconstruction of Kuwait's and Iraq's production. The greatest unknown that would influence supply in 1992 was the oil production level of the CIS,[78] with economic disorder there liable to further reduce production, which was already weakened. Experience showed, however, that the political disturbances in 1991 did not bring about a collapse in production. In the longer term, some analysts envisaged a major role in the world oil market for the Russian oil industry if it were able to exploit Western capital and know-how optimally.[79]

Saudi Arabia resumed its hegemony over Opec, and, accounting for one third of the organization's production, dictated production and price policy. This served the interests of the consumer states, primarily the US, and achieved one of the aims of the war in the Gulf — to ensure the supply of oil from the region. The Saudis, claiming that the crisis in the Gulf and the war that followed cost them close to $60bn., depleting their already diminishing foreign currency reserves, indicated that they needed to produce 8m. b/d in the future in order to increase their income.[80] The Saudi minister of oil vowed that the kingdom would never again act as a swing producer.[81]

The connection between Saudi Arabia and its markets is one of "reciprocal security." This may explain its entry into new downstream operations in South Korea and Japan in 1991. The internationalization of the Saudi oil company and of other national oil companies (for example, Venezuela's and Abu Dhabi's) began at a time when oil prices were low in order to ensure a permanent and reliable market for oil. This was in the consumers' interest as well, and marked the establishment of a new set of relations between consumers and producers.

The conclusion of the war in the Gulf led to more intensive activity in Opec in the upstream field, with supply and demand forecasts indicating that the organization would be called upon to fill most of the increased world demand for oil in the future. This meant, in essence, that the burden would fall on the Gulf states, which contained the largest reserves, and explained the vigorous approach to Western oil companies to increase production potential. Ironically, the oil producers had struggled for a long time to force the Western companies out of the oil-producing countries, but in 1991 tried wooing them back. The dialogue that resumed after a long break between consumers and producers in 1991 in the conferences in Isfahan (27–29 May) and Paris (1–2 July), intended to promote cooperation between the two sides, reflected this effort to improve mutual trust.

FIGURE 1: SPOT CRUDE OIL PRICES, JANUARY-FEBRUARY 1991

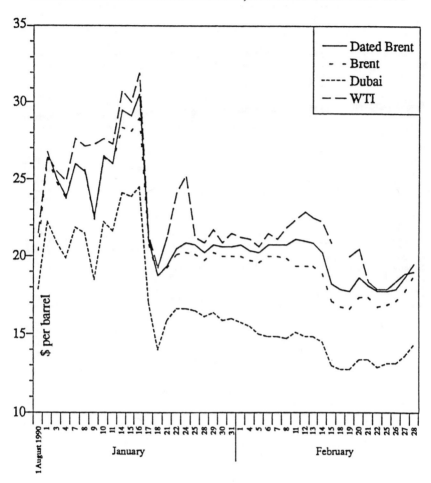

NOTE: Based on data from Table 2 below.

TABLE 1: 1991 CRUDE OIL PRICES (Dollars per barrel)*

Date	Dubai Fateh	Brent	Date	Dubai Fateh	Brent
2 January	22.45	26.85	3 July	15.75	18.50
9 January	18.70	22.65	10 July	16.15	19.25
16 January	24.60	30.55	17 July	16.50	20.00
23 January	17.75	22.05	24 July	16.05	19.30
30 January	16.00	20.75	31 July	16.40	19.70
7 February	15.25	20.80	7 August	16.25	19.40
13 February	15.10	21.05	14 August	16.20	19.20
20 February	13.55	18.70	21 August	16.40	19.55
27 February	13.70	18.65	28 August	16.85	20.00
6 March	15.15	19.85	4 September	17.30	20.30
13 March	14.95	20.00	11 September	17.25	20.00
20 March	14.40	18.85	18 September	17.40	20.55
26 March	14.50	18.40	25 September	17.75	20.70
3 April	14.50	17.75	2 October	18.13	21.35
10 April	15.25	19.35	9 October	18.80	22.50
17 April	15.75	19.85	16 October	18.98	22.30
24 April	15.45	19.50	23 October	18.65	22.35
1 May	15.75	19.70	30 October	18.55	22.00
8 May	16.10	19.85	6 November	19.25	22.05
15 May	15.90	18.80	13 November	18.00	21.40
22 May	15.85	18.60	20 November	17.50	20.60
29 May	15.90	18.75	27 November	16.85	19.65
5 June	15.55	18.50	4 December	16.35	19.20
12 June	15.40	17.75	11 December	15.15	18.25
19 June	15.15	17.85	18 December	14.90	18.15
26 June	15.27	18.10	30 December	14.75	18.00

* A middle spot price.
SOURCE: *MEED*, 1991–92, various issues.

TABLE 2: SPOT CRUDE OIL PRICES OF DATED BRENT, BRENT, DUBAI AND WEST TEXAS INTERMEDIATE, JANUARY–FEBRUARY 1991
(Dollars per barrel)*

Date	Dated Brent	Brent	Dubai	WTI	Date	Dated Brent	Brent	Dubai	WTI
1 August 1990	—	20.40	17.85	21.55	1 February	20.75	20.10	15.80	21.35
1 January 1991	26.80	26.45	22.35	26.50	4 February	20.40	19.75	15.55	21.14
3 January	25.00	24.85	20.95	25.50	5 February	20.25	19.60	15.05	20.65
4 January	23.95	23.85	19.95	24.90	6 February	20.75	20.10	14.85	21.50
7 January	26.05	25.95	21.95	27.65	7 February	20.85	20.10	14.85	21.20
8 January	25.70	25.60	21.55	27.15	8 February	20.75	19.90	14.75	21.90
9 January	22.55	22.45	18.55	27.25	11 February	21.20	19.45	15.15	22.45
10 January	26.55	26.40	22.35	27.70	12 February	21.05	19.40	14.90	22.95
11 January	26.10	26.00	21.70	27.30	13 February	20.95	19.40	14.95	22.55
14 January	29.55	28.40	24.20	30.80	14 February	20.25	18.90	14.55	22.30
15 January	29.20	28.20	23.90	30.05	15 February	18.25	17.20	13.00	20.90
16 January	30.50	29.10	24.50	32.00	18 February	17.90	16.80	12.75	**
17 January	21.10	20.80	17.05	21.45	19 February	17.80	16.70	12.75	20.00
18 January	18.75	18.75	14.05	19.25	20 February	18.65	17.40	13.45	20.50
21 January	19.35	19.30	15.90	21.30	21 February	18.20	17.40	13.45	18.45
22 January	20.50	20.20	16.60	24.20	22 February	17.75	16.75	12.85	17.85
24 January	20.95	20.30	16.60	25.30	25 February	17.80	16.85	13.20	17.95
25 January	20.80	20.20	16.50	21.35	26 February	17.95	17.15	13.20	18.35
28 January	20.35	19.80	16.10	20.95	27 February	18.60	17.75	13.60	18.85
29 January	20.85	20.25	16.40	21.85	28 February	19.55	18.80	14.40	19.09
30 January	20.65	20.05	15.90	20.95					
31 January	20.65	20.05	16.05	21.55					

* Dated Brent is for delivery within 15 days to the British terminal of Sullum Voe. Apart from prices for August, Brent is for February delivery up to 11 January, for March delivery from 12 January–8 February, and for April delivery from 9 February. WTI is for February delivery up to 28 January, for March delivery from 29 January–22 February, and for April delivery thereafter.

** New York market was closed for a public holiday.

SOURCE: *AOG*, 16 January, 1, 16 February, 1, 16 March 1991.

TABLE 3: SPOT QUOTATIONS OF OPEC REFERENCE BASKET
FOR JANUARY–DECEMBER 1991 (Dollars per barrel)

	Saharan Blend	Minas	Bonny Light	Arab Light	Dubai	Tia Juana Light	Isthmus	Basket
January	25.00	23.96	24.55	20.70	19.65	20.95	21.85	22.38
February	21.10	20.03	20.25	15.31	14.26	15.46	16.46	17.55
March	20.48	17.50	19.36	15.94	14.84	15.36	16.88	17.19
April	19.80	17.19	19.24	16.31	15.23	16.11	17.78	17.38
May	19.72	18.14	19.53	16.59	15.92	16.41	18.14	17.78
June	18.74	18.46	18.53	16.13	15.40	15.83	17.44	17.22
July	20.07	19.07	19.81	17.02	16.22	16.69	18.48	18.20
August	20.46	19.16	20.18	17.38	16.60	16.80	18.75	18.47
September	21.50	19.10	21.03	18.28	17.75	17.44	19.21	19.19
October	23.29	19.60	22.81	19.64	18.85	18.41	20.34	20.42
November	22.20	20.58	21.74	19.03	18.39	17.40	19.23	19.79
December	19.59	19.44	18.98	16.25	15.31	15.28	16.59	17.35
Year								
1991	21.07	19.42	20.59	17.47	16.62	16.90	18.53	18.66
1990	24.34	23.25	24.16	20.82	20.38	20.78	22.05	22.26
1989	18.53	17.63	18.50	16.21	15.64	16.94	17.72	17.31
1988	15.14	15.10	15.11	13.40	13.18	13.58	14.19	14.24

SOURCE: *MEES*, 6 January, 10 February 1992.

TABLE 4: OPEC COUNTRIES' ESTIMATED OIL PRODUCTION* IN 1991
(Volume in million barrels per day)

Country	January	February	March	April	May	June	July	August	September	October	November	December
Saudi Arabia	8.1	8.3	8.1	7.4	7.7	8.2	8.2	8.4	8.4	8.3	8.4	8.4
Iran	3.0	3.1	3.5	3.3	3.3	3.4	3.5	3.3	3.4	3.3	3.4	3.6
Iraq	0.3	0.1	0.1	0.1	0.3	0.3	0.3	0.3	0.3	0.4	0.4	0.4
UAE	2.5	2.5	2.5	2.5	2.4	2.3	2.3	2.3	2.3	2.4	2.5	2.5
Kuwait	0.1	0.0	0.0	0.0	0.0	0.03	0.1	0.1	0.2	0.3	0.3	0.4
Neutral Zone	0.1	0.0	0.0	0.0	0.0	0.1	0.2	0.1	0.3	0.3	0.3	0.3
Qatar	0.4	0.4	0.4	0.4	0.4	0.4	0.4	0.4	0.4	0.4	0.4	0.4
Nigeria	1.9	1.9	1.9	1.9	1.9	1.9	1.9	1.9	1.9	1.8	1.9	1.9
Libya	1.5	1.5	1.5	1.5	1.5	1.5	1.5	1.5	1.5	1.5	1.6	1.6
Algeria	0.8	0.8	0.8	0.8	0.8	0.8	0.8	0.8	0.8	0.8	0.8	0.8
Gabon	0.3	0.3	0.3	0.3	0.3	0.3	0.3	0.3	0.3	0.3	0.3	0.3
Venezuela	2.4	2.4	2.3	2.3	2.3	2.3	2.3	2.4	2.4	2.4	2.4	2.4
Ecuador	0.3	0.3	0.3	0.3	0.3	0.3	0.3	0.3	0.3	0.3	0.3	0.3
Indonesia	1.4	1.5	1.5	1.5	1.4	1.5	1.5	1.4	1.4	1.4	1.4	1.4
Opec crude oil	22.9	23.0	23.2	22.3	22.6	23.3	23.5	23.5	23.9	23.9	24.3	24.5

* Exluding natural gas liquids (NGLs). Totals may not add up due to rounding.

SOURCES: *AOG* according to IEA; *Oil and Gas Journal*, 1991–92, various issues.

TABLE 5: OPEC QUOTAS
(million barrels per day)

Country	Highest Production August 1990-February 1991*	April-September 1991**	% Share of Total	October-December 1991+	August 1990++	% Share of Total
Saudi Arabia	8.457	8.034	36.03		5.380	23.92
Iran	3.387	3.217	14.43		3.140	13.96
Iraq	—	—	0.00		3.140	13.96
UAE	2.442	2.320	10.40		1.500	6.67
Kuwait	—	—	0.00		1.500	6.67
Qatar	0.420	0.399	1.79		0.371	1.65
Nigeria	1.937	1.840	8.25		1.611	7.16
Libya	1.500	1.425	6.39		1.233	5.48
Algeria	0.803	0.827	3.71		0.827	3.68
Gabon	0.300	0.285	1.28		0.197	0.88
Venezuela	2.353	2.235	10.02		1.945	8.65
Ecuador	0.287	0.273	1.22		0.273	1.21
Indonesia	1.519	1.443	6.47		1.374	6.11
Total[0]	23.404	22.298	100.00	23.650	22.491	100.00

* Represents highest production figures compiled by the Opec Secretariat since August 1990, from secondary sources, and direct communication for February 1991 production in respect of Indonesia, Nigeria and Venezuela.

** Proposed second-quarter production based on a 5% cut from highest production level, except for Algeria. Fixed by the agreement of 12 March 1991, and retained for the third quarter by the agreement of 4 June 1991.

+ Fixed by the agreement of 25 September 1991.

++ Fixed by the agreement of 27 July 1990 but suspended on 29 August 1990 because of the Gulf crisis.

0 Totals may not add up due to rounding.

SOURCE: *MEES,* 18 March, 10 June, 30 September 1991.

TABLE 6: OIL SUPPLY AND DEMAND, 1991
(million barrels per day)

	First Quarter	Second Quarter	Third Quarter	Fourth Quarter	1991	1990	1989	1988
World Oil Demand	67.5	65.1	65.4	67.8	66.3	66.2	66.0	64.9
Non-Opec Supply	42.0	41.2	40.9	41.3	41.4	41.8	42.2	43.0
Additional Requirements	25.5	23.9	24.5	26.5	24.9	24.4	23.8	21.9
Implied Call on Opec Crude	23.6	21.9	22.5	24.5	22.9	22.4	21.8	20.0
Opec Production								
Crude	23.1	22.7	23.5	24.1	23.4	23.1	21.7	19.8
NGL	2.0	2.0	2.0	2.0	2.0	2.0	2.0	1.9
Total	25.1	24.7	25.5	26.1	25.4	25.1	23.7	21.7
Supply/Demand Balance	-0.5	+0.8	+1.0	-0.4	+0.5	+0.7	-0.1	-0.2

SOURCE: IEA's OMR, end-January; MEES, 13 April 1992.

TABLE 7: CRUDE SUPPLY AND DEMAND IN THE US, 1982-91
(Volume in thousand barrels per day)

	1991*	1990	1989	1988	1987	1986	1985	1984	1983	1982
Supply										
Crude Imports**	5,780	5,894	5,843	5,107	4,674	4,178	3,201	3,426	3,330	3,488
Crude Production	7,385	7,355	7,613	8,140	8,349	8,680	8,971	8,879	8,688	8,649
Unaccounted-for Crude	260	258	200	196	145	139	145	185	114	71
Total Supply	13,425	13,507	13,656	13,443	13,168	12,997	12,317	12,490	12,132	12,208
Demand										
Crude Refinery Runs	13,250	13,409	13,401	12,246	12,854	12,716	12,002	12,044	11,685	11,774
Crude Used Directly, and Loss	37	24	28	40	34	49	61	65	66	62
Crude Exports	125	109	142	155	151	154	204	181	164	236
Crude for SPR	-47	27	56	51	73	48	118	195	234	175
Total Demand	13,365	13,569	13,627	13,492	13,112	12,967	12,385	12,485	12,149	12,247
Crude Stock Change (Industry)	60	-62	29	-49	56	30	-68	5	-17	-39
Crude Stocks (million barrels)										
Primary (Industry)+	345	323	341	330	349	331	320	345	343	350
SPR	569	586	580	560	541	512	493	450	379	294

*   Preliminary.
** Includes imports for the SPR.
+   Includes Alaskan crude in transit.

SOURCE: Oil and Gas Journal, 27 January 1992.

TABLE 8: US CRUDE OIL IMPORTS,* 1990–91
(Volume in thousand barrels per day)

Exporting Country	1991**	1990	% Change, 1990–91
Saudi Arabia	1,679	1,195	+40.5
Canada	773	643	+20.2
Mexico	766	689	+11.2
Venezuela	670	666	+0.6
Nigeria	635	784	-19.0
Angola	237	236	+0.4
UK	126	155	-18.7
Colombia	122	140	-12.9
China	93	77	+20.8
Indonesia	90	98	-8.2
Iran	61	0	
Algeria	46	63	-27.0
Kuwait	11	79	-86.1
Oman	2	36	-94.4
UAE	0	9	-100.0
Libya	0	0	—
Iraq	0	514	-100.0
Others	469	510	-8.0
Total	**5,780**	**5,894**	**-1.9**
Imports from the ME	1,799	1,896	-5.1
ME Share	31.1%	32.2%	

*   Includes imports for the SPR.
** Preliminary.

SOURCE: *Oil and Gas Journal*, 27 January 1992.

TABLE 9: ESTIMATED OIL PRODUCTION: THE MIDDLE EAST AND NORTH AFRICA, 1990–91
(million tonnes)

	1990	1991	% Change 1990–91	% Share in Total World Production 1990	1991
Saudi Arabia*	321.928	409.839	+27.31	10.21	13.02
Iran	157.084	166.024	+5.69	4.98	5.27
UAE:					
Abu Dhabi	79.301	95.117	+19.94	2.51	3.02
Dubai	20.901	20.901	—	0.66	0.66
Sharja	1.802	1.922	+6.66	0.06	0.06
Iraq	100.681	14.876	-85.22	3.19	0.47
Libya	65.990	73.567	+11.48	2.09	2.34
Kuwait*	58.729	9.567	-83.71	1.86	0.30
Algeria	56.673	58.454	+3.14	1.80	1.86
Egypt	43.805	45.264	+3.33	1.39	1.44
Oman	32.848	34.857	+6.12	1.04	1.11
Syria	20.292	24.638	+21.42	0.64	0.78
Qatar	19.125	19.085	-0.21	0.61	0.61
Yemen	9.931	9.932	+0.01	0.31	0.32
Tunisia	4.491	5.192	+15.61	0.14	0.16
Turkey	3.773	4.925	+30.53	0.12	0.16
Bahrain	2.084	2.096	+0.58	0.07	0.07
Total	**999.438**	**996.256**	**-0.32**	**31.69**	**31.64**
World Total	**3,153.730**	**3,148.913**	**-0.15**	**100.00**	**100.00**

*   Including shares of production from the Neutral (Partitioned) Zone. All were allocated to Saudi Arabia, during August 1990-January 1991.

SOURCE: *PE,* January 1992.

TABLE 10: ESTIMATED PROVEN OIL RESERVES:
THE MIDDLE EAST AND NORTH AFRICA, 1 JANUARY 1992
(Volume in thousands of barrels)

Country	Volume	% Share in Total World Reserves
Abu Dhabi (UAE)	92,200,000	9.30
Algeria	9,200,000	0.93
Bahrain	83,490	0.01
Dubai (UAE)	4,000,000	0.40
Egypt	4,500,000	0.45
Iran	92,860,000	9.37
Iraq	100,000,000	10.09
Israel	1,289	0.00
Jordan	5,000	0.00
Kuwait	94,000,000	9.49
Libya	22,800,000	2.30
Morocco	2,139	0.00
Neutral Zone	5,000,000	0.50
Oman	4,250,000	0.43
Qatar	3,729,000	0.38
Ra's al-Khayma (UAE)	400,000	0.04
Saudi Arabia	257,842,000	26.02
Sharja (UAE)	1,500,000	0.15
Sudan	300,000	0.03
Syria	1,700,000	0.17
Tunisia	1,700,000	0.17
Turkey	540,450	0.05
Yemen	4,000,000	0.40
Total ME and North Africa	**700,613,368**	**70.70**
Total Gulf*	**655,864,490**	**66.18**
Total World	**991,011,448**	**100.00**

*   Including Bahrain, Iran, Iraq, Kuwait, Neutral Zone, Oman, Qatar, Saudi Arabia and the UAE.

SOURCE: *Oil and Gas Journal*, 30 December 1991.

NOTES

For the place and frequency of publications cited here, and for the full name of the publication, news agency, radio station or monitoring service where an abbreviation is used, please see "List of Sources." Only in the case of more than one publication bearing the same name is the place of publication noted here.

1.   *AOG*, 16 January 1991.
2.   Ibid.
3.   *MEED*, 11 January; *MEES*, 18 February; *FT*, 28–29 December 1991.
4.   *Oil and Gas Journal*, 21, 28 January; *AOG*, 1 February. For the IEA emergency plan, see particularly *MEES*, 21 January 1991.
5.   *AOG*, 1 February 1991.
6.   Ibid.; *FT*, 28–29 December 1991.
7.   *MEED*, 15 February; *AOG*, 1 March 1991.
8.   Ibid.; *MEES*, 4 February; *AOG*, 16 March 1991. Only 600,000–700,000 b/d of the 2m. b/d that the IEA committed itself to release into the markets from the stocks were actually withdrawn. Moreover, there was not much indication that the other emergency measures

(demand restraint, fuel switching and others) were implemented. The IEA suspended its emergency plan on 6 March.

9. *MEES*, 21 January; *MEED*, 15 February 1991.
10. *MEED*, 15 February; *FT*, 28–29 December 1991.
11. *MEED*, 1 March 1991.
12. *AOG*, 1 November 1991.
13. *MEED*, 15 March 1991.
14. *AOG*, 16 March 1991.
15. *AOG*, 1 April 1991.
16. *AOG*, 16 May 1991.
17. *MEED*, 19 April 1991.
18. Ibid.; *AOG*, 16 April 1991.
19. *MEED*, 10, 17 May 1991.
20. *MEED*, 17 May 1991.
21. *Oil and Gas Journal*, 29 July 1991.
22. *AOG*, 16 June 1991.
23. *MEES*, 22 July; *AOG*, 1 August 1991; for the stocks, see IEA's *OMR* for end-January 1992.
24. *MEED*, 17 January 1992.
25. *Memo*, 2 August 1991.
26. *MEED*, 17 January 1992.
27. *AOG*, 1 September 1991.
28. *MEED*, 2, 9 August 1991.
29. *MEES*, 19 August 1991.
30. *NYT*, 20 September 1991.
31. *FT*, 18 December 1991.
32. *MEED*, 30 August; *PE*, September 1991.
33. *MEED*, 30 August 1991.
34. *MEED*, 6 September; *PE*, September 1991.
35. *AOG*, 16 September 1991.
36. *AOG*, 1 November 1991.
37. *AOG*, 16 October; *MEED*, 25 October 1991.
38. For the prices on 23 December, see *AOG*, 1 January 1992.
39. *AOG*, 1 November 1991.
40. *FT*, 11 February 1992.
41. *MEED*, 22 November 1991.
42. *MEED*, 17 January 1992.
43. *MEED*, 20 December 1991.
44. *MEES*, 16 December; *FT*, 20 December 1991; *MEED*, 10 January 1992.
45. *FT*, 27 December 1991.
46. *Oil and Gas Journal*, 27 January 1992.
47. IEA's *OMR* for end-January 1992.
48. *MEES*, 11 March 1991.
49. *AOG*, 1 March 1991.
50. *MEES*, 18 March 1991.
51. *MEED*, 22 March 1991.
52. *Memo*, 29 March 1991.
53. *MEES*, 18 March 1991.
54. *MEES*, 22 April; *MEED*, 3 May 1991.
55. For full details on the conference, see *MEES*, 10 June 1991.
56. *MEED*, 14 June 1991.
57. *MEED*, 26 July; *MEES*, 26 August 1991.
58. *MEES*, 26 August, 2, 9 September 1991.
59. *IHT*, 25 September; *MEED*, 4 October 1991.
60. *IHT*, 24 September; *AOG*, 1 October 1991.
61. *AOG*, 1 October 1991.
62. Ibid.

63. *JP*, 27 September; *PE*, December 1991.
64. *MEES*, 30 September 1991.
65. E.g., *AOG*, 16 November 1991.
66. *MEED*, 22 November 1991.
67. *MEES*, 2 December 1991.
68. *AOG*, 1 December 1991.
69. Ibid.; *MEED*, 6 December 1991.
70. OPEC NA, 28 November — DR, 2 December 1991.
71. *MEED*, 10 January 1992.
72. *FT*, 18 December 1991.
73. *The Economist*, 17 August 1991.
74. *MEED*, 18 October; *PE*, November 1991.
75. *ME*, February 1992.
76. *AOG*, 16 April, 16 November 1991; IEA's *OMR* for end-January 1992. For Soviet oil exports based on Russian news agency "Interfax" see *MEES*, 17 February 1992.
77. IEA's *OMR* for end-January 1992.
78. *Oil and Gas Journal*, 27 January 1992.
79. E.g., *Newsweek*, 21 October 1991.
80. *FT*, 30 January 1992.
81. *FT*, 18 December 1991.

Trends in Demographic Development in Syria, 1986-90

ONN WINCKLER

Syria's population increased rapidly during the 1980s, with an average rate of natural increase during 1986-89 of 38 per thousand. This high rate resulted from a very high birthrate (c. 46 per thousand) and a low mortality rate (7 per thousand). These figures reflect the high proportion of young people in the population: Syrians aged 15 and younger comprised about half the total population of the country at the end of the 1980s. Both the natural increase rates and the proportion of the young in the Syrian population were among the highest in the Middle East at the end of the 1980s.

Also significant during this period was the high concentration of population in the cities and regions of Damascus, Aleppo and Homs, which contained c. 51% of the country's total population in 1990. The population distributed by region remained stable throughout the 1980s. There was, in fact, a significant slowing down in the urbanization process and, in particular, in rural migration to the primary cities. In 1988 the urban population constituted 50% of the total population, a proportion that was maintained until the end of the decade. Similarly, the migration of Syrians seeking employment in other economies in the ME and beyond also declined. Particularly noticeable was the decline in the negative migration balance to the Arab oil states. This decrease in internal migration as well as in emigration may be explained by the government's economic and demographic policies, together with economic changes in Syria itself and in neighboring countries.

POPULATION GROWTH

Syria's population at the end of 1990 was estimated at 12.5m. Twenty years earlier, its population was half that size, 6.3m. (see Table 1). The rapid growth of the population was the result of a high natural increase, which underwent an upward trend throughout the 1960s and 1970s, stabilizing at a high level — one of the highest in the world — during the 1980s. The average annual rate of natural increase for 1981-89 was 38 per thousand. At the end of the 1980s a decline in this rate had not yet begun (see Table 2).

High gross birthrates, on the one hand, and a low gross mortality rate, on the other, continued in the 1980s, which explains the high rate of natural increase. A noteworthy feature was the stability of the gross birthrate throughout the 1980s: 45 to 46 births per thousand inhabitants, with no decline in these rates by the end of the 1980s, according to the available statistics. The data on fertility rates, however, indicate a different trend. In 1989 this rate was 6.6, whereas a decade earlier it had been higher, 7.0.[1] Forecasts for the 1990s prepared by research departments of international agencies indicated a continued decline in fertility rates. A forecast by the World Bank, based on data from the UN Population Division, predicted a fertility rate of 5.5 for the year 2,000.[2] This projected rate is high in comparison with the rates that were prevalent in a number of Muslim countries in the late 1980s (Turkey — 3.9, Tunisia — 4.0 and Egypt — 4.2).[3] Still it would appear that Syria has been in a "fertility transition" stage since the 1970s and perhaps earlier, although the rate of change, or decrease, in average fertility was slow.

The reduction in the fertility rates during the period under discussion was not the result of a government family planning policy (there was none) but of socioeconomic changes in Syrian society during the last generation. Perhaps the most important of these was the increase in the proportion of women with high school education (partial or complete), as well as an increase in the proportion of urban women among the total number of women in their childbearing years (see Table 3). A comprehensive demographic survey carried out during 1976–79 indicated that women in these two categories (educated and urban) were more likely than other women in Syria to use birth control and to plan the size of their families.[4]

The high rates of natural increase in Syria, which had been ongoing for over two decades, explained the wide base of Syrian society's age structure, i.e., the large proportion of children under 15 years within the total population. In 1990 this age group numbered c. 6.2m. (49.2% of the total population), and was larger than the working-age population group (15–64 years), which was 5.8m. (46.4% of the total population; see Table 4).

ETHNIC AND RELIGIOUS MINORITIES

The authorities did not publish data on the ethnic breakdown of the population after the Ba'th's advent to power in 1963. Unofficial estimates published in recent years allow for rough guesses only, and can provide a basis for only the major ethnic and religious minorities.

The Kurds were Syria's largest ethnic minority, comprising (according to figures relating to the late 1970s) c. 9% of the total population. Approximately 40% lived in the rural areas of the Tartus region and another 40% in the Jazira region.[5] The Armenians were estimated at 2.3% of the total population residing mostly in Aleppo, Damascus and several other cities.[6]

The 'Alawites, Druzes and Isma'ilis were the most prominent religious minorities. At the end of the 1980s the 'Alawites comprised c. 15% of the total population. Most of them lived in the rural areas of the Ladhiqiyya region, while some lived in Damascus where they had migrated during the 1970s.[7] The Druzes were estimated to make up 3% of Syria's total population at the end of the 1980s, the majority of them living in the Suwayda region.[8] The Isma'ilis formed about 1.5% of the total population. Most of them were concentrated in the Hama region, although sizable groups had migrated to the large cities in the early 1970s.[9]

POPULATION DISTRIBUTION AND INTERNAL MIGRATION

In 1990 approximately 60% of the total Syrian population was concentrated in four regions (*muhafazat*): Damascus (city and region), Aleppo (city and region), Homs and Hama. The Jazira, or, according to the Syrian administrative term, the "eastern region," which included Hassaka, Dayr al-Zur and Raqqa regions, constituted about 16% of the country's total population in 1990 (see Table 5).

Official Syrian demographic statistics clearly show that there was no change in population distribution by region during the 1970s and 1980s, with the exception of a decline in the relative share of the Damascus population within the total (from 13.3% in 1970 to 11.4% in 1990). Particularly notable was the stability of the relative share of the populations in the three Jazira regions (15.8% in 1970 and 15.6% in 1990), and in the Ladhiqiyya region (6.2% in 1970 and 6.0% in 1990), despite the fact that these regions had been earmarked by the central government for intensive development and construction during the 1970s and 1980s (see Table 5).

After about three decades of an intensive urbanization process, this trend changed at the end of the 1980s. In 1960 the urban population (i.e., the population living in settlements with 20,000 or more inhabitants) had constituted about 37% of the total population. From then until the late 1980s, the relative share of the urban population increased. In 1988 the urban population formed 50% of the total. This relative share remained unchanged for the next two years (see Table 1).

The slowing of the urbanization process at the end of the 1980s was also reflected in data on population size in the main cities. The number of inhabitants in Damascus increased during 1986–89 from 1.22m. to 1.34m. The population in Aleppo increased from 1.19m to 1.31m. Similar growth rates were recorded during these years for Homs, Ladhiqiyya and Hama (see Table 6). Significantly, these rates of increase were lower than the rates of increase for the total urban population, and even lower than the rates of natural increase for the Syrian population as a whole (urban and rural) during the same years (see Tables 1 and 2).

The moderate increase in the population of the major cities during the late 1980s may be explained by growing rural migration to small and medium-sized cities with populations of a few thousand. This was particularly evident with regard to the towns at the periphery of Damascus and Aleppo, and in the Dar'a, Hassaka and Raqqa regions. For example, the relative share of the urban population in Hassaka increased between 1985 and 1991 from 32.5% to 38.1% and in Raqqa from 52.4% to 64.8% (see Table 5).

These changes reflected two processes that occurred simultaneously: the pulling force of Syria's two major metropolitan centers weakened, while forces pushing peasants to leave their villages also weakened. It would appear that the decline in internal migration was the result of ongoing government policy formulated in light of the urbanization process of the 1960s and 1970s.

The 1960s witnessed a high rate of migration from the villages to the cities, with the percentage of the urban population in the total population increasing from 37% to c. 44% during the decade. Most of the peasants who left their villages moved to the main cities: the population of Ladhiqiyya increased by 85%, that of Damascus and Homs by about 58% each, and that of Aleppo by 50% (see Tables 1 and 6). This migratory movement was the outcome mainly of demographic pressures in the villages, which resulted, inter alia, from the restricted allocation of resources by the central government for rural development and from great inequality in the ownership of arable lands during a period of over 60 years — throughout the Mandate and the first 35 years of Syrian independence.[10] Simultaneously, there were pull forces by the big cities, some of which expanded as a result of the political and economic changes in

Syria after independence. However, the weight of the pull forces in fueling the migration process was marginal; the push from the villages was the primary cause for internal migration during the 1960s.[11]

The rapid population increase in Syria's main cities was accompanied by the growth of slums, poor housing conditions, high unemployment rates and strain on the physical and social service networks.[12] Most seriously, the concentration of hundreds of thousands of peasants in the main cities added to the political instability that characterized Syria in the 1950s and 1960s. This was one of the major factors impelling the government to change its policy on rural and agricultural development. From the beginning of the 1970s, the government initiated several rural development programs focused on investment in infrastructure and social services — the development of the water and electricity systems, and the improvement of the educational and health systems. In addition, large sums were allocated for the expansion of arable lands.

A series of five-year plans for developing social services in rural areas budgeted £SY389,000 in 1971–75, £SY4.8m. in 1976–80, and £SY7.1m. in 1981–85 (at current prices).[12] In the 1986–90 five-year plan, 20% of the total amount was set aside for developing irrigation systems in rural areas and preparing new lands for cultivation.[13]

In addition to these activities, the government aimed at raising the income level of the peasants by increasing the amounts the authorities paid for their produce. According to official Syrian data, this rise in payments, made in the late 1980s, exceeded the inflation rate, thus contributing to a real increase in the peasants' income.[14] It would appear that the government's rural development policy and the steps taken to raise the income level of the peasants slowed the migratory trend away from the villages. Another area of government policy — the priority given to comprehensive development of the Jazira region — accounted for the peasants' preference for moving to the cities in the Jazira region itself rather than to Syria's major cities.

EXTERNAL MIGRATION

Syria is one of the ME countries characterized by a negative external migration balance (i.e., the number of Syrian nationals leaving the country exceeded the number of those entering it) during long periods of this century. A negative migration balance existed during the late 1980s as well. Though the Syrian authorities did not publish data on the extent and nature of this migration, the main trends could be verified.

Migratory movement continued in the late 1980s to two destinations that could be defined as "traditional": countries in North and South America (to which migratory movement began in the late nineteenth century), and closer destinations — the Arab oil states, principally Kuwait, Saudi Arabia and Libya (to which significant migration began following the oil price rise of 1973). However, the migratory movement to these areas in the 1980s was moderate in comparison with earlier periods. For example, the number of Syrian citizens who received permits for extended stays or full citizenship in the US from 1980–88 was 16,500.[15] The migration balance for workers to the Arab oil states was also marked by a sharp downturn. At the end of the decade, the (net) number of Syrian immigrants to Kuwait and Saudi Arabia was only a few thousand per year,[16] as compared to an average of 47,000 immigrants per year during 1980–84.[17]

The decline in the number of immigrants at the end of the 1980s resulted primarily from changes in the economic situation of the migration-absorbing countries, especially the Arab oil states. The sharp fall in revenues from oil exports in these countries led to a marked slowdown in development and construction programs, as well as a decline in overall economic activity, resulting in decreased demand for foreign workers. Nevertheless, the movement of Syrian workers abroad in search of employment did not cease in the late 1980s, although the country had gradually eased out of its mid-decade economic crisis. The pressure to emigrate came from two categories of workers:. (1) unskilled or semiskilled laborers, and (2) those with higher education, who were dissatisfied with wages in Syria (i.e., physicians and engineers).[18] A new migration destination had opened up for the first group, offering employment at relatively high wages: the Greek economy. By the end of the decade, the number of Syrian workers in this country had probably reached 125,000.[19] The migration of Syrians with higher education to traditional destinations in the ME and the Western hemisphere continued, although once the Syrian economy began to recover from its crisis of the 1980s, the government sought to curb the emigration of this group, particularly in the field of engineering. Several measures were adopted to restrict the emigration of these workers. In July 1988, President Hafiz al-Asad ordered the formation of a special public committee to examine the economic position and employment situation of university graduates in general, and engineering and medicine graduates in particular, in order to analyze the causes of emigration by graduates in these professions.[20] That same year, a law was passed guaranteeing employment in the public sector for a period of at least five years for engineering graduates who could not find work in the private sector. In actuality, however, many of the engineers employed in the public sector as a result of this law found themselves in administrative positions because of a lack of suitable jobs in their profession.[21]

CONCLUSION

Demographic developments in Syria in the late 1980s were marked both by continuity and by a change in trends that had been ongoing for many years. On the one hand, the high rates of natural increase continued. While the fertility rate did decrease slightly, it was not enough to reduce the gross birthrate because of the age structure of the population. These high rates of increase were expected to be maintained for most of the 1990s, and were the basis for a population forecast of 18m. by the year 2000.[22] On the other hand, a significant reduction in population movement, both internal and external, began. Unlike most Third World countries in which accelerated population growth was accompanied by massive migration from rural areas to the main cities and by emigration from the country itself over a long period, in Syria these processes, which had been intensive during the 1960s and the 1970s, weakened considerably in the 1980s. Despite high rates of population growth, rural migration and emigration abroad were not a dominant phenomenon in Syrian society.

An important factor in slowing the rate of migration from the villages to the cities and in reducing the emigration rates of skilled workers, especially in the professions which were in short supply in Syria itself, seemed to have been the social and demographic policies which the Syrian Government had applied since the 1970s. In addition, the economic recession in those economies that had absorbed most of

Syria's workers in the 1970s and early 1980s also accounted for the decline in migration abroad.

Thus in the late 1980s, a period marked by the beginning of recovery from its deep economic crisis earlier in the decade, Syria was one of the few Third World countries that had both high rates of natural increase and low rates of urbanization and emigration. There were signs, however, that the authorities were aware that this demographic-economic balance could not continue for very long. The government came to the conclusion in the 1980s that a family planning policy must be instituted.[23] This change in position regarding the country's rapid population growth could prove to have an important influence on Syria's demographic development in coming years.

NOTES

For the place and frequency of publications cited here, and for the full name of the publication, news agency, radio station or monitoring service where an abbreviation is used, please see "List of Sources." Only in the case of more than one publication bearing the same name is the place of publication noted here.

1. The World Bank, *World Development Report 1981* (New York: Oxford University Press, 1981), p. 168, Table 18.
2. *World Development Report 1991*, p. 256, Table 27.
3. Ibid., pp. 256–57, Table 27.
4. Syria, Central Bureau of Statistics, *Syria, Fertility Survey, 1976–1979, Principal Report* (Damascus, 1982), p. 91.
5. Richard F. Nyrop, *Syria — A Country Study* (Washington, DC: The American University, 1979), p. 58.
6. Ibid., p. 59.
7. *Country Profile, Syria,* 1990, p. 11; Nyrop, p. 87.
8. *Country Profile, Syria,* 1990, p. 11.
9. Ibid., Nicolaos Van-Dam, *The Struggle for Power in Syria* (London: Croom Helm, 1979), pp. 23–24.
10. Ziad Keilany, "Land Reform in Syria," *MES,* Vol. 16 (1980), pp. 209–10.
11. *Al-Ba'th* (Damascus), 24 March 1977; *al-Bayan* (Dubai), 25 November 1987.
12. *Al-Ittihad* (Abu Dhabi), 19 September 1987; *al-Bayan* (Dubai), 25 November 1987.
13. *Al-Ittihad* (Abu Dhabi), 14 March 1988.
14. *Al-Thawra* (Damascus), 15 January 1988; *Tishrin,* 30 March 1988.
15. *Al-Ahram,* 13 January 1989.
16. *Country Profile: Syria,* 1991–92, p. 19.
17. *Oman,* 14 January 1985.
18. *Al-Thawra* (Damascus), 28 June 1988.
19. *Al-Yawm al-Sabi',* 2 October 1989.
20. *Al-Muharrir,* 9 July 1988.
21. *Al-Thawra* (Damascus), 28 June 1988.
22. *World Development Report 1991,* p. 254, Table 26.
23. *Tishrin,* 21 May 1985.

TABLE 1: SYRIA. POPULATION BY URBAN AND RURAL SETTLEMENTS, 1960–91

	Total		Urban		Rural	
	'000	%	'000	%	'000	%
1960(C)[1]	4,565	100.0	1,685	36.9	2,880	63.1
1970(C)[2]	6,305	100.0	2,741	43.5	3,564	56.5
1980(E)[3]	8,797	100.0	4,189	46.7	4,608	53.3
1981(C)[3]	9,050	100.0	4,264	47.1	4,786	52.9
1982(E)[3]	9,295	100.0	4,370	47.0	4,925	53.0
1983(E)[4]	9,611	100.0	4,587	47.7	5,024	52.3
1984(E)[4]	9,934	100.0	4,783	48.1	5,151	51.9
1985(E)[4]	10,267	100.0	4,991	48.6	5,276	51.4
1986(E)[4]	10,612	100.0	5,208	49.1	5,404	50.9
1987(E)[4]	10,969	100.0	5,428	49.5	5,541	50.5
1988(E)[4]	11,338	100.0	5,672	50.0	5,666	50.0
1989(E)[4]	11,719	100.0	5,855	50.0	5,864	50.0
1990(E)[5]	12,116	100.0	6,087	50.2	6,029	49.8
1991(E)[6]	12,529	100.0	6,355	50.7	6,194	49.3

NOTES: Urban settlement — over 20,000 residents.
C — Census
E — Estimate

SOURCES:
[1] UN, *Demographic Yearbook 1963* (New York: UN Publication, 1963), p. 147.
[2] *Demographic Yearbook 1975*, p. 175.
[3] *Demographic Yearbook 1984*, p. 177.
[4] *Demographic Yearbook 1989*, p. 155.
[5] Syrian Arab Republic, Office of the Prime Minister, *Statistical Abstract 1990* (Damascus: Central Bureau of Statistics, August 1990), p. 61.
[6] *Statistical Abstract 1991*, p. 60.

TABLE 2: SYRIA. NATURAL INCREASE RATES, 1960–89
(per thousand)

	Crude Birthrate	Crude Deathrate	Natural Rate Increase
1960[1]	47	18	29
1965[8]	48	16	32
1975[1]	46	14	32
1980[2]	45	8	37
1981[3]	47	8	39
1982[4]	46	7	39
1983[5]	46	7	39
1984[6]	45	8	37
1985[7]	44	8	36
1986[8]	45	8	37
1987[9]	47	7	40
1988[10]	45	7	38
1989[11]	45	7	38

SOURCES:
[1] The World Bank, *World Development Report 1978* (New York: Oxford University Press, 1979), p. 104.
[2] *World Development Report 1982*, p. 145.
[3] *World Development Report 1983*, p. 187.
[4] *World Development Report 1984*, p. 257.
[5] *World Development Report 1985*, p. 213.
[6] *World Development Report 1986*, p. 231.
[7] *World Development Report 1987*, p. 257.
[8] *World Development Report 1988*, p. 277.
[9] *World Development Report 1989*, p. 217.
[10] *World Development Report 1990*, p. 231.
[11] *World Development Report 1991*, p. 256.

TABLE 3: SYRIA. WOMEN'S FERTILITY RATES BY AGE GROUP, 1973–87
(per thousand women)

	Age Groups						
	15–19	20–24	25–29	30–34	35–39	40–44	45–49
Level of Education							
Illiterate	448	474	432	390	301	163	58
Literate (primary education)	445	459	385	270	155	66	11
Post-primary	452	419	322	223	147	63	—
Residence Category							
Urban	458	433	357	292	203	106	27
Rural	441	481	451	401	332	189	75
Region of Residence							
Damascus City	459	386	326	244	136	60	12
Aleppo City	422	438	377	296	229	119	29
Northeast	429	458	418	376	324	221	101
West	472	491	424	334	284	129	9
Center	513	451	401	375	287	163	54
South	410	518	462	384	305	149	60
Total	**449**	**459**	**402**	**341**	**262**	**148**	**51**

SOURCE:
Syrian Arab Republic, Office of the Prime Minister, *Statistical Abstract 1990* (Damascus: Central Bureau of Statistics, 1990), p. 55.

TABLE 4: SYRIA. POPULATION BY AGE 1960–91
(in thousands)

	Total		0–14		15–64		Over 65	
	'000	%	'000	%	'000	%	'000	%
1960[1]	4,565	100.0	2,111	46.3	2,234	48.9	220	4.8
1970[2]	6,305	100.0	3,106	49.2	2,923	46.4	276	4.4
1981[3]	9,046	100.0	4,385	48.5	4,372	48.3	289	3.2
1984[5]	9,934	100.0	4,894	49.2	4,605	46.4	435	4.4
1985[5]	10,267	100.0	5,060	49.3	4,758	46.3	449	4.4
1986[6]	10,612	100.0	5,229	49.2	4,920	46.4	463	4.4
1987[7]	10,969	100.0	5,405	50.6	5,085	45.0	479	4.4
1988[8]	11,338	100.0	5,586	49.6	5,257	46.0	495	4.4
1989[9]	11,719	100.0	5,773	49.2	5,432	46.4	514	4.4
1990[10]	12,116	100.0	5,968	49.2	5,616	46.4	532	4.4
1991[11]	12,529	100.0	6,169	49.2	5,812	46.4	548	4.4

SOURCES:
[1] UN, *Demographic Yearbook 1970* (New York: UN Publication, 1970), pp. 296–97.
[2] *Demographic Yearbook 1975*, pp. 240–41.
[3] Syrian Arab Republic, Office of the Prime Minister, *Statistical Abstract 1990* (Damascus: Central Bureau of Statistics, 1991), p. 51.
[4] *Statistical Abstract 1984*, p. 72.
[5] *Statistical Abstract 1985*, p. 68.
[6] *Demographic Yearbook 1986*, pp. 210–11.
[7] *Statistical Abstract 1987*, p. 69.
[8] *Statistical Abstract 1988*, p. 60.
[9] *Demographic Yearbook 1989*, pp. 210–11.
[10] *Statistical Abstract 1990*, p. 60.
[11] *Statistical Abstract 1991*, p. 60.

TABLE 5: SYRIA. URBAN AND RURAL POPULATIONS BY REGIONS, 1960–91
(in thousands)

Region		1960[1]	1970[1]	1981[1]	1984[2]	1985[5]	1987[4]	1988[5]	1990[6]	1991[7]
Damascus City	T	530	837	1,112	1,196	1,227	1,292	1,361	1,397	1,434
	U	530	837	1,112	1,196	1,227	1,292	1,361	1,397	1,434
	R	—	—	—	—	—	—	—	—	—
Damascus Region	T	473	621	917	1,013	1,050	1,127	1,210	1,254	1,302
	U	74	182	332	387	409	456	499	527	557
	R	399	439	585	626	641	671	711	727	745
Aleppo	T	957	1,317	1,879	2,058	2,126	2,269	2,421	2,501	2,587
	U	474	708	1,122	1,262	1,316	1,431	1,541	1,607	1,676
	R	483	609	757	796	810	838	880	894	911
Homs	T	401	546	815	903	936	1,007	1,084	1,124	1,167
	U	150	254	408	461	481	525	568	593	620
	R	251	292	407	442	455	482	516	531	547
Hama	T	324	515	737	807	834	890	949	981	1,013
	U	118	175	248	272	281	300	320	330	341
	R	206	340	489	535	553	590	629	651	672
Ladhiqiyya	T	527	390	555	607	627	668	712	735	758
	U	111	149	232	259	270	281	303	315	328
	R	416	241	323	348	357	387	409	420	430
Dayr al-Zur	T	221	293	409	445	458	487	517	533	549
	U	58	89	125	136	140	149	159	164	170
	R	163	204	284	309	318	338	358	369	379
Idlib	T	333	384	580	644	669	721	777	807	838
	U	51	85	122	133	138	147	158	163	169
	R	282	299	458	511	531	574	619	644	669
Hassaka	T	353	468	670	735	759	810	865	894	929
	U	58	96	194	232	247	281	310	331	354
	R	295	372	476	503	512	529	555	563	575
Raqqa	T	178	244	348	382	395	422	450	465	475
	U	15	39	135	175	207	259	300	304	308
	R	163	205	213	197	188	163	150	161	167
Suwayda	T	100	140	199	218	225	240	256	264	272
	U	24	39	57	63	65	70	75	78	82
	R	76	101	142	155	160	170	181	186	190
Dar'a	T	168	232	363	407	424	460	499	520	543
	U	22	33	77	96	104	121	136	147	159
	R	146	199	286	311	320	339	363	373	384
Tartus	T	..	302	443	489	506	542	581	602	623
	U	..	55	89	101	106	116	125	131	137
	R	..	247	354	388	400	426	456	471	486
Qunaytra	T	..	16	26	30	31	34	37	39	39
	U	..	..	..	..	..	..	..	..	..
	R	..	16	26	30	31	34	37	39	39
Total	T	4,565	6,305	9,053	9,934	10,267	10,969	11,719	12,116	12,529
	U	1,685	2,741	4,253	4,783	4,991	5,428	5,855	6,087	6,335
	R	2,880	3,564	4,800	5,151	5,276	5,541	5,864	6,029	6,194

NOTES: T= Total; U = Urban; R = Rural.

SOURCES:

[1] Syrian Arab Republic, Office of the Prime Minister, *Statistical Abstract 1985* (Damascus Central Bureau of Statistics, 1985), pp. 54–55.
[2] *Statistical Abstract 1984*, p. 73.
[3] *Statistical Abstract 1985*, p. 70.
[4] *Statistical Abstract 1987*, p. 70.
[5] *Statistical Abstract 1989*, p. 61.
[6] *Statistical Abstract 1990*, p. 61.
[7] *Statistical Abstract 1991*, p. 61.

TABLE 6: SYRIA. POPULATION IN FIVE MAJOR URBAN CENTERS, 1960-89

City	1960[1]	1970[2]	1981[3]	1982[4]	1985[5]	1986[6]	1987[7]	1988[8]	1989[9]
Aleppo	425,467	639,428	976,727	985,413	1,145,117	1,191,151	1,216,000	1,216,000	1,308,000
Damascus	529,963	836,668	1,251,028	1,112,214	1,196,710	1,219,448	1,292,000	1,326,000	1,343,000
Hama	110,809	137,421	176,640	177,208	193,000	198,160	214,000	222,000	229,000
Homs	136,474	215,423	354,508	354,508	409,326	427,500	431,000	447,000	464,000
Ladhiqiyya	68,000	125,716	196,791	1,967,791	229,944	239,533	241,000	249,000	258,000

SOURCES:
1   UN, *Demographic Yearbook 1963* (New York: UN Publication, 1963), p 248.
2   *Demographic Yearbook 1975*, p 266.
3   *Demographic Yearbook 1982*, p. 255.
4   *Demographic Yearbook 1984*, p. 272.
5   *Demographic Yearbook 1985*, p. 270.
6   *Demographic Yearbook 1986*, p. 285.
7   *Demographic Yearbook 1987*, p. 311.
8   *Demographic Yearbook 1988*, p. 320.
9   *Demographic Yearbook 1989*, p. 266.

The Palestinians: Demographic and Economic Developments, 1986–90

GAD GILBAR

The world Palestinian population at the end of 1989 was estimated at 5.18m. This figure was based only in part on data derived from censuses held in the 1980s. The rate of natural increase of the Palestinian population at the end of the 1980s was estimated at 32–36 per thousand. Toward the end of the decade the migratory movement from the West Bank and the Gaza Strip to Jordan and the Arab oil states in the Gulf declined.

The Palestinian population in 1989 consisted of the following main communities: the West Bank and Gaza Strip — 30%; Jordan — 25%; Israel — 16%; Syria and Lebanon — 12%; the Arab oil states in the Gulf — 12%; other countries in the Middle East and elsewhere — 6%.

Population growth among the Palestinians in the occupied territories and in Israel was at the heart of extensive public debate during the late 1980s. Discussions on the political implications of this demographic development took place both in Israel and within the PLO. However, the mass Jewish migration from the Soviet Union to Israel in late 1989 and throughout 1990 took the edge off this issue.

The late 1980s and 1990 were years of economic crisis for major Palestinian communities, primarily those in the territories, but also in Jordan, Kuwait and Israel. This crisis was due to several unrelated developments: the Intifada, the economic crisis in Jordan, the Iraqi invasion of Kuwait, and the increase in unemployment in Israel. By the end of 1990 large sections of the Palestinian population were in serious economic straits.

THE SIZE OF THE PALESTINIAN POPULATION

The most recent census covering the entire Palestinian (Muslim and Christian Arab) population was conducted by the mandatory government in Palestine in 1931.[1] The data presented in this chapter on the size of the total number of Palestinians in the late 1980s, therefore, like other demographic data relating to this population as a whole, is based on estimates. In the absence of general censuses, the size of the Palestinian population can only be assessed by summing the established or estimated sizes of the various Palestinian communities wherever they exist.

According to Israel's Central Bureau of Statistics (CBS), 2.37m. Palestinians resided in Israel and the occupied territories at the end of 1989. Of these, 843,000 (including Druzes, Bahais and "others") lived in Israel, 915,000 lived in the West Bank, and 612,000 lived in the Gaza Strip (see Table 1). Of these figures, only the statistics relating to the Arabs of Israel are based on a reliable census, which was held fairly recently (1983). The last census in the West Bank and the Gaza Strip was

311

conducted by the CBS in September 1967. It has been argued that that census suffered from several flaws, chief among them being undercounting in the West Bank. Since the data for the late 1980s is a cumulative update of the 1967 census, it has been claimed that the CBS figures for recent years are lower than the actual population figures in the West Bank by at least 14%.[2]

Such sources as were available for calculating the size of the Palestinian population in Israel and the territories did not exist for any other large Palestinian community; hence estimates and evaluations had to be relied on heavily. The number of Palestinians in Jordan (East Bank) at the end of 1989 was estimated at about 1.3m.[3] This figure referred to Palestinians actually residing in Jordan, and did not include those Palestinians holding Jordanian passports who lived outside Jordan, principally in the Gulf states. The Jordanian authorities have never published any data on the size of the Palestinian population in Jordan. However, they maintained in the 1980s that the Palestinians constituted about 40% of the total population of the East Bank.[4] This proportion was lower than that widely cited outside Jordan: 55% (1.3m. out of a total population of 2.4m.).

Relatively large Palestinian populations resided in two other areas of the ME in the late 1980s:

(1) Syria and Lebanon. Estimates based on corrected UNRWA data indicated a figure of 270,000 Palestinians in Syria and about 340,000 Palestinians in Lebanon.[5] Hence, at the end of 1989 there were about 610,000 Palestinians in these two Arab states bordering on Israel.

(2) The Gulf states: Kuwait, Saudi Arabia and the United Arab Emirates (UAE). Kuwait conducted systematic and comprehensive data collection in the 1970s and 1980s, publishing the results of censuses held every five years in its *Statistical Abstracts*. However, these publications made no distinction between Jordanians and Palestinians. Moreover, a substantial number of Palestinians apparently lived in Kuwait illegally. Hence, it is difficult to arrive at the exact size of the Palestinian community in the late 1980s even in Kuwait. A widely cited estimate, accepted by the Kuwaiti authorities as well, was 350,000 at the end of 1989.[6] The number of Palestinians in Saudi Arabia and the UAE together was estimated at about 250,000,[7] although unlike Kuwait, this figure was not based on any census. It was perhaps the least reliable of all the estimates of sizes of major Palestinian populations in the Arab states at the end of 1989.

There were smaller Palestinian communities in other Arab states, mainly Egypt and Iraq. Outside the ME there were Palestinian communities in central and western Europe, the US and Latin America. At the end of 1989, the number of Palestinians in all these countries together was estimated at about 300,000.[8]

On the basis of the figures, estimates and evaluations on the size of the various Palestinian communities worldwide, the total Palestinian population at the end of 1989 amounted to 5.18m. Of this number, 45.8% lived in Israel and the territories, 36.9% lived in three of the Arab states bordering on Israel (Jordan, Syria and Lebanon), and 11.6% lived in the oil states of the Arabian Peninsula (see Table 2).

Other scholars have arrived at similar estimates, with a variation of ±5%.[9] There were, however, other significantly higher assessments. For example, Yasir 'Arafat claimed that the Palestinian population was 6m. in the late 1980s.[10] This figure was an overestimation. It did not tally with estimates on the size of the Palestinian population in 1947 (1.3m.)[11] and the probable rates of natural increase of this population in recent decades (3.2%–3.6%).[12]

RATES OF NATURAL INCREASE

Data on the rates of natural increase of the Palestinian population were to be found only for the Arabs of Israel. The CBS also published figures on the gross birth and mortality rates in the West Bank and Gaza Strip. Owing to difficulties in collecting data in the territories, however, the rates published by the CBS for the late 1980s were only estimates. The data for the number of births and deaths in the UNRWA camps in Syria were greatly biased, mainly because of obvious underscoring of the number of deceased. No data had been published on the rates of natural increase for the Palestinian communities in the other Arab states.

Available figures, however incomplete, lead to the conclusion that the Palestinian population continued to grow at a high rate in the late 1980s. The average rate of natural increase of the Muslim population in Israel in 1988–89 was 32.5 per thousand, while the average rate of natural increase in the territories in 1987 and 1988 was even higher: in the West Bank 34.9 per thousand, in the Gaza Strip 43.5 per thousand.[13] The decline in the rate of natural increase of the Arabs in Israel (particularly the Muslim population) that had occurred between 1975 and 1984 came to a halt after 1985; in 1988–89 there was actually a moderate rise in these rates (see Table 3). In the territories, as far as may be concluded from the CBS figures, the rise in the rate of natural increase that occurred in the 1970s continued into the late 1980s as well. In the Gaza Strip this rate was extremely high — close to the record among Muslims in Israel, which was reached in the 1960s (45.1 per thousand on average during 1960–69).[14] The difference in the rate of natural increase between the Arabs in Israel and those in the West Bank and the Gaza Strip reflected different stages in the process of modernization experienced by these three communities. During the 1980s the Arabs of Israel experienced a decline in mortality rates that was paralleled by a decline in birthrates. By contrast, in the West Bank and Gaza Strip the major change was a decline in mortality rates with no decline in birthrates.[15]

The Palestinian communities in the Arab states apparently did not experience a decline in natural increase rate in the late 1980s. According to a study completed in 1986 by the US Bureau of Census on the demographic development of the Palestinians, the average rate of natural increase of the total Palestinian population during 1975–84 stood at 32 per thousand (weighted rates).[16] These rates may be taken as the lower limit for 1986–89 as well. On the other hand, there was evidence to support a higher assessment of the rate of increase in the late 1980s (see above). A reasonable upper limit would be a rate of 36 per thousand.

In light of assessments of the size of the total Palestinian population and its rate of natural increase in 1989, it appeared that this population increased by 160,000–180,000 persons during 1990.

EMIGRATION

In the late 1980s, there was a steep drop in the scope of Palestinian emigration from the West Bank and the Gaza Strip to Jordan, and thence to the oil states of the

Arabian Peninsula, for shorter or longer periods (see below). The drop was due chiefly to the economic recession in the oil states that began in 1983 and peaked in 1986 because of the sharp decline in income from oil exports. This decrease in income was accompanied by a slowdown in investment in development projects. As a result, the demand for both skilled and unskilled foreign workers, including Palestinians, decreased.

The decline in emigration was enhanced in 1988-89 by a development in the territories that was related to the Intifada: the growing adherence to the idea of *sumud,* meaning clinging to one's place and land however difficult the circumstances. Departure from the territories, which until 1987 had not been considered wrong, became reprehensible thereafter as new winds began to blow in the West Bank and Gaza Strip. Emigration was equated with weakness and desertion in battle. The migratory movement of the 1970s and 1980s was portrayed as a serious error because it decimated the most important asset at the disposal of the Palestinians in their struggle with Israel — rapid population growth.[17] Data on the migration balance for the territories showed a steep decline in 1982–86 and a further fall in 1987–88 (see Table 4). This decrease in migration from the West Bank and the Gaza Strip contributed to the economic crisis in the territories, and hence to the outbreak of the Intifada.[18]

In 1990 a reversal of direction occurred in the migratory movement of the Palestinians. From August 1990, following the Iraqi invasion of Kuwait, until the outbreak of the war in January 1991, 100,000–150,000 Palestinians left Kuwait.[19] Most went to Jordan where they could stay indefinitely.

THE DEBATE ON THE SIZE OF THE POPULATION IN THE REFUGEE CAMPS

About 764,000 people still lived in refugee camps administered by UNRWA in June 1989.[20] Not all residents of the camps were Palestinian refugees. There were many cases of residents of nearby villages or urban neighborhoods who for economic reasons — low rentals — leased housing that had been vacated by the refugees.[21]

According to UNRWA reports, there were 61 refugee camps at the end of the 1980s. Of these, 28 were in the West Bank and the Gaza Strip, and 31 in Jordan, Syria and Lebanon.[22] Of the 764,000 camp residents, 47% lived in camps located in the West Bank and the Gaza Strip, 25% in Jordan, 19% in Lebanon and 9% in Syria. Based on these figures, Palestinians still living in UNRWA camps at the end of the 1980s constituted about 15% of the total Palestinian population. The proportion of camp residents in the Palestinian population in Lebanon and the Gaza Strip was much higher.

Despite programs designed to phase out the refugee camps, very little was done in this area. A program initiated by the Government of Israel in the 1970s that thinned out the refugee camps in the Gaza Strip by relocating families in new neighborhoods nearby[23] was discontinued in the 1980s. Population density and economic hardship in the refugee camps in the territories worsened at the end of the 1980s, especially in the Gaza Strip.

THE DEBATE ON THE "DEMOGRAPHIC BALANCE"

The rapid growth of the Palestinian population in the territories and in Israel, on the one hand, and the slower growth of the Jewish population in Israel during most of the 1980s, on the other, raised the issue of "demographic balance" between Jews and Arabs in Eretz Israel/Palestine. A debate ensued in the Jewish public as well as among the Palestinian leadership on the political implications of this demographic development. The debate was influenced not only by trends during the 1970s and 1980s, but also by forecasts published by the CBS projecting the size of the Palestinian population in Israel and the territories in the 1990s and at the start of the twenty-first century. A CBS "intermediate" forecast (published in 1987) predicted that the proportion of the Arab population in Israel would rise to 21.5% in the year 2000 and that the Palestinians would constitute 50% of the total population in Israel and the occupied territories by 2015.[24] This forecast was based on several assumptions, the most important being little change in the birth and mortality rates of the Palestinian and Jewish populations, along with the continuation of 1985–87 trends regarding population movement of both Jews and Palestinians (small positive and negative migration balances).

The demographic issue elicited diametrically opposed conclusions within the Israeli public. On the one hand, current demographic developments strengthened the conviction of those who believed that the territories had to be abandoned by Israel wholly or in part, and that local government in one form or another had to be instituted, principally in the main Palestinian population centers in the Gaza Strip and the West Bank.[25] On the other hand, these same developments, along with the CBS forecasts, reinforced the position of those who favored population "transfer" — enforced or "voluntary" — and the "Jordan-is-Palestine" approach.[26] A new party, Moledet, advocating the "voluntary transfer" of Palestinians from the territories, won two seats in the elections to the 12th Knesset held in November 1988 (see *MECS* 1988, pp. 549, 571).

The PLO also focused increasingly on the implications of demographic developments in the territories and in Israel during the 1980s, its reactions largely a mirror image of attitudes in Israel. PLO leaders, especially in the Fath, regarded the changing proportions of the Jewish and Arab populations not only as a welcome development but also as an important tool in the Palestinian struggle against Israel. As such, demography was an effective weapon even in the short term, in that it threatened Israel and fomented serious disagreement within it. According to this approach, the threat of Palestinian demographic growth was likely to bring about an Israeli recognition that there was no escape from the establishment of a Palestinian state in the territories. In the long term, the Palestinian demographic advantage would lead to the diminution of Israel to the point of its disappearance as a Zionist state.[27] 'Arafat voiced this approach in a statement in November 1987, which became a Palestinian slogan in the territories: "They [the Israelis] are concerned about our children and the Palestinian woman, who bears yet another Palestinian every ten months....[She] is a biological bomb threatening to blow up Israel from within."[28] A variant of this approach was the hope that the Palestinian, and the larger Arab, human mass would overwhelm Israel in the military arena as well.

Yet, in the Palestinian camp, too, there was debate over the political implication of demographic development in the territories. Fears mounted in the PLO that the graver the demographic menace to Israel, the greater the threat of mass deportation from the territories. This anxiety intensified in the late 1980s when the idea of "transfer" was overtly articulated in Israel. The PLO feared that inflated use of the demographic argument to influence political positions in Israel vis-à-vis the national goals of the Palestinians was a double-edged sword. Moreover, the Democratic Front for the Liberation of Palestine and the Popular Front for the Liberation of Palestine, and to some extent Fath, claimed that overdependence on the demographic advantage as a means of bringing about change in the Palestinian situation was dangerous because it could lead to inaction among Palestinians generally and the population in the territories in particular.[29] Hence, after several years of intense promotion of the promise inherent in demographic development, PLO leaders adopted a more restrained position on the "biological bomb."

The mass immigration of Jews from the Soviet Union to Israel that began at the end of 1989 (see *MECS* 1990, chapter on Israel) generated a profound change of heart on the demographic issue on both sides. In Israel, the great wave of immigration in 1990 (about 200,000 immigrants), and the assessment that tens of thousands or even hundreds of thousands more would continue arriving annually in subsequent years, seemed to have taken the sting out of the demographic threat, even though Israeli demographers pointed out in 1990 that the immigration would merely delay the point of numerical equality between Jews and Arabs in Israel and the territories by a few years.[30] Conversely, on the PLO side, the large wave of immigration in 1990, together with other developments in the political arena — notably the marked decline of the Soviet Union as a superpower — struck a note of deep anxiety. The Palestinian demographic advantage, hitherto considered a source of strength in the conflict with Israel, seemed to be severely undermined. Palestinian leaders were particularly alarmed that Soviet Jewish immigration was likely to renew the drive to increase Jewish settlement in the territories either directly or indirectly.[31] Palestinian leaders and several heads of Arab states applied pressure on the Soviet Government to stanch the flow of Jewish migration to Israel. Simultaneously, Arab leaders attempted to prevail upon the Administration in Washington to increase substantially the number of immigration permits for Jews from the Soviet Union. In 1990, neither of these efforts seemed to have had much effect.

ECONOMIC DEVELOPMENTS

Data on economic developments in the Palestinian communities was even sparser than that available in the demographic sphere. The little that had been published consisted of CBS figures on the Arab population in Israel and the occupied territories. Even this information had become scarcer since the outbreak of the Intifada, as the CBS could barely collect data on economic activity in the territories. As for the Arab countries, there was not a single official publication that cited economic developments in the Palestinian communities. All that was available from the Arab countries were press reports describing the economic situation in one or another Palestinian community, mainly in times of crisis and distress.

Two basic characteristics of Palestinian economic development remained unchanged in the late 1980s:

(1) The major portion of the Palestinian work force in Israel, in the territories, and probably in the Arab states as well, continued to be employed in the service sector. There was no significant rise in the proportion of employees in the industrial or agricultural sectors.[32]

(2) Widespread acquisition of secondary and higher education by young men and women (aged 15–29) continued.[33] However, this process was slowed down in the West Bank and the Gaza Strip during the period in question because of the prolonged disruption of studies from the start of the Intifada onward. Apparently there was also a moderate decline in enrollment rates of Palestinians at universities in Jordan and other Arab states in the late 1980s, probably as a result of reduced demand for academically trained personnel in the Arab oil states, especially in the Arabian Peninsula.

While there were marked differences in income level and living standards among the various Palestinian communities, there was at least one common trend among the Palestinians in Israel, the occupied territories, Jordan and Kuwait during part or all of the 1987–90 period: an absolute or relative decline in average per capita income for considerable sectors of the population. Income levels and living standards were affected most adversely in the territories, where the gross national product fell at a cumulative rate of 30%–40% in 1988–90.[34] This decline was a result of the decrease in the number of workdays on the part of laborers from the territories in Israel, damage to crops, primarily in the West Bank, and a drop in income in the service sector[35] — all largely attributable to the Intifada. Added to this were negative developments in the Jordanian and Israeli economies, which further exacerbated the hardship in the West Bank and the Gaza Strip. In Jordan, an economic crisis that peaked in April-May 1989 reduced the demand for workers from the territories.[36] In Israel, the addition of immigrants from the Soviet Union to the work force began to be felt: there was a drop in demand for workers from the occupied territories, chiefly in the service sector.[37]

The economic situation in the territories worsened in the closing months of 1990, following the invasion of Kuwait by Iraq, due to the falloff in the remittance of cash by Palestinian workers to their families in the territories. According to an estimate by the Kuwaiti authorities, these remissions amounted to $120m.–$150m. annually during 1988 and 1989.[38] In addition, the flow of grants approved by Kuwaiti funds (such as the Arab Fund for Economic and Social Development and the Kuwaiti Fund for Arab Economic Development) ceased as of August 1990. Prior to the conquest, Kuwaiti aid to the territories had amounted to about $70m. annually. Grants from Saudi Arabia and the UAE to residents of the territories also plummeted with the onset of the Gulf crisis.[39] Lastly, developments in the Jordanian economy, with the onset of the crisis, also contributed to exacerbating economic distress in the territories — for example, the 20% drop in the exchange rate of the Jordanian dinar.[40]

The recession in the Jordanian economy from 1988 onward affected the Palestinian community living in Jordan as well. Their situation also worsened as a result of the overall crisis experienced by Jordan in August-December 1990. Many Palestinian households in Jordan, as in the territories, depended on remissions by family members working in Kuwait and the other oil states in the Arabian Peninsula. Moreover, about 100,000 Palestinians returned to Jordan from the Gulf states — mostly Kuwait — during the last months of 1990,[41] most of them joining the already large body of unemployed in Jordan. According to a survey conducted in Jordan, the number of people living below the poverty line (monthly income of $120 or less) increased from 600,000 in 1988 to about 1m. in 1990,[42] the majority estimated to be Palestinians.

The economic damage to the Palestinian community in Kuwait as a result of the Iraqi invasion and the events that followed in August-December 1990 was grave. It was estimated that the 100,000–150,000 Palestinians who left Kuwait by the end of 1990 abandoned property there (including bank accounts) valued at the start of 1991 at $10bn.–$12bn.[43]

The economic situation of the Arabs of Israel also deteriorated, although in a different context and in different circumstances. Unemployment rose from 1985 onward. In 1985 and 1986 the rate of unemployment in the Arab work force was 9.5% and 10.5% respectively (see Table 5), reaching 11% in 1990 (about 1% higher than in the Jewish work force that year).[44] Reports published in the Arabic and Hebrew press in Israel in late 1990 and early 1991 quoted even higher rates of unemployment in Nazareth, Umm al-Fahm and in many villages.[45]

CONCLUSION

The 1986–90 period was marked by a widening gap between demographic growth and economic development in some of the large Palestinian communities for which data or reliable estimates were available.

The Palestinian population continued to grow at a very high rate, among the highest rates in the ME. Rates of natural increase in the West Bank and the Gaza Strip were especially high, and could continue rising in the early 1990s. Even if the weighted rate of natural increase of the total Palestinian population did not grow during the 1990s, the population was expected to reach 6.5m.–7m. by the year 2000.

Simultaneous with increased demographic growth, there was a decline in per capita income within a sizable sector of the Palestinian communities. The complex economic balance in sources of income of the larger Palestinian populations in the ME that had evolved since the 1960s was upset in 1988–90. Many Palestinian households, particularly in the West Bank, had been compensated for relatively low income levels and limited employment opportunities by migration and employment in the oil states of the Arabian Peninsula. This source of income shrank continuously as a result of the economic recession that the oil states experienced, and dropped further following the Iraqi invasion of Kuwait and the support by PLO leaders and by Palestinians in Kuwait itself for the Iraqi move. The rapid reduction of the Palestinian community in Kuwait dealt a serious blow to Palestinian society, which was dependent on it financially. The other economy that had absorbed Palestinian labor — Israel — also reduced its demand for it, both because of the Intifada and increase in violent incidents between Arabs and Jews within Israel proper, and because of mounting pressure to employ Jewish immigrants. The cumulative result of these economic developments in Kuwait, Jordan, the occupied territories and Israel was the most severe economic crisis experienced by the Palestinians since 1967.

TABLE 1: PALESTINIAN POPULATION IN ISRAEL,[a]
THE WEST BANK AND GAZA STRIP, 1965–89
(Population in thousands at end of year)

	Israel[b]	West Bank	Gaza Strip	Total
1965	299.3	..	..	..
1970	440.0	607.8	370.0	1,417.8
1975	533.8	675.2	425.5	1,634.5
1980	639.0	724.3	456.5	1,819.8
1985	749.0	815.5	527.0	2,091.5
1986	769.9	837.7	545.0	2,152.6
1987	793.6	868.1	565.6	2,227.3
1988	817.7	895.4	588.5	2,301.6
1989	842.5	915.0	612.0	2,369.5

SOURCE: CBS, *SA 1990,* p. 38, Table 2.1; p. 708, Table 27.1.
NOTES: [a] Including Druzes and other religious minority groups.
          [b] Including census adjustments and addition of Arab population of East Jerusalem in 1967 and Druze population of the Golan Heights in 1982.

TABLE 2: THE PALESTINIAN POPULATION ACCORDING TO COUNTRY/REGION OF RESIDENCE, 1989[a]

	Thousands
Israel	843
The West Bank	915
Gaza Strip	612
Jordan	1,300[b]
Lebanon	340[b]
Syria	270[b]
Kuwait	350[b]
Saudi Arabia and UAE	250[b]
Elsewhere	300[b]
Total	5,180[b]

SOURCES: See text.
NOTES: [a] At end of year.
          [b] Estimate.

TABLE 3: THE PALESTINIAN POPULATION:
RATES OF NATURAL INCREASE, 1975–89
(per thousand)

| | Israel | | West Bank | Gaza Strip |
	Muslims	Christians		
1975–79	39.5	18.2	32.0	36.6
1980–84	33.6	14.5	33.0	38.2
1985	31.3	13.1	33.7	38.4
1986	30.4	16.4	33.3	40.3
1987	31.0	17.0	34.8	42.5
1988	32.0	16.4	34.9	44.4
1989	32.9	17.4	..	..

SOURCE: CBS, *SA 1990*, pp. 103-4, Table 3.1; p. 708, Table 27.1.

TABLE 4: PALESTINIAN POPULATION:
BALANCE OF MIGRATION, 1975–89
(in thousands)

	Israel	West Bank	Gaza Strip
1975	-0.3	-15.1	-3.5
1976	0.4	-14.4	-4.2
1977	0.4	-10.2	-2.9
1978	0.1	-9.4	-4.7
1979	0.4	-12.6	-4.8
1980	1.0	-17.3	-5.1
1981	-1.2	-15.7	-5.3
1982	0.1	-7.9	-3.1
1983	1.2	-2.7	-1.0
1984	0.7	-5.8	-4.8
1985	0.0	-5.0	-2.9
1986	-0.1	-5.1	-3.6
1987	1.3	+0.7	-3.3
1988	0.4	-3.5	-2.7
1989	-0.4	..	..

SOURCE: CBS, *SA 1990*, p. 40, Table 2.2; p. 708, Table 27.1.

**TABLE 5: ISRAELI ARABS: CIVILIAN LABOR FORCE,
TOTAL AND UNEMPLOYED, 1980-89**

	Total	Unemployed	
	Thousands	Thousands	%
1980	132.0	5.6	4.2
1981	139.7	6.7	4.8
1982	146.7	9.3	6.3
1983	151.9	8.4	5.5
1984	158.9	10.5	6.6
1985	166.9	16.2	9.5
1986	169.4	17.8	10.5
1987	171.7	13.6	7.9
1988	182.4	15.3	8.4
1989	191.8	19.6	10.2

SOURCES: CBS, *SA 1985*, p. 349, Table XII/25; CBS, *SA 1990*, p. 358, Table 12.26.

NOTES

For the place and frequency of publications cited here, and for the full name of the publication, news agency, radio station or monitoring service where an abbreviation is used, please see "List of Sources." Only in the case of more than one publication bearing the same name is the place of publication noted here.

1. E. Mills, *Census of Palestine 1931* (2 vols; Alexandria: Government of Palestine, 1933).
2. Meron Benvenisti and Shlomo Khayat, *The West Bank and Gaza Atlas* (Jerusalem: The West Bank Data Base Project, 1988), pp. 27-29.
3. Cf. *Emirates News,* 22 February 1986; *al-Usbu' al-Jadid,* 15 September 1989; Lisa Hajjar, "The Palestinian Journey, 1952-1987," *MERIP Middle East Report,* Vol. 17, No. 3 (May-June 1987), p. 10; Gad Gilbar, "Trends in the Demographic Development of the Palestinians, 1870-1987," *Occasional Papers,* No. 108 (Tel Aviv: The Moshe Dayan Center, 1989; in Hebrew), pp. 32-33.
4. *Al-Dustur* (Amman), 17 April 1987.
5. Cf. *L'Orient Le Jour,* 9 July 1990; Gilbar, ibid.
6. *Al-Usbu' al-Jadid,* 15 September 1989.
7. Ibid.
8. Ibid.
9. Hajjar, p. 10.
10. See, e.g., "Yasir 'Arafat's Speech before the 43rd Session of the United Nations General Assembly on the Palestine Question, Geneva, 13 December 1988," *MECS* 1988, p. 267.
11. Roberto Bachi, *The Population of Israel* (Jerusalem: The Institute of Contemporary Jewry, 1977), pp. 397-401.
12. Gilbar, p. 30.
13. CBS, *SA 1990,* pp. 103-4, Table 3.1; p. 708, Table 27.1.
14. Ibid., p. 103, Table 3.1.
15. Ibid., pp. 103-5, Table 3.1; CBS, *JSGAS,* Vol. 17 (1987), No. 1, pp. 83-84, Tables 1 and 2.
16. *Emirates News,* 22 February 1986; Gilbar, pp. 29-30.
17. Dr. Hisham 'Awartani of al-Najah University (Nablus) in a colloquium on "The Palestinian National Movement — In the Wake of the Intifada," Tel Aviv: The Moshe Dayan Center, 5 April 1989.
18. Gad Gilbar, "The Demographic and Economic Origins of the Intifada," in idem and Asher Susser (eds.), *At the Core of the Conflict: The Intifada* (Tel Aviv: Hakibbutz Hameuhad, 1991; in Hebrew), pp. 23-26, 31-33.
19. *Al-Majalla,* 20 March 1991.

20. *Report of the Commissioner-General of the United Nations Relief and Works Agency for Palestine Refugees in the Near East, 1 July 1988–30 June 1989,* General Assembly, 44th Session (New York: UN, 1989), p. 37, Table 2.
21. Ibid.
22. Ibid.
23. Sara M. Roy, *The Gaza Strip: A Demographic, Economic, Social and Legal Survey* (Jerusalem: The West Bank Data Base Project, 1986), pp. 136–37.
24. CBS, *Special Report,* No. 802 (1987).
25. Yehoshafat Harkabi, *Fateful Decisions* (Tel Aviv: Am Oved, 1986; in Hebrew), pp. 60–69.
26. See "Transfer: Pro and Con," *Ha-Umma* (in Hebrew), Vol. 25, No. 88 (1987), pp. 11–19.
27. Matti Steinberg, "The Demographic Factor in the Conflict with Israel — the PLO Viewpoint," *Medina, Mimshal ve-Yahasim Beynleumiyim* (in Hebrew), No. 31 (1989), p. 38.
28. *Al-Akhbar,* 3 July 1987.
29. Steinberg, pp. 31, 36.
30. *Ha'aretz,* 25 May; *JP,* 5 October 1990.
31. Yasir 'Arafat, quoted by VoP (San'a), 27 February — DR, 2 March 1990.
32. CBS, *SA 1990,* p. 352, Table 12.19; p. 728, Table 27.20.
33. Jamil M. Tahir, "An Assessment of Palestinian Human Resources: Higher Education and Manpower," *JPS,* Vol. 14, No. 3 (1985), pp. 33–35.
34. CBS, *JSGAS,* Vol. 19 (1989–90), p. 19, Table 2; p. 27, Table 9.
35. Ibid., p. 144, Table 17.
36. *Al-Ahali* (Nicosia), 1 May 1991.
37. *Yedi'ot Aharonot,* 10 July 1991.
38. *Al-Majalla,* 20 March 1991.
39. Ibid.
40. Ibid.
41. Ibid.
42. Ibid.
43. Ibid.
44. CBS, *MBS,* May 1991.
45. *Ha'aretz,* 14 November, 7 December 1990; *al-Sinara,* 12 April 1991.

PART TWO:
COUNTRY-BY-COUNTRY
SURVEY

Middle East Countries
Basic Data

Country	Capital	Most Important Natural Resources	Area 1,000 sq. km.	Population in millions (mid-1990)	GNP per capita ($US 1990)
Bahrain	Manama	Crude Oil	1	0.503	..
Egypt	Cairo	Cotton, Crude Oil, Fruits, Vegetables, Iron	1,001	52.1	600
Iran	Tehran	Crude Oil, Natural Gas	1,648	55.8	2,490
Iraq	Baghdad	Crude Oil, Dates, Cement	438	18.9	..
Israel	Jerusalem	Fruits, Vegetables, Potash	21	4.7	10,920
Jordan	Amman	Phosphates, Vegetables, Fruits	89	3.2	1,240*
Kuwait	Kuwait	Crude Oil	18	2.1	..
Lebanon	Beirut	Fruits, Citrus Fruits, Vegetables, Forests	10	..	..
Libya	Tripoli	Crude Oil, Vegetables, Fruits	1,760	4.5	..
Oman	Muscat	Crude Oil	212	1.6	..
Qatar	Doha	Crude Oil	11	0.439	15,860
Saudi Arabia	Riyadh	Crude Oil	2,150	14.9	7,050
Sudan	Khartoum	Cotton, Gum, Cereals	2,506	25.1	..
Syria	Damascus	Cotton, Crude Oil, Vegetables, Fruits, Livestock, Phosphates	185	12.4	1,000
Turkey	Ankara	Cotton, Wool, Tobacco, Chrome, Copper	779	56.1	1,630
United Arab Emirates	Abu Dhabi	Crude Oil	84	1.6	19,860
Yemen	San'a	Coffee, Cotton, Sorghum, Fish, Fruits, Vegetables, Tobacco	528	11.3	..

* East Bank only.
.. not available.
SOURCE: *World Development Report 1992* (New York: Oxford University Press for the World Bank, 1992).

Currencies

Country	Currency Unit	US Dollar	Pound Sterling	Deutsche Mark	Swiss Franc	French Franc
			*Approximate Equivalent in Other Currencies**			
Bahrain	Bahraini Dinar (BD) = 1,000 Fils	2.68	1.52	4.53	3.84	15.31
Egypt	Egyptian Pound (£E) = 1,000 Milliemes	0.30	0.17	0.51	0.43	1.71
Iran	Iranian Riyal (IR) = 100 Dinars	0.015	0.008	0.025	0.021	0.086
Iraq	Iraqi Dinar (ID) = 1,000 Fils	3.23	1.83	5.46	4.63	18.45
Israel	New Israeli Shekel (NIS) = 100 Agorot	0.44	0.25	0.75	0.63	2.51
Jordan	Jordanian Dinar (JD) = 1,000 Fils	1.56	0.88	2.63	2.24	8.91
Kuwait	Kuwaiti Dinar (KD) = 1,000 Fils	..	..	..	..	..
Lebanon	Lebanese Pound (£L) = 100 Piastres	0.0011	0.0006	0.0018	0.0016	0.0063
Libya	Libyan Dinar (LD) = 1,000 Dirhams	3.54	2.00	5.98	5.11	20.22
Oman	Omani Riyal (OR) = 1,000 Baiza	2.62	1.48	4.42	3.75	14.97
Qatar	Qatari Riyal (QR) = 100 Dirhams	0.28	0.16	0.47	0.40	1.60
Saudi Arabia	Saudi Riyal (SR) = 100 Halalas	0.27	0.15	0.45	0.39	1.54
Sudan +	Sudanese Pound (£S) = 1,000 Milliemes	0.088	0.050	0.15	0.13	0.50
Syria	Syrian Pound (£SY) = 100 Piastres	0.045	0.026	0.076	0.064	0.257
Turkey	Turkish Lira (TL) = 100 Kurus	0.00027	0.00015	0.00045	0.00039	0.00154
United Arab Emirates	UAE Dirham (UAEDh) = 100 Fils	0.27	0.16	0.46	0.39	1.54
Yemen (North)	Yemeni Riyal (YR) = 100 Fils	0.077	0.044	0.130	0.110	0.440
Yemen (South)	South Yemeni Dinar (SYD) = 1,000 Fils	2.18	1.23	3.68	3.12	12.45
$US rate $1		—	0.5652	1.6889	1.4330	5.7122

* As quoted by the *Financial Times* in London on 8 April 1991.
.. not available.
+ Financial rate.

Bahrain

(Al-Bahrayn)

UZI RABI

The early part of 1991 was a deeply unsettling period for Bahrain. The battle for the liberation of Kuwait recalled memories dating back to the eight-year Iraqi-Iranian War, and reminded the tiny island-state of its own vulnerability and inability to cope with such eventualities. In the event, Bahrain had no compunction in inviting the Allied forces to use its territory as a staging post for operation "Desert Storm." However, the challenges created in the Gulf by the crisis and its aftermath drove Bahrain to take a stronger, more independent stand.

The Gulf crisis exposed the weakness of the Gulf Cooperation Council's (GCC) concept of collective security and the tiny island-state realized that a collective arrangement could no longer be the solution for regional security. The idea of "every nation for itself" seemed to take over. With this in mind, Bahrain moved to unleash its pro-American sentiment to the full, concluding a bilateral security pact with the US in October.

Bahrain was a member state of the GCC, and, faithful to the US efforts to establish a "new world order," Bahrain took part in the GCC delegation to the Middle East Peace Conference in Madrid,[1] asserting that the world was "on the verge of a major breakthrough in the peace process in the Middle East."[2]

It is clear that events in the Gulf led to fundamental changes in Bahrain's relationships with other countries in the region. For example, relations with Egypt and Syria, which had opposed Iraq's aggression, greatly improved; whereas relations with the PLO and Jordan deteriorated in an unprecedented manner, because of their support for Baghdad. It is not surprising that references to the ME peace process omitted any mention of a role for the PLO, the onetime "sole, legitimate representative of the Palestinians." Another important change was Bahrain's improved relations with Iran, which could serve to allay a deep-rooted anxiety of further Iranian subversive activity.

As Bahrain matured as an independent state, a set of challenges confronted the Al Khalifa family. As one of the major casualties of the Kuwait crisis, on the economic front, Bahrain could well suffer irreversible consequences to its former status as the regional banking center. Within the GCC, difficulties with Qatar over the simmering territorial dispute loomed on the horizon. The challenges to the very existence of the ruling Al Khalifa family, which were triggered by the crisis, posed an even more alarming threat to the regime.

The credibility of the political structures in the Gulf, including Bahrain's, had been seriously eroded and this, in the minds of many, emphasized the absence of democratic decision-making institutions. The question which came to the fore was not whether

328

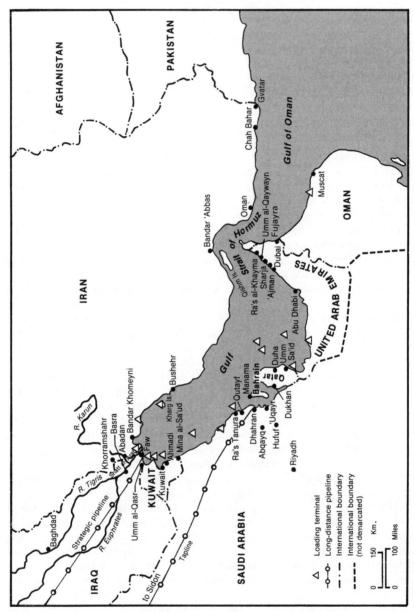

The Gulf

Legend:
△ Loading terminal
―o―o― Long-distance pipeline
―··―··― International boundary
― ― ― International boundary (not demarcated)

Scale:
0 — 150 Km.
0 — 100 Miles

Labels on map:
AFGHANISTAN
PAKISTAN
IRAN
IRAQ
SAUDI ARABIA
KUWAIT
OMAN
UNITED ARAB EMIRATES
Qatar
Bahrain
Gulf of Oman
Strait of Hormuz
Gulf

Baghdad
R. Tigris
R. Euphrates
Strategic pipeline
Umm al-Qasr
to Sidon
Tapline
Riyadh
Hufuf
Abqayq
Dhahran
Ra's Tanura
Qutayf
Manama
Dukhan
'Uqayr
Umm Sa'id
Duha
Abu Dhabi
'Ajman
Sharja
Ra's al-Khayma
Qeshm Is.
Bandar 'Abbas
Oman
Umm al-Qaywayn
Fujayra
Dubai
Muscat
Chah Bahar
Gvatar
Bushehr
Kharg Is.
Bandar Khomeyni
Abadan
Basra
Khorramshahr
R. Karun
Shatt al-'Arab
Faw
Ahmadi
Mina al-Sa'ud
Kuwait

Bahrain would survive regional threats, but whether the regime would adopt new, adequate measures to cope with the postcrisis challenges.

BAHRAIN AND THE GULF CRISIS

Iraq's invasion of Kuwait served as a painful reminder that Bahrain's road to security and prosperity was still fraught with danger. The fact that the danger came from Iraq made the reality even more painful. In actual fact, it had been Iran, not Iraq, which had given the Bahraini regime cause for concern since the summer of 1979, as a result of propaganda and threatening activities, such as the Iranian-sponsored coup attempts in 1981 and 1987 (for details see *MECS* 1981–82, pp. 490–92, and 1988, pp. 429–30). The traumatic vision of Kuwait, a fellow GCC member state, wiped out in a very short space of time by Iraq, a country that Bahrain had fervently supported, caused Bahrain considerable disorientation and loss of confidence. It thus came as no surprise that Bahrain became an integral part of the anti-Iraqi coalition: joining in the orchestrated denouncement of Iraq's aggression; demanding compliance with the decisions of the GCC, the Arab League and the UN, calling for the unconditional withdrawal of Iraqi troops from Kuwait; and insisting on the restoration of Kuwaiti legitimacy under the ruling Al Sabah family.[3]

Bahrain maintained its former links with Kuwait, asserting that its embassy in Kuwait would remain open, and that Bahrain "does not recognize any situation resulting from Iraq's occupation of Kuwait."[4] Kuwaiti ministers in exile were officially received by their Bahraini counterparts, and Shaykh Jabir Al Sabah, the Kuwaiti ruler, was greeted by Shaykh 'Isa, the Bahraini ruler, on Kuwait's 30th National Day,[5] as though the invasion of 2 August had never happened.

Although Bahrain's confidence was markedly bolstered by the mounting array of military equipment in the region, Bahrain was growing nervous about hints of a negotiated settlement. The tiny island, which had taken the calculated risk of exposing itself to possible taunts by Arab nationalists because it hosted foreign troops, was not ready to see them leave after only a compromise solution. As the crisis intensified, Bahrain became more aware of the hazards that it could anticipate, if the Iraqi challenge were not properly met. Consequently, from Bahrain's perspective, the buildup to the 15 January deadline was a nerve-racking time. During this period, a state of emergency was declared in Bahrain, and arrangements were made to guarantee the safety of its citizens. The population was given guidance on how to act in case of air raids and gas masks were made available.[6] The 25 km. King Fahd causeway, linking Saudi Arabia and Bahrain, was closed.[7]

Bahrain greeted the outbreak of hostilities with a certain degree of relief: the war had finally dispelled the uncertainty that had seriously affected business confidence on the island.[8] Effects of the fighting were felt in Bahrain. Situated en route between Iraq and Saudi Arabia, Bahrain had to contend with the possibility that Iraqi *Scud* missiles aimed at Saudi Arabia could land in its territory as well. In fact, several *Scud*s were reportedly intercepted by *Patriot* antiballistic missiles situated in Bahrain.[9]

Bahrain's actual participation in the conflict was marginal, of a more symbolic nature than anything else. Several Bahraini Defense Force units, initially deployed in Saudi Arabia, were recorded present on the outskirts of Kuwait City in the course of its liberation from Iraqi subjugation.

THE POSTWAR ERA: QUEST FOR REGIONAL SECURITY

Shortly after the fighting ended, amidst the general euphoria, there were signs of unease. The GCC states, including Bahrain, faced two basic dilemmas. The first was how to deal with Iraq, the main culprit, so to speak, held responsible for the break of regional calm, that had been so arduously achieved in 1988. The second was the nature of future Gulf security. Bahrain could not help but draw negative conclusions on the GCC's effectiveness. This inevitably called into question the way in which Bahrain and the other Gulf states would organize regional security arrangements in the postwar period.

There was a general desire among the GCC states to see Iraq rid of its leader, Saddam Husayn, and his regime, but not at the cost of a politically balkanized Iraq, with a Shi'i-controlled territory in southern Iraq. Since Iraq had a potentially flammable and vast Shi'i community, Bahrain, in particular, would feel very uneasy at such a possibility. Hence, Bahrain tried to juggle two incompatible policy objectives — Saddam's fall and Iraq's political and territorial integrity.

Bahrain could not resist the temptation of making its own comments of satisfaction on the evaporating prestige of the Iraqis. The media sarcastically noted that the Iraqi regime was due for condolences on the "death of the mother of all battles."[10] The alleged Iraqi infiltration of the Kuwaiti island of Bubiyan in August (see chapter on Kuwait) was hastily condemned by Bahrain, before it was even proved to have existed.[11] Bahrain also made clear its desire to see Iraq — and any other party for that matter — disarmed of its nonconventional weapons. Consequently, it greeted the US initiative to reduce nuclear weapons as "positive steps [which] contribute to a considerable extent in alleviating the world's fears."[12] Bahrain was happy to serve as the regional headquarters of the US special committee charged with the task of disarming Iraqi nonconventional weapons. However, at that stage, Bahrain refrained from calling on the Allied forces to finish the job by dealing further blows to the already battered country.

Toward the end of 1991, the Bahraini tone became more strident. By then, Bahrain had concluded its bilateral security pact with the US (see below) and felt more protected. Negative descriptions of the Iraqi regime's isolation began to appear in the media, most probably orchestrated by the higher echelons of the Bahraini regime, specifically calling to topple Saddam Husayn. "It all points to an imminent military coup," claimed the *Gulf Daily News*, which went on to demand that "the US-led Allies must be totally prepared to assist senior Iraqi officers when the attempt [to revolt] is made."[13]

A more complicated issue was that of a regional security system. By the end of October, Bahrain and the US had concluded a bilateral defense accord. The pact was probably discussed during the May visit to Bahrain of US Secretary of Defense Richard Cheney and given the seal of approval when Shaykh 'Isa visited Washington in mid-October. Bahrain had emerged from the crisis relatively unscathed, but was the most war-traumatized GCC state (after Kuwait). Consequently, security remained "a fundamental and very important element."[14]

As of early March, when the guns fell silent, rumors were spread that Bahrain was to allow the establishment of a formal headquarters of the US Central Command on its territory.[15] Although Bahraini officials denied giving their permission for the headquarters, they were only too happy to inform the Western press of the Bahraini willingness to cooperate with the US on the issue of regional security. "Bahrain has always shown a willingness to cooperate with the US," asserted Information Minister Tariq al-Mu'ayyad, and added that "we feel that as small as we are, we have a role to play and would like to contribute to the security of the region."[16] It transpired that for Bahrain the issue of regional security was clearly tantamount to US presence in the region.

It was only toward the end of October that the Bahraini-US pact was finally concluded. The fact that the pact was not made immediately after the cessation of hostilities, but only in late 1991, was worthy of note. It would appear that Bahrain allowed the GCC a great deal of latitude to reach some sort of solution that would be both tangible and acceptable to all member states, although Bahrain was quick to draw the negative conclusions about the Iraqi invasion with regard to the GCC. The six-state GCC military force could not, under any circumstances, deter, let alone contain, this sort of threat by itself. The concept of its military force had been eliminated by the invasion without even being put to the test. The six states were left defenseless and, from August 1990, this point was well understood in Manama. "There is no place in the world today for weak groupings or isolated states," noted Shaykh Khalifa Ibn Salman Al Khalifa, the prime minister. A different security system was essential in order to protect the six countries and prevent a recurrence of such events, he said.[17]

Accordingly, Bahrain welcomed the "Damascus declaration" signed in March by the foreign ministers of the six and their Egyptian and Syrian counterparts[18] (see chapter on inter-Arab relations). The declaration proclaimed the intention "to build a new Arab order to bolster joint Arab action."[19] It was proposed that Egyptian and Syrian troops already deployed in Saudi Arabia and neighboring states constitute "the nucleus for an Arab peacekeeping force to be prepared so as to guarantee the security and safety of the Arab states in the Gulf region."[20] However, the Arab "six plus two" alliance gradually faded away, due to differences within the GCC and between the six and their Arab partners.[21] No agreement was reached about the size, structure or command of the force. During the year, there were no signs that the plan would be started up again. It was the same with joint security arrangements with Iran, although, at least in this regard, the subject was raised, from time to time, throughout the year.

The only course of action the GCC states could agree upon was for each of them to seek military help from its allies when necessary. Bahrain was back at square one. The Bahraini unease was further exacerbated as, amidst the lengthy procedure to sort out an acceptable settlement on regional security, Arab and Western troops began evacuating the region. The Egyptian troops left in May and the last RAF *Tornado* aircraft flew out of Bahrain at the end of June, signaling the end of Britain's Gulf War presence in the country. Furthermore, the simmering territorial dispute with Qatar over the Hawar islands had flared up again and the two GCC member states were at loggerheads (for details, see chapter on Qatar). It was, perhaps, the difficulties with Qatar that served as a turning point for Bahrain, causing it to unleash its pro-American sentiment to the full.

The tiny island-state must have felt left alone to face its destiny and again came to draw some negative conclusions. It could no longer hope that a solution for regional security could be found on a collective basis. The situation had returned to its prewar state and a repetition of a similar scenario could indeed occur. Speaking to the London-based *Sawt al-Kuwait al-Duwali,* Shaykh Khalifa noted that "the concepts and versions of security agreements differ from one state to another. This is because every state has its own circumstances and requirements."[22] He went on to hint at an "every nation for itself" situation. The individual channel was gaining the upper hand. In October, the Bahraini-US bilateral security pact became a fact.

THE BAHRAINI-US SECURITY PACT

The Bahraini-US security pact of October 1991 was an improvement and formalization of a long-standing friendship. The island-state was a veteran Western ally, having hosted US navy ships over a period of 50 years. The Iraqi-Iranian War, and even more so the Gulf crisis, fostered a closer intimacy between both states. "Bahrain has been a firm friend and a close ally for half a century, but never more than in this past year, as we have stood together to turn back aggression," enthused US President George Bush.[23] Having gained a great deal of respect in the West, in general, and in the US in particular, for its steadfast assistance to the anti-Iraqi coalition, the island-state was seen more than ever before as a politically and militarily secure base in a volatile region. Given the sensitivity in the Gulf concerning relations with the US, especially with Tehran, details of the pact were not released. However, it most probably comprised a US commitment for the defense of Bahrain, paralleled by a Bahraini commitment for a supportive role such as the one it had played during the Gulf War, and the provision of naval facilities for US ships. Bahrain became the second GCC state after Kuwait to sign a defense pact with the US (for details, see chapter on Kuwait). The fact that Bahrain followed the Kuwaiti move was no coincidence: in the months after Kuwait's liberation, intense exchanges of visits indicated a special cementing of relations. The two countries had a great deal in common. They were in close proximity to the war front and, more than the other four states, suffered from internal instability.

RELATIONS WITH IRAN

Another result of the Gulf crisis and its aftermath was a positive development in Bahrain's relations with Iran. Their relations had been strained during the Iraqi-Iranian War and clouded by the alleged Iranian involvement in several coup attempts on the island in the 1980s. However, after the crisis, there was a significant improvement in relations with Tehran. In November 1990, a Bahraini diplomatic delegation to Tehran had agreed to upgrade relations from chargés d'affaires status to ambassadorial level. This led to the nomination of Iran's Javad Torkabadi as the ambassador to Bahrain in January; the island-state reciprocated by appointing Hamad Ahmad 'Abd al-'Aziz al-'Amr as its new ambassador to Tehran in April.[24] Officials from both countries maintained close contacts and held consultations during the course of the crisis and thereafter.

Bahrain made every effort to avoid friction with Iran. Bahrain wanted to preserve the positive feelings between the two countries and took into account Iran's eagerness to play a major role in the region and its rejection of any foreign presence in the Gulf. A supporter of Saudi policies, Bahrain must have felt relieved when the kingdom resumed its diplomatic ties with Iran in March. Bahrain called it "a positive step...aimed at enhancing security and stability in the region."[25] The good relations also had a positive influence in the economic sphere. For the first time since the outbreak of the Iraqi-Iranian War, a new maritime trade link was officially inaugurated between the two countries, in March.[26] Air links were also resumed with Iran Air, which made its first flight to Manama in December. In September, both countries signed a letter of understanding on trade development, mainly in the oil and gas industries.[27]

BAHRAIN AND THE COLLAPSE OF THE SOVIET UNION

Having established diplomatic relations with the Soviet Union only as recently as September 1990, Bahrain maintained the facade of orderly relations with the disintegrating empire. Accordingly, it welcomed the failure of the August coup and the reinstatement of Mikhail Gobachev as the legitimate Soviet leader, in the hope that this "will help the Soviet Union occupy its important position and play its positive role in the international arena, including the causes of peace in the world."[28] However, a mere two weeks later Bahrain recognized Estonia, Lithuania and Latvia — the Baltic states — as independent and sovereign entities. The final salute to the collapsing empire was given in late December, when Bahrain recognized the new commonwealth according to the Alma-Ata agreement. In the meantime, Bahrain continued to branch out diplomatically among the former East European allies of the Soviet Union. Ties were established with Romania and Poland in March and April, respectively.[29]

INTERNAL AFFAIRS

THE ECONOMIC RAMIFICATIONS OF THE GULF WAR

The Bahraini economy was one of the major casualties of the crisis. Virtually all sectors of the economy were affected in some way by the loss of business confidence, and despite some initial recovery since the end of hostilities, most still remained in depression.

The crisis seriously jeopardized Bahrain's chance to claim the title of the region's financial center, since the banking industry was badly hit by the flight of capital and reputation, which, in turn, led to serious retrenchment, also aggravating the island's already growing unemployment problem.[30] According to official estimates, the damage to the local economy was in the vicinity of $2bn. Half the amount was borne by the banking sector, which was compelled to make provisions for loan losses and was granted less favorable lending opportunities. This even affected the grants and aid given annually to Bahrain by some of its neighboring GCC states (c. $100m.).[31] The higher oil prices, due to the war, were of little consolation to Bahrain, which was among the poorer GCC oil-producing states. In fact, 84% of its crude consumption was piped from neighboring Saudi Arabia. One positive spin-off was the huge inflow of cash from the international force parking in the Gulf.[32]

The government introduced a series of confidence-building initiatives, in order to lift the gloom. It concentrated on traditional methods to stimulate the economy, as well as somewhat radical ones. It resumed issuing government securities in the shape of treasury bills and bonds, although fewer than previously. This had been suspended in August 1990 to reduce the strain on bank liquidity. The government also increased its own expenditure by renewing projects which had been frozen in late 1990, and announced new ones. Hence, the second crossing from Manama to Muharraq was given the go-ahead.[33] In anticipation of a return to normality for Gulf shipping, the Arab Shipbuilding and Repair Company renewed work on the installation of the two dry docks in its yard at al-Hidd.[34] Other projects included increasing electricity and desalination capacity.

In a more radical attempt to revive the economy, the cabinet decided to allow foreign-owned companies to be established in Bahrain, thus waiving the previous stipulation that any venture on the island should be at least 51% Bahraini owned.[35] The move, which was unprecedented among the usually suspicious GCC states, bore two preconditions: that any such project would "attract new technologies in new fields" and that it "be useful for the economy and create employment for Bahrainis." In order to further facilitate industrialization, the government also approved the establishment of a finance instrument, Bahrain's Development Bank, which was to provide a range of "development finance products, venture capital subscriptions, working capital and seed capital loans for small businesses."[36] The move was also meant to deal with the problems of unemployment. With large-scale retrenchment and widespread job losses, particularly in the banking sector (which was a major employer of Bahrainis), employment became an immediate issue of concern for the regime, which was also fearful that it might not be able to cope with the challenge of providing sufficient employment opportunities for the large number of nationals who were going to enter the market in the coming years.[37] Given the island's usual sensitivity to popular discontent, the issue was sure to receive further attention.

THE ECOLOGICAL DAMAGE

The oil spill in the Gulf waters, caused by deliberate sabotage on the part of the Iraqis, constituted a severe threat to Bahrain's marine ecology. Its fishing grounds, an important source of food for the island-state, were expected to be ruined.[38] Another, though far less likely danger, emanated from the proximity of the oil slick to Bahraini desalination plants located at Sitra and al-Dawr.[39] Bahrain was ready for preventative action, calling on the international community to help tackle the danger, which threatened the 33-island archipelago. In response to its outcry, Britain supplied Bahrain with six heavy-duty skimmer machines, used to separate oil from water.[40] UN, French and other missions also visited the island, in an attempt to combat the pollution. An emergency response center was set up on the island and calls were made to recruit local volunteers.[41]

THE DEMAND FOR POLITICAL REFORM

At a seminar for GCC intellectuals, hosted in Kuwait in December, the blame for the GCC's failings was laid on the ruling regimes, particularly the lack of public participation in decision-making. This was perhaps a sign of the times. Prominent among the participants at the seminar was a Bahraini professor of Islamic Studies at Bahrain University, Shaykh 'Abd al-Latif Mahmud, who argued that the autocratic rulers of the six overstepped their rightful powers and should be restrained by elected legislative assemblies. In addition to calls for implementing the freedom of expression and the rule of law, al-Latif insisted that there should be a clear distinction between the state's public finances and the private wealth of its ruling family.[42] Upon his return to Manama, al-Latif was immediately arrested. This testified to the high degree of sensitivity of the Al Khalifa ruling family to any questioning of its legitimacy. Unlike other GCC states, Bahrain did not promise, during the crisis, to introduce political reforms. In fact, Bahrain was the second state in the Gulf to create an elected parliament, but the first to suspend it. The short-lived experiment of the National Assembly (*al-majlis al-watani*, 1973–75) served to indicate the regime's anxiety that it might provide a stage for radical opposition to the Al Khalifa ruling family.

Hence, although the Gulf crisis allowed many earlier taboos on semipublic debate to be broken, it seemed only to reconfirm Bahrain's perpetual fear that opening up the political process would increase rather than contain the pressure on the ruling family.

NOTES

For the place and frequency of publications cited here, and for the full name of the publication, news agency, radio station or monitoring service where an abbreviation is used, please see "List of Sources." Only in the case of more than one publication bearing the same name is the place of publication noted here.

1. AFP, 19 October — DR, 21 October 1991.
2. *NYT,* 16 October 1991.
3. GNA, 19 August — DR, 22 August 1992.
4. Ibid.
5. GNA, 25 February — DR, 28 February 1991.
6. GNA, 8, 14 January — DR, 9, 14 January 1991.
7. AFP, 19 January — DR, 22 January 1991.
8. *FT,* 19 January 1991.
9. *FT,* 22 January; GNA, 24 January — DR, 24 January 1991.
10. *Akhbar al-Khalij, al-Ayyam,* 1 March 1991.
11. GNA, 1 September — DR, 3 September 1991.
12. GNA, 1 October — DR, 2 October 1991.
13. *Gulf Daily News,* 12 December 1991.
14. Interview given by Shaykh Khalifa to *Sawt al-Kuwait al-Duwali,* 12 October 1991.
15. *NYT,* 25 March; *JP,* 31 March 1991.
16. *NYT,* 25 March 1991.
17. GNA, 24 December — DR, 24 December 1990.
18. GNA, 10 March — DR, 11 March 1991.
19. R. Kuwait, 10 March — DR, 11 March 1991.
20. *MEI,* 31 May 1991.
21. E.g., *al-Khalij* (Sharja), 16 September 1991.
22. *Sawt al-Kuwait al-Duwali,* 12 October 1991.
23. USIS, 15 October 1991.
24. GNA, 9 April — DR, 9 April 1991.
25. GNA, 24 March — DR, 25 March 1991.
26. E.g., interview given by the director of customs, Khalil Ibrahim al-Mutawwa to *Gulf Daily News,* 1 September 1991.
27. IRNA, 4 September — DR, 5 September; GNA, 11 December — DR, 12 December 1991.
28. GNA, 22 August — DR, 23 August 1991.
29. GNA, 10 March, 22 April — DR, 14 March, 23 April 1991.
30. *FT,* 3 July 1991.
31. *CR,* Bahrain, No. 2, 1991.
32. *MEED,* 11 January 1991.
33. *CR,* Bahrain, No. 2, 1991.
34. *MEED,* 27 September 1991.
35. *The Gulf States,* 15 July 1991.

Egypt
(Jumhuriyyat Misr al-'Arabiyya)

URI M. KUPFERSCHMIDT

The Gulf War and the subsequent liberation of Kuwait from Iraqi occupation had a far-reaching impact on Egypt, which emerged from the crisis with its international standing strengthened, its regional role buttressed, and its economic prospects improved. According to an assessment by *The Financial Times,* "Mr. Mubarak may have gained more from the successful completion of the Gulf mission than any Western leader, including President George Bush. His prestige domestically has been enhanced. He acted decisively and with conviction, qualities which he had not often previously demonstrated."[1]

In economic terms, Egypt reaped important economic benefits from the Gulf War, due to what *Le Monde* termed *"une aubaine"* — a stroke of good luck. A long-sought agreement with the International Monetary Fund (IMF) and political generosity on the part of Egypt's creditors made possible the writing off of half its foreign debt.[2] This was as much the result of American efforts to compensate Egypt for its stand in the Gulf crisis as of global concerns to safeguard domestic stability in Egypt.

The upshot, especially of the IMF conditions, was that a new momentum appeared to develop domestically with regard to economic reforms that aimed at freeing the economy from its etatist bonds of the past while at the same time attempting to limit most of the adverse effects of these necessary measures on the population. A US Embassy report reportedly spoke of "golden opportunities for the first time in years" for reform.[3] President Mubarak optimistically declared at the end of the year:

> The reforms that began this year have enjoyed progress and success because of the policy of speaking frankly to the people and giving them the facts, and the people's understanding of the economic situation and their belief that economic reform is inevitable....The first year of the economic reform program was the most difficult.[4]

It remained to be seen whether this momentum would have a long-term effect. Certainly the domestic economic situation had not improved to the extent that the population — 57m. on 30 June 1991[5] — and particularly the poorer sectors experienced any major improvement in their lives by year's end. The contrary might have been true in terms of price rises, taxes and inflation. The implementation of reform measures deemed necessary in the shift from a semi-socialist to a free market economy was likely to cause additional social pressure.

With the focus on such sensitive questions as Arab and Islamic solidarity and the peace process between Israel and the Arabs during the course of the year, antigovernment opposition might have been expected to be more violent. In fact, the

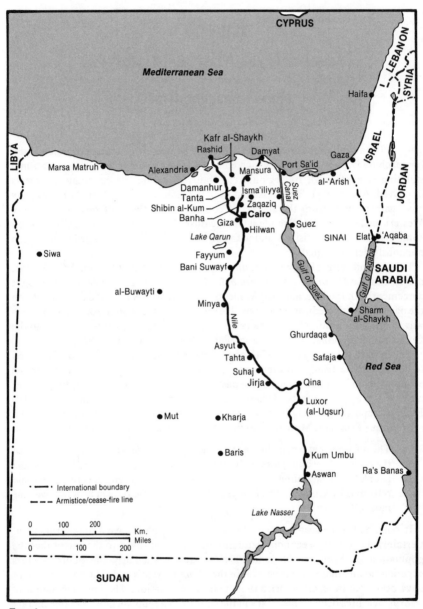

Egypt

authorities consciously allowed limited opposition to be expressed regarding the Gulf War, the Madrid peace conference, and government policy, but this did not cause major upheavals or affect overall stability. Although there were recurring clashes with extremist groups, their significance was local or limited and they did not appear to threaten the regime. Still, several ongoing trials against Muslim militants were a reminder that the government was not without enemies. Earlier, in a trial of a different violent group named "Egypt's Revolution" that had killed and wounded several US and Israeli diplomats and embassy personnel (see *MECS* 1985, p. 283; 1986, p. 336; 1988, pp. 393–94, 404; 1989, p. 298), a dozen defendants received stiff prison sentences ranging from 25 years to half a year, although Khalid Jamal 'Abd al-Nasir, the 40-year-old son of the former president and an engineer and professor at Cairo University, was acquitted.[6] Nevertheless, the government did not appear overly concerned about the domestic reactions to the Madrid peace conference scheduled for October, even though Minister of Interior 'Abd al-Halim Musa admitted that from the outbreak of the Gulf crisis in August 1990 until September 1991 no fewer than 49 attempts "to undermine Egypt's security" had been discovered and dealt with, involving the arrests of Iraqis, Palestinians, Jordanians and Sudanis in Egypt, along with Egyptians.[7]

Egypt's Gulf crisis diplomacy, its unqualified involvement in the ensuing war, President Mubarak's political steadfastness and skillful diplomacy, and the active role he and his government played in paving the way for the peace conference bore out Egypt's vision of its regional role: a leading regional power cooperating closely with the US, while carefully cultivating relations with all the countries in the region, including Israel, and reaping recognition and prestige from the whole world as attested by the steady stream of foreign heads of state, political leaders, parliamentarians and other dignitaries who visited Egypt in 1991.

Egypt's self-image was further bolstered by the election of two prominent ministers to high international office: Foreign Minister 'Ismat 'Abd al-Majid to the office of secretary-general of the Arab League, and erstwhile minister of state for foreign Affairs Butrus Butrus-Ghali to that of secretary-general of the UN. *Al-Ahram Weekly* readers, polled about the major events of the year, rated these events more important than the Gulf War and the Madrid peace conference.[8] 'Abd al-Majid's election was a logical outcome of the return of the Arab League headquarters and related agencies to Cairo on 1 January 1991, a long-awaited event preceded by the resignation of Chedli Klibi in September 1990 over the Gulf crisis. As such, it reflected the return of an Egyptian to this position, which had been Egypt's bailiwick from 1945–79, and a return as well to the tradition of a former foreign minister holding the post.[9] The election of Butrus-Ghali in November, hailed by the press as a victory for Egypt, had been preceded by several months of intensive diplomatic lobbying, with the African bloc in the UN serving as a springboard for the necessary support.[10]

Of more than domestic importance as well was the passing away of the famous singer and composer Muhammad 'Abd al-Wahhab, "the father of modern Arab music."[11] Other prominent persons who died were writer Yusuf Idris and literary critic Louis Awad, as well as former free officer 'Ali Sabri, who had been jailed in 1971 under President Sadat for conspiracy, thus reducing the number of surviving members of the 1952 coup to five.[12] Egypt embarked on several ambitious projects during 1991. It hosted the fifth All-Africa Games in the hope of enhancing its chances to host the

Olympics at some future date, which accounted for President Mubarak's emphatic rejection of criticism regarding the considerable expenses involved. Another prestigious project was the start of construction of a large library in Alexandria, scheduled to be completed in 1995, thereby renewing the renowned library that had existed there in Hellenistic times.[13]

EGYPT AND THE GULF WAR

EGYPT'S POSITION AND ITS IMPACT ON THE DOMESTIC FRONT

The Gulf War marked the first time that Egypt participated in actual fighting since 1973; the first war not fought against Israel since 'Abd al-Nasir's Yemenite adventure in 1967; and the first time Egypt emerged unequivocally on the winning side. President Mubarak, in a New Year's message, appeared extremely concerned about the possibility of war with the 15 January ultimatum to Iraq approaching. He warned of "a merciless hell...in which heads will turn white, minarets will bend, and the mutilated bodies of victims will be scattered in seas of blood."[14] At a meeting in Misurata, Libya, with the leaders of Syria, Sudan and Libya on 4 January, he still expressed hope "that Saddam Husayn will spare his people and the Arab region the calamities of the impending destructive war."[15] Apart from the issue of the dangers of the war itself, Mubarak was struggling with the difficult challenge of balancing international, regional and domestic interests as well as public opinion. Addressing parliament after the war, he referred to "the hardest and most severe days of responsibility" in his presidential career.[16]

From the beginning of the Gulf crisis until the end of the war, Mubarak relayed no less than 32 messages to Saddam Husayn, at first attempting to prevent the war and later attempting to achieve an early Iraqi withdrawal. An additional message in July 1991 admonished Iraq to take the Security Council resolutions seriously. Even after government circles were quoted in the press around 8 January that there was "no room for any appeasement," the Egyptian Government still pinned its hope on the crucial meeting between US Secretary of State James Baker and Iraqi Foreign Minister Tariq 'Aziz in Geneva on 9 January[17] (see chapter on the Gulf War and on the US and the Middle East.) As late as 16 January, Mubarak implored Saddam Husayn to respond to the peace appeals, but, according to a government statement, "the Iraqi leadership persisted in its intransigence, causing the war to break out."[18] Once the actual fighting began on 16 January, regular meetings of the cabinet as well as of the "ministerial group in charge of monitoring the war to liberate Kuwait," were held, chaired generally by Prime Minister 'Atif Sidqi.[19] Intensive contact was maintained with the US and the other allies. Government policy was debated and endorsed by the People's Assembly, which consistently expressed support for Mubarak's policy "in all his efforts and steps to tackle the crisis in order to achieve peace, avert bloodshed, prevent the outbreak of hostilities, safeguard legitimacy, repulse aggression and liberate the State of Kuwait." The assembly passed a resolution "salut[ing] our valiant armed forces...who defend the security and safety of our brothers in Arabism and Islam."[20]

As the war over Kuwait progressed into successive phases there was some nervousness on the part of the Egyptians that it would drag on, or that it would expand into Iraq. Minister of Information Safwat al-Sharif emphasized on 20 January that Egypt's basic aim was confined to "the liberation of Kuwait and the restoration of the legitimate authority there."[21] President Mubarak went to great lengths to justify the war, in light of Arab uneasiness, referring to Egypt's obligations under the charters of the Arab League and the UN and stressing that he had received "pledges from President George Bush to look into the Palestinian problem once the Gulf War was over."[22]

One of the consequences of the Gulf crisis and the war was the return of hundreds of thousands of Egyptian migrant workers to their homeland[23] (see also *MECS* 1990, chapter on Egypt). Some 10,000 of them, having escaped from Kuwait, were stranded in the desert, necessitating somewhat delicate logistic and financial arrangements for overland transport with Jordan, perceived as siding with Iraq.[24] Egyptian students at universities in such sensitive countries as Algeria, Yemen, Jordan and the Sudan also had to be brought home.[25]

Simultaneously Cairo became a center of Kuwaiti refugees who domiciled themselves in the city's sumptuous hotels but, like other nationals from the Gulf countries, did not always enjoy popularity among the Egyptian population.[26] Indeed, there was some negative sentiment in Cairo against "the corrupt monarchies" in the Gulf, even if these had provided Egypt with financial help in the past and were expected to continue doing so in the future. The Kuwaiti refugees in Cairo kept a low profile throughout the war, emerging more visibly only upon the announcement of the Iraqi withdrawal, when they organized a motorcade victory celebration.[27]

Although Egypt's active involvement in the Gulf War was not enthusiastically acclaimed by its own citizens, there was basic support for it, stemming mainly from aversion to Saddam Husayn's regime. Arab solidarity with Iraq as a country and as a people, however, remained intact and overt signs of support for the war, or outright enthusiasm, were rare, reflecting a certain pan-Arab predicament, if not embarrassment.[28] Still, a legal opinion (*fatwa*) issued by the mufti of Egypt, Shaykh Muhammad Sayyid 'Atiyya al-Tantawi, endorsed the Saudi stand, explicitly stating that "religion does not forbid the reliance on non-Muslim forces against an external aggressor."[29] The government received the support of other establishment 'Ulama in favor of the liberation of Kuwait, and some were also quoted as calling for the formation of an Islamic army to defend the holy places in Saudi Arabia.[30] A typical advertisement in the national secular press warned of a "disaster brought on the Islamic nation by dictator Saddam Husayn."[31]

Although the confrontation arena in the Gulf was far away, Egypt also felt threatened at home. Precautionary security measures were taken at the High Dam, partly in response to veiled Sudanese threats to bomb the dam, and a daily mine sweeping was carried out at the Suez Canal, while two Honduran ships loaded with cement were denied access to the canal for fear that they would be sunk as an Iraqi act of sabotage. Flights to the Gulf were halted, security at airports and border crossing-points was tightened, and visa requirements were instituted for citizens of the Maghrib countries, apparently meant to deny entrance to Islamic activists from Algeria and Tunisia who could possibly endanger Egyptian security under the impact of Saddam Husayn.[32] Moreover, after anti-Egyptian demonstrations took place in Khartoum on 17 January, Egypt closed its educational and cultural institutions, and the local Egypt Air office there. The Egyptian Embassy in San'a was closed as well following anti-Egyptian demonstrations there.[33]

On 30 January, Minister of Interior Muhammad 'Abd al-Halim Musa announced that Egypt's security services had arrested 17 Iraqis, Palestinians and others who had planned "to carry out acts of sabotage and terrorism in Egypt in retaliation for the country's stand on this brutal invasion [of Kuwait]." Later it was stated that a detailed plan was uncovered envisioning attacks against American, Saudi and Kuwaiti embassies and firms, and the sum of $42,000, apparently meant to finance the operations, was found. During the following weeks there were additional disclosures to the effect that several other groups of Iraqis or "pro-Iraqis" — which could mean Egyptians as well as Palestinians — had been apprehended. The scant details given about them included the information that some of them had attempted to enter Egypt at the Red Sea ferry harbor of Nuwaybi' and that a few of them had been supplied with money by Iraq. In May, the minister of interior reported to the People's Assembly that a total of 100 saboteurs had been caught.[34]

Domestic Opposition to the War

Domestic opposition, which was permitted to be expressed to some extent, emanated from the left and from Islamist circles. Part of this opposition was straightforward and part was implicit. Some of it was directed simultaneously against the Western components of the coalition forces and against the person of Saddam Husayn (as evidenced by numerous caricatures in the press), though generally not against Iraq itself.[35] Some support for Saddam Husayn was later said to exist after he succeeded in striking Israel and preserving his power against all odds, or at least against Egyptian expectations. Judging by a foreign press report, latent opposition to government policy may have been stronger than what was apparent. For example, the opposition newspaper *al-Sha'b* was reported, by a Moroccan paper in February, to have tripled its daily circulation from 70,000 to 200,000 copies during the days of the war.[36]

Small signs of dissent had become visible even before the outbreak of hostilities when the political opposition tried to organize a march to the 'Abidin palace. When police prevented this, the opposition mounted a demonstration in front of the Socialist Labor Party (SLP) headquarters, with participants shouting "Death to America" and "No to Aggression against Iraq." Police, who reportedly outnumbered the demonstrators, nevertheless allowed several of the organizers to deliver a petition calling on the government to stop "the war and aggression against the Iraqi people."[37] During the following weeks, small-scale demonstrations took place from time to time, and anti-Mubarak pamphlets were distributed, which led to what was apparently the preventive detention of several dozen people, among them SLP members and other opposition activists.[38] At one opposition meeting, Saddam Husayn was called upon to divert his troops from Kuwait to Palestine.[39]

A certain shift in public pro-government attitude became apparent around 24 January after the destructive effects of the Allied bombings of Iraq were publicized and the ground war was in full swing (see chapter on the Gulf War), with beds in Cairo hospitals rumored to be readied for mass casualties.[40] Although the opposition parties showed some confusion, owing to what one paper termed "the contradictions of the Egyptian street," it called for a cease-fire in order to make negotiations possible. National Progressive Unionist Grouping (NPUG) leader Rif'at al-Sa'id, speaking for the opposition parties, announced the circulation of a petition to end the war which was described as "a savage American attack on the Iraqi people." Anti-American sentiments were also predominant in Islamist circles.[41] Several professional organizations, journalists and others held sit-ins and rallies denouncing "American aggression" and calling for an immediate cease-fire.[42]

By far the most vehement and the largest demonstrations against the Gulf War and against Egypt's involvement in it took place on university campuses in mid-February after the semester break, which had purposely been extended by two weeks. In fact, student unrest coincided with the last days of actual fighting in the Gulf, before the cease-fire of 28 February.[43] The demonstrations that took place at Cairo University, 'Ayn Shams, Asyut, Alexandria and Mansura universities, were initially orderly, with security forces cordoning off the campuses and refraining from interfering so long as the demonstrators remained within campus limits. The moving forces behind these demonstrations were apparently leftist and fundamentalist groups of varying degrees of anti-government intensity, some of them as critical of the coalition forces, and of Israel, as of Saddam Husayn. Portraits of the Gulf coalition leaders, as well as American and Israeli flags, were burned, and cries of *Allahu Akbar* voiced. President Husni Mubarak was branded as a "coward" and an "American agent." The atmosphere became more heated on 25 February when 10,000 students demonstrated on the Cairo University campus "in solidarity with their Iraqi brothers who are being subjected to death and annihilation." The demonstrators cheered for the long life of the Iraqi people and called for "the downfall of the American-Israeli scheme to destroy Iraq." Media reports described a "virtual battleground" when a police force stormed the main building, using tear gas, smoke bombs and rubber bullets for a period of three days.[44] When a student was killed, the demonstrations became even more violent and dozens of students were wounded. An unknown number of students were arrested.[45] By the beginning of March, however, student unrest over the Gulf situation had died down.[46]

Expectations and Debate in the Aftermath of the War

Skepticism expressed in the media during the last weeks of fighting over Iraq's preparedness to withdraw, on the one hand, and America's ulterior objectives in Iraq, on the other, soon turned into a debate on the future of Iraq. A certain amount of media consensus emerged regarding the necessity of Saddam Husayn's removal,[47] but there was also the feeling that Iraq must not be divided, and that its defense capability had to be safeguarded for the future.[48] Moreover, opposition to further Allied military action and to maintaining the boycott against Iraq continued to be voiced after the fighting had ended.[49] Though initially rather mixed feelings among the Egyptian troops were reported on their being stationed in the Gulf, the forces had performed their duties quite well.[50] For a force numbering 35,000 men (or more, according to nonofficial sources), casualties were low: eight officers and men killed — "martyred," according to the religious term employed in official announcements — and 74 wounded.[51] Egyptian soldiers who had fallen into Iraqi captivity were soon released.

By the end of the war, a discussion of future regional security arrangements emerged. Egyptian officials argued that "the crisis has shown that Egypt is indispensable" and hoped for postwar security arrangements that would leave a sizable Egyptian presence in the Gulf.[52] However, talks with the Gulf Cooperation Council (GCC) and with Syria failed to produce agreement on this issue, with Kuwait seen as preferring a Western rather than an Egyptian-dominated presence (see below), and at the end of April Egypt began quietly to withdraw its troops.[53] In a volte-face on the Damascus declaration (signed and released in July and endorsed by the Egyptian cabinet in August), which had envisaged more cooperation and coordination among the members of the GCC, even the idea of a token contingent of 3,000 Egyptians within a larger security force in the Gulf was abandoned.[54]

A transition to new approaches on regional strategic issues appeared to be taking place at the war's end. Public debate was waged in the media and in political and academic circles on the issue of peace with Israel and on the role which the US should play in that context.[55]

ECONOMIC DEVELOPMENT: THE IMPACT OF THE WAR

THE DIRECT ECONOMIC IMPACT

The state of the Egyptian economy had been generally depressed in 1990, to the extent that some observers predicted that Egypt's foreign debts and loss of credibility would prevent it from being able to import necessary food and raw materials. Initially, the Gulf War heightened fears that the situation would become even worse. While overall losses due to the Gulf crisis and war were initially estimated at $10bn., a later IMF estimate put them at $27bn.[56] These included a virtual halt to the remittances of Egyptian migrant workers in Iraq and Kuwait, the return home and subsequent unemployment of migrant workers, and losses in income from tourism and trade.

From the beginning of the Gulf crisis, an estimated 400,000–500,000 Egyptian migrant workers returned from Iraq and Kuwait.[57] Workers' remittances had amounted to $3.4bn. in 1989, and had declined to $2.3bn. in 1990, and were completely frozen by Iraq when the Gulf crisis started. An estimated outstanding Iraqi debt to Egypt amounting to $1bn. was similarly frozen[58] (for their partial freezing by Iraq prior to the crisis see *MECS* 1989, pp. 312–15). The large number of repatriates exacerbated the existing unemployment problem in Egypt by as much as 25%, according to one source. International Labor Organization (ILO) representatives, examining the problem of creating jobs for high school and university graduates in Egypt, cited 3m. unemployed and forecast an increase in unemployment from 15%–17% in the near future, with an estimated additional 5% due to public sector employees losing their jobs as a result of privatization.[59] The war, therefore, accounted only for a part of the problem.

Losses in tourism were estimated as exceeding $2.5bn. immediately after the war, of which $1.25bn.–$1.5bn. were direct losses to the tourist sector, such as to hotels, tour operators and others dependent on tourists for their livelihood, and the rest resulting from a decline in purchases by rich tourists from the Gulf countries in Egypt.[60] However, tourism picked up again soon after the hostilities ended[61] with an annual income from tourism projected at $2.6bn.[62]

Surprisingly, the impact of the war on revenues from the Suez Canal was positive. In spite of a slack in international traffic, more warships than usual passed through the canal, paying high tariffs that had been raised considerably over a period of years. Income from the canal was reported to have risen by 18.2% over the 1990 total of $1.6bn.[63] Trade losses, however, were reported, especially by companies in the public sector.[64] There were also difficulties in maintaining overland exports during the war, e.g., of fruits and vegetables to the Gulf countries.[65] On the other hand, somewhat ironically, Egypt, which went to war with Iraq, nevertheless derived a 200% increase in oil revenues from the cycle of global price rises that had been set in motion by the crisis (see chapter on oil developments). By June 1991, Egypt reported $2.53m. in revenue from petroleum exports, 70% more than anticipated while increasing production by only 4%.[66] On the other hand, cotton exports, once a major source of Egypt's foreign currency, and a focus of reform plans, were stalled due to massive local consumption.[67]

RESCHEDULING DEBTS

Egypt had much to gain by its stand in the war with regard to its foreign debt, estimated at $48.8bn. and possibly even $55bn., which was the most critical aspect of the country's economy.[68] Considerable concern was also voiced about Egypt's domestic debt, although this problem was less urgent.[69]

A process of partial debt forgiveness had begun in November 1990 (see also *MECS* 1990, chapter on Egypt), when the US remitted Egypt's military debt of $6.7bn. and added extra military and economic grants amounting to $2.1bn.[70] Egypt's military debt had been growing since the 1970s, with interest alone amounting to $780m. in 1991, so that, already by the beginning of the year, *Le Monde* aptly referred to "*un cadeau imperial*" — befitting a world power — amounting to a total of no less than $8bn.[71] In July, another long-term financial agreement with a generous interest rate was concluded with the US.[72] Saudi Arabia and the United Arab Emirates (UAE) followed suit, writing off a further $7bn. in debts and promising new loans and investments: Saudi Arabia forgave $2bn. and announced $200m. in investments, while the UAE promised to forgive $500m. and Abu Dhabi granted $85m.[73]

A chain of developments was thereby set into motion that involved European countries and Japan writing off or suspending part of Egypt's debts. The US played a crucial diplomatic role in this process by overcoming initial resistance on the part of the seven great industrial countries (G7).[74] On 5 February, an agreement was signed with the European Community (EC) for a grant of $240m. to compensate Egypt for the negative effects of the Gulf War and to aid it in importing commodities and spare parts as well as in creating jobs. A later protocol, signed in November in Cairo by EC President Jacques Delors, granted $700m. in long-term loans.[75] In February, France, which was Egypt's largest European creditor with an outstanding loan of over $5bn., agreed to furnish FFr2m. ($400m.) as a grant for the purchase of food and for a supercomputer.[76] Germany, which had earlier suspended aid to Egypt due to differences of opinion but which sought to disprove Egyptian accusations that its aid to Israel created an "unbalanced" situation, decided to waive half of the $5bn. debt. Foreign Minister Hans-Dietrich Genscher, on a visit to Cairo in February, declared that "we have assured President Mubarak that Egypt can now rely on Germany."[77] Similar debt remission moves were undertaken by the UK, the Netherlands, Denmark and Finland.[78]

The US secretary of the treasury, Nicholas Brady, after discussions in Cairo in April on Egypt's economic policies and debt relief, declared himself satisfied and pledged: "We will now work with our colleagues in the Paris Club and elsewhere to see if we can extend the debt reduction to other [creditor] countries."[79] The next phase came on 24 May when the Paris Club, the consortium of creditor countries to which

Egypt owed 90% of its foreign debt, decided in principle to reduce Egypt's outstanding debt by 50%. In an extremely lenient arrangement, similar only to what Poland had been granted, 15% of Egypt's debt was to be waived as of 1 July 1991, another 15% 18 months later, and the remaining 20% in 36 months, thus reducing the debt to $20.2bn. to be paid over an extended period of 25–35 years.[80] Dr. Salah Hamid, governor of the Central Bank, returned from Paris elated, declaring that the Paris Club move reflected "appreciation for President Mubarak's efforts and honorable stand during the Gulf crisis and for the daring steps taken to reform the Egyptian economy."[81] The Paris Club decision was soon imitated by nonmember countries such as Switzerland, which granted Egypt SFr60m and canceled SFr44m. in debts.[82]

While the process of debt rescheduling was made possible as a result of arduous deliberations with the IMF, undoubtedly it was the Gulf War that accelerated ongoing negotiations that had dragged on for over three years, ever since a prior agreement on a $250m. loan in 1987 had collapsed that same year. It is arguable whether agreement would have been reached at all if not for the political and economic benefits that Egypt derived from the Gulf crisis and the war. Still, reaching an agreement with the IMF required highly delicate economic and diplomatic exercises, for the cut in subsidies and other reform measures demanded by the IMF threatened to evoke a repeat of the serious 1977 food riots that erupted following IMF-inspired price increases.

The signing of the agreement was preceded by several IMF missions, in January, and again after the war, in March, whose purpose was to formulate a letter of intent on monetary and economic reforms, in particular a liberalization of exchange and interest rates; a reduction of the budget deficit to less than 10% of the gross national product (at the time it was 17%); a cut in subsidies of basic foodstuffs, household commodities and energy; and the introduction of a new sales tax.[83] Most of the far-reaching reform measures demanded by the IMF, and introduced during the year, were announced by Prime Mister 'Atif Sidqi as early as January,[84] with the exception of an IMF recommendation in March to dismiss a certain proportion of personnel in the governmental and public sectors that was rejected by the Egyptians.[85] This initial agreement was embodied in a letter of intent signed on 9 April, that served as the basis for further deliberations with the IMF in Washington and with the Paris Club.[86] President Mubarak spoke of "difficult negotiations," but of an agreement "whereby the Egyptian economy can fulfill its development requirements." Later, in his May Day speech, when the agreement with the IMF was already certain, he emphasized that the government had preferred a three-year delay before instituting any of the difficult measures demanded.[87] Opposition newspapers predicted steep price rises, and establishment-inclined al-Ahram Weekly ran a headline: "Debt relief is costlier than expected."[88]

With a crucial meeting scheduled for May, the cabinet discussed the proposed IMF agreement on 14 April, after which Prime Minister Sidqi stated that it was compatible with "Egypt's economic reforms, the state's higher interests, the country's abilities and the need to preserve the standard of living of the poorer sections of society."[89] IMF Executive Director 'Abd al-Shakir al-Sha'ban, arriving in Cairo on 11 May, showed much diplomatic sensitivity by declaring that the economic reform program was "completely Egyptian" and that "the IMF's role was confined to helping draw up the program to reach its required goal."[90] With the IMF in Washington finally agreeing to the terms of Egypt's letter of intent, the final move was made at a Paris Club meeting on 20–24 May in Paris, which endorsed the agreement.[91]

The road was thus formally opened for agreements with other international parties, some of which had anticipated this development. A loan of $168.5m. by the World Bank to the Bank for Industrial Development had been agreed on in February.[92] The World Bank had agreed to supply $550m. in loans for economic liberalization measures in early April,[93] and by the end of March a loan was obtained from the World Bank for restructuring key public sector areas of the economy, including price policies.[94] By fall, however, the World Bank showed caution in supplying further loans until it received more data on the Egyptian economy.[95] Another loan of $70m. on easy terms was supplied by the International Development Authority to the Egyptian Social Development Fund, a newly established body dealing with social security, the creation of some 150,000 new jobs over the next four years, job training and reducing unemployment.[96] An even larger loan of $4bn. was pledged at a meeting of 30 creditor countries in Paris bringing total grants and loans at reduced interest to $8bn.[97] Moreover, additional loans could be solicited from the US, such as a five-year $1bn. loan, for infrastructural development in the rural areas, based on the existing loan framework.[98]

ECONOMIC REFORM MEASURES

From the onset, it was clear that canceling debts alone would not offer long-term solutions. President Mubarak himself warned in March that "the Gulf crisis does not mean cash will start flowing to us from every direction and there will be prosperity."[99] A prominent Egyptian economist, agreeing in his analysis with the views of the country's foreign creditors, pinpointed three basic "biases" in the Egyptian economy: the external debt, uneconomical pricing and heavy subsidies that weighed down on the budget, and the low level of productivity in the public sector as well as corruption, all of which had to be rectified.[100]

New economic reform measures were initiated throughout the year. Monetary changes were introduced and bank interest rates were liberalized in January, which had the effect of increasing deposits by 14% in deposits and loans by 18.5%. New treasury bills were issued, a move that was welcomed by Egyptian economists.[101] A new sales tax of 10% was introduced in May, which had been recommended by the IMF and which was modeled on the value added tax (VAT) principle. Initially, however, it failed to generate positive effects, and it was reported to have contributed to price increases, caused considerable confusion in its application, and produced disappointing revenues.[102]

In line with the efforts to bring about a general liberalization of the economy, the exchange rate of the Egyptian pound was floated for the first time in December 1990 and it appeared to be relatively stable during the year at £E3.30 to the dollar. Also reflecting liberalization was a hard-currency supermarket which was opened in Cairo.[103] Another obstacle to liberalization, differential rates for official and private (including tourist) transactions, was removed on 8 October, four months ahead of schedule, with the introduction of a unified exchange rate. While Egyptian spokesmen tended to ascribe the prompt move to the overall success of the monetary measures already implemented, it may have also been meant to impress a visiting IMF mission, "compensating for failures in other fields."[104] Another new measure, implemented in

June, was a mandatory ceiling on credit expansion and limits on bank credits imposed by Egypt's Central Bank.[105] A proposed new banking law aimed at instituting more centralized supervision over the activities of banks (also, apparently, those working according to Islamic principles) as did a veto by the government on the appointment of their executives.[106]

Ongoing price increases constituted a sensitive problem, with the success of the reforms dangerously dependent on the reaction of the population. The government vacillated between the hammer of the IMF and the anvil of the ability of large segments of the population to cope. Just how many people were living below the poverty line was the subject of public debate.[107] In May, gas had reportedly gone up by 30%, kerosene by 50%, and telephone and electricity rates by 30%–50%. By July, the Cairo Chamber of Commerce reported price increases of 4%–85% of basic foods, commodities and services.[108] However, the price of bread, a major political issue remained stable at 5 qirsh ($0.015) per loaf, much below its real cost of 13 qirsh ($0.04), due to government subsidies amounting to £E1bn. The same artificial stability applied to sugar.[109]

The outcome of reforms in the public sector was equally uncertain. It still controlled c. 75% of industry, 80% of foreign trade and 90% of banking, and employed some 4m., about a third of the total labor force. One of the most basic structural reforms begun in 1991 was the enactment of the public sector law, intended to limit government involvement in the public sector and give management more freedom in economic and financial decisions; float shares; link wages to productivity; and partially share profits with the workers.

A law envisaging the privatization of 373 public companies as a first stage was passed in June to take effect in July. The law was supported by the National Democratic Party (NDP) and Wafd but opposed by the leftist NPUG and by the Muslim Brothers — both sides of the political spectrum — who were fearful of increased foreign involvement.[110] The NPUG, anxious to protect the Nasserist heritage, also appeared to be apprehensive of layoffs in the governmental and public sectors.[111] It claimed that the law would lead to the "opening of the door to multinational companies... and an increase in the suffering of the people when they face sharp price increases."[112] The actual auctioning of several of the smaller public companies began on a modest scale in July. The shares of four luxury hotels were floated for the first time as well, and two large oil companies went private.[113]

By early October local economists and diplomats observed that "the real test in the public sector reforms is still to come," and that commitment would be measured "when and if heads begin to roll at every level, right up to the cabinet." Rumor had it that the cabinet was divided between "reformists" and "gradualists" and that there was serious infighting on reform among the political-economic elite of the country. According to the press, "vested interests" and the "resistance of the Egyptian system to change" were also not conducive to speedy reform.[114]

Although it did not protest, the general population did not appear to be happy with these developments. The Wafd opposition newspaper, *al-Wafd,* reported in June that the public was depressed by economic developments, eliciting a response by veteran *al-Akhbar* editor Mustafa Amin exhorting the youth in particular to redouble its economic efforts.[115] The NPUG, in an official party statement predicting price rises and a freeze on salaries, proposed the encouragement of local production and a limit on imports as an alternative to the IMF conditions.[116] Significantly, the Muslim Brothers took a similar line on a broad range of economic issues: instead of the IMF-imposed measures, Ma'mun al-Hudaybi, spokesman of the Muslim Brothers, proposed an austerity program and the transfer to Egypt of monies deposited abroad.[117] The Brothers opposed the public sector law and the sales tax because they reflected IMF directives forced upon Egypt by a Western body, putting additional burdens on the population.[118]

Visits by World Bank and IMF missions to Egypt in the fall of 1991 were accompanied by statements that were generally full of praise for the degree of reform and liberalization attained in Egypt.[119] However, there was ample reason for skepticism. By the end of the year, when another IMF mission visited, it appeared that not all targets had been attained, partly because tax revenues had been lower than expected, thus increasing the budget deficit. It was already clear by then that the IMF goal of pushing the budget deficit under the 10% GDP line would not be reached.[120] Still, it was anticipated that the IMF would take a lenient attitude. On the other hand, the World Bank continued to delay a $300m. loan for structural reforms owing to disagreements with Egypt regarding the low procurement price for cotton paid to the *fellahin* (peasants) and the wavering implementation of the public sector law.[121]

THE DOMESTIC POLITICAL SCENE

GOVERNMENT AND PARLIAMENT

President Husni Mubarak's tenth anniversary in office, on 14 October, offered an occasion to publish numerous lengthy articles in the press, mainly enumerating achievements in all fields of government, though evoking also some predictably critical appraisals in the opposition press. Significantly, the issue of democracy and freedom, which was discussed both by the government's supporters and its opponents, revealed a considerable gap in interpretation between the two.[122]

A long-awaited government reshuffle, if not complete overhaul of the cabinet, to improve the performance of the economic ministries and to restructure the country's cumbersome bureaucracy generally, evoked considerable speculation in the press, but ultimately turned out to be disappointing.[123] The weekly *al-Musawwar,* in an article entitled: "Does Egypt Need 22 Ministries?" in May, calculated that there were dozens of deputy ministers, hundreds of administrative organizations and 5,000 directors-general in the governmental and public sectors.[124] Establishment journalist Musa Sabri, in an article in *Akhbar al-Yawm,* proposed appointing Mubarak as prime minister, implying that only the president had the required prestige to push through the necessary reform measures. Mustafa Amin ascribed the limited changes to the inability to find the necessary 24 suitable candidates to fill the cabinet posts.[125]

Limited personnel changes in the government were announced on 20 May. Dr. Butrus Butrus-Ghali moved up from the Foreign Ministry to the position of deputy prime minister for foreign relations, emigration and Egyptian affairs abroad. The post of foreign minister, previously held by 'Abd al-Majid, went to a career diplomat and lawyer by training with wide experience in the UN and in negotiations with Israel, 'Amr Mahmud Musa. Lt. Gen. Muhammad Husayn al-Tantawi Sulayman, a veteran of all the wars fought by Egypt since 1956 and previously the head of the army's operations branch, replaced Gen. Yusuf Sabri Abu Talib as minister of defense. Other appointments included Dr. Mahmud Sayyid Ahmad Sharif, a surgeon, previously governor of Cairo, as minister of local government; Dr. Husayn Kamil Baha al-Din, a pediatrician teaching at Cairo University, as minister of education; and Dr. Hamdi 'Ali 'Abd al-Wahhab al-Banbi, as minister of petroleum and mineral resources.[126] By September, rumors circulated about a restructured government of only 15 ministries, manned by "75% new faces", according to al-Ahali, and four deputy prime ministers, with the formation of ministerial groups to deal with different sectors of the economy. These rumors, however, were denied by President Mubarak.[127]

The elections of November and December 1990 (see MECS 1990, pp. 322–28) had produced a rather malleable People's Assembly dominated by the NDP, a party that originated in the establishment and remained firmly anchored in it. The boycott of the elections by most opposition parties represented in earlier assemblies, the failure of other opposition parties to gain sufficient votes, and the election of a significant number of so-called independent members — some of them with unconcealed party affiliations — set the scene for a rather anomalous opposition. As against 348 NDP deputies, there were only six formal NPUG deputies, with the rest of the assembly consisting of 10 nominees of the President and 85 so-called independents. Although some of the independents aligned themselves with the opposition, inevitably it was weak. Speaker Dr. Fathi Surur, however, emphasized that "all [political] directions were represented in the assembly."[128]

The new assembly began under a shadow, to some extent because of at least 256 complaints from the public questioning the validity of the elections owing to irregularities. One complaint even pertained to the election of Speaker Fathi Surur. Most of the cases were rejected by the assembly's Legislative Committee, while others went to a special judicial body.[129] Several deputies were also accused of having violated building regulations, one was involved in a bribery and another in a misdemeanor case. The matter of 10 deputies accused of narcotics trafficking was of far greater consequence, for the problem of drugs had received more attention from the government and from the press in recent years than in the past, and the accusations reflected upon the prestige of the assembly and the NDP. The matter was first exposed by the press, including the opposition al-Wafd in April.[130] Although initially Minister of Interior 'Abd al-Halim Musa stated that "everyone is innocent until proven guilty," Surur had little choice but to request that the relevant files be sent from the prosecution to the assembly. There the Ethics Committee tried to put off at least some of the accusations, but by September legal action was unavoidable and all the cases were referred to the prosecutor.[131] On 29 November, three of the accused NDP deputies were expelled from the assembly by an overwhelming majority although they had not yet been tried, thus demonstrating the assembly's sensitivity to public criticism.[132]

PARTY ACTIVITY AND OPPOSITION TACTICS

The NDP, though appearing to be comfortably in control of the political and administrative processes, never enjoyed wide popularity. At one point, Prime Minister 'Atif Sidqi came under such heavy criticism from deputies of his own party at an NDP parliamentary committee meeting that he left "soaked in sweat" while "his ministers had to run after him to escape the NDP deputies' wrath." As the editor of the Wafd opposition newspaper wrote: "This is the real calamity in Egypt: the country lives under a government which is rejected at the parliamentary level and a People's

Assembly which is rejected at the popular level."[133] The NDP, painfully aware that it had never succeeded in adapting its previous Arab Socialist Union structure and image to the post-Nasserist pluralist era, embarked on a democratization and rejuvenation effort during the year to broaden its base.[134] It announced internal party elections on all levels, starting with villages and urban quarters in October 1991, which would culminate in a major party convention projected for July 1992 to coincide with the 40th anniversary of the Free Officers' Revolution.[135] Reports in the press predicted intense internal competition, with the possibility that no fewer than 85% of the district secretaries might be deposed.[136] The actual election process at the district level started in December.[137]

As a result of the People's Assembly elections in 1990, and the boycott of the elections by most of the parties, the NPUG was the only formal opposition party in the assembly, albeit with a mere six seats in the 454-member assembly. It thus became the leader of an unofficial opposition bloc consisting of several independent deputies who identified with the Wafd, the SLP, several Nasserist deputies, and one Liberal. Efforts by erstwhile Free Officer Khalid Muhyi al-Din, who had made a political comeback in the assembly, to attain formal recognition for a 34-member opposition faction, or to form an even larger bloc of 64 deputies, failed.[138] Both the NPUG and the SLP, which was not represented in parliament, tried unsuccessfully to form a bloc with a group of independent Nasserist deputies.[139] The Wafd might have controlled a bloc of 14 independent deputies but refused to do so because of its decision to maintain the election boycott.[140] The Young Egypt Party, claiming a base of 20,000 members, "mostly lawyers," according to its own newspaper, kept aloof from these parliamentary deals, indicating that it preferred future cooperation with new, small parties such as the Greens and the Democratic Union.[141]

The opposition parties, including those which had boycotted the elections, although not represented in the assembly, tried to develop a degree of extraparliamentary cooperation and solidarity in the face of certain government policies, while seeking to avoid violence so as not to be susceptible to forceful repression by the government. In January, representatives of most opposition parties met to discuss the situation in the Gulf, although the Wafd took exception, declaring that it had already "expressed its opinion...and does not need to sit with these parties, while the government fulfills its duty as well as possible."[142]

One bitter criticism shared by all the opposition groups was the continued existence of the emergency law, enacted in 1981 by President Sadat just before his assassination essentially in order to facilitate large-scale arrests, and extended several times since.[143] The law also had critics within the assembly.[144] With the law coming up for another three-year extension in May, most opposition parties staged a sit-in at Wafd headquarters on that day,[145] issuing a statement that "the continued imposition of the emergency law is politically unjustified and that the claim that the aim of the law is to confront terrorism is baseless....The crimes and political assassinations have all taken place with the emergency law still in force" — the latter being an allusion to the assassination of Assembly Speaker Mahjub the year before (see *MECS* 1990, chapter on Egypt).[146] Advancing the argument that the law constituted an impediment to the development of pluralistic democracy, SLP leader Ibrahim Shukri claimed that it led to the inability of the opposition to act.[147] Muslim Brotherhood spokesman Ma'mun al-Hudaybi asserted that "the governmental system is based on oppression and dictatorship, which is why it hides behind emergency laws."[148] NPUG secretary-general Rif'at al-Sa'id's view was that "the government acted in all sorts of ways with the aim, on the one hand, to break up the parties from within and deny them their real strength, and on the other, to thwart their public activity by [imposing] a series of [restrictive] measures."[149] All this criticism, however, was dismissed as "easy opportunistic activity" by the establishment newspaper *al-Jumhuriyya,* whose editor admonished the opposition parties "to live with the public, to help it and give it guidance in fulfilling its duties before inciting it with regard to its rights."[150] President Mubarak signed a decree extending the emergency law by another three years in May.[151]

In a related but potentially more far-reaching move, the opposition parties drew up guidelines in May for a new constitution to replace the existing one dating from 1971, which was deemed unsuitable for a pluralistic regime and a liberalized economy.[152] The proposals, drawn up by a group of opposition leaders, the most prominent being Dr. Muhammad Hilmi Murad of the SLP, university professors, trade union leaders and other public figures, were contained in 10 paragraphs stressing human and civic rights, freedom of the press, and certain limits on the president's powers.[153] However, the proposals could not bridge the gap between the Muslim Brotherhood's demand for "a hundred percent Islamic constitution" and the NPUG's desire to retain the "achievements of the 1952 Revolution."[154]

With the gradual return to multiparty politics from the late 1970s onward, the tendencies toward political fragmentation and personal rivalries characteristic of the interwar era also seemed to resurface. The tripartite coalition of the SLP, the Muslim Brotherhood and the Liberal Party, in disarray for some years, became even looser. After one independent deputy had openly identified himself with the Liberal Party, party leader Mustafa Kamil Murad declared that the joint election boycott "had ceased with the beginning of work in parliament," but he still failed to set up a parliamentary faction of his own.[155] The Muslim Brotherhood was upset by what it viewed as increasing socialist-Nasserist tendencies in the SLP, and the Brotherhood's venerated Guidance Bureau was reported to have decided to leave the alliance with the SLP at one stage after SLP activist 'Adil Husayn appeared to be trying to establish a new Islamic party modeled on the militant Sudanese Islamic Front.[156] The SLP, indeed, had been internally divided between Islamist and socialist factions ever since 1989, and this was reflected in fierce rivalry between leaders Ibrahim Shukri, Ahmad Mujahid and 'Adil Husayn, which accounted for a postponement by six months of a party convention scheduled for September.[157] Feelers were apparently put out by the Muslim Brotherhood to the Liberal Party in October regarding a bilateral arrangement,[158] while members of the SLP allegedly sounded out the NPUG and the Nasserists at various times during the year about an alliance.[159]

Various rumors continued to circulate during the course of the year about efforts by the Muslim Brothers to circumvent the ban on religious parties and set up a full-fledged party of its own, with a nonreligious charter or with a token proportion of Christian members (the latter possibility was explicitly denied).[160] One weekly asserted that Brotherhood spokesman Ma'mun al-Hudaybi "was only waiting for the right moment."[161] There was even gossip the Muslim Brothers were planning to buy "a small party" with a bribe of £E250,000.[162] Nevertheless, Hudaybi denied that there was a schism in the three-way alliance, stating in September that "the common goal of application of the Shari'a still stands." A deal involving the Brotherhood subsidizing a new press for the SLP's *al-Sha'b* in return for SLP cover for another newspaper may have accounted for the survival of the alliance, however problematic.[163]

Most of the other opposition parties were also beset by internal strife, whether ideological, personal, or as a result of a generation gap between old-guard politicians and younger activists.[164] The generation gap was particularly apparent in the Wafd, where old-time leader Fu'ad Siraj al-Din, anyway pressed by a group within the party for a more outspoken stand on the Gulf crisis, was derogatorily labeled by a faction calling itself the Wafdist Vanguard (*al-Tali'a al-Wafdiyya*) "Fu'ad Pasha" for having ignored an annual memorial day honoring the late Sa'd Zaghlul and Mustafa al-Nahhas.[165] Liberal Party leader Mustafa Kamil Murad was criticized by younger members of his party for his vacillating stand on the Gulf War and by the party's Democratic Front, a radical wing pushing for extensive economic and administrative reforms.[166] The Misr al-Fatat Party was fragmented because of personal rivalry over leadership in several branches.[167]

A former faction, the Arab Socialist Misr Party, made a formal comeback in 1991 and became the 10th licensed party, immediately joining the opposition. The reconstitution of the party followed protracted litigation in the administrative court in order to nullify a merger with the NDP that had been forced upon it by President Sadat 13 years earlier,[168] although the redistribution of branches, offices and property, including a share in the newspaper *al-Misr,* still remained to be negotiated with the NDP and other former fellow parties.[169] The chairman of the Arab Socialist Misr Party, Jamal al-Rabi'a, claimed that the party had 250 active branches and the support of some several unspecified deputies in the assembly. Describing it as the "party of the future and the young," he outlined a program to fight illiteracy and a commitment to regional security in the face of the Israeli threat, which was perceived as the main danger.[170] Other political parties awaited formal recognition as well. The chances that the Muslim Brotherhood would be recognized were nil owing to the rule that no "religious or communal parties" were allowed. The Nasserists, however, insisted that they had a separate identity, and complained that they suffered from unjustified discrimination as a result of the legal objection of "ideological closeness to one of the existing parties."[171] The party claimed that it had the support of seven deputies in the assembly, although it was still in the process of formation.[172] Other political groupings that attempted to gain formal recognition were the Arab Democratic Party, the Islamic-oriented Awakening (*sahwa*) Party, the Egypt Socialist Party, the People's (*sha'b*) Democratic Party and the liberally inclined Future (*mustaqbal*) Party led by the anti-fundamentalist agronomist and intellectual Faraj Fawda.[173]

THE RADICAL-ISLAMIC FACTOR

Islamic Associations and the Muslim Brothers

Militant Islam in Egypt continued to be characterized by a high degree of fragmentation as in the past. One Egyptian observer made the distinction between the "quantity" of the Muslim Brotherhood and the "quality" of the multiple small Islamic associations (*jama'at*), which had the advantage vis-à-vis the authorities of being difficult to pin down.[174] Islamist student societies at most university campuses continued to constitute a significant element in militant Islam. Commenting on the fragmentation, Shaykh 'Abdallah al-Samawi, recognized as the spiritual leader by certain adherents of the militant Jihad movement, explained that while there were no real differences between the "thousands" of groups, fragmentation originated in the fact that "everybody wishes to be a leader [of one]."[175]

Of earlier waves of militant Islamic activity, only partly suppressed by the authorities, one of Sadat's assassins, 'Abbud al-Zumur, was still serving a life sentence. An official statement in July indicated that 1,225 Jihad members were under arrest, of whom 305 had been put on trial.[176] The blind "ideologue" of the movement (the Egyptian authorities consistently referred to a single movement), 'Umar 'Abd al-Rahman, acquitted of charges of subversion in 1990, was living in New York, and apparently was no longer a cause for concern to the regime.[177]

The trial of the assassins of Assembly Speaker Rif'at al-Mahjub, which opened on 12 October 1990, served as a reminder that the protracted confrontation with the Jihad militants was far from over[178] (see *MECS* 1990, p. 322). Only 13 of the 25 accused were present, the others having evaded capture. One had been killed in a shoot-out at his hiding place in Giza, another had been wounded while resisting arrest, and the most important defendant, Safwat 'Abd al-Ghani, who was the leader of the organization's military wing, had escaped while being escorted to exams at the university in Bani Suwayf, although later, in July, he was caught again, in Upper Egypt.[179] One of the defendants confessed that the Jihad "had weapons and explosives and is planning to create chaos and forcefully overthrow the regime. This operation is based on the rule of Islamic jurisprudence decreed by the organization's prominent leaders that makes it a duty to personally remove any vice."[180] Another defendant, the leader of the Jihad in Alexandria, confessed that the movement had destroyed stores and a church by arson, instigated the murder of a policeman, possessed arms illegally, and falsified identity cards.[181] The arrest and trials of Jihad members continued throughout the year.[182]

A relatively new type of crime carried out by the more violent Islamic associations, including Jihad, was armed robberies of jewelry stores — a large number of them owned by Copts — and luxury villas in Cairo and Alexandria in broad daylight, with the perpetrators often dressed in police uniform.[183] A new association engaging in this type of operation, although later officially pronounced eliminated, was the *Wathiqun min al-nasr* ("Those who have trust in the victory" — apparently an allusion to the Gulf War). It included a group of Islamic militants who had been arrested in the 1980s for demonstrating and perpetrating violence and were since released. They were thought to have split away from the Jihad movement in January 1991, possibly after they received a *fatwa* allowing armed robbery of non-Muslim property for the purpose of funding the purchase of arms.[184] Members of another militant group that split away from the Jihad, the *Shawqiyyun,* who also robbed jewelry stores, were caught in June.[185]

Reports published by the leftist newspaper *al-Ahali* in October about some of the poor quarters of greater Cairo, which lacked social services and had become centers of crime, suggested that whole areas had passed out of the control of the authorities and were dominated by Islamic groups.[186] However, it appeared that most of the Islamic-inspired turbulence continued to be focused in Upper Egypt. Searches and arrests among various Islamic groups, often involving shoot-outs, were ongoing features, occurring mostly in the cities but sometimes in villages as well.[187] The London-based

Sawt al-Kuwait al-Duwali published in May an extensive investigative report on Islamic activity in Upper Egypt, ascribing the ongoing tensions both to poverty and to a strained Muslim-Coptic relationship. According to the paper, many of the members of the militant organizations were young people from villages and small towns who had migrated to larger provincial centers, primarily in order to attain higher education. The article estimated the number of members of militant associations aged 15–37 at 5,000, probably an underestimation. It differentiated between the moderate Muslim Brotherhood, the Islamic Jihadiyya Association, the even more radical Jihad itself, the secretive *Salafiyyun* (those taking the path of the *salaf,* the venerated forefathers), and dozens of small groups that had split off from the Jihad, such as *al-Najun min al-nar* (those saved from hell), and some others called *al-Shawqiyyun, al-Harakiyyun,* and *al-Tawaqquf,* all active to one extent or another in the towns of Upper Egypt.[188]

The leaders of Egypt's most veteran fundamentalist movement, the Muslim Brotherhood, appeared to lean over backward in an effort to project a moderate rather than revolutionary image. Questioned about the Brotherhood's solidarity with Iraq during the Gulf War, spokesman Ma'mun al-Hudaybi asserted:

> If you screen our statements you will not find a single sign of identification with the person of Saddam Husayn. What is more, we even opposed him before, when he went to war against Iran....Saddam Husayn is a Ba'thist and I am a Muslim Brother, and he still murders Muslim Brothers. However, Saddam Husayn is one thing, and the Iraqi people another.[189]

Defending himself after returning from an Islamic conference in Sudan in August — a questionable visit against the background of tensions between Egypt and Sudan — he denied any links with Hasan al-Turabi's fundamentalist Islamic National Front and made it clear that the Brotherhood was not interested in the overthrow of governments.[190] Earlier, he had declared that the Brotherhood had "opposed violence since the 1940s."[191] He was even more explicitly moderate in explaining that the Brotherhood demanded civil government and not a religious government composed of 'Ulama. "We will receive Christian brothers into the party, and if one day we will form a government, we will include Christians in it as well, as it will be the government of all Egyptians."[192] The Islamic movements, essentially different from one another in character, and appealing to different social segments of the population, occasionally came into conflict, with incidents occurring between the Muslim Brothers and some of the smaller militant Islamic associations, in certain quarters in Cairo, such as Bulaq, 'Ayn Shams and Imbaba. However, there was also speculation in the press about a possible rapprochement between the militant and moderate streams.[193]

With Muslim Brotherhood Supreme Guide Muhammad Hamid Abu al-Nasr's health declining, speculation in the press about his successor surfaced, or rather resurfaced, inasmuch as his election following the death of his predecessor, 'Umar al-Tilmisani, had never been fully accepted. The likely contender was Mustafa Mashhur, like Abu al-Nasr a veteran member of the Guidance Bureau, but apparently he was unacceptable to the influential Sayf al-Din al-Banna and Ma'mun al-Hudaybi, both of whom were sons of former supreme guides.[194] Interestingly, the name of Muhammad al-Ghazzali was put forward as a possible successor. Ghazzali, a renowned 'Alim but not a leading activist in the Brotherhood, had taken an unambiguous stand against the Iraqi occupation of Kuwait and the Gulf War, unlike the leaders of the Brotherhood.[195]

An ongoing court case that had begun in 1990, and that continued to stir Islamic emotions, was the trial of the Rayan brothers, owners of a bankrupt Islamic investment company. There were hopes that mysterious buyers abroad would finally allow for the repayment to an estimated 800,000 depositors, but there were no concrete developments by the year's end.[196]

As in the past, the government linked Islamic violence with drugs and crime but failed to come up with solutions for the Islamic predicament.[197] Measures were increased to bring private mosques under government control or to turn them into integrative community centers, to limit the length of the sermons (*khutbas*) and, in general, to launch an educational drive that would moderate Islamic extremism.[198] As in the recent past, the government continued to sponsor symposia and public meetings led by Azharites and other establishment 'Ulama with the aim of offsetting Islamic militancy, or more specifically of defending government policy (e.g., the peace conference).[199] However, the arrest and conviction of author 'Ala Ahmad, who wrote a supposedly heretical book, and of his publisher, showed an inconsistency in policy.[200]

Intercommunal Tensions

Intercommunal relations between Egypt's Muslim majority and its Coptic minority, which comprised 6% of the population, had been strained ever since 1979 due to the emergence of Islamic fundamentalism (see *MECS* 1979–80, pp. 329–32), and intermittently previously as well. The Copts chafed at gross underrepresentation in the assembly, with only seven deputies (five of them presidential appointees), the continued imposition of Ottoman restrictions on the construction of churches, and discrimination in the civil service.[201] While Muslim-Coptic friction was a constant feature in the towns of Upper Egypt, for the first time since 1981 serious disturbances took place in Cairo itself during 1991. Tension had been building up for some time in Imbaba, a mixed neighborhood of southern rural migrants in the Giza district, erupting in violent clashes after the feast of the Virgin Mary on 20 September and lasting for three days. There was no agreement as to who had started the violence, with Islamic activists accused of having attacked Copts and their property as a result of a Coptic butcher playing cassettes of Christian liturgical songs too loudly, or as a result of alleged immoral video showings in a Coptic coffee shop. Others claimed that a Coptic butcher had shot a Muslim customer. Minister of Interior Musa, in an attempt to play down the disturbances, ascribed them to "a simple scuffle between a Christian and a Muslim...over a money dispute," and the governor of the Giza district described them as "sporadic and insignificant incidents," but Coptic spokesmen cited false rumors that a Christian had killed a Muslim. Tension was raised during the days of the rioting by certain provocative Islamist sermons, an Islamist procession during which such slogans as "Copts are the enemies of Allah" were shouted, and attacks on Coptic pedestrians. By the time the wave of incidents had ended, some 18 people were wounded, one church was burned down and another was damaged as a result of arson, several stores and coffee shops were vandalized, and apartments were wrecked. Although several policemen had been injured as well, apparently the police had been slow to interfere.[202] Limited criticism of the government for ignoring "religious extremism" appeared in the press, as did an appeal by NPUG leader Rif'at al-Sa'id to President Mubarak to visit the neighborhood in order "to lay the cornerstone for the rebuilding of the church that was burned down."[203] The appeal was unanswered.

There were, however, several local Muslim-Coptic meetings held in an effort at conciliation.[204]

FOREIGN RELATIONS

EGYPT AND THE ARAB AND ISLAMIC WORLDS

The Gulf War undoubtedly inflicted new pains on the minds of those striving for Arab unity, proving that the gap between ideals and realities was as great as ever. Egypt, maneuvering skillfully on the diplomatic level, tried to maintain its regional leadership and enhance whatever historical prestige it enjoyed on the pan-Arab level, while keeping open all possible options for reconciliation with its rivals in the future.

The Arab League Council, with Iraq participating, met in Cairo in March, returning to its historic headquarters after 12 years, which Egypt's official press agency, MENA, hailed as "a major step down the road of restoring Arab solidarity and opening a new chapter in intra-Arab relations." Former Foreign Minister 'Ismat 'Abd al-Majid, elected in May as secretary-general, committed himself to solving such regional problems as the food gap, inadequate water supply and technological development. And significantly, proposals were put forward by the Egyptian Consultative (*Shura*) Council, a body mainly composed of experienced politicians, to revise the League's charter and turn it into a more effective organization. Such ideas were not yet discussed by the League, but clearly reflected the trauma of the Gulf crisis. They envisaged holding Arab summit conferences under the auspices of the League, forming an Arab parliament modeled on the European example, and establishing an Arab defense council.[205]

Egypt had hoped, during and after the Gulf War, to use the framework of the "six-plus-two" military coalition — the six members of the GCC, Syria and Egypt — to lay the foundations for postwar regional security and economic cooperation (see also chapter on inter-Arab relations). It expected to play a dominant role in a future regional peacekeeping force by supplying the largest contingent of troops, with Western troops and navies remaining "over the horizon," not immediately visible but available on call. This "new order" in the ME was outlined in the Damascus declaration, drawn up in Damascus on 16 March, which focused on coordination and cooperation in political and security affairs among the "six-plus-two," the holding of a regional peace conference, disarmament of weapons of mass destruction, and regional socioeconomic development. Several meetings were held in Cairo, Damascus and elsewhere, and intensive diplomatic contacts, including several short visits by President Mubarak to the Gulf states, centered around this issue along with bilateral matters such as financial aid.[206]

However, the Damascus declaration soon became an empty vessel. Egypt, hoping to achieve recognition of its regional military hegemony, felt rebuffed by the US, which opposed the exclusion of non-Arab powers from future security arrangements in the Gulf. Egypt also felt betrayed by the Gulf states, in particular by Kuwait, which essentially endorsed the American position, with the exception of advocating a different, more cautious, approach to the role of Iran.[207] "They want blue-eyed soldiers to protect them," an Arab journalist remarked, reflecting a sense of bitterness in Egypt, but basically Egypt accepted the new situation with self-respect and speedily withdrew its forces from the Gulf, drawing the correct conclusion that its presence had "to be accepted, invited and welcomed." As a senior Egyptian official explained, "pride is very important."[208]

This disappointment, if not setback, did not enhance the Gulf states' popularity, and particularly Kuwait's, in Egypt's view. Historical, psychological and economic factors were also involved. Some mutual disdain of "pure Arabs" as the Arabs of the peninsula felt themselves, versus "7,000 years of civilization," of which the Egyptians could boast, had always been extant. However, Egyptian resentment was exacerbated by a perception of ingratitude in the Gulf and a tendency there to play down Egypt's contribution to the war, even though the emir of Kuwait publicly expressed his gratitude on several occasions.

Disappointment with Kuwait was compounded when no significant financial assistance was forthcoming after the war as Egypt had anticipated, with the Gulf states adhering generally to restrictive World Bank conditions. Egypt also had hoped to get a share of the postwar reconstruction work in Kuwait, both in terms of contracts and labor opportunities, but Egyptian contractors were bypassed in favor of American and European ones. "After the Gulf War, a new war broke out over reconstruction contracts," commented the weekly *Ruz al-Yusuf* in late March. *Akhir Sa'a* reported in October that only 90,000 Egyptians had returned to Kuwait, as compared to 230,000 who had worked there before the war, and that not all of them had steady jobs as before. Relations were further marred by the treatment accorded to some of the Egyptian workers because of suspected collaboration with the Iraqis or because of technical transgressions, a topic raised by Egypt several times in frequent high-level bilateral talks between the two countries.[209] Kuwait's image vis-à-vis Egyptian public opinion was further damaged by the arrest in Cairo of Talal Nasr Al Sabah, a nephew of the emir, for drug trafficking, which also reflected a more assertive attitude by the authorities after the Gulf War and according to *The New York Times*, "a departure from the Egyptian policy of tolerance towards visiting Arab royal figures."[210]

Though formal relations with Iraq remained strained as a result of the war, they were more modified at the unofficial level. Media commentators made a fine distinction between Saddam Husayn and the Iraqi people. "The leadership that planned the adventure of the occupation of Kuwait, defied the entire world, destroyed all the bridges with the East, the West, the North and the South, went into a miscalculated battle against forces stronger than its own, and exposed the country to devastation and humiliation, cannot in any circumstance whatsoever continue to wield power," said Radio Cairo in a commentary in late March. The press speculated as to a possible successor, with some support said to be given by Egypt to Iraqi opposition groups in Cairo. There were even suggestions, such as that put forward by veteran journalist Mustafa Amin, to try the Iraqi president for war crimes.[211] Nevertheless, it was clear that Egypt wished to keep the option of a future rapprochement open or at least did not wish to punish Iraq beyond liberating Kuwait. President Mubarak, in his 33rd message of the year to President Saddam Husayn, in July, urged him to comply with the UN resolutions and warned the Iraqi people against more "unwarranted and unequal battles." The press also published unequivocally negative reactions to a possible second round of US bombings.[212] Similarly, commentators and politicians urged lifting the economic sanctions against Iraq as an act of sympathy with its people, not its leader, during the months following the war.[213] No meaningful rapprochement was initiated in 1991, however, even though Iraqi representatives did attend meetings of the Arab League and its related organizations in Cairo.

Relations with Jordan suffered badly from King Husayn's pro-Iraqi stand in the war, which was perceived in Cairo as outrageous, and thereafter by the King's White Paper published in August which constituted a defense of his policy. However, the relationship gradually improved after a visit to Cairo by Jordanian Foreign Minister 'Abdallah al-Nusur in September. Part of this improvement was due to Egypt's desire to coordinate positions with regard to the upcoming peace conference[214] (see below).

Egypt continued to be considerably concerned about the developments in Sudan, its southern neighbor, traditionally a focus of interest and anxiety. Relations that had been ambivalent for some time ever since the regime of Gen. 'Umar al-Bashir had taken an Islamic course and Hasan al-Turabi's Islamic Front had become powerful, were exacerbated by Sudan's position during the Gulf War. An *al-Jumhuriyya* editorial lashed out at the Sudanese ruler with the question: "Do Islamic principles encourage bloodshed and do they incite people to attack their own brothers and abandon human ethics and values?" President Mubarak demonstrated his disapproval by refusing to engage in a direct dialogue with President Bashir at a quadripartite meeting, involving Syrian President Hafiz al-Asad and Libyan President Mu'ammar al-Qadhdhafi, held in Misurata in January.[215] The outbreak of the war elicited explicit Egyptian warnings to Sudan against positioning Iraqi missiles or fighter planes on Sudanese soil, which could threaten the Aswan Dam. Moreover, following demonstrations in Khartoum in January, mutual deportations took place.[216] Mutual recriminations appeared in the media of both countries during the year, but the desire to improve the poor relationship and reach some form of dialogue was also expressed. This hope, however, was frustrated when Sudan initiated a rapprochement with Iran in the fall.[217]

Relations with Yemen, too, deteriorated as a result of its stand during the Gulf War, manifested in anti-Egyptian demonstrations in San'a and the expulsion of Yemen's ambassador in Cairo after he had insulted an Egyptian bank employee. However, Egyptian-Yemeni relations began to improve in the spring following a secret visit to Cairo by Yemeni President 'Ali 'Abdallah Salih in April, as well as by Foreign Minister Dr. 'Abd al-Karim Iryani in May.[218]

One of the more conspicuous developments in Egypt's regional position was the ongoing improvement in relations with its western neighbor, Libya, with which it had had an abortive union, sharp conflict and even a war, within the two previous decades. In a strange convergence of interests, a rapprochement emerged which, although falling short of President Qadhdhafi's dream of unity with Egypt, was significant nevertheless. After three summit meetings with Qadhdhafi (see *MECS* 1990, chapters on Egypt and Libya), Mubarak paid his first official visit to Tripoli in April, followed by additional visits to Libya later in the year, including attendance at the inauguration of the great man-made river project (see chapter on Libya). Qadhdhafi reciprocated with several visits to Egypt, despite a past commitment not to set foot in Cairo so long as the Israeli flag flew there. The talks centered on bilateral issues such as the back payments to Egyptian workers who had been expelled from Libya in 1985, plans for cooperation in technology, industry, oil drilling, trade, and manpower supply, and the peace process with Israel, a major topic on which the two continued to disagree.

An attack during a public appearance by Libyan Vice President 'Abd al-Salam al-Jalud on the Camp David accords and on the late President Sadat in October led to some tension between the two countries, with an immediate negative impact expressing itself in harassment at the border, but a major crisis was avoided.[219]

The closure of the Libyan-Egyptian border in 1977, and its formal reopening in May 1989 (see *MECS* 1989, p. 545) had to a large extent reflected the past relationship between the two countries. In April, Libya symbolically demolished its border gate near al-Salum, and the Libyan-Egyptian border was opened with no restrictions in August. Later that month, 16,000 Egyptians and Libyans were reported to be crossing the border daily in both directions, with an attendant brisk exchange of commodities.[220] Possibly the most important aspect of the open border, however, was that it marked the beginning of a new episode in Egypt's attempts to solve its population problem by settling *fellahin* abroad. After unhappy earlier experiences in resettlement in Sudan, Syria, Libya itself, and most recently with Iraq and Kuwait, the great man-made river project (although the subject of debate by experts in Egypt owing to the possibility that it might result in the salination of groundwater in Upper Egypt) held out the hope that within a year, no fewer than 1m. Egyptians could be settled in Libya. The project was to start with 100 *fellahin* and 400 professional families settling on plots of 15 *feddan* (15.5 acres) each, at a token cost to the settlers, in new rural communities along the Libyan-Egyptian border.[221]

In view of Egypt's improved ties with Libya, and its enhanced prestige vis-à-vis the US, Egypt, playing the role of regional power broker, urged the US in March to revise its negative attitude toward Libyan President Qadhdhafi, who, it argued, was "showing signs of restraining his militant behavior." The new relationship between Egypt and Libya was demonstrated even more explicitly in November and thereafter when the Lockerbie affair led to renewed Western pressure on Libya, as well as a military threat (see chapter on Libya), evoking strongly worded warnings in the Egyptian media against another American military attack on Libya. President Mubarak, concerned that an American attack would "torpedo the peace conference," phoned President Bush to counsel restraint and stood by Libya, "a new state that calls for achieving stability and condemns terror throughout the world." Egypt's opposition parties similarly expressed their "full support for the Libyan people in its stand against the threats of aggression by the US and Great Britain."[222]

Egypt's earlier rapprochement with Syria, begun in 1989, resulted in frequent high-level contacts between the two countries on the Gulf crisis and the Madrid peace conference, and new agreements on trade, technological cooperation, and educational and cultural exchange, but no broader political alliance. Nevertheless, after cooperating with Syria in the Gulf War coalition, Egypt, along with the US, could claim some success in influencing Syria to adopt a more flexible position and participate in the Madrid peace conference and the ensuing bilateral talks with Israel under the conditions worked out by Secretary of State Baker.[223]

PLO Chairman Yasir 'Arafat, more than any other supporter of Saddam Husayn, including Jordan's King Husayn, became a particular target of Egyptian wrath. *Al-Jumhuriyya* columnist Muhammad al-Hayawan, in an open letter, called for his resignation, charging: "Your crime against the Palestinian people is worse than what Saddam did against the Iraqi people and army; Saddam acts in stupidity but you function deliberately." An even more extreme statement was issued by the renowned establishment journalist Musa Sabri: "You are a corrupt war criminal, you clown. You betrayed those who fed you and meanly stabbed those who helped you. You are the clown of every circus....It is time you retire...away from us, you treacherous bloodsucker." But in spite of these bitter outbursts, Egyptian spokesmen were aware that "no solution of the Palestinian cause is possible without the PLO's participation."[224] The Palestinian issue remained high on the Egyptian agenda, reflected in frequent press articles on the Intifada and on Israeli policy in the occupied territories.

Top-level PLO delegations, though not led by Yasir 'Arafat himself, resumed frequent visits to Cairo from May onward after having shunned Egypt during the Gulf crisis and war, and participated in political deliberations in connection with the peace process. The first encounter between Mubarak and 'Arafat after the Gulf crisis took place at Benghazi on 29 August, on the occasion of the great man-made river inauguration, with Mubarak making it clear in typically Egyptian diplomatic idiom that "Egypt was the one that sought consultation with the Palestinians when there appeared signs on the horizon of a possible political solution to the Palestinian problem." As an outcome of this meeting, an ad hoc joint Egyptian-Palestinian committee was established as a vehicle for talks during the coming months. 'Arafat visited Cairo on 22 October and 9 November and was received by President Mubarak and Foreign Minister 'Amr Musa. While the performance of the Palestinian delegation in Madrid was praised by journalist Anis Mansur in *al-Ahram* for its effectiveness, Egyptian delegates advised the PLO not to reject the idea of autonomy for the occupied territories, with the Foreign Ministry dispatching two advisers to the Palestinian delegation to share its experience in peacemaking with Israel.[225]

Developments in Algeria during 1991, in particular the growing strength of the Front Islamique du Salut (FIS), elicited divided reactions by the Egyptian public. Part of it blamed the ruling Front de Libération National (FLN), while the fundamentalists condemned the Algerian Government's suppression of the Islamic movement, as well as the Tunisian Government's measures against its Islamic opposition, and sympathized with the FIS. The Muslim Brothers stopped short of outright practical support, thus forestalling any accusations of insubordination by the Egyptian authorities. Muslim Brotherhood Supreme Guide Muhammad Hamid Abu al-Nasr, declaring himself shocked by developments in Algeria and Sudan, exhorted: "Rulers should not oppress!"[226] Spokesman Hudaybi, however, at least in public, took issue with the FIS, as well as with the Sudanese Islamic Front.[227] There was also a measure of anxiety in Egypt over the possible impact of the developments in Algeria.[228] An editorial in the government-sponsored *al-Jumhuriyya,* published on the occasion of a visit to Cairo by Tunisian Prime Minister Hamid Qarawi, reflected the prevailing feeling in Egypt by pointing out that "both countries adhere to Islamic principles, but it is no secret to anyone that the extremists, hiding behind a religion that does not acknowledge them, harbor a blatant enmity to democracy and to the pillars of civil society."[229]

Diplomatic relations with the Islamic Republic of Iran were formally restored in March after a break of 12 years, ever since the late President Sadat had refused to extradite the Shah and had branded Ayatollah Khomeyni a madman. Relations had been tense under Mubarak as well, although there had been a measure of rapprochement from late 1989 onward. The decision to renew diplomatic ties was undoubtedly accelerated by the Gulf War, although Iranian ambitions, both in the Gulf and in the global Islamic context, continued to be viewed circumspectly in the Egyptian press. Indeed, Iran's negative attitude toward the Camp David accords and toward the peace conference, in addition to its views on security in the Gulf, prevented any further development in relations.[230]

Egypt's own involvement in Islamic affairs was conservative, aimed at emphasizing its pivotal role in this arena too, but at the same time rejecting radical views. The government-sponsored Supreme Council for Islamic Affairs convened in Cairo in April with the participation of *waqf* ministers from abroad, while Egypt's Foreign Minister 'Amr Musa participated in meetings of the foreign ministers of the Islamic Conference Organization (ICO) held in Istanbul and Dakar, proposing an Islamic nonaggression pact at the latter meeting.[231]

RELATIONS WITH ISRAEL AND THE PEACE PROCESS

The "cold" peace between Egypt and Israel continued to be strained by mutual recriminations, but was kept up nevertheless because of important regional and global interests on both sides, as was indeed illustrated by the Gulf crisis and the peace process. "It is not the peace we hoped for," wrote a senior journalist for the *Jerusalem Post*. "Twelve years after Egypt and Israel signed their historic peace treaty many Egyptians still share a cold, even hostile indifference to Israel — like neighbors who keep the blinds pulled because they find the family next door unpleasant," commented a *New York Times* correspondent.[232] How precarious relations between the two countries were, and how carefully Egypt still had to balance its connections with Israel vis-à-vis the Arab arena, became clear during the UN General Assembly vote of 16 December 1991 on canceling the 1975 resolution which equated Zionism with racism. Egypt, though pressed by Israel and the US to vote in favor, declined to take part in the vote. Resentment in Israel on this issue, juxtaposed with Egypt's critical attitude toward Israel's peace policy generally, reflected the differences in expectations that both countries had on the peace issue.[233] There was a subtle, though not always schematic, distinction between Egypt's official spokesmen and the establishment media, which tended to focus on major political differences between Egypt and Israel on the occupied territories and on Palestinian issues, and the opposition parties and press, which often expressed themselves in a rather less diplomatic way.

The Gulf War served to divert attention from the bilateral relations between the two countries, with Egypt intently concerned about keeping Israel out of the war, with American assistance, lest active Israeli involvement complicate the situation.[234] President Mubarak stated that "he had warned the US...stressing that the situation would change completely if Israel intervened," by which he undoubtedly meant an Israeli military advancement into Jordan.[235] Initially, Mubarak denied that Iraq had the capability to strike Israel, but when *Scud*s actually hit Israel, anxiety in Egypt was heightened. The *Scud* attacks, while not openly condemned at first, were later criticized in the press as "political missiles" with the aim of provoking Israel.[236] When Israel did not retaliate, opposition circles, perennially critical, interpreted its restraint as a further strategy "to reap the benefits of Iraqi stupidity." Israel, in the view of some Arab strategic experts, had made gains it had never dreamt of, such as gaining an antimissile air defense system from the US, complete muting of the Intifada, and acquiring a new image internationally as a country besieged.[237] Exceptional as a publicly expressed opinion was the view of Nobel prize laureate Najib Mahfuz, who praised Israel for its "superior wisdom."[238]

"The joint predicament of the Arab world and Israel during the Gulf War should form a starting point for a political settlement that will end the Arab-Israeli conflict," wrote the noted historian and columnist, 'Abd al-'Azim Ramadan, soon after the war was over.[239] Indeed, the prevailing feeling in both the Egyptian and Israeli establishment during March and April was that options for new regional arrangements had been created.[240] The partial neutralization of Iraq's weapons of mass destruction led to a greater focus on Israel's nuclear potential as well, and criticism by establishment newspapers of renewed American ideas suggesting the transforming of Israel into a permanent emergency base, thereby "stockpiling weapons and bypassing peace," as one paper described it.[241] In Egyptian thinking, new regional arrangements required Israel to make concessions, give up its "outdated [security] concepts," and refrain from "provocations [against the Arabs]."[242]

Egypt's diplomatic efforts during the post-Gulf War period were directed at obtaining Israel's consent to holding a peace conference. Simultaneously, there was general condemnation in the press of Israel's "intransigence" and "sabotage" of peace efforts,[243] part of which related to controversy over the sensitive issue of Palestinian representation at the conference, in particular representation from East Jerusalem[244] (see also chapter on the ME peace process). Considerable criticism in the political establishment, as well as in the press, focused on the issue of the settlements in the occupied territories throughout the year. They were seen as "barring peace," "provocations," and as one of "those weapons Israel will use as a last resort to stop the wheel of peace."[245] However, President Mubarak's proposal that "if Israel halts building settlements in the occupied Arab territories, it is possible that the Arab countries would take a corresponding step and end the Arab boycott of Israel" was not taken up by Israel. In his Revolution Day speech on 23 July, Mubarak called upon Israel to show responsibility, and in November he charged that the settlements were being set up for the purpose of haggling, which, he said, "is the Israeli nature."[246]

The influx of new immigrants from the Soviet Union and Ethiopia to Israel was observed with much anxiety, lest the need for land and water would radically change the status of the territories or even lead to a population "transfer." Foreign Minister 'Amr Musa on several public occasions urged Israel not to settle new immigrants in the occupied territories. This anxiety was played up by the opposition, with the parliamentary chairman of the Wafd, Yasin Siraj al-Din, describing immigration to Israel as "one of the most dangerous problems of the twentieth century," at a symposium on the subject.[247] The export of bricks from Egypt to Israel, supposedly being used for the building of new settlements, was scathingly criticized in the opposition press.[248] Israel's imposition of curfews and deportations, and its conduct regarding the Intifada generally, were also repeatedly condemned by official sources.[249] A search for illegal material undertaken by Israeli police in the East Jerusalem Shari'a Court in November evoked heated reactions in Egypt, with the establishment *al-Akhbar* accusing Israel of being a "renegade state."[250] Egyptian spokesmen were also "extremely concerned" about the Israeli presence in Southern Lebanon and condemned raids and bombings several times, adding to the strained atmosphere.[251]

By June, existing bilateral cultural exchange agreements between the two countries

— the sort of agreements often used as diplomatic leverage — were under considerable strain, eliciting a denial by Foreign Minister Musa that Egypt was cutting back on them,[252] while rumors circulated about the recall of Ambassador Basyuni from Tel Aviv.[253] The US continued to play a pivotal role in Egypt's relationship with Israel, advising both countries against worsening relations and publicly indicating support for the Arab position on the question of the settlements.[254] In this context, there was a certain amount of praise in the press for President Bush's withholding of loan guarantees that Israel had requested for absorbing new immigrants.[255] Bilateral trade relations were kept at a minimal level, with Egypt's exports to Israel, excluding oil, amounting to only $11,000, or 1% of its total exports, in 1991,[256] although a pilot farm project which Israel sponsored away from the limelight was reported to be developing well.[257] Tourism from Israel to Egypt (100,000 Israelis visited Egypt in 1990, while 3,000 Egyptians came to Israel), down during the Gulf crisis, was quick to recover.[258]

In the atmosphere of the crucial issues at stake in the region during the year, occasional incidents between the two countries assumed only secondary importance. In July, Egyptian authorities arrested 12 Israeli ocean scientists on a ship in the Red Sea, accusing them of violating Egyptian territorial waters but they were soon released.[259] Negotiations over family reunification in the border town of Rafah, which had stalled when Egypt halted payments, were resumed in October.[260] Long-standing Egyptian charges that Israel removed antiquities from the Sinai when it was under Israeli rule were officially raised for the first time by an Egyptian delegation visiting Israel in November, but the matter remained pending.[261] Mutual border violations were discussed at periodic meetings of the joint military committee. According to the Egyptians, in October, the number of cases was on the decline.[262] However, on 12 November, four Arab infiltrators were killed near Mount Harif in the Negev by an Israeli patrol, the first such incident in a year (see *MECS* 1990, p. 344). Egypt denied any responsibility, claiming that there was no proof that the four had crossed the border from Egypt.[263]

An invitation to Israeli Foreign Minister David Levy to visit Egypt on 29–31 July was obviously intended as a means to achieve progress on the peace process, as Levy was deemed to be more pliable than Shamir. "There is a golden opportunity now to make peace. We want to know if the Israeli Government really means peace or not," an Egyptian official declared.[264] Levy's visit was the first by an Israeli government minister since then-defense minister Rabin had been invited to Egypt in September 1989, and the first by a Likud minister since then-foreign minister Moshe Arens had been there in February of that year, and was covered extensively by the Egyptian media in widely divergent terms ranging from the positive to the negative. Levy met with his counterpart 'Amr Musa, Deputy Prime Minister Butrus-Ghali, members of the People's Assembly, and twice with President Mubarak on "all aspects of the peace process," and, while he appeared to establish considerable personal rapport with the Egyptian leaders, there was no breakthrough on the peace process, nor on the issue of Palestinian representation at the forthcoming peace conference in particular. "I have not come to discuss a compromise, and essential positions are not subject to negotiation," Levy stated.[265] In a later meeting at the UN, Levy and Musa "agreed to disagree" on the issue of freezing the establishment of new settlements.[266]

An invitation to seven younger-generation Labor members of the Knesset (MKs) to visit Egypt in June and meet with a number of cabinet ministers and other dignitaries, which according to Egyptian sources was "intended to contribute to the stalled peace process," came under considerable attack from opposition Knesset members who charged Egypt with domestic interference and a preference for "Labor doves," while a parliamentarian from the right-wing Tehiya Party attacked the delegation itself for its "act of national irresponsibility."[267] The result of the criticism in Israel was that, unprecedentedly, a Likud delegation was also invited and held a similar round of talks in Cairo. Its leader, party spokesman Gil Samsonov, expressing his view that the delegation had contributed to the chances for peace, declared that "it is now clear to the Egyptians that they had erred for the past eight years by ignoring the Likud government."[268] Another Likud delegation, consisting of veteran Israeli MKs, arrived in Cairo in October, after the visit had been delayed as a result of a scathing attack on Housing Minister Ariel Sharon in the Egyptian press following Sharon's announcement of the establishment of new settlements around Jerusalem.[269] At the year's end, Israeli Minister of Religious Affairs Avner Shaki, a member of the National Religious Party, visited Cairo at the invitation of Minister Butrus-Ghali and met with dignitaries such as the Mufti of Egypt, Shaykh al-Tantawi and the Coptic Pope Shenuda.[270] However, the effect of these visits on the existing positions of the various Israeli coalition parties was minimal.

President Mubarak sent several messages to Prime Minister Shamir during the course of the year, urging Israel to agree to a peace conference and show greater flexibility.[271] In an interview with the prominent Egyptian journalist, Anis Mansur, Shamir expressed his conviction "that Egypt has a major role to play in the peace process because it is the largest Arab state, it has experience in dealing with Israel, and President Mubarak enjoys widespread respect."[272] However, no meeting materialized between the Egyptian president and the Israeli prime minister, who had not met since September 1982, although it was advocated strongly by Israeli spokesmen.[273] While Israeli newspapers speculated that Mubarak feared "embarrassing statements" from Shamir, it was also clear that there was a lack of chemistry between the two, or, as a prominent Egyptian psychiatrist said, "One is stubborn in a positive way, the other in a conservative way."[274] Mubarak displayed pessimism, bordering on criticism and irritation about the Israeli prime minister's intentions regarding the peace process, predicting in July that Shamir would come to the peace conference but would then promulgate elections and stall the peace process.[275] In November, Mubarak granted a rare interview to Israeli television, prompting an idle demand by Shamir to get "equal time" on Egyptian television.[276] Earlier, NDP Secretary-General and Agriculture Minister Yusuf Wali, meeting with the younger-generation Likud delegation in Egypt, was reported to have extended an "open invitation" to Prime Minister Shamir, but it was not taken seriously.[277]

Most of the visits by Egyptian dignitaries to Israel were kept in low profile. Egypt's deputy foreign minister Fawzi al-Ibrashi delivered a speech at Tel Aviv University in which he urged the halting of Israel's settlement policy.[278] Deputy chairman of the NDP Mustafa Khalil, a former prime minister, attended the Israeli Labor Party's congress in November and also met with Foreign Minister Levy. Levy also received a delegation of five Egyptian parliamentarians that month.[279] However, an invitation extended by Levy to Musa did not materialize in a visit, nor did a planned visit by Minister of Tourism Fu'ad Sultan take place.[280]

Israel's image in the Egyptian media, particularly in the opposition press, remained negative on the whole. Prime Minister Shamir was consistently depicted as evil and predatory and was the subject of numerous personal attacks and vituperative caricatures, which, for example, labeled him "another Saddam Husayn," or a terrorist.[281] A portion of the press also continued to publish bizarre accusations and conspiracy stories, as in previous years. A columnist in the Wafd newspaper alleged that Israel permitted the *Scuds* to penetrate its airspace in order to have an excuse to occupy the East Bank and continue using the West Bank for its settlements, while letting Saddam Husayn have the Gulf.[282] Even an establishment newspaper, *Akhir Sa'a*, ran an article predicting that Israel would bomb the Aqsa Mosque and claim it had been hit by Iraqi missiles.[283] Other articles accused Israel of trying to harm Egyptian agriculture and its tourism industry, undermining the economy by means of counterfeit dollars and society by drugs or Aids, planning to deplete Egypt's water reserves, and using the Israel Academic Center in Cairo for espionage purposes. The trial of Ayman Hasan, the Egyptian soldier who had crossed into the Negev and murdered four Israelis and wounded another 24 on the highway a dozen kilometers north of Eilat in November 1990, and his subsequent sentencing to 12 years of imprisonment and hard labor, evoked a certain amount of empathy for the accused, especially in Islamic circles. Similarly, Sayyid Nusayr, the Egyptian who had murdered Kach leader Rabbi Meir Kahana, received sympathetic coverage during his trial in New York.[284] When questioned about the hostile anti-Israel tone in the press, Egyptian spokesmen generally referred to the freedom of the press and democratization.

THE PEACE CONFERENCE IN MADRID

The convening of the peace conference in Madrid from 30 October till 1 November was the outcome of numerous overt and secret contacts, principally reflecting the efforts of US Secretary of State James Baker (for a detailed discussion, see chapter on the ME peace process). Ultimately, it refuted the skepticism as to the feasibility of bringing together all ME parties expressed by the press and by politicians during the months following the Gulf War. Egypt, having successfully concluded a peace agreement with Israel, and considering itself the leading diplomatic force in the region, took the lead in consulting, coordinating and promoting the idea of the conference. However, it had to take conflicting Arab interests as well as domestic opposition into account, and so it tried to function essentially as a catalyst. "If somebody is in need of help, we will help," Mubarak declared.[285]

Egyptian expectations, as reflected in numerous articles in the press, ranged in tone from skeptical (especially owing to Israel's stand) to realistic. A prominent commentator wrote: "Although the Madrid peace conference received the support of the overwhelming majority of Egyptian public opinion-molders, this overwhelming majority itself continues to suspect the objectives of the Israeli leadership and the degree of its preparedness to take steps forward to peace." However, the same journalist, in an optimistic mood, drew attention to changes in the international climate that were favorable to the Arabs.[286] "Peace is no luxury, but a need," said Foreign Minister 'Amr Musa, expressing the regime's position. Reactions in the street appeared to be passive, but government spokesmen constantly felt a need to defend Egypt's prominent role in the conference, brushing aside opposition attacks with the argument that the Palestinians themselves participated in this conference with Israel.[287]

President Mubarak, speaking at an NDP meeting in November, urged "patience" and "determination."[288]

Significantly, Egypt's delegation to Madrid, led by Foreign Minister 'Amr Musa, included several personalities who had been former adversaries of the Camp David accords, such as veteran leftist journalist Lutfi al-Khuli. Interviewed by Israeli television, he spoke sarcastically about "Israel and its Arab neighbors now being trapped in the peace cage." Sometime later he commented that "negotiations at the conference are nothing but the conduct of conflict through new means, but they do not form a substitute for the means of negotiations which are in fact used between the [Palestinian] people and the occupation."[289] Most of the opposition welcomed the peace conference in principle, although they did so reservedly and not all in the same voice.[290]

Of all the opposition forces, the Islamic groups, and particularly the Muslim Brotherhood, were the most adamantly antagonistic. They argued that the conference represented "a submission to the Zionist entity," that the US would satisfy Israeli territorial demands, that the Jerusalem issue would be removed from the conference table, and that the Palestine question would be circumvented. According to Muslim Brothers' spokesman Ma'mun al-Hudaybi, the conference would simply lead to a document "which would efface the name of Palestine and abolish the [Arab] boycott, thereby increasing the penetration of the Zionist entity into the Arab countries and Islamic states." The Palestinian question could be settled only by Jihad, which, according to Hudaybi, was not only a matter of battle but of money and manpower as well.[291] The Brotherhood convened a mass meeting in Helwan on Friday 25 October, under the slogan: "Islam does not sanction peace with usurpers of Islamic lands and holy places," and Supreme Guide Muhammad Hamid Abu al-Nasr published statements accusing the US of "taking advantage of our Islamic nation's weakness" and "selling out the Palestine question...for the benefit of the Jews." Abu al-Nasr emphasized: "We have not, do not and will not negotiate in any way on the Land of Palestine....It would be negotiating our faith and our holy places, denying our fallen, our heroes and our history."[292] Hudaybi, too, warned against "submission to the Zionist entity."[293] Mustafa Mashhur, another Brotherhood leader, revived an old theme when he claimed in an article that the peace conference constituted a foreign conspiracy [against Islam and the Arabs]. Hafiz Salama, a popular and influential preacher although not a Muslim Brother, also saw the peace conference as an American conspiracy.[294]

Spokesmen of the Islamically inclined SLP, although declaring themselves not opposed to the peace conference — only fearful of its results — took an even more blatantly anti-American position.[295] The party's newspaper, al-Sha'b, claimed to have received hundreds of letters opposing the peace conference.[296] In the same vein, the nationalist Young Egypt (Misr al-Fatat) Party accused the Americans of plotting a conspiracy against the Arab people and Islam. The Liberal Party merely called for a closing of the ranks in the hope that American and Soviet pressure would ultimately enforce UN Security Council Resolutions 242 and 338. The Liberals, together with some of the other opposition parties and with physicians' and engineers' associations, organized a mass rally in Alexandria on 27 October, only one of a series of opposition meetings held in those days.[297]

The Physicians' Union organized another mass rally under the slogan "False Peace and Lost Rights," reportedly attended by 20,000 and addressed by leaders of the Muslim Brotherhood, among others.[298] Reportedly 185 persons were arrested during this period, including 15 Muslim Brothers for putting up anti-Jewish posters and others for distributing leaflets opposing the peace conference.[299] Moreover, Minister of Interior 'Abd al-Halim Musa announced the arrest of 67 persons for distributing pamphlets promoting "the idea that killing those who supported the peace conference was legal," identified more explicitly by the weekly *al-Usbu' al-'Arabi* as a *fatwa* by a group of unidentified religious personalities.[300]

The left-wing NPUG was skeptical and internally divided on the peace conference, with Secretary-General Dr. Rif'at al-Sa'id opposed and others in favor. Nevertheless, the party acquiesced to Egypt's participation in the conference, provided that the government would insist on Israeli withdrawal from the occupied territories, and that there was an end to Israeli settlement there, an amendment to the Camp David accords on the creation of an independent Palestinian state, and freedom of speech for opponents of the peace conference.[301] The Nasserists called for Arab unity, while the Wafd, skeptical from the start, saw the conference primarily as an Arab capitulation to US and Israeli interests "to impose peace and to liquidate the Palestinian question," and called for more pressure on Israel instead.[302]

The demonstrations against the peace conference involved a broader spectrum of the population than the opposition to the Gulf War. Several took place at mosques, and cases of anti-Jewish graffiti on walls were reported.[303] The major Islamic demonstrations, however, took place on university campuses, such as at al-Azhar Mosque, where demonstrators took to the street, and in Asyut.[304] Over 3,000 students rallied at Cairo University, chanting antigovernment slogans. They staged a mock procession with Israeli flags and with dozens of participants dressed in rabbinical attire, their heads covered with yarmulkas (Jewish headgear), shouting: "O Jerusalem, do not fear, we love the color of blood. To Jihad, to Jihad, on the way to martyrdom."[305] The events, confined to the university campus, did not elicit violence, and security forces did not interfere. Later, in November, the university was the venue of more balanced public debates on the questions of peace.[306]

The peace conference was considered by some sectors of Egyptian society to be a tactical breakthrough in exposing Arab flexibility as against Israeli obstinacy. "The Arabs gained a great victory at the conference," *May,* an establishment weekly, concluded, "Shamir proved that Israel is based on aggression and expansion."[307]

RELATIONS WITH THE MAJOR POWERS AND THE EUROPEAN COMMUNITY

The Gulf crisis and war and subsequent negotiations to bring about a peace conference involved intensive diplomatic contacts with the US, with relations between the two countries becoming more intense and to some extent closer, though mutual criticism was also leveled from time to time. Egypt made a determined effort to present itself as the major regional power, with constructive ideas on the role and position of other countries as well.

US Secretary of State James Baker paid a total of eight visits to Egypt during the year, in addition to holding talks with his Egyptian counterpart in the US and elsewhere. The first visit, on 12 January, was devoted mainly to a review of the Gulf crisis, with Baker declaring that "once again we join our Egyptian friends and call on Iraq to withdraw [from Kuwait]." He also used the opportunity to call for a ME peace conference "at an appropriate time." During later visits following the war, attention increasingly shifted from regional security arrangements in the Gulf to the promotion of a peace conference, to which Baker devoted extensive shuttle diplomacy and perennially optimistic public statements. In June, US Secretary of Defense Richard Cheney toured the region to examine the question of security in the Gulf.[308]

Baker's arduous negotiations ultimately led to the opening of the conference in Madrid on 30 October. It had been preceded by a great deal of time and effort on his part to solve procedural questions and differences of opinion between the Arab states and the Palestinians with Israel. Some Egyptian commentators criticized this protracted effort as indicating American backing for Israeli intransigence, accused the US of applying "double standards" (e.g., on the issue of disarmament), and called for applying more pressure on Israel.[309] Later, when the American stand was perceived to move closer to Egypt's, as against Israel's position, the establishment press praised President Bush and Secretary of State Baker extensively. Baker, in a diplomatic tour de force involving all the parties, gradually succeeded in persuading Egypt to relax some of its initial positions, such as its insistence on collective rather than bilateral negotiations, its perception of a regional conference only as a preliminary format to a full-scale peace conference (the Israeli Government had insisted on a onetime "regional" peace conference, to be followed immediately by bilateral negotiations with the Arab countries), and, for the time being, its a priori demands that Israel halt settlement in the occupied territories and recognize Palestinian national rights.[310]

On the bilateral level, Baker, and the US Administration generally, declared themselves "encouraged" by the progress made on economic reform, and backed Egyptian demands in the IMF and the World Bank. A visit by US Secretary of the Treasury Nicholas Brady for this purpose took place in April. American aid to Egypt featured sending specialists on fiscal reform to setting up technological and agricultural projects and manpower training.[311] Ongoing bilateral military cooperation included a $1.6bn. deal announced in April by which the US would sell 46 F-16 fighter planes to Egypt to be delivered starting in November 1993.[312]

While the effect of the Gulf crisis and the war on the relegation of the Soviet Union to a secondary status was arguable, undoubtedly these events did change Egypt's relations with the declining superpower, and with the former Eastern Bloc generally to the level of secondary political importance, especially since the Soviet Union failed to play a decisive role in the Gulf crisis.[313] Cairo received leaders from Eastern Europe on an ongoing basis. Such was also the case with regard to dignitaries from almost all the major countries in the world, including Japan, China and the Latin American countries, all of whom visited the region in the wake of the war, calling on Israel as well. The essence of these visits was confined to bilateral matters, with the major exception of visits by Soviet Foreign Minister Bessmertnykh in May and by his successor, Boris Pankin, in October, as well as a visit by President Mubarak to Moscow in September, in preparation for the peace conference, to be cochaired by the now defunct superpower.[314]

The abortive coup against President Mikhail Gorbachev in August, which was almost immediately hailed by several Arab governments and by the PLO, elicited a cautious reaction by Egypt, with President Mubarak declaring himself "astounded how quickly the failed coup found Arab supporters." On 22 August, Mubarak, expressing "profound satisfaction" at Gorbachev's return to power, congratulated him and Russian President Boris Yeltsin, the latter "for his courage shown."[315] However, the media voiced anxiety and misgivings regarding the emerging new global system. Commentator Muhammad Jalal, for instance, wrote in *al-Akhbar*:

> We hoped that communism would collapse for the benefit of peoples and of progress, but it collapses for the benefit of Israel and the completion of American hegemony over the world. Our joy is mixed with deep concern for the future, which is completely open for the monkey [Israel] and the party which carries it on its shoulder [the US].

Another commentator wrote in the opposition paper, *al-Wafd*: "The Soviet Union has lost its independence to the US....Soviet policy is one of the factors accounting for Israel's intransigence, as 100,000 Jews came to change the West Bank, Gaza, East Jerusalem and the Golan." Similarly, even the Muslim Brothers, who consistently rejected Communist ideology, viewed developments in the USSR with mixed feelings, stating with regret: "The Islamic nation...benefiting by US-USSR antagonism... favored a balance of power."[316]

The future of trade relations between Egypt and the Soviet Union, 90% of which was with Russia alone (according to one estimate), appeared in doubt owing to noncompliance with export contracts on the Soviet side. This gave rise to Egyptian concern, but by the end of the year, when Egypt recognized the new Commonwealth of Independent States, a new trade memorandum was signed.[317]

The increasing importance of Europe, and particularly the EC, within the global system was reflected in a steady flow of mutual visits by government ministers and parliamentarians. Apart from bilateral topics such as economic aid and trade, and the signing of several new agreements, as well as "expressing appreciation for the Egyptian position," in the words of Britain's Prime Minister John Major on a visit during the Gulf War, these frequent talks underlined the role that the European countries themselves expected to play in the peacemaking process with regard to the Arab-Israeli conflict, an aspiration less welcome to the US and Israel but viewed positively by Egypt. "Europe can use its ties with the world and Israel to play a useful role in the ME process," French Foreign Minister Roland Dumas asserted in April.[318] President Mubarak embarked on several European tours during the year and addressed the European Parliament in Strasbourg in November, where he revealed a plan for a new cooperative framework, which he called the Mediterranean Forum, to include the European as well as the Arab countries of the Mediterranean littoral. The plan, probably stemming from fears of the ill effects of the forthcoming European economic union, and possibly also from competition from Israel, aimed to remove trade barriers, encourage economic cooperation and the transfer of technology, and possibly also develop some form of regional European-Mediterranean security guarantees.[319]

NOTES

For the place and frequency of publications cited here, and for the full name of the publication, news agency, radio station or monitoring service where an abbreviation is used, please see "List of Sources." Only in the case of more than one publication bearing the same name is the place of publication noted here.

1. *FT*, 24 June 1991.
2. *Le Monde*, 27 February 1991.
3. *Al-Wafd*, 19 July 1991.
4. R. Cairo, 30 December 1991, after President Mubarak personally chaired a meeting on the economic reform program.
5. The figure is from *al-Ahram International*, 5 July 1991.
6. R. Cairo, 2 April; *FT, JP, Ha'aretz*, 3 April 1991.
7. *JP*, 3, 5 September; MENA, 4 September; *al-Ahram Weekly*, 31 October 1991.
8. *Al-Ahram Weekly*, 2 January 1992.
9. On 'Abd al-Majid's election and biography, see *al-Ahram Weekly* (extensively); *NYT, JP, Ha'aretz*, 16 May; *Le Monde*, 17 May 1991.
10. *Al-Ahram Weekly*, 16 May–28 November 1991.
11. *JP*, 5 May; *Ha'aretz*, 5, 6 May; *Le Monde*, 6 May. For a negative note, see *al-Ahram Weekly*, 25 July 1991.
12. On Yusuf Idris see *al-Ahram Weekly*, 8 August, on Louis Awad, ibid., 19 September; on 'Ali Sabri, see *JP* and *Ha'aretz*, 4 August, and *Le Monde*, 6 August 1991, according to which the survivors were: Zakariya Muhyi al-Din, Khalid Muhyi al-Din, Husayn al-Shafi'i, 'Abd al-Latif al-Baghdadi and Kamal al-Din Husayn.
13. *Al-Ahram Weekly*, 18 July 1991.
14. *NYT, FT*, 2 January 1991.
15. MENA, 4 January 1991.
16. R. Cairo, 3 March. See also *Ha'aretz*, 13 June 1991.
17. MENA, 8, 15 January 1991.
18. MENA, 17 January 1991. According to R. Monte Carlo, 16 January, Mubarak also asked the US to postpone military action.
19. See, for instance, R. Cairo, MENA, 19 January, 17 and 19 February 1991.
20. R. Cairo, MENA, 26 January 1991.
21. *Al-Ahram International*, 21 January; *FT*, 22 January; *WSJ*, 23 January. Minister of State Butrus-Ghali declared: "If he [Saddam Husayn] will withdraw from Kuwait, we will be able to coexist and even to cooperate with him"; *JP* and *NYT*, 28 January. Similarly, British Foreign Secretary Douglas Hurd emphasized at a press conference in Cairo that Britain and Egypt were not seeking "to expand war aims"; *JP*, 10 February. When Iraq's withdrawal began, Mubarak pledged that Egypt would not enter Iraq, *JP*, 25 February 1991.
22. *IHT, NYT*, 25 January 1991.
23. According to *al-Ahali* (Cairo), 7 August 1991, 232,000 Egyptian workers returned from Iraq. Earlier, in March 1991, *al-Fallah al-Misri* estimated that there had been 450,000 Egyptian workers in Iraq, 85,000 of them *fellahin* engaged in agriculture in the Basra area.
24. MENA, 16 January; *al-Wafd*, 23 January 1991.
25. *Al-Wafd*, 8 February 1991.
26. *Le Monde*, 18 January; *JP*, 6 February 1991.
27. *Le Monde*, 27 February 1991.
28. *Ha'aretz*, 6 January 1991, translated from *WSJ*.
29. *Al-Jumhuriyya* (Cairo), 27 February 1991.
30. *Akhbar al-'Alam al-Islami*, 7 January. See also Khalid Muhammad Khalid in *al-Musawwar*, 1 February 1991.
31. *Al-Masa*, 12 January 1991.
32. AFP, 3, 14 January; MENA, 17 January; *JP*, 17 January, 10 February; *Akhir Sa'a*, 23 January; *IHT*, 31 January 1991.
33. *FT*, 22 January 1991.

34. MENA, 30 January, 11, 12, 13, 28 March; *JP*, 10, 19 February; AFP, 26 February, 11 March; *Ha'aretz*, 15 March, 30 May; *al-Jumhuriyya* (Cairo), 20 March 1991.
35. The Egyptian Scientific Society even conducted a public trial against Saddam Husayn, *al-Wafd*, 16 February 1991.
36. *Al-'Alam* (Rabat), 17 February 1991.
37. R. Monte Carlo, 7 February; *IHT, FT, JP*, 8 February; *al-Siyasi*, 17 February 1991.
38. *JP*, 29 January; R. Monte Carlo, 29 January; *Qarun al-Mu'arada*, 10 February; *Ha'aretz*, 18 February 1991.
39. *Al-Wafd*, 17 January. The SLP also published a statement to the effect that Palestine was the central Arab problem, *Qarun al-Mu'arada*, 20 January. Opposition spokesmen also called for the defense of Islamic shrines in Saudi Arabia; *NYT*, 28 January 1991.
40. *NYT*, 24, 28 January; IHT, 26, 28 January; *al-Jumhuriyya* (Cairo), 3 February; *JP*, 6 February 1991.
41. *Qarun al-Mu'arada*, 20 January; *Misr al-Fatat*, 21 January; MENA, 22 January, 7 February; *al-Ahali* (Cairo), 23 January; *NYT, IHT*, 25 January; *al-Ahram International, al-Akhbar*, 26 January; *al-Wafd*, 27 January; *al-Sha'b* (Cairo), 29 January; *al-Jumhuriyya* (Cairo), 5 February; *al-Siyasa*, 17 February. On different emphases in Islamic circles see, *Ruz al-Yusuf*, 18 February; *Le Monde*, 19 February 1991.
42. R. Monte Carlo, 29 January 1991.
43. R. Baghdad, INA, 13 February; *WP*, USIS, 18 February; R.Monte Carlo, 19 February. The last source reported a sit-in of 4,000 students at 'Ayn Shams, a rally of 3,000 students at Asyut, and smaller demonstrations at Cairo and Mansura universities. See also *FT*, 20 February; *JP*, 24 February; *NYT*, 25 February 1991.
44. R. Monte Carlo, 15 February. Another demonstration took place at 'Ayn Shams on the same day. See also AFP, 25 February; *Le Monde*, 27 February 1991.
45. AFP, 27 February; *JP*, 27, 28 February 1991.
46. A ministerial committee found that the university situation had been exaggerated in the media, MENA, 26 February. Although MENA stated on 28 February that classes were normal and there were no demonstrations, two student demonstrations, in Cairo and Alexandria, were reported during the last days of February; *JP*, 1 March; R. Cairo also mentioned a small demonstration by "extremist students" at 'Ayn Shams on 5 March 1991.
47. *NYT*, 24 February; *al-Wafd*, 27 February; *JP*, 1 March. However, Liberal Party leader Mustafa Kamil Murad called on "brother" Saddam Husayn to set up a democratic regime; *al-Ahrar*, 11 March 1991.
48. *Al-Wafd*, 30 January, 7 March; *al-Ahram International*, 4 February; *al-Sha'b* (Cairo), 12 February 1991.
49. *Al-Sha'b* (Cairo), 26 March; MENA, 30 March, quoting from *al-Ahram*. See also letter by Muslim Brotherhood Supreme Guide Abu al-Nasr, *al-Sha'b* (Cairo), 2 April 1991, in which he also blamed the war that had befallen Iraq on the abandoning of Islamic precepts.
50. *IHT*, 17 February; *Ha'aretz* (translated from *Le Monde*), 18 February. For a military assessment of the war, see interview with Chief of Staff (*fariq*) Salah Halabi in *al-Difa'* (Cairo), October 1991.
51. R. Cairo, 28 January; MENA, 5 March. *Le Monde*, 16 March 1991, estimated that over 800 Egyptian civilians had been killed in Kuwait as well.
52. *NYT*, 1 March 1991.
53. AFP, 30 April; MENA, 9, 10, 19, 26, 27 May; *JP*, 9 May. See also *al-Ahram Weekly*, 11 April, 16, 30 May, 20 June 1991.
54. MENA, 6 August. However, following talks with King Fahd in Jidda, President Mubarak pledged military assistance should the security of the Gulf states be threatened; *al-Ahram Weekly*, 3 October 1991.
55. *Al-Wafd*, 12 March; *al-Akhbar*, 15, 22 March 1991. *Al-Ahram al-Iqtisadi*, focused on the role of the Palestinians as well. *Misr al-Fatat*, 3 June 1991, claimed that with the destruction of Iraq, only Israel remained as a threat in the region and the US now imposed a new relationship with that country.
56. *Al-Akhbar*, 11 January; *al-'Alam* (London), 19 January. The *WSJ*, 12 February, quoted an estimate by Prime Minister 'Atif Sidqi of $13.7bn. Cf. *Le Monde*, 12 April 1991, which specified a loss to the state in foreign currency of $12bn., a loss of $3bn. in remittances,

$2bn. in tourism and $500m. in revenues from the canal, as well as the sum of $7,500 required to support each unemployed returnee.

57. Estimates of the number of returnees differed: the *WSJ,* 12 February, estimated 500,000; *Ha'aretz,* 21 November, as well as other sources, quoted 400,000; *al-Ahali* (Cairo), 7 August 1991, cited 232,000 returnees from Iraq.

58. *Al-'Alam* (London), 19 January; *Ruz al-Yusuf,* 15 July 1991, however, cited lower remittances.

59. MENA, 2 April; *al-Ahram Weekly,* 11 April; *al-Wafd,* 15 July and 6 October 1991. In reality unemployment was already higher, according to the *NYT,* 10 March 1991, well over 20%.

60. Statement by Sayyid Musa, head of the Tourism Promotion Authority, *al-Musawwar,* 15 February. See also *al-Musawwar,* 18 January 1991.

61. *Al-Akhbar,* 27 February; *al-Ahram,* 9, 26 March; *al-Ahram International,* 9 May 1991.

62. *Al-Ahram,* 22 May 1991.

63. *Al-'Alam* (London), 19 January 1991.

64. *Al-Wafd* estimated public company losses at $3bn.–$5bn. (18 February 1991), and trade losses to Arab countries at £300m. (26 February 1991).

65. *Al-Ahram,* 22 January 1991.

66. *Al-Ahram,* 10 August 1991.

67. *Al-Ahrar,* 18 February; *al-Wafd,* 23 February, 5 August; *FT,* 9 August; *al-Ahali* (Cairo), 28 August 1991.

68. Egypt had the fourth largest external debt in the world, after Brazil, Mexico and Argentina; *IHT,* 11 April 1991.

69. *Al-Ahram Weekly,* 26 September, 26 December 1991.

70. More agreements with the US were signed, e.g., regarding a grant of $150m. for imports, raising the total amount of benefits to $810m.; *al-Ahram,* 12 February 1991.

71. *Le Monde,* 1 January 1991.

72. Egypt would pay $4.5bn. over 20 years, beginning in four years, with interest not exceeding 2.8%; MENA, 25 July. See also *al-Ahram,* 20 July; *IHT, JP,* 22 July 1991.

73. MENA, 18 June 1991.

74. *FT,* 15 January; *Ha'aretz,* 11 April 1991.

75. R. Cairo, 5 February; *al-Ahram,* 6 February; *al-Ahram Weekly,* 16 May; *Akhir Sa'a,* 13 November 1991.

76. *Al-Ahram,* 12 February. *Le Monde,* 2 March 1991, reported the arrival of a French mission in Cairo to discuss details of an agreement involving FFr1bn. which had been signed in October 1990.

77. *JP,* 12, 13 February; *Ha'aretz,* 12 February. On the defreezing of DM381.5m. in loans, *Ruz al-Yusuf,* 11 March. In September, the German minister of economic cooperation came to Cairo for talks on rescheduling debts; *al-Ahram Weekly,* 19 September. In October, following three days of talks between Egyptian and German diplomats, a new financial protocol was initialed involving DM225m. in aid (of which DM25m. was a grant); *al-Akhbar,* 27 October 1991.

78. R. Cairo, 18 April, reported that the UK was prepared to cancel some of Egypt's debts; *Ha'aretz,* 25 April 1991, summed up the waiving of debts and promises of additional financial aid as follows: Germany DM1m., the Netherlands Fl30m., Denmark Kr130m.

79. *JP,* 21 April 1991.

80. MENA, 24 May; *al-Ahram Weekly,* 30 May 1991. The latter also discussed some of the remaining differences with the US and Japan.

81. MENA, 27 May 1991.

82. *Al-Akhbar,* 19 July; *al-Haqiqa,* 26 October 1991.

83. *Al-Ahram,* 7 January; *al-Wafd,* 13 January, 6 February; *Akhbar al-Yawm,* 19 January; *al-Jumhuriyya* (Cairo), 22 January. Cf. *Ha'aretz,* 25 April 1991.

84. *JP,* 29 January 1991.

85. MENA, 27 March 1991.

86. MENA, 9 April; *FT,* 10 April; *IHT,* 11 April; *Le Monde,* 12 April 1991.

87. *Al-Ahram Weekly,* 11 April; MENA, 16 April 1991.

88. *Al-Ahram Weekly,* 11 April (which, however, also cited the liberal *al-Ahrar* predicting an

economic boom); *JP,* 17 April; *IHT,* 19 April; *al-Wafd,* 10 May 1991.
89. Cairo, 14 April 1991.
90. MENA, 11, 12 May; *FT,* 13 May 1991.
91. *Al-Ahram Weekly,* 16 May 1991.
92. *Al-Ahram,* 12 February 1991.
93. *Ha'aretz,* 20 March 1991.
94. R. Cairo, 28, 31 March 1991.
95. *Al-Wafd,* 30 October 1991.
96. *Ha'aretz,* 26 March, reported that President Mubarak announced launching the fund with $400m. capital; *al-Ahram International,* 25 May, 20 June, 11 July 1991.
97. *Al-Ahram Weekly,* 11 July; *Le Monde,* 12 July; *al-Ahram,* 24 July 1991.
98. *Al-Ahram,* 31 October 1991.
99. *NYT,* 18 April 1991.
100. Article by Dr. Sa'id al-Najjar, lecturer at Cairo University and UN adviser, in *al-Akhbar,* 1 August 1991.
101. *Al-Ahram Weekly,* 15 August 1991.
102. *Ha'aretz,* 25 April; *al-Wafd,* 25 August; *al-Ahram International,* 12 September 1991.
103. *Al-Ahram Weekly,* 11 April 1991.
104. *Ha'aretz,* 3 October; *al-Ahram,* 8 October; *FT,* 9 October 1991.
105. *Al-Ahram Weekly,* 13 June 1991.
106. *JP,* 19 August 1991.
107. The World Bank estimated 10%-25% below the poverty line, but the government quoted 47%, a figure that may have been inflated in order to persuade international bodies to grant economic aid; *al-Haqiqa,* 7 December 1991.
108. *Al-Ahram Weekly,* 25 July; *NYT,* 28 July. A list of additional items that had become more expensive appeared in *al-Siyasi,* 15 September, which ascribed some blame to the new VAT and to increased demand for certain foodstuffs by foreigners returning home, and by Libyans, again visiting Egypt. *Al-Wafd,* 25 September, blamed the liberalization of exports; *al-Jumhuriyya* (Cairo), 23 November 1991, estimated that the average family spent 40% of its income on vegetables alone.
109. *Al-Masa,* 31 August 1991.
110. *Al-Wafd,* 12, 16 June; *al-Ahram Weekly,* 20 June, 4 July; *al-Siyasi,* 21 July 1991.
111. *Al-Ahali* (Cairo), 27 March 1991.
112. *Al-Ahram Weekly,* 4 July 1991.
113. *Al-Ahram Weekly,* 1, 22 August. Disagreements were reported over the sale of public companies in the outlying districts; *al-Wafd,* 19 September. On the hotels, see *al-Ahram Weekly,* 12 September, 5 December 1991.
114. *JP,* 2 October; *FT,* 18 October 1991.
115. *Al-Wafd,* 12 June; *al-Akhbar,* 14 August 1991.
116. *Al-Ahali* (Cairo), 8 May 1991.
117. *Al-Usbu' al-'Arabi,* 8 July 1991.
118. *Al-Haqiqa,* 4 May 1991.
119. *Al-Ahram Weekly,* 3 October, 28 November; *FT,* 13 November. The governor of the Central Bank, Dr. Salih Hamid, also declared that the IMF was satisfied. *Ha'aretz,* 27 December 1991, in an article translated from *Die Zeit.*
120. On the budget for 1991-92 (£E54.4bn.) see R. Cairo, 29 April; *al-Ahram,* 7 May; R. Cairo, 5 June; *al-Wafd,* 24 June. The first indication that the effort to curtail expenditure was not succeeding appeared in *al-Sha'b* (Cairo), 6 August 1991.
121. *Al-Ahram,* 13 November. A report by the World Bank expressed skepticism about Egypt's economic future because too many external factors were involved; *al-Ahram Weekly,* 12 December 1991.
122. *Al-Ahram, Akhir Sa'a,* 16 October; *al-Wafd,* 17 October; *al-Sha'b* (Cairo), 12 November 1991.
123. *Ha'aretz,* 26 March; *al-Ahram Weekly,* 11 April, 30 May; *al-Sha'b* (Cairo), 21, 28 May 1991.
124. *Al-Musawwar,* 3 May. Also *October,* 5, 12 May, 2 June 1991.
125. *Akhbar al-Yawm,* 11 May 1991.

126. R. Cairo, 20 May; *al-Ahram* (with the relevant biographies), *FT, Ha'aretz* and *JP*, 21 May 1991. In addition, Lt. Gen. Salah Muhammad 'Atiyya Halabi, who had commanded the Egyptian forces in the Gulf War, became the new chief of staff.

127. *Al-Ahali* (Cairo), 11 September. Still, rumors of a comprehensive reshuffle continued; cf. *Ruz al-Yusuf,* 21 October; MENA, 22 October 1991.

128. *Al-Hawadith,* 12 July 1991.

129. Interview with Dr. Fathi Surur, *al-Jumhuriyya* (Cairo), 21 November. Earlier, over 300 election complaints were cited, ibid., 24 April. A panel of High Court judges rejected appeals challenging the legality of the election law itself, *al-Wafd,* 2 December 1991.

130. *Al-Wafd,* 10 April. See also *Ha'aretz,* 15 April 1991.

131. *Al-Wafd,* 22 May, 1 and 9 November; *al-Akhbar,* 11 September, 10 November; MENA, 25 September; *al-Jumhuriyya* (Cairo), 12, 21 November; *al-Nur,* 27 November; *al-Ahram Weekly,* 26 September, 31 October, 7, 14, 21, 28 November 1991.

132. *Al-Wafd,* 13 November; Egyptian Space Channel, 29 November; R. Cairo, 30 November. President Mubarak himself was severely criticized in the opposition *al-Wafd* for thwarting the prosecution of the deputies, 6 December 1991.

133. *Al-Wafd,* 21 November 1991.

134. According to *al-Wafd,* 25 September, President Mubarak had received a report that the NDP had only 612,000 members (including 44,000 in Cairo, 86,000 in Giza, and 51,000 in Alexandria to mention only the largest urban concentrations) but that some branches lacked even the required 200 members to properly constitute a branch. Youngsters were particularly encouraged to join, *al-Siyasi,* 10 November 1991.

135. *Al-Akhbar,* 10 May; *al-Ahram,* 22 May, 12 June; *Ruz al-Yusuf,* 17 June, 9 September; *al-Siyasi,* 23 June, 7 July; *al-Sha'b* (Cairo), 1 July; *al-Ahram Weekly,* 5 September, 3, 31 October; *al-Jumhuriyya* (Cairo), 22 September 1991.

136. *Al-Haqiqa,* 17 August, 26 October. Prominent journalist Musa Sabri proposed that first a new leadership should be molded from above by President Mubarak; *al-Akhbar,* 8 May. There were also warning voices against holding a ballot; *al-Ahram Weekly,* 31 October 1991.

137. *Al-Siyasi,* 7, 22 December; *al-Ahram,* 22 December; *al-Haqiqa,* 28 December. On alleged irregularities, see *al-Sha'b* (Cairo), 12 December, and *al-Akhbar,* 25 December 1991.

138. *Al-Dawliyya,* 9 March 1991.

139. *Al-Siyasi,* 23 June 1991.

140. *Ruz al-Yusuf,* 1 April 1991.

141. See statement by party chairman Mahmud al-Malij, *al-Ahram International,* 20 July. For data on its membership and ideology, see ibid., 1 June, and *Misr al-Fatat,* 24 June 1991.

142. *Al-Ahram International,* 26 January; *al-Sha'b* (Cairo), 29 January. The Muslim Brothers were represented by the SLP.

143. *Ha'aretz,* 30 May 1991.

144. Deputy Kamal Khalid pointed to a contradiction between the government's drive for democratization and the existence of the emergency law; *al-Wafd,* 16 March 1991.

145. Wafd leader Fu'ad Siraj al-Din, however, expressed disappointment over the poor participation in the sit-in, particularly by the Muslim Brothers; *Ruz al-Yusuf,* 17 June 1991.

146. *Al-Sha'b* (Cairo), 8 April 1991. See also *al-Shira',* 1 July 1991.

147. *Al-Sha'b* (Cairo), 2 April; *al-Ahram,* 25 May 1991.

148. *Al-Haqiqa,* 20 April 1991.

149. *Al-Ahram,* 13 July. The leftist NPUG, having come under criticism by other opposition parties for not participating in the joint sit-in, announced it had prepared a draft bill on political rights; *al-Ahram International,* 15 June 1991.

150. Article by Mahfuz al-Ansari in *al-Jumhuriyya* (Cairo), 3 June 1991.

151. *Le Monde,* 10 May 1991.

152. *Al-Wafd* editor Jamal Badawi had called for constitutional reform as early as 14 February 1991, once the Gulf War ended.

153. *Al-Haqiqa,* 18 May, 1 June; *al-Sha'b* (Cairo), 21 May, 1, 30 July; *al-Ahram Weekly,* 16 May, 11 July; *al-Wafd,* 7 June, 9, 26 July; *al-Akhbar,* 10 July. The Liberal Party and the Wafd, however, carried on a separate campaign for a new constitution; cf. *al-Ahrar,* 28 October, and *al-Wafd,* 21 December 1991.

154. *Al-Ahram Weekly,* 18 July 1991.
155. *Al-Hayat* (London), 21 January. The constituent parties made some attempt at conciliation in November, apparently in vain; *al-Siyasi,* 24 November 1991.
156. *Ruz al-Yusuf,* 20 May; *al-Siyasi,* 8, 15 December 1991.
157. *Ruz al-Yusuf,* 1, 7 April, 6, 20 May, 8 July, 9 September; *al-Sha'b* (Cairo), 1 July; *al-Siyasi,* 7 April, 9, 23 June, 28 July, 10, 15 September, 1, 15, 22, 29 December; *al-Ahram,* 13 July; *al-Ahram International,* 20 July 1991.
158. *Al-Siyasi,* 6 October 1991.
159. *Al-Siyasi,* 29 May, 4 August 1991.
160. *Al-Ahram al-Iqtisadi,* 22 April; *al-Siyasi,* 12 May, 15, 29 December 1991.
161. *Al-Siyasi,* 9 June 1991.
162. *Al-Siyasi,* 9 June, 15 September, 27 October 1991.
163. *Al-Ahram International,* 14 September. *Ruz al-Yusuf,* 9 September, also reported a temporary conciliation, but according to *al-Siyasi,* 24 November, the Labor leadership opposed extending formal invitations to Muslim Brothers to speak at their upcoming party convention. On the alleged press deal, see *al-Jumhuriyya* (Cairo), 12 December 1991.
164. For a survey of internal party conflicts, see *al-Siyasi,* 7 July 1991.
165. *Ruz al-Yusuf,* 6 May, 9 September 1991.
166. *Al-Jumhuriyya* (Cairo), 5 February; *al-Siyasi,* 28 July, 6 October, 15 December; *Ruz al-Yusuf,* 9 September 1991.
167. *Al-Ahram International,* 7 September; *al-Siyasi,* 15 September, 15, 22 December 1991.
168. *Al-Hayat* (London), 24 February; *al-Ahram Weekly,* 20 June, 19 September; *al-Ahram al-Iqtisadi,* 24 June 1991.
169. *Al-Ahram al-Iqtisadi,* 24 June; *al-Balagh,* 1 August; *al-Haqiqa,* 4, 31 August 1991.
170. *Al-Siyasi,* 16 June; *al-Ahram International,* 14 September 1991.
171. *Al-Siyasi,* 9 June. Similarly, the Nasserists rejected an offer of an alliance with the SLP due to its "Islamic character"; *Ruz al-Yusuf,* 9 September 1991.
172. *Ruz al-Yusuf,* 6, 20 May 1991.
173. *Ruz al-Yusuf,* 20 May; *al-Ahram al-Iqtisadi,* 24 June; *al-Ahram Weekly,* 27 July; *al-Akhbar,* 28 July; *al-Ahali* (Cairo), 11 December 1991.
174. Baha al-Din Shu'ayb in *al-Ahram al-Iqtisadi,* 7 June 1991.
175. *Al-Ahrar,* 28 July 1991.
176. *Al-Nur,* 24 April, published a letter by 'Abbud al-Zumur calling from jail for a united Islamic front in Egypt. On the Jihad, see *al-Ahram Weekly,* 18 July 1991.
177. Having married an American woman, 'Umar 'Abd al-Rahman was said to have sent his first wife in Asyut two checks amounting to $140,000 in contributions collected in the US, but Minister of Interior 'Abd al-Halim Musa did not appear to be worried about him anymore; *al-Ahram Weekly,* 31 October. See also *al-Usbu' al-'Arabi,* 11 November. 'Umar 'Abd al-Rahman, visiting Saudi Arabia, spoke out against the "elimination" of Islamic societies and the "torture of youngsters" by the authorities; *al-Nur,* 11 September 1991.
178. *Al-Nur,* 20 February. In an allusion to initial official announcements that the murder was perpetrated by "non-Egyptians" (i.e., Iraqis), the defense asked for the release of those arrested. Complaints about torture were raised to suggest the innocence of those standing for trial; cf. *Le Monde,* 6 August 1991.
179. MENA, 20 April, 8, 10 June, 7 July; *Le Monde,* 25 April; *Ha'aretz,* 30 May; *al-Ahram Weekly,* 20 June, 18 July, 8, 22 August, 17 October 1991.
180. *Al-Ahram al-Masa'i,* 10 June 1991.
181. *Al-Jumhuriyya* (Cairo), 22 May 1991.
182. E.g., *al-Wafd,* 15 July, reported the arrest of 137 Jihad members in Tukh, Shibin al-Qanatir and Khanaqa in the area north of Cairo; *al-Ahram al-Masa'i,* 18 July, mentioned a shoot-out between police and Jihad members in the 'Ayn Shams area; AFP, 4 August, covered the trial of 27 Jihad members accused of robbing Christian jewelers in 'Ayn Shams and Shubra al-Khayma; *al-Ahram al-Masa'i,* 19 September, reported that 19 Jihad members were under investigation for robberies and related crimes; *al-Musawwar,* 4 October 1991, ran a story on the leader of an Islamic association in Mansura who claimed he had a religious injunction for robbing banks.
183. *Le Monde,* 25 April; *al-Watan al-'Arabi,* 18 July 1991.

184. *Al-Sharq al-Awsat* (London), 22 May; *al-Ahali* (Cairo), 25 October 1991.
185. *Al-Ahrar,* 3 June 1991.
186. *Al-Ahali* (Cairo), 9, 25 October 1991. The inhabitants of these quarters referred generally to the "Suniyyun," but also mentioned certain associations by name, e.g., the *Faramawiyyun* and the *Salafiyyun.*
187. *JP,* 11 January; *al-Ahram,*13 January, 3 September; *Ruz al-Yusuf,* 25 February; *Ha'aretz,* 6 March; MENA, 20 April, 25 May; *al-Siyasi,* 28 April; *al-Masa,* 11 May 1991, 19 June; *al-Ahram al-Masa'i,* 27 May; *al-Masa,* 11 July 1991; *al-Nur,* 19 June, 10 July; *Le Monde,* 29 June; *al-Ahali* (Cairo), 30 July, 7 August; R. Monte Carlo, 3 September; *al-Haqiqa,* 20 October; *al-Wafd,* 20 November 1991.
188. *Sawt al-Kuwait al-Duwali,* 23 May. Cf. *al-Ahali* (Cairo), 23 October 1991, describing incidents during the summer months in the Aswan district.
189. Interview in *October,* 10 March. See also *Ruz al-Yusuf,* 29 July 1991.
190. *Al-Ahram Weekly,* 15 August. Cf. an earlier interview in *Ruz al-Yusuf,* 29 July 1991, in which he denied that the Muslim Brotherhood had any formal international links and quoted Hasan al-Banna as having said at the fifth congress in 1939 that revolution would cause damage to Egypt.
191. *Al-Haqiqa,* 20 April 1991.
192. *Al-Ahram al-Iqtisadi,* 22 April 1991.
193. E.g., *al-Usbu' al-'Arabi,* 8 July 1991.
194. *Ruz al-Yusuf,* 17 June 1991.
195. *Ruz al-Yusuf,* 8 July. In a remarkable statement, Shaykh Ghazzali declared at a Cairo University debate that "to convince the world of our problems at a peace conference is part of jihad. The Prophet too negotiated with enemies and unbelievers"; *al-Jumhuriyya* (Cairo), 10 November. For other statements by him on the peace conference (some of them ambiguous), see *al-Ahram International,* 28 October; *al-Haqiqa,* 2 November; *al-Sha'b* (Cairo), 5 November; *al-Nur,* 6 November 1991.
196. *Al-Ahram Weekly,* 13 June, 11, 18 July, 1 August, 17 October, 21 and 28 November; *al-Jumhuriyya,* 18 July. Another Islamic investment company, al-Sa'd, was also in trouble and its owner fled the country, *al-Wafd,* 17 December 1991.
197. Examples of articles linking religious extremism with drugs appear in *al-Ahram Weekly,* 28 November 1991.
198. *Al-Ahram,* 6 March, 21 August; MENA, 20 July; *al-Ahram International,* 22 August; *al-Sha'b* (Cairo), 27 August; *al-Nur,* 18 September; *al-Sharq al-Awsat,* 3 August 1991.
199. *Al-Ahali* (Cairo), 10 May; *al-Nur,* 22, 29 May; *al-Siyasi,* 10 November; *al-Ahram Weekly,* *al-Liwa al-Islami,* 21 November 1991.
200. *Le Monde,* 30 December 1991.
201. *JP,* 9 January; *al-Ahram Weekly,* 27 June, 11 and 18 July; *al-Akhbar,* 19 July; *al-Watani,* 10 November 1991.
202. *Le Monde,* 25 September; *Ha'aretz,* 6 October; *Misr al-Fatat,* 7 October, reported that security in Imbaba was still heavy two weeks after the incidents, but 60 persons had been released from prison and Islamic activists had disappeared from the neighborhood. See also *NYT,* 22 October; *JP,* 23 October; *Ha'aretz,* 24 October; *al-Ahram Weekly,* 31 October 1991.
203. Columnist Baha al-Din Shu'ayb in *al-Ahram al-Iqtisadi,* 14 October; Rif'at al-Sa'id's criticism in *al-Ahali* (Cairo), 9 October 1991.
204. *Al-Ahram,* 8 October; *al-Jumhuriyya* (Cairo), 16 October 1991.
205. MENA, 28 March; *JP,* 31 March; *al-Jumhuriyya* (Cairo), 30 April; *al-Haqiqa,* 29 June 1991.
206. For the full English translation of the Damascus declaration, see *al-Ahram Weekly,* 8 August 1991.
207. *Ha'aretz,* 16 May; *al-Sha'b* (Cairo), 12 March, 21 May; *Le Monde,* 17 May.
208. *Le Monde,* 10 May; *WP,* 11 May. In an analysis of the reasons for the Gulf states' position, the *JP,* 2 June 1991, cited, inter alia, the weakening of the Iraqi threat, the high cost of maintaining a large Egyptian force, and the fear that the Egyptian troops might become a disruptive element.
209. *Al-Ahrar,* 18 February; *al-Ahram,* 26 February, 24 March; *FT,* 8 March; *al-Jumhuriyya*

(Cairo), 12 March; *Ruz al-Yusuf,* 25 March; R. Monte Carlo, 25, 27 March; MENA, 28, 30 March, 10 April; *NYT,* 16 May; *al-Ahram Weekly,* 26 September; *al-Akhbar,* 27 September; *Akhbar al-Yawm,* 28 September; *Akhir Sa'a,* 23 October, 2 November 1991.

210. *NYT,* 15 April; *Ha'aretz,* 13 May 1991.

211. *Al-Jumhuriyya* (Cairo), 28 February, 16 November; *al-Akhbar,* 5 March, 18 April; *al-Dawliyya,* 9 March; R. Cairo, 24 March; *al-Wafd,* 31 March, 25 August; *al-Ahali* (Cairo), 18 December 1991.

212. MENA, 13 July; *JP,* 14 July; *al-Jumhuriyya* (Cairo), 18 July; *al-Ahram,* 16, 21 July; *al-Sha'b* (Cairo; statement by nine opposition leaders); *Ruz al-Yusuf,* 23 September 1991.

213. *Al-Ahram,* 17, 20, 23 July; *NYT, JP,* 22 August; *al-Ahali* (Cairo) (report on a solidarity rally organized by the NPUG), 6 November; *Misr al-Fatat,* 18 November 1991.

214. MENA, 11 September; *JP,* 12 September; *al-Musawwar,* 13, 20 September; *al-Ahram Weekly,* 11 July, 12 September 1991.

215. *Al-Jumhuriyya* (Cairo), 12 January. Mubarak was also reported to have rejected a later Libyan mediation effort to arrange a meeting with Bashir, *al-Wafd,* 26 June; *al-Ahram Weekly,* 4, 7 July, 28 November. Eventually, Mubarak did receive Sudanese Minister of Interior al-Zubayr Muhammad Salah for talks on bilateral relations; ibid., 5 December 1991.

216. *JP,* MENA, 23 January; R. Monte Carlo, 24 January; *IHT,* 31 January, 6 February. On alleged anti-Egyptian activity by the Sudanese Islamic Front, see *Ha'aretz,* 18 June 1991.

217. On relations with Iran, see *al-Ahram, al-Wafd,* and R. Monte Carlo, 22 December; *Ruz al-Yusuf,* 31 December 1991.

218. MENA, 1, 19, 20 January, 1, 15 May, 18 August; *al-Wafd,* 2 February; *al-Haqiqa,* 9 February; *Ha'aretz,* 4 February, 6 March; GNA, 5 April; *al-Sharq al-Awsat,* 5 April; *NYT,* 14 April 1991.

219. *Al-Jumhuriyya* (Cairo), 2, 9, 11 November; *al-Ahram, al-Akhbar,* 3 November; *al-Sharq al-Awsat,* 4 November 1991.

220. MENA, 3 April; *al-Jumhuriyya* (Cairo), 16 May, 7 August; R. Cairo, 6 August; *al-Ahram Weekly,* 8, 22, 29 August; *al-Haqiqa,* 17 August 1991.

221. *Al-Ahram,* 14 February; *Qarun al-Mu'arada,* 12 May; MENA, 7 September; *al-Ahram,* 16 August; *al-Ahram Weekly,* 17 October; *Akhir Sa'a,* 23 October 1991.

222. *NYT,* 6 March; *al-Wafd,* 14 May; R. Monte Carlo, 15, 17 November; MENA, 17, 29 November, 4, 5, 7, 17 December; AFP, 17 November; *al-Jumhuriyya* (Cairo), 17 November, 5 December; *al-Sha'b* (Cairo), 19, 25 November; *al-Ahram,* 24 November; *Misr al-Fatat,* 25 November, 2 December; *al-Ahram Weekly,* 21 November, 5 December; *Akhbar al-Yawm,* 30 November; *al-Ahrar,* 23 December 1991.

223. MENA, 31 March, 1 April, 5 June, 17 July, 12, 27 October; *FT,* 6 June, 26 November 1991.

224. *Al-Jumhuriyya* (Cairo), 21 January. In another attack, al-Hayawan called 'Arafat "an ugly face" and insisted that "he also go," ibid., 15 July; *JP,* 6 March, quoting from *al-Akhbar,* 5 March. For another editorial with the term "clown," see *al-Akhbar,* 18 March 1991.

225. *JP,* 21 February, quoting Foreign Minister 'Abd al-Majid. Also see R. Monte Carlo, 29 August; *Misr al-Fatat,* 2 September; *al-Ahali* (Cairo), 4 September; MENA, 22 October, 7 November; *al-Ahram,* 4, 6 November (the Mansur article appeared in the latter); *Ha'aretz,* 28 November 1991.

226. *Al-Ahram Weekly,* 11 July 1991.

227. *Ruz al-Yusuf,* 29 July 1991.

228. *Al-Ahram Weekly,* 13 June, 11 July; *al-Ahali* (Cairo), 14 August, summarizing Islamic reaction in Egypt to developments in Algeria; *al-Ahram al-Iqtisadi,* 14 October 1991.

229. *Al-Jumhuriyya* (Cairo), 20 December 1991.

230. MENA (press summaries): 14 March, 16, 7 July, 1 , 9 September; *Le Monde,* 22 March; *al-Ahram al-Iqtisadi,* 25 March; *al-Musawwar,* 10 May; *al-Jumhuriyya* (Cairo), 11 May, 22 November; *al-Ahram,* 4 June; ; *Akhir Sa'a,* 2 October; IRNA, 30 October, 5 November; R. Cairo, 6, 11 November; *al-Akhbar,* 19 November 1991.

231. *Al-Thawra* (Damascus), 24 April; *JP,* 5 August; *al-Ahram Weekly,* 5, 12 December. The opposition newspaper *Misr al-Fatat,* 16 December 1991, criticized the "suppression" of the word jihad from the final Dakar communiqué.

232. Y. Goel in *JP,* 3 May; W. E. Schmidt in *NYT,* 4 August 1991.

233. MENA, 19 May, 26 September, 3 October, 18 December; *JP*, 3 October, 17, 18 December; VoI, 3, 5 October (when Egypt was expected to support canceling the resolution); *Ha'aretz*, 4, 6 October, 15 December; *al-Masa, al-Jumhuriyya* (Cairo), 8 December; *al-Akhbar*, 10 December 1991.

234. See article by the al-Ahram Center for Strategic Studies summing up Egypt's war aims, *al-Ahram*, 16 February 1991.

235. *Al-Wafd*, 9 January; *NYT*, 10 January; cf. R. Monte Carlo, 16 January 1991.

236. *Al-Ahram*, 22 January; *al-Ahram International*, 23 January; *Ha'aretz*, 28 January; *al-Akhbar*, 30 January 1991.

237. *Al-Wafd*, 22 January; *al-Akhbar*, 30 January 1991.

238. *Akhir Sa'a*, 12 February 1991.

239. *Al-Wafd*, 11 March 1991.

240. Cf. Shimon Shamir in *Ha'aretz*, 4 April; *al-Ahram*, 11 April 1991.

241. *Al-Wafd*, 6 February; *Ha'aretz*, 17 April, 9 July; R. Cairo, 5 May; MENA, 22 May, 23 September. On Israel as a military base, see *JP*, 3 June; MENA, 4 June; *al-Ahram*, 5 June 1991.

242. R. Cairo commentary by Anwar Zahir, 17 April; speech by Ambassador Basyuni at the International Center for Peace in the Middle East in Tel Aviv, *Ha'aretz*, 14 May. Cf. an article by Taha al-Maghdub of the Ahram Center for Strategic Studies in *al-Ahram*, 17 December 1991.

243. *Al-Ahram*, 7 February 1991.

244. *Ha'aretz*, 31 July; *JP* and VoI, 8 August 1991.

245. MENA, 24 March, 6 November; *JP*, 25 March, 13 December; *al-Ahram*, 17 April; *al-Jumhuriyya* (Cairo), 17 April, 8 November; *NYT*, 19 October; R. Cairo, 7 November; *al-Ahram International*, 7 November; *Ha'aretz, JP*, 13 December 1991.

246. MENA, 19 July; *NYT*, 20 July; *IHT*, 20–21 July; *Le Monde*, 22 July; *al-Akhbar*, 21 July; cf. *Ha'aretz*, 5 November 1991.

247. *October*, 13 January, on "transfer"; *Davar*, 5 May; *al-Ahram*, 14, 29 May, 11 June; *al-Wafd*, 29 May, accusing the US for allegedly assisting the Ethiopian airlift, 1, 15 July, quoting Siraj al-Din; *JP*, 30 May, on Musa's statement; *al-Musawwar*, 10 May; *al-Sha'b* (Cairo), 9 July 1991.

248. *Al-Sha'b* (Cairo), 3 September, 26 November, 3 December 1991; *Ha'aretz*, 21 November. The Engineers' Association ordered an investigation, *al-Wafd*, 3 December 1991.

249. *JP*, 15 February; *al-Ahram*, 11 March; R. Cairo, 24 March 1991.

250. MENA, 20 November; *al-Ahram Weekly*, 21, 28 November 1991.

251. MENA, 5 June, 8 November; *al-Sharq al-Awsat*, 2 July 1991.

252. VoI, 14 June; *NYT*, 15 June; *JP*, 16 June. Nevertheless, the Israeli Medical Association later protested that Egypt was preventing Egyptians from participating in congresses organized by Israel; *Ha'aretz*, 18 October 1991.

253. *Yedi'ot Aharonot*, 14 June 1991.

254. *Ha'aretz*, 11 June; VoI, 19 June; *al-Ahram*, 22, 23 June 1991.

255. MENA, 7 September; R. Cairo, 9, 10 September; *Akhir Sa'a*, 18 September 1991.

256. *JP*, 1 March, 14 June; *al-Sha'b* (Cairo), 6 August 1991.

257. *Le Monde*, 29 October 1991.

258. *JP*, 13 March, 23 April. As early as April, 36,183 tourists crossed the Egyptian border from Israel, the second largest contingent after Egypt's other neighbor, Libya, *Misr al-Fatat*, 13 May 1991.

259. *JP*, 4, 5 July 1991.

260. *Ha'aretz*, 29 September, 23 October 1991.

261. Ibid., 20 September. Israel allegedly was prepared to return the artifacts, *JP*, 20 October, 15 November 1991.

262. *Ha'aretz*, 23 October 1991.

263. VoI, 12 November; *Ha'aretz*, 12, 14, 21 November; *al-Ahram al-Masa'i*, 14 November 1991.

264. *JP*, 21 March 1991.

265. *Ha'aretz*, 29, 30, 31 July; R. Cairo, 29 July; *JP*, 30 July; MENA, 30, 31 July; *NYT*, 1 August; *Le Monde*, 2 August; *Yedi'ot Aharonot*, 5 August 1991.

266. MENA, 3 October; *JP,* 4 October 1991.
267. The preference for "Labor doves" also referred to a visit to Egypt by Eliezer Granot and MK Ya'ir Tzaban of the left-wing Mapam Party in March, when they were received by Minister Butrus-Ghali, MENA, 18 March 1991. *JP,* 9, 12, 16 June; MENA, 12, 13 June; VoI, 11 and 14 June. Former Israeli ambassador Moshe Sasson called the selection of the Labor delegation "a grave Egyptian mistake" for not "maintaining contacts on the highest level with the Israeli Government"; *Ha'aretz,* 10 June 1991.
268. *JP,* 13, 16, 18, 25 August; *Ha'aretz,* 19 August; *Ma'ariv, Yedi'ot Aharonot,* 23 August 1991.
269. *JP,* 30 August, 1 September: VoI, 30 August; MENA, 2 October 1991.
270. R. Cairo, 17 December; *Ha'aretz,* 19, 24 December 1991.
271. *Ha'aretz,* 31 March; *JP,* 7 April; MENA, 22 April, 10 July. Minister Butrus-Ghali, meeting with Shamir in Paris, conveyed the same message, MENA, 12 September. Minister of Foreign Affairs 'Amr Musa reportedly delivered a similar message to Shamir in Madrid, R. Monte Carlo, 31 October 1991.
272. *Al-Ahram,* 22 April 1991.
273. See Defense Minister Arens's forceful statement in the Knesset, *Ha'aretz,* 1 May, and the editorial, ibid., the following day. See further, *Davar,* 3 November; R. Monte Carlo, 24 December 1991.
274. *Yedi'ot Aharonot,* 12 July; *Ha'aretz,* 1 August 1991.
275. *Ha'aretz,* 28 July 1991.
276. *JP,* 14 November 1991.
277. Ibid., 20 August 1991.
278. *JP, Ha'aretz,* 21 July 1991.
279. VoI, 19, 27 November; *Ha'aretz,* 20 November. Mustafa Khalil summed up his impressions in a thoughtful interview to *October,* 1 December 1991.
280. On Musa, see *al-Ra'y* (Amman), 22 August. On Sultan, see *October,* 15 September; *JP,* 18 October, 6 November 1991.
281. *JP,* 14 March, 25 October; *Ha'aretz,* 13 June; *al-Akhbar,* 1 November 1991. There were also several attacks on other Israeli government ministers (Sharon and Levy) and on military figures.
282. *Al-Wafd,* 20 January 1991.
283. *Akhir Sa'a,* 30 January 1991.
284. On Ayman Hasan, see a critique by the anti-fundamentalist intellectual Faraj Fawda of "cheap arguments" used by the opposition, see *May,* 21 January; *al-Yasar,* January, October 1991; *al-Sha'b* (Cairo), 8 January; *al-Haqiqa,* 12 January; *Misr al-Fatat,* 14 January; *al-Ahali* (Cairo), 16 January, 13 February; *al-Nur,* 13 March; *Ha'aretz, JP,* 7 April. On the Sayyid Nusayr affair, see *al-Musawwar,* 24 May, 27 December; *Ha'aretz,* 9 July; *al-Wafd,* 26 July 1991.
285. *Ha'aretz,* 31 October 1991.
286. 'Abd al-Latif al-Hanafi in *al-Ahram al-Masa'i,* 11 November. For surveys of press comment, see *al-Ahram Weekly,* 24, 31 October, 7 November. *Al-Musawwar,* 12 December 1991, commented on "a turnabout in American public opinion."
287. *Ha'aretz,* 18 November 1991.
288. *Al-Ahram Weekly,* 14 November 1991.
289. *JP,* 8 November; *al-Ahali* (Cairo), 11 December 1991.
290. On the political parties' stand in general see *al-Ahram International* and *al-Haqiqa,* 12 October; *Ruz al-Yusuf,* 28 October; *al-Sha'b* (Cairo), 29 October, 5 November. See also *al-Liwa,* 16 November 1991.
291. *Ruz al-Yusuf,* 29 July; *al-Nur,* 18 September. The SLP, though as a party with strong Islamic inclinations favoring Jihad, started to oppose only Israel's conditions on which the conference was convened; *Ruz al-Yusuf,* 28 October. For the positions of other Muslim Brotherhood spokesmen, see *al-Sha'b* (Cairo), 24 September, 5 November, 3 December; *al-Haqiqa,* 5 October; *Ruz al-Yusuf,* 28 October; *al-Nur,* 6 November 1991.
292. *Al-Mukhtar al-Islami,* October. See also *al-Ahram Weekly,* 31 October, and a statement sent to Arab and Muslim rulers in *al-Sha'b* (Cairo), 29 October 1991.
293. *Al-Sha'b* (Cairo), 29 October 1991.

294. *Al-Hayat* (Beirut), 9 August. On Salama, see *al-Haqiqa,* 2 November 1991.
295. *Al-Ahram International,* 12 October; *Qarun al-Mu'arada,* 21 October; *al-Sha'b* (Cairo), 5 November 1991.
296. *Al-Sha'b* (Cairo), 12 November 1991.
297. *Al-Ahrar,* 29 July, 4 November; *al-Nur,* 6 November 1991.
298. *Al-Wafd,* 2 November; *al-Sha'b* (Cairo), 5 November; *al-Ahram Weekly,* 7 November 1991. *Al-Wafd* reported the arrest of eight doctors for opposing the peace conference on the basis of a *fatwa* issued by Shaykh Muhammad Sayyid 'Atiyya al-Tantawi, the mufti, "which forbids conciliation with Israel."
299. VoL, 28, 29 October; *Ha'aretz,* 29 October; *JP,* 30 October. In addition, some 300 arrests of intellectuals were reported, including two former members of the People's Assembly and the editor of *Liwa al-Islam; Ha'aretz,* 31 October 1991.
300. *Al-Wafd* (Cairo), 1 November; *al-Usbu' al-'Arabi,* 11 November 1991.
301. *Al-Ahali* (Cairo), 23, 30 October, 6, 27 November, 11 December. Muslim Brotherhood spokesman Hudaybi attacked NPUG supporters of the peace conference, ibid., 9 November. NPUG-leader Khalid Muhyi al-Din asserted that Israel was not interested in peace but merely in wringing concessions from the Arabs and gaining legitimacy for holding onto the Palestinian territories, *al-Liwa,* 4 December 1991.
302. *Al-Haqiqa,* 12 October; *al-Wafd,* 15, 28 October; *Ruz al-Yusuf,* 28 October 1991.
303. *Ruz al-Yusuf,* 28 October. See also *al-Ahram Weekly,* quoting from *al-Sha'b* (Cairo), 7 November 1991.
304. *Ha'aretz,* 24 November 1991.
305. *Le Monde,* 30 October; *JP,* 30 October; MENA, 31 October. *Ruz al-Yusuf,* 11 November 1991, drew a comparison between the Cairo fundamentalist students' demonstration in Cairo and Jewish extremism in Israel.
306. *Al-Jumhuriyya* (Cairo), 10 November 1991.
307. *May,* 11 November 1991.
308. Baker's visits took place on 12 January, 11–12 March, 10–11 April, 20–21 April, 12–14 May (during which he also met with Soviet Foreign Minister Alexander Bessmertnykh), 19 July, 17 September, and 13–14 October (see relevant MENA statements, *NYT* and Egyptian press). Cheney's visit took place on 1–5 June 1991.
309. E.g., *al-Ahram,* 21 March, 19 June, 9 July, 15 November, 22 December; *Akhbar al-Yawm,* 13 July 1991.
310. *NYT,* 11 April; *Le Monde,* 17 April 1991.
311. *Al-Haqiqa,* 3 February, 6 April; *NYT,* 12 March; MENA, 19 April; *al-Sha'b* (Cairo), 30 April; *al-Musawwar,* 24 May; *al-Wafd,* 26 May; *al-Ahram International,* 5 July; *al-Akhbar,* 21 August; *al-Jumhuriyya* (Cairo), 10 September; *al-Ahram,* 4 October; *Ha'aretz,* 11 October 1991.
312. *FT,* 7 March; *Le Monde,* 4 April; *Ha'aretz,* 10 April. On Cheney's talks in Cairo, see MENA, 1 June; *Ha'aretz,* 2 June; *JP,* 3 June 1991.
313. MENA, 14 January 1991.
314. MENA, 10, 11, 13 May, 26 September, 21 October; R. Cairo, 11 May, 2 October 1991.
315. MENA, 19–22 August; R. Cairo, 20 August; *JP,* 21, 23 August 1991.
316. *Al-Akhbar,* 10 September; *al-Wafd,* 16 May. See also *al-Ahram Weekly,* 29 August, and *al-Sha'b* (Cairo), 27 August 1991.
317. *Al-Ahram,* 2 February; *al-Wafd,* 1 June; *al-Musawwar,* 6 September; *Ruz al-Yusuf,* 23 September; *al-Haqiqa,* 2 November; R. Cairo, 22, 28 December; MENA, 25, 30 December. On trade and economic cooperation, see also *al-Ahram Weekly,* 11 July, 12, 26 September, 3, 24 October, 26 December 1991.
318. MENA, 5 February, 23 April 1991.
319. R. Cairo, 20 November, *al-Ahram Weekly,* 21 November; *FT,* 2 December 1991.

Iran

(Jomhuri-ye Islami-ye Iran)

DAVID MENASHRI

After seizing power in 1979, the clerics who took control in Tehran concentrated on two main goals for the first 12 years of their rule: first, the consolidation, institutionalization and, as far as possible, perpetuation of their rule; and second, the implementation of Ayatollah Ruhollah Khomeyni's revolutionary ideology, which, in turn, would further legitimize and consolidate their hold on power. While fairly successful in stabilizing their rule during the initial years, they were much less effective in implementing their dogma or resolving the mounting social, economic, political and other intricate problems that had initially led to the revolution.[1] To advance such goals more effectively they had to deviate again and again — often considerably — from their doctrine and adopt more pragmatic policies to cope with the exigencies of daily life.[2]

Such deviation was by no means unique to the Iranian revolution. As a natural progression, revolutionary movements are often led to depart from their radical doctrine once they have made the transition from opposition to power. The Islamic revolution was no exception. As long as Ayatollah Ruhollah Khomeyni had led an opposition movement, he had depicted a "new Iran" as being modeled on early Islam. Once in power, he — and even more so his successors — realized that they could not rule by means of revolutionary slogans, especially not those drawn from seventh-century thought. They were now called upon to manage, rather than just discuss, affairs of state. Soon they were forced to compromise with realities, not because of a new-found moderation, but due to a pragmatism consonant with the exigencies of their situation.

The first signs of pragmatism date back to the early years of the revolutionary regime. A close scrutiny of its policy shows a gradual move away from ideological purity toward expedient practicalness. Revolutionary leaders' appeals for cautious pragmatism initially related to specific and narrow issues, such as the employment of professionals who might have served the monarchical regime (see *MECS* 1981–82, pp. 546–47). Later, when the regime felt more secure, and became more aware of the areas of public resentment, appeals for moderation came to deal with broader issues. By 1984 Khomeyni had actively adopted a policy of slowing down Islamization (see *MECS* 1983–84, pp. 446–50).

Gradually this same tendency also extended to foreign policy. Here again, the overall trend was first given legitimacy by the Imam and then spelled out in greater detail and more specific terms by Speaker (later President) 'Ali Akbar Hashemi Rafsanjani. The initial notion that Iran did not need foreign countries and could do well without ties with foreign states (see *MECS* 1980–81, pp. 557–58), gave way to the

383

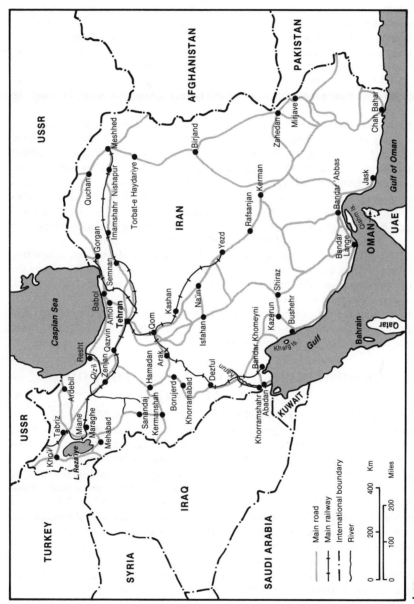

Iran

realization that any country, including Iran, needed contacts with the world powers (see *MECS* 1984–85, p. 449).

In 1991, there were clear signs that Tehran was aspiring to normalize its foreign relations. The revolution had passed its initial stage, in which it was necessary to compose slogans to attract popular support and unify the revolutionary camp. Now Tehran needed to live with the other countries of the world and dispense with the notion of permanent conflict with them. Moreover, after its war with Iraq, Tehran needed to expand its foreign ties in order to relieve serious economic problems (see below). And, following the 1991 Gulf War, Tehran needed to establish closer ties with the Gulf countries to secure its strategic and economic interests. Thus, 1991 saw the beginning of a new trend of expansion of relations.

At the same time, however, other significant factors contributed to the formation of a contrary approach. First, the actual improvement of such ties often necessitated deviation from dogma, and was therefore fiercely opposed by Rafsanjani's more radical rivals. Second, Iran's foreign relations, although successfully removing some major obstacles and reflecting significant ideological "concessions," were not without their basic disagreements and often proved to be fragile and vulnerable to setbacks even with those countries with which it maintained cordial ties, such as Syria and certain European states. The very nature of revolutionary Iran and its ideology — or what was left of it — were still sufficient to create delicate situations.

All these domestic and foreign relations issues caused ideological frictions within the regime. Thus, fierce rivalries colored the developments of 1991. These were the combined result of divergent doctrinaire convictions, contradictory political considerations, personal rivalries and pure struggle for power.

Examining the developments of the year through the prism of these divergent approaches by the various revolutionary camps, this survey also attempts to detect the nature and depth of the differences between them.

THE DOMESTIC SCENE UNDER THE SHADOW OF INTERNAL RIFTS

THE STRUGGLE FOR IDEOLOGICAL AND POLITICAL SWAY

Western opinion, by and large, viewed the struggle rather simplistically as being between factions of "moderates" and of "extremists." In fact, the situation was much more complex, and tracing the affinity of individual leaders with one group or another was not an easy matter. For one thing, the various competing groups were never organized into clear-cut factions, let alone political parties, and had no collective coherent ideology: actually, all proclaimed loyalty to the Imam's "line." It was also impossible to differentiate between personal rivalries and ideological controversy. Moreover, some protagonists on the domestic scene appeared to be moderate on one issue yet extremely radical on another. It was a common occurrence for the same people to speak at times in more pragmatic language, while at others to voice extremely radical views. Further complicating the situation was the fact that in their public statements these leaders — their doctrinaire differences and personal rivalries notwithstanding — often chose to compliment, and express personal affection for each other and, more often than not, claimed that disagreements did not exist between them at all.[3] Also, as the *Echo of Iran* wrote: "Iranian officials are speaking sweet words in English to foreigners, but it's strictly Satan-as-usual when they speak Farsi on the home front." Referring to Rafsanjani's hard-line statements to domestic audiences, it added, in a somewhat flowery fashion: "That does not necessarily mean the kinder, gentler foreign policy is a hoax. It may only signal that Rafsanjani and his aides know the new policy riles the radicals and feel they must be fed some red meat to keep them at bay."[4] All these factors made it difficult for outsiders to characterize such groups with certainty. Yet, taking their entire vision and their cumulative statements throughout the revolutionary (and earlier) era, a classification of these leaders as "pragmatists" and "radicals" seems perhaps inevitable.

Being well aware of the pitfalls of error and inaccuracy, one could propose the following general distinction: those holding executive power who shared the burden of running the state were generally more pragmatic; while those outside the Administration made up the bulk of the radicals. In a way, this marked the inherent tension between the interests of the *revolution* and the distress of the *state*.[5] Gradually, the latter had clearly gained supremacy over the former.

Leader Seyyed 'Ali Khamene'i's periodic exhortations to the various "camps," "trends" or "currents" (as they were often depicted) to maintain their unity could be an indication of the intensity of domestic rivalries (for earlier such counsels by Khamene'i, see *MECS* 1989, pp. 360–61; 1990, p. 353). The figureheads of these groups also often asserted that basic disagreements existed (see below).

While still aligned to Khomeyni's radical doctrine, the practical problems of the day-to-day running of the government and of perpetuating the Islamic rule tinged the establishment's thinking with a belated pragmatism. With time, as the problems facing the regime grew, the ranks of the pragmatists swelled and their tendency toward pragmatism became more marked. Rafsanjani led this trend. His Friday sermon of 20 December gave a typical example of his approach. He said that the country needed at that stage *tadbir,* "a prudent policy," both in domestic and foreign matters "so that we can help people without being accused of engaging in terrorism, without anyone being able to call us fanatics." There was no need any more, he added, "to speak fanatically," or "to chant impractical slogans."[6] This, however, did not mean total rejection of acts of terror. Rafsanjani only wished that his country would not be identified with such actions and not be viewed as fanatic. This was the nature of his "pragmatism," if this was the correct word for such an approach. The government generally supported his line. Yet, he too admitted that different attitudes did in fact exist. In March, he said: "There are two currents in our country — a radical one and a more moderate one."[7]

And indeed other prominent revolutionary figures continued to preach the same old ultraradical policies. An important example of this group — eventually to become the token figure of fundamentalist or, rather, the anti-Rafsanjani trend — was the former minister of the interior (and currently a Majlis member) Hojjat ul-Islam 'Ali Akbar Mohtashami. Others supporting similar views were Hojjat ul-Islam Mohammad Musavi Kho'iniha (Majlis member, former prosecutor-general and proprietor of the new radical daily *Salam*), Hojjat ul-Islam Sadeq Khalkhali (Majlis member who at the outset of the revolution was the intimidating head of the revolutionary courts), Majlis Speaker Mehdi Karubi and more often than not Khomeyni's son, Ahmad.

Mohtashami himself alluded to just how deep such disparities ran. Explaining the need to publish his new monthly, *Bayan,* he said in March that following Khomeyni's demise Iranian society was plunged into a deep despondency since the true "revolutionary and Hizbollah forces...no longer had a voice in the country's executive system and [in fact] ...were being eliminated from the scene." *Bayan,* he said, was published to represent "the voices from the hearts of these mobilization forces, of the martyrs' families, of the oppressed masses of the people," thus implying that the government was no longer sufficiently sensitive to the genuine revolutionary sentiments. He carefully accused "some members of a particular action [who] spread venom and distorted facts to prevent us from continuing our rightful course."[8]

Khamene'i, although politically closer to Rafsanjani and giving him staunch support whenever it seemed essential (see below), held certain more radical views than Rafsanjani (on such issues as relations with the US, or the export of the revolution), although less so than his rivals.

In 1991, the faction led by Rafsanjani seemed to wield greater power. However, the radicals continued to offer a challenge. Not sufficiently powerful to obstruct government policy, they nevertheless often proved capable of checking the process of pragmatism and delaying some practical government programs. Aware of the popular appeal of his rivals' claims (always basing their arguments on Khomeyni's doctrine), Rafsanjani often seemed to follow a contradictory line: proclaiming loyalty to radical convictions, yet virtually steering the country toward greater pragmatism.

All these factors led to seeming inconsistencies in the president's policy to the point of obscuring his "real" views. What was then his genuine view? *Ideologically,* Rafsanjani seemed to possess no cohesive or clear ideology (nor a commitment to any given worldview) — he frequently altered his stance according to the circumstances.[9] *Politically,* there was a clear difference between his statements directed at the domestic audience and his declarations meant for foreign ears. *Tactically,* while challenged by his rivals, he habitually preferred to delay action rather than openly confront them. He wished to maintain popular support, and therefore he seldom put aside his real intentions and (even declared) policies, but waited for a more opportune time to advance them.

From time to time, Rafsanjani tried to test popular opinion on some controversial questions, in order to decide his policy. He often had his associates carry out this task for him. Thus, in April 1990 Vice President 'Ata'ollah Mohajerani wrote an article in *Ettela'at* advocating the establishment of ties with the US. This invoked an extremely negative response and consequently the president's associates publicly claimed that Mohajerani was expressing only his own views, and not those of Rafsanjani (see *MECS* 1990, p. 363). Such considerations in 1991 may have led Sa'id Raja'i Khorasani to advocate "aggressive diplomacy," including his highly controversial bid to renew ties with South Africa (see below). Another example was the allusion by Mohammad Larijani, in an interview with *The New York Times,* to some common interests between Washington and Tehran and his motion that the two could enjoy a "marriage of convenience" (see below). Be that as it may, Rafsanjani's shrewdness was, as one source suggested, in his "correct perception of the [domestic] public opinion as well as his ability to adapt himself to the international developments."[10] Yet, even if the above-mentioned assertions were not coordinated with Rafsanjani, they were viewed by his rivals as representing the danger of the establishment's realpolitik, and succeeded in inciting their fury.

Rafsanjani and his government were severely criticized, particularly after the 1991 Gulf War, mostly because of their failure in domestic (especially economic) policies. Rafsanjani now required Khamene'i's support, which the leader was willing to give him. Yet, by supporting Rafsanjani, he also exposed his vulnerability and continued need for the backing of the "leader."

The radicals often chose to criticize individual ministers and direct attention toward their failure to solve the problems facing the nation. They thus seemed to criticize Rafsanjani as well, albeit indirectly. After successfully dismissing Minister of Health Iraj Fazel through a vote of no-confidence (13 January 1991), Minister of Education Mohammad 'Ali Najafi was questioned by the more radical Majlis members (23 April) on charges including "mismanagement" and appointment of "incompetent personnel."[11] Najafi gained the confidence of the House. (For the radical composition of the third Majlis, see *MECS* 1988, pp. 489–92.)

The government, though not the president personally, was systematically criticized for its failure to meet popular expectations. Kho'iniha harshly criticized the government through his paper *Salam* as did Mohtashami in his own *Bayan,* while other Majlis members used the podium to raise similar arguments. The government was clearly on the defensive. In February, Rafsanjani claimed that some (unidentified) elements were attempting to sow discord by implying that "affairs are being conducted in a faulty fashion and that *gerani* [exorbitant] prices existed."[12] In May, Majlis deputy Movahedi Savoji warned the government's adversaries against making accusations so freely and questioning all foreign and domestic policies. Musavi Tabrizi responded that those (radicals) who (unlike the other group) followed the Imam were not afraid of threats and intimidation.[13] When the criticism became more intense and frequent, to the point of obstructing government policy or even threatening the government's stability — not to mention the president's authority — Rafsanjani took up the offensive. In an attack on his critics in a Friday sermon on 24 May, he gave an account of the heavy burden of the (Iraqi-Iranian) war, the influx of refugees, inflation and the insufficient budget to explain the concrete difficulties facing the government. He went on to blame "certain elements" that were trying to shake popular confidence in the government and who set out to "fan the fire of public expectations cunningly."[14] According to some sources, he even threatened to resign.

Immediately after his speech, statements of support flooded the media. However, even these could not hide the intense rivalries and mutual accusations continued. Rafsanjani's supporters even revealed incidences of corruption among those who had hidden behind loyalty to the Imam. According to the *Echo of Iran,* they "shrewdly succeeded in compiling evidence of embezzling by such individuals as Ayatollah 'Abdul-Karim Musavi Ardebili [head of the judiciary], Hadi Ghaffari [Majlis member and leader of the Iranian Hizbollah], Hasan Karubi [the speaker's brother], Asadollah Bayat [deputy Majlis speaker]...and Sadeq Khalkhali...and presenting some of these evidences, indirectly to the public to destroy their image."[15] *Salam* disclosed that some of the government's critics (such as Majlis member Qorban-'Ali Salehabadi, who condemned the government for renewing ties with Saudi Arabia and Britain) were summoned to Evin prison and warned to keep quiet and not make life difficult for themselves. Salehabadi's interrogation was labeled "another action of the moderate faction for discrediting the Majlis."[16] Khalkhali concluded that the government's attempt to hold criticism in check "breeds dictatorship."[17]

Another source of controversy was a statement made at the end of the year by Raja'i Khorasani, a pragmatist, who, until March 1989, served as ambassador to the UN, and then headed the Majlis's committee on foreign relations. In a Majlis speech early in November he called upon the government to reestablish ties with Egypt, Morocco and even South Africa. (Revolutionary dogma, it should be recalled, forbade the establishment of ties with South Africa, the US and Israel.) It was former Egyptian President Sadat, said Khorasani, who had made peace with Israel, and he had received his due punishment, while Mubarak's error (his participation in the peace conference; see below) was no different from that of Syria, Jordan and Lebanon. "Should we sever ties with these countries as well?" he asked, dismissing those radicals who "imagine that since the performance of a certain government is not endorsed [by Iran]...relations between the two countries should be severed." He went on to accuse the "others" of "sensationalism." Echoing Rafsanjani's pragmatic line to a certain extent, and candidly criticizing the other group's methods, he concluded that foreign policy should be dealt with "by precisely analyzing the realities," not by "methods that consume the foreign policy issues for domestic cliquism."[18] He reiterated these points early in December, calling for "aggressive diplomacy" aimed at renewing ties with foreign countries with whom Tehran did not have relations, including, again, South Africa.[19] Not surprisingly his statements were severely criticized in the Majlis. In the press, too, his proposal was condemned, though it was possible to detect some differences — such as between the harsh tone used by *Jomhuri-ye Islami*[20] and the somewhat friendlier exhortations voiced by (the pragmatic) *Resalat*.[21]

Another issue over which the radicals severely criticized the government was its attempt to attract investments by exiled Iranian capitalists and to invite fugitive professionals to return. A delegation headed by Minister of Economy and Finance Mohsen Nurbakhsh and Governor-General of the Central Bank Mohammad Hoseyn 'Adeli visited the US for this purpose and invited Iranian emigrants to return home and help reconstruct the economy. This time, the government's critics were supported by Ahmad Khomeyni, who went so far as to claim that the very act of holding such meetings had turned the country into "the Iran of the Shah's era."[22] This was the harshest accusation that could be directed against any revolutionary leader. Others, such as Majlis member Zabihollah Safa'i, claimed that such an initiative went against the Imam's path. Those *taqutis* (arrogant persons), he said, echoing the typical revolutionary terminology, exploited the nation. They were currently leading corrupt lives in the West, and were mostly spies. Their return, therefore, was tantamount to deviation.[23] Khalkhali similarly criticized Rafsanjani for such a move.[24]

Mohtashami condemned the holding of a seminar on Persian carpets in Germany (by the Ministry of Commerce) which, he said, cost the government $100,000 and was attended by big capitalists.[25] He similarly criticized the oil minister for inviting representatives of American oil companies to deal with Iran, evidently referring to a conference on oil and gas held in Isfahan. On what authorization, he asked, were the Americans invited to Iran?[26]

Some of the infighting at the close of the year may be seen as signaling the resumption of the campaign for the Majlis elections, scheduled for April 1992: the radicals wished at least to preserve their power, while the more pragmatic camp was attempting to check their influence. Rafsanjani, who had served as speaker for nine years (1980–89) and had helped mold the politicized nature of the Majlis, now seemed to wish it had operated more as a legislative than a political organ.

All these factors led Rafsanjani frequently to express radical statements to demonstrate his loyalty to the Imam. He felt obliged to reassert his government's ideological purity to "placate its radical opponents."[27] This was important to meet the challenge posed not only by his critics, but also by the growing power of the occasionally more radical "leader."

Since his succession of Khomeyni, Khamene'i aspired to imitate the Imam and follow his style. This led him to adopt some of Khomeyni's more radical views, but at the same time — again, in keeping with Khomeyni's style — to back the president. Their old friendship notwithstanding, relations between the two had not been without tension and setbacks throughout the revolutionary era. However, on the whole, since the reinstitution of the revolutionary organs in 1989 — when Rafsanjani became president and Khamene'i the leader — the trend had been toward closer coordination.[28] (For their cooperation following Khomeyni's death, see MECS 1989, pp. 359–62.) Khamene'i seemed to realize that Rafsanjani's failure could endanger the regime's stability. Rafsanjani, for his part, was often in need of Khamene'i's support to implement his policy and overcome domestic criticism. Nevertheless, a measure of competition between the two was inevitable: Khamene'i wished to play (at least partially) the role of Khomeyni; while Rafsanjani wanted to limit Khamene'i's political involvement and did not acknowledge his religious credentials. Rafsanjani claimed, for example, that although he succeeded Khomeyni, Khamene'i could by no means be considered a marja'-e taqlid[29] (source of religious imitation; see also below). Nevertheless, as long as the threat of the more extreme radicals existed, the two leaders were ultimately in need of each other. As long as their alliance held, they seemed more powerful together than any combination of their rivals, at least from the perspective of 1991. Yet, this too forced Rafsanjani to be more sensitive to Khamene'i's more radical views.

Another challenge was posed for Rafsanjani by Ahmad Khomeyni. The two were once close confidants, but their views had often clashed. There was so much speculation about their rivalry, that when Rafsanjani attacked his rivals in May, many thought that he was referring to Ahmad. The speculation intensified when unlike most prominent figures, Ahmad did not publish a statement of support. Rafsanjani had to publicly deny that he was referring to Ahmad. He described him as a friend and colleague who rendered great services to the revolution.[30] Ahmad said that on main principles "we share the same opinion and style."[31] Clearly, their opinions differed on Ahmad's right to criticize publicly the executive: Ahmad believed this was his right and duty, whereas Rafsanjani wished him to express his views more discreetly. In any case, in order to gain Ahmad's support, it was necessary for Rafsanjani to show greater loyalty to Imam Khomeyni's approach.

At the end of the year a new challenge emerged for both Rafsanjani and Khamene'i — this time from supporters of Ayatollah Hoseyn 'Ali Montazeri who was once Khomeyni's heir apparent, but was eliminated from succession in March 1989. There are still insufficient sources available to make a firm judgment about this issue. However, in November, a group of Majlis members reportedly composed of 80–100 members, including Mohtashami, visited Montazeri in Qom to brief him on the results of the Palestine conference (see below). The group was led by the deputy Majlis speaker, Hojjat ul-Islam Hoseyn Hashemian, who was later summoned to a special court dealing with clerical matters to explain his activities against the Islamic regime.

The visit to Qom rapidly turned into a great political incident.[32] *Resalat* criticized the meeting as being politically motivated and violating instructions of the Imam.[33] Deputy Morteza Alviri defended Montazeri in a Majlis speech (17 November), disclosing that about 100 Majlis members, including himself, still considered Montazeri their *marja'*.[34] Mohtashami's *Bayan* claimed that the very act of publicizing the issue may have been "a calculated step aimed at opening an arena of deviation in the existing legitimate and useful political struggle."[35]

Some observers claimed that the meeting was the radicals' means to indicate to Khamene'i that he lacked the necessary qualifications for being a *marja'*. This could also be implied from Alviri's above-mentioned speech. Alviri said that some people interpreted the meeting that way, but that they should bear in mind that the 1989 constitution in fact distinguished between the *rahbar* (leader) and *marja'*.[36] (For such stipulations in the constitution, see *MECS* 1989, pp. 348–49. For similar assertions about his lack of religious qualification to be considered a *marja'*, see *MECS* 1990, p. 354.) Such a meeting could also be a hint by the radicals directed at Khamene'i's friend and ally, Rafsanjani. Yet, this could also antagonize Ahmad Khomeyni, who often supported the radicals, and consistently expressed critical views against Montazeri. Whether or not the meeting indicated Montazeri's intention to become more involved in politics was impossible to judge at this stage.

While factional rivalries continued to present a challenge, the challenge from the opposition gradually diminished. The opposition's main hope seemed to be that the regime would be weakened by the growing internal difficulties. However, they seemed to have lost faith that coordinated action on the part of the exiled opposition could achieve this. From time to time there were reports — mainly by the opposition and sources with a vested interest — of growing popular resentment leading to outbursts of rage and demonstrations in Tehran and other large cities (see below), although the scope of such developments was difficult to establish. However, in 1991, they seemed far from endangering internal stability.

As far as the exiled opposition was concerned, the main development in 1991 was Shahpur Bakhtyar's assassination in Paris in August. By that stage, however, his elimination could have only had a minor, if any, impact on Iran. It had long been clear that the exiled opposition was weak and ineffective (see *MECS* 1981–82, pp. 557–60), and Bakhtyar's movement was no exception. Apparently his assassination was considered a punishment rather than a reflection of the government's concern about his challenge.

Overall, the most crucial challenge facing the regime was still that presented by the harsh exigencies established in the 12 years of revolutionary rule. These exigencies led to growing popular disillusionment with and negative feeling for the regime. Social and economic problems constituted one of the main areas of popular discontent, possibly the most significant area.

ECONOMIC AND SOCIAL REPERCUSSIONS

Since the founding of the Islamic regime, the revolutionary process and the resultant insecurity had led to a gradual, but progressively serious, deterioration of the economy. Unemployment increased; prices rose; investment virtually ceased both by local businessmen and by foreign interests and the brain drain constantly increased. From 1980 onward, the war exacerbated these problems and they became a growing threat, generating other problems, namely costly military imports; the destruction of the economic infrastructure immediately behind the front line (one of the most highly industrialized areas of the country); and the growing number of refugees from the war zones. Furthermore, the world oil glut and the sharp decline in oil prices made it difficult for Iran to increase its revenue from oil as a means of advancing the economy and the state. All these problems posed a growing threat because of the accelerated population growth, from around 38m. in 1979 to nearly 60m. in 1991, and rapid urbanization (the population of Tehran doubled since the mid-1970s). Above all, the revolution had not yet eased the burden on the *mostaz'efin* ("dispossessed"). For the Islamic regime, which had pledged to serve the unprivileged strata, this was not only frustrating but also potentially dangerous.[37]

These problems combined to form a gloomy economic scene, leaving the regime torn between its desire to initiate radical long-term planning for the Islamization of the economy, and the necessity to take short-term measures for the immediate relief of the acute economic imbalances. The programs the government had were embodied in the first five-year economic plan (see *MECS* 1989, pp. 362–64). In a July sermon Rafsanjani encapsulated his government's design as transforming "our centralized, war-time economy into [a] balanced, peace-time one." The country, he admitted, was in "a dangerous" situation during the war and was still facing momentous problems.[38] Others simply claimed that "our biggest problem...is the economy."[39]

In 12 years of Islamic rule, little progress had been made toward the execution of the main socioeconomic plans. The most fundamental of these, among them land reform and the nationalization of foreign trade, had been vetoed by the Council of Guardians. Vital plans, such as preventing the influx into the cities and boosting agriculture more than industry, had failed totally. Moreover, legislation regarding such important issues as taxation and the regulation of the private sector's freedom continued to stir fierce doctrinal and political debate. Promises to improve housing, education, and health had came to nothing. In fact, in many cases there had been a change for the worse.

The most severe problems were the shortages in a number of basic commodities and the government's inability to distribute fairly the amounts available among the different classes and the different regions. Hoarding and profiteering increased tremendously, while soaring prices placed many commodities beyond the means of the *mostaz'efin*. The black market continued to boom even after the war, and speculators carried on prospering. Price control proved ineffective: buying sprees created extra demand and forced up prices even higher. The few, already rich individuals grew richer, while the poorer class carried the real burden of the economic depression.

High prices for rental and home purchase continued to be a principal cause of discontent in the early 1990s, as had also been the case a decade earlier. Most heavily hit by unemployment were high-school graduates, whom the education system, being geared to scholastic achievement, had failed to prepare for any form of employment. Another potential area of social and political unrest was created by the large number of high-school graduates, prevented from achieving higher education because of the limited number of university admissions.[40] With professionals continuing to leave the country, the government's attempts to reinvigorate the economy and improve public services were severely set back. More substantial government initiatives, such as the privatization of the economy, the use of foreign loans and expertise, and attempts to attract the return of fugitive professionals (see above) were hampered by the more radical groups on the basis of dogmatic purity.

Public criticism of the economic situation grew constantly and some members of the leadership came to fear that the political success of the revolution would be jeopardized by economic hardships. Reviewing such difficulties, *Jomhuri-ye Islami* wrote that even if the problems were not less sensitive than they had been during the war, they certainly had not improved: while people had limited expectations during the war, their expectations had naturally risen since it ended.[41] (For Rafsanjani's indictment of the fanning of such expectations by his rivals, see above.) The former policy, *Resalat* lamented, did not lead toward closing the gap between rich and poor.[42] One Iranian source, hiding behind what was customarily termed as "public opinion," wrote that people in Iran believed that "instead of providing means for the welfare of the deprived classes," the revolution had "only provided more facilities for the profit seekers and the well-to-do classes."[43]

The government continued to fight hoarding and profiteering mainly by exhortation and indoctrination. Preachers sermonized that such practices were not acceptable in Islam; official spokesmen stressed that they constituted "economic sabotage." They tried to impress upon the public that prices would necessarily be brought down by reduced demand. The attempt to keep prices in check through teams of market inspectors had also proven ineffective. A vigorous campaign against hoarders and profiteers continued. However, even with all these measures, the main problems were not eased, let alone solved.

Expatriate opposition quarters speculated that economic difficulties were on the point of shaking the regime. In fact, there were signs of growing disillusionment among the poorest classes in 1991. While the government pledged "revolutionary patience," it was obvious that patience was wearing thin. On several occasions, more than in previous years, people took to the streets demonstrating against economic hardships. Criticism of the government for raising the prices of many goods and services was stepped up in early July after hundreds of people demonstrated in different parts of the capital against the raising of bus fares. The protest escalated into a clash between angry travelers and the police. (In response to the demonstration, the bus company canceled the price increase.) A week earlier, hundreds of students at the Open University in Tehran and Karaj had held sit-ins over a reported doubling of tuition fees and demanded that they be allowed to present their complaints to the president.[44] Disturbances were also reported in the Tehran Bazaar on several occasions during the year. Nevertheless, the government's measures proved sufficient (if only barely) to prevent absolute economic chaos in 1991. As in previous years, the economy was kept running by oil revenue.

For its part, the government tried to explain, or explain away, the economic problems and continued to counter criticism by using the two excuses: revolution and the war.[45] Economic distress was the price Iran had to pay for having launched its anti-imperialist struggle and for remaining loyal to its dogma. More practically, Rafsanjani — as Khomeyni had occasionally done — publicized his instructions to the officials in order to lessen the burden on the *mostaz'efin*. Similarly, the government tried — again, in line with Khomeyni's policy — to lower material expectations, urging the people not to expect swift gains and advising them against consumerism.

The steep increase in the cost of living was felt mainly at the beginning of the Persian year (March 1991), after the removal (in April) of government subsidies from many basic items. The price of a loaf of bread jumped by 50% and poultry prices increased threefold. The cost of gas for heating and cooking rose by 150%, while electricity rates climbed by 250%. Analysts said that Tehran adopted this austere economic program in order to meet guidelines set by the International Monetary Fund and the World Bank, which made loans conditional on privatization programs and the removal of subsidies.[46]

Official statistics, too, showed a rise in inflation rates. 'Adeli said in November that not only would the rate of inflation not drop in the coming year, it would be likely to double — from 9%–18%.[47] Another official report, in which levels of income and expenditure were compared, showed a "disturbing gap between the two. If this gap is not filled before long, Iran will be in a dreadful situation. A situation where Iran will become one of the poorest nations of the Third World."[48]

Despite these serious difficulties the government usually painted an optimistic picture, quoting figures which showed a notable improvement at least on paper. For example, early in July Nurbakhsh said that Iran's economy for the calendar year ending on 20 March 1990 had grown by a robust 10.1% and inflation eased to 9% (compared with 17.4% the previous year).[49] Opposition camps quoted totally different figures. One such source, quoting official statistics, claimed that Iran's gross domestic product fell to less than one half the prerevolutionary figure.[50]

The economic failures were constantly criticized by the government's rivals: both by the exiled opposition, and by the radicals at home, particularly from the Majlis podium, which was more dangerous for the government. Rafsanjani's sermon of 24 May was one tangible sign of this delicate problem. Aware of popular discontent, Khamene'i, in a meeting with the heads of the three branches of government in mid-August, urged them to avoid asraf (squandering) and tajamolgara'i (sumptuous) expenses. He took up the offensive against those officials who, on the pretext of security, traveled in expensive cars; conducted lavish marriage ceremonies, as in the previous regime; and occupied the luxurious houses of the ministers and capitalists of the previous regime.[51] Referring to the same issue in his Friday sermon (22 November), Ayatollah 'Ali Meshkini called for those holding sensitive state office to have even "a lower standard of life than other people." He asserted that those officials who drive cars costing 20m. toman to travel to their homes worth 70m. toman, should keep in mind the practices of Imam 'Ali.[52] The resort to such exhortations by revolutionary leaders could only imply that exasperation was taking over.

Although the government started a campaign against excessively luxurious living, an Iranian source — again, hiding behind unidentified "observers" — said that "the observers believe" that these problems were too deeply rooted and therefore unlikely to be removed by "such superficial affections," because "some of the government's authorities and MPs are the prominent examples of such a kind of living." The paper added that such occurrences as those to which Khamene'i was referring had in fact "provoked the general hatred and indignation of the public" against some of the authorities.[53] Kayhan furiously posed the question as to which class of society a government agent who traveled in a $10m. Mercedes was serving, or how a Majlis member could justify his lavish way of living.[54] (For a long time, people in Tehran had used the term "Ayatollah Benzi," i.e., Ayatollah who rides in a Mercedes Benz, to denounce such practices.)

Nevertheless, in mid-November, Rafsanjani publicly emphasized "the main points of our [economic] achievements." He stressed the reduction of direct governmental intervention in the economy; the removal of obstacles to domestic and foreign investment; the liberalization of foreign trade and the creation of proper grounds for expanding the public sector's activities; the liberalization of the banking system; the expansion of private sector ownership by putting on the market shares of state-owned and nationalized companies, as well as activating the stock exchange; and movement toward balancing the budget. He also said that "inflationary pressures were considerably reduced."[55] Rafsanjani reiterated these points while presenting his government's budget for 1991–92 to the House on 7 December. He then said that Iran had succeeded in bringing about "basic changes in the economic scene" and singled out, among other things, the "notable increase in production," paying "special attention to the society's vulnerable strata," and managing to keep the budget deficit at the level envisaged by the economic plan.[56]

His domestic rivals continued to assail him for the economic setbacks and the government's policy. For example, Ebrahim Asghari, a Majlis member, pointed out that the budget deficit had increased in the past year and blamed the government for being chiefly responsible for the increase in inflation.[57] However, when the government wished to ease some of the problems by raising foreign loans, or improving foreign ties, these same groups fiercely opposed such moves.

FOREIGN RELATIONS: NEW DYNAMICS

THE UNITED STATES, FRANCE AND WESTERN EUROPE
Relations with the US
For some time, Rafsanjani seemed to have been convinced of the advisability of opening channels of negotiation with the US and bring about a change at least in the atmosphere of bilateral "relations." However, he was not powerful enough to bring about a significant change. Current American politics in the region — the war, the continued American military presence in the region in its aftermath, and the US role in the Middle East peace initiative — in addition to the massive obstacles still in the way of bilateral relations, i.e., the freezing of Iranian assets in the US and the hostages kept in Lebanon, still prevented any significant change. The fierce opposition by the radicals to any such initiative made the situation all the more complicated. While there was some progress in solving bilateral problems, there was little change in the general view of the US as the Great Satan.

During the war, there were signs that the two states had maintained some channels of communication. Rafsanjani disclosed that the Swiss Embassy was providing services in this respect.[58] At that time, establishment anti-American statements were milder (see below), sometimes even revealing a measure of understanding for US war policy. However, after the war there was a return to business as usual. The main barrier facing Rafsanjani was not so much the strength of his rivals, but rather the delicate nature of the issue. Breaking ties with Washington in fact became one of the symbols of revolutionary Iran. It would therefore demand a strenuous effort to produce a significant — let alone formal — change. His rivals could, as they in fact often did, raise the issue to gain further popular support, not commensurate with their real influence over the people.

Exposed to conflicting pressures, Rafsanjani made several contradictory statements on the issue, to the point of obscuring his genuine opinion. He did, however, see that there were some grounds for change. First, he was aware that, for economic reasons mainly, Tehran needed to improve its relations with the outside world, including the West, and probably even with the US in the longer run. Second, the change in the world order similarly encouraged him to improve ties with Washington, now the only superpower. Third, he was probably aware that to ultimately stabilize the revolution and perpetuate it, Tehran would do better to appear less revolutionary and more cooperative with the outside world (see above). However, other important considerations dictated the contrary. Public opinion, by and large, still considered the US as the Great Satan, and the legacy of Khomeyni's policy on this issue was crystal-clear and still widely supported. If Rafsanjani were to institute change, the extremists could use such a blatant deviation as an excuse to oppose his reform programs altogether.

Rafsanjani therefore decided to make a distinction between his practical (pragmatic) policy and public (more radical) statements. Consequently, in 1991, he helped in "closing the file" of the American hostages in Lebanon, and continued to deal with the Americans to resolve the outstanding financial disputes (see below). At the same time, he continued to close ranks with his domestic foes, although he was careful not to sound as radical as they. For example, unlike his rivals, he systematically avoided declaring that the animosity with the US was eternal. As one Iranian source maintained, he did not state that Iran "will never establish relations" with the US. He only stressed that "as long as...[its] hostility continues, we will not establish relations... ."[59]

As for the American presence in the Gulf area, Rafsanjani stated that, although it was "not useful" it "did not constitute a threat" to Iran.[60] When a journalist remarked that it seemed that he had given up Khomeyni's "implacable attitude toward the West," Rafsanjani did not deny it. "The preconditions," he said, "have changed," and "our policy corresponds to these changed conditions."[61] In a way, this sums up Rafsanjani's pragmatist approach.

Yet, even those willing to see an improvement in relations with the US believed it was up to Washington to prove its goodwill by making some meaningful practical gestures toward Iran. Late in April, Velayati bitterly complained that the US had not yet taken any such steps. As examples of such possible "positive measures" he "offered" the unfreezing of Iranian assets.[62] As such gestures did not materialize and, equally important, opposition to the government's pragmatism became more intense, Rafsanjani publicly ruled out the possibility of the resumption of ties in early May. He said "We are in no way ready [yet?] to establish ties with the US and we do not think about it."[63] Tehran laid the blame for continued hostility at Washington's door. "The American policy toward us has not changed," said Velayati on 4 May. Hence "we don't think there is any different climate in our relations."[64]

Yet, from time to time appeals for reconciliation were made, mainly in statements aimed at foreign audiences. For example, Mohammad Javad Larijani, an adviser of the minister of foreign affairs and a pragmatist, said in May that there were some common interests between Tehran and Washington, such as in the security of the Persian Gulf. He suggested that while Tehran's domestic politics precluded formal relations, both countries could enjoy a "marriage of convenience." Alluding to the fact that some Iranians were willing to see ties restored, he said that even they were suspicious of American intentions and thought "that the US wants to fool Iran, dominate Iran, interfere in Iran."[65] It was up to the US, according to this logic, to prove that the contrary was in fact the case.

Khamene'i was more radical on this point than the president and his associates. For example, in his message on the anniversary of Khomeyni's death (an occasion when revolutionary zeal was in any case at a high pitch), he maintained that the slogan of "Neither the East nor the West" was still crucial in Iranian politics. He added that his country rejected any ties with the US which were "the manifestation of bullying, unjust domination and the symbol of cruelty....Iran will *never* establish ties with that regime."[66]

The radicals were even more hostile. Mehdi Karubi stated in mid-May that Tehran would under no circumstances renew ties with the US.[67] He added that the US was "even worse than a wolf" and that Iran "could never have good relations with it." This, he said was "one of the principles of the revolution." Consequently, when an American plane landed in Iran to bring supplies destined for Kurdish refugees, Ahmad Khomeyni said, "I was terribly ashamed."[68] *Abrar* wrote in March that Iran would continue fighting American imperialism, and would keep "in a state of constant struggle against the values of world arrogance headed by American imperialism."[69]

The ME peace conference provided the main issue on which anti-American sentiments were focused in the fall (see below). However, on a variety of other occasions, most notably around the anniversary of the Imam's exile (in 1964) and the seizure of the American Embassy (1979), both on 4 November, anti-American feelings were also expressed. A careful analysis of these statements indicates varied nuances. Those who were usually more radical voiced the harshest accusations; Khamene'i's anti-American statements approached the radicals' in their severity; while Rafsanjani was relatively the most moderate.

Not surprisingly, it was Mohtashami who again led the radical camp, repeatedly calling for the targeting of all the US objectives throughout the world (see also below).[70]

However, it was Khamene'i's statements which attracted the most attention, both because of his leadership position and because of his radical tone. Meeting martyrs' families on 9 October, he accused the US of aiming to "control this important, sensitive and vital region." Their primary motive, he continued, touching upon a highly sensitive point, was their animosity toward Islam. He said: "They are the very dangerous enemies of Islam, the Iranian nation and humanity....They intend to enslave the [Muslim] nations of the region."[71]

However, even then, when Rafsanjani discussed regional problems he chose to accuse Israel first and foremost. Although he criticized the US, his tone sounded less threatening: he only advised the US that it was committing a strategic mistake by "setting aside" 1.2bn. Muslims "for a few million Zionists."[72] This was not meant to signify an amicable attitude toward the Americans. On one occasion (31 October), for example, Rafsanjani went so far as to state that the US "must be made" to give up its thoughts on regional affairs.[73] Nevertheless, on consideration of his statements in their entirety, and given the anti-American atmosphere in Iran, his statements could still be thought of as relatively pragmatic.

All these various harsh statements notwithstanding, there were greater indications

of some mutual understanding behind the scenes. As one Iranian source claimed —
rather overoptimistically — although "no hope is expressed in Tehran on the
resumption of diplomatic relations...it is confirmed that the ice is melting... tension
between the two sides is decreasing noticeably."[74] At the end of the year several such
signs could in fact be detected. One was the visible trend toward removing some of the
immediate obstacles, mainly the hostage problem and the Iranian assets frozen in the
US. While claiming that it did not have control over those who had taken the
hostages, Tehran made it clear that it did have significant leverage over them and was
willing to use its influence under certain conditions. An official in Washington said
there were some indications that Tehran wanted "to rejoin the community of nations.
We will await the next steps."[75] In fact, there were indications immediately after the
1991 war that Tehran wished to get the hostage issue out of the way. Velayati said that
the hostages should be released "as soon as possible."[76] Deputy Foreign Minister
Mahmud Va'ezi said in May that all hostages, irrespective of their nationality, should
be released immediately.[77] Tehran, for its part, still expected the US to take the first
step by demonstrating its own goodwill. But by the end of the year most Western, and
all American, hostages had been released (see chapter on the US and the ME). There
was also some information on a mutual understanding to unfreeze part of the Iranian
funds kept in the US.[78] Another example of American goodwill was the fact that it
cleared Iran of the allegations that it was involved in the Pan Am aircraft disaster of
1988.

Relations with France and Western Europe
With the decline in Soviet power, Tehran realized that there was no alternative but to
turn to the West in its search for financial assistance and expertise to rebuild the
country after the long war with Iraq. Iran endeavored to strengthen ties with France,
Germany and Japan in the hope of advancing the Iranian economy. Signs of
improvement in bilateral relations were discernible in 1991, especially in relations
with Paris.

Relations between Iran and France improved significantly after Velayati's visit to
Paris the previous year. The two states signed several agreements on cooperation in
the fields of the economy, oil, gas, petrochemicals and heavy industry during a
two-year period. The central banks of both countries came to an agreement that credit
reportedly of $2.6bn. would be placed at Iran's disposal, to be used to purchase
technical equipment. According to the same sources, further credit of $2.2bn. would
also be placed at Iran's disposal for the implementation of petrochemical projects.
Referring to this, an Iranian commentary stated that France had been actively
participating in the implementation of Iran's economic plan.[79]

Early in May, French Foreign Minister Roland Dumas visited Tehran. Bilateral
relations as well as regional and international issues were discussed. The two sides also
concluded an agreement in principle on the financial dispute inherited from the
Shah's era, which had been marring bilateral relations for over a decade. At the heart
of the dispute was a $1bn. loan made by the late Shah to the French nuclear energy
authority, of which the French Government had already paid back $630m. (see
below). Velayati stated that reaching an understanding on this issue was the most
important result of the visit.[80]

Early in July, the French reciprocated by hosting Velayati in Paris. President

Mitterrand then announced that he would visit Iran later in the year.[81] (Meanwhile, President Kurt Waldheim of Austria, who visited Tehran in June, was the only Western head of state who had visited Iran since 1979.) Iranian officials promised to arrange the dates for a return visit by Rafsanjani, which was also intended as the Iranian president's first visit to a major Western country. However, none of these visits materialized in 1991. The French president had to postpone his visit following Bakhtyar's assassination (see above). Still, relations continued to improve during 1991.

Early in October, Velayati stated that historical and cultural ties constituted the backbone of Iranian-French relations.[82] *Tehran Times* pointed out the "long history of mutual cooperation in the cultural, economic and political fields" between the two countries.[83] On 25 October, the two states announced that they had reached a final agreement regarding their 12-year-old loan dispute.[84] This, Va'ezi concluded, would remove all obstacles restricting the development of bilateral ties and establish a clear framework for mutual cooperation in the future.[85] Finally, late in December, when French deputy foreign minister François Scheer visited Tehran, a memorandum of understanding for resolving the financial dispute was signed (29 December). According to its stipulations, within two days from the signing, the French Government would pay $550m. and another $450m. would be paid in three installments during the course of 1992. (Since France had already paid Iran $630m., payments to Iran totaled $1.63bn.).[86]

Although relations continued to improve, they were not without tension and setbacks. Tension mounted in December following the French request to hand over to its authorities an Iranian citizen detained by the Swiss Government in connection with Bakhtyar's assassination while in the Iranian Embassy in Switzerland.[87] Although the immediate clash was with the Swiss, the incident soon clouded relations between Tehran and Paris as well. Tehran believed that the detention took place at the request of the French. *Jomhuri-ye Islami* made this point in so many words, writing that there was "little reason" why the Swiss should want "to partake of the problem of France."[88]

Following Dumas's visit in May, his West German counterpart, Hans-Dietrich Genscher, arrived in Tehran. Genscher emphasized Tehran's "important role" in the creation of "a peace order" for the region.[89] He too conveyed an invitation from President Kohl to Rafsanjani to visit Germany.[90] However, tension crept into the relations with Germany as well, the disputed issue being the refusal by the Germans to construct the Bushehr power station.[91]

Relations with Britain were restored in September 1990 (see *MECS* 1990, p. 365), having been broken off following Khomeyni's death sentence against Salman Rushdie. In mid-May, a British parliamentary delegation visited Tehran. Later that month, Velayati met with the British foreign office minister, Douglas Hogg, in London, where they discussed the hostage issue, among other matters.[92]

IRAN, THE WAR AND THE GULF STATES
Iran and Iraq: The War and its Aftermath
Iran was a major beneficiary of the war, since its two major enemies, the US and Iraq, confronted each other. Tehran gained two important advantages from this confrontation. Immediately following the Iraqi invasion of Kuwait, Saddam Husayn

made considerable concessions to Iran. Furthermore, the destruction of Iraqi military power also served Iranian interests: their major regional rival was weakened; Iran had a better opportunity to become a central power in the Gulf; and it improved its image in the West and enhanced its ties with the outside world, particularly with states in the region.

When analyzing Tehran's war policy, a clear distinction should be made between Iran's public statements and its sincere interests, since these two often seemed not only inconsistent, but even contradictory. Consequently, although often conveying support for certain Iraqi positions, Tehran denied Iraq any significant concrete backing. Tehran gave the impression of wishing to avoid war, yet ultimately longed for, and at least implicitly encouraged coalition members to engage in war (for Iranian interests and policy prior to the actual fighting, see *MECS* 1990, pp. 368–75).

A close look at Iran's policy throughout the war shows that it in fact followed a fairly consistent line aimed at serving its interests in the best possible manner. Tehran's main aim was to use the war to secure Iran's position as the major force in the Gulf region after the war was over. In this regard, it wished to see both Iraq and the US suffer severe blows and neither of them emerge victorious. Its policy was therefore twofold: to see the Iraqi military might broken, and to guarantee the withdrawal of the foreign troops after the war. This approach remained consistent throughout the crisis.

In order to fulfill its war aim, Iran resorted to several measures. Gestures of goodwill were made toward the Iraqi people, as opposed to the regime, in a bid to prepare the ground for improved relations with Iraq in the future, and possibly also to influence its future regime (or at least to exert influence in certain parts of the country). Iran also insisted that the Western powers withdraw from the region following the war in order to avoid a decisive *political gain* by the US. This, in turn, was aimed at guaranteeing Tehran a greater role in future regional security arrangements. Furthermore, Iran used the opportunity of the war to end its diplomatic isolation by turning its capital into a major center for diplomatic activities. Iranian leaders, mainly Velayati, made many diplomatic overtures during this period, thus presenting Iran not only as an important (perhaps the most significant) country in the Gulf region, but also as a peace-seeking country, contributing to the stability of the region.

While consistently adhering to its principled opposition both to the Iraqi occupation of Kuwait and to any foreign presence in the Gulf, especially after the war, Tehran's actual policy was otherwise quite flexible, to the point of sometimes appearing contradictory. It took some steps that could have been seen as lending a measure of support to Iraq, but stopped short of significantly or openly supporting the Iraqi regime. The following gestures of goodwill, all primarily serving Iran's own interests, are worthy of note.

From the time of the invasion of Kuwait, Tehran responded positively to Iraqi gestures, such as those made in August 1990, and strengthened bilateral ties. Tehran welcomed the Iraqi planes that requested "parking" permission in Iran. Although it was not yet clear what motivated the pilots to flee to Iran (cf. chapter on the military dimension of the Gulf War), Tehran's positive response to their request for permission to land there has been commonly interpreted as a pro-Iraqi gesture. Again, this was not necessarily Tehran's intention. There were clearly other reasons motivating Iran:

first, Iran could use this in the future to prove to the Iraqis — once again, the people and not the regime — that they had come to their aid in their hour of need; and second, while parked in Iranian territory the planes were of no military value anyway. It is also possible that Iran intended to keep the planes after the war as the first installment in Iraqi reparations to Iran for the Iraqi-Iranian War.[93]

Iran began intensive diplomatic activity when it became clear that the Iraqis had suffered "sufficiently," ostensibly in order to "help out" Baghdad. This, too, was primarily aimed at serving Iran's own interests. Tehran benefited by acquiring the image of a stable country concerned with establishing peace and stability. It further demonstrated Iran's central role in the region. Tehran also wished to have some influence on the terms of the termination of the war. However, when proposals, such as Karubi's[94] for a cease-fire prior to the land operation were rejected, Tehran was not disappointed, since the ground war was likely to serve its interests even better. The grievance voiced by Tehran was no more than a case of crocodile tears.

This is not to say that Iran had not rendered certain favors to Iraq. It permitted the import into Iraq, through Iranian territory, of certain goods, mainly food and medicine, in amounts as yet impossible to ascertain. (Baghdad later claimed that Iran used this opportunity to smuggle arms to the Shi'is in southern Iraq.) No less important was the fact that Iran, as a major Muslim state, remained neutral, albeit with some pro-Iraqi — or rather, anti-American — tilt, which was extremely beneficial to Baghdad. However, the fact that Tehran refused to lend Iraq the kind of support that could have been really meaningful, such as backing Baghdad's claim that this was an Islamic war (see *MECS* 1990, p. 374), was the most significant point. Similarly, Iran continued to insist that Iraq withdraw from Kuwait.

Rejecting Iraq's claim that it was waging an Islamic war, Ayatollah Mohammad 'Ali Yazdi argued that this was by no means a war of Islam against heresy; its essence was simply a struggle for *qodrat* (power) and *tajavoz* (aggression), which had nothing to do with "religion and divine piety."[95] Rafsanjani similarly rejected the claim that it was a war between *haqq* (truth) and *batel* (falsehood) — had this been the case, Tehran would have participated, and in fact led it.[96] Ahmad Khomeyni went so far as to claim that, on the contrary, the Iraqi invasion of Kuwait only proved that Baghdad was unfaithful to Islamic law and doctrine.[97]

The war did not create a major internal rift as far as the domestic struggle for power was concerned. Prior to the actual fighting, the more radically oriented, mainly Mohtashami and Kho'iniha, did advocate a more active Iranian approach against the US. They continued to raise such arguments in the first week or two of the war. Typical of their approach was that they did not view the war as being fought for the liberation of Kuwait, nor that it was fought for oil only. They viewed it primarily as a war conducted by the US to fight Islam. They did not argue, of course, that Saddam for his part was leading a campaign *for Islam,* rather that the US was leading a campaign *against Islam.* This being the case, the radical argument went on, it was the duty of Iran to lead such a struggle.

Thus, for example, on 19 January Sadeq Khalkhali said, "we cannot leave the Iraqi nation alone in this brave battle." He suggested that Iran put aside the history of the Iraqi invasion of Iran, because now "the fate of Islam is at stake." He requested Khamene'i to declare *jehad* (holy war) against the US and its Western allies.[98] Similarly Mohtashami claimed (20 January) that faced with Western aggression, it was the religious duty of the Muslim nations of the region — but particularly that of the Iranians — "to rise for a holy *jehad*...against the infidel forces of the US, Nato and Zionism."[99] Elsewhere he made clear (on 23 January) that his arguments in this regard "did not concern Saddam...it was about the attack waged...against the Muslim nation of Iraq."[100] He concluded: "It would be simpleminded to think that America has come to repel [an Iraqi] aggression and believe its promise to leave the Persian Gulf after driving Iraq out of Kuwait. America has come to uproot Islam and the Muslims."[101] (It is important to note that after the first ten days of the war — when the Iraqis had suffered heavy blows and the radicals could have been expected to preach for greater Islamic solidarity and support — one could not find similar statements by the radicals reported in the leading Iranian press.) It was eventually against such a background that Rafsanjani conceded that some (unidentified) groups had then advocated an Iranian engagement in the war against America, but he dismissed them as insignificant.[102] The pragmatists, for their part, did not go that far.

On the whole, however, during the war no major disagreements were registered. Statements made by the establishment revealed only marginal differences in attitude. For example, Ahmad Khomeyni's approach seemed to be more anti-Iraqi and emotionally motivated. He often recalled the mistreatment of his father by the Ba'th regime while his father was in exile there and the expulsion of the Imam from Iraq in 1978.[103] Rafsanjani seemed more determined to show his country's neutrality.[104] But on the main policy lines there was an agreement.

All Iranian officials criticized Saddam Husayn for having invaded Kuwait and denounced the anti-Islamic nature of his rule.[105] They therefore all wished to see Saddam weakened. Ahmad said that Saddam would never be a "human being," and as long as he retained power there would be no peace and tranquillity in the region.[106] Rafsanjani predicted that the Ba'th regime would not be able to put the country back on its feet (thus indirectly encouraging the regime's downfall), and "advised" the Iraqi Government to "yield to popular will" (and resign).[107] Khamene'i stated simply that the Ba'th regime did not have the right to rule,[108] and Ardebili called on Saddam to resign in order to avoid the further shedding of Muslim blood.[109]

At the same time, Tehran openly accused the US of misusing the UN resolutions to destroy the Iraqi economic infrastructure and its cultural centers.[110] All officials accused Washington of striving to sustain its power in the region and stated that Tehran would not put up with such an ambition. Karubi was speaking for most of his colleagues — certainly for the radicals — when he stated that the very presence of American troops in the region was a disgrace to all Muslims, and therefore should not be accepted.[111] Iranian officials also shared the opinion that fighting should be stopped (even before the land operation started) to avoid further shedding of Muslim blood and additional damage to a Muslim state.[112] Moreover, they all expressed support for maintaining the territorial integrity of Iraq,[113] and stated that Tehran would not deny support for the Iraqi *people*.[114]

Following the war, developments in Iraq continued to occupy an important place in Iranian policy. Attention was focused on these major issues: new regional arrangements for the security of the region (see below); the attitude toward Saddam's domestic rivals (mainly the Shi'is); and reparations from Iraq for the Iraqi-Iranian war damage.

With regard to the last issue, Tehran insisted on receiving its due reparations.[115]

Rafsanjani set the amount now demanded at $900bn. ($600bn. for direct and $300bn. for indirect damages).[116] The *Tehran Times* claimed that Kuwait stood only "next after Iran" in its right for reparations.[117]

While denouncing the Iraqi suppression of the Shi'is in Iraq, Tehran nevertheless stated that it would not interfere in Iraq's domestic affairs. Ayatollah Mohammad Reza Golpaygani led the criticism, maintaining that Iraq's policy vis-à-vis the Shi'is showed that it had no respect whatsoever for religious principles. He asked Muslims to show their disgust at sacrilege to the holy places, the massacre of Muslims, and the oppression and injustice on the part of the Ba'th rulers against the Iraqi people.[118] However, although all Iranian leaders criticized the suppression of the Shi'is and the demolition of some holy places, they also made it known that Iran viewed this as an Iraqi internal issue, and would therefore not interfere (but cf. above). In stressing this policy of expediency, however, Rafsanjani expressed the hope that developments there would favor the Iraqi people and Islam.[119] He stated that "we do not hesitate to prove our moral and political solidarity with the Iraqi people. Yet we will not intervene through the use of arms."[120] This, he continued, did not contradict the declared aim of exporting the revolution, which only concerned the *enteqal-e afkar* ("transfer of ideas") anyway.[121] Khamene'i concluded in March that although the continuation of Saddam's rule was "dangerous and detrimental...to the interests of the Muslims," and while he wished that "an Islamic and truly popular government... will come to power" in Iraq, Iranian intervention was "not recommended."[122] Karubi, Ardebili and Yazdi similarly expressed the hope that the future of Iraq be determined by its own people alone.[123]

In connection with this issue, Iran criticized the Ba'th regime's treatment of Grand Ayatollah Abul-Qasem Kho'i, who had been brought by Saddam to Baghdad in the midst of the Shi'i uprising (see chapter on Iraq). Khamene'i blamed Baghdad for transferring him under duress and behaving shamefully against his eminence.[124] His detention was criticized in equally harsh terms by Ayatollah Mohammad 'Ali Araki, Golpaygani, Ahmad Khomeyni, Meshkini and other individuals and groups.[125]

From the Iranian point of view, there seemed to be several basic differences between the Shi'is and the Kurds: Tehran had considerably more interests in, and apparently more leverage among the Shi'is and would sincerely have liked them to have succeeded. Yet, apparently there were difficulties in attaining such a goal, especially as the Shi'is, unlike the Kurds, lacked a tradition of military struggle, and were more vulnerable to Baghdad's countermeasures. The likelihood of their success, Tehran seemed to have concluded, was minimal. Tehran, therefore, was caught in a dilemma: it wanted to support the Shi'is, but did not make its support public for fear that they would ultimately fail, in which case Tehran was likely to lose some of the advantages it had gained during the crisis. As in so many other instances, the pragmatic interests of the state also seemed to carry more weight than the dogmatic philosophy of the revolution — yet another sign of Iran's realpolitik.

Nor was Tehran's attitude to the Kurdish struggle without its basic dilemmas. The Kurds seemed to have a better chance of success than the Shi'is, but Tehran had little incentive to help them realize such an aim. A Kurdish victory could have had some advantages, but also contained potential threats for Tehran. On the one hand, Kurdish success could further diminish Baghdad's power and force Iraq to concentrate on its domestic problems; on the other hand, however, the Kurds' triumph in Iraq could have repercussions on Iranian Kurds — provoking them either to strive for a similar status in Iran, or to join their brothers across the border. Both were detrimental from an Iranian perspective.

The Security of the Gulf Following the War

Iran made it known even before the war, and more forcefully in its aftermath, that it wished to play a key role in any strategic arrangement in the region. Rafsanjani said that although Iran did not wish to become a hegemonic power, and while it was willing to be on friendly terms with all regional states and "together" create "a new security system," it should also be clear that Tehran wished to be one of the main influences involved in maintaining the region's security.[126] His more radical associates were even more forceful. According to *Abrar,* since Iran was the "strongest and biggest country" in the region, no security system could be established without it.[127] *Jomhuri-ye Islami* concluded, from the same premises, that any arrangement which did not include Tehran, which had the longest border with the Gulf, would simply be "meaningless."[128]

The Iranian stance on the Gulf's security was, broadly speaking, crystal clear, and remained consistent throughout the revolutionary era. Iran believed that the Gulf's coastal states should be responsible for the security of the Gulf and that the Gulf should be free from foreign interference. The Iranians felt that they should have a share in the security of the Gulf proportional to the country's power, and its long border with the Gulf. Based on these premises, Tehran was now also opposed to any Arab security system, and objected to any of the nonregional Arab states participating in security arrangements. Despite the significant changes in overall Iranian politics, and given the disagreements among the revolutionary camps on so many issues, these precepts were adhered to throughout the revolutionary era and all domestic groupings agreed with them unanimously.

Nevertheless, certain developments led to a somewhat greater governmental pragmatism. First, in keeping with the general trend of growing pragmatism, Tehran seemed more intent on improving its relations with the Gulf coastal states (see below). Second, the Gulf War of 1991 and the consequent weakening of Iraq removed — at least temporarily — the threat of its most powerful rival in the Gulf who was striving for hegemony and threatening Iranian interests. Third, a change in the Iranian approach was influenced by the changes in the world order and the weakening, to the point of ineffectiveness, of the Soviet Union's position in the region, with the consequent benefits for the American position.

While there was unanimous agreement on the principal questions, the various camps nevertheless differed on more minor, yet significant, issues, such as the kind of relations Iran should maintain with other coastal states; how forceful Iranian opposition should be to other coastal states' initiatives to invite foreign powers; and what the actual Iranian policy in exporting its revolution to such countries should be.

Once again, while the radicals wished to keep to revolutionary dogma, those who were more pragmatic, and the government as such, favored greater realism aimed at better understanding and closer ties with such states as Saudi Arabia and the United Arab Emirates. According to one of Rafsanjani's advisers, at a meeting with Khamene'i at the end of the year the president defended his government's policy of bolstering relations with the Gulf states and launched a campaign against the hard-liners who, he said, wanted to isolate Iran from its environment and from the world.[129]

The government expected to be invited by the Gulf Cooperation Council (GCC) to take part in the Gulf security arrangements. In order to prepare the ground for such a development, Velayati visited Riyadh late in April. However, it would appear that these efforts did not lead to any meaningful agreement. Iran was therefore left with no choice other than to engineer a key role for itself in the security of the Gulf and to prevent all-Arab arrangements, and even more so superpower involvement. As one Iranian source put it, Tehran "is playing its hand in a poker game with very high stakes. The name of the game is *Realpolitik*."[130] When Kuwait invited the US to establish a station on Kuwaiti soil, Tehran voiced its opposition, though "in a mild tone, which was more advisory than quarrelsome."[131] It seemed that Tehran was aware of Kuwait's apprehension, yet it was not willing to tolerate an American presence.

Greater Pragmatism in Exporting the Revolution

As with so many other dogmatic principles, Tehran's policy concerning the export of the revolution changed considerably after the Islamic regime came to power.[132] Although all leaders continued to express support for the idea, the pragmatic interests of the state gained supremacy over the radical philosophy of the revolution in the course of time. The vision was not abandoned; but, practical calculations took priority over its implementation. Khomeyni himself was forced to change his order of priorities by the lack of spontaneous Muslim response, on the one hand, and the exigencies of the Iraqi-Iranian War on the other. The export of the revolution had to give priority to the consolidation of the revolution in Iran to set an attractive example that might be emulated elsewhere. In fact, Khomeyni's theories of Islamic unity that had characterized his thought since the late 1960s, were disseminated much more loyally by his followers outside Iran (i.e., the Hizballah in Lebanon and al-Da'wa in Iraq) than by his disciples at home. Here too, Iran was compelled to operate within the constraints of realpolitik.

Nevertheless, in tactical terms, Tehran continued to progress toward its goal using different methods, wherever the opportunity presented itself, i.e., in Lebanon, Sudan and Algeria. In this sense the actual policy of the Islamic regime was not very different from the historical Shi'i tradition of attempting to "export" its ideas whenever the opportunity presents itself. However, even in places where it may have been possible to successfully "export," Tehran worked with great caution, so as not to jeopardize its national interests. One such example was its attitude toward the Shi'i uprising in Iraq (see above); another was its expedient policy toward the Muslim people of the USSR in the fall of 1991. In both cases Tehran wished first and foremost to protect its national interests.

In these, as in other instances, the revolutionary establishment adopted a more conciliatory tone when appealing to governments, although certain more radical segments of the leadership continued to operate among Muslim extremist movements with greater fervor, as in Lebanon, the Gaza Strip, Algeria and Sudan. For leaders such as Mohtashami, Kho'iniha, Khalkhali and Meshkini, commitment to exporting the revolution remained as firm as ever.[133] The government used the victory of the Islamic Salvation Front in Algiers as an example both of the kind of export they now had in mind as well as proof of the influence of the Iranian revolution beyond its frontiers. Some 170 Majlis members addressed a letter to the Front, asserting that their victory showed in fact the extensive influence of Islamic movements — inspired by Iran — throughout the Muslim world[134] (see chapter on Islamic affairs).

Here, too, Rafsanjani led the pragmatists. Thus, when referring to the Iraqi Shi'is, he said that the export of the revolution only meant the transfer of ideas, nothing more (see above). Similarly, in mid-July he said that such an aim could not be achieved by force and that the best way to export the revolution was to concentrate on domestic policy. Only by solving Iran's internal problems could the revolution set an example for other communities to emulate.[135] Yet, such pragmatism notwithstanding, Iran continued to advocate military measures against Israel, and Israeli interests throughout the world. Similarly, as stated above, they were actively engaged in supporting Islamic movements in different localities, such as in Sudan.

Relations with Saudi Arabia and Qatar

The Hajj has always been a suitable measure by which to judge relations between Tehran and Riyadh. Its approach has often signaled, rather than caused, the existing tension in bilateral relations. Each of the countries had its own interpretation of the pilgrimage's significance and this had led to harsh mutual criticism in the past.[136] However, in 1991, the circumstances were different. As a consequence of the developments since the 1991 Gulf War, both sides wished to improve the atmosphere. They therefore endeavored to solve this problem well before the pilgrimage season began and to prepare the ground for the resumption of full political ties.

Since 1987, Tehran had not participated in the annual pilgrimage and this of course was unacceptable to Tehran for three main reasons. As the "most important country" in the Gulf area, Iran had to take part in the most important Islamic event of the year. Moreover, Iran considered itself the leader of the Islamic world and therefore its presence was essential. Iranian participation was equally important as part of its bid to export the revolution. Saudi Arabia now had its own reasons for wanting to see Tehran participating (see chapters on Saudi Arabia and Islamic affairs).

As far as the Hajj itself was concerned, the main problems had always concerned the quota of Iranian pilgrims and the fact that the Iranians demanded the right to hold "political" demonstrations. The Saudis did not wish to agree to the Iranian demands, but were now clearly willing to reach a compromise. According to an agreement reached in mid-March, Iran was allowed to send some 110,000 pilgrims (Tehran had wished to send 150,000) who would be entitled to hold a gathering (outside of Mecca) to express their distinctive views. This was an important step in the normalization of bilateral relations, which opened the way for more constructive discussions to reestablish ties, since — as *Jomhuri-ye Islami* wrote — Tehran always viewed its relations with Saudi Arabia "within the framework of the Hajj rituals and other Islamic precepts."[137]

Tehran agreed to renew relations, while at the same time stressing that the hostile attitude in the past could not be forgotten.[138] Following the official announcement of the resumption of ties on 26 March, the Iranian foreign ministry's director for Persian Gulf affairs, Mostafa Fumani-Ha'eri, left for Saudi Arabia on 30 March. The main topics of his discussions were issues related to the pilgrimage as well as other aspects of bilateral and regional relations.[139]

At the end of April, Velayati visited Saudi Arabia and met with the king, the foreign minister and other officials. The Hajj was again a major topic of discussion; however, bilateral issues as well as regional security questions were also at the forefront. Early in June, Saudi Foreign Minister Sa'ud al-Faysal returned the visit. In his meeting with the guest, Velayati expressed satisfaction with the cooperation that already existed between the two states, and said that they had opened a new page in their relations.[140] Rafsanjani conveyed similar satisfaction.[141] Sa'ud al-Faysal invited Rafsanjani to visit Riyadh and added that the recent warming of Saudi-Iranian relations would "have important effects for the [entire] Islamic community."[142]

For the first time since 1987, Iranian pilgrims took part in the Hajj in 1991. Although unable to persuade the Saudis to agree to all their demands in terms of sending a larger contingent, and turning the Hajj into a major political event, Iran nevertheless had a remarkable representation (some 117,000 pilgrims, the largest group from any Muslim community) who were allowed, with certain restrictions, to voice their particular ideas about the Hajj and other "Islamic" matters (i.e., Israel and the US).

Despite differences, bilateral relations continued to develop and the atmosphere improved considerably. In June, Velayati paid another visit to Riyadh, holding two meetings with King Fahd as well as other meetings. Velayati stated that bilateral relations were developing in an extremely positive way.[143] King Fahd's present to Rafsanjani (a piece of the black cloth that drapes the Ka'ba) was seen as another token of improving ties, with Radio Tehran expressing gratitude for this "precious gift."[144] True, there still were significant disagreements to work out. These included the security of the Gulf; disagreements regarding the future government of Afghanistan; the peace process between the Arabs and Israel; their different attitudes toward the US; and their competition for influence over the Soviet Muslims. Their basic abiding differences on the interrelation between Islam and politics remained another area of potential contention. Yet, with all these important areas of possible clashes of interests, both sides seemed willing to mend their fences and establish closer ties in 1991.

The four-day official visit to Tehran of Qatar's heir apparent (7–11 November) and his support for the Iranian stance vis-à-vis the Gulf security system was regarded as a significant success by Iran.[145] The two sides signed five agreements for cooperation in the fields of education, labor, air transportation, trade and economy and the transfer of Iranian fresh water to the shaykhdom.[146] In a joint communiqué both sides stressed that the interests of all parties in the region would be best served if the security and stability of the region was maintained. They also called for closer relations between Tehran and the GCC, and announced readiness to expand bilateral relations.[147]

THE MIDDLE EAST AND SOUTHEAST ASIA
Relations with Turkey and Syria
Late in April, Rafsanjani left for a six-day state visit to Damascus and Ankara. The idea was to bring about closer relations between Iran and Syria, and Turkey following the war. The main emphasis of his discussions in Turkey was on the economic ties between the two states and mutual relations in the light of the Gulf War. In Syria they also focused on the questions of Palestine and Lebanon.

Revolutionary Iran and Turkey had several common interests, which could have made them suitable allies. The two Muslim states shared certain economic interests and had a more or less similar approach to the Gulf War, although, unlike Tehran, Turkey participated in the coalition. However, following a short period of smooth running early in 1991, tension in bilateral relations reemerged later in the year.

Certain characteristics of Turkey seemed to work against their alliance. Its being the most secular Muslim country; its alliance with the US with Nato bases on its territory (near the Iranian border); and its being the only Muslim state other than Egypt, to maintain diplomatic relations with Israel. Furthermore, both countries differed in their attitudes to the Kurdish problem in Iraq, which Tehran feared might be used as a pretext by Ankara to invade northern Iraq. Developments in the Soviet Union in the latter part of 1991 further clouded mutual relations, with both countries "competing" to win the hearts of the Muslims there — Iran for Islamic considerations, and Turkey for pan-Turkish reasons. In October, the tension reached its peak.

On 22 October, the Turks seized the cargo ship, *Cape Maleas,* which was bound for Iran, in the Bosphorus, suspecting it carried cargo which might have been destined for an unnamed terrorist organization. Although outraged, the Iranian Government thought it unwise to react severely, and the foreign minister "was satisfied" with recalling the ambassador for "consultations."[148] The radicals called for more extreme action, claiming that the Turks had seized the ship on orders from Washington and in a move to serve Israeli interests.[149] *Kayhan* wrote that Turkey had always acted as "the threatening tongue of the West."[150] *Tehran Times,* which often expressed pragmatic stances, similarly stated that Turkey was acting against Iran's interests and in the service of Washington.[151] (In March 1992, a Turkish court ruled for the confiscation of the cargo, thus adding to Iranian outrage.)

There had always been a significant ideological disparity between Damascus and Tehran.[152] Nevertheless, since the Islamic regime came to power, these strange bedfellows had been each others' best, if not sole, allies in the region. In 1991, relations between these unlikely friends were soured by two developments: Syria's participation in the American-led coalition against Iraq at the beginning of the year, and its participation in the ME peace conference at its end. In both instances the two allies had different approaches. Yet, despite Tehran's provocative statements, there seemed to be at least some measure of understanding for the Syrian policy, both because of Tehran's own mixed feelings about the Iraqi regime and its policy (see above), and because Tehran was aware of the domestic as well as international considerations which forced Damascus to participate in the peace conference (see below). For these reasons, Tehran was hesitant to go beyond a mild response, given its lack of allies.

New Dynamics in Relations with Southeast Asia

In 1991 Tehran endeavored to cultivate its ties with the countries of southeast Asia, mainly China and India as well as the Muslim nations of that region. This was in line with the recent trend of expanding foreign relations, and motivated by the difficulties Iran was having with the Western states (see above).

Since the late summer there had in fact been "heavy traffic" between Tehran and capitals of southeast Asia's Muslim countries, with visits to Tehran by the foreign ministers of Bangladesh and Indonesia and the deputy prime minister of Malaysia among many others. Velayati saw a great possibility of economic and strategic cooperation between these countries.[153] From Iran's point of view, this became even more imperative due to the unipolarization of the world. Tehran now wished for a more extensive cooperation in political, economic and military issues with such countries as China, India, Indonesia, Malaysia and Pakistan. Velayati stated that the world system should not remain unipolar, and that "the Third World in general and the Islamic world in particular should form an independent group."[154] What he implied was, in fact, that this new alliance should replace the void left by the USSR.

Iran saw China as the most important nation in southeast Asia, a balancing power in the world system, leading the developing countries. Relations did in fact prosper, as growing official contacts might have suggested. The most important of these official contacts was the Chinese president's visit to Tehran (30 October–2 November). The Chinese prime minister had already visited Tehran in July; he was followed by a Chinese parliamentary group, in September; the Chinese minister of construction, in mid-November; and the Chinese minister of machine-building and the electronics industry, early in December.[155]

Referring to the change in the world order during the Chinese president's visit, Rafsanjani said that such developments gave China — a powerful and nonaligned country — a heavier responsibility.[156] He singled out China's support for Iran during the Iraqi-Iranian War and his own visit to China in 1985 (see *MECS* 1984–85, pp. 451–52), adding that his country viewed China as "one of our sincere partners."[157] Both states denied secret cooperation on an Iranian nuclear weapons program, although China confirmed that it had a nuclear cooperation program with Iran for peaceful purposes.[158] Western sources maintained that China sold Iran more military weaponry than had been published, and that China provided Tehran with nuclear technology. The available sources did not permit any definitive conclusions as to the scope of their cooperation in this field. However, there were also important disagreements between Iran and China. For example, China refused to condemn the ME peace conference, and openly expressed its intention to establish relations with Israel, as in fact it did on 24 January 1992.

From 8–12 November, the Indian foreign minister visited Tehran. Although negotiations on economic questions were eventually successful, they were less so on political issues. In the field of politics, major disagreements overshadowed attempts to establish firmer relations. Iranian support for the Kashmir rebels was one obstacle in the way of better relations, with India calling on Tehran to refrain from supporting them, and Tehran maintaining that it was only providing humanitarian assistance. India also reneged on its nuclear commitment to Iran, causing Iranian outrage.[159] Indian support for the ME peace conference, as well as rumors of the possible establishment of ties with Israel, caused further disagreement. (Relations between India and Israel were established early in 1992.) However, despite all these problems, the two countries expressed their pleasure at the visit and signed five memoranda of understanding. These included the transfer of technical expertise; increased trade in industrial goods; joint investments and the possibility of exporting manufactured goods to other markets; and the exchange of commercial delegations.[160]

IRAN AND THE MIDDLE EAST PEACE PROCESS
Iran was totally against the US initiative in organizing the ME peace conference (for a discussion of the conference, see chapter on the ME peace process). Its policy was

based on several considerations. Tehran regarded itself as the major anti-American force and saw it as its duty to oppose any American-led initiative aimed at strengthening US control over the region. Iran similarly viewed itself as the major enemy of "America's unlawful son" (i.e., Israel), and felt it was its responsibility to oppose any initiative aimed at legitimizing its existence. By leading the opposition to the conference, Iran saw another way to show the world as a whole, the Muslim community and the population at home that Iran was the leading Muslim state.

To advance its policy Tehran missed no opportunity to criticize the US and present it as an archenemy of the Muslim world; to denounce Israel and deny its right to exist; and to criticize the Arab states participating in the conference. An international conference on Palestine, held in Tehran in October, was Iran's main attempt to unite under its leadership all the radical movements opposing the US-initiated peace conference in Madrid.

By and large, all internal factions agreed unanimously on these three reasons why Iran opposed the peace process. Rafsanjani articulated the sentiments of the entire leadership when, in a Friday sermon in mid-July he claimed that it was impossible for Muslims to trust America's good intentions: "One cannot accept that you want to make peace, while...you take Jews from Ethiopia, Albania, Yugoslavia, the Soviet Union...[and] airlift them to Israel. We would not believe it."[161] *Jomhuri-ye Islami* wrote that "the ME sector of America's new world order only means domination and, ultimately, the exploitation of the ME."[162] It also added that the US wished to use the conference to strengthen Israel, and that the Arabs would receive nothing in return but "disgrace and contempt."[163] Ahmad Khomeyni said the US wished to draw the Arabs into a humiliating compromise with Israel, having in mind only to undermine Islam.[164]

Tehran's criticism of Israel was similarly uniform. In a Friday sermon early in August, Ayatollah Ardebili said that the US wished to make Israel the "absolute lord of the region so we [Muslims] become the servant of the servant of America."[165] A similar approach was taken in its condemnation of the "reactionary" Arab states participating in the peace process. They, *Jomhuri-ye Islami* wrote, had bowed down before the US, which now wanted them to grovel before Israel as well.[166] Khamene'i threatened that any Arab leader negotiating with Israel would find his position among his people shaken.[167]

The October conference provided Tehran with an occasion to demonstrate its unity. However, closer study of the arguments, tone and language used by the various leaders revealed the same basic disagreements dividing the radicals from their more pragmatic associates. Thus, while Mohtashami and his colleagues went so far as to call for concrete action against American interests, Rafsanjani and his associates stopped short of calling for immediate action — neither against the Arab leaders participating in the conference, nor against the Americans. As with so many other issues, Khamene'i held the middle ground.

As might have been expected, Mohtashami was the most radical. In an interview with *al-Diyar,* he said it was part of Iran's "doctrine and duty" to struggle against the US and Israel, and maintained that all Muslims "must use various means to obstruct this [peace] conference."[168] In a Majlis speech (30 October), he denounced the "criminal US," the "hireling Arab leaders," certain "traitorous Palestinian leaders," and Israel. Arguing that participating in the conference was a "declaration of war against Islam," he warned that the revolutionary and martyr-nurturing offspring of Khomeyni would turn the world into a graveyard and an inferno for the Americans, the Zionists and their mercenaries. He went on to say that, "based on the Shari'a, all participants in the Madrid conference are considered *mohareb* [those who wage war on Islam] and they must face a death sentence. It is the duty of Muslims in the world to carry that out."[169] Based on the same considerations, he said elsewhere (21 October) that it was necessary to "target all the US objectives throughout the world."[170]

A similarly radical tone was used by Ardebili. In a Friday sermon (4 October), he called for resistance cells to be formed to fight against American interests, wherever they were, promising that whoever was killed in this struggle would "definitely be a martyr."[171] In late November, he used another Friday sermon to call on people to "kill Americans."[172] The radical paper *Jahan-e Islam* also called for a worldwide Islamic mobilization to inflict blows on American interests all over the world.[173]

Although critical of the conference, Rafsanjani did not go that far. His approach was typified by his "threat" (9 August) that even if the peace talks resulted in an agreement, the Arabs would never give up Palestine, and that one day the "Muslims will rise up against the Israeli mischief, and America will be left with [Muslim] spite and hatred forever."[174] *Kayhan International* suggested that such a plot be countered by the "effective role of diplomacy and publicity."[175]

Khamene'i was more radical than Rafsanjani, but less so than Mohtashami. On 25 August, he called on the Arabs to foil this plot with all their might. But from the context of his speech it was clear that what he had in mind was using "the active political publicity measures," not necessarily the use of arms. The only threat he was willing to make was that if the conference did in fact convene, "the devoted faithful Palestinian combatants should continue to stay on the scene."[176] Later (30 October), he went on to reiterate that those participating would be "hated by their nations," and suffer their wrath.[177]

While Tehran did not expect the other Arab states to take a different stance, it was greatly disappointed by Syria's participation. The Iranian approach to this also revealed the inherent dichotomy in Tehran's domestic rivalries. The more radical *Abrar* warned that Syria had already lost its credibility as an anti-imperialist power while participating in the war, and that it was now committing another mistake by taking part in the conference.[178] *Ettela'at* was more tolerant toward the Syrian move, describing the objective (mainly economic) difficulties facing Syria, and the change in the global order as the main reasons that compelled Syria to participate.[179]

NOTES

For the place and frequency of publications cited here, and for the full name of the publication, news agency, radio station, or monitoring service where an abbreviation is used, please see "List of Sources." Only in cases where there is more than one publication bearing the same name is the place of publication noted here.

1. For a discussion of their initial success in consolidating their rule, see David Menashri, "The Islamic Revolution in Iran: The Consolidation Phase," *Orient*, 4/84, pp. 499–515. See also idem, *Iran: A Decade of War and Revolution* (New York: Holmes & Meier, 1990), pp. 4–11.
2. For discussion of the gradual, but significant deviation from some major doctrinal

convictions of the revolutionary movement, see: David Menashri, "Iran: Doctrine and Reality," in Efraim Karsh (ed.), *The Iran-Iraq War: Impacts and Implications* (London: MacMillan, 1989), pp. 42–57. Also idem, *Iran: A Decade of War and Revolution,* pp. 366–69.

3. Rafsanjani said of Ahmad Khomeyni and 'Ali Akbar Mohtashami: they are "of the best people of the country." His policies, he added, are coordinated with Ahmad (*Ettela'at,* 27 March 1991). Ahmad, for his part, described Rafsanjani as "being in the line of the Imam. He is a great revolutionary" (*Ettela'at,* 2 February 1991). However, there were many differences between them (see below).

4. *Echo of Iran,* No. 41 (June 1991), p. 17.

5. Such a distinction has already been made by Ayatollah Hoseyn 'Ali Montazeri in 1986 when explaining the differences dividing his associates and the government. In an interview with the Beirut paper *al-Shira'* (3 November 1986) he said: the philosophy of my office "is different from yours. You are a state [*dawla*] with relations that you must preserve. The office is a revolution [*thawra*]." See also Menashri, *Iran: A Decade of War and Revolution,* pp. 379–80.

6. R. Tehran, 20 December — DR, 23 December 1991. It should be noted, that these phrases in his speech were deleted from the reports on his sermon, otherwise reported in length in the following day's papers: *Kayhan* (Tehran), *Ettela'at* and *Abrar,* for example. For Rafsanjani's pragmatic approach in 1984, see Menashri, *Iran: A Decade of War and Revolution,* pp. 323–25.

7. *Der Spiegel,* 25 March as quoted in *Ettela'at,* 27 March and DR, 26 March 1991.

8. *Salam,* 17 March, as quoted in DR, 8 April 1991.

9. In his interview with *Der Spiegel* (quoted in *Ettela'at,* 27 March 1991), Rafsanjani maintained that he was not changing his views, what was changing were the circumstances (see below).

10. *Echo of Iran,* No. 40 (May 1991), p. 19.

11. *Ettela'at,* 25 April; IRNA, 23 April — DR, 24 April 1991.

12. *Ettela'at,* 5 February 1991.

13. R. Tehran, 21 May — *Echo of Iran,* No. 40 (May 1991), p. 14.

14. *Kayhan* (Tehran), 25 May; *Echo of Iran,* No. 40 (May 1991), pp. 12–13; No. 41 (June 1991), p. 10.

15. *Echo of Iran,* No. 40 (May 1991), p. 19.

16. *Salam* as quoted by *Echo of Iran,* No. 40 (May 1991), p. 14.

17. Tehran TV, 2 June — *Echo of Iran,* No. 41 (June 1991), p. 12.

18. *JI,* 6 November; IRNA, 5 November — DR, 6 November 1991.

19. *Salam,* 10 December; IRNA, 9 December — DR, 11 December 1991.

20. *JI,* 9 November. For more criticism see, *Ettela'at,* 5 December 1991.

21. *Resalat,* 9 November 1991.

22. *Echo of Iran,* No. 40 (May 1991), p. 13.

23. *Echo of Iran,* No. 43 (August-September 1991), p. 18.

24. Tehran TV, 2 June — *Echo of Iran,* No. 41 (June 1991), p. 12.

25. *Salam,* 6 June — *Echo of Iran,* No. 41 (June 1991), p. 12.

26. *Echo of Iran,* No. 41 (June 1991), pp. 12–13.

27. *Echo of Iran,* No. 46 (November 1991), p. 17.

28. For their relations in earlier years, see Menashri, *Iran: A Decade of War and Revolution,* pp. 264, 307–9, 350–52, 390.

29. *Ettela'at,* 22 April 1991. He then also confessed that the fact that Khamene'i was lacking such qualifications could cause difficulties for the regime. Faced with such delicate problems, Khomeyni could instantly solve them by issuing a *fatwa* (religious decree); Khamene'i lacked the religious credentials to do the same.

30. *Ettela'at,* 1 June; *JI,* 1 June — *Echo of Iran,* No. 41 (June 1991), p. 11.

31. *Ettela'at,* 18 July; R. Tehran, 18 July — DR, 19 July 1991.

32. *Resalat,* 18 November; *Bayan,* 22 November–21 December — DR, 31 December 1991.

33. *Resalat,* 18 November 1991.

34. Ibid.

35. *Bayan,* 22 November–21 December — DR, 31 December 1991.

36. *Resalat,* 18 November 1991.
37. For such problems in the first years of the revolutionary regime and their effect on growing public resentment, see Menashri, *Iran: A Decade of war and Revolution,* pp. 197–98, 230–34, 277–78, 280, 325–27, 355–59. For an example of the accelerated growth of the population and the ensuing social and economic difficulties, as well as the government's current attempts to block the growth, see a report in *Ettela'at,* 14–23 October 1991.
38. *Resalat,* 13 July 1991.
39. These were the words of Majlis deputy Karim Malek-Asa on 15 September; *Resalat,* 16 September 1991.
40. The discrepancy between high-school graduates and numbers of university admissions grew from 10,000 in 1961–62 to over 250,000 in 1978–79. In each of the last three years of the Shah's rule, between 250,000 and 300,000 youngsters applied for university admission; the highest actual admission figure (that of 1978–79) was just under 30,000. For this and its consequent political implications for the Shah's regime, see: David Menashri, *Education and the Making of Modern Iran* (Ithaca: Cornell University Press, 1992), in particular pp. 205–9. In 1984/85 there had already been over 500,000 applicants who were denied university admission (see *MECS* 1987, p. 402). In 1990 the number grew to as many as 700,000 (*Jahan-e Islam,* 31 July — DR, 9 August 1991).
41. *JI,* 9 July 1991.
42. *Resalat,* 13 July 1991.
43. *Echo of Iran,* No. 43 (August-September 1991), pp. 11–12.
44. *NYT,* 3 August 1991.
45. See, e.g., a broadcast over R. Tehran, 19 November — DR, 20 November 1991.
46. *NYT,* 3 August 1991.
47. *MEED,* 8 November 1991; *Echo of Iran,* No. 46 (November 1991), p. 12.
48. *Echo of Iran,* No. 46 (November 1991), p. 12.
49. *JP,* 5 July 1991.
50. *Kayhan* (London), 6 June 1991.
51. *Ettela'at,* 15 August; *Echo of Iran,* No. 43 (August-September 1991), p. 12.
52. *Resalat,* 23 November; R. Tehran, 22 November — DR, 26 November 1991.
53. *Echo of Iran,* No. 43 (August–September 1991), p. 12.
54. *Kayhan* (Tehran), 18 August 1991.
55. Tehran TV, 19 November — DR, 22 November 1991.
56. *Ettela'at,* 7 December; R. Tehran, 7 December — DR, 13 December 1991.
57. *Echo of Iran,* No. 45 (October 1991), p. 11.
58. *Ettela'at,* 22 April; IRNA, 22 April — DR, 23 April 1991.
59. *Echo of Iran,* No. 40 (May 1991), p. 18.
60. *Der Spiegel,* 25 March as quoted in *Ettela'at,* 27 March and DR, 26 March 1991.
61. See an interview with him in *Der Spiegel,* 25 March as cited in *Ettela'at,* 27 March and DR, 26 March 1991. Rafsanjani did not deny that there were people in the Iranian leadership who held more radical views, but dismissed them as not being "a powerful trend" (*jaryan-e qavi*).
62. *JI,* 22 April; IRNA, 21 April — DR, 22 April 1991. At the same time, Rafsanjani, too, suggested that Washington should prove its goodwill by action, not words (*Ettela'at,* 22 April 1991).
63. *Ettela'at,* 6 May 1991.
64. *NYT,* 7 May 1991.
65. *NYT,* 26 May; *Echo of Iran,* No. 41 (June 1991), p. 18.
66. *Ettela'at,* 3 June; R. Tehran, 3 June — DR, 7 June 1991 (emphasis added).
67. *Ettela'at,* 2 June; *Ha'aretz,* 22 May 1991.
68. *Kayhan* (Tehran), 1 May 1991.
69. *Abrar,* 12 March — DR, 25 March 1991.
70. IRNA, 22 October — DR, 23 October 1991.
71. *Ettela'at,* 10 October; R. Tehran, 9 October — DR, 10 October 1991.
72. *Ettela'at,* 12 October; R. Tehran, 11 October — DR, 18 October 1991.
73. R. Tehran, 31 October — DR, 1 November 1991.
74. *Echo of Iran,* No. 41 (June 1991), p. 8.

75. *NYT,* 28 May 1991.
76. *JP,* 5 May 1991.
77. *TT,* 12 May 1991.
78. *Echo of Iran,* No. 46 (November), p. 10. According to *NYT* (21 November 1991), Washington was to undertake to pay Iran $275m. as partial compensation for the military equipment Tehran had paid for, which had been frozen since the revolution. It seemed hard to believe that the timing of such negotiations, following the release of the hostages, was a pure coincidence. For more on American payments to Iran for undelivered weapons, see *FT,* 4 December 1991.
79. R. Tehran, 4 May — DR, 6 May 1991.
80. *Soroush,* 18 May — DR, 28 May 1991.
81. *IHT,* 4 July 1991.
82. R. Tehran, 6 October — DR, 7 October 1991.
83. *TT,* 7 October 1991.
84. R. Tehran, 26 October — DR, 28 October 1991.
85. *JI,* 4 November — DR, 5 November 1991.
86. R. Tehran, 29 December — DR, 30 December 1991.
87. *JI,* 31 December — DR, 31 December 1991.
88. *JI,* 26 December — DR, 26 December 1991.
89. IRNA, 6 May — DR, 6 May 1991.
90. IRNA, 7 May — DR, 7 May 1991.
91. R. Tehran, 15 July — DR, 16 July 1991. For the expanding commercial ties between the two countries see article in *Der Spiegel,* 15 July 1991.
92. *FT,* 26 May 1991.
93. In a number of statements and interviews, Rafsanjani made the point that their arrival was not coordinated with Tehran, and that Iran did not want them to come. He stressed that they would not be allowed to go back as long as the war continued, but denied that they would be kept as a partial reparation for the Iranian losses in the Iraqi-Iranian War: see, e.g., *Ettela'at,* 3, 4 February, 27 March 1991.
94. For his proposed scheme for a cease-fire, see *Ettela'at,* 27 January 1991.
95. *Ettela'at,* 28 January, 2 February 1991.
96. *Ettela'at,* 26 January 1991.
97. *Ettela'at,* 17 January 1991.
98. R. Tehran, 19 January — DR, 22 January 1991.
99. R. Tehran, 20 January — DR, 22 January 1991.
100. R. Tehran, 23 January — DR, 24 January 1991.
101. R. Tehran, 24 January — DR, 24 January 1991.
102. An interview with *Der Spiegel,* 25 March as cited in *Ettela'at,* 27 March 1991.
103. See, e.g., his statement on this subject quoted in *Ettela'at,* 2 February 1991. (Yet, at the same time he also criticized Kuwait for denying his father asylum there at that time.)
104. He repeatedly made it clear that as long as his country's neutrality was honored, Iran would not take part in the war (*Ettela'at,* 4 and 5 February 1991). "We would never shed our blood to enable the US to achieve its aims nor for Iraq's remaining in Kuwait," he added (ibid., 21 February 1991). Even when asked whether Iran would take part in the war in case of Israeli involvement, all he had to say was that the Iranian National Security Council had not discussed this issue yet: *Ettela'at,* 4 February 1991.
105. See, e.g., statements by Khamene'i (*Ettela'at,* 26 January) and Ahmad Khomeyni (ibid., 28 January and 6 February 1991).
106. *Ettela'at,* 28 January 1991.
107. *Ettela'at,* 9 March 1991.
108. *Ettela'at,* 3 March 1991.
109. *Ettela'at,* 16 March 1991.
110. See typical statements on this matter by Khamene'i (*Ettela'at,* 26 January) and Karubi (ibid., 7 February 1991).
111. *Ettela'at,* 17 January 1991.
112. See statements on this issue by Rafsanjani (*Ettela'at,* 21 January), Karubi (ibid., 27 January) and Ahmad Khomeyni (ibid., 28 January 1991).

113. See, e.g., statements by Karubi and Rafsanjani quoted in *Ettela'at*, 29 January and 11 March, respectively.

114. See, e.g., statements on this topic by Karubi (*Ettela'at*, 27 January), and Ahmad Khomeyni and Khamene'i (both quoted in *Ettela'at*, 2 February 1991).

115. See, e.g., statement by Velayati to this effect, *Ettela'at*, 3 March 1991.

116. See Rafsanjani's interview with *Der Spiegel* (25 March) as quoted in *Ettela'at*, 27 March and DR, 26 March 1991.

117. *TT*, 17 March 1991.

118. *Ettela'at*, 19 March; R. Tehran, 18 March — DR, 19 March 1991.

119. *Ettela'at*, 11, 12, 13 March 1991.

120. *Der Spiegel*, 25 March — DR, 26 March 1991.

121. From his interview with *Der Spiegel* (25 March) cited in *Ettela'at* (27 March 1991).

122. IRNA, 18 March — DR, 19 March 1991.

123. See their statements quoted in *Ettela'at*, 10, 16 and 30 March 1991, respectively.

124. R. Tehran, 21 March — DR, 22 March. The office of the leader issued a statement labeling the act as anti-Islamic; *Ettela'at*, 25 March 1991.

125. R. Tehran, 21, 22 March — DR, 22, 25 March; Tehran TV, 22 March — DR, 25 March; *Ettela'at*, 25 March. See also statement signed by some 160 Majlis members, ibid., 25 March 1991.

126. *Der Spiegel*, 25 March — DR, 26 March 1991.

127. *Abrar*, 13 March — DR, 25 March 1991.

128. *JI*, 16 March 1991.

129. *Sawt al-Kuwait al-Duwali*, 14 November 1991.

130. *Echo of Iran*, No. 40 (May 1991), p. 17.

131. R. Tehran, 1 September — *Echo of Iran*, No. 43 (August–September 1991), p. 4.

132. This issue was discussed in great detail in David Menashri, "Khomeyni's Vision: Nationalism or World Order?" published in idem (ed.), *The Iranian Revolution and the Muslim World* (Boulder, Col.: Westview Press, 1990), pp. 40–57.

133. See, e.g., recent extremist ideas raised by Mohtashami in his interview with *al-Diyar*, 28 October 1991.

134. R. Tehran, 29 December — DR, 30 December 1991.

135. *Ettela'at*, 17 July; IRNA, 17 July — DR, 17 July 1991.

136. For the contradictory approaches of the two states to this issue, see Jacob Goldberg, "Saudi Arabia and the Iranian Revolution: The Religious Dimension," in Menashri, *The Iranian Revolution and the Muslim World*, pp. 155–70. For previous occasional tension on the eve of the Hajj, see Menashri, *Iran: A Decade of War and Revolution*, pp. 209, 245–46, 293–94, 332–33. For an improved atmosphere on the eve of the 1985 Hajj, see ibid., 366–67.

137. *JI*, 26 March 1991.

138. Ibid.

139. *Ettela'at*, 31 March; R. Tehran, 30 March — DR, 2 April 1991.

140. R. Tehran, 5 June — DR, 6 June; *Ettela'at*, 8 June 1991.

141. R. Tehran, 6 June — DR, 6 June; *Ettela'at*, 8 June 1991.

142. *FT*, 7 June 1991. The invitation to Rafsanjani was renewed in December; *Ettela'at*, 5 December 1991.

143. Riyadh TV, 23 June — DR, 24 June 1991.

144. *Echo of Iran*, No. 46 (November 1991), pp. 7–8.

145. *Ettela'at*, 6, 7 November; *Echo of Iran*, No. 46 (November 1991), p. 8.

146. IRNA, 10 November — DR, 13 November; *Ettela'at*, 11 November 1991.

147. R. Tehran, 10 November — DR, 13 November 1991.

148. *Echo of Iran*, No. 46 (November 1991), p. 5.

149. *JI*, 11 November 1991.

150. *Kayhan* (Tehran), 10 November 1991.

151. *TT*, 10 November 1991.

152. For the political alliance between the two states, their conflicting ideologies and the vicissitudes of their relations since the revolution, see: Yosef Olmert, "Iranian-Syrian Relations: Between Islam and Realpolitik," in Menashri, *The Iranian Revolution and the*

Muslim World, pp. 171–88. See also Menashri, *Iran: A Decade of War and Revolution,* pp. 103, 210, 253, 294–95, 333–34, 362, 368–69.

153. *JI,* 26 August 1991.
154. *Echo of Iran,* No. 43 (August–September 1991), p. 10.
155. R. Tehran, 8, 14 December — DR, 9, 16 December 1991.
156. *Ettela'at,* 2 November; R. Tehran, 31 October, 1 November — *Echo of Iran,* No. 46 (November 1991), p. 10; DR, 5 November 1991.
157. *Ettela'at,* 31 October; R. Tehran, 30 October — DR, 1 November 1991.
158. *FT* and *NYT,* 1 November 1991.
159. *FT,* 21 November 1991.
160. R. Tehran, 11 November — DR, 13 November 1991.
161. R. Tehran, 12 July — DR, 15 July 1991.
162. *JI,* 20 July 1991.
163. *JI,* 23 July 1991.
164. R. Tehran, 6 August — DR, 6 August; *Ettela'at,* 6 August 1991.
165. R. Tehran, 2 August — DR, 5 August. Similarly, *Ettela'at,* 3 August 1991.
166. *JI,* 23 July 1991.
167. R. Tehran, 31 July — DR, 2 August; *Ettela'at,* 1 August 1991.
168. *Al-Diyar,* 28 October 1991.
169. R. Tehran, 30 October — DR, 30 October; *Abrar, FT, JP,* 31 October 1991.
170. *Abrar,* 22 October; IRNA, 22 October — DR, 23 October 1991.
171. R. Tehran, 4 October — DR, 7 October; *Ettela'at, FT,* 5 October 1991.
172. R. Tehran, 22 November — DR, 25 November; *Ettela'at,* 23 November 1991.
173. *Jahan-e Islam,* 2 November 1991.
174. *Ettela'at,* 10 August; R. Tehran, 9 August — DR, 9 August 1991.
175. *KI,* 27 October 1991.
176. *Ettela'at,* 26 August; IRNA, 25 August — DR, 27 August 1991.
177. *Ettela'at, FT,* 31 October; IRNA and R. Tehran, 30 October — DR, 31 October 1991.
178. *Abrar,* 5 August 1991.
179. *Ettela'at,* 29 July 1991.

Iraq
(Al-Jumhuriyya al-'Iraqiyya)

MEIR LITVAK

The year 1991, marked by defeat in the Gulf War and by civil war, was the most turbulent year in the history of modern Iraq. Unwilling to compromise over the occupation of Kuwait, President Saddam Husayn was willing to risk a war with the the US-led coalition, viewing a military defeat as politically less harmful than bowing to Western pressure.

Aware of his military inferiority vis-à-vis Allied air power, Husayn relied on a combination of political moves and propaganda in order to divide the Allied coalition from within and create public pressures in the West to end the war. His unwillingness to compromise led to the Allied ground attack, which overwhelmed the Iraqi army and drove it out of Kuwait. Husayn succeeded in escaping total defeat by publicly accepting all UN resolutions regarding Kuwait before his army was annihilated, although he never relinquished his claim to Kuwait.

Husayn's defeat elicited a mass uprising (Intifada) during March 1991 by the long-oppressed Shi'is in the south and Kurds in the north. The Shi'i Intifada, the largest popular movement in Iraqi history, proved to be the greatest domestic challenge the Ba'th regime had ever faced. With the core of the Iraqi army remaining loyal to Husayn, the rebellion was quelled within two weeks and the regime applied harsh, repressive measures in the entire Shi'i south throughout the year to put down sporadic armed resistance.

The Kurdish Intifada was crushed by late March. Terrified of the regime's retribution, c. 2m. Kurds fled to the mountainous Turkish and Iranian border areas. The suffering of these stranded refugees prompted the Allies, who had hitherto ignored the Kurdish plight, to establish safe zones for them in the northwestern region of Iraqi Kurdistan. However, even though the safe zones offered temporary humanitarian relief, they did not solve the Kurdish political problem.

In that the Shi'i and Kurdish rebels confined their aims to Iraq alone, rather than seek a supraterritorial solution, their defeat demonstrated the strength of the Iraqi territorial entity and that of the regime. Yet the sectarian nature of both rebellions, and the rallying of the Sunnis behind Husayn, revealed the resilience of religious and ethnic loyalties despite the regime's attempts to forge Iraqi patriotism by force. Ultimately, the brutal suppression of the rebellions further diminished prospects for reconciliation and national cohesion.

Husayn's major strategy after the war was to bide for time during the Allied withdrawal from Iraq, in order to overcome the external and internal challenges to his rule. In an attempt to allay popular discontent, he promised, and actually initiated various measures ostensibly leading to democratization, including the formation of a

417

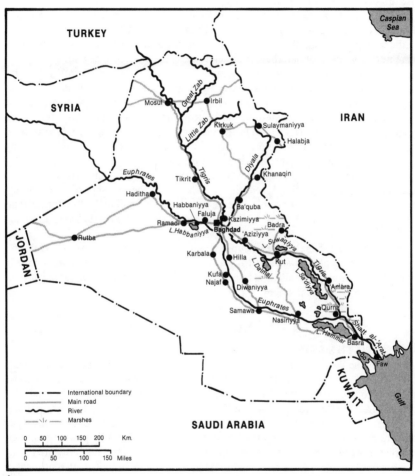

Iraq

new government under his Shi'i lieutenant Sa'dun Hammadi. Concurrently, he conducted a campaign to revitalize the Ba'th Party, which had been a prime target of popular hatred and which had failed as an instrument of control during the uprisings. The convening of the tenth Ba'th congress in September at which Husayn denounced Western liberalism, and Hammadi's subsequent dismissal marked the end of the pseudo-democratization process.

Husayn's real intentions were also revealed in negotiations he held with the Kurdish leadership from April to July. Procrastinating until the Allies had completed their withdrawal from Iraq, Husayn then presented the Kurds with a limited autonomy scheme that would have left them completely at his mercy. When the Kurds rejected it, he renewed his military offensive and imposed a blockade on northern Kurdistan.

Following its defeat, Iraq was required by the UN to dismantle its arsenal of unconventional weapons. While claiming to comply with the UN demand, Iraq attempted to conceal information and impede the working of the UN inspection teams, hoping that the UN would be forced to give up its efforts. The UN responded by maintaining sanctions against Iraq in the anticipation that economic hardship would stir opposition to Husayn within the Iraqi elite.

While Iraq made considerable progress in reconstructing its infrastructure during the course of the year, the Allied blockade hindered the recovery of its economy. Husayn, rejecting any compromise to ease the sanctions, exploited the suffering of his people to demonstrate Western brutality as well as to starve the rebellious Shi'is and Kurds.

Although the regime's base of support narrowed during the year and Husayn's control of the periphery was less firm than before, he could justifiably claim success in overcoming the major challenges to his regime. The prospects for the people of Iraq, however, did not appear bright.

IRAQ AND THE GULF WAR

GOING TO THE BRINK

As seen by the West, Iraq refused to display any flexibility in order to avert war during the two weeks in January preceding the war. While declaring its desire for a peaceful solution to the crisis, Iraq sought to deter the US from launching an attack by threatening to inflict unbearable casualties upon the attackers and by hinting that it would employ terror against Allied targets all over the world.[1] Concurrently, Iraq tried to drive a wedge between the US and its European allies by pointing up their conflicting economic interests in the region.[2] It also sought to exert pressure on the Arab states to withdraw from the coalition by appealing to the pan-Arab sentiment of the Arab masses and by cultivating opposition groups in various Arab states.[3] Iraq presented itself in these appeals as defying the US in the service of the Palestinian cause. Moreover, it portrayed the US-led effort as instigated by Israel in order to destroy Iraq, and threatened, therefore, that Israel would be its first target should war break out.[4]

Husayn also portrayed himself as the champion of Islam against Western imperialism. The culmination of these efforts was the convening of the International Islamic Popular Conference on 9 January, attended by representatives of Islamic movements from all over the world (see also chapter on Islam). In another show of piety, Husayn ordered the redesigning of the Iraqi flag on 14 January so as to include a drawing of the Islamic slogan *Allah akbar* (God is greatest).[5]

Iraq intensified its efforts to mend fences with Iran in preparation for the military conflict. On 8 January, a high-level Iraqi delegation headed by 'Izzat Ibrahim (al-Duri), deputy chairman of the Revolutionary Command Council (RCC), visited Iran, and the two states announced a mutual pullback of their forces to create a buffer zone of c. 1 km. along their common border. On 13 January, an Iranian delegation arrived in Baghdad, and the two sides signed an accord permitting mutual visits to the holy places in both countries. Iran also repatriated 166 prisoners of war (PoWs) to Iraq. These efforts, however, did not effect a profound change in the basic Iranian position on the Gulf crisis[6] (see chapter on Iran).

When an intense haggling by Baghdad with Washington over dates and locations that was intended to force the US to go beyond its ultimatum deadline failed, Iraq accepted President Bush's proposal for a meeting between the foreign ministers of the two states (see chapter on the US and the Middle East). Husayn, however, showed no intention of negotiating, but rather demonstrated his resolve to stand up to the US. Refusing to discuss withdrawal from Kuwait, Iraqi Foreign Minister Tariq 'Aziz insisted on the priority of the Palestinian question, and declined to accept a personal letter from President Bush to Husayn.[7] A last-minute mediation attempt by UN Secretary-General Javier Pérez de Cuellar, who arrived in Baghdad on 13 January, also failed to have any effect on Husayn.[8]

In order to boost the morale of his troops and of the population at large, Husayn presented his case as transcending the question of Kuwait and having become "a symbol of the whole nation...and an area of honor." The "mother of all battles" which had united Kuwait with Iraq, he declared, would also liberate Palestine, defeat American "tyranny," and drive "the forces of atheism from the holy lands of the Muslims." Justifying his refusal to budge, Husayn insisted that the US sought not peace, but Iraq's capitulation.[9]

Husayn's emphasis on Arab honor would appear to explain his unyielding stance. Initially he apparently believed that the US would not attack for fear of heavy casualties. He may have also viewed the internal debate in the US as a sign of weakness characteristic of democratic regimes. In addition, he probably expected the Allied coalition to break up from within prior to 15 January because of lack of resolve or internal conflicts. When he realized the inevitability of war, Husayn presumably hoped that even if defeated, his army would exact a heavy price from the Allied forces that would either force them to stop the war unilaterally, or at the very least turn him into a hero among the Arab masses. Thus, he would transform a military loss into a political victory as a leader who had defied the West, just as Egypt's President 'Abd al-Nasir had done in 1956. Backing down under an American ultimatum without war, on the other hand, would be regarded in Iraq as a greater humiliation and would pose a more serious threat to his leadership.

IRAQI POLICY DURING THE WAR
The outbreak of the war on 17 January at dawn took Iraq by surprise for Husayn had apparently fallen victim to his own propaganda regarding the West's lack of resolve (see chapter on the Gulf War). Aware of Allied air superiority, Husayn adopted a strategy of waiting until the ground assault in order to inflict heavy casualties on the

Allied forces, which optimally would force them to halt the war or at least give Iraq a heroic image. Concurrently, he hoped by the effective use of political maneuver and propaganda to divide the Allied coalition from within and create public pressure in the West and in the Arab world to end the war.

As soon as hostilities began, Iraq portrayed itself as a victim of ruthless Western aggression charging that the Allies were bombing mainly civilian, economic and religious targets. By the end of the war, Iraq claimed that c. 50,000 civilians had been killed. A delegation from the European Parliament visiting Iraq in March estimated the number as ranging between 3,000–10,000 civilian deaths.[10]

The Iraqi authorities brought foreign journalists, who had hitherto been restricted in their coverage of the war, to the site of a shelter that the Allies had bombed on 13 February in the belief that it was a military communications center, killing according to Iraq's claim c. 700 civilians, so that the charred bodies would be photographed as a manifestation of Allied brutality.[11] This publicity indeed had a shocking effect worldwide. Another propaganda feat showing captured Allied pilots on Iraqi television in order to demonstrate the price of war to the Allied public backfired: the clear evidence that the pilots had endured torture only enhanced support for the war in the US.

Focusing on Arab and Muslim audiences, Iraq accused the Allies of bombing mosques and enlisted its religious leaders to appeal to the Islamic world to "save Iraq and its holy places from the aggression of the infidels." Of particular importance were Iraqi allegations of the bombing of the sacred tombs of the Shi'i Imams 'Ali and Husayn in Najaf and Karbala, made with the intention of turning Iran against the West and winning it over to Iraq's side. However, the allegations failed to convince the Iranians and were refuted by an Iranian delegation which visited both towns.[12] The landing of 104 Iraqi planes in Iran seeking refuge from Allied bombing beginning on 26 January raised speculation of a secret agreement between the two countries, which was firmly denied by Iran.[13]

In appealing to the Arabs and Muslims, Husayn portrayed the war in terms that were current among Muslim writers, namely as a conflict between the spiritual Islamic civilization and the materialistic West. He contrasted himself "the faithful slave of God," with Bush, "the enemy of God and colleague of the devil."[14] Iraq also sought to enlist the support of Third World countries by posing as their champion in the struggle against Western imperialism.[15] As the champion of Islam, Husayn urged the Arabs and Muslims to wage a jihad against the Allies. He also called upon them to eliminate the "treasonous" and "cowardly" Arab rulers, referring particularly to King Fahd of Saudi Arabia and Presidents Mubarak and Asad. Here, too, Husayn miscalculated, apparently confusing emotional solidarity with Iraq in its defiance of the West with a willingness to make sacrifices for its sake. Realizing the futility of these tactics to win the Arab states to his side, Iraq severed its diplomatic relations with the US, Britain, France, Italy, Egypt and Saudi Arabia.[16]

A major component of Husayn's strategy was missile attacks launched at Israeli population centers with the expectation of achieving two goals. First, he hoped that Israeli retaliation would transform the war against Iraq into an Israeli-Arab war, which would force the Arab states to withdraw from the coalition under pressure of Arab public opinion. The war would then be seen as a Western assault on the Arabs as a whole, which would deny the legitimacy of the US to pursue it any further. Iraq justified the missile attacks by alleging that Israeli planes had participated in the bombing of Iraq, and more importantly by charging that the entire war was the result of a Zionist conspiracy against Iraq.[17] Israel's decision against retaliation, however, foiled Husayn's calculation. Although Iraq had the technical capacity, Husayn refrained from striking Israel with chemical weapons, presumably fearing a nuclear counterstrike by Israel.

Husayn's second goal in attacking Israeli cities was to earn the admiration of the Arab world as the first Arab leader to inflict a heavy blow on Israel and expose its weakness, thereby restoring Iraqi morale and that of its supporters in the face of Allied superiority. Judging from popular reactions in various Arab states, this goal was largely achieved. Iraqi propaganda continuously reiterated that the missile attacks had "broken a psychological barrier" for the Arabs, and that "the countdown has begun for the demise of the so-called State of Israel."[18]

Iraq also issued repeated threats that it would resort to "commando" and "suicidal" acts against Allied interests throughout the world. Apparently, Iraq hoped that the PLO and various fundamentalist Islamic organizations would launch terrorist campaigns, but to no avail, although US intelligence sources did charge Iraq with the responsibility for at least three terrorist acts against US interests in the Philippines, Thailand and Tanzania.[19]

On 22 January, Iraqi troops began igniting Kuwaiti oil wells, resulting in a heavy smoke screen that hampered Allied air movement. On 27 January, they opened Kuwaiti oil pipelines, letting massive quantities of oil flow into the Persian Gulf, apparently in order to foil an anticipated Allied sea landing. Iraq responded to subsequent worldwide indignation, by first contending that the oil spill resulted from Allied bombings, and later that it was a "legitimate right to self-defense."[20] On 21 January, Iraq announced that Allied PoWs would be held as human shields in strategic sites, arguing that the Allies themselves had violated the Geneva convention by bombing civilians and by failing to apply the convention on the situation of the Palestinians under Israeli occupation.[21]

Parallel with his efforts to magnify Iraq's suffering to the outside world, Husayn had to dispel growing doubts domestically in view of Iraq's obvious military inferiority. He claimed in a speech on 20 January that Iraq had used only a small part of its force, and that once the ground war began, Iraq would inflict heavy casualties on the enemy, opening the door for the liberation of Palestine, Lebanon, the Golan and Mecca.[22] The Iraqi media claimed that Iraq had, in fact, won the first round of the war by its steadfastness, which destroyed American expectations for a quick victory, and also warned the US that Iraq would resort to using unconventional weapons.[23] However, this rhetoric could not hide the worsening domestic situation following the destruction of Iraq's civilian infrastructure (see below). In late January, with the Allied bombings exacting an increasingly heavy toll, Husayn announced a new definition of victory — "gaining the satisfaction of God." The US, he argued, had been defeated because it had made a morally wrong decision by attacking Iraq, while Iraq had won a moral victory.[24]

After enduring four weeks of bombing, and failing to attain his goals, Husayn nevertheless rejected an Iranian initiative to end the war that involved Iraq's withdrawal from Kuwait and US withdrawal from the Gulf. Deputy Prime Minister Sa'dun Hammadi, who was dispatched to Tehran, argued that the problem was no

longer Kuwait, but American aggression against Iraq.[25] Husayn also declined a Soviet
initiative launched during the second week of February, insisting on linking any peace
proposal to a comprehensive solution to all other problems in the region, particularly
the Palestine problem.[26]

TURNING A MILITARY DEFEAT INTO A POLITICAL VICTORY?
By mid-February, Husayn began to weaken under the ongoing pressure of the Allied
bombings. On 15 February the RCC, probably to deflect direct responsibility from
Husayn himself, announced "Iraq's readiness to deal with Security Council Resolution
660 with the aim of reaching an honorable and acceptable political solution to the
crisis, including a withdrawal." This vague pledge, however, was made dependent
upon the fulfillment of several conditions, including: (1) a comprehensive cease-fire;
(2) the revocation of all Security Council resolutions regarding Kuwait, primarily the
sanctions against Iraq; (3) the withdrawal of all coalition forces and equipment from
the region, including the weapons provided to Israel during the war (primarily the
antimissiles defense system); (4) an Israeli withdrawal from all the occupied territories
and South Lebanon, with the imposition of sanctions against Israel should it fail to
comply; (5) the guarantee of Iraq's historical rights (in Kuwait); (6) a political
settlement in Kuwait based upon "the people's will" and not upon the rights acquired
by the Al Sabah family; (7) compensation to Iraq for damages incurred during the
war; and (8) the annulment of all Iraqi debts to the Gulf states and to other members
of the coalition.[27]

The statement did not come close to complying with the relevant UN resolutions, as
it did not pledge withdrawal from Kuwait even if the conditions it enumerated were
met. Rather, it seemed to propose a discussion of withdrawal, or perhaps a partial
withdrawal. Clause 6, for example, assured Iraq of indirect control over Kuwait even
after a withdrawal in view of the intensive policy of Iraqization carried out there (see
MECS 1990, pp. 402–5). In all, the conditions put forward more closely resembled
those dictated by a victor than those accepted by the vanquished.

The Iraqi statement was welcomed by the USSR but rejected by President Bush,
who termed it a "cruel hoax." It was also rejected by the coalition's eight Arab
members, who called upon Iraq to withdraw unconditionally from Kuwait. An
equally worrisome reaction, from Husayn's point of view, was the jubilation in
Baghdad following the cease-fire offer, indicating little support for the war and
possibly also for the regime.[28]

Rebuffed by the US, Iraq responded positively to Soviet mediation efforts and
peace proposals, hoping to avoid direct capitulation to US demands. It sought a
formula with Soviet aid, during the week of 18–26 February, which would end the war
with minimum concessions, as well as save the Iraqi army from destruction, so that it
would be able to claim political victory. It announced its acceptance of Security
Council Resolution 660 on two separate occasions in late February, conditional upon
certain timetables and the revoking of the 11 other resolutions on the crisis. The US,
however, rejected these gestures as insufficient. In the end, the RCC rejected Bush's
ultimatum to Iraq to commence withdrawal from Kuwait on 24 February, whereupon
Bush authorized the ground assault, which began that night.[29]

Iraq's rhetoric notwithstanding, the Iraqi army was overwhelmed by the Allied
forces within 24 hours. The Iraqi high command sought to disguise the collapse of the

army and avert the annihilation of its forces by ordering them "to withdraw in an organized manner" from Kuwait on 25 February. Prior to their retreat, the Iraqi troops ignited over 600 oil wells in Kuwait.[30] In compliance with Bush's demand, Husayn himself announced the withdrawal in a speech broadcast on 26 February. He called on the people to "shout for victory," explaining the withdrawal as merely the technical outcome of Allied military pressure. He also vowed that Iraq would never forget the annexation of Kuwait, and left the door open for future attempts to realize Iraq's claims to the principality.[31]

As the announcement on 26 February, and an additional attempt to achieve a cease-fire by circumventing the undesirable Security Council resolutions ultimately failed, Foreign Minister 'Aziz notified the UN on 28 February of Iraq's acceptance of all 12 resolutions. Several hours later, the US forces ceased aggressive action, thereby sparing the Iraqi army from total annihilation. Claiming a military victory, the Iraqi high command also proclaimed a cease-fire.[32]

Husayn's first priority was to get the Allied forces to withdraw from Iraq as soon as possible, even at the price of accepting humiliating terms. On 3 March, an Iraqi military delegation unconditionally accepted the cease-fire terms dictated by the Allied commanders, pledging to rescind the annexation of Kuwait, release all Allied PoWs and Kuwaiti civilian detainees, and return all plundered Kuwaiti property. The RCC revoked all previous decisions regarding Kuwait on 5 March, although it did not relinquish Iraq's historical claim to it. All Allied PoWs were released within a week and several thousand Kuwaiti detainees were released during the following months, although thousands of other Kuwaitis who had been taken to Iraq remained unaccounted for and were assumed murdered.[33] Claiming to be the wronged party, Iraq demanded that the UN annul the sanctions imposed upon it and grant compensation for Iraqi loss of life and property caused by the Allied bombing. Likewise, Iraq submitted daily complaints to the UN throughout the year about the continued Allied presence and Allied flights within its territory.[34]

On 6 April, Iraq officially accepted Security Council Resolution 687 stipulating the terms of the truce. The next day, Allied troops began their withdrawal from Iraq,[35] having rendered the Iraqi-Kuwaiti campaign the greatest failure of the Ba'th regime, which exacerbated the country's strategic and economic position at a high human and material cost. Furthermore, it had triggered a war between the majority of the population in Iraq and the regime.

CIVIL WAR IN IRAQ

THE SHI'I INTIFADA

Sporadic antigovernment demonstrations by the Shi'i population broke out in Basra and Diwaniyya in mid-February but were apparently dispersed. On 2 March, however, as the Iraqi army was retreating, antigovernment riots erupted again in Basra and within days spread throughout southern Iraq as far as Hilla, c. 50 km. southwest of Baghdad. Sporadic riots in the Shi'i neighborhoods of Baghdad were dispersed by loyalist troops who killed and wounded c. 100 people.[36]

Although they constituted a majority of the population numerically (c. 55%), the Shi'is had been largely excluded from power in Iraq and were generally in an economically inferior position to the dominant Sunnis. While the Ba'th regime made

some effort to improve their lot, and promoted Iraqi patriotism encompassing both
Sunnis and Shi'is, it simultaneously restricted the Shi'i religious leadership and
suppressed all attempts to enhance the Shi'i identity (see *MECS* 1988, pp. 519–20).
The Shi'is had been politically quiescent because of their history of defeats and
repression. However, following Iraq's military defeat, when Husayn's fall seemed
imminent, they gave vent to their long-suppressed resentments. Notwithstanding the
decades-long struggle for autonomy waged by the Kurds, the Shi'i Intifada by virtue
of size of the Shi'i population and its location in the southern and central regions of
Iraq, including in the capital, Baghdad, became the largest popular rebellion in Iraqi
history and the most serious internal challenge the Ba'thist regime had ever faced.

The rebels comprised disaffected soldiers retreating from Kuwait, outraged
citizenry, and eventually a number of religious leaders. They numbered some tens of
thousands, but apparently enjoyed widespread support within the population. For a
period of two weeks in March, the rebels controlled the south, and anarchy reigned.
Government and Ba'th party buildings were burned, and an unknown number of
government and party officials were executed.[37]

The infiltration from Iran of the Badr Brigade, an Iranian-trained force of former
Iraqi PoWs and exiled Shi'is, seriously harmed the Intifada. The Badr fighters
executed captured and surrendering army troops, thereby putting an end to surrenders
and defections which were crucial to the success of the revolt.[38] Moreover, fortunately
for Husayn, the elite units of the Republican Guard, which had been spared by the US
at the end of the war, remained loyal to the regime and played a major role in
suppressing the rebellion. Additional army units were moved from the Kurdish north
to join the Republican Guard units in quelling the more dangerous threat to the
regime. The rebels, lacking effective leadership, organization, experience and
equipment could not withstand the intensive onslaught of the Republican Guard.[39]

The Shi'i rebellion was brutally suppressed by means that included the use of gas
and napalm against the civilian population. Entire neighborhoods were razed in order
to deprive the rebels of sanctuary and to punish the population. Captured rebels were
hanged from lampposts and from tank gun barrels. The regime's professed piety
notwithstanding, the army shelled and heavily damaged the sacred Shi'i shrines in
Najaf and Karbala. On 6 March, Iraq expelled the remaining Western journalists in
Baghdad, apparently to remove unwanted witnesses.[40]

The regime made use of Shi'i clerics to legitimize its policies. It went to the extreme
of showing the most prominent Shi'i leader in Iraq, 94-year-old Grand Ayatallah Abu
al-Qasim Kho'i, who was known for his aversion to politics, on Iraqi television on 20
March, sitting with Husayn and thanking God for enabling the Iraqi president "to
quell the sedition." Kho'i reportedly accused the rebels of vandalism and wanton
murders in violation of religious law. Shi'i opposition groups, however, charged that
Kho'i had been abducted and forced to make the statements. Although Kho'i denied
the charges, he had apparently been put under house arrest in Najaf. Several members
of his family were arrested as well, and possibly executed. Whether or not the
abduction achieved its purpose is questionable, but it did contribute to a chill in Iraq's
relations with Iran.[41]

By most accounts, civilian casualties during the civil war in the south and in
Kurdistan were higher than those that resulted from the Allied bombings, with
estimates varying from c. 6,000–30,000.[42] Terrorized by the military, c. 40,000 Shi'i

civilians and army deserters fled to the Allied-held zone in southwestern Iraq. When the US army withdrew from Iraq, c. 19,000 refugees were moved into Saudi Arabia. Approximately 70,000 refugees crossed the border into Iran, and an unknown number of thousands fled to the marshlands in al-Ahwar beyond the reach of mechanized army units.[43]

By 8 March, a week after the outbreak of the revolt, the army regained control over Basra, by 15 March it controlled Karbala, and on 27 March the government reported that all areas in the southern governorates "enjoy tranquillity and stability."[44] However, although the mass rebellion was crushed, sporadic armed resistance in the south continued throughout the year, with rebels claiming control of various towns from time to time. These reports could not be confirmed.[45]

During May and June, the Shi'i opposition and the Government of Iran warned of a planned campaign by the Iraqi regime to annihilate the many thousands of Shi'is who had taken refuge in the Ahwar marshlands. The US did not react, but both Britain and Germany warned Iraq against taking such an action. Under pressure by a UN official, Sadr al-Din Agha Khan, who visited Iraq at the time, the regime withdrew its forces and enabled the refugees to leave the area, while denying the charges. After Agha Khan's departure, Iraq sealed off the area and prohibited the entry of UN food convoys. Opposition reports of renewed action against the marshland refugees in November could not be verified.[46]

The regime continued to apply tough measures in the south throughout the year, taking advantage of the absence of the Western media there. Escaping refugees reported that thousands of Shi'is were executed during the year. Towns and villages where military confrontations took place were bombed by napalm and were severely punished. Concurrently, it intensified contacts with Shi'i tribal shaykhs, previously described as reactionaries, in order to gain their support, an indication that tribal loyalties were still entrenched in Iraq. Although the Shi'i 'Ashura mourning rites were reportedly banned in order to prevent antigovernment incitement, the heavily damaged shrines in Najaf and Karbala were rebuilt with wide publicity "under Husayn's personal supervision."[47]

By the end of the year, it was clear that the Sunni-Shi'i divide in Iraq was wider than ever. While the Intifada was not the product of an Islamic Shi'i ideology, the Shi'i identity played a major motivating role in it. Ultimately, during a period of crisis, sectarian and religious identity combined with socioeconomic disparity proved to be more powerful than the sense of Iraqi patriotism that the regime had attempted to inculcate for years.[48]

THE KURDISH REBELLION AND ITS DEMISE

Aware of their costly defeats in the past (see *MECS* 1988, pp. 521–25), the Kurdish opposition leadership hesitated to move against the regime, but the Kurdish population was carried away by the Iraqi defeat in the war and by reports of the Shi'i Intifada. A spontaneous uprising broke out on 4 March in the town of Raniyya and spread throughout Iraqi Kurdistan within days, augmented by the mass defection of hitherto pro-government Kurdish militiamen and by the removal of army units from Kurdistan to the south. Unwilling and unable to oppose popular pressure, the leaders of the two main Kurdish factions, Mas'ud Barazani of the Democratic Party of Kurdistan and Jalal Talabani of the Patriotic Union of Kurdistan threw their weight behind the rebellion. The Kurdish leadership was misled into believing that the US supported their cause because of appeals to the Iraqi people by President Bush and by a CIA-operated radio station to topple Husayn.[49]

By 20 March, the Kurds took control of most of Iraqi Kurdistan up to Khanaqin, 150 km. north of Baghdad — an area that included the major Kurdish cities, and that constituted a goal they had never dared try to achieve before. They also put the city of Mosul under siege. Unlike the Shi'is, the Kurds set up a provisional government and began to provide basic services for the population. An illustration of their new status was an unprecedented meeting by a Kurdish delegation led by Talabani with President Özal of Turkey on 8 March.[50] However, Talabani and Barazani repeatedly emphasized that the Kurds had abandoned the dream of Kurdish independence as unrealistic in order to allay fears among Iraq's neighbors of irredentism among their own Kurdish populations. Returning to Iraq after a long exile, Talabani declared in Zakho that the Kurds would continue their fight until "the whole of Iraq is liberated."[51]

Kurdish euphoria, however, was short-lived. Having subdued the Shi'is, Husayn moved c. 100,000 troops to the north during the last week of March. The city of Kirkuk, the strategic key to the north, fell to the troops on 28 March after two days of heavy shelling and fierce battles. According to Kurdish sources, an unknown number of civilians were slaughtered by the troops.[52]

With the Kurdish fighters — the Peshmerga — unable to repel the army, they withdrew from the cities in order to carry on the fight in the mountains and spare the civilian population from further casualties. Repeated Kurdish appeals to the US to put an end to Iraqi air attacks went unanswered (for US policy, see chapter on the US and the ME). The towns of Dahuk and Irbil were taken by the army on 31 March, Zakho and Sulaymaniyya the next day.[53] Simultaneously with the attacks, the regime orchestrated demonstrations of support by loyalist Kurdish tribal chiefs and by the government-sponsored Kurdistan Democratic Party in an effort to show that the rebellion was confined to a small renegade faction.[54]

The Refugees and the Safe Havens

The ferocity of the army's attack, combined with fears of brutal reprisals evoked by the memory of the poison gas attacks on Halabja in 1988, caused mass panic among the Kurdish population. An unprecedented mass exodus took place as Kurds, joined by Christians and Turkomans, fled to the mountains mostly on foot. The Iraqi air force staged fake chemical attacks on the fleeing refugees to intensify their panic, possibly in the hope of driving them out of Iraq permanently. With the Syrian border sealed by the army, c. 1.2m. refugees headed toward Iran, and c. 800,000 toward Turkey.[55] But Turkey closed its borders on 3 April, after having allowed 100,000 refugees to enter, maintaining that it could not handle any more. Apparently, Turkey feared that if the refugees were allowed to enter, sustained by the UN they would remain in Turkey indefinitely. Iran also sealed its border, on 7 April, after taking in over half a million refugees. Stranded in the mountains, the refugees suffered from harsh weather and from lack of food, water and shelter. These factors combined with poor sanitary conditions, led to a daily mortality of c. 1,000, mostly children, during the month of April.[56]

As a result of extensive media coverage, Western public opinion pressured their governments, which hitherto had paid little attention to the Kurdish plight, to provide aid to the refugees. President Bush ordered the US air force to drop food and supplies to refugee areas in the mountains and promised aid to Turkey and Iran. European governments and aid organizations also pledged assistance during April. But difficult terrain and a lack of proper transportation resulted in a delay of several weeks until sufficient aid arrived. Most of the aid was delivered to Turkey where Allied air bases were located and less was received in Iran.[57]

Although the US assumed the main burden of the humanitarian effort, it declared its determination not to be involved in the civil war. The European Community (EC), on the other hand, proposed on 8 April to create safe havens for the Kurds in northern Iraq to be supplied and protected by the UN. The US went along reluctantly, issuing an ultimatum to Iraq on 10 April to cease all military activity north of the 36th parallel. A day later, the Allies agreed on establishing "informal safe havens where aid would be given to the Kurds." The phrasing was intended to sidestep potential problems of international law and regional sensitivities about the legal and political nature of the zone by precluding all possible claims for statehood by the Kurds. The US also agreed to dispatch troops to take charge of the distribution of the aid supplies in the havens.[58]

In addition to regaining full control in Kurdistan, Husayn was concerned with minimizing the Allies' intervention in this area. To attain this goal, he had to create quickly a semblance of resumed normalcy by reorganizing local governmental and party machinery. On 5 March, the RCC declared an amnesty for all Kurds and security forces personnel (i.e., those who had defected), except for acts of murder and rape committed during the rebellion. Visiting the north himself, Husayn urged the refugees to return to their homes. But the amnesty, which was extended three more times on 11, 20 and 29 April, encompassing the Shi'is in the south as well, was officially rejected by all Kurdish organizations, and failed to convince most refugees to trust the regime with their lives.[59]

The Iraqi Government denounced the safe haven scheme as a violation of international law and of Iraq's sovereignty, and vowed to resist any foreign military effort to establish them. In an effort to refute the need for the Allied activity, the Iraqi media began publicizing data about growing numbers of Kurds returning to their homes. In order to limit the Allied presence on its soil and, more important, to preclude any possibility of the emergence of an official Kurdish entity, Iraq signed a "memorandum of understanding" with the UN on 18 April providing for UN help for the refugees in northern and southern Iraq.[60]

Iraq complied with the Allied ultimatum to cease military operations north of the 36th parallel, withdrawing its troops from the town of Zakho and its environs near the Turkish border on 21 April. The following day, Allied troops entered the region to set up camps for the refugees. In a pattern that was to be repeated elsewhere (see below), Husayn sought to test the Allies' determination by sending a police force of c. 200 men to Zakho in defiance of the ultimatum. The police began harassing the returning Kurdish refugees presumably to demonstrate that Iraq was still sovereign there, but withdrew following an additional Allied ultimatum.[61]

Reassured by the Allied presence, thousands of Kurds descended from the mountains to Zakho, with some even returning to cities held by the Iraqis. During May, the Allies extended the safe zone eastward to the provincial capital of Dahuk in order to accommodate the flow of refugees. There too, as in Zakho, the Iraqis withdrew only after an explicit Allied ultimatum. By mid-May, c. 230,000 refugees had settled in camps surrounding Zakho. The establishment of the safe zone, however, did not solve the problem of the refugees in Iran. Although most of them returned to the safe zone or the border strip controlled by the Peshmerga, c. 400,000 still remained in Iran by early July.[62]

Initially criticizing the safe zone as an insufficient solution, the Kurdish leadership acquiesced to the limits of Allied support and repeatedly requested the Allies to extend the zones over all of Iraqi Kurdistan. Various Kurdish organizations set up checkpoints throughout the zone, the result of internal Kurdish power struggles as well as the first step toward de facto Kurdish autonomy. They also forced many Arabs who had been settled there by the Iraqi regime to leave. In addition, the Peshmerga kept up guerrilla warfare against the Iraqi army, seeking, according to Western observers, US intervention on their behalf.[63]

By mid-May the UN assumed control of the civilian administration of the camps, and was to be entrusted by the Allies with the security of the zones as well. Iraq initially rejected this new arrangement, but on 23 May signed an agreement with the UN stipulating the deployment of no more than 500 UN troops to guard the safe zone. Thousands of Kurds, however, demonstrated in Dahuk against the Allied withdrawal, threatening to return to the mountains. Although the US feared further entanglement in the Kurdish problem, on 25 June it accepted an EC proposal to establish a rapid deployment force of 5,000 troops based in Turkey to be used in case of Iraqi reprisals against the Kurds. The last Allied troops left Iraq on 12 July.[64]

The Negotiations on Kurdish Autonomy

Soon after crushing the Kurdish rebellion, Husayn secretly offered the Kurdish leadership an opportunity to "open a new chapter" in mutual relations based on the 1970 autonomy agreement. Like other gestures after the war, Husayn's magnanimity was designed first and foremost to preclude Allied intervention on behalf of the Kurds as well as to divide the opposition to his regime. The Kurdish leaders responded favorably in order to mitigate both the unprecedented extent of the suffering of their people and the danger of permanent displacement from their homeland. In addition, they believed they could extract favorable terms from Husayn in light of his defeat in the war.[65]

After obtaining a cease-fire agreement, a Kurdish delegation headed by Talabani arrived in Baghdad on 19 April to negotiate with Husayn. On 24 April, Talabani announced that an agreement in principle had been reached on the establishment of autonomy for Iraqi Kurdistan based on the 1970 accord with the final draft to be concluded in negotiations shortly afterward. He urged all refugees to return to Iraq. The accord was received with skepticism among many Kurdish activists, in view of Husayn's poor record of keeping promises and their fear that eventually he would outmaneuver the Kurds.[66]

Husayn's tactic in the negotiations was procrastination. He counted on the Allies' desire to speed up their withdrawal from Iraq, as well as on the absence of a military option for the Kurds and the pressure of the refugees' misery, all of which would force the Kurds to accept his terms. Simultaneously, he sought to create false hopes among the Kurds by issuing periodic announcements on an imminent breakthrough in Kurdish government negotiations, although he did not accede to any of their demands.[67]

After two months of negotiations, Barazani, who led the Kurdish delegation, announced in late June that a draft agreement on autonomy had been reached.[68] However, the two published documents — the Kurdish proposal, and the autonomy law as approved by the RCC — revealed significant gaps on practically every major autonomy issue, similar to the disagreements that had led to the demise of the 1970 accord. These issues included the boundaries of the autonomous region, with the regime refusing to include the districts of Kirkuk, Khanaqin and Mandali in the region; the extent of legislative and executive authority delegated to the autonomous region; the extent of Kurdish participation in the central government; and the autonomy's sources of revenue, particularly the share of revenues from the Kirkuk oil wells and allocations from the national budget.[69]

In addition, the Kurds demanded a massive reconstruction effort in their region and the repeal of all anti-Kurdish measures enacted by the government. The government's proposal, on the other hand, contained a secret appendix demanding a commitment by the Kurds to support the regime against internal opposition and foreign threats; disband the Peshmerga; hand over all radio stations to the government; end any cooperation or contacts with foreign states; and denounce the foreign intervention in northern Iraq.[70]

In a setback for Barazani, a summit meeting of the Kurdistan Front (see *MECS* 1989, p. 399) attended by c. 300 tribal and guerrilla leaders in the town of Shaqlawa north of Irbil on 27–30 June rejected the government's demands. Confident that the creation of an Allied rapid-deployment force in Turkey would prevent Husayn from persecuting the Kurds, the Front called for additional negotiations before signing an agreement. While dropping a demand for international guarantees for the autonomy agreement, in view of the Allies' reluctance to offer it, the meeting did demand that the government should ratify the agreement in an official document submitted to the UN.[71]

Once the withdrawal of the Allies from Iraq had been completed, Husayn hardened his position and insisted that the Kurds accept his terms unconditionally. The Kurds, however, insisted on comprehensive democratization in Iraq as the barometer of the regime's sincerity in keeping with the autonomy agreement.[72] The Allied withdrawal also led to a deterioration on the ground. Antigovernment riots erupted in Sulaymaniyya on 18 July and led to armed clashes between the Peshmerga and the army, resulting in c. 500 Kurds dead and injured. The Iraqi garrison of 2,500 soldiers in Sulaymaniyya surrendered to the Peshmerga, who seized control of the town. The poor performance of the Iraqi troops led Husayn to order the army to withdraw from Irbil and Khanaqin as well as various other towns.[73]

In August and early September, clashes again broke out in Kirkuk and elsewhere, including areas north of the 36th parallel where the Allies had prohibited Iraqi military activity. The Allies, however, did not respond, enhancing Husayn's confidence. According to the Kurdistan Front, the regime had carried out mass arrests and forced evictions of Kurds during the previous months, and intensified the Arabization of Kirkuk and Irbil. Turkoman leaders complained of similar repressive measures directed at their community as well.[74]

As part of Husayn's general policy of tightening his control in Iraq (see below), in early October the army mounted a large-scale offensive against the Kurds in the northeastern region of Kurdistan, but after experiencing several setbacks was forced to withdraw its forces from Sulaymaniyya and Irbil.[75] Changing its tactics to a slow and gradual advance, the army overran 52 villages and small towns and surrounded the major cities by the end of November. Fleeing the attacks, c. 200,000 Kurds headed for the mountains again, further stretching the meager UN resources allocated to the refugees. In an effort to spare the civilians from additional suffering, the Kurdistan Front ordered all Peshmerga units to redeploy outside the cities and towns.

Concurrently, the army imposed a tight blockade on the Kurdish areas to force them into submission. In addition, Husayn refused to extend the UN mandate to provide aid to the refugees, which was due to expire on 31 December 1991. The regime also reneged on agreements reached with the Kurds to lift the blockade in return for the Peshmerga's withdrawal to the border region. Husayn made several minor conciliatory gestures regarding the future autonomy agreement, successfully sowing discord among the Kurds (see below). In late November, Iran allowed the UN to transport aid to Kurdistan via its territory in response to the mounting suffering of the Kurds. As winter approached, the Iraqi army halted its offensive and withdrew to its previous positions, allowing the harsh climate to take its toll on the Kurds.[76]

The renewed crisis aggravated divisions within the Kurdish leadership. Barazani, persisting in his efforts to reach an accord with the regime, initially portrayed the antigovernment attacks as the outcome of local misunderstandings. A summit meeting of the Kurdistan Front held in Qulijan on 12 August adopted his position ordering the Peshmerga to avoid confrontations with the army, allow government troops to return to certain positions from which they had been driven out, and return government prisoners.[77] Talabani, on the other hand, accused the government of provocation, and voiced doubts about the possibility or the usefulness of any settlement in light of Husayn's intransigence.[78] In response, Barazani argued that the Kurds had no better alternative to the agreement he was negotiating. He also opposed Talabani's efforts to renew the alliance with the non-Kurdish opposition asserting his reluctance to use the Kurdish issue as a bargaining chip by foreigners to pressure Baghdad. Exasperated by Talabani's criticism, Barazani in late October called for an electoral test of strength to decide which course to take. A premature announcement by Barazani in mid-November that an agreement had been reached with the government, prompted the Kurdistan Front to hold a referendum on the matter, but it never took place in view of complex technical, military and political circumstances.[79] Thus, at the end of the year, the Kurds faced the dilemma of an unsatisfactory autonomy agreement that left them at Husayn's mercy or a de facto autonomy in the mountains at the cost of great suffering and uncertainty.

THE IMPOTENCE OF THE IRAQI OPPOSITION IN EXILE
The exiled opposition, particularly the Shi'is, were torn during the war between hatred of Husayn and hostility to the US (for a background on the opposition see *MECS* 1990, pp. 414–15, 417–19). They hoped that the war would bring down the regime, but feared that it would rally the population behind Husayn as the defender of Iraq. Thus, while calling for Iraq's immediate withdrawal from Kuwait, they criticized the Allied attacks as punishing the Iraqi people rather than the regime. The leader of the Supreme Assembly of the Islamic Revolution in Iraq, Hujjat al-Islam Muhammad Baqir al-Hakim, declared that his supporters would fight the Allies should they invade Iraq. The opposition accused Husayn of destroying Iraq by his insistence on fighting, thereby seeking to demonstrate their patriotism.[80]

The opposition received some support from Saudi Arabia and Egypt before and during the war, after years of disregard by most Arab states, and was allowed to operate clandestine radio stations from these countries. It was also given wide coverage in the Western media but none of this could compensate for its total powerlessness inside Iraq.[81]

When the Shi'i Intifada broke out, the Iranian-backed opposition groups claimed they were assisting and guiding the rebels, while denying any role for Iran, for fear of alienating the Sunnis of Iraq. In contrast to the opposition's previous boasts of its power (see *MECS* 1990, p. 415), the actual military aid provided to the rebels was limited and even counterproductive. The repeated exhortations to the army to rebel against Husayn merely revealed the opposition's own impotence. Moreover, its efforts to gain American support were rebuffed, as the US was counting on an internal coup against Husayn.[82]

A conference held by the opposition on 11–13 March in Beirut was attended by c. 300 delegates representing 25 organizations and independent individuals. Officially meeting to discuss ways and means of supporting the Intifada, it also hoped to convince the Allies of its credibility as an alternative to the regime. However, aside from agreeing on the necessity of toppling Husayn, and on broad principles for a future regime in Iraq, the conference exposed the deep divisions within the opposition and failed to agree on a concrete plan of action.[83]

The opposition's frustration with the suppression of the rebellions was heightened by the willingness of the Kurds to enter into negotiations with the regime. The non-Kurdish opposition organizations accused the Kurdish leaders, particularly Talabani, of promoting their own personal interests, of short-sighted naïveté in trusting Husayn, and of giving respite to Husayn's besieged regime. Claiming that they themselves had rejected similar Iraqi overtures, they persisted in urging the Kurds to end negotiations and return to the ranks of the opposition.[84]

The opposition suffered a further split when the pro-Syrian and pro-Iranian organizations called their own conference in Damascus in early July, officially under the guise of the Steering Committee that had been established in December 1990. As a consequence, several small nationalist groupings and independent individuals backed by Saudi Arabia and Egypt organized a conference of their own in London. These two conferences revealed a division within al-Da'wa, originally the largest and most active Shi'i organization, which was caused by the resentment felt by various activists at the excessive Iranian control of the movement and their desire to enhance its Iraqi character in order to heighten its appeal in Iraq.[85]

HUSAYN REASSERTS HIS RULE

SUPPRESSION AND PSEUDODEMOCRACY

Iraq's military defeat, combined with the uprisings in the south and the north, posed the most serious threat that Husayn and the Ba'th regime had ever faced. The Iraqi army had been defeated by the Allies, while the two other key components of the regime had suffered severe setbacks during the rebellions. Of the three, the support of the army, and particularly of the elite units of the Republican Guard, was the most crucial for Husayn to remain in power. Since the party and the security apparatus were the primary targets of the people's rage, their support for Husayn was ensured as their fate was inextricably bound to his. The army, however — the only body capable of both saving and threatening the regime — had good reason to resent Husayn, who was responsible for its humiliating defeat. Consequently, Husayn's first priority of reconstruction was directed toward the military.

The RCC, seeking to regroup and marshal its battered troops, declared an extraordinary amnesty for deserters and absentees on 4 March, provided they rejoined their units within a few days. Concurrently, 15 army divisions, which had been routed in battle and probably ceased to exist as units, were disbanded in two stages, and all reservist soldiers born during the years 1953–60, i.e., the generation of soldiers which spent its youth in two wars, were demobilized. This move was probably made to appease the embittered troops. On 6 March, all military salaries were raised, with the Republican Guard receiving a double allowance. The Popular Army, which had served as the Ba'th party militia and functioned as a counterbalance to the army, was abolished on 26 April, presumably in view of its failure during the rebellions and possibly also to placate the military. Its property was transferred to the Defense Ministry.[86]

Revitalizing the internal security, Husayn appointed his cousin, 'Ali Hasan al-Majid, as interior minister on 6 March. Majid's record as the official responsible for gassing the Kurds in Halabja and as governor of Kuwait served as an indication of Husayn's determination to crush his opponents by any means. While the appointment of a relative to such a sensitive post might have signified a certain narrowing of Husayn's base of support, forcing him to trust only close relatives, it might have also suggested his unlimited power to appoint whomever he desired. Majid's old portfolio, the Ministry of Local Government, was merged with the Interior Ministry, augmenting his power.[87]

Husayn replaced almost all of the 19 provincial governors during the course of the year, in an effort to restore the government's full authority. Six army officers, rather than party officials, were appointed as governors in the south, indicating a weakening of the party's position vis-à-vis the military.[88]

Husayn also utilized political means to rally the population behind him. On 16 March, in his first speech since the end of the war, Husayn portrayed himself as the sole bulwark against sectarian efforts aiming at fragmenting and Lebanonizing Iraq, which would endanger the status of the Sunni minority, thus playing on Sunni fears of Shi'i domination. He also stressed Iran's backing for the Shi'i and Kurdish revolts.

While vowing to crush sedition, Husayn offered a "new phase" in Iraq's national life. He explained that his previous efforts to introduce democratization (see *MECS* 1989, pp. 378–79, and 1990, pp. 381–84) had been thwarted by "foreign aggression," declaring that his determination to build a "democratic society" based on the rule of law and political pluralism was "irrevocable." In addition, he promised to give top priority to reconstruction and the provision of basic services to the population.[89]

As he had promised in his speech, Husayn appointed a new government, which he announced on 23 March. In a gesture to the Shi'is, he appointed Sa'dun Hammadi, his most prominent Shi'i lieutenant, as the new prime minister, a post he himself had hitherto held. Another Shi'i, Muhammad Hamza al-Zubaydi, was appointed deputy prime minister. Two days earlier, Taha Yasin Ramadan, first deputy prime minister, was promoted to the vice presidency to elevate him above the ministers. Foreign Minister 'Aziz was removed from his ministry, but retained his post as deputy prime minister, while Information Minister Latif Nusayf Jasim was demoted, both apparently made scapegoats for the failure of Iraqi propaganda during the war. The rest of the ministers were mostly technocrats.[90] On 6 April, Husayn appointed his cousin, Husayn Kamil Hasan, as defense minister instead of Sa'di 'Abbas Tu'ma, a Shi'i, presumably in order to ensure tighter control over the military.[91]

Hammadi's appointment as prime minister was also aimed at demonstrating Husayn's commitment to implementing reforms, as Hammadi had been known among the Iraqi leadership as the most consistent advocate of reform (see *MECS*, 1990, pp. 383). In a series of statements during March and April, Hammadi pledged to advance democratization based on the "supremacy of the law." He expressed his wish to reform the system of government from "revolutionary institutions to constitutional ones" and to permit the press to criticize the system.[92]

During the following two months, a series of measures was announced that appeared to be leading toward democratization. On 23 March, National Assembly Speaker Sa'di Mahdi Salih declared that the Assembly had completed its debate on the new constitution, which upheld the democratic principles (on the draft of the constitution, see *MECS* 1990, pp. 382–83). Information Minister Hamad Yusif Hammadi declared on 12 April that presidential elections would be held "soon," although no concrete steps were taken in that regard. On 23 April, the RCC delegated some of the constitutional powers hitherto held by the president to the government ministers. However, a law defining the authority of the cabinet, which went into effect on 13 June, limited it to proposing and executing government policy, and excluded shaping it. The real power still lay in Husayn's hands. On 17 May, the revolutionary courts, responsible for the prosecution of the regime's opponents, were abolished. On 21 July, the RCC granted amnesty to political prisoners, to citizens who fled the country for political reasons, and to army deserters. Simultaneously with this much-publicized liberalization, the suppression of the Shi'is in the south continued unabated.[93]

According to foreign journalists, the new policy was greeted by the population, with a blend of skepticism and cautious hope. According to some Arab observers, the defeat and the new measures that were announced somewhat decreased the fear which had prevailed in Iraq, leading people "for the first time in many years" to "raise questions and think aloud" about the government's policies and mistakes.[94]

A new party law approved by the RCC on 27 June aptly illustrated the regime's concept of democracy. New parties were prohibited from involving religion in politics. They could be dissolved by the Interior Ministry if they "undermined" national unity and security. Only the Ba'th Party was allowed to operate within the armed and security forces. The new law was passed by the National Assembly on 25 August with the addition of several amendments, allowing religious parties but banning any party founded on "atheism, sectarianism, racism, regionalism or anti-Arabism."[95] Such provisions in effect meant the disappearance of all opposition or the obliteration of their identity in total subservience to the regime.

REORGANIZING THE BA'TH

Widespread popular hostility toward the Ba'th Party during the Shi'i and Kurdish rebellions and the party's inadequate performance then prompted Husayn to launch a campaign to revitalize this essential pillar of his rule. The lack of contact between the party and the population, and between the party leadership and its rank and file was unofficially pinpointed by senior party officials probably directed from above as a major problem. The growth of the party apparatus had been mostly confined to the security services and the army, leading to a stifling bureaucratization and lack of initiative. The bloated party membership of c. 1.5m. out of a population of c. 17m. was also criticized as having become essentially a career channel for opportunists and uncommitted members.[96]

As in the past (see *MECS* 1982–83, pp. 561–63), Husayn took a leading role in castigating the party's weaknesses, presumably in order to deflect criticism from himself. On 27 March, he called for the separation of the party from the government in order to prevent bureaucratic duplication and improve the government's functioning. In a speech on 7 May, he chided party officials for lethargy and for preferring their personal comfort to assuming a vanguard role during the war and the Intifada.[97]

The main thrust of the revitalization process involved the holding during the following months of allegedly free internal elections at all party levels, the first since Husayn's seizure of power in 1979. Several senior government officials were reportedly defeated as a consequence of neglecting party work for years. Resignation from the party was allowed. An unknown number of members were purged for disloyalty and some were arrested.[98]

In a show of confidence by the regime, the tenth Ba'th congress, named the "Congress of Jihad and Construction," was convened on 12–13 September after a 10-year hiatus. Unlike in the last congress, Husayn was unanimously elected as secretary of the Regional Command and as general secretary of the Ba'th by the entire congress rather than by the Command members only, probably in order to demonstrate his popularity.

For the first time, the congress proceedings were published manifesting the new atmosphere of openness. Elections for the Regional Command were held for the first time by secret ballot. Of the 42 candidates for the 16-member Command, only 11 won more than the required 50%, headed by deputy secretary-general, 'Izzat Ibrahim and Interior Minister 'Ali Hasan al-Majid. Four members of the previous Regional Command, most notably Prime Minister Hammadi who received an exceptionally low number of votes and RCC member Hasan 'Ali Nassar, were not reelected, Only after an additional five rounds of voting was the entire 16-member Command elected. It included seven new members, apparently all Sunnis[99] (see Appendix).

In light of the emergency circumstances of the postwar period, the congress unanimously adopted Husayn's opening speech as its concluding political statement. This decision suggested some difficulty in the party's functioning as well as Husayn's absolute control over it. The campaign to restructure and democratize the party was revealed as hollow inasmuch as Husayn would not allow the party to serve even as a debating platform, let alone as a decision-making body.

Husayn's speech combined self-congratulation for having overcome all challenges to his rule, assurances that the leadership had made the right decisions during the crisis, and exhortations for perseverance during the difficult period of reconstruction. Presumably these remarks were designed to stave off prevalent doubts in light of Iraq's defeat and its postwar difficulties. Reverting to a doctrinaire party line, Husayn asserted that Iraq's steadfastness in the war had exposed the fallacies of Western liberalism and capitalism, and consequently would hasten their demise. By contrast, the Ba'th mission, correct principles and moral direction were vindicated with greater vigor and clarity than before during the wars against Iran and the US. While committing himself to work toward democratic elections for the National Assembly, Husayn criticized liberal democracy and a free market economy as Western ideas designed to subjugate the Arabs and as systems that prescribed the domination of the many by the few. Extolling Ba'thist socialism, he assailed those who admired Western ideas, warning that they could have no place inside the Ba'th Party. On a practical level, he stressed the need to mobilize the party in order to address the emerging social problem of increasing delinquency, alienation and indifference among the youth, and warned against the entry of opportunists into the leadership ranks.[100]

GOVERNMENTAL RESHUFFLING
With the adjournment of the Ba'th congress on 13 September, Husayn sacked Sa'dun Hammadi as Prime Minister and replaced him with his deputy, Muhammad Hamza al-Zubaydi. Furthermore, Hammadi and 'Ali Hasan Nassar, the other Shi'i member of the RCC, were ousted from the RCC allegedly as a consequence of the party elections. More significantly, since Hammadi was known for his advocacy of greater political pluralism and economic liberalization, his dismissal just after Husayn's explicit rejection of liberal democracy at the party congress signified Husayn's growing conviction that he no longer needed to maintain the facade of liberalization in order to wield absolute power.

Zubaydi's main qualifications for the post apparently were his Shi'i origin and his total subservience to Husayn. On 5 October, he was promoted to the RCC together with Interior Minister 'Ali Hasan al-Majid and Mizban Khidr al-Hadi, a Shi'i and secretary of the central bureau of the popular and professional organizations. Hadi's appointment was probably designed to preserve the Shi'i representation of two members in the RCC even though he had received less votes in the congress than other contenders. In early November, Hammadi was appointed as an adviser to the president with the rank of minister, signifying that he still enjoyed Husayn's personal favor.[101]

On 6 November, Husayn ordered another reshuffle, dismissing Defense Minister Husayn Kamil Hasan and replacing him by 'Ali Hasan al-Majid. Three days later the daily *Babil* and the weekly *al-Rafidayn,* edited and managed by Husayn's son 'Uday, were closed. A week later Husayn appointed his half-brother, Watban Ibrahim al-Hasan, formerly head of one of the security services, as the new interior minister.[102] The reshuffle involving Husayn's two most powerful ministers and cousins (for his family tree, see *MECS* 1989, pp. 382), along with 'Uday's temporary eclipse evoked a wave of speculations about an internal power struggle within Husayn's family, which allegedly threatened the foundations of his rule. Opposition and foreign sources claimed that Husayn Kamil and 'Uday were seeking to establish a combined center of power that threatened Husayn's position. However, Husayn Kamil's reappearance at Husayn's side in top-level meetings seemed to discredit these speculations.[103]

A more plausible explanation was the necessity to address growing resentment in the army against Kamil's appointment as defense minister, thereby passing over senior officers. Another reason might have been Kamil's failure to effectively control the army. Since the army was the only body that could pose a threat to Husayn's rule, the appointment of 'Ali Hasan al-Majid, who was known for his toughness, was probably aimed at tightening Husayn's control over it.[104] There were various indications of problems in the army ever since the war's end. On 20 June, Chief of Staff Lt. Gen. Husayn Rashid, who had been appointed only seven months earlier, was replaced by Lt. Gen. Iyad Futayh al-Rawi, commander of the Republican Guard. The chief of military intelligence, Maj. Gen. Wafiq Jasim al-Samara'i, was dismissed after serving only two months and was replaced by Brig. Gen. 'Abd al-Khadir Salman Khamis, who was related to Husayn. Reports of coup attempts and of executions and dismissals of army officers were issued by the opposition regularly, but could not be verified. Generous financial and property benefits were granted to army officers twice during August and September, while salaries of all military personnel were raised by 40%. In order to ease discontent over prolonged stints of service, conscripts born in 1961–66 and reserve officers born in 1924–33 were demobilized.[105]

'Uday's eclipse, which may have been designed to placate the army, was short-lived. A press campaign, probably approved by Husayn himself, called for the reopening of the two newspapers that had been closed. As in an earlier incident involving 'Uday (see *MECS* 1988, pp. 507–8), Husayn complied with these requests, and two weeks later both papers resumed publication.[106]

By the end of the year, Husayn displayed concern over the mounting difficulties in Iraq, but also growing self-confidence in his ability to overcome the challenges to his rule. In a series of public ceremonies, he granted his closest aides and army generals medals and awards for their valor during the war and the ensuing rebellions. He mocked the reports circulating in the West about a possible military coup against his regime. Summing up the events of the year in a Christmas message to Iraq's Christian community, he justified his invasion of Kuwait as a legitimate act of defense of Iraq's national interests in the face of a Western-Zionist conspiracy against it. He vowed that Iraq would overcome the sanctions and expressed his confidence that God would provide Iraq "with a great public victory."[107]

RECONSTRUCTION OF THE ECONOMY

The war and the ensuing Shi'i and Kurdish rebellions further exacerbated the already difficult state of the Iraqi economy (see *MECS* 1990, pp. 384–85) with the industrial and oil sectors, electrical, water and sewage, transportation and telecommunications systems all heavily damaged. An epitome of the country's distress was the rationing of gasoline during March and April even though Iraq had been a major oil exporter before the war. Official figures on the overall loss to the country's economy varied from $200bn.–$300bn. These may have been inflated, in order to prove the Allies' brutality and to aggrandize the government's subsequent reconstruction achievements.[108]

The economic blockade imposed by the UN prevented Iraq from exporting its oil to cover its losses and from purchasing the food, machinery and spare parts it needed for reconstruction. Unemployment rose because of the partial paralysis of industry and the demobilization of soldiers, which was intended to save costs and reduce discontent in the military. Hidden unemployment in the semi-idle industries reportedly rose to c. 70%. Declining revenues forced a reduction of 24.7% in the 1991 investment budget. The Ministry of Industry announced that the military industries had been relegated to a lower priority than the civilian sector, a claim which could not be verified and seemed unlikely in view of the regime's past record of awarding rearmament a priority over civilian reconstruction[109] (see *MECS* 1990, p. 384).

Nevertheless, Iraq's pace in reconstructing its infrastructure was remarkable, according to foreign observers, even though some government reports were probably exaggerated. (In July, for instance, Iraq announced that 81 bridges had been rebuilt, but in September the figure was lowered to 50.) By mid-May, the government declared that all the governorates had been reconnected to the national grid, although production of electricity was only c. 37% of its prewar level by mid-August. With high priority given to the oil industry, Iraq claimed by December that it was capable of exporting 1.5m. barrels per day. However, since a considerable part of the reconstruction involved cannibalizing existing equipment and risky makeshift repairs, its long-term viability was questionable without the massive import of machinery and spare parts.[110]

American and Iraqi opposition sources asserted that Iraq was financing its reconstruction with the aid of secret government funds deposited in foreign banks years before the war, and that it circumvented the UN sanctions by utilizing fictitious Western and Jordanian companies as intermediaries for purchasing equipment and raw materials. A US Senate report concluded that Jordan permitted the transit of Iraqi exports — primarily refined oil products — and imports through its territory. Opposition sources claimed that Jordanian banks laundered Iraqi funds deposited in Swiss banks, and provided Iraq with credits amounting to several billion dollars. Large-scale sanction-breaking trade also took place along the Turkish border, with goods shipped into Iraq and fuel shipped to Turkey, while the Kurdish organizations apparently sold Iraqi construction materials to Iran in return for food.[111]

The major problem was food shortages. Agricultural production, insufficient before the war, declined by 70%–75% compared with 1990 because of lack of fuel and spare parts for agricultural machinery. Despite imports of grain from Canada and Australia (0.5m. and 1m. tons respectively) and rice from Thailand (200,000 tons), allowed by the UN for humanitarian reasons, food rationing had to be introduced. The government-supplied rations, however, met less than 50% of the average family's needs, increasing the pressure on the free market, where prices were soaring. Flour mills and bakeries, which had been privatized in the later 1980s, were renationalized in order to prevent widespread pilfering of grain.[112]

In an effort to stimulate the economy, as well as enhance its own popularity, the government issued licenses for imports that could be paid for with funds held outside Iraq, without inquiring as to the source of the funds or the nature of the deals. In August, food importers were exempted from income tax for one year, whereupon wealthy Iraqis living outside Iraq exported considerable quantities of food and goods to Iraq via Jordan. As a further incentive, in December, the government offered to pay all freight charges to truck drivers coming from Jordan.[113] Industrialists were allowed to travel abroad and import raw materials without having to supply foreign currency. In August, the RCC approved the establishment of a stock exchange in Baghdad.[114]

Shortages led to spiraling inflation, estimated at 250% during the first half of 1991. The removal of a restriction on withdrawals from bank accounts as of July increased the supply of money and further exacerbated inflationary pressures. Although food subsidies jumped from ID500m. in 1990 to ID2.15bn. in 1991, American economists visiting Iraq in August put the rise of food prices between 1,500% and 2,000%, while real earnings had fallen to between 5%–7% of the pre-August 1990 level. The official currency rate was $3.2 to the dinar, but the dinar was worth only $0.12 on the black market. Prices of goods and services provided by the public sector were frozen for a year in order to curb inflation, but Husayn ordered pay raises ranging from 10%–55% to all government employees in September, as their support was crucial to his rule.[115]

The economic crisis led to an unprecedented rise in crime and corruption. With the lifting of travel restrictions, a massive flow of Iraqis arrived in Jordan seeking to emigrate or merely to enjoy a short respite from the difficulties at home. Government propaganda about Iraq's achievements in the face of the blockade apparently failed to improve the discouraged mood of the population. Former information minister Latif Nusayf Jasim warned in a newspaper article in October that excessive complaints about shortages, high prices and corruption created frustration and doubt, which played into the hands of the enemy, who was constantly waging psychological warfare.[116]

By the end of the year, both government and foreign sources reported increasing malnutrition within the population, particularly among children and pregnant women, due to the sanctions, a poor summer harvest and an inefficient rationing system. Moreover, the combination of malnutrition, unclean water and shortages of medicine (which was not subject to the sanctions) had led to a sharp increase in mortality, particularly child mortality. The Iraqi health ministry put the cost of the blockade in human life from August 1990-September 1991 at 68,093, although this was probably an inflated figure designed to serve Iraq's propaganda needs.[117]

The UK and various other Western sources claimed that by the end of October Iraq had imported and received from international organizations more than 4m. tons of food — a quantity which, coupled with smuggling and various other sanctions-busting measures, provided Iraq with adequate food supplies. Moreover, it was argued that malnutrition was largely confined to the Shi'i and Kurdish regions, whereas the Sunni regions around Baghdad, the backbone of Husayn's regime, and particularly the ruling elite enjoyed adequate food supplies.[118]

Although Iraq accused the Allies of inhumanity for refusing to lift the sanctions, it prohibited international relief organizations from distributing food and medicine, particularly in the Shi'i south, except by channeling it through the government rationing system. Husayn rejected the UN compromise proposal on the sale of oil, preferring, apparently, to starve the hostile Shi'i and Kurdish populations and thereby weaken their opposition to his regime. UN officials accused Iraq in June of diverting at least 3,000 tons of UN food shipments earmarked for the Kurdish refugees to the Sunni regions, particularly Tikrit, Husayn's hometown. Concurrently, Husayn dramatized his people's plight for the benefit of Western public opinion in order to break the blockade against his regime.[119]

IRAQ AND THE WORLD

THE CAT-AND-MOUSE GAME OF DISARMING IRAQ

Security Council Resolution 687, adopted on 3 April, aimed at eliminating the Iraqi military threat to the Gulf region in the future. It required Iraq to accept the destruction of its nuclear, chemical and biological weapons, as well as "all ballistic missiles" in addition to all support and production facilities of these weapons systems. Iraq was ordered to enumerate the locations, amounts and types of these weapons and agree to a UN-supervised destruction of them within 120 days. It also had to undertake not to use, develop or acquire any of these weapons in the future. Although the arms embargo remained intact, the resolution prescribed a gradual lifting of the economic sanctions, conditional upon Iraq's full compliance with its terms. The Security Council also decided in June that Iraq must pay the costs of the entire weapons-destruction operation.[120]

Repeatedly pledging compliance with the resolution throughout the rest of the year, Iraq nevertheless consistently attempted to conceal information and obstruct the working of the UN inspection teams.[121] It kept on testing the Allies' determination, making gradual and partial concessions within its nuclear arsenal only under Allied threats of military action. Husayn, seeking to preserve his military strength, also apparently feared that the presence of UN teams in Iraq would be perceived domestically as an indication of his weakness and would undermine his position. He was biding his time, a policy he pursued vis-à-vis the Kurds as well, hoping that the UN would eventually either accept his figures on Iraq's unconventional military capability, or abandon the effort to destroy it.

Iraq was, nevertheless, forced to reveal the existence of several secret nuclear facilities during the May-August period. It also admitted possessing quantities of uranium far higher than previously reported to the International Atomic Energy Agency (IAEA), and of having engaged in uranium enrichment procedures usually utilized for the development of nuclear weapons. Likewise, it reported that it had extracted 3 grams of plutonium required for making a nuclear bomb, claiming that its efforts had been intended for peaceful purposes only. These revelations constituted admissions of previous deception of the UN by Iraq, and of breaching its obligations as a signatory of the nuclear weapons nonproliferation treaty. Husayn avoided provoking the hesitant Allies into taking military action by releasing piecemeal information from time to time.[122] Conceding the success of Iraq's policy of obstruction, Ambassador Rolf Ekeus, who was in charge of the UN operation, observed that while the inspectors gathered "a lot of facts," they lacked understanding of Iraq's "master plan."[123]

Within the nuclear uproar, UN teams also worked on tracking down Iraq's other unconventional weapons. The destruction of the *Scud* missiles that were reported by Iraq was completed by mid-July, according to UN sources, but hundreds of other missiles remained concealed, and UN inspectors charged as well that Iraq was building new *Scud* carriers at an intensive pace. Much larger quantities of chemical weapons than previously reported by Iraq were also found. On 19 July, Iraq admitted to having built two superguns, which were subsequently destroyed by the UN team. In contradiction to earlier denials, Iraq conceded in early August that it had conducted experiments in biological warfare, but claimed to have halted them in the autumn of 1990 for fear of air attacks.[124]

The most serious confrontation between Iraq and the UN occurred on 24 September, when Iraqi troops detained a UN team as it seized secret documents at a nuclear plant, and made the release of the UN inspectors conditional upon the return of the documents. These documents constituted the first tangible evidence of the scope and components of Iraq's overall nuclear development plan. When the Security Council demanded that Iraq free the detained inspectors, Deputy Prime Minister 'Aziz accused the leader of team, David Kay, of spying for the CIA and indirectly for Israeli intelligence. After a four-day standoff and renewed Allied threats, Iraq agreed to release the detained inspectors in return for receiving a complete inventory of the documents seized and photocopied by the UN team.[125]

Based on its findings the IAEA concluded that the Iraqi nuclear effort had gone on for several years, at a cost of over $10bn., employing more than 10,000 scientists and technicians. The program had used two systems for enriching uranium: electromagnetic isotope separation (EMIS), and the more advanced centrifuge isotope separation. Though cumbersome, the EMIS system, which had been used by the US during World War II, did not require specialized imported equipment and was, therefore, easier to conceal. In addition, Iraq was engaged in producing Lithium 6, used only for the production of hydrogen bombs.

Iraq used hundreds of foreign companies as suppliers, making parallel acquisitions of equipment at quantities below the ceiling required for reporting to the IAEA. A large secret network of facilities for the production of nuclear equipment was spread all over Iraq. The scope and achievements of the Iraqi effort exposed the total failure of the IAEA's regular inspection policy, as well as of Western intelligence efforts. Even if all existing facilities in Iraq were destroyed, IAEA officials conceded, they could be rebuilt within a third of the original time if Iraq were not closely monitored. Moreover, the technical knowledge acquired by the Iraqis could not be erased. Iraq, in fact, had been only months away from producing a nuclear device prior to the outbreak of the war.[126] In this context, Husayn's decision to invade Kuwait and risk war was a major mistake from his point of view.

In view of Iraq's nuclear buildup and its obstructionism, the Security Council passed Resolution 715 on 11 October which placed Iraq's military industry under UN control for an indefinite period of time and allowed UN inspectors unrestricted access to all sites. While IAEA teams located additional major components of the Iraqi nuclear program, the cat-and-mouse game played by Iraq continued till the end of the year. In view of the concerted UN effort, the IAEA considered it unlikely but possible that Iraq could still be actively engaged in the development of a nuclear capability at that time.[127]

THE POLITICS OF STARVATION

The payment of reparations by Iraq to all those harmed by its conduct during the crisis and war required by Security Council Resolution 687 was held up because of disagreements among the Allies over the proportion of Iraq's oil revenues to be earmarked for reparations and disagreements over the priorities of the claimants. Meanwhile, Iraq asked the UN in April to lift the ban on food and medicines purchased before 2 August 1990, and to allow it to sell $942.5m. worth of oil to finance additional food imports. In early May, it requested a five-year reprieve on all reparations citing the need to restore its devastated economy and service its $75bn. debt. Security Council Resolution 692, passed on 20 May, rejected these requests and established a compensation commission to supervise Iraq's payment of reparations.[128]

Iraq denounced the resolution as a violation of international law and justice, and as a conspiracy to plunder its oil and impoverish its people.[129] On 11 June, following a 60-day review period, the Security Council decided against lifting the sanctions in view of Iraq's failure to comply with several provisions of Resolution 687. The resolution was a compromise between the US and British demand to link the lifting of sanctions to the removal of Husayn from power, and the call of several other members to relax them, thereby offering Husayn hope that steadfastness and procrastination would enable him to outlast the Allied coalition.[130]

In July, Iraq again requested permission to export oil, citing food shortages and claiming that 6,000 children had already died of malnutrition and 170,000 more were expected to die by the end of the year should the sanctions continue.[131] In view of the civilians' plight, the Security Council passed two resolutions on 15 August which partially complied with the Iraqi request while simultaneously tightening international control over Iraq's economy. Resolution 705 established a 30% ceiling from the projected Iraqi oil revenue to be allocated for the payment of reparations, while Resolution 706 permitted Iraq to sell $1.6bn. worth of oil for six months under UN supervision, with all proceeds channeled to a UN-controlled escrow account. Of the $1.6bn. revenues, $1.05bn. was to be spent on imports, $480m. on reparations, $60m. on financing Iraqi weapons destruction and $10m. on other UN operations in Iraq.[132]

Iraq, however, rejected both resolutions as an affront to its sovereignty. Husayn stated on 12 October that "Iraq can live 20 years under the blockade without asking anybody to give it anything," and Minister of Trade Muhammad Mahdi Salih announced that the Iraqi people were prepared to "eat dates and barley" in order to defend the country's independence. Concurrently, in an effort to mobilize Western and Arab public opinion against the sanctions, Iraqi spokesmen continuously stressed the issue of the death of thousands of civilians, particularly children, due to shortages of food and medicine caused by the blockade.[133]

FOREIGN RELATIONS

Iraq's first foreign-policy priority after the war was to restore its central position in the Arab arena, so that it could enlist Arab support in repelling Allied pressures and sanctions. In April, Prime Minister Hammadi declared Iraq's firm support for strengthening the Arab League and Arab solidarity, and its readiness "to apologize, to turn over a leaf" in its relations with all the Arab states. The Iraqi media urged the Arab League to play a key role in removing "the injustice that has befallen Iraq as a result of US hegemony."[134]

Iraq participated in the Arab League sessions held in Cairo during April and May and, in an attempt to restore normal working relations in the Arab world, did not oppose the transfer of the League's offices to Cairo despite Egypt's position during the war. In April, Iraq sought to warm its relations with the Maghrib states dispatching envoys with personal messages to their leaders.[135]

While Iraq enhanced its ties with Jordan, Yemen, Sudan and the PLO, which had supported it during the war, its diplomatic efforts in the rest of the Arab world were largely a failure. Relations with the Arab Gulf countries remained especially acrimonious. Iraq accused them of betraying the Arab nation by collaborating with the US, and urged their people to topple their corrupt rulers. The Gulf states, however, remained within the anti-Iraqi coalition and provided tacit support for the Iraqi opposition in exile. The unresolved fate of the Kuwaiti prisoners taken to Iraq also aggravated mutual hostility. The only success Iraq achieved was establishing closer relations with Libya toward the end of the year (see chapter on Libya). Iraq also renewed its campaign of courting Arab opposition parties and intellectuals to plead its case that the Western nations were trampling on Arab pride in Iraq.[136]

During the course of the year, Iraqi troops disguised in civilian clothes made several clandestine attempts to enter the demilitarized zone between Iraq and Kuwait in order to gather abandoned weapons. By October, at least 26 Iraqis were reportedly killed during these attempts. The most serious incident took place on 29 August when Iraqi boats landed several dozen troops in mufti on the Kuwaiti island of Bubiyan. Kuwaiti forces sank one boat and captured three others, taking 45 prisoners. Responding to a Kuwaiti complaint to the UN, Iraq denied that the affair had taken place, and accused "some Arab regimes" of serving "the imperialists" in order to harm Iraq and the entire Arab nation.[137]

Turkish bombings of Kurdish guerrilla camps in Iraq in early August aggravated relations between the two states (see chapter on Turkey). Although presumably Iraq was not overly distressed over the punishment inflicted on the Kurds, it was nonetheless upset with the violation of its sovereignty, and condemned Turkey. Likewise, it denounced the West's double standard for its concern about the Iraqi Kurds while ignoring the plight of the Kurds in Turkey.[138]

Relations with Iran fluctuated sharply during the course of the year. Iraq accused Iran of supporting the Shi'i Intifada and of meddling in the Kurdish problem. Iran, for its part, condemned Iraq's treatment of the Shi'is and Shi'i holy sites. Iran's refusal to return the Iraqi planes that had sought shelter there during the Gulf War elicited further Iraqi accusations of treachery. Both countries also accused each other of violating the 1988 cease-fire agreement.[139]

By late July, however, Iran signaled its readiness to improve relations. In response, Iraq expressed its desire "to establish a comprehensive and permanent peace" based on its offer of 12 August 1990 (see *MECS* 1990, pp. 406–8). Following a visit by Iraqi deputy foreign minister Sa'd 'Abd al-Majid al-Faysal to Tehran during late August, the two countries set up joint committees to discuss the issues of the refugees, PoWs, border demarcation and the Iraqi planes. In a goodwill gesture, Iran released 400 PoWs and expressed its willingness to release the remaining Iraqi prisoners provided Iraq reciprocate by releasing all Iranian PoWs.[140]

The brief rapprochement ended, however, when UN Secretary-General Pérez de Cuellar submitted to the Security Council on 10 December his conclusions on the Iraqi-Iranian War naming Iraq as the aggressor. Hailing the decision, Iran demanded reparations of a trillion dollars based on Security Council Resolution 598 — a demand, evidently, with little more than a declaratory value. Incensed at this new diplomatic setback, Iraq rejected the report and the reparations claim, charging Iran as being the true aggressor. Mutual recriminations between the two countries continued until the end of the year.[141]

Iraq played on the anti-Israeli theme after the war, as during the war, in order to improve its image among the Arab masses. In an effort to turn its isolation and exclusion from the Arab-Israeli peace process into an asset, it denounced the Madrid conference in October (see chapter on the ME peace process) as a ploy to impose the "Zionist entity" on Arab land, and contrasted Iraq with the "treacherous" Arab regimes which attended it. Likewise, it condemned the repeal of the 1976 resolution by the UN General Assembly, passed on 16 December, branding Zionism as racism, as a "disgrace in the history of humanity" and a manifestation of the American domination of the UN.[142]

Resentful of the changing circumstances in the global arena, Iraq welcomed the conservative coup in the USSR in August as an event that would restore "the correct international balance" and put an end to American hegemony and aggression. The Iraqi media criticized Gorbachev for reversing traditional Soviet support for the Arabs and for backing Israel, as well as for collaborating with the US during the Gulf crisis. *Al-Jumhuriyya,* in August, expressed hope for the emergence of a new world order "built on the debris of the international Zionist conspiracy."[143] Iraq's hastiness in supporting the coup, however, aggravated relations with the new democratic Russian state.

Despite Husayn's attacks on the US throughout the year and his obstruction of the implementation of the UN resolutions, he put out occasional feelers for a reconciliation with the US. In July, Defense Minister Husayn Kamil Hasan informed former US attorney general Elliot Richardson, who was visiting Iraq, of Iraq's desire to improve its relations with the US. On 15 August, *Babil* and *al-'Iraq,* dailies published by Husayn's son 'Uday, called for the normalization of ties with the US. Referring to Iran's growing power, the newspapers argued that the weakening of Iraq would harm international interests in the region and demanded that the US stop insisting on Husayn's removal from power.[144] None of these initiatives bore much fruit, although Iraq did score one success when Britain released $125m. in frozen Iraqi funds in return for the release of a British businessman long imprisoned in Iraq.[145]

APPENDIX I: REGIONAL COMMAND OF THE BA'TH ARAB SOCIALIST PARTY[146]

Saddam Husayn	Sunni	General Secretary
Muhammad Yunis al-Ahmad*	Sunni	Secretary of the Central Organization Bureau
'Izzat Ibrahim al-Duri	Sunni	Deputy Secretary of the Regional Command
'Abd al-Rahman Ahmad 'Abd Rahman al-Duri*	Sunni	Secretary of the al-Euphrates Organization Bureau
Khidr 'Abd al-'Aziz Husayn 'Ali al-Duri*	Sunni	Secretary of the Northern Region Bureau
Muzhar Matni al-'Awwad al-Hardan al-Dulaymi*	Sunni	Secretary of the Baghdad Organization Bureau
Tariq 'Aziz	Christian	Deputy Prime Minister
'Abd al-Ghani 'Abd al-Ghafur*	Sunni	Secretary of the Foreign Relations Bureau
Mizban Khidr al-Hadi	Shi'i	Secretary of the Central Bureau of the Vocational and Popular Organizations
'Ali Hasan al-Majid	Sunni	Interior Minister (later appointed as Defense Minister)
Taha Yasin Ramadan	Sunni	Vice President of the Republic
Kamil Yasin Rashid	Sunni	
Muhammad Zimam 'Abd al-Razzaq al-Sa'dun*	Sunni(?)	Secretary of the Southern Organization
Sa'di Mahdi Salih	Shi'i	Speaker of the National Assembly
Nuri Faysal Shahir Shahir 'Abd al-'Aziz al-Hadithi*	Sunni	Secretary of the Students' and Youth Bureau
Fawzi Khalaf Ruzayq Mahmud al-Tikriti*	Sunni	Secretary of the Salah al-Din Organization
Muhammad Hamza al-Zubaydi	Shi'i	Prime Minister

Reserve Members:
'Abd al-Rahim Hamid
Khalil Ibrahim
Mawlud Dhiban

* New members.

APPENDIX II: THE IRAQI CABINET
MARCH–SEPTEMBER 1991[147]

Prime Minister	Sa'dun Hammadi[b]
Deputy Prime Minister	Tariq 'Aziz
Deputy Prime Minister	Muhammad Hamza al-Zubaydi[c]
Agriculture and Irrigation	'Abd al-Wahhab Mahmud 'Abdallah al-Sabagh
Awqaf and and Religious Affairs	'Abdallah Fadil 'Abbas
Culture and Information	Hamid Yusif Hammadi[a]
Defense	Husayn Kamil Hasan[d]
Defense (Minister of State)	'Abd al-Jabbar Shinshal
Education	Hikmat 'Abdallah al-Bazzaz[a]
Finance	Majid 'Abd Ja'far[a]
Foreign Affairs	Ahmad Husayn Khudayr[a]
Foreign Affairs (Minister of State)	Muhammad Sa'id Kazim al-Sahhaf
Health	'Abd al-Salam Muhammad Sa'id
Higher Education and Scientific Research	'Abd al-Razzaq al-Hashimi[a]
Housing and Reconstruction	Mahmud Dhiyab al-Ahmad[a]
Industry and Military Industrialization	'Amir Hammadi al-Sa'di[a]
Interior	'Ali Hasan al-Majid[e]
Justice	Shabib al-Maliki[a]
Labor and Social Affairs	Umid Midhat Mubarak
Oil	Usama 'Abd al-Razzaq al-Hiti[a]
Planning	Samal Majid Faraj
Trade	Muhammad Mahdi Salih
Transport and Communication	'Abd al-Sattar Ahmad al-Ma'ini[a]
Minister of State without Portfolio	Irshad Ahmad Muhammad al-Zibari

[a] New minister.
[b] Replaced by Muhammad Hamza al-Zubaydi in the September reshuffle.
[c] Appointed prime minister in September.
[d] Succeeded Lt. Gen. Sa'di Tu'ma 'Abbas on 6 April. Replaced by 'Ali Hasan al-Majid on 6 November 1991.
[e] Succeeded on 6 November by Watban Ibrahim al-Hasan.

NOTES

For the place and frequency of publications cited here, and for the full name of the publication, news agency, radio station or monitoring service where an abbreviation is used, please see "List of Sources." Only in the case of more than one publication bearing the same name is the place of publication noted here. In the present chapter, however, all references to *al-Thawra* and *al-Jumhuriyya* are to the Baghdad papers of these names.

1. *Al-Qadisiyya,* 1 January; *Baghdad Observer,* 3 January; *al-Thawra,* 4, 7, 10, 13 January; *al-Jumhuriyya,* 15 January 1991.
2. INA, 3 January — DR, 4 January; *NYT,* 1, 5 January; *IHT,* 7 January 1991.
3. AFP, 4 January — DR, 5 January; INA, 12 January — DR, 14 January 1991.
4. INA, 2 January — DR, 3 January; 'Aziz's statement in INA, 4 January — DR, 7 January; Hammadi to *al-Tadamun* (London), 7 January; R. Baghdad, 6 January — DR, 8 January; *al-Jumhuriyya,* 16 January 1991.
5. R. Baghdad, 9, 11, January — DR, 9, 11 January; *al-Thawra,* 11, 15 January 1991.
6. *NYT,* 9 January; INA, 8, 15 January — DR, 9, 15, 16 January 1991.
7. *NYT,* 3, 10 January 1991.
8. *NYT,* 13, 14 January. See the Iraqi version of the minutes of his talks in *al-Dustur* (Amman), 9 February 1991.
9. INA, 7, 13 January — DR, 7, 14 January 1991.

10. R. Baghdad, 17 January — DR, 18 January; *NYT,* 11 February; IRNA, 19 February — DR, 19 February; AFP, 6 March — DR, 7 March 1991.
11. IRNA, 14 February — DR, 19 February 1991.
12. R. Baghdad, 22 January, 2 February — DR, 22 January, 4 February; *Alif Ba,* 30 January; INA, 1 February — DR, 4 February; R. Tehran, 18 February — DR, 19 February 1991.
13. R. Tehran, 26 January — DR, 28 January; *Hürriyet,* 31 January; *Le Monde,* 31 January; IRNA, 31 January — DR, 1 February 1991.
14. *Al-Thawra,* 18 January; R. Baghdad, 20 January — DR, 22 January 1991.
15. R. Baghdad, 27, 31 January — DR, 28 January, 1 February 1991.
16. R. Baghdad, 27, 28, January, 8, 11 February — DR, 28, 29 January, 11, 12 February; INA, 6 February — DR, 7 February 1991.
17. Text of Husayn's letter to Bush in *al-Thawra,* 18 January; R. Baghdad 18, 25 January — DR, 18, 28 January; Husayn to CNN, cited in *NYT,* 31 January 1991.
18. R. Baghdad, 25, 29 January — DR, 28, 30 January; *al-Jumhuriyya,* 20, 24 January 1991.
19. R. Baghdad, 19, 26 January, 6 February — DR, 22, 28 January, 6 February; *IHT,* 29, January, 1 February; *FT,* 7 February; TASS, 11 February — DR, 11 February 1991.
20. *IHT,* 23 January; R. Baghdad, 28 January — DR, 28 January; Husayn to CNN, cited by *NYT,* 30 January 1991.
21. The Press Association, 21 January — DR, 22 January; INA, 22 January — DR, 23 January 1991.
22. R. Baghdad, 20 January — DR, 22 January 1991.
23. R. Baghdad, 17, 21, 22 January — DR, 17, 22 January; *al-Qadisiyya,* 29 January, 2 February 1991.
24. JT, 23 January; R. Baghdad, 23 January, 2 February — DR, 23 January, 6 February; *NYT,* 2 February 1991.
25. IRNA, 2 February — DR, 4 February; *al-Jumhuriyya,* 9 February; *al-Qadisiyya,* 10 February; *NYT,* 11 February 1991.
26. R. Baghdad, 12 February — DR, 13 February; *NYT,* 14 February 1991.
27. R. Baghdad, 15 February — DR, 15 February 1991.
28. *IHT,* 16–17 February; *NYT,* 16, 17 February 1991.
29. *NYT,* 19, 22, 24 February; R. Baghdad, 22, 23 February — DR, 25 February; *FT,* 24 February 1991.
30. *IHT,* 23-24, 25 February; R. Baghdad, 25, 26 February — DR, 26 February; USIA, 26 February 1991.
31. R. Baghdad, 26 February — DR, 26 February 1991.
32. R. Baghdad, 27, 28 February — DR, 27 February, 1 March; *IHT,* 27, 28 February, 1 March 1991.
33. *IHT,* 4, 8, 14 March; INA, 5 March — DR, 6 March; AFP, 21 March — DR, 22 March 1991.
34. R. Baghdad, 1, 3, 4 March — DR, 1, 4 March; INA, 1 April — DR, 2 April 1991.
35. R. Baghdad, 7 April — DR, 8 April; *NYT,* 7 April 1991.
36. *NYT,* 14, 25 March; *JT,* 23 March; *WSJ,* 26 December 1991.
37. *NYT,* 4, 5, 8, 10, 22 March; Peter Galbraith, *Civil War in Iraq: A Staff Report to the Committee on Foreign Relations, United States Senate,* May 1991, p. 1; *Middle East Report,* July/August 1991, p. 10.
38. *NYT,* 5 March; R. Damascus, 5 March — DR, 6 March; Galbraith, ibid.
39. Galbraith, ibid; *NYT,* 13 March; *IHT,* 14 March; *al-'Alam* (London), 16 March 1991.
40. *WP,* 10 March; *NYT,* 7, 14, 22, 28 March; *FT,* 16–17 March; VoIO, 19 March — DR, 19 March; AFP, 22 March — DR, 25 March; *IHT,* 27 March; R. Tehran, 7 April — DR, 9 April 1991; Galbraith, ibid.
41. INA, 20 March — DR, 21 March; R. Tehran, IRNA, 21 March — DR, 21 March; VoRI, 21 March — DR, 22 March; IRNA, 21, 24, 28 March, 4 April — DR, 21, 25, 29 March, 5 April; VoFI, 22 March — DR, 25 March; R. Monte Carlo, 23 March — DR, 25 March; *al-'Alam* (London), 20 July 1991.
42. *Al-Hayat* (London), 16 June; *Middle East Report,* July-August p. 10; *al-Ittihad* (Abu Dhabi), 8 August; *WSJ,* 26 December 1991; *Le Monde,* 13 January 1992.
43. *NYT,* 22 March; *IHT,* 13–14 April; *FT,* 16 April; WF, 15 May 1991; Galbraith, ibid.

44. *NYT*, 22, 28 March; *al-Jumhuriyya*, 27 March 1991.
45. SANA, 1 April — DR, 2 April; VoIO, 26 October — DR, 28 October; *CR*, Iraq, No. 2, 1991.
46. VoIO, 23 May, 1 June — DR, 24 May, 5 June; *TT*, 11 June; IRNA, 11 June — DR, 12 June; R. Baghdad, 12 June — DR, 13 June; *IHT*, 12 June; *NYT*, 12 July; VoIP, 7, 24 November — DR, 8, 26 November 1991.
47. R. Tehran, 7, 29 April, 15 July — DR, 9, 30 April, 16 July; IRNA, 16 May — DR, 16 May; *MEI*, 14 June; *Sawt al-Kuwait al-Duwali*, 6 July; *al-Thawra*, 17 July; *Liwa al-Sadr*, 4 August; *Alif Ba*, 25 September; VoIP, 6 November — DR, 7 November 1991.
48. On this policy, see Amazia Baram, *Culture, History and Ideology in the Formation of Ba'thist Iraq, 1968–89* (Basingstoke: Macmillan, 1990).
49. AFP, 4, 12 March — DR, 5, 18 March; *NYT*, 12, 13 March, 7 April 1991; Galbraith, op. cit.
50. *Al-Safir*, 13 March; *IHT*, 19 March; *FT*, 21 March; *Time*, 15 April; Galbraith, op. cit; *CR*, Iraq, No. 2, 1991.
51. *Der Spiegel*, 25 March; *NYT*, 27 March; *al-Musawwar*, 29 March; *Time*, 15 April 1991.
52. *IHT*, 26 March; *NYT*, 29 March; *Time*, 15 April 1991; Galbraith, op. cit.
53. *NYT*, 26, 31 March; AFP, 28 March — DR, 29 March; *IHT*, 1 April; *Time*, 15 April 1991; Galbraith, op. cit.
54. INA, 16, 17 March — DR, 18, 19 March; R. Baghdad, 17 March — DR, 19 March 1991.
55. *NYT*, 31 March; *Time*, 15 April 1991; Galbraith, op. cit.
56. *NYT*, 5, 8, 16 April; *Time*, 15 April; *WF*, 16 April 1991; *CR*, Iraq, No. 2, 1991.
57. *NYT*, 8, 13, 16 April; *The Economist*, 20 April 1991.
58. *NYT*, 9, 12, 13 April; *IHT*, 11 April 1991; *CR*, Iraq, No. 2, 1991.
59. R. Baghdad, 20 April — DR, 22 April; INA, 5, 11, 13, 29 April — DR, 5, 12, 15, 30 April; *IHT*, 6 April 1991.
60. INA, 7, 10, 16, 23 April — DR, 8, 10, 17, 25 April; *al-Thawra*, 11, 16, April; R. Baghdad, 18 April — DR, 19 April 1991.
61. *IHT*, 21, 22, 23, 24, 27–28 April 1991; *CR*, Iraq, No. 2, 1991.
62. *NYT*, 2, 3, 13, 23, 25 May; *IHT*, 6, 11, 30 May; *MEI*, 17 May; *The Economist*, 18 May; AFP, 7 July — DR, 8 July 1991.
63. *IHT*, 23 April; *MEI*, 17 May 1991; *CR*, Iraq, No. 2, 1991.
64. *FT*, 29 April, 26 June; *NYT*, 23 May, 3 June, 13 July; *IHT*, 17, 20 June, 12 July; *WP*, 23 June 1991.
65. AFP, 19 April — DR, 22 April; *Sawt al-Kuwait al-Duwali*, 24 April; *IHT*, 26 April 1991.
66. *FT*, *NYT*, 26 April; INA, 29 April — DR, 30 April 1991.
67. See Hammadi's statements in *NYT*, 6 June 1991.
68. VoPK, 17 June — DR, 18 June; *NYT*, 24 June; *Milliyet*, 27 June 1991.
69. See the Kurdish proposal in *al-Hayat* (London), 26 June. For the Iraqi draft, see *al-Sharq al-Awsat*, 29 June 1991.
70. *Sawt al-Kuwait al-Duwali*, 25 June; *Sawt al-Ittihad* cited by *Ha'aretz*, 28 June; *al-Sharq al-Awsat*, 29 June 1991.
71. *Al-Sharq al-Awsat*, 29 June; *Milliyet*, 30 June; VoIK, 2, 15 July — DR, 2, 17 July; *al-'Alam* (London), 13 July 1991.
72. *Sawt al-Kuwait al-Duwali*, 9 July 1991.
73. *IHT*, 22 July; *NYT*, 4 August 1991.
74. VoPK, 12, 25 August — DR, 15, 26 August; *Günaydın*, 2 September 1991; *CR*, Iraq, No. 4, 1991.
75. AFP, 9 October — DR, 10 October; *NYT*, 9 October; *IHT*, 10 October 1991.
76. *IHT*, 18 October; VoPK, 13 November — DR, 14 November; *NYT*, 17, 26 November; AFP, 5 December — DR, 6 December; VoIP, 8 December — DR, 9 December 1991.
77. *IHT*, 21 July; VoPK, 9, 10, 29 September — DR, 10, 13 September, 1 October 1991.
78. *IHT*, 21 July; *Sawt al-Kuwait al-Duwali*, 31 July; *NYT*, 4 August 1991.
79. *Al-Sharq al-Awsat*, 16 October; *NYT*, 29 October; AFP, 15, 21 November — DR, 18, 22 November. For Talabani's criticism, see *al-Sharq al-Awsat*, 10 October; VoPK, 10 November — DR, 13 November; *Sawt al-Kuwait al-Duwali*, 21 December 1991.
80. *FT*, 21 January; AFP, 26 January — DR, 29 January; IRIB TV, 1 February — DR, 4 February; VoFI, 9, 12 February — DR, 12, 21 February 1991.

81. *FT,* 5 March; *al-Ahram,* 6 March 1991.
82. IRNA, 4, 10 March — DR, 5, 13 March; WF, 5 March; *al-'Alam* (London), 16 March 1991.
83. SANA, 12 March — DR, 13 March; AFP, 14 March — DR, 18 March; *IHT,* 14 March; *al-'Alam* (London), VoFI, 25 March — DR, 26 March 1991.
84. VoFI, 20 April — DR, 22 April; IRNA, 21 April — DR, 22 April; *IHT,* 31 May; *al-'Alam* (London), 1 June 1991.
85. *Al-Shira',* 1 July; *al-'Iraq al-Hurr,* 19 June, 10, 13 July 1991.
86. R. Baghdad, 2, 4, 6, 8, 9 March — DR, 4, 6, 7, 8, 11 March; INA, 26 April — DR, 29 April 1991.
87. R. Baghdad, 6 March — DR, 6 March 1991.
88. *JT,* 16 July; R. Baghdad, 4 November — DR, 4 November 1991.
89. *Alif Ba,* 20 March 1991.
90. *Le Monde,* 26 March 1991; *CR,* Iraq, No. 2, 1991.
91. *NYT,* 7 April 1991.
92. INA, 30 March, 25 April — DR, 1, 26 April; *Alif Ba,* 17 April 1991.
93. INA, 23 March, 23, 26 April, 21 July — DR, 25 March, 23, 29 April, 22 July; *al-'Alam* (London), 1 June; R. Baghdad, 13 June — DR, 14 June 1991.
94. *JT,* 24 March; *al-Hadaf* (Damascus), 26 May; *al-Ittihad* (Abu Dhabi), 8 August 1991.
95. INA, 27 June, 3 September — DR, 28 June, 3 September; *al-Jumhuriyya,* 2 July, 25 August 1991.
96. *JT,* 24 March; *FT,* 1 August; *al-Hadaf* (Damascus), 18 August 1991.
97. INA, 27 March — DR, 28 March; *al-Qadisiyya,* 9 May 1991.
98. *CSM,* 1 August; *al-Hadaf* (Damascus), 18 August 1991.
99. R. Baghdad, 14 September — DR, 16 September; *Alif Ba,* 18 September 1991.
100. R. Baghdad, 16 September — DR, 18 September 1991.
101. *Alif Ba,* 18 September; INA, 5 October — DR, 7 October; *Babil,* 6 November 1991.
102. INA, 6, 13 November — DR, 7, 13 November 1991.
103. VoIO, 8, 11 November — DR, 12 November; *Sawt al-Kuwait al-Duwali,* 21 November; WSJ, 26 December; INA, 29 December — DR, 30 December 1991.
104. *Al-Watan al-'Arabi,* 15 November 1991.
105. *IHT,* 21 June; AFP, 9 July — DR, 9 July; R. Baghdad, 15 August, 8 September — DR, 16 August, 9 September; *al-Thawra,* 16 September; *al-Qadisiyya,* 16 July, 26 December 1991.
106. *Al-Jumhuriyya,* 17 November 1991.
107. *Al-'Iraq,* 22 October; *al-Thawra,* 15 December; INA, 14 December — DR, 16 December; R. Baghdad, 24 December — DR, 26 December 1991.
108. R. Baghdad, 14 March — DR, 15 March; *Sawt al-Sha'b* (Amman), 20 April; INA, 1 May — DR, 2 May; *NYT,* 24 June; *al-Shira',* 1 July; AFP, 6 September 1991.
109. INA, 2, 8 May, 18 August — DR, 3, 10 May, 19 August; *al-Hadaf* (Damascus), 18 August; *Alif Ba,* 18 September 1991.
110. INA, 13 May, 31 July, 19 December — DR, 14 May, 1 August, 20 December; AFP, 6 September 1991; *CR,* Iraq, No. 3, 1991.
111. *Al-'Iraq al-Hurr,* 3 July; *WP,* 10 December; AFP, 13 December — DR, 16 December; *WSJ* cited in *Ha'aretz,* 17 January 1991.
112. *CR,* Iraq, No. 3; R. Baghdad, 3 June — DR, 4 June; *MM,* 14 October 1991.
113. R. Baghdad, 11 August — DR, 14 August; *MM,* 14 October; *al-Jumhuriyya,* 4 December 1991.
114. INA, 8 May — DR, 10 May; R. Baghdad, 11 August — DR, 14 August 1991.
115. *CR,* Iraq, Nos. 2 and 3; *Alif Ba,* 21 August, 11 September; *MM,* 14 October; *FT,* 23 October; *al-Sharq al-Awsat,* 5 November 1991.
116. *JT,* 30 July; *al-Ahali* (Cairo), 25 September; *al-Thawra,* 13 October; R. Baghdad, 19 June, 15, 22 December — DR, 20 June, 6, 23 December 1991.
117. *CR,* Iraq, No. 4, 1991.
118. *NYT,* 24 June; INA, 26 November — DR, 27 November 1991.
119. *CR,* Iraq, No. 4; *MEI,* 14 June; *Le Monde* quoted in *Ha'aretz,* 31 October; *NYT,* 3 November 1991.
120. WF, 4 April; *IHT,* 19 June 1991.
121. WF, 27 June; INA, 28 June — DR, 1 July; *NYT,* 29 June, 3 July 1991.

122. *NYT,* 12 July, 3 August; INA, 15, 17 July — DR, 16, 18 July; WF, 16 July; *IHT,* 29 July; *CR,* Iraq, No. 3, 1991.
123. *NYT,* 12 September 1991.
124. *IHT,* 21 July, 6 August, 19 September; *NYT,* 31 July, 12 September 1991.
125. *NYT,* 23, 24, 28 September; INA, 25 September — DR, 26 September 1991.
126. *Profil,* 16 September; *FT,* 3, 4 October; WF, 10 October 1991.
127. *CR,* Iraq, No. 3; *FT,* 10 June; *IHT,* 20 July; *NYT,* 30 July 1991.
128. *NYT,* 17 April; INA, 2 May — DR, 3 May; WF, 20 May 1991; *CR,* Iraq, No. 2, 1991.
129. R. Baghdad, 21 May — DR, 23 May; *FT,* 4 June 1991.
130. WF, 11, 12 June 1991.
131. *IHT,* 13 July; *NYT,* 17 July; *FT,* 25 July 1991; *CR,* Iraq, No. 3, 1991.
132. WF, 15 August 1991.
133. *Alif Ba,* 2 October; R. Baghdad, 13 October — DR, 17 October; *NYT,* 21 October, 3 November 1991.
134. INA, 25 April — DR, 26 April; *al-Qadisiyya,* 11 May; *al-Thawra,* 14 May 1991.
135. *CR,* Iraq, No. 2; AFP, 10 April — DR, 11 April 1991.
136. R. Riyadh, 8 June — DR, 10 June; *al-Thawra,* 18 July; KUNA, 27 August — DR, 29 August; INA, 30 August, 12 December — DR, 30 August, 13 December; *NYT,* 24 October; SUNA, 3 November — DR, 5 November 1991.
137. *IHT,* 29 August; R. Baghdad, 30 August — DR, 3 September; AFP, 6 October — DR, 7 October 1991.
138. *NYT,* 8 August; *al-Qadisiyya,* 12 August 1991.
139. INA, 11 April, 9 May — DR, 11 April, 9 May; IRNA, 28 April — DR, 29 April; IRIB, 20 May — DR, 21 May; R. Tehran, 2 June — DR, 4 June; Taha Yasin Ramadan to *al-Hadaf* (Damascus), 2 June; *al-Qadisiyya,* 21 July; *al-Thawra,* 22 July 1991.
140. *Monday Morning,* 5 August, 2 September; INA, 28, 29 August — DR, 29 August; IRNA, 12, 16 November — DR, 13, 18 November 1991.
141. IRNA, 11 December — DR, 12 December; INA, 13, 17 December — DR, 16, 17 December; R. Baghdad, 30 December — DR, 31 December 1991.
142. INA, 27 August, 30 October, 2 November, 19 December — DR, 29 August, 1, 4 November, 20 December 1991.
143. R. Baghdad, 19 August — DR, 19 August; *al-Qadisiyya, al-Jumhuriyya, Babil,* 20 August 1991.
144. *WP,* 14 July; *Babil,* 15 August; *al-'Iraq* quoted by *Ha'aretz,* 16 August 1991.
145. *NYT,* 24 November 1991.
146. R. Baghdad, 14 September — DR, 16 September; *Alif Ba,* 18 September 1991.
147. *Al-'Iraq,* 24 March 1991.

Israel

(Medinat Yisrael)

GAD BARZILAI and ELIE REKHESS*

The looming shadow of the Gulf crisis and the traumatic events of the Gulf War had a considerable effect on Israeli politics in 1991, although the country's public life was influenced by other factors as well. Both the large-scale immigration of Jews, particularly from the republics of the former Soviet Union, and the continuing Intifada waged by the Palestinian residents of the occupied territories had significant consequences for the Israeli political scene. These three principal developments — the Gulf War, the necessity to absorb hundreds of thousands of new immigrants rapidly, and the ongoing threats posed by the country's Arab neighbors and the Palestinians — meant that Israel confronted a difficult combination of challenges in security, politics and economics. Moreover, 1991 was characterized by severe internal political crises arising from the coalition government's fundamental instability, aggravated by sharp disputes within the public at large and between the political elites over the issue of reforms in the governmental and electoral systems.

DOMESTIC POLITICAL AFFAIRS

ISRAEL DURING THE GULF WAR

The Gulf War brought into sharp relief the interaction between the country's internal politics and its international relations, on the one hand, and between wars and the society's relationship to its regime, on the other. Thus, for example, even though the majority in Israeli society found no fault with its government's decision not to respond militarily to Iraqi missile attacks on its cities, it nevertheless revealed itself to be fully prepared to do battle with the enemy if need be. In addition, although certain of the country's democratic features were temporarily suspended within its "Green Line," pre-1967 borders, no significant impairment of democratic principles was permitted. Moreover, though the events of the Gulf War did much to reinforce the views of those elements in Israeli society that have always advocated resorting to arms most vociferously, the latter stopped short of articulating an express demand that military force be implemented against Iraq, so that the country as a whole remained essentially passive over the issue.

Despite the fact that the Gulf War was brief and did not take place close to Israeli territory, it managed to elicit a profound change in the Israeli political scene — a sharp split between the Jewish and the Arab political left. A prime example of this was the falling out between Arab and Jewish members of the Progressive List for Peace Party. Several of its Jewish members left the party, ostensibly on account of their opposition to its support for the Iraqi invasion. While the real reasons for their

---

* All sections of this chapter were written by Gad Barzilai, except for that dealing with the Israeli Arabs, which was written by Elie Rekhess.

449

450

Israel, the West Bank, and the Gaza Strip

departure were open to interpretation, the crisis gave them the excuse they may have sought to make their break.[1]

A general state of apprehension over what might occur caused almost everyone in Israel's Jewish population, irrespective of individual political views, to start talking very much the same political language. The ruling party — the Likud — did all it could to encourage this trend, emphasizing the fact that, in light of probable ongoing serious threats to its security, Israel had no alternative but to rule out any form of withdrawal from the territories. The Likud's task was aided considerably by the fact that the mass media both in Israel and worldwide gave extensive publicity to the PLO's unreserved support for Iraq.

The development of consensus, and the enhanced degree of governmental involvement in the lives of the citizens, were two major Israeli phenomena on the eve of the Gulf War. Governmental interference in daily life became even more pronounced when the first *Scud* missiles began landing on population centers, particularly in the Tel Aviv area, starting from the night of 16–17 January. A state of emergency was declared and civil defense regulations were activated, so that management of the country's civilian life was effectively taken over by the army and other security forces. The state of emergency did not derive from an acquiescence by the political echelon to demands issued by the military, but rather from the active desire of the political echelon to obtain the military's assistance in increasing the degree of governmental control over the public (which involved military legislation, among other things). This control was considered essential by the government, as well as by the army, in order to ensure achieving the country's defense aims.

The emergency regulations particularly affected the country's social and cultural life. Restrictions regarding the hours during which people were permitted to work, and the ban on holding public gatherings after dusk, enabled the government to maintain control of the population's movements with a minimum of disruption. It applied this control without seeking the Knesset's approval and failed to heed an established Israeli law which prescribes that resort to emergency regulations should not be intended to improve the efficiency of the executive branch other than in circumstances where getting a law passed rapidly in the Knesset is simply impossible. Rather than taking steps to amend the Civil Defense Law, which would have enabled the Knesset to exercise a reasonable degree of public control over the emergency legislation, the government simply authorized the minister of defense to institute emergency regulations. He began to activate these regulations about two weeks after the outbreak of the Gulf War, thereby becoming invested with the authority to declare the onset of a special period of civil defense, to restrict freedom of movement, and to oblige every citizen to take refuge either at home or in a public shelter. Most of the public actually gave little thought to the legality of these regulations and, being occupied with concern for personal protection and generally inclined to consensus, would probably not have protested about them even if they had realized that their legality was somewhat dubious.

Israel's indigent Arab population was severely cautioned by Police Minister Roni Milo against displaying any signs of active political support for Iraq (as, for example, via demonstrations) or interfering in any manner with Israel's preparations for dealing with the military threat it was confronting. This served to widen still further the chasm that existed between the country's Jewish government and the demographic reality of two distinct peoples, Israeli Jews and Israeli Palestinian-Arabs.[2]

If, in periods of "no war, no peace," the boundaries of nationality in Israel had always been defined in terms of religion and in terms of the mutual attitudes between the country's Jewish and Palestinian communities, those boundaries suddenly became even more pronounced in view of the general suspicion that the Arabs in Israel and in the territories might identify closely with Iraq and take advantage of the war to commit acts of sabotage.[3]

The state of public anxiety that accompanied the Gulf War was carefully exploited to achieve certain internal political aims, especially regarding the Palestinians in the territories. One was the attempt made to subdue the Intifada by harassing its leaders, especially the placing under house arrest of Sari Nusayba, a prominent Palestinian, by order of the minister of defense. The order was issued on the strength of the allegation that Nusayba had cooperated with Iraq by faxing it information on Israel's defense arrangements against Iraqi missile attacks. If the government possessed evidence to substantiate those charges, it refused to disclose it, claiming that such disclosure would cause serious damage to state security. In the event, to avoid revealing the reasons for Nusayba's arrest, the government agreed, at hearings conducted at the Jerusalem District Court, to shorten the period of Nusayba's detention from six to three months.

The government's attitude was also reflected in its decision to coopt the Moledet Party on 5 February 1991, thereby granting an appreciable degree of legitimacy to that party's "transfer" policy. In acting to bring Moledet into the government, the Likud aroused serious suspicions among Zionist and non-Zionist parties alike that its policy thenceforth might include the forcible expulsion of the Palestinians living in the territories and possibly also of the Israeli Arab population itself. For the first time since the Gulf War began, stormy debates took place in the Knesset and severe criticism was leveled at the government and at Prime Minister Yitzhak Shamir. But the Likud seemed to know what it was doing. Nine years previously, in 1982, it had similarly exploited the public's preoccupation with national security issues (during the Lebanon War) to take the controversial step of bringing the Tehiya Party into the government. This time, however, because of Moledet's "transfer" platform, the Likud's act aroused more intense controversy than before. For the Arab parties, this represented a grave signal. Their spokesmen in the Knesset articulated the view that Moledet's accession to the government was likely to cause the political system to deteriorate drastically, even to the point of civil war.[4]

The government did all it could to avoid having to respond to public criticism. Only a limited number of cabinet ministers — chiefly members of the ministerial committee on security matters — were provided with data and informed about decisions made on national security issues. In fact, the prime minister and defense minister made most of the important decisions on their own, without really consulting with any of their colleagues in the government, and very often without even informing them of what had been decided. But this type of decision-making process was quite typical of Israel, particularly in wartime and during serious security crises. During the Gulf War, as during previous wars, various politicians proposed the establishment of new political decision-making forums. One such proposal was to reinstate the previous National Unity Government. But personal rivalries, especially that between Yitzhak Shamir and Labor's Shimon Peres, as well as the still-unhealed wounds resulting from the crisis that had brought about the fall of the National Unity Government in March 1990, put paid to that notion fairly quickly. In any case, since Shamir had succeeded in establishing a government sufficiently strong to survive even the pressures of war, and had consolidated his power base even further by the inclusion of Moledet, the Likud hardly considered a national unity government worthwhile. A proposal that did receive some genuine consideration, however, concerned setting up a national security council — an idea that had appeared on the national agenda many times in the past. But the general public was essentially incapable of appreciating the significance of the suggestion, while each of the two political contenders, Likud and Labor, quickly made it clear that they basically opposed the formation of a body whose influence on policy-making might undermine that of the majority party currently in power. In any case, as has been proven in other countries such as the US, special decision-making forums are generally not very successful in reducing the alienation between government and the public. Some even end up serving as tools for promoting political interests instead of restricting themselves to recommending policy on matters of national security.

The Gulf War experience constituted an example of how far a ruling power would go to prevent the public from comprehending the significance of both the decisions that it makes and those that it fails to make, thereby protecting or even enhancing its own position. The government scarcely bothered to report on its activities to the Knesset during the war and the prime minister abstained from providing information to the Knesset and its committees. The Knesset Foreign Affairs and Defense Committee, in charge of supervising the activities of the security forces, found itself helpless in the face of the obstinate refusal of government ministers and senior officials to supply it with substantive information beyond what was published in the mass media. The media, for its part, was wholly subject to military controls imposed particularly by the army spokesman's office and the military censor. The country's two radio stations were temporarily merged for the duration of the war, so that the limited degree of pluralism that characterized the electronic media during less pressured times became even further restricted. For the more militant elements in the society, it was entirely acceptable that during the period of crisis which Israel was undergoing all matters relating to national information efforts and to instructing the public on how to conduct itself be placed in the hands of the military authorities.

Public opinion surveys conducted during the period indicate the degree of consensus that developed. About 90% of the public concurred with the consolidation of the radio stations.[5] The astonishing fact that the public was prepared to waive its right to more than a single source of news could be attributed to the extraordinary degree of importance that the population attached to various national symbols during wartime and security crises. For a period of a month and a half, Israel's civilian population had no real air cover against repeated missile attacks, yet suppressed nearly every inclination to question the wisdom of instructions that they take shelter in "sealed" rooms which, in the event of a conventional attack, actually offered very little protection, particularly in the event of a direct hit. Although rumors about the defectiveness of many of the gas masks that were distributed began to spread while the war was still in progress, they were rapidly and effectively silenced. The army and other security forces issued emphatic, and somewhat pretentious, denials of any defects, insisting that the population had been provided with effective protection against a chemical or biological attack.[6]

As a result of censorship restrictions, the public was given only partial information, which was very general and included no more than the data provided by the CNN television broadcasts. Reports issued by the army spokesman's office were also usually very general in nature and provided a fragmented picture of the real situation. The ban imposed on senior army officers against granting press interviews was a clear indication of how far the government was prepared to go in controlling information released to the public. The distribution of civil defense kits to each citizen in itself contributed to establishing a consensus. This was because it reinforced the mounting fears of the public, on the one hand, while giving the impression that the government was taking the necessary defense measures, on the other. Even political parties as dovish as the Citizens' Rights Movement (CRM, or Ratz), theretofore sharply critical of the government on a wide range of issues, supported its policy of military passivity and praised Prime Minister Shamir on the way he was leading the nation. Convincing evidence that many civil defense kits and gas masks were either wholly or partially defective was made available only after the war had ended. Reports prepared by the State Comptroller's Office, published soon after the war's termination, showed that many such kits could not have provided even a minimal degree of protection in the event of a chemical or biological attack. This constituted further evidence that the phenomenon of public consensus, rather than being a positive development, can sometimes lead to a risk of serious damage.[7]

The Israeli public conducted itself with considerable discipline during the war. In most of Israel's previous wars, a large proportion of the population had been drafted into the army — a fact which had impeded extraparliamentary opposition to those wars. Where the call-up had been restricted in scale (as during the Lebanon War), protest groups organized themselves more easily. During the Gulf War, recruitment took an entirely different form. Most soldiers in the reserves were not called up, but instead, about 200,000 workers employed in various vital fields were informed that temporarily they would be working subject to the special emergency regulations.

In democratic societies, the public generally does not manifest opposition to the government during the early stages of a war, as there is a collective assumption that the government deserves a certain period of grace in which to prove the correctness of its war-management policy. Moreover, the population tends to shun controversy at a time when the country faces serious security danger. It was precisely this form of "permissive consensus" that emerged during the Gulf War. Although the civilian population was directly hit by missile attacks, casualties were relatively light (only one person was killed as a result of the *Scud* attacks) and the government managed to convey the impression that it was handling the crisis firmly and efficiently. Most of the public was unaware that the government's decision not to respond militarily to Saddam's attacks was the result of heavy American pressure.[8] Few people, therefore, reminded themselves about the repeated pledges made earlier by the defense authorities and the prime minister that Israel would respond militarily and would not make do with self-defense measures only, such as the *Patriot* batteries. In fact, about 94% of the public felt that the government was handling the security situation either "well" or "very well."[9]

Within the army, by contrast, there was considerable awareness of what the real situation was, and some senior officers demanded taking military action against Iraq. Many of them felt Israel to be unacceptably exposed to attack by both conventional and nonconventional weapons, and considered that the country ought to respond militarily in order to maintain its deterrent capacity. However, since the army was, as always, controlled entirely by the political echelon, its controversies with the government on this issue were not permitted to be made public.

The fact that the war ended without Israel having suffered unsustainable damage contributed to the widespread conclusion by the population that the country's democratic system had proven to be viable. At the same time, Israel's traditional confidence in its ability to repel any aggressor singlehandedly — an assumption which had begun to erode previously — gave way to a more realistic appraisal. The entire population, including all political groups, seemed to accept and even to support the government's decision to deviate from time-honored tradition and meet a military threat to the country by reliance on foreign intervention in order to protect Israel's skies and its civilian population — a strategic first since the Suez campaign of 1956.

What had occurred, in fact, was a shift in the perception of an external threat. More Israelis than ever before became convinced that Israel's military power was not limitless. While thousands of citizens displayed Israeli flags and affixed "We Are All Patriots" stickers to their vehicles — evidence of the rapid emergence of a sense of solidarity rarely seen in periods of relative calm — that solidarity derived from an acute case of national nerves: about 40% of the public admitted that they suffered from attacks of anxiety either "often" or "sometimes" during the war. In late January 1991, 36% were afraid that they might not be able to cope with the stresses of the war if *Scud* missiles were to continue to land on Israeli population centers,[10] with tension highest in those areas that were hit by missiles — the Tel Aviv region and Haifa. This was a clear indication — the clearest ever in the history of Israel's many wars — of an unmistakable decline in the Israeli public's ability to withstand the pressures of an external threat. Some of those who felt themselves buckling under the strain traveled overseas, either permanently or temporarily, seeking respite. Others sought shelter elsewhere in the country, at least during the fateful nighttime hours when most of the *Scud* missile attacks on the country's population centers took place. Still, most of the population supported the government's stance. It is important, in this context, to clarify that the war actually produced a relatively low toll in Israeli civilian casualties. Iraq attacked Israel with about 40 salvos of *Scud* missiles, mostly consisting of a single missile, though on two occasions a salvo of eight *Scuds* arrived simultaneously. Yet, as indicated, there was only a single fatality, plus a few hundred wounded. Most of the injury was occasioned to property, with thousands of buildings damaged.

The Gulf War was the first military confrontation since 1949 that involved the country's civilian population in hostilities directly, with part of the population actually on the front line bearing the brunt of the enemy's attack. In contrast with the victorious euphoria which swept over the country in 1967; the political dilemmas brought on by Israel's "Goliath-like" strength since 1967; or the self-doubts about the country's identity caused by the growing dominance of the conflict with the Palestinians, fundamental questions of ethnic, communal and social identity emerged in the public's self-awareness.

One manifestation of changed perceptions in Israeli society during the Gulf War related to the issue of the definition of patriotism. During most of Israel's previous wars, the criterion for measuring patriotism was military service or some form of volunteerism in the war effort. During the Gulf War, however, the criterion became cooperation in taking the necessary survival measures, a passive acceptance of whatever fate might bring, and a willingness to stay put in the face of missile attacks. Slogans such as "We'll get through this, too," which appeared on street posters and were aired on the radio repeatedly, reflected the consensus, which was based on an awareness that there was no alternative in sight. The self-imposed night curfews which a large proportion of the population experienced for about a month and a half, and which brought cultural life and entertainment to a standstill, manifested the atmosphere of reconciliation to a gray reality and intensified the public's sense that Israel was paying a high price for having been dragged into an international confrontation. Thus, even political groupings on the left, which had initiated considerable protest activity during the Intifada, were relatively silent when stiff curfews were imposed on the Arab residents of the territories. Groups such as Peace Now, as well as gatherings of intellectuals, issued calls to peace movements throughout the world to support Israel and its policies during the crisis.[11] Their message was that occupying a country by force was an act that must be opposed, but that, once the war was over, they would redouble their efforts to end the Intifada by the granting of self-determination to the Palestinians. They stressed, however, that first, Saddam Husayn's regime had to be crushed. Broadly, their stance was that Israel had ceased to be an all-powerful conqueror, probably for all time, and had become a victim.

What was proved once again, therefore, was that involvement in wars tended to strengthen symbols in a democracy at the expense of basic values. In Israel's case, it reinforced the regime's Jewish elements, while the problems faced by its minorities were shunted to a side. To have attempted to solve these problems during the war would have been regarded as contradicting the nation's "logic."

Still, a certain amount of relatively marginal activity was undertaken by small leftist groups and by Jewish and Arab intellectuals who called on the US to end its military involvement in the Gulf immediately and to insist that the solution of the Palestinian problem was Israel's principal task. The most prominent of these groups was one which prior to the outbreak of the Gulf War had called itself "A Moment Before War" and which, during the course of the war, changed its name to "Enough." It declared the need to establish linkage between ending the Gulf War and the Palestinian crises respectively; accused the US of harboring motives for its involvement in the Gulf; demanded that the US leave the region forthwith; and called for comprehensive solutions, including the establishment of a Palestinian state, to be found for all of the Middle East problems.[12] However, their protest activity while the war was still in progress, aimed at arousing a demand by the Israeli public for government initiative in this area, diverged appreciably from the general consensus and produced no results whatsoever, largely because the rules of the political game as played by Israel's society were simply far too powerfully entrenched.

A comparison with the Six-Day War of 1967 would indicate the extent to which consensus played a significant role during the Gulf War. Just as in 1967, the country in 1991 was gripped by anxiety over the chances of survival and by a certainty that its population centers stood a serious likelihood of being hit. However, while in 1967 the national consensus had favored going to war, the reverse was the case during the Gulf crisis. One of the reasons for the pervasive reluctance to go to war was that there was no immediate threat to the country. Whereas in 1967 the existential danger was considered to be close to Israel's borders, in 1991 it was regarded as being far away.

Another reason was the public awareness of the fact that this time a superpower had taken most of the military burden upon itself. Furthermore, and probably most important of all, the Israeli population was inclined to identify with the government on matters of national security. Notwithstanding the damage to residential areas as a result of the missile attacks, 80% of the public felt that Israel "ought to stay in calm control and not react for the moment."[13] This manifestation of national forbearance emerged despite the fact that most of the people interviewed were aware of the possibility that the war might last for a relatively protracted period — as long as two months in duration — and that population centers were likely to sustain severe damage. This phenomenon of the emergence of a consensus in a traditionally fighting society does not necessarily mean the society is militant in nature and therefore automatically supportive of the idea of going to war. In the case under review, it demonstrated a preparedness on the part of the population to follow the government's lead. This compliance, which was translated into an acceptance of the decision not to take military action, was especially noteworthy given the repeated warnings by senior army officers, including the chief of military intelligence, that Iraq possessed chemical and even binary weapons,[14] and declarations by Iraq's leaders that they intended to strike a lethal military blow to Israel in response to the "Zionist plot" against their country and to US bombings of Baghdad and the Iraqi people.

In comparison with the Intifada, which was an intercommunal encounter, the Gulf War was an international war. While the Intifada exposed the Israeli difficulty in defining national identity, the Gulf War strengthened tendencies to unite around a national identity determined by the criterion of Jewishness. A danger deriving from an external source, Iraq, assisted in crystallizing that identity. In actual fact, the Gulf War diverted the Israeli public's attention away from the painful Palestinian aspect of its country's protracted struggle and toward another issue that was part of Israel's identity — the conflict with its external neighbors. The energetic support given by Yasir 'Arafat to Saddam Husayn provided Israel at that time with a convenient pretext for evading the necessity to define its permanent borders and the prescribed geographical area within which the Israeli nation would choose to reside.

Once again, the Palestinians were conveniently branded by the political leadership, and by most of the public, as a satanic enemy working hand in hand with elements bent on bringing Israel to ruin. In point of fact, while the war was still in progress, and in contrast with the attitudes held by most of the Palestinians, in the occupied territories a few manifestos were actually published and a few hesitant voices raised against Iraq's aggression, expressing the fear that Saddam Husayn's occupation of Kuwait might result in damage to Palestinian interests. Moreover, several Palestinian Arab leaders publicly accused Iraq of forcibly transferring Palestinians from Kuwait. But these phenomena of protest, limited in number, made practically no impression on the Israeli political system.

The declaration of a state of emergency in Israel helped deter criticism of the many foul-ups which occurred in the economy. Although some 300,000 wage-earners were forced to absent themselves from work for three days following the initial *Scud* missile attacks (17–21 January 1991), the government did not arrange for compensation for loss of income. Many sectors of the economy (for example, education), involving tens of thousands of workers, were effectively paralyzed for most of the war, but no measures were taken to provide alternative forms of employment. It was only about three weeks after the war began that the Ministry of Finance, the Histadrut-General Federation of Labor and the employers' associations started to coordinate activities in an attempt to guide the economy through the crisis. Some wage earners, particularly working mothers who had no option but to remain at home to look after their children, began to feel financial pressure. However, the issue elicited no extraparliamentary protest and was raised for discussion by only a few Knesset members and a number of Histadrut functionaries. In this respect, too, the Gulf War differed from previous wars, especially from the Yom Kippur War (1973), when the Israeli economy had adjusted to cope with a period of extreme national emergency. This time, many things seemed to go wrong, including the fact that functionally the economy did not adjust well to the new circumstances. However, the ongoing nature of the interaction between the society and the state, as well as the positive consensus that had developed, prevented the emergence of major public controversies over these issues both during the Gulf War and thereafter.

Once the Gulf War ended, Israeli society returned to normal. State control of the broadcasting stations was reduced, the economy resumed its regular activity, and most of the population resumed its former life-style. It became apparent that the democratic system had not been put to any grave test, and that, at least on the surface, the government had demonstrated reasonable efficiency in dealing with a crisis situation of major proportions.

It was still unclear whether the Gulf War had any long-term impact over basic political attitudes. Once the war was over, for example, public debate resumed over the issue of how much strategic depth Israel required, but there was no apparent alteration in the former positions of the political parties. If anything, those positions seemed to have become even more entrenched. The Likud put forward the argument that the Iraqi assault on Kuwait, as well as its missile attack on Israel, was proof of what was likely to happen if a pro-Iraqi Palestinian state were to come into existence alongside Israel. By contrast, the Labor Party's view was that the Gulf War had clearly proven the degree to which Jordan's stability was vital to Israel's security and the extent to which the Hashemite Kingdom was capable of granting Israel the real strategic depth it needed. According to Labor's chairman, Shimon Peres, the "Jordanian option" should therefore now be revived, meaning that it was time to return to the notion of solving the Israeli-Arab conflict on the basis of territorial compromise with Jordan, with the participation of a Palestinian delegation. Political doves both within the Labor Party and to its left argued that the Gulf War had provided further evidence that the notion of strategic depth was nothing more than a myth and that in an era of advanced military technology, no strategic advantage could be gained by holding on to the west bank of the River Jordan — the territories. They claimed, moreover, that maintaining the status quo on the territorial issue would be likely to tempt the Arabs to launch yet another war. The best form of strategic depth that Israel could hope for, they asserted, would be that achieved by entering into a stable peace agreement and granting the Palestinians the right to political self-determination.

The parties situated to the right of the Likud, however, stressed that the PLO's unreserved identification with Iraq proved that it was now vitally urgent to take measures that would amount to incorporating the territories into Israel, although a formal annexation would probably be undesirable. This was to be accomplished by undertaking massive settlement activity in Judea and Samaria. The right also asserted that it was equally necessary to categorically deny granting the least legitimacy to the notion of an independent Palestinian political entity.[15]

It appeared that the Gulf War had made the public entrench itself even more firmly in the views it had maintained before the Gulf crisis broke out.[16] There was a sense, however, that Israelis might be less inclined than before to rely on the country's military capability as a means of maintaining its presence in the ME. The possibility arose that even the political elites would be obliged to moderate their positions in an unprecedented fashion, given these developments: the massive acceleration in the regional arms race, the growing likelihood, or even probability, that nuclear weapons would become part of the ME scene, the determination shown by the US to neutralize the capability of the ME to upset its vision of a new international world order, and Israel's relative vulnerability to ballistic weapons. A trend toward moderation of this kind had begun to manifest itself in the Israeli public even previously during the course of the Intifada.

THE INTIFADA AND THE PROBLEM OF THE TERRITORIES

By and large, 1991 was characterized by considerable disparity in the various positions on possible political solutions to the issue of the occupied territories and how the Arab-Palestinian-Israeli conflict should be solved. There was no clear public preference, and every indication that a political leadership which evinced genuine preparedness to try to break the long-standing diplomatic deadlock over the territorial status quo would probably win significant public support.

Only 2.1% of the public favored the existing territorial status quo as a solution to the conflict. A total of 28.5% supported solutions of a dovish character, itemized as follows: 9.8% backed the parties on the left wing of the Israeli political spectrum which called for the establishment of a Palestinian state alongside Israel that would occupy the entire West Bank and Gaza Strip; 7.5% favored a variation on that theme, endorsed by moderate elements within the Labor Party, that a Palestinian state be created in the Gaza Strip only; and 11.2% supported Labor's long-established concept of some form of territorial compromise with Jordan. These percentages could be augmented by two additional options which generally conformed to platforms of dovish groups within the Labor Party and on the political left: 6% favoring the idea of a Palestinian-Jordanian confederation, and 14.1% who backed the establishment of a Palestinian-Jordanian state in the territories. In summary, it could be stated that 48.6% of the Israeli public approved of solutions based on significant territorial compromise and on a recognition of Palestinian sovereignty, at least in a sizable proportion of the territory of the West Bank.[17]

By contrast, 16.7% of the general public advocated as the most suitable permanent solution the concept of Palestinian autonomy under Israeli rule, while an additional 5.2% supported the idea of Palestinian autonomy under joint Israeli-Jordanian rule. These two proposals comprised the basis for the formal policy of the Likud Party and of the Shamir government. Generally speaking, indeed, the option of Palestinian autonomy, which preserved maintaining Israeli dominion in the area of national security, was the sole proposal acceptable to the Israeli public in 1991. It was perceived as a pragmatic solution which did not entail surrendering too much and which guaranteed that Israel would maintain its strategic depth. Granting the

Palestinians autonomy was regarded by relatively many Israelis as the formula that would enable their country to control the Palestinians while not actually annexing their territory to Israel. More hawkish solutions, endorsed by parties on the radical right, mustered less support: 2.6% favored the notion of giving the Palestinians certain civil rights but annexing the West Bank and Gaza Strip to Israel; 1.8% favored annexation without granting of civil rights; and 11.2% backed the idea of annexing the territories after forcibly transferring the Palestinian population to neighboring Arab countries.[18]

According to a majority of Israel's public, the possibility existed of arriving at some sort of solution to the problem of the territories and of eventually achieving peace with the Arab countries and the Palestinians. Only 5.5% maintained that the interstate and intercommunal conflicts were insoluble, while another 6.3% declared themselves to be at a loss as to what form such solutions could take. Thus, the majority of Israelis continued to maintain some degree of trust in the potential ability of their political leaders in 1991 to solve the Palestinian problem.[19]

Yet, during the course of 1991 Israel in fact failed to terminate the Palestinian uprising and the bitter, violent struggle between Jews and Arabs for control of the West Bank (including East Jerusalem) and the Gaza Strip continued. The more protracted the Intifada, the more pronounced the government's determination became to settle the territories by Jews (the great majority of whom did not come from among the new immigrants to the country.) The financial year 31 March 1990 to 31 March 1991 witnessed investment in the territories of over NIS1bn. In total, about 20% of the Housing Ministry's budget was allocated to the construction of about 12,000 new housing units in the territories during that period. Guided by Housing Minister Ariel Sharon, a prominent leader of Israel's political right, the process of de facto annexation of the territories was undoubtedly accelerated. The number of permanent Jewish settlers in the territories increased from 90,000 to 120,000 (compared with 1.7m. Palestinians during the financial year 1990–91.) Taking into consideration Jewish settlement in the Golan Heights and East Jerusalem as well, the overall number of Jews residing in the territories captured during the Six-Day War (1967) rose to c. 225,000.[20] Plans for the construction of c. 24,000 additional housing units in the West Bank, designed to accommodate c. 90,000 more Jews, were drawn up by the Housing Ministry in 1991.[21] These plans were backed by Prime Minister Yitzhak Shamir, who went on record as saying that Jewish settlement in the entire territory of Judea and Samaria was an urgent matter of policy and that no force in the world, including the US, would be capable of halting it.[22]

Differences of opinion in the country over the judiciousness of Jewish settlement activity in the occupied territories were clearly manifested at the beginning of October 1991, a few days before the impending visit to Israel of US Secretary of State James Baker. Several dozen religious Jewish students at a rabbinical college decided to establish a settlement in Silwan village, a part of East Jerusalem, known in Jewish history as Kfar Shilo'ah. Arriving at Silwan one night (9 October), accompanied by several right-wing Knesset members, they expelled Arab residents from a number of buildings and occupied them. This act angered several cabinet members of moderate disposition, including Foreign Minister David Levy, who warned about the damage to Israel's international image, and particularly to its relations with the US, which was likely to follow. Labor Party leaders and almost all the parties on the left reacted agitatedly, characterizing the Silwan settlement as a deliberate provocation, orchestrated by the right with the intent to thwart any possibility of real dialogue between Palestinians and Jews.[23]

The year 1991 witnessed a more than usual amount of friction between the Israel Defense Forces (IDF) and the Jewish settlers residing in the 142 settlements in the territories. The settlers were apprehensive that Secretary Baker's trips to the area might lead to the establishment of a Palestinian state or Palestinian autonomy, which could result in a cessation of further Jewish settlement in the territories. They intensified their appeals to the army not to interfere with the widespread Jewish settlement activity in progress, which included settlement in areas densely populated by Arabs, such as within and close to Nablus, Hebron and Jerusalem. Issuing repeated allegations of mounting Palestinian violence, they warned that if the army failed to clamp down on Palestinian troublemakers, they would resort to using firearms and inflict collective damage on Palestinian settlements. Tension between the army command in the territories and the settlers increased to the point that Minister of Defense Moshe Arens, although well known for favoring Israeli rule in the territories, issued a stern warning to the settlers against taking the law into their own hands.[24]

Not only did the battle for security in the face of the Palestinian Intifada fail to level off, it deteriorated during the course of 1991. At the beginning of the year, four Palestinians who were active in the Hamas Islamic fundamentalist movement were deported;[25] despite the prolonged curfews imposed on the territories during the Gulf War, violent incidents there continued, though less frequently than in the past, leading to the detention of more than 5,000 Palestinian residents.[26] During and immediately following the Gulf War, a variety of severe restrictions were placed on the Palestinian population, including strict curtailment of their freedom to travel to places of work in Israel.[27] There was also an increase in the number of instances of arrests of Palestinian journalists and Palestinian newspaper offices in the territories were shut down.[28] The murder, with a dagger, of four Jewish women in Jerusalem by a Palestinian from the Gaza Strip on 10 March signaled that the outcome of the Gulf War had not diminished, and may even have exacerbated the hatred toward Jews and Israelis that prevailed in the territories. The murders stirred up disputes within the Israeli political leadership over the most effective way of contending with the Intifada, with spokesmen for the Likud and for parties to its right calling for wholesale deportation of the Palestinian leadership from the territories. Labor and left-wing party leaders, though stopping short of endorsing that demand, responded to the murder in a manner that suggested that continued acts of violence would be likely to lead to a greater degree of hawkishness within the country's leftist camp and within the Labor Party in particular.[29]

All elements within the political system, apart from the Arab parties, endorsed in March 1991 a proposal to limit the number of Palestinians permitted to travel from the territories to work in Israel. The Labor Party, the Likud and parties on the right (Moledet, Tehiya and Tsomet) hoped that a move of that sort would serve to pressure the PLO and other Palestinian organizations in the territories to abstain from acts of terrorism. The parties on the left (the CRM, Mapam and Shinui) were hopeful that a reduction in the number of Palestinians working in Israel would have the long-range effect of reestablishing the Green Line which had delineated Israel's geographical boundaries prior to 1967 and would help lead to the de facto establishment of a Palestinian state in the territories.[30]

When on 12 October two Israeli soldiers were deliberately run down and killed at the Tel Hashomer intersection in the Tel Aviv area by a motorist from Qibya (an Arab village on the West Bank), all the old disputes over security policies erupted in the political system once again. Spokesmen for parties on the right demanded that the offender's family, and all similar offenders in the future, be punished by deportation. Some rightists accused the left of having created an atmosphere in which politically motivated murderers could commit their crimes without fear of paying with their lives. Several politicians within the ruling Likud Party demanded the imposition of the death penalty for terrorists irrespective of whether or not they used firearms to commit murder. By contrast, spokesmen for the Labor Party and the left expressed their fervent hope that the murder of the soldiers would not cause the disruption of the dialogue then currently taking place between the Arab states, the Palestinians and Israel. Labor Party Chairman Shimon Peres declared that only genuine peace negotiations were capable of ensuring that similar acts of murder would not recur.[31]

THE RULE OF LAW

Continued control of the occupied territories subjected Israel's rule of law to ongoing strains. On 3 January 1991, President Chaim Herzog announced his decision to adopt recommendations put forward by the Ministry of Justice and the government to pardon three Jewish underground activists who in 1984 had been found guilty of the murder of Palestinians from the territories and sentenced to life imprisonment. When arrested, the activists had admitted their intention to cause grievous bodily harm to a large number of Palestinians, as well as attack a mosque, in order to promote Jewish domination of the territories. The president justified his decision by stating that prolonged incarceration was an ineffective form of punishment, that the accused had expressed regret for their deeds, and that the Jewish underground movement to which they belonged had been dismantled in any case.[32] The reaction of the country's top political echelon, for the most part, was agreement with the president's position. Minister of Justice Dan Meridor, who defended the president's decision during the Knesset debate on 7 January, expressed the view that Herzog's reasoning was entirely consistent with legal principles in Israel. Spokesmen for the opposition, however, claimed that the clemency decision was a mistake because it implied that Jews deserved more favorable treatment than Arabs.[33]

The question of compliance with Israeli law in the context of Israel's rule of the territories rose yet again upon the conviction in October of Abie Nathan, an Israeli peace activist. Nathan was found guilty of breaching a law (passed in 1986) which prohibited all meetings between Israelis and members of the PLO. He was sentenced to three years' imprisonment, of which 18 months were suspended. One of the court's allegations in support of its verdict was that in a democratic society there were a sufficient number of other ways for opponents of government policy to express their views without taking the extreme step of breaking the law. For his part, Nathan, who had previously been imprisoned in 1990 for the identical crime of meeting with PLO representatives, made it clear after the court announced its sentence that he did not regret his action and that immediately upon his release he would resume his meetings with Palestinians, including representatives of the PLO. He stated his belief that his actions actually contributed to the possibility that the Israeli Government would eventually agree to conduct meetings with the PLO.[34]

Subsequent to Nathan's conviction, yet another Israeli left-wing activist was tried and sentenced in October 1991 to nine months in prison. This prompted Israeli spokesmen on the right to urge that the provisions of the law be expanded to include prohibitions on meetings with Hanan 'Ashrawi and Faysal Husayni, Palestinian leaders who were residents of the territories. This demand attested to the ambiguity of the existing law which, though ostensibly proscribing discrimination between Jews and Arabs, appeared nevertheless to require bringing charges against members of the PLO for holding meetings with other representatives of that organization. Indeed, by virtue of that absurdity, the attorney general's office decided to refrain from prosecuting either 'Ashrawi or Husayni on charges of their having met with the PLO leadership in Algeria, justifying its position by claiming that there was insufficient substantiating evidence. Overall, the political establishment in Israel appeared to have learned through bitter experience that formalizing restrictions on democratic rights by turning them into laws tended to have damaging repercussions.[35]

The president's decision to reduce the jail sentences of the members of the Jewish underground, and the reasons he cited to support it, continued to elicit questions about Israel's rule of law when the High Court of Justice convened to debate an appeal against the security authorities submitted by four activists belonging to the Hamas Islamic fundamentalist movement. The four, residents of the occupied territories, had been convicted of religious incitement against Jews and calling for a holy war against Israel, and had been ordered to be deported on the grounds that they were a threat to state security. The evidence against them was submitted to the High Court by the Israeli army and the General Security Services and, according to the provisions of Israeli law regarding evidence against persons suspected of security crimes, became privileged information. Thus, the application by the defense counsel for the deportees for permission to view the evidence was rejected by the High Court for reasons of national security. The appellants then decided that there was no point in pursuing their appeal and were subsequently deported from the territories.[36]

A serious controversy among various government departments over the issue of equality between the Jewish and Arab populations erupted on the eve of the Gulf War. The Ministry of Defense and the army decided that even though the country faced the possibility of attacks by missiles with chemical warheads, civil defense kits would not be distributed to the Arab residents of the occupied territories, on the grounds that the territories were far less likely than Israel proper to be a target for such attacks. When residents of the territories applied to the High Court of Justice, adducing the principle of equality in support of their right to be equipped with the means to protect themselves, the defense establishment countered with the claim that the issue was solely one of security considerations, preempting interference by the High Court. However, this argument was rejected by the High Court, which, led by Justice Aharon Barak, ruled in favor of the Palestinians' appeal on the grounds that the army was discriminating between Arabs and Jews. The court declared:

> Even when the guns are firing, military commanders are obliged to abide by the law. A society's ability to defend itself against its enemies is founded on the recognition that it is fighting for values worth defending. The rule of law is one of those values. A military commander's obligation to conduct himself

impartially toward all residents of the area should not become impaired when tension rises. His duty in that respect is an ongoing duty, which is incumbent on him all the time.[37]

However, in light of the defense establishment's subsequent claim that the number of civil defense kits available (particularly those suitable for small children) was limited, the High Court prescribed that initially the equipment would be distributed to people residing in areas in the territories closest to the Green Line (Israel's pre-1967 borders) and to those living in proximity to Jerusalem.[38] In so ruling, the High Court was stating its opinion that even in circumstances where Israel's security was being threatened by Arab action; even in a situation of crisis or war; and despite the fact that the Palestinians in the territories were displaying outright sympathy for Israel's enemies, the state (including its security forces) was duty-bound to treat all of its Arab residents, including the Palestinians living not in Israel but in the occupied territories, as impartially as it treated its Jewish population.

Another challenge to the rule of law in Israel stemming from the country's jurisdiction over the territories emerged in the form of a draft bill submitted for legislation by two Knesset members (MKs) — Reuben Rivlin (Likud) and Hanan Porat (National Religious Party) — granting pardons to all soldiers facing conviction for criminal acts against Palestinians during the first three months of the Intifada. The implication of the bill was that constitutional immunity would be granted to soldiers committing crimes. The bill was vigorously contested, mainly by MKs from the Labor Party and parties on the left. Yitzhak Rabin, who had served as minister of defense during the three months concerned, declared that he opposed the bill, and that never before had Israeli law provided wholesale immunity from prosecution to violators of army regulations. The proposed legislation was also condemned by most senior representatives of the Israeli legal community (e.g., judges and lawyers), including even the (Likud) minister of justice, who stated that the bill would be misinterpreted as implying that a great many soldiers, and not only the few actually found guilty, had committed offenses during the period in question. Notwithstanding the support for the bill by many right-wing MKs and ministers (estimated as totaling as many as 50), the bill failed to secure formal governmental backing and was therefore never sent to the Knesset for debate.[39]

What spurred MKs Rivlin and Porat to propose the legislation were disturbing revelations emerging from the trial of Col. Yehuda Meir which shed light on the extent of violence committed by IDF soldiers against Palestinian residents of the territories (for an analysis of the trial see *MECS* 1990, chapter on Israel). At the beginning of April, Col. Meir was convicted of ordering his men to commit crimes of grievous bodily assault against Palestinians in the Arab villages of Beita and Hawarra. All the claims submitted in his defense — that he had been a loyal officer, that he had only carried out the orders of the O.C. Central Command, Gen. Amram Mitsna, and that he had executed the policy articulated by Defense Minister Yitzhak Rabin — were rejected. The court's ruling was:

A commander holding the rank held by the accused who causes his men to entirely ignore considerations of what is seemly and moral can certainly be said to have acted in a manner unbefitting his rank and status within the army. The army is entitled to expect from someone of such rank that he remain alert to his duty and that he constantly guard against permitting behavior which would stain the army's reputation.[40]

Col. Meir was punished harshly: he was reduced to the rank of private and deprived of the rights to which he had been entitled as an officer. The most significant part of the court's verdict was the following:

> We regard infringement of the fundamental value of respecting other persons, whoever they may be, as constituting such a serious breach of military procedure, that it is inconceivable that a commander bereft of that value, or one who fails to consider it important, should be permitted to serve as an officer and to command units of the IDF. It is an officer's obligation to abide by and maintain all the basic values, which simply expand and grow in importance the higher that he himself rises in rank and position.[41]

DOMESTIC SOCIAL AFFAIRS

IMMIGRATION AND ABSORPTION

By the end of 1990, 200,000 Jews had immigrated to Israel from the Soviet Union, with the Israeli authorities drawing up a nationwide master plan preparing for the anticipated arrival of hundreds of thousands more. The economic collapse of the new Commonwealth of Independent States (CIS) and the threat of civil war within those states spurred the Israeli Government, and the Ministry of Absorption in particular, to gear itself for the emergency absorption of huge waves of immigration from these areas. The plan was based on the premise that by the year 2010 Israel's population would reach a total of 7m., while the occupied territories would still be retained.[42] In the event, the rate of immigration continued apace, even during the Gulf War. In fact, a total of 1,500 immigrants landed in the country on one day during the war.[43] Approximately 3% of those arriving settled in the territories, while the remainder found accommodation within the Green Line borders (pre-1967 Israel).[44] All told, some 170,000 immigrants from the former Soviet Union came to Israel during 1991, along with 15,000 Jews from Ethiopia who were airlifted into the country in "Operation Moses," executed by Israel's Air Force in coordination with the Ethiopian Government.

The integration of the immigrants followed a policy of direct absorption, limiting the contribution of the government and the Jewish Agency to providing the immigrants with financial grants and with loans on easy terms. This policy of governmental nonintervention in absorption, however, resulted in a rise in the number of unemployed immigrants to a total of 80,000. Most of these were academically trained individuals who were unable to enter the Israeli labor market because it was too limited in scope to offer sufficient employment opportunities for the technologically sophisticated labor force arriving from Eastern Europe.[45] The situation was especially grim for the immigrants who arrived in 1991. Not a single family member managed to find employment in 70% of the immigrant families that year. In addition, only in 16.4% of families arriving did at least one family member succeed in securing full-time employment.[46] Overall, the rate of unemployment among immigrants who arrived from the former Soviet Union since 1989 reached about 40%.[47] The economic plight of former Soviet Jews in Israel became so bad that many of them began to organize themselves politically, supported in their political efforts by volunteer organizations acting on behalf of the immigration absorption drive. The protest demonstrations that the immigrants organized had the effect of forcing the government to involve itself somewhat more actively in matters related to housing and absorption for new immigrants.[48]

But governmental intervention was problematical. In order to absorb all the newcomers effectively, the government realized that certain far-reaching economic reforms would be necessary. Cabinet ministers involved in the economic area declared that sizable economic growth was necessary if the country were to create as many as half a million new jobs in the course of only three or four years. The gross national product would have to grow by 12% and exports would have to double.[49] Finance Minister Yitzhak Moda'i stated that the anticipated population growth of about 30% during the forthcoming four years meant that the Israeli economy would require investment amounting to $50bn., which it was unlikely to procure from its own resources.[50] Treasury officials therefore drew up plans for financing the immigrant absorption effort by asking world Jewry for substantial financial contributions and by requesting the US Government for loan guarantees of $10bn. over a five-year period so as to reduce the interest costs entailed in borrowing from commercial sources.[51] Toward the end of the year, however, Israeli Government officials appeared to have become increasingly pessimistic over the country's capacity to absorb the immigration of Soviet Jews. Minister of Immigration and Absorption Yitzhak Peretz went so far as to liken the phenomenon of mass immigration to a calamitous natural disaster, while Prime Minister Yitzhak Shamir also expressed genuine concern over Israel's ability to absorb the wave of immigrants.[52]

The large-scale immigration promised to have significant electoral repercussions. Overall, the number of immigrants who arrived in Israel during the 1989–91 period was sufficient to determine as many as eight seats in the Knesset in the 1992 general elections. In a country where the two main parties, Likud and Labor, had for many years run neck and neck, and where a marked polarity of views existed, this demographic development was of genuine significance. It was clear, moreover, that if the immigrants — particularly those from the Soviet Union — were to decide to set up a new political party of their own, that party could have an enormous impact on future attempts to form a governmental coalition, and possessed the potential of eventually becoming a major party itself.

Indeed, the political community devoted considerable attention to trying to predict how these Soviet immigrants would vote. It could be expected, on the one hand, that being almost exclusively of "Ashkenazi" (European) extraction, irreligious, educated and, typically, trained in a profession, they would incline toward the Labor Party or perhaps even to a party to its left, such as the CRM. On the other hand, having escaped, often after great suffering, from a Communist regime and gratefully identified instead with the State of Israel which happened to be dominated by the Likud at the time, it was equally possible that their sympathies would lie with the Likud. Moreover, the fact that they had never known an Israel that did not incorporate the occupied territories was seen as an additional factor likely to steer them toward the Likud, or even a party to its right.

The many public opinion surveys conducted among Soviet Jewish immigrants during 1991 revealed that many of them — about 40% — had not yet developed any clear political orientation. Of the remainder, c. 38% indicated that they would vote for the Likud or for other political parties on the right, while c. 22% stated that their vote would go to the Labor Party or to parties on the left. As many as 41% of the Jewish immigrants from the former Soviet Union declared that if an immigrants' party were formed, they would back it at the polls. However, a finding that emerged in all the surveys conducted was that the longer the period that elapsed after the immigrant's arrival, the less likely he was to express a preference for an immigrants' party.[53]

RELATIONS BETWEEN THE SECULAR AND RELIGIOUS COMMUNITIES

No fundamental change occurred during 1991 in the nature of relations between Israel's secular and religious communities and, as in the past, there were particular occasions when the tensions and conflicts between them came to the fore. One such instance, early in the year, was when 93-year-old Rabbi Eliezer Schach, spiritual leader of Israel's ultra-Orthodox "haredi" community, declared that the Holocaust had occurred only because Jews had failed to adhere to the commandments of the Torah, and predicted that if Israel's Jews, under their secular leadership, were to persist in ignoring the dictates of the Bible, a further holocaust was likely to befall them. This statement, interpreted as a violent condemnation of Zionism, aroused an uproar of protest among the secular community. Labor MK Shevah Weiss, a Holocaust survivor, accused Schach of suggesting that Hitler and his Nazi followers, who had so brutally slaughtered the Jewish people, had acted as emissaries of the Almighty. During the bitter parliamentary debate which ensued, haredi MKs defended the rabbi's statement by claiming that by virtue of its ignorance, the secular community had incorrectly interpreted their leader's statement, which had only sought to explain that Judaism provides both reward and punishment. Was it even conceivable, asked Rabbi Schach's defenders, that, having lost his own family in the Holocaust, he would justify the Nazis' deeds?[54]

Another matter that aroused sharp controversy was the issue of special government budgetary allocations to the various institutions sponsored by the religious political parties. These allocations amounted to about NIS400m. during the 1991 financial year, c. NIS90m. more than the religious parties had received the previous year.[55] A sharp dispute broke out between the haredi parties and the National Religious Party (NRP, or Mafdal) during the final stages of the budget debate when the matter of the special allocations came up for discussion in March. The haredi parties, exploiting the increase in their electoral strength, which had brought them a total of 13 Knesset seats in the 1988 elections, managed to get the government coalition to agree to providing them with inflated budgetary allocations, while the Mafdal, smaller numerically and thus less vital to the coalition, failed to secure similar allocations. This led the Mafdal to threaten to bring about a coalition crisis, which was averted only when the Mafdal was itself promised a special allocation amounting to about NIS10m.[56]

These sizable allocations outraged the secular parties, including those who were members of the governmental coalition. All of them issued statements condemning the special allocations, and many secular MKs declared that they viewed the growth of the special allocations as a gross violation of the accepted religious status quo in the country.[57]

More friction occurred in April when the haredi political parties proposed shutting down Ben-Gurion Airport, Israel's main international airport, on the Sabbath and on religious holidays. The proposal aroused bitter controversy between the secular and ultrareligious elements within the ruling government coalition. The Likud eventually made it plain that the haredi initiative was unacceptable, and that if the haredi parties failed to shelve it, the Likud would have no alternative but to propose special legislation to ensure the continued operation of the airport on the Sabbath and holidays.[58]

Fierce altercations between the secular and religious parties erupted yet again in June over the manner in which new immigrants from the Soviet Union were being absorbed. The cabinet minister responsible for immigration and absorption, Yitzhak Peretz, himself a member of the haredi community and a former leader of the haredi Shas Party, accused the country's Kibbutz movement of deliberately dissuading those immigrants who had elected to make their homes on Kibbutz collective settlements from embracing Jewish tradition and a Jewish religious way of life. Peretz heatedly charged that the Kibbutz movement was thus ensuring that the new immigrants would lose all contact with Judaism. The media gave considerable publicity to these accusations partly because of ethnic slurs hurled by Peretz, a prominent leader of the Sephardi community (comprised of Jews of North African and Asian ancestry), at Ashkenazis (originating from Eastern and Central Europe generally). Peretz alleged that in the 1950s, too, the various kibbutzim had improperly absorbed North African immigrants by depriving them of the opportunity to lead a traditional Jewish way of life. Representatives of the Kibbutz movement responded furiously, accusing Peretz of unstatesmanlike behavior and of exploiting his cabinet post for party ends. They reiterated their traditional grievance that while many fine young people from the kibbutzim had lain down their lives in the defense of their country, the young people in the haredi community were consistently encouraged to seek exemption from military service in order to engage in protracted study of the Torah. Denouncing the minister for hypocrisy in claiming to have the welfare of new immigrants at heart, the kibbutz spokesmen demanded that he resign. Had he done so, the fragile government coalition would have been jeopardized. Peretz, therefore, did not resign;[59] but the bitter controversy engendered by him once again exposed the dimensions of the deep-seated conflict between the secular Zionist and the haredi non-Zionist communities. The former advocated an emancipated, secular Jewish life-style, while the latter wanted, above all, to preserve fundamentalist-religious values. Emotions were so stirred up that representatives of the Kibbutz movement threatened to launch a moral war against the country's haredi sector.[60]

These and similar events, including violent demonstrations organized by haredis seeking to have certain roads in Jerusalem closed to traffic on the Sabbath, prompted the Labor Party Congress to propose a draft bill promulgating the separation of religion from state (November 1991). This was a surprising development for Labor, which, since the end of the 1930s, had maintained close political ties with the country's Zionist religious parties. These parties had consistently supported Labor, while Labor, in return, had backed the religious status quo, pursuant to which Judaism was recognized as the state religion. A similar understanding had also been reached between Labor and the haredi religious non-Zionist parties from the late 1940s onward. For the first time in the country's political history, Labor advocated complete severance of religion from the state. Despite intensive efforts by Peres and Rabin to cancel the proposed reform (out of fear that it might prejudice future relations between Labor and potential coalition partners from the religious camp), it continued to form part of the Labor Party's political platform.

POLITICAL REFORMS

A considerable proportion of the secular public, perceiving the religious, and particularly the haredi, parties as behaving in an extortionist manner, stepped up demands for changes in the governmental and electoral systems. The underlying assumption of this view was that direct election of the prime minister by the voting public without intervention by the party apparatus would probably result in a marked decline in the political power wielded by the religious parties, which would be unable to dictate the condition of special financial allocations in return for joining a coalition. This would be because a system of direct election of the prime minister would grant the elected prime minister considerable freedom of choice in forming his government, with much less dependence on the Knesset. Since Israel lacked a constitution and had no written mechanism for insuring personal and civil rights, a significant portion of the secular public entertained the hope that a system of direct election of the prime minister would constitute an alternative means for producing the end result of separating religion from state.

The issue was hotly disputed by both the left and right while the draft bill to reform the system of government was being prepared by the Constitution, Law and Justice Committee for its second and third reading in the Knesset. The Labor Party, which, since 1977 and apart from its participation in two National Unity Governments (1984–88, and 1988–1990), had been out of power by virtue of alliances forged between the Likud and the haredi parties, did all it could to encourage the passage of the proposed reform. The haredi parties had, in fact, consistently refused to join parliamentary coalitions headed by Labor from 1952 to 1977. In 1977 they agreed to become part of the Likud coalition largely because they considered that party to represent closer identification with Jewish traditional values, as well as because of the Likud's hostility to the secular "socialism" represented by Labor. It was against this background that Labor leader Yitzhak Rabin made a far-reaching statement in June rejecting the haredi parties as potential partners in any future government headed by Labor. The system of government, he added, was urgently in need of reform so as to put an end to the haredi parties' extortionist practices.[61]

The Likud's political interests regarding the reform bill were completely opposite. The support of the religious, and particularly the haredi, parties was vital to the Likud's goal of insuring the maintenance of a political bloc capable of preventing Labor from establishing a governmental coalition. Accordingly, despite the opposition of certain liberal-minded Likud members who backed the reform, political considerations motivated Prime Minister Shamir and his closest colleagues to oppose it. Shamir, who had beaten his Labor opponents in the 1988 general elections, apparently realized that the existing rules operated in his favor and that altering them might play into the hands of more attractive candidates for the premiership, such as Yitzhak Rabin. An odd situation thus arose in the Knesset in which Likud MK Uriel Lynn, chairman of the Constitution, Law and Justice Committee, found himself arguing with members of his own party, principally those closest to the prime minister, in an attempt to persuade them to support the reform bill despite the prime minister's views.[62]

The Shamir loyalists, possibly hard put to produce convincing arguments justifying their steadfast opposition to the bill, resorted to dredging up the specter of the "Arab threat," claiming that changing the system would assist the Arab sector to increase its political strength and make the Arabs potentially important partners in a Labor takeover.[63] In an effort to add legitimacy to Shamir's antireform stand, his colleagues, well aware of the great respect still commanded by former prime minister Menahem Begin, asserted that Begin himself opposed the reform.[64] However, supporters of the bill argued that if the electoral system were not reformed to provide for the direct election of the prime minister, the haredi parties would simply continue to raise their price for agreeing to take part in coalitions and thereby endanger the entire democratic process.[65] Lynn expressed his views as follows:

> Our present system is honeycombed with flaws and it has failed. Following elections, we don't even know who the prime minister is going to be. The bargaining for a coalition cabinet takes no less than 60 days. It can take even longer. During this process, the majority loses to the minority. Decisions which should be taken by the government are set aside because of the interests of the small coalition partners. Our continual government crises, while providing drama, are unhealthy for the country.[66]

In light of the prime minister's adamant stand, the Likud ultimately imposed strict discipline on its members in the Knesset and instructed them to vote en bloc against the bill in its second and third readings. In a letter addressed to the 3,200 members of the Likud Center (who were in the midst of the debate over the proposed reform), the director general of the Prime Minister's Office, Yossi Ahimeir, wrote on Shamir's behalf: "From our point of view, the most important thing is to do whatever we can to insure that the Likud remains the ruling party and to prevent the possibility that, through this bill being approved by the Knesset, Labor succeeds in returning to power by the backdoor."[67]

Extraparliamentary groups of all shades of opinion applied considerable pressure on MKs from all parties to support the reform proposals. They articulated the great frustration of a large segment of the public over the continuing inability of the politicians to solve the country's chronic economic and security problems, as well as deep public distress over corruption in the government. It was their expectation that electoral reform, in addition to considerably reducing the political power of the haredi community, would result in elected representatives having far more answerability to the voters and a far greater degree of concern for their needs and aspirations.[68] Ultimately, however, as was traditionally the case in Israeli politics, it was the power of the political parties themselves, and not pressure by extraparliamentary groups, that determined the public agenda. The battle over the reform proposal was to continue into 1992. Its sponsors failed to get the draft bill approved on its second reading even though the opponents to the bill had succeeded in watering it down by eliminating or amending some of its most important clauses. At that point, the bill was returned to the Constitution, Law and Justice Committee for further discussion.

THE ISRAELI ARABS**

The Gulf War had contradictory repercussions for the Arab population in Israel. Unlike previous wars in Israel's history, the entire civil population, Jews and Arabs alike, came under direct attack by a foreign Arab military force. The fact that Arab villages in Israel were bombarded by an Arab army significantly sharpened the Israeli

** This section was written by Elie Rekhess.

Arabs' dilemma in terms of their national identity. Under the peculiar circumstances of the war, they found themselves torn, perhaps more acutely than hitherto, between conflicting loyalties to Israel, Palestine, the Arab nation and the world of Islam.

The immediate response of the vast majority of Israeli Arabs to the outbreak of war in January 1991 was support for Saddam Husayn. Unlike the invasion of Kuwait, which elicited divided reactions by the Arab minority, the massive air and ground attack against Iraq evoked nearly unanimous support for Saddam Husayn and the Iraqi nation for raising the flags of the Arab struggle against an alien Western coalition. Likewise, nearly all political parties and organizations were united in blaming the US for the eruption of the war.[69] The Americans, charged the Israeli Arab Communist daily *al-Ittihad,* were motivated by their imperialist interests, namely their goal of gaining control over the Arabs' economy and oil resources. The alleged American concern for Kuwait, it argued, was only a pretext; the real goal was to superimpose Western neocolonialism on the Arab nation.[70] Similarly, MK Muhammad Mi'ari, head of the Progressive List for Peace (PLP), described the US as the "Great Satan" whose main objective was the destruction of Iraq's economic structure.[71] The National Committee of Heads of Arab Local Councils (NCHALC) also issued a strongly worded statement criticizing the American move and called upon the US to stop the "aggressive war and withdraw from the region."[72]

The Islamic movement perceived the war as a crusaders' invasion. Highlighting the religious aspect, its spokesmen condemned the US for having contaminated Islam's holiest cites in Saudi Arabia. The war, Islamic leaders charged, was yet another Western device to ruin Islamic civilization and dominate the Muslim ME.

Yet, the reaction of the Arabs in Israel simultaneously reflected another facet of their national identity. As Israelis they were exposed to the repeated attacks of Iraqi *Scud* missiles, which hit densely populated residential areas, making no distinction between Arabs and Jews. Their acute human dilemma was best epitomized by Israeli Arab actor Makram Khouri, Israel Prize Laureate. "When I hear about the [tragedy of the] Baghdad Bunker," he said, "I am outraged, but I immediately remind myself that the *Scud*s have destroyed houses here, have wounded and killed [here]."[73]

When the first *Scud* attacks began, Israeli Jews were mistrustful of the local Arabs' intentions. The Israeli authorities feared that radical nationalist elements might take advantage of the confusing circumstances and act as a "fifth column," serving the Arab cause in secret. Minister of Police Roni Milo issued a warning to the Arab public against subversive activity. Several Israeli Arabs were, in fact, arrested and charged with treason and espionage, but these cases were not representative of the general mood.[74] On the whole, despite their generally favorable position toward Iraq, the vast majority of Israeli Arabs demonstrated civic loyalty to the State of Israel.

The war revealed the shared fate of the Arabs and Jews. The first victim of the missile attacks on Israel was an Arab baby from the village of Tayba, who suffocated in her gas mask. Arab authorities, public figures and private citizens volunteered aid to the Jewish sector by donating blood, rebuilding destroyed houses and hosting Jewish families made homeless by the *Scud*s. This atmosphere of cooperation was best expressed by the mayor of Shafa-'Amr, Ibrahim Nimr Husayn, who said: "We are now in the same boat. We are brothers and it is the duty of brothers to help each other."[75]

Nevertheless, the Israeli Arabs felt discriminated against and humiliated because of delays in the distribution of gas masks and the serious lack of shelters and alarm sirens in many Arab settlements. Arab leaders sharply criticized the Israeli defense authorities for these shortcomings. Thus, for example, Muhammad Mana', the head of the local council of Majd al-Kurum, an Arab village in the Western Galilee, claimed that most of the masks distributed in the Arab sector were found unfit. He demanded the establishment of an inquiry committee to investigate what he regarded as the government's misconduct.[76] Moreover, the Jewish public's expectation of the Israeli Arabs to reaffirm their loyalty to the state explicitly was dismissed out of hand. As Mayor Husayn said, "We have had enough of these loyalty tests. There is no need to declare our loyalty to the state every other day."[77]

The Gulf crisis had also upset the delicate political relations between the Arabs and the Jews in Israel. The Jewish-Arab partnership in at least two political parties, the PLP and the Israeli Communist Party (ICP), was undermined as a result of the different reactions on the part of its Arab and Jewish members. Hayim Hanegbi, the Jewish secretary of the PLP, resigned from the party allegedly because of his Arab colleagues' pro-Iraqi position. Similarly, Arab politicians expressed their deep disappointment at the position of the Israeli peace camp, which refrained from condemning the civilian casualties in Iraq.

Reactions to the *Scud* attacks also underscored the difference between the Israeli Arabs and the Arabs in the territories. The majority of the Israeli Arabs showed dismay at the *Scud* attacks, while the Arabs in the territories openly demonstrated their satisfaction. Despite this discrepancy, the Israeli Arabs extended aid to the Palestinian residents of the West Bank serious shortages of basic commodities, while the Arab MKs and the NCHALC appealed to Prime Minister Shamir and Minister of Defense Arens to lift the curfew.

Israeli Arab leaders welcomed the end of the war and expressed hope that it would lead to new diplomatic initiatives in the region. However, there were disappointment and frustration in some quarters with the Iraqi army's humiliating defeat and Saddam Husayn's failure to fulfill his pledges.[78] The disillusionment over the outcome of the war caused a state of disorientation which was reflected on 30 March, the fifteenth anniversary of Land Day.[79] Unlike in past years, this event, which commemorated the March 1976 clashes between Arab protesters and Israeli security forces over land expropriation, was marked quietly with an exceptionally low rate of attendance at the public demonstrations.

THE ARAB POLITICAL PARTIES IN CRISIS

The low-keyed mood on Land Day was attributed firstly to the disarray and widespread confusion following the war. A second factor was the firm police policy. In past years, security forces stayed out of the Arab localities in order to avoid unnecessary provocation, intervening only when riots occurred. In 1991, however, police headquarters reversed its past strategy and deployed sizable forces in key Arab towns and villages, as a preemptive act. Undoubtedly, the massive police presence deterred potential Arab militants.

A third reason was internal division within the Arab political parties. Controversies over the question of how to commemorate Land Day had recurred since the late 1970s. The debate was between radical elements, including the ultranationalist Sons of the Village (*Abna al-balad*), who opted for a militant line, and a more moderate viewpoint such as espoused by the Communists. In 1991, the dispute focused on the composition and control of the countrywide Committee for the Defense of Arab Lands. The ICP-led organization, founded in 1976 to coordinate protest activity, organized the first Land Day that year. From the late 1980s, the Islamic movement attempted to gain control of the committee's central bodies and reduce Communist influence in them. In 1991, the conflict intensified to the point that the Islamic movement decided to boycott the official Land Day activities and arrange a program of their own. While the Communists took part in public rallies and processions held in several Arab localities on 30 March, representatives of the Islamic movement paid condolence visits to the families of the six Arabs killed on the first Land Day in 1976, held special prayers in mosques, and planted thousands of olive trees.[80]

The Land Day controversy illustrated the political crisis that was occurring in the Arab sector, namely, the diminishing strength of the Communist Party and the growing status of fundamentalist Islam. In mid-May, ICP secretary-general Tawfiq Tubi drew a gloomy picture of the party's standing, stating that the ICP faced "diminishing activity by a substantial number of party members, irregular meetings of party cells in various branches, difficulties in collecting contributions, [and] a delay in renewing and recruiting subscriptions to [the party periodicals] *al-Ittihad* and *al-Jadid.*"[81]

The ICP position was weakened not only because of resurgent Islam; it had been losing ground ever since the advent of *perestroika* and *glasnost* and the collapse of East European Communist regimes. Like Communist parties elsewhere, the ICP was severely affected by the deep structural crisis of communism. However, it proved perhaps the most rigidly conservative of the Communist parties. Its veteran leaders appeared unwilling or unable to participate in the current ideological revolution, thereby alienating the younger generation of party cadres. While they carried out limited organizational reforms, under severe internal pressure, these steps were seen as merely cosmetic. The effect of developments in Eastern Europe was drastically compounded by the dilution of Soviet patronage in the Arab world, by Soviet-Israeli rapprochement, and by the beginning of mass immigration of Soviet Jews to Israel, stripping the party of vital assets that had been important props of its electoral appeal until then.

Not surprisingly, when conservative elements in the USSR attempted a coup d'état to regain power in August 1991, the ICP reaction was favorable. While not supporting the conspirators openly, the party leaders hoped that a successful coup would bring about a return to the former staunchly pro-Arab, pro-Palestinian Soviet position, a change which could help the ICP reestablish its monopoly position. Later, when it appeared that the coup would fail, the party leadership reversed its stance and condemned the coup attempt as undemocratic. Yet the fact that the ICP failed to dissociate itself initially from the abortive coup further eroded the party's standing within the Arab sector. Significantly, it led veteran Communist activist Emile Habibi to resign from the party, sending a resounding signal to many young cadres to leave the party as well.[82]

The worst damage to the party was in the area of Jewish-Arab relations within its ranks. Since the mid-1980s, Arab dissatisfaction with the hold on party power by a small group of Jewish leaders, as well as with the party's irresolute stand on issues of Arab nationalist concern, became more vocal. Open references to the numerical preponderance of Arab party members, as contrasted with the limited Arab representation at the leadership level, became more frequent. Eventually, this criticism did register with the Jewish leaders, and Arabs gained a majority in all central party bodies. However, this crisis was superseded by another: the gap between the leaders' ideological inflexibility and the reality of collapsing socialist regimes was unbridgeable, with the argument that the class struggle would eventually solve the national conflict between Jews and Arabs losing much of its credibility.

The binational communist ideology that had governed Arab politics in Israel was gradually being replaced by a single national framework for political action. MK 'Abd al-Wahhab Darawsha's Arab Democratic Party (ADP), established in 1988, was the party to set itself up as an exclusively Arab grouping from its inception. Islamic leader, Shaykh 'Abdallah Nimr Darwish noted that the consequences of the war proved the failure of the Jewish-Arab experiment in political cooperation, and the lesson to be learnt was that the Arabs needed a unified Arab list of their own.[83] With the announcement of Knesset elections in 1992, Darwish made concerted efforts to form a united Arab list comprising Islamic movement activists, Darawsha's ADP, Mi'ari's PLP and a group of independent leaders active in the municipal sphere.

Shaykh Darwish's involvement marked a new tendency in the Islamic movement's political approach: a gradual shift from municipal to parliamentary politics. His views, nevertheless, were not shared by an influential oppositional Islamic faction within the Islamic movement, generally identified with Shaykh Ra'id Salah, mayor of Umm al-Fahm, who rejected the idea of active Islamic participation in the Knesset. Following a heated internal debate, the Islamic movement adopted a compromise decision in September 1991 not to enter the 1992 elections race independently, yet not to boycott the elections altogether. A month before the elections, it was announced, the movement would instruct its followers and supporters which candidates to support.[84]

SOCIOECONOMIC ISSUES

In the year under survey, the government failed to meet the pressing socioeconomic needs of the Israeli Arabs. For example, the Ministry of Education and Culture, while drawing up a five-year plan for developing the Arab educational system, admitted that it addressed itself to minimal needs only and that in order to bridge the gap between Arab and Jewish schools, larger investments were required.[85]

Studies published in 1991 also illustrated the extensive gap in the poverty level between Arabs and Jews. Research conducted by "Sikkuy" ("Chance"), an Israeli nonprofit equal opportunity organization, showed that 60% of all Arab children in Israel lived below the poverty line, as compared to 10% of all Jewish children. Moreover, the housing conditions of the Israeli Arabs had deteriorated over a period of ten years as a result of uncompleted ordinance plans and a shortage of approved building areas. As a result of these limitations, illegal construction proliferated, countered occasionally by government demolition orders.[86]

In the summer of 1991, a meaningful breakthrough was made toward eliminating one of the major grievances harbored by the Israeli Arabs: the gap between governmental budget allocations to Arab and Jewish municipal authorities. By 1991, the discrepancy between the per capita grant to the two sectors had reached a peak of 10:1, and was even higher with regard to development budgets. This discriminatory governmental policy had nourished deep feelings of bitterness and alienation and was the source of ongoing protest campaigns and a lengthy series of general strikes, hunger strikes and sit-ins since the mid 1980s.[87]

A 1991 protest campaign proved productive when in August the government endorsed a proposal submitted by the ministers of interior and finance for a four-year program designed to eliminate existing municipal budgetary gaps. The plan called for an immediate government allocation of NIS140m. to the Arab municipalities — an increase of 240% over current levels. An additional sum of NIS76m. was expected to be immediately collected by the local authorities themselves. The proposal also called for the expansion of the development budget for the Arab sector by NIS370m. over a period of five years. This long-awaited step was warmly received. "Blessed are those who took this decision to equalize the government grants," said Ramiz Jara'isi, deputy mayor of Nazareth.[88] Others were more cautious, maintaining that the test of the plan would come when it was implemented.

REACTIONS TO THE MADRID PEACE CONFERENCE

The Madrid conference (see chapter on the ME peace process) was warmly welcomed by the majority of Israeli Arabs, who shared a sense of pride and satisfaction with their brothers in the territories. The mainstream Arab political parties, namely the ICP, PLP and ADP, were outspoken in their support for the participation of the Palestinian delegation in the peace conference. Endorsing the Palestinian position, spokesmen for these parties strongly criticized what they considered the obstinate stance of the Israeli Government in rejecting official PLO participation and doubted its intentions. Lasting peace could not be achieved, argued Lutfi Mash'ur, editor of the Nazareth weekly al-Sinara, unless there was international and, more important, Israeli recognition of the right of Palestinians to self-determination. "This is the minimum that is required to end the conflict," he said. Other leading personalities reportedly felt the Palestinians had made enough concessions and feared "another Camp David."[89]

Prime Minister Shamir's speech in Madrid was seen by Israeli Arab leaders as "hard and inflexible." "Hopefully this was more of a propaganda speech and [did] not represent the final Israeli position," commented Muhammad Zaydan, spokesman for the NCHALC.[90] Some public figures, Tawfiq Zayad, the mayor of Nazareth among them, argued that, in fact, it was the Palestinian delegates who represented the Arab minority in Israel and not the official Israeli delegation headed by Prime Minister Shamir.

While no official representation of the Arab population was included in the Israeli delegation to Madrid, MK Muhammad Mi'ari of the PLP traveled independently to Madrid and maintained intensive contacts with the Palestinian representatives. He claimed that this activity was essential because the Israeli Arabs made up one fifth of the Palestinian nation and therefore ought to have a presence in a conference in which the Palestinian fate was discussed.[91]

Following the first round of talks, most leaders of the Arab community in Israel expressed cautious optimism. The prevalent mood was best described by Muhammad Zaydan who explained that the Arabs of Israel, perhaps more than any other group, were interested in the accomplishment of peace "because we live and are citizens of a country that is essentially in a state of war with our [Palestinian-Arab] people." "This

[was] a historic moment which none of the sides [could] afford to miss," he concluded.[92]

Less enthusiastic leaders of the Arab community cautioned against overoptimism. Most radical in their opposition were the more militant elements in the Islamic movement and the rejectionist Sons of the Village organization which regarded the Madrid conference as a sellout of Palestinian rights in return for a vague agreement which in effect enabled Israel to maintain its grip over the occupied territories.[93]

"Before, we had only one Sadat," wrote the Islamic movement's official organ, *Sawt al-Haqq wal-Hurriyya,* "but now we have hundreds of 'Sadats' ready to sell out the homeland." "In this campaign the rifles turned into whiskey glasses, the blood and tears of the Palestinian children became ammunition [used by the Madrid negotiators] and the battlefield is no other than the hotels and the bars," the weekly further ridiculed the Madrid gathering.[94]

FOREIGN AFFAIRS

The year 1991 witnessed a marked improvement in Israel's relations with the international community. This resulted in part from the Gulf War, during which Israel was perceived as the victim of unprovoked aggression, and in part by acceleration of the regional peace process initiated and supported by the US. Israel's relations with the UN improved in unprecedented fashion during the Gulf crisis. For the first time since occupying the territories in the 1967 Six-Day War, Israel was perceived by the UN as justly defending itself against Arab aggression. This new perception was symbolized by a visit to Israel of UN General Assembly President Guido de Marco, who expressed warm sentiments toward his hosts and whose general attitude was welcomed in Jerusalem. He indicated that the UN saw no direct connection between the Palestinian problem, on the one hand, and the Gulf crisis, on the other. No artificial linkage should be made, he implied, between the possibility of granting eventual political self-determination to the Palestinians and securing the immediate unconditional withdrawal of Iraq from Kuwait.[95] This message had the effect of temporarily easing the pressure heretofore applied by Western European countries on the Israeli Government to alter its policies regarding the West Bank, the Gaza Strip and East Jerusalem.

At the same time, diplomatic coordination between Israel and the Western powers, particularly with the US and Great Britain, intensified. Israel utilized various diplomatic channels to signal its acceptance of the position adopted by the US and its allies, for example, a visit to Israel by a British parliamentary delegation in early January, which was informed that Israel was prepared to refrain from initiating any preemptive strike against Iraq.[96] Nevertheless, Jerusalem harbored suspicions, subsequently proved well founded, that once the Gulf crisis was over it would be obliged to make a number of painful concessions so that the US could compensate its Arab allies for their support during the Gulf crisis.[97]

The damage inflicted by Iraqi *Scud* missiles on Israeli population centers, particularly in the Tel Aviv area, produced a wave of sympathy for Israel throughout the West, with the apparent exception of France, which continued to advocate linkage between the solutions to the Gulf and Palestinian problems. This led to a further worsening of relations between the two countries.[98] That exception apart, though, Israel's status in the international community had implications far beyond mere sympathy.

The US made available military aid in the form of a consignment of *Patriot* antimissile missiles, which were manned by American crews, marking the first occasion since 1956 (during the Suez campaign) that foreign troops landed on Israeli soil for the purpose of participating in the country's defense. Despite the improved relationship with the US, however, a solution to the "loan guarantees" issue (for the absorption of Russian immigrants) remained illusive. When Israel's ambassador to Washington, Zalman Shoval, attacked the Administration for failing to make these guarantees available, he was sharply rebuked by the US State Department.[99]

The German Federal Republic, several of whose scientists had assisted Iraq in developing its weapons industry, announced that all German companies found guilty of illegally shipping weapons to Iraq would be severely punished. It also offered Israel financial aid amounting to the equivalent of $166m.[100] The fact that Israel agreed to remain militarily inactive and backed US policy and military strategy during the Gulf crisis earned it further international prestige.[101] The EC, for example, which had previously tended to dispute Israel's policies regarding the territories and solving the conflict generally, decided to provide it with financial aid of $170m. as compensation for the damage caused by the Iraqi missile attacks.[102]

Once the Gulf War was over, the Israeli Government, reckoning the time might be ripe to take advantage of the points scored from its recent close cooperation with the world's last remaining superpower, requested increased civilian grants and more massive military financing from the US, but was given clear signals that the US would reject these requests. One of the primary American interests in the post-Gulf War period was to form a regional alliance with the more moderate Arab states (Saudi Arabia, Egypt and Jordan, though relations with the latter were perceived as problematic because of its close relations with Iraq during the course of the Gulf crisis). Overall, the US seemed to be broadcasting the message that Israel ought to be feeling more secure following the Gulf War, and therefore was not in need of special additional aid.[103]

The perception by the US that Israel was less of a strategic asset than before became increasingly apparent as differences in political outlook between the Shamir government and the Bush Administration widened. The US became increasingly insistent that Israel adopt the formula of territorial compromise in return for peace, a proposal utterly rejected by Shamir. A further, related, reason for the differences between the two countries was the issue of Israel's settlements in the territories. The Shamir government policy was to settle the territories intensively so as to forestall any chance of the establishment of a Palestinian state. This policy in particular prompted President Bush to announce to Congress that he opposed granting Israel the $10bn. in loan guarantees it was seeking for the purpose of funding immigrant absorption, a position he would alter only if Israel undertook to end settlement activity in the territories, he declared.[104]

The deterioration in relations with the US spurred Israel's drive to improve ties with other countries which it thought might be prepared to assist it. The year 1991 witnessed considerable progress in the improvement of Israel's contacts with states in the Eastern Bloc. Representatives of Israel's Foreign Ministry visited Moscow to prepare the ground for the resumption of diplomatic relations with the Soviet Union.[105] After several exchange visits by diplomats and businessmen from both countries, Israel and the Soviet Union announced the resumption of full diplomatic relations on 28 March 1991.[106] From the standpoint of the Soviet Union (and of its successor, Russia), this promised to be a worthwhile step, for renewing its ties with Israel, despite Israel's small size, Soviet participation was assured, alongside that of the US, in the formulation and negotiation of any international arrangements for the future of the ME. Israel, too, clearly stood to benefit from the resumption of diplomatic relations in terms of expanded cultural, economic and diplomatic cooperation with the Eastern Bloc and a further increase in the immigration of Jews from the republics comprising the new CIS. Indeed, the new atmosphere of optimism in Israeli Government circles regarding the future course of relations with Russia contrasted with the mood that had prevailed ever since the 1950s when, against the background of the Korean War, Israel had effectively aligned itself with the Western Bloc. The dawn of this new diplomatic era was symbolized by the Madrid conference (October 1991), jointly chaired by US Secretary of State James Baker and Soviet Foreign Minister Alexander Bessmertnykh (see chapter on the ME peace process). A significant result of the dramatic change that had occurred in Israel's international standing was support by the Soviet Union, the Ukraine, Latvia and Lithuania for the draft proposal to annul UN Resolution 3379, passed in 1975, which had condemned Zionism and equated it with racism.[107] Because of this support, and largely by virtue of the dissipation of the Cold War, the resolution was annulled on 16 December 1991.[108]

Overall, Israel's international position improved significantly, primarily because of the Gulf War, the collapse of the Soviet Union, the end of the Cold War and progress forged in the US-sponsored peace process. In addition, the resumption of full diplomatic relations in mid-1991 between Israel and Hungary symbolized a bridge of renewed cultural and economic links between the West and Eastern Europe. There was also some positive movement toward establishing trade relations between Israel and China, accelerated by the visit to China of a large Israeli commercial delegation in November 1991[109] and by an announcement by Chinese Foreign Minister Qian Qichen that China and Israel were gradually moving toward establishing full diplomatic relations.[110]

SUMMARY

Few states or societies had to contend simultaneously with the challenges of sudden and radical population growth (resulting from mass immigration), palpable threats to national security, and the major task of creating a sound economic infrastructure, as did Israel in 1991. Its efforts to meet this concurrence of challenges turned the country into what might be described as a fascinating political-social case history. That thousands of new immigrants had to be equipped with gas masks immediately upon landing at Ben-Gurion International Airport was a painful indication of the bitter realities of life in Israel in 1991. Nevertheless, the country achieved some genuine successes during the year: its refusal to become actively entangled in the Gulf War, the considerable improvement of its international position, and the absorption of about 200,000 new immigrants accompanied by a massive building program. On the debit side, the year ended with the Arab-Palestinian-Israeli conflict appearing to be as far from solution as ever and with the territorial status quo (including Israel's control of the occupied territories) still entirely unaltered.

NOTES

For the place and frequency of publications cited here, and for the full name of the publication, news agency, radio station or monitoring service where an abbreviation is used, please see "List of Sources." Only in the case of more than one publication bearing the same name is the place of publication noted here.

1. See interview with Gen.(Res.) Matti Peled, formerly one of the leaders of the Progressive Party for Peace, in which he stated that Haim Hanegbi, despite his protestations, did not leave the party out of wholly ideological motives and decidedly not on account of the party's "identification" with Saddam Husayn's invasion. *Hadashot,* Supplement, 8 February 1991, pp. 18–19.
2. For an expanded analysis of this topic, see G. Barzilai and Y. Shain, "Israeli Democracy at a Crossroads: A Crisis of Non-Governability," *Government and Opposition,* XXVI, 3 (Summer 1991), pp. 345–67.
3. Ibid.
4. See Knesset debates over MK Rehav'am Ze'evi joining the government, 2 May 1991, Protocols of Knesset Debates, pp. 2030–55.
5. Ze'ev Segal, Gad Barzilai, "An Administration Bereft of Goodwill," *Ha'aretz,* 14 February 1991.
6. G.Barzilai, *A Democracy in Wartime: Conflict and Consensus in Israel* (Tel Aviv: Sifriat Poalim, 1992) pp. 275–90 (in Hebrew).
7. *Annual Report of the State Comptroller,* Report No.41 (Jerusalem, 1991) p. 974; *Annual Report of the State Comptroller,* Report No.42 (Jerusalem, 1992) p. 923. In these reports, State Comptroller Judge Miriam Ben-Porat stated that the findings of examinations and ongoing professional follow-up indicated that most of the civil defense kits were defective and would not have provided the population with appropriate protection against chemical weapon attacks.
8. E.Inbar, "Strategic Consequences for Israel," in G.Barzilai, A.Klieman and G.Shidlo (eds.) *The Gulf Crisis and its Aftermath* (London: Routledge, 1993) (forthcoming).
9. Shlomit Levi, "Support for the Government: As During the Six-Day War," *Ma'ariv,* 1 February, in which the author reports on surveys conducted by the Institute for Applied Social Research, Jerusalem. See also the report on a telephone survey conducted by the same institute, *Ha'aretz,* 28 January 1991.
10. Ibid. (*Ma'ariv* and *Ha'aretz*).
11. *Ha'aretz,* 7 February, 29 January 1991.
12. Ibid.
13. Shlomit Levi, op. cit.
14. See, e.g., the declaration by the chief of military intelligence, Gen. Amnon Shahak, *Yedi'ot Aharonot,* 15 February 1991.
15. See: S. Peres, "Peace Comprises Strategic Depth" and: B. Z. Begin, "A Zionist Attitude" in N. Shaham and Z. Raaman (eds.) *War in the Gulf* (Tel Aviv: Sifriat Poalim, 1991) pp. 23–31, 33–46 (in Hebrew).
16. See the report by Roni Shaked on the survey conducted by the Institute for Applied Social Research, Jerusalem, dated June 1991, in *Yedi'ot Aharonot,* 7 June 1991. Similar conclusions emerge from a research study compiled from questionnaires distributed to Knesset members and from public opinion surveys: Gad Barzilai, Giora Goldberg and Efraim Inbar, "Israeli Leadership and Public Attitudes Toward Federal Solutions for the Arab-Israeli Conflict Before and After Desert Storm," *Publius,* XXI, 3 (Summer 1991), pp. 191–209.
17. For further analysis of these findings, see Barzilai *et al., ibid.*
18. Ibid.
19. Ibid.
20. *Ha'aretz,* 9 April; *NYT, FT,* 11 April 1991.
21. *Ha'aretz,* 11 May 1991.
22. VoI, 18 June — DR, 19 June 1991.
23. *Ha'aretz,* 10 October 1991.

24. Ibid., 19, 25, 30 December; VoI, 27 December — DR, 27 December 1991.
25. Ibid., 9 January 1991.
26. Ibid., 15 February 1991.
27. Ibid., 11 February, 4 March 1991.
28. Ibid., 27 February 1991.
29. Ibid., 11 March 1991.
30. Ibid., VoI, 25 March — DR, 25 March 1991.
31. *Ha'aretz,* 13, 29 October 1991.
32. *JP,* 4 January 1991.
33. Knesset debates, 7 January, Protocols of Knesset Debates. For commentaries on Knesset debates, see *Ha'aretz,* 8 January 1991.
34. *Ha'aretz, NYT,* 7 October 1991.
35. *Ha'aretz,* 9, 28 October, 19 November; *NYT,* 16 November 1991.
36. *Ha'aretz,* 4 January — DR, 7 January; *JP,* 7 January 1991.
37. See High Court of Justice 37. 22, 168/91, Murcus vs. the Minister of Defense (still unpublished, verdict handed down on 14 January 1991).
38. Ibid.
39. *Ha'aretz,* 19, 20 February 1991.
40. *Ha'aretz,* 9 April 1991.
41. Ibid., 24 April 1991.
42. Ibid., 8 January 1991.
43. Ibid., 25 January 1991.
44. Ibid., 11 April 1991.
45. See statements by the chairman of the Knesset Absorption Committee, MK Michael Kleiner, *Ha'aretz,* 24 April 1991.
46. *Ma'ariv,* 28 April — DR, 1 May 1991.
47. *Ha'aretz,* 2 August. See the findings of a manpower survey conducted by the Central Bureau of Statistics, ibid., 18 December 1991.
48. Ibid., 8 May 1991.
49. See address of the minister of trade and industry to the Knesset, *Ha'aretz,* 8 May 1991.
50. R. IDF, 13 June — DR, 13 June 1991.
51. *Ha'aretz,* 26, 27 June 1991.
52. Lily Galilee, "Towards a Crisis in Immigration," *Ha'aretz,* 12 December 1991.
53. See Yaron London, "The Immigrants are Tending to the Right," *Yedi'ot Aharonot,* 28 June; *Ha'aretz,* 2 August 1991.
54. See report on debates in the Knesset, *Ha'aretz,* 3 January 1991.
55. Ibid., 20 March 1991.
56. See report on Knesset debates on the state budget, ibid., 22 March 1991.
57. Ibid., 21 March 1991.
58. Ibid., 23, 30 April 1991.
59. *JP,* 14 June 1991.
60. *Ha'aretz,* 17 June 1991.
61. Ibid., 26 June 1991.
62. Ibid., 10, 12 June 1991.
63. Ibid., 17 July 1991.
64. Ibid., 29 July 1991.
65. Uriel Lynn, ibid., 12 October 1991.
66. Uriel Lynn, "Politics and the Personal Element," *JP,* 13 December 1991.
67. *Ha'aretz,* 15 December 1991.
68. See article by Avi Kadish, a leader of the pro-reform protest groups, "The State Cannot be Stolen from Us," *Ma'ariv,* 9 August 1991.
69. *Ha'aretz,* 18, 21 January, 8 February 1991.
70. *Al-Ittihad* (Haifa), 16 January 1991.
71. *Al-Sinara,* 1 February 1991.
72. Ibid.
73. *Ma'ariv,* 22 February 1991.
74. *Ha'aretz,* 22 February 1991.

75. VoI, 24 January 1991, cited in Sara Osotsky and Asad Ghanim, *Skirot,* 6, May 1991, p. 8.
76. *Ha'aretz,* 6 February 1991.
77. Ibid.
78. *JP,* 1 March 1991.
79. See, e.g., interview with Lutfi Mashur, *JP,* 4 April 1991.
80. *Ha'aretz,* 28, 29 March, 19 April 1991.
81. *Zo Haderech,* 29 May 1991.
82. Ibid., 20 August; *Ha'aretz,* 21, 23, 25, 28 August; *al-Ittihad* (Haifa), 28 August 1991.
83. *JP,* 15 March 1991.
84. *Sawt al-Haqq wal-Hurriyya,* 20 September; *al-Watan* (Nazareth), 27 September 1991.
85. *Ha'aretz,* 2 January, 20 February, 30 June 1991.
86. *Al-Ittihad* (Haifa), 20 December 1991.
87. Yosef Goel, "Apathy and Achievement," *JP,* 8 September 1991.
88. *Ha'aretz,* 26, 28 August; *JP,* 13 September 1991.
89. *JP,* 18 October 1991.
90. Ibid., 1 November 1991.
91. Cited in Sara Osotsky and Riyad Kabha, "The Madrid Conference in the Eyes of the Arab Press in Israel," *Skirot,* 7 December 1991, p. 8 (in Hebrew).
92. *JP,* 1 November 1991.
93. *JP,* 18 October, 1 November; *al-Watan* (Nazareth), 1, 8, 15 November 1991.
94. *Sawt al-Haqq wal-Hurriyya,* 1 November 1991 cited in Osotsky-Kabha, *Skirot,* 7, p. 14.
95. VoI, 3 January — DR, 3 January 1991.
96. VoI, 7 January — DR, 8 January 1991.
97. See, e.g., the interview with Prime Minister Yitzhak Shamir, *Davar,* 8 January 1991.
98. *Ha'aretz,* 21 January 1991.
99. Ibid., 16 February 1991.
100. Ibid., 24 January 1991.
101. See Yitzhak Shamir's broadcast in support of US President George Bush, VoI and R. IDF, 5 February — DR, 5 February 1991.
102. *Ha'aretz,* 5 February 1991.
103. See, e.g., the declaration by US Secretary of Defense Richard Cheney.
104. WF, 14 November 1991.
105. *Ma'ariv,* 25, 26 March; VoI, 26 March — DR, 26 March 1991.
106. *Ma'ariv,* 28 March 1991.
107. VoI, 11 November — DR, 12 November 1991.
108. *IHT,* 18 December 1991.
109. *Yedi'ot Aharonot,* 13 November 1991.
110. *IHT,* 29 November 1991.

Jordan
(Al-Mamlaka al-Urdunniyya al-Hashimiyya)

ASHER SUSSER

Major regional events such as the Gulf War and the revived peace process dominated Jordanian domestic and foreign affairs in the year under survey. Popular support for Iraq during the war and opposition to the peace process after the war by the Islamist right and the radical secular left, and continued economic difficulties, led to sustained political disquiet throughout the year.

No serious threat was posed to the stability of the regime, but the frequent changes of government (in January, June and November) were a reflection of the regime's difficulty in contending with domestic opposition. The composition of the cabinet underwent radical changes as the regime engaged in exercises of trial and error alternating between co-optation and exclusion of the Muslim Brethren.

The approval of the national charter, which created an agreed quasi-constitutional framework for the guided liberalization process, and the bailing out of the economy, mainly by Japan and the European Community (EC), both had a stabilizing effect. Jordan, however, still faced major domestic problems. The challenge of Islamic radicalism and structural economic problems were far from being overcome. New doubts about the king's health, after his hospitalization in June with a heart complaint, lent a certain urgency to questions about the succession and the long-term future of the kingdom without the dominant unifying figure of Husayn. Even the king himself claimed to have briefly considered reducing his responsibilities in the government.

In the meantime, the monarchy remained secure and confident enough to pursue the peace process with Israel, despite domestic opposition. The peace process was, in the king's view, a window of opportunity that had to be exploited for the sake of regional stability and the long-term strategic and economic well-being of the kingdom itself.

DOMESTIC AFFAIRS

POLITICAL AND ECONOMIC RAMIFICATIONS OF THE GULF WAR
The Popular Anti-Western Mood
All sectors of the Jordanian population, both houses of parliament, the press and political parties and organizations all expressed overwhelming support for Iraq in its confrontation with the US and its allies. As opposed to the more nuanced approach of the regime, popular sentiment was consistently and blatantly anti-American. King Husayn's own, albeit more measured, condemnation of the US and its allies (see below) set the tone for the entire population. Popular anti-US sentiment was

482

Jordan

undoubtedly deeply felt and the king's own position indicated that an explicit anti-American stance would be tolerated by the regime.

Upon the outbreak of war in mid-January, the Chamber of Deputies strongly condemned the "savage aggression" of the US and its allies against the "fraternal Iraqi people" and urged Arabs and Muslims everywhere to strike at American interests. The chamber also appealed to the peoples of the Arab and Muslim states allied with the US — Egypt, Saudi Arabia, Syria, Turkey, Bangladesh and Pakistan — to prevent their rulers from participating in the "tyrannical aggression" against Iraq. It similarly urged Iran to take a stand befitting its own doctrines on the "Great Satan" that threatened not only Iraq but all Muslims.[1]

Jordan's mufti, Shaykh 'Izz al-Din al-Khatib al-Tamimi, declared that the war against Iraq was yet another link in the chain of "Crusader-Jewish hostility" toward the Muslim people and called for Jihad (holy war) to "win the strength of this world and paradise in the hereafter."[2]

Political parties and groups representing all strands of the domestic scene, from the left-wing Jordanian Arab Nationalist Democratic Alliance (JANDA; see *MECS* 1990, p. 464) to the religious right (the Muslim Brethren, the Islamic Liberation Party, Hamas and the Islamic Jihad), issued statements and organized rallies to condemn the US and its European and Arab allies and to appeal to Arabs and Muslims to strike at American interests in the region or to wage Jihad.[3]

Editorials and articles in the Jordanian press throughout the war were similarly supportive of Iraq, initially assuring their readers of inevitable US defeat;[4] justifying the Iraqi *Scud* attacks on Israel, which was termed an "advanced aggressive base" of the US in the region;[5] and, when the tide of war appeared to be shifting against Iraq, condemning the "Zionist West" for uncivilized barbarism similar to that of Hulagu's Mongol hordes that had ravaged Baghdad in 1258.[6]

In the pervasive anti-American mood, frequent rallies and demonstrations were held in support of Iraq in Amman and other cities, some with as many as 10,000 people in attendance. Anti-American outrage was especially evident after Jordanian truckers were killed in Allied bombing raids on the Baghdad-Amman highway (late January and early February). This was also the case after the bombing of the shelter in the Amiriyya quarter of Baghdad (see chapter on Iraq) and the loss of more Jordanian lives when a bus of evacuees from Kuwait was hit in an Allied air attack on its way from Baghdad to Amman, killing 30 people (mid-February).

Demonstrations were generally peaceful but the authorities took the precaution of not allowing mass demonstrations to approach the US Embassy in Amman for fear of an outbreak of violence. In contrast to the cautious official reaction (see below), demonstrators welcomed the Iraqi *Scud* attacks on Israel and even urged Saddam Husayn to use his chemical arsenal against the Israelis.[7]

On 6 February, a convoy of Turkish and Syrian trucks on their way to Saudi Arabia and other Gulf states was attacked by angry Jordanian civilians in the northern border town of Ramtha. The crowd, however, responded to appeals from the authorities not to interrupt transit trade through the kingdom and to warnings that strict measures would be taken to enforce law and order.[8]

The Jordanian public was said to have been astonished by Iraq's decision at the end of February to withdraw from Kuwait[9] and to accept a cease-fire. The press and the public were reluctant to admit that Iraq had been defeated. A massive demonstration in solidarity with Iraq was held on 28 February where President Bush's call for a cease-fire was jubilantly hailed as proof of Iraq's victory.[10] Political organizations from left to right cabled congratulatory cables to Saddam Husayn, but within a few days the reality of defeat began to sink in. Statements issued by both houses of parliament in early March, though clearly supportive of Iraq, reflected a sober recognition of the new reality.[11] Bitterness toward the West remained profound. Drawing lessons from the crisis, Prof. Kamil Abu Jabir (who became Jordan's foreign minister in October), condemned the speed with which the "Zionist West [had] resorted to the use of naked and brutal force," thereby exposing the "near primitive nature of a civilization almost always ready to revert to the law of the jungle." In the "so-called civilized West...technological advances [had] far outstripped the capacity of the Western soul to absorb and tame the primeval human tendency toward violence." The Arabs, he observed, should "Just think: if that [was] what the West [was] willing to do under the slogan of the 'liberation of Kuwait,' what would it do should Israel be really threatened?" Another lesson to be drawn, Abu Jabir contended, was that the centrifugal forces within the Arab world were, in fact, far stronger than the popular support for unity. The Middle Eastern state system was, therefore, "here to stay."[12]

Jordan's Oil Supply Problems During the War

Allied air attacks on oil tankers on the Baghdad-Amman highway in late January and early February disrupted regular oil supplies from Iraq to the kingdom. Jordanian officials rejected US charges that its continued imports of Iraqi oil were in violation of the international sanctions against Iraq. Iraq, they argued, did not benefit financially from these supplies as they were made in settlement of an Iraqi debt of $310m. to Jordan, without any cash remuneration. Moreover, Jordan had no suitable alternative source of supply, particularly since Saudi Arabia had cut off all oil supplies to Jordan in September 1990 (see *MECS* 1990, pp. 475, 487). Without Iraqi oil, Jordan's economy would "come to a standstill," the officials said. Jordan had previously informed the UN Sanctions Committee that it would continue to import oil from Iraq (see *MECS* 1990, p. 487) and had not been informed of any objections. The US itself, they argued, had previously given Jordan to understand that, while it did not approve of the Jordanian position, it did not object to it either. Jordan also rejected US charges that Iraqi war material had been transported in convoy with the Jordanian civilian oil trucks. The Allied attacks were seen by Jordan as a new American position designed to punish the country for its "refusal to join the war camp against Iraq."[13] The official US explanation was that it was not coalition policy to attack the oil tankers even though the oil exports to Jordan were a violation of the sanctions. But the evidence, according to US sources, that military transports were among the oil trucks made the convoys a legitimate target.[14]

The disruption of oil supplies, and concern that they may be cut off altogether, prompted the Jordanian Government to seek alternative, albeit more expensive, sources of supply. In early February, the government purchased a 100,000-ton oil tanker to be stationed permanently in 'Aqaba and thus serve as a storage vessel to ensure a sufficient supply of crude oil. Shortly thereafter, Jordan concluded agreements with Syria and Yemen to purchase crude oil and refined petroleum products at market prices.[15]

By early February, imports from Iraq had dwindled from some 40,000 barrels per day (b/d) before the war to about 5,000 b/d after the air strikes on the Baghdad-Amman highway.[16] In addition to energy conservation measures taken in October 1990 (see *MECS* 1990, p. 475), the government introduced stricter fuel-conservation measures, including restrictions on private car use that aroused considerable public criticism.[17]

In early March, immediately after the end of the Gulf War, official sources announced that Jordan intended to resume oil imports from Iraq,[18] and the emergency conservation measures were canceled shortly thereafter.[19] Jordan continued to receive Syrian oil until the regular supply from Iraq was resumed, but in early June it was reported that Jordan had decided to halt oil imports from Syria.[20] At the same time, it was also reported that Jordan had informed the UN Sanctions Committee of the resumption of its imports from Iraq.[21]

Allied Interception of 'Aqaba-Bound Shipping

The number of ships docking at the port of 'Aqaba was drastically reduced as a result of the imposition of sanctions on Iraq following its invasion of Kuwait (see *MECS* 1990, p. 475). Before the Gulf crisis, 70% of the cargo handled at 'Aqaba had been normally destined for Iraq. US and other Allied naval forces therefore regularly intercepted ships in the Red Sea on their way to 'Aqaba to ensure that they carried no Iraqi cargo.[22] Jordanian shippers complained that the US navy was stopping and inspecting 'Aqaba-bound ships even in cases where the entire cargo was destined for local Jordanian consumption and not for reexport to Iraq.[23] There was no way the US could verify such claims. The Allied blockade was never complete, but ships were still subjected to Allied interception even after the Gulf War cease-fire, due to the continuation of sanctions against Iraq.[24] 'Aqaba-bound vessels were often diverted to other ports to be off-loaded for inspection, causing delays in delivery that, according to Jordanian shippers, inflicted losses of up to $200,000 per vessel.[25] King Husayn complained that 401 ships had been intercepted, delayed, turned back or diverted to other ports from August 1990 until early September 1991, and that Jordan's trade with its traditional markets had consequently been adversely affected. No other state neighboring Iraq had been similarly treated, he said.[26]

Jordan's repeated complaints to the US Government in this regard had no effect and the stringent enforcement of the blockade continued until the end of the year as part and parcel of the UN attempt to maintain effective sanctions against Iraq. According to Jordanian sources, 'Aqaba port had provided a regular net revenue of about JD44m. a year. The blockade, however, was costing Jordan about JD14m. a year.[27]

The Socioeconomic Pressure of the Returning Expatriates

Shortly after the Iraqi invasion of Kuwait, over 200,000 Jordanian expatriate workers and their families returned to the kingdom from Kuwait and other Gulf countries. In July 1991, an official Jordanian source stated that 269,744 persons had returned to Jordan between 2 August 1990 and 15 July 1991.[28] Another 29,574 Jordanians returned from Kuwait in August and September, bringing the total of returnees to some 300,000.[29] The exact figure was never ascertained. For example, in September the minister of planning noted that only 230,000 had returned by the end of August 1991.[30]

Most of the returning Jordanians were of Palestinian extraction. While in the past it had been difficult to discern whether Palestinians were a majority on the East Bank, with the influx of returnees from the Gulf it would appear that Palestinians had indeed become a majority on the East Bank. Though this could have long-term political ramifications, in the short term the main problems were the extreme pressures that the returnees imposed on Jordan's social services and its already faltering economy. Jordan's expatriate workers, who had formerly buoyed the country's economy with their remittances, were suddenly transformed, for the most part, into needy dependents of the state. Only about 10% of them were said to be reasonably well off. The rest were in "dire need."[31]

Fahd Fanik, one of Jordan's leading economic analysts, noted that "the mother of all economic problems" that Jordan faced was the imbalance between resources and population. This imbalance was now seriously exacerbated by the sudden increase of population by some 10%.[32]

Nearly 80% of the returnees settled in the overpopulated metropolitan area of Amman-Zarqa. This "shocking increase" of population was expected to lead to a further deterioration in the existing levels of social and other services.[33] The sudden influx of returnees created a housing crisis. Rents rose sharply, leaving "many Jordanians struggling to find a place to live."[34] Providing housing, medical services and education was a heavy burden on the state. Moreover, the additional population taxed Jordan's limited water and food resources.[35]

The returnees also aggravated the already serious level of unemployment which, according to King Husayn, soared to an unprecedented rate.[36] Planning Minister Ziyad Fariz claimed that Jordan would need $4.5bn. over a period of five years to absorb the returnees.[37]

However, not all the effects of the influx of the returnees were negative. The housing crisis for some was a real estate and construction boom for others. In fact, the government encountered difficulties in convincing private contractors to engage in low-cost housing projects as they were "not short of business."[38] Many of the better-off returnees were involved in an "investors' rush" in a variety of commercial and industrial ventures,[39] which had a certain revitalizing effect on the economy.

Foreign Aid and the Performance of the Economy

Pessimistic forecasts of imminent economic collapse in Jordan because of the impact of the Gulf crisis proved to be incorrect. The Jordanian Government, it appeared, had deliberately exaggerated the losses it was expected to incur as a direct consequence of the Gulf crisis (see *MECS* 1990, pp. 473–76). This had the desired effect and produced more than enough emergency foreign aid to forestall the collapse of Jordan's fragile economy.

Foreign aid was received especially from Japan, Germany and other EC countries, Canada, Taiwan and the World Bank in amounts that exceeded initial expectations for 1991. Thus, for example, Japan provided Jordan with a soft loan of $450m. further to a similar loan of $250m. made in 1990;[40] Germany offered a grant of DM150m. in addition to a similar grant of DM180m. it had made in 1990,[41] making Jordan the highest per capita recipient of German aid;[42] and the EC provided Jordan with grants worth $210m. to compensate for losses incurred by adherence to sanctions against Iraq.[43]

Both Japanese and German officials explained their largesse toward Jordan in terms of its importance to regional stability and to the eventual solution of the Palestinian problem.[44] While Jordan's role as a buffer state was at times a severe liability exposing it to conflicting political pressures, its contribution as a buffer to regional stability was also clearly an asset, recognized by interested outside powers which were willing to bail out the Jordanian economy regularly.

At the end of May, it was reported that Jordan had received emergency assistance totaling some \$1.1bn. in soft loans and grants since the beginning of the Gulf crisis.[45] Foreign currency reserves in 1991 were at their highest level ever, \$878m.[46] The Jordanian dinar (c. \$1.5) remained stable and inflation dropped from 16.1% in 1990 to just over 8% in 1991.[47]

Jordan's economic stability was also made possible by the renewal of concessionary Iraqi oil supplies, which were only briefly interrupted (see above), and by the suspension of much of Jordan's foreign debt service. Part of the damage done to Jordanian exports by the loss of markets in Iraq, Kuwait and Saudi Arabia was redressed by an agreement to sell phosphates to Iran worth \$66m. Simultaneously, imports declined as a result of uncertainties over the Gulf situation and problems arising from the blockading of 'Aqaba.[48] The gross domestic product (GDP) for 1991 increased by 1%, in comparison to the 8% decline in the GDP in 1990.[49]

Jordan still required massive foreign aid to maintain a modicum of economic equilibrium and to generate growth. The International Monetary Fund (IMF) and the World Bank continued to encourage the government to cut expenditure and reduce the deficit in the state budget. Accordingly, the JD1.27bn. budget for 1992 projected a deficit of JD107m., compared to JD351m. in 1991. The budget was part of a seven-year "revival and restructuring" plan, which won the approval of the IMF and therefore enabled Jordan to reschedule its foreign debt yet again and obtain new loans. The 1992–98 program aimed to steadily reduce the budget deficit (from about 18% of the GDP in 1991 to 5% at the end of the period) and to gradually increase the GDP, starting with 3% growth in 1992 (as opposed to the 1% growth achieved in 1991).[50] According to Minister of Finance Basil Jardana, the program was a comprehensive economic framework that guaranteed continuous and healthy growth. This would provide increased employment opportunities, tackle internal and external imbalances, ease the problem of poverty, reduce the burden of foreign debt and increase confidence in the national economy.[51]

Whether these ambitious objectives would ever be reached remained to be seen. In the meantime, however, the government and society had to contend with some harsh realities and cutbacks in public spending. The government was forced to reduce the military budget. King Husayn spoke of the need to reorganize the armed forces with an emphasis on "quality and balance rather than quantity."[52] In practice, this meant the reduction of manpower from some 130,000 to 107,000; the intended abolition of conscription;[53] and serious cutbacks in arms procurement, such as the cancellation in August of a FFr5bn. order for 12 French *Mirage* 2000 fighter aircraft.[54]

The structural imbalance between resources and population took a heavy toll on Jordanian society. Unemployment soared with the influx of the returnees and layoffs from Jordanian businesses suffering from the impact of the Gulf War.[55] According to official figures, unemployment rose from 18% to 24%.[56] According to unofficial sources it was even higher, possibly as much as 35%.[57] Unemployment was especially high among professionals. Addressing this problem, the government invested in the expansion of domestic health facilities, creating over a thousand jobs for doctors and other health workers. Jordan also signed agreements with Libya to employ 2,000 Jordanian engineers, doctors and teachers, and similar agreements were sought with Yemen.[58]

According to a study conducted by the Ministry of Social Development, at least 20,000 families in Jordan lived in abject poverty and might have faced starvation had it not been for government-sponsored and voluntary charities. The study confirmed an earlier survey conducted by Unicef, which found that about a third of Jordan's population lived below the poverty line[59] (cf. *MECS* 1990, p. 475).

The demographic, and consequent socioeconomic, pressures were not expected to decline in the near future. Economic growth still lagged behind population growth, which continued to be about 3.5% a year. Jordan's population (including the returnees) of 3.5m. was expected to rise to about 4.8m. by the turn of the century and to close to 5.7m. by the year 2005.[60] According to Jawad al-'Anani, former minister of industry, trade and tourism and a leading economic analyst, Jordan's entire future depended on the Middle East peace process. If peace were not achieved, he argued, Jordan could be threatened by an Israeli-inspired "forced migration of Palestinians" from the occupied territories,[61] which Jordan would not be able to sustain either economically or politically.

GOVERNMENT, PARLIAMENT AND POLITICAL LIBERALIZATION
Cabinet Rotation and Parliamentary Opposition
Jordan had three different cabinets during the course of the year, a rare occurrence in its more recent history and an indication of considerable domestic political disquiet. On 1 January, at the height of the Gulf crisis, Prime Minister Mudar Badran reshuffled the cabinet he had formed in December 1989 (see *MECS* 1989, pp. 465–66, 473) for the second time. The first reshuffle, in June 1990, was minor and of marginal political significance. The second, however, was a major political event. In what appeared to be an effort to conciliate and co-opt the Islamic trend, in the midst of a regional crisis that had created considerable domestic uneasiness, Badran included five representatives of the Muslim Brethren and three independent Islamists in the new cabinet. The cabinet also included deputies of the loyalist National Bloc and other loyalist deputies, more or less reflecting their relative weight in the Chamber of Deputies, but excluded any representative of the leftist Democratic Bloc (see Table 1). The inclusion of the Muslim Brethren as a representative political organization and the relatively large number of Islamists in the cabinet, constituted a new departure in Jordanian politics. The formation of the new cabinet had come after weeks of intensive negotiations between Badran and the Muslim Brethren. In contrast with negotiations that had failed prior to the formation of Badran's cabinet in December 1989, he now agreed to the Brethren's demand to take over the Ministry of Education, although he denied their request to have the Ministry of Higher Education as well.[62] Another change in the cabinet was the replacement of Marwan al-Qasim by Tahir al-Masri as foreign minister, reportedly as a result of Qasim's reluctant endorsement of Jordan's policy in the Gulf crisis[63] due to his growing concern about Jordan's isolation.[64]

With the end of the Gulf crisis, the soothing of the domestic scene and the start of intensive preparations for the revival of the Arab-Israeli peace process (see below), the Muslim Brethren in the cabinet became more of a liability than an asset. Staunchly opposed to any form of negotiation or settlement with Israel, their influential presence in the cabinet became an impediment. On 17 June, Mudar Badran resigned to pave the way for a new cabinet to be headed by the Palestinian Tahir al-Masri. Masri was not Jordan's first premier of Palestinian origin, but his predecessors had usually been appointed for brief transitional terms at times of crisis between the regime and the country's Palestinian population. Masri's appointment was clearly related to the renewed peace process, and was intended, at least in part, to pave the way for solid coordination in a joint delegation between Jordan and the Palestinians in the anticipated negotiations. On the domestic front, Masri's cabinet, founded on a secular coalition, was designed to further the liberalization process and to counter the influence of the Islamist groups inside and outside parliament.

Masri's cabinet, formed on 19 June, was therefore of markedly different composition from the one formed by Badran. The Islamist influence was replaced by that of the secular left, in a departure no less unusual than Badran's previous inclusion of the Muslim Brethren. In some respects the composition of Masri's cabinet was even more radical. He included leftists associated with the JANDA coalition not simply on an individual basis but as representatives of JANDA itself which incorporated parties such as the Ba'th and the Communists, as well as the Popular Democratic Unionist Party (PDUP) and the Popular Democratic Party (PDP). These last two were essentially extensions of the more radical factions of the PLO — the Popular Front for the Liberation of Palestine and the Democratic Front for the Liberation of Palestine respectively — which in the not too distant past had been the mortal enemies of the regime. Though the PDUP and the PDP themselves were not represented in the cabinet, they took part in selecting the five JANDA members who did join.[65] The inclusion of five members of JANDA, as well as Salim al-Zu'bi, an ultranationalist left-winger, was "tantamount to a coup d'état in contemporary Jordanian politics," according to one Jordanian observer.[66] Though Masri also included four members of his own parliamentary National Bloc ('Abdallah al-Nusur, 'Abd al-Karim al-Kabariti, Sa'd Surur and Samir Qa'war) and three independent Islamists, the cabinet had an obvious left-wing tilt, further reinforced by the total exclusion of the Muslim Brethren. Masri had briefly negotiated with the Brethren before he formed the cabinet but there had been no basis for agreement, as he refused to offer them the education portfolio, which was and remained their essential precondition for joining.[67] Actually, he may have had no genuine intention of including them. Indeed, there was hardly a place for the Brethren in a government committed to the ME peace process, which they opposed in principle. The spiritual leader of the Brethren, 'Abd al-Rahman Khalifa, had stated publicly that his movement would not join a government that intended to enter negotiations with Israel.[68] While Ahmad Qutaysh al-Azayida, spokesman for the Brethren's parliamentary bloc, the Islamic Movement Bloc, denied that the education portfolio had anything to do with their decision, he confirmed that the Brethren's ministers in Badran's cabinet had committed themselves to withdraw from the government if it took any practical steps toward "negotiations [with] the Jews."[69]

The Masri Cabinet Crisis

The composition and timing of the new cabinet, obviously the work of the king and Masri in tandem, was not coincidental, coming shortly after the end of the Gulf War and the approval of the National Charter (see *MECS* 1990, pp. 468–69, and below) and on the eve of the anticipated ME peace negotiations. The composition of the new cabinet contained a message to the Islamists, who appeared to be losing ground once the Gulf War ended, and in light of the rather poor performance of their ministers in Badran's cabinet (see also below). That message was that the regime would not allow them to dominate the liberalization process, as was the case, for example, in Algeria. An unnamed "seasoned observer" said that the king had drawn a red line for the fundamentalist and ultraconservative groups, i.e., that Jordan would not tolerate the Algerian kind of violent experience, and whoever ignored the rules would do so "at his own peril."[70]

Masri faced considerable opposition from the very outset. Though he enjoyed the unquestioned support of the king, the wide range of potential opponents of the government could sidestep confrontation with the monarchy itself by directing all their criticism at Masri and his cabinet, with the king remaining above the fray. Some of Masri's opponents were, in fact, staunch loyalists from the East Bank establishment who disapproved of the Palestinian prime minister and his leftist cabinet. Together with the Islamists they proved to be a force too formidable for Masri's government. After just five months at the helm, Masri had no choice but to resign.

Though not required by the constitution to do so, Masri had decided at the start of his term of office to obtain an immediate vote of confidence by the Chamber of Deputies. The regular session of the chamber had ended in mid-March. In response to the request of the speaker of the chamber, the king called for an extraordinary session of the chamber to begin in early July. Masri chose to obtain the confidence of the chamber immediately rather than wait until the next regular session, scheduled for October. To improve Masri's chances of success, on 7 July Husayn endorsed a recommendation by the government to repeal martial law, which had been in force since 1967.[71] The king and Masri thus fulfilled a prior commitment made by Mudar Badran shortly after the November 1989 elections as part of the general liberalization policy (see *MECS* 1989, p. 466).

In his policy statement to the chamber on 11 July, Masri reiterated the commitment of his government to democracy, political pluralism and the rule of law. He noted its determination to pass new legislation to formally legalize the activity of political parties as well as a more liberal press and publications law and urged the chamber to enact the necessary legislation to allow for martial law to "be fully repealed."[72] Masri's policy statement was generally cautious, focusing on uncontroversial domestic social and economic issues. He made only brief mention of Jordan's long-standing support for a solution to the Palestinian question based on international legitimacy, a subject to which he devoted as much time as he did to public works, housing and a host of other domestic matters.[73] As some deputies pointed out, this was merely a tactic to avoid any confrontation over specifics.[74] In the debate that followed the most severe criticism of the government came, as expected, from the Islamic Movement Bloc. The Muslim Brethren had already announced prior to the debate that they intended to vote no confidence in the government.[75] The spokesman for the Islamic Movement Bloc, Ahmad Qutaysh al-Azayida, accused the government of two major failings: its intention to seek a peaceful solution of the Palestinian problem and its desire to curtail "the Islamic awakening in Jordan."[76] The Brethren were joined in their criticism by the independent Islamist deputy, 'Ali al-Faqir, a former minister of Awqaf and Islamic affairs in one of Mudar Badran's previous cabinets (see *MECS* 1989, p. 473), who attacked Masri's government for ignoring the Shari'a (Islamic law) and for attempting to uproot Islam in Jordan.[77] Another independent Islamist deputy, the outspoken Layth Shubaylat, delivered a somewhat milder but no less substantive critique of the government and the regime, calling for constitutional reform to alter the balance of power between the chamber and the monarchy in favor of the former.[78]

Masri's reply to his Islamist critics was rather apologetic. He assured them of his government's respect for civil liberties and his intention to abolish all remnants of martial law; of the government's commitment to abide by Jordan's traditional policies on the Palestinian question, as defined by King Husayn, from which it would not and could not deviate; of its firm commitment to the constitution and the national charter (cf. below), according to which Islam was the religion of the state and the Shari'a the main source (*al-masdar al-ra'isi*) of legislation; and of its intention to uphold the Islamic heritage as a central component of the state's education system.[79] However, this had no effect on the Islamic Movement Bloc and other Islamist deputies who had decided in advance to vote against the government.

Not all the blocs formed in the Chamber of Deputies after the November 1989 elections were entirely stable. The most consistent were the ideological Islamic Movement Bloc and the left-wing Democratic Bloc, whereas the composition of the nonideological loyalist blocs tended to be far more flexible (see *MECS* 1990, p. 463). On the eve of the vote of confidence in Masri's cabinet the distribution of seats between the blocs was as follows:

Islamic Movement Bloc — 23; National Bloc — 17; Constitutional Bloc — 13; Democratic Bloc — 9; Independent Islamic Bloc — 6; Liberal Bloc — 5; unaffiliated independents — 7.[80]

Masri had the assured support of just over 30 deputies from his own pro-establishment National Bloc and the left-wing Democratic Bloc together with a few liberal and independent deputies, of a total of 80 deputies in the chamber. It was the Constitutional Bloc, a newly formed 13-member group, that held the power, in combination with the Islamist opposition, to unseat him and thereby deal a severe blow to the prestige of the king who had just appointed him. This conservative bloc, formed in mid-July,[81] was headed by the veteran East Bank establishment politician Dhuqan al-Hindawi, a former chief of the royal court, deputy prime minister and minister of education. Though initially dismissed as a group of disgruntled "pretending ministers" (*mustawzirin*),[82] who had been excluded from Masri's cabinet, the bloc had certain substantive grievances against Masri's Palestinian-led and left-leaning cabinet.

Several Muslim Brethren deputies unsuccessfully pressured independent deputies to sign a letter of opposition to the cabinet in the hope of mustering a majority of 41 before the confidence session and thus force Masri to resign.[83] This possibility of a no-confidence vote raised the specter of palace intervention and the exercise by the king of his constitutional prerogative to dissolve parliament at any time. In the one precedent in which a government in Jordan had been forced to resign by a no-confidence vote (Samir al-Rifa'i's government in April 1963) the king had indeed dissolved the Chamber of Deputies. Shortly before the confidence vote King Husayn met with members of the Constitutional Bloc and apparently persuaded them to vote for the government. Members of the bloc denied that they had been swayed by pressure from the king,[84] though Hindawi subsequently explained that his bloc had decided not to join the opposition in order to prevent the dissolution of the chamber. Israel, he contended, would have exploited the situation to "create chaos in Jordan." His bloc, therefore, decided to support the government for the sake of national unity rather than out of support for the cabinet, which did not meet with their approval.[85] On 18 July, with the support of most of the Constitutional Bloc, Masri won the confidence vote by a handsome margin of 47 to 31.[86]

His troubles, however, were far from over. At the end of July, the Chamber of Deputies issued a statement rejecting the US-inspired peace conference that was to include direct negotiations with Israel. The government, nevertheless, accepted the US initiative and agreed to attend the conference. Masri was assailed in the Chamber of Deputies by both the Islamist right and the pan-Arab left for having ignored the will of the elected representatives of the people. With opposition mounting in the chamber, Masri's own coalition began to fall apart. Two of his leftist ministers, Muhammad Faris al-Tarawina and Salim al-Zu'bi, threatened to resign if and when negotiations with Israel actually took place.[87]

Radicals from the left and the right expressed their opposition to the peace process at a time when the Arabs, in the aftermath of the Gulf War, were in disarray and relatively weak. This, they argued, would allow Israel to dictate the rules. Masri tried to convince parliament that in the prevailing circumstances Jordan had little choice if it wished to avoid regional isolation, economic pressure from the West and a possible further influx of Palestinians from the West Bank if a solution to their problem was not found.[88] He met with little success, however, and parliamentary support for his government steadily eroded.

The extraordinary session of parliament came to a close in early September. At the end of September King Husayn issued a royal decree postponing the next ordinary session from 1 October to 1 December, presumably to allow for the convening of the controversial peace conference while parliament was in recess and to give Masri some extra time to get his house in order. Left-wing opposition to Masri grew as the date for the scheduled peace conference approached. At the end of September, two left-wing deputies affiliated with the Democratic Bloc, Fakhri Qa'war and Mansur Murad, appealed to Masri to resign,[89] while Ministers Faris Tarawina and Salim al-Zu'bi decided to resign from the cabinet. They were soon joined by three other members of the cabinet — Ra'if Najm, an independent Islamist, and 'Abdallah al-Nusur, of Masri's own parliamentary faction, who resigned for reasons related to the peace process, and Muhammad al-Hammuri, who resigned apparently for private reasons. While Najm opposed the peace process in principle,[90] Nusur, the foreign minister, appeared to have been intimidated by the parliamentary opposition to the peace process, resigning after Masri turned down his request to appoint a minister of state for foreign affairs to lead Jordan's delegation to the peace conference in his stead.[91]

On 3 October, Masri reshuffled his cabinet and replaced the five ministers who had resigned. The most noteworthy new appointees were Kamil Abu Jabir, a well-known political science professor, who was named foreign minister, and Mahmud al-Sharif, editor in chief of the daily *al-Dustur* since its establishment in 1967, who became minister of information[92] (see Table 1).

Inexplicably, representatives of the Constitutional Bloc were excluded yet again from the cabinet. Masri thereby sealed the fate of his government, for the Constitutional Bloc, which had by then grown to 18, finally turned against him,[93] joining the Muslim Brethren and the faction of the Democratic Bloc that had crossed over to the opposition, in order to unseat him.

On 7 October, 49 members of the Chamber of Deputies (the Islamic Movement Bloc, the Constitutional Bloc, four members of the Democratic Bloc and four independents)[94] signed a petition calling for the resignation of Masri's cabinet. On 24 October, yet another of Masri's left-wing ministers, 'Abd al-Karim al-Dughmi, resigned.[95] Efforts by Masri to reshuffle his cabinet once again and arrive at an understanding with the opposition were fruitless. The Muslim Brethren flatly rejected the notion of participating in any cabinet that supported the peace process.[96] JANDA similarly refused to rejoin a reshuffled cabinet, and no understanding was reached with the Constitutional Bloc either.[97] By mid-November it was clear that Masri would not be able to secure a majority in the chamber by the time it convened for its next ordinary session at the beginning of December.

On 16 November, Masri tendered his resignation to the king. Simultaneously challenging the Muslim Brethren along with a significant segment of the East Bank establishment, while supported by a fickle and insecure leftist coalition, proved to have been a gross miscalculation, especially against the background of the controversial peace process with Israel.

Ibn Shakir Restores the Traditional Balance

Masri was succeeded as prime minister by the chief of the royal court, Sharif Zayd Ibn Shakir,[98] who formed a new cabinet on 21 November. Ibn Shakir, a sharif (claiming descent from the Prophet), a member of the Hashemite family, cousin and close confidant of the king, a former commander in chief of the armed forces and prime minister after the April 1989 riots (see *MECS* 1989, p. 456), was, as opposed to Masri, an archrepresentative of the very core of the East Bank elite. Ibn Shakir also offered, in the words of a Jordanian source, a "forcefulness of leadership" and determination that Masri, a more "refined politician," seemed to have lacked.[99]

Ibn Shakir's cabinet was aptly described as right of center,[100] in contrast to Masri's cabinet which was decidedly leftist. Like most of his predecessors since the 1989 elections, Ibn Shakir included ten deputies in his cabinet. However, as opposed to Badran's last cabinet, which included significant Muslim Brethren representation, and Masri's, in which leftist groups were prominent, Ibn Shakir's cabinet rested on the strictly loyalist Constitutional Bloc (which Masri had excluded) and the National Bloc. Each had four representatives in the cabinet, with the leader of the Constitutional Bloc, Dhuqan al-Hindawi, who had been instrumental in Masri's downfall, appointed deputy prime minister and minister of education. An independent Islamic deputy ('Atif al-Butush) and an independent loyalist deputy (Jamal Haditha al-Khuraysha) were also included in the cabinet.[101] Both the Muslim Brethren and the leftist Democratic Bloc were excluded. Ibn Shakir's cabinet had fewer Palestinians than previous cabinets, presumably to placate the East Bank loyalist establishment and to stress the separate Jordanian and Palestinian identities in light of the start of the new process of Arab-Israeli peace negotiations.

In his letter of appointment to Ibn Shakir on 21 November, and in his speech from the throne at the opening session of parliament on 1 December, King Husayn reiterated the regime's support for the Arab-Israeli peace negotiations as well as for the continuation of the liberalization process in Jordan. He also noted, however, that democracy entailed "responsible behavior" and criticized the "unstable relationship" between the legislative and executive authorities, suggesting that this relationship ought to be one of cooperation in the service of the homeland and not of "contention, disturbance and obstruction."[102]

In their replies to the speech from the throne both the Chamber of Deputies and the Senate adopted a conciliatory tone, expressing unswerving loyalty to the monarchy.[103] Ibn Shakir requested that the Chamber of Deputies regard the speech from the throne as the government policy statement, thus placing potential opponents in the uncomfortable position of appearing to oppose the monarchy itself if they chose to vote against the government in the vote of confidence. On 16 December, Ibn Shakir won the confidence of the chamber with a comfortable majority of 46 to 27. He was opposed by almost the entire Islamic Movement Bloc, several independent Islamists and six members of the leftist Democratic Bloc. Their major complaints against government policy were its continued involvement in the peace process and its agreement with the IMF on the management of Jordan's economic problems.[104] Obtaining a similar majority in the vote on the budget, Ibn Shakir's government appeared to be firmly in control.

The speakership of the chamber remained in the hands of the Muslim Brethren, with the outgoing speaker, 'Abd al-Latif 'Arabiyyat, reelected on 1 December without opposition. He was, however, initially opposed by 'Abd al-Majid al-Shurayda, who had the support of the loyalist National and Constitutional Blocs as well as a number of independents. Shurayda had a fair chance of defeating 'Arabiyyat, but he withdrew from the race as part of a deal between Ibn Shakir and the Islamist opposition whereby the Muslim Brethren could retain the speakership unchallenged, provided they toned down their opposition to the government.[105] Following the vote of confidence, in which the Islamic Movement Bloc had not supported the government, 'Arabiyyat found it necessary to clarify that those who had voted against the government were no less loyal to the homeland and the throne than those who had supported it.[106] It was obvious that neither the government nor the Islamist opposition had any interest in an outright confrontation.

CONTENDING WITH THE ISLAMIC CHALLENGE

In the aftermath of Iraq's defeat in the Gulf War, the Islamic movement in Jordan appeared, at least temporarily, to have lost some of its popular appeal. The message disseminated during the crisis by the Muslim Brethren, that Iraq would be delivered by divine providence, undermined their credibility in the popular mind. As one Jordanian observer put it, "mythology had lost to technology," and the Islamic groups paid a price politically. Mosque attendance dropped considerably in the immediate aftermath of the war and this was said to have reflected a mood of disappointment with the religious message.[107]

Joining Mudar Badran's cabinet in January also proved to have been a costly exercise for the Muslim Brethren. The movement itself was divided on the question of participation in government. Some opposed the notion of participation in any government that was not Islamic in character, as this accorded legitimacy to regimes that were *jahili* (ignorant of Islamic teachings, and therefore religiously and politically illegitimate). The evolutionary Islamization of the state would not be achieved by joining a non-Islamic government, it was argued. Others noted that the participation of deputies in the cabinet undermined their role as parliamentarians whose duty was to effectively control or oppose the government. Abandoning this role, they asserted, damaged their credibility with the public that had elected them to perform this function in the first place.[108] Indeed, the Brethren did face a certain measure of public criticism for having abandoned their previously single-minded quest for political and economic reform.[109]

Muslim Brethren participation in the government also gave rise to controversy when decisions made by some of their representatives in the Badran government were deemed offensive or reactionary by segments of the secular public. Yusuf al-'Azm, the minister for social development, issued instructions to segregate male and female employees in his ministry. Minister of Education 'Abdallah al-'Akayila dismissed a number of senior employees who were said to have been liberal-minded. He also banned male sports teachers from instructing female students in state schools and subsequently disallowed male parents from watching their daughters perform in shorts in school sports.[110] Public controversy on these issues subsided with the exclusion of the Muslim Brethren from the Masri government.

Still disappointment on the part of the Brethren's own following and condemnation by secularists did not result in a lasting decline of Islamic popularity. The secular public lacked both the political organization and any alternative ideology to effectively contend with the Islamic trend, which had made such remarkable inroads in the wake of the apparent universal failure of left-wing ideologies. The Brethren remained the most influential and best organized of all political groups in the country.

An indication of the continued Islamist popular appeal could be found in elections held in the professional unions. Although in March a JANDA representative won election as President of the Bar Association, in late May and early June, Islamists won leading posts in elections in the medical and pharmacists' associations, traditional bastions of the left wing.[111]

There remained but one effective bulwark against Islamic radicalism — the state and the power wielded by the regime. King Husayn issued repeated public statements against politicized religion and religious extremism, which he portrayed as a threat to the democratic system. Democracy, he noted in his speech from the throne at the opening of parliament in December, did not "confer on any single group a claim of monopoly over wisdom or truth. Nor [did] it provide a license to justify encroachment on the rights and liberties of the vast majority of the people."[112] The principal role of preachers in the mosques was to educate the people and promote the values of virtue and tolerance rather than the dissemination of "fanaticism, bigotry and narrowmindedness."[113] Arab ethics, the king contended, could not tolerate "abuse, slander and intellectual and psychological terrorism." Encouraging youth to believe that suicide was martyrdom was an "unforgivable crime" that had "nothing to do with religion, responsibility or morality."[114]

In its attitude toward the various Islamic groups, the regime tended to distinguish between parliamentary and extraparliamentary organizations, showing considerably more tolerance for the former. The Muslim Brethren and even the two members of the independent Dar al-Qur'an group, Layth Shubaylat and Ya'qub Qirsh, who were especially outspoken in their condemnation of the government and the regime, were allowed considerable though not entirely uninhibited, freedom. The Muslim Brethren, for their part, consistently reaffirmed that their opposition to any particular government's policies should not be construed as opposition to the regime itself.[115] Moreover, they pledged, however serious their opposition to any particular government in Jordan, they would not resort to violence,[116] and they condemned in no uncertain terms any use of violence against the regime by other Islamic groups.

During the Gulf crisis and thereafter, the Muslim Brethren held political rallies condemning the US and Israel, which did not conflict with government policy at the time. Their political rallies, however, assumed a different character after the Brethren left the government and began to censure its policy in regard to the ME peace process. The peace process, based on UN Security Council Resolutions 242 and 338, was totally rejected by the Muslim Brethren and other Islamic groups. According to the Brethren, "recognition for the Jews on any inch [shibr] of Palestine was impermissible on [grounds of] faith and religion."[117] These resolutions, they argued, stipulated that the Arabs had to "give up 77 per cent of the land of Palestine and to negotiate with the Jews on the remaining 23 per cent." Moreover, the negotiations were expected to produce an agreement on autonomy for the West Bank and Gaza, which "meant that all of the land of Palestine belonged to the Jews and the people of the [West] Bank and the [Gaza] Strip would rule themselves while they lived on land that was not theirs."[118]

In October, the Masri government banned a rally organized by the Muslim Brethren that was timed to coincide with King Husayn's address to the nation on Jordan's support for the peace process — timing that was perceived by the regime as an intolerable provocation. The government also banned the distribution of the Brethren's weekly al-Ribat (printed in Greece) because of its opposition to the peace talks. An unnamed cabinet minister warned the Islamic movement against entering a "losing battle" with the government, asserting that there would be "no wavering on the government's commitment to safeguarding the rule of law and protecting higher national interests." Democracy, according to another government source, did "not mean anarchy."[119] Ultimately, the Brethren shied away from a head-on confrontation with the regime, deciding not to defy the ban and expressing their determination to pursue their campaign against the peace process by democratic and "constitutional means."[120] The Brethren declared a day of mourning when the Madrid peace conference convened on 30 October but reiterated their opposition to violence, noting that "any conflict with the government will only be harmful to the cause."[121] A student strike and rally called by the Islamic movements at the University of Jordan was effectively thwarted by student supporters of the regime and its peace policy.[122] This came only two days after a rally in Amman organized by Islamist and left-wing opponents of the peace process had degenerated into a violent confrontation between supporters and opponents of the government. Layth Shubaylat, one of the most outspoken Islamist deputies, hinted at government involvement in the rally, charging that the whole "charade was organized to sabotage the rally. It [was] a conspiracy."[123]

Despite the obvious tension between the regime and the Muslim Brethren, the government continued to demonstrate calculated tolerance and restraint toward the

Brethren. This was not the case, however, in regard to other, more radical, groups such as the extraparliamentary Islamic Liberation Party or the Islamic Jihad groups. Members of these organizations were occasionally arrested and were generally harassed by the regime more intensively than the Muslim Brethren. In March, police raided the offices of the Liberation Party and the Islamic Jihad-Bayt al-Maqdis group led by Shaykh As'ad Bayyud al-Tamimi. Two of Tamimi's sons were arrested in connection with an incident of infiltration into Israel, and members of the Liberation Party were detained for the illegal distribution of leaflets.[124] Shortly thereafter, the spokesman for another wing of the Islamic Jihad, the al-Aqsa Battalions, was also arrested.[125]

In July, following a series of acts of sabotage in different parts of the country, about 150 suspects who were said to belong to the Army of Muhammad (*jaysh Muhammad*) were arrested and accused by the authorities of having acquired arms to carry out "criminal acts to destabilize Jordan."[126] They were said to have formed the group initially in support of the Afghan mujahidin, but turned it into an antigovernment organization in 1988.[127] The spiritual leader of the Muslim Brethren, Shaykh 'Abd al-Rahman Khalifa, refused to comment on the arrests but condemned all acts directed against state security. Both the Islamic Liberation Party and the Islamic Jihad-Bayt al-Maqdis faction denied any connection with the group.[128] Layth Shubaylat, however, accused the government of cracking down on this particular group (with which he said he had no association) as part of a campaign against all Islamist groups. All were targeted, he contended, because of their opposition to the peace process.[129]

In early September most of the suspects were released as an "expression of leniency and forgiveness," while 20 were brought to trial (two in absentia) before a special State Security Court in October. Almost all the accused were of Palestinian origin. More surprising, however, was the fact that the initial group of suspects included 17 Circassians. Though they were released, the very fact that they were apparently involved in some way with the group was an indication that Islamic radicalism had also penetrated this traditionally loyal ethnic minority.[130]

In November, the court sentenced eight of the accused to death and four to life imprisonment. Following an appeal by Amnesty International, all the death sentences (except for the two sentenced in absentia) were commuted to life imprisonment and the other prison sentences were reduced.[131] This was seen as a gesture toward the Islamic trend in general and to the Muslim Brethren in particular. Together with the deal made with the Brethren over the speakership in the Chamber of Deputies (see above), it indicated that the government had redrawn the dividing line between the permissible and the intolerable. Opposition was acceptable provided that it did not challenge the regime directly nor resort to violence. According to an "official source," the Islamic movement was being suppressed throughout most of the Arab world, with Jordan the "last remaining lung through which it [could] breathe." He was therefore convinced that it would not act in a manner that would jeopardize the movement's status.[132]

THE NATIONAL CHARTER AND THE LIMITS OF DEMOCRATIZATION
In April 1990, King Husayn had appointed a royal commission to draw up a national charter that would govern political life in the country and lay the quasi-constitutional

foundations for the democratization process (see *MECS* 1990, pp. 468–69). The commission was chaired by Ahmad 'Ubaydat, a former prime minister and director of General Intelligence, and represented a broad spectrum of political trends, from the secular left to the religious right (excluding the Islamic Liberation Party, which refused to recognize the legitimacy of any secular government and called for the reinstatement of the caliphate).[133] Although the commission had completed the draft of the charter and presented it to the king in December 1990, the Gulf War crisis caused a delay, and it was only in June 1991 that the charter was brought before a specially convened national conference for ratification.

On 9 June, the 2,000 delegates to the national conference, selected by the regime to represent all political trends and walks of life in Jordan, ratified the charter by acclaim.[134] Ratification by a conference of selected delegates was a way both of circumventing parliament and of avoiding any serious debate over the charter, for although the charter had been drawn up by a fairly representative 60-member commission, it still had opponents who regarded it as restrictive.

The charter began with a rather sketchy historical survey of Jordan from pre-Islamic times to the present, laying special emphasis on Jordan's contribution to the Arab cause, particularly in Palestine. This was followed by eight sections dealing with the objectives of the charter; the law-abiding state and political pluralism; national security; the economy; society; culture, education, science and information (*i'lam*); Jordanian-Palestinian relations; and Jordan's relations with the Arab and Islamic worlds and with the international community.

The charter reaffirmed the nature of the Hashemite Kingdom as a parliamentary, constitutional, hereditary monarchy. In defining the role of religion in the state the charter went beyond the constitution, which had only stipulated that Islam was the religion of the state, and added that the Islamic Shari'a was the main source (*al-masdar al-ra'isi*) of legislation. This and other concessions to the Islamic trend, however, were interwoven with other principles that emphasized Jordan's cultural pluralism. Jordan's Arab Islamic cultural identity, the charter noted, was exposed to the universal civilization of mankind, and Jordanian society was characterized by tolerance that rejected political or social violence, religious coercion, fanaticism, confessionalism or regionalism. Multiparty political and ideological pluralism was the foundation for Jordanian democracy and the establishment of a balanced civil society.

Jordan, the charter confirmed, was a law-abiding state (*dawlat al-qanun*), subservient to the rule of law, deriving its legitimacy and its authority from the will of the people. A highly detailed section of the charter paid special attention to the question of political parties. The people had the right to form and join political parties provided these were legal and did not engage in anticonstitutional activity. Political parties, however, could not have organizational or financial ties with any foreign party and could not receive instructions or guidance from any other state or outside party. These restrictions were obviously inspired by the regime's fear of a repetition of its experience in the mid-1950s when pro-Nasserite and other pan-Arab parties almost overthrew the monarchy. The charter did, however, concede that parties that expressed support for Palestine, Arab unity or Islamic solidarity would be considered to be serving Jordanian patriotic interests. This addition was intended to constrain the regime from banning pro-Palestinian, pan-Arab and Islamic parties simply because of their views rather than their actions. Furthermore, parties were not permitted to engage in any activity in the military or security forces nor to form any military or paramilitary forces of their own, a reminder that the regime had no intention of allowing the democratization process to degenerate into the kind of anarchy that plagued Jordan in the period between 1968 and 1970, culminating in the "Black September" civil war.[135]

The charter represented a political compromise and the definition of a broad common ground between the regime and the political community and between the left and the right. All political factions represented in the drafting commission had accepted the unchallenged legitimacy of the monarchy in exchange for a pluralist political system that was to operate within certain confines to reduce the probability of domestic destabilization. Political pluralism allowing participation from the far left to the far right was also intended to stem the tide of Islamist prominence in Jordanian politics. A leading critic of the charter, the independent Islamist deputy Layth Shubaylat, argued, however, that it left far too much authority in the hands of the king. The king, he explained, was constitutionally the head of both the executive and the legislative branches and had the right to dissolve parliament. The charter, he complained, left all these prerogatives intact.[136]

Shortly after the ratification of the charter, in July, King Husayn issued a royal decree repealing martial law "to complete the structure of democracy," although the actual implementation of the repeal remained incomplete until such time as all the necessary legislation to "eliminate all remnants of martial law"[137] had been passed. In December, the Chamber of Deputies ratified the repeal of the 1953 anti-communist law[138] which had already been abolished by the cabinet in early 1990 (see *MECS* 1990, p. 459). More controversial, however, was the new Defense Law which empowered the government to declare a state of emergency and impose emergency laws. In December 1990, despite government objections, the Chamber of Deputies had passed the law with an amendment empowering parliament to revoke a state of emergency declared by the regime (see *MECS* 1990, p. 463). The senate (an appointed body, and therefore loyal) then referred the amendment to the Higher Council for the Interpretation of the Constitution, which rejected the amendment, and the Defense Law was passed by the Chamber of Deputies in its original form without the amendment in December 1991. Consequently, the king could still declare a state of emergency upon the recommendation of the cabinet,[139] unfettered by parliamentary limitations.

Key legislation related to the liberalization process included a new law permitting the activity of political parties, a new press and publications law and a new election law. These laws, in various stages of preparation, had not been passed by the end of 1991.[140]

The regime's management of the liberalization process was cautious. The prerogatives of the monarchy remained outside the bounds of political reform and the process of liberalization was both gradual and limited. King Husayn and Crown Prince Hasan had a distinctly instrumental approach to democratization. Democratization was a means to "guarantee the stability of the Hashemite Kingdom"[141] at a time of prolonged domestic crisis. Political pluralism and openness were the "safety valve in Jordan"[142] and democracy was "one of the most important pillars of national security."[143] Intended to secure stability, the democratic process could hardly be allowed to develop into a threat to the status quo. Husayn noted that in the democratic experience "the homeland must come first." In veiled references to the Islamic trend, he warned that democracy should not be construed as an "umbrella providing cover for intellectual terrorism or a means whereby a larger sector dominates a smaller sector." This, he contended, would mean "chaos...and the ruin of society and the country."[144] No one would be allowed "to exploit democracy to liquidate it."[145] Political pluralism, in Husayn's view, was not only a safety valve but also an instrument to hold the Islamist movement in check.

The Islamist movement, well represented in the Chamber of Deputies, frequently attacked government policy on domestic and foreign affairs. This was particularly the case in reference to Jordan's participation in the ME peace process and the mounting parliamentary opposition to Tahir al-Masri's government (see above). Husayn, disturbed by what he perceived as undesirable parliamentary encroachment on the powers of the monarchy and the government, reiterated the importance of the separation of powers pursuant to the constitution. It was his own task, he said, as head of all three branches of power, to make sure that there was no encroachment of one branch on another.[146] In a speech before the Chamber of Deputies, Prime Minister Zayd Ibn Shakir elaborated on this theme, explaining that the three branches of power should not dominate one another nor assume each others' responsibilities. Their role, he noted, was to cooperate in harmony rather than engage in rivalry.[147] In its reply to Husayn's speech from the throne, the chamber, taking heed of the regime's admonition, reassured the king of its unquestioned loyalty, its intention to shoulder its "primary responsibility — legislation," and its resolve to "cooperate with the executive authority."[148]

King Husayn at times deliberately undermined the legitimacy of the parliament as a genuine representative of the popular will. In his letter of appreciation to outgoing Premier Badran, the king noted his understanding of the prime minister's difficulty in dealing with an inexperienced chamber elected by only some 40% of the people.[149] Significantly, the national charter was not ratified by parliament but rather by a specially summoned national conference (see above). The king similarly circumvented parliament by choosing to deliver his major speech to the nation on Jordan's role in the peace process to a national congress summoned for that purpose in October.

The uneasy relationship between the regime and parliament was exacerbated by charges of government infringement of the democratic process leveled by members of the Chamber of Deputies. A report made in August by the chamber's committee for public freedoms (dominated by Islamist deputies) accused the government and the security services of repeated violations of the law and of human rights abuses in their treatment of detainees. The report referred specifically to the *jaysh Muhammad* suspects (see above) who, the report contended, had been tortured and generally mistreated by agents of General Intelligence (*mukhabarat*). The report also accused the government of failing to comply fully with commitments it had undertaken in the past to release political prisoners, to reinstate officials dismissed for political reasons, and to cease withholding or confiscating passports from citizens suspected of political opposition to the regime[150] (see *MECS* 1990, p. 459).

Although the Ministry of Interior categorically denied the charges of torture made by the committee,[151] matters did not rest there. In mid-September, Layth Shubaylat, who was a member of the public freedoms committee, summoned a press conference to deliver a scathing attack against both the government for dismissing the report, and the local media for largely ignoring it. Shubaylat concluded that the democratization process in Jordan was no more than "a superficial democratic facade" that had changed nothing of substance in the style of government. As for the media, he charged, they were merely pliant collaborators of the regime who were unable to do anything but align themselves with the executive authority.[152] Jordan's three dailies, *al-Ra'y, Sawt al-Sha'b* and *al-Dustur,* were still owned in large part by the government, which did indeed produce a rather compliant local press. Newspapers printed elsewhere, whether Jordanian (as *al-Ribat,* printed in Athens) or foreign, were frequently prevented from being distributed in Jordan.[153]

Both the left and the Islamists complained that the domestic security services still played a far too central role in Jordanian politics.[154] King Husayn, however, asserted that democracy did not provide a license to "question the importance of the role of the national security bodies entrusted with protecting the interests of the homeland and the people. Such conduct can only be construed as undermining the security of the homeland and the people."[155]

FOREIGN AFFAIRS

JORDAN'S POSITION IN THE GULF WAR

Jordan's Uneasy Neutrality

From the outset of the Gulf crisis in the summer of 1990, Jordan had sought a peacefully negotiated solution to the conflict (see *MECS* 1990, pp. 487–89), pursuing efforts in this regard unabatedly until the actual outbreak of hostilities on 17 January 1991. In early January, King Husayn visited London, Bonn, Luxembourg and Rome for talks with European leaders in a desperate last-minute effort to avert war. Feeling increasingly exposed and vulnerable as the 15 January deadline approached, Husayn consistently warned of the devastating political, economic and ecological consequences of war that would be "very cruel to all of us."[156]

Jordan claimed to have adopted a neutral position in the crisis, declining to recognize Iraq's annexation of Kuwait, while simultaneously refusing to join the anti-Iraqi coalition. However, as the crisis deteriorated into war Jordan's public posture became increasingly supportive of Iraq.

Premier Mudar Badran and the Jordanian press accused the US and its Western allies of succumbing to Israeli pressure to launch a war against Iraq instead of seeking a solution based on the implementation of UN resolutions not only regarding the Kuwaiti problem but regarding the Palestinian question as well.[157]

On 17 January, when Allied air strikes on Iraq began, Jordan denounced the "brutal onslaught against an Arab and Muslim people" and warned the members of the anti-Iraqi coalition that they would "bear the responsibility before God, people and history for attempting to crush a military, scientific and human Arab power."[158] In a news conference on 19 January, King Husayn contended that the crisis and the outbreak of war could have been avoided had his initial diplomatic efforts not been scuttled by the Arab League. Husayn repeated the argument he had made in the early phases of the crisis that he had obtained an Iraqi commitment to withdraw from Kuwait shortly after the invasion, provided that Iraq would not be condemned by the Arab League (cf. *MECS* 1990, pp. 487–88). Arab condemnation, he argued, followed by the series of anti-Iraqi UN Security Council resolutions and the deployment of foreign forces had prevented a peaceful solution. He appealed to all the parties to the conflict to halt military action, if only for a limited period, and to resume dialogue and diplomacy in order to solve the Kuwaiti problem. Then, he noted, there also ought to be movement to solve the Palestinian question and to tackle other regional issues as well, such as the removal of weapons of mass destruction and the assurance of "freedom, democracy, human rights, peace and security for all." It was "naive to think that there was absolutely no connection" between the Kuwaiti and Palestinian problems, he said.[159]

Jordanian appeals for a cease-fire, however, were ignored. Popular frustration in the country mounted with the continued bombardment of Iraq and the loss of Jordanian lives in the bombing raids on the Baghdad-Amman highway (see above). Jordanian fears of being drawn into the conflict were exacerbated by the possibility of Israeli retaliation against Iraq for the *Scud* attacks on its cities. On 6 February, a desperate and frustrated King Husayn launched an unprecedented verbal assault on the US. In a speech to the nation, designed both to represent and define the manifestations of anti-US sentiment, Husayn denounced the "all-out ferocious war [that had been] imposed on fraternal Iraq." Abstaining from any mention of Iraqi responsibility for the crisis, Husayn accused the US and its allies of seeking "to destroy Iraq and to rearrange the regional state of affairs." The Allied objectives, he argued, were more damaging to the Arabs than the infamous Sykes-Picot agreement between the British and the French in 1916 to divide the Arab ME into spheres of influence. The Arab "homeland, nation, aspirations and resources" were to be placed "under direct foreign hegemony," he charged. In "a call from a Hashemite Arab," Husayn appealed to "all honorable Arab and Muslim leaders to do all in their power to save the Iraqi people and the Arabs in general from the plots against them" and to put an end to the war. By "destroying Iraq" the war had "exceeded the limits set by the UN resolutions." The US and its allies, therefore ought to accept a cease-fire and embark upon "responsible dialogue" to achieve peace.[160]

Husayn's speech, and particularly the fact that he had made no reference to the Iraqi invasion of Kuwait, was met with sharp criticism by the US Administration. Husayn then backtracked somewhat, clarifying that his failure to mention the invasion of Kuwait was only because he had already done so "zillions of times before." Jordan, he noted, had always been opposed to the occupation of territory by war and that applied to the case of Kuwait as well.[161] Crown Prince Hasan, too, restated Jordan's position of neutrality in the war, noting that Kuwaiti sovereignty was "beyond dispute," although he added that Iraqi territorial claims on some Kuwaiti territory were "not without foundation." Hasan also justified Iraqi accusations against Kuwait for overproduction of oil in violation of Opec quotas. The "catastrophic effects of such overproduction" on Iraq's economy were not only incontestable, but there was even "some evidence" to suggest that this was part of "an international attempt to weaken Iraq." If true, he noted, this could have been construed as "economic aggression" against Iraq.[162]

In late February, as it became increasingly apparent that Iraq faced certain defeat, King Husayn welcomed the Soviet initiative for an Iraqi withdrawal in order to bring an end to the war (see chapter on the Soviet Union and the ME), despite the fact that it included no linkage to the Palestinian question. This was seen by diplomatic sources in Amman as an expression of Husayn's frustration with Iraq's intransigence and a certain distancing of Jordan's position from that of Iraq.[163] Jordan took advantage of the Soviet initiative to launch yet another diplomatic effort to end the war, and Foreign Minister Tahir al-Masri was hastily dispatched to Europe for talks with EC ministers. But Jordan's "peace offensive" was stopped short by the ground attack against Iraq which the US and its coalition partners launched on 24 February.[164] Jordan could do no more than denounce the ground assault and continue to call for a cease-fire and for support for the Soviet initiative. Undoubtedly relieved, Jordan welcomed the cease-fire on 28 February.[165] The worst of all scenarios had been avoided — Jordan was not drawn into the war, and in that respect emerged from the crisis unscathed.

Military Preparedness

King Husayn's rather frantic diplomatic efforts to prevent or at least shorten the war were motivated first and foremost by the fear of devastation if Jordan were to become the "killing ground" in a confrontation between its two powerful neighbors — Iraq and Israel (see *MECS* 1990, p. 488). Preparing for the worst, Jordan took a series of military and political precautions. On the eve of the outbreak of war, King Husayn was said to have "reopened channels of communication" with Israel. His objective was to remove any possible misunderstandings that might have played into the hands of those on the Israeli side who sought an opportunity to take military action to transform Jordan into a Palestinian state.[166] Israel's Prime Minister Yitzhak Shamir and Chief of Staff Lt. Gen. Dan Shomron issued public assurances to Jordan that it had nothing to fear from Israel. All the same, by early January, Jordan had deployed most of its forces on the mountains overlooking the Jordan Valley and the frontier with Israel in what Israeli military sources described as a defensive posture.[167]

King Husayn and other senior spokesmen repeatedly contended that Jordan would do its utmost to prevent the violation of its sovereignty in the air or on land by any of the potential protagonists.[168] Jordan would "not be a corridor for anyone," according to Crown Prince Hasan.[169] Mudar Badran announced in early January that Jordan had assurances of Syrian assistance if it were attacked by Israel. Jordan, he noted, would also ask for Iraqi and Egyptian help in such an eventuality.[170] Jordan, however, had agreed with Iraq that Iraqi forces would not enter Jordan unless by official Jordanian request and only for the purpose of defending Jordan against attack from Israel. Badran, at the same time, also noted that Jordan had received assurances that it would not be attacked by Israel in the event of Israeli retaliation against Iraq.[171]

With the approach of the 15 January deadline, King Husayn declared that Jordan would defend itself at all costs and Jordan's armed forces were placed on the highest alert since the beginning of the crisis.[172] Following the outbreak of war, King Husayn and Crown Prince Hasan, in contrast to the popular mood of praise and jubilation, cautiously refrained from either condemning or condoning the Iraqi *Scud* missile attacks on Israeli cities. Keenly aware of Jordan's vulnerability and "geopolitically thankless position," they expressed their concern and alarm in public statements, but explained that Jordan had no capability of intercepting *Scud* missiles.[173] A major reason for Israel's failure to retaliate against Iraq for the *Scud* attacks was its disinclination to draw Jordan into the conflict. Husayn was subsequently reported to have said that he had been encouraged by Israel's restraint and by the fact that Israel had done nothing to exploit the situation to implement the "Jordan is Palestine" notion, which Jordan had feared so profoundly.[174]

The Issue of Sanctions Against Iraq

Jordan began to comply with the resolution imposing sanctions on Iraq only after a while (see *MECS* 1990, pp. 486–87), and persistent charges were leveled against Jordan, for violating the sanctions. At the close of the war, American troops in Iraq were said to have found proof that Jordan had supplied weapons to Iraq long after the imposition of sanctions. Jordan rejected the charges as "totally untrue," explaining that it had assisted Iraq in the procurement of arms only during the Iraqi-Iranian War.[175] In April, a press report claimed that Iraq had set up a purchasing operation in Jordan to buy armaments and advanced technologies from certain Asian countries. This was similarly denied by the Jordanians.[176] In both cases, US official sources said they had no evidence to substantiate the reports.[177]

The London *Observer* published figures of Iraqi-Jordanian trade for the year between April 1990–April 1991 citing a figure of $665m. as proof of sanctions violations on an enormous scale. The Jordanians contended that those figures included some $400m.–$500m. worth of Iraqi oil that Jordan continued to receive with the tacit approval of the UN Sanctions Committee, and that legal Jordanian exports of food, medicine and other humanitarian supplies, and transport fees from 'Aqaba, accounted for the rest. The US State Department pointed out that the trade figures included the period before the Iraqi invasion of Kuwait when sanctions did not apply and affirmed that the announced policy of the Government of Jordan was to adhere to the UN sanctions against Iraq.[178]

Several hundred trucks transported supplies daily from Jordan to Iraq.[179] However, according to the US Administration, most of the 3,000 tons of goods that were transported daily were permitted under the sanctions guidelines, and the "seepage" of illicit imports (said to include various types of machinery, spare parts and communications equipment) was relatively insignificant.[180]

JORDAN, THE PALESTINIANS AND THE PEACE PROCESS
Jordan's Sense of Urgency

Immediately after the cease-fire that brought an end to the Gulf War, King Husayn appealed to the international community to deal with the Palestinian question with the same "enthusiasm and commitment" that it had dealt with the issue of Kuwait.[181] Jordan, therefore, welcomed the statement made by US President Bush in early March in which he called for a solution to the Arab-Israeli conflict on the basis of Security Council Resolutions 242 and 338, the exchange of territory for peace, the recognition of the legitimate political rights of the Palestinian people, and the recognition of Israel and its need for security[182] (see chapter on the US and the ME).

According to the Jordanian analysis, the regional balance of power had, on the whole, shifted in Israel's favor. While Israel was less important to US strategic interests as a result of the end of the Cold War, the Arabs had lost far more ground. They were no longer capable of effectively wielding the oil weapon, they had lost militarily in the Gulf War, they were disunited, and they had lost the traditional support of the Soviet Union as a major world power.[183] Israel was "undoubtedly very strong now," while the Arab world was "still in turmoil." Even if this balance were to change in the future, without a peaceful settlement the region could only drift into further conflict from which neither the Arabs nor Israel would gain.[184] According to Husayn, the status quo was not static. It changed constantly, and consistently for the worse. Since the US, "the only country that decides matters," now appeared to be firmly committed to deal effectively with the Arab-Israeli conflict, there "was no room for procrastination."[185] There was "a window of opportunity that may never come again," the king contended, and there was "simply no other alternative" to a peaceful settlement "except disaster."[186]

Demographic concerns intensified Jordan's sense of urgency. The exodus of Jordanians of Palestinian origin from the Gulf placed a heavy economic, social and potentially dangerous political burden on the kingdom (see above). The Jordanians also expressed the fear that massive Soviet Jewish immigration to Israel would result in expanded Jewish settlement of the occupied territories. This would not only create a situation in which there would be no territory to talk about,[187] but could also eventually result, the Jordanians argued, in the massive expulsion of Palestinians by Israel to Jordan.[188] The Jordanians therefore hoped that the resolution of the Palestinian-Israeli conflict would defuse the "potentially explosive demographic situation" that confronted Jordan.[189] Husayn, therefore, encouraged the Arabs to abandon "taboos and clichés" in the hope that possible future face-to-face contacts with Israeli leaders would dispel many of the fears that both sides had of each other.[190]

The Acceleration of the Peace Process

Jordan's sense of urgency and its appraisal of the regional balance of power inspired a revision of long-standing Jordanian positions on the Arab-Israeli peace process. As the US embarked upon an intensive effort to revive the peace process in the immediate aftermath of the Gulf War, Jordan proved to be particularly accommodating to its suggestions for progress.

In the past Jordan had consistently called for the convening of an international conference under the auspices of the UN and the five permanent members of the Security Council, to which all regional parties to the conflict, including the PLO, would be invited (see *MECS* 1987, pp. 496–97; 1988, p. 596; and 1990, pp. 479–80). In the initial phase after the Gulf War, Jordan continued to support the concept of an active role by the UN and the convening of an international conference as "the ideal conduit" for resolving the Palestinian question. Jordan also reaffirmed that Palestinian representation at such a forum could come only "through the PLO," which remained the sole legitimate representative of the Palestinian people.[191] Jordan therefore criticized the US approach to the process, which, along with Israel, opposed an international conference and PLO involvement. According to Foreign Minister Tahir al-Masri, this was an example of the double standard applied by the US and its allies, who in the case of Iraq, by contrast, had insisted on working through the UN Security Council.[192]

US-Jordanian relations remained strained during the first few weeks after the end of the Gulf War. US Secretary of State James Baker did not visit Jordan in March, on the first of his frequent visits to the region to revive the ME peace process. However, at the conclusion of his second visit to the region, in early April, he met with Foreign Minister Masri in Geneva, followed shortly thereafter by a meeting with Husayn in

'Aqaba. By this juncture it was clear that Jordan had abandoned its adamant support for the old international conference formula and that it was willing to accept what was, in effect, a US-inspired process for direct negotiations with Israel. The American idea, accepted by Jordan, was for a conference that would promote "dual track" negotiations between Israel and the neighboring Arab states and between Israel and the Palestinians. This was made more acceptable by the redefinition of the parley as a "peace conference" rather than a "regional conference" as the US had initially suggested.[193] The new phraseology paved the way for Soviet and European involvement in the process, albeit marginal and of little practical consequence. More significantly, it was at least symbolically closer to Jordanian and Arab conceptions of such a conference. Though Jordan continued to publicly call for a major Soviet and European role in the process,[194] this could not alter the reality that the process was clearly dominated by the US. Tahir al-Masri admitted that Jordan was "trying to cooperate with American ideas," even though they did "not correspond to what [Jordan] would like." The Arabs, he noted, were not in a position "to dictate conditions" and Jordan had little choice but to accept a "semi-international" conference in which there would be no direct role for the PLO.[195] In July, King Husayn declared that Jordan was ready to attend the peace conference as suggested by the US.[196]

Jordan similarly demonstrated flexibility on the issue of Palestinian representation at the conference. In this matter, however, as opposed to the nature of the peace conference, Jordan's support for US ideas more closely reflected Jordan's own interest in playing a central role in determining the political fate of the Palestinians.

The declining international stature of the PLO in the wake of the Gulf crisis prompted Jordan to take a more active role in pursuit of a partnership with the Palestinians in the negotiating process. Jordanian spokesmen repeatedly emphasized the pivotal importance of Jordanian involvement in the peace process because of its unique association with the Palestinian question in the past and the potential effect of any Palestinian settlement on Jordan in the future.[197]

Jordan had territorial claims of its own that did not relate to the West Bank — a small area at the confluence of the Jordan and Yarmuk rivers and a larger area along the border with Israel in the Wadi 'Araba region. Both areas combined did not exceed 400 sq. km.[198] However, it was none other than the Jordanians themselves who explained that their main interest in the peace conference was not in this relatively insignificant territorial dispute.[199] As King Husayn noted, Jordan's entire political history and its social and economic situation had been shaped by the consequences of the Palestinian question. Jordan's geographic proximity and demographic reality rendered the separation of Jordan's fate from that of Palestine impossible.[200] Jewish settlement in the occupied territories impinged directly on Jordanian national security and the social, economic and environmental interests of Jordan's population. The constant drain on its water supplies threatened the population on both sides of the river.[201] Jordan, therefore, intended to follow developments in the Palestinian negotiation closely, in close coordination with the Palestinians.[202] It was also deeply concerned with regional issues that were to be addressed in the multilateral negotiations, such as the scarcity of regional water resources, regional security and refugees (many of whom were Jordanian citizens or residents).[203] All these had immediate ramifications for Jordan's security and economic well-being.

As opposed to its position after the disengagement from the West Bank (see *MECS* 1988, p. 596), Jordan now took a far more favorable attitude toward the idea of joint Jordanian-Palestinian representation at the peace conference. This was not only an effort to overcome Israeli objections to direct PLO involvement, but also served Jordan's own desire for an influential role in Palestinian matters. The Jordanians, however, made it abundantly clear from the outset that they were not a substitute for the Palestinians.[204] They were willing to consider a joint Jordanian-Palestinian delegation, if the PLO asked for it.[205] If such a delegation were to be formed, Jordan stipulated, the Palestinian representatives would have to be chosen by the Palestinians themselves. Furthermore, it would be the Palestinian component that would deal with the Palestinian-Israeli track and the Jordanian component would address Jordan's interests.[206]

While Jordanian spokesmen frequently reaffirmed their recognition of the PLO as the sole legitimate representative of the Palestinians,[207] old Jordanian ambiguities on this subject were also revived and efforts were made by Jordan to pressure the PLO to cooperate with it. Husayn and Hasan, in an effort to legitimize Palestinian representation from the West Bank and Gaza (rather than through the PLO itself), condemned those who hid behind "a facade of patriotism" when the true patriots were not those "pontificating from outside" but those who remained steadfast on their land in the occupied territories.[208] Husayn consequently urged the PLO not to raise problems that might delay the convening of the peace conference and to accept the Israeli demand that the Palestinian representation exclude the PLO. It was, after all, the people in the occupied territories who had the "right for us to be concerned about their conditions," while the PLO was "by definition a temporary body" whose purpose was to recover Palestinian rights.[209]

Shortly before the convening of the peace conference in Madrid in October, Jordan and the PLO came to an agreement on the formation of the joint Jordanian-Palestinian delegation. The delegation was composed of 28 members, 14 from each side, headed by Jordanian Foreign Minister Kamil Abu Jabir. All the members of the Palestinian component of the delegation came from the West Bank and Gaza, as required by Israel, and none were formal representatives of the PLO, nor was there any representation from East Jerusalem or the Palestinian diaspora. To compensate for these limitations Jordan included a number of Jordanian citizens of Palestinian origin, who were either born in Jerusalem or represented the Palestinian diaspora, in its part of the delegation.[210]

Jordan at the Madrid Conference

Before the opening of the peace conference in Madrid, Jordan and the Palestinians, like the other participants in the process, were given assurances by the US on the nature of the process as understood by the Americans. The assurances to Jordan and the Palestinians reaffirmed long-standing US positions on territorial issues, i.e., that the US interpreted Resolution 242 as requiring territorial concessions by Israel in exchange for peace on all fronts and that the US did not recognize Israel's annexation of East Jerusalem.[211]

When the peace conference convened in Madrid at the end of October, Jordan's Foreign Minister Abu Jabir declared that Jordan's vision was "not merely an end to hostility" but a "comprehensive, just and permanent peace." Jordan took heart from the fact that "this whole enterprise is firmly anchored in international legitimacy" as embodied in Resolutions 242 and 338 "providing for the exchange of land for peace." More land did not mean more security, and Israel's occupation, the building of settlements and the expropriation of land were all illegal. Jordan, therefore, demanded total withdrawal of Israeli forces from occupied Jordanian, Palestinian, Syrian and Lebanese lands. Arab sovereignty had to be restored to Arab Jerusalem, illegal settlements had to be removed and not augmented, and the issue of the Palestinian refugees of 1948 and those displaced after 1967 had to be solved in accordance with the relevant UN resolutions. The Palestinian people had to be allowed to exercise their right to self-determination in their ancestral homeland. Jordan, Abu Jabir emphasized, was not Palestine. For peace to be permanent and comprehensive, he said, the regional issues of arms control and security, settlements, the distribution of water resources, the fate of the refugees, and the establishment of economic balance between the peoples of the area all had to be satisfactorily addressed.[212]

Jordan laid particular emphasis on the need for Israel to withdraw from all the occupied territories. Israel could either have land or peace, but it could not have both, according to Abu Jabir.[213] Jordan was only prepared to consider what King Husayn defined as "minor reciprocal adjustments," reached by agreement between the parties.[214] Jordan similarly attached special importance to the refugee issue, which had direct implications for Jordan's own increasing demographic and socioeconomic pressures. According to the Palestinian Affairs Department of the Jordanian Foreign Ministry, 960,212 Palestinian refugees (and/or their descendants) from the 1948 and 1967 wars were registered with the UN as resident in Jordan. Of these, 430,083 were from the 1948 war and the rest were displaced in 1967 and thereafter. Regarding those displaced in 1967, Jordan intended to insist that they return to the West Bank to join the new political entity expected to emerge at the end of the peace talks. As for the 1948 refugees, Jordan called for the application of UN Resolution 194 of December 1948, which offered the refugees a choice between repatriation and compensation. Most Jordanian officials did not actually expect these refugees to be allowed by Israel to return, but they did expect to win "hefty compensation" for the refugees and for Jordan for past and future public services rendered by the state to this population.[215]

Issues of procedure rather than substance dominated the talks in the first rounds of negotiations. A first round of bilateral talks was held in Madrid in early November, immediately after the opening session of the conference, during which the joint Jordanian-Palestinian delegation met with their Israeli counterparts to discuss the venue and other procedural matters related to the bilateral negotiations.[216] The second round of bilateral negotiations convened in Washington in December. Matters were soon bogged down over a disagreement between Israel and the Jordanian-Palestinian delegation on procedural issues. Israel refused to negotiate with the Jordanians and the Palestinians separately, regarding the joint delegation as essentially one unit. The Palestinians and the Jordanians, however, regarded the joint delegation as two delegations under one "umbrella" and expected Israel to negotiate with each component separately. Before the convening of the Madrid conference, Jordan and the PLO had agreed that the Jordanian and Palestinian tracks would be negotiated separately, with one or more coordinating members from the Jordanian side participating in the Palestinian-Israeli negotiation and the same for the Palestinians in the Jordanian-Israeli negotiation.[217] According to the head of the Jordanian delegation, 'Abd al-Salam al-Majali, the Palestinians and the Jordanians were two independent parties, and Jordan could not negotiate on the Palestinians' behalf.[218] After days of haggling in the US State Department, the Israelis, Palestinians and Jordanians left Washington with no final agreement on the matter (see also chapter on the ME peace process).

Reduced Tension Along the Border with Israel

Since 1989, there had been a marked deterioration in the security situation along Jordan's border with Israel (see *MECS* 1990, pp. 478–79). During the first half of 1991, there were numerous incidents of armed infiltration from Jordanian territory or of shots fired across the border from Jordan. However, with the end of the Gulf War, the revival of the peace process and action taken by the Jordanian authorities to reinforce the border area and to suppress Islamic militants (see above), incidents along the border with Israel in the second half of the year had ceased almost completely.[219]

Perceptions of Future Relations with the Palestinians

Jordan's national charter devoted a special section to Jordanian-Palestinian relations stressing the distinguished (*mutamayyiza*) historical and cultural ties between the Jordanian and Palestinian peoples. These ties, the charter noted, ought to be reinforced in order to confront the "Zionist, racist imperialist danger" that threatened both Jordan and Palestine. The Jordanian and Palestinian national identities, though separate, complemented one another and did not, and ought not conflict with each other. As for the future, a unitary relationship (*'alaqa wahdawiyya*) between the two states of Jordan and Palestine was essential.[220]

This was actually an endorsement of the idea of confederation that Jordan and the PLO had agreed upon in 1985 (see *MECS* 1984–85, pp. 514, 523), and, with the revival of the peace process, King Husayn made it clearer than he had for a number of years that this was the solution he envisaged for the future.[221]

Jordan's agreement to enter into a joint delegation with the Palestinians was, according to Husayn, only the latest example of Jordan's "pan-Arab and principled commitment to the Palestinian Arab people."[222] The Palestinians and the Jordanians, he said, were "one people bound by strong links. Both adhere to their identity, but they represent two wings of one body. They practically represent individuals of one family." Reverting to formulations he had used in the early 1970s, Husayn argued that, all along, Jordan had endeavored to retrieve the occupied territories not for itself but for "their kinfolk and owners" who would then exercise their right to self-determination.[223] He recalled that in the early 1970s he had offered the Palestinians a choice between reunification, independence or federation "or some form of confederation, in today's language."[224] Husayn seemed to be deliberately blurring the distinction between a federation and a confederation. Indeed, he also said that if a confederal government were to be agreed upon between Jordanians and Palestinians, it would probably be along the lines of the federation plan he had suggested in the early 1970s: two local governments, two local parliaments, and at the higher level a central government representing both peoples.[225]

INTER-ARAB AND INTERNATIONAL REALIGNMENT

Jordan's support for Iraq during the Gulf crisis had upset its traditional alliance with Saudi Arabia, Kuwait and other Gulf states as well as with its Western benefactors, particularly the US.

In the immediate aftermath of the Gulf War, Jordan appealed to its Arab brothers to forgive and forget and to begin a new chapter of fraternity and cooperation. Reminding the Gulf states of the ever-increasing gap between the poor and wealthy states in the region, Jordan urged them to opt for cooperation based on mutual respect and the common benefit of all.[226] Jordan, according to Crown Prince Hasan, was "not asking for handouts" but rather "for a contract between manpower exporting countries and the hinterland of oil."[227] Jordan, therefore, appealed especially to Saudi Arabia and the other states of the Gulf Cooperation Council to restore Arab solidarity, resume "quiet dialogue" and reestablish normal relations.[228]

In August, on the first anniversary of the Iraqi invasion of Kuwait, Jordan issued a "white paper" explaining its policies during the crisis. The "white paper" recalled Jordan's opposition to the Iraqi invasion and annexation of Kuwait and its efforts to achieve a peaceful Arab solution to the crisis so as to prevent foreign intervention. As proof of Jordan's neutral stand in the crisis, the "white paper" included the text of a letter from King Husayn to Saddam Husayn from 22 September 1990, in which he had explained that neither Jordan nor any of the other Arab states could accept the acquisition of territory by force, especially if it meant "the elimination of a state which is a member of the Arab League and the UN."[229]

Jordan's professions of neutrality in the crisis, however, did not improve its inter-Arab relations. Though the Jordanians had in fact opposed the conquest of Kuwait by Iraq (see *MECS* 1990, p. 484), they failed to convince their Arab critics that a peaceful Arab solution was ever really possible and that Iraq could have indeed been made to withdraw from Kuwait without the use of foreign force. Jordan's position was therefore seen by the Saudis, the Kuwaitis and even the Egyptians to some extent as a form of collusion or at least collaboration with Iraq. The Egyptians were specifically aggravated by the Jordanian suggestion that had it not been for Egypt's leading role in Arab censure of Iraq, a peaceful settlement could have been attained[230] (cf. *MECS* 1990, pp. 487–88). Condemnation in the Jordanian press of Egypt's "treasonous role" during the crisis[231] made matters worse, and the Egyptian and Jordanian media launched a campaign of mutual recrimination in early September.[232] Shortly thereafter, however, Jordan's foreign minister, 'Abdallah al-Nusur, was received by President Mubarak and, with the upcoming Arab-Israeli peace conference, Jordanian-Egyptian relations appeared to be taking a turn for the better.[233]

The Saudi and Kuwaiti sense of betrayal was far more difficult to overcome. Husayn, however, rejected the Saudi demand for an apology for Jordan's stance during the war. Prime Minister Zayd Ibn Shakir declared that Jordan would "not bow to any...pressure....Hunger with honor [was preferable to] being overfed with humiliation."[234] Trade between Jordan and Saudi Arabia and Kuwait declined dramatically during the year,[235] and economic aid was cut off. In October, Saudi Arabia opened its border to Jordanian vehicles, thus allowing for the resumption of transit trade which had been suspended since late 1990.[236] Though Jordan expressed the hope that this was "the beginning of real détente,"[237] it proved not to be so. Saudi Arabia did not return its ambassador, who had been recalled in October 1990, and

Husayn's expression of "nothing but love for [Jordan's] relatives and brothers in the Kingdom of Saudi Arabia"[238] changed nothing in the frosty relationship.

Relations with Kuwait were not only strained but were further exacerbated by the trials of Palestinians (many of whom were Jordanian nationals) in Kuwait after the war, as well as by human rights violations. The Kuwaitis rejected a formal Jordanian request to reopen its embassy in the emirate[239] and showed no signs of seeking any form of reconciliation.

Jordan's relative isolation was eased somewhat by the continuation of normal relations with Syria and a brief improvement in relations with Iran. Asad and Husayn continued to meet frequently, and though they had their differences during the Gulf War and on the peace process, this did not impinge upon their political or economic ties. Jordan and Iran resumed diplomatic relations in January after a break of ten years.[240] Both states claimed neutrality during the Gulf War, while trade relations improved with the conclusion of a $66m. deal for the sale of Jordanian phosphate to Iran.[241] The relationship with Iran, however, did not appear to have a very solid foundation. As soon as the Gulf War ended, the Jordanian press repeatedly attacked Iran for conspiring against Iraq and for threatening its integrity in collusion with the US and its Western and Arab allies in the Gulf.[242] Jordan was clearly apprehensive about Iranian regional influence at Iraq's expense.

Jordan had few illusions about pan-Arab or pan-Islamic solidarity as a determinant of foreign policy. In a speech in May, King Husayn championed Jordan's *raison d'état* without hardly any qualification:

> Every state has its own national interests that stop at the boundary of the national interests of others....Each Arab state has its own national priorities. Under the umbrella of the Arab League and until the outbreak of the Gulf crisis, national priorities had been adapted or made in harmony with the supreme pan-Arab interests. In the 'fifties and 'sixties, pan-Arab interests prevailed to the extent that they governed to a great degree the national priorities of every country. The Gulf crisis, however, gave birth to a new phenomenon in which pan-Arab interests were sacrificed in favor of national priorities.[243]

Jordan's position in the Gulf War, its refusal to join the anti-Iraqi coalition, and its harsh censure of the US and its allies created a rift in the traditionally friendly relations between the US and Jordan. However, neither Jordan nor the US were interested in a rupture. Relations reached a low point in early February after Husayn's speech in which he condemned the US and its allies for seeking to destroy Iraq (see above), but the rift was not lasting. The US Administration, though critical of Husayn for having abandoned his neutrality and for having "moved...way over"[244] into the Iraqi camp, showed considerable understanding for Jordanian regional and domestic constraints. It attached much importance to Jordan's geopolitical role as a stabilizing buffer in the region,[245] and saw "no attractive alternative"[246] to the Hashemite regime. The US also recognized the importance of a key role for Jordan in the peace process that was envisaged for the region in the aftermath of the Gulf War. Jordan, for its part, fully realized that in the unipolar post-Cold War era, a firm relationship with the US was probably more important than ever. When Secretary of State Baker met with Husayn for the first time after the war in April in 'Aqaba, the meeting was immediately hailed by the Jordanians as the beginning of a new chapter in US-Jordanian relations after both sides had agreed to "let bygones be bygones."[247]

Congress, however, was less tolerant than the Administration toward Husayn's behavior in the Gulf War. After Husayn's February speech, Baker called for a review of US aid to Jordan, but a month later, in March, when the Gulf War was over, the Bush Administration strongly opposed legislation in Congress to cut aid to Jordan. Spokesmen for the Administration explained that Jordan was "critical politically [and] geographically" and its stability was important to the region as a whole, to Israel and to the advancement of the peace process.[248]

A cut in aid ($55m.) was eventually approved by the president after a compromise was reached whereby the aid would be restored if the Administration could certify to Congress that Jordan had taken steps to advance the peace process. The cut, however, did not affect $246m. of aid to Jordan that was already in the pipeline in the form of pending contracts,[249] and once Jordan expressed its willingness to join the peace negotiations the suspended aid was restored. By the end of the year, US-Jordanian relations were back to normal. Though Congress remained critical of Jordanian violations of the sanctions against Iraq, the Administration chose to turn a blind eye, dismissing the violations as negligible[250] (see above).

While Jordan did not expect the declining Soviet Union to play a major role in the region, it expressed the hope, nevertheless, that the USSR would become involved in the peace process. In particular, Jordan hoped for Soviet pressure on Israel through the halting of Jewish emigration.[251] The decline of the Soviet Union as a great power was widely seen in Jordan as disadvantageous to the Arab cause. The abortive coup against Gorbachev in August was initially welcomed by the Jordanian press and leftist political circles as the possible beginning of a new era in which the USSR would be restored to its former status as a world power and undercut the US monopoly on the ME peace process.[252] The king and the government, however, prudently abstained from any comment on the matter.[253]

At the end of December, Jordan officially recognized the Russian Federation as well as the independence of the other states that joined the federation in forming the Commonwealth of Independent States.[254]

TABLE 1: JORDANIAN CABINETS 1991

Portfolio	1 January	19 June	3 October (Reshuffle)	21 November
Prime Minister and Defense	Mudar Badran	Tahir al-Masri (P)[c]		Zayd Ibn Shakir
Deputy Prime Minister	Salim Masa'ida	'Ali Suhaymat		'Ali Suhaymat
Interior	Salim Masa'ida	Jawdat al-Subul		Jawdat al-Subul
Foreign Affairs	Tahir al-Masri (P)[c]	'Abdallah Nusur[c]	Kamil Abu Jabir	Kamil Abu Jabir
Minister of State for Parliamentary Affairs	'Abd al-Baqi Jamu[a]	'Abd al-Salam Furayhat[a]		'Atif al-Butush[a]
Minister of State for Prime Ministry Affairs	Hikmat al-Sakit	Muhammad Faris al-Tarawina[e]	Qasim 'Ubaydat	Ibrahim 'Izz al-Din
Information	Ibrahim 'Izz al-Din	Khalid al-Karaki	Mahmud al-Sharif	Mahmud al-Sharif
Culture	Khalid al-Karaki	Khalid al-Karaki		Mahmud al-Samra (P)

Portfolio	1 January	19 June	3 October (Reshuffle)	21 November
Youth	Khalid al-Karaki	Salih Irshidat[f]		Salih Irshidat[f]
Tourism and Antiquities	Da'ud Khalaf (P)	'Abd al-Karim al-Kabariti[c]		Yanal Hikmat
Justice	Majid Khalifa[b]	Taysir Kan'an (P)		Yusuf al-Mubayyidin[c]
Education	'Abdallah al-'Akayila[b]	'Id Duhayyat		Dhuqan al-Hindawi[c**]
Higher Education	Sa'id al-Tall	Muhammad al-Hammuri	Khalid al-Karaki	'Awad Khulayfat
Transport and Communications	Jamal al-Sarayira[a]	'Ali Suhaymat		Jamal al-Sarayira[c***] 'Ali Suhaymat
Industry and Trade	Ziyad Fariz	'Ali Abu al-Raghib[f]		'Abdallah al-Nusur[c]
Energy and Mineral Resources	Thabit al-Tahir (P)	Thabit al-Tahir (P)		'Ali Abu al-Raghib[f]
Awqaf and Islamic Affairs	Ibrahim Zayd al-Kaylani[d]	Ra'if Najm (P)[g]	'Izz al-Din al-Khatib al-Tamimi(P)	'Izz al-Din al-Khatib al-Tamimi (P)
Health	'Adnan al-Jaljuli(P)[d]	Mamduh al-'Abbadi[f]		'Arif al-Batayina
Social Development	Yusuf al-'Azm[b]	'Awni al-Bashir[a]		Amin Mashaqba
Public Works and Housing	'Abd al-Ra'uf al-Rawabida[c]	Sa'd al-Surur[c]		Sa'd al-Surur[c]
Water and Irrigation	Sa'd al-Surur[c]	Samir Qa'war[c]		Samir Qa'war[c]
Agriculture	Muhammad al-'Alawina[a]	Subhi al-Qasim (P)		Fa'iz al-Khasawna
Supply	Ibrahim Ayyub	'Ali Abu al-Raghib[f]		Muhammad al-Saqqaf
Finance	Basil Jardana	Basil Jardana		Basil Jardana
Planning	Khalid Amin 'Abdallah (P)	Ziyad Fariz		Ziyad Fariz
Labor	'Abd al-Karim al-Dughmi[e]	'Abd al-Karim al-Dughmi[e*]		'Abd al-Karim al-Kabariti[c]
Rural, Municipal and Environmental Affairs	Muhammad 'Addub al-Zabn[c]	Salim al-Zu'bi[e]	'Abd al-Razzaq Tubayshat	'Abd al-Razzaq Tubayshat
Minister of State		Jamal Haditha al-Khuraysha[c]		Sultan al-'Adwan[c]
Minister of State				Jamal Haditha al-Khuraysha[c]

NOTES

(P) Of Palestinian origin.

a   Deputy — Independent Islamist.

b   Deputy — Muslim Brethren.

c   Deputy — Loyalist.

d   Muslim Brethren, but not a member of the Chamber of Deputies.

e   Deputy — Leftist.

f   Leftist (JANDA), but not a member of the Chamber of Deputies.

g   Islamist but not a member of the Chamber of Deputies.

*   Also Minister of State for Prime Ministry Affairs.

**   Also Deputy Prime Minister.

***   Transport and Communications were separated in Ibn Shakir's cabinet. Sarayira, previously an Independent Islamist, joined the Constitutional Bloc.

NOTES

For the place and frequency of publications cited here, and for the full name of the publication, news agency, radio station or monitoring service where an abbreviation is used, please see "List of Sources." Only in the case of more than one publication bearing the same name is the place of publication noted here.

1. *Sawt al-Sha'b* (Amman), 19 January 1991.
2. *Al-Ra'y* (Amman), 23 January 1991.
3. *Al-Ra'y* (Amman), 20, 29 January; *JT,* 22 January; *Filastin al-Muslima,* February; *al-Dustur* (Amman), 20 February; *al-Ra'y* (Amman), 22, 27 February; JNA, 25 February — DR, 27 February; *Sawt al-Sha'b* (Amman), 25 February 1991.
4. *Sawt al-Sha'b* (Amman), 18, 31 January 1991.
5. *Sawt al-Sha'b* (Amman), 27 January 1991.
6. Editorial in *al-Ra'y* (Amman), 6 February; Kamel S. Abu Jaber, "Latter Day Hordes," *JT,* 16 February 1991.
7. *FT,* 19 January, 9, 15 February; *JT,* 31 January-1 February, 9, 12, 13, 16 February; R. Monte Carlo, 14 February — DR, 14 February 1991.
8. *JT,* 7–8 February 1991.
9. R. Monte Carlo, 26 February — DR, 27 February 1991.
10. *JT,* 1 March 1991.
11. JNA, 4 March — DR, 5 March; R. Amman, 9 March — DR, 11 March 1991.
12. *JT,* 16 March 1991.
13. *JT,* 3, 6 February; *Sawt al-Sha'b* (Amman), 4 February 1991.
14. *JP,* 5 February; *JT,* 6 February 1991.
15. *FT,* 13 February; *JT,* 24 February 1991.
16. *JT,* 10–11 January; *FT,* 4 February 1991.
17. *JT,* 4 February; R. Amman, 4 February — DR, 5 February 1991.
18. *JT,* 9 March 1991.
19. *JT,* 14–15, 17, 18 March 1991.
20. *Al-Ra'y* (Amman), 2 June 1991.
21. *Al-Ra'y* (Amman), 9 June 1991.
22. *JT,* 27 January 1991.
23. *Al-Dustur* (Amman), 29 January 1991.
24. *Al-Ra'y* (Amman), 31 January; *JT,* 25 March 1991.
25. *JT,* 12–13 September 1991.
26. *JT,* 17 November 1991.
27. *Al-Ra'y* (Amman), 4, 7 May; *JT,* 25 August 1991.
28. *JT,* 28 July 1991.
29. *JT,* 26–27 September 1991.
30. *JT,* 10 September 1991.
31. *JT,* 25–26 April 1991.
32. *JT,* 14 April 1991.
33. *JT,* 19–20 September 1991.
34. *JT,* 22 September 1991.
35. *JT,* 25 August 1991.
36. *JT,* 12–13 September 1991.
37. *JT,* 10 September 1991.
38. *JT,* 25 August, 25 September 1991.
39. *JT,* 25 August 1991.
40. *JT,* 27 April 1991.
41. JNA, 14 February — DR, 15 February 1991.
42. *JT,* 4 December 1991.
43. *JT,* 29 January 1991.
44. *FT,* 15 February; *JT,* 16 February, 4 June 1991.
45. *FT,* 31 May 1991.
46. *JT,* 17 March; *al-Ra'y* (Amman), 12 December 1991.
47. *JT,* 22 September 1991.

48. *JT,* 6 January, 23 February 1991.
49. *JT,* 9-10 May; *al-Ra'y* (Amman), 12 December 1991.
50. *Al-Ra'y* (Amman), 12 December; *JT,* 12-13 December; *JT, FT,* 31 December 1991.
51. *JT,* 12-13 December 1991.
52. *Al-Dustur* (Amman), 20 June 1991.
53. Chief of Staff Fathi Abu Talib to *Defense News,* quoted in *Ha'aretz,* 26 November 1991.
54. *JT,* 28 August 1991.
55. *JT,* 4 March 1991.
56. *JT,* 6 March 1991.
57. *The Economist,* 6 April; *JT,* 14 October 1991.
58. *JT,* 28, 30 September, 21 October 1991.
59. *JT,* 23 October 1991.
60. *JT,* 11-12 April 1991.
61. *JT,* 1-2 August 1991.
62. *JT,* 2 January 1991.
63. *MEI,* 11 January 1991.
64. *NYT,* 6 January 1991.
65. *JT,* 20-21 June 1991.
66. Ibid.
67. R. Monte Carlo, 19 June — DR, 20 June; *al-Dustur* (Amman), 29 June 1991.
68. *JT,* 19 June 1991.
69. *Sawt al-Sha'b* (Amman), 30 June 1991.
70. *JT,* 20-21 June 1991.
71. *JT,* 8 July 1991.
72. R. Amman, 11 July — DR, 12 July 1991.
73. Ibid.
74. *JT,* 13 July 1991.
75. *JT,* 15 July 1991.
76. *JT,* 17 July 1991.
77. *JT,* 18-19 July 1991.
78. *JT,* 17 July 1991.
79. R. Amman, 18 July — DR, 19 July 1991.
80. *JT,* 16 July 1991.
81. *Sawt al-Sha'b* (Amman), 15 July 1991.
82. *JT,* 15, 16 July 1991.
83. *JT,* 15 July 1991.
84. *JT,* 17 July 1991.
85. *JT,* 27 August 1991.
86. R. Amman, 18 July — DR, 19 July 1991.
87. *JT,* 25-26 July 1991.
88. *JT,* 3 August 1991.
89. *JT,* 29 September 1991.
90. *JT,* 26-27 September 1991.
91. *JT,* 5 October 1991.
92. Ibid.
93. *JT,* 6 October 1991.
94. *Sawt al-Sha'b* (Amman), 7 October; AFP, 7 October — DR, 8 October; *JT,* 8 October 1991.
95. R. Amman, 24 October — DR, 25 October 1991.
96. *Al-Ra'y* (Amman), 7 November 1991.
97. *JT,* 12. 13 November 1991.
98. Ibn Shakir was replaced by 'Adnan Abu 'Awda, long-standing political adviser to the king, as chief of the royal court (*JT,* 23 November 1991).
99. *JT,* 17 November 1991.
100. *JT,* 23 November 1991.
101. Ibid.
102. R. Amman, 21 November — DR, 22 November; Jordan TV, 1 December — DR, 4 December 1991.

103. R. Amman, 7 December — DR, 13 December 1991.
104. *JT,* 16 December 1991.
105. *JT,* 2 December; *MEI,* 20 December 1991.
106. *Al-Dustur* (Amman), 24 December 1991.
107. *JT,* 4–5 April; *The Economist,* 13 April 1991.
108. *Al-Liwa,* 10 April, 12 June 1991.
109. *JT,* 4–5 April 1991.
110. *JT,* 2 April, 23–24 May; *al-Ra'y* (Amman), 9 May 1991.
111. *JT,* 17 March, 2, 8 June 1991.
112. *JT,* 4 June; Jordan TV, 1 December — DR, 4 December 1991.
113. Jordan TV, 1 December — DR, 4 December 1991.
114. King Husayn in his letter of designation to Tahir al-Masri, *al-Dustur* (Amman), 20 June 1991.
115. *JT,* 9 October 1991.
116. Spokesman of the Islamic Movement Bloc, Ahmad Qutaysh al-Azayida, to *Filastin al-Muslima,* November 1991.
117. *Filastin al-Muslima,* November 1991.
118. Statement by the General Guide of the Muslim Brethren published in *al-Ribat,* 13 June 1991.
119. *JT,* 10–11 October 1991.
120. *JT,* 12 October 1991.
121. *JT,* 31 October 1991.
122. Ibid.
123. *JT, al-Dustur* (Amman), 29 October 1991.
124. *JT,* 20 March 1991.
125. R. Monte Carlo, 27 March — DR, 27 March 1991.
126. R. Amman, 25 July — DR, 26 July; *JT,* 8 October 1991.
127. *JT,* 26 November 1991.
128. *JT,* 27 July 1991.
129. *JT,* 15 September 1991.
130. *Al-Dustur* (Amman), 31 July 1991.
131. R. Amman, 4 December — DR, 5 December; *JT,* 5–6, 7 December 1991.
132. *JT,* 10–11 October, 14 December 1991.
133. *Filastin al-Thawra,* 16 June 1991.
134. *JT,* 10 June 1991.
135. The full text of the charter appeared in *al-Dustur* (Amman), 30 December 1990.
136. *Filastin al-Thawra,* 16 June 1991.
137. Jordan TV, 7 July — DR, 8 July; *JT,* 17 December 1991.
138. *JT,* 23 December 1991.
139. Ibid.
140. *JT,* 17 December 1991.
141. Hasan to *Le Monde,* 23 January; similarly King Husayn in *JT,* 1 July 1991.
142. Hasan quoted on R. Amman, 1 October — DR, 3 October 1991.
143. Husayn in letter of designation to Tahir al-Masri, *al-Dustur* (Amman), 20 June 1991.
144. Husayn in speech to national charter conference, R. Amman, 9 June — DR, 10 June 1991.
145. Husayn in *al-Ra'y* (Amman), 8 December 1991.
146. R. Amman, 21 November — DR, 22 November; *al-Ra'y* (Amman), 8 December 1991.
147. R. Amman, 16 December — DR, 17 December 1991.
148. R. Amman, 7 December — DR, 13 December 1991.
149. Jordan TV, 19 June — DR, 28 June 1991. The figure Husayn used was correct and referred to the percentage of eligible voters who had participated in the election in 1989 (see *MECS* 1989, p. 463).
150. *Al-Ribat,* 10 September 1991.
151. Jordan TV, 11 September — DR, 12 September 1991.
152. *Al-Ribat,* 17 September; *JT,* 18 September 1991.
153. *Al-Ribat,* 3 December 1991.
154. *MEI,* 22 November, 20 December; *JT,* 18 December 1991.

155. Jordan TV, 1 December — DR, 4 December 1991.
156. *JT,* 13 January 1991.
157. R. Amman, 9 January — DR, 10 January; *al-Ra'y* (Amman), 11, 13 January 1991.
158. R. Amman, 17 January — DR, 17 January 1991.
159. R. Amman, 19 January — DR, 22 January 1991.
160. R. Amman, 6 February — DR, 7 February 1991.
161. *JT,* 11 February 1991.
162. *JT,* 13 February 1991.
163. *JT, FT,* 23 February 1991.
164. *JT,* 26 February 1991.
165. R. Amman, 24, 28 February — DR, 25 February, 1 March; *JT,* 27 February, 1 March 1991.
166. *Ha'aretz,* 1 March 1991.
167. *IHT,* 2 January; *Ha'aretz,* 6, 13 January 1991.
168. *JT,* 13, 14 January 1991.
169. BBC TV, 17 January — DR, 23 January 1991.
170. R. Amman, 9 January — DR, 10 January 1991.
171. *JT,* 12 January 1991.
172. *JT,* 15 January 1991.
173. R. Amman, 19 January — DR, 22 January; *JT,* 19 January; *IHT,* 23 January; London ITV, 24 January — DR, 29 January 1991.
174. *Ha'aretz,* 20 February 1991.
175. *IHT, JT,* 1 March 1991.
176. Jordan TV, 29 April — DR, 30 April; *JT,* 1 May 1991.
177. *NYT,* 16 March; *JT,* 1 May 1991.
178. *JT,* 26 June 1991.
179. *ME,* July 1991.
180. *IHT,* 10 December; *JT,* 11 December 1991.
181. R. Amman, 1 March — DR, 1 March 1991.
182. *JT,* 9 March, 24–25 May 1991.
183. Tahir al-Masri in *al-Usbu' al-'Arabi,* 6 May; similarly King Husayn in his speech to the nation, R. Amman, 12 October — DR, 16 October, and *al-Ra'y* (Amman), 8 December 1991.
184. Tahir al-Masri in *La Repubblica,* 18 June — DR, 24 June 1991.
185. Husayn in *JT,* 24-25 May, and Masri on Jordan TV, 12 August — DR, 14 August 1991.
186. R. Amman, 9 May — DR, 10 May; *JT,* 1 July 1991.
187. Hasan in *JT,* 20 July; Foreign Minister Nusur in *Akhbar al-Usbu',* 22 August 1991.
188. Tahir al-Masri on Jordan TV, 12 August — DR, 14 August; Husayn in speech to the nation, R. Amman, 12 October — DR, 16 October 1991.
189. Crown Prince Hasan in *JT,* 2 July 1991.
190. Husayn's interview with *Le Point,* as translated in *JT,* 4 June 1991.
191. JNA, 13 March — DR, 14 March; *JT,* 14–15 March; R. Amman, 30 March — DR, 1 April 1991.
192. *JT,* 14–15 March 1991.
193. *JT,* 20 April 1991.
194. *JT,* 25 April; R. Amman, 2 May — DR, 3 May 1991.
195. *La Repubblica,* 18 June — DR, 24 June; *al-Hayat* (London), 31 July 1991.
196. *NYT,* 22 July 1991.
197. *JT,* 5 March, 28 July; R. Amman, 9 May — DR, 10 May 1991.
198. Tahir al-Masri on R. Monte Carlo, 9 November — DR, 12 November 1991.
199. Masri on Jordan TV, 12 August — DR, 14 August 1991.
200. Husayn in speech to the nation, R. Amman, 12 October — DR, 16 October 1991.
201. 'Abd al-Salam al-Majali quoted in *JT,* 11 December 1991.
202. *JT,* 5 November 1991.
203. *JT,* 27 July 1991.
204. *NYT,* 13 March 1991.
205. *JT,* 23 March 1991.

206. *JT,* 4 June, 22–23 August 1991.
207. *JT,* 5 March; *al-Musawwar,* 20 September; Jordan TV, 1 December — DR, 4 December 1991.
208. *Al-Dustur* (Amman), 20 June; *JT,* 20 July 1991.
209. *NYT,* 30 July 1991.
210. *JT,* 23, 27 October 1991.
211. *Al-Hayat* (London), 27 September; *JT,* 28 October 1991.
212. *JT,* 1 November 1991.
213. *JT,* 2 November 1991.
214. *Al-Ra'y* (Amman), 8 December 1991.
215. *JT,* 5 November 1991.
216. R. Amman, 4 November — DR, 5 November 1991.
217. *Al-Sharq al-Awsat,* 27 October; R. Amman, 2 December — DR, 3 December 1991.
218. MBC TV, 5 December — DR, 6 December; *JT,* 10 December 1991.
219. *Ha'aretz,* 24 October 1991.
220. Text of charter in *al-Dustur* (Amman), 30 December 1990.
221. *IHT,* 30-31 March; *JT,* 4 June 1991.
222. R. Amman, 29 November — DR, 2 December 1991.
223. Jordan TV, 29 November — DR, 3 December 1991.
224. Jordan TV, 26 October — DR, 28 October 1991.
225. *JT,* 26 November 1991.
226. R. Amman, 1 March — DR, 1 March 1991.
227. *JT,* 3 March 1991.
228. *Al-Hayat* (London), 31 July; R. Amman, 21 November — DR, 22 November 1991.
229. The Government of the Hashemite Kingdom of Jordan, *White Paper — Jordan and the Gulf Crisis, August 1990–March 1991* (Amman, August 1991), pp. 32–36.
230. *White Paper,* pp. 4–5; MENA, 14 August — DR, 15 August 1991.
231. E.g., *al-Ra'y* (Amman), 12 February, 26 August 1991.
232. *Al-Dustur* (Amman), 3 September; MENA, 4 September — DR, 5 September 1991.
233. *Al-Musawwar,* 20 September 1991.
234. *NYT,* 13 March; R. Amman, 16 December — DR, 17 December 1991.
235. *JT,* 27 May 1992.
236. *JT,* 19 October 1991.
237. R. Amman, 21 November — DR, 22 November 1991.
238. Jordan TV, 29 November — DR, 3 December 1991.
239. *Al-Dustur* (Amman), 13 June 1991.
240. R. Amman, 15 January — DR, 15 January 1991.
241. *JT,* 12 February 1991.
242. *Al-Dustur* (Amman), 11, 13, 19 March; *JT,* 7 May 1991.
243. R. Amman, 22 May — DR, 23 May 1991.
244. *NYT,* 9 February 1991.
245. Ibid.
246. *JP,* 11 February 1991.
247. *JT,* 23 April 1991.
248. *NYT,* 21 March; *JT,* 23 March 1991.
249. *NYT,* 23 March 1991.
250. *JT,* 11 December 1991.
251. *JT,* 9-10, 11 May 1991.
252. *Al-Ra'y—*(Amman), *al-Dustur* (Amman), *JT,* 20 August 1991.
253. *JT,* 20 August; R. Amman, 20 August — DR, 21 August 1991.
254. Jordan TV, 28 December — DR, 30 December 1991.

Kuwait

(Al-Kuwayt)

JOSEPH KOSTINER

For Kuwait, the beginning of 1991 was marked by images of destruction brought about by the Iraqi occupation and the subsequent Gulf War. In addition to mass robbing, kidnapping and physical abuse perpetrated by the Iraqis against the Kuwaitis before the war, Iraqi acts of destruction, burning and looting of Kuwaiti infrastructure, institutions and oil fields intensified during the war. It was therefore surprising that Kuwait's physical reconstruction, including the restoration of basic services; the extinguishing of more than 700 oil well fires; and the reopening of state institutions and rebuilding of roads, was achieved relatively quickly (by fall 1991), and at a considerably lower expense than was expected. There were three reasons for this: the broad support for reconstruction shown by all Kuwaitis; the assistance of Western experts; and the liberal financial outlay of the Al Sabah-dominated government on the restoration of Kuwaiti life.

Yet, by focusing on reconstruction, the authorities failed to come to grips with their difficulties in other areas. One of these problems was sociodemographic: the Kuwaitis wanted to expel foreigners, notably Palestinians, who had constituted the majority of the population before the Iraqi invasion. They also wanted to punish the Palestinians for their alleged assistance to the Iraqis during the occupation. Partisan vigilante beatings and murders took place and, on a more organized level, there were detentions, deportations and trials. The Kuwaitis thereby reduced the number of foreigners to a minority of 250,000. These methods earned them worldwide condemnation for human rights abuse and, still worse, weakened their previously foreign-dominated managerial and administrative ranks. Moreover, by late 1991, they had not succeeded in persuading the majority of the c. 350,000 Kuwaitis living abroad to return. Consequently, their aspirations to retain a Kuwaiti majority proved problematic in the long run.

Kuwait was also beset by a major political problem. Before the Iraqi invasion, there had been opposition to the Al Sabah government. This now reemerged for several reasons: Kuwaiti leaders had continuously made promises to restore the National Assembly that was suspended in 1986 and had not fulfilled these promises; the manner of the Iraqi occupation and the restoration of services after the occupation elicited widespread accusations of mismanagement on the part of the rulers; furthermore, since the anti-Iraqi underground had gained confidence during the occupation, this seemed certain to enhance opposition activity. However, the opposition feared an internal rift, and were unwilling to confront the US-supported Al Sabah government. Consequently, the opposition made a widely supported but rather limited bid to restore the National Assembly and hold elections. Initially, the authorities tried to

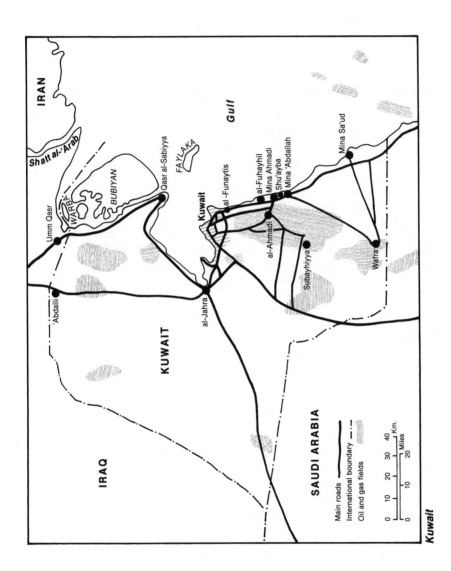

Kuwait

satisfy the opposition by establishing a new government, in late March. Apart from strengthening Crown Prince Sa'd 'Abdallah's family branch, it otherwise failed to satisfy the different opposition groups. In the following months, the government set an election date for the National Assembly in October 1992, when restoration and demographic problems would be fully resolved. This was a limited, but significant achievement for the opposition, and was accomplished without forcing revolutionary changes on the system.

Kuwait preferred to rely on Western forces for a new defense arrangement and concluded security agreements with the US, Britain and France in the fall. Kuwait objected to the plan, based on the "Damascus declaration" of March 1991, to station the forces of Syria and Egypt on its soil. Kuwait's pro-West leaning reflected its frustration with the failure of Arab parties to prevent the Iraqi invasion by their unimpressive performance in the war in comparison with that of Western troops, and with their financial demands. The security agreements concluded with Western powers provided defense from an immediate military escalation and assistance of future Western intervention against any invader.

Kuwait's relations with its anti-Iraqi allies, Syria and Egypt, were slightly strained by its reluctance to enter into defense pacts with these states, but basically remained cooperative and friendly. Kuwait continued to maintain a strong anti-Iraqi attitude and viewed Saddam's regime as its main and constant source of danger. It was also highly critical of the PLO and significantly reduced its support for the Palestinian cause. Kuwait also supported the US-initiated Arab-Israeli peace process, thereby throwing in its lot with the US.

KUWAIT AND THE WAR

ATTITUDE TOWARD THE WAR

Kuwaiti leaders, who were in exile in Ta'if, Saudi Arabia, were not willing to compromise over Kuwait's absolute liberation. Heir Apparent Sa'd 'Abdallah rejected the idea of any possible compromise, stating that Kuwait would neither "concede a single inch of its territory" nor would it accept any solution "inconsistent with the Arab summit and the UN Security Council resolutions."[1] An independent Iraqi decision to withdraw from Kuwait and avoid war was not expected. Consequently, the result of the meeting between US Secretary of State James Baker and Iraq's Foreign Minister Tariq 'Aziz, on 9 January in Geneva, was viewed by the Kuwaiti media as a manifestation of Saddam's continuous use of his "twisted logic of terrorism."[2] Thus, a full-scale allied attack on Iraq was inevitable; Kuwaiti leaders urged the US Congress to authorize US President Bush's plan to use force against Iraq. The emir, Jabir Al Ahmad, explained to James Baker during the latter's visit to Ta'if on 11 January, that it was imperative to use force to evict the Iraqis from Kuwait.[3] Moreover, the proposals for a compromise made by Iraq during the last two weeks of the war were not sufficient in the view of the Kuwaiti leaders and they urged the coalition to keep fighting for Kuwait. Foreign Minister and Deputy Prime Minister Sabah Al Ahmad stressed that "the liberation war cannot witness any truce" before Kuwait's full reoccupation.[4]

Kuwait's role in the actual fighting showed both its strength and its weakness. On the one hand, Kuwait had the financial resources to pay for some of the coalition's expenses. Kuwait had various investments in the West, and the London-based Kuwait Investment Office had channeled diverse sums to several destinations. Thus, Kuwait had pledged to pay the US $5bn. to cover the costs of "Desert Shield" (the initial deployment) and had paid half of this amount by the end of 1990. Kuwait pledged a total of $13.5bn. to the US for Operation Desert Storm (the war itself) and a further $1.3bn. to the UK. Kuwait also provided unspecified sums to France and to Arab states in the coalition, and granted the Soviet Union a $1bn. credit line.[5] Moreover, a Syrian paper reported that a Syrian-Kuwaiti committee would donate £SY20,000 to every Syrian citizen who had legally worked in Kuwait before the invasion.[6]

On the other hand, Kuwait's role in the planning and operations of Desert Storm reflected the fact that it was an occupied state whose army had numbered only 18,000 men before the Iraqi invasion. On their way to the battle zone, Western heads of state stopped in Ta'if to meet Kuwaiti leaders. However, there were no reports of actual Kuwaiti participation in high-level policy-making either before or during the war. The participation of several Kuwaiti air force units in air raids against Iraqi targets was described by Kuwaiti Minister of State for Cabinet Affairs 'Abd al-Rahman al-'Awadi as "a symbol that we...have the will to fight to liberate our country."[7] However, they were not much more than symbolic. Kuwaiti spokesmen reported with pride on the sorties of Kuwaiti air force units into Kuwait and Iraq, notably against artillery battalions ("the Kuwaiti sky eagles"). But such sorties were not very frequent.[8] There were only a few reports of Kuwaiti underground resistance activities. As in the previous year underground actions, notably attacking Iraqi positions and patrols, continued[9] (see *MECS* 1990, pp. 513–14) but were overshadowed by reports on the preparation for the war and the war itself.

Other Kuwaitis, mostly students in the US, were trained for a limited but significant role in the war: c. 300 were annexed to US ground forces to work as interpreters, help interrogate Iraqi prisoners, and identify possible Iraqi soldiers who had abandoned their uniforms.[10] Kuwaitis in Saudi Arabia also helped the coalition forces by operating a radio station, which instructed those Kuwaitis who had remained at home on how to defend themselves against the Allies' air raids and broadcast morale-boosting speeches by Kuwaiti exiled leaders about the up-and-coming liberation.[11]

CONDITIONS UNDER THE IRAQI OCCUPATION AND THE WAR
During the Iraqi occupation, there were reports about continual atrocities perpetrated against the Kuwaiti population by Iraqi soldiers (see *MECS* 1990, p. 512). As it became evident that the Iraqis would eventually be driven out of Kuwait, they exploited the occupation more and stepped up their activities against the local population. There were reports of systematic stealing of medical equipment from hospitals, even at the expense of suffering patients.[12] There were numerous reports of Iraqi soldiers raping individuals and families, murdering, torturing and insulting Kuwaitis, as well as looting Kuwaitis' private cars and electronic appliances.[13] Toward the end of the war, Kuwaiti sources reported that the Iraqi authorities had arrested 7,000 citizens during the fighting; they had also ordered Kuwaitis to remain indoors and subsequently arrested and detained those found in the streets, notably when they tried to raise Kuwaiti flags.[14] A cautious estimate by Western sources said that up to 15,000 Kuwaitis were reported to have been taken from Kuwait to Iraq. (Kuwaitis claimed a total of 33,000.)[15]

During the lead-up to the war, Iraqi forces became entrenched in Kuwait.[16] Consequently, the Kuwaitis were expecting war and air raids on their country and were reported to be "haunted by war" and busy preparing shelters.[17] During the fighting, Iraqi troops often came out of their fortified positions and moved into populated areas, mining the fields and drawing the Allies' fire after them.[18] Both Kuwait City and several provincial towns, notably coastal port towns, were hit; and some of the streets and houses, including gas and electricity facilities, were destroyed.[19] During the first weeks of the war, the Iraqis started destroying Kuwait's oil facilities. Toward the war's end, while retreating, the Iraqis tried to hamper the Allies' progress by burning over 732 oil wells. They also destroyed the National Assembly building, as well as other official institutions and installations.[20]

Kuwaitis in Exile
Most of the c. 500,000 Kuwaitis, who had left their state either before or after the Iraq invasion, barely participated in Kuwait's liberation. In Cairo, for example, most Kuwaitis led a luxurious lifestyle. With the exception of a group led by a former member in the National Assembly, Ahmad al-Nafisi, which focused on vocational training for youth, most Kuwaitis in Cairo were known for their participation in the night-life and squandering money.[21] In Ta'if and London, the political and financial leaders focused on the distribution of allowances to exiled Kuwaitis (see *MECS* 1990, p. 514) and, from the initial stages of the war, on the planning of restoration and reconstruction projects to be carried out after the liberation[22] (see also below). The leaders were obviously concentrating exclusively on the postliberation period, and made no effort to exert a moral code of behavior for exiled Kuwaitis or to encourage them to utilize their efforts toward liberating Kuwait.

INTERNAL AFFAIRS AFTER LIBERATION

Although after the liberation, on 25 February, an atmosphere of joy prevailed in Kuwait, the liberation also served to accentuate the tremendous problems involved in restoring an independent and organized regime in Kuwait. The difficulties that had to be overcome could be divided into three categories: (a) There was the problem of reactivation of daily services and basic administration. It was necessary to restore running water, electricity, adequate roads and streets; to extinguish the burning oil wells; and to provide immediate law and order. The situation was further complicated by the fact that, during the week following the liberation, the leading members of the ruling family were still absent. (b) There were financial problems resulting from Kuwait's immediate contribution to war expenses (c. $2.2bn.). During the first few days after the liberation, the destruction and cost of reconstruction was estimated at c. $100bn.[23] (c) There were major sociopolitical problems. In the light of Kuwait's defeat by Iraq, and the difficulties encountered after liberation, it was questioned whether the Al Sabah family was fit to rule, and a demand for changes in the nature of Kuwaiti government was voiced.

These problems compounded other serious issues. The demographic balance was severely upset by the fact that hundreds of thousands of Kuwaitis and non-Kuwaitis had fled the country. There was growing tension between indigenous citizens and foreigners due to the Kuwaitis' desire for revenge against alleged pro-Iraqi foreigners, notably Palestinians.

Kuwaiti leaders were aware that solutions to sociopolitical issues, hinging upon the careful cooperation between Kuwaitis and non-Kuwaitis and between society and the rulers, could only develop over a longer term. They therefore gave first priority to the reconstruction of services, administration and internal security. These were essential both for the actual provision of minimal living conditions and for the regime's popularity. In the words of Minister of Planning Sulayman al-Mutawwa', "the important thing is to provide services and to achieve stability for everyone."[24]

RESTORATION OF SERVICES AND CONTROL

The problems of physical reconstruction and the restoration of administration were quite serious. The 732 burning oil wells were not only an economic pitfall, but also presented an urgent pollution problem,[25] since they produced 765,000 tons of smoke daily. There were difficulties in restoring running water and electricity, aggravated by the lack of generators (many of which had been destroyed by the Iraqis) and by c. 500,000 Iraqi-laid land mines. Due to damaged roads and impaired communications, which hindered access to the relevant areas, garbage disposal was grossly inadequate. Moreover, gangs of Kuwaiti youths, notably those belonging to the former underground, were imposing their own type of law and order on the cities, mainly by committing vigilante actions against pro-Iraqi Palestinians. Kuwaitis were also concerned about those of their compatriots who had been captured and kidnapped by the Iraqis before the liberation.[26]

During the early days after the liberation, the outlook for solving or alleviating these problems seemed rather bleak. Both Kuwaitis and Westerners sought to stress the malevolent nature of Iraq's activities and exaggerated the pictures of destruction. The delayed return of the ruling family (the crown prince and Prime Minister Sa'd 'Abdallah on 4 March, and the emir, Jabir Al Ahmad, on 14 March) created the impression that there was no firm leadership in Kuwait, and fueled the concern that reconstruction was going to take a long time.

On the other hand, there were several factors which eased physical reconstruction. There was a consensus of opinion among Kuwaiti political groups over the need for reconstruction. As early as 28 February, the emir issued a decree establishing a supreme security committee to formulate an internal security policy. Sa'd 'Abdallah then met former underground leaders to reinstate the armed forces' responsibility for internal security. He also declared a state of martial law for three months, to facilitate the government's activities. In addition, Kuwait was helped by international firms, such as the US-based Bechtel consortium (which employed 5,000 workers) to restore services, and 27 international companies (notably that of the Texan Red Adair) to cap the burning oil wells. Kuwait's wealth, much of which was held in Western banks, was used to pay for these types of assistance.[27] Hence, although it took several weeks for reconstruction to get under way, by late spring and early summer most basic services were provided free of charge; the roads repaved; one port reactivated; 62,000 mines dismantled; and scores of bank branches reopened to the public.[28]

Early estimates of time quoted for extinguishing the wells turned out to be grossly exaggerated, either because of genuine overassessment or in order to blacken Iraq. Initial estimates were that c. 6m. barrels per day (b/d) were being burnt (at the cost of about $100m.–$200m.); and that 80% of Kuwait's oil infrastructure and 10%–15% of its reserves had been damaged or even corroded. It was also estimated that extinguishing operations would last three years.[29] However, by early November, all fires had been extinguished at the cost of $1.5bn.; and only about 3% of Kuwait's reserves had been damaged.[30] By late summer, most kidnapped Kuwaitis had been freed and Iraq had officially returned c. 5,000 Kuwaitis in prisoner exchanges.

In late May, Sa'd 'Abdallah made it clear that partisan vigilante activities would be banned, and that all arms held by private citizens should be handed in by 2 July. From April (the end of the extended period of martial law), instead of arbitrary partisan punishment, the Ministry of Justice commenced investigations against 628 people suspected of war crimes, treason, espionage or collaboration with Iraq during the occupation, and 450 were put on trial. By the end of June, 325 had been tried: 29 (mostly Palestinians, Iraqis and stateless) were sentenced to death, and the rest to various terms of imprisonment. The trials themselves lacked appropriate defense procedures, and were characterized by the handing down of heavy punishments for trivial offenses. Consequently they were criticized by Western human rights organizations (on 20 May, they drew critical remarks from President Bush). The Kuwaitis then decided to permit court appeals, and in late June decided to commute the death sentences to life imprisonment.[31] However, the conducting of these trials was advantageous in that the law enforcement and legal systems, including the police, were able to restore their authority.

ECONOMIC CONDITIONS

In mid-March, a UN fact-finding mission, led by UN Deputy Secretary-General Maartti Ahtisaari, estimated that Kuwait had suffered $23bn. worth of damage (including $8.5bn. in lost oil production) during the occupation. Although Kuwait's own initial estimates (based on the overestimated period required to extinguish the oil wells), which assessed the damage at c. $100bn., were discarded in late spring, the Kuwaitis included the reconstruction costs in their damage assessment, and set the total at more than $30bn. In addition, they estimated the inclusive expenditure on its liberation, and on its allies was about $23bn.[32]

Kuwait encountered difficulties in financing this cost. Reluctant to draw excessively on Kuwaiti reserves in foreign banks, which had reached a low of $45bn., Kuwaiti leaders had little choice but to borrow. In early July, a special decree issued by the emir permitted the government to borrow up to a ceiling of $34bn. In early October, the government decided to borrow $5bn. (as an unsecured, syndicated loan), coordinated by the US bank, J. P. Morgan.[33] In late July, Kuwait resumed its oil exports, although at a low level. Plans to increase oil production were realized only after the oil well fires had been extinguished. By the end of 1991, when production had reached c. 510,000 b/d, the refinery at al-Ahmadi was working at full capacity. However, even then, Kuwait was still producing considerably less than the Opec quota of July 1990 (1.5m. b/d), and could not yet generate desirable revenues. According to Western sources, total costs for rebuilding Kuwait's oil infrastructure and restoring production to the preinvasion level were estimated to be $7.16bn., and it was expected that the process would take several years.[34]

In addition to the difficulties in reactivating economic enterprises, such as its oil industry, the Kuwaiti economy was also affected by short-term developments, such as the declining population (see below). Development of banking and local business activities slowly returned. This was encouraged by the decision of banks, in April, to write off the debts of 180,000 citizens. There were also food shortages which, in late spring, caused short-term but severe inflation as high as 32%.[35] Consequently, recession was still evident in 1991.

SOCIOPOLITICAL DEVELOPMENTS

Demographic Issues

The crisis provided Kuwait with the opportunity to curb its alien population and prevent a return to the pre-occupation situation when Kuwaitis were a minority of 40% (and 30% of the work force) in their own country. Without being very specific on details, government officials noted that both for security reasons and economic self-reliance, they estimated a target population of 1m.–1.2m. people, 800,000 of whom would be Kuwaitis (compared with a preinvasion population of 2.1m.). Palestinians would number less than 200,000 (compared with over 350,000 before the Iraqi occupation), and Egyptians and Turks would replace the Palestinians in management positions.[36]

There were various problems in fulfilling this plan. The return of about 450,000 Kuwaiti citizens, who had left Kuwait before and during the invasion, was essential to the plan; but the authorities failed to implement this part of the plan efficiently. Only on 2 April, after the resumption of basic services, were the first permits issued for returning Kuwaitis. It then became evident that most of the Kuwaitis in exile were not tempted to return by the free return flights offered by the authorities. They feared disorder and the lack of business opportunities; were concerned about the declining educational system; and were worried about what they would face in the aftermath of the destruction caused by the war. By the end of the year, there were c. 400,000 Kuwaitis in Kuwait, while about 250,000 were estimated to have remained abroad (notably in Egypt and in Western states). At first there were reports of tension between the Kuwaitis who had stayed during the Iraqi occupation and those who returned afterward. The former viewed themselves as tough and resolute and thought of the latter as soft and weak. However, as time passed, such reports of conflict grew fewer, and the two groups were eventually united by their other troubles.[37]

The prevailing situation triggered two contradictory Kuwaiti responses. One focused on the government's intention to implement carefully the employment of foreign workers. In March, Minister of Planning Sulayman al-Mutawwa' stated the need to either maintain or reemploy non-Kuwaitis and review all the laws concerning their continued stay in Kuwait. In late October, the government declared a plan to form a committee of "competent citizens" to define a naturalization policy for non-Kuwaitis.[38] Apparently, no such policy evolved. The other response which ultimately prevailed, was overtly supported by the Kuwaiti citizens and tacitly also by the leaders. It focused on an indiscriminate purge of Palestinians and other foreigners. Since it was impossible to draw a clear distinction between those Palestinians who had helped the Iraqis, and others who had remained pro-Kuwait during the Iraqi occupation, most Kuwaitis displayed feelings of vengeance against all Palestinians for their alleged pro-Iraqi stand. In broader terms, the Kuwaitis harbored basic suspicions of all foreigners, whom they deemed potentially disloyal, or had not supported Kuwait.

This purge consisted of the persecution, beating up, and harassment (including torture) of Palestinians. Some 1,600 of them were officially "asked to leave" Kuwait and several hundreds more sentenced to various terms of imprisonment. The stateless residents or *bidun* ("without") of local bedouin or mixed Arab origins, including those who had served in the Kuwaiti army and had even been prisoners of war in Iraq, were held in refugee camps, tried and expelled. Moreover, after 16 May, which was the "deadline for registration of foreign residents," foreigners of various nationalities who were not properly registered were also forced to leave. Palestinians were the first to be expelled from jobs and have their employment contracts renounced. Without means of financial support, they were obliged to leave Kuwait.

Consequently, by the end of the year there were only c. 50,000 Palestinians, 50,000 stateless, and a similar number of returning Egyptians left in Kuwait. Together with other Arabs and Asians, the number of non-Kuwaitis was 350,000. The Kuwaitis thus achieved their goal of reducing the number of foreigners to less than that of the Kuwaitis, but at a high price to the state bureaucracy, private business and households which had been manned by foreigners.[39]

GOVERNMENT AND OPPOSITION
The Opposition Demands
Opposition groups, either Islamic fundamentalists, leftists or middle-of-the-road reformists put forward several major demands for change in the Kuwaiti regime but, interestingly, did not back them up with a meaningful show of force. The main demand focused on earlier concerns, that had characterized the previous four years. This was to restore the National Assembly (suspended by the emir in 1986) and permit elections, according to the 1962 constitution (see *MECS* 1990, pp. 502–6). The manner in which Kuwait had been defeated by Iraq and the way in which its government had restored services after the liberation, provided the opposition with additional grievances. Thus, the former military attaché to Iraq, Col. Sa'id Matar, accused the government of having ignored intelligence reports of the forthcoming Iraqi invasion. In addition, while members of the Kuwaiti resistance movement (such as paratroop commander Jabir Al Sabah, a brother of the emir) stayed to fight, most members of the Kuwaiti royal house fled the country. While in exile and after the liberation, the royal family negotiated with opposition members, but did not form a national unity government with them. The late return of the crown prince and the even later return of the emir, together with rumors of his being depressed and rather dazed since the invasion, added to the grievances. The declaration of martial law by the emir's unilateral decree (justified, as it was, by postwar conditions) triggered a response from the opposition. On 1 April, the opposition groups submitted to Jabir a declaration, signed by 89 notables. It called for the restoration of the National Assembly; elections on a fixed date; the appointment to cabinet positions of capable individuals, who also reflected political trends in Kuwait; the right to free press and assembly; reform of the civil service; and an independent judiciary.[40]

While these demands showed how critical the opposition was of the authorities, they also attested to the fact that the opposition was reluctant to overthrow the Al Sabah rule, but wished only to reform it. There were several reasons for their relative moderation. The people who traditionally fought for democratization and had led the opposition after the liberation were notables — wealthy and well-educated businessmen, who shared their social origins and interest in stability with the Al Sabahs and who did not question the latters' inherent right to rule. In the words of a Western observer, "what styles itself a democracy movement here is really an oligarchy movement." The businessmen wanted a stronger say in the decision-making process; a merit-system-based government; and more opportunities for the private sector. The realization of the above-mentioned demands would have been sufficient for them.[41] Moreover, the postliberation conditions encouraged the relatively moderate businessmen's approach: it was clear to all opposition groups that the US supported the restoration of the Al Sabah rule; and although Washington encouraged the latter to democratize, it would not have tolerated the collapse of the Al Sabah regime. In addition, there were fears of internal deterioration in the event of a strong political struggle. In early March, an assassination attempt which culminated in injury to the banker 'Abd al-Hamid al-Ja'wan, a leading opposition leader, was construed by the opposition as an attempt by the ruling family (notably its peripheral branches and not the emir) to defend its supremacy with blood — a development which was not desired by all parties.

In addition, despite similar social origins, there was the opposition's own fear of internal ideological rifts: fundamentalist leaders (such as the former deputy of the National Assembly, 'Abdallah al-Nafisi) heralded the role of their people in the anti-Iraqi underground and wrote articles against Kuwait's nepotism.[42] Shi'i groups and leftist-Nasserist former deputies also demanded political change. The Kuwaitis who had remained in the country during the occupation, fought the Iraqis and acquired a taste of power and self-rule, were the most vociferous regardless of their ideology. The banker 'Abd al-'Aziz al-Sultan declared: "those of us who stayed are not willing to put up with anything less than democracy...we have suffered, we have seen terror, we are not afraid."[43] His emphasis on democracy demonstrated that, by avoiding an extremist manifesto and by establishing a common interest in a moderate parliamentary democracy, these groups had managed to bridge their differences and were in agreement over the above-mentioned demands. Their main goal, as emphasized by the chairman of the chamber of commerce, 'Abd al-'Aziz al-Saqr, was to cooperate with the government in order to effect a peaceful reform.[44]

Government Initiatives and Opposition Responses
Kuwaiti leaders were committed, in principle, to the restoration of parliamentary activity (see *MECS* 1990, pp. 515–16) and reiterated this commitment after Kuwait's liberation. However, their methods of implementing what was commonly perceived as democratization could not possibly have won the opposition's cooperation. In mid-March, contrary to the opposition's aims, the authorities stated that elections for a new National Assembly would take place within a year. In the leaders' view, as expressed by the Kuwaiti envoy to the US, Sa'ud Nasir Al Sabah, until all exiled Kuwaitis returned and services were restored, democratization would be on "pause."[45] Women were still barred from voting and the preinvasion relatively small electorate (c. 65,000 citizens) was not expanded. The authorities apparently wanted to regain popular support first by providing reasonable living conditions and bringing back exiled Kuwaitis who would back their compatriots, the Al Sabahs, vis-à-vis the Kuwaitis who had remained in Kuwait during the invasion. The government explained

this policy as being an expression of consideration and equality. The opposition, in its turn, failed to convince the authorities to hold elections before the leaders had reestablished popular support for themselves. In the words of an opposition leader: "This beginning does not bode well for the future."[46]

The authorities preferred instead to change the government. They presumably thought that the opposition would be satisfied and the critics silenced by a new Al Sabah-led government, which would also include representatives of the main political groups and appear to be a "national salvation" government, and which would focus on the resolution of immediate reconstruction problems. Hence, on 20 March, Sa'd 'Abdallah's government, which had been formed before Iraq's invasion, resigned. This, however, did not satisfy the opposition and its struggle with the government did not abate. Irritated by the delay in holding elections for the National Assembly, opposition members did not cooperate in forming the new government. Leftist politicians (who then formed a body called "the democratic forum" [al-minbar al-dimuqrati], such as the Nasserist veterans, Ahmad al-Khatib and Jasim al-Qattami, the Sunni fundamentalist editor of the journal al-Mujtama' Isma'il al-Shatti, and the middle-of-the-road politician, former National Assembly speaker, Yusuf al-'Adsani, were consulted by Sa'd 'Abdallah, but did not join in forming a new government, and on 1 April, only reiterated their above-mentioned demands.

In the new government, formed on 20 April, the number of Al Sabah members was reduced from seven to five, reflecting an attempt to win the opposition's support, but even more, attesting to a latent power struggle within the ranks of the royal family over whom should be blamed and punished for the invasion and the inadequate leadership during reconstruction efforts. Thus, the new Sa'd 'Abdallah-led government had two members of the emir's Al Ahmad branch (compared with four in the earlier one) and three of Sa'd 'Abdallah's Al Salim branch (as in the former government). It did not include the former deputy prime minister and foreign minister, Sabah Al Ahmad, Jabir's brother and a leader of the Al Ahmad branch in the royal family. His exclusion removed an ambitious rival from Sa'd 'Abdallah's path. Another brother and prominent Al Ahmad member, former minister of defense Nawwaf Al Ahmad, became minister of social affairs and labor. The strengthening of the Al Salim branch was also marked by the appointment of Salim al-Sabah Al Salim, a former governor of al-Ahmadi and an ally of Sa'd 'Abdallah, to deputy prime minister and foreign minister. 'Ali Al Salim became minister of defense. From his new position, Nawwaf could still affect demographic policies, but the emir's branch basically lost power.

Other than these changes, there were nine (non-Al Sabah) newcomers in the new government, including former civil servants, a judge and a professor. Another prominent non-Al Sabah was the oil minister (and former minister of power and water), Hamud al-Ruqba. Sa'd 'Abdallah thus excluded the former finance and oil ministers from the new government. This not only underlined the prominence of his family branch, but also that of non-royalist technocrats with professional skills[47] (see Appendix).

The opposition's response throughout the whole period was unsympathetic. Two days after the former government's resignation, over 1,000 people gathered in a demonstration organized by the Sunni fundamentalist Social Solidarity Committee, to urge the release of Kuwaiti prisoners of war (POWs). The leftist democratic forum demanded the exclusion from the new government of members of the former failing government and that the banning of an Al Sabah member from being prime minister should be seriously considered. The emir's passion for new young wives was mocked. Furthermore, a pledge Jabir had made on 7 April to hold elections "next year" and study women's rights in this context was depicted by the leftist former National Assembly member, 'Abdallah Nibari, as "partly positive" but he remained skeptical over the realization of this pledge. The new government was described by former assembly speaker Ahmad al-Sa'dun as manifesting "no change" but only "a constitutional vacuum."[48]

The government then resorted to enforcing its authority. In April, during Secretary of State James Baker's visit and his advice to Kuwaiti leaders to strengthen the course of democratization in Kuwait, an opposition press conference was banned. This press conference had been called to express the objections by all the opposition groups to the government's policies.[49] In mid-May, five Islamic activists were arrested[50] during a demonstration they had staged to welcome returning Kuwaitis.

In early June, in response to opposition and US pressure, Jabir proclaimed that elections for the National Assembly would be held in October 1992. A month later, the authorities also reconvened the National Assembly inaugurated before the invasion. The opposition, which advocated the reestablishment of a 1986-type assembly, had continuously objected to the 1990 progovernment, partly appointed body (see *MECS* 1990, pp. 504–5). The government's activities were viewed as "a facade of democracy" and an attempt to stall for time and ultimately form "a parliament they like."[51] The emir's decision to delay the elections prompted a major opposition rally.

In the following weeks, the tension between the government and opposition abated. The government's ultimate success in restoring services and returning Kuwaiti POWs; its allocation of financial assistance to Kuwaiti citizens; and the Al Sabah's continued dominance (regardless of family branch), prevented a transfer of power to the opposition, and ensured the government's supremacy.

The opposition, in turn, lost its postliberation momentum. It failed to stir up mass support; it did not succeed in changing election rules and the electorate; and it failed to either join or topple the government. In summer 1991, opposition groups started to prepare for the October 1992 elections and to institutionalize their organizations. Thus, in December, the leftist democratic forum declared itself a political party. By so doing, the forum broke Kuwait's law, and it remained to be seen whether it would be suppressed by the authorities or if it would gain antigovernment momentum. The opposition's main achievement was to force new elections on the government, even if with some delay, and in so doing maintain cooperation among all its groupings, despite their basic differences. Moreover, in August, under opposition pressure, the government introduced to the highly unpopular existing National Assembly a draft bill, giving Kuwaiti women the right to vote for the first time.[52]

FOREIGN AFFAIRS

GULF SECURITY
Kuwaiti leaders were determined to prevent another invasion of their country and sought to establish the best possible security arrangements. In Sa'd 'Abdallah's words:

"Security comes before anything else."[53] However, during the first weeks after liberation, they encountered difficulties in deciding on a proper strategy. On the one hand, they had to put into practice a massive and immediate security system to compensate for their obvious military weakness, which was symbolized by Kuwait's defeat and destruction by Iraq. In the rulers' opinion, the need for such a strategy was particularly valid, since Saddam's Iraq was still a threat[54] and, in contrast to the preinvasion period, they were not willing to risk their state being left undefended. Unlike the Saudis, the Kuwaitis openly displayed their feelings of support and gratitude toward the Americans.[55] They trusted the US forces' effectiveness and therefore wanted to keep a sizable number of US forces along Kuwait's border for six months to a year. During Secretary of Defense Richard Cheney's meeting with Kuwaiti leaders in early May, it was agreed to station a US brigade of 3,700 armored troops in Kuwait as a temporary measure.[56]

On the other hand, Kuwait participated in the initiative to align the Gulf states with Egypt and Syria, and establish a Gulf security pact with US support embodied in the 6 March Damascus declaration (see chapters on inter-Arab relations and Saudi Arabia). The foreign minister, Salim al-Sabah Al Salim, praised the "closeness of the eight states." Sa'd 'Abdallah stressed that the Gulf states, being members of the Gulf Cooperation Council (GCC) should develop a cooperation "to include all concepts."[57]

Like Saudi Arabia, however, Kuwait had doubts about the value of such a pact. First and foremost, it had come to distrust inter-Arab cooperation which had failed in the face of Iraq's aggression. In addition, its leaders doubted the effectiveness of Arab forces, compared with that of Western troops, and did not look favorably upon Egypt's and Syria's high financial demands. Kuwait, therefore, insisted on ongoing military cooperation with the US, in addition to an Arab Gulf defense force. Consequently, in May, Egypt decided to withdraw its forces from the Gulf. Kuwait had no wish to alienate Cairo, and intimated its gratitude to Egypt. During President Mubarak's visit to Kuwait in mid-June, he reiterated Egypt's commitment to defend the Gulf states, which was aimed at reestablishing Egypt's military role in Gulf security (see chapter on Egypt). However, while interested in improving bilateral relations with Egypt, Kuwait remained hesitant about an Arab security pact. Kuwaiti spokesmen stressed that patience and judicial considerations should precede the making of the pact; that the states in question should aim at achieving no less than a comprehensive cooperation; and that Kuwait's military cooperation with the US should be acknowledged and accepted by Syria and Egypt.

The more time that elapsed from the initial Damascus declaration, the less Kuwait was interested in its realization, for the above reasons.[58] The plan that the parties concerned finally drafted focused on stationing a 26,000-member force in Kuwait, which would include only a token presence of 3,000 troops each from Egypt and Syria, 10,000 men from Saudi Arabia and another 10,000 men from Kuwait and the other GCC states. However, at a meeting of the foreign ministers of the Damascus declaration states, held in Kuwait from 15–17 July, they failed to reach an agreement. There were several reasons for this failure (see chapter on inter-Arab relations), but Kuwait's role was apparent. Its preference for maintaining Western troops as its principal form of protection eventually angered Egypt and Syria. Moreover, Oman, one of the participants in these negotiations, insisted that Iran be included in a security pact (see chapter on Oman), and this prompted Kuwait to distance itself from the security initiatives of other Gulf states, with the exception of Saudi Arabia. Although Kuwaiti spokesmen did not deny that their state was committed to the Damascus declaration, Salim al-Sabah played down its significance. He stressed that "the role played by forces that came to help liberate Kuwait is no longer necessary" and that rather than massive participation, it was the principle of participation in the pact that really counted.[59]

In early August, Kuwait was decisively persuaded to cooperate with Western forces in the establishment of a valid security arrangement, after Iraq made several night incursions into Kuwaiti territory to retrieve weapons left there before Kuwait's liberation. National Assembly deputies even suggested that the former preinvasion opposition to the establishment of Western bases in Kuwait might be reversed.[60] During August, representatives from Kuwait, the US, Britain and France discussed the issue. On 3 September, an agreement with the US was announced by the Kuwaiti Government. The parties were ultimately reluctant to agree to the permanent deployment of US contingents at Kuwaiti bases on a large scale, which would have been tantamount to a US assumption of responsibility for Kuwait's security, a commitment that Washington was not prepared to make and that Kuwait did not want to concede. The parties therefore agreed to stockpile US military equipment on Kuwaiti soil, including aircraft and naval units for the next 10 years, and to maintain American technical teams at air and naval bases. A small number of US troops would also remain in Kuwait. The two parties would hold joint military maneuvers. Kuwait would provide logistical assistance to the US forces, but Washington would underwrite the cost of stockpiling its weapons, with the provision that it would be able to use them to defend any other country requesting protection, without objection from Kuwait. The two parties thus decided on a limited military cooperation which left sufficient leeway for each to fulfill other commitments. The pact did not include provision for permanent US bases in Kuwait. However, it included means for Kuwait's immediate as well as long-term defense, in the form of provisions for instant and future US intervention. Salim al-Sabah did not rule out a return of US forces to the region in case of an emergency. The pact was signed by the defense ministers of both states on 20 September, in Washington.[61] Kuwait subsequently contracted to purchase 40 US-made F-18 aircraft to strengthen its redeveloping air force.[62]

Kuwaiti leaders went on to establish security pacts with Britain and France. During Jabir's visit to Britain on 4 October, he and British Prime Minister John Major concluded a Kuwaiti-British agreement which focused on joint military maneuvers, training for Kuwaiti forces by Royal Air Force teams, and the maintenance of a British naval presence in the Gulf. The agreement did not provide for pre-positioning of equipment, or for leaving a permanent force in place, and was not limited to a specific period. Jabir's visit to Paris during the same week led to a similar pact with France. The French undertook to defend Kuwait if required, and to dispatch military equipment and sophisticated weapons in the meantime, as well as stage training and maneuvers with Kuwaiti forces.[63] On 11 November, Kuwait and US forces began joint military exercises, involving amphibious landings and air support sorties.[64] This was also an opportunity for the remnants of the Kuwaiti army to regroup and train its men.

Kuwait sought to reestablish good relations with Iran, as an additional step toward regional stability. Iran's embassy in Kuwait was reopened on 11 March and both states engaged in continuous discussions over Gulf affairs. Kuwait considered Iran a neighbor whose policies were crucial to Gulf stability and conveyed its appreciation for Iran's neutrality during the war, which had contributed to the victory of the anti-Iraqi coalition. Salim al-Sabah Al Salim viewed Iran as a partner for consultation over Gulf issues, but he still distrusted Iran's revolutionary leanings. Kuwait was further dissuaded from entering into a security pact with Iran by its cooperation with the US and Egypt, both of which distrusted Iran's role.[65] In Kuwaiti eyes, Iran's neutrality was in itself sufficient to ensure Gulf security.

Kuwait responded to Tehran's fierce criticism of Kuwait's reliance on foreign forces, as evident in its security agreement with Western states (see chapter on Iran), by stressing that its security agreements were only directed against Iraq. Consequently, Tehran showed willingness to improve relations. Iran Air resumed its direct flights to Kuwait and Tehran approved the return of six Kuwaiti airbus aircraft which had been confiscated by the Iraqis and then flown to Iran for safekeeping. On 22 September, Iran's Foreign Minister 'Ali Akbar Velayati and Jabir met in New York and the same positive atmosphere prevailed.[66] Kuwait thus succeeded in keeping Iran friendly and cooperative, even without a pact.

Kuwait's security strategy was coordinated on a regular basis with that of Saudi Arabia. Both states maintained continuous contacts and usually displayed similar positions. However, Kuwait was more assertive over embarking on security agreements with the West. There are several reasons for this. Kuwait was more fearful of renewed anti-Kuwaiti activity by Iraq; less hesitant than the Saudi Wahhabis about hosting foreign troops on their soil; and, as inhabitants of a small state, less concerned with other regional parties' response (see chapter on Saudi Arabia). Hence, during the second half of 1991, Kuwait in fact played the role of a pioneer among the GCC states by seeking actual security pacts with Western states and influencing others, such as Bahrain, to follow suit (see chapter on Bahrain). Saudi Arabia's hesitation prevented the formation of an all-embracing Western-dominated regional security pact. The Kuwaiti leaders' priority was obviously aimed at achieving solid defense arrangements for the prevention of another invasion, and although a comprehensive pact embodying all the GCC states did not materialize, their strategy was nevertheless quite effective.

However, Kuwait was still concerned about several Iraqi-initiated small-scale problems that were not tackled by its grand strategy and thus relied on the UN for the return of its stolen property. By August, Iraq had returned 42 tons of gold stolen from the Kuwait Central Bank and c. $4bn. in notes. Kuwait maintained that Iraq still had to return more gold and more money, c. $1.25bn. at least, which, by the end of 1991, it had failed to do.[67] Thanks to the efforts of the Red Cross, Iraq released a slow but continuous trickle of Kuwaiti citizens and residents who had been held in Iraqi prisons. In late July, according to sources in Kuwait's Ministry of Justice, 1,857 Kuwaitis and 619 non-Kuwaitis were still being held by Iraq,[68] and, by the end of 1991, the numbers were almost the same.

The biggest grievance was Iraq's infiltrations. Some of these were made by stateless persons, who had gone to Iraq during Kuwait's occupation and were trying to return to Kuwait. There were also attempts by Iraqi forces to recapture stockpiles of arms and military equipment or simply to harass the Kuwaitis. The UN patrols that were supposed to be supervising a 15 km.- wide demilitarized zone were quite ineffective. Consequently, in June, the government announced that it would build a 175 km.-long fence along the Iraqi border to prevent infiltrations. According to Kuwaiti sources, the incidents escalated in August. On 27 August, a party of 80 Iraqi marines landed at the north of Bubiyan Island (east of Kuwait's shore), backed by small Iraqi vessels. Their aim was to collect abandoned ammunition. Kuwaiti forces sank several Iraqi vessels and captured 47 Iraqis. Kuwait further complained that, on 15 September, Iraqi military squads attempted and failed to occupy the border post, al-Abraq and, on 11 October, another group of 55 soldiers was intercepted trying to infiltrate the north coast. Despite their limited scope, these incidents proved to Kuwaiti rulers the vulnerability of their northern border in relation to Iraqi infiltrations or attack.[69] They were, therefore, encouraged to conclude the above-mentioned security pacts with Western states. However, this did not completely put an end to other such attempts by Iraq.

ATTITUDE TOWARD OTHER MIDDLE EASTERN PARTIES

Anti-Iraqi Coalition Parties

Egypt's hopes for tangible benefits in reward for fighting for Kuwait against Iraq were frustrated in the weeks following the liberation. Kuwait chose security pacts with Western forces rather than with Arab ones, a decision which obviously dismayed Egypt (see also chapter on Egypt). In addition, due to the chaos and xenophobic atmosphere which prevailed in Kuwait during this period, other Egyptian interests were harmed. At the end of March, the Egyptian ambassador in Kuwait, Amin Nimr, confirmed that 4,400 Egyptian citizens were stranded on the Iraqi-Kuwaiti border with inadequate food and medical care and at least 300 Egyptians were said to have been held and tortured by the Kuwaiti authorities. In November, he reconfirmed that there were between 400 and 500 Egyptians under Kuwaiti arrest. He admitted that most of them had breached the Kuwaiti immigration and employment laws. By then, however, Kuwait was apparently already trying to resolve the issue, and either permitted these Egyptians' reemployment by Kuwaitis or their transfer to Egypt. These arrangements were agreed upon during the visit to Kuwait of Egypt's prime minister, 'Atif Sidqi, in late October.[70]

After Kuwait's liberation, the Kuwaiti authorities promised to compensate "coalition nationals" for lost property and bank savings and to exempt them from any contract infractions. According to Egyptian sources, the combined sum Kuwait owed to Egyptians was $20bn.[71] The issue remained outstanding. Following Egyptian complaints that only Western firms had obtained Kuwaiti reconstruction contracts, Egypt received in June a contract worth c. $1bn. to participate in building work on Faylaka Island and in other regions.[72] This was not sufficient to satisfy the Egyptians. In view of the deteriorating security ties and other problems, the Egyptian People's Assembly rejected a Kuwaiti fund loan to Egypt. After September, the Kuwaiti authorities realized the depth of Egypt's frustration and tried to compensate Egypt by granting up to 4,000 entrance visas weekly to Egyptians who sought work in Kuwait.[73] For the rest of 1991, Egyptian-Kuwaiti relations remained cooperative, but constrained.

Syria played a lesser role in the contemplated Damascus declaration security pact than Egypt. Moreover, Damascus's interests were focused on the Arab-Israeli arena, rather than on the Gulf. Its response to Kuwait's security pacts with the West was not as sensitive and bitter as Egypt's. Hence, in March and April, Syria accepted both a

Kuwaiti Arab Development Fund generous credit line and direct assistance of $250m. for four different projects. In July, Kuwait gave Syria a $60m. development loan for 20 years.[74] In the following weeks, alongside its cooperation with the West, Kuwait continued to use economic assistance to maintain a friendly relationship with Syria. During Jabir's visit to Damascus in September, he not only thanked President Asad for Syria's assistance against Iraq, but also emphasized Kuwait's willingness to help Syria further in economic development, notably by encouraging its foreign trade. An agreement to this effect was concluded on 18 September, during a visit by Syria's Prime Minister, Mahmud Zu'bi, to Kuwait[75] (see also chapter on Syria).

Attitude Toward the PLO and Related Issues

Palestinian leaders, such as the deputy speaker of the Palestine National Council, Salim al-Za'nun, noted in March that the PLO's position during the Gulf crisis was only neutral and not pro-Iraqi.[76] The Kuwaitis, however, saw the situation differently. Kuwaitis on the streets openly said that, since it was impossible to distinguish between a "good Palestinian" who did not collaborate with the Iraqi occupiers and a "bad Palestinian" who did, they should all be punished. The press published articles analyzing both the Palestinian population's and the PLO's ingratitude by demanding that the "fate of Kuwait be linked with that of Palestine." Kuwaiti leaders' standpoint was that they would not abandon the Palestine cause; but the PLO leaders, notably Yasir 'Arafat, had proved to be incompetent and had been internationally rejected, and should therefore step down.[77]

While Kuwaiti persecution of Palestinians continued for the rest of 1991 (see above), so did Kuwait's criticism of their organizations and leaders. Thus, Foreign Minister Salim al-Sabah Al Salim stated in June that the "Palestine cause belonged to all the Arabs" rather than being under exclusive PLO representation. He urged that it should not be forgotten that the PLO, Yemen, Jordan, Tunis and Sudan had condoned Iraq's occupation of Kuwait: "I am afraid the time for this [forgetting and forgiving] has passed," he said.[78] The PLO was also accused by the Kuwaiti press of preparing "terrorist acts" against Kuwait.[79] The Palestinians suffered a further blow when Kuwaiti nationality was withdrawn from Khalid al-Hasan, a member of the PLO's Central Committee.[80]

Kuwait supported the ensuing Arab-Israeli peace process. It was encouraged to that position by the US sponsorship for the process, Egyptian and Syrian participation, and the possibility of stabilizing the Arab-Israeli arena, which would, in turn, help stabilize the Gulf region. Moreover, either because of Israel's support of the anti-Iraqi coalition and/or its anti-PLO attitude, Kuwait somewhat improved its attitude toward Israel. The media remained critical of what they considered Israel's stubbornness, but encouraged the start of negotiations. In mid-November, after continuous denials, its director-general of customs and excise, Ibrahim Ghanim, admitted that Kuwait had eased the Arab boycott on Israel. Kuwait, thereby, not only strengthened the US-peace initiative, but also made it possible for more Western firms (which were no longer boycotted) to bid for a share in Kuwait's reconstruction.[81]

ATTITUDE TOWARD WESTERN STATES

Since Kuwait maintained close security cooperation with the US, Britain and France, it was not surprising that its attitude on other issues concerning Western states was friendly and cooperative. Kuwait's dependence on Washington's help, combined with its gratitude toward the US, led to a wide-ranging cooperation. Thus, starting with Bechtel, American firms won the lion's share of Kuwait's reconstruction, in all spheres. In June, 60 American companies staged the first Kuwaiti postliberation trade fair. Continuous contacts were maintained between Jabir and the White House. In the wake of the US sensitivity to human rights violations, the Kuwaiti emir called President Bush to report and explain internal affairs — a fact which helped win Washington's support for Kuwait's policies.[82] The earlier-mentioned security pact, the joint military exercises and the purchase by Kuwait of US-made F-18 aircraft brought the cooperation between the two states to a peak in 1991.

British firms received a small but significant share of Kuwait's reconstruction, notably, in industrial work. Britain's most impressive contribution occurred in May, when British firms undertook to supply Kuwait with equipment and advice to enable it to reopen its school system.[83] During 1991, British and French high-ranking officials visited Kuwait several times.

APPENDIX: SA'D 'ABDALLAH'S NEW GOVERNMENT, APRIL 1991

Prime Minister	Crown Prince, Sa'd 'Abdallah Al Salim Al Sabah
Deputy Prime Minister and Foreign Minister	Salim al-Sabah Al Salim
Minister of State for Municipal Affairs	Ibrahim Majid al-Shahin
Minister of Interior	Ahmad Hamud Al-Jabir
Minister of Planning	Ahmad 'Ali al-Jassar
Minister of Electricity and Water	Ahmad Muhammad Salih al-'Adsani
Minister of Information	Badr Jasim al-Ya'qub
Minister of Communications	Habib Hasan Jawhar Hayat
Minister of Petroleum	Hamud 'Abdallah al-Ruqba
Minister of Education	Sulayman Sa'dun al-Badr
Minister for Cabinet Affairs	Dhari 'Abdallah al-'Uthman
Minister of Commerce and Industry	'Abdallah Hasan al-Jaralla
Minister of Public Works	'Abdallah Yusuf al-Qutami
Minister of Health	'Abd al-Wahhab al-Fawzan
Minister of Defense	'Ali Sabah Al Salim
Minister of Higher Education	'Ali 'Abdallah al-Shamlan
Minister of Justice and Legal Affairs	Ghari 'Ubayd al-Shammar
Minister of Waqf and Legal Affairs	Muhammad Saqar al-Ma'usharji
Minister of State for Housing	Muhammad 'Abd al-Muhsin al-'Usfur
Minister of Finance	Nasir 'Abdallah al-Ridan
Minister of Social Affairs and Labor	Nawwaf al-Ahmad al-Jabir Al Sabah

SOURCE: KUNA, 20 April — DR, 22 April 1991.

NOTES

For the place and frequency of publications cited here, and for the full name of the publication, news agency, radio station or monitoring service where an abbreviation is used, please see "List of Sources." Only in the case of more than one publication bearing the same name is the place of publication noted here.

1. *Al-Anba* (Cairo), 30 December 1990.
2. *Sawt al-Kuwait al-Duwali,* 10 January 1991.
3. WF, 10 January; KUNA, 11 January — DR, 14 January 1991.

4. KUNA, 15 February — DR, 19 February; *Sawt al-Kuwait al-Duwali*, 25 January 1991.
5. WF, 2 January; *FT*, 23 January, 4 February 1992; *CR*, Kuwait, No.1, 1991, pp. 14–15.
6. *Al-Ba'th*, 21 January 1991.
7. *FT*, 18 January 1991.
8. KUNA, 28 January — DR, 29 January 1991.
9. Cf. R. Riyadh, 20 January — DR, 22 January 1991.
10. *NYT*, 25 January 1991.
11. *NYT*, 30 January 1991.
12. *IHT*, 2 January; WF, 13 February 1991.
13. Cf. *IHT*, 2 January — WF, 11 February; KUNA, 12 February — DR, 13 February 1991.
14. KUNA, 23 February — DR, 26 February 1991.
15. *CR*, Kuwait, No. 1, 1991, p. 8; No. 2, 1991, p. 8.
16. The Press Association, 8 January — DR, 9 January 1991.
17. *JP*, 15 January 1991 (a Reuters report).
18. KUNA, 14 February — DR, 15 February 1991.
19. AFP, 20 February — DR, 22 February 1991.
20. KUNA, 25 February — DR, 26 February 1991.
21. *WSJ*, 20 February 1991.
22. Cf. *IHT*, 26 January 1991.
23. Cf. *FT*, 27 February 1991.
24. Mutawwa''s interview, *al-Majalla*, 27 March 1991.
25. *Ha'aretz*, 3 March; *NYT*, 16 March 1991.
26. *NYT*, 2, 3 March; *WP*, 7 March; *al-Majalla*, 27 March, 3 April; *al-Watan al-'Arabi*, 22 March 1991.
27. Cf. KUNA, 7 March — DR, 11 March; *JP*, 9 March; *IHT*, 17 October 1991.
28. Cf. *WP*, 25 June; KUNA, 25 November — DR, 26 November 1991.
29. *Ha'aretz*, 8, 11 March; *IHT*, 14 March; *WP*, 3 June 1991.
30. KUNA, 5 November — DR, 6 November 1991.
31. *NYT*, 21 May, 19 June; *IHT*, 21 June 1991.
32. *IHT*, 14 March 1991; *CR*, Kuwait, No. 2, 1991, pp. 14–15; No. 3, pp. 10–11.
33. *CR*, Kuwait, No. 3, 1991, pp. 10–11; *FT*, 16 July, 11 October, 4 November; *Le Monde*, 12 October 1991.
34. *NYT*, 19 October; *FT*, 25 October; *CR*, Kuwait, No. 4, 1991, pp. 8–11.
35. Ibid.; *FT*, 10 April 1991.
36. *CR*, Kuwait, No. 2, 1991, p. 15; *FT*, 15 March, 22 May 1991.
37. *CR*, Kuwait, No. 4, 1991, p. 9; Riyadh TV, 2 April — DR, 5 April; *NYT*, 19 April, 12 May; *Le Monde*, 14 May 1991.
38. R. Kuwait, 25 March — DR, 27 March; KUNA, 29 October — DR, 29 October 1991.
39. *CR*, Kuwait No. 4, 1991, pp. 9–10; *al-Watan al-'Arabi*, 29 March; R. Kuwait, 19 May — DR, 20 May; *NYT*, 31 May, 16 July; AFP, 7 July — DR, 9, 12 July 1991.
40. *CR*, Kuwait No. 2, 1991, p. 9; *NYT*, 25, 28 February; *IHT*, 8 March 1991.
41. *NYT*, 31 March; *FT*, 5 March; *WP*, 10 March 1991.
42. *NYT*, 10 March; *Sourakia*, 12 August 1991.
43. *NYT*, 12 March 1991.
44. Saqr's interview, *Sawt al-Sha'b* (Amman), 11 March; Ja'wan's interview, *al-Ittihad* (Abu Dhabi), 14 March 1991.
45. Sa'ud Nasir quoted by WF, 24 February; *NYT*, 10 March 1991.
46. *NYT*, 28 February, 10 March; *Sawt al-Kuwait al-Duwali*, 10 April 1991.
47. R. Kuwait, 21 April — DR, 22 April; *al-Watan al-'Arabi*, 19 May, 20 June 1991; *CR*, Kuwait, No. 2, 1991, pp. 9–11.
48. *NYT*, 23, 27 March, 22 April; AFP, 8 April — DR, 8 April 1991.
49. *IHT*, 23 April 1991.
50. *FT*, 15 May 1991.
51. *IHT*, 3 June; *NYT*, 10 July 1991.
52. *IHT*, 2 August, 31 December 1991; *CR*, Kuwait, No. 4, 1991, p. 7.
53. Sa'd 'Abdallah's interview, *al-Wafd*, 6 July 1991.
54. *Sawt al-Kuwait al-Duwali*, 17 May 1991.

55. *NYT,* 12 May 1991.
56. *IHT,* 18 May 1991.
57. Salim al-Sabah's interview, *al-Shira',* 2 July 1991.
58. KUNA, 15 May — DR, 16 May; Sa'd 'Abdallah's interview, *al-Wafd,* 6 July; *NYT,* 8 July 1991.
59. Salim al-Sabah's interview, *al-Shira',* 2 July 1991; *CR,* Kuwait, No. 3, 1991, pp. 7–8.
60. *IHT,* 24 August 1991.
61. AFP, 14 September — DR, 16 September; KUNA, 30 September — DR, 23 September; *FT,* 20 September 1991; *CR,* Kuwait, No. 4, 1991, p. 6.
62. *Al-Watan,* 7 October 1991.
63. *FT,* 4, October; *Le Monde,* 6 October; *Misr al-Fatat* (Jiza), 7 October 1991.
64. KUNA, 11 November — DR, 14 November 1991.
65. IRNA, 17 March — DR, 18 March; *al-Shira',* 22 July 1991.
66. KUNA, 22 September — DR, 23 September 1991; *CR,* Kuwait, No. 4, 1991, p. 7.
67. AFP, 17 August — DR, 22 August 1991.
68. KUNA, 30 July — DR, 31 July 1991.
69. *NYT,* 29 August; *Sawt al-Kuwait al-Duwali,* 31 August, 16 September; KUNA, 12 October — DR, 15 October 1991.
70. *Akhir Sa'a,* 2 November 1991; *CR,* Kuwait, No. 2, 1991, p. 13.
71. *Al-Anba* (Cairo), 29 March; *al-Wafd,* 23 May 1991.
72. *Sawt al-Kuwait al-Duwali,* 12 June 1991.
73. Kuwaiti Ambassador to Egypt 'Abd al-Razzaq al-Kandasri's interview, *Sawt al-Kuwait al-Duwali,* 29 September 1991.
74. *Al-Thawra* (Damascus), 27 March; R. Damascus, 21 April — DR, 22 April; KUNA, 22 July — DR, 23 July 1991.
75. R. Damascus, 19 September, 18 December — DR, 20 September, 19 December 1991.
76. Za'nun's interview, *al-Dustur* (Amman), 7 March 1991.
77. *Sawt al-Kuwait al-Duwali,* 12 March; *NYT,* 9, 14 March; *al-Siyasa,* 30 March 1991.
78. *Al-Shira',* 26 July 1991.
79. *Sawt al-Kuwait al-Duwali,* 21 June. One Palestinian fundamentalist group, led by As'ad al-Tamimi, indeed permitted the killing of Kuwaiti leaders; AFP, 3 July — DR, 3 July 1991.
80. KUNA, 15 December — DR, 16 December 1991.
81. *NYT,* 16 November 1991.
82. *IHT,* 30 May; WF, 4 June 1991.
83. *FT,* 24 May 1991.

Lebanon
(Al-Jumhuriyya al-Lubnaniyya)

WILLIAM W. HARRIS

In 1991 Lebanon assumed its place in the "new world order" — an ineffectual satellite of the Syrian Ba'thist regime. As a direct consequence of the Syrian-American rapprochement following the Iraqi occupation of Kuwait, and the October 1990 Syrian operation against Gen. Michel 'Awn, the entire Lebanese official apparatus was subjected to the will of Damascus, for the first time since the original 1976 Syrian military intervention in Lebanon.

The formal foundation for Syrian Ba'thist domination already existed in the American-Saudi promoted Ta'if agreement between Lebanese parliamentarians of October 1989 (see *MECS* 1989 and 1990, chapters on Lebanon). Through 1991, the semifeudal Lebanese upper class of all sects, in alliance with militia elements that had developed establishment tastes, hastened to translate the Ta'if document into whatever specific arrangements for Lebanese-Syrian integration were transmitted to them from Damascus. Not surprisingly, the one issue on which Syria hesitated was that of reciprocal economic access, the only point on which Lebanese national interests might be served.

In Beirut, Syrian President Hafiz al-Asad worked through the subservient regime of President Ilyas al-Hirawi and Prime Minister 'Umar Karami, neither of whom could ever have hoped for high office except via Syrian agency. Asad had preserved both the regime and the class it represented from the populist 'Awnist movement and, in the Shi'i sector, from the radical challenge of Hizballah. The Hirawi-Karami government, which was both incompetent and corrupt, could never aspire to more than minimal public acquiescence on the basis of a security quietening — and it was well known that such quietening was not produced by a regime headed by ineffectual leaders, but by a changed international environment and Lebanese exhaustion.

Events in South Lebanon indicated the shakiness of the post-1990 stabilization, and its dependence on non-Lebanese geopolitics. In 1991, South Lebanon assumed a particular significance as a barometer of crosscurrents affecting the American-coordinated Middle East peace effort. It represented a "no-man's-land" on which a variety of parties could test each other, play for diplomatic advantage, and maneuver for position in a continuing strategic competition. At this stage, the chief movers were Syria, Israel and Iran, with the US periodically exerting itself, and the Palestinians and Hizballah reduced to subplots by Syria's general advance in Lebanon. Syria was deterred from a direct appearance by the Israelis and deployed its hegemony in Beirut and the southward spread of the Lebanese army, to bid for a steering role over the Palestinian presence in Sidon and Tyre, and over Hizballah activities. Increased influence on the Palestinians and more weight in the Syria-Iran-Hizballah "triangle"

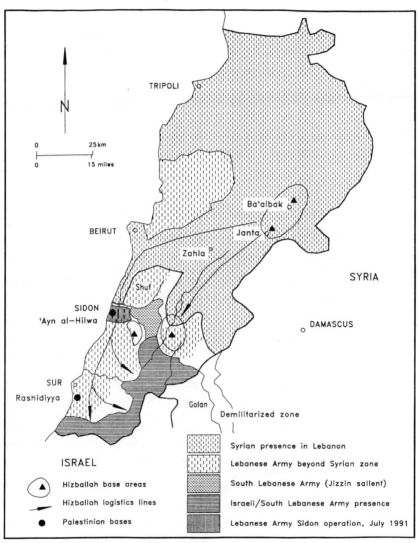

N

0   25km

0   15 miles

TRIPOLI

Ba'albak

BEIRUT

Janta

Zahla

SYRIA

Shuf

SIDON

'Ayn al-Hilwa

DAMASCUS

SUR

Rashidiyya

Golan

Demilitarized zone

Syrian presence in Lebanon

Lebanese Army beyond Syrian zone

South Lebanese Army (Jizzin salient)

Israeli/South Lebanese Army presence

Lebanese Army Sidon operation, July 1991

ISRAEL

▲ Hizballah base areas

Hizballah logistics lines

● Palestinian bases

Lebanon: Geopolitical Conditions, 1991

could be used either in diplomatic haggling or for future confrontation with Israel. The Lebanese regime had made itself irrelevant for the duration of its new relationship with Syria; it abdicated autonomy concerning its own territory in the "Brotherhood, Cooperation and Coordination Pact" made with Damascus in May 1991.

No whim of Damascus was questioned in Beirut. With 'Awn out of the way, the Lebanese army subverted, and the Maronite presidency of the republic in his pocket, Asad lost no time in having the old militias cut down to size. By mid-1991, the Christian Lebanese Forces (LF), the Druze Progressive Socialist Party (PSP) and the Shi'i Amal had all been removed from Greater Beirut and substantially disarmed. Only Hizballah remained unreduced, although the religious radicals shifted their Beirut military apparatus southward, where they could concentrate on antagonizing the Israelis. As for the others, the LF was humiliated in return for collaboration with Syria; the PSP became isolated in the Shuf, demoralized by the evaporation of its Moscow link, while Damascus considered currying favor with the Maronites by patronizing a Christian refugee return to the Druze heartland; and Amal, worn down by years of service to the Syrians, faced oblivion.

However, despite the Syrian successes and the obsequiousness of the regime, the Syrian hegemony could not be assured of what Damascus knew it still lacked, even by 1992 — a stable longevity. Sooner or later, Syria would have to face pressure on its military presence in the Lebanese capital, regardless of the loopholes Damascus had deliberately insinuated into the Ta'if document. Within Lebanon, both the regime and the Syrians stimulated deep popular malice. Also, eventually the international environment favoring the Syrian hegemony would change, perhaps coinciding with the test of a post-Asad transition in Syria.

Despite loud protestations about their eagerness to leave Beirut,[1] the Syrians needed more time to exploit their expanded access to the Lebanese official machine in order to institutionalize coordination and stabilization. First, the basic political and socioeconomic grievances of the Shi'is had not been settled by the Ta'if pact, while new resentments had arisen amongst the Maronites and Druzes. Although the constitutional elevation of the prime minister was a visible gain for the Sunni community, it did nothing positive for intersectarian relations, as regards either Muslims or Christians. Communal frustrations thus continued to fester under the "lid" represented by Syria and Ta'if, threatening the destabilization of Syrian hegemony, if Damascus relaxed its grip. Second, complexity and passive resistance within the Lebanese bureaucratic, military and financial sectors set limits on the conversion of intergovernment agreements into solid Syrian "coordination." Remote-control hegemony, of the extent desired in Damascus,[2] was probably impossible without a large Syrian presence in Beirut.

BEIRUT AND DAMASCUS: THE CONTOURS OF SYRIAN HEGEMONY

A brief examination of the new Lebanese "National Unity" Government of December 1990 (see *MECS* 1990, chapter on Lebanon) suffices to indicate the improbability of its exhibiting either probity or independence. Seven of the 30 ministers were militia chiefs, with a further five from parties intimately associated with militias. Only the three ministers from the LF-Kata'ib bloc could be expected to question orders from

Damascus openly, and they themselves had demonstrated readiness to trade national sovereignty for Maronite sectional interests. The two personalities responsible for security matters, Defense Minister Michel al-Murr and Interior Minister Sami al-Khatib, were on good terms with the Syrian leadership, while the assignment of other portfolios represented a distribution of sinecures, unrelated to experience or technical competence. The 'Awnist movement, Lebanon's only cross-sectarian populist tendency, was excluded. Hizballah, populist but narrowly sectarian, chose not to participate. After 15 years of death and destruction, Lebanon received an unsatisfactory replica of the prewar ancien régime.

What made the Hirawi regime viable? This issue did not just relate to the Syrian-American partnership which produced it, but to the interests of the Lebanese haute bourgeoisie as a resurgent ruling class, with the retreat of the militias, and to communal circumstances in the early 1990s. The upper social strata had changed in shape during Lebanon's war, and not for the better. The pre-1975 rural and commercial leadership, semifeudal and corrupt, had mutated into a combination of bits of the old order melded with wartime mafiosi, nouveaux riches and Lebanese agents of foreign powers. Representatives of the old class with personal integrity or real feeling for Lebanon had either been murdered — principally by the Syrians, for example Dani Chamoun, Mufti Hasan Khalid and Kamal Junblat, or become ineffectual, like Salim al-Huss.

The haute bourgeoisie of 1991, Christian and non-Christian, wanted security from the frustration of the middle and lower orders, which had been badly hit by the currency collapse of the late 1980s. It also sought protection from the instability caused by militia conflict and Hizballah populism. It cared little for national sovereignty, and so welcomed the Ta'if pact and the Syrian security umbrella. Having integrated militia elements, who saw more profit in joining the status quo than in challenging it, this class became impatient over a dissolution of militias.

PSP leader Walid Junblat, a maverick in enforced connection with the regime, correctly noted "how they hate us [the militias], those that accepted Ta'if — it is because they derive from the old generation, the generation which behaves as if the war never happened, or as if this period must be expunged from history."[3] Damascus could rely on segments of the haute bourgeoisie, particularly those Maronite, Sunni and Shi'i traditionalists who felt exposed to 'Awnism or Islamic radicalism, to support parliamentary elections under heavy Syrian influence. Asad shielded these people from the abyss.

As regards the Lebanese communities in 1991, Hizballah mentor Muhammad Husayn Fadlallah mixed reality with conspiracy theory when commenting:

> The American Administration aimed to expel Europe from Lebanon — especially France, recognized with the Vatican as godfather of the Lebanese Christian openness to Europe — and in this matter it was necessary, from the American standpoint, to fragment the Christian people, as the Islamic people had already been fragmented, because America wishes a shattering of Lebanon's balances so that it can restructure the country to its own satisfaction. And this can only be via the splintering of the the two great Lebanese sects, the Shi'is and the Maronites.[4]

Naturally, Fadlallah did not dare speculate on a Syrian interest in such a development, being careful to cite Syria only as a victim.[5]

In the Shi'i and Christian sectors — about three quarters of Lebanon's population — leadership had failed; no political center of gravity existed; and the public mood was bitter. However, tiredness predominated.[6] The vacuum provided a temporarily congenial environment for the Hirawi regime. Political collapse was particularly marked in East Beirut, where the defeat of 'Awn after two years of extreme tension left an atmosphere of hopelessness. Hirawi was despised as a Syrian puppet[7] and lived under Syrian guard in West Beirut, but the regime had no local Christian challenger. The East Beirut public saw the surviving formal opposition — the LF/Kata'ib bloc — as heavily responsible for the 1990 disaster; hence, whatever their illusions, Samir Ja'ja' and George Sa'ada had no chance of popular legitimacy.

Amongst Shi'is, the brutal tussle between Amal and Hizballah for supremacy in the south and the Beirut suburbs had discredited much of the younger nontraditional leadership, and opened the way for a traditionalist recovery. Despite continuing vigor and generous Iranian support, Hizballah could never have more than a partial attraction in a culturally open, substantially Westernized population. The organization held widespread respect as an indigenous expression of Shi'i impatience with the world, but many were fed up with its high-handed behavior in southern villages and saw little point in unproductive provocation of the Israelis. Amal attracted similar opprobrium for splitting the community, and lacked Hizballah's dynamic zeal. It decayed into a variety of poorly coordinated groups, while its leader, Nabih Barri, came to be viewed as a lightweight personality.

The traditionalists gained from rudderlessness and conservative money-making sentiment in the community. One old Shi'i notable, Kamal al-As'ad, eclipsed for years by his association with the Jumayyil regime, resurfaced as a pole of influence in the south. Parliamentary speaker, Husayn al-Husayni, who had achieved de facto equality with the Maronite president and the Sunni prime minister in the "reformed" regime, overshadowed Barri in Beirut and as linkman with Damascus. Even the Higher Shi'i Islamic Council, an appendage of Amal throughout the 1980s, emerged more in its own right. This buttressed the role of the respected moderate religious personality, Muhammad Mahdi Shams al-Din, a firm opponent of Hizballah,[8] though it did not affect the regard for Fadlallah as the community's preeminent religious authority (*marji'a*).

With the Lebanese haute bourgeoisie under its control, the major communities debilitated, and a permissive international environment, Damascus looked to consolidate its hegemony. Command of the National Unity Government would be the the mechanism for erosion of nonregime power centers on Lebanese territory; for subordination of the Lebanese security apparatus; and for supervision of official institutions. In 1991, issues dominating relations between Beirut and Damascus encompassed the extent of Syrian direction of the Lebanese regime, and the effectiveness of the regime as a Syrian mechanism. Up to early 1992, the Lebanese-Syrian interaction passed through three phases: buttressing the National Unity Government with militia dissolutions and parliamentary appointments; defining "privileged relations" in formal agreements; and the practical test of Lebanese-Syrian coordination as the two states entered negotiations with Israel after October 1991.

CONSOLIDATION OF THE REGIME, JANUARY-APRIL 1991
Until the Gulf crisis ended with the Iraqi collapse, in late February 1991, the Syrians

cautiously guarded their recent Lebanese gains, but held back on new initiatives. The Lebanese Government received firm support for "battening down the hatches" in Greater Beirut, with joint Syrian-Lebanese policing of 15 January directives (which coincided with the American air offensive against Iraq), restricting party offices and political activities. The government also went ahead with personnel changes in senior bureaucratic positions, and started a drastic restructuring of the army.[9] Every aspect entailed close consultation with Syria, including joint committees for army reform. On the latter subject, change aimed at sectarian mixing of brigades and a reduction of 'Awnist influence in the officer corps.[10]

Syria was distracted by events in the Gulf. Walid Junblat's resignation from the government on 11 January, and a boycott of the regime by the disgruntled LF brought virtually no reaction; these were affairs which could be rectified later. Damascus vacillated on plans to deploy the Lebanese army to parts of South Lebanon.[11] The Lebanese army command and Shi'i ministers wanted an early demonstration of regime initiative, however superficial, whereas the Syrians preferred caution. The army move went ahead without incident on 7 February (see below), but a Syrian official commented to Lebanese Foreign Minister Faris Buwayz that: "It would have been better to finish the strengthening of Greater Beirut before sending the army south."[12]

Immediate assertion of Syrian will came in March, with Iraq's military defeat and nervous relief in Damascus. On the one hand, Asad made important pan-Arab gains through Saddam Husayn's strategic miscalculation. On the other hand, the end of the Cold War and US global dominance left Syria, a former Soviet client and known sponsor of terrorists, in an uncomfortable position. As the US intimated that it intended to exert itself in the Arab-Israeli arena to establish regional stability, Syria looked to cement its assets as a key player. Most immediately, loose ends on the Lebanese western flank had to be tied up. Sarkis Na'um of *Al-Nahar*, a conduit for "sources close to Damascus," summarized the Syrian outlook: Junblat and the LF had been "betting on an upset to Syria — at this delicate moment Syria does not want islands in Lebanon outside its hegemony"; Damascus "fears" that such islands would reflect on the Syrian position in the new order and "doesn't want the US to see any weakening in the Syrian hold."[13]

In the first instance, Syria was determined to maintain the Ta'if agreement date of 21 March 1991 for the formal government decision on dissolution of militias. On 28 February, President Hirawi returned from a summit with Asad talking about "finishing with the [LF and Junblati] boycott" and speeding up the army reorganization.[14] Syrian Vice President 'Abd al-Halim Khaddam laid down the law to Lebanese parliamentarians about regime appointment of deputies instead of elections: "Ta'if says appointment — the parliamentarians agreed to Ta'if — what has changed?"[15]

Junblat adapted to reality on the day of the Gulf cease-fire. In place of his publicity against Ta'if, against parliamentary appointments and in favor of Iraq, he now wished to start afresh with Damascus and, on 3 March, returned to the government "to improve the nationalist situation."[16] Thus were the Druzes reduced. The LF in East Beirut also came under intensifying pressure, and similarly had no basis for resistance. Encroachment by the army, Syrian intelligence and rival Christian parties had already sapped LF organizational effectiveness in Christian areas, and no internal or external allies remained. At a session with Buwayz in Damascus, US Secretary of State James Baker reiterated support for Ta'if "in letter and spirit,"[17] a solid endorsement of the Syrian approach. Directly after Baker's visit, on 17 March, Khaddam descended on Beirut, proclaiming that: "The Lebanese do not have any choice" about executing Ta'if; "We do not expect any serious obstacle to any operational step to close the Lebanese file in all its aspects."[18]

The three ministers from the LF-Kata'ib bloc duly assumed their cabinet seats in time for the 20 March cabinet session, which unanimously endorsed the "principles" of militia dissolution and appointment of deputies. Samir Ja'ja', who gave up his seat for his representative Roger Deeb, lamely indicated that: "The LF will try to modify what it is possible to modify from within the government."[19] More humiliation followed; a 28 March cabinet meeting set 1 May as the final date for the militia surrender of heavy and medium weaponry, and decided on legislation to allow the parliamentary appointments, brushing aside the attempt by Deeb and Sa'ada to have appointments linked to a Syrian pullback from Beirut. Disbandment of Lebanese militias became detached from action regarding the Palestinians. A government statement, delivered by Ba'thist minister 'Abdallah al-Amin, threatened that any problem would bring a "calling on Syria" and "use of force."[20]

LF stalling through April extracted a government commitment to recruit 20,000 militiamen into the army and state security organs, mainly because this was also an insistent demand from the PSP, Amal and other Syrian-connected parties. Palestinian recalcitrance (see below), which the LF hoped might upset the general program, did not affect the division of priorities between Lebanese and non-Lebanese armed groups. No comfort came from US Ambassador Ryan Crocker, who dismissed appointment of members of parliament as a "matter of detail not concerning us or any other foreign country"[21] — Syria apparently was not a foreign country — and remarked that: "The presence of Palestinian weaponry in Sidon is not a threat to the Christians."[22] Adjusting to the inevitable, the Kata'ib demonstrated its democratic principles by a swift policy change to appointment of members of parliament provided the Kata'ib got its share,[23] while the LF consoled itself with lucrative arms sales on the international black market — some sources estimated the proceeds at $280m. by mid-April.[24]

Other indigenous militias bowed without fuss. Like the LF, the Druzes sought to preserve their political-social organization, and stashed away lighter weaponry in hideouts; Amal had little organized capacity left worth preserving; and, immune in the south and with Iranian cover in the Biqa', Hizballah reordered its military geography in these two directions.

Barri announced Amal's end as a military body. Junblat made sympathetic comments comparing the predicaments of the PSP and the LF, and refused to deliver heavy weapons to what Druzes still regarded as a suspect military institution. Instead, the PSP transferred most equipment to the Syrian army, the original owner of PSP tanks and artillery. Apart from sales, the LF, as with other militias, was required to return Lebanese army property and to store the residue at designated depots or ship it out of the country. Thus, on the night of 10 May, a large shipload left Junya,[25] probably a return of equipment to Israel. The movement of Lebanese army brigades into the Kisrawan, Jubayl and the Kura (LF and Faranjiyya areas), and into the Druze Shuf took place, as planned, on 1 May.

Consolidation of the Ta'if regime, under Syrian guidance, had passed a significant test with the reduction of organizations that had ruled Beirut in the mid-1980s. The Ta'if provision about establishing Christian-non-Christian equivalence through the packing of the legislature with appointees came next: to reward militia leaders for their cooperation; for distribution of favors to friends of the regime and Damascus; and to institutionalize executive control of parliament. Syrian Vice President Khaddam, who joined Hirawi, Karami and Husayni to sift through the lists of "candidates," attacked the existing parliament as having lost "representative legitimacy" because of self-voted extensions since 1972[26] — an interesting reflection on the Syrian definition of the same parliament as "legitimate" when voting in Ta'if and the Hirawi presidency. The government rammed through the enabling law on 9 May, and the first to submit official candidacies to the Ministry of the Interior were Junblat and Prime Minister Karami. A former (Sunni) prime minister commented sarcastically on the rush of those who had made a virtue of opposition: "It's not just that the train is moving, but everyone is moving with the train."[27]

On 7 June, the cabinet chose the 40 new deputies to make a 108-member chamber, filling 31 vacancies and the nine new non-Christian seats. The 40 names had already been cleared with Damascus, with a final vetting by Ghazi Kan'an, chief of Syrian military intelligence in Lebanon.[28] All except the one-tenth LF-Kata'ib allotment had close connections with the Syrian regime. Thirteen ministers assured themselves of places, while 15 of the new parliamentarians had militia backgrounds. Very few of these would have even the slightest prospect in free elections, which would be a landslide for 'Awnism and Hizballah, thus explaining the lack of US interest in Lebanese democracy. Whether in appointments past or managed ballots to come, Syria looked to have the green light for a free hand.

"BROTHERHOOD, COOPERATION AND COORDINATION"
Syria's crowning Lebanese prize of 1991 came in the 22 May "Treaty of Brotherhood, Cooperation and Coordination" (see Appendix 1) and the 7 September "Defense and Security Pact" (see Appendix 2), which together represented the written elaboration of the call for Syrian-Lebanese "privileged relations" in the Ta'if agreement. Hafiz al-Asad had good reason to refer effusively to the Brotherhood Treaty as a "brilliant token" (*zahira sati'a*), "dissipating the thick clouds which have enclosed us."[29] Despite interpretations to the contrary, these were not mere pieces of paper, unimportant in comparison with the shifting balance of forces. Nor did they approximate to general world trends toward more interstate collaboration. For the first time, the Lebanese regime was officially bound to joint institutional arrangements with Syria for foreign, security, socioeconomic and even cultural affairs. The May treaty formally invited and legitimized deep Syrian intrusion in Lebanon's policy-making, while in the security sphere, the September pact emasculated Lebanese sovereignty in depth and in detail. This was in no way the same, as Prime Minister 'Umar Karami tried to assert,[30] as relations between democracies in the European Community. In a formal bond between a small fragmented polity and a predatory dictatorship, all the stylized reciprocity was no more than a cruel joke.

Lebanese-Syrian discussions on concretizing "privileged relations" began with a decision at the 20 March cabinet meeting in favor of a Lebanese government committee to consider "relations with Syria." Under strong Syrian pressure, the drawing-up of the first draft of a treaty proceeded at speed and was shrouded in secrecy, one of the few newspaper indications being a cryptic note in *al-Nahar* of 10 April that: "The privileged relations draft will be studied soon." The extent of Syrian dictation proved too much even for some on the regime committee, who leaked unattributed complaints that the draft transgressed the spirit of Ta'if on mutual respect for independence and sovereignty.[31] This elicited the comment from Khaddam that certain committee members were handling the matter "with the mentality of a well-known Maronite monk."[32] It seems that the Syrians desired to insert the terms "unification" and "integration," but dropped these in favor of "coordination" when the Americans saw the text and protested.[33] The Syrians were not concerned about such minor details, since in essence they got everything they wanted.

All Lebanese ministers except two attended the 22 May signing ceremony of the Brotherhood Treaty in Damascus. The treaty established a Higher Council between Syria and Lebanon, comprising the most senior political personalities and supported by a general secretariat. This Higher Council would oversee an institutional structure of four permanent interstate committees: for prime ministerial "coordination," foreign affairs, economic and social affairs, and defense and security. The text of the treaty contained vague but ominous references to interstate committees taking decisions "that are effective as soon as issued"; to "coordinating the foreign policies of the two states and defining their relationships with all other states"; to "coordination of social activities in the two states"; to "joint measures to confront disturbances and riots" (entirely an internal issue on any definition of sovereignty); and to follow-up agreements to come, even in "education."

Very few Lebanese had the courage to dissent publicly. Only Deputy Albert Mukhaybir, previously praised by Junblat for his autonomy, voted against the treaty when it was submitted to parliament for rubber-stamp ratification. Two months earlier, a "former minister" had painted a "black future" for Lebanon: "Free Lebanon is a dream — as East Europe comes out of hegemony and autocracy, Lebanon goes in until an unknown time — the US sees that Lebanon cannot run itself and is not against someone else running it."[34] Otherwise reaction varied between fawning praise of Damascus and what commentator Sarkis Na'um described as "the difficulty in saying no."[35]

Syria's hegemonic scheme was now so blatant that Prime Minister Karami himself felt obliged to make such statements as: "It is clear to all that Syria has no ambitions in Lebanon and does not wish, as some see it, to swallow Lebanon and to colonize it and take its revenues."[36] Triumphant Syrian officials had no need for this sort of double-talk. Defense Minister Mustafa Talas stressed the approach of "unity between Lebanon and Syria," while Foreign Minister Faruq al-Shar' flatly observed that: "The majority of people in Lebanon and Syria are with unification, but [Damascus] is content for the present time with coordination." As for opposition, "we do not hear any respectable Lebanese speaking in that fashion."[37]

After the Brotherhood Treaty, the Syrians were diverted for a time by the Palestinians in South Lebanon and by maneuverings associated with the American initiative for a ME conference. Apart from the July army operation in Sidon, the Lebanese regime occupied itself with squabblings over prerogatives between Hirawi, Karami and Husayni, and toying with a purge of the Administration. It carefully left activity in the Arab-Israeli conference controversy to Damascus. However, in mid-July

Asad decided to accept the American framework (see chapter on the ME peace process), leaving Lebanon as the only one of Israel's neighbors still hanging back.

On this issue, the Lebanese Government found itself in an embarrassing position, experiencing conflicting pressures and unable to get clear guidance from Damascus. One segment of the cabinet, which included the Shi'i ministers, argued that UN Resolution 425 demanded unconditional Israeli withdrawal from South Lebanon, and that attending the proposed conference would confuse the matter with wider Arab-Israeli issues. Shi'i radicals outside the regime went further, denouncing the conference and threatening anybody who had ideas of participating in it. The Syrians were unenthusiastic about a separate Lebanese role at the conference, viewing their own attendance as sufficient for both states. However, since they did not wish to offend the Americans, they refrained from clarifying their attitude, even to Beirut.

On the other hand, the Lebanese regime, particularly its Christian component, was well aware of its low popular rating and was nervous about the consequences of not participating in a major international event relevant to Lebanon's future. Washington pressed for a positive Lebanese decision, indicating that Beirut could not expect action on Resolution 425 if it did not shoulder minimal international responsibilities. At a Cairo encounter on 19 July, Secretary of State Baker dismissed Foreign Minister Buwayz's arguments for Lebanese delays, responding that "even Syria agreed without reservation."[38] As a result, the Lebanese Government, assuming tacit Syrian permission, announced compliance with American wishes.

Syria swiftly indicated its irritation with even this degree of Lebanese autonomy. First, Hirawi was regarded as having been insufficiently diligent in following the Brotherhood Treaty requirement for foreign-policy coordination. Second, Syria wanted freedom to use South Lebanon as a "card" for its own strategy, and was suspicious that Israel and the US desired a Lebanese presence in negotiations for purposes of splitting. On 27 July, Hirawi, Karami, Husayni and Defense Minister Michel al-Murr were summoned to Damascus, to be told that Lebanon would restrict itself to demanding implementation of Resolution 425 and must avoid any concept of bilateral "peace" with Israel or any digression into wider regional affairs. Syria also exploited jostlings within the Lebanese regime to teach Hirawi a lesson. In early August, a cabinet meeting was held without Hirawi for the first time — following the literal text of Ta'if — and House Speaker Husayni questioned whether Lebanon's conference attendance had really been decided. In a dispute with Karami over senior appointments in the Lebanese Foreign Ministry, Hirawi was reduced to consulting Asad via his son, Basil al-Asad. Hirawi went to Ladhiqiyya to pursue the question, and was jocularly rapped over the knuckles by the Syrian president, who told him that "You are sometimes cheeky and problematic, but I am reliable, oh Abu George."[39]

The conference issue stimulated the Syrians into renewed urgency over tying down Lebanese decision-making on security, the arena most critical to Damascus. On 22 August, a draft agreement prepared by a joint committee of the two countries was approved by the Lebanese Government without ministers even seeing the written text.[40] The defense and interior ministers of Syria and Lebanon then signed the "Defense and Security Pact" at Shtura on 1 September. The regime maintained silence to prevent media comment, and the text did not become public knowledge until a week later.

The "Defense and Security Pact" translated the generalities of the Brotherhood

Treaty into detailed interstate obligations. The aim of the Syrians was to attach the subordinated Lebanese army, intelligence services, security agencies and Interior Ministry to the Syrian apparatus. For example, Lebanon committed itself "to exchange information related to all security and strategic matters, national and internal, to exchange officers — including exchange of military instructors — to achieve the highest level of military coordination." An extraordinary clause demanded "banning any activity or organization in all military, security, political and information fields that might endanger and cause threats to the other country." This put an end to the possibility of a free election campaign in Lebanon, and covered the option of controlled elections if Syria came under early Western pressure to leave Greater Beirut. In addition, the degree of Lebanese-Syrian integration raised doubt as to whether Lebanon remained a free agent to honor other international accords — such as the 1949 Armistice Agreement or any replacement treaty between Lebanon and Israel.

THE REGIME AT HOME AND ABROAD, AUGUST-DECEMBER 1991

After mid-1991, regime activities assumed a consistent pattern. In the economy and Administration, corruption prevailed (see section on economic and social degradation, below). Overall, within parameters established by Syrian interests and the play of Syrian and American influences, different elements within the Lebanese Government pursued their own agendas. The main axes of friction were: first, competition for sectarian precedence between the Maronite president, the Sunni prime minister and the Shi'i parliamentary speaker (termed the "troika" by the Lebanese media); and second, discontent amongst the main former militia leaders (Walid Junblat, Nabih Barri and Samir Ja'ja'), regarding the regime's neglect of their priorities.

For the Syrians, these frictions involved manipulatory opportunities and management inconveniences. A stream of Lebanese ministers and officials visiting Damascus for mediation in every imaginable Lebanese internal squabble gave a gratifying demonstration of Lebanese dependence, and assisted Syrian penetration of Lebanon's regime apparatus. However, it also meant that Syrian leaders were bombarded with tiresome minutiae at a time of important ME developments.

In part, friction within the government and dependence on Syria reflected sensitivity about the regime's total lack of popular legitimacy. Publicly, the government scorned the continuing "'Awnist phenomenon" on both sides of Beirut as a sentiment of no practical relevance that would decline with time. Privately, President Hirawi feared 'Awn as a "Christian and Lebanese Khomeyni"; the regime tried to outlaw "the blowing of car horns in a politically significant manner" and diligently tracked down 'Awnist activists and printeries.[41] On 26 August, the French were permitted to remove 'Awn from their Beirut embassy to exile in Marseilles. Despite the conditions of the "amnesty," 'Awn began an inflammatory publicity campaign which found support in all Lebanese communities[42]: Lebanon had "a puppet government which has delivered the country to the [Syrian] occupier and the charge of treason will follow it."[43]

Karim Bakraduni, an astute East Beirut chameleon, in a new manifestation as contributor to the West Beirut daily *al-Safir* guessed that the "'Awnist phenomenon" would grow in direct relation to "the negligence of the regime in caring for basic needs of the population — and its incapacity to cope with the aspirations of the people."[44] The haute bourgeoisie had nothing but contempt for the ordinary citizen. However, the matter was of more than theoretical significance, as the traditional class would have to steer itself through general elections in the foreseeable future. The preferred solution was repression, as evidenced by a banning order against *al-Nahar* when it tried to print extracts from a new book about Gen. 'Awn in early 1992.

The transfer of most executive prerogatives from the presidency to the cabinet, as agreed at Ta'if, left the regime with no clear center of gravity. Of the three leading personalities, President Hirawi wished to retain a degree of initiative, as he was vulnerable to the charge of betraying the Maronite political position; prime minister Karami sought to reinforce his enlarged functions as cabinet head; and the parliamentary speaker, Husayni, who regarded himself as "godfather" of Ta'if, special confidant of Damascus and senior political spokesman of Lebanon's largest sect, was anxious to exert moral supremacy. In late September, all three went to the UN General Assembly session in New York, and made a joint visit to President Bush. Bush cut their interview short; the Americans were not impressed with their provincialism; and the three returned to Beirut with no concrete results on either South Lebanon or financial aid.

Hirawi attracted criticism from Karami and Husayni, and came under Syrian suspicion as he tried to show a coldly hostile Christian public that a Maronite presidency still meant something. He and his son-in-law, Foreign Minister Buwayz, struggled to keep for themselves what little was left of Lebanese foreign policy after Syrian dictation. Following the troika's American fiasco, Hirawi went alone in October to France, Italy and the Vatican. Karami resented this as a transgression of the prime minister's primacy in managing regime policy under the new constitution, and Syria perceived Hirawi as becoming ensnared in a French bid to recover influence in Beirut. When French Foreign Minister Roland Dumas came to Lebanon in December, with only a short subsequent stopover scheduled for Damascus, Asad refused to receive him.

Relations between Hirawi and Husayni involved common interests in their home area, the Biqa', especially for prospective parliamentary elections, as well as competition. Husayni attempted to establish his own Christian base by posing as cover for the Christians with Syria.[45] Jockeying in the Biqa' and between the legislative and executive branches of the regime were mixed together when, in November, Hirawi blocked a parliamentary measure backed by Husayni in favor of municipal elections. Hirawi had already encountered resistance from the Zahla municipality when he moved to appoint a new city leadership. Husayni sought influence in the Christian west Biqa', either with or against Hirawi, to buttress his Shi'i standing. His Christian "group" included Biqa'is such as Information Minister Albert Mansur and regional governor Simon Karam, as well as deputies John 'Ubayd and Nasif Lahhud and even Kata'ib minister George Sa'ada.[46]

Although Hirawi wriggled within the Syrian embrace, there was never a chance that he could emulate the escape act of President Ilyas Sarkis of the late 1970s — not while Asad lived. Both the Maronites and the presidency had declined decisively, largely through self-mutilation, while Hirawi's performance as a Syrian agent left him with no communal legitimacy. Any move by Hirawi to acquire Christian depth or to cooperate with the Americans immediately brought him up against Syrian interests. Feeble maneuverings by the Lebanese regime for Israeli assent to army deployment in Jizzin and for a clamp on Hizballah activities went counter to Syrian policy to keep a range of options in South Lebanon. Any sign of autonomy in international relations — for example regarding the US, France and Egypt — invited swift Syrian truncation. Despite providing himself with a circle of advisers with "American" proclivities, Hirawi was weak and of limited abilities. As one commentator diplomatically claimed: "President Hirawi possesses political characteristics which distinguish him from others, especially his predecessors Presidents Ilyas Sarkis and Amin Jumayyil, and which he has displayed since the day of his election."[47] Another simply noted: "Hirawi will stand with Syria if [it has] any difference with the US."[48]

The antics of militia chiefs, who were alarmed at their declining standing after the dissolution of the military wings of their organizations, added to the confusion of the regime. Damascus guarded the integrity of the government, and exhibited annoyance with anything it viewed as an unnecessary perturbation.

On 31 August, Amal ministers Nabih Barri and Muhammad Baydon withdrew from the cabinet, declaring themselves affronted by a visit to Libya by Karami and Buwayz on the anniversary of the 1978 disappearance in Libya of Shi'i leader Musa Sadr. This action expressed Shi'i resentment of Sunni and Maronite advantages in the regime, and of the haute bourgeoisie resurgence, including that within the Shi'i community. Reactions from Syria and the government leadership were frigid. Amal hardly figured any more in Syrian calculations concerning South Lebanese Shi'is. These concentrated on Hizballah or a new "pole" being worked on by Ba'thist Shi'i minister 'Abdallah al-Amin, to embrace traditionalists and other party elements.[49] On 16 September, Khaddam suddenly appeared in Beirut to announce that "Barri continues and will continue to carry out his national responsibilities by working in the cabinet."[50] The following day, Barri and Baydoun dutifully returned to their posts.

One issue bothering Barri, Junblat and Ja'ja' was lack of progress on absorption of militia personnel into the army and internal security force, as this affected their credibility amongst their followers. The army procrastinated because it was not enthusiastic about accepting militiamen, and relatively few LF men came forward, due to their fear of 'Awnist officers. A shortage of Christians meant delays with non-Christians, as there was supposed to be communal balance. The government eventually considered a conscription plan, mainly because an exemption fee for the wealthy promised a profitable kickback.[51] Such cavalier schemes, together with disdain from the traditionalist politicians, caused Junblat and Ja'ja' to boycott and snipe at the regime, though Damascus made sure that the opposition was ineffectual.

Disputes over the return of displaced people to their homes presented a more serious difficulty, as this encompassed approximately one quarter of Lebanon's population and involved the basic credibility of Ta'if, the regime and the peace process. Platitudes aside, the LF and PSP could not be comfortable contemplating a refugee return that would stand against future options for militia cantons or federalism. On the other hand, support for a restoration of the Christian presence in the Druze Shuf was politically mandatory in East Beirut, while the PSP had to make careful demographic calculations regarding the Druze position between the Maronites and the Shi'is.

For the Syrians, the refugee issue had potential for opportunism. First, support for refugees gave the appearance of virtue, and could be used to browbeat recalcitrant militias. Second, patronizing the case of the c. 150,000 displaced Shuf Christians offered a chance to mend fences with the Christian communities. A well-informed source, close to the Lebanese regime, indicated to the author in early 1992 that mass Maronite alienation from the regime and from Syria disturbed Damascus.[52] Hints of rival repatriation ideas came from Elie Hubayka, involving refugee return under a Syrian security umbrella, and from the Vatican envoy in Lebanon, Pablo Puente, who suggested to Junblat an arrangement between Druze and Christian leaders, to circumvent the Syrians.[53]

Despite the pressures, Junblat proved resistant. The PSP was angry about being a target while there was less attention to Muslims displaced from East Beirut,[54] many Shuf Druzes were using refugee property, and Junblat possibly wished to bargain for financial inputs from foreign Christian agencies. In November, Junblat rejected refugee repatriation before "a new national pact," and accused the Maronites of trying to sell "international coordination [to Syria] in exchange for continued advantages internally."[55]

This was a blow to the regime — especially its traditionalist Christian component — on a matter of populist sensitivity. However, Damascus looked to playing several sides of the game. A long drawn-out trickle of repatriation would promote Christian dependence on Syrian "good offices," while favorable terms for Junblat and highlighting of Druze vulnerabilities would intensify Druze links with Syria. Also, with regard to hegemonic goals, Damascus still balanced between the regime and other forces, including the residual militia apparatuses. The idea was both to deter the regime from autonomous thinking, and to keep options open, in case the regime ever proved unviable.

Syria's main mechanism for ensuring good behavior was the Brotherhood Treaty. On 17 October, the Higher Council of the two countries held its first meeting in Damascus. From the Syrian perspective, the purpose was to terminate even minor divergences between Syrian and Lebanese positions before the opening of the ME peace conference at the end of the month. In addition to Lebanon's "mistake" in joining the American initiative with insufficient "coordination," Damascus wished to deal with the 15 October US letter of assurances to the Lebanese Government. The letter annoyed the Syrians by referring to "the withdrawal [from Lebanon] of all non-Lebanese forces," without making a clear distinction between the Israeli and Syrian presences.

At the Higher Council, Syria and Lebanon stressed total coordination on the stand that UN Resolution 425 for Israeli withdrawal from Lebanon would not be connected with any other matter, including Syria's own presence in Lebanon or wider ME "land for peace" discussions under UN Resolutions 242 and 338. As regards contacts with Washington, the Lebanese side "submitted" all correspondence and records of "communications," while the Syrians merely reviewed the "various stages" of Syrian/American interactions.[56] In formulating a response with "reservations" to the US assurances, the Lebanese regime tried to find a balance between Syrian dictation and the desire not to offend the Americans. The chief Lebanese reservation was "that emphasis on the Ta'if pact does not necessarily bring the Syrian army into consideration, in the instance of mentioning withdrawal of all foreign forces from Lebanese territory," coupled with "the appreciation of the Lebanese Government for the interest indicated by Washington in supporting the sovereignty and independence of Lebanon."[57]

As a result, the Lebanese-Israeli sessions at the bilateral Arab-Israeli talks of

November and December 1991 were characterized by Lebanese rigidity about not discussing any peace arrangements before unconditional Israeli withdrawal. Syrian guidance was illustrated by Lebanese rejection of American suggestions about a partial deal for Jizzin, previously a pet project of Hirawi's advisers. The Lebanese now insisted on the indivisibility of Resolution 425, and that armed resistance could be called off only after the end of "the occupation."[58] Such a line ensured sterile Lebanese-Israeli discussions.

Syrian constraint was reinforced by unhappiness in the Shi'i community regarding negotiation with Israel. Backed by Iranian leader Rafsanjani's "moderates," Hizballah opposed the talks and bullied Lebanese participants. The initial head of the Lebanese delegation, Zafir al-Hasan, resigned after threats caused his wife to have a nervous breakdown and fearful neighbors in their apartment building asked them to move.[59] Foreign Ministry Secretary-General Suhayl Shammas took over from December.

In late 1991, there was no doubt about Syrian command of the Lebanese Government. However, it did not yet mean that Syria had stable control of Lebanon. Under Syrian directives, the regime had rushed into a program to break up old army units, including old loyalties and personal associations, and to smash links between brigades and particular communities or regions. This, however, could not change the alienation from the Syrians of the bulk of the officer corps — not just 'Awnists or Christians.[60] Closure of the Lebanese army academy and direction of army personnel to Syria for "training" stimulated irritation rather than fraternalism. Further, the Americans for once exerted themselves and made clear that they opposed Syrian penetration of the army.[61] The military institution had to do what the Syrians required, but it was a Syrian subordinate more through unwilling compulsion than through conversion and coordination.

Hirawi, Karami, Husayni and the upper class gave the Syrians whatever was demanded without too much fuss, mainly because of self-interest. They could not, however, be serviceable beyond their limited capacity. They could not deliver something as significant as metropolitan Beirut into permanent bondage. They could not guarantee Syrian remote control of the disorganized Lebanese official apparatus. Also, Syria's divide-and-rule approach may have smoothed out faint autonomous urges in the Lebanese regime, but it also compounded the ruling class's natural indigence. At the end of 1991, the Syrians had two questions to consider: whether to honor the Ta'if stipulation about military withdrawal from Beirut in September 1992, and what to do about pressure for parliamentary elections.

For Damascus, which regarded control of Beirut as critical to Syrian domination elsewhere in Lebanon, and which wanted a lot more time for taming Beirut, the answers presented no difficulty. Parliamentary elections would be conducted under close Syrian management in 1992. A House of Deputies at once elected and selected would be a crucial cornerstone of longer-term strategic hegemony. Consent would be extracted from the Lebanese for perpetuation of a Syrian presence in Beirut, perhaps with some cosmetic redeployment for the foreign audience. The only problem was that the Americans, to whom the Syrians had to pay more attention than previously, demurred. Washington indicated an initial preference for a Syrian pullback in September 1992, and for parliamentary elections after, not before, this pullback. However, these things depended on wider Arab-Israeli issues. Syrian flexibility on the ME level might be rewarded with an allowance of extended hegemony in Lebanon.

Hiccups in adapting Beirut and Washington to the Syrian view of the world caused frustration in Damascus. The Syrian leadership interpreted its post-Ta'if strategic understanding with the US as meaning de facto federalism between Syria and Lebanon, and in late 1991, suspected American backsliding. Signs of increased American influence with the regime and army,[62] and of American cultural weight symbolized by recovery at the American University of Beirut (AUB), were all unwelcome. It was a noteworthy coincidence that this phase saw a return of the car bomb to the Lebanese capital; on 8 November, a massive explosion demolished the AUB administration building, and on 30 December, another blast killed 20 in the Basta markets of West Beirut. The standard accusations ensued against the Islamic fundamentalists and the Israelis. However, it is worth stressing that the two bombs were in areas dominated by Syrian military intelligence; that the explosions serviced arguments for prolonging Syrian security "protection" in Beirut; and that the AUB event certainly set back any American return to Lebanon.

THE SOUTH, THE SHI'IS AND THE HOSTAGES: LEBANON AS REGIONAL COCKPIT

Even in the violence and intricacy of the ME, South Lebanon had a unique significance. Nowhere else did so many confrontations come together in such a small space. In South Lebanon, geography and demography combined to draw in the greater and lesser players of a variety of ME dramas, and hence to attract the attention of the international community.

From a geographical perspective, South Lebanon possessed important characteristics as part of the Arab-Israeli conflict zone. First, it lay between Israel and Syria, the two regional powers of the Levant. For both it had critical strategic value, whether defensive or as a platform for forward probing. Second, it was the only section of the Arab-Israeli front where the Palestinians were able to maintain an autonomous military capacity, for leverage in either the Arab-Israeli conflict or inter-Arab affairs, particularly in facing Syrian pressure. The weakness of Lebanese regimes and the availability of Lebanese allies and proxies gave the Palestinians, Syria and Israel freedom to maneuver, though Syria and Israel began to indicate a preference for stronger central authority.

As regards demography, the local population distributions attracted intense external interest. Adjacent to the coastal cities of Sidon and Sur, the large Palestinian refugee camps of 'Ayn al-Hilwa and Rashidiyya provided a congenial base for a substantial Palestinian military infrastructure, rapidly restored after the 1985 Israeli withdrawal. Otherwise, South Lebanon was the heartland for Lebanon's Shi'i community, which comprised at least 60% of the population between the Awali River and the Israeli border. Lebanon's Shi'is gave the Islamic regime in Iran a window on the Arab-Israeli conflict and a strategic extension in the depth of the Arab world. At the same time, however, preeminent influence amongst the Shi'is was critical for Syria's hegemonic ambitions in Lebanon. Thus in 1991 in South Lebanon, two contests involved the Shi'i community: an open struggle between the radical Islamic Hizballah and the Israelis, and a veiled maneuvering within the community between Hizballah, secular Shi'i elements, Iran and Syria.

The outcome of the 1991 Gulf War and the opening of Arab-Israeli negotiations changed power relationships in South Lebanon, sharpening some local conflicts and eclipsing others. Syria's bid to convert Gulf crisis gains into assets in the Arab-Israeli arena represented a new dynamic. Gains encompassed Syrian command of Beirut and the Lebanese regime; a Syrian-American understanding about Syrian stabilization of Lebanon; and the isolation of 'Arafat's Palestinians after their support for Iraq. Aware of the wasting value of such advantages, Damascus wished to translate them into greater mastery of the Lebanese and Palestinian "cards" in Arab-Israeli negotiations. In South Lebanon, this meant asserting more Syrian influence in the neighborhood of the Israeli deployment, and putting a hand on the Palestinian camps in order to limit 'Arafat.

Due to Israeli reservations and a preference for putting proxies on front lines, Syria did not move its own army southward. It operated through its intelligence services and the Lebanese army. The 1991 deployment of Lebanese regular units toward the Unifil and Israeli zones served several purposes from the Syrian perspective. It introduced a new instrument for pressure on the Palestinians and Hizballah; the appearance of government authority would serve in international fora to challenge the Israeli presence; the Israelis could be embarrassed through collisions with the Lebanese army; and diversion of Lebanon's security forces southward, especially Christians, removed possible trouble from Beirut and provided an argument for prolonged Syrian security in the Lebanese capital. The only difficulty was that the Lebanese army had its own agenda for bringing stabilization to the south, and restoring popular respect for legitimate authority. Syria patronized the army spread to broaden, not to constrain, its options — stabilization was only one of those options, and heightened local prestige for the Lebanese military was not necessarily convenient.

For the late 1991 Arab-Israeli discussions, Damascus had a twin-track policy: dangling the prospect of a quiet northern border in front of the Israelis, and promoting continued mischief to demonstrate the cost of sidelining Syria. This required delicacy: Syria needed to indicate simultaneously its ability to curtail the various Palestinian and Shi'i radicals, to avoid curtailment except when Syrian interests required it, and to keep a distance from provocative operations by allies and clients, thus blurring responsibility. Syrian maneuvering had to be conducted in a constantly shifting setting, as the Palestinians and Hizballah themselves pursued programs that were only erratically concurrent with Syrian policy. Backed by Iran, Hizballah emphasized perpetual confrontation with the Zionist "enemy," and viewed Syria's flirtation with peace negotiations unfavorably. The Palestinians wanted to make a deal with the US and Israel that Damascus suspected might neglect Syrian interests — hence, the Palestinian position in Lebanon became an important hostage to ensure good behavior.

Armed clashes in South Lebanon in 1991 were either between the Lebanese army and the Palestinians, as the army deployed in Sidon and Sur, or on the fringes of the Israeli-dominated "security zone," between the Israelis and the South Lebanese Army (SLA) on one side and an assemblage of radical Palestinian and Lebanese organizations (especially Hizballah) on the other. The cleavages within the Shi'i community and between Palestinians and Shi'is, which had racked South Lebanon through the late 1980s were no longer significantly disruptive. After the Syrian capture of the Lebanese regime in 1990, Amal had lost much of its utility to Damascus, whether for policing the Shi'i community or for checking the Palestinians — the regime and army could perform these functions. This, added to Shi'i exhaustion and Syrian coordination with Hizballah, brought an Amal-Hizballah settlement.

Unlike Amal, Hizballah had the energy and coherence to preserve a status quo position in a less hospitable environment. Popular Shi'i disapproval of the Hizballah role in internecine conflict, and Syrian and Iranian adjustments to Western preeminence in the "New World Order," forced a degree of flexibility. Hizballah adapted to the Rafsanjani trend in Tehran; accepted Asad's opening to Washington; and finally collaborated in releasing most of the Western hostages held in Lebanon. However, cooperation with Syria was conditional on confrontation with Israel. In the end, Hizballah was still Iran's Lebanese extension, and its leadership would be truculent the moment its interests diverged from those of Damascus.

Through the dramatic events in Lebanon and the ME in the early 1990s, Israel maintained an unchanging geostrategic supremacy in South Lebanon. Locally, this was based on a direct presence in the "security zone" (see map), a hold on the topographically commanding Jizzin hills and the SLA — a well-equipped proxy militia of 2,800 Christians, Shi'is and Druzes. In the absence of an independent Lebanese partner willing to establish a peace arrangement to replace the 1949 armistice, Israel was inclined to sit tight and, like Syria, to link concessions in Lebanon to broader issues, i.e., reduction of the Syrian strategic presence in Lebanon or the future of the Golan Heights. In 1991, the Israelis easily warded off all political and military challenges to their position. The Americans reiterated their support for UN Resolution 425, but told the Lebanese that Israeli withdrawal could not come before subjection of the Palestinians and Hizballah to the Lebanese security forces, which the Syrians were unwilling to allow.

For a more detailed consideration, South Lebanon and Shi'i issues could be divided between aspects involving the Palestinians, the Shi'i-Iran-Syria "triangle" and the Israelis.

THE PALESTINIAN DIMENSION
Although the first stage of the Lebanese army movement into South Lebanon on 7 February related mainly to defusing inter-Shi'i problems in the Tuffah region (see *MECS* 1989, chapter on Lebanon), it entailed a clear Syrian "message" to the PLO in Sidon.[63] In late January, at the height of the US-led aerial bombardment of Iraq, the PLO tried to antagonize the Israelis by firing rockets into the "security zone." The PLO was probably targeting the Lebanese Government more than Israel, to impel the regime to negotiate for recognition of the Palestinian position in South Lebanon.[64] 'Awn's demise and the settlement of the Amal-Hizballah conflict had made the PLO nervous even before Iraq's defeat. The rocket firings and Israel's vigorous retaliation undoubtedly had repercussions in Damascus and Beirut that were detrimental for the PLO.

In 1990–91, changes in Lebanon, the ME and worldwide stripped away much of the internal and international cover for the Palestinian redoubts on the South Lebanese coast. Iraq and the Soviet Union were gone, and financial flows from the Gulf oil states were interrupted. The Ta'if blueprint, backed by the international community, referred only to the Palestinian political-military presence as part of a conglomerate of "non-Lebanese militias" that were to be "dissolved." Lebanese and Syrian approaches regarding the Palestinian presence did not entirely coincide, but neither boded well for the PLO. The Lebanese Government simply wanted the PLO out in order to help obtain an Israeli withdrawal. Damascus had a more convoluted program: Syria wanted the PLO's presence circumscribed for use as a Syrian pawn to cause trouble for the Israelis or to make trade-offs. The PLO felt constrained to be concessionary toward Syria, which might at least enable it to preserve an infrastructure in Lebanon.

Since the PLO was isolated internationally, it had no choice but to bow to the move made by the Lebanese army in February, which required the Palestinian surrender of a geographical extension into the Tuffah hills used as a "mediator" between Amal and Hizballah. The precedent of retreat angered some Fath personnel and, in mid-February, the commander in the Tuffah, 'Abd al-Ra'uf Za'rura, rebelled against 'Arafatist orders and briefly kidnapped the Fath military leader, 'Ala Afandi. The rebellion also reflected discontent over the austerity imposed by the cutoff of Gulf Arab funds, and the PLO managed to quell it only after a tough battle, leaving more than 30 dead.

PLO headquarters in Tunis faced a dilemma: the organization was not in a good position to defy Syrian-Lebanese demands, but prestige considerations and the mood of Sidon personnel dictated opposition to military "dissolution." In exchange for accepting army deployment in Sidon — the next step for the Lebanese regime in the south — PLO representatives insisted that the government treat Palestinian units as "the army of a sister state," not a militia, and acknowledge the Palestinian right to maintain capacity "to continue the armed struggle."[65]

Whatever uses Syria might see in a contrite PLO, the existing Palestinian disposition in the Sidon area could not persist; the contradiction with the Ta'if program was too blatant. First, the decision of the Lebanese Government for dissolution of militias, on 28 March, could not be reconciled with immunity for the PLO. This would leave an open door for later resurgence of armed factions. Second, Palestinian elements intersected supply and communication lines between Beirut and the new Lebanese army positions south of Sidon (see map). Even in January, "some near Damascus" suggested an operation similar to the Syrian-promoted sieges of Tripoli in 1983 and 1985: an assault force comprising the Lebanese army and Palestinian dissidents, backed by Syrian artillery and intelligence.[66]

Between February and late June 1991, the affair drifted toward a crisis. Following the Gulf War, a rigid Syrian line brought a satisfactory Palestinian genuflection, in the form of a visit to Damascus by PLO foreign relations spokesman, Faruq Qaddumi.[67] Thereafter, the Syrians looked for a "mixed solution."[68] A Lebanese army entry to Sidon would mean more control over Palestinian groups, an appearance of fulfilling Ta'if requirements, and deflection of American pressure. Retention of some Palestinian military capacity would guard options regarding Israel, the US and PLO-Syrian relations in case ME talks were unsuccessful. The fact that "mixed solutions" did not impress the Israelis did not bother Damascus; perpetuation of Israeli intractability in Lebanon suited Syrian purposes at the time.

In early April, Khalid Fahum, titular head of the Syrian-backed Salvation Front, observed that Damascus had not yet decided on collection of Palestinian weapons in Lebanon, although according to a Lebanese "ministerial source," a green light had been received for Lebanese-Palestinian contacts.[69] From this point, Muhsin Ibrahim, head of the Communist Action Organization and close to a range of Palestinian factions, acted as mediator between Beirut and PLO headquarters in Tunis, watched carefully by Syria.[70] Bizarre interactions proceeded between the PLO, the Lebanese Government and the Syrians.

At the PLO-Lebanese level, basic standpoints remained widely separated. The PLO sought to be treated as a state, with diplomatic representation in Beirut and a privileged Palestinian military role. Syrian insistence extracted Palestinian agreement to the Lebanese army takeover of Sidon, but the PLO introduced the notion of military coexistence in Sidon and the south. The Lebanese demanded full subjection to army security before any political dialogue. Syria propelled both parties toward a fudged outcome, which was in keeping with its own interests.

The Lebanese were thus induced to see the advantage of leaving a limited Palestinian presence as a lever on Israel,[71] while the Palestinians made cooperative comments about reducing their distribution outside the camps. *Al-Safir* commented that "The issue of the Palestinian weapon will not be pushed urgently at this stage, and a space of three months would suffice to test regional intentions."[72] In the meantime, Syria forced most of its Palestinian clients in the Salvation Front to disengage from the Shuf, while leaving behind Ahmad Jibril's PFLP-GC.[73] Coordinating with Syria, the Lebanese set 30 June as a deadline for the army move into Sidon and, in mid-June, the regime felt sufficiently confident about a smooth outcome to delegate minister Muhsin Dallul and the internal security chief, Nabih Farhat, to negotiate the final technicalities with PLO local commanders.

In fact, Palestinian-Syrian convergence on the "mixed solution," with the camps removed from Lebanese access, encouraged the PLO to try its luck in a fight with the Lebanese army. For 'Arafat, simple surrender promised recrimination inside his apparatus: a show of resistance, however irrelevant, was the softer option, especially with the fallback position guaranteed. In late June, orders went out from Tunis for PLO fighters not to hand over any sites or arms before PLO-Lebanese agreement "on all matters."[74] The crisis had a preset course, the Lebanese serving as a Syrian device in forcing PLO adjustment to a ME balance more favorable to Syria.

Dallul and Farhat, for the Lebanese side, were well warned about the discontent of Palestinian officers and ranks over the loss of the PLO alignment east of Sidon. The Lebanese ignored these warnings, believing that they had had the Palestinian "secret word" from a meeting hosted by Mustafa Sa'd, head of the Nasserite Popular Army.[75] The Lebanese Government was also buoyed by a go-ahead for army deployment given in a telephone conversation between Asad and Hirawi.[76] On the verge of accepting the US project for Arab-Israeli negotiations, Asad calculated the strategic moment to exhibit his power over the Palestinians in Lebanon.

A total of 6,000 Lebanese troops, including commandos, were assembled north and south of Sidon for the operation — a force markedly superior to PLO dispositions outside the camps.[77] Syrian officers carefully watched everything from Rumayla in the Shuf,[78] and Damascus made sure that the Sidon Palestinians got no support from elsewhere. When the army moved into the east Sidon hills on 1 July, PLO units fought back, but radicals, such as the Abu Nidal group and religious fundamentalists, did not resist. After two days of clashes, with more than 60 Palestinians killed against only three from the army, the Lebanese troops overran the whole of the Sidon area up to the refugee camp limits, and were enthusiastically welcomed by the Sidon population.

On 4 July, the Palestinians requested a cease-fire, committing themselves to withdraw into the camps and to hand over medium and heavy weaponry. A week later, an army force blockaded the three refugee camps near Sur (Rashidiyya, Burj al-Shimali and al-Buss), demanding that weaponry be removed.

Eventual results were very limited for the Lebanese — up to 6,000 Palestinian fighters remained in the Sidon and Sur camps, retaining personal and light weapons and hiding other stocks. Some heavy weapons, for example field artillery, were ostentatiously transferred to the Biqa', but even conservative estimates indicated that much of the medium category (mortars, missiles, etc.) was missed.[79] In Lebanon, the PLO had a large Palestinian population of at least 250,000 within which to adapt its infrastucture for more clandestine activity. Damascus itself stipulated that the South Lebanon camps were a "red line" which the Lebanese regime could not cross.[80] In early August, one report noted that the weapons issue had, for the meantime, been shelved.[81]

On political matters, the government, its self-importance inflated by the army performance, refused to discuss anything beyond Palestinian civil rights, and intimated that it would sit only with a joint delegation of Palestinian factions — not with the PLO alone. The PLO reacted by freezing dialogue, certainly until the fate of the Arab-Israeli negotiations became clearer.[82] Little countervailing pressure came from Syria, which was indifferent provided the PLO understood the lesson of the Sidon operation, and coordinated with Damascus on the Arab-Israeli level. In December 1991, 'Arafat made a supplicatory visit to the Syrian capital. He was received by Asad and praised Syrian "democracy." The Syrians had heard it all before, but for the moment it was an adequate obeisance. *Plus ça change, plus c'est la même chose.*

HIZBALLAH, IRAN AND SYRIA

In their relations with Lebanese Islamic radicalism, Iran and Syria had to juggle contradictory elements. Both states had little choice but to mend fences with the West: Iran because of its devastated economy and declining living standards; and Syria to avoid unviable isolation in facing Israel. On the other hand, there remained the desire to have instruments for confrontation: in Iran, domestic politics was split between the more and less pragmatic outlooks, although the former held the high ground in the regime; and in Syria, Asad wanted to keep bargaining strength for difficult phases.

Iran and Syria each saw its connection with South Lebanon and the Lebanese Shi'is as a valuable tool for enticement or extortion on the international level. The two matters on which this tool might prove advantageous were the Western hostages detained by Shi'i radicals, and the strategic location of South Lebanon for stirring the Arab-Israeli conflict. In 1991, Iran and Syria converged as regards their tactical approaches, but matching longer-term interests was more problematic, and each viewed itself as the rightful primary influence on Lebanese Shi'is.

Syria exhibited conflicting impulses in its dealings with Hizballah. Damascus understood the utility of a proxy whose activities were both a nuisance to the Israelis and removed from direct Syrian responsibility. However, the proxy was of use only if its activities could be switched off when Syria felt assured of the right price — and Hizballah did not want to be switched off. In terms of pressure, Syria could exert its own presence in Beirut and the Biqa', but had to rely on balances of proxies in the south. The Lebanese army, Shi'i secularist tendencies and traditional leaders were all serviceable. From the Syrian perspective, tighter supervision of Hizballah was the main purpose of the February 1991 Lebanese army entry to the Tuffah area, a Hizballah stronghold bordering Israeli/SLA-controlled zones. Syrian coordination with Iran ensured Hizballah acceptance, but Iran only cooperated because it sought to reassert influence in the Shi'i community beyond Hizballah, influence which had been degraded due to Iranian association with Hizballah during the inter-Shi'i fighting of 1988–90. Iran wanted a wider base in Lebanon, precisely because it was suspicious of Syria's international maneuverings, first in the Gulf and later in the Arab-Israeli arena. Syria might have to contend with Iranian opposition if it tried to manipulate the Lebanese army in order to curtail Hizballah actions against Israel.

Hizballah knew very well that its survival depended on its own resourcefulness. Syria could not be trusted and Iran was too far away. As "the most prominent fundamentalist source" put it, Iran "cannot extend protection because it doesn't border Lebanon and even the Revolutionary Guard [in the Biqa'] does not represent 1% of the force that the media reckons."[83] In an interview for the weekly al-Hawadith, Hizballah mentor Fadlallah made vague but uncomplimentary references to Syria when analyzing the army entry to the Tuffah and the potential fate of the Sidon Palestinians: "The aim was to cool the Lebanese situation so there would be no hotbed of tension other than the Gulf — will Sidon become another Tripoli?"[84] Mention of Tripoli meant an accusing finger pointing toward Damascus. The May 1991 dissolution of militias in central Lebanon led to heavy reinforcement of Hizballah forces in the south,[85] as Shi'i radicals strengthened resistance against Israel in order to reject equivalence to other militias, gravitated toward an area where Israeli strategic deterrence allowed freedom from Syria, and buttressed their alignment in advance of the Lebanese army's Sidon operation. Hizballah military strength south of Sidon rose from a few hundred to 1,000–2,000,[86] with a core that was increasingly well trained by Iranian revolutionary guards.[87]

Hizballah adapted to the slippage of the radical faction in Tehran, to Rafsanjani's tactical approach of not offending Syria and to popular Shi'i tiredness with violence, by making organizational and policy shifts. At the Hizballah general assembly in May 1991, secretary-general Subhi Tufayli lost his position to the more pragmatic 'Abbas Musawi, reputedly closer to the Rafsanjani trend. This was followed by the emergence of what one "major Lebanese source" defined as "a realistic policy paralleling that predominating in Tehran."[88] For example, Hizballah replaced its outright opposition to Resolution 425 with criticism of the government's method in trying to secure implementation of 425. At the same time, there was no change in its attitude of rejection of the Ta'if Accord, which obstructed "the abrogation of sectarianism and the building of a struggler society."[89] Hizballah shifted a little toward the wider Shi'i outlook, balancing its hostilities between Israel and the Lebanese regime. The party realized that it had to be careful about "relations between the resistance and the people of the south;"[90] this heightened the utility of Iranian aid to the civilian population. In strategic terms, adaptation aimed at preserving Hizballah's value to Tehran, and at maintaining the organization's strength in South Lebanon, with regard to Syria and Israel.

In 1991, interactions between Hizballah, Iran and Syria were best illustrated by the manner in which the saga of the Western hostages ended, and by responses to moves toward Arab-Israeli negotiations.

In the early part of 1991, Iran decided that the Westerners held by Hizballah offshoots in Beirut must be released, and a major barrier to improved economic and political relations with the outer world thereby removed. For Rafsanjani and others — who were not moderates in any meaningful sense, but who could at least read the winds of the world — the demonstration of Western power in the devastation of Iraq undoubtedly had a catalytic effect. As for Syria, the rapid transfer of American attention from the Gulf to Arab-Israeli affairs made judiciously timed hostage releases, via the "good offices" of President Asad, an imperative interest. At first, a great play was made of connecting the Western hostages to Lebanese Shi'is detained by Israel or the SLA, which eased Hizballah cooperation. However, in the end, Syria and Iran insisted that release of Westerners proceed independently. Between August and December, all nine American and British hostages were freed and handed over to the Syrian army, being then displayed at media rituals in the Syrian capital.

The process began after the May Hizballah leadership change. The hostages were in the hands of Hizballah intelligence, which used such cover names as Islamic Jihad and the Revolutionary Justice Organization, but not necessarily under people sympathetic to Rafsanjani's style of pragmatism. To produce action from Hizballah, Iran's initial price list included the unfreezing of Iranian deposits in American banks. Lack of American response delayed matters for more than two months;[91] the Americans had the whip hand, and the first two hostages appeared in early August, without any return except some Israeli flexibility over Shi'i detainees. A radical faction reflecting the hard-line Mohtashemi camp in Iran immediately tried to stall the process by kidnapping a Frenchman — a direct challenge to the international credibility of Rafsanjani and Syria. Extreme Iranian and Syrian pressure had the Frenchman freed within hours, a revealing indication of both capability and urgency from the two states. The Syrians were intimately involved in the contacts leading to the initial releases, "at the side of Tehran in the 'joint operations room'."[92]

Talks on further releases continued tortuously over the following months, with the intervention of UN Secretary-General Pérez de Cuellar to try to arrange a broad deal including Israeli servicemen missing in Lebanon and Shi'is held by the Israelis. The Israelis made some gestures in return for information, but refused a general prisoner release in advance of settlement of their concerns. Hizballah would not have been able to satisfy Israel, even if it had wished to do so, as the whereabouts of the lost Israelis also encompassed the Syrians and Palestinians. By October, with the ME conference looming, the Syrians became impatient, and clearly willing to decouple the Western hostages from the Israeli dimension, which could more safely be retained for later exploitation. On a six-day visit to Tehran in early October, Syrian army Chief of Staff Hikmat Shihabi tried to press upon the Iranians the "necessity" of having the Westerners released "with speed, to serve stability and quiet in Lebanon."[93] Iran concurred, and by mid-November the Lebanese kidnappers indicated that Terry Waite and the remaining Americans would be liberated unconditionally. Consequently, Hizballah capitulated, but only because, under the changed circumstances, the Western hostages were losing their insurance value and becoming an embarrassment.

On Arab-Israeli developments, Syria and Iran sought to smooth over differing perspectives. Iran continued loudly to reject Israel's existence; Syria could not afford to take such a line and felt pressured to participate in American-sponsored talks, albeit showing a marked lack of enthusiasm. Syria needed Iran and Hizballah for bargaining purposes. Iran and Hizballah needed to keep Syria happy for as long as possible in order to hold their position in Lebanon. Syria feared the ingenuity, commitment and reach of the Iran-Hizballah combination. Iran and Hizballah suspected that Syria might attempt to sell them off, and prepared to be disruptive. The alliance of the three was a strange affair, natural yet unnatural, strained yet durable.

When Rafsanjani visited Damascus in April 1991, the Syrians reversed their post-Ta'if inclination to restrain military activity against Israel from South Lebanon, Khaddam clarifying that "the resistance to Israel in Lebanon will continue until the liberation of the south."[94] Rafsanjani responded by putting the Iranian presence in Lebanon at Asad's disposal and, later in the year, Iran reduced the number of revolutionary guards stationed in the Biqa'. This proved inconvenient for Hizballah, which had to contend with a local challenge from the Shi'i Ja'far clan, probably encouraged by Syria.

Despite opposition to the Arab-Israeli peace conference, Iran and Hizballah did not oppose Syrian participation. A Lebanese fundamentalist source expressed the view that Syria's move was "tactical not strategic" and designed to expose Israel as "obstructing peace."[95] In late October, "fundamentalist currents" seemed uncertain about Syrian deployment of the "resistance" card in Arab-Israeli maneuvers. Confidence prevailed that the "card" would not be given up soon or easily. There was also, however, awareness of a possible split if the conference made progress on Arab-Israeli compromises: that parleying existed over constricting Hizballah and other radicals by "strengthening the role of the Lebanese army in...areas of passage to zones under Israeli occupation."[96]

ISRAEL'S ALIGNMENT IN LEBANON

For Israel, a residual alignment in Lebanon provided cover for the northern border; gave a minimal strategic projection in relation to the Syrian deployment; and extended bargaining possibilities in Arab-Israeli discussions. Realistically, the alignment could be given up only in one piece, since a partial retreat — even with regard to SLA control of Jizzin — would gravely compromise the remainder. For a full withdrawal, Israel expected nothing less than total disbandment of hostile armed groups, a solid peace with a credible Lebanese regime, and decisive reduction, if not removal, of the Syrian presence. Withdrawal with acceptance of Syrian hegemony in Lebanon might not be inconceivable, but would presumably involve a price for the Syrians on the Golan Heights. There was no detectable interest in the Litani water resource in the Israeli stance, which concentrated on strategic military concerns. Throughout 1991, Syria tried to use its enhanced capabilities, particularly concerning the Lebanese regime and Hizballah, to embarrass the Israelis, and even to prepare the ground for a forced Israeli retreat without fulfillment of basic Israeli requirements. Israel sought to preserve its alignment until a worthwhile alternative came into view.

The Israeli-Syrian balance in Lebanon in 1991 was worthy of careful study, as the appearance of Israeli disadvantage was deceptive, provided the Israelis played a subtle diplomatic game. In Syria's favor, the collapse of East Beirut eliminated a diversion in central Lebanon; resurgence of regime authority made it more difficult to assert a regime vacuum as an argument for the Israeli presence; and the Ta'if document gave the Syrian alignment Lebanese and international legitimacy — its

Israeli counterpart had neither. However, in trying to make life difficult for Israel, whether in military or diplomatic terms, the Syrians faced a double dilemma.

First, machinations with proxies in South Lebanon could cause mischief but nothing more, and mischief alone could not move Israel. Indeed, continued activity by Hizballah and the Palestinians contradicted Lebanese and Syrian claims about the new capacity of the Lebanese army and state. Second, causing Israel serious difficulty with the US depended on persuasive evidence that Syria and Lebanon were willing and able to keep their side of a bargain — delivering lasting peace along the Israeli border. Here, Syria had a credibility problem. The Syrian fondness for preserving "cards" and for two-track policies, as demonstrated in both the Lebanese army Sidon operation and the Syrian participation in peace talks at the same time as encouraging Hizballah, did not promote Syrian sincerity. Certainly, Syria would have to pay a high price for repressing the proxies: a break with the Iranian Islamic regime and Arab radicalism, and coping with the ferocity and cunning of a cornered Hizballah. Was Ba'thist Syria capable of such things? In 1991, a positive answer was not assured.

From an Israeli perspective, longer-term considerations did not seem so unfavorable. Senior Israeli officials dealing with Lebanon doubted that Syria could ultimately sustain hegemony in Beirut against the underlying will of the vast majority of Lebanese.[97] Also, the larger question of the future of the Syrian regime loomed: could the Ba'thist apparatus live through a post-Asad transition? In brief, despite all the international changes and the beginnings of ME peace negotiations, in 1991 the Israelis saw little reason to do other than hold to their Lebanon stance set in the mid-1980s.

The Israeli response to challenges in Lebanon after the February 1991 Gulf War was of the usual hard-line variety, though with some debate and later, regarding Hizballah actions and disappointment in the hostage affair, a distinct acerbity. As for hostilities, there was an increase in tempo compared to the two preceding years; early June air raids on the Sidon Palestinians were the heaviest since 1982. However, casualties were relatively low and incidents were of the normal intermittent type. Along the fringes of the "security zone" and the Jizzin salient, nine Israelis and 17 Islamic resistance or Palestinian fighters died during 1991, while 22 Israeli air raids caused c. 45 fatalities[98] — for comparison, twice the very low 1990 toll, but about half the 1988 figure. Eighteen of the raids were against assorted Palestinians, including the 'Arafatists, three against Hizballah, and one against Amal. Toward the end of the year, the Israelis resorted more to artillery bombardment in relation to Hizballah.

Syria's moves of mid-1991, involving the Brotherhood Treaty with Lebanon and the constriction of the Sidon Palestinians using the Lebanese army, elicited a mixed Israeli reaction. Defense Minister Moshe Arens described the Brotherhood Treaty as an *Anschluss* in Syria's favor,[99] and there was concern that it might unravel the tacit military understandings limiting Syria's Lebanon alignment — the "red lines" banning a Syrian army spread into South Lebanon and Syrian introduction of air power or surface-to-air missiles. The unusually severe June air raids around Sidon, unconnected to any immediate provocation, served as a message to Syria that "acquiescence in conversion of Lebanon into a Syrian protectorate does not hold regarding the south of the country."[100]

The Lebanese deployment in Sidon was initially a stimulus to debate about possible Israeli territorial flexibility, especially with hints from Washington for a gesture in

Jizzin. From one outlook, Jizzin, which had not been part of the original "security zone" and involved an Israeli umbrella rather than a presence, could be treated separately.[101] Symbols of Lebanese sovereignty, such as the army, might be allowed to enter as a goodwill measure, perhaps useful for wedging the Lebanese regime a little away from Damascus in future. Some "IDF sources" suggested that it would be "a mistake to continue declaring an Israeli obligation to Jizzin under the SLA."[102] Another view was that any Israeli weakening "will send undesirable messages to Damascus,"[103] and that concession over Jizzin would show the SLA and the "security zone" population that Israel was on the way out, thus threatening the Israeli alignment. It was even said that compromising a real strategic asset, like the position in South Lebanon, for no concrete return, to support obstinacy on the West Bank, was a serious error.[104]

When it became clear that Syria had designated the Palestinian camps as no-go areas for the Lebanese, and that Hizballah remained immune from restraint, Israeli uncertainties vanished and toughness prevailed. This had been the constant line of the Israeli coordinator for Lebanon, Uri Lubrani, who saw no relevance in Lebanese army moves unless areas were "cleared of terrorists" and who had never believed that Jizzin could be distinguished from the "security zone."[105] Israel had little interest in Palestinian "heavy and medium weaponry," as infiltration actions involved the "light weapons" which the Palestinians were officially permitted to retain. Despite flirtations with the Jizzin option, the US tended to the Israeli side, from mid-July onward, telling the Lebanese that a conclusive clampdown on Hizballah and the Palestinians must come before — not after — implementation of Resolution 425.[106]

From July 1991, Israel's Lebanese affairs had three faces: Lebanese aspects of the Arab-Israeli talks, worries about the increasing sophistication of Hizballah activities, and wranglings over prisoners and hostages. The three were intimately connected, as each also involved the Syrians. The Israeli team that sat with the Lebanese negotiators after the November Madrid conference knew that the sessions would be indefinitely unproductive due to Syrian controls, but nonetheless tried to deal with the Lebanese as if they had some autonomy.[107] Israeli officials stressed that they would not discuss Lebanon with Syria; indicated flexibility for a settlement, as long as security was adequately addressed; and avoided mention of the ill-fated 17 May 1983 agreement, which they knew would provoke the Lebanese. The Israelis absolutely rejected Lebanese demands for unconditional withdrawal accompanied by vague Lebanese promises, replying that 425 could be carried through only within a peace arrangement, and pointing to the existence of UN Resolution 520, calling for withdrawal of all foreign forces. Israel aimed at a balance between making what in Israeli eyes was a credible offer, and limiting corrosive morale effects on the SLA.

Hizballah set about sabotaging the Arab-Israeli process. Iranian revolutionary guards assisted with instruction about tactics and remote-controlled booby traps. For Iran, "the conflict with Israel will remain open even if Israel withdraws from South Lebanon."[108] Syria adopted a permissive attitude, implying an ambiguity toward peace talks, which annoyed Israel, and the Lebanese army cohabited with Hizballah. The Israelis noted that the Syrians were able to rein in other Lebanese and Palestinian elements, and that they specifically told the Lebanese army only to allow passage to Hizballah.[109] Hizballah concentrated on the vulnerable neck of the Jizzin salient, which offered suitable rough topography and was flanked by Hizballah bases in the Tuffah and south Biqa' areas.

Late in the year, paralleling the Arab-Israeli talks, Hizballah launched an electronic campaign with radio-directed roadside bombs, killing six Israelis. Israel experimented with radio jamming and in early November, carried out a selective artillery bombardment of villages used by Hizballah, preceded by warnings to the local population. The shelling precipitated mass flight — pressure intended to split civilians from the militiamen. In fact, most civilians were already long tired of Hizballah, but they had no influence on it.[110] The Israeli response was therefore fatuous: thrashing around in South Lebanon, while leaving the Iranian and Syrian logistic structure untouched, gratified — rather than deterred — Hizballah's backers. This was particularly the case with a tendency, by early 1992, for Hizballah to use the deep rear in the Biqa', inside territory under direct Syrian occupation, as its main military base, and for the Tuffah and south Biqa' to be forward operational staging areas (see map).[111]

On the hostage issue, Israel found itself sidelined in December, as the last British and Americans were freed. At this stage, Israel had the deaths of three of its missing servicemen confirmed, but the fate of four remained unknown, including that of the pilot, Ron Arad, shot down over Sidon and probably alive in Syria or Iran. Israel felt deceived by Iran and the UN, and an angry phone conversation between Uri Lubrani and the UN Secretary-General set a sour tone.[112] It was obvious that Syria and Iran intended to play with the matter.

ECONOMIC AND SOCIAL DEGRADATION

THE ECONOMY

"The Lebanese Administration today is beset by every variety of disease — corruption rules at all levels and in all places, most notably in the very institutions which people have to deal with in their everyday lives."[113] Lebanon entered 1991 with a devastated infrastucture and a government with no competence in economic management. It entered 1992 with no serious infrastructural repair, a population almost driven to spontaneous rebellion by a regime of carpetbaggers, and on the verge of fiscal collapse. Damages caused by fighting since 1975 required an estimated $3bn. emergency rehabilitation investment,[114] just to create a skeletal basis for economic recovery. Only foreign aid could provide the money, and up to early 1992, there seemed no prospect of more than a few hundred million dollars, not even equivalent to the needs of public sector wage rises.

During 1991, the economic picture had two aspects: a superficial holding of pressures, due to the security lull and the Central Bank's technical manipulations; and a deepening malaise exacerbated by corruption and fiscal irresponsibility. On one side, restoration of regime control over the ports, enhanced customs revenues, imposition and collection of increased taxes and other charges and the Central Bank's raising of interest rates on treasury bills and the acquisition of foreign currency, together enabled a temporary stabilization of the Lebanese lira. Through the year, the lira retained a value of c. LL900:$1. However, this did not bring any improvement in the lot of the ordinary citizen. The monthly minimum wage, which, since 1982, had declined to Third World levels — from the equivalent of $240 to $50, remained the same in real terms. This reflected a general lack of adjustment, and even deterioration, in the real value of wages and salaries. In such a context, an impoverished middle class and an angry, growing underclass had to cope with the massive rises in taxes, fines and school fees, and reductions in subsidies on, for example, wheat. The population "suffered from the peace more than in the war,"[115] and was well aware that ministers, officials and the Syrians took hefty cuts from improved revenues.

Regarding infrastucture, the main interest of the regime was not in normal services, such as water, electricity, road-building and telephones, but in a speculative project to mobilize foreign and Lebanese investment in reconstructing the Beirut city center. The electricity network alone needed half a billion dollars in order to restore it to modern standards; water provision was beyond disaster conditions, with 80% of sources polluted and only 10% of chlorine pumping stations operational.[116] By early 1992, little or nothing had been done in the sphere of basic services.[117]

The city center plan, involving a private company to acquire compulsorily the properties of a multitude of smallholders in exchange for shares, epitomized the outlook of the Lebanese haute bourgeoisie. It envisaged a freewheeling capitalist venture, with 50% of shares owned by new investors, including foreigners, and the old smallholders and renters swamped by big money. In the Lebanese environment, endless prospects opened up for fraud and kickbacks, doubtless with a large Syrian rake-off. In early 1992, the scheme remained on the drawing board.

Three features of the regime's relationship with the economy in 1991 indicated an unpromising economic future for "Ta'if Lebanon," at least if the welfare of the population was considered relevant. Certainly they were enough to produce wariness amongst potential aid donors and outside investors, whether foreigners or diaspora Lebanese.

Fiscal irresponsibility: Despite the partially successful attempts to increase state income, the spendthrift character of the Karami government ensured that revenues stayed at about 20% of expenditures. An official report to the Central Bank in June estimated 1991 government outlays at LL2,000bn. and income at LL440bn.[118] In December, the government decreed a 120% pay increase for public sector employees, an outlay of $600m. — equal to total annual state revenue.[119] Such blowouts on the budget deficit, even for the more worthy causes, doubled the national debt in 1991 to $4bn. One official source told *al-Nahar* that "the expenditures of this presidency exceed those of any previous period, including that of Jumayyil."[120] In consequence, despite a relatively stable lira exchange rate, inflation amounted to 40% for the year, quickly eroding wage adjustments.

Continued reckless printing of money with no productive underpinning eventually guaranteed a dramatic new run on the lira, depleting Central Bank reserves and bringing a further collapse of the national currency.

Regime corruption: Financial irregularities were viewed benignly, even in public statements, by the circle around Hirawi and Karami. One of the president's sons, George al-Hirawi, blandly noted that "corruption and bribery have become a feature of public administration — what the government gives to officials as salaries and benefits is not enough to cover their requirements."[121] For example, people could not have property ownership documents registered in some districts "without paying a foreign currency surcharge, usually in American dollars."[122] An official in the Ba'abda land registry, well known for collecting large "cuts" on office business, was said to distribute proceeds to four ministers. A contact of the author watched the official sitting with these ministers at West Beirut's Summerland Hotel.[123] Another instance with direct relevance for foreign aid donors concerned a grant from a Gulf state for road repairs. So much of the money disappeared in kickbacks that the contractor was forced to use materials which washed away in the first winter storms.[124] If anything resembling such attrition applied to regular government spending, it would indicate losses through corrupt practices, perhaps entirely discounting state revenues.

Syrian penetration: Syria had no intention of allowing free economic interchange between itself and Lebanon. The Syrian Ba'thists feared and resented Lebanon's commercial expertise and "free market," and were determined to use their domination of the Beirut regime to control, degrade and reorient Lebanon's economy in line with Syrian Ba'thist interests.

First, Syria gained free access to "Ta'if Lebanon" for transit trade and dumping of cheap products, but without reciprocity. Syrian imports swiftly wrecked the Lebanese textile industry, one of Lebanon's growth sectors in the late 1980s.[125] Only in August 1991 did Asad even allow Lebanon to export to Syria all the commodities already permitted to enter from other countries.[126] A hopeful Lebanese delegation that visited Damascus to buy oil was coldly offered the world market price.[127] In September, Syria increased the charge on Lebanese private cars crossing the border from $65 to $85 — the border, of course, had no significance for crossings in the other direction.

Second, Syria stalled on concrete arrangements for economic cooperation, in which concessions for Lebanese private business would be difficult to avoid. Damascus rejected ideas from a Lebanese ministerial committee for economic "privileged relations" in the Brotherhood Treaty.[128] The treaty text referred to economic coordination and joint planning — in crude terms, Syrian control mechanisms — but nowhere mentioned freeing of trade. Negotiations for a detailed economic agreement became protracted, with no result in 1991 — a sharp contrast to the political-security dimension. It seems the Syrians preferred establishment of monolithic joint trading companies, while the Lebanese simply sought lifting of barriers on trade by existing private firms.[129] The Syrians exhibited concern about "Lebanese economic advantages."[130]

Third, Lebanon's water resources, a major reservoir within the Arab world, provided a prominent target for "the joint projects and development plans" of the Brotherhood Treaty. Syrian-Lebanese talks on sharing "common waters" began in Shtura in late July, concentrating on the Orontes and al-Nahr al-Kabir. 1991 being a year of drought, Syria emphasized the use of irrigation, but hydroelectricity was also an interest. Damascus did not conceive of a separation between Syrian and Lebanese waters: there were only "Arab waters" and Arab countries "required every drop — dam construction will enable water collection for the benefit of each of the sisterly regions [Syria and Lebanon]."[131]

Overall, "Ta'if Lebanon" was Syria's Wild West, a land of opportunity for diverse Syrian social strata. Swarms of Syrian peddlers displaced the Lebanese poor from the street trade, especially along West Beirut's airport highway. These also had their uses as low-grade spies. In West Beirut neighborhoods, Syrian troops had a "station" in apartment buildings every few hundred meters, rather like the militias before them. At the other end of the spectrum, high-level Syrian personnel were reputed in both parts of Beirut to take a 45% portion of state revenues from the Beirut port[132] — if accurate, not a good omen for the security of investment money.

Against the general background of national degradation, fortunes and perspectives varied somewhat between the regions of Lebanon. East Beirut, with economic facilities shattered by the 1990 fighting and stripped of any credible political reference point, was particularly depressed, in mood and reality. Christian capitalists overseas were even less willing to invest in the Ta'if era than their non-Christian counterparts.[133] South Lebanon, with an injection of funds from such varied sources as diaspora Shi'is, Iran and Israel, witnessed a tentative economic remission, albeit a hostage to ME political developments. It was not all bad to be the geopolitical cockpit of the Levant. Parts of the Biqa' even prospered from making the best out of Syria's peace. Zahla turned its back on earlier rebelliousness to profit as an entrepôt for the Syrians; the city's exports surged to $17m. in the first half of 1991, up from $8m. for the same period in 1990.[134] To impress the Americans, the Syrians occasionally conducted publicized burnings of hashish and opium fields, but visitors to Hirmel and Ba'albak in August observed that hashish planting had "returned to its former levels."[135]

A 1991 opinion survey of 1997 "representative Lebanese" throughout the country, conducted by the Lebanon citizen's movement, with the support of Unicef-Lebanon, demonstrated the regional differentiation.[136] The majority of those surveyed saw political and socioeconomic conditions as "bad," but economic pessimism was most marked in East Beirut and the southern suburbs — an interesting combination. Responses from West Beirut, South Lebanon and northern areas, though still unfavorable, indicated rather less discontent. Shuf respondents gave the only "acceptable" rating for the socioeconomic situation, but, with East Beirut, were the most pessimistic about Lebanon's future. This reflected Druze insulation and insecurity.

SOCIAL AND CULTURAL AFFAIRS: A CONCLUDING COMMENT

A Central Bank study of early 1992 indicated that 450 individuals controlled at least 55% of all assets in the Lebanese banking system.[137] With the decimation of the middle class, 16 years of war had changed Lebanon's social order only for the worse. In preliminaries for possible Syrian-supervised elections in late 1992, the haute bourgeoisie behaved as if the population did not even exist. Through the first months of 1992, small coteries of upper-class and traditional families groped toward blocs and alliances. Political strategies were shaped by feudal tendencies and sectarianism, with Syrian tinkerings: domination of the Biqa' by a Husayni-Hirawi link; Mount Lebanon split into two districts to satisfy the Druzes; and Sunni blocs in Beirut and Sidon, backed by the Saudi-derived wealth of Rafiq al-Hariri. The main inconveniences disturbing Damascus were amongst the Shi'is and in East Beirut — somehow 'Awnism and Hizballah had to be brought to heel. For the Syrians any elections had to serve the higher priority of cementing Syrian control of Beirut.

In 1991, clear indications could be detected that Syria's intentions for Lebanon went beyond strategic control, political supervision and economic coordination. For Syrian Ba'thists, the tattered but potent remnants of Lebanon's liberal media traditions and pluralist education system were deeply offensive — an alien Western intrusion in the heart of the Arab world. Here, Damascus knew that it was threatening vital elements of Lebanon's separate identity, and that it could expect automatic social resistance, including among the haute bourgeoisie.

The first moves were therefore experimental, designed to test the resistance — prefatory probes for the longer-term surgery. The Ta'if agreement set in place some modest openings; it referred to needs "to unify history and civic education textbooks" and stipulated that "all the media shall be reorganized in line with the law and within the framework of responsible freedom."[138] In November 1990, the Hirawi regime pushed through Law No. 29, committing Lebanon to adhere to the charter of the Arab Organization for Education, Culture and the Sciences. This charter aimed at monolithic "Arab" education, with standardized interpretations of Arab culture and displacement of foreign languages by Arabic to the maximum feasible extent. The legislation caused an uproar from private schools and colleges and the regime drew back, promising no drastic change. However, Law No. 29 remained in the statute book.

Syria's distaste regarding Lebanese laxity with the media came to the surface in the mid-1991 Brotherhood Treaty and Security Pact. Apparently, a preliminary draft of the Brotherhood Treaty demanded that: "To improve relations between Lebanon and Syria, all media distortions must be banned."[139] This clause did not survive to the final version, which left such details to "bilateral agreements." The Security Pact required a ban on any "information activity" which might be a threat to Syrian interests. In August 1991, Information Minister Albert Mansur formulated measures to regulate and license private radio and television stations, which continued to multiply. Although the proposal was superficially unexceptional, the underlying drive was exposed when a high official intimated that private radio and television would be forbidden to broadcast news.[140] As with education, the regime drew back when widespread protest ensued, including from affected commercial and militia elements. Anyway, self-censorship had already substantially emasculated all the media in the general environment of Syrian mastery after October 1990.

In the end, the tension between the rigid Arabism of the Syrian interior and the cosmopolitanism of the Mediterranean coast was a point of contention within every Lebanese community, as much as between Lebanon and a particular Syrian apparatus. Certainly, the anarchy and sprawling complexity of Lebanese society gave this society a ramshackle but powerful resilience. Yet, many Lebanese believed that serving Damascus served their own interests, and commitment to a Lebanon above sect and below wider identification was uneven. International indifference, the venality and mediocrity of the ruling class, and the long shadow of Asad's autocracy had a slow deadening effect.

APPENDIX I: TREATY OF BROTHERHOOD, COOPERATION AND COORDINATION CONCLUDED BETWEEN LEBANON AND SYRIA ON 22 MAY 1991[41]

The Lebanese Republic and the Arab Republic of Syria, motivated by the brotherly and distinctive bonds between them that draw strength from their geographic propinquity and their common history, allegiance, fate and mutual interests, and confident that realizing the widest cooperation and coordination shall serve their mutual interests, guarantee their progress and development, ensure their national security, secure their prosperity and stability, enable them to confront all regional and international developments, and fulfill the ambitions of the peoples in both countries in line with the Lebanese National Reconciliation Pact approved by [the Lebanese] Parliament on 5 November 1989, have agreed on the following:

Article One
The two countries shall seek the highest levels of cooperation and coordination in all fields, including political, economic, security, educational, scientific and others, with the aim of promoting the mutual interests of the two sisterly states within the framework of their respective sovereignty and independence. This will enable them to exploit to the maximum their political,

economic and security resources in order to ensure prosperity and stability in a way that guarantees their national security and boosts their common interests, and consolidates their brotherly relations in facing their common future and fate.

Article Two
The two countries shall seek coordination and cooperation in all sectors of the economy, including agriculture, industry, trade, transport, customs and communications, and shall engage in joint projects and development plans.

Article Three
The interconnectedness between the security of both countries requires that Lebanon should not be a source of threat to Syria's security and vice versa under any circumstances....Therefore, Lebanon shall not become a transit way or a base for any power, state or organization which seeks to undermine Syria's security, while Syria, keen to preserve Lebanon's security, unity and independence, shall not allow any action that would constitute a threat or danger to Lebanon's security.

Article Four
After the political reforms have been approved and endorsed in a constitutional manner in line with the provisions of the Lebanese National [Reconciliation] Pact and after deadlines fixed in the pact have expired, the Lebanese and Syrian governments shall decide on the redeployment of Syrian troops in the Biqa' valley, and the entrance to the western Biqa' at Dahr al-Baydar, up to the Hammana-Mudayriji-'Ayn-Dara line, and, should the need arise, in other points to be determined by a joint Lebanese-Syrian military committee. The two governments shall have also to agree on the size and duration of stay of the force that will be redeployed and define the relationship between this force and the Lebanese authorities.

Article Five
The Arab and foreign policies of the two countries shall be based on the following principles:
(1) Lebanon and Syria are two Arab states committed to the charter of the Arab League, the Treaty for Arab Defense and Economic Cooperation, and all other agreements signed within the League's framework. They are also members of the UN and committed to its charter as well as the charter of the Nonaligned Movement.
(2) The two states have a common fate and common interests.
(3) Each country shall assist the other in matters related to its security and national interests according to the terms of the treaty. As such, the governments of the two countries shall seek maximum coordination in formulating Arab and foreign policies and in taking positions in Arab and international organizations regarding all regional and international questions.

Article Six
In order to achieve the objectives of the treaty, the following bodies and organs shall be created in addition to other possible institutions to be decided by the Higher Council.
(1) The Higher Council
(a) This council shall be composed of the presidents of the two countries in addition to the speaker of the house, the prime minister and the deputy prime minister in the Lebanese Republic, and the head of the People's Assembly, the prime minister and the deputy prime minister in the Syrian Arab Republic.
(b) The council shall meet once a year and when the need arises at a location which shall be agreed upon.
(c) The council shall formulate the general policy of coordination and cooperation in the political, economic, security, military and other fields, and shall oversee its application. It shall also endorse plans and proposals put forward by the Follow-up and Coordination Committee, the Committee for Foreign Affairs, the Committee for Economic and Social Affairs, the Committee for Security and Defense, and any other committee that might be set up at a later stage.
(d) The decisions of the Higher Council are binding and effective within the framework of the two countries' respective constitutions and laws.
(e) The Higher Council shall define the questions and subjects that are to be discussed by the specialized committees and over which the committees may take decisions that are effective as soon as issued, provided they do not contradict the norms and constitutional provisions in each country.

(2) Follow-up and Coordination Committee
This committee shall be made up of the prime ministers of the two states and a number of concerned ministers. Its task shall consist of:
(a) Following up on the implementation of decisions and policies taken by the Higher Council, and preparing reports on the course and phases of implementation which shall be submitted to the council.
(b) Coordinating recommendations put forward by the specialized committees and referring the proposals to the Higher Council.
(c) Holding meetings with the various committees whenever needed.
(d) The committee shall meet once every six months and when the need arises at a location which shall be agreed upon.

(3) The Committee for Foreign Affairs
(a) This committee shall consist of the foreign ministers of the two countries.
(b) The committee shall meet once every two months and when the need arises in one of the two countries consecutively.
(c) The committee's task shall consist of coordinating the foreign policies of the two countries and defining their relationships with all other states. It shall also coordinate their activities and positions within Arab and international organizations, and shall prepare plans for that purpose which shall be submitted to the Higher Council for endorsement.

(4) The Committee for Economic and Social Affairs

(a) This committee shall consist of the concerned ministers in the economic and social sectors in the two states.

(b) The committee shall meet once every two months and when the need arises in one of the two countries consecutively.

(c) Among the committee's tasks is the coordination of the economic and social activities in both states and the preparation of recommendations aimed at boosting cooperation and coordination in this respect.

(d) The recommendations made by the committee shall be considered binding and effective after being approved by the Higher Council, taking into account the constitutional norms in each country.

(5) The Committee for Defense and Security

(a) This committee shall group the defense and interior ministers of the two countries.

(b) It specializes in studying and exploring means for ensuring the security of both states, and proposing joint measures to confront any possible aggression or threat to their national security or disturbances and riots that would jeopardize internal security and stability in each of the two countries.

All plans, recommendations, and proposed measures prepared by the committee shall be submitted to the Higher Council for approval and endorsement taking into consideration the constitutional requirements in each of the two states.

(6) General Secretariat

(a) A general secretariat shall be set up to oversee the implementation of the terms of the treaty.

(b) The secretariat shall be headed by a secretary-general to be appointed by the Higher Council.

(c) The secretariat's headquarters, prerogatives, cadres, and budget shall be defined by the Higher Council.

Concluding terms

(1) Bilateral agreements shall be signed between the two countries in all fields covered in the treaty, including economic, defense, educational and others, taking into account the constitutional norms in each of the two states. They shall be considered a complementary part of this treaty.

(2) The treaty shall become effective after ratification by the concerned authorities in the two countries in line with constitutional rules and regulations.

(3) Each of the two governments shall abrogate present laws which contradict the terms of the treaty without violating the constitutional norms of each country.

APPENDIX II: DEFENSE AND SECURITY PACT BETWEEN SYRIA AND LEBANON, 1 SEPTEMBER 1991[42]

In accordance with the Treaty of Brotherhood, Cooperation and Coordination between the Lebanese Republic and the Syrian Arab Republic, signed in Damascus on 22 May 1991, and approved by the Lebanese Parliament on 27 May 1991, especially the third, fifth, and sixth articles, the following has been decided and approved:

(1) *Organizational Structure:* A Committee for Defense and Security Affairs will be set up, grouping the defense and interior ministers in both countries. The committee will meet every three months in Beirut or Damascus or any other location, and whenever there is need for a meeting. The committee may seek the help of any department related to the concerned ministries. The army commands, security organs, and other concerned departments should meet monthly to put into effect the recommendations and programs approved by the Committee for Defense and Security [Affairs] and then supervise implementation.

(2) *Missions:* The Committee for Defense and Security Affairs will concentrate on studying means for ensuring the security of the two countries, and putting forward proposals and joint plans to counter any aggression or threat against their national security and to curb disturbances that could jeopardize their internal safety and security. Conforming to the content of Article Three of the Treaty of Brotherhood, Cooperation and Coordination which provides that Lebanon should not be a source of threat of Syria's security and Syria should not be a source of nuisance and threat to Lebanon, the military and security organs and departments in each of the two countries should take the necessary measures to achieve the following:

— Banning any activity or organization in all military, security, political, and information fields that might endanger and cause threats to the other country.

— Each side should commit itself to avoid becoming a passage, base or stronghold for any force, state or organization seeking to undermine the other country's security, and should extradite criminals sought by the other country if that is requested.

— To enable military and security institutions in each of the two countries to carry out their tasks in implementing the above-mentioned policies, officials from these institutions should meet periodically in order to exchange information and data related to all security and strategic matters, national and internal, including drug issues, financial crimes, terrorism and espionage.

— On the defense level, the defense ministers in the two countries and the concerned organs should meet periodically every three months and whenever there is a need for a meeting in order to trade information regarding security concerns in each country, and should pursue aggressive activity with the aim of reaching a common perception of dangers and eliminating threats through cooperation and coordination.

— The interior and defense ministers in the two countries should work on increasing the exchange of individuals and officers within the framework of training sessions in different fields, including exchange of military instructors in military academies, in order to achieve the highest level of coordination between military personnel to face common threats and dangers.

— The Committee for Defense and Security Affairs should put forward plans for boosting and developing exchange on the level of civil defense in both countries.

(3) *Concluding Clauses:* In addition to its mission, the Committee for Defense and Security Affairs should achieve the following:

— Watch closely the full and complete implementation of the pact's terms and provide directives for smoother application.

— Suggest bases, principles and norms for implementing the agreement in a complete and efficient manner to the Higher Council.

NOTES

For the place and frequency of publications cited here, and for the full name of the publication, news agency, radio station or monitoring service where an abbreviation is used, please see "List of Sources." Only in the case of more than one publication bearing the same name is the place of publication noted here. However, all references to *al-Nahar* in this chapter are to the Beirut paper of that name.

1. Voice of the Mountain, 28 March — DR, 1 April 1991; Khaddam to Ministers Sa'ada and Deeb.
2. *Al-Nahar*, 20 March 1991. Sarkis Na'um's report on Washington interpretation of "Syria's efforts to put its own Lebanese implants (*murtakizat*) into most institutions, arising from the wish to withdraw and secure its back thereafter."
3. *Al-Safir*, 9 September 1991, Junblat interview with Joseph Abu Khalil.
4. *Al-Safir*, 16 September 1991, Fadlallah interview with Joseph Abu Khalil.
5. Ibid.
6. Observation by the author from visits to East Beirut and the Shi'i southern suburbs, January-February 1992.
7. The author noted colorful graffiti to this effect in East Beirut backstreets in early 1992. One Arabic scrawl in Antelias alluded disparagingly to Hirawi's prominent lips, proclaiming that: "Hirawi was suckled by his father."
8. Author's interview with Shams al-Din, February 1992.
9. *The Lebanon Report*, February and March 1991 (Lebanese Center for Policy Studies, Beirut) provides a good summary on these matters.
10. *Al-Nahar*, 11 April 1991, gives a full list of 269 resignations and dismissals in the officer corps.
11. *Al-Nahar*, 8 February 1991, quotes visitors to Damascus: "Everyone is returning with different information."
12. *Al-Nahar*, 7 February 1991.
13. *Al-Nahar*, 16 February 1991, Sarkis Na'um's column.
14. *Al-Nahar*, 28 February, 1 March 1991.
15. *Al-Nahar*, 5 March 1991.
16. *Al-Nahar*, 1, 4 March 1991.
17. *Al-Nahar*, 15 March 1991.
18. *Al-Nahar*, 18 March 1991.
19. *Al-Nahar*, 21 March 1991.
20. *Al-Nahar*, 29 March 1991.
21. *Al-Nahar*, 2 April 1991.
22. *Al-Nahar*, 22 April 1991.
23. VoL, 9 April — DR, 11 April 1991: "Phalangist leader Minister George Sa'ada proposed that the deceased partisan deputies be replaced by persons chosen by their parties, as parties are a mainstay of democracy."
24. *Al-Safir*, 18 April, 29 June 1991. Rumored destinations included Armenia, southern Sudan, Somalia and "one of the Yugoslav republics."
25. *Al-Safir*, 7 June 1991 — LF "compelled" by Israel to send some of its weaponry to the "security zone." Also *al-Nahar*, 11 May 1991.
26. *Al-Nahar*, 4 May 1991.
27. *Al-Nahar*, 14 May 1991.
28. *Al-Nahar*, 7 June 1991.
29. *Al-Nahar*, 23 May 1991.

30. *Al-Nahar*, 11 May 1991.
31. *Al-Nahar*, 6 May 1991.
32. *Al-Nahar*, 15 May 1991.
33. *Al-Nahar*, 21 May 1991, Sarkis Na'um's column.
34. *Al-Nahar*, 28 March 1991.
35. *Al-Nahar*, 29 May 1991, Sarkis Na'um's column.
36. *Al-Nahar*, 6 May 1991.
37. *Al-Nahar*, 10, 24 May 1991.
38. *Al-Nahar*, 24 July 1991.
39. *Al-Nahar*, 5 September 1991.
40. *The Lebanon Report*, October 1991.
41. *Al-Nahar*, 20 June 1991. In early August, there was a series of night raids and detentions "without arrest documents from the prosecutor general's office" (ibid., 6 August 1991). In October, just before Independence Day, official Defense Ministry posters appeared with "'Awn independence" printed on them (ibid., 26 October 1991).
42. As regards the Shi'i community, the author discussed this in early 1992 with sources both in the Beirut southern suburbs and in the Higher Shi'i Islamic Council.
43. An open letter from 'Awn appeared in *al-Nahar*, 3 September 1991. It seemed that *al-Nahar* had a degree of protection in such matters from connections with Saudi Arabia and the prominent Lebanese billionaire, Rafiq al-Hariri, who had acquired an ownership interest in the paper.
44. *Al-Safir*, 12 October 1991.
45. Author's discussion with knowledgeable Zahla source, Beirut, January 1992.
46. Zahla source, January 1992.
47. *Al-Safir*, 10 October 1991, Muhammad Shuqayr's column.
48. *Al-Nahar*, 10 October 1991, Emil Khoury's column.
49. *Al-Nahar*, 11 September 1991, Sarkis Na'um's column.
50. *Al-Nahar*, 17 September 1991.
51. *The Lebanon Report*, December 1991. It was estimated that this device could bring the government $200m. from the first draft.
52. Discussion with member of the regime's "Higher Economic Committee," Beirut, February 1992.
53. As heard by the author from reliable East Beirut sources, February 1992.
54. *Al-Anwar*, 25 June 1991.
55. *The Lebanon Report*, December 1991.
56. *Al-Safir*, 19 October 1991, 'Arif al-'Idd's report on Higher Council meeting.
57. *Al-Safir*, 24 October 1991, Muhammad Shuqayr's column.
58. *The Lebanon Report*, January 1992.
59. *Al-Nahar*, 27 November 1991, Sarkis Na'um's column.
60. Several Shi'i officers made this clear to a Shi'i contact of the author, Beirut, February 1992.
61. Lebanese regime source to author, February 1992. Also *al-Nahar*, 13 November 1991, Sarkis Na'um's column.
62. *Al-Nahar*, 13 November 1991, Sarkis Na'um's column.
63. *Al-Nahar*, 15 February 1991.
64. *Al-Safir*, 1, 2 February, Muhammad Shuqayr's column.
65. *Al-Nahar*, 11 February, 5 April 1991.
66. *Al-Nahar*, 20 January 1991.
67. *Al-Safir*, 22 June 1991, Muhammad Shuqayr's column.
68. *Al-Nahar*, 3 April 1991.
69. *Al-Nahar*, 3, 11 April 1991.
70. R. Beirut, 8 April — DR, 9 April 1991.
71. *Al-Nahar*, 2 May 1991.
72. *Al-Safir*, 22 June 1991, Muhammad Shuqayr's column.
73. AFP, 29 April — DR, 30 April 1991.
74. *Al-Nahar*, 25 June 1991.
75. *Al-Safir*, 28 June 1991, Muhammad Shuqayr's column.
76. *Al-Nahar*, 18 June 1991, Sarkis Na'um's column.

77. *Al-Nahar,* 1 July 1991, quoted 800 Palestinians on the main Qurayya-Kafr Fulus line.
78. *Al-Nahar,* 3 July 1991. Lebanese army chief Emil Lahhud also oversaw developments from the Syrian observer office for South Lebanon, the head Syrian field representative being a Col. "Ziyad."
79. *Al-Nahar,* 9, 16 and 18 July 1991. The army assessed that only 10%–20% of medium and heavy weaponry had been collected from the Sur camps. SLA commander, Antoine Lahad, asserted that the situation was not much different for Sidon.
80. *Al-Nahar,* 18 July 1991.
81. *Al-Nahar,* 7 August 1991.
82. *Al-Safir,* 12 August 1991, Muhammad Shuqayr's column.
83. *Al-Nahar,* 9 August 1991, comment to Sarkis Na'um.
84. *Al-Hawadith,* 29 March — DR, 4 April 1991.
85. *Al-Nahar,* 14 June 1991.
86. *Al-Nahar,* 7 July 1991. FR, 5 December 1991, estimated an increase in the south, by late 1991, to c. 1,900 militiamen, with a semiprofessional core of about 400.
87. Reuven Pedehtsur in *Ha'aretz,* 19 July 1991.
88. *Al-Safir,* 17 October 1991, comment to Muhammad Shuqayr.
89. Ibid., and *al-Nahar,* 13 March 1991.
90. *Al-Safir,* 22 October 1991, Muhammad Shuqayr's column.
91. *Al-Safir,* 9 August 1991.
92. *Al-Safir,* 10 August 1991.
93. *Al-Safir,* 17 October 1991.
94. *Al-Nahar,* 5 May 1991, sources close to Islamic radical currents to Sarkis Na'um.
95. *Al-Nahar,* 8 October 1991, comment to Sarkis Na'um.
96. *Al-Safir,* 22 October 1991, comment to Muhammad Shuqayr.
97. Senior Israeli source to author, January 1992.
98. Numbers derived from *al-Nahar, The Lebanon Report* and *Ha'aretz.*
99. *Ha'aretz,* 21 May 1991.
100. Reuven Pedehtsur in *Ha'aretz,* 6 June 1991.
101. Ze'ev Schiff in *Ha'aretz,* 12 July 1991.
102. *Ha'aretz,* 8 July 1991.
103. A. Schweitzer in *Ha'aretz,* 12 July 1991.
104. Ibid., and Ephraim Sneh in *Davar,* 12 July 1991.
105. Lubrani to VoI, 1 July — DR, 2 July 1991. Discussion with author, January 1992.
106. *Al-Nahar,* 19 July 1991, observation by "the ambassador of a big Western power" that no room existed for talk about the return of Jizzin until the completion of weapons withdrawal from the Palestinians and Hizballah.
107. Israeli participant to author, January 1992.
108. *Al-Nahar,* 27 October 1991, Sarkis Na'um's visit to Tehran, reporting on "the international conference to support the Islamic revolution of the Palestinian people."
109. Ze'ev Schiff in *Ha'aretz,* 13 December 1991.
110. Israeli officials knew this. See Reuven Pedehtsur in *Ha'aretz,* 4 November 1991: "In the security structure and the IDF there are no illusions. Senior sources in the IDF say the attacks will continue, and almost certainly their pace will accelerate. There is a direct connection between what is happening in the political sphere and Hizballah operations."
111. Ze'ev Schiff in *Ha'aretz,* 26 May 1992.
112. *Hadashot,* 15 December — DR, 16 December 1991.
113. *Al-Nahar,* 27 June 1991, Sarkis Na'um's column.
114. Bechtel-Dar al-Handasa study of Lebanese reconstruction needs, *The Lebanon Report,* December 1991.
115. *Al-Nahar,* 16 October 1991, Emil Khoury's column.
116. *The Lebanon Report,* June and December 1991.
117. Personal observation by the author in Beirut and the southern suburbs, January 1992.
118. *Al-Nahar,* 24 June 1991.
119. *The Lebanon Report,* December 1991.
120. *Al-Nahar,* 18 September 1991.
121. *Al-Anwar,* 2 November 1991.

122. *Al-Nahar,* 27 June 1991, Sarkis Naʻum's column.
123. Comment to author, January 1992.
124. *CSM,* 26 March 1992.
125. East Beirut industrialist to author, January 1992.
126. *Al-Nahar,* 20 August 1991.
127. *Al-Nahar,* 14 June 1991.
128. *Al-Nahar,* 17 May 1991.
129. *The Lebanon Report,* November 1991.
130. *Al-Nahar,* 17 August 1991, Sarkis Naʻum's column.
131. *Al-Anwar,* 29 July 1991. See also R. Beirut, 28 July — DR, 30 July 1991.
132. Heard by the author from a government official in the southern suburbs, January 1992.
133. *Al-Nahar,* 5 August 1991, Sarkis Naʻum referring to "no economic input from Christian capitalists."
134. *Al-Nahar,* 14 August 1991.
135. *Al-Nahar,* 22 August 1991.
136. *Le Liban du Citoyen,* December 1991.
137. *The Lebanon Report,* April 1992.
138. Taʼif agreement sections on "education and teaching" and "the media."
139. *FR,* 16 May 1991.
140. *Al-Nahar,* 17 December 1991.
141. English translation from *The Lebanon Report,* June 1991; Arabic text in *al-Anwar,* 17 May 1991.
142. English translation from *The Lebanon Report,* October 1991; Arabic text in *al-Nahar,* 7 September 1991.

Libya
(Al-Jamahiriyya al-'Arabiyya al-Libiyya al-Sha'biyya al-Ishtirakiyya al-'Uzma)

YEHUDIT RONEN

In 1991, Libya's attention was largely focused on foreign affairs. At least, such was the impression given by the Libyan and foreign media's coverage of the Jamahiriyya. Tripoli invested a great deal of effort in nurturing a twofold policy in the Arab arena: the advancement of its political and economic rapprochement with Egypt, and the continuation of the fine balance of creative neutrality in the Gulf crisis during the war and in its aftermath. Tripoli's success in its relations with Cairo was reflected in increased diplomatic exchanges between Libya and Egypt, highlighted by a series of seven meetings that inspired positive feelings between their heads of state on the political level, and also projected the growing pace of economic cooperation. Mu'ammar al-Qadhdhafi skillfully maneuvered a balanced stand vis-à-vis the Gulf conflict. He managed to toe the line with Egypt, while supporting Iraq against the US, and also backing Kuwait against Iraq. He also successfully reversed the pro-Iraqi sympathies of Libyan circles and their implicit criticism of his passive role, and turned these feelings into a pro-Arab, patriotic campaign, with himself playing the role of guardian of all-Arab interests. Thus, not only did he gain political advantages on the home front and in inter-Arab politics, but he also scored bonus points with the international community, although only of potential significance at that stage. His Gulf policy enabled him, to a certain extent, to dispel his image as the region's enfant terrible.

Tripoli's political interests shifted toward the Mashriq in 1991. Qadhdhafi's earlier dreams of "the great Maghrib unity" seemed to have apparently turned into a nightmare in 1991, following the alarming rise of Islamic fundamentalism in Sudan, Algeria and to a lesser extent also in Tunisia, and Qadhdhafi feared it might spill over into the Jamahiriyya.

Another foreign arena in which Tripoli invested a great deal of diplomatic effort was relations with the West, in particular with the US. However, Libya's endeavors yielded little result. Tripoli repeatedly received a negative response to its overtures to Washington designed to defuse bilateral tension. The Bush Administration resolutely continued its campaign against Qadhdhafi, renewing economic sanctions early in the year and, later in the spring, blacklisting many firms accused of trying to sidestep US economic sanctions against Tripoli. However, despite its rage toward Washington, on the one hand, and the obsessive fear of a US military attack against it, on the other, Tripoli kept a low profile on the US role in the Gulf crisis, and, surprisingly enough, even went so far as to justify it. Unfortunately for Qadhdhafi, his efforts were fruitless.

578

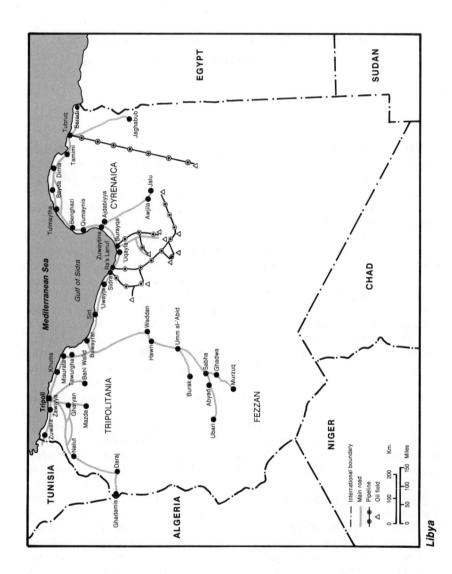

Libya

Furthermore, as the year drew to a close, hostility reached new heights, following US (and UK) accusations that Tripoli was responsible for the explosion of the Pan Am airliner over Scotland in 1988. Libya categorically denied any responsibility, but the new escalating crisis threatened Tripoli's ties with Washington and London even further.

There was a short-lived improvement in Libya's relations with France in the first part of 1991, but they deteriorated later in the year, following the French issue of arrest warrants for Libyan citizens suspected of being involved in bombing the French Union des Transports Aériens (UTA) DC-10 airplane over the Sahara in 1989.

Tripoli openly declared its apprehension of the Soviet Union's disintegration, yet this was tinged with malicious pleasure. Qadhdhafi drew two major conclusions from the new dramatic developments: that the Arabs had no other ally than from among themselves, and that his "Third International Theory" had been proven justified (for Qadhdhafi's theory, see *MECS* 1977–78, pp. 629–33). Qadhdhafi mourned over and worried about the new international circumstances, whereby the world was suddenly being led by one superpower only.

Tripoli was annoyed about the campaign led by the West against Libya's alleged manufacturing of chemical weapons. But it was even more worried about foreign accusations that Tripoli was involved in terror and made an intensified effort to dispel its image as a leader of international terrorism, fearing military retaliation by the US. At the same time, Libya's top officials took every opportunity to present to the world the Jamahiriyya's own revolutionary-style perception of the concept of terrorism.

There was no change in Qadhdhafi's rejection of the existence of Israel. It was in keeping with his hitherto-held stance that he was opposed to the Arab-Israeli peace conference held in Madrid in late October.

The regime's preoccupation with external affairs came at the expense of attention to the home front. Under the tight control of the regime's security apparatus, the domestic arena remained calm, displaying the smooth and welcome inertia shaped and nursed by Qadhdhafi since the seventies, within the system of "People's Power." Tripoli also derived a great deal of satisfaction from the impotence of the opposition, both within the country and abroad.

Economic conditions improved during 1991. Financial liquidity was better due to the increase in oil exports and the rise in oil prices following the Gulf War. This enabled Tripoli to introduce new dynamics into the country's socioeconomic system, and to complete the first phase of the ambitious great man-made river project, designed to transfer water from aquifers under the Sahara desert to the dense, urbanized Mediterranean coastline. This seemingly impressive achievement coincided with Qadhdhafi's 22nd year in power, which was, in itself, a major success.

INTERNAL AFFAIRS

PHASE I OF THE GREAT MAN-MADE RIVER COMPLETED

Against the background of the West's incessant, annoying attacks on Libya for its alleged involvement in terrorism and the production of chemical weapons, the celebrations marking the completion of the first phase of the great man-made river were like a breath of fresh air for Qadhdhafi. On 28 August, precisely eight years after publicly announcing the grandiose plan, the Libyan leader celebrated the realization of the first phase of his dream. The project, he reiterated during the year, "is the world's eighth wonder" and "the twentieth century miracle."[1]

In keeping with the political and economic importance of the event, the celebrations were "a star-spangled, laser-lit, orchestra-thumping production,"[2] widely covered by the local and international media. Thousands of Libyans were taken off to the desert for the occasion, and many high-ranking, foreign diplomats and officials attended the spectacular ceremony, including some heads of state, mainly from neighboring countries. Using the "historic" and "immortal" occasion to enhance his regime's political prestige, Qadhdhafi stated that "the noise that the great man-made river is making now is much stronger than the noise of any fleet or any other force on earth. This one is life; that one is death." The Libyan leader elaborated in the same euphoric tone upon opening the pipeline's flow near Benghazi: "These waters will have traveled one 1,000 km. when they arrive today....The wires used in the manufacture of these pipes, if we wrap them around the globe, would go around 250 times."[3]

But despite its impressive engineering and technological achievements, the project also elicited criticism. Foreign critics regarded the project as "a monument to vanity" that made little economic sense in a country where the UN Development Program claimed that 94.6% of territory was desert wasteland. The critics further argued that no one knew for sure how long the underground aquifers would feed the pipeline. They also feared the negative environmental influence. The project had hitherto cost $5bn. and an evaluation of its completion estimated the cost at an additional $20bn.– $25bn. According to some assessments, the Libyans could have built up to five desalination plants, each producing nearly 4m. liters of water a day for the cost of $5bn.[4]

Whatever the project's political and economic benefits in the medium and long term, it had already proved its political value in the short term. It placed local and international attention on what appeared to be an impressive success, counter-balancing, to a certain extent, other internal shortcomings, not to mention external pressures and difficulties in relations with the West.

THE OPPOSITION'S IMPOTENCE
One reason why Qadhdhafi was able to direct most of his energies toward foreign affairs, was the inefficacy of the Libyan opposition. Not even when 400 Libyan prisoners of war (PoWs) from Chad joined the expatriate opposition ranks, early in the year, was it activated.[5] The US had trained and equipped the PoWs in Chad during the late 1980s, aiming both to shake Qadhdhafi's regime and induce him to loosen his grasp on the Chadian arena, in exchange for freeing the PoWs from PoW camps.[6] In the spring of 1991, they were moved to the US, which became the central base for the main expatriate opposition movement, the National Front for the Salvation of Libya (NFSL) having lost its political support in Egypt, Sudan and Chad. The contacts reportedly held between the NFSL military wing, the Libyan National Army, the Pentagon and the Defense Intelligence Agency officers[7] gave cause for concern in Tripoli, particularly as tension with the US reached its peak (see below).

During the course of the year, Tripoli's apprehension proved to be somewhat exaggerated, although Libyan security authorities announced the exposure of two cases of subversion. It was not known whether the NFSL or the Muslim Brothers, who were also opposed to the regime, had any connection with the reported subversive actions. In the spring, a foreign source claimed that the Libyan security authorities foiled a plan for collaboration between the outlawed and severely persecuted Libyan Muslim Brothers and Sudanese fundamentalist elements. The plan was designed to overthrow Qadhdhafi.[8] However, the information was not corroborated by any other domestic or foreign source. On 30 November, another foreign source exclusively claimed that an army officer and a civilian official planned a military coup, which the security authorities had caught just in time.[9] The Libyan ambassador in Beirut denied that this had happened.[10]

Whether or not such subversive actions took place, it became evident during the year that the Islamic fundamentalists irritated Qadhdhafi. He called them "the lackeys of the Americans and the Israelis" who "sabotaged Islam."[11] Qadhdhafi was perhaps trying to calm his own fears, which increased with the aggressive upsurge of fundamentalism in Libya's backyards, namely Sudan, Algeria and Tunisia. Consequently, he somewhat understated that the issue of the Islamic movement "is one of history's cycles; it runs its course and then it ends."[12] Tripoli made increased efforts during the summer to give the impression that there was no danger of fundamentalism in the Jamahiriyya, following the eruption of fundamentalist turmoil in neighboring Algeria. "We should not speak of fundamentalist movements in the Arab Maghrib," a senior official stated:

> There are political movements seeking to reach power. These movements are a product of an accumulation of factors resulting from the economic crises,...the absence of a strong Arab plan, and the lack of Arab unity. They have received aid from foreign quarters which also helped to train their members in acts of violence, sabotage and terrorism. The main aim of these movements is to seize power. There is no fundamentalist phenomenon in Libya. The Libyan people have no economic crisis, no social crisis, and no government crisis. There is no logical or historical reason for that devilish phenomenon to appear in Libya.[13]

Qadhdhafi likewise emphasized:

> What we are seeing today is a relaunch of these movements, which will soon disappear. They have survived for a certain time because they appeal to people who have suffered from an ideological void caused by imperialism, colonialism and reaction. But it will not be long before they return to reality and abandon these movements.[14]

THE ISSUE OF LIBYA'S CHEMICAL WEAPONS CAPABILITIES

In 1991, international attention was still drawn to the controversy over the Rabta plant, which allegedly manufactured chemical weapons, and over Libya's additional planned projects to produce weapons of mass destruction, i.e., biological (see *MECS* 1990, pp. 559–60). However, several other events were the focus of international attention, and the issue of chemical weapons occupied an inconspicuous place among them.

Nevertheless, in the early part of the year, reports originating in the West claimed that Libya was building near Tripoli "the biggest underground arsenal for chemical and nuclear weapons in the Middle East"[15] Whether or not this was so, such a large underground storage area could also be used to store Libya's huge stock of conventional weapons, and to shelter its top political and military personnel in case of an American military attack, which was Tripoli's obsessive fear at the time. It might, therefore, be assumed that Qadhdhafi had learnt a lesson from the US air attack on Libya in 1986, and also from American action toward the destruction of Iraq's military arsenal.

Libya repeatedly denied producing weapons of mass destruction, while simultaneously calling for a ban on the manufacture, storage and use of any such weapons.[16] These calls contradicted official statements of previous years, which had justified, and even urged all Arab countries to manufacture or purchase urgently weapons of "total destruction" as a right and a duty. The impression given by these different attitudes was that the changes might be for tactical reasons more than anything else.

On 6 March, a year after fire allegedly broke out and damaged the Rabta industrial complex (see *MECS* 1990, p. 559), Tripoli announced that it was negotiating with some European states for their assistance in repairing the plant and renewing pharmaceuticals production.[17] To lend further credibility to its persistent claim that the plant was designed solely for the manufacture of medicines, Qadhdhafi took his guest, the Egyptian president, to the plant on a visit which was widely covered by the Libyan media in April (see below).

Meanwhile, Western research intelligence services repeated their claims that Libya planned a second chemical-weapons plant west of Sabha, in the depths of western Libya.[18] In addition, American satellites photographed a new complex of buildings, spreading over 12 sq. km., near the allegedly existing chemical-weapons complex in Rabta. A German high-technology firm reportedly supplied sophisticated measuring and laser technology for the new buildings.[19]

Libya's immediate interests were seriously damaged by further claims that it was increasing production of chemical weapons. The West simultaneously intensified its accusations of terrorism, and the likelihood increased that the US would launch a military attack on Libya. It was obviously with this in mind that Qadhdhafi declared his support for "the UN proposal to conduct a UN-sponsored international inspection...to remove nuclear, chemical and biological weapons and ban their manufacture, sale and use."[20]

TERRORISM: ALLEGED INVOLVEMENT AND LIBYA'S OWN PERCEPTION
In the second half of 1991, the Western media intensified their accusations of Libya's responsibility for the two bomb explosions, of the Pan Am Boeing 747 airliner over Lockerbie, Scotland, in 1988, and of the French UTA DC-10 over the Sahara in 1989. More than 300 people were killed in the two incidents. Those making such claims quoted intelligence sources as saying that both explosions were planned at a meeting in Tripoli in the fall of 1988: the first in revenge against the US for its 1986 air bombing of Tripoli and Benghazi and the second against France for backing Chad in its war against Libya.[21] Such Western media allegations contradicted earlier suspicions that a Syrian-sponsored Palestinian group, the Popular Front for the Liberation of Palestine-General Command, was responsible for the Lockerbie incident acting on orders from Iran. Iran's grudge against the US was a result of the shooting down of an Iranian airbus over the Gulf by a US warship in July of that year, which claimed the lives of 29 people.

The British made a breakthrough in the Lockerbie investigation in 1991, when UK experts uncovered the remains of a detonator equipped with an electronic timer at the site of the explosion. The timing device contained a chip of a type delivered to Libya by a Swiss-based firm.[22] Naturally, Libya was swift to deny the accusation categorically.

This new barrage of accusations came at a bad time for Qadhdhafi — at the height of his campaign to dispel his image as the world's leading backer of terrorism. The West's outrage against him undid all the good and seemed to have put an end to any benefits he had hoped to gain from the West and the US in return for his policy of good conduct during the Gulf crisis. In response, Qadhdhafi stepped up his propaganda efforts to dissociate his regime completely from terrorism: "I condemn blind and irresponsible attacks, bombs in public places, big stores and stations [and] airports," he stated in one of the many references of that kind. However, in the same breath, he continued: "Do not lump terrorism together with the violence which is inseparable from a just and sacred struggle for freedom."[23] In other words, violence was legitimate when the cause was sacred. The same point was further elaborated upon by Qadhdhafi on a later occasion. "We must differentiate terrorism from armed struggle which we support. We are against terrorism and we hate terrorism [but] we support the sacred struggle for just issues like the Palestinian issue; the liberation of the peoples; their unity and their independence."[24] One of the Jamahiriyya's best diplomats, who was mobilized by Tripoli to help refute the West's accusations, further clarified: "Terrorism is a matter of definition, not only between Libya and the US, but also between the Third World in general and the US....Yes," he stressed, "we help legitimate liberation movements, but we don't help take hostages or hijack planes. We are strongly against all actions aimed at civilians."[25]

FOREIGN AFFAIRS

THE ARAB WORLD

Continued Rapprochement with Egypt and the Effects on Libya's Inter-Arab Position

There were frequent diplomatic exchanges between Libya and Egypt, and much solidarity was displayed in meetings between Qadhdhafi and Mubarak, showing a strengthening of relations. On 3 January, Mubarak arrived in Misurata, Libya's third-largest town on the Mediterranean coast. He participated, together with the Syrian, Sudanese and Libyan heads of state, in the Arab minisummit hurriedly convened by Qadhdhafi. Their talks concentrated on the Gulf crisis in the countdown to the 15 January deadline.[26] For Qadhdhafi, it was highly significant that the three leaders participated in his conference at a highly volatile and potentially explosive phase in inter-Arab affairs, and for the second time in less than a year (for their quadrilateral meeting in March, see *MECS* 1990, p. 567). It served as a public acknowledgment of Qadhdhafi's growing influence at the center of the Arab camp. Furthermore, by bringing together Mubarak and Bashir, despite their strong mutual antagonism and differences concerning the Gulf crisis, Qadhdhafi not only enhanced his position as a mediator — an important step toward gaining more influence in inter-Arab politics — but it also served as a shrewd tactic for attesting to Tripoli's professed neutrality toward the Gulf crisis. Because of the sharp contrast between Egypt's and Sudan's stances vis-à-vis the Gulf crisis, the release of a joint communiqué, agreed by all four participants, was aborted in advance and thus the Libyan host was spared a great deal of embarrassment (for Libya's relations with Sudan, see chapter on Sudan).

From 13–16 February, Qadhdhafi returned Mubarak's visit. The discussions between the two leaders centered around the Gulf War and its regional repercussions, as well as the nurturing of bilateral relations.[27] Qadhdhafi took advantage of the opportunity to highlight the "urgency of forging unity" between Libya and Egypt, stressing that "circumstances are favorable for such a development."[28] He also tried to use the visit to ease tension between Cairo and Khartoum, but to no avail. In exchange for his services as mediator, the Libyan leader had hoped that Cairo would plead his case in restoring relations with Washington and mediate in returning home the Libyan PoWs from African countries (see below). However, he was unsuccessful on both counts.[29] At the same time, Qadhdhafi also hoped that his rapprochement with Egypt would provide him with a protective shield against a US military attack, which he feared at that stage.

On 9 April, Qadhdhafi and Mubarak held another round of talks, this time in Tripoli. Their meeting, which came "within the framework of regular consultations," dealt with postwar security and political effects and with the bolstering of bilateral relations.[30] It was during that visit that Qadhdhafi scored an important propaganda and political victory, when Mubarak accompanied him on a tour, widely covered by the local media, to the plant in Rabta, which allegedly manufactured chemical weapons. Though no official statement was made, Mubarak's presence on the tour could be interpreted as signifying his approval of Tripoli's persistent claim that the plant was designed solely for the manufacture of pharmaceuticals.

On 19 May, Mubarak arrived on a one-day visit at the city of Ra's Lanuf, where he and Qadhdhafi toured the town's huge petrochemical industrial complex.[31] At a joint press conference, both reaffirmed the close relations between the "single Arab people in the two fraternal countries," adding that these relations "have never been better."[32] This congenial spirit was further promoted by Libya's foreign minister, stating that his country's "pan-Arab objective is to establish an Egyptian-Libyan unity."[33]

On 28 March, Qadhdhafi added a new dimension to bilateral relations, when he unilaterally announced that "the artificial border" with Egypt, including restrictions on travel and customs on trade, had been abolished. In a symbolic gesture, on the same day, using a tractor he knocked down the border post in the Masa'id area.[34]

On 2 July, Qadhdhafi arrived in Alexandria, en route from Sudan. The main purpose of his visit was to reconcile the regimes of Cairo and Khartoum. "Egypt, Libya and Sudan form the golden triangle of the Arab nation," stated Libya's foreign minister, further stressing the importance of tripartite connections.[35] Qadhdhafi and Mubarak also discussed the Gulf War security arrangements in the aftermath of the war.[36]

Meanwhile, economic cooperation grew. Libya was rich in oil, but in dire need of petroleum technology, which the long-standing American sanctions had denied it. Libya also desperately needed a variety of consumer goods, including food. Tripoli hoped to profit from the surplus of Egyptian manpower, especially skilled labor, for various services and fields of production, particularly agriculture. It should be recalled that Qadhdhafi offered agricultural land to be reclaimed by the great man-made river to 1m. Egyptians to settle on (see *MECS* 1990, p. 567). However, in 1991, the ambitious settlement was still only at the visionary stage.[37]

The growing pace of cooperation was further exemplified in the joint Libyan Egyptian higher committee meeting, held in Benghazi from 6-8 July. Qadhdhafi attended one of the sessions in accordance with the importance of the occasion, affirming his determination to "work with Egypt side by side until the end....The end is unity and strength." Furthermore, on his way from Sudan through Egypt in July, he elaborated that he had seen that "in reality, integration and real unity should involve the three countries. 'Abd al-Nasir himself had entrusted me with it. We were sitting with the map of the Arab world in front of us and he said to me: look Mu'ammar, this is the great state — Libya, Egypt and Sudan."[38]

On 4 August, Mubarak paid an unannounced two-day visit to Libya within the framework of the two countries' "constant consultation." The then scheduled Israeli-Arab peace conference was at the top of the two leaders' agenda of talks.[39] Though neither side made reference to the fact, Qadhdahfi apparently promised his counterpart not to complicate Egypt's position on that issue. Mubarak's opening of the Egyptian side of the border with Libya, on 6 August, further corroborated that alleged promise.

From 27–29 August, Mubarak once again visited Libya, this time attending the celebrations marking the inauguration of the first stage of the great man-made river. Qadhdhafi utilized the opportunity to reaffirm that Arab unity was "inevitable" and to initiate a tripartite meeting between him and the Sudanese and Egyptian heads of state, hoping to "clear the air" between Cairo and Khartoum.[40]

From 9–10 October, Qadhdhafi paid a private visit to Egypt. He met Mubarak and again they discussed the scheduled Arab-Israeli peace conference. The Libyan leader used their meeting, once again, to try to diffuse tension between Cairo and Khartoum,[41] but there were no tangible results of his efforts.

Skillful Political Maneuvering in the Gulf Crisis

Immediately after the outbreak of the Gulf War, Qadhdhafi stated: "We wish Iraq to triumph and America to be defeated....That would be nice."[42] This statement was totally out of line with the well-calculated and relatively muted anti-American attitude. It showed Qadhdhafi's deep aversion to, and fears of Washington. By making such a statement Qadhdhafi also paid important lip service to Baghdad, as well as Arab and especially Maghribean countries, which he felt obligated to do in an attempt to counter their criticism for not taking a tougher anti-American and pro-Iraqi stand. Qadhdhafi's statement also paid lip service to pro-Iraqi circles in Libya. According to an unconfirmed report, a huge crowd demonstrated in front of the Saudi Embassy in Tripoli on 18 January, chanting support for Saddam Husayn.[43] Although the Libyan state-controlled media completely ignored the demonstration, one could read between the lines of one of Qadhdhafi's speeches that there was pressure from within the country to take part in the war, or at least to declare support for Baghdad.

> The war is not clear. If it were only Iraq being threatened by America, we would all have gone to Baghdad and declared our stand by her....However, now if you are fighting on Iraq's side, it means that you are fighting the people of [many Arab countries]. It [also] means you are saying I am supporting Iraq whether she is right or wrong.[44]

His message apparently also reflected his anger toward, and possibly even his avenging spirit against Iraq, who had significantly contributed to his army's defeat in the Chad war in 1987. Further demonstrating his delicately maneuvered neutrality, Qadhdhafi cunningly encouraged "a 1m.-people demonstration" in the streets of Tripoli and other towns on 19 January. The Libyan demonstrations coincided with other mass pro-Iraqi ones, held on the same day in various Arab capitals. However, in contrast to the others, the Libyans confined their message to the "immediate stop to the war," adding that "a third world war decided by mad individuals [Saddam Husayn? George Bush?] should not be allowed to erupt." The demonstrations organized by Qadhdhafi further showed his neutrality by demanding "a halt to the bombing of Baghdad," while at the same time stressing "the Kuwaiti people's right to self-determination."[45] The Libyan leader further stated that the war "is an imperialist mission and a hatred against the Arabs, apart from an aggressive stand toward Iraq, Arabs and Islam [and in any case], not for the sake of Kuwait."[46] Qadhdhafi repeated his call to end the war and to find "an Arab solution" to the crisis, "away from any foreign interference."[47]

In mid-February, Qadhdhafi resumed his peace efforts, which had not met with success in the prewar period (see *MECS* 1990, pp. 564–67). He focused his activities on the UN, urging it to forbid the anti-Iraq coalition to continue fighting beyond the liberation of Kuwait. He expressed his support for the "Iraqi Government's compliance with UN Security Council Resolution 660 and readiness to withdraw from Kuwait in accordance with limited conditions."[48] The Libyan leader skillfully manipulated the Iraqi announcements (see chapter on Iraq) for his own political gains, stating, during the second half of February, that he felt "happy that Libya's efforts to convince Iraq to withdraw from Kuwait have been successful so that the Kuwaiti people can decide its fate." Qadhdhafi also warned that "we do not accept that Kuwait be delivered from one occupation to another," i.e., from Iraqi to American. The way to prevent such an eventuality, he added, "is to establish Arab unity from the Gulf to the ocean."[49] Qadhdhafi demanded that the UN Security Council should exclusively supervise the Iraqi withdrawal, ensuring that Kuwait was "effectively liberated."[50]

Qadhdhafi made sure that his campaign to take care of the interests of both Iraq and Kuwait and the whole Arab nation against the "colonialist military campaign in the Arab homeland,"[51] was widely publicized. This was another step on his diplomatic tightrope walk. The Libyan leader strongly rejected the terms of the UN cease-fire "in the Gulf," terming them as "humiliating and contemptuous."[52] At the same time, Tripoli also expressed its annoyance with Baghdad, stating that "nobody ever believed that Iraq would accept this humiliating resolution, even if it means its disappearance from the world map."[53] In the same vein, the Libyan media continued to denounce Iraq's "irresponsibility," its role in "the farce resulting in catastrophe that is totally illogical from beginning to end."[54]

The postwar security arrangements in the Gulf did not give Tripoli rest: "The Arabs must take responsibility for pan-Arab security. There is no need for foreign troops [i.e., American] in the Gulf after the liberation of Kuwait." These forces came "to implement the principle of international legitimacy," but now after Kuwait had been liberated they needed to remain no more.[55] "The only efficient, and acceptable security arrangement in the Gulf," Qadhdhafi stressed, "should be an Arab union."[56]

On 27 August, Taha Yasin Ramadan, the Iraqi Revolution Command Council member and vice president arrived on a three-day visit to Libya, to attend the celebrations marking the inauguration of the first stage of the great man-made river. The Iraqi gesture gave Qadhdhafi political satisfaction and, apparently, was interpreted by him as clear evidence of his successful Gulf policy.

The Maghrib: A Declining Interest; Growing Fears of the Mounting Algerian Fundamentalism

On 1 January 1991, Qadhdhafi became the president of the Arab Maghrib Union (AMU) for a six-month period, in accordance with the organization's charter (for the AMU's formation, its aims and activities, which, in 1991, were still mainly confined to procedural matters, see *MECS* 1989, pp. 144–47 and 1990, pp. 569–70).

The Libyan media let Qadhdhafi's new appointment pass almost unnoticed. This near silence could be explained by the fact that the AMU's political and economic value had dropped considerably from Tripoli's point of view, mainly as a result of the shift in its own political and economic emphasis from the Maghrib arena to the Mashriq, and more specifically to Egypt. Furthermore, the Gulf crisis exposed the AMU members' different stances and highlighted the fact that the AMU countries' common denominator was relatively narrow politically (for details on the various positions of the AMU countries toward the Gulf War and on the further activities of the AMU later in the year, see chapter on inter-Arab relations).

Meanwhile, in the summer, there was an eruption of violent political turmoil in Algeria, a key member of the AMU, which wrecked the imminent AMU meeting, scheduled to be held in Tripoli on 9 June. The latter's reactions toward the turmoil in Algeria were restrained. Nevertheless, the stunning victory of the Algerian Islamic fundamentalists in the first round of the December parliamentary elections, and Algeria's immediate plunge into new and potentially explosive political and military uncertainty, caused a great deal of concern in Tripoli, which had steadily held its own threatening Islamic fundamentalists in check.

STRENUOUS EFFORT TO IMPROVE IMAGE IN THE WEST

Libya and the US

During 1991, the hostility in relations between Libya and the US was not overcome, even in the slightest. There was a strong sense of déjà vu in bilateral relations when Washington extended its economic sanctions against Tripoli in early January. The US sanctions were first imposed in 1986 and then renewed on an annual basis, because of the "unusual and extraordinary threat" posed by Libya to American "national security and foreign policy."[57] Though not stated explicitly by the Bush Administration, Washington's decision to renew sanctions was based on its suspicion of Tripoli's role in the Pan Am airplane bomb explosion (see above), and its wish to deter Libya from further terrorist and subversive actions.

As expected, Libya strongly denounced "the American aggressive policy."[58] Qadhdhafi was particularly outraged because he was dependent on American technology for the prosperity of his country's oil industry. There was, no doubt, significant relief for the Libyan regime over the increased oil revenue in 1991, as a direct consequence of the Gulf conflict. Nevertheless, more than ever before, the limitations in the country's capacity for oil production became apparent. Oil production capacity was seriously cut back by the long-standing American embargo on spare parts and technological know-how, as well as the departure of the majority of US oil industry personnel. Thus, Tripoli was both humiliated and worried by its desperate need for, and dependence on the US, particularly as the Soviet Union's superpower position was rapidly declining.

The Libyan leader had good reason to be angry with the Bush Administration. In early December 1990, amidst the change of leadership in Chad, the US swiftly evacuated 600 Libyan PoWs from Chad to other African countries (see above), completely ignoring Libya's demand that they be able to return home. While 250 of them eventually returned to Libya, those remaining were scattered by the Americans to undisclosed locations in the US in late spring.[59] This American operation, repeatedly referred to by Tripoli as an "act of piracy," and as the "practicing of state terrorism,"[60] particularly infuriated Qadhdhafi. In contrast to his relatively restrained anti-American reactions concerning the Gulf crisis, Qadhdhafi seemed to have lost his self-discipline with regard to the PoW issue. His series of vehement verbal assaults spoke for themselves. "America is not committed to ethics or international law....This is the behavior of any superpower in the world, like Hitler, Mussolini, Genghis Khan, Napoleon, Alexander of Macedon, Reagan and Bush. They all belong on one list," stated Tripoli in a typically venomous tone.[61]

Meanwhile, the US continued its actions against Libya. On 30 April, it blacklisted 48 banks, companies and organizations around the world as being "front agents" for Libya, trying to sidestep US economic sanctions against Tripoli.[62] "Libya's continued refusal to disavow terrorism as a tool of international policy makes such a listing particularly useful in redirecting public attention to the comprehensive sanctions program in place against Libya," Washington stated.[63] Tripoli repeatedly rejected the US claim that it was involved in terrorism, stating the accusation "completely lacks credibility and objectivity."[64]

At the same time, Tripoli continued with its restrained reaction toward the US role in the Gulf conflict. While reiterating on the one hand its wish to see the American troops' immediate withdrawal from the Gulf region,[65] on the one hand, Qadhdhafi also pointed out that the US intervention "was not a bilateral problem between Iraq and the US" and that it "was justified by the decisions made within the Security Council."[66] Qadhdhafi's relatively muted anti-American statements were born not only of his severe economic pressure, but also, and to an even greater extent, of his obsessive fear that the US was planning a military attack on Libya. "Libya is on the blacklist as far as America is concerned," he stated during the Gulf War.[67] "When the Americans finish destroying Iraq's infrastructure," he further claimed, "they will turn their attention to Libya and search for anything to strike...."[68]

At the same time, Libya intensified its efforts, albeit discreetly, to restore relations with the US. Not only did Tripoli desperately need the US to increase the volume of its oil output and to unfreeze more than $2bn. of its assets in US banks,[69] but it was also aware that rapprochement with the US would dispel its tarnished image as a supporter of terrorism. Thus, Libyan top officials repeatedly stressed their country's wish "to create a language of logical political dialogue" and establish diplomatic ties with the US, on condition that it be based on "equal footing..., on mutual respect and mutual benefits, and on noninterference and nonencroachment."[70] Libya's efforts toward reconciliation were conducted through intermediaries, mainly Egypt, and through its battery of top, pragmatic officials. A leading figure in formulating the Libyan pragmatic stance toward the US was Ahmad Qadhdhaf al-Damm, the Libyan leader's cousin, who was also the driving force behind the successful rapprochement with Egypt. He stayed in Cairo from where he courted American officials,[71] trying to revive bilateral ties with Washington from their long-standing stalemate.

However, in the fall of 1991, bilateral tension increased, as the US reiterated its claim that Libya was responsible for the Pan Am airplane explosion. The insistence of the US on Libya's role, "is no more than a continuation of the official terrorism...and a pretext for aggression against [the Libyans] to prevent them... from living their own life with their complete freedom and will," Tripoli responded in familiar style.[72] Qadhdhafi seemed on the verge of panic, fearing an imminent military attack by the US. In an attempt to defuse the mounting tension, he stated: "We have no desire to antagonize America, and America cannot be proud of antagonizing a small state like Libya by attacking it."[73]

On 14 November, the US (and Britain) officially charged two Libyan agents for the Lockerbie disaster. Two weeks later, they demanded that Tripoli accept responsibility for the incident, extradite the two, and pay compensation. Libya still persistently denied any connection with the disaster, stressing that both Washington and London had "failed to supply proof to substantiate their claim."[74] In a bid to defuse the mounting damaging pressure from the West, Tripoli announced that the two citizens had been placed in "precautionary detention" in early December, adding, however, that it was a pity that the "real culprit is laughing."[75] At the same time, Libya declared its willingness to allow judges from the US and the UK to participate in the Libyan investigation of the case, and even agreed to accept the appointment of any judge chosen by the UN and the Arab League.[76] This affair lingered into 1992.

Relations with the UK

Libya's overtures to restore diplomatic ties with Britain, in 1991, proved futile. Britain had broken off diplomatic relations in 1984, in response for the killing of a British policewoman and the injuring of several others by shooting them from inside the building of the Libyan embassy in London (see *MECS* 1983–84, pp. 592–93). In 1986, tension had increased, following Britain's permission for US F-111s to fly from bases in Britain to attack Libya (see *MECS* 1986, pp. 514–15).

Throughout the year reviewed, the Libyans went out of their way to bring about a normalization in relations with London.[77] However, Tripoli repeatedly denied that it was responsible for the death of the policewoman,[78] and also claimed that it did not support the outlawed Irish Republican Army (IRA).[79] Tripoli even added that it disagreed with the operations of the IRA, to which it had hitherto referred as the "heroic Irish revolution" which was leading "a struggle for liberation." However, in the same breath, Tripoli declared that "the Irish people...have the right to self-determination."[80]

In a further bid to thaw relations, Libya made an extraordinary gesture of goodwill, offering to endow a sum of £250,000 ($404,000) to a British police fund for widows and orphans.[81] However, the British Foreign Office dismissed Libya's obvious overture as "little more than blood money."[82]

Qadhdhafi eventually took offense at the constant British rejection of his efforts at reconciliation. He furiously declared: "To hell with Britain and relations with it until the day of judgment."[83] Foreign Minister Bishari was more contained in his reaction, stating that Libya made "enough gestures.... It cannot give more than it has offered and the ball is now in the British court."[84]

From the middle of the year, bilateral tension increased, following Britain's demand that Libya extradite both the gunman responsible for the killing of the policewoman and the Libyans suspected of bombing the Pan Am airliner. Libya, who categorically denied any connection with either case, did not meet London's demands. Relations therefore remained frosty and Qadhdhafi claimed that Britain was applying against "the Arab Jamahiriyya a form of anti-Semitism."[85]

Libya and France

Libya and France were on good terms throughout most of 1991, in sharp contrast to the tension in relations of the 1980s. In the 1980s, there had been political and military frictions between them, even an indirect military confrontation, in the Chadian civil war. But with the Chad war over, relations had improved. From 22–24 April 1991, the French Foreign Minister Roland Dumas paid an official visit to Tripoli. He praised Qadhdhafi's stand during the Gulf crisis, and expressed his country's interest in promoting "cooperation in all fields."[86] Tripoli was well pleased with this upward turn in bilateral relations, a comforting reality in view of the stalemate in relations with Washington, and Qadhdhafi hoped his good ties with France could somehow generate a thaw in these relations. Tripoli also hoped Paris would help it to enhance its political and trade ties with the EC.

However, toward the end of 1991, the wheel turned once again. On 30 October, a French judge, Jean-Louis Bruguière, responsible for investigating terrorist cases, issued arrest warrants for four Libyan government officials, suspected of blowing up the French UTA DC-10. Once again Libya denied any connection and called for an end to the crisis by means of "dialogue" and "a peaceful solution."[87] It seemed that the French magistrate's action embarrassed the Quai d'Orsay. The French foreign minister was quoted as saying that "the case against Libya was far from cast-iron,"[88] while his Libyan counterpart emphasized his "eagerness to find a formula for judicial cooperation to obtain the truth."[89] In the meantime, however, the damage had been done to bilateral relations, and the process of rapprochement was slowed down, to some extent.

APPREHENSION, AND MALICIOUS PLEASURE, AT THE SOVIET UNION'S DISINTEGRATION

The dwindling power of the USSR and its eventual disintegration, elicited intensive verbal reaction from Tripoli, with emphasis on two major lessons: the Arabs "have no ally apart from themselves";[90] and Qadhdhafi's "revolutionary" ideology had been proven justifiable.[91]

It was mainly during the Gulf War and immediately thereafter that Qadhdhafi blatantly expressed his awareness of and alarm over the Soviet Union's bankruptcy, both as a superpower and as a pro-Arab prop. "Why did the Soviet Union not say it was impermissible to crush Iraq and annihilate it once she left Kuwait, despite the fact that there is a treaty of friendship and cooperation" between Moscow and Baghdad? Such a treaty, the Libyan leader elaborated, "compels the Soviet Union to stand by the side of Iraq if...aggression is waged against it...."[92] As for the second point,

Qadhdhafi maintained that the "basic transformations which the Green Book predicted more than 15 years ago, that is, the nationalities will triumph and the masses will triumph," was happening in the Soviet Union.[93]

Libya's strong support for Gennady Yanayev's coup against Mikhail Gorbachev in August (see chapter on the Soviet Union and the ME), was not at all surprising. Libya labeled the coup a "brave historical action," adding that it "will save the Soviet Union from the fatal crisis in which it was involved as a result of a large scale imperialist plot....It is very vital," Tripoli further noted, "that the Soviet Union stands united as a second world power," thus reducing US exclusiveness as a superpower.[94] In the summer, Qadhdhafi further claimed that "we Arabs are interested in seeing the Soviet Union stand on its own feet and restore the balance. This is an important matter which will affect the question of Palestine, the issue of Arab unity, and will put an end to imperialist arrogance."[95]

Qadhdhafi was embarrassed by the successful countercoup, which brought Gorbachev back to power. Qadhdhafi resorted to verbal acrobatics, explaining that his support of the aborted coup was on a "political and not ideological basis." He utilized the failure of the coup to highlight the "magnificent victory" of his "revolutionary" theory, which affirmed that "the popular masses are stronger than tanks and jets." Qadhdhafi made it clear that the congratulatory message he had sent to the aborted coup leaders was merely "a political bill," in defense of the dignity of the Soviet Union and, as further implied by his statement, as revenge against Gorbachev for not backing Libya immediately after the American military attack against it in 1986.[96]

Later in the year, Qadhdhafi referred to the downfall of communism, and to the Soviet Union's final dismantling, arguing that communism was an "impractical theory and ideal." Thus, he added, "it cannot succeed ideologically, because it is a theory suitable only for implementation through its bureaucratic nature. It was its bureaucratic nature which destroyed the revolutionary regimes. This happened because governments under communism run everything and monopolize leadership. That may be fine for them," he concluded, "but it is unrealistic."[97]

At the end of the year, Libya welcomed the declaration of independence of the Soviet republics, which suited the Libyan belief "in the right of these nations for self-determination and choice of proper national options by themselves."[98]

PERSISTENT REJECTION OF THE EXISTENCE OF ISRAEL
Qadhdhafi did not let up in his crusade for the elimination of the State of Israel, the "Zionist entity" in his words. "We wish that today or tomorrow the Iraqis will hit the Israelis and destroy Tel Aviv,"[99] he declared. The existence of the Jewish state continued to be an open wound for Qadhdhafi. "We will never be quiet nor our minds at rest until we avenge the Palestinian people, and see it return to its homeland Palestine, from the river to the sea." He added that "there will be no state other than the State of Palestine, the existence of which is mutually incompatible with any intruding usurping and imposed entity."[100]

As expected, in early summer, Libya strongly condemned the upcoming peace conference, describing it as an attempt "to rob the Arab citizen of his choice, of his patronage over his present and to assassinate his future...."[101] Qadhdhafi referred to the peace conference as "empty words," as an American political maneuver in the face of the coming presidential elections in the US. According to Qadhdhafi, the Americans "have inspired the conference...so that President Bush will get votes as the reconciler who achieved peace between the Arabs and Israel."[102] Accordingly, on 30 October, angry demonstrators marched in Libyan cities and villages against the "so-called peace conference" in Madrid. The marchers carried placards denouncing the conference and declaring that there was an "absolute impossibility of coexistence between the Arabs and the Zionists." They further called for "the liberation of Palestine from the river to the sea."[103]

NOTES

For the place and frequency of publications cited here, and for the full name of the publication, news agency, radio station or monitoring service where an abbreviation is used, please see "List of Sources." Only in the case of more than one publication bearing the same name is the place of publication noted here.

1. *Risalat al-Jihad*, September; Tripoli TV, 4 January — DR, 7 January 1991.
2. *LAT*, 10 September 1991.
3. Tripoli TV, 28 August — DR, 3 September 1991.
4. *FT*, 29 August 1991, quoting Angus Henley, who monitored Libyan affairs for the London-based *MEED*.
5. Interview with Khalifa Haftar, the head of the opposition Libyan National Army, *al-Hayat* (London), 19 December 1991.
6. *NYT*, 12 March 1991.
7. *AC*, 8 November 1991.
8. *Al-Wafd*, 31 March 1991.
9. *Al-Hayat* (London), 23 December 1991.
10. R. Beirut, 24 December — DR, 26 December 1991, quoting Ambassador 'Ashur al-Furtas.
11. Tripoli TV, 1 August — DR, 6 August. See also Tripoli TV, 17 October — DR, 25 October 1991.
2. Interview with Qadhdhafi, *al-Hawadith*, 25 October 1991.
13. Interview with Ibrahim Bishari, secretary of the Libyan external liaison and international cooperation (i.e., foreign minister), *al-Hayat* (London), 13 July 1991.
14. Interview with Qadhdhafi, *Monday Morning*, 4–10 November 1991.
15. E.g., DPA, 6 February — DR, 8 February 1991.
16. E.g., JANA, 6 February, 10 September — DR, 8 February, 10 September and Tripoli TV, 5 June — DR, 6 June 1991.
17. JANA, 7 March — DR, 8 March 1991.
18. *Ha'aretz*, 26 March; DPA, 11 April — DR, 12 April; *FT*, 18 November 1991.
19. *NYT*, 7 March; *Newsreport*, May-June 1991.
20. Interview with Qadhdhafi, *al-Ahram*, 7 December 1991.
21. *Der Stern*, 25, 26 June; *WP*, 27 June; *IHT*, 28 June 1991.
22. *LAT*, 24 June; *Der Stern*, 25 June 1991.
23. Interview with Qadhdhafi, *Le Figaro*, 4 July 1991.
24. Speech on the occasion of the 22nd anniversary of the revolution, Tripoli TV, 31 August — DR, 4 September 1991.
25. *ME*, July 1991, 'Ali al-Turayki, ex-foreign minister, ex-delegate to the UN and the then Libyan representative to the Arab League.
26. *Al-Fajr al-Jadid*, January. For more details on the summit discussions, see *al-Usbu' al-'Arabi*, 14 January 1991.
27. *Al-Fajr al-Jadid*, 15 February 1991.
28. MENA, 16 February — DR, 19 February 1991.
29. *Al-Usbu' al-'Arabi*, 22 February; *al-Dawliyya*, 23 February; *al-Hayat* (London), 5 August 1991.

30. *Al-Fajr al-Jadid,* 10, 11 April 1991.
31. The Ra's Lanuf petrochemical complex was the most successful industrial project in the country. For more details on the complex, including data regarding its production capacity, see *al-Fajr al-Jadid,* 9 May 1991.
32. R. Tripoli, 19 May — DR, 20 May 1991.
33. *Al-Ahram al-Masa'i,* 28 May 1991.
34. *Al-Fajr al-Jadid,* 2 April 1991.
35. *Al-Hayat* (London), 13, 26 July; for another similar statement of Bishari, see *al-Hawadith,* 9 August 1991.
36. R. Monte Carlo, 5 July — DR, 9 July 1991.
37. For details on the project's status in 1991, see *Akhir Sa'a,* 17 April, 23 October; *Qarun al-Mu'arada,* 12 May; *al-Hawadith,* 9 August 1991.
38. R. Tripoli, 7 July — DR, 10 July 1991. For the joint communiqué issued at the end of the committee's meeting, see JANA, 9 July — DR, 10 July; see also *al-Jumhuriyya* (Cairo), 29 July 1991.
39. MENA, 4 August — DR, 5 August 1991.
40. JANA, 28 August — DR, 29 August; R. Monte Carlo, 29 August 1991.
41. *Al-Hawadith,* 18 October 1991.
42. Tripoli TV, 17 January — DR, 18 January 1991.
43. *CR,* Libya, No. 2, 1991.
44. Qadhdhafi's speech at a meeting with secretaries of vocational unions in Tripoli, Tripoli TV, 26 January — DR, 28 January 1991.
45. *Al-Da'wa al-Islamiyya,* 23 January. Qadhdhafi reiterated that message on subsequent occasions, e.g., JANA, 27 January — DR, 28 January; *al-Hawadith,* 8 February 1991.
46. JANA, 27 January — DR, 28 January 1991, quoting Qadhdhafi's interview with the BBC.
47. Tripoli TV, 14 February — DR, 15 February 1991.
48. R. Tripoli, 16 February — DR, 19 February 1991.
49. JANA, 15 February — DR, 19 February 1991.
50. Tripoli TV, 10 March — DR, 12 March; JANA, 23 February — DR, 25 February 1991.
51. R. Tripoli, 28 March — DR, 28 March 1991.
52. JANA, 27 March — DR, 27 March 1991.
53. R. Tripoli, 7 April — DR, 8 April 1991.
54. Tripoli TV, 27 April — DR, 30 April 1991.
55. Statement by Foreign Minister Bishari, *al-Ahram al-Masa'i,* 28 May 1991.
56. R. Monte Carlo, 5 July — DR, 9 July 1991.
57. USIS, 14 January 1991, quoting President Bush's statement to Congress.
58. Tripoli TV, 6 January — DR, 7 January 1991.
59. *Africa Report,* May-June 1991.
60. E.g., Tripoli TV, 6, 9 January, 4, 11, June — DR, 7, 14 January, 7, 12 June; JANA, 11, 12 February — DR, 12, 15 February 1991.
61. *Al-Fajr al-Jadid,* 7 June 1991.
62. USIS, 2 May 1991. The list was issued by the US Treasury Department's Office of Foreign Assets Control in Washington.
63. USIS, 12 May 1991.
64. E.g., JANA, 1 May — DR, 3 May; R. Tripoli, 8 May — DR, 9 May 1991.
65. E.g., Qadhdhafi's interview, DPA, 8 February — DR, 11 February 1991.
66. Interview with Qadhdahfi, *Le Figaro,* 4 July 1991.
67. Tripoli TV, 17 January — DR, 18 January 1991.
68. Qadhdhafi in a meeting with Arab lawyers in Benghazi, *JP,* 29 April 1991, quoting Reuters.
69. *FT,* 18 November 1991. According to the same source, some \$2bn.-\$4bn. assets of American oil companies were frozen in Libya.
70. TANJUG, 28 May — DR, 29 May; for similar statements, see also *al-Usbu' al-'Arabi,* 10 June; *al-Majalla,* 9–15 October 1991.
71. *ME,* June; interview with al-Damm, *al-Majalla,* 9–15 October 1991.
72. JANA, 19 December — DR, 20 December. For other statements of that kind see, e.g., JANA, 27 June, 23 September — DR, 28 June, 24 September; *al-Mawqif al-'Arabi* (Nicosia), 7 July 1991.

73. Interview with Qadhdhafi, *al-Ahram*, 7 December 1991.
74. JANA, 15 November — DR, 15 November 1991. The Libyan official position was vociferously reiterated, e.g., Tripoli TV, 16 November — DR, 18 November; interview with Qadhdhafi, *al-Ahram*, 6 December 1991.
75. Interview with Libya's new intelligence chief, Col. Jabri, *al-Sharq al-Awsat*, 4 December 1991.
76. Turayki in a news conference in Cairo, MENA, 7 December — DR, 9 December 1991.
77. E.g., statements by Foreign Minister Bishari in *Mideast Mirror*, quoted in TANJUG, 28 May — DR, 29 May; *al-Usbu' al-'Arabi*, 10 June 1991.
78. JANA, 8 June — DR, 10 June 1991.
79. Statement by Foreign Minister Bishari, JANA, 9 June — DR, 10 June; a two-part interview with Qadhdhafi, *al-Ahram*, 6, 7 December 1991.
80. Foreign Minister Bishari, quoted by JANA, 9 June — DR, 10 June 1991.
81. *The Economist*, 14 June 1991. The donation was offered to be made via the British Conservative MP for Southend, Teddy Taylor, who paid a private visit to Libya in May.
82. *The Economist*, 28 June 1991.
83. Qadhdhafi's speech at a session of the Libyan General People's Congress, formally the Jamahiriyya's highest political authority, *JP*, 19 June 1991, quoting AP.
84. JANA, 8 June — DR, 10 June 1991.
85. Interview with Qadhdhafi, *al-Hawadith*, 25 October 1991.
86. TV Tripoli, 22 April — DR, 23 April 1991, broadcasting Dumas's speech.
87. Interviews with Turayki, *al-Ahram Weekly*, 12 December; MENA, 7 December — DR, 9 December 1991.
88. *MEI*, 22 November 1991.
89. JANA, 29 November — DR, 2 December 1991.
90. Interview with Foreign Minister Bishari, *al-Wafd*, 11 September 1991.
91. JANA, 2 September — DR, 4 September 1991.
92. Qadhdhafi's speech to military graduates in Benghazi, Tripoli TV, 31 August — DR, 4 September 1991.
93. R. Tripoli, 28 March — DR, 28 March 1991.
94. R. Tripoli, 19 August — DR, 20 August 1991.
95. Qadhdhafi's interview with the BBC, R. Tripoli, 20 August — DR, 21 August 1991.
96. JANA, 2 September — DR, 4 September 1991.
97. Interview with Qadhdhafi, *al-Hawadith*, 25 October 1991.
98. JANA, 25 December — DR, 27 December 1991.
99. Tripoli TV, 17 January — DR, 18 January 1991.
100. E.g., R. Tripoli, 11, 28 March — DR, 12, 28 March 1991.
101. R. Tripoli, 4 August — DR, 6 August 1991.
102. *Monday Morning*, 4–10 November 1991.
103. R. Tripoli, 30 October — DR, 31 October 1991.

Oman
('Uman)

UZI RABI

During the course of 1991, Oman's self-conscious aloofness and open-minded approach in foreign policy affairs was clearly in evidence and proved to be particularly profitable. Oman showed the ability to remain on good terms with all sides, thereby keeping all channels of communication open. The sultanate's defense pacts with the West — previously criticized by its fellow Gulf Cooperation Council (GCC) states, Kuwait in particular — were vindicated by similar moves on the part of Bahrain and Kuwait, and Oman was in the fortunate position of being able to sit back and watch them adjust their foreign policy stances, bringing them closer to its own.

By virtue of its long-standing and valuable understanding with Tehran, forged during the Iraqi-Iranian War, the sultanate emerged unscathed from the "six-plus-two" alliance fiasco and was furthermore able to bring about the long-awaited reconciliation between Tehran and Riyadh. Ironic as it may seem, even the shelving of Qabus's proposal for a united GCC army, a subtle counterbalance to the Arab "six-plus-two" alliance and a sophisticated maneuver in itself, gained the sultanate prestige and credibility, both regionally and internationally. Overall, the successful harvest left Oman's outlook basically unchanged, best characterized by a foreign observer who said that the Omanis see "no change in what they do, but a greater willingness to be seen doing it."[1] It thus came as no surprise that although the sultanate expressed its unanimity with the anti-Iraqi consensus, its stance was somewhat different from that of the other GCC states. While they adopted an outright hostile attitude toward Iraq and were willing to contemplate a military solution, Oman opted for a more moderate approach, which reflected its desire to maintain a neutral posture. As during the eight-year Iraqi-Iranian War, Oman sought to keep all channels of communication open, thereby retaining an open Iraqi embassy — the only GCC state to do so.

Nonetheless, the Al Sa'id ruling family was still confronted by a set of challenges. The sultanate's economic future was fraught with difficulties, especially in view of its rising population growth and the supposedly diminishing oil reserves. The threats to the very existence of the Gulf ruling families, triggered by the Gulf crisis, were even more alarming. The credibility of the political structures in the Gulf had been seriously eroded and, in the minds of many, this served to emphasize the absence of democratic decision-making institutions. In acknowledgment of lessons learned from the crisis, Oman was the first of the GCC states to move ahead with political reform and, in December, it inaugurated the State Consultative Council (SCC), a vehicle for increased popular participation in political affairs.

THE DILEMMA OF REGIONAL SECURITY:
THE OMANI PLAN

After the Gulf crisis, the six GCC states realized that unless they took the postwar realities more seriously, their future well-being could be at stake. The most important issue for Oman, and indeed for all the GCC states, was the problem of regional security, i.e., the measures that were needed to prevent another powerful state from bullying its weaker neighbor. High priority was given to the need for new measures, since it was widely acknowledged after the Gulf crisis that the GCC's much appraised 12,000-strong Peninsula Shield force (*Dir' al-jazira*) was, in effect, a failure. Despite the GCC's continuous efforts to secure the Gulf, first by relying on a joint Arab force and then through self-reliance, by the close of 1991 the issue of regional security was still unresolved.

In March, a rather vaguely worded defense pact was concluded in Damascus (see chapter on inter-Arab relations) between the six GCC states together with Egypt and Syria (often depicted as the "six-plus-two" group), by which a joint Arab force, comprising Egyptian and Syrian contingents, would remain stationed in the Gulf in exchange for financial aid. However, a major obstacle was that Iran was excluded from the plan and was consequently angered that its desire to have a major say in any plan for safeguarding the future stability of the region had been disregarded. The Iranian indignation was especially worrisome for Oman which, since the Iraqi-Iranian War, had been considered the GCC country closest to Tehran and had often served as a go-between for the Islamic Republic with the Arab world and even the West (see, e.g., *MECS* 1989, p. 562). Clearly, Oman stood to be the ultimate loser should Iranian-GCC relations again turn sour. The sultanate had already attempted to preempt such a scenario, when Oman's minister of state for foreign affairs, Yusuf Ibn 'Alawi Ibn 'Abdallah, had visited Tehran during the fighting to discuss Iran's integration in future security arrangements in the region.[2] However, Oman remained the only viable party to tie up the loose ends due to its vested interest and diplomatic capabilities. Hence it intensified its efforts to relieve the animosity that existed between Tehran and the Cairo-Riyadh axis. But despite Muscat's partial success, in March, to have Iranian-Saudi relations restored (see below), Iran remained outside the "six-plus-two" alliance, mostly due to Egypt's objection. Qabus's visit to Cairo in May and his discussions with Egypt's President Mubarak did not help soften the latter's attitude.

Omani representatives made every effort to play down the GCC-Tehran tension and attributed it to a mere "lack of knowledge of details and orientations."[3] Shuttling between Tehran and Muscat, 'Alawi reiterated the need for an "all-out cooperation and coordination"[4] stressing that Muscat, for its part, openly supported the idea of an Iranian say in any security structure devised for the region in the postcrisis era.[5]

Oman's diplomatic capabilities were simultaneously demonstrated on the other side of the line, where the GCC encountered Syria and Egypt over the issue of the "Damascus declaration." Differences arose over the size and the role of the proposed force. However, with the wartime threat diminishing, the GCC states were no longer as receptive as before to the idea of a substantial Arab military presence on their soil. In an attempt to clear the heavy atmosphere created between the GCC and its senior would-be Arab partners, Oman's minister of information, 'Abd al-'Aziz al-Rawwas, explained that there were "...no differences as such but an exchange of views."[6] Qabus, who traveled to Riyadh and Cairo in May, was probably expected to tie up the loose ends, but his mission was unsuccessful. By late May, the last Egyptian soldier left the Gulf. The Arab "six-plus-two" alliance, which threatened to be a trap for Oman, gradually disintegrated, but true to its diplomacy of avoiding abrupt endings, Oman kept trying to be seen as reviving the plan in order to appease the disenchanted Arab allies. Consequently, in July, when Qabus asserted that the forthcoming GCC summit in December would discuss the issue of relations with Egypt and Syria, he was merely paying lip service to the proposition, by then no longer valid.[7] However, Oman was led to push forward its proposal for self-reliance, both out of a desire to end the tension between Iran and Egypt, but also because it genuinely wished to provide the GCC with a practical defense plan.

The Omani plan for self-reliance was a last all-out effort to resolve the vexed and complicated issue of regional security. The sultanate suggested the creation of a 100,000-strong force, drawn exclusively from each GCC state "...not from quota but from Gulf citizens."[8] The force was to have an integrated command and, once committed to action, would operate as a rapid response force. Qabus further proposed that each member state could have separate bilateral military agreements with Egypt, Syria and the leading Western states, thus providing the would-be participants with an element open to great flexibility. The focal point of the proposal and its uniqueness, explained 'Alawi, was that it afforded GCC residents "...for the first time the opportunity to defend themselves, their own sons, their countries and their resources."[9] For a while, Oman's plan seemed to be gaining momentum. Extraordinary GCC chief-of-staff meetings, convened in August and October, decided on the means required for its implementation, and its formal approval was expected to take place at the December GCC summit. However, the plan's odds for success became markedly bleaker when Kuwait and Bahrain each concluded a bilateral security pact with the US in September and October respectively. Furthermore, Saudi Arabia, the GCC's leading country, became the strongest opponent of the plan.[10] Consequently, it was not surprising that by the close of the December summit, Oman's proposal for a joint GCC army had been effectively shelved. There were simply too many obstacles impeding effective coordination on Gulf security, which was demonstrated by a vote of no confidence initiated by Kuwait and Bahrain. There was no state strong enough to seriously contest the US role of chief protector.

No GCC leader, least of all a visionary yet realistic statesman such as Qabus, was deluded into thinking that the GCC states could effectively manage their own security under the circumstances. However, the Omani plan for a joint GCC army, the high point of the sultanate's foreign policy in 1991, had its compensations. First and foremost, as mentioned above, Muscat emerged unscathed from the uneasy position between the Iranian hammer and the Egyptian anvil. Relations with Egypt remained cordial, and an Omani-Syrian memorandum dealing with exchange of medical information and manpower was concluded.[11] Muscat also managed to tighten its bilateral relations with Tehran, best evinced by the stream of mutual visits and economic agreements concluded. Moreover, the sultanate's image remained untainted in Western eyes, since the US and Britain had also been urging the GCC states to draw up a collective security system, albeit under a Western umbrella. Oman's prowess in regional security matters was openly acknowledged at the summit. Qabus was singled out, in the final communiqué, and especially thanked for his efforts. He was also entrusted, for the second consecutive year, with the task of leading the GCC's security committee.[12]

However, with the plan effectively shelved, Oman was left far from its ambition to contain the financial wastefulness engendered by defense duplication among the six. Clearly, in the absence of full security coordination, Oman could not afford to be profligate in the area of defense which already consumed about 20% of its yearly budget.[13] It was, therefore, probably likely that Qabus would pursue his efforts to persuade the reluctant GCC states to go beyond their individual reliance on the West, by seeking to secure the Gulf from within. Meanwhile, Oman pursued an independent policy in security matters, backing up its security agreements with the West with more training exchanges and joint maneuvers. Omani and British troops were to conduct a joint air force exercise in the sultanate between January and April 1992. In spite of its budgetary limitations, Oman upgraded its navy with British corvettes and its armory with US M-60A3 tanks.[14] Furthermore, the US was set to upgrade its base at Thamarit, in the framework of the "access agreement" initially concluded in the early 1980s, and was allowed prepositioning rights for troops refueling and supplies in Oman. The Western presence in Oman proved beneficial to both sides. Large in terms of territory but small in terms of power, Oman could feel a sense of security with such a presence on its soil. The sultanate's strategic value to the West was emphatically underlined by the access given to Western troops to Saudi Arabia via Omani air bases after Iraq's invasion of Kuwait. "The links with the West proved their value last year and we see no need for change," concluded one top-level Omani official.[15]

OMAN AND ITS NEIGHBORS
Iraq's failed attempt to annex its tiny neighbor seemingly spurred the GCC states on to settle their own intraregional problems. It became clear that, in the absence of competition between superpowers for influence in the Gulf, the only remaining viable cause of friction was border disputes. 'Alawi corroborated that view, stressing that not only the military outcome of the war, but also the political one should be taken into consideration.[16] Accordingly, geographic considerations came to be seen as far less important than the "bonds that should link neighbors, on the one hand, and peoples of the region, on the other."[17]

Within the GCC, the first meeting of the joint Omani-UAE Higher Committee, which followed a visit of UAE ruler, Shaykh Zayid, to Muscat in May, took place in Abu Dhabi in November. Its declared purpose was to upgrade bilateral relations by resolving the remaining "technical issues" with each emirate separately.[18] However, in the interim, these problems were clearly not seen as an obstacle to closer relations. As of early 1992, nationals of the two states could move freely on the mutual border on presentation of their identity cards.[19] Oman and Saudi Arabia ratified a border treaty which appeared to have resolved outstanding frontier questions between the two countries.[20] The issue had been particularly acute for Oman, since the disputed land skirted some of its most productive oil fields. Eventually, Qabus and King Fahd personally concluded a deal whereby the border line was left where originally drawn.[21]

On its southern front, the sultanate's long-awaited border demarcation treaty with Yemen, originally expected to have been signed and sealed by the end of 1990, seemed to be running into problems. Yemeni opposition accused the San'a government of planning to transfer to Oman 15,000[2] km. of territory in the sparsely populated area of al-Mahra.[22] However, the talks reportedly made significant strides following Rawwas's visit to Yemen, in November, reciprocated by a high-level Yemeni delegation visit to Oman in the same month.[23] Although portraying an atmosphere of optimism in view of the continued consultations, Omani officials claimed they were "...waiting for the Yemenis to decide their final position."[24] There remained a proposed visit by Qabus to Yemen in early 1992, pending the settlement of differences.

Postwar realities were marked by the desire for a new "Arab order," in which old animosities were to be patched up and new alliances created. In this respect, the sultanate's pragmatic and cool-headed approach was most advantageous. It no doubt allowed Oman a certain degree of maneuverability to bridge the gap between the various Arab and Muslim dissenters. 'Alawi's untypically pretentious remark in early March, that "...we should be the leaders in that context because we are more capable than others of having an insight into the future,"[25] served to indicate that the sultanate had taken up the gauntlet.

The thorniest problems were the Iranian-Saudi rivalry, which erupted following the 1987 Mecca incident (see *MECS* 1987, pp. 601–2), and the long-standing Iranian-Egyptian rivalry, engendered by the struggle for influence in the Gulf. After several fruitless attempts to mend fences between Saudi Arabia and Iran since the Mecca incident, the Omani mediation effort this time was brief and successful. In March, Saudi and Iranian foreign ministers met in Muscat and agreed on a compromise which was followed by an announcement on the restoration of diplomatic relations (see chapters on Iran and Saudi Arabia).[26]

In contrast, the protracted campaign to render a similar service to Iranian-Egyptian relations did not meet with success, and these relations remained deadlocked. "When the matter concerns two big countries in our Islamic world, such as the Islamic Republic of Iran and the Arab Republic of Egypt, we will be happy to do all we can to ease tension in the relations between the two countries," 'Alawi announced enthusiastically.[27] 'Alawi himself visited both Tehran and Cairo in September. On his return from Tehran he sounded fairly optimistic, saying that Iranian-Egyptian relations could be developed "...in the interest of both peoples."[28] However, despite his optimism, his efforts in Cairo were apparently futile, probably due to Egypt's adamant rejection of Iranian participation in any Gulf security arrangements. Even Qabus, who visited Cairo in May before 'Alawi, could do nothing to change Egypt's attitude. He received a sympathetic welcome by the local media — which again highlighted the Egyptian gratitude for Oman's refusal to break relations with Egypt following the Camp David accord with Israel — but came back empty-handed. The disenchanted Omanis could do no more than blame the press for releasing "incorrect" information, claiming Oman's efforts "have achieved nothing."[29]

Muscat also expected to rebuild the bridge between Arab dissenters from the Gulf War and the rest of the GCC. Having accused Amman of colluding with Baghdad, the GCC reacted sharply by various sanctions, such as cutting off aid and oil supplies to Jordan (see chapter on inter-Arab relations).[30] Qabus was the GCC leader closest to King Husayn, and the latter visited Qabus and attempted to enjoin him to intercede in mending relations between Jordan and the GCC. Muscat was also expected to offer some aid to Jordan to help it weather the economic crisis that had been exacerbated by wartime measures.

Oman found it easier than other Arab states to adopt a more flexible attitude toward Israel in the postwar era. In this respect, the sultanate's approach toward Israel in the years preceding 1991 was surprisingly moderate, perhaps even unique (see, e.g., *MECS* 1988, pp. 451–53). Omani representatives called on the two sides that constituted the core of the conflict — Israel and the Palestinians — to make every effort to resolve it. Oman supported the Egyptian proposal to end the Arab boycott of Israel in exchange for Israel's halting the building of settlements in the "occupied Arab territories";[31] convening an international peace conference; and starting negotiations on the basis of the relevant UN resolutions. A withdrawal to the 1967 borders was a must "sooner or later,"[32] specified 'Alawi. However, Oman offered that guarantees be given to Israel in order to strengthen its sense of security, make it feel an integral part of the Middle East and enable it to "coexist with its Palestinian and Arab neighbors." 'Alawi warned that if Israel missed such an opportunity to make peace with its neighbors, "it could not be able to live in security among the Arab peoples."[33]

In the same manner, Oman spared no remorse for the behavior of the Arab side in the conflict. "Experience shows that we have been in pursuit of the impossible [regarding the conflict] in this world," 'Alawi lamented, calling on the Arabs to aspire "within the limits of the possible and viable."[34] With these words, he no doubt meant that Israel was a fact, and the Arabs as a whole must accept it. True to the GCC's vengeful attitude toward the PLO, Oman made no mention of the organization as being instrumental with regard to the peace process. Indeed, the sultanate's moderate approach and farsightedness were vindicated with the convening of the Madrid peace conference in November, in which it took part through the GCC's general secretary, 'Abdallah Bishara.

INTERNAL AFFAIRS

THE FORMATION OF THE STATE CONSULTATIVE COUNCIL

As on the issue of military integration, Oman also took the lead in the sociopolitical issue. The reformed State Consultative Council (*Majlis al-shura*), first announced by Qabus in a speech marking the sultanate's 20th anniversary on 18 November 1990 (see *MECS* 1990, chapter on Oman), became operational in December 1991.[35] While lacking the powers of a proper legislature, the new-look SCC was likely to enjoy considerably more clout and credibility than its predecessor. The reformed SCC was to be allowed a certain measure of free debate and even criticism to some extent and to take over from the existing State Consultative Chamber (*al-Majlis al-istishari lildawla*), the sultanate's first experiment in popular participation, which was established in 1981. The latter, a body of 55 appointed members with no legislative power, met several times a year to discuss, often in a somewhat halfhearted manner, a predetermined agenda.

The composition of the new Majlis — a crop of new faces apparently in keeping with the wishes of Qabus — suggested the possibility of an improvement on its predecessor in several key areas.[36] First, government officials and civil servants were no longer eligible to sit on the new Majlis in an official capacity, therefore preventing the possibility of any conflict of interest. The common characteristic of Omani officials, to be active in business as well as politics, evolved with time to be a dominant "business oligarchy" within the government, provoking resentment among some

Omanis.[37] Second, candidates could be selected by friends or even nominate themselves and be endorsed by top government officials. Third, the Majlis would be empowered to call ministers to account. Automatic consultation on legislation and issues of the day were to become the norm rather than the exception, as with the old body. One indication of its projected scope of activity was that, for the first time, the Omani Government would have to postpone new laws or revise them should the Majlis deem it fit.

Criticism was nevertheless leveled at the new assembly, most notably for the fact that its representation of the various vilayets (provinces) was disproportionate. Each vilayet was represented by one member, irrespective of the size of its population.[38] The full powers and functions of the Majlis were still unclear. Yet undeniably it was the very formation of this institution that represented another step forward in Qabus's slow and cautious experiment at broadening Oman's political base. Nineteen years previously, a year after assuming power, Qabus had stated that Oman was "not ready for democracy."[39] In 1991, he described the SCC as initiating a new era, suggesting that further reforms could follow. In a broader view, the move was in keeping with steps elsewhere in the Gulf toward greater democracy within traditional Arab terms of reference. Its composition seemed to assure that the SCC was not going to follow its Kuwaiti and Bahraini counterparts, which were shut down for embarrassing their respective regimes. The other Gulf ruling families — among them Kuwait's aiming to hold national elections, and Saudi Arabia's proposing a national consultative council — were no doubt watching events in Oman with the keenest of interest.

CABINET RESHUFFLE
In December, in addition to increasing popular participation in state affairs and within the framework of preparing the state administrative apparatus, Qabus announced a major cabinet reshuffle. The wide ministerial changes and the amalgamation of some ministries as well as the creation of new departments were aimed at cutting down famous Omani bureaucracy and making the system more efficient.[40] The ministry of environment was merged with the ministry of regional municipal affairs, as were the ministries of labor and social affairs. Important changes were also introduced in senior civil service positions and two new bodies, the Vocational Training Organization and the General Organ for Sport and Youth Affairs were created. However, the changes in personnel did not seem to indicate any shift in foreign or domestic policy. Rather, they reflected Qabus's desire to bring some new and younger blood into the sultanate's Administration. The holders of the four top portfolios — interior, minister of state for foreign affairs, information, and palace affairs — retained the positions they had held for over a decade.

ECONOMIC AFFAIRS: THE YEAR OF INDUSTRY
Whatever hardships the Gulf War may have brought to Oman, the year under review was one of almost unequaled good news for the sultanate's oil-based economy. Oman's oil revenues, which made up 80% of government income, were given a boost during 1991.[41] However, the relative prosperity and development of Oman's basic infrastructure, achieved over the previous 20 years, were not expected to last for long. Various estimates claimed that despite intensive, sometimes fruitful discoveries, levels

of oil production could not be sustained.[42] Another tough hurdle the sultanate had to overcome was the population increase, the result of which would be that more than 100,000 Omanis would enter the job market between 1991 and 1995.[43] The government attempted to cope with this set of challenges by putting into operation the five-year plan, announced by Qabus in early 1991.[44] This plan was essentially realistic, specifying that the oil and gas sectors would continue to be the mainstay of the economy, and that unlike other Gulf countries, Oman did not propose to end its dependence on oil by diversifying into heavy investment in "grandiose" projects. The practical reason for this was that there was no guarantee that such projects would earn more money than they would drain from state coffers. Given Oman's shortage of other marketable resources and the modesty of its budget, in Gulf terms, the sultanate focused on adding value to its agricultural and fishing products; making tentative steps toward encouraging tourism; and building heavily subsidized light industrial parks. The first of these, at Rusayl, already had 60 units, making soap, biscuits, copper, cables, etc.[45] Moreover, in order to increase the external surplus in the long term, industrial incentives were provided to encourage the private sector to look increasingly to nontraditional markets outside the Gulf, such as Eastern Europe. The Muscat stock exchange, which was inaugurated in 1989 and already soaring far higher than originally expected, also had a prominent role. The government announced the launching of the first state development bonds, which, it hoped, would raise $11bn. over the five years of the plan. The bonds were designated to finance the capital spending on various development projects outlined in the five-year plan.[46]

In contrast with the sultanate's aim to minimize outside influence, the government considered allowing foreign investors, including expatriates living in Oman, to buy stock in local companies.[47] These policies were well corroborated with the announcement by Sultan Qabus at Oman's National Day celebrations, that the year of industry, originally 1991, would be extended through 1992.[48] Nor was the issue of trade neglected. Export earnings rose in confirmation of the increase in transshipment traffic, as Oman became a more attractive entrepôt for the Arabian Peninsula in the wake of the Gulf War. Consequently, Mina Qabus was set to be expanded, while the plan to set up a new port at Suhar was shelved, probably due to the high cost involved.[49] Among its Gulf partners, the sultanate's political pragmatism toward Iran (and to some extent Iraq) could well pay off. The recent opening of direct air and sea links with Iran was expected to increase cargo and passenger traffic between the two, thereby boosting Oman's potential to integrate in the potential market of 60m. people.[50] For the time being, however, nearby Dubai, with its capacious Jabil 'Ali free port, was still a more attractive option for the vast majority of shipping.

DIFFICULTIES ON THE ROAD TO "OMANIZATION"
Oman's attempts to create jobs for its rapidly growing population, that is, the policy of making the work force Omani, represented perhaps the most aggressive drive for indigenization within the GCC states. The plan, which had been initiated in recent years (see *MECS* 1989, p. 560), was broadened and intensified in 1991 in the framework of the five-year plan. With targets set for specified proportions of Omani citizens in each sector and the inducement of subsidized pay for new Omani recruits, the government hoped to gradually cut its reliance on expatriates to a minimum and overcome the overwhelming preference of most Omanis for employment in

government sectors. The plan was greeted by leading industrialists as creative and innovative, yet there was still a long way to go. "Zeal has its limits," lamented one senior Omani official.[51] For example, the banking sector, where Omanis were supposed to be 90% of the work force by 1993, had only c. 70% at the end of 1991.[52] Given the youth and inexperience of the new Omani workers in that branch, the hope of quickly fitting them into senior positions seemed somewhat farfetched. In the oil industry, the figure was nearer to 60%. However, the hardest task facing the government was to persuade Omanis to enter trade and industry, which constituted only 23% of the private sector work force in Oman at the end of 1991. It was hoped that this would increase to 45.2% by 1995, when the five-year plan was due to fully materialize. Meeting the 1991–95 five-year plan targets was merely the first hurdle of many. Qays 'Abd al-Mun'im al-Zawawi, the finance and economics minister, may not have been unduly pessimistic when he predicted that the problem would "greatly multiply after the year 2000."[53]

NOTES

For the place and frequency of publications cited here, and for the full name of the publication, news agency, radio station or monitoring service where an abbreviation is used, please see "List of Sources." Only in the case of more than one publication bearing the same name is the place of publication noted here.

1. *FT,* 20 November 1991.
2. GNA, 22 February — DR, 28 February 1991.
3. 'Alawi's interview with R. London, 1 May — DR, 2 May 1991.
4. IRNA, 1 July — DR, 3 July 1991.
5. 'Alawi's interview with R. London, 1 May — DR, 2 May 1991.
6. Rawwas's interview with *Oman Daily Observer,* 20 November 1991.
7. Qabus's interview with Kyodo, 4 July — DR, 5 July 1991.
8. Rawwas's interview with *Oman Daily Observer,* 20 November 1991.
9. 'Alawi's interview with *al-Hayat* (London), 25 October 1991.
10. *FT,* 20 November 1991.
11. *Al-Thawra* (Damascus), 2 October 1991.
12. *CR:* Oman, No. 1, 1992.
13. Ibid.
14. *The Gulf States,* 2 December 1991.
15. *FT,* 20 November 1991.
16. GNA, 2 March — DR, 6 March 1991.
17. Ibid.
18. Interview of Fahd Ibn Mahmud Al Sa'id, the deputy prime minister, with *al-Hayat* (London), 25 February 1991; R. Muscat, 25 February — DR, 26 February 1991.
19. *CR:* Oman, No. 2, 1992.
20. 'Alawi's interview with Oman News Agency, 2 March — DR, 6 March 1991.
21. *FT,* 20 November 1991.
22. *CR:* Oman, No. 2, 1992.
23. Rawwas's interview with *Oman Daily Observer,* 20 November 1991.
24. R. Muscat, 25 February — DR, 26 February 1991.
25. 'Alawi's interview with Oman News Agency, 2 March — DR, 6 March 1991.
26. *The Gulf States,* 25 March 1991.
27. GNA, 12 September — DR, 13 September 1991.
28. GNA, 13 September — DR, 18 September 1991.
29. 'Alawi's interview with *al-Hayat* (London), 25 October 1991.
30. *JP,* 31 March 1991.
31. GNA, 21 July — DR, 22 July 1991.

32. 'Alawi's interview with *al-Hayat* (London), 25 October 1991.
33. Ibid.
34. GNA, 2 March — DR, 6 March 1991.
35. *MEED*, 29 November 1991.
36. *Al-Watan al-'Arabi*, 29 November 1991.
37. *FT*, 20 November 1991.
38. Ibid.
39. Ibid.
40. *Sawt al-Kuwait al-Duwali*, 12 December; *al-Hayat* (London), 13 December 1991.
41. *MEED*, 27 September 1991.
42. *FT*, 20 November 1991.
43. Ibid.
44. *Al-Watan al-'Arabi*, 1 March 1991.
45. *MEED*, 23 August 1991.
46. *The Gulf States*, 15, 29 July 1991.
47. *The Gulf States*, 11 February 1991.
48. *Al-Usbu' al-'Arabi*, 4 March 1991.
49. *MEED*, 20 September 1991.
50. *CR:* Oman, No. 1, 1992.
51. *FT*, 20 November 1991.
52. *CR:* Oman, No. 1, 1992.
53. *FT*, 20 November 1991.

Qatar

UZI RABI

Qatar had a special reason to celebrate on 3 September 1991, its 20th anniversary of independence, for this date coincided with another momentous event, the inauguration of the first phase of the North Field gas project. Qatar successfully endured the Gulf War, watching Iraq's ominous military might being shattered. Qatar's share in the fighting — the victory over Iraqi troops at al-Khafji — gave a tremendous boost to Doha's pride and sense of security. Another benefit was the improvement of relations with other important countries, namely Iran and the US.

Qatar's relations with Arab countries were also influenced by the Gulf crisis. After the Iraqi invasion of Kuwait, on 2 August 1990, Qatar and other Gulf states were forced to adopt a stand different from that taken by some of their long-standing allies. Qatar's relations with the PLO and Jordan deteriorated, as a result of their support for Baghdad; while relations with Egypt and Syria, members of the anti-Iraqi coalition, greatly improved.

The Thani ruling family was confronted by a set of challenges. In the sphere of foreign affairs, difficulties with Bahrain loomed on the horizon. The long-standing territorial dispute over a cluster of coral reefs flared up again and the two neighboring states were at loggerheads. On the economic front, problems still lay ahead. The cabinet reshuffle of 1989, aimed at providing a fresh, greater impetus to the decision-making process, did not live up to its expectations. The threats to the very existence of the ruling Al Thani family, triggered by the Gulf crisis, were even more alarming. The credibility of the political structures in the Gulf was seriously eroded. The royal families of the Gulf states were clearly shown as incapable of preserving national sovereignty. A petition was handed to Shaykh Khalifa Ibn Hamad Al Thani, the Qatari ruler, expressing an eagerness for a more open, less paternalistic form of government, which could be considered as a sign of things to come. How was the regime to handle these problems? In the postwar period Qatar had to face the challenge and decide whether it was necessary, and possible, to adopt new, adequate mechanisms in order to cope with its problems.

FOREIGN AFFAIRS

QATAR AND THE GULF WAR

Like the other Gulf Cooperation Council (GCC) states, Qatar was caught unprepared by the Iraqi invasion of Kuwait. Yet, despite its usually conservative decision-making policy, Qatar proved that it could act in an effective manner when circumstances required. Doha fully endorsed the Arab and international decisions condemning the Iraqi invasion and demanding restoration of Kuwaiti legitimacy under the Al Sabah ruling family.[1] It also supported UN Security Council Resolution 678, which authorized the council to use force if Iraq refused to withdraw from Kuwait by 15

January 1991.[2] Doha had no compunction in allowing the Allied forces staging facilities, although it was the last GCC state to do so. The Qatari support for the anti-Iraqi coalition had its advantages. The security provided by the presence of the US, French and other foreign troops on its soil gave a boost to local confidence, and to the stagnant economic situation. Both these factors helped the authorities to cope with the outbreak of hostilities.

Qatari participation in the actual fighting was marginal (for further details, see chapter on the Gulf War). The air force conducted a number of combat sorties against Iraqi targets inside Iraqi-occupied Kuwait.[3] The high point of the conflict for Qatar was its involvement in the battle of Khafji, in late January. In the course of the Iraqi attack over the Saudi border town, Qatari land forces, supported by US helicopters, destroyed several Iraqi tanks, took prisoner a number of Iraqi soldiers, and caused the rest to flee.[4] Furthermore, the Qatari forces suffered no losses. The fact that tiny Qatar managed to inflict a blow on neighboring Iraq, albeit a very limited one, inflated Qatar's self-confidence. For the first time, Qatar had a military victory of its own to its credit. Official statements noted "with pride" the role played by Qatari troops in the battle of Khafji.[5] The media glorified the "crushing defeat" dealt to Iraq, claiming it constituted a lesson "in military tactics and strategic coordination."[6] Qatari myth was in the making.

THE POSTWAR ERA — THE QUEST FOR REGIONAL SECURITY
When the guns fell silent, Qatar turned to the task of restoring "business as usual" in all aspects of life at home and abroad. With the announcement of Kuwait's liberation, Qatari forces were recalled and Doha's embassy in Kuwait quickly resumed full functioning.[7] On more important matters, however, Qatar readopted a conservative "wait-and-see" policy regarding decision-making, namely, its traditional artful indecision. Apart from swift denunciations of Iraq's alleged attempt to invade the Kuwaiti island of Bubiyan in August,[8] there were no media attacks on Iraq. The ousting of the Iraqi leader, Saddam Husayn, was no longer a desirable objective, since this could lead to a southern Iraqi political entity under Shi'i control, which Qatar did not want at all.

Despite the crucial importance, particularly in the postwar era, of the issue of regional security, Qatar's approach to it was similarly indecisive. Like the other five GCC members, Qatar was quick to draw negative conclusions regarding the GCC's concept of security. Addressing the opening session of the extraordinary meeting of GCC foreign ministers, held in May in Kuwait, Qatari Foreign Minister Mubarak 'Ali al-Khatir, stressed that the Iraqi invasion of Kuwait had "explicitly [revealed] loopholes in our [the GCC's] defense and security systems." Khatir went on to conclude that it had become essential to "modernize our defense means and coordinate our military structures."[9] However, when it came to taking more practical steps toward achieving that goal, Qatar's position remained rather ambiguous.

As early as March, the six GCC member states, together with Syria and Egypt, conferred to issue the "Damascus declaration," which pointed to the permanent presence of an Arab force in the region, made up predominantly of Egyptian and Syrian contingents (for further details see chapter on inter-Arab relations). This declaration led to a clash of interests in Qatar's approach toward Egypt and Iran, two of the most important countries in Doha's foreign policy. These two countries were locked in open rivalry, both vying to become the GCC's main regional protector and fill the power vacuum left by Iraq. Iran was excluded from the declaration.

Qatar became one of the keener GCC states in pushing for better ties with Iran. It welcomed the resumption of diplomatic relations between Saudi Arabia and Iran in March[10] (see chapter on Saudi Arabia), marking the ongoing Iranian integration in the region. Doha openly advocated that Iran have a say in any security structure devised for the region in the postcrisis era. This view was voiced by the heir apparent, Shaykh Hamad Ibn Khalifa Al Thani, who was the highest-ranking member of a GCC state to visit Iran following the Gulf War (in November). During the visit a number of cooperation agreements were concluded in the sphere of education and economics. The most prominent issue discussed was the feasibility of constructing a 2,000km., fresh water pipeline, extending from Iran's Karun River to Qatar, whose cost was initially estimated at $13bn.[11] Aware of its escalating territorial dispute with Bahrain (see below), Qatar had another reason to be keen to promote relations with Tehran. Qatar's huge gas reserves known as the North Field and Iran's South Pars field came from the same geological formation.[12] In 1989, Iran had claimed that at least 30% of the field was within its territorial waters (for further details, see *MECS* 1989, p. 569). Wary of complications that might endanger the further development of the field, Doha had adopted a strictly no-comment policy on the issue ever since this claim was made. However, in 1991, there were reports, according to which Tehran was making exploratory drills in its field, and it became clear that a low-profile Qatari policy could no longer suffice. A collision course between the neighbors could seriously affect Qatar's soft economic belly. Qatar, therefore, wished to see Iran integrating in the region and the continuous talks regarding oil and gas ventures, topped by a bilateral agreement,[13] were meant to ease a potential source of friction.

The Egyptian Government was rather upset by Doha's diplomatic approaches to Tehran, as it was firmly opposed to any Iranian involvement in regional security arrangements. Since Qatar was indebted to Egypt for participating in operation Desert Storm, it tried to appease Cairo, mostly through economic compensation. For example, Doha was the first GCC capital to cancel its portion of Egypt's debts to the Gulf Development Agency and allow access to Egyptian companies in industrial projects in Qatar.[14] However, this did not seem to clear the atmosphere of unease in Cairo toward Doha.

By the end of 1991, Qatar's dilemma between Tehran and Cairo became far less relevant. The "Damascus declaration" gradually faded into oblivion, due to differences between the signatories over the size and command of the proposed force. The issue of a framework for collective Gulf security remained open. Individual rather than collective activity seemed to become a more feasible option, especially with the conclusion of the US-Kuwaiti and US-Bahraini bilateral pacts in September and October respectively (for details, see chapters on Kuwait and Bahrain). Qatar likewise took the individual path, albeit on a much smaller scale. Seeking to increase its own feeling of security, Qatar embarked on purchasing additional "most sophisticated weaponry"[15] and upgraded land and sea facilities.

THE QATARI-BAHRAINI DISPUTE

The simmering territorial dispute, which again flared up between Qatar and Bahrain, constituted another chink in the armor of regional security. The dispute over the sovereignty of several unpopulated islets, Fasht al-Dibal, Hawara and al-Jarada, legally regarded as Bahraini territory, had long since been a source of tension between the neighboring emirates. The disputed area was in close proximity to Qatar's North Field gas project and this only served to raise the stakes and increase the tension that had erupted in 1986. At the time, Qatar had raided the man-made islet of Fasht al-Dibal, capturing foreign workers who were reclaiming it from the sea. According to another version, the workers were constructing a Bahraini coast-guard station on it.[16] The workers were subsequently released and Saudi Arabia had initiated mediation attempts to defuse the tension ever since, but to no avail.

In the wake of the Gulf War, amidst Qatari preparations to inaugurate the first phase of the North Field gas project, the dispute resurfaced as Doha referred the issue to the International Court of Justice in the Hague on 8 July. Angered by Qatar's unilateral move, Bahrain rejected the allegations and the court's jurisdiction, demanding that Saudi Arabia should be allowed to resolve the problem or that both sides "jointly agree on international arbitration."[17]

Meanwhile, matters seemed to get out of hand, with both countries reporting alleged incursions into each other's territorial waters. In August, Bahrain submitted an official protest to the Qatari Government, claiming that one of its warships had violated Bahraini territorial waters. The vessel was reportedly escorted out by a Bahraini coast-guard ship.[18] Qatar was also accused of detaining Bahraini fishermen. For its part, in mid-September, Doha claimed that a Bahraini gunboat fired on one of its vessels.[19] The dispute took a further twist when Qatar reportedly ordered a dozen howitzers from South Africa, thereby putting Bahrain's Shaykh 'Isa air base within artillery range. Despite Doha's prompt denials, Bahrain's predicament was well publicized in the media, which expressed deep concern about the "escalation of events" and noted that, against the background of the Gulf crisis, "one lesson should have been more than enough."[20] Effects on the diplomatic front were also evident, when Bahraini representatives failed to show up at the ceremonial inauguration of Qatar's North Field in September. Qatar retaliated by withdrawing its representatives from Bahrain's biannual Middle East oil show in November.[21]

It was only a matter of time before the ongoing tension between two of the GCC member states would affect the organization. Oman, for example, stood by Qatar, openly claiming that the latter should have sovereignty over the islets.[22] Several meetings of the GCC were postponed due to differences on the issue. Fortunately for the GCC, its annual summit in December was not disrupted, as had been feared. Doha stopped lobbying to raise the matter at the summit when Bahrain threatened to walk out altogether.[23] Despite continued pressure on both sides to show some restraint, the issue remained unresolved and cast a heavy shadow over the GCC.

QATAR AND THE US
Qatari-US relations, which had kept a very low profile following the *Stinger* missiles imbroglio in 1988 (see *MECS* 1988, p. 459), showed a marked improvement in 1990–91. The vital role of the US in forcing Iraq out of Kuwait and thereby eliminating an ominous threat to the whole region did not go unheeded. Like its neighbors, Qatar realized that the new geopolitical realities made the US "the unchallenged superpower."[24] It was quite clear that, henceforth, Washington was to become a focus of attention in Qatar's foreign policy, although Britain and France were to continue to play important roles.

In May, as a gesture of gratitude, Qatar bestowed on Gen. Norman Schwarzkopf, commander of the US forces in the Gulf, the Sash of Independence (the highest Qatari medal), for the "heroic role" he played in the liberation of Kuwait.[25] This was an example of Qatar's changing attitude. The wartime military coordination had been maintained even after the war, through a stream of high-ranking US officials, including Secretary of Defense, Richard Cheney, who arrived in June. The Qatari media, which had hitherto incessantly denounced US policy toward the region, reflected the change in the relationship in a drastic reversal of attitude. It praised the US drive to achieve a "new world order" and resolve the Arab-Israeli conflict.[26] There were no allegations made of a biased US attitude toward Israel.

QATAR AND THE MIDDLE EAST PEACE PROCESS
Qatar had a seemingly broad-minded approach toward the Arab-Israeli conflict. This was best exemplified by its presence (represented by GCC General Secretary 'Abdallah Bishara) at the Madrid peace conference in November 1991[27] (see chapter on the ME peace process). Qatar acted cautiously, yet made the surprising claim that it was ready to reconsider joining in an "appropriate step to stop the Arab boycott" of Israel should the latter stop building settlements.[28] This willing attitude was clearly due to the effect of the Allied forces' victory and the change in geopolitical realities. The media stressed that it was time to resolve other conflicts, including the Arab-Israeli one, in order to "ensure security and peace" for everyone.[29] However, it was stressed that the new approach was by no means a "political victory" for Saddam in his attempt to bind the Kuwait crisis to the Palestinian issue.[30]

Qatar was in no way favorably disposed toward the PLO. The organization had sided with Iraq throughout the Kuwait crisis and thus tremendously angered the GCC states, including Qatar. In April, the GCC retaliated by suspending all aid to the PLO and Jordan, both of which had heavily relied on Gulf states' subsidies. Furthermore, Qatari references to the peace process omitted any mention of a role for the PLO, which in the past had been referred to as "the sole legitimate representative of the Palestinians."[31]

INTERNAL AFFAIRS

INAUGURATION OF THE NORTH FIELD
On 3 September 1991, at a festive ceremony, Shaykh Khalifa inaugurated the world's largest-known nonassociated gas field with recoverable reserves, estimated at 150 trillion cu.ft. According to estimates, such quantities could meet the needs of a country the size of France for the whole of the next century.[32] The event, which coincided with Qatar's 20th National Day, marked a watershed in Qatar's development of gas to replace oil (which was due to be depleted early in the next century), as the long-term base of the economy. With the huge field in operation, Qatar would be in a position to develop its domestic industrial base of aluminum, fertilizers and petrochemicals, as well as providing energy for local consumption.

Production of the first phase was aimed at providing the fuel requirements for domestic gas-based industries and as fuel for the utilities.[33] However, despite the boost provided by the offshore gas project, the long-term outlook was not so positive, due to uncertainties over government policy, to the extent that the ambitious plan might be shelved. Past experience and inherent conservatism made Qatar wary of borrowing in the international market, even for a project as important as the North Field. Even the sharp rise in oil revenues, in the latter part of 1990, was not translated into increased government spending. The biannual budget, in April, clearly indicated that caution again reigned supreme.[34] There was an obvious sense of nervousness about the scale of the scheme for such a small country. Even the mid-1989 cabinet reshuffle (for details see *MECS* 1989, pp. 567–68), which aimed at providing greater impetus to the decision-making process, evidently failed to take the country into the next phase of development.

The combination of a generally conservative economy and a hesitant cabinet began to take its toll. There was a considerable waste of resources and frustration on the part of investors, as rival industries competed for approval.[35] Numerous plans were put forward, but few were implemented. The aluminum smelter at Umm Sa'id was still under consideration.[36] Accordingly, output of the first phase was, as yet, underutilized, with only half the field's output being used by domestic industries. Unfortunately for Qatar, the first phase already had a bad start. Although constantly denied, it encountered technical difficulties caused by leaking wellheads. Since the outbreak of the Gulf crisis, the absence of much-needed foreign workers further burdened Qatar, whose own local human resources were meager.

The second phase of the project — to export dry gas to regional states as well as Pakistan — seemed to be held up. Negotiations with Dubai for the sale of gas to fuel energy-intensive industries in Jabil 'Ali free zone were being protracted. The pipeline to Dubai and the pipeline to pipe natural gas to Pakistan were stuck at the stage of contingency plans.[37] The state of affairs could be summed up by the saying: "All talk and no action."

However, there were some encouraging developments which would be interpreted as on the road to a change in Doha's policy. A contract was signed with Japan's Chubu Electrics, by which 4m. tons of liquefied natural gas (LNG) would be supplied yearly for 25 years. This marked a significant step for the third phase, which was expected to be launched by the end of the century. The purchase added greater urgency to implementation of LNG installation plans.[38] Tenders were issued for the supply of LNG carriers to lift the output to Japan and for building a new port to Ra's Laffan to accommodate those vessels.[39]

Another encouraging sign was Doha's attitude toward raising finance. "Qatar welcomes all serious partners in the gas field," stressed Shaykh Hamad, adding that "there is no limit to the level of this participation....We want to attract foreign investment and we are ready to consent to many beneficial advantages with regard to tax exemptions, infrastructure and the price of gas."[40] It could not be verified whether Shaykh Hamad's proposal gained the seal of a royal decree or law.

ECOLOGICAL LESSONS OF THE KUWAIT CRISIS

Another ramification of the Gulf crisis, and one of the most damaging, was in the field of ecology. The huge oil spill caused by Iraq (see chapter on the Gulf War), which it was assumed would reach the shores of Qatar, posed a major threat to the island's desalination plants. Among the world's poorest in water resources, Qatar tried desperately to protect its water purifying plants. German and French experts were flown in to advise the government on an efficient course of action. Although the threat did not materialize, lessons were learnt in Doha. Once again, pretentious contingency plans to pipe fresh water from the mainland were under study. The construction of another desalination plant was started. Furthermore, efforts began to locate fresh water springs on Qatari soil.[41]

CABINET CHANGES

There were some changes of personnel in the government which, as had been the case in the past, could mean that a cabinet reshuffle was on the cards. Such a step had already been taken in 1989 (see *MECS* 1989, pp. 567–68). The 11 newcomers were expected to manage ministries more efficiently and generate new ideas after the passing of the old guard. Nonetheless, little seemed to have changed: the government was slow to provide the lead required to take the country into the next phase of economic development, and the results started to affect the North Field. The changes at ministerial level in 1991 could have indicated a forthcoming broader reshuffle. The health minister, Shaykh Khalid Ibn Muhammad Ibn 'Ali Al Thani, resigned and no successor was appointed. The communication and transport minister, 'Abdallah Ibn Salih al-Mana, was referred to by the press as acting economy and trade minister, although no official announcement was made to that effect.[42]

DEMAND FOR POLITICAL REFORMS

For the first time in the history of Qatar, as far as can be ascertained, 50 prominent families petitioned Shaykh Khalifa urging for a more democratic, elected, rather than designated, legislative council. The petition expressed "worry and disappointment" over what was regarded as "the abuse of power in Qatar,"[43] in particular, the stagnant state of the economy, which was run in a way that did not serve "the interests of the homeland" and was utilized for the exclusive benefit of influential people from within the government and administration.[44]

Other issues which came under fire were the lack of freedom of speech, the inequitable health system and the stagnant education system. The signatories concluded that an elected council with "legislative powers and widened controlling body" were the only means to guarantee "effective participation of the people."[45]

The petition seemingly reflected an authentic mood within Qatar's upper echelon and mirrored an eagerness for a more open, less paternalistic form of government. It was probably affected by the mood of democracy triggered by the Gulf crisis. That very same wave had already produced what seemed to be the beginnings of change in other GCC countries, prompted more by the changing realities than by self-motivation. The Kuwaiti ruling family, as such, had promised to hold parliamentary elections in late 1992. Saudi Arabia indicated its readiness to set up a consultative council after years of unfulfilled promises (see chapters on Kuwait and Saudi Arabia). Since 1972, Qatar had a consultative council made up of 40 members designated by the ruler. However, more was apparently expected from the rulers. But the Qatari leadership did not seem willing to go any further than that. Hence, although the Gulf crisis allowed many earlier taboos on semipublic debates to be abolished, it seemed to reconfirm Qatar's fear that introducing a more liberal political system would increase rather than contain the pressures on the Thani ruling family.

NOTES

For the place and frequency of publications cited here, and for the full name of the publication, news agency, radio station or monitoring service where an abbreviation is used, please see "List of Sources." Only in the case of more than one publication bearing the same name is the place of publication noted here.

1. GNA, 15 August — DR, 16 August 1990.
2. Riyadh TV, 25 January — DR, 28 January 1991.
3. GNA, 3 February — DR, 4 February; AFP, 7 February — DR, 7 February 1991.
4. GNA, 2 February; SPA, 3 February — DR, 4 February 1991.
5. GNA, 27 February — DR, 28 February 1991.
6. *Al-'Arab, al-Sharq,* 4 February 1991.
7. GNA, 2 March — DR, 5 March 1991.
8. SPA, 30 August — DR, 3 September 1991.
9. KUNA, 5 May — DR, 6 May 1991.
10. GNA, 21 March — DR, 21 March 1991.
11. *The Gulf States,* 24 April 1991.
12. *CR,* Qatar, No. 1, 1991.
13. IRNA, 6 January — DR, 7 January 1992.
14. GNA, 12 March — DR, 13 March 1992.
15. *Al-Raya* (Doha), 13 January 1992.
16. AFP, 29 July — DR, 30 July 1991.
17. GNA, 24 August — DR, 26 August; GNA, 4 October — DR, 7 October 1991.
18. *Al-Hayat* (London), 15 August 1991.
19. GNA, 20 September — DR, 20 September 1991.
20. GNA, 24 August — DR, 26 August 1991.
21. *CR,* Qatar, No. 1, 1992.
22. AFP, 29 July — DR, 30 July; *al-Hayat* (London), 8 October 1991.
23. *CR,* Qatar, No. 1, 1992.
24. GNA, 9 October — DR, 10 October 1991.
25. GNA, 1 April — DR, 3 April 1991.
26. GNA, 9 March — DR, 11 March; *al-'Arab,* 9 October 1991.
27. SPA, 27 October — DR, 29 October; *FT,* 31 October 1991.
28. GNA, 21 July — DR, 22 July 1991.
29. *Al-Sharq,* 9 March 1991.
30. Ibid.
31. See, e.g., *al-Usbu' al-'Arabi,* 23 October 1989; *The Gulf States,* 8 April 1991.
32. *MEED,* 11 January 1992.
33. *CR,* Qatar, No. 4, 1991.
34. *MEED,* 4 November 1991.
35. *CR,* Qatar, No. 4, 1991.
36. *The Gulf States,* 7 October 1991.
37. *MEED,* 22 March; *al-Watan al-'Arabi,* 26 March 1991.
38. *MEED,* 8 March 1991.
39. *The Gulf States,* 23 September 1991.
40. *ME,* 11 October 1991.
41. *The Gulf States,* 18 November 1991.
42. *MEED,* 4 October 1991.
43. AFP, 18 January — DR, 22 January 1992.
44. *Al-Dunya,* 23 January 1992.
45. *AFP,* 18 January — DR, 22 January 1992.

Saudi Arabia
(Al-Mamlaka al-'Arabiyya al-Sa'udiyya)

JOSEPH KOSTINER

During the course of 1991, the Saudi authorities were forced to cope with the impact of the Gulf War, which shattered some of the Saudi kingdom's basic infrastructure. Both the changes resulting from the war, and the subsequent attempts by the government to cope with them, turned the year 1991 into a watershed in Saudi Arabia's development.

During the war, the kingdom fought hard and, together with the coalition forces, overpowered the Iraqi enemy. The impact of the war was evident in several spheres, both during and after the fighting. There were problems of internal unrest, such as terrorist attempts, abandonment of border settlements and economic recession, as well as the low morale and questionable efficacy of the armed forces. There was also skepticism over Saudi Arabia's future, resulting from the presence of foreign Western forces on Saudi soil and Riyadh's dependence on the coalition troops for its security. These problems, alongside moral shortcomings, which characterized some of the royal princes' behavior (notably the taking of commission on business deals), prompted a renewed debate about the preferred course of development of the Saudi state. The debaters were mostly members of the growing "middle class," namely, an educated stratum which did not belong to the royal family (students, 'Ulama, professionals or officials who constituted the kingdom's administrative and professional backbone), and the debate threatened to spread throughout Saudi society. Some wanted Saudi Arabia to adopt a modernist-liberal policy, while others leaned toward an orthodox-fundamentalist course. For the first time, both parties openly petitioned the king, published their arguments in the media, and organized public rallies.

Regional security constituted another major problem. Iraq's invasion of Kuwait and its subsequent threat to Saudi Arabia proved the futility of the old security system in the Gulf, and the Saudis had to rethink their position in this respect. They faced difficult choices: they could rely on an unprecedented but effective cooperation with US forces; a less effective but more traditional cooperation with Arab coalition states, such as Syria and Egypt; or a combination of the two. During 1991, Saudi leaders grappled with these problems, seeking suitable formulas to stabilize their kingdom.

The Saudi authorities obviously regarded the first set of problems as the most urgent. They took advantage of the swift and successful conclusion to the war to devise a series of tactics to overpower terrorism and calm the population, which involved embarking on an ambitious plan to enlarge and strengthen the army. They were presumably less worried about the functioning of their Administration and made relatively few changes in the government. Moreover, despite differences of

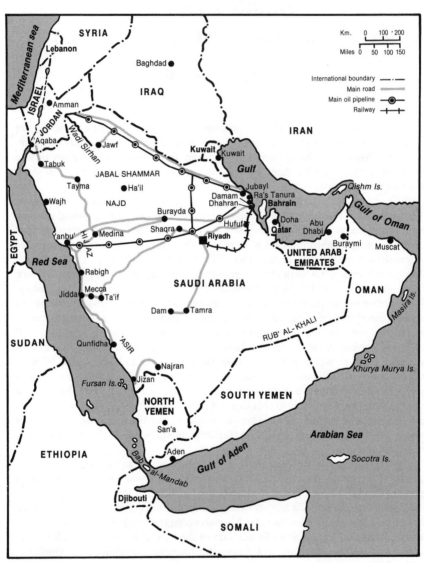

Saudi Arabia

opinion among Saudi royal leaders, they maintained unity of ranks and there were no changes of positions among the top leaders. The only incident, in this context, was the dismissal by King Fahd of Khalid Ibn Sultan, the leader of the Arab and Islamic forces (for unclear reasons), during the Gulf War, and this incident passed without repercussions.

The government's response to ideological and sociopolitical problems was less assertive and less effective. Fahd made a firm commitment to establish an appointed consultative council (*majlis shura*) which was aimed at satisfying, at least in part, the thirst of the different groups for representation. However, the postwar winds of change and the controversial cooperation between Saudi Arabia and the US only deepened the rift between modernists and fundamentalists. The two groups formed clearly defined contradictory platforms: the modernists strove to strengthen society's political and human rights, the fundamentalists wanted a full and effective implementation of the Shari'a.

The fundamentalists succeeded in inciting the population in provincial regions and were more critical of the authorities, particularly of their pro-Western and elitist policies. The government, in its turn, dispersed some of the leading fundamentalist rallies and managed to turn the leading, traditional 'Ulama against the active fundamentalists. However, they were unable to stop their antigovernment activities.

Immediately after the war, the Saudi authorities were interested in devising a security policy based on a combined strategy, utilizing Syrian and Egyptian ground forces under a regional US security umbrella. In early summer, it became clear that Saudi Arabia (and other Gulf states) were having reservations about the Arab forces' effectiveness and reliability. This prompted Riyadh to adopt a policy of security that relied almost exclusively on US protection in the Gulf. Riyadh's cooperation with Washington motivated Saudi leaders to lend their support for peace in the Arab-Israeli arena. They also continued to cooperate with the kingdom's wartime allies, Egypt and Syria.

POLICY IN THE GULF WAR

MOTIVES AND INTERESTS

Saudi Arabia regarded an Allied attack on Iraq as mandatory. Like the other coalition members, it feared that Iraq, with its conventional and chemical arsenal, would remain a constant threat to Saudi Arabia itself and to the entire Gulf, if it were not defeated. Moreover, Saudi leaders feared that if Saddam's forces became entrenched in Kuwait, and the world became used to Iraq's occupation there, Iraqi rule in Kuwait would be legitimized and its utilization of Kuwaiti oil, finances and ports would eventually become a fait accompli. This would most probably lead to Iraq's economic rivalry and military threat to the Gulf states. This problem had already manifested itself in the Iraqi forces' proximity to the Saudi Eastern Province, its oil fields and water desalination plants. The Saudis were also very worried about Iraq's chemical weapons.[1] On the war's eve, Saudi spokesmen stressed that their intensive diplomatic efforts to prevent war had reached an impasse. In Fahd's own words: "God knows that we have knocked on every door for peace and proceeded along every brotherly dialogue and understanding," but these efforts were rejected by Saddam. The latter also defied the international community's resolution to end the crisis; "he alone should today face the responsibility of his position," said Fahd.[2] Fearing Iraq's immediate and future wrath, and after all peaceful means to effect an Iraqi retreat from Kuwait had failed, Saudi leaders decided that there was no way to defeat Iraq other than by warfare, which would remove these dangers for a long period of time. In fact, on the eve of the war Fahd told Western reporters that, like President Bush, he too feared the possibility of Saddam's last minute withdrawal from Kuwait, which would prevent war and leave Iraqi forces intact for future aggression attempts.[3] Fahd sought a decisive battle.

The Saudis did not just aim to achieve the official UN goal, which was to liberate Kuwait from Iraqi occupation, but like most coalition partners, they were also eager to see Saddam's war machine destroyed and his potential to harm any Gulf state in the future curtailed. However, the Saudis did not seek Iraq's complete devastation. This would have prompted endless feelings of revenge in Iraq and would very likely have split the coalition, with some of its member states refusing to participate in the destruction of Iraq's military might.[4]

SAUDI ARABIA AND THE ANTI-IRAQI COALITION

As host and main client of the anti-Iraqi coalition, it was reported in early January that Saudi Arabia had contributed enormous sums toward the Gulf states' defense in general, and the maintenance of the coalition forces. Unofficially, the Saudis were reported to have given friendly governments more than $6bn. in grants and government-guaranteed loans to offset the cost of the crisis.[5] In late January, Saudi Arabia pledged another $13.5bn.[6] (For detailed and official figures, see below).

Saudi leaders understood that their security hinged upon the coalition's effectiveness. The military superiority of the coalition forces was essential for Saudi existence. A huge US arms sale to Saudi Arabia (estimated at $15bn.) was discussed between Riyadh and Washington (a $7.3bn. deal had already been approved by Congress in October 1990). The US had agreed that the resolution of the Gulf crisis was Washington's first priority.[7] King Fahd and US President Bush held constant telephone conversations to coordinate strategic affairs;[8] US Secretary of Defense Richard Cheney and chairman of the US Joint Chiefs of Staff, Gen. Colin Powell, came to Ta'if on 9 February for further coordination. There was full cooperation on the field level between the US commander in chief, Gen. Norman Schwarzkopf, and the Saudi commander of the Joint Islamic Task Force, Gen. Khalid Ibn Sultan. In Ibn Sultan's words: "[We] appreciated each other's command."[9] US intelligence officers even participated in the interrogation of Iraqi prisoners of war (POWs) conducted by the Saudis, to establish a joint intelligence assessment.[10] Saudi leaders also met and coordinated with Britain's Foreign Secretary Douglas Hurd and with French Minister of Defense Pierre Joxe. The relationship between US armed forces and the Saudis they encountered in the kingdom's northeastern regions were characterized by mutual discovery of each others' different and seemingly strange cultures and practices (see *MECS* 1990, pp. 616–17). However, the Saudis and Western soldiers displayed mutual respect and cooperation in their daily social and business interactions and no disputes were reported.[11]

During the war, the Saudis deferred all major operational decisions to the US, although during the last two weeks of February, the Saudis, like the other Gulf states, pressed President Bush to counter Soviet peace proposals with an absolute insistence that Iraq fully comply with the relevant UN resolutions and withdraw from Kuwait, prior to any cease-fire.[12] The Saudis pressed for the ground attack to take place and, in Western observers' view, to drive Saddam into a humiliating unconditional withdrawal and, ultimately, to his downfall.[13] The Saudis were definitely influential in the US decision to launch a ground attack on 24 February. Several days later, in the wake of Iraq's defeat, the Saudis feared that Iraq would disintegrate into small units, including a pro-Iranian Shi'i fundamentalist entity along the Saudi border, which would endanger the Saudi kingdom. It was unclear whether, at that time, the Saudis actually wanted to stop the war, but they evidently started seeking alternative solutions to Iraq's disintegration by war, namely, the toppling of Saddam's regime. They took it upon themselves to prepare a valid political alternative to Saddam's rule. In early February, they hosted a four-member delegation representing the 17 Iraqi political groups in exile, who were at that time regrouping in Damascus. The Saudi Government also approached certain former Iraqi military and political leaders in exile, as possible members of an alternative government.[14] While these attempts did not produce any immediate results, they probably influenced Bush in his decision to stop the fighting, as he did on 28 February, before Iraq's army and government disintegrated totally.

Saudi Arabia maintained close relations with its Arab coalition partners. These partners, whose forces were less experienced than Western forces and numbered only c. 100,000, were obviously less important to the Saudis in purely operational terms, but their participation gave the coalition an Arab and Islamic legitimacy, and also facilitated specific tactical operations, such as negotiating with the Iraqi opposition. The Saudis termed their own participation in the war as being part of an effort on the part of the Gulf states incorporated within the Gulf Cooperation Council (GCC; see also chapters on the Gulf states and inter-Arab relations).

The Saudis considered the GCC as the body actually responsible for regional security and for Gulf states' relations with other Arab states. The GCC secretary-general, 'Abdallah Ya'qub Bishara, often represented the Saudi standpoint in the Western press, and the GCC summit, which took place in Qatar's capital Doha in December 1990, formulated the Gulf states' assistance policy for other Arab states.[15] Soldiers from other GCC countries also joined the Saudi forces in specific patrol and fighting missions.

Saudi cooperation with Syria and Egypt had an immediate operational impact, since the forces of these states were responsible for operating major battle zones in the arena. Moreover, Saudi Arabia was particularly keen on cooperating with these two major Arab states, in order to demonstrate the broad and substantial inter-Arab consensus against Iraq. Riyadh maintained almost daily contact with Damascus and Cairo at the highest levels, with foreign ministers and heads of state. Fahd consulted with Syrian President Asad and Egyptian President Mubarak about the operational roles of Arab armies and policy lines toward Iraq (i.e., coordinating the Damascus-based Iraqi opposition groups) and Iraq's Arab allies. Riyadh also took positive steps toward improving bilateral relations with these states: on 6 February, the Saudis and Syrian representatives decided to establish a bilateral coordination committee to discuss political, economic and social affairs of interest to both states. The first session began the next day.[16] At the same time, Riyadh wrote off Egypt's debt of $4bn. and went so far as to pay Egypt $1.5bn. to compensate it for military expenses and war losses (notably the return of Egyptian workers from Iraq and Kuwait; see also chapter on Egypt). Saudi Arabia also undertook to increase its investments in Egypt.[17]

Riyadh's attitude toward Iraq's Arab allies was another way in which Saudi Arabia showed its support for the coalition. The leaders of Jordan, the PLO and Yemen were described as "dwarf rulers."[18] The Saudi ambassador to Washington, Prince Bandar Ibn Sultan, called King Husayn of Jordan "lost"; PLO chairman Yasir 'Arafat "a clown"; and Yemeni President 'Ali 'Abdallah Salih an "ignoramus."[19] The media of these states reported that the Saudi authorities, who had already cut their aid and expelled c. 900,000 Yemeni workers (see *MECS* 1990, pp. 613–14) were, in fact, banning Jordanian, Palestinian, Sudanese and Yemeni nationals, even those with valid visas, from entering the kingdom.[20]

The Saudis tried to maintain coordination and good relations among the main coalition members and set them apart from the pro-Iraqi group. This was Riyadh's main contribution to the war effort.

SAUDI ARABIA'S WAR OPERATIONS

Saudi forces played an active role in the war operations, though not a leading role, due to limited battle experience and relatively small numbers (an army of c. 60,000 and the internal militia and national guard totaling c. 45,000). Saudi (and other Arab) forces were never meant to participate in a ground invasion into Iraq, but only to liberate Kuwait and/or defend Saudi territory. Given these limitations, the role of the Saudi forces was evident only in the following instances: from 28 January-2 February, Saudi units (mainly the national guard), fought Iraqi units that had infiltrated the Saudi border town of al-Khafji after intensive artillery shelling. Together with units from Qatar, the Saudis fought a bloody street battle with the Iraqis and suffered 15 killed, 32 wounded and four missing. With the help of US helicopter and ground forces, Khafji was recaptured.[21] During the following days, Saudi ground forces were intermittently occupied in intercepting Iraqi armored and commando units which attempted to infiltrate Saudi territory. According to Saudi spokesmen, with the help of Syrian artillery, their forces overpowered the Iraqi units.[22] Saudi towns, notably Riyadh and Dahran were the target of 37 Iraqi *Scud* attacks, which failed to cause major destruction or casualties (with the exception of the destruction of a US soldiers' residence in Dahran) during the war.[23] The most impressive Saudi actions were the operation of the air force. Saudi airplanes carried out 6,061 out of the 110,573 sorties by the coalition air forces.[24]

INTERNAL AFFAIRS

THE GULF WAR'S IMMEDIATE EFFECT (JANUARY-MARCH); CHALLENGE AND RESPONSE

The prewar preparations and then the war itself posed immediate challenges to the Saudi authorities. First, there were acts of sabotage and terrorism, perpetrated by the kingdom's enemies. Second, there were signs that, due to the daily pressures, some of Saudi Arabia's fundamental institutions, such as the army and the economy, were failing to operate adequately and that the authorities' ability to keep control over society was shaken, with the consequent ever-present danger of internal instability. Third, there was the dilemma of whether to introduce more changes and innovations into public life, or to reaffirm the traditional lifestyle. This dilemma was the result of the encounter with foreign troops and exposure to daily hardships and it generated conflicting social expectations. The following section attempts to shed some light on both the nature of these challenges and on the Saudi Government's endeavors to surmount them (see also *MECS* 1990, chapter on Saudi Arabia).

Coping with Terror

There were continuous reports about various terrorist attempts: Yemeni residents were reported to be instigating civil unrest in the south of the kingdom, and Iraqi squads were infiltrating Saudi Arabia to sabotage and attack Saudi leaders. The authorities were particularly worried about the intensification of these attempts toward 17 March, which was the beginning of Ramadan.[25] The Saudi authorities usually acted swiftly to either prevent and/or block these attempts. The Yemeni threat was neutralized by anti-Yemeni policies, which had forced c. 900,000 Yemenis to leave Saudi Arabia in 1990, and were still effective in 1991. Reinforced national guard patrols intercepted the majority of infiltrating Iraqi agents. In addition, the minister of internal affairs, Na'if Ibn 'Abd al-'Aziz, warned all foreign residents that "any offense or access, or any disturbance...will receive the ultimate punishment as stipulated by the Islamic Shari'a."[26] Apparently, the government effectively applied a variety of defensive measures against terrorists (in mid-February, more than 12 people were detained on this charge),[27] and successfully controlled potentially dangerous groups of the population.

Consequently, only one serious terrorist attack was reported during this period. In early February, three people (two US soldiers and one Saudi security guard) were injured by flying glass when a gunman fired at a shuttle bus in Jidda. The authorities subsequently reported intercepting the sniper and his associates. The associates were described as unspecified "residents," namely, foreigners living in Saudi Arabia.[28]

Surmounting Administrative and Economic Difficulties

Several days before the war, parts of the population in the regions affected by the militaristic build-up started to panic. Increasing rumors that Iraq would use chemical weapons, accompanied by inadequate civil defense drills, and insufficient distribution of civil defense equipment, led to massive public desertion. In Dahran, non-Saudis (mostly Asians) were reported to be fleeing. One man complained to a US reporter "what are we to think when we see you, Americans, even going to dinner with your gas masks, while we have none?"[29] In towns located near the Iraqi border, those running away included indigenous Saudis. Thus, before and during the fighting, the town of Khafji, Saudi Arabia's main border crossing with Kuwait (45,000 inhabitants), and Khafar al-Batin, which was located near the new King Khalid military town, 50 miles west of the Kuwait-Iraqi-Saudi border (30,000 inhabitants), were reported to be deserted. Not all the border settlements suffered a similar war syndrome; the people of Zulfi, located in northern Najd, were reported to have engaged in profitable business activities with foreign soldiers.[30] However, it was clear that the Saudi authorities feared losing control over the border regions, leading to more panic and desertion among the local civil population. Moreover, they also feared that panic could affect the population of the capital, al-Riyadh, which, like Dahran, was hit by Iraqi *Scud* missiles.

Although the Saudis participated on the side of the victorious coalition, the performance and morale of the Saudi armed forces proved to be less than desirable. Saudi leaders praised the national guard's performance in the battle of Khafji, calling it courageous and proving "the Saudi people's readiness to fight for their homeland." However, it was public knowledge that the Saudis had sustained 15 dead and had only managed to liberate Khafji with substantial assistance by US marines.[31] American evaluation rated the Saudis as brave individual fighters, but lacking initiative and technical ability; overcautious and hesitant in battle; and given to obstructive attitudes when placed in organized formations. The soldiers' own awareness of their lack of combat experience, American criticism, and their evident inability to defend their country alone, rendered the Saudi infantry's morale low. Only the performance of the Saudi air force was regarded by the Western coalition parties as equal to that of their own air forces.[32] The authorities' response focused on a transformation and enlargement of the army during the postwar period (see below).

The Saudi authorities also faced major economic problems. The economy was severely strained by the kingdom's payments to frontline states and allies, and by the flight of capital away from Saudi banks (see also *MECS* 1990, pp. 623–24). In addition to the $13.5bn. cash pledge made to the US soon after the war started, Saudi spokesmen in the US showed detailed accounts proving that Riyadh had paid about $20bn. extra in 1990 toward war expenses. This was in response to US Congress jibes that the Saudis were not contributing enough toward the costs of the war. Saudi Arabia claimed to have paid for regional aid to neighboring frontline states and for Saudi armed forces and arms purchases, which constituted 85% of the undisputed amount of $20bn.[33] In early 1991, the Saudis also reaffirmed their future commitments in this regard.[34] Unofficial reports quoted Saudi war-related expenses as high as $48bn.[35]

There were reports of industrial and commercial groups that had to curtail their business, both because of currency problems and dormancy in the formerly prosperous and presently war-ridden Eastern Province. The private sector had to alter production lines to manufacture commodities demanded by the public during the war. Moreover, private employers were also forced to adapt to the expulsion or evacuation of hundreds of thousands of foreign workers (Yemenis, Palestinians, Asians and others) and to the readmission of others under strict security control.[36] Internal markets were further burdened by higher prices of goods and services, high insurance costs and inevitable supply bottlenecks, even in regions located far from the war, such as Jidda.[37] Moreover, the Saudis stressed that even the rise in oil prices in the early months of the Gulf crisis, yielding a revenue of $12bn.–$15bn., did not cover the increasing expenses, and left the kingdom with a major deficit for 1991.[38]

The economic difficulties became evident as early as January 1991, when the Saudi authorities decided to postpone publication of the annual budget. In mid-February, it was announced that Saudi Arabia had raised its first commercial loan, worth $4.5bn. (originally $3.6bn.) from a close US banking associate, J. P. Morgan.[39] The borrowed finances enabled the authorities to activate business and various social services in society.

Despite the severity of these problems, the Saudi authorities were able to deal with them successfully. There were several explanations for their success: first, the security forces were in a state of alert against any internal disturbance. Second, the Saudi media abstained from any overt criticism of the government's military or administrative faults. According to Western reports, this policy, which had been formulated by King Fahd himself,[40] successfully prevented public panic and dissatisfaction with the authorities from spreading any further. Third, the war effects were mostly limited to the kingdom's northeastern regions, and consequently most of the Saudi population, located in more distant areas, did not feel the direct impact of the war. Fourth, because the war was short and ended with the anti-Iraqi coalition's triumph, the authorities' policies were proved victorious and forestalled the development of any serious crises.

The authorities' ability to take advantage of these conditions and use effective means to stem immediate problems should not be underestimated. They successfully regained control of the entire population all over the kingdom despite severe challenges. Since the late 1960s, under kings Faysal and Khalid, the central government had been able to keep control; make further development in construction and the economy; and establish bureaucracy and organization in all provinces. In the 1970s and 1980s, the government had successfully surmounted crisis situations in various Saudi provinces by applying "stick-and-carrot" tactics, namely, control and suppression, combined with administrative and economic improvement for any dissatisfied group. The authorities gained experience in introducing administrative changes and utilizing financial aid to these ends. Hence, despite the unusual circumstances and the problems that had evolved in Saudi institutions and the social fabric, the government demonstrated enough resilience and resourcefulness to tackle the war-related problems.

Despite some Western reports of disagreements among the leading emirs, the government's executive ability was also demonstrated by the resilience and uniform performance of the royal family. Crown Prince 'Abdallah, who was dissatisfied with the Saudi war strategy, suggested relying more on Arab mediation in tackling the Gulf problems and criticized King Fahd's and Defense Minister Sultan's all-out pro-American line. The younger emirs, sons of the king and his brothers, such as Foreign Minister Sa'ud al-Faysal (King Faysal's son), Gen. Khalid and Ambassador Bandar (sons of Sultan), were reported to be skeptical of the older leaders' abilities to cope with the war, and expected to have to step in and curb them.[41] However, these problems did not surface: Fahd remained the supreme leader and, despite disagreements, 'Abdallah and the younger emirs complied with and supported Fahd's policies.

Ideological and Sociopolitical Rifts

As the war approached and throughout its duration, there was a splintering in Saudi society between more conservative, Islamic fundamentalists and liberal-modernist groups. The split occurred over the kingdom's future character and course of development. Unlike the administrative, economic and military problems, which the government could tackle by drawing on earlier experience and on its ability to enhance central control and economic development, socioideological rifts were more difficult to contain: first, because Saudi Arabian society was, on the whole, characterized by regional and tribal divisions. Although these groups were loyal to the royal family, which often intermarried with their nobility, and were bound by a common interest in benefiting from Saudi wealth, they remained differentiated by kin ties.

Second, there were socioeconomic tensions, involving educated professionals, teachers, students and officials, sometimes referred to as the middle class or the nonroyalists. Although these educated professionals were a "strategic elite," responsible for operating managerial, economic, health, administrative and teaching institutions, they were nevertheless barred from participating in policy-making at the top. Since they already constituted more than 8% of the work force (a percentage which had bred revolutionary movements in other Arab states), and had occasionally criticized the less-able but more influential emirs, Saudi leaders had good reason to worry about these groups. Third, the former nomadic tribesmen, who had been undergoing a transition into an urban population, became unskilled, lower-class workers, already a factor for political unrest.[42] Both the social divisions themselves and their political implications were difficult to contain.

The social problems were compounded by ideological confusion. The Saudi authorities have had an ongoing problem trying to establish a delicate balance between two main contradictory systems of value: the pious and austere, deriving from the dominant Wahhabi belief, and the modernist-affluent, inspired by technological change and oil wealth. The establishment of such a balance had always been difficult: in the 1920s, the resistance of traditional and zealous tribal groups (*Ikhwan*) was encountered during the kingdom's unification, the pacification of its borders and governmental centralization. Only their defeat in 1930 facilitated the building up of the Saudi Administration in the following decades. The introduction in the 1960s of bureaucratic institutionalization and media (notably television) facilities by King Faysal, stirred up demonstrations by 'Ulama, tribesmen, officials and even an emir (whose death during a violent demonstration against the introduction of television in 1964, which was dispersed by force, prompted a relative to assassinate King Faysal in 1975).

Saudi leaders, and society in general, perceived the period of the Gulf crisis as another such historical crossroad, when the Saudi future course of development was questioned. This perception resulted from the difficulties in maintaining the old order: there were foreign soldiers on Saudi soil; old concepts of security collapsed; a new strategic alliance with Western states against another Arab state was formed; and the royal family had difficulty in ruling the kingdom peacefully. The modernist camp hoped for change: for more governmental consideration of Western-styled human rights and political representation. On the other hand, the traditionalist-fundamentalists sought to impose a strict Wahhabi value-system on the government and the public (see below).

Both camps increased their activities in the weeks leading up to the war. The "moral police" (a body supervised by the Ministry of Interior, responsible for the proper behavior of society in public, in keeping with the Wahhabi code) displayed growing zeal in punishing women for indecent dress and men for neglecting their prayers. In response to this development, some women held a demonstration in November 1990, where they deliberately performed the illegal act of driving. They were subsequently dismissed from their jobs and barred from holding passports (see *MECS* 1990, pp. 621–23). This indicated that the modernist-liberal camp was also trying to affect public behavior.

The authorities' reaction focused on King Fahd's pledge, in early November 1990, to reopen a consultative council (*majlis shura*), an institution that had been active in the 1920s and early 1930s in the Hijaz Province, and although not officially dissolved, had not operated since. Such a council would give the notables and elders in society a forum to consult and advise the king, thereby satisfying their political interest, but would not strip the king of any executive or legislative authority. Despite the minimal powers vested in this body, the reestablishment of a *shura* was regarded by both the authorities and the public as an acceptable means to overcome periods of social unrest. Fahd, who last pledged to reestablish a *shura* after his coronation in 1982, had avoided doing so, in order to maintain the status quo. However, at the current crossroad, he found it expedient to make this promise once more.[43] This announcement did not satisfy the aspirations of the two camps but only raised their expectations for sociopolitical change.

POSTWAR CHANGES
Attempting to Reinvigorate the Economy
In the summer of 1991, Western sources estimated the Gulf War's total cost for Saudi Arabia at $37.5bn. ($12.5bn. in 1990, and $25bn. in 1991). The earnings during this period, mainly from oil, were estimated at $39.5bn. (According to earlier-mentioned Saudi sources, their war expenses were higher.)[44] Hence, the economic difficulties affecting the kingdom for the rest of 1991 did not result from massive financial losses, but rather from an immediate partial stagnation in local business activities and more significantly, from a severe currency shortage. The currency shortage was the result of Riyadh's immediate payments to the US and other coalition allies for their participation in the war and to cover parts of its Gulf neighbors' military reinforcements. Furthermore, the reserves of the kingdom's state bank, the Saudi Arabian Monetary Agency, had declined from $20bn. in 1988, to $10bn. in mid-1990, and continued to fall after that. The budget deficit was estimated at $13.3bn. and that of the balance of payments at $6.5bn.[45]

The Saudi authorities viewed the prevalent economic difficulties as temporary and transient. Their main aim was to spread the message that the basis of the Saudi economy was solid, and that economic development should therefore be encouraged. For example, in November, King Fahd stressed that Saudi Arabia had to pay "some 33 states [which] sent their youth, troops, tanks and aircraft." Expenditure was therefore expected and "it is not strange for a state to be in debt in extraordinary circumstances." The Saudi economy was nevertheless strong: "approved projects continued unhampered...the funds allocated, worth thousands of millions, will be available...there is banking freedom and freedom of transaction...I think the debt will be settled within two or three years. No projects will be affected and we will not resort to cuts."[46]

Riyadh's main efforts focused on obtaining a continuous increase in oil revenues. It wanted a relatively high production quota from the Organization of Petroleum Exporting Countries (Opec), to enable increased oil sales for a reasonable price of no more than $23 a barrel. This policy served several aims: politically, it was in keeping with the interests of the main oil consumers, the kingdom's Western anti-Iraqi allies for whom a reasonable oil price was a vital interest. Moreover, Saudi Arabia succeeded in finding common ground with Iran over this policy. Economically, this policy not only enabled Riyadh to benefit from oil revenues, but also to overpower smaller producers who wanted production cuts and higher oil prices, and thus to maintain a dominant position in Opec. Saudi policy was beneficial to its own and Western interests and to Opec's stability (see also chapter on oil developments).

From 11–12 March, during the convention of the informal Opec Ministerial Committee in Geneva, Oil Minister Hisham Nazir suggested and obtained a small cut of 5% from the maximum production level of each country, reached during the war. This was a token gesture in serving "a postwar normalization in production," to stave off demands for more severe cuts and price increases. At Opec's June conference in Vienna, this decision was officially endorsed, setting Opec's total production at c. 22.3m. barrels per day (b/d), of which the kingdom kept producing the highest share of around 8.2m. b/d. In another Opec Ministerial Committee meeting, Riyadh successfully argued that the Opec quota for the last quarter of 1991 should be 33.65m. b/d, setting its own production quota on an increased amount of 8.5m. b/d, at $21 per barrel.[47]

In addition to oil revenues, Saudi leaders encouraged foreign and local business enterprises to disregard passing difficulties and, in the spirit of King Fahd's words, accelerate their economic activities. In May, the government took another loan of $2.5bn. from local banks.[48] A leading local business expert then explained that the current cash-flow difficulty was a "limited problem and is manageable given Saudi Arabia's resources." In the same month, major business families, such as al-Gosaibi and Kanoo (al-Qusaybi, Kanu) announced their intention to expand and invest in Saudi Arabia.[49] In the following months, major development projects were announced: a plan to establish a free zone at Yanbu' port along the Red Sea, backed by a joint stock company; and projects by the Saudi Iron and Steel Company and the Saudi Electricity Company, to expand their activities, based on loans raised earlier (of $133m. and $200m., respectively).[50]

By the end of 1991, no significant improvement in the Saudi economy had taken place. However, both the government and the business community showed their confidence in the economy and, at the risk of taking loans, were committed to reactivate it.

Organizational Change

The Saudi authorities attempted a series of improvements in the Administration and the armed forces in the weeks before and during the war, in order to overcome the difficulties faced. King Fahd and other supreme leaders wanted to maintain stability and continuity in the top echelons and therefore made only a few changes in the cabinet and the supreme military command. Despite reports of occasional disagreements between them, the status quo between Crown Prince 'Abdallah and King Fahd prevailed, permitting the king to maintain his supreme position and rely on the cooperation of other princes and nonroyal government members.

On 31 July, a royal decree announced three minor cabinet changes including the filling of two posts that had not had full-time occupants for some time. 'Abd al-Wahhab 'Attar became minister of planning, taking over from the oil minister, Hisham Nazir, who had held the post in an acting capacity. Khalid al-'Anqari was moved from his position as minister of municipal and rural affairs to become minister of higher education, a post held in an acting capacity by Minister of Education 'Abd al-'Aziz al-Khuwaytir. A senior official, 'Abd al-'Aziz al-Shaykh (of Ibn 'Abd al-

Wahhab's family), was appointed minister of municipal and rural affairs. Shaykh was regarded an expert technocrat, which perhaps accounted for his appointment to the sensitive position of controlling Saudi Arabia's municipal and rural affairs. Other than these, only a handful of new appointments were made at the levels of deputy minister and director general. The reshuffle seemed to be on a very limited scale; a Saudi businessman commented "the mountain went into labor and gave birth to a mouse...a very small mouse."[51]

The efforts to improve lower-level services and control over society won higher priority. An evident result was the successful Hajj season in early June, in which the kingdom accommodated hundreds of thousands of pilgrims including Iraqis and Iranians.[52]

After the war, the need to reinforce the armed forces and to improve their fighting skills and morale led to a new policy. In his 'Id al-Fitr speech in mid-April, King Fahd announced his intention to strengthen and enlarge the army. At a later date, Minister of Defense Sultan clarified that the program would focus on the building of at least eight divisions of ground forces. Western observers estimated that under this arrangement, the army (including reservists) would number c. 200,000 men (nearly triple the present size). They further estimated that similar levels of expansion were planned for the Saudi sea and air forces. No details were given about the growth of the national guard.[53] The authorities nevertheless still objected to nationwide, compulsory conscription: Sultan explained that the army's training facilities would not be able to absorb the masses.[54] It was obvious that the authorities actually feared the potential internal political dangers generated by a huge and modern army.

Plans for new arms sales were made. The US Congress had hitherto approved proposed arms sales to Saudi Arabia of $7.3bn. Plans to purchase 24 F-15 and 90 F-18 aircraft, four Awacs surveillance planes, 2,400 Maverick air-to-air missiles, and more M-1 Abrams tanks were still waiting for approval. The Saudis also went ahead with the building of a modern airfield, al-Yamama. The US role in this scheme would be to assist in training Saudi forces to become a highly mobile, offensive force.[55] However, the impact of these efforts on the Saudi army remained to be seen.

A major personnel change concerning the armed forces was the dismissal, on 24 September, of Lt. Gen. Khalid Ibn Sultan from his position as commander of the Joint Arab-Islamic Task Force, immediately after he had been promoted to full general. Observers speculated as to whether Fahd had looked unfavorably upon Khalid's reputation, his popularity with the Western media or his ambition to become chief of staff, a post that was not traditionally given to a member of the ruling family (in place of Gen. Muhammad Salih Hammad, who had been ill for the previous couple of years). There were also speculations that Khalid's dismissal resulted from an interroyal family struggle over taking commission charges from business deals.[56] There were no reports of subsequent unrest in the armed forces.

POSTWAR POLITICAL AND IDEOLOGICAL UNREST
The Question of Representation
After the Gulf War, the quest for the establishment of a majlis shura was voiced nationwide. In late February, a group of 43 businessmen, academics and officials, who could be described as liberal-modernists, submitted a petition to Fahd. They

demanded the establishment of a constitution, a consultative council and the revival of municipal and provincial councils. A second petition, signed by c. 100 senior 'Ulama, was submitted to Fahd in mid-May, similarly demanding a consultative council. On 1 August, the petitioners published an additional explanatory letter abroad, in the London-based *al-Quds al-'Arabi,* reiterating their demands. They explained the king's obligations and need (according to Islam) for consultation with free, unpressured specialists in the relevant fields.[57] In April, in his *'Id al-Fitr* speech, the king reiterated his pledge to establish a consultative council. He explained that a recently appointed committee, chaired by his full brother, the Minister of Interior Na'if, was in the process of preparing a basic law for the functioning of government, a consultative council and district councils.[58] Fahd repeated this pledge in June and November, emphasizing that Na'if's committee would soon finish its work and submit its conclusions.[59]

The Saudi authorities were apparently now more ready than in the early 1980s to establish a consultative council and also provincial councils. Fahd sought the support and expertise of the elite and middle-class groups, who were eager to participate, at least partially, in the political process. Both these considerations led him to adopt a *shura* policy. However, this did not mean that the king and the petitioners had reached common ground. Fahd wanted to follow the Muslim tradition of utilizing the people's qualities for the benefit of his own rule, in return for giving them the right of participation (*musharaka*) in consultation and political discussions that had tribal origins. However, he did not intend to include them in final policy-making. Judging by their petitions, both political camps demanded full implementation of the religious laws, the Shari'a, in Saudi Arabia's public life. While the Shari'a was a common norm in the kingdom, its effective implementation in politics would have forced Fahd to conform to a transcendental command, to consult and consider the *shura*'s voice in all political spheres, including policy-making.[60] Yet despite these shortcomings, in 1991, the authorities and both nonroyalist camps agreed on the reestablishment of a consultative council for the first time since the early 1930s. An execution date for the plan was not set in 1991.

The Modernist-Religious Rift

The above-mentioned petitions attested to the growing awareness of political circles toward influencing future Saudi development. The liberals' ideas were evident from other demands that they included in their petition: they asked the government to reconsider women's role in society; freedom of the press and education; an independent judiciary; control of the moral police; and the establishment of district councils. In Western observers' views, this was the group "with whom the foreign diplomatic corps can easily see eye-to-eye."[61]

The liberal-modernist group personified the willingness of the so-called Western-educated, nonroyalists to go public and try to influence King Fahd. Among their leaders were former cabinet ministers, Muhammad 'Abduh Yamani and Ghazi al-Qusaybi, holding the portfolios of information and health respectively. In 1982, Qusaybi was dismissed from his cabinet post for criticizing the royal family members' practice of taking commission in business deals with Western companies (see *MECS* 1983–84, p. 622). As the kingdom's ambassador to Bahrain (which he later became), he wrote a book entitled, *To Avoid Sedition (Hatta la takun fitna),* which was published in 1991, and focused on the dangers he saw in fundamentalism: he condemned the new wave of fundamentalist teachings as a stimulus for the reintroduction of antimodern practices, and superstition, which would set back the kingdom's technological progress and its health and education services. He also warned against the formation of a hostile rejectionist coalition (*rafida*) with Iran, against Saudi Arabia.[62] Women also sometimes expressed their frustration with Saudi fundamentalists, notably the harassment they suffered at the hands of the moral police.[63]

The fundamentalists, in their turn, demanded that all government policies and activities should be conducted according to moral and Islamic principles. Thus, they demanded strict government control of state officials' honesty and integrity; equal rights and justice for all people; fair distribution of public funds; and the abolishment or reduction of burdensome taxes and fees. In their explanatory letter in August to *al-Quds al-'Arabi* (see above), the fundamentalists stressed their interest in minimizing the economic monopoly of the royal family and other elite families; appointments to important posts through favoritism and nepotism; and the imposition of high, unnecessary taxes. In this respect, the fundamentalists expressed a clear antiroyal family drive and popular antielite feelings. In addition, they demanded that the kingdom's propaganda, foreign and military policies would aim to incorporate only Islamic principles and that it should avoid engaging in anti-Islamic alliances. This was in clear opposition to Riyadh's current policies. They also called for the development of the kingdom's missionary and religious institutions. Finally, they criticized Riyadh's borrowing of Western money as being illegal from the Islamic standpoint.[64]

In the following weeks, the fundamentalists reiterated their main ideological convictions, reflecting a clear antigovernment message, which, in many respects, contrasted with the modernists' views. They stressed that the government only professed to implement the Shari'a. Unlike the modernists, who wanted protection for women and for the media according to Western liberal rights (including the control of the moral police), the fundamentalists insisted that Islamic law and principles should dictate Saudi lifestyle, policies and institutions: namely, that a strict Wahhabi regime be established. While the modernists sought to limit the authorities' power, and secure protection and greater uninhibited freedom for society, including relatively free action for provincial councils and the proposed *majlis shura,* the fundamentalists wanted to restrict the authorities in making non-Islamic patrimonial appointments, taking commissions on business deals, and imposing what they regarded as arbitrary taxes. The fundamentalists also demanded that the royal princes would behave strictly according to the Shari'a, in order to prevent them from indulging in unworthy conduct. The modernists saw at least a partial model for the kingdom to follow in Western regimes, and did not criticize Riyadh's alliance with the West against Iraq. In Qusaybi's view, any other alliance, detached from the West and based on fundamentalist Islam, was considered rejectionist. As against this, the fundamentalists, although critical of Saddam's Iraq, objected to Saudi security and foreign policies. They regarded the presence of foreign troops on Saudi soil as a sin against Islam (even if restricted to certain regions); rejected Riyadh's proposal to abolish the Arab boycott against Israel; and, later, condemned Riyadh's support of the Arab-Israeli peace process (see below). They rather advocated a more traditional policy, supporting Palestinian rights and anti-Israel actions.[65]

The discourse concerning the kingdom's future character became more complex during the summer of 1991, when the fundamentalist camp showed signs of internal rift. Supreme 'Ulama, either descendants of the founder of the Wahhabi denomination, Muhammad Ibn 'Abd al-Wahhab, or of the other well-known urban families, had for centuries intermarried with the royal, Al Sa'ud family, enjoyed economic benefits, and constituted part of the elite. The Saudi leading scholar 'Abd al-'Aziz Ibn Baz was befriended by all contemporary Saudi kings. Hence, despite their own strict Wahhabi convictions and fundamentalist teachings (Ibn Baz stated in 1965 that the planet earth was flat), the supreme 'Ulama were also receptive to the government's pressures and respectful of the royal family's political superiority. On 3 June, after princes and security officers had visited some of the leading 'Ulama who had signed the April petition, some of these 'Ulama and others, who had not signed the petition, published what Western observers viewed as an open enforced apology. The official board of senior Islamic scholars and the higher judicial council (a body which, according to the April petition, had to be reformed) thus ruled that a Muslim's right to advise his government did not include pressuring the king with petitions, or publicizing these petitions in order to incite the public. The signatories of the June letter did not criticize the fundamendtalists' petition because of its contents, but rather because of the manner in which it had been delivered. Nevertheless, the leading 'Ulama no longer constituted part of the fundamentalist opposition.

In the ensuing weeks, attempts were made to reunify the ranks. The renewed petition of 1 August was supposed to explain why leading 'Ulama, including Ibn Baz, had signed the first petition. It was unlikely that the latter and his senior colleagues would have taken part in reformulating an opposition statement, published as it was in London, especially since the renewed petition hardly reflected their opinions. In November 1991, senior 'Ulama once more found common ground with other fundamentalists, when they jointly criticized the government's support of the Arab-Israeli peace process, notably the ensuing contacts between Saudi leaders (especially Bandar), and leaders of the American Jewish community.[66] However, there was no organizational or ideological cooperation between the two groups. The senior 'Ulama were elitist and apparently more friendly toward the royal family and less prepared to incite the public than other elements that had engaged in fundamentalist activities. As in earlier periods of crisis (i.e., in 1979–80, when Khomeyni-inspired antigovernment activities spread throughout the entire Gulf region), the established 'Ulama hesitated somewhat in moving against the fundamentalists' religious convictions, but politically supported the government. In fact, Ibn Baz tried to dissociate himself and his established colleagues from fundamentalist deeds. In late December, he published a religious ruling (fatwa), in which he referred to "those brothers who have detracted from the honor of the preachers...what we have written or said has corrupted the hearts of some youth, filled them with grudges and rancor...by gossip, by talk against this one and that one...[relating to accusations against royal family members] and a search for what they consider to be errors by others...."[67]

The active fundamentalists were thus another manifestation of a grass-root, provincial, nonconformist, uncontrolled form of Wahhabi creed, which, like the Ikhwan movement in the 1920s or the Juhayman al-'Utaybi group that tried to capture the grand mosque in Mecca in November 1979, had appeared on the Saudi public scene during ideological confusion. The 1991 fundamentalists gained their main strength in the Qasim (north-central) and 'Asir (southeastern) provinces rather than the kingdom's main urban centers. Their prominent ideologues were rising, but still nonprominent 'Ulama, such as A'id al-Qarni in Abha in the 'Asir Province, and Sulayman Ibn 'Awda in Burayda in the Qasim Province. According to opposition sources, only about 15% of the 'Ulama held extremist views and participated in fundamentalist activities; other participants included students, active and former servicemen, officials and others.[68] The moral police, which included many fundamentalists, personified their main power base and activity, controlling society's public behavior, punishing indecent dress or religious laxity. Moreover, to carry out antigovernment activities, the fundamentalists arranged mass rallies, openly called for changes in government policies, and distributed cassettes and leaflets, to incite the public.[69] These activities had an antiestablishment and antiroyal flavor.

The Government's Response

King Fahd and other leaders were surprised by the widespread ideological discussions concerning Saudi Arabia's future. In order to counter their public vehemence and destabilizing effect, Saudi leaders tried to play off the political camps against each other, thereby exploiting their mutual adversity. The modernist camp did not attempt to stir up the public, or enforce unwanted policies upon the government. The authorities' main priority was therefore to weaken the fundamentalists, who performed the most daring acts of opposition and who commanded the utmost ability to influence the public.

The government's first main initiative was to place a buffer between the senior 'Ulama and the other, more peripheral fundamentalists. As mentioned earlier, this had a considerable effect, since the fundamentalists could no more rely on the support of their senior peers.

In the face of fundamentalist demonstrations in 'Asir and Qasim, in the summer and fall, which were organized in response to Riyadh's pro-Western policies, the authorities cracked down on the demonstrators and moved to limit the teaching, free gatherings, and cassette distribution by 'Ulama such as al-Qarni, 'Awda and their followers. Students, university lecturers and officials who sympathized with the fundamentalists were put under surveillance.[70] In December, after the fundamentalists had branded members of the liberal women's movement as prostitutes, among them princesses and employees in higher education, the government was provoked to a more decisive response. Ibn Baz's earlier-mentioned *fatwa* was part of this response, followed by a speech by the emir, Turki, son of King Faysal, who openly challenged the fundamentalists to prove their allegations, or be held accountable for making them. Delivered by the chief of the Saudi intelligence services and an important emir, Turki's speech was a clear sign to the fundamentalists. A Saudi businessman assessed that the royal family thus informed the fundamentalists, "you have gone too far."[71]

The authorities achieved mixed results. Their efforts limited fundamentalist activities and questioned their legitimacy. The royal family could continue running the kingdom's foreign policy, administration and economy, regardless of the fundamentalists' demands. The government accommodated only two minor fundamentalist demands: taxes and fees on motor vehicles and other consumer goods were reduced; and liberal rights for women were uncompromisingly negated, despite the fact that Fahd was secretly helping the women of the November 1990 protest to obtain compensation for being dismissed from their jobs and to renew their passports.[72] The government thereby maintained a basic popular and orthodox image, which helped defy any contrasting criticism directed against it.

However, the authorities, fearing a sociopolitical backlash, did not completely ban or outlaw the fundamentalists' preachings and activities. In 1991, the latter definitely influenced the modes of thinking and behavior of Saudi society. An Arab envoy in Riyadh thus noted that the fundamentalists "are making a forceful effort to get to the front line of this [ideological] debate — making sure they are heard first, loudly and surely."[73]

FOREIGN AFFAIRS

THE SEARCH FOR A NEW GULF SECURITY ARRANGEMENT

The obvious conclusion that Riyadh drew from the Gulf War was that it should devise a new security arrangement in the Gulf, to prevent the possible recurrence of a threat, such as Iraq's invasion of Kuwait. Riyadh saw the need to discard the previous pillars of security and make new arrangements. These previous pillars were reliance on pan-Arab solidarity and good-neighborly relations with surrounding states, and the utilization of Western forces only as a last resort.[74] Riyadh wanted a stronger and more comprehensive military cooperation with the West, whose forces rescued the kingdom, and a more binding inter-Arab cooperation, after the earlier mode, denoted by the media as "pretense of fraternity and common fate," had disappointed the Saudis.[75]

The Damascus declaration of 6 March (based on a meeting which included the GCC states, Syria, Egypt and the US; see chapter on inter-Arab relations), should have provided a framework for fulfillment of the new principles. On the one hand, Egyptian and Syrian troops could remain in the GCC states in a defensive role, for as long as the GCC states so desired. By so doing, Saudi Arabia spared itself radical Arab criticism, since Arab-Muslim forces, rather than Westerners, would be its defenders. Moreover, by undertaking to increase economic cooperation among the participants, the Damascus declaration seemed to have provided for Saudi economic assistance to Egypt and Syria, to satisfy these states' needs. This, in turn, would enable the establishment of regional stability. As this declaration was supported by the US, it seemed to be a blueprint for a new comprehensive order to create security in the Gulf. However, Khalid Ibn Sultan's visit to Cairo on 13 March, for military talks with his Egyptian counterparts, revealed some of Riyadh's immediate reservations about the new scheme: a united Arab army consisting of the GCC states, Egypt and Syria, Sultan explained, "is realistic if it is related to joint training." An Arab force, merely to be deployed "in a certain region or state without reason or objective...is unrealistic and difficult to implement."[76] In the following weeks, it became evident that Saudi Arabia and the other GCC states were having difficulty in accommodating the deployment of the Egyptian and Syrian forces, the financial remuneration for their states, and long-term cooperation with an Arab radical state, as Syria was believed to be.[77]

In negotiations with US leaders, which also evolved at the same time, Saudi leaders initially supported the Damascus declaration security scheme. Secretary of State James Baker's visit to Saudi Arabia in March and his discussions about further major arms deals (see above), highlighted the assumption that the US would play a limited role in the defense of the kingdom, by being only the provider of strategic weapons. However, the visit of President Bush's national security adviser, Brent Scowcroft, in early April, had further implications. He discussed with Saudi leaders the pre-positioning of enough military equipment in Saudi Arabia to provide for a US division; increasing the frequency of joint exercises; and placing a US regional headquarters in Bahrain (which is connected by a causeway with Saudi Arabia). In later discussions, it also became evident that US forces would carry out frequent air, land and sea exercises combined with Arab Gulf forces. In addition, an integrated air defense system, relying mainly on US-made aircraft, radar and other equipment, would be established over the six GCC states. US experts would also carry out security surveys for Saudi Arabia and the other Gulf states.

Consequently, in late April, Saudi leaders were more ready to view the US military contingent in the Gulf as a main strategic defender whose role would be more important than that of the Arab forces. First and foremost, they were prompted by feelings of trust in the US and gratitude for its performance in the war. Moreover, in Saudi eyes, the weakening of Saddam's regime and the dependence of even Arab radical forces, such as Syria, on the US (in the aftermath of the collapse of the Soviet Union), considerably neutralized Syria's or the PLO's wrath and ability to harm the kingdom. Therefore, the Saudi leaders' confidence to host US forces and cooperate with them openly continued to develop.[78] In March, Sultan stressed: "The United States is a friendly country. It responded to the call of duty and contributed effectively."[79] Fahd also wholeheartedly reiterated his gratitude to the US and his expectation of further cooperation.[80]

In addition, Saudi leaders also hoped for substantial progress toward ending the Arab-Israeli conflict, not just for the sake of the peoples involved in the conflict (see also below), but also as a means to help stabilize the Arab world, restrain Palestinian and Syrian radicalism (which had threatened the kingdom in the past), and demonstrate the implementation of UN resolutions in regions other than the Gulf. In Riyadh's view, Washington was capable of influencing Israel to make concessions that would fuel the peace talks. Furthermore, the fact that Saddam was capable of using weapons of mass destruction (revealed by the UN during early summer 1991), further prompted Gulf leaders, including the Saudis, to rely heavily on direct US assistance, rather than on any other Arab defense. This was illustrated by the deployment of additional US-made *Patriot* antirocket missiles on Saudi soil.[81]

Due to a combination of all these reasons, Saudi leaders tended to minimize its strategic dependence on Syria and Egypt, and Riyadh ran into difficulties in its discussions with Cairo and Damascus. In early May, President Mubarak decided to pull out the 38,500 Egyptian troops from the Gulf.[82] Thus, despite continued Saudi economic and strategic cooperation with Egypt and Syria, the participation of these Arab states in the Gulf's defense was replaced by an alternative option.

During the rest of the year, only minimal progress was achieved over the pre-positioning of weapons for a US force. The question was not resolved during Secretary of Defense Richard Cheney's visits to Riyadh in May and July; the parties then disagreed over the quantities of weapons and who would pay for them, the Saudis objecting to the inclusion of these weapons in their $13.3bn. long-term arms request.[83] The Saudis then showed growing reluctance to settle these differences. This might have been because they were trying to be accommodating toward Iran's objection to the presence of foreign forces in the Gulf (see below) and, in any case, wanted to develop their own army before accommodating US forces. These considerations became evident in the following months.

There were reports that Saudi reservations toward assisting in a possible further US military strike against Iraq (accentuated by Iraq's resistance to permit UN inspectors to search and destroy Iraqi nuclear facilities) caused further tension between Riyadh and Washington. In September, Sultan clarified that such a strike should not look like a "Saudi-American operation"; that Kuwait should participate; and that the US should not dispatch more troops for this purpose. This caused tension in negotiations between the two states.[84] In addition, the Saudis decided to set new priorities: they wanted to enlarge their army to c. 200,000 troops, to compensate for the missing coalition forces. The Saudis also wanted an agreement to upgrade their armed forces prior to any pre-position conclusions.[85] The Americans, for their part, feared immediate massive arms sale deals that would entangle the US Administration in difficulties with Congress.[86] Despite such disagreements, however, it became evident that, during 1991, the US became Saudi Arabia's patron, and Riyadh's security designs became closely associated with those of Washington.

Saudi Arabia considered the improvement of its relations with Tehran as an additional component of the Gulf states' security. Iran's attitude toward Iraq during the war appealed to Saudi leaders and prompted them to start a dialogue with Iran (see chapters on Iran and on the Gulf War). At a meeting held in mid-March, between Foreign Minister Sa'ud al-Faysal and his Iranian counterpart 'Ali Akbar Velayati, they agreed to resume diplomatic relations (which the Saudis had broken off in 1988). For its part, Iran did not want to be excluded from a forthcoming security arrangement in the Gulf. Thus, in April, the Saudis welcomed Velayati's visit to Riyadh,[87] and Sa'ud al-Faysal visited Tehran in early May. Arab observers noted that, during this visit, Faysal met the Iranian-backed radical leader of Iraq's Shi'is, Muhammad Bakr al-Hakim and the two reached an agreement to overthrow Saddam's rule, maintain Iraq's territorial integrity, and establish a regime on Iraqi territory which would reflect all sectarian, political and ethnic trends.[88] Although there was no other information to corroborate this report, it appeared to be genuine, insomuch as Riyadh was indeed interested in toppling Saddam, but without decimating Iraq. Saudi-Iranian relations warmed further in June when, in marked contrast to the clashes between Iranian pilgrims and Saudi security forces in 1987, Velayati led a large group of 115,000 Iranian pilgrims to Mecca[89] on a peaceful pilgrimage (see also chapter on Iran).

Saudi leaders thus sought to utilize the improved connections with Iran to strengthen the anti-Saddam Gulf forces and to influence Tehran to stop Shi'i insurgency against Gulf states. However, they could not reach full agreement over other aspects of Saudi strategy, as Tehran opposed the presence of Arab and US forces in the Gulf. Consequently, in 1991, although Saudi-Iranian relations did not become a new strategic partnership across the Gulf, they certainly helped ease Saudi security problems. Crown Prince 'Abdallah met Iranian President Rafsanjani during the Islamic conference held in Dakkar in December and reported that they had had a successful meeting.[90]

During this period, Saudi Arabia maintained close contacts with the other GCC states. Not only was the Kuwaiti royal family hosted in Saudi Arabia during the war, but Fahd was among the first to congratulate the Kuwaiti ruler, Jabir al-Ahmad Al Sabah on his country's liberation, and visited Kuwait in June. Saudi leaders also contributed their good offices to mediate a border dispute over the Hawr peninsula and two small adjacent islands, between Qatar and Bahrain. Riyadh's intervention prevented a major deterioration in relations between Qatar and Bahrain, but failed to produce a solution to the problem, which continued to plague inter-GCC relations (see chapters on inter-Arab relations, Qatar and Bahrain).[91] Riyadh itself had its own disagreements with other GCC states, notably Kuwait and Bahrain, over strategic issues. Since these states were smaller in size and more vulnerable than Saudi Arabia, they were quicker than the kingdom to disregard Arab and Iranian viewpoints and engage in military defense cooperation with the US (see chapters on Kuwait and Bahrain). The Saudis were influenced by the smaller states' initiative, but did not conclude a comprehensive defense pact with Washington.

ATTITUDE TOWARD OTHER REGIONAL ISSUES
Arab-Israeli Settlement
The Saudis were interested in settling, or at least easing the tensions of the Arab-Israeli conflict. In Riyadh's view, the war proved that Israel could cooperate with Arabs for the benefit of the latter's interests, and hence, that a settlement with Israel was within reach. It also proved that a settlement, or a lull in the Arab-Israeli conflict, could help stabilize other Middle East arenas, including the Gulf. Saudi leaders also believed that the postwar atmosphere of goodwill and, particularly, the strong US position in the entire region, could provide an effective impetus for peace negotiations. However, they did not envisage a leading role for Riyadh in this process: they supported US initiatives for peace and helped behind the scenes to coordinate the standpoints of Syria and Egypt — Riyadh's partners in the Damascus declaration.[92]

Saudi Arabia's tactics varied: its initiatives were sometimes covert and diplomatic, and at other times overt and declarative. In April, while Scowcroft was visiting Riyadh, Saudi businessmen in the US suggested investing in economic projects in the Gaza Strip, as a means to advance Palestinian-Israeli cooperation.[93] However, Riyadh's main role was to accompany the US in their initiatives. In April, Riyadh informed Baker that it would send an observer to participate in the Madrid peace conference on behalf of the entire GCC states. This decision disappointed Israel and other Western observers who had hoped for a more forthright Saudi approach (influenced by rumors of visits by Saudi personalities to Israel). However, Riyadh could thus perform its traditional inter-Arab mediating activities, using financial and diplomatic pressures and incentives.[94]

During the summer, Saudi papers occasionally published anti-Semitic articles, depicting the Jews as usurpers who contaminated Islamic holy places.[95] Although these articles demonstrated Saudi identification with Israel's Arab negotiators, King Fahd nevertheless put forward a new suggestion to encourage peace: in July, he told Baker that, if Israel suspended settlement activity, Riyadh would act to cancel the Arab economic boycott against Israel.[96] This was a Saudi attempt to encourage Arab negotiating parties to adopt confidence-building measures vis-à-vis Israel. The Israeli Government rejected the suggestion (see chapter on the ME peace process).

Saudi leaders welcomed the Madrid conference as a means to achieve peace and stability. After a formal cabinet meeting, their wholehearted blessings were published by the Saudi official press agency.[97] The participation of Ambassador Bandar as an observer in Madrid, indicated that Saudi Arabia regarded the conference seriously; the ambassador actually helped to soften Syria's position toward Israel during the meetings. Riyadh especially tried to convey the public relations message, which was so significant in an international conference, that, as opposed to the Israelis, the Arabs were interested in making progress toward peace. Saudi newspapers therefore regretted Israel's "irrational approach" at the conference.[98]

On 18 November, the Saudis carried out a spectacular feat in the encouragement of peace, when Bandar met openly with American-Jewish leaders in New York. Bandar gave the impression that, by negotiating with Jews, the Saudis were ready to break a taboo and were therefore committed to the peace process. By stressing that Israel's right to exist was now unquestioned, and that the Arabs would stop objecting to new immigration to Israel if further settlement activity would cease, he evinced goodwill and interest in peace. His emphasis that he was expressing King Fahd's views gave his words political credibility, and lent encouragement to the future of the peace process.[99]

Relations with Egypt and Syria

Saudi Arabia maintained good relations with its non-Gulf Arab coalition partners. Despite Riyadh's reluctance to establish its strategy for Gulf security by relying on the presence of Egyptian and Syrian forces in the Gulf, it shared two common interests with Cairo and Damascus. The first was support for a broadly based peace process in the ME, led by the current US initiative, and the second was regional economic development, with Saudi Arabia playing the role of financier of economic aid development projects in Egypt and Syria. It could be argued that Riyadh used its economic capacity as a lever to urge other Arab states, notably Syria, to maintain and even strengthen their interest in peace and stability in the ME. Moreover, as radical Arab parties' reliance on the Soviet Union was eliminated during the course of 1991, Saudi Arabia's economic assistance remained their almost exclusive source of aid, thereby augmenting Riyadh's influence on their policies (see chapter on inter-Arab relations).

Saudi leaders viewed Egypt as a state with which they shared common views and with which they could cooperate. Fahd and Mubarak continued communicating with each other by telephone, Sa'ud al-Faysal visited Cairo in mid-May and the Egyptian minister of defense, Lt. Gen. Muhammad Husayn Tantawi, reciprocated in June. Despite the disagreements between the two states about Egypt's future role in the Gulf which then became evident, Emir Sultan denied having any "different views" from Egypt.[100] Mubarak's visits to the kingdom in early September and, again, one month later, indicated continuous Saudi cooperation with Egypt. Fahd and Mubarak coordinated their views on most regional issues.

Riyadh offered various economic compensations to Egypt for its cooperation with the anti-Iraqi coalition and for its exclusion from an overt and established role in Gulf security. By the end of April 1991, the number of Egyptian workers in Saudi Arabia had reached 1.25m., constituting c. 50% of the foreign workers in the country (double the prewar number). Their arrival was welcomed by the Saudi authorities and businessmen.[101] In addition to these workers' remittances, there was an increase in

Egyptian-Saudi commerce across the Red Sea and a first meeting of the two states' commercial lodges in mid-June.[102] Riyadh also extended its aid in corn from 800,000 to 1m. tons.[103]

Saudi Arabia's cooperation with Syria was not as straightforward as with Egypt, and was only achieved after exerting pressure and attempts to persuade Syria to participate in the ME peace process; thereafter, coordination between President Asad and King Fahd became frequent. Saudi-Syrian relations were still based on Riyadh's playing the role of stimulator and energizer of Syria's participation in the process, along with Secretary Baker's initiatives. The Saudis undertook to aid Syria, by helping to finance the development of a huge gas field near Palmyra in Syria,[104] and by attracting Arab investments into that country.[105]

Relations with the Former Pro-Iraqi Parties

The Saudi leaders' attitude toward Iraq was still based on their perceptions, which were typical of the last stages of the war: they opposed Iraq's disintegration, but sought to topple Saddam's regime, and directed their efforts toward this aim. After the war, Fahd expressed the hope that Saddam would meet an "ominous end,"[106] which reflected the Saudi attitude. Under Saddam, Iraq was perceived as subjugated and unworthy of a true cease-fire.[107] In the meantime, while the Saudi press condemned Saddam's action against the Kurds, there were reports that the Saudi authorities were cultivating both Kurds and Saddam's former aides, now turned enemies.[108] The Saudis also agreed to absorb Shi'i refugees from southern Iraq.[109] Furthermore, in August, Saudi Arabia accused Iraq of holding five to six Saudi POWs, and ignoring calls to exchange them.[110] Relations did not improve during 1991 (see also chapter on Iraq).

Saudi policy toward Yemen remained hostile. Riyadh continued to suspect the Yemeni leaders' policy of inter-Arab neutrality as tantamount to supporting Iraq, and feared the possibility of Yemeni nationals' sabotage activities within the kingdom. Consequently, Saudi leaders did not renew economic aid to San'a or entrance visas to the hundreds of thousands of Yemenis who sought employment in the kingdom[111] (see also chapter on Yemen).

Saudi leaders and its media were also critical of Jordan, stressing that the "we had no choice" explanations for Jordan's pro-Iraqi position during the war and promises "to turn over a new leaf" in its aftermath were not good enough.[112] Riyadh was persuaded to normalize its relations with Jordan somewhat, probably because of Jordan's significant position in the ensuing peace process and Amman's renewed cooperation with the US in this respect. In March, normal travel was reported at Jordanian-Saudi border crossings.[113] In April, Saudi airspace was reopened to Jordan.[114] In May, an agreement concerning Jordanian participation in the pilgrimage was signed,[115] and in September, Riyadh lifted a ban on granting transit visas to Jordanians willing to return to their jobs in the Gulf states and Yemen.[116] In return, Jordan was reported to have surrendered to Saudi Arabia a Saudi religious opposition figure, Muhammad al-Fasi, who had been living in Jordan.[117]

Riyadh kept wavering between its support for the Palestinian cause and its exasperation with the PLO for its pro-Iraqi stand. In March, a leader of the daily 'Ukaz even called for Yasir 'Arafat's dismissal from his leading Palestinian position, as a punishment for the damage he had caused his own people.[118] His resignation was deemed expedient in order to advance the Palestinian issue in the peace process.[119] Israeli reports even indicated that Riyadh started cultivating 'Arafat's more radical Palestinian rivals (including Abu Nidal), as a way of weakening his position.[120]

In order to ease the tension, a high-ranking PLO official, Hani al-Hasan, visited Riyadh in April; and in June, the Palestinian envoy to Riyadh, Subhi 'Ali Abu Kharsh, praised the kingdom and Fahd for supporting the Palestinian cause.[121] Saudi Arabia eventually partially resumed its assistance to the PLO, probably because of such a pleading attitude, and in the wake of Palestinian consent to participate in the peace process. In September, only $9m. collected from Palestinians employed in the kingdom (who contributed 5% of their salaries to the PLO) was delivered. Toward the end of 1991, reports of a possible détente between Saudi Arabia and the PLO appeared to be an issue that would continue to occupy Riyadh during the following year.[122]

RELATIONS WITH OTHER PARTIES

The United States

The Saudi-US strategic cooperation influenced other, bilateral issues. Thus, the Saudi authorities were anxious to complete a $21bn. arms deal; only $7.3bn. had been approved by the US Congress in October 1990. In January, the $13.7bn. package (including fighter jets, and helicopters, tanks and other items; see also above) was indefinitely postponed. US reluctance resulted both from the pro-Israel lobby's objection to selling sophisticated weapons to Riyadh, which might be used against Israel, and from Pentagon sources' objection to selling arms "that will take years to deliver," when both "the threat and the enemy might be completely different."[123] However, the Saudis wanted the new weapons as a means of defense against any (even if currently invisible) potential enemy, and in order to upgrade their own army. Their dependence on the US during the war motivated them to use sophisticated propaganda tactics (to paraphrase Bandar's words, typical of the pro-Israeli lobby),[124] to struggle patiently and continuously to clinch the deal.

In order to avoid difficulties with Congress, the US Administration decided to split up the above-mentioned major arms deal into considerably smaller deals, which Congress would be less reluctant to approve. In July, the Administration notified Congress of a delivery of bombs worth $365m., which was again criticized, but not rejected by Congress.[125] This fell short of Saudi hopes, but it was not reported that Riyadh objected to the US Administration's tactics.

Saudi-US bilateral cooperation was also demonstrated at the UN, when, on 17 September, with the help of the US, Saudi Arabia's UN representative, Samir Shihabi, was elected president of the 46th General Assembly.[126]

During a meeting of the US treasury secretary and Saudi Minister of Finance Muhammad Aba al-Khayl, in April in Jidda, the parties discussed the Saudi commitment to pay the $US 13.5bn. for operation "Desert Storm," an issue that did not cause difficulties in the relations between the two states.[127]

Saudi media, which usually served a pro-Arab line, often actively criticized the US for supporting Israel and demanded Washington's firmness in dealing with it.[128] However, in contrast with previous years, it also publicized Saudi support for the US-led peace process and welcomed it. The achievement of regional peace, thanks to US efforts, became an official Saudi propaganda issue.[129]

The Soviet Union

The resumption of full Saudi-Soviet diplomatic relations, announced on 17 September 1990, stimulated the Saudis to embark on an actual improvement of relations with Moscow. Riyadh wanted to encourage Gorbachev's policy of winding down Moscow's subversive policies in the ME, which at present were deemed in Riyadh as friendly and useful.[130] Moreover, during the war, Moscow's views as expressed by its chargé d'affaires in Riyadh, that "Saddam's obstinacy...is regrettable and [he] will be responsible for what happens in this war,"[131] was well received in Riyadh. Saudi leaders were less pleased with Soviet attempts to save Saddam's polity.[132] The speedy and successful termination of the war allayed Saudi suspicion toward Moscow, and Fahd even sent Gorbachev a message praising the Soviet stance in the war.[133] In May, Foreign Minister Sa'ud al-Faysal visited Moscow. The visit focused mainly on economic and technical cooperation. In the following weeks, the Saudis initiated several projects, notably a bank in Uzbekistan. However, because of the political changes there, they were slow to implement investment.[134]

The collapse of the Soviet Union prompted Riyadh to try to prevent demoralization among the Soviet-Muslim peoples, and Iran's interference there. Saudi leaders were interested in maintaining the stability of the status quo, or to emerge as an ally to the Soviet Muslims. Following a short visit by Bandar to the former Soviet Muslim republics in September, Riyadh decided to contribute $1bn. of humanitarian aid (in addition to an earlier $1.5bn. worth of aid) and to send Islamic preachers into the Muslim republics.[135] This was an innovation that opened up a new avenue for Saudi policy in the following year.

Britain and France

The Saudi authorities maintained close contacts with these two coalition members. British and French leaders, notably prime ministers John Major and Michel Rocard, visited Riyadh during and after the Gulf War and met Fahd and other Saudi leaders. However, the nature of Saudi cooperation with these two states indicated that they were of secondary importance to the kingdom, and less significant than the US. Thus, Britain's main involvement in the Saudi security buildup was preliminary bids by British contractors to participate in the building of a large military complex located in the empty quarter, c. 500km. south of Riyadh.[136]

NOTES

For the place and frequency of publications cited here, and for the full name of the publication, news agency, radio station or monitoring service where an abbreviation is used, please see "List of Sources." Only in the case of more than one publication bearing the same name is the place of publication noted here.

1. *NYT*, 9 January; R. Riyadh, 22 January — DR, 22 January; SPA, 26 January — DR, 28 January; *IHT*, 1 March 1991.
2. R. Riyadh, 19 January — DR, 23 January 1991.
3. *NYT*, 9 January 1991.
4. Ibid.
5. *NYT*, 11 January 1991.
6. *JP*, 28 January 1991.
7. *IHT*, 5 January; *NYT*, 7 February 1991.

8. SPA, 2 February — DR, 4 February 1991.
9. SPA, 9 February — DR, 11 February 1991.
10. *IHT,* 20 February 1991.
11. Cf. *NYT,* 11 February 1991.
12. SPA, 19 February — DR, 19 February 1991.
13. *CR,* Saudi Arabia, No. 1, 1991, p. 7.
14. Op. cit., p. 7; *WSJ,* 16 March 1991.
15. *NYT,* 9 January; *CR,* Saudi Arabia, No. 1, 1991, p. 7.
16. SPA, 6 February — DR, 6 February 1991.
17. *JP,* 6 December 1990; *al-Akhbar,* 7 March 1991. .
18. R. Riyadh, 15 February — DR, 19 February 1991.
19. *NYT,* 27 February 1991.
20. Cf. *al-Ra'y* (Amman), 28 January 1991.
21. *FT,* 2 February; *IHT,* 6 February 1991.
22. See R. Riyadh, 5 February — DR, 6 February 1991.
23. *CR,* Saudi Arabia, No. 1, 1991, p. 7.
24. R. Riyadh, 1 March — DR, 4 March 1991.
25. *CR,* Saudi Arabia, 1991, No. 1, p. 11; *JP,* 1 January; Riyadh TV, 15 April — DR, 16 April 1991.
26. *CR,* Saudi.Arabia, No. 1, 1991, pp. 11–12.
27. *NYT,* 13 February 1991.
28. *FT,* 7 February; SPA, 10 February; *LAT,* 13 February 1991.
29. *NYT,* 14 January 1991.
30. *NYT,* 29, 30 January 1991.
31. SPA, *NYT,* 2 February; *CR,* Saudi Arabia, No. 1, 1991, p. 9.
32. *NYT,* 17 February 1991.
33. *CR,* Saudi Arabia, No. 1, 1991, pp. 11–12.
34. *IHT,* 28 January; *NYT,* 1 February 1991.
35. Riyadh TV, 15 April — DR, 16 April 1991.
36. R. Algiers, 13 February — DR, 19 February 1991.
37. *CR,* Saudi Arabia, No. 1, 1991, p. 12; *NYT,* 16 January; *FT,* 23 January 1991.
38. *FT,* 28 January; SPA, 12 February — DR, 14 February 1991.
39. SPA, 17 February — DR, 22 February; *NYT,* 17 February; *FT,* 14 May 1991.
40. *NYT, FT,* 2 February 1991.
41. *NYT,* 17 February 1991.
42. M. Heller and N. Safran, *The New Middle Class and Regime Stability in Saudi Arabia,* Harvard Middle East Papers, No. 3 (Cambridge, MA: Harvard University, 1985).
43. *CR,* Saudi Arabia, No. 1, 1991, p. 8.
44. *CR,* Saudi Arabia, No. 3, 1991, p. 14.
45. Ibid.; *ME,* 25 December 1991.
46. Fahd's interview, MBC TV, 14 November — DR, 19 November 1991.
47. *CR,* Saudi Arabia, No. 2, 1991, p. 16; No. 3, 1991, pp. 18–20; No. 4, 1991, pp. 20–21.
48. *CR,* Saudi Arabia, No. 3, 1991, p. 14.
49. *MEED,* 24 May 1991.
50. *ME,* 25 December 1991.
51. *CR,* Saudi Arabia, No. 4, p. 9; *NYT,* 3 August 1991.
52. Na'if's interview, SPA, 15 June — DR, 17 June; *al-Bilad,* 15 June 1991.
53. AFP, 15 April; R. Riyadh, 29 June; *CR,* Saudi Arabia, No. 2, 1991, p. 10.
54. R. Riyadh, 29 June 1991.
55. *CR,* Saudi Arabia, No. 2, 1991, pp. 10–12; No. 4, 1991, pp. 11–13.
56. *CR,* Saudi Arabia, No. 4, p. 12; *NYT,* 3 August; *Misr al-Fatat,* 7 October — DR, 10 October 1991.
57. *CR,* Saudi Arabia, No. 2, p. 10; No. 3, p. 7; *al-Quds al-'Arabi,* 1 August — DR, 22 August 1991.
58. *CR,* Saudi Arabia, No. 3, 1991, p. 10.
59. *Al-Hawadith,* 21 June; *al-Khalij* (Abu Dhabi), 4 November 1991.
60. *Al-Duwaliyya,* 27 November 1990.

61. *CR,* Saudi Arabia, No. 2, 1991, p. 10.
62. Ghazi al-Qusaybi, *Hatta la takun fitna* (n.p., 1991)
63. *JP,* 31 July; *NYT,* 15 November 1991.
64. *Al-Quds al-'Arabi,* 1 August — DR, 22 August 1991.
65. *Al-Jazira al-'Arabiyya,* August 1991.
66. *CR,* Saudi Arabia, No. 3, 1991, p. 7; *al-Jazira al-'Arabiyya,* December 1991.
67. Riyadh TV, 27 December — DR, 31 December 1991.
68. Al-Qusaybi, op. cit.; *al-Jazira al-'Arabiyya,* July, August 1991.
69. *MEI,* 14 June; *al-Jazira al-'Arabiyya,* July, August 1991.
70. *Al-Jazira al-'Arabiyya,* August 1991.
71. *NYT,* 31 December 1991.
72. Cf. *NYT,* 11 November; *JP,* 23 December 1991.
73. *NYT,* 11, 13 November 1991.
74. On the crystallization of this strategy, see, N. Safran, *Saudi Arabia, Ceaseless Quest for Security* (Cambridge, MA: Harvard University Press and Belknap, 1985).
75. *Al-Sharq al-Awsat,* 4 March 1991.
76. MENA, 14 March — DR, 18 March 1991; *CR,* Saudi Arabia, No. 1, p. 8.
77. *IHT,* 9, 10 March; and see the analysis in *Ha'aretz,* 10 September 1991.
78. *NYT,* 2 April; *WP,* 21 April 1991.
79. SPA, 12 March — DR, 13 March 1991.
80. R. Riyadh, 21 April — DR, 22 April 1991.
81. *CR,* Saudi Arabia, No. 3, 1991, p. 11.
82. *IHT,* 9 May 1991.
83. *JP,* 6 August 1991.
84. *Ha'aretz,* 29 September 1991.
85. *Ha'aretz,* 14 October; *IHT,* 26 October; *NYT,* 13 December 1991.
86. *NYT,* 18 March; *FT,* 19 March 1991.
87. *FT,* 26 April 1991.
88. R. Monte Carlo, 13 May — DR, 16 May 1991.
89. R. Riyadh, 23 June — DR, 24 June 1991.
90. *'Ukaz,* 10 December 1991.
91. *Al-Hayat* (London), 29 July 1991.
92. *Ha'aretz,* 22, 27 March (articles by Jacob Goldberg and Mordechai Abir, respectively); *'Ukaz,* 9 April; *WP,* 24 April 1991.
93. *Ha'aretz,* 3 April 1991.
94. Cf. letter of 50 Senators to Fahd, *Ha'aretz,* 26 April 1991.
95. *Al-Madina,* 5, 6 July 1991.
96. SPA, 20 July — DR, 22 July; *Ha'aretz,* 21 July 1991.
97. SPA, 21 October — DR, 24 October 1991.
98. *'Ukaz,* 3 November; *al-Madina,* 3 November 1991.
99. *JP,* 19, 22 November 1991.
100. SPA, 11 June — DR, 12 June 1991.
101. *Al-Wafd,* 16 May 1991.
102. *Al-Wafd,* 12 June 1991.
103. *Al-Haqiqa,* 6 July 1991.
104. *MEED,* 23 August 1991.
105. *'Ukaz,* 31 August 1991.
106. *IHT,* 7 March; see also *'Ukaz,* 16 March 1991.
107. *Al-Jazira,* 17 March 1991.
108. *WSJ,* 10 April 1991.
109. *NYT,* 25 April 1991.
110. SPA, 14 August — DR, 15 August 1991.
111. *Al-Shira',* 18 November 1991.
112. See Qusaybi's article, *al-Sharq al-Awsat,* 3 March 1991.
113. *Al-Dustur* (Amman), 6 March 1991.
114. *Al-Ra'y* (Amman), 5 April 1991.
115. R. Amman, 6 May — DR, 7 May 1991.

116. R. Monte Carlo, 4 September — DR, 5 September 1991.
117. *Ha'aretz,* 13 October 1991 (quoting *DT*).
118. *'Ukaz,* 6 March 1991.
119. *Al-Majalla,* 20 March 1991.
120. *JP,* 8 March; *Ha'aretz,* 9 August 1991.
121. SPA, 17 June — DR, 19 June 1991.
122. *Al-Dustur* (Amman), 11 November 1991.
123. *NYT,* 5 January 1991.
124. *Ha'aretz,* 27 February 1991.
125. *Ha'aretz,* 1 August; *JP,* 4 August 1991.
126. *NYT,* 18 September 1991.
127. *JP,* 17 April; SPA, 20 April — DR, 23 April 1991.
128. *'Ukaz,* 8 June 1991.
129. Sa'ud al-Faysal's interview, SPA, 21 July — DR, 22 July 1991.
130. *FT,* 5 January 1991.
131. *Al-Sharq al-Awsat,* 15 February 1991.
132. Cf., *al-Sharq al-Awsat,* 26 February; *al-Madina,* 22 February 1991.
133. R. Riyadh, 10 March — DR, 11 March 1991.
134. SPA, 14 May — DR, 15 May; *'Ukaz,* 27 August 1991.
135. *NYT,* 9 October 1991.
136. *FT,* 7 June 1991.

Sudan
(Jumhuriyyat al-Sudan)

YEHUDIT RONEN

In 1991, the regime of the National Islamic Front (NIF) marked its second year in power under the leadership of 'Umar Hasan Ahmad al-Bashir. This was a major, and perhaps even somewhat surprising, achievement, considering the regime's relatively narrow political base and its failure to solve, or even relieve, any of the country's main problems.

Stumbling from crisis to crisis, the NIF leadership "buried its head in the sand," lifting it for only one double goal — turning Sudan into a fully Islamic state, and simultaneously tightening its grip on power. There were three noticeable signs of the process toward achieving this goal, namely the implementation of the Shari'a (Islamic law); the support of Islamic fundamentalist groups abroad; and the widespread dismissal of non-NIF civil servants in the state machinery's political, economic and military positions and their replacement with NIF loyalists.

However, the regime paid a high price for adhering to its priorities, when it had to face growing political and socioeconomic restiveness throughout the country. The NIF leadership's hope to to reverse the trend in Sudanese politics and break the dominance of the traditional politico-religious parties, failed dismally and these parties remained active in opposition, assuming a low profile under the tough security. Backed by the military opposition group, code-named *Ana al-Sudan* (I am the Sudan), they launched a series of subversive activities. However, all of them were suppressed. Famine and the refugee problem peaked in 1991, but such human suffering did not shake the regime's priorities. Bashir's consistent denial that famine existed and his simultaneous imposition of Shari'a law in many ways recalled the Numayri regime's last years in power. The political impasse in the armed conflict between Khartoum and the southern Sudanese People's Liberation Army (SPLA) was also reminiscent of Numayri's "swan song" period. Not only was no progress made toward peace talks, but Bashir also failed to capitalize militarily from the SPLA's dramatically worsening position.

The regime's foreign relations, shaped basically by its urgent need for economic and military aid to secure its survival, were increasingly colored with ardent Arab Islamic zeal. Khartoum virtually doomed its relations with the pro-American Arab countries, from where a great deal of its financial assistance was coming. This came about as a result of Sudan reinforcing its political reliance upon, and ideological and emotional identification with what it regarded as the three pillars of Arab and Islamic power and anti-American sentiments, namely Tripoli, Baghdad and Tehran. Furthermore, Khartoum's growing Islamic radicalism, to the extent of supporting Islamic fundamentalist elements abroad, only served to further damage its already poor

642

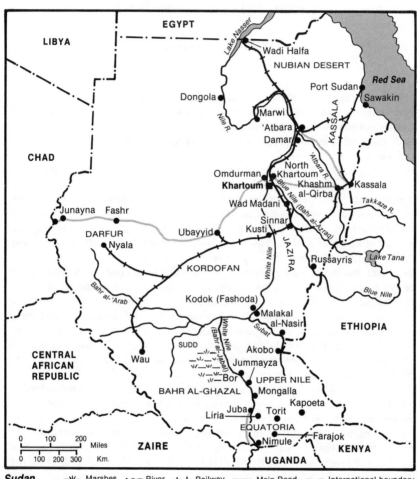

EGYPT

LIBYA

Lake Nasser

Wadi Halfa

NUBIAN DESERT

Red Sea

Port Sudan

Sawakin

Dongola

Nile R.

Marwi

KASSALA

'Atbara

Damar

CHAD

'Atbara R.

North
Khartoum

Omdurman

Khartoum

Khashm
al-Qirba

Kassala

Blue Nile (Bahr al-Azraq)

Wad Madani

Takkaze R.

Junayna

Fashr

Sinnar

DARFUR

Ubayyid

Kusti

Nyala

JAZIRA

White Nile

KORDOFAN

Russayris

Lake Tana

Bahr al-'Arab

Blue Nile

Kodok (Fashoda)

Malakal

al-Nasir

ETHIOPIA

Subat

White Nile (Bahr al-Jabal)

Akobo

SUDD

Wau

Jummayza

CENTRAL
AFRICAN
REPUBLIC

Bor

UPPER NILE

BAHR AL-GHAZAL

Mongalla

Kapoeta

Liria

Juba

Torit

EQUATORIA

Farajok

0   100   200   Miles

Nimule

0   100   200   300   Km.

ZAIRE

KENYA

UGANDA

Sudan   –ᴸ⁄– Marshes   ⌒⌒ River   ┼┼ Railway   —— Main Road   –·— International boundary relations in the Arab arena. Most severe was the harm caused to Sudan's relations with Egypt and Tunisia.

Even relations with Libya, the main lifeline of the Bashir regime, were tainted with suspicion, since Qadhdhafi feared that the Sudanese fundamentalists' influence would penetrate into Libya. The shadow this cast on bilateral ties further strengthened Tripoli's awareness that Sudan was a poor political and strategic-military asset.

Sudan strongly supported Iraq in the Gulf crisis, thereby dooming its relations with Kuwait. Khartoum's pro-Iraqi and anti-Kuwaiti stand remained unchanged during the whole year. Khartoum's staunch and vociferous support of the Palestinian cause was in keeping with the regime's pan-Arab and pan-Islamic ideology. The regime rejected the existence of the Jewish state and denounced what it called American imperialism of which, it maintained, Israel was a by-product.

Khartoum's interest in the surrounding Black African countries was minimal and limited to its neighbors only. Khartoum concentrated its main diplomatic energies on this front in establishing good ties with the new leadership in Addis Ababa.

INTERNAL AFFAIRS

FURTHER MOMENTUM IN THE ISLAMIZATION PROCESS

The Implementation of the Shari'a

Perhaps the most powerful driving force motivating the NIF regime was the desire to turn Sudan into a fully Islamic state. Thus, Bashir's announcement, on New Year's Eve of 1991, that the Shari'a, or Holy Law, was to be implemented throughout the country, excluding the south, came as no real surprise. In the southern region, Bashir stated, the legal system would remain unchanged "in the meantime." However, Bashir did not elaborate on this definition of time, nor did he clarify whether the Shari'a would apply to the millions of non-Muslims living in the north. He emphasized that the implementation process would be carried out promptly, without inconvenience or delay, "in compliance with Allah's clear ordinance and in compliance with the popular will."[1] The announcement was greeted in Khartoum by masses of people enthusiastically taking to the streets, probably NIF zealots. This reflected the fundamentalists' euphoria stirred by the implementation eventually, of Islamic law for which they had long aspired. It should be recalled that Shari'a law had already been imposed eight years previously by the former president, Ja'far al-Numayri. But after the overthrow of his regime in 1985, Shari'a law had been suspended and virtually shelved, despite the NIF's persistent demand that it should be reimplemented. Though not in force during a period of almost six years, since Numayri's overthrow, the Shari'a issue had been a source of a political-religious controversy. The southern SPLA's major demand to repeal the Shari'a law formally, as a prerequisite to any negotiation with Khartoum, was one of the most important manifestations of this political-religious controversy.

During the first few months of 1991, the state-controlled media played an intensive role in projecting the impression that the country was entering a new, promising phase, depicting the people being swept up by a powerful Islamic wind. In the spirit typical of the media, one of the official dailies stated that Sudan had been turned into a *dawla 'uzma* (a great state), having become closer to Allah.[2] Intensive gestures of *mubaya'at* (oath-of-allegiance ceremonies) for *qa'id al-umma* (leader of the [Islamic] nation) swept the country. Not only did they strengthen the impression of a growing Islamic tide, coming from the grass-roots layers, but, even more important to the country's leadership, the Revolutionary Command Council for National Salvation (RCCNS), they projected the impression that the NIF had broadened its relatively narrow political base.

On 22 March, the new penal code, based on the Shari'a, came into force in all six northern provinces.[3] It replaced the criminal code introduced in 1983, which was now formally abolished. The Sudanese leadership was keen to make sure that the new Shari'a law had no relation to the law implemented by Numayri.[4] (For Numayri's process of applying the Shari'a law, including the punitive system, see *MECS* 1983–84, pp. 639–44.)

In the spring, the government raised the sum of $440m. for a special fund to further enhance Islamic spirit and standards throughout the country. As officially stated, the fund was earmarked for stamping out corruption, the setting up and running of religious schools, and generally improving living standards.[5] In April, the fund announced the distribution of £S200m. to "poor people."[6] This fund had a very significant political value, although its socioeconomic aspect should, by no means, be underestimated. Through the fund's money, the NIF regime could attract the support of various circles of Sudanese society that hitherto had not identified themselves with the NIF and thereby broaden its political base. Hitherto, the NIF had drawn its political backing mainly from petty traders in the urban areas in general, and the capital in particular, as well as from student circles. As the 1986 elections to Sudan's first democratically chosen Constituent Assembly indicated, the NIF emerged as the country's third political force; the Umma Party (UP) and the Democratic Unionist Party (DUP) were significantly more powerful (see *MECS* 1986, pp. 576–78). The NIF regime was duly aware of the major importance of gaining support in the UP's and DUP's potential constituencies. The regime could not ensure its hold on power by military force while relying solely on a relatively narrow base. This threatened its continued existence. The formation of the above fund and distribution of resources came in part to address that need for broader popular support.

The Alleged Exporting of the Islamic Revolution
During 1991, an increasing number of reports indicated that the NIF regime was involved in supporting Islamic fundamentalists abroad, mainly in the Maghriben arena. Sudanese and foreign opposition sources accused the government of providing Islamic, militant, non-Sudanese leaders with diplomatic passports. One example was the case of Rashid Ghannushi, leader of the Tunisian Islamist Nahda (revival) movement, who was said to have traveled on a Sudanese diplomatic passport while in exile. 'Abbas al-Madani, the chief ideologist and a central leader in the Algerian opposition Front Islamique du Salut was reportedly also provided with a Sudanese diplomatic passport.[7] The Tunisian authorities officially protested to Khartoum, drawing the Sudanese reaction that "there is no homeland for the Muslims."[8]

The Sudanese regime was also allegedly involved in subversive activities, aimed at overthrowing the Tunisian and Algerian regimes and helping the fundamentalists to seize power.[9] Ideologically, these activities were completely in line with the aspirations of the NIF regime. Politically, however, public reports of such subversive acts, whether or not they took place, was detrimental to Khartoum's already poor foreign relations. The US, Egypt, Saudi Arabia, Tunisia and Libya were duly alarmed by what seemed to be an aggressive outburst of Islamic radicalism under their noses, so to speak. The Egyptian and Tunisian authorities even went so far as to translate their concern into threatening to take diplomatic punitive measures (see below). However, Khartoum denied any intervention in "other countries' internal affairs."[10]

CHANGES IN THE CABINET, THE RCCNS AND THE ARMY COMMAND

On 20 January, Bashir once again made cabinet changes. The cabinet had already been reshuffled twice since its formation in summer 1989 (see *MECS* 1990, pp. 636–37). The changes, comprehensive in scope and essence, introduced eight new faces into the government, all outstanding NIF figures. One of the noteworthy new appointments was that of Salah al-Din Muhammad Karar, an RCCNS member and a well-known NIF loyalist. He brought the number of RCCNS members in ministerial posts to four, two of them holding the key portfolios of defense and the interior. Along with his new position in the cabinet, Karar continued to function as head of the RCCNS's economic committee, a position of powerful political influence. 'Ali al-Hajj Muhammad, another NIF zealot and close confidant of the NIF veteran leader, Hasan 'Abdallah al-Turabi, was appointed adviser to Karar's committee, thereby reinforcing the NIF's control over the country's economic pulse. Among the changes in the cabinet's structure most worthy of note was the setting up of the ministry of coordinating provincial affairs (*tansiq shu'un al-wilayat*) to implement the process of federalism (for more details regarding changes in personnel and composition, see cabinet table below).

As in the case of earlier cabinet reshuffles, this latest shake-up was not accompanied by any official explanation. However, the January reshuffle could be construed as an indication of growing discontent and even strong differences of opinion among the cabinet and RCCNS members. The major bones of contention seem to have been internal policies, primarily the recently implemented Shari'a law, and the vehement Sudanese support for Iraq in the Gulf War (see below).

On 14 April, the latent conflicts within the country's top leadership erupted when Bashir dismissed two RCCNS members in the first purge of its kind since his advent to power. Those dismissed were the interior minister, Faysal 'Ali Abu Salih, and the head of the RCCNS political committee, 'Uthman Ahmad Hasan. The two were replaced the same day by other RCCNS members: Deputy Prime Minister Muhammad Salih al-Zubayr, known as a major proponent of the implementation of the Shari'a, assumed the interior ministry, and Pio Yukwan, a southerner, became head of the RCCNS political committee. In accordance with their policy of no public reference to any discord within the inner circle, the authorities again remained silent. However, foreign sources provided some explanations. One of them argued that the dismissed interior minister, hitherto in charge of internal security, failed in preventing, and then in suppressing, the violent demonstrations staged by NIF zealots near the Egyptian Embassy in Khartoum in late January, in protest against its position in the Gulf War.[11] However, that version contradicted another report according to which the authorities had encouraged the demonstrations (see below). Another source pointed in an entirely different direction, suggesting that Salih was dismissed because he had strongly criticized Bashir's way of conducting the country's affairs in general, and his execution of 20 officers several days earlier-on charges of attempting a coup, in particular. The same source also reported that Salih had been under house arrest.[12] This time the authorities deviated from their consistent silence, and publicly denied categorically that an attempted coup had taken place and that Salih had been placed under house arrest.[13] The same foreign source further claimed that Salih and Hasan had harshly criticized Bashir's decision-making process. They particularly resented the unofficial body they called *majlis thawra siriyya* (the secret revolutionary council) headed by the NIF leader Turabi, which functioned behind the scenes as the real deciding force in shaping the country's domestic and foreign policies.[14] The government ignored these allegations. However, several months later, while holding a closed joint meeting of RCCNS and cabinet members, Bashir himself referred to the conflicting opinions within the top political echelon vis-à-vis Khartoum's position in the Gulf crisis. At the meeting, the justice minister and attorney general, Ahmad Mahmud Hasan, protested against the appointment of 'Ali 'Uthman Taha, deputy general secretary of the NIF and a lawyer by profession, to the post of legal adviser to the official delegation to the negotiations with the SPLA,[15] thus eroding his own political and professional status. The appointment further attested to Bashir's tough, centralized handling of Sudanese politics. Above all, it mirrored Bashir's untiring efforts to consolidate the NIF radicals' control over the country's key political functions.

Meanwhile, there were other signs of growing discord within the regime's core. The reported resignation of the southerner, Martin Malwal Arap, from the RCCNS in mid-April,[16] and repeated reports of sharp disagreement between the economy minister, 'Abd al-Rahim Hamdi, a veteran NIF member and one of the government's most powerful men, and Karar, the influential interior minister and head of the RCCNS's economic committee (see below), supported the impression that personal and political rivalries were being waged within the RCCNS, the cabinet and in their dealings with each other. While Hamdi was regarded as a supporter of free enterprise, Karar was known as a fierce proponent of state control over the economy. An additional source of discord between them was disagreement over the issue of handling the famine disaster, which both chose to call "a food gap." Karar represented the hard-line trend within the country's leadership which refused to acknowledge publicly the existence of a famine, so as not to admit that the RCCNS had failed to fulfill the most basic needs of the people. Hamdi belonged to the more pragmatic camp, arguing that Khartoum should formally admit to the acute shortage of food and set about receiving urgent aid.[17] The tightly controlled media did not publicize any of the alleged controversies. It was, therefore, not surprising that the media made no mention of the rumor that Hamdi was threatening as an act of protest to return to London to his former position as senior bank adviser.[18] It was not known whether there was a crisis in relations between Hamdi and Bashir. Nevertheless, Hamdi continued to hold his ministerial post until the end of the period reviewed.

The increasing rumors of growing internal conflict prompted powerful RCCNS member, Muhammad al-Amin Khalifa, to release a formal statement, stressing the solid (*mutamasik*) nature of the RCCNS and assuring the public that "there is not the slightest power struggle" within the organization.[19] In May, the Ministry of Culture and Information was reorganized. This, like Khalifa's statement, was also aimed at strengthening the image of the country's leadership, as being coordinated and united, and dispelling the widespread impression that it was in decline. The government clearly stated that the changes were designed to enable the ministry, i.e., the propaganda machine, "to do its job in a more revolutionary way than it does now."[20] Bashir held up the "revived life in the media" as a shining example of a major achievement, although the changes really only served as a means of tightening the regime's control over the pipes conveying information to the people. These changes, he stated, will "consolidate national unity, encourage production, present facts to the citizens and conduct constructive dialogue."[21]

Nevertheless, even the efficient silence of the state media could not conceal the escalating rivalries within the country's top leadership. On 7 July, the chief of staff, Lt. Gen. Ishaq Ibrahim 'Umar, who was not an NIF loyalist, was sacked on his return from a trip to London.[22] Officially, he was retired, and was replaced by Lt. Gen. Hasan 'Abd al-Rahman 'Ali, 'Umar's deputy and loyal to the NIF.[23] Later in the month, 368 officers of various ranks, including eight colonels, were also "retired."[24] In this case, too, no reason was given for the "retirements." One might have assumed that purges of the army's high command were aimed, first and foremost, at avoiding the concentration of military power in the same few hands, thereby reducing the danger of any coup being attempted. At the same time, and still within the context of the same supreme goal, the regime steadily reinforced the NIF militia, the Popular Defense Forces (PDF), in the army, thereby weakening the effect of the non-NIF elements. Between 15,000–20,000 NCOs and enlisted men and "more than 1,000 officers" had been dismissed since mid-1989,[25] while tens of thousands of PDF simultaneously flooded the armed forces (see also *MECS* 1990, p. 636). Not only did the PDF serve as a supervising eye on the military, from the security point of view, they also fought against the SPLA in the south of the country, and were engaged in mopping-up activities in the Nuba mountains in central Sudan,[26] which although not a part of the south, was nevertheless a focus of potential subversive activities against the regime.

The purges in the military leadership further reflected the growing impact of NIF extremists, led by Zubayr. In late July-early August, Bashir was in the UK for medical treatment[27] and speculation mounted that he would not return home. In his absence, Zubayr assumed the position of acting chairman of the RCCNS. He took advantage of the opportunity to carry out a minor reshuffle, demoting al-Tayyib Ibrahim Muhammad Khayr from his post as minister of presidential affairs and appointing him governor of the Darfur region. The previous governor and RCCNS member, Faysal Madani Mukhtar had reportedly resigned about a week earlier, in protest at the NIF dominance over the country's political foci.[28] The same source also reported, in early August, the resignation of another RCCNS member, Sulayman Muhammad Sulayman, from his post as governor of the central region. 'Awad Ahmad al-Ghaz, hitherto the trade, cooperation and supply minister, took up Khayr's previous post. Ghaz's post was filled by the NIF economic spokesman, Ibrahim 'Ubaydallah. This source claimed that Zubayr had also appointed 'Abd al-Wahhab Sulayman, another NIF economic spokesman and formerly director of the Islamic Insurance Company, as head of the Energy and Mining Ministry. On 3 August, the southern RCCNS member and the head of the political committee, Pio Yukwan was announced dead "after a short illness."[29]

In early November, Bashir made further changes in the Culture and Information Ministry's leadership, dismissing the minister and appointing him an ambassador.[30]

No official reason was given. However, several days later, Bashir announced that the media "were not reflecting the true face of the national salvation revolution," which showed his strong disapproval of that minister's functioning.[31]

In 1991, the composition of the cabinet was as follows:

Portfolio	Incumbent, 20 January	Incumbent, August
Prime Minister and Defense	'Umar Hasan Ahmad al-Bashir[f]	Unchanged
Presidential Affairs	Al-Tayyib Ibrahim Muhammad Khayr	'Awad Ahmad al-Ghaz
Foreign Minister	'Ali Sahlul	Unchanged
Interior	Faysal 'Ali Abu Salih[f]	Muhammad Salih al-Zubayr[g]
Justice and Attorney General	Ahmad Mahmud Hasan	Unchanged
Culture and Information	'Abdallah Muhammad Ahmad[a,h]	Unchanged
Finance and National Economy	'Abd al-Rahim Hamdi	Unchanged
Agriculture and Natural Resources	Ahmad 'Ali Qunayif	Unchanged
Planning	'Abd al-Wahhab Hamza[a]	Unchanged
Irrigation and Water Resources	Ya'qub Abu Shura	Unchanged
Energy and Mining	Hasan Wahhab Dahawit[a]	'Abd al-Wahhab Sulayman
Industry	Tajj al-Sirr Mustafa[a]	Unchanged
Education	'Abd al-Basit Sirat[a]	Unchanged
Construction and Public Works	'Uthman 'Abd al-Qadir 'Abd al-Latif[a]	Unchanged
Trade, Cooperation and Supply	'Awad Ahmad al-Ghaz	Ibrahim 'Ubaydallah
Welfare and Social Development[b]	Husayn Sulayman Abu Salih[a]	Unchanged
Relief and Refugees	_[e]	
Transport and Communications	Salah al-Din Muhammad Karar[a,d,f]	Unchanged
Labor and Social Insurance	George Kinga	Unchanged
Guidance	'Abdallah Deng Lual	Unchanged
Health[c]	Shakir al-Sarraj	Unchanged
Youth and Sports	Ibrahim Nayil Idam[f]	Unchanged
Higher Education[b] and Scientific Research	Ibrahim Ahmad 'Umar[a]	Unchanged
Coordination of States' Affairs[b]	Natali Ambu	Unchanged

NOTES

a   New faces in the cabinet.
b   Newly formed ministries.
c   Reorganized ministries.
d   In March, 'Ali Ahmad, the dismissed minister of transport and communications was appointed an adviser to the same ministry, maintaining his rank of minister.
e   Peter Orat Adwar, a non-Muslim and the minister since the cabinet's original composition, was sacked. No replacement was announced. A short while later, Bashir abolished the ministry, delegating its former responsibility for the refugees to the Interior Ministry, its responsibility for displaced persons to the Welfare and Social Development Ministry, and relief to the Trade Ministry.
f   RCCNS members.
g   On 14 April, Muhammad Salih al-Zubayr replaced Faysal 'Ali Abu Salih as interior minister.
h   He was dismissed in early November, and Bashir assumed his duties.

ECONOMIC-POLITICAL INTERACTIONS

The 1990–91 Gulf crisis further accelerated the deterioration of Sudan's already plagued and weakened economy. The acute chronic economic problems were exacerbated by the collapse of expatriate remittances and the suspension of economic aid from Saudi Arabia and the Gulf states. The situation was further aggravated by the rises in the cost of oil imports. The minister of the economy, Hamdi, estimated early in 1991 that the Gulf crisis would cost Sudan "$750m.–$1bn. per year,"[32] probably alluding to future aid payments from the West and the Gulf states.

The regime tried to tackle the problems through its National Economic Salvation

Program for 1990–93. This program defined three goals: food self-sufficiency; stricter budgetary control and deficit reduction; and the privatization of parastatals and liberalization of trade.[33] The economy minister, Hamdi, and the RCCNS member and head of the RCCNS economic committee, Karar, were the mainstays of this program. Although they did not agree on all economic issues (see above), they were both interested in the NIF's plan to attract new socioeconomic circles to its ranks, especially from the lower and middle bourgeoisie. Hamdi and Karar also had another major common interest: damaging the UP's and the DUP's economic bases, as well as that of the SPLA. The latter had allegedly counterfeited a great deal of money.[34]

On 6 May, a change of currency was officially announced, essentially prompted by political considerations. Hamdi's statement emphasizing that the move was "purely economically motivated,"[35] and the strong criticism made by the UP leader, al-Sadiq al-Mahdi, against the change of currency,[36] seemed to confirm the political motivation. Hamdi further claimed that the move was "a strategic overall remedy to the economy through controlling money supply."[37] The uncontrolled circulation of Sudanese money within Sudan and outside the country, estimated at c. £S17bn. ($3,800m.), constituted a serious problem as the banks possessed only £S2bn. ($440m.).[38] In addition to the declared goal of this measure, it was also officially aimed at controlling inflation. In spring 1991, inflation was estimated at 200%–300%.[39]

On 7 October, the regime took another tough economic measure, devaluating its new currency and reducing subsidies on basic commodities, including sugar and fuel. The Sudanese pound was devaluated to an official exchange rate of 15 to the US dollar.[40] These measures improved Khartoum's strained relationship with the International Monetary Fund. The latter had repeatedly threatened to expel Sudan for its failure to introduce economic reforms that would be acceptable to the fund (see *MECS* 1990, p. 637).

GROWING INTERNAL UNREST

In mid-January, a foreign source reported that the authorities had foiled "sabotage operations" planned against them by the outlawed Communist Party (CP). No further details were given and the information was reported by one source only.[41] Whether or not that report was true, it certainly mirrored the situation between the regime and the CP. Although the regime attempted a reconciliation, the two continued to be embroiled in sharp political conflict.[42]

On 13 April, a military coup was allegedly foiled by Khartoum's security network. Once again, one foreign source published the report, which added that, immediately following the attempted coup, 20 army officers were executed and there were extensive arrests.[43] However, these allegations were categorically denied by Khartoum.[44]

On 12 June, "mass demonstrations" took place in various neighborhoods of Khartoum against the economic conditions in the country, in particular the change of currency. The NIF central reserve police force used tear gas and clubs to disperse the demonstrators.[45] Security measures in the capital were further stepped up toward the anniversary day of the regime's seizure of power on 30 June. Given the mounting popular resentment, this move was not surprising. As the day approached, the regime canceled the military parade and celebrations were muted. Bashir made a speech to the nation from the heavily defended Friendship Hall in Khartoum which was the highlight of the celebrations.

Civilian unrest continued to spread. In July, a student was killed in clashes with riot police over protests against the university's new accommodation arrangements. One hundred students were arrested,[46] and 12 others were expelled "for trying to turn the accommodation issue into a political cause."[47] This incident sparked off a week of demonstrations and the subsequent closing of Khartoum University in mid-July.[48] The demonstrations also spread to Kosti, Wad Madani and other towns. It was even reported by a foreign anti-Sudanese source that Bashir was forced to cut short his visit to the eastern region and return to Khartoum "posthaste."[49]

On 23 August, the government announced that an attempted coup had been foiled at its "early stage." Ten army officers, both serving and retired, and a few civilians had been arrested. The statement further claimed that the attempted coup of 21 August was "instigated and financed by certain foreign powers," but Khartoum did not identify them.[50] Foreign sources named senior UP leader, 'Abd al-Rahman 'Abdallah, and Maj. Gen. (ret.) Muhammad 'Abdallah Khalifa, apparently another UP member, as the leaders of the attempted coup.[51] Even if the UP was not involved, the fact that the regime cast suspicion on it at such an early stage of the coup interrogation, showed how afraid the regime was of its opposition. Despite the release from prison, in the spring, of the most senior UP leader, al-Sadiq al-Mahdi, as a gesture of goodwill on the part of Bashir, the party continued to antagonize and threaten the regime. In addition to the UP, another foreign source also named Fathi Ahmad 'Ali, the leader of the opposition movement code-named *Ana al-Sudan*, as being responsible for the attempted coup[52] (for details on the movement, see *MECS* 1990, p. 635). However, the UP opposition denied any involvement in the alleged coup attempt.[53] Since the authorities did not elaborate on the incident, the possibility existed that the whole affair had been used as a pretext for the regime to launch further drastic purges of the top echelons in the army and the opposition. It was reported that 30–50 people were arrested.[54] Later in the fall, 13 officers and two UP civilians were sentenced to death for their alleged role in the attempted coup.[55]

THE HUMAN DISASTERS OF FAMINE, DISEASES AND REFUGEES

Foreign sources estimated that the number of Sudanese who were at risk of starvation in early 1991 was 7m.–11m. people.[56] Sudan had suffered in recent years from a problem of acute food shortages, and starvation was not a new phenomenon. However, foreign relief agencies considered the situation in 1991 as the most extensive and severe ever, even worse than the 1984–85 famine, which had claimed over 200,000 lives.[57] In 1991, there was widespread starvation in the war-torn south and in the eastern and western peripheries, especially in the Kordofan region, where "a minimum of 200–300 deaths were reported each day."[58]

The hunger crisis was significantly aggravated by many factors: the government's gross mismanagement of the national economy and food affairs, together with the failure to replace Sudan's major cash crop, cotton, with wheat; droughts throughout the country and in Kenya and Uganda, which supplied food to southern Sudan; government bombing in southern SPLA-held territory and insecure supply lines to SPLA and government-held towns in the south; and the government's selling-off of substantial grain reserves in order to earn foreign currency to pay for weapons which were desperately needed to continue the war in the south.[59]

Bashir's government further contributed to the escalating starvation — the "food gap," as it persistently labeled the problem[60] — by refusing to appeal formally to the international community for urgent assistance. Khartoum's leadership feared that such a move would be tantamount to acknowledging publicly that it could not feed its people, which might further erode its political position. That was precisely the reason why the US and other Western countries insisted upon such a procedure. Khartoum exacerbated the crisis by harassing and obstructing international relief agencies and destroying indigenous institutions capable of responding to the famine.[61] It further alienated Western and Arab states which could be sources of assistance, especially in the Gulf, by staunchly supporting Iraq in the Gulf crisis and dissociating itself from the pro-American Arab regimes (see below), while increasingly tending toward radicalism.

The government endeavored to divert attention away from its domestic crisis and its own ineffectiveness in relieving the situation. At the same time, it emphasized what it considered the rosier aspects of the "NIF revolution." Sudan "is not about to be struck by famine. It is about to become an Islamic paradise," a Sudanese official stated in a typical reference.[62] Moreover, according to another Sudanese top official, the famine issue was "a Western-inspired conspiracy" designed to undermine the regime. "It offends Sudan's people and government," he concluded.[63] The Sudanese head of state summed up the external pressure to declare Sudan a famine zone as aimed at "insulting Sudan and make it kneel."[64]

Meanwhile, the south was plagued by widespread diseases. Many southerners died from meningitis and leishmaniasis epidemics. Tragically, however, international medicine and food-relief efforts were hindered by the conflicting sides, which used them as weapons in their war (for details on the civil war, see below).

In the middle of the year, another dimension was added to the Sudanese human tragedy. There was a huge influx of southern Sudanese refugees into Sudan's eastern territory from Ethiopia in the aftermath of the overthrow of the Mengistu Haile Mariam regime. In June, the Sudanese authorities estimated the number of refugees as fluctuating from 150,000–195,000. Foreign sources assessed as much as double that number.[65] The Sudanese Government seized upon the opportunity of the new crisis to further its own interest in mobilizing urgent relief aid from the international community, while, at the same time, diverting international attention away from the famine to the refugee issue. Top Sudanese officials repeatedly requested that the world render immediate assistance to what Khartoum insisted on calling the "Ethiopian refugees,"[66] even though the overwhelming majority were returning southern Sudanese.

THE CIVIL WAR
The Course of Fighting
In the early months of 1991, the army took advantage of the dry season and initiated a series of "successful heavy attacks" on SPLA positions in the regions of the Upper Nile and western Equatoria. The army also launched a "successful" series of assaults against the SPLA in southern Kordofan,[67] a strategically and economically important area outside the south's informal border (for the SPLA's attempts, and partial success in gaining a foothold in southern Kordofan, see *MECS* 1987, p. 624; 1989, p. 526; and 1990, p. 638).

However, the army's successes were of negligible significance compared with the SPLA's military achievements. On 22 March, the SPLA captured the important garrison town of Maridi in western Equatoria. It claimed to have killed many army soldiers and to have seized large quantities of weapons.[68] Several days later, Garang's forces also captured Mundiri, another important garrison town, located on the main road of Wau-Rumbek-Juba road, and the Leri and Rokon garrisons, on the Juba-Yambio road.[69] Consequently, in spring, Juba was cut off from almost every army-controlled area, leaving the small garrison near Jabel Lado, a prominent rock about 27 km. north of Juba, to protect the town's airport. "Juba remained naked" and the SPLA would hit the town "from any direction any time from now," Garang stated in a euphoric tone in late March.[70]

The SPLA's series of significant victories sent further shock waves through Bashir's government. At that stage, it seemed that the army was losing the war. It was, therefore, not surprising that Khartoum made concerted efforts to reinforce the armed forces and boost the morale of the troops. On 17 March, the imposition of three-year's national service was formally announced, and ten days later, Bashir paid an extraordinary visit to the south. While meeting the officers' cadre in the Upper Nile region, Bashir delivered an optimistic message to all army troops, telling them that "the coming battle against the outlaws will be decisive" and that there "will be no rebellions after this year."[71]

Whether encouraged by Bashir's moves, or merely taking advantage of the beneficial conditions of the dry season, the army launched a new offensive in early April. Its main aim was to weaken the SPLA's stranglehold over Juba, Wau and Malakal, which had been reinforced since March by over 1,000 Fertit militiamen from western Bahr al-Ghazal.[72] Until March, the Fertit people, like other southern militia tribes, such as the Toposa and Latoka, both from Equatoria, had been used by the government as an eroding force in the Dinka, the major tribal base of the SPLA. These militias were integrated into the PDF units which fought the SPLA.

The SPLA Loss of its Ethiopian Patron

In late May, there was a dramatic turn of events, to the SPLA's detriment. Ironically, this started in the month the SPLA celebrated its eighth anniversary and when it was closer than ever before to gaining complete control of the south. Tragically, for Garang's forces, its devoted supporter, the Ethiopian regime of Mengistu, was overthrown. This event dealt a serious blow to the southern Sudanese protégé, which lost its political and military backing, including its headquarters in Addis Ababa. It also lost its rear bases, its supply routes and the highly important facility of continuing to operate its radio station from Ethiopian territory.

There was great relief in Khartoum that the SPLA radio station was no longer operating. The government cynically stated that with the silencing of SPLA broadcasting, the latter lost "more than 50% of its true strength."[73] The paralysis of the SPLA's transmitter, which had operated since the fall of 1984, marked the end of its sole, highly effective channel of communication both internally and externally. Not only had SPLA broadcasts delivered messages to its fighters in the field, issued propaganda for its cause, and worked to enhance its political standing throughout the country and abroad, but they had also been used to viciously attack the Khartoum "junta" and erode its prestige. By putting its broadcasting facilities during 1990–91 at the disposal of the northern opposition to the Sudanese regime, especially that of 'Ali Fathi (see above), the SPLA had largely strengthened its position. In mid-1991, when hundreds of thousands of southern Sudanese refugees fled from Ethiopia to Sudan and faced a serious plight, the SPLA could no longer report their misery, and this prevented them from receiving urgent aid. Although the damages should be viewed, first and foremost, in human terms, a political blow was also dealt to the SPLA, exposing its failure to look after the people who provided its actual or potential support.

The top officials of the SPLA found safe refuge: some went to Kenya, some remained in the Ethiopian embassy in Kenya, and others reached Kapoeta, the SPLA's eastern Equatoria stronghold.[74] Garang escaped to Kenya, and later arrived in Kapoeta. About 700 "elements of the SPLA" were reportedly killed by "Ethiopian rebels."[75] However, it was absolutely clear that this last crisis, which the SPLA had just endured, was by no means the end of their troubles.

A Short-Period Suspension of Fighting; Renewal of Mediation Efforts

Meanwhile, Bashir took advantage of the circumstances and launched an intensive propaganda campaign, aimed at highlighting his image as a peace-seeking leader. In June, the government declared an amnesty to those rebels who were willing to stop fighting and invited them to join the special villages it was setting up in order to enable them to lead a "normal life."[76] Khartoum manipulated the new crisis atmosphere and exercised its well-oiled propaganda machine to persuade the rebellious southerners to lay down their weapons and join the amnesty process. One foreign source even claimed that Bashir's government doubled the financial incentive to every SPLA deserter and estimated it at £S20,000 (about $1,500).[77]

At the end of 1991, the two conflicting sides remained as far away from the negotiating table as they had been before, despite the fact that, during the summer, Khartoum had reiterated its calls for the beginning of negotiations, and despite the US's and Nigeria's mediation attempts.

The Struggle for Power within the SPLA Leadership

On 30 August, three Upper Nile commanders, Riek Mashar, Gordon Loang Chul and Lam Akol Ajawin (longtime senior aide and official spokesman for Garang), announced that the SPLA leader had been ousted. They claimed that their action was to save the SPLA struggle from collapse. The dissidents also said that their move was "for renewal and democratization within the movement" and for the "attainment of a peaceful settlement of the civil war." They accused Garang of running the movement "alone, in a very dictatorial, autocractic manner," turning "a popular struggle into a reign of terror." They claimed "widespread support" adding that out of the 13 members of the SPLA High Command, seven supported them.[78]

It quickly appeared that the dissidents' statement had been premature. Later that same day, Garang's close aides, Justin Arop, the SPLA representative in West Africa, and Mario Mure arrived in Nairobi on behalf of their leader, for the purpose of refuting his overthrow and to make it clear that Garang was still firmly in control.[79]

This event publicly exposed the political and ideological controversies within the inner circle of the SPLA leadership, as well as personal and tribal rivalries. Akol and Mashar, both members of the SPLA High Command and both holding a PhD in engineering, were of Shiluk and Nuer origin. Chul, also of the Nuer tribe, was one of the leaders of the Anyanya II, a separatist movement established in 1983 to fight the government. However, it became embroiled in a violent confrontation with the SPLA. Eventually, most of its people joined Garang's forces (see *MECS* 1983–84, p. 661).

Whatever motivated the three to challenge Garang's leadership, their attempted putsch was clearly not a mere struggle between individuals or tribes. The highly sensitive issue of ideology also played a role. While Garang consistently advocated a solution within a united Sudan, the three insurgents favored separatism.

FOREIGN AFFAIRS

SUDAN AND THE GULF

Iraq

Sudan's support for Iraq in the Gulf crisis became more fervent and vigorous after the outbreak of the war in mid-January. Bashir and Khalifa were ardent supporters of Saddam Husayn's regime. Sudanese leaders did not miss any public occasion to hail the Iraqi "valiant steadfastness" in facing "the Atlantic aggression." They also repeatedly glorified Baghdad's contribution to "the pride of the Arab Islamic nation."[80]

Khartoum did not limit its support to verbal activities. On 19 January, "hundreds of thousands" of Sudanese marched the streets of the capital under the instigation, albeit behind the scenes, of the RCCNS. The incensed masses, swept along by forceful pro-Iraqi sentiments, burned effigies of US President George Bush, and the US, Egyptian and Israeli flags. They also strongly denounced Egypt's role in the war (see below). The Iraqi ambassador to Sudan, Tariq Yahya, praised the demonstrators. Harping on the Islamic strings, he further stirred up their feelings by stressing that "this war...will restore Muslims and Arabs to their rightful place among the peoples and nations of the world."[81]

The strong solidarity of the Sudanese people and government with their Iraqi counterparts was further shown by the number of volunteers, once again organized by the Sudanese authorities. It was reported that "more than 1,000" members of pro-government employees' trade unions volunteered to help Iraq. However, this was merely another propaganda ploy and a repetition of a similar move made by Khartoum during the Iraqi annexation of Kuwait in August 1990. With the same motives in mind, Sudan sent a medical team to Iraq during the war, which arrived in Iraq on 4 February.[82]

Khartoum flatly denied rumors that Iraq had stationed *Scud* missiles and combat aircraft on Sudanese territory, calling them "lies" and "fabrications."[83] It likewise denied "foreign media reports" claiming that Sudan had agreed to store Iraqi nuclear and chemical weapons on its territory.[84]

On 8 February, Iraq's deputy premier, Sa'dun Hammadi, arrived in Khartoum on one leg of a tour of several Arab countries. Khalifa, a staunch supporter of Iraq within the RCCNS leadership, headed a massive public gathering he had especially called for the occasion, using the event to reiterate Sudan's support for Iraq.[85] Other public rallies and marches in support of Iraq took place on the streets of Khartoum later in February. Throughout the year, other Iraqi and Sudanese high-ranking officials exchanged visits. However, the Sudanese authorities did not release details about the visits, nor about their outcome.

Kuwait

Once Sudan declared its firm support for Iraq in the Gulf crisis, its relations with Kuwait were doomed. Bilateral links between the two countries were at their lowest ebb during the war and immediately after it. It was, therefore, surprising that Khartoum released an official statement in March, implicitly indicating to the Kuwait Government that it wished to defuse the bilateral tension. "Sudan was eager to see the freedom, independence and territorial integrity of Kuwait," the statement read.[86] Another official reference made by RCCNS member Arop expressed Sudan's satisfaction at Kuwait's liberation and "restoration of its legitimacy."[87]

Possibly, these sporadic gestures reflected some of the confusion and dissension prevailing among RCCNS members over the stand Sudan should take vis-à-vis the Gulf crisis. It is also possible that such moves were an expression of the widely held opinion among RCCNS members that it was imperative to resume good relations with Kuwait in order to receive, once again, its desperately needed economic assistance.

However, the Kuwaitis had their own valid reasons for not responding positively to Sudan's overtures. Sudan reacted by verbally attacking Kuwait. Khartoum accused Kuwait of torturing (in one case to death) Sudanese expatriates residing in the Kuwaiti capital.[88] At the same time, Khartoum also seized all Kuwaiti government property and investments in Sudan in order to pressure Kuwait to compensate those Sudanese who had been working in Kuwait at the time of Iraq's invasion. In retaliation, Kuwait recalled its ambassador and downgraded relations with Sudan to the level of chargé d'affaires.[89]

RELATIONS WITH EGYPT, LIBYA AND TUNISIA

Egypt

Throughout 1991 the tension, which had crept into Sudan's relations with Egypt since Bashir's advent to power, increased significantly (for the sources of mutual disenchantment, see *MECS* 1990, pp. 642–43). Most of the concern and the grudges emanated from Cairo. This was clearly shown by the refusal of Egypt's president, Husni Mubarak, to hold any direct talks with his Sudanese counterpart,[90] when they both attended the quadrisummit conference in the Libyan town of Misurata on 3 January (see chapter on Libya). Khartoum did not publicly refer to the insulting affair, swallowing its pride. But Bashir soon found a way to express his anger. On 19 January, massive, violent pro-Iraqi and anti-Egyptian demonstrations were staged in Khartoum's streets by NIF activists. The demonstrators called for the destruction of the Aswan High Dam and the pyramids "in retaliation for Egypt's position in the Gulf War." The demonstrators threw stones at the Egyptian Embassy and set fire to the Egyptian flag.[91]

The anti-Egyptian riots were not only severe, but it was also the first time in recent memory that negative emotions had reached such an extreme between the two countries. Cairo ended its policy of restraint toward Khartoum and immediately retaliated with a series of punitive measures. It closed down the Egyptian educational schools in Sudan as well as the Khartoum branch of Cairo University, and stopped flights between the two countries. It also deported 500 Sudanese nationals charged with "trying to create unrest and instability" in Egypt.[92] Sudan reacted by cutting off the Nile River transport link between Wadi Halfa in northern Sudan and Aswan. It also deported five Egyptians, including a diplomat, who were on a mission in Khartoum. They were held for 48 hours and "badly treated" at Khartoum airport.[93]

Bashir was alarmed by the mounting crisis, especially as Cairo stepped up its warnings to Khartoum against any attempt to station Iraqi missiles or airplanes within its territory,[94] and he tried to relieve some of the friction. On 23 January, at a meeting with Egypt's ambassador in Khartoum, initiated by Sudan, the Sudanese foreign minister, Sahlul, pointed out that the anti-Egypt demonstrations, or the "excesses" according to his reported message, did not "reflect the views of the Sudanese Government or people."[95] However, given the tightly controlled internal security and the huge demonstrating masses, one could not but have the impression that the demonstrations were organized and controlled by the regime's well-oiled machine. A foreign source even alleged that official cars toured the capital encouraging people to demonstrate against Egypt.[96]

In sharp contrast to the authorities' mild and barely apologetic stand toward the anti-Egyptian turbulence, the Sudanese opposition unequivocally condemned the demonstrations.[97] The opposition was deeply involved with Cairo and increasingly dependent on it for its survival. The government was indeed seriously troubled by the growing rapprochement between the Sudanese opposition and Egypt, and went so far as to request that Cairo ban the opposition's activities. The request was rejected.[98]

A further example of Egypt's enmity and suspicion toward Khartoum was Cairo's refusal, in July, to officially receive the Sudanese militant Islamic fundamentalist NIF leader Hasan 'Abdallah al-Turabi, who traveled on a Sudanese diplomatic passport.[99] In retaliation, Khartoum expelled 84 Egyptian lecturers and their dependents, who were on their way to reopen the Khartoum branch of Cairo University. This game of mutual punitive measures continued with more than 800 Sudanese nationals denied entry into Egypt.[100]

In the late summer, Bashir publicly expressed his desire to make up with Egypt. The relentless hostility between the two countries had become increasingly damaging, with no benefits to any Sudanese interest. Bashir sensibly feared that Cairo might become involved, or even initiate, subversive activities against his regime. Bashir also hoped that if the situation with Cairo were improved, this would pave the way for bettering the intensely strained relations with the US and the Gulf states and, consequently, improve the regime's political and economic prospects. "We do not want our term of office to be marked by estrangement or tension with the northern part of the Nile Valley," Bashir stated, adding that even "a husband and wife can disagree." Thus, he elaborated, "we must discuss matters calmly.... We must always remember that there are foreign forces seeking to divide us." He concluded by stressing his government's supreme efforts to contain the crisis.[101] However, by the end of the period reviewed, neither Sudan's willingness nor Libya's mediation had succeeded in bridging the wide gap and profound disagreement that overshadowed relations between the two countries.

Libya

The friendly spirit that had colored Khartoum's relations with Tripoli in 1989–90 was still very much in evidence in 1991. There was, however, a growing uneasiness and tension brewing under the surface. This change of mood came about as Libya realized that Sudan was becoming an ineffective political and strategic-military asset. The

Bashir regime was unpopular, both at home and abroad, and its Islamic radicalism was growing. Sudan was becoming an increasing economic burden on Tripoli. In addition, Libya did not need the Sudanese card anymore to win the political and military "games" in neighboring Egypt and Chad. All these factors contributed to making Khartoum less attractive.

The Sudanese regime's declining value in Qadhdhafi's eyes was reflected by Libya's diminished aid, both in scope and essence. Bashir, for his part, was very much aware of Libya being a vital and almost the only lifeline of his regime, and went to great lengths to placate Tripoli. The Sudanese leadership and the state-controlled media never missed an opportunity to praise "the internationalist leader"[102] personally, and to laud him ideologically and politically. They glorified the Qadhdhafi-born political system of Jamahiriyya (People's Power) and also expressed their wish to adopt some of his "revolutionary" ideas. One of these was the removal of the formal "imaginative borders" between Sudan and Libya, as reported by Khartoum in early 1991, and regarded by it as "a step toward Islamic unity."[103]

Throughout the year Bashir and other RCCNS officials paid several visits to Tripoli. This attested to the importance that was attached to Libya as an essential component in strengthening the regime's prospects of survival. Qadhdhafi returned the visit to Khartoum from 29 June–2 July and was guest of honor at the celebration marking the Bashir regime's second anniversary in power. He was the only head of state from the Arab world to attend — a clear indication of Khartoum's isolation in this arena. Although he said that the day was "dear to us all,"[104] the Libyan leader did not take advantage of the special occasion to make any noteworthy gesture of goodwill. Neither did he pay any compliments to the Sudanese leadership. However, Bashir did not waste the opportunity and utilized the event to enhance his own political standing, while at the same time making sure not to overshadow his high-ranking guest. Thus, he invited Qadhdhafi to join him in bulldozing the gates of the Kubar prison in Khartoum and releasing "more than 2,000 prisoners."[105] The event echoed the Libyan-style act of demolishing the gates of Tripoli prison three years earlier (see *MECS* 1988, p. 647).

It is not known whether Sudan adopted various Libyan "revolutionary" symbols because they reflected its own ideological and political identity, or were merely tactics aimed at drawing a greater share of Libyan aid. Toward the end of the year, bilateral relations were marred by a "silent crisis." The most conspicuous evidence of this was that Libya cut off its oil supplies to Sudan.[106] Qadhdhafi's reservations toward Khartoum grew further with the strengthening of Libya's ties with Egypt. Cairo was highly critical of Bashir's regime, and both Libya and Egypt were increasingly worried about Bashir's militant Islamic fundamentalism.

Tunisia

During the course of 1991, Sudan's relations with Tunis became significantly strained. Tension culminated in Tunisia's recalling its ambassador to Khartoum on 15 October. The Sudanese described the Tunisian move as "regrettable,"[107] without providing any details or explanation for the crisis in their relations. Tunisia repeatedly claimed that Sudan had provided the outlawed Tunisian Nahda (Revival) Islamic fundamentalist movement with backing and facilities. Tunis accused Khartoum specifically of providing the Nahda leader, Rashid Ghannushi, with a Sudanese diplomatic passport (see above), and of training Tunisian opposition elements in Sudanese camps, thereby jeopardizing stability in Tunisia.[108]

RELATIONS WITH IRAN
Besides Libya and Iraq, Khartoum considered Iran a very attractive ally. Not only was Iran a leading component in the radical Islamic camp, with which Khartoum strongly identified, but it also remained one of the very few sources of political and perhaps also economic and military support left for the Bashir regime.

However, Khartoum was cautious not to cause political tension with Iraq, Egypt or the US and, consequently, the Sudanese state-run media kept coverage on its cooperation with Iran low-key, focusing exclusively on aspects of culture and Islamic guidance. Furthermore, Khartoum made no mention of other sensitive areas of cooperation, such as internal security and military assistance. In contrast, the intensive exchange of high-level, official delegations between the two capitals preoccupied the Sudanese media's headlines throughout the whole year. In December, Iran's president, Hojjat ul-Islam 'Ali Akbar Hashemi Rafsanjani paid a state visit to Khartoum, which further reflected the growing ties between the two countries.

STAUNCH SUPPORT FOR THE PALESTINIAN CAUSE
Bashir was vocally dedicated to the Palestinian cause. This logically emanated from his strong identification with the militant Arab Islamic camp, on the one hand, and his firm rejection of the "Zionist entity," on the other. Khartoum provided the Palestinians with moral and political backing, and was therefore one of the preferred residing places of PLO Chairman Yasir 'Arafat. The country's media were put at his disposal, and he utilized them to broadcast his political messages to the world. Khartoum also raised the PLO's diplomatic status to that of "embassy of the Palestinian state" in Khartoum.[109] The Bashir regime simultaneously utilized the intensive visits of 'Arafat to Khartoum to enhance its prestige at home and in the Arab world.

Sudan strongly denounced the Madrid peace conference (see chapter on the Middle East peace process). A protest demonstration was staged by the NIF in Khartoum on 30 October. The foreign minister stated that the massive protest was clear proof that "the flame of struggle is still kindling inside the hearts of the Arab Muslim peoples who are at maximum alert to defend at any time the interests of the Arab Muslim nation." He further emphasized that his country would not accept "from that conference anything less than imposing a total withdrawal of the Israeli troops from the Arab occupied lands" and "the establishment of an independent Palestinian state, with Jerusalem its eternal capital."[110] Turabi, the powerful fundamentalist leader, condemned the "peace conference" including its title, arguing that it was an American fait accompli, aimed at persuading the parties involved to sign Washington's document, in line with its own interests.[111]

THE AFRICAN ARENA: A QUEST FOR IMPROVED RELATIONS
Ethiopia
Sudan's relations with Mengistu's regime, which had long been demolished, reached a new low ebb in the spring of 1991. In late March, Ethiopia expelled Sudan's military attaché and consul (along with two Libyan diplomats), for "engaging in activities

incompatible with their diplomatic status." Several days later, Khartoum retaliated by deporting two Ethiopian diplomats.[112] Addis Ababa reportedly charged Khartoum with orchestrating a plot in support of the Eritrean People's Liberation Front and the Tigrayan People's Liberation Front. The same source also reported that Sudanese forces were believed to be preparing for blowing up the Abbai bridge across the Blue Nile.[113] Other unconfirmed reports claimed that Sudanese troops took part in the capture, at the end of May, of the Ethiopian town of Gambela, near their common border, which was carried out by the Oromo Liberation Front (OLF).[114] (The OLF, along with other Ethiopian rebel groups, enjoyed Khartoum's support.) Khartoum repeatedly denied any role in Mengistu's overthrow at midyear, counterclaiming Ethiopia's active support for the SPLA.[115]

As expected, Khartoum welcomed the new regime in Addis Ababa. It brought immediate and highly significant relief for Sudan. The official spokesman of Khartoum's government stated that the change of guard in Ethiopia had already "solved 50% of the problem in southern Sudan";[116] his statement was understandable since the Ethiopian People's Revolutionary Democratic Front (EPRDF), formerly backed by Sudan, headed the new government in Addis Ababa. The EPRDF and Khartoum had shared a common interest in overthrowing the Mengistu regime, each for its own reasons. Bashir hoped that the EPRDF would cooperate with him in further destroying the SPLA. Khartoum made a statement affirming its support for "the right of the Eritrean people to self-determination."[117] This statement, aimed at persuading the new Ethiopian regime to collaborate with it, was somewhat ironic in view of Khartoum's absolute rejection of any self-determination, or separatist tendencies in its own multiethnic and religious state.

The official visit to the Sudanese capital in early July of EPRDF leader and president of Ethiopia, Meles Zenawi, strengthened Khartoum's expectations for increased cooperation with Addis Ababa. A Sudanese official delegation, headed by Khalifa, returned the visit in the same month. There were soon tangible results. In the fall, the two countries canceled the requirement of entry visas, and about 50,000 Ethiopian soldiers were repatriated.[118] Another example of the growing rapprochement was Bashir's visit to Ethiopia from 19–25 October. During the visit, the two countries signed several bilateral agreements.

Chad

Sudan's relations with Chad, which had long been hostile, improved significantly in the immediate aftermath of the change of guard in Ndjamena in December 1990. Libya presumably played the role of go-between, trying essentially to further its own interests through a Sudanese-Chadian reconciliation (see chapter on Libya). A foreign source hinted that Sudan had provided military facilities to Idris Deby, the Chadian president, when the latter took up the offensive against Habré and toppled his regime. This was a reasonable assumption, considering Libya's interest in overthrowing the Hissène Habré regime in Chad, on the one hand, and Libya's influence in Khartoum's politics, on the other. Bashir refuted the insinuation.[119]

The Sudanese regime was swiftly rewarded by Tripoli and Ndjamena. In mid-January, immediately after Deby's seizure of power, Chad announced the closure of the SPLA office in Ndjamena and a ban on any Sudanese opposition activities within its territory.[120] There was soon a wide range of contracts between them covering various fields of cooperation.

Later in the year, however, the volume of bilateral activities diminished considerably, reflecting the fact that the two devastated, war-torn countries had very little to offer each other. The presence of Chadian President Deby as a guest of honor, alongside Qadhdhafi, at the anniversary celebrations of the Bashir coup in Khartoum at the end of June, was utilized by Khartoum to emphasize that the regime had gained new friends in its near geographic vicinity, thereby trying to dispel the widespread impression that it was largely isolated.

NOTES

For the place and frequency of publications cited here, and for the full name of the publication, news agency, radio station or monitoring service where an abbreviation is used, please see "List of Sources." Only in the case of more than one publication bearing the same name is the place of publication noted here.

1. *Al-Inqadh al-Watani,* 5 January 1991.
2. *Al-Inqadh al-Watani,* 6 January 1991.
3. On 4 February, Bashir decreed a new federal system in the country, dividing it into *wilayat* (provinces) as follows: Khartoum, Central, Darfur, Kordofan, Northern, Upper Nile, Bahr al-Ghazal and Equatoria. The responsibility of the new governments was defined as handling the day-to-day local administration. For details, see R. Omdurman, 9 February — DR, 12 February; for the names of the governors, apparently all NIF members, see R. Omdurman, 27 May — DR, 4 June 1991. As the year drew to a close, it became evident that the federal-rule system was becoming increasingly impotent. It was thus reminiscent of the earlier abortive implementation of federalism in the country in 1980 by Numayri (see *MECS* 1980–81, pp. 766, 768–69).
4. Justice Minister and Attorney General Ahmad Mahmud Hasan in a press conference on 3 January in Khartoum, stressed that the "Shari'a now was not the same as in 1983." Then, he emphasized, the regime did not truly believe in it and Numayri used it as "a cover-up for remaining in power." SUNA, 3 January — SWB, 5 January 1991.
5. *Al-Quwat al-Musallaha,* 2 April 1991.
6. *Al-Quwat al-Musallaha,* 24 April 1991. The estimated official exchange rate (average) £ per $1 in 1990 was 4.50. *CR,* Sudan, No. 3, 1991.
7. *Ha'aretz,* 7 August, quoting *Der Spiegel; al-Wafd,* 25 August 1991.
8. R. SPLA, 11 April — DR, 16 April 1991, quoting the acting under secretary for foreign affairs and a staunch NIF supporter, 'Abd al-Rahman Muhammad Sa'id.
9. *Al-Wafd,* 2 June; *Ha'aretz,* 7 August 1991, quoting *Der Spiegel.*
10. Interview with Bashir, *al-'Alam* (London), 10 August; statement released by the Sudanese Embassy in Tunis, *al-Hayat* (London), 11 August; Ghannushi himself denied the allegations, *al-Sha'b* (Cairo), August 1991.
11. *Sourakia,* 22 April 1991.
12. *Al-Wafd,* 20 April 1991.
13. Interview with 'Ali Sahlul, Sudan's foreign minister, R. Amman, 21 April — DR, 22 April 1991.
14. *Al-Wafd,* 19 May 1991.
15. *Al-Wafd,* 28 July 1991.
16. R. SPLA, 18 April — DR, 19 April 1991.
17. *AR,* March-April; *MEI,* 3 May 1991.
18. *Al-Wafd,* 21 April 1991.
19. *Al-Inqadh al-Watani,* 17 April 1991.
20. R. Khartoum, 19 May — DR, 22 May 1991. For more details regarding the changes, see *al-Hayat* (London), 22 May 1991.
21. R. Omdurman, 20 June — DR, 5 July 1991.

22. *AC,* 12 July 1991.
23. *Al-Quwat al-Musallaha,* 8 July 1991.
24. *Al-Wafd,* 18 July 1991.
25. Interview with 'Abd al-Rahman Sa'id, former deputy commander in chief and the deputy leader in the *Ana al-Sudan* opposition movement, *al-Majalla,* 13–19 March 1991.
26. 'Amid Babakr 'Abd al-Mahmud, the commander of the PDF, asserted that these forces took an active role in the army's fighting in the south. E.g., *al-Inqadh al-Watani,* 22 March, 2 July; *CR,* Sudan, No. 1, 1991.
27. R. Omdurman, 3 August — DR, 6 August 1991.
28. *Al-Wafd,* 11 August 1991.
29. R. Omdurman, 3 August — DR, 6 August 1991.
30. SUNA, 6 November — DR, 12 November 1991.
31. SUNA, 16 November — DR, 19 November 1991.
32. *ME,* January 1991.
33. *CR,* Sudan, No. 1, 1991.
34. *Al-Sha'b* (Cairo), 4 June 1991.
35. Ibid.
36. *Al-Wafd,* 30 June; *Akhbar al-Sudan,* 15 July 1991.
37. SUNA, 8 May — DR, 10 May 1991.
38. Ibid; *MEED,* 24 May 1991.
39. R. Omdurman, 6, 15 May — DR, 10, 23 May; *MEED,* 8, 17 May 1991.
40. SUNA, 7 October — DR, 10 October 1991. For more details, see *MEED,* 18 October 1991.
41. *Al-Hayat* (London), 11 January 1991, quoting "Sudanese reliable sources."
42. In the spring the regime released the CP leader, Ibrahim Nuqud, from prison, where he had been detained since Bashir's advent to power. For reconciliation efforts, of which the climax was the meeting between Bashir and Nuqud, see *al-Shira',* 4 November 1991.
43. *Al-Wafd,* 20 April 1991.
44. R. Amman, 21 April — DR, 22 April, quoting Sudan's Foreign Minister Sahlul. See also *al-Sudan al-Hadith,* 22 April 1991.
45. *Al-Wafd,* 16 June 1991.
46. *Al-Sharq al-Awsat,* 18 July 1991.
47. *New African,* October 1991.
48. Ibid.
49. *Al-Wafd,* 28 July 1991.
50. MENA, 23 August — DR, 26 August 1991, quoting staff Maj. Gen. Muhammad Tulba 'Uwayda, official spokesman for the Sudanese army.
51. *Al-Hayat* (London), 22 August; *al-Wafd,* 25 August 1991.
52. *Al-Sha'b* (Cairo), 27 August 1991.
53. BBC, 22 August — DR, 23 August, in the "Focus on Africa" program; *al-Sharq al-Awsat,* 17 October 1991.
54. *Al-Wafd,* 31 August; *al-Sharq al-Awsat,* 4, 23 September; *MEI,* 13 September 1991.
55. *Sawt al-Kuwait al-Duwali,* 1 October 1991.
56. *NYT,* 17 January; *AR,* January-February 1991.
57. *FT,* 9 January 1991, estimated the 1984–85 number of deaths at 250,000.
58. *CR,* Sudan, No. 2, 1991.
59. Foreign sources reported the export of 300,000–600,000 tons of food in 1990. *AR,* January-February; *FT,* 9 January 1991. In 1991, Sudan's grain needs were estimated at 1.2m.–1.5m. tons; USIS, 25 April, 14 August 1991.
60. E.g., R. Omdurman, 21 April — DR, 23 April 1991.
61. For example, the Red Crescent Society, one of the most effective nongovernmental agencies, had its constitution dissolved in 1990 and all its senior staff dismissed. *FT,* 9 January. See also *New African,* March and *AR,* March–April 1991.
62. Ahmad Kamal al-Din, the editor in chief of Sudan's two English-language publications, *New Horizons* and *Sudanow.* See *Atlanta Journal/Atlanta Constitution,* 10 March 1991.
63. SUNA, 5 January — DR, 4 February 1991, Maj. Gen. al-Zubayr Muhammad Salih, the deputy chairman of the RCCNS.
64. SUNA, 1 February — DR, 4 February; see also an inerview with Bashir, *al-'Alam* (London), 10 August 1991.

65. SUNA, 9 June — DR, 10 June; *AC*, 14 June; *New African,* October 1991.
66. E.g., *al-Inqadh al-Watani,* 3, 9, 16, 17 June 1991.
67. *Al-Quwat al-Musallaha,* 11, 15, 18 March 1991.
68. R. SPLA, 22 March — DR, 26 March 1991.
69. R. SPLA, 1 April — DR, 8 April 1991.
70. R. SPLA, 25 March — DR, 26 March 1991.
71. *Al-Quwat al-Musallaha,* 28 March 1991.
72. R. SPLA, 16 March — DR, 21 March 1991.
73. R. Omdurman, 15 June — DR, 21 June 1991.
74. *AC,* 14 June 1991.
75. AFP, 28 May — DR, 30 May 1991, quoting Sudan's culture and information minister.
76. E.g., *al-Sudan al-Hadith,* 9 July; *al-Inqadh al-Watani,* 18 July 1991.
77. *Al-'Alam* (London), 27 July 1991.
78. BBC, 30 August — DR, 3 September 1991. Their statement was given to the BBC East Africa correspondent, Colin Blane, who had been especially invited to southern Sudan by the dissidents in order to deliver their message to him.
79. *JP,* quoting AP from Khartoum, 1 September 1991.
80. E.g., *al-Quwat al-Musallaha,* 20 January, 8, 13 February; R. Omdurman, 6 March — DR, 8 March 1991.
81. AFP, a report from Khartoum, 19 January — DR, 22 January 1991.
82. SUNA, 27 January — DR, 28 January; AFP, a report from Khartoum, 4 February — DR, 5 February 1991.
83. *Al-Inqadh al-Watani,* 6 February 1991.
84. Sudanese culture and information minister at Cairo airport while en route to Amman, MENA, 25 July — DR, 26 July 1991.
85. *Al-Inqadh al-Watani,* 15 February 1991.
86. R. Omdurman, 14 March — DR, 18 March 1991.
87. PANA, 6 March — DR, 7 March 1991.
88. R. Khartoum, 26 March — DR, 27 March 1991. The number of Sudanese in Kuwait was estimated at 15,000 by Sudan's economy minister; *ME,* January 1991.
89. *CR,* Sudan, No. 3, 1991.
90. *Al-Jumhuriyya* (Cairo), 10 January 1991.
91. *Al-Sharq al-Awsat,* 23, 29 January 1991.
92. MENA, 23 January — DR, 24 January 1991.
93. R. Monte Carlo, 24 January — DR, 25 January 1991.
94. *Al-Sharq al-Awsat,* 24 January 1991.
95. MENA, 23 January — DR, 25 January 1991.
96. Opposition leaders' responses as appeared, e.g., in *al-Hayat* (London), 27 January 1991.
97. See R. Cairo, 23 January — DR, 24 January; *al-Wafd,* 27 January; *al-Madina,* 2 February; *al-Yasar,* March 1991.
98. *Al-Wafd,* 9 April 1991.
99. *CR,* Sudan, No. 3; for details on his visit, see *al-Sudan al-Hadith,* 30 July 1991.
100. *CR,* Sudan, No. 3, 1991.
101. Interview with Bashir, *al-Sha'b* (Cairo), 9 July 1991.
102. E.g., SUNA, 4 January, R. Omdurman, 1 July — DR, 4 January, 2 July 1991.
103. SUNA, 5 January — DR, 8 January 1991.
104. R. Tripoli, 29 June — DR, 2 July 1991.
105. R. Omdurman, 1 July — DR, 2 July 1991.
106. *Al-Majalla,* 11–17 December 1991.
107. *Al-Hayat* (London), 17 October 1991, quoting the minister of information and culture and acting foreign minister, Ahmad.
108. R. Tunis, 15 October — DR, 17 October; MENA, 9 November — DR, 12 November, quoting a Tunisian publication; *al-Hayat* (London), 7 December; *al-Wafd,* 15 December 1991.
109. E.g., *al-Inqadh al-Watani,* 10 February; SUNA, 12 March — DR, 18 March 1991.
110. SUNA, 31 October — DR, 1 November 1991.
111. Interview with Turabi, *Kayhan al-'Arabi,* 5 November 1991.

112. *Al-Inqadh al-Watani,* 25 March; *al-Nahar* (Beirut), 26 March 1991.
113. *CR,* Sudan, No. 2, 1991.
114. *MEI,* 14 June 1991.
115. E.g., SUNA, 20 June — DR, 24 June 1991.
116. *Akhir Sa'a,* 5 June 1991.
117. *Al-Sudan al-Hadith,* 29 May 1991.
118. R. Omdurman, 21, 25 September — DR, 23, 30 September; *al-Inqadh al-Watani,* 4 August 1991.
119. R. Omdurman, 31 December 1990 — DR, 3 January 1991.
120. *Al-Inqadh al-Watani,* 13 January 1991.

Syria

(Al-Jumhuriyya al-'Arabiyya al-Suriyya)

EYAL ZISSER

Syria was influenced by two major events during the course of 1991: the weakening of the Soviet Union and the eruption of the Gulf crisis in the wake of Iraq's takeover of Kuwait. The Gulf crisis evolved into full-scale war in the early part of the year, while the rapid disintegration of the Soviet Union during the latter part of the year led to its final collapse on 31 December. These two developments facilitated progress in the Middle East peace process, which toward the end of the year overshadowed most other events in Syria, as in the region at large.

Syria's position regarding the Gulf crisis, its siding with the US against Iraq, and its willingness to join the peace process reflected a dramatic change in its foreign policy and stood in striking contradiction to the ideological principles of its regime. While the disintegration of the Soviet Union was a major cause of this change, it was not the only one. A wide array of domestic and foreign problems that had been plaguing Syria since the early 1980s had become exacerbated toward the end of the decade. Domestically, the Syrian regime found itself in a predicament caused by an economic crisis and a growing demand for political reform in the wake of the changes in Eastern Europe. Regionally, Syria confronted a dead end in Lebanon because of its inability to enforce its authority over the various power elements in the country. In the inter-Arab arena, Syria continued to be isolated, while an unmistakable Iraqi threat began looming on its horizons after the Iraqi-Iranian War came to an end in 1988. Internationally, Syria was obliged to deal with the collapse of the East European Communist regimes, especially the Soviet Union, and the concomitant emergence of the US as the single world power.

As a result of these problems, Syria began forming a new policy in the late 1980s designed to improve its status and ensure its survival in the new US-dominated world order, with minimal concessions ideologically. The implementation of this policy led to the renewal of diplomatic ties with Egypt in 1989 and to a gradual warming of relations with Western Europe and the US during 1990. Syria's joining the anti-Iraq coalition in the course of the Gulf crisis, therefore, was the product of an ongoing process of change in policy. Joining the coalition, in fact, accelerated this process, as it helped improve Syria's status especially vis-à-vis the Gulf states, the US and Western Europe.

From Syria's point of view, this policy yielded several immediate gains, not least in the inter-Arab and regional arenas. For example, after a number of years of stagnation, Syria was able to force a solution of its liking to the problem of Lebanon, which seems to have been achieved with American backing. It also improved relations with Egypt and the Gulf states — receiving generous economic aid from the latter. Syria's status

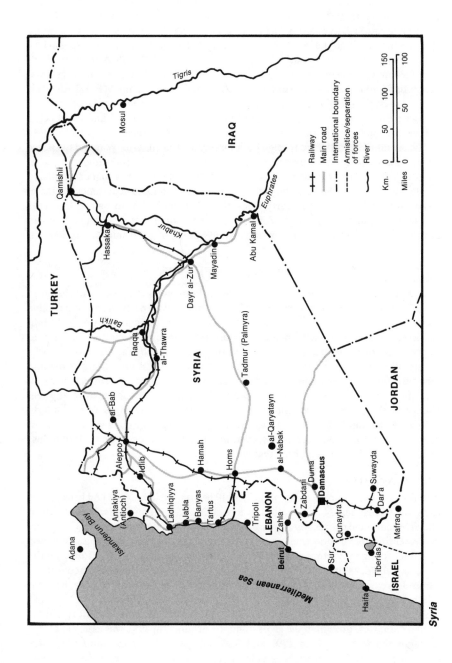

Syria

in the international arena improved considerably as well. Although it did not achieve close relations with the US, its need to reach an understanding with the US precipitated some moderation in its position on the Arab-Israeli conflict, at least ostensibly. Syria seems to have realized that the importance accorded by the US to this issue could be a key to improve bilateral relations. Syria also assessed the Bush Administration's regional policy as being more congenial to Syria than that of its predecessors, prompting it to consent to take part in negotiations for peace in the ME. Whether this attested to Syria's preparedness to accept the legitimacy of the State of Israel and sign a peace treaty with it, or simply reflected a desire to placate the US and avoid being blamed for the failure of the peace process, remained to be seen.

The prominence in 1991 of foreign policy issues such as the Gulf War and the peace process underscored the striking absence of any change in Syria's domestic scene. Although the regime was clearly hard put to adopt a foreign policy that contradicted its ideological principles, the country was politically calm and economically stable. Asad's reelection to office in early December 1991 marked a fitting end to a year whose eventfulness in the inter-Arab and international arenas did not have an immediately adverse effect on domestic stability or cause governmental ferment.

DOMESTIC AFFAIRS

Like the preceding year, 1991 was marked by an almost complete absence of change in Syria's social and economic systems. This situation was particularly remarkable inasmuch as the domestic arena had been a major cause for concern for the Syrian Ba'th regime during the past few years because of the ongoing economic crisis as well as pressures for political and economic reform precipitated by the dramatic changes taking place in Eastern Europe. The regime had adopted a program of slow and gradual economic liberalization and democratization as a solution to its problems. In fact, the democratization measures lacked substance and did not involve any real change in the power balance in Syria, and the economic changes were similarly limited. Apparently, the lesson drawn by the Syrian regime from events in Eastern Europe was that substantial reforms, even slow and gradual ones, would lead to loss of control and the collapse of the regime.

THE ECONOMY

As a result of the economic crisis of the mid-1980s, the Syrian regime had been forced to devote a great deal of its attention to economic affairs. It made vigorous efforts to alleviate economic distress by slowing down military buildup to some degree and by implementing liberalization measures (at the cost of ideological compromise) designed to attract foreign investors and encourage private enterprise. These efforts and the discovery and development of oil fields in eastern Syria, which enabled the country to export increasing quantities of oil and thus improve its commercial balance, brought relative economic stability as early as 1989. Stability was maintained in 1990 and 1991, and the economy even showed further improvement, as indicated by official Syrian data. Real growth in the gross domestic product for 1991 was assessed at 5%, as compared with 13.7% in 1990 and 3.2% in 1989.[1] A similar annual rise was anticipated for the coming years — a major objective of Syria's seventh five-year plan for 1991–96. The surplus in Syria's commercial balance for 1991 was assessed at some

$944m. ($3,706m. in export and $2,760m. in import), as compared with a surplus of $1,814m. in 1990 ($4,212m. in export and $2,400m. in import); a surplus of $991m. in 1989 ($2,812m. in export and $1,821m. in import); and a negative balance in preceding years.[2]

The dramatic improvement in Syria's commercial balance, and consequently in its overall economic situation, was mainly the result of a growth in oil production and export. In 1991, oil production in Syria reached some 470,000 barrels per day (b/d), as compared with 410,000 b/d in 1990 and only 300,000 b/d in 1989. Syria's oil production was expected to reach some 550,000 b/d in 1992. The country's oil export in 1991 was assessed at a value of $1,597m., as compared with $1,470m. in 1990 and $814m. in 1989, with an anticipated value of $2,250m. for 1992.[3]

The balance of expenditures and revenues in the Syrian budget was also positive in 1991, standing at £SY2,848bn. ($220m.): £SY60,437bn. ($5,375m.) in revenues, and £SY57,993bn. ($5,155m.) in expenditures.[4] This positive balance was mainly the result of an increase in tax revenues due to the growth in economic activity in Syria. It should also be borne in mind that Syria received generous grants of $2.5bn.–$3bn. during the course of the Gulf War, which, although not in the official data, improved Syria's economic situation considerably.[5]

Syria's foreign debt hardly rose at all in 1990, standing at $5,287m. at the end of the year, as compared with $5,202m. at the end of 1987.[6] The rate of inflation in Syria in 1990 was 20%, as compared with 11.4% in 1989, 34.6% in 1988 and as high as 59.4% in 1987.[7] The rate of inflation for 1991 was expected to increase as in 1990, and to reach 25% due to the curtailing of subsidies and the growth in the scope of economic activity.[8]

Some 100,000 Syrian workers returned from Kuwait to Syria during the course of the Gulf crisis, causing pressure on the Syrian job market, with unemployment rising to more than the 6% reported in official data. There was also less transfer of foreign currency into Syria as a result of the war.[9] On the whole, however, it would seem that the war caused no more than temporary and sectorial damage to the Syrian economy.

The improvement in Syria's economic situation was manifested in its consumer markets, with an abundance of goods available in 1991, and in the disappearance of the chronic shortages in staples that had characterized previous years. The regime continued implementing liberalization measures in an effort to take advantage of the relative economic stability and encourage private enterprise and foreign investment. A clear example of this was Investment Law No. 10, passed in May 1991, which was designed to make it easier for both local and foreign entrepreneurs to invest in the country. The initial impression, however, was that while the law encouraged private initiative on the part of Syrian investors, it did not bring the sought-after wave of foreign investment. It would seem that uncertainty concerning the prospects of economic stability in Syria, the country's awesome bureaucracy and the ideological vacillation of the regime prevented large-scale investment in Syria.[10]

The impressive (mainly official Syrian) economic data notwithstanding, Syria managed to do no more than block further economic deterioration and stabilize its market. It was unable to accomplish more since, as in previous years, there was no substantial change in the structure of the Syrian market, which was still controlled by government bureaucrats, and since a large portion of the budget and of the grants received by Syria continued to be allocated to security expenditure. Arms deals which

Syria apparently concluded with the Soviet Union alone were worth some $1.5bn.–$2bn. According to the official budget, Syria's expenditure on national security (army, police and internal security forces) in 1991 totaled £SY27,520bn. ($2,446m.) or 32.5% of the budget, as compared with £SY23,500bn. ($2,088m.) or 34.8% of the budget in 1990.[11] These factors prevented any significant improvement in Syria's economic situation in 1991.

THE POLITICAL SYSTEM AND THE STABILITY OF THE REGIME
During 1990, under the pressure of events in Eastern Europe, including the fall of Ceauşescu's regime in Romania, the Syrian regime began adopting ostensibly democratic measures. For example, it allowed new parties to be established and demonstrated relative openness in the elections to the People's Assembly in May 1990 (see *MECS* 1990, p. 654). Municipal elections were held on 21 February 1991 and there was a referendum to approve Hafiz al-Asad's candidacy for a fourth term of office on 2 December. These steps, however, seemed to have been little more than a facade which did not signify any real change in Syria's domestic scene. Apparently, the lesson which the Syrian regime learned from the collapse of the Soviet Union was that it should endeavor to prevent such a change at all costs.

Presidential Elections
With Asad's third seven-year term in office as president of Syria due to end on 12 February 1992, a constitutional amendment was passed in 1991 allowing the approval of his candidacy for a fourth term to be brought forward. Following Syrian constitutional provisions for a two-stage presidential election, i.e., the selection of the candidate by the People's Assembly followed by the approval of his candidacy by referendum, the People's Assembly on 17 November unanimously nominated President Asad as the sole candidate for the presidency.[12] The nomination followed an official recommendation by the Ba'th Party Regional Command, which declared that in nominating Asad it was "responding to a comprehensive popular consensus in support of his outstanding leadership, affirming the historic role he played in leading the people's march toward reconstruction and liberation."[13] Asad's candidacy was approved by an overwhelming majority in a referendum held throughout Syria on 2 December. According to official Syrian data, 6,727,992 Syrians, comprising 94% of the eligible voters, participated in the referendum, with 99.98% voting for Asad's candidacy. Only 396 individuals, less than 0.005% of the voters, voted against it.[14] However, the referendum, conducted with voters marking their ballots in full view of the ballot-box officials, was not a truly democratic procedure and could not indicate the real extent of support for Asad's regime.

The regime utilized the referendum for a propaganda campaign aimed at stirring up its supporters and the Syrian population at large. The media praised the president extensively, and mass demonstrations of support were organized throughout the country, with more than 2m. Syrians participating in them, according to official accounts.[15] Even the small Jewish community in Damascus was enlisted to express loyalty to the president.[16] The government-orchestrated demonstrations reflected the regime's desire to project a spirit of business as usual in the face of threats to its stability posed by the collapse of East European communism and the government's participation in a peace process with Israel.

The Failure to Convene the Ba'th Party Congress

The Ba'th Party congress, scheduled to be held once every four years, was last held in January 1985 and from 1989 onward was postponed annually without explanation. Nor did it take place in 1991, although rumors about its imminent convention had been current since late 1989. There appeared to be two reasons for the postponements. First, the government wished to avoid confronting the ideological quandary posed by the collapse of East European communism and the contradictions between its traditional positions and the steps it had taken in the recent past, such as participating in the anti-Iraq coalition and in the peace process. Second, the regime wished to avoid dealing with issues that could destabilize the domestic balance of power in the country. In this connection it should be noted that although the brothers Hafiz and Rif'at al-Asad had met in Geneva in November 1990, their relationship had not improved sufficiently to allow for Rif'at to return to Syria. Meanwhile, Asad's son, Basil, was gradually gaining power and influence, although he had perhaps not yet reached political maturity.

The Stability of the Regime

The regime maintained its stability and its control over the country throughout the year. The few disturbances that did occur took place at the beginning of the year and derived from the Gulf War.

Most of the reports on disturbances in Syria came from Iraqi sources and were repeated by Jordanian ones but were rarely confirmed by other sources. One report taht received wide publicity alleged that 80 Syrian writers and artists, who had signed a letter of protest expressing solidarity with Iraq and objecting to the war against it, had been arrested, but the Syrian regime published a firm denial of the story, as did several of the Syrian intellectuals alleged to have been arrested.[17]

The Iraqi and Jordanian media also focused on statements critical of the Syrian regime made by opposition bodies, some of them, such as the Muslim Brothers, based abroad. For example, in mid-January the Jordanian media quoted statements by the Syrian Muslim Brothers and the Syrian National Party (Jordan and Palestine legation) expressing support for Iraq's "struggle against Zionist-American aggression."[18] Iraqi radio also broadcast an appeal by the Syrian Muslim Brothers, published in Amman, "for the overthrow of Hafiz al-Asad's regime because of its plots against Iraq and its siding with the enemies of Iraq and the Arab people."[19] Such reports from Amman and Baghdad, however, were clearly tendentious and therefore unreliable. In fact, the Jordanians soon stopped publicizing such reports after being reprimanded by the Syrian media (see section on relations between Syria and Jordan below).

Despite the potential disruptive impact of the momentous events in Eastern Europe, Syria remained calm domestically during the entire year. Even its involvement in the peace process did not precipitate the signs of dissatisfaction or protest that the regime feared. The relative calm in the Syrian streets, in comparison with previous years, probably resulted from economic stability as well as from acceptance of the regime's foreign policy, in the face of international change.

But although there was no concrete or immediate threat to its stability, the Syrian regime felt pressured during the course of the year, primarily because of the dissonance between its ideology and its actual policy. This ideological quandary was reflected in the fact that Asad refrained from delivering the main speeches on Revolution Day on

8 March, the anniversary of the October War on 6 October, and Corrective Revolution Day on 16 November. It was also manifested by extensive efforts to explain the government's foreign policy in the Syrian media, among party activists and to senior officials, as well as numerous rallies held toward the end of the year to enlist support for Syria's participation in the peace process (see section on the conflict with Israel below). Another sign of the regime's unease was extensive media activity surrounding Asad's reelection for a fourth term.

The message the regime delivered by means of rallies and propaganda campaigns was clear: Syria's policy was sound and unchanged; at most, the state was making certain tactical adaptations to the new world order, but without budging from its traditional ideology. Syrian propaganda also portrayed Syria's participation in the peace process as an achievement and as a logical continuation of its long-term policy (see section on Syria and the conflict with Israel, below). Dealing with the collapse of East European communism, which posed a considerable challenge to the regime, the Syrian media maintained that since the country's approach was the only true road to socialism, the disintegration of the East European regimes should have no bearing upon it. A *Tishrin* editorial stated:

> The collapse of the regimes that used to call themselves socialist in Eastern Europe does not mean the end of socialism and the collapse of socialist thinking. Rather it signals the collapse of a pattern of socialist practice that will be rightly judged and assessed by history....The importance of the Corrective Movement led by struggler Hafiz al-Asad can be seen. This movement advanced the principle of political and economic pluralism almost two decades ago. It also devised methods for political and social development that proved capable of withstanding the toughest foreign pressures.[20]

Another step taken apparently to assure domestic peace was the general pardon announced at the end of the year on the occasion of Asad's reelection, a move that could be viewed as a sign of the regime's self-confidence. The pardon, which involved the release of 2,864 prisoners convicted of violating state security, reportedly was decided upon in order to demonstrate goodwill toward Islamic groups in Syria, to which most of the released prisoners belonged, and in response to a request by a Jordanian Muslim Brothers' delegation that visited Syria as guests of the regime. Indeed, in a statement published in Amman, the chairman of the political bureau of the Muslim Brothers in Syria commended the step as "positive."[21]

FOREIGN AFFAIRS

RELATIONS WITH THE UNITED STATES

One of the major developments of 1991 was the growth of US influence and power in the ME and in the world at large. America's leadership of the anti-Iraq coalition during the Gulf War and its active involvement in the peace process were impressive examples not only of its military and political capabilities but of its status as the dominant power in the region. (For further discussion of this, and other issues surveyed in this section, see chapter on the US and the ME.)

This American rise to dominance, precipitated by the collapse of the Soviet Union, obliged Syria to try to improve relations with Washington, so as to enable Syria to continue playing a role in the emergent new world order with minimal ideological and political concessions. Moreover, the Syrians hoped that closer ties with the US would bring political and economic gains.

Their rapprochement, begun during 1990, was accelerated by the US need for Syria's cooperation during the Gulf crisis and its subsequent interest in guaranteeing Syrian participation in the peace process. However, the process of rapprochement between the US and Syria proceeded slowly, mainly because the US insisted that it be contingent upon Syria ceasing to foster terrorism, ending the involvement of senior officers in the cultivation of drugs in the Lebanese Biqa', and adopting a more moderate stance toward Israel. Implicitly, the US also expected Syria to respect human rights, including the rights of minorities such as the Jews, and to institute political freedom. Similarly, American economic aid was made contingent upon structural reforms in the Syrian economy.[22]

Attempting to comply with some of the American demands during the course of the year, Syria reportedly withdrew support from several terrorist organizations. Indeed, in the course of the Gulf War the US implicitly complimented Syria for its contribution in minimizing terrorist attacks against Western targets.[23] Moreover, the findings of the investigation of the 1988 Pan Am explosion published in 1991 did not include any evidence of Syrian involvement, a conclusion that was criticized by Israel, by the victims' families, and even by some of the press in the US.[24] Toward the end of the year, the Syrians, acting together with Iran, were involved in achieving the release of all the Western hostages held in Lebanon, including the five Americans, and won the gratitude of the US (see chapter on the US and the ME).

Yet, this was not perceived by the US to be sufficient. The State Department's annual report for 1990 on "Patterns of Global Terrorism," published in April 1991, once again named Syria as a country that supported terrorism.[25] Even after Syria was cleared of involvement in the Pan Am disaster, American Administration spokespersons reiterated that Syria was still on the list of countries sheltering terrorist organizations.[26]

The Syrians repeatedly denied any connection with the cultivation of drugs, and gave considerable publicity to reports on operations aimed at preventing or curtailing the smuggling of large quantities of drugs from Lebanon to Syria.[27] Here too, however, there is no indication that its efforts satisfied the American Administration. In addition, in a hearing of the Congressional Human Rights Caucus held on 24 April, Syria was once again accused of violating civil rights and of persecuting the Syrian Jews. At the hearing, caucus chairman Tom Lantos quoted the 1990 State Department Human Rights Report on Syria according to which: "Major human rights abuses including torture, arbitrary arrest and detention and denial of freedom of speech, press and association and the right of citizens to change the government continued to characterize the regime's record in 1990." Tom Lantos further said that the US should insist that Syria end its human rights violations before improving relations.[28] Toward the end of the year Israel and American Jewish organizations condemned the Syrian regime's treatment of the Jewish community, which was given prominent exposure in the media. All of this seemed to have detracted from Syria's image among the American public and with American decision-makers.

A closer understanding between the US and Syria was attained on the issue of the ME peace process, which became the main focus of American involvement in the region after the Gulf War. The Syrians seemed to have understood that their stand on this issue would determine their relationship with the US and hoped that even limited progress in the peace process would serve to improve their relations with the US. Furthermore, the Syrians felt that the Bush Administration's position was closer to theirs than that of its predecessors, giving cause for optimism that a resolution to the conflict — especially regarding the future of the Golan Heights — would be more favorable for them than any other alternative.

Syria therefore welcomed President Bush's March declaration officially launching the new stage in the peace process, which established the principle of land for peace as its basis. According to *Tishrin,* this declaration was "positive and enhances the chances of attaining a just and comprehensive peace in the region."[29]

Nevertheless, it took American Secretary of State James Baker eight visits to Damascus, between March and May, during which he conducted extensive discussions with President Asad and other senior officials, to pave the way for Syria's participation in the peace process. On 1 June, Baker delivered a letter to Syrian Foreign Minister Faruq al-Shar' in Lisbon containing President Bush's proposal for the convening of a peace conference. Asad's response, received by the US only on 14 July,[30] reflected not only a willingness to negotiate with Israeli representatives, but also a concession in the form of waiving the traditional Syrian demand that the ME conflict be resolved by an international conference attended by the five permanent members of the UN Security Council, with Europe and the UN having a special status. Nevertheless, the Syrians made it clear that they would not participate in the multilateral talks that were scheduled to be held about a month after the Madrid Peace Conference. They intimated that the reason they had responded positively to the conference idea was that the US had promised them that they would regain sovereignty over the Golan Heights. The US made it clear, however, that promises made to Syria did not conflict with those offered to Israel on any point. Baker emphasized at a press conference in Damascus that all that the US conveyed to Syria was the traditional American position, i.e., that UN Resolution 242 applied to the Golan Heights and that the annexation of the Golan Heights by Israel did not meet with US approval.[31] Syria's positive response was welcomed by the US, with both President Bush and Secretary of State Baker describing it as a "breakthrough."[32]

Although the Syrians had reached an understanding with the US Administration on some issues on the agenda, and were satisfied with some of the American decisions (such as postponing discussion of the loan guarantees for Israel, which the Syrians viewed as proof of the seriousness of President Bush's peace initiative),[33] they made no effort to conceal their frustration with the fact that the American position was still far from serving their interests. Syria continued attacking the US for its massive support for Israel, stipulating that US credibility would be tested on this issue specifically.[34] It also viewed American hints about the desirable resolution to the ME conflict with great suspicion. For example, it was dissatisfied with the speech delivered by President Bush at the Madrid conference in which he stressed the need for changes in Israel's borders in order to guarantee its security, as well as the importance of ending the conflict by signing peace treaties between the parties, without addressing the principle of land for peace.[35] The Syrians also rejected a proposal for arms control in the ME that Bush made in May, arguing that it would perpetuate Israel's military superiority and thus not contribute to resolving the major problem in the ME — Israel's aggressive policy.[36]

Furthermore, although talks between Syrian and American officials were intensive, they were not especially warm, and no close relationships developed between the presidents and foreign ministers of the two countries. Even the appointment in mid-June of US Ambassador to Damascus Edward Djerejian as assistant secretary of state for Near Eastern and South Asian affairs, making him one of the leading figures in the peace process, which was perceived by the Syrians as a position sign, failed to help warm relations with the US.[37]

That the understanding between Syria and the US was limited to certain issues and could not transcend the wide political and psychological gap between them was illuminated when, toward the end of the year, the US named Libya as responsible for blowing up the Pan Am plane over Lockerbie, Scotland, in 1988. The Syrians were satisfied with their being acquitted from such responsibility, and attempted to use their newfound relationship with the US to defuse the tension between it and Libya. Having failed in that, however, they sided with Libya and criticized the campaign in the West against it, which Vice President 'Abd al-Halim Khaddam called a "campaign against Syria and all pure people of the Arab nation."[38] Thus, while Syria's motivation to strengthen relations with the US grew, the gap between the two countries still remained wide in many spheres.

SYRIA AND THE SOVIET UNION

During the previous few years, the Syrians had endeavored to ignore the changes in the Soviet Union and give their relations with it a business-as-usual air. Damascus continued to portray the Soviet Union as a political, military and economic backer and as a true friend of the Syrian regime. But events finally persuaded the Syrians that the Soviet Union could no longer be considered a real backer. The Soviet passivity during the Gulf War, its secondary role to the US regarding the peace process in the ME, and its eventual disintegration confirmed this conclusion. Ultimately, the official Syrian media ceased its efforts to present the Soviet Union as a stable source of support. Syria's reaction to the abortive coup of 19 August in the USSR typified the attitude it had developed toward the Soviet Union: the Syrian media reported the coup but refrained from any commentary or analysis.[39]

Nevertheless, the two states maintained the same scope of military cooperation as in previous years. The number of Soviet advisers in the Syrian army remained almost unchanged. Exchange visits by military officials continued, albeit on a smaller scale, with the deputy defense minister visiting Syria in May and the commander of the Soviet Navy visiting in September.[40] The Syrians continued viewing the Soviet Union as a potential weapons supplier, and even hoped to profit from Russia's economic distress, which, they thought, might make it more interested in selling weapons. Syrian Minister of Defense Mustafa Talas visited the Soviet Union from 3–7 February with the aim of finalizing a new arms deal[41] (see section on Syria and the conflict with Israel, below), but the final collapse of the Soviet Union in late 1991 raised doubts about the realization of this deal and forced Syria to search for alternative weapons suppliers, such as North Korea and China. The level of economic ties, too, remained similar to that of previous years, with the Soviet Union continuing to be a preferred destination for Syria's commercial export. In 1990, 44.3% of Syria's export went to the Soviet Union.[42]

The continuation of close military and economic ties between the Soviet Union and

Syria contrasted sharply with the decline in their political relations. The only political visits during 1991 were those by Syrian Foreign Minister Shar' to Moscow on 3–5 April, during which he met with Gorbachev, and two visits by Soviet foreign ministers to Syria: Bessmertnykh on 8–9 May and Boris Pankin on 18–19 October[43] — a stark contrast to the intensive contacts between the two countries in the past and another sign of the Soviet Union's decline in value to the Syrians. Even the few visits that did take place were connected with the American initiative to promote the peace process, accentuating the decline in the status of the Soviet Union in the region.

RELATIONS WITH WESTERN EUROPE AND
THE EUROPEAN COMMUNITY
Relations between Syria and the European Community (EC) countries continued to improve during 1991. Syria's effort to develop these relations stemmed both from economic interests and from a desire to counterbalance American dominance in the ME, especially concerning the peace process, in view of the fact that the EC position was more sympathetic to Syria than the US one.

Syria's relations with the EC improved both in the economic and in the political spheres. During the course of the Gulf War, the EC reapproved £100m. in economic aid to Syria that it had suspended since 1986. Syria was also promised loans by several of the EC countries individually.[44] The fact that in 1990, for example, almost half of Syria's export went to EC countries and over 60% of its import originated there also attested to these countries' economic centrality for Syria.[45]

In the political sphere, Syria pressed for European representation in the peace talks. Radio Damascus wondered: "How can Europe be distanced from the peace conference when Europe is linked to the Middle East by a series of vital, strong historical bonds?"[46] This position, and the concomitant recognition by Western European countries of Syria's centrality to the peace process, in which they wished to play a part, elicited visits by European foreign ministers to Damascus at a rate that the Syrian capital had not witnessed in many years. During the course of 1991, the foreign ministers of most of the EC countries visited Syria individually or in groups, as did the Italian prime minister as well, while Foreign Minister Shar' visited the EC headquarters in Brussels and a number of other European capitals in late May.

Most remarkable was the improvement in relations between Syria and Britain. Diplomatic ties between them had been renewed in 1990 (see *MECS* 1990, p. 658), and ambassadors were exchanged in February 1991. This led to intensive political contacts between the two states, most of them at foreign-minister level: Shar' visited London on 6–7 February[47] and British Foreign Office Minister Douglas Hogg reciprocated in February, March and June.

Noteworthy, too, was the improvement in Syria's relations with Germany, which was becoming increasingly prominent among the European countries. The improvement was reflected in a visit to Damascus by German Foreign Minister Hans-Dietrich Genscher during the Gulf War, on 13–14 February.[48]

In contrast, Syria's relations with France remained strained as a result of long-standing disagreements regarding Lebanon. The French were opposed to the dominance that Syria had attained in Lebanon, and although they reluctantly recognized the legitimacy of the brotherhood and cooperation treaty signed between Syria and Lebanon, they asserted in an official communiqué that as part of the Ta'if agreement Syria should withdraw its forces from Lebanon (as should Israel) and enable free elections to be held there.[49] Relations between the two countries were further strained by the issue of the fate of Gen. 'Awn, who spent most of the year sheltered in the French Embassy in Beirut. In early September, the Hirawi regime reached an agreement with France, which allowed 'Awn to leave Lebanon. However, in violation of this agreement, 'Awn, upon arriving in Paris, attacked Syria and, in an interview with *Le Figaro* called for a general revolt against it (see also chapter on Lebanon).[50] The tension between the two countries was reflected in the cancellation of a visit to Damascus by French Foreign Minister Roland Dumas, which had been scheduled for December, leaving Dumas practically the only EC foreign minister not to have visited Damascus in 1991. The Syrians claimed that the visit had been canceled on their initiative.[51] The only visit by a French statesman to Syria during the year was that of François Scheer, secretary-general of the French Ministry of Foreign Affairs, which took place on 8 February in the midst of the Gulf War.[52]

On the whole, however, the year was a positive one in terms of Syria's relations with Western Europe. The release of most of the Western hostages held in Lebanon, including Britons John McCarthy, Jack Mann and Terry Waite, which signaled the Syrian (and Iranian) desire for more positive relations with the West, was a fitting end to the year.

THE INTER-ARAB ARENA

Syria's standing in the inter-Arab arena continued to improve in 1991. It expanded cooperation and coordination with Egypt during the Gulf War early in the year, and developed its ties with the Gulf states, which were grateful for Syrian support. Syria's participation in the peace process in a key role during the latter part of the year also led to an improvement in its relations with Jordan and the PLO.

SYRIA, THE GULF WAR AND RELATIONS WITH IRAQ
Early in the Gulf crisis, Syria placed itself firmly in the US-led anti-Iraq camp. Its commitment to the anti-Iraq coalition grew as the crisis peaked during the war itself, when Syrian troops participated in the fighting for the liberation of Kuwait. (For details on the fighting, see chapter on the Gulf War.)

Press reports in the West disparaged the capability and motivation demonstrated by the Syrian forces in the Gulf. Syria dispatched only ground troops to the Gulf, and its participation in the war was limited to artillery fire in response to an Iraqi attack on Syrian positions and to ground combat against Iraqi forces retreating from Kuwait. According to reports (denied by the Syrians), Syrian artillery fire intentionally missed the Iraqi targets it was supposed to hit.[53]

All this, however, did not detract from the significance of Syria's participation alongside the US in the fighting against another Arab country, a development which was difficult for the regime to explain both at home and in the Arab world. Relative calm was maintained throughout the war domestically, but there was also criticism of the regime, some of which was inflated beyond proportion by Iraqi and Jordanian media. Countering this criticism, Syria devised a clear-cut information line which laid the blame for the war on Saddam for rejecting all compromise proposals and causing real damage to the interests of the Arab nation. Hinting at their concept of Iraq as a strategic force in a prospective confrontation with Israel,[54] the Syrians declared that the damage Saddam caused to Iraq's army and to its political and economic infrastructure detracted from the resources and capabilities of the Arab nation as a whole. Syria also portrayed the Iraqi Government as having shattered Arab unity and accused it of harming the "sacred" Palestinian cause by undermining Arab claims against Israel.[55] Reacting to Saddam's use of Islamic motifs, Syria emphasized that his struggle had nothing to do with Islam. Syria's decision to join the anti-Iraq camp, it explained, was prompted by the need to protect Arab interests that might otherwise be taken over by "foreign elements," and was grounded in resolutions by international forums (the UN) and inter-Arab bodies (the Arab League).[56]

This line was reflected in a letter sent by Asad to Saddam Husayn on 12 January, on the eve of the war, which was given wide publicity in the Syrian media. Asad called upon the Iraqi president to accept the demands of the international community and withdraw from Kuwait for the sake of the Arab nation. He promised that should Iraq be attacked after withdrawing, Syria would take its side. He also pointed out that the only party to benefit from the crisis was Israel.[57] Vice President Khaddam joined the Syrian propaganda effort when, in a speech to a convention of high-ranking officials of the Ba'th Party and other organizations in Syria during the war, on 10 February, he settled on a long historical account with Iraq's leaders going back to the Hashemite period. Khaddam gave a lengthy account of all the disputes that had broken out between Syria and Iraq in the course of recent history, blaming Iraq for them all. He also accused Iraq of fomenting the Muslim Brothers' rebellion in Syria in the early 1980s. Khaddam reiterated that Iraq's actions rendered objections to Israeli aggression illogical. Syria could not stay neutral in the conflict, he stressed, because Arab resources were endangered and unless Arab forces took action in the Gulf, foreign forces would do so instead.[58]

Iraq's missile attacks on Israel were hardly mentioned in the Syrian media except in terms of the benefit derived by Israel from them. Syria pointed out that Israel received generous economic and military aid from the West and its international image soared as a result of the attacks, while the Palestinian uprising was pushed to the sidelines. A bus accident would have caused the same damage as the Iraqi missiles, *Tishrin* argued.[59] The Syrian news agency asserted that "the Iraqi regime will not deceive Arabs by firing a few missiles against occupied Palestine," and that "such a game will not liberate land nor restore displaced people to its land. The only target of such a game is to expand the scale of the fire and to involve the Arab nation at the wrong time and place. The game is an Israeli demand which serves the enemy's interest at this particular time more than ever."[60]

Undoubtedly, these views in the Syrian media reflected the position of Syria's leaders. Indeed, Khaddam, Shar' and Defense Minister Mustafa Talas made it clear that they would not allow Iraq to involve Syria in a war with Israel. Shar' went so far as to declare that Syria would not alter its position even if Israel retaliated against Iraq.[61]

In early March, when the collapse of Saddam's regime seemed imminent, Syria was forced to consider the possible replacements for it, none of which seemed attractive: American patronage, Iranian involvement (which could entail the rise to power of Shi'ite fundamentalism), or Turkish involvement (which might entail the dismemberment of Iraq in its extant form). Two responses to this dilemma emerged.

One was a call for the liquidation of Saddam's regime (including in the literal sense) voiced not only by Iraqi oppositionists based in Damascus, but also by an editorial in *al-Thawra* calling for Saddam's assassination.[62] The editorial apparently went too far for the government's taste, prompting Syrian Minister of Information Muhammad Salman to explain that it expressed the personal opinion of its author only and not an official appeal on the part of the government.[63] Simultaneously, Syria tried to make use of exiled Iraqis, some of whom had been especially summoned to Damascus to foment a revolt in Iraq. However, the exiles lacked a power base and were divided among themselves, so that Syria retracted its idea of organizing them to overthrow Saddam's regime and settled for utilizing them for counterpropaganda purposes.[64] Iraqi refugees who fled to Syria toward the end of the war in search of food and shelter were utilized for similar purposes.

Yet Syria also made a considerable effort to preserve Iraq's independence and territorial integrity. For example, it warned Turkey unequivocally in light of Turkish territorial claims in northern Iraq not to interfere with Iraq's territorial integrity, which, Syria, declared, it viewed as holy.[65]

Once the situation in Iraq stabilized, in April, the anti-Saddam propaganda campaign in the Syrian media was reduced in intensity. Apparently, Syria considered Saddam's remaining in power unthreatening and preferable to any other alternative once the war was over.

RELATIONS WITH SAUDI ARABIA AND THE GULF STATES

Syria's siding with Kuwait, Saudi Arabia and the other Gulf states during the course of the Gulf crisis made them morally and materially indebted to it. Syria began collecting this debt in late 1990, when it received $2.5bn.–$3bn. from Kuwait and Saudi Arabia in compensation for having sent troops to the Gulf and for economic damage it incurred as a result of the Gulf crisis.[66] Relations between Syria and the Gulf states remained close after the war with the parties working together, alongside Egypt, on future security arrangements in the Gulf. The security formula that was worked out, known as the Damascus declaration, was published in early March following talks between the foreign ministers of the countries involved.[67] Although the declaration also dealt with economic cooperation, it concentrated on security arrangements, stipulating that Syrian as well as Egyptian troops would remain as permanent defense forces in the Gulf in return for generous economic aid from the Gulf states.[68]

Later, however, the declaration was rendered null and void, as the Gulf states, as well as Syria, reconsidered their position, possibly as a result of Iranian pressure. The Syrians began a rapid withdrawal of their forces from the Gulf in June and suspended plans to replace them with other forces.[69]

Syria and the Gulf states disagreed on the peace process as well. Despite considerable pressure exerted by Syria on the Gulf states not to make any goodwill gesture toward Israel that could be interpreted as recognition of its existence, the Gulf states (as several North African states) sent an observer — 'Abdallah Bishara, secretary-general of the Gulf Cooperation Council — to the Madrid conference. They also declared their willingness to participate in the multilateral talks in Moscow, which Syria refused to attend.[70]

Nevertheless, on the whole, relations between Syria and the Gulf states continued improving, to the mutual benefit of both sides. Intensive contacts between their foreign ministers attested to the importance accorded by both sides to diplomatic coordination, while visits to Damascus in September by the emir of Kuwait, Shaykh Jabir al-Ahmad Al Sabah, and United Arab Emirates' President Shaykh Zayid Ibn Sultan Al Nuhayan[71] further highlighted the close relations between the parties.

RELATIONS WITH EGYPT

The Egyptian-Syrian axis, which began forming in 1990, remained a focus of Syria's activity in the inter-Arab arena in 1991 as well. Syria needed coordination with Egypt on the Gulf War, the ensuing security arrangements, and the peace process. Moreover, while the West tried to use Egypt to achieve some flexibility and moderation on the Syrian side, Syria regarded Egypt as a means for attaining friendship with the West, and with the US in particular. Cooperation between Syria and Egypt was manifested mainly in meetings between their two presidents, who developed warm personal ties, meeting five times during the year (on 1 April, 5 June, and 12 October in Cairo, and on 19 May and 17 July in Damascus). The foreign ministers of the two countries also met frequently, further strengthening relations. Egypt and Syria acted together to consolidate future security arrangements in the Gulf during the early part of the year, and when the Gulf states reneged upon the agreement reached on this issue, Egypt and Syria (which came to have second thoughts) jointly withdrew their forces from the Gulf. During the latter part of the year, Egypt made vigorous efforts to moderate Syria's position regarding the peace process and to increase Syria's commitment to it.[72] It would seem, however, that although there was a mutuality of interests between the two countries, and although their leaders developed good personal relations, Mubarak could not manage to exert much influence on Asad, who continued to act entirely in his own interests. In fact, Asad tried exploiting his relations with Egypt in order to promote Syrian interests in the inter-Arab arena and vis-à-vis the US.

RELATIONS WITH THE PLO

After years of stagnation, relations between Syria and the PLO improved dramatically during 1991. This rapprochement was precipitated by the regional peace process, which prompted Syria to coordinate with all the Arab elements involved, but even more so by Syria's fear (which had already become obvious the previous year) that the Palestinians would reach a separate peace treaty with Israel and leave Syria behind. It was primarily as a result of this fear that Syrian abandoned its traditional policy regarding the PLO and its manifest aversion to its leader, Yasir 'Arafat, and set in motion a process of gradual rapprochement with the PLO. The declared purpose of this process was to coordinate political positions with the PLO, but in fact it was designed to harness the PLO to the Syrian wagon. The official PLO leadership, for its part, was interested in rapprochement with Syria in order to improve its status, which had declined considerably as a result of the Gulf crisis, as well as to integrate into the peace process. It was also implicitly interested in ensuring that the Syrians did not reach a separate agreement with Israel regarding the Golan Heights at the expense of the Palestinian issue.

During the first few months of the year, the polarized positions which Syria and the PLO had held in the course of the Gulf crisis continued to cast a heavy shadow on their relations (see *MECS* 1990, p. 665). However, after the inception of the peace process in the region, the Syrians, in a gesture of goodwill, released in March some 300 members of Fath who had been jailed in Syria for various offenses.[73] In April, high-level contacts began between Faruq Qaddumi, head of the PLO's political department, who had always been regarded as close to the Syrians, and Syrian officials such as Vice President Khaddam and Foreign Minister Shar'. On 26 May, Qaddumi visited Syria at the head of an official PLO delegation and met with Asad, as well as with Khalid al-Fahum, chairman of the National Salvation Front, with which the PLO had a long-standing dispute. At the end of the visit, both sides declared that they were turning over a new leaf in their relations.[74] Qaddumi returned to Damascus in July for another round of talks and again in October for the conference of the five Arab foreign ministers held in preparation for the Madrid conference[75] (see chapter on inter-Arab relations).

Rapprochement between Syria and the PLO peaked with a series of visits by 'Arafat to Syria, for the first time since his deportation from the country in 1983. On 29 August, 'Arafat met with Syrian Vice President Khaddam in Benghazi, Libya. On 19 October, he arrived for a visit in Damascus, where he met with Asad. Shafiq al-Hut, head of the PLO executive committee, defined the talks with the Syrians as "long-desired" talks which had been "amiable, intimate and genuine," and "produced agreement to coordinate moves between Syria and the PLO concerning the peace conference."[76] Two additional visits to Damascus were made by 'Arafat on 7 November and 2 December.

The thaw — at least formally — in Syria's relations with the PLO was also manifested in the Lebanese arena where, obeying Syrian orders, the Lebanese army eased its pressure on the Palestinian organizations deployed in the southern refugee camps. The Syrian orders were issued as well because some of the organizations deployed in the camps, such as the Popular Front for the Liberation of Palestine and the Democratic Front for the Liberation of Palestine, reestablished their base in Damascus and despite disagreements over the Gulf crisis continued to enjoy its patronage.[77]

RELATIONS WITH JORDAN

Relations between Syria and Jordan deteriorated to some extent early in the year because of Jordan's clear and unequivocal support for Iraq during the Gulf crisis. This disrupted the ongoing and mutually beneficial improvement in relations between the two countries that had occurred since 1986. Relations reached their lowest point in the course of the war itself, mainly because the Jordanian media, having become a vehicle for Iraqi propaganda, published tendentious reports on opposition in Syria to Asad's Gulf crisis policy. Syria reacted harshly. A *Tishrin* editorial declared that the policy being pursued by Jordan, which "claims concern for Iraq, embroiled the Iraqi rulers in the current crisis by publicizing the enormity of Iraqi military capabilities and fanning Saddam's conceit, thus prompting him to refuse to yield to the Arab and international community['s will] and [to] escalate matters to the point of catastrophe."[78] According to a report (later denied by both Syria and Jordan), Syria also expressed its dissatisfaction with Jordanian policy by imposing restrictions on the entry of Jordanian citizens into Syria.[79]

Nevertheless, Syria was careful not to sever its ties with Jordan completely, and even promised to aid it should it be attacked by Israel.[80] Syria also expressed its preparedness to supply much-needed oil to Jordan after the Iraqi oil artery — the Baghdad-Amman road — had been damaged by allied bombings and the Saudis refused to supply oil to Jordan.[81] Contacts on a ministerial level, too, continued as before. Political contacts as well as mutual visits of ministers and even telephone calls between King Husayn and President Asad took place before and during the war,[82] as did commercial and economic relations between the two countries.

Relations improved after the Gulf War, largely as a result of the peace process and the consequent need felt by the Syrians to close ranks with the Jordanians, whom they considered to be the weak link in the Arab world because their increased dependence on the US after the war made them, Syria believed, likely to reach a separate peace agreement with Israel. After seven months of communication by phone alone, Asad and King Husayn met in Damascus on 25 March, followed by two more visits by Husayn on 18 May and 19 August.[83] Syria seemed to understand that its ability to influence Jordan's policy on the peace process was limited by Jordan's total dependence on the US and therefore concentrated its political efforts on influencing the Palestinian side.

SYRIA AND THE LEBANESE ISSUE

From Syria's point of view, one of the most positive consequences of its rapprochement with the West was the improvement of its status in Lebanon. During the course of the year, Syria achieved legitimacy for this status in Lebanon itself, in the inter-Arab arena, and even in the US and Europe (excluding France). After 15 years of largely futile Syrian involvement in Lebanon, there was now a widespread international consensus concerning the vital role Syria was playing in maintaining stability in the country as well as in rehabilitating it.

On 13 October 1990, Syrian troops had taken over the enclave held by Gen. 'Awn around Ba'abda palace in Beirut, thus clearing away the last obstacle to control of the country by Syria's protégé, Ilyas al-Hirawi, which in effect meant Syrian hegemony over Lebanon (see *MECS* 1990, chapter on Lebanon). Hirawi, indeed, immediately entrenched himself around Beirut and in other areas of Lebanon, with American encouragement and with Israel's silent consent, while Syria's presence and influence in Lebanon grew stronger, leading eventually to the signing of the Treaty of Brotherhood and Cooperation between Syria and Lebanon on 22 May. The treaty, which legitimized Syria's special status in Lebanon, declared that "the bilateral relations between Lebanon and Syria are designed by historical and geographical considerations which go deep." Because "Lebanon may be the source of aggression against Syria," the treaty sanctioned Syrian involvement in Lebanon's security and foreign policy. The scope and duration of the presence of Syrian forces in Lebanon, it stipulated, would be decided by the Supreme Council (of the presidents of Syria and Lebanon) — in violation of the Ta'if Accords of 1989, which specified that Syrian forces were to be removed from Beirut six months after the militias were disbanded and security reforms instituted.[84] Addressing this issue, President Hirawi later asserted that Syrian forces would indeed withdraw by September 1992.[85] The treaty also indicated that the governments of Syria and Lebanon would "coordinate their economic, agricultural, industrial, commercial, transport, communications and customs sector, undertake joint prospects, and coordinate their development plans."[86]

The importance that Syria accorded the treaty was stressed in the speech delivered by President Asad on the occasion of its signing:

> [Syria] did not create what is between Syria and Lebanon. It was created by God. It was a common history, a common geography, and a united blood. Therefore, what we are building today together between the two countries is part of what is reflected by the common heritage, which can neither be removed nor erased with the passage of time, because it is a living fact that is unrelated to whether we live in one political entity or in two separate political entities.[87]

The Brotherhood and Cooperation treaty, reflecting as it did a Syrian takeover of Lebanon, was received with great misgiving in Israel. Defense Minister Moshe Arens stated that it posed a danger to Israel, expressing special concern over the article in the treaty that permitted Syria to keep its forces in Lebanon indefinitely and deploy them everywhere. The treaty, he declared, was in fact a Syrian anschluss of Lebanon.[88]

The US, too, was far from enthusiastic about the treaty. Initially, State Department Spokesperson Margaret Tutweiler said that the US did not consider the treaty to be a Syrian annexation or takeover of Lebanon and believed that it would enhance Lebanon's independence.[89] In late June, the State Department stated that the treaty was a cause for concern and that the US would keep a close watch over its implementation. Assistant secretary of state John Kelly warned explicitly that the US did not wish to witness a development that would lead to an annexation or takeover of Lebanon.[90]

Nevertheless, Syria and Lebanon signed on 1 September a defense and security agreement that was defined as a sequel to the treaty. Syrian Defense Minister Talas stated, in a speech delivered on the occasion of the signing of the new agreement, that it gave Syria the "right to prevent Israeli attacks against Lebanon."[91]

Although the Treaty of Brotherhood and Cooperation was widely considered a Syrian takeover of Lebanon, it did not reflect any change in Syria's attitude toward, or activity in Lebanon. At most, it legitimized an existing state of affairs. Essentially, it reflected long-standing Syrian goals in Lebanon: the preservation of Lebanese independence, and the establishment of a stable central regime under Syrian influence. In the course of the year Syria extended much aid to Lebanon precisely in order to further these goals. It was involved in the disarming of the militias in Lebanon in late April, and backed the deployment of the Lebanese army in various areas of the country, mainly in the vicinity of Beirut and south of it. Syria supported the army in clashes with Palestinian organizations in the refugee camp areas of Sidon. Yet, in light of inter-Arab pressure, and apparently in its own self-interest as well, it did not permit the Lebanese army to eliminate the Palestinian armed presence in Lebanon and compelled it to settle for forcing the Palestinians into the refugee camps and appropriating their massive weapons arsenal.

The army's firmness toward the Palestinians contrasted with the restraint it showed toward the Hizballah. Syria, which was clearly behind this moderation, followed this policy apparently because of pressure from Iran, with which it coordinated its activity in Lebanon (see below).

Although Syria's aspiration was to let the Lebanese regime handle its domestic issues on its own, it found itself inextricably involved in them. 'Abd al-Halim Khaddam, the senior Syrian official in charge of Lebanese matters, devoted much time and effort to mediation efforts in petty squabbles involving the Lebanese president, prime minister, speaker of parliament and various ministers. Although annoyed by its increasing involvement in such matters, Syria considered it a temporary necessity. The extent of attention which it was obliged to devote to Lebanon was reflected by the extensive scope of visits to Damascus by Lebanese officials, including the president, the prime minister and various other ministers. President Hirawi, for example, visited Damascus on 27 February, 16–17 May, 22 May, 27 July, 17–18 October, 5 November and 5 December, and the prime minister and other Lebanese officials visited Damascus as frequently.

Syria's hegemony over Lebanon was clearly reflected in the ME peace process: Syria had bound Lebanon to it in such a way that Lebanon was forced to seek Syrian approval for every move it wished to make in this process. Although there were relatively few bilateral disputes between Israel and Lebanon, progress in Israeli-Lebanese talks appeared to be entirely conditional upon parallel progress between Israel and Syria.

Overall, then, the year 1991 brought Syria closer to realizing its long-range strategic goals in Lebanon: the establishment of a stable regime under Syrian influence that would insure peace and stability on Syria's western flank and grant Syria control without domestic embroilment. Nevertheless, there were still obstacles to the full realization of these objectives. First, Lebanon's nearly complete acquiescence to Syria's presence in Lebanon derived from (and was therefore conditional upon) narrow and local considerations by the traditional leadership of most of its communal groups. Moreover, radical Shi'ite factions in Lebanon, such as Hizballah, not only rejected the Ta'if Accords, which denied the rights of the Shi'ite community, but objected to the very existence of Lebanon as it was constituted politically, aspiring to establish an Islamic republic. Syria did not act as vigorously as it could have to suppress these organizations, both because it wished to make use of them for operations against Israel and because its ally, Iran, was their patron. Nor could Syria help Lebanon eliminate the Palestinian presence on its territory, which was another destabilizing factor in the country. So long as the conflict with Israel continued, Syria considered the Palestinians an important pawn both in the inter-Arab arena and vis-à-vis Israel. Last, the achievement of stability in Lebanon and the establishment of a stable regime were encumbered by the condition stipulated by Israel for the withdrawal of its forces from the Jizzin area and the security zone: the withdrawal of Syrian troops from Lebanon or at a minimum the attainment of a new understanding with Syria on the question of Southern Lebanon.

THE REGIONAL ARENA: TURKEY AND IRAN

RELATIONS WITH TURKEY

The relationship between Turkey and Syria did not change significantly during 1991. The basic problems pending between the two countries continued to be the Euphrates waters, the province of Alexandretta and Syrian assistance to Turkish underground organizations. Another issue was added, however, which dominated Syrian-Turkish relations at the beginning of the year: Turkey's intentions toward Iraq. Syria feared that Turkey would take advantage of the Gulf crisis to alter its southern border with Iraq, while Turkey was concerned about the rebellion of the Kurds in Iraq, supported by Syria, because of the ramifications it could have for the Kurds in Turkey. During the Gulf War and for a short while thereafter, Syria made substantial efforts to persuade the Turks not to take any steps toward realizing their aspirations in northern Iraq. Turkish Foreign Minister Ahmet Kurtcebe visited Damascus during the war, on 11–13 February, and about a month later, on 18–19 March, Syrian Foreign Minister Shar' visited Ankara. The Syrians stressed their objection to any violation of Iraq's integrity during both visits and also articulated the same message in the official media. The issue seemed to have been resolved as both sides described the discussions as constructive and useful. Shar' even stated that "the two countries' views on international and regional questions [were] identical" and that "Turkey and Syria [were] eager to preserve Iraq's territorial integrity."[92]

No development occurred in the course of the year in the dispute over the Euphrates waters and both countries refrained from bringing this issue up. Toward the end of the year, an American nonprofit research group wished to hold an international conference on water in Turkey. The conference was eventually canceled after Syria announced that it would not participate should Israel be invited. The Turkish Government did not intend to invite Israel in light of the Syrian threat, but when the US Government indicated its disapproval of this move, the conference organizers felt obliged to cancel the event.[93]

RELATIONS WITH IRAN
Despite the change in Syria's policy toward the US and the Arab-Israeli conflict (see below), which predictably elicited Iran's disapproval, relations between the two countries continued to be warm.

Ongoing friendship and cooperation with Iran were vital to Syria for two main reasons. First, Syria wished to cultivate Iran as a military, political, and economic ally in view of global and regional changes. Second, Iran's goodwill and assistance were necessary to Syria in order to promote its objectives in Lebanon, specifically to remove the obstacles posed by Iranian clients such as Hizballah.

However, the issue which dominated Syria's relations with Iran in 1991 was postwar security arrangements in the Gulf. Iran was clearly dissatisfied with the proposed arrangements, declaring that it would accede neither to an Arab nor a Western presence in the Gulf unless consulted. It hoped to gain support for its position from Syria, which had played a central role in the formulation of the Damascus declaration — the accepted plan for security arrangements in the Gulf for a time (see above). Iranian Vice President Hasan Habibi arrived for a visit to Damascus on 7 March, and President Rafsanjani arrived on 27 April for his first presidential visit there. The question of security arrangements in the Gulf was widely discussed during both visits.[94] The tension between Iran and Syria on this issue dissipated as it became clear that Egypt and Syria would withdraw their troops from the Gulf and that the Damascus declaration would not be implemented.

The Iranian officials also devoted part of their discussions with the Syrians to the question of Lebanon. Iran apparently agreed to help soften the resistance of its allies in Lebanon to the enforcement of Hirawi's rule and the deployment of the Lebanese army throughout the country, in return for Syrian agreement to let Hizballah continue functioning.[95] In addition, both Syria and Iran played an important role in the release of Western hostages held in Lebanon. In this context, Iran helped Syria project an image of moderation, so essential for winning US approval, which Iran, too, was interested in attaining. It appeared, however, that ultimately the implementation in Lebanon of the Ta'if Accords, which largely ignored the status achieved by the Shi'ite community, could cause tension between Iran and Syria and force the latter to make a choice between the full attainment of its objectives in Lebanon and its close friendship with Iran.

Another issue was Syria's attempt to rely on Iran strategically, in view of the new conditions in the ME and the world at large. During the course of the year, and especially toward the year's end, there were reports on Syrian-Iranian cooperation in the military and technological spheres. A visit by Syrian Chief of Staff Hikmat Shihabi to Iran on 25 September was accompanied by rumors (denied by both sides) about the signing of an agreement between Syria and Iran for the joint production of surface-to-surface missiles.[96] Shihabi's visit was clearly intended for the purpose of discussing military cooperation, a subject whose importance was undermined by reports about Iran's intention to develop a nuclear weapons.[97]

Syria's joining the peace process with Israel did not cause friction with Iran. In fact, just a short while before arriving at the Madrid conference, Syria sent a parliamentary delegation to attend the Palestine conference convened by the Iranians in Tehran in order to protest the peace process.[98] It would seem that Iran had more or less accepted Syria's explanation for joining the process and perhaps also its commitment not to diverge from positions acceptable to Iran. Nevertheless, Iran monitored this process carefully, realizing perhaps that, like the question of Lebanon, it harbored potential friction for Iranian-Syrian relations.

SYRIA AND THE CONFLICT WITH ISRAEL

Syria, in reassessing its basic positions of a variety of issues, also initiated the beginnings of a change in policy on the conflict with Israel, although the significance of this change could not yet be assessed. Syria expressed preparedness to participate in the peace process and meet with Israeli negotiators face-to-face, thus showing an understanding that progress in this process was vital to improving its status internationally and its relations with the US in particular. On the other hand, the regime had difficulty abandoning its traditional policy regarding Israel, mainly for emotional reasons but possibly also because of fear of domestic repercussions. This difficulty was clearly manifested in official statements and in the Syrian media, which continued to take an extreme anti-Israel position. It also reflected Syria's attempts to thwart the efforts to nullify the UN resolution equating Zionism with racism, which it called a "harmful precedent in the history of the UN."[99]

Unofficial signs regarding Syria's preparedness to alter its position on the conflict and reach an agreement with Israel that would include the returning of the Golan Heights to Syrian sovereignty had begun emanating from Damascus in 1990 through various American and European envoys and visitors. It is doubtful, however, whether these hints had been serious ones, and in any event they did not elicit a response from Israel.

After the Gulf War, under heavy American pressure, Syria consented to take an additional step forward and participate in the peace process, which was highlighted by the Madrid peace conference and a round of direct talks in Washington between

Syrian and Israeli delegations. Considering the outright refusal of the various Syrian Ba'th regimes since 1963 to negotiate with Israel directly (and thereby, in their view, implicitly recognize Israel's existence), Syria's agreement to participate in the peace process was highly significant (see above).

The Madrid conference, which began on 31 October, marking the official opening of the new stage in the peace process between Israel and its neighbors, was less than satisfactory from Syria's point of view. Syria was far from content about President Bush's speech in which he recognized the security needs of Israel, and refrained from mentioning the formula of land for peace (see above). Moreover, Syria's efforts to achieve inter-Arab coordination in preparation for the conference had failed. Although the foreign ministers of the confrontation states, Egypt and the PLO had met in Damascus on the eve of the conference, intergovernmental coordination had not been achieved.

Syrian Foreign Minister Faruq al-Shar''s performance at the conference catered primarily to Syrian public opinion. Shar' adopted a tough stance, reiterating traditional Syrian positions. At the end of his first speech he said:

> [The Syrians] have come [to Madrid] for a just and honorable peace that rests on right and international legitimacy, not for a fake peace that reflects the conditions of the aggressor and the weight of the occupation. We have come for a real peace that includes all the fronts of the Arab-Israeli conflict, not for a peace that deals with one aspect of the conflict, and creates new conflicts and tensions in the region. Out of our belief in this peace, we announce, with confidence and determination, our resolve to work for a peaceful, just and comprehensive settlement to the Arab-Israeli conflict that liberates territory and ensures the national rights of the Palestinian people and security for all.[100]

The second speech that Shar' delivered to the conference continued this line and dedicated to a fierce personal attack against Israeli Prime Minister Shamir, whom Shar' portrayed as a terrorist, as well as anti-Semitic insinuations about the double identity of American Jews.[101]

The Syrian media depicted the Madrid conference as a disappointment, with Radio Damascus stating that it had "accomplished nothing toward the restoration of Arab rights." However, it pointed out, the conference had "exposed Israel's intransigent positions that reject peace, revealed its hostile nature, and created the beginning of a rift within Zionist society itself." Moreover, the conference had focused international attention on the ME problem and, therefore, Radio Damascus claimed, the Arabs had won in Madrid after all.[102]

Despite Syria's disappointment, Syrian officials met with Israeli officials in Madrid for discussions on 3 November, after delays caused by the Syrian side, followed by another round of talks on 10 December in Washington. While neither side expected these talks to be productive, both the Syrians and the Israelis described them as a step forward. The Syrians viewed the start of discussions by both parties on UN Security Council Resolution 242 as a substantive and an indication of progress. At the same time, Syria made it plain that it expected the US to take a more active role in the process because, it claimed, Israel was determined not to make any progress, was dragging its feet, and refused to discuss withdrawal from occupied Arab lands.[103]

Syria's change of policy on the conflict with Israel obliged it to reformulate its official line on the issue and undertake an information campaign. Following President Asad's positive reply to President Bush on 14 July regarding the peace process, the Syrian regime made intensive efforts to explain its position, especially to key groups of supporters such as party activists, government workers, heads of communal organizations and unions, mainly by means of mass rallies.[104] The new official line reflected the contradictions in Syrian policy: an awareness of the need to proceed toward peace with Israel, on the one hand, and an unwillingness to, and fear of, changing its traditional position, on the other. Along with praise for peace in the Syrian media, Israel continued to be portrayed as an aggressive and devious country. The message was that Syria's policy on the conflict with Israel had not actually changed, and that joining the peace process was simply the natural outcome of Syria's policy ever since Asad's accession to power in 1970. The Syrians even claimed that the Madrid conference, which they regarded as an international forum, reflected their traditional demands and therefore represented a triumph for their policy.

While the Syrian media dealt extensively with the peace process and the attainment of peace in the region, it did not refer to the form the peace would take, i.e., a treaty with Israel and the establishment of political, economic and other ties with it. Rather, it depicted the peace process as helping Syria and the Arabs at large to regain the territories conquered by Israel in 1967 and restore the rights of the Palestinian people — an implicit reference to Palestinian rights of return and self-determination.

Although aware of Israel's refusal to withdraw from the Golan Heights, as well as of American insistence on border amendments, the Syrians reiterated their demand for full Israeli withdrawal. They were also aware of the possibility that progress would be made in other channels of the peace talks, such as the Jordanian-Palestinian-Israeli one, and therefore coordinated policy with Jordan and the PLO, stressing the necessity to achieve a comprehensive peace.

The position adopted by Syria was explicitly articulated in a series of interviews which Asad granted such foreign media as *The Washington Post,* ABC, CNN and *Newsweek.* In an interview to *The Washington Post,* he stated: "For almost 20 years we have been saying we want peace...perhaps others thought we were not serious. But now they think we are serious."[105] Equally remarkable was his statement in an interview to the American ABC television network: "From our point of view, they [the Israelis] are to benefit the most from peace. Peace does not destroy: it builds. I seek peace not destruction" — a remark never before heard in the Syrian media.[106] On the other hand, Asad consistently avoided replying to the question of whether he was prepared to recognize the existence of the State of Israel. For example, in his interview with *The Washington Post,* he said that the acceptance of the existence of the Jewish state in the ME "has to be put forward in the conference. All parties will go to the conference and this and other subjects will be put on the table for discussion."[107]

While participating in the peace process, Syria also continued to acquire advanced weapons, some of them procured as a result of lessons learned from the Gulf War. Most of the economic aid granted to Syria by the Gulf states in return for its support was used to finance arms deals, including a $1.5bn. transaction with the Soviet Union for the purchase of MiG-29 and Su-24 planes, T-72 tanks, advanced SAM missiles and other equipment, and a $300m. contract with Czechoslovakia for the purchase of 300 additional T-72 tanks.[108] The highlight of Syria's procurement efforts was a transaction with North Korea for improved *Scud*-C missiles with a 600 km. range.[109]

In addition, the Syrians negotiated with China on the purchase of M-9 surface-to-surface missiles.[110] There were also reports of an agreement reached with Iran on a project for the joint production of SSMs, as well as of Syria's intention to procure a miniature neutron source reactor from China, and American efforts to prevent the deal.[111]

Syria's procurements were designed to improve its ability to defend itself against a possible Israeli attack along the lines of the Allied attack on Iraq's economic infrastructure and to achieve parity with Israel's technological and alleged nuclear capabilities. With the concept underlying Syria's military acquisitions a basically defensive one, Syria was naturally critical of President Bush's initiative to limit the arms race in the area (see above).

Israel made considerable efforts to block Syria's procurement activity, for example, by trying unsuccessfully to persuade Czechosovakia to call off its deal with Syria. Similar pressure exerted on Poland was successful and, following a visit to Israel, Polish President Lech Walesa announced that the Polish-Syrian deal would not be carried out.[112] In late October, there were rumors that Israel planned to attack ships carrying *Scud* missiles from Korea to Syria, giving rise to warnings by the US to Israel to refrain from such action.[113]

The Israeli-Syrian border continued to be one of the quieter Israeli borders, especially in comparison with the Israeli-Lebanese one, where terrorist activity mounted. Nevertheless, on 3 July, a terrorist squad infiltrated into the Mount Hermon stronghold in Israel (according to Israeli sources, from Syrian territory), killing one Israeli soldier. Israel warned Syria that it considered it responsible for preventing such activity from its territory. However, the attack, which was not conclusively proven to have emanated from Syrian territory, could not be considered a change in Syria's attitude toward terrorist activity against Israel from its territory or even a change in the status quo along the Israeli-Syrian border on the Golan Heights.[114]

NOTES

For the place and frequency of publications cited here, and for the full name of the publication, news agency, radio station or monitoring service where an abbreviation is used, please see "List of Sources." Only in the case of more than one publication bearing the same name is the place of publication noted here.

1. *CR,* Syria, No. 4, 1991, p. 7.
2. *CR,* Syria, No. 3, 1991, p. 3.
3. *CR,* Syria, No. 4, 1991, p. 7.
4. *Country Profile, Syria, 1991–92* p. 45.
5. *Al-Hayat* (London), 6 July 1991.
6. *Country Profile, Syria, 1991–92* p. 53.
7. Ibid., p. 21.
8. Ibid., p. 5.
9. Ibid.
10 Ibid.; *al-Thawra* (Damascus), 4 July 1991.
11. *Al-Jarida al-Rasmiyya,* 20 November 1991.
12. Syrian TV, 17 November — DR, 18 November 1991.
13. Syrian TV, 16 November — DR, 18 November 1991.
14. R. Damascus, 3 December — DR, 4 December 1991.

15. DR, 27 November 1991.
16. *Ha'aretz,* 28, 29 November 1991.
17. INA, 4 February; SANA, 4 February — DR, 5 February 1991.
18. *Sawt al-Sha'b* (Amman), 22, 23 January — DR, 24, 25 January 1991.
19. R. Baghdad, 23 January — DR, 23 January 1991.
20. R. Damascus, 2 October — DR, 4 October 1991.
21. *Al-Ribat,* 24 December — DR, 31 December 1991.
22. *WT,* 11 March; *CSM,* 12 March 1991.
23. Ibid.
24. *NYT,* 24 November 1992.
25. *JP,* 1 May 1991.
26. *Ha'aretz,* 15 November; *NYT,* 24 November 1991.
27. SANA, 13 July — DR, 15 July; Syrian TV, 27 July — DR, 29 July 1991.
28. *JP,* 25 April; USIS, 24 April 1991.
29. *Tishrin,* 8 March 1991.
30. *JP,* 2 June; Syrian TV, 14 July — DR, 15 July 1991.
31. *JP,* 26 July; R. Damascus, 19 September — DR, 19 September 1991.
32. *NYT,* 18 July 1991.
33. R. Damascus, 28 September — DR, 30 September 1991.
34. R. Damascus, 28 September — DR, 1 October 1991.
35. R. Damascus, 30 October — DR, 31 October 1991.
36. *Ha'aretz,* 3 June; R. Damascus, 2 June — DR, 3, 5 June 1991.
37. *Ha'aretz,* 18 June 1991.
38. Libyan TV, 18 November — DR, 19 November; *JP,* 21 November 1991.
39. Syrian TV, 22 August — DR, 23 August 1991.
40. SANA, 18 May — DR, 20 May; Syrian TV, 12 September — DR, 13 September 1991.
41. R. Damascus, 7 February — DR, 8 February 1991.
42. *CR,* Syria, No. 3, 1991, p. 23.
43. R. Damascus, 5, 25 April, 19 October — DR, 5 April, 3 May, 21 October 1991.
44. *FT,* 6 February 1991.
45. *CR,* Syria, No. 3, 1991, p. 23.
46. R. Damascus, 14 May — DR, 14 May 1991.
47. *FT,* 6 February 1991.
48. R. Damascus, 13 February — DR, 14 February 1991.
49. *Ha'aretz,* 30 May 1991.
50. Ibid., 8 September 1991.
51. RFI, 19 December — DR, 20 December 1991.
52. R. Monte Carlo, 8 February — DR, 11 February 1991.
53. R. Monte Carlo, 7 February — DR, 8 February; *IHT,* 6 February; *'Ukaz,* 24 February 1991.
54. *Tishrin,* 14 January 1991.
55. R. Damascus, 7 January — DR, 8 January 1991.
56. R. Damascus, 19 January — DR, 24 January 1991.
57. R. Damascus, 12 January — DR, 14 January 1991.
58. *Tishrin,* 22 February 1991.
59. *JP,* 21 January 1991.
60. SANA, 19 January — DR, 22 January 1991.
61. *IHT,* 22 January 1991.
62. *Al-Thawra* (Damascus), 5, 9 February — DR, 14 February 1991.
63. R. Monte Carlo, 19 February — DR, 11 February 1991.
64. *NYT,* 17 February 1991.
65. R. Damascus, 22 February — DR, 28 February 1991.
66. *Al-Hayat* (London), 6 July 1991.
67. *Tishrin,* 7 March 1991.
68. R. Damascus, 6 March — DR, 6 March; *JP,* 7 March 1991.
69. R. Damascus, 2 June — DR, 5 June 1991.
70. *Ha'aretz,* 17 October; R. Damascus, 1, 2, 24 October — DR, 1, 3, 25 October 1991.

71. R. Damascus, 18, 19 September — DR, 18, 19 September 1991.
72. *Ha'aretz,* 6 June 1991.
73. *FT,* 13 March 1991.
74. R. Monte Carlo, 27, 28 May — DR, 28, 30 May 1991.
75. R. Damascus, 22 July — DR, 23 July 1991.
76. Ibid., 19 October — DR, 21 October 1991.
77. *Ha'aretz,* 23 December 1991.
78. SANA, 21 January — DR, 23 January 1991.
79. *JT,* 28 January 1991.
80. AFP, 20 January — DR, 22 January 1991.
81. *JT,* 3 February 1991.
82. R. Damascus, 12, 24 January, 22 February — DR, 14, 25 January, 22 February 1991.
83. R. Damascus, 25 March, 18 May, 19 August — DR, 26 March, 20 May, 20 August 1991.
84. *FT,* 20 May 1991.
85. R. Beirut, 19 November — DR, 19 November 1991.
86. *JP, FT,* 20 May 1991.
87. R. Damascus, 22 May — DR, 23 May 1991.
88. *FT,* 18–19 May; *Ha'aretz,* 21 May 1991.
89. *Ha'aretz,* 26 May 1991.
90. Ibid., 28 June 1991.
91. *JP,* 2 September 1991.
92. R. Damascus, 12 February, 18 March — DR, 12 February, 20 March 1991.
93. *JP,* 8 October 1991.
94. R. Damascus, 7 March — DR, 7 March 1991.
95. Ibid., 29 April — DR, 30 April 1991.
96. Tehran TV, 25 September — DR, 26 September 1991.
97. *Ha'aretz,* 1 October 1991.
98. IRNA, 22 October — DR, 23 October 1991.
99. R. Damascus, 18 December — DR, 19 December 1991.
100. Jordan TV, 31 October — DR, 1 November 1991.
101. R. Damascus, 1 November — DR, 1 November 1991.
102. R. Damascus, 5 November 1991.
103. R. Damascus, 19, 23, 28 December — DR, 20, 23, 30 December 1991.
104. *Tishrin,* 1 August, 11 September — DR, 20 September 1991.
105. *WP,* 28 July 1991.
106. R. Damascus, 20 September — DR, 20 September 1991.
107. *WP,* 28 July 1991.
108. *Ha'aretz,* 22 July 1991.
109. Ibid., 5 July 1991.
110. Ibid., 8, 17 March; *JP,* 22 November 1991.
111. *Ha'aretz,* 1 October; *JP,* 29 November 1991.
112. VoI, 21 May — DR, 22 May 1991.
113. R. Damascus, 25 November — DR, 27 November 1991.
114. *Ha'aretz,* 5 July 1991.

Turkey
(Türkiye Cumhuriyeti)

WILLIAM M. HALE

The year 1991 produced several important changes for Turkey, both internationally and domestically. For the first two months, it was inevitably affected by its frontline status in the war against Iraq. Fortunately, it managed to stay out of the war, but was sucked into its aftermath by the tragedy of the Kurdish refugees. Later on, its external horizons were dramatically affected by the unsuccessful coup in Moscow in August and the collapse of the USSR. This brought important opportunities, as well as dangers, to the east and north. It was remarkable, however, that while the government was gaining a higher profile internationally, it was losing ground at home — a development which suggested that, in Turkey as in some other countries, foreign policy success does not always translate into domestic popularity. The main cause of the decline of the internal fortunes of the ruling Motherland Party (*Anavatan Partisi*) was its failure to bring down inflation, and infighting and leadership changes within the party. When the government opted for early general elections in October 1991, the party was ousted from power for the first time since its foundation in 1983. The successor government was a coalition under Süleyman Demirel, the veteran conservative leader of the 1960s and 1970s. On paper, the coalition did not look well founded: in practice, however, it was able to provide a far more stable government than many had expected. On these grounds, Turkish democracy seemed to be more firmly based than in the recent past, even if it still faced innumerable problems.

DOMESTIC POLITICS

THE GOVERNMENT AND PARLIAMENT
At the beginning of 1991, the position of the government and parliamentary parties was full of paradoxes. On the one hand, the ruling Motherland Party had a large majority, with around 280 of the 450 seats in the Grand National Assembly, Turkey's unicameral legislature. This was a legacy of its resounding victory in the last general elections, held in 1987 (see *MECS* 1987, pp. 667–68). On the other hand, the government was seriously weakened by a sharp loss in its popularity since 1987, mainly caused by its failure to reduce inflation. It was also hampered by ideological and personal rivalries within the Motherland Party, by the ambiguous position of President Turgut Özal, and the evident weakness of the Prime Minister, Yıldırım Akbulut.

The contradictions in President Özal's role derived from the fact that his personality and political experience clashed with Turkey's constitutional rules and traditions. Under the constitution, the president is supposed to be a neutral, nonpartisan figure

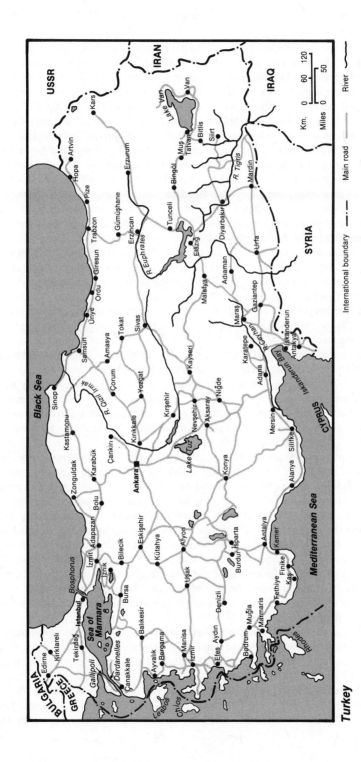

Turkey

who acts as the head of state but not of the government — in fact, he is legally obliged to sever any links he may have with any political party before he can assume the office.[1] Moreover, all Özal's predecessors as president since 1961 had been retired military commanders, with no background in party politics and little or no personal following in parliament or the country. Özal's political persona was strikingly different, because he had been the dominant figure in Turkish politics since the latest return to a civilian regime in 1983. He had founded and led the Motherland Party, had served for six years as prime minister, and was probably Turkey's best-known politician on the international scene. Although he had stuck to the letter of the constitution by officially resigning from the Motherland Party in 1989, he was still popularly identified as its unofficial leader and did little to disabuse people of this notion. From the start, Prime Minister Yıldırım Akbulut had inevitably been overshadowed by the president — in fact he was generally, and not incorrectly, regarded as a colorless stand-in for Özal, and had probably been chosen for precisely that reason.

This situation created two bases for an unofficial opposition to Özal from within the Motherland Party. Firstly, the party's backbenchers, as well as several government members, strongly resented the president's frequent interventions in the work of the government, which were seen as contrary to the constitution. Özal's tendency to appoint members of his own family to top positions strengthened complaints that he was trying to turn the state into a sort of dynastic fiefdom. Secondly, several alternative leaders from within the Motherland Party felt that they could do a much better job than Akbulut as premier, and sought to project themselves as such. Chief of these was Mesut Yılmaz, a former foreign minister who had resigned from the cabinet in February 1990, alleging constant interference in the work of his ministry by the president and other ministers. During 1990, Yılmaz had emerged as the leader of the anti-Akbulut faction within the ruling party, and had capitalized on popular opposition to Özal's pro-American policy in the Gulf crisis to enhance his standing in parliament (see *MECS* 1990, pp. 672–73, 685).

These personal rivalries were sharpened and complicated by divergent ideological currents in the Motherland Party. The dominant trend within the party could be broadly defined as pro-Western liberal, attached to the vision of a democratic, modernized and capitalist Turkey aligned with the Western powers, while preserving its national traditions. Against this was a more distinctly pro-Islamic tendency, which supported the preservation of religious values in education and other spheres of public life. It was linked with a third, ultranationalist faction in what was known as the Holy Alliance. The latter had gained strength in November 1989 when four of its members had entered the cabinet, following Kenan Evren's retirement from the presidency. This had stiffened the resistance of the liberals, of whom Mesut Yılmaz became the main leader. Hence, the ideological battle came to overlap the personal rivalries in the party.

A saving grace for the government was that, even if its own ranks were disunited, the opposition was also fragmented into a miscellaneous array of center-right, center-left, Islamic conservative, ultranationalist and Kurdish ethnic parties. The biggest opposition party in parliament was the Social Democrat Populist Party (SDPP; *Sosyaldemokrat Halkçi Parti*) led by Erdal İnönü, which had around 80 MPs, followed by the center-right True Path Party (TPP; *Doğru Yol Partisi*) under Süleyman Demirel, with just under 60 seats. In terms of policies and ideology, there was little to distinguish the Motherland and True Path Parties, since both represented the center-right tradition in Turkish politics. The main difference between them was the sharp personal conflict between Özal and Demirel, which derived from the fact that Demirel had been kept out of the political ring by the military when Özal had come to power in 1983. Nevertheless, Demirel enjoyed the advantage that his party was the most likely choice of conservative voters dissatisfied with the Motherland Party's performance in office. In addition, he had a personal reputation as a doughty political warrior and former premier who had twice been ejected from office by the military (in 1971 and 1980) and had come back fighting on both occasions. The SDPP enjoyed broad support from followers of the center-left and pro-secularist tradition in Turkish politics, reinforced by the fact that its leader, Erdal İnönü, was the son of İsmet İnönü, Atatürk's right-hand man and president of the republic between 1938 and 1950. On the other hand, İnönü's distinguished pedigree could not overcome the problem that he failed to impress the public as a sufficiently dynamic or forceful party chief, and had faced repeated challenges to his leadership from Deniz Baykal, a former secretary-general of the party.

Among the other opposition parties, the Democratic Left Party (DLP; *Demokratık Sol Partisi*) led by Bülent Ecevit, had failed to win any seats in the 1987 elections, but now had the support of a handful of MPs who had defected from the SDPP. The relationship between Ecevit and İnönü mirrored that between Demirel and Özal: there was little to choose between their two parties in terms of policies, but Ecevit had been prevented from competing in the 1983 elections by the military, and İnönü's party had slipped into the vacant slot in the political spectrum. On the right were two smaller parties which had won no seats in 1987, but enjoyed scattered local support. Of these the Welfare Party (WP; *Refah Partisi*) led by Necmettin Erbakan, enjoyed the support of the antisecularist segment of the Turkish electorate. Further to the right, Alparslan Türkeş carried on as the stormy petrel of the ultranationalist fringe of Turkish politics and the leader of the Nationalist Endeavor Party (NEP; *Milliyetçi Çalışma Partisi*). Finally, the People's Labor Party (PLP; *Halkın Emek Partisi*) acted as a thinly disguised Kurdish party; it had been formed by a group of deputies who had originally been elected as Social Democrats in 1987, but had been ejected from the SDPP by İnönü in 1989 (see *MECS* 1989 p. 657).

During the first half of 1991, political interest in Turkey naturally centered on the Gulf War and its tragic aftermath which is described below (see section on Foreign Relations). Nevertheless, the struggle for power within the Motherland Party absorbed much domestic attention.[2] The high point of the contest was the party's national convention, which was eventually held on 15 June. Its significance derived from the fact that the convention delegates elect the chairman of the party, and that the latter is virtually certain to take over the premiership, if the party is in power. During the long run-up to the convention, the rival factions in the party jostled for position, in an attempt to ensure maximum support among the 1,154 delegates who were to be elected by local party branches. The most prominent of the expected delegates was Mrs. Semra Özal, the wife of the president, who presented herself as a prospective member of the Istanbul delegation. Mrs. Özal had never previously sought political office but, as a former chair of the Foundation for Promoting and Strengthening Turkish Womanhood (popularly known as "the Daisies") she had won plenty of press coverage, and effectively projected herself as the champion of the modernist, liberal wing of the party. More crucially, although Turgut Özal stoutly maintained that he was not giving her orders, she could be assumed to acting as his instrument. At an early stage of the skirmishing, her candidacy was hotly opposed by Hüsnü Doğan, the minister of defense (ironically, the Özals' nephew) who was dismissed from the cabinet after a fierce quarrel with the president on 22 February. Other members of the Holy Alliance, notably Mehmet Keçeciler, joined in the criticism of Mrs. Özal's prospective launch into party politics. Nonetheless, she was chosen as the leader of the Istanbul delegation to the convention on 28 April. Her election must have come as bad news to Akbulut, since it suggested that President Özal would probably be lending his indirect support to Yılmaz in the forthcoming leadership race.

As the opening of the convention drew near, it became clear that two rivals would challenge Akbulut for the party chairmanship, and thus the prime minister's office. Of these, the first, Hasan Celal Güzel, was expected to be a rank outsider: he had failed to garner more than a few votes when he had contested Akbulut's original election to the party leadership in November 1989, and his reputation had since been smeared by a complex, if rather indeterminate scandal involving himself and a junior female official of the Foreign Ministry (see *MECS* 1990, p. 672). As a result, the only effective challenge came from Yılmaz. In response, Akbulut, who had previously held aloof from the conservative-versus-liberal debate, was projected as the standard-bearer of the conservative faction.

When the delegates gathered in Ankara on 15 June, the first round of balloting for the leadership resulted in confusion: Yılmaz took 580 delegate votes to Akbulut's 557, with 20 for Güzel, but there had evidently been some irregularity, since the number of recorded votes was three more than the total number of delegates. In the second round, Güzel withdrew, and Yılmaz won a convincing majority over Akbulut with 631 votes to 523. It was assumed that most of Güzel's erstwhile supporters had switched to Yılmaz in the second round, but it also appeared that around 30 delegates had transferred their votes directly from Akbulut to Yılmaz. In the aftermath of defeat, Akbulut claimed that fierce lobbying by Mrs. Özal had cost him as many as 150–200 delegate votes — in effect, that his overthrow had been engineered by the president.[3] While he may well have exaggerated the effect of Mrs. Özal's intervention, it was nevertheless clear that Turgut Özal must have decided to drop him from the leadership, and that this was the decisive factor for many delegates.

President Özal's motives in seeking this change were not hard to find. Akbulut's lackluster performance was evidently costing the party much of its former electoral support and a new chairman was needed to revive its popularity. Yılmaz had the advantage of relative youth (he was 43 at the time), previous ministerial experience, and the fact that public opinion polls suggested that he was more popular than Akbulut among the voters at large. He stepped into his new position with alacrity. Akbulut formally resigned as premier on 16 June, and Yılmaz was invited to form a new government on the following day. His cabinet, which was announced on 23 June, signaled a clear victory for the liberals. Of the 30 cabinet members, only eight were carried over from the Akbulut government, and 18 were new faces. The remaining four were rebels who had resigned from the previous government. Besides the premier himself, they included Ekrem Pakdemirli, formerly minister of finance, who now became a minister of state with special responsibility for the economy; Safa Giray, now foreign minister and Doğan's predecessor as defense minister and Fahrettin

Kurt, now another minister of state and formerly minister of energy and natural resources. Only two of the remaining ministers — that is, Vehbi Dinçerler and Barlas Doğu — were identified as Akbulut supporters, and neither turned out to wield much influence in the new government. In spite of threatened rebellions by some pro-Akbulut diehards, the new government comfortably won a vote of confidence.

THE GENERAL ELECTIONS, AND THE POSTELECTION GOVERNMENT

On assuming office, Yılmaz and his team faced two urgent questions. Firstly, when and how should they try to bring down the surging rate of inflation, which was then running at around 65% per year? Secondly, given that parliament's term would run out in November 1992, should they call early general elections?[4] These two questions were interconnected, since it was clear that an anti-inflationary program would involve a sharp reduction of public expenditure, and possible increases in taxation, neither of which would be at all palatable to the voters. Hence, the government had two options: either to introduce an anti-inflationary program immediately, and hope that it had enough time to work by November 1992, delaying the elections to the last possible moment, or to pump up the economy into a preelection boom, hold general elections within a few months, and thus delay the nasty economic medicine until after the voters' verdict had been delivered.

It does not seem to have taken Yılmaz more than a few weeks to decide on the second option. In making this decision, he evidently concluded that an immediate anti-inflationary package would cost him too much support, and was unlikely to be effective much before November 1992 anyway. There was also the consideration that even if he lost the elections, then the odium of taking unpopular belt-tightening measures would be passed on to the successor government, which would in turn leave the Motherland Party in a strong position in the following elections. Accordingly, a motion calling for early elections was passed by the Motherland Party parliamentary caucus on 16 August, and a bill presented to and passed by parliament eight days later, fixing the polling day as 20 October.

Prior to the elections, some important developments occurred in the ranks of the opposition parties. In the first place, the SDPP plunged into yet another round of its seemingly interminable leadership quarrels. On 27–28 July, the party held its regular annual national convention, at which İnönü's leadership was again challenged by Deniz Baykal. The main difference between the two was a personal rivalry, as Baykal and his supporters criticized İnönü for having insufficient popular appeal. However, Baykal also presented himself as being to the right of İnönü in policy terms (in particular, the party's links with Kurdish nationalism — tenuous as they were — were criticized by Baykal and other more Turkish-nationalist members of the party). In the event, İnönü survived the challenge, but in a hard-fought contest: after three rounds of balloting he won the race by 534 delegate votes to 451.[5] Hikmet Çetin, who sided with İnönü, was confirmed in office as the party's secretary-general. İnönü's supporters also won a clear majority of seats in the 44-member party assembly, which is the SDPP's main policy-making body. Subsequently, Baykal took a back seat in the party's election campaign. Nevertheless, this recent memory of discord in its ranks cannot have helped the party's efforts to persuade the electorate that it was a convincing alternative government.

The SDPP's fortunes were also affected by its relations with the PLP. During the summer, the PLP's deputies evidently decided that they had little chance of reelection if they contested the elections as a separate party, since the electoral law stipulates that no party is entitled to any parliamentary seats if it wins less than 10% of the national vote. The PLP had scant hope of surmounting this barrier, given that it was unlikely to win seats outside the Kurdish-inhabited provinces of southeastern Anatolia, which only account for about 10%–15% of Turkey's total population. There was also a legal obstacle, in that the PLP had not held a national convention within six months of the polling day, which was a condition for entering the elections. Hence its members decided to rejoin the election lists of the SDPP. İnönü and his colleagues accepted the deal — partly because they were prepared to support moderate Kurdish demands for greater cultural rights anyway, and partly because this alliance could be expected to bring them a valuable harvest of votes in the southeast. This was a two-edged weapon, however, since many center-left voters outside the southeast were likely to be alienated by the suggestion that the SDPP had become allied to Kurdish nationalism. Bülent Ecevit's DLP, which strongly opposed Kurdish separatism, was the most probable beneficiary of this Turkish nationalist backlash. On the other hand, a third contender on the left, the tiny Socialist Party (*Sosyalist Parti*) led by Doğu Perincek, offered a more openly pro-Kurdish program, though to little effect.

This re-alliance on the left was accompanied by a similar movement on the right. Here, the Welfare and Nationalist Endeavor parties faced the same dilemma as the PLP — fighting singly, they both ran the risk of failing to clear the 10% hurdle. An electoral alliance, in which the smaller NEP entered candidates on the WP lists, was the obvious answer. The marriage was not an easy one, since some members of the NEP took a strongly secularist line, clashing with the WP's attachment to "Islamic values." On the other hand, it suited both parties' electoral interests. The alliance was then joined by the Reformist Democracy Party (*İslahatçi Demokrasi Partisi*), a minuscule party of the right which had competed separately in the 1987 elections, but had won only a tiny fraction of the vote. As a result, the WP became the rallying point for a diverse collection of alienated right-wing voters who wanted to register a protest against both Özal and Demirel, the established leaders of the center-right. Nevertheless, the weakness of the alliance was demonstrated by the fact that, soon after the elections, 19 ex-NEP members of the WP resigned from the party, to become independents. Türkeş was reelected chairman of his old party on 29 December, and the NEP was, in effect, re-formed.

Officially, the election campaign began at the end of September, once the parties had announced their lists of candidates for each constituency; in practice, however, the party leaders began campaigning as soon as the election bill had been passed by parliament. The campaign was keenly fought, but generally calm: there was no violence outside the southeastern provinces, where the continued campaign by the armed militants of the PKK (see below) could have been expected anyway, elections or no elections. The generally relaxed atmosphere was taken as an encouraging sign of political maturity: the fact that, for instance, rival party marchers sometimes encountered one another, but passed each other by with friendly waves, was a comforting contrast with election campaigns of the 1970s, in which violent clashes had been the order of the day.

This atmosphere of consensus was probably strengthened by the fact that a remarkable degree of convergence had developed between the main parties on most of the major policy issues. Of these, the state of the economy was easily the most important. Following the collapse of communism in eastern Europe, virtually all parties favored strengthening the market system, even though there were some divergences as to how this could be done. All the parties recognized that the reduction of inflation was the main demand of the electorate, and promised to bring it down. Although the party programs tended to be vague on detail, privatization of loss-making state industries and reform of the tax system were widely supported methods of reducing the public sector deficit, which was generally agreed to be the main engine of inflation.

During the summer, the government allowed large pay increases for civil servants and other public sector workers, besides sharply increased minimum prices for agricultural products, without commensurate increases in taxation. This was almost the exact opposite of an anti-inflationary policy. Nevertheless, the Motherland Party's program promised to reduce inflation to below 10% p.a. by 1996, besides raising the period of compulsory education to eight years, increasing credits to small traders and artisans, and providing more resources for public housing.[6] In response, Mrs. Tansu Çiller, the chief economist in Demirel's team, promised to reduce inflation to an annual rate of 30%–40% within one year, and to increase gross national product (GNP) by 7%–8% annually: she argued that a TPP government would reduce the public sector deficit by privatizing the state-owned industrial sector and reforming the tax system.[7] Tax reform was also supported by the SDPP, which promised to exercise tighter control over public spending and to cut out wasteful state sector projects, besides launching new programs in the fields of education, health and housing. Finally, Bülent Ecevit claimed that he had now abandoned the attachment to state enterprises which had marked the former Republican People's Party, which he had once led: as he admitted, "I used to be an étatist — but now I support the market economy."[8] Like the other party leaders, he supported privatization in principle, but urged that it should be achieved by selling state enterprises to their employees, rather than to existing private firms.

Of the other issues in the election campaign, foreign policy was a notable absentee, in spite of Turkey's enhanced international role in the Gulf crisis. This was probably due to the fact that the crisis had subsided by the time the elections took place. At the same time, there did seem to be general agreement that Turkey had followed the right policies, by strictly abiding by UN decisions, and supporting the campaign against Saddam Husayn without becoming militarily involved. The Kurdish issue was more controversial, however; on this score, the SDPP promised to withdraw the emergency regime in the southeast, which gives special powers to the regional governor and police, and to encourage the revival of Kurdish culture in Turkey. The other parties were less specific on this issue, though they all promised to improve Turkey's human rights regime. Finally, for both Demirel and İnönü, the main target of attack was Turgut Özal: they both claimed that if they won the election, this would show that the President had lost his legitimacy, and that he should be replaced (though how, or by whom, was unclear).

During the campaign, public opinion polls had consistently given the TPP a clear lead, with the Motherland Party and SDPP vying for second place. Of the other parties, the polls predicted that the DLP and the WP alliance would just clear the 10% hurdle. These predictions proved remarkably accurate — in fact the only surprise was the strength of the WP vote, which had generally been underestimated by the pollsters.[9] In the event, the TPP came out ahead of the Motherland Party, though not by a substantial margin; with 179 seats, Demirel was well short of the 226 which he needed to form a government on his own. Certainly, the results were a setback for Yılmaz and Özal, but not a rout. The election returns showed that the TPP had taken over much of the Motherland Party's former vote in rural areas of western and central Turkey, but the Motherland Party still came out well ahead in Istanbul (which returns 50 of the total of 450 MPs) and the two parties were neck and neck in Ankara.

The results were also a serious disappointment for the SDPP, which was left with fewer seats than it had won in 1987, in spite of the government's unpopularity. Part of the explanation was the stronger showing of the DLP, which won over the loyalty of many potential SDPP supporters, especially in Istanbul, and in a string of provinces along the Black Sea coast. The poor performance of the SDPP in Istanbul's municipal administration, which it had captured in 1989, combined with the constant leadership wrangles in the party, had probably accounted for this. The SDPP did well in southeastern Anatolia, where it was aided by its re-alliance with the PLP, but may well have lost votes in other regions due to its association with the Kurdish cause. Finally, the WP alliance enjoyed a strong showing in Konya, a traditionally religious area, but its strength was otherwise limited to eastern Anatolia, where conservative Turkish-Sunni voters were probably attracted to the Islamic and ultranationalist banner by the presence of large Alevi (in effect, Shi'ite) and Kurdish communities in the same districts. It is also likely that the relative isolation and lack of development in the east inclined local voters to support what was, in effect, a party of protest against the Westernized, capitalist vision espoused by both Demirel and Özal.[10]

TABLE 1: TURKISH GENERAL ELECTION RESULTS, OCTOBER 1991

Party	Percentage of votes	Seats
True Path Party (TPP) (*Doğru Yol Partisi*)	27.0	179
Motherland Party (*Anavatan Partisi*)	24.0	112
Social Democrat Populist Party (SDPP) (*Sosyaldemokrat Halkçı Parti*)	20.8	91
Welfare Party (WP) (*Refah Partisi*)	16.9	61
Democratic Left Party (DLP) (*Demokratık Sol Partisi*)	10.8	7
Independents and others	0.5	—
	100.0	450

SOURCE: final results, as issued by Supreme Election Board, Ankara:
percentages rounded to nearest 0.1%. The discrepancy between each party's share of the votes, and its share of seats, is explained by the fact that the electoral system biases the results in favor of the bigger parties.

While the election results gave the pundits plenty of material for analysis, they also presented the politicians with some urgent problems, since it was clear that a coalition government was now inescapable. This was not an encouraging outlook, given Turkey's disastrous experiences of coalitions in the 1970s, when weak governments had succeeded one another with dizzying rapidity, and general chaos resulted. As the leader of the biggest party, Demirel was asked by the president to form a government, and was faced with a number of options. At first glance, a coalition between the True Path and Motherland Parties may have seemed logical, and was supported by the business community, since both parties had similar policies. However, it was ruled out by the rivalry between Özal and Demirel. Similarly, a coalition between the TPP and WP was likely to be wracked by arguments between Demirel and Erbakan, who had proved a very unreliable and demanding coalition partner in the 1970s. This left a TPP-SDPP coalition as the only workable alternative. As a reconciliation between the center-right and center-left, the alignment had historical significance. It was also facilitated by the convergence of the two parties' economic policies, even though there were still important differences of emphasis. Finally, Demirel and İnönü were united in their opposition to Özal, and their determination to liberalize the political system as a whole.

On this basis, Demirel and İnönü, with their respective colleagues, entered into an intense period of negotiation, ending with the announcement of their new government

TABLE 2: MEMBERS OF THE COUNCIL OF MINISTERS, APPOINTED ON 20 NOVEMBER 1991

Prime Minister	Süleyman Demirel (TPP)
Deputy Prime Minister	Erdal Inönü (SDPP)
Ministers of State	Cavit Çağlar (TPP)
	Tansu Çiller (TPP)
	Ekrem Ceyhun (TPP)
	Ibrahim Tez (SDPP)
	Akın Gönen (TPP)
	Güler Ileri (SDPP)
	Gökberk Ergenekon (TPP)
	Orhan Kilercioğlu (TPP)
	Mehmet Kahraman (SDPP)
	Ömer Barutçu (TPP)
	Mehmet Ali Yılmaz (TPP)
	Erman Şahin (SDPP)
	Şerif Ercan (TPP)
	Mehmet Batallı (TPP)
Ministers:	
Justice	Seyfi Oktay (SDPP)
Defense	Nevzat Ayaz (TPP)
Foreign Affairs	Hikmet Çetin (SDPP)
Interior	İsmet Sezgin (TPP)
Education	Köksal Toptan (TPP)
Health	Yıldırım Aktuna (TPP)
Finance	Sümer Oral (TPP)
Public Works	Onur Kumbaracıbaşı (SDPP)
Trade and Industry	Tahir Köse (SDPP)
Agriculture	Necmettin Cevheri (TPP)
Energy	Ersin Faralyalı (TPP)
Transport	Yaşar Topçu (TPP)
Labor	Mehmet Moğultay (SDPP)
Culture	Fikri Sağlar (SDPP)
Tourism	Abdülkadir Ateş (SDPP)
Forestry	Vefa Tanir (TPP)
Environment	Doğancan Akyürek (SDPP)

SOURCE: *Milliyet*, 21 November 1991.

on 20 November. In the coalition cabinet, the TPP had 20 members to the SDPP's 12 — a ratio roughly proportionate to the parliamentary strength of the two parties. Members of Demirel's party occupied most of the crucial economic posts, as ministers of finance, energy, and agriculture. Tansu Çiller, as one of 14 ministers of state, was also set to play a central role in economic policy-making. On the other hand, Erdal İnönü became deputy prime minister, with Hikmet Çetin as foreign minister. The SDPP also had its fair share of other ministries, by holding the portfolios of public works, trade and industry, justice, labor, culture and tourism. Given their performance in the elections, both parties could be reasonably content with this distribution of power, though it was noticed that İnönü had pointedly excluded Baykal's supporters, as well as former members of the PLP, from cabinet seats.[11]

The coalition government presented its program to parliament on 25 November, and duly received a vote of confidence. The most important part of the program concerned economic policy: on this score, Demirel and his colleagues undertook to work toward a balanced budget, to reduce the size of the public sector and make it more efficient, through restructuring and privatization where necessary. The government also promised to reform legislation on human rights, so as to bring Turkey into line with Western democratic standards, to tackle terrorism in the southeast, and to grant greater cultural rights to the Kurdish minority (see below). More immediately, it also had to decide what attitude to adopt toward President Özal. In spite of their campaign promises to depose him, Demirel and İnönü quickly realized that they would be unable to do so, at least in the short run. Even assuming they had been able to find a constitutionally acceptable formula for ending his term of office, any change in his status would necessitate a constitutional amendment. This would require a three-fifths supporting majority in the assembly, plus approval in a national referendum, but the government did not command the former and could not be sure of winning the latter.[12] Hence, the two coalition leaders were driven to the conclusion that, like it or not, they would have to learn to live with Turgut Özal. On his side, the president was determined to make full use of his constitutional powers, and did so on several occasions in December 1991 by returning bills to parliament, though not on politically crucial issues.[13] In effect, the two sides were driven into a state of uneasy live and let live, in which the government's business was delayed, but not fatally sabotaged.

CIVIL RIGHTS AND THE KURDISH PROBLEM

The most serious criticism of the Turkish political system is that, while it certainly has a democratically elected government, its legal code contains provisions which are quite incompatible with democratic norms, since they restrict the freedoms of association and expression to an unacceptable degree. Police are also entitled to hold suspects for up to 30 days without charge, and torture is regularly resorted to. Until recently, the Kurdish ethnic minority, which probably accounts for around 15%–20% of the total population, has been denied even the most limited cultural rights, let alone the right to self-determination. These restrictions are not just a heritage from earlier and less liberal regimes, but also reflect the powerful sense of national solidarity which is a striking feature of Turkey's political culture. On the other hand, as political liberalization has proceeded, cultural values have changed, so that there is now a far greater realization of the need for wider civil liberties than was formerly the case. For their part, the Turkish Kurds have become increasingly aware of their separate identity, and less prepared to accept the old structures of tribal control through which they were traditionally co-opted into the Turkish political system. Finally, governments have realized that if they are to integrate Turkey into the Western political community, then the human rights regime must be made to match up to Western standards. For all these reasons, reform of legislation affecting civil liberties has become a major issue for governments of all party colorings.

On 12 April 1991, the Motherland Party government took an important step in this direction when it issued a Law for the Struggle Against Terrorism. As its title suggests, the main part of this law introduced increased punishments for "terrorist" activities, which were widely defined, and could hardly be classified as liberal in direction. On the other hand, the end of the law contained the vital addition that, henceforth, Sections 140, 141, 142 and 163 of the Turkish Penal Code would be withdrawn.[14] The significance of this derived from the fact that Sections 140–42 had been objects of constant criticism from liberal opinion, both in Turkey and abroad. Article 141, in particular, had laid down heavy punishments for anyone who "attempts to establish or establishes, or arranges and conducts and administers the activities of, societies...with the purpose of establishing the domination of a social class over the other social classes, or exterminating a certain social class or overthrowing any of the established basic economic or social orders of the country." Section 142 had specified slightly lighter punishments for those convicted of "making propaganda" to the same effect. Thanks to their catchall wording, these two sections had frequently been used to prosecute anyone accused of allegedly communist or antistate activities, defined in the widest sense. Even where convictions had not resulted, protracted trials and long periods on remand had meant serious suffering for those affected. Section 163, meanwhile, had been used to prosecute supposed Islamic fundamentalists: it had provided for heavy punishments for anyone who, "contrary to laicism, establishes, organizes, regulates or administers societies with the purpose of adapting, even partially, the basic social, economic, political or judicial orders of the state to religious principles and beliefs."[15] By withdrawing these clauses, the government showed that it was prepared to liberalize freedom of expression for those espousing radical views at opposite ends of the political spectrum.

The same legislation included a long overdue reform affecting the cultural rights of the Kurdish minority. Under the Law regarding Communications in Languages other than Turkish,[16] which had been enacted by the former military regime in 1983, the use of any language which was not the official language of a state recognized by Turkey (in other words, Kurdish) was made illegal, including — in theory — its use in everyday speech. Under the Law for the Struggle Against Terrorism, this legislation was also withdrawn. It had not only been a flagrant denial of human rights, but was also quite absurd, since Kurdish is the first language of several million Turkish citizens.[17] The withdrawal of the law meant that Turkey's Kurds could no longer be prosecuted for speaking their language, though, at this stage its use in publications or broadcasting was still banned. A step had at least been made toward the recognition of the Kurdish identity. Nonetheless, any form of propaganda, meetings or publications supporting Kurdish separatism (in the words of the statute, "aiming to damage the indivisible integrity of the Turkish Republic, with its territory and nation") remained strictly illegal.[18]

Along with these changes, the new statute also provided for early release of 43,000 prisoners, including those convicted on political charges, although not those found guilty of terrorism or other acts of serious violence. This was expected to free the big majority of those imprisoned for political reasons; in fact, by early 1992 Amnesty International reported that there were now no prisoners of conscience in Turkey. It was also decreed that the 256 prisoners who were currently held on death sentences would not be executed, although the death penalty would not be formally abolished (in fact, no death sentences have been carried out in Turkey since 1984). Finally, political exiles who had been deprived of their citizenship would have it restored, provided they returned to Turkey within two years.[19]

Unfortunately, the withdrawal of the notorious Sections 140–42 from the Penal Code still left the civil rights regime in Turkey more restrictive than in the Western democracies, since provisions in the Law on Political Parties repeated many of the bans which had been contained in the Penal Code; in other words, what was now permitted to individuals or societies was not necessarily permitted to political parties. The existing law on trades unions also banned any links between the unions and political parties and prevented civil servants from becoming union members.[20] Similar restrictions are included in the constitution, though how binding they could be without specific legislation is doubtful.[21] Finally, under a law passed in 1987, eight Kurdish-inhabited provinces in southeastern Anatolia had been classified as a State of Emergency Region, in which the police and army enjoyed specially enlarged powers, under the regional governor. Although it was not officially classified as such, the region could be said to be under a regime close to permanent martial law.

During the election campaign, the SDPP put particular emphasis on removing these restrictions on civil liberties, primarily by altering the constitution so as to increase the freedom of the press, and lift the ban on union membership by civil servants and union-party links. On the Kurdish issue, İnönü's party promised to end the special regime in the southeast, and to secure "the protection and development of the language, traditions, folklore and personality of the population."[22] For his part, Demirel joined İnönü in demanding reform of the constitution, and promised to end torture and other maltreatment of prisoners by the police; a TPP television commercial claimed that cell walls would be "made of glass" if the party won the elections.[23] These commitments were reflected in those contained in the official program of the coalition government which stated that "our government will ensure that human rights in Turkey come to be on a par with our country's international undertakings, its political system and its desire to integrate with the civilized world....all principles in our legal system that run counter to universal democracy will be amended." Similarly, the program promised to extend Kurdish cultural rights, stating that "it is the basic right and freedom of everyone to research, protect and develop his mother tongue, culture, history, folklore and religious beliefs," though Turkey's borders and its official language "cannot be questioned."[24]

As an earnest of its aim to work for reconciliation with moderate Kurdish opinion, the new government made it clear that henceforth it would be possible to publish books and newspapers in Kurdish, to address meetings and organize classes in the language, and to mount other activities such as Kurdish cultural festivals. Demirel and İnönü also paid a well-publicized visit to the southeastern provinces on 7–8 December, in the company of the chief of the general staff, in which they stated that the government now accepted the separate cultural identity of the Kurds in Turkey and that (to quote Demirel) "the people in the southeast are our brothers....Turkey must recognize the Kurdish reality."[25] Early pronouncements by the new government also suggested that it would reform, if not withdraw, the "emergency" regime in the southeast. The difficulty for the coalition leaders was to persuade their more conservative followers (especially in the TPP) to go along with this liberalization and, for the SDPP, to simultaneously retain the loyalty of its more radical Kurdish MPs. An early sign that this would be difficult occurred on 6 November, when the new MPs were being sworn in to the assembly. Several Kurdish members sported mufflers, handkerchiefs and headbands in the Kurdish national colors of yellow, green and red. Two of the SDPP members for Diyarbakır, Hatip Dicle and Mrs. Leyla Zana seized the opportunity to create a rumpus by shouting Kurdish nationalist slogans. Subsequently, the two MPs announced their resignation from the SDPP, to become independents. By the end of the year, other resignations by members of the ex-PLP group within the SDPP were expected. It thus seemed likely that the alliance between the Social Democrats and the more radical Kurdish representatives would be a very fragile one.

The kind of accommodation which Demirel and İnönü were evidently looking for was made far more difficult by a continued campaign of violence by the PKK (*Parti Kerkeren Kurdistan* or Kurdistan Workers' Party). This is the main Kurdish guerrilla organization in Turkey, and was supported by Syria with bases in Lebanon, besides financial and other assistance. The PKK opposed participation in the Turkish political system (and was in any case an illegal organization in Turkey) although it claimed in 1991 that it had abandoned the goal of full independence in favor of autonomy within Turkey. PKK attacks continued throughout the year and were, if anything, intensified by the Kurdish tragedy in Iraq since the PKK was able to obtain weapons and ammunition from retreating Iraqi forces, and benefited from a general upswelling of sympathy for the Kurds. Its attacks in Turkey also led to cross-border operations into Iraq by the Turkish army and air force. On 4 August, a PKK gang killed nine Turkish gendarmes stationed at Samanlı, in the remote southeastern province of Hakkari, and carried off another seven to their base in Iraqi Kurdistan. In response, Turkish air and ground forces launched a counterattack which lasted until 19 August. By official accounts, they penetrated only 10 km. into Iraq and killed at least 35 PKK fighters without causing civilian casualties: however, UN officials confirmed that around 30 innocent Kurdish civilians had actually been killed.[26] The counterattack severely damaged Turkey's international image, and caused sharp criticism from the German Foreign Minister Hans-Dietrich Genscher, who condemned the Turkish operations as a "serious violation of international law and of humanity."[27]

In the event, the cross-border operation did not seem to have made any effective dent in the PKK's operational strength. PKK attacks continued during the following months, causing a steady death toll among the Turkish security forces, as well as "village guards" (that is, anti-PKK Kurdish militiamen who had been armed by the government). On 9 December, at a village in Diyarbakır province, nine people, including one gendarme, were killed when security forces opened fire on a crowd of mourners at a funeral of PKK militants. The PKK struck back on the following day by fire-bombing a department store in the Istanbul suburb of Bakırköy, killing 11 people, including a two-year-old child. This caused a shocked reaction, since it suggested that the PKK now had the ability to launch terrorist attacks in the big cities of western Turkey (possibly in collaboration with ultraleftist Turkish urban-guerrilla groups). Although none of the Turkish parties favored concessions to Kurdish political demands, it was hard to see how the violence could be ended without some sort of dialogue between the government and Kurdish nationalist opinion, and a substantial improvement in the human rights regime in the southeast — neither of which seemed very likely, in spite of the government's commitments.

FOREIGN RELATIONS

THE GULF WAR AND ITS AFTERMATH

Following Saddam Husayn's invasion of Kuwait in August 1990, Turkey had fully applied economic sanctions against Iraq. It could reasonably claim to have played a major role in making them effective, granted that the oil pipeline from Iraq's northern oil field at Kirkuk to the Turkish Mediterranean coast at Yumurtalık was the normal route for around half Iraq's oil exports, and that Iraq normally depended on Turkey for transit routes to the West and an important part of its food supplies. Thanks to parliamentary pressure from his own backbenchers as well as the opposition parties, President Özal had been prevented from sending Turkish troops to join the coalition forces facing Saddam in the Gulf, but at the end of 1990 Turkey had begun a substantial buildup of troops along its 150-mile border with Iraq. This move was taken primarily for defensive purposes, but it also had the important effect of pinning down around 100,000 Iraqi troops in the north of the country, which would have otherwise been available for deployment on the southern front. By the end of 1990, as a war between the coalition powers and Iraq looked increasingly probable, the main question facing the government in Ankara was whether it should allow the US and other coalition air forces to use bases in Turkey to launch sorties against Iraq, which would give the coalition a big advantage in establishing air supremacy (see *MECS* 1990, pp. 685–86).

The question was not an easy one for the government to answer. On the one hand, if Turkey refused the use of its bases, then it would do serious damage to its long-term relations with the Western powers. Özal's claim that, in spite of the end of the Cold War, Turkey had not lost its strategic value to the West would have looked completely hollow. On the other hand, although Saddam had few supporters in Turkey, there was little public enthusiasm for a war against him. Several large cities in eastern Anatolia were within range of Iraq's *Scud* missiles, and would have been very vulnerable if Saddam had decided to retaliate. On all these grounds, the government delayed its decision until the last minute. Finally, on 17 January, parliament voted to give the government special war powers, including permission to the coalition air forces to use bases in Turkey for attacks on Iraqi targets. The air war against Iraq began on the following day, as US planes took off from İncirlik. Initially, the Foreign Ministry claimed that they were purely on "training missions," but this pretense was later dropped, and the raids continued right up to the time of the cease-fire in the Gulf on 28 February.[28] Fears that Saddam Husayn might retaliate against Turkey proved unfounded, as the Iraqi ruler evidently realized that opening up a second front in the north would be suicidal. The guns along the Turkish-Iraqi frontier thus stayed silent, and Turkey remained uninvolved in the land war, to the general relief of both sides.

Following Iraq's defeat in Kuwait, and its acceptance of the cease-fire, the government in Ankara could feel pleased with the success of its policy. Turkey had given vital support to the coalition cause, but had not fired a shot in anger. As President Özal claimed in a television broadcast on 2 March: "Our country has passed a test with flying colors and has proved to the world at large that it is a country that can be trusted, increasing its prestige abroad."[29] However, this fanfare of success was to prove all too brief, as Turkey rapidly found itself embroiled in the tragedy of the Kurdish population of Iraq. Following Saddam's brutal suppression of the Kurdish uprising of March 1991, a huge exodus of refugees began toward the Turkish and Iranian borders, with as many as 500,000 gathering along the Turkish frontier, and even more along that with Iran.

This tidal wave of human misery presented the Turkish Government with an acute problem. On the one hand, it could not refuse to do anything: the sight of hundreds of thousands of refugees, undergoing appalling sufferings, which appeared every day on the world's television screens, awoke universal sympathy, in Turkey as elsewhere. On the other hand, if the government allowed the refugees free entry to Turkish territory, then it would require legal responsibility for caring for them, long after the attention of the world's media had moved on to other problems. The effects of such a huge refugee presence on Turkey's own Kurdish minority was another worrying threat for the government, even though it was less likely to advertise this abroad.

Initially, during early April, the government stalled: the refugees were cooped up along the Iraqi side of the mountainous border, as a relief effort began. Before long, however, it became obvious that this policy was unsustainable. The Turkish Red Crescent, local villagers and international aid workers did their best to cope, but it was obvious that the scale of the problem made much more radical measures essential. Moreover, the topography of the region made the problem far worse: there were few roads, appalling weather conditions, and no regular organization for distributing such supplies as were available. The fact that it was Saddam Husayn who had caused this suffering was overshadowed by the sight of Turkish soldiers pushing back desperate refugees onto bleak mountainsides. Much of the international credit which Turkey had gained during the Gulf War evaporated. By the second week of April it was becoming accepted that the only solution to the crisis would be to move the refugees back to their homes. However, there was no chance that they would do so unless they were offered protection against further vengeance by Saddam.

For Turkey, this meant going back on what had hitherto been a fixed point of foreign policy — that is, complete opposition to any form of partition of Iraq, either explicit or implied. Nevertheless, President Özal decided to grasp the nettle on 7 April, when he proposed that UN forces should establish a security zone in northern Iraq, to which the refugees could return.[30] This idea was taken up by British Prime Minister John Major, and eventually by President George Bush. At the end of April, some 17,000 coalition troops moved into northern Iraq, and the Iraqi-Turkish border zone, and the refugees began to move back to their homes. "Operation Bring Comfort" was remarkably successful: by the end of May, virtually all the refugees had returned to their homes, and a regular system of relief supply had begun. In July, the first phase of the operation was succeeded by "Poised Hammer," in which coalition forces were withdrawn from Iraqi territory, but replaced by a small multinational ground force at Silopi, on the Turkish side of the border, supported by a coalition air detachment at

İncirlik. This was allowed for by a special mandate from the Turkish parliament, which had to be renewed at six-month intervals. During the autumn, the Silopi force was gradually withdrawn, but the air presence at İncirlik served its purpose, by preventing the Iraqi air force from operating in northern Iraq, and thus launching another attack on the Kurds.

On the Turkish side "Poised Hammer" did not enjoy wholehearted support, since Turkey had always been very wary of any involvement by outside powers in the Kurdish problem. On the other hand, it was recognized that, without the coalition presence, the refugee crisis could not have been solved, and that if it were withdrawn there might be another exodus. Hence, "Poised Hammer" was accepted as much the lesser of two evils. Its mandate was duly renewed at the end of September, and then by the new parliament in December 1991. The establishment of what was, in effect, a semi-independent Kurdish administration in northern Iraq also forced Turkey into a reluctant recognition of the Iraqi Kurdish leadership. This had begun in March when Jalal Talabani, leader of the Patriotic Union of Kurdistan, and Muhsin Dizah'i, an assistant of Mas'ud al-Barazani of the Kurdistan Democratic Party, paid an unpublicized visit to Turgut Özal (the fact that the meeting had taken place at all was not admitted by Özal until almost a week later). This was a dramatic reversal of policy for Turkey, which had hitherto avoided any high-level contact with the Kurdish leaders, but as Özal put it, "everyone else is talking to them, why not us? We must be friends with them as much as possible."[31] Talabani paid another visit to Turkey in June (ostensibly, to attend a meeting of the Socialist International in Istanbul) and had further talks with Özal. Talabani and Dizah'i were back in Ankara in early August, coinciding with Turkey's attack into Iraqi Kurdistan. Their main purpose was to secure food and other supplies from Turkey, and to end the Turkish military operation as soon as possible, so as to prevent further civilian casualties. However, it was noticed that they did not publicly condemn the Turkish attack, and undertook to prevent the PKK from launching raids into Turkey from their territory. In effect, they seemed willing to trade material assistance for a common front against the PKK.

Thanks to these developments, by the end of the year the Turkish Government could at least feel that the immediate crisis provoked by the Gulf War had subsided. Nonetheless, the medium-term outlook was far from promising. Hopes that Saddam Husayn's defeat in Kuwait would lead to his overthrow in Iraq had been dashed: the economic embargo was still in place, but there was no proof that it would produce the desired political effects. In Iraqi Kurdistan, both the coalition powers, the Kurdish leadership and Turkish policymakers were still stuck in a potentially dangerous impasse. There was no sign that the protracted talks between Barazani and Talabani on the one side, and the Iraqi regime on the other, would produce a viable agreement on Kurdish autonomy, and the Kurds could only survive with the help of Western aid and air cover, which might not continue indefinitely.

The relationship between Ankara and the Iraqi Kurdish leaders was also fraught with problems. Turkey was closely interested in the situation in Iraqi Kurdistan, but had little ability to control it. In the meantime, the position of the PKK was the most immediate source of friction. The Iraqi Kurdish leaders had officially denied that they supported the PKK, but their physical ability to suppress it was limited. On the other hand, so long as PKK attacks continued, there would be pressure within Turkey for renewed counterattacks into northern Iraq, which would almost certainly bring international criticism. Hence, Turkey needed to address the problem by continuing a dialogue with the Iraqi Kurds, and by making some attempt to tackle the root causes of Kurdish discontent within Turkey.

GLOBAL AND REGIONAL CHANGES, AND THEIR IMPLICATIONS

At the beginning of 1991, international recognition of its positive role in the Gulf crisis, and the end of the Cold War, meant that — for the first time since World War II — Turkey was able to develop good relations with both the US and the USSR simultaneously. This became evident on 11 March, when Turgut Özal arrived in Moscow for talks with Presidents Gorbachev and Yeltsin (the latter in his capacity as President of the Russian Federation). This was followed by visits to the then Soviet republics of Ukraine, Azerbaijan and Kazakhstan. While in Moscow, Özal signed a 20-year Treaty of Friendship and Cooperation, recalling the very first treaty which Turkey had signed with the infant Soviet state in 1921. Other agreements on the strengthening of economic links were negotiated with Ukraine and Kazakhstan, and arrangements made for direct airline flights between Istanbul and Baku, the Azeri capital.[32] All this suggested that Turkey's support for the US in the Gulf War had not damaged its relations with Moscow — rather the reverse, since the USSR appeared to welcome Turkey's enhanced international standing, and was keen to strengthen economic relations.

One strategy for achieving this was the proposal to establish a Black Sea Economic cooperation zone. The Turkish Government (and Özal in particular) had taken the lead in this project, partly because it helped to give another boost to the country's international profile and, more materially, because it offered important potential economic advantages. In particular, the value of Turkey's imports from the USSR had increased from $597m. in 1989 to $1,247m. in 1990 (mainly through the development of natural gas imports via a newly constructed pipeline) whereas Turkey's exports to the Soviet Union had actually fallen from $705m. to $531m.[33] The main cause of this was the USSR's shortage of hard currency, and disruption and bureaucratic confusions on the Soviet side. On these grounds, any scheme which promised to make mutual trade easier seemed worth exploring. Apart from this, Turkey's relations with both Bulgaria and Romania had improved dramatically, following the overthrow of the dictatorships of Zhivkov and Ceaușescu, and it seemed important to turn this to economic and political advantage (see *MECS* 1990, p. 681).

In line with this plan, the four countries had held a preliminary meeting in December 1990 at which they agreed to work toward establishing free movement of persons, goods, capital and services, to cooperate in developing infrastructure projects in transport and communications, and to establish a Black Sea Development Bank. Their delegates met again in Moscow in July 1991 to produce a memorandum of understanding on trade cooperation and the free movement of capital and businessmen (the idea of free movement of labor having been abandoned). Greece and Yugoslavia sent observers to the meeting, and the Greeks later applied to join the project.[34] Progress was then delayed by the break-up of the USSR, and could not be resumed until 1992. The question of how Turkey could fit in new trade commitments to the Black Sea states with those it had already undertaken to the EC was also unanswered as yet, though the authorities in Ankara emphasized that the Black Sea project was supplementary to their links with the Community, and not a replacement.

Meanwhile, Özal was also busy cultivating his relations with the US, visiting Washington on 22–24 March. In talks at Camp David, he apparently reached agreement with President Bush on a wide range of regional issues, in particular the need to maintain the territorial integrity of Iraq. More concretely, the US Congress agreed to make an emergency appropriation of $200m. in aid to Turkey, to compensate for the losses it had incurred as a result of the trade embargo on Iraq. It was also expected that the Administration would sanction an extra $280m. in military aid to Turkey.[35] In spite of potential tensions in the Turkish-US relationship arising from the allied intervention in northern Iraq, the mood of mutual support continued during the rest of 1991. It was symbolized by President Bush's visit to Turkey on 20–22 July — the first by a US president since that of Dwight Eisenhower in 1959. The two presidents had had ample opportunity to talk to one another by telephone, at other international conferences, or on Özal's frequent visits to Washington, so the encounter had a mainly symbolic significance. Nevertheless, it was a good opportunity for Özal to advertise the friendship to the rest of the world, and to the Turkish public, and the visit was generally well received by the Turkish press.

Apart from the ending of the Gulf crisis, the failure of the anti-Gorbachev coup in Moscow was almost certainly the most momentous event affecting Turkey's international position during 1991 — as it was for all the neighbors of the former USSR. On 19–20 August, as initial news of the coup was coming in, the Turkish reaction was cautious, although Prime Minister Mesut Yılmaz made it clear that "our political philosophy does not allow us to condone such interventions, whatever their causes."[36] Naturally enough, the collapse of the coup was greeted with great relief in Ankara. A return to the Cold War might have reasserted Turkey's old importance within the Western alliance, but this doubtful gain would have been more than outweighed by a return to the old tensions, and the economic and political cost of hostility from the USSR. On the other hand, the subsequent collapse of the Soviet Union did not provoke an immediate or radical reorientation of Turkish foreign policy. This may partly have been because its full implications were not fully assessed at the time, but more probably because the wind had been blowing in this direction for some time. With the collapse of the Warsaw Pact, the end of the Cold War, and the attempted reform of the Soviet system by Mikhail Gorbachev, Turkey had already begun building closer relations with the eastern European countries and Central Asia, before the Soviet Union finally collapsed. In effect, the breakup of the USSR came as the last installment in a series of incremental changes.

This radical transformation of the external environment had two important implications for Turkey. In the first place, it implied the need for a basic reform of its defense structure. This had hitherto been based on the maintenance of massive conventional land forces, facing the Balkan and Transcaucasian frontiers, which had been designed to block any Warsaw Pact attempt to take over the Turkish straits or eastern Anatolia (and thus the Middle East). Hence, in mid-1991, the Turkish armed forces had some 579,000 men, of whom 470,000 were in the army, and 498,000 were conscripts performing their 18-months military service.[37] In the new conditions, such large forces were no longer necessary — moreover, the Gulf War of 1991 had shown that huge conscript armies were no match for smaller and more professional forces, armed with the latest hardware. Hence, in November 1991, it was announced that by 1996 the armed forces would be reduced to a total of 470,000 men, of which 70,000 would be in the gendarmerie, 120,000 in the navy and air force, and the remaining 280,000 in the army. The period of compulsory service would be reduced accordingly.[38]

The second effect of the collapse of the USSR was to open political and economic opportunities for Turkey in the newly independent republics of the Commonwealth of Independent States (CIS). This particularly affected Turkey's relations with the states of Transcaucasia and Central Asia, which had already begun to develop during the latter stages of Gorbachev's presidency (see *MECS* 1990, pp. 680–81). For more extreme nationalists in Turkey, the end of the Soviet state heralded the future realization of the pan-Turkish dream — that is the political union of all the Turkic peoples, stretching from the Mediterranean to the deserts of Sinkiang, in the extreme west of China. Certainly, there was considerable sympathy in Turkey for the peoples of Central Asia, most of whom share the Muslim religion and speak languages related to that of Turkey. This was reflected in coverage of the topic in the Turkish press. On the other hand, the government and Foreign Ministry tended to take a far more cautious attitude, based on Turkey's wider international interests. These rested on the fact that Turkey needed to maintain good relations with the Slavic as well as Muslim republics of the CIS, granted that Russia and the Ukraine had inherited the vast majority of the human and physical resources of the former USSR, and are likely to be of crucial political and economic importance to Turkey. Moreover, the Ankara government was very unwilling to be drawn into an open contest for power in Central Asia with Iran, another important neighbor and trade partner.

Pan-Turkism also tended to ignore or underestimate the physical and cultural barriers between the Turkic peoples of Central Asia — the fact that, for instance, their languages are related, but are far from identical, or even mutually comprehensible in several cases (thus, for instance, a Turk from Turkey can understand the spoken language of Azerbaijan, but will be hard put to it to hold a conversation with an Uzbek or Kazakh). Equally, the economies of the Central Asian and Transcaucasian republics were still overwhelmingly dependent on that of Russia. Thirdly, the Ankara government was fully aware of the innumerable ethnic and religious conflicts within the former USSR, and most unwilling to get sucked into them. Hence, both the Motherland Party government and its successor stuck to the line that they fully respected the independence and territory of all the CIS states and were not looking for a contest with Iran, Russia or any other country. Turkey would hope to develop economic cooperation with all the republics: it might have particularly important cultural ties with the Turkic-Muslim nations, but all that it aimed to do was to act as the model of a successful transition to democratic politics and the market economy. In short, Turkey might have a special relationship with the Turkic republics, but no more than that. In the economic sphere, it was also realized in Ankara that Turkey lacked the huge capital resources which the new republics needed for their economic transformation: these could only come from the advanced economies of western Europe, north America and Japan. In this respect, as in others, Turkey's new international role could only be realized in collaboration with the Western powers — in fact, one of the main advantages of the new avenues open to Turkey was precisely the fact that they increased the value of its friendship to the West.

On this basis, one of the last acts of the Yılmaz government was to declare that it was prepared to recognize the independence of Azerbaijan. This was confirmed by the Demirel government, and an official protocol establishing formal diplomatic relations was signed on 14 January 1992. Meanwhile, the government announced that it would also recognize all the republics of the former USSR, and would establish diplomatic relations with them in due course. As a first sign of these new opportunities, the presidents of Uzbekistan, Turkmenistan and Kirghizia all paid official visits to Ankara during December. For Turkey, the closest links were with Azerbaijan, but these were also the most problematic, due to the continuing contest between Azerbaijan and Armenia over the status of Nogorno-Karabagh, the Armenian-inhabited enclave in Azeri territory. Although the government supported the Azeri position that Nogorno-Karabagh was constitutionally part of Azerbaijan, it was realized in Ankara that Turkey could not afford a confrontation with Armenia, let alone military commitments to Azerbaijan. Once more, the reason was Turkey's wider interest — in particular, the need to maintain good relations with the US, which is the home of a large Armenian diaspora. As a sign of this, a high-level delegation from Armenia was received by Ekrem Pakdemirli, deputy prime minister in the Yılmaz Administration. Equally, when a crisis in Armenian-Azeri relations erupted in December, following the crash of an Azeri helicopter carrying government officials over Nogorno-Karabagh, Prime Minister Demirel sent an open message to the Azeri Premier Hasan Hasanov, urging him not to take precipitate action. In effect, Demirel was warning Azerbaijan that it could not expect Turkish support if it provoked an all-out war with Armenia.

ECONOMIC TRENDS

Thanks to external instability, and continuing defects in Turkey's economic structure, 1991 was a difficult year for the Turkish economy. These problems were exacerbated by internal political uncertainties, and the failure of the Motherland Party government to take effective remedial measures. The result was a low rate of growth in the economy, and a high and rising rate of inflation which severely undermined the confidence of both businessmen and consumers. Paradoxically, Turkey's external accounts were a good deal stronger than had been expected, though this was partly explained by lower domestic growth and the inflow of emergency assistance, mainly from the Arab oil-exporting states.

According to semiofficial figures issued in mid-1992, gross domestic product (GDP) rose by only 1.1% in 1991, or well below both the 8.4% GDP growth recorded in 1990 and the annual population growth rate of 2.17%. Moreover, due to a fall in net factor income from abroad, mainly emigrants' remittances, GNP grew by a mere 0.3%. The low rate of growth in the domestic economy was partly explained by a fall in agricultural output of 0.8%: this in turn derived from one of the basic weaknesses of the economy, which is the dependence of the important agricultural sector on uncertain weather conditions. These were evidently less favorable in 1991 than they had been in 1990 (see *MECS* 1990, pp. 686–87). More importantly, the industrial sector, which now accounts for around 28% of GNP, also grew at the low rate of 3.2% in 1991, compared with 9.1% in the previous year. Here the main explanation was that the economy had begun to experience fairly serious overheating at the end of 1990, and that some reaction was predictable. There was also a decline in the construction sector, where value added fell by 1.9%. Finally, the level of activity in the main productive sectors inevitably affected the services sector, which grew by only 1.1%, after the 9.4% growth rate recorded in 1990.[39]

Quarterly figures for national income add detail to this picture, and help to give some explanations of the disappointing performance. During the first and second quarters of 1991, GNP fell by 1.1% and and 0.6% respectively, compared with the same quarters of 1990. Output at the beginning of the year was hit by a series of industrial disputes. These had begun on 30 November 1990 when the miners of the Zonguldak coal basin (Turkey's main source of hard coal) came out on strike. During January 1991 the miners were joined by workers in the metal-working and paper industries. All these strikes were suspended by the government on 25 January, following the start of the war against Iraq. The workers' wage claims were then settled by arbitration, but by this time a good deal of production had been lost. In the following weeks, worries about the Gulf crisis caused further falls in production, which lasted for some time after the war against Iraq was over. Confidence was somewhat restored during the third quarter of the year, when GNP grew by 2.7% compared with the same period of 1990, and was probably further encouraged by the steep rises in state sector wages and agricultural support prices which were decreed by the government (see below). However, during the election and postelection periods, domestic political uncertainties and a relatively poor harvest again affected the economy, as GNP growth fell back to 0.8%.[40]

This low rate of growth was accompanied by further increases in Turkey's already high inflation rate. As measured by the national consumer prices index, the monthly rate of inflation ran at 4.4%–6.6% during the first four months of the year. This fell during the following three months, to reach a low point of 1.3% in July, but this reduction in the monthly rate was only to be expected, and is normally repeated every summer as fresh food supplies come onto the market. During the following three months, inflation climbed back up, to reach a rate of 6.6% in October. There was then a slight fall to 4.4% in December, but these monthly increases still left the overall rise in the index at 71.1% for the year as a whole. This compared with a rate of 60.3% in 1990, and was the highest rate recorded since 1989, when inflation had touched 75.4% on the same index.

Sometimes it was suggested that Turks had come to regard galloping inflation as normal, but it was hard to believe that they accepted it, since the relentless rise in prices put constant pressure on wage earners, farmers and businessmen. Employees in both the public and private sectors were periodically granted large wage hikes, but these only occurred at yearly or six-monthly intervals, so there were long periods in which real incomes were falling for many families. Equally, businessmen found it very hard to plan ahead, and were forced to pay astronomical interest rates for borrowed funds. Since banks had to offer depositors a reasonable real rate of return, interest rates for medium- and long-term loans ran at around 105% p.a. during the year. Under this pressure, as well as the low rate of economic growth, fixed capital investment contracted by 1% in real terms. All this had critical political effects. Public opinion polls showed that inflation was the major concern in the minds of voters, and its failure to bring it down was almost certainly the principal reason for the Motherland Party's defeat in the general elections.[41]

It was generally accepted that the main cause of inflation was lax fiscal and monetary policy by the government which, in effect, was constantly printing new money to make good its deficits. These, in turn, were caused mainly by three factors: first, the shortcomings of the tax system, which allowed many businesses and self-employed people to escape with very low direct taxes; second, the fact that a large proportion of government expenditure — around 50%–55% of the total — was devoted to civil service wages, which the government was periodically obliged to increase in line with inflation; third, the large financial losses chalked up by most of the state sector industries (known in Turkey as State Economic Enterprises, or SEEs) which were made up by state subsidies. Inefficiencies in the SEEs were, in turn, mainly the result of underinvestment and overmanning in many state factories, basic structural defects like mislocation, and the reluctance of the government to allow the SEEs to increase their prices in line with costs, in an attempt to hold down the consumer prices index.

These defects were illustrated by the government's fiscal performance in 1991. The state budget for the year planned for total expenditure of TL104,780bn. (around $35bn. at the January 1991 exchange rate) compared with planned revenues of TL84,130bn., leaving a deficit of TL20,650bn., or about 20% of expenditure and 4.5% of forecast GDP. As had been widely expected, the outturn was far worse than this: actual revenues reached TL99,105bn. ($17.7bn. at the January 1992 exchange rate) but expenditures climbed to TL130,865bn., and the budget deficit to TL31,760bn. or about 7% of GDP.[42] Moreover, the state budget figure failed to tell the full story of government expenditure, since subsidies to SEEs are often made through extra budgetary payments: as a result the total public sector borrowing requirement, which takes these payments into account, reached around 12% of GDP.

Government policies during the year increased this inflationary pressure. In spite of frequent declarations, the government failed to make the necessary reforms to the tax system, so as to increase its revenues in real terms. Deficit financing of the state sector continued, so that Central Bank loans to the public sector increased by 262% over the level of 1990.[43] Although the government was officially committed to privatizing the SEEs, little was achieved. This was partly due to that fact that few private investors were willing to take over obvious loss makers, and partly to the slackness in the Istanbul stock market, which failed to make up more than a part of the severe losses it had suffered in the aftermath of the Gulf crisis. Sadly, government policies during the run up to the election made the problem of state finances far worse. Civil service wages are normally raised in January and July of each year: the first half rise was modest, at around 15%, but during the second half a 40% rise was granted, giving a total increase of about 60%. Moreover, some 600,000 workers in SEEs were given far higher wage rises. Initially, the Akbulut government had planned to hold the rise in minimum prices paid to farmers by state purchasing agencies at around 35%–40%, but in August the Yılmaz government decreed price rises of about 60%–75% for most crops. The clear intention was to buy both urban and rural votes in the forthcoming elections. This largesse was expected to cost the government around TL40,000bn. gross: even allowing for the fact that some of the extra cash would be recouped through the tax system, the net cost to the Treasury was still expected to reach about TL25,000–27,000bn.[44]

In contrast, the foreign accounts were the one bright spot in the economic record. Exports grew in 1991 by just under 5% over the 1990 total, to reach $13.7bn., whereas the value of imports fell by 7%, at $21bn. Dollar income from services was affected by a decline in tourism revenues, which fell from $3.2bn. in 1990 to $2.7bn. in 1991, mainly as a result of the Gulf War and its aftermath. However, this loss was offset by an increase in other service earnings, such as transport, transit trade and contractors' remittances: taking outflows into account, Turkey had a credit balance on services of just under $2.5bn. In addition, remittances from Turkish expatriates working in western Europe and the ME brought in $2.9bn. The trade accounts were also affected by the economic embargo of Iraq, of which the direct costs to the Turkish balance of payments probably ran at the rate of around $2bn. p.a.[45] On the other hand, the balance of payments account for 1991 shows a net inflow of $2.2bn. for public unrequited transfers — that is, mainly compensation aid from Saudi Arabia and Kuwait for the cost of applying sanctions against Iraq. As a result, there was a positive balance on current account of $272m., compared with the deficit of $2.6bn. recorded in 1990.[46]

The decline in imports was largely accounted for by the lower rate of domestic economic growth, which reduced demand for imported machinery, spare parts and raw materials like chemicals. However, Turkey also benefited from the low price as well as volume of oil imports (the latter being caused partly by a higher level of domestic oil production). The increase in exports was also a creditable achievement, granted the effects of the Gulf War and difficult world trading conditions. Sales to the OECD countries recorded only a small increase of 2.4%, but exports to the Islamic countries as a whole increased by 11.6%, as the collapse of exports to Iraq was more than made up by a stronger performance in other Middle Eastern markets. Exports to the CIS and eastern Europe rose by 15.7%, indicating that Turkish exporters had been quick to take advantage of the opening up of these economies, in spite of the severe internal dislocation many of them were undergoing. Exports were also aided by a steady fall in the exchange rate, resulting in a nominal rate of devaluation over the year of 71.6% against the deutsche mark, and 73.8% against the dollar, or slightly more than the rate of domestic inflation.[47] The fact that Turkey was still paying its way internationally, in spite of external upsets, showed the importance of the structural adjustment policies which Turgut Özal had originally introduced at the beginning of the 1980s, even though the same approach had certainly not been applied in the regulation of the domestic economy.

NOTES

For the place and frequency of publications cited here, and for the full name of the publication, news agency, radio station or monitoring service where an abbreviation is used, please see "List of Sources." Only in the case of more than one publication bearing the same name is the place of publication noted here.

1. Turkish Constitution (1982) Article 101.
2. This narrative is based on contemporary Turkish press reports. Specific references are given only for other sources, or for statistics and quotations.
3. *Milliyet,* 16–17 June 1991.
4. Under the constitution, parliament is elected for a five-year term; the previous general elections had been held in November 1987. However, parliament may pass a bill decreeing early general elections. Effectively, this gives the power to the government, assuming it has a clear majority and the support of its own backbenchers. The president can unilaterally order early elections, but only in certain complicated circumstances which did not apply in this case (Turkish Constitution, Articles 77 and 116).
5. Voting figures from *Milliyet,* 30 July 1991.
6. Party programme summarized in ibid., 22 September 1991.

7. Ibid., 9 September 1991.
8. Quoted, ibid., 8 September 1991.
9. See, for instance, the poll conducted by the Konda organization for *Milliyet*: the full series appears in the issue for 10 October 1991.
10. This analysis is based on the maps and commentary published in *Cumhuriyet* after the elections.
11. The full cabinet list was published in the Turkish press on 21 November 1991.
12. Under Article 175 of the constitution, as amended in 1987, constitutional amendments may be effected by either (a) a three-fifths majority in the Assembly, plus approval in a national referendum or (b) a two-thirds majority in the Assembly. In the latter case, the president may order a referendum, but it is not obliged to do so. However, if he were threatened with dismissal, it can be assumed that President Özal would exercise his constitutional powers to the full — in other words, that a referendum would be virtually inevitable.
13. The measures concerned were, firstly, a bill delaying certain local elections and, secondly, decrees making appointments to the civil service. According to the constitution (Article 89) the president is obliged to promulgate a law passed by the Assembly within 15 days, or to return it to the Assembly within the same period. In the latter case, if the Assembly repasses the law unamended, and by a simple majority, the president is bound to promulgate it immediately. The president's signature is also necessary for government decrees which do not have the status of acts of parliament. However, if he refuses to sign a decree, it is still open to the government to have it passed by the Assembly and thus convert it into an act of parliament (although it may still then be subject to the delaying procedure outlined above). To summarize, the president has powers of delay over legislation (which in some cases can prove crucial) but no veto. Moreover, he has no delaying powers over the budget.
14. *Terörle Mucadele Kanunu* No.3713, Section 23(c): text published in *Official Gazette* (*Resmi Gazete*) No. 20843, 12 April 1991.
15. *Türk Ceza Kanunu* No. 765: English translation published as *The Turkish Criminal Code* (South Hackensack, NJ: Fred B. Rothman & Co.; London: Sweet & Maxwell, 1965).
16. *Türkceden başka Dillerle Yapılıcak Yayınlar hakkinda Kanun* No.2932, 22 October 1983. See Christian Rumpf, "Das Sprachenverbot in der Turkei unter besondere Berücksichtigung ihrer volkerrechtlichen Verpflichtungen," *Orient,* No. 3, 1989.
17. Law No. 3713 (see Note 14) Section 23(e). To be strictly accurate, the Turkish Kurds speak two separate languages, Zaza and Kermanji.
18. Ibid., Section 8.
19. Ibid., Temporary Sections 1–5.
20. *Siyasi Partiler Kanunu,* No. 2820; *Sendikalar Kanunu,* No. 2821.
21. Article 14 of the constitution states that "None of the rights and freedoms embodied in the constitution shall be exercised with the aim of damaging the indivisible integrity of the state with its territory and nation...or of establishing the hegemony of one social class over others." Article 26 adds that "No language prohibited by law shall be used in the expression and dissemination of thought," while Article 28 states that "Anyone who writes or prints any news or articles which threaten the internal or external security of the state or the indivisible integrity of the state with its territory and nation...shall be held responsible under the law relevant to these offenses." Lastly, Article 52 repeats the ban on "political" activities by trades unions.
22. Quoted, *Milliyet,* 22 September 1991.
23. *The Independent,* 10 October 1991.
24. Government program, as broadcast on Turkish TV, 25 November — SWB, 28 November 1991.
25. *Milliyet,* 9 December 1991.
26. *The Guardian, The Independent,* 14 August 1991.
27. *The Independent,* 10 August 1991.
28. *FT,* 18 January; *The Times,* 19 January 1991.
29. Turkish TV, 2 March — SWB 4 March 1991.
30. *The Independent,* 8 April 1991.
31. Quoted, ibid., 15 March 1991.
32. Hugh Pope, "Turkey and the USSR," *MEI,* 22 March 1991.

33. Data from *Economic Indicators of Turkey*, 1987–1991 (Ankara: Türkiye İş Bankası, 1992) p. 10.
34. *Turkey Confidential*, September 1991, pp. 27–28; *Briefing*, 29 July 1991, p. 14.
35. *Le Monde*, 26 March 1991.
36. R. Ankara, 19 August — SWB, 21 August 1991.
37. *The Military Balance*, 1991–1992 (London: Brasseys, for the International Institute of Strategic Studies, 1991) pp. 73–75.
38. *Milliyet*, 24 November 1991.
39. Data from *The Turkish Economy in 1991*, pp. 3–4, and *Review of Economic Conditions, 1992/1*, p. 20, both published by Türkiye İş Bankası, Ankara, 1992.
40. *Turkish Economy in 1991*, p. 3.
41. *Review of Economic Conditions, 1992/1*, p. 28; *Turkish Economy in 1991*, p. 4; *Economic Indicators of Turkey, 1987–1991*, pp. 16–17.
42. *Turkish Economy in 1991*, p. 5
43. Ibid., p. 6.
44. *Turkey Confidential*, September 1991, pp. 21–22; *Briefing*, 29 July 1991, pp. 11–12, 19 August 1991. p. 11.
45. Writer's estimate for the Economist Intelligence Unit, London. It was made up as follows: direct exports to Iraq, $800m.; pipeline royalties, $300m.; other invisibles (transit trade, contractors' earnings, etc.) $700m.–$1bn.
46. *Briefing*, 27 July 1992, p. 24. Figures are rounded to nearest $100m.
47. Exchange rates from ibid., 10 February 1992, p. 26. If domestic inflation is calculated on the basis of the Wholesale Prices Index, which is probably a more accurate indicator of TL export prices, then the real rate of devaluation works out at c. 10%–13%.

United Arab Emirates
(Al-Imarat al-Arabiyya al-Muttahida)

UZI RABI

With the 20th anniversary celebrations of the state's independence on 2 December 1991, the United Arab Emirates (UAE) drew the curtain on a year that had proved unusually rich in unexpected developments. Throughout the Gulf crisis, the UAE leadership had confidently steered the federation through the diplomatic minefield. The UAE helped to contain Iraq's ambitions by coming out forcefully in favor of the anti-Iraqi coalition and inviting Western forces onto its soil. The UAE survived the Gulf crisis relatively unscathed, and at the conclusion of the crisis was able to see Iraq's military might eroded. As the guns fell silent, the fortunes of the UAE became brighter. Postwar realities allowed the country to enter into a process of carving out a more prominent economic role for itself in the region, as it expected to take a leading role in rebuilding Kuwait. With the danger of regional havoc removed, the UAE could well anticipate a more calm, secure region. The country now readopted a pragmatic line of decision making on crucial matters. Like the other five Gulf Cooperation Council (GCC) member states, the UAE was quick to draw negative conclusions with regard to the GCC's concept of security. It was clear that the six-state GCC military force could not, under any circumstances, deter, let alone contain, by itself the sort of threat that Iraq had posed. A different security system was essential in order to protect the six and prevent a recurrence of such events. However, in the final analysis, the GCC states managed only to agree that each could seek military help from its allies when necessary. Kuwait and Bahrain, for example, opted for an overt security pact with the US. Relations between the UAE and the US improved markedly and seemed smoother than ever before. However, although the UAE was grateful for the Western assistance, the federation made it clear that it was against any long-term presence on its soil. In fact, the UAE chose to conclude a modest military agreement with France.

But if the UAE had hoped to escape the headlines after Iraq's defeat, it was quickly disappointed. Barely six months later, it was implicated in the downfall of the 77% Abu Dhabi-owned Bank of Credit and Commerce International (BCCI), which aroused worldwide financial turmoil, highlighted financial mismanagements, and threatened to tarnish the emirates' credibility. The scandal marred the 25th anniversary of the accession to the throne of the UAE ruler, Shaykh Zayid Ibn Sultan al-Nuhayan, and soured relations with Britain, a long-standing and well trusted ally.

Nevertheless, although the Gulf crisis and the BCCI downfall preoccupied Abu Dhabi, the federal structure was quietly maturing. By their very nature, the two crises helped to erode parochial loyalties and create national symbols. After two decades of independence, the seven emirates and their rulers became more committed to the success of the federation. Areas of disagreement between emirates still existed, particularly over oil policy. However, as one Western diplomat noted, there was "much less disagreement about what direction the federation is going in."[1]

THE UAE, THE GULF CRISIS AND ITS REPERCUSSIONS

The Iraqi invasion of Kuwait was a bitter blow for the UAE, which was still in the process of developing an atmosphere of stability and economic confidence in the aftermath of the Iraqi-Iranian War. It was very traumatic for the UAE to realize that it, too, could be a victim of Iraq's ambitions, especially after Iraq singled out the UAE (together with Kuwait) for "stabbing Baghdad in the back."[2]

Despite its usually low-key policy in international affairs, the UAE came out forcefully in favor of the anti-Iraqi coalition. It fully endorsed the Arab and international decisions condemning the invasion and demanding the restoration of Kuwaiti legitimacy under the Al Sabah ruling family.[3] Accordingly, the seven-state federation allowed the anti-Iraqi forces staging facilities on its soil. In another move aimed at checking Iraqi ambitions, the UAE became a major financial contributor to the war effort, pledging nearly $6bn. in cash and in kind services to the US, Britain and regional states affected by the crisis.[4] Although these commitments were no small undertaking, they were still manageable. The UAE also helped to compensate for the drop in oil output caused by Kuwait's occupation, and the embargo placed on Iraq by the UN after the crisis erupted in August 1990.[5]

The UAE also took a share in the military burden, albeit on a much smaller scale. Its air force conducted numerous combat sorties against Iraqi positions in occupied Kuwait,[6] and UAE ground forces were present on Kuwaiti territory during the course of its liberation by the Allied forces. The UAE's losses in the fighting were as low as six dead and 15 wounded.[7] On the announcement of Kuwait's liberation, in late February, the federation's armed forces were recalled and ceremoniously received by senior military figures.[8]

THE POSTWAR ERA — THE QUEST FOR REGIONAL STABILITY

With the danger of regional havoc halted, the UAE returned to projecting its "business as usual" image. This aimed, first and foremost, to revitalize its economy, which had become stagnant during the war (see below). At the same time the federation readopted its traditional low-key policy in foreign affairs, best reflected in its indecisive attitude toward the postwar dilemmas and the issue of regional security. The first dilemma dealt with the attitude toward postwar Iraq. Singled out (together with Kuwait) by Saddam Husayn (see *MECS* 1990, chapter on the UAE), the UAE had every reason not to be compassionate toward the defeated Iraqi regime. In fact, the UAE wished very much to see Saddam ousted, but not at the price of a politically balkanized Iraq, partly under Shi'i control. The outcome was an indecisive, middle course. There were many manifestations of hostility in the federation toward the Iraqi regime (but not the Iraqi people). Iraq's alleged attempted invasion of the Kuwaiti island of Bubiyan in August (see chapter on Kuwait) was strongly denounced. The media urged that "stringent conditions" be imposed to ensure that the food supplied to Iraq (under the embargo) did not end up in "the ruling Ba'th Party's elite stomachs" alone.[9]

On the other hand, the UAE did not wish to appear as though it were instigating an antigovernment revolt in Iraq or advocating foreign interference in that country's affairs. "It is necessary that Iraq remains a united, stable and prosperous country,"[10] asserted UAE Defense Minister Muhammed Ibn Rashid al-Maktum. On one point, however, the UAE was adamant. There would be no dealing with Iraq under Saddam's leadership. The ruler, Shaykh Zayid, stated that, under the current leadership, dealing with Iraq was like "taking poison with our own hands and that is inconceivable."[11]

Despite the crucial importance of regional security, this issue was subject to a similar pragmatic approach. Like the other five GCC member states, the UAE was quick to draw the inescapable negative conclusion with regard to the GCC's effectiveness. Foreign Minister Rashid 'Abdallah diplomatically remarked that there was a need for "establishing a security and safety fence" with which the Gulf states could feel secure.[12]

As early as March, the GCC states, together with Syria and Egypt, concluded the "Damascus declaration," which pointed to the permanent presence of an Arab force, made up predominately of Egyptian and Syrian contingents, in the region (for further details, see chapter on inter-Arab relations). For a while, it seemed as though the Iraqi invasion of Kuwait had helped to create the idea of an Arab collective security plan. However, the declaration led to a clash of interests in the federation's relationship with Egypt and Iran: Iran strongly objected to Egypt's military presence, seeking for itself the role of the GCC's main regional protector and thus filling the power vacuum left by Iraq. The two were perhaps the most important figures in the federation's foreign policy.

Since Iran was strongly opposed to foreign involvement in the region, and was excluded from the would-be security pact embodied in the Damascus declaration, the UAE's involvement in the Damascus declaration could have only negative repercussions for the improved relations the UAE sought to cultivate with its powerful neighbor. The UAE, more than any other GCC state, had better connections and was better placed to take advantage of Iran's reemergence as an important force in the region. Iran's first deputy foreign minister, 'Ali Muhammad Besharati, visited Abu Dhabi in November to discuss the bolstering of economic and trade relations, financial and banking cooperation and joint investments in Iran's economic and industrial development project.[13] Shaykh Zayid was quoted saying that the good neighborly relations between the two countries were "a major factor in regional peace."[14] It was, therefore, not surprising that the UAE was less than willing to jeopardize these achievements. Egypt, on the other hand, was a long-standing, well-trusted ally, to which the UAE felt indebted for the positive role it had played throughout the Gulf crisis. Consequently, the UAE also wished to avoid antagonizing Cairo.

Given the circumstances, the UAE tried to take a middle, even contradictory course. Rashid 'Abdallah did his best to juggle the two options, ensuring those concerned that the forthcoming defense pact "does not seek to hurt any party" but affirming that Tehran "has a basic role to play in the security arrangements."[15] Zayid, for his part, perhaps even slightly in favor of Egypt, said that it was not acceptable that Iran "does not have good relations with Egypt" and that it was not in the Gulf states' best interests.[16]

In time, the whole dilemma of maneuvering between Tehran and Cairo became less relevant, much to Egypt's dismay, as the Damascus declaration gradually faded from existence due to differences between its signatories. The GCC states gradually moved away from their initial plan to rally other Arab nations to their future defense, leaving open the fraught and complicated issue of regional security. The GCC states were, in effect, each left free to steer its individual course. Since the exodus of foreign troops from the region had left the area as defenseless as it had been previously, the most likely outcome was a shopping spree in search of highly sophisticated weaponry. The UAE ordered $500m.-worth of guided missiles from Britain. It also planned to purchase 20 *Apache* helicopters from the US, but the issue brought about an objection in Congress.[17] Another prospective deal of M-1A1 tanks was shelved until 1992 (see below).

Nevertheless, none of the GCC states, the UAE included, was deluded into thinking that it could effectively manage regional security alone, and they sought a replacement for the failed security pact. Kuwait and Bahrain opted for an overt security pact with the US, and Saudi Arabia chose to rely just as heavily on American alliance but without such a contract (see chapters on Bahrain, Kuwait and Saudi Arabia). The UAE seemed hesitant to follow suit, since it had its pan-Arab reputation to consider. Shaykh Zayid was no doubt grateful for the Western "God-given aid that exceeded our hopes,"[18] but made it clear that he would "never accept the permanent presence of foreign bases." Kuwait, he continued, "may feel an urgent need for this military accord to safeguard its security against foreign aggression, but we don't have the same reasons for having foreign troops, even from friendly nations."[19]

This, however, this did not mean that the UAE antagonized Washington. On the contrary, with the improved relationship forged in the course of the crisis, the outlook for bilateral relations seemed brighter and far less volatile than it had been for a long time. One example of the cordial relations was given in April, when Gen. Norman Schwarzkopf, commander of the US Central Command in the Gulf, ceremoniously decorated UAE officers.[20] The UAE backed various US initiatives, such as the liquidation of nuclear arms. For the first time, the US was not denounced for its "biased" attitude toward Israel. Yet, the UAE had to be careful not to cause Arab antagonism by being too closely aligned with the US. Therefore, as pressures mounted in Abu Dhabi, Zayid concluded a relatively modest defense accord with France during a visit to the French capital in September.[21] France was the UAE's most important arms supplier, providing more than 80% of the UAE's defense equipment. Details of the agreement were not made public, but it was assumed to contain provisions for joint maneuvers and military consultation. Military hardware sales were also discussed during the visit.

RELATIONS WITH OTHER ARAB STATES

The Gulf crisis influenced the UAE's behavior in the Arab arena. Relations with those countries which had sympathized with or taken part in the anti-Iraqi coalition took a turn upward, while relations with others, whose stance was rather ambivalent or clearly pro-Iraqi, deteriorated. In March, the UAE joined the rest of the GCC states in suspending all aid to the PLO (and Jordan), both of which heavily relied on subsidies from the Gulf states.[22] Clearly, the PLO, whose "betrayal" angered the UAE, was the most affected by this. The UAE media emphasized the "terrible shortsightedness of some Palestinian leaders who thought that establishing a link between the invasion of Kuwait and the Israeli occupation of Arab lands could yield results."[23]

The UAE spared no efforts to play down the importance of the organization's leadership in Tunis, claiming that the focal point had shifted to the West Bank and Gaza.[24] This did not mean, however, that the UAE did not pursue its sympathetic rhetoric toward the Palestinian issue, but in all such messages of support, it refrained from mentioning the PLO.

Another result of the Gulf crisis was a more broad-minded approach toward the Arab-Israeli conflict, best reflected by the UAE's presence at the Madrid peace conference in November, represented by the GCC's general secretary, 'Abdallah Bishara. This was clearly another expression of gratitude to the US for its assistance during the Gulf crisis, as well as recognition of the new geopolitical realities. In this context, Syria was praised for its willingness to participate in a Middle East peace conference. UAE references to the peace process also omitted any mention of a role for the PLO, which in the past had been referred to as "the sole legitimate representative of the Palestinians."[25]

THE BCCI IMBROGLIO

Abu Dhabi failed to escape the headlines after Iraq's defeat. Barely three months after the end of fighting the emirate was implicated in an international banking scandal, when, on 5 July, the Luxembourg-registered BCCI, which was 77% owned by the UAE ruler, the heir apparent and the government, was shut down in most international centers. The move followed an overall accounting review, issued by the Bank of England (BoE), which uncovered "prima facie evidence of widespread fraud at the BCC group."[26] Further details of the report revealed that huge losses at BCCI had been systematically concealed for many years, using virtually every trick in arithmetic: fictitious deposits and loans, unrecorded transactions, falsified records and transfers of money from one subsidiary to another. In effect, the BCCI had been running a "bank within a bank," whose purpose was to use fraudulent tricks to preserve a sound and healthy appearance for the bank as a whole.[27] There were far more severe allegations that the bank knowingly dealt with laundered cocaine money, covert arms transactions and peddling around the globe, through a web of complex businesses, which had been operated at least in six main countries — the US, Luxembourg, France, Spain, the Cayman Islands and Switzerland.[28] It was clear that so much illegal activity, so far removed from the conservative nature of a financial establishment, could only have been carried through with the collaboration, or at least the tacit agreement, of the bank's top officials. The decision to close the bank down was swift, perhaps even hasty. In the space of three days, the banking authorities in all financial centers orchestrated a worldwide swoop, dated for Friday, 5 July.[29] Within days, BCCI operations in most of the 69 countries where it was represented had been suspended.

Ironically, the shutdown came just as Abu Dhabi was putting the final touches to a reorganization plan which had been under preparation since April 1990, when the emirate had increased its share from 36% to 77%, to become the major shareholder. The BCCI Central Service Organization had already been relocated from London to Abu Dhabi, and a new management team appointed. The swoop occurred on the very day that a BCCI board meeting was held to finalize the rescue plan, which had been approved in principle by the BoE.[30]

Before they had time to take stock, the Abu Dhabi authorities, together with

Shaykh Zayid, were involved up to their necks in the biggest banking fraud in history and exposed, not only to unprecedented embarrassment, but even worse, to scrutiny. Inquiries were set up in the major financial centers, most important in Washington, where Congress was investigating several aspects of the affair, and in New York, where the BCCI group, as a whole, was prosecuted.[31] Caught unprepared by the sudden swoop, it was not surprising that Abu Dhabi was particularly angered by the BoE's decision to seize BCCI assets without notifying the major shareholder. Shocked by the abrupt closure, the Abu Dhabi authorities severely criticized the accounting firm, Price Waterhouse, for not having uncovered the "irregularities" earlier.[32] Claims were made — though not by official sources — that the clampdown was part of a plan to undermine a flourishing, Arab-owned Third World enterprise which competed with Western banks.[33]

Abu Dhabi's indignation had as much to do with reputation as with money. A main oil producer within the federation, Abu Dhabi could bear the potential loss of several billions of dollars in revenue, more than the negative publicity surrounding the scandal. Reflecting the general mood in Abu Dhabi, one local businessman lamented that "the reputation of Abu Dhabi is being ruined."[34]

The BoE, for its part, claimed that the shutdown was purely a banking matter and the decision had been taken in concert with regulatory authorities in other countries. Furthermore, the BoE stated that, under the circumstances, it was "the only way to protecting the remaining bank assets."[35] The Abu Dhabi authorities were not convinced that the shutdown was for commercial motives only, and this led to a souring of the UAE's relations with Britain. A British low-key goodwill mission, which visited the emirate in August, brought back reports which indicated the "depth of anger against the British Government."[36] The assessment of Britain's Minister of State for Foreign and Commonwealth Affairs, Douglas Hogg, who visited Abu Dhabi in October, that relations "will remain excellent"[37] did not prove to be the case.

The frostiness in relations with Britain stood in marked contrast to the blossoming of a new closeness with France. Zayid made his second-ever state visit to France in September. It soon became clear that the visit was, in effect, a policy statement. Its most important outcome was the UAE-French military agreement (see above). It was highly likely that this development stemmed, at least in part, from Abu Dhabi's wish to get back at Britain for the latter's high-handed behavior over the BCCI affair.

Another result of the imbroglio was in the UAE's relations with the US, where two of Zayid's 19 sons and two of his close advisers were allegedly used as a BCCI front in an illegal takeover of a US bank in Washington. The emirate took great pains to reassure Washington of its cooperation with officials from the Federal Reserve Board and the US Department of Justice, and to assure the US that it was conducting its own investigation of the problems uncovered "under the most stringent proceedings."[38] Nonetheless, some damage had already been done. Abu Dhabi's sensitivity to US criticism led the emirate to suspend the purchase of 337 M-1A1 tanks until 1992, fearing that Congress would make an objection.[39]

Shaykh Zayid was the biggest loser in the whole fiasco. The BCCI scandal not only marred the celebrations of his 25th anniversary of accession to the throne, but it was also, apparently, the largest single disaster in his 75-year life. While his integrity remained unimpeachable, Zayid had every reason to feel betrayed. He had been behind the bank since its inception in 1972, in person as well as in finance. In April

1990, he had harnessed Abu Dhabi to a rescue operation of the bank, during which the sum of at least $1bn. was injected into the establishment. Moreover, Zayid had entrusted his vast personal fortune — the entire share of Abu Dhabi's oil revenues over a period of several years during the early 1980s — to BCCI headed by his long-standing friend, BCCI general manager, Hasan 'Abadi. The bank repaid him by looting c. $2bn.[40] of the amount owed. He must have felt a deep sense of betrayal and anger at the fraud, engineered by men he had trusted with his money and, as he saw it, with his honor as well. His only consolation was that he had been taken for a ride. It was not so much the financial loss that rankled, as the loss of trust. Moreover, it was not the first time that Zayid, who showed little interest in finance, had been robbed by well-trusted advisers. In the wake of the 1973 Opec oil price rises, Zayid had committed his wealth to speculation on the copper market — with calamitous results.[41]

Abu Dhabi's involvement in the whole affair, particularly the final stages, was one of the hardest aspects of the saga to understand. It was interesting to note that the emirate had decided to increase its stakes in the bank and mount a rescue operation, instead of pulling out altogether, at a time when billions of dollars were at stake and evidence of fraud abundant. The explanation for this basically concerned the character of Zayid, which was formulated in the desert where tribal pride was a dominant factor. It was a culture where face-saving was all important and problems were brushed under the carpet. It was, therefore, not surprising that, in the end, Abu Dhabi was more worried about its tarnished reputation than the financial losses. "It would have made more sense to try to paper over the cracks than suffer the indignity of being associated with public failure," concluded one local businessman.[42]

Once the scandal was made public, it became even more imperative to effect a complete shutdown. This seemed to be the only way for the emirate to distance itself from the fated bank and somehow make up for its damaged reputation. In September, much to the chagrin of the bank employees and creditors worldwide, it was announced, on behalf of the shareholders, that there was "little real prospect of reconstructing the bank as originally envisaged."[43] By that time, massive layoffs of bank staff were already in progress. The only portion of the BCCI to be saved was its local affiliate in Abu Dhabi, the Bank of Credit and Commerce Emirates (BCC(E)), which survived the scandal. As a sign of the times, the name of the BCC(E) was changed, by a royal decree, to United National Bank (*Bank al-Ittihad al-Watani*).[44] In another move, some 30 BCCI executives, among them Salih Naqri, the former chief executive, were rounded up and detained by Abu Dhabi police, and some of them were to be formally charged.[45]

Toward the end of the year, Abu Dhabi indicated that it was prepared to undertake the moral task of making up some of the depositors' losses, about $125m., since some of them stood to lose their life's savings. Having been personally and closely involved with the BCCI, Zayid took a personal interest in the plan. By early 1992, negotiations to that effect, held between Abu Dhabi and the provisional liquidators, had reportedly become no more than "a signature away" from completion.[46]

Still other painful lessons for Abu Dhabi were yet to be learnt. The emirate's exposure to the BCCI scandal was estimated to have cost it a staggering $9.4bn. The immense cost highlighted the inability of one of the wealthiest countries in the world, whose rulers regarded the oil which sprang from the earth as theirs by right, to cope with modern financial systems. Having been self-governed for only 20 years, the UAE did not have a wealth of experience from which to draw: appointments were made to assuage the pride of important families, rather than on the basis of suitability for the job. Clearly, the banking sector required thorough reorganization, but little had been done in this respect previously. The BCCI debacle perhaps proved to be a turning point. Steps were being taken to strengthen the sector's main supervisory body, the Central Bank. A new governor, Sultan Nasir al-Suwaydi, considered to be the most capable local banker, was nominated to replace the former governor, 'Abd al-Malik al-Hammar.[47] This nomination, as well as other new appointments to the governing board, could be seen as an effort to introduce international banking expertise to the country's banking industry.

INTERNAL AFFAIRS: ON THE ROAD TO A MORE COHESIVE FEDERATION

The Gulf crisis had its positive effects on the structure of the seven-state federation. By its very nature, the crisis helped to erode parochial loyalties and create national symbols. The emirates had united in a combined effort to face the Iraqi challenge. The only voice heard throughout the war to mirror the UAE's attitude came from Abu Dhabi, the capital. Signs of the storm which befell the UAE during and after the attempted coup in Sharja in 1987 (see *MECS* 1987, pp. 386–87) were no longer seen or heard. Western observers estimated that "there is much less disagreement about what direction the federation is going in."[48] The most prominent feud that threatened to overshadow the development of the federation — the Abu Dhabi-Dubai rivalry — was gradually dying down, a fact that was leaving its mark on day-to-day activities. At the ministerial level, Dubai ruler and prime minister of the UAE, Shaykh Maktum Ibn Rashid, was now attending most cabinet sessions, thereby helping to consolidate the country's credibility to the outside. Another encouraging sign was that, after years of inordinate delays, the federal budget, to which Abu Dhabi and Dubai were the major contributors, was approved at an early stage, with the aim of easing planning and payment difficulties. Even the decision of Dubai-owned Emirate Airlines to fly for the first time from Abu Dhabi, as of January 1993, was considered a political issue. "There is a feeling now that Dubai is not so detached,"[49] enthused a local banker. With the passage of time — especially after enduring regional threats, such as the Kuwait crisis — the possibility of anything replacing the federal structure clearly became increasingly remote. However, areas of disagreement still existed, particularly over oil policy — a long-standing bone of contention — and this remained a troublesome issue for the leading emirates. Dubai, which was not an Opec member, continued to run an assertive oil policy, pumping the maximum possible quantity of oil, thereby compelling Abu Dhabi to serve as swing producer. In practice, this meant that Abu Dhabi was to safeguard the Opec quota set for the entire UAE by cutting back its own.

Other developments, also triggered by the crisis, indicated that the federal structure was quietly maturing. In a move rarely seen in the conservative societies of the Arabian Peninsula, the UAE authorities began enlisting and training women to serve in the army. In neighboring Saudi Arabia, for example, women were still not allowed to drive cars or even walk the streets alone (see chapter on Saudi Arabia). The incentive to recruit women was said to have been the initiative of Fatima, Shaykh Zayid's favorite wife, who was considered to be a promoter of women's rights. The

1,200 volunteers were handpicked, according to criteria such as education, fitness and motivation, and trained by US army women officers. This revolution in policy was fully attributed to the Iraqi invasion of Kuwait. "Saddam Husayn made this happen" asserted one new woman cadet.[50] However, the invasion of Kuwait was not the only reason for this dramatic change. The UAE had long been looking to expand its army of 50,000 men, or at least reduce the armed forces' dependence on expatriates. This could be achieved only by a more effective use of the population. Accordingly, several years previously, the UAE had begun sending teenagers to paramilitary courses, and indeed, throughout the Gulf crisis, drew on these reserves. Enlisting women was only an elaboration of this trend. "There was no way to do it without the participation of our local ladies," asserted a top military official.[51] This move was also generally in keeping with postwar realities, which reflected a stronger influence of Western values in the region. By enlisting women, the UAE proved that it was, to some extent, receptive to some of these values.

Nevertheless, one postwar lesson did not appear to have been received in the UAE. Like the other Gulf ruling families, UAE leadership was closely monitoring the political reforms taking place in Kuwait. In the wake of the Gulf crisis, the royal families in the GCC states were shown up as clearly incapable of preserving national sovereignty. Throughout the region, there were demands for a more open, less paternalistic form of government, affected by the mood of democracy triggered by the Gulf crisis. That same wave of demands had already led to some minor changes in some of the six. The Sultanate of Oman reformed the structure of its consultative council (*Majlis al-shura*) into a body which was to be elected rather than nominated; by the end of 1991, Saudi Arabia announced that the long-awaited nominated council would very soon be established.

The UAE, which had already had a nominated consultative council since 1972, did not seem willing to go any further than that. "If this democracy is compatible with the Qur'an and the teachings of the prophet," Zayid claimed, "we welcome it."[52] Hence, although the Gulf crisis allowed many earlier taboos on semipublic debate to be abolished, it seemed to openly reconfirm the UAE's perpetual fear that liberating the political process would increase, rather than contain, the pressure on the ruling family.

THE ECONOMY

The postwar era allowed the UAE to enter into a process of carving out a more prominent economic role for itself in the region. The UAE was not as badly affected by the crisis as was initially assumed. Since the political stability in the region increased, greater business initiative had been encouraged by the announcement of new government spending plans and the revival of projects that had been suspended during the crisis. The only real remnant of the crisis was the 1991 budget, announced around June, which was in deficit mainly due to the UAE war pledges.[53] The UAE could, therefore, seek to capitalize on the new opportunities available. Firstly, the UAE was considered a major party in Kuwait's reconstruction. Almost all the initial demands for goods in the UAE came from the Kuwaiti Government and this was supposed to continue until the Kuwaiti sector became fully operational. Moreover, the Kuwaiti Government stressed that a large percentage of the products it planned to purchase was to be routed through Dubai and that it planned to transship most of its imports through the UAE port of Jabil 'Ali, until its own deep-water port of Shuwayka was fully operational.[54]

The UAE trend of prospective development was further bolstered as Iran's rehabilitation progressed. By nature, the UAE was better connected and better placed to take advantage of Iran's reemergence as an important economic force, than any other GCC state. Dubai's long-standing ties with Iran provided plenty of opportunities for UAE firms. It also provided a useful base in terms of geographic proximity and infrastructural facilities for international banks and companies seeking to deal with Iran.[55]

The Ecological Damage

One of the most potentially damaging effects of the Gulf crisis was the appearance of the huge oil slick, caused by Iraq, which threatened the GCC states' desalination plants, which, in turn, provide the bulk of their sweet water. The general alarm in the region was understandable, since the GCC states were among the world's poorest in terms of water resources, and its biggest consumers. As the vast slick was reported to be drifting toward its soil, the UAE authorities hurried to surround their desalination plants with booms to block off the crude oil. Although the threat did not materialize, some lessons were learnt by the GCC states, and they upgraded the issue of environmental damage on their agenda.[56] Accordingly, a GCC-sponsored conference was held in Dubai in October, with the aim of exchanging technical expertise and promoting cooperation in future environmental disasters. Drawing its own conclusions, the UAE began enlarging its network of desalination plants; the forerunner of which was the Tawila base power and desalination plant which was in the process of construction.[57]

NOTES

For the place and frequency of publications cited here, and for the full name of the publication, news agency, radio station or monitoring service where an abbreviation is used, please see "List of Sources." Only in the case of more than one publication bearing the same name is the place of publication noted here.

1. *MEED*, 29 November 1991.
2. See, for example, INA, 24 June — DR, 28 June; *The Gulf States*, 20 August 1990.
3. R. Abu Dhabi, 9 August — DR, 10 August 1990.
4. *MEED*, 29 November 1990.
5. *MEED*, 22 February 1991.
6. GNA, 18 February — DR, 20 February 1991.
7. GNA, 26 February — DR, 28 February 1991.
8. GNA, 11 March — DR, 15 March 1991.
9. *Gulf Daily News,* 27 July 1991.
10. AFP, 3 April — DR, 4 April 1991.
11. *MEED*, 29 November 1991.
12. Rashid 'Abdallah's speech during his visit to Qatar. GNA, 21 May — DR, 23 May 1991.
13. IRNA, 12 November — DR, 14 November 1991.
14. Ibid.
15. Rashid 'Abdallah, GNA, 21 May — DR, 23 May 1991.
16. Shaykh Zayid's interview to *Ruz al-Yusuf,* 23 September 1991.
17. *JP*, 2, 14 June 1991.
18. *MEED*, 29 November 1991.

19. *MEI,* 13 September 1991.
20. GNA, 4 April — DR, 5 April 1991.
21. *MEI,* 27 January 1992.
22. *JP, Ha'aretz,* 31 March 1991.
23. *Al-Bayan* (Dubai), 9 March 1991.
24. *Al-Khalij* (Dubai), 17 October 1991.
25. SPA, 27 October — DR, 29 October 1991. See, e.g., *al-Bayan* (Dubai), 30 October 1991.
26. *CR,* UAE, No. 3, 1991.
27. *FT,* 8 July 1991.
28. Ibid; *WP,* 18 August 1991.
29. *FT,* 8 July 1991.
30. *MEED,* 19 July 1991.
31. *Ha'aretz,* 31 July 1991.
32. *CR,* UAE, No. 3, 1991.
33. *FT,* 2 August 1991.
34. *FT,* 11 July 1991.
35. *MEED,* 8 November 1991.
36. *MEED,* 6 September 1991.
37. *MEED,* 8 November 1991.
38. *FT,* 20 September 1991.
39. *Ha'aretz,* 31 July 1991.
40. *FT,* 11 November 1991.
41. *FT,* 14 November 1991.
42. *WP,* 18 August 1991.
43. *MEED,* 18 October 1991.
44. R. Abu Dhabi, 3 August — DR, 5 August 1991.
45. *FT,* 11 September; *WSJ,* 25 November 1991.
46. *FT,* 3 February 1992.
47. *IHT,* 13 December 1991.
48. *MEED,* 29 November 1991.
49. Ibid.
50. USIS, 8 August 1991.
51. Ibid.; *al-Bayan* (Dubai), 1 November 1991.
52. *The Gulf States,* 8 April 1991.
53. *CR,* UAE, No. 3, 1991.
54. *The Gulf States,* 20 May 1991.
55. *CR,* UAE, No. 2, 1991.
56. GNA, 28 January — DR, 28 January 1991.
57. *The Gulf States,* 29 July 1991.

The Republic of Yemen
(Al-Jumhuriyya al-Yamaniyya)

ANAT LAPIDOT

The year 1991 was characterized by a strong influence of Yemen's foreign affairs on its domestic arena. The Gulf War came at a bad time for Yemen, and the official line adopted by the government regarding the Gulf conflict made its situation even worse. The economic and social effects of the coalition's retaliatory measures against Yemen were harsh. The newly united country's economy, weak from the start, was highly dependent on foreign aid and on Yemeni workers' remittances from the Gulf states and Saudi Arabia. The results of the punitive measures were manifested in high inflation, price increases, shortages in housing and in basic goods and a high rate of unemployment, signifying a serious economic crisis. This crisis was exacerbated by the return of masses of Yemenite workers from Saudi Arabia and the other Gulf states.

The poor economic situation impeded ongoing government efforts to stitch together the two former Yemeni regimes and to pursue the process of democratization. The social and economic crises were exploited by the opposition — mainly by the Islamic opponents — who utilized the new relatively pluralized political system to organize unprecedented large violent demonstrations in October. Criticism of the government on economic issues as well as foreign policy was also leveled by the Saudi-backed tribal chiefs. Nevertheless, despite these difficulties, the government managed to make some progress in its democratization process, successfully passing a referendum on the constitution in May 1991 in a vote that was boycotted by the Islamic parties.

When the Gulf crisis erupted, Yemen took what it considered a neutral stand and supported the creation of a nonaligned front. While it did not unequivocally back the Iraqi invasion, and condemned the annexation of Kuwait, it was hostile to the US intention to drive Iraq out of Kuwait, whether by sanctions or by force. This position was perceived as pro-Iraqi both in the West and in such Arab countries as Syria, Saudi Arabia, Egypt and the Gulf states.

The allied reaction was immediate and decisive. The US, which led the coalition forces, cut most of its grant aid to Yemen for 1991. Saudi Arabia cut off all aid and expelled a million Yemenites from the kingdom. Other Western countries also demonstrated their discontent with Yemen's policy by discontinuing aid.

Once the war ended, the government acted to improve the country's economic situation and relations with Western countries and the Arab world, with the goal of regaining financial support. Toward this end, particular efforts were made to improve relations with Oman in the hope that it would intervene in Riyadh on Yemen's behalf. Regaining financial aid, the government hoped, would give it a better chance to solve, or at least ease, the economic crisis and thus prevent social unrest.

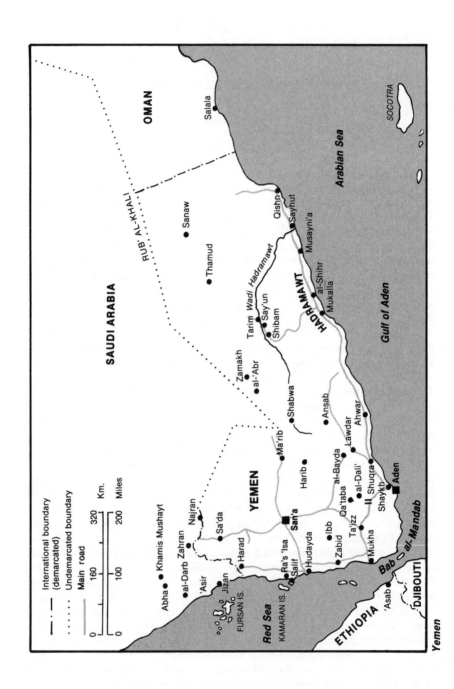

Yemen

DOMESTIC AFFAIRS

Though the challenge of stitching together a single administration from the two old regimes seemed to have been handled relatively smoothly, Yemen's unity was still fragile. There were still two different currencies, the riyal and the dinar, although the government planned to replace both currencies with the dirham.[1] There were different passports as well. While some of the obstacles to complete unification were technical, there appeared to be basic and growing dissatisfaction with unification in the south, focusing on the issue of Aden. Although the government continuously repeated the promise to turn Aden into a free zone, it postponed passing the necessary law, which had been scheduled to be approved in 1991, several times. Significantly, the government body in charge of the project was named the "Committee for the Development of Free Ports in Yemen," which suggested that Aden might not be chosen as the free port site. The delays began to worry the southerners, who viewed the possibility of replacing the Aden site by a northern port, possibly Hudayda, as an attempt by the central government to weaken the south or the Yemeni Socialist Party (YSP) position in the south.[2] Generally, it seems that there was growing criticism in the south toward government policy, which was perceived as keeping the south in a permanent state of underdevelopment.

THE ECONOMIC CRISIS

The Crisis

Yemen's economic problems were partly the result of the unification process involving the two Yemens, and partly the result of the Gulf War. When the People's Democratic Republic of Yemen (PDRY) and the Yemeni Arab Republic (YAR) merged in May 1990 they had a combined foreign debt of $8bn. and a negative trade balance. With the country's economy highly dependent on foreign aid and workers, remittances from the Gulf states and Saudi Arabia, the government took a great risk and ultimately paid a heavy price by choosing to adopt a neutral position during the crisis and war. Before the war erupted, Yemen's regime had received development aid from the West, Saudi Arabia, the Gulf states, and Iraq, with which it had close links. This foreign aid had been the mainstay of the Yemeni economy. Once the war began, project funding from Saudi Arabia, Kuwait and the Gulf states virtually dried up, while US grant aid to Yemen in the fiscal year starting October 1990 was cut to $2.9m. from an anticipated $20.5m. Moreover, Yemen also lost the remittances of the Yemeni workers in the Gulf, an important source of income. Government estimates put the country's losses as a result of the Gulf crisis at $3bn.

Up until August 1990, Saudi Arabia had permitted Yemeni nationals to live and work in the kingdom without visas. Yemeni workers enjoyed access to the Saudi job market. Many Yemenis owned businesses in Saudi Arabia, a privilege not granted to other foreigners. The problem of the return of these expatriates actually preceded the Gulf crisis, for with the decrease in the world demand for oil and the cutback in aid programs by the wealthy countries, many Yemeni workers abroad lost their jobs and were forced to return home. However, the problem of the return intensified with the expulsion of over a million Yemeni expatriates by the Saudis who abolished the special rights held by Yemeni workers. Official figures showed that in Hudayda the population rose from 154,000 before the Saudi move to 504,000 thereafter.[3] Many of the returnees were forced to live in poverty in shantytowns, constituting a heavy burden on Yemen's weak economy.

The return of the expatriate population meant an increase in domestic demand for staples and jobs. At the same time, the sudden injection of supply capital into the domestic market as a result of the return also heightened inflationary pressures and raised consumer prices. A scarcity of dollars drove up the unofficial riyal exchange rate and led to rising inflation, estimated at 45% annually.[4] Moreover, a large proportion of the newcomers could not find employment. Unemployment overall was as high as 35%, constituting a potential source of social unrest.

Government Response to the Economic Crisis and the Promise of Oil

Alleviating the country's economic problem was the government's first priority. In a speech to the General People's Congress (GPC) committee in August, President 'Ali 'Abdallah Salih stated that the government would deal immediately with the problem of inflation, set fixed prices, stop speculation on the dollar, guarantee the provision of foodstuffs and other essential goods, develop oil resources, activate industrial production, expand the scope of investment, and encourage national capital to assume its role and contribute to the national economy.[5]

Hoping to attract both Arab and foreign capital, the government issued an investment law, which took effect in July, designed to encourage and channel the investment of local, regional and Western capital mainly into industry, agriculture, tourism, technical training, transport, construction and housing.[6] In addition, measures were taken to reduce the budget deficit by increasing taxation, reducing government spending, and cutting back on diplomatic missions abroad, and on teachers' salaries by half.[7] To ease the difficulties caused by the repatriation of Yemenite workers, the government, aided by the World Bank, initiated a $245m. emergency project to create jobs and provide services for the returnees. In addition, the International Development Association undertook to provide $33m. in aid.[8] Presenting a new economic liberalization program in September, Prime Minister Haydar Abu Bakr al-'Attas declared that Yemen was aiming for a free market economy in an effort to encourage the necessary foreign investment, to improve the country's economy.[9]

Commercially viable quantities of oil were first discovered in North and South Yemen in 1984 (see previous *MECS* chapters on Yemen). Until the unification, concession rights in the south were controlled by Technoexport, a Soviet production company. Soon after unification, the Yemeni Government capitalized on competition among oil companies for exploration rights throughout the country, selling rights to 18 companies after the end of 1990. Positive news about the country's oil potential — the hope for Yemen's economy — was often used by the government to calm public discontent with the worsening economy. On 26 September, Yemen's independence day, President Salih announced the discovery of a major new oil field at Masila, in eastern Yemen, with potential reserves of some 490m. barrels. However, even if this discovery enabled Yemen to become a significant oil producer in time, the lag of three to five years between the discovery of oil and production in commercial quantities meant that oil was not the immediate solution to the country's economic crisis.

THE DEMOCRATIZATION PROCESS

The unification process was accompanied by fundamental political liberalization involving the establishment of a multiparty system. Efforts at democratization in Yemen halfway through the designated 30-month transition period produced relatively open debate throughout the country on the exact nature of political structure. A draft law establishing freedom of the press, which had been proposed upon unification, was ratified and a number of new periodicals and newspapers appeared in 1991, bringing the total to four daily newspapers and about 30 weekly and monthly magazines. Political debates were televised for the first time during the year. The former YAR radio and television stations were merged with their PDRY counterparts to form the Yemen Radio and Television General Corporation. Parliamentary debates were broadcast on the radio with only minor censorship.

Political Parties

Yemen was governed from San'a by a five-member presidential council, a 39-member cabinet, and a 301-member house of representatives. Some 38 new political parties were reported to have been formed since unification. The ruling party was the former Aden-based YSP, led by 'Ali Salim al-Bayd, which merged with the northern GPC. The new parliament (*Majlis al-nuwwab*), consisted of 159 members from the former North Yemeni Consultative Assembly, 111 from the old South Yemeni Supreme People's Council, and another 31 places were reserved for the opposition. The leading opposition parties were the Democratic Unionist Party, sympathizers of 'Ali Nasir Muhammad, the former president of the PDRY; and the National Democratic Front, which was in opposition to the government of the former YAR. They had five and four delegates respectively, in the House of Representatives. Other popular opposition parties were the Ba'thist, Aden-based Nasserite Unionist Organization formed as a legal party in 1989 and the Yemeni Unionist Party (YUP), founded in 1989 by liberal intellectuals and politicians from the former YAR and PDRY with the aim of protecting human rights, lead by Muhammad 'Abd al-Rahman and 'Umar al-Jawi. The Yemen Reform Group (YRG) was a major conservative party, founded in September 1990, by leading parliamentarians and political figures from both north and south, whose policies were based on adherence to Islamic law and whose members were reportedly involved in organizing antigovernment demonstrations. Merging with the Islamic Revival Party (IRP) in September 1991, the YRG further strengthened its base.

The introduction of a multiparty system was perceived in Yemen as an important step in the democratization process. However, in a country traditionally characterized by tribal and religious factionalism, this step was charged with danger and, in combination with economic unrest, could aggravate existing tensions. Several political assassinations were reported toward the end of the year. On 10 September, Hasan Huraybi, director general of the Central Highlands Rural Development Bank and the oppositionist official in San'a, was killed in what was widely considered a political assassination.[10] At the time of the attack he had been accompanied by 'Umar al-Jawi, secretary-general of the YUP and a newspaper editor in the south, who might have been the attackers' target. The YUP had been sharply critical of Iraq and of the government's position during the crisis,[11] while Jawi was known as an outspoken critic of Muslim fundamentalism. The incident triggered a chain of assassination attempts which continued until the end of the year, with the opposition accusing the government of responsibility for them and mass antigovernment demonstrations on this issue taking place from 20 October onward.

The Referendum on the Constitution

The government headed by President Salih was officially termed transitional and was set up in order to implement democratic reforms by November 1992. A draft constitution for the united Republic of Yemen, based on that endorsed by the legislatures of the former YAR and the PDRY, was adopted in 1990 following unification (see *MECS* 1989, chapters on the two Yemens, and 1990 chapter on Yemen). Article 29 of the draft constitution issued by the unification government stipulated a general referendum in order to validate the constitution.[12] The referendum was postponed several times by the government, which blamed the Gulf crisis, as well as the need to consolidate the new state, for the delay. It was finally held, on 16 May, and proceeded without a major incident, although it was boycotted by the Islamic circles because the constitution posited Shari'a law not as the sole source of legislation in the new state but only as the "principal" source (Article 3). According to official figures, only 1.89m. voters registered for the referendum, out of a total electorate of 4m. The vote on the constitution was 1.34m. in favor and 20,409 against.[13]

The main principles of the constitution, which was not published in full, were: (1) The Republic of Yemen is an independent, indivisible and fully sovereign state. The Yemeni people are part of the Arab nation and the Islamic world (Article 1); (2) Islam is the official state religion and Arabic the official state language (Article 2); (3) The Islamic Shari'a is the principal source of legislation (Article 3); (4) The people are the source of all authority, which is exercised directly, through referenda and general elections, and indirectly, through the legislative and executive bodies, through the judiciary, through elected local councils (Article 4); (5) The economy of the state is based on the principles of Islamic social justice and protection of private ownership (Article 6).

Opposition to Democratic Reforms

From the outset of its establishment in May 1990, the transitional government faced considerable opposition from Yemen's Islamic fundamentalists, a fairly small but irritating force. The fundamentalists opposed the multiparty system, the new constitution and the referendum. On 12 May, three days before the scheduled referendum, over 20,000 supporters of the YRG and the IRP demonstrated in the streets of San'a,[14] chanting Islamic slogans and condemning the constitution as secular and socialist. They waved copies of the Qur'an and banners that demanded the supremacy of the Shari'a. A statement read by one of the leaders demanded the veto of any law violating the Shari'a principles, as well as the adoption of serious measures to ease the burdens of the suffering Yemeni people as a result of the economic crisis.

The poor economic and social situation, mainly unemployment and high inflation, was exploited by the fundamentalists' opposition. This was especially evident during an incident in the San'a area on 19 October, when an army colonel shot and killed a traffic policeman who had stopped him for failing to stop at a red light.[15] The shooting, which took place in an area of high unemployment, became an instant catalyst for rising frustrations, with crowds gathering at the scene, burning the officer's car and refusing to disperse. Islamic leaders instigated riots of an unprecedented scope, in which two civilians were killed, according to an official report (nine, according to foreign observers) and many were wounded. Demonstrations organized by the YRG continued the next day as well.[16]

Besides opposing the government's social and economic policy, Islamic opposition leaders also criticized its not entirely consistent policy during the Gulf War.[17] During the Gulf crisis, a prominent shaykh, 'Abdallah al-Ahmar, had simultaneously deplored Salih's pro-Iraqi position and entered into a coalition with the Muslim Brotherhood, which itself supported Iraq despite its links with Saudi Arabia.

Tribal-Government Tensions
The new multiparty system was slow to change the country's social structure, which was based on tribal identity. On the contrary, the system gave the tribes a new avenue of self-expression, which proved more effective during the course of the year. Tribal division was directed into the tribal-based parties, as was the case with the YRG, a northern-based party of tribal origin and the League of the Sons of Yemen, a southern party bound by tribal connection. The government, aware of how the new system was enhancing the power of the tribal shaykhs, tried to invalidate their political nominations.[18]

Saudi and Egyptian sources reported on strong opposition to the government from tribal shaykhs of the Hashid and Bakil confederacies in the northern part of the country under Saudi influence throughout the year.[19] In a memorandum submitted to the government in early February, these northern opposition elements, led, according to foreign sources, by such chiefs as Muhsin al-Surayhi, 'Abdallah Abu Sur'a, 'Ali al-Qajl and others, expressed their discontent with the social and economic situation and condemned the president's policy, which, they claimed, damaged relations with Saudi Arabia, thereby leading to the economic crisis.[20] A significant alliance between the tribes and the fundamentalists was achieved in the south although it failed to establish itself in Aden, where secular traditions were strong.[21]

FOREIGN AFFAIRS

YEMEN'S POSITION ON THE GULF CRISIS
Iraq's invasion of Kuwait in August 1990 put the new government of Yemen in a difficult position. Yemen faced a conflict between loyalty to the Arab and Muslim cause and its interest in maintaining links with the West. (For more discussion of the Yemen's reaction at the early stage of the crisis, see *MECS* 1990, chapter on Yemen).

Domestically, there was widespread, often violent, popular support for Saddam Husayn during the crisis and the war in the form of large rallies involving thousands of Yemenites demonstrating in the streets and repeatedly stoning the American, Saudi, British and Egyptian embassies in San'a. At the beginning of the crisis, during August and September 1990, these demonstrations took place mainly in the southern part of the country and in the major cities,[22] while in the north, a region of Saudi influence, a number of key tribal leaders supported Saudi Arabia's anti-Iraqi position. This support weakened, however, with the Saudi expulsion of hundreds of thousands of Yemenite workers from September 1990 onward.

Yemen's immediate response to the invasion was support for Iraq. With a seat in the

UN Security Council, Yemen had a high-profile role to play in the crisis. However, when Iraq invaded Kuwait on 2 August 1990, the council voted the same day to condemn that action and to impose economic sanctions on Iraq, Yemen chose to abstain. During the next three months up until the start of the Desert Storm operation, Yemen acquired a pro-Saddam image by voting against, or abstaining, in major Security Council resolutions condemning Iraq, although in late September the government attitude in fact started to shift to a more moderate position.

Yemen voted in favor of the Security Council resolution to impose an air embargo on Iraq, on 25 September, but for the coalition forces it was too little and too late. Similarly, from September onward Yemen tried to play a role of mediator in the crisis, manifested by visits of top Yemeni officials to Jordan, Algeria and Iraq. In mid-January, a few days before the war started, Yemen sponsored a diplomatic initiative delivered to the Egyptians, the Americans, the Soviets, the French, the Germans and the Omanis, but with no results. On 14 January, President Salih presented his proposed six-point peace plan: (1) The Iraqi forces were to be withdrawn from Kuwait; (2) Arab and international forces were to take over the area in dispute under the supervision of the Arab League and the UN; (3) foreign forces in the region were to be pulled out upon Iraq's acceptance of the principle of withdrawal from Kuwait; (4) the UN would commit itself to implementing its resolution on the Arab-Israeli conflict; (5) the states that had troops in the region would pledge not to use force against Iraq; and (6) on acceptance of all this by the disputing parties the economic blockade against Iraq should be ended.[23] Although US Secretary of State James Baker acknowledged Yemen's efforts to develop some sort of proposal on 14 January, a day before the expiration of the ultimatum, another senior US official later explained that the US could not support the Yemeni proposal because it linked the Gulf crisis with the Palestinian problem and a proposed international conference.[24]

The launching of the coalition offensive in January was condemned in the Yemeni press, in parliament and in statements by state bodies such as the cabinet and the Presidential Council. The latter termed it an aggression against the Islamic nation and was convinced, according to Radio Aden, that if the US wanted to contribute to settling the dispute peacefully it could, and that the war was unnecessary, a view which seemed to have reflected the general feeling in Yemen.[25] President Salih was quoted later in denouncing what he described as a "US plot against Iraq" and said the war "is not aimed at solving the Kuwaiti problem, but at destroying Iraq".[26]

A mass demonstration two days after the offensive began (19 January) drew up to an estimated 500,000 people, marking the start of an escalation of violence that included the use of automatic weapons in attacks on US, French, Italian, Japanese and Turkish embassy facilities.[27] The Presidential Council issued an official statement on 21 January, calling for the immediate implementation of the following six-point plan: (1) A UN Security Council resolution calling for a halt to all military activity to take effect immediately; (2) allowing Arab and Islamic mediation efforts to end the dispute between Iraq and Kuwait; (3) a UN Security Council resolution calling for the withdrawal of foreign forces from the region; (4) a new Security Council resolution canceling Resolution 661 that imposed the comprehensive blockade of Iraq; (5) a confirmation by the UN of its commitment to implement previous resolutions relating to the Arab-Israeli conflict; and (6) reaching a comprehensive agreement for removing weapons of mass destruction throughout the region.[28]

A stronger official reaction to the offensive was channeled through a conference held by the Association of Yemeni 'Ulama at the time, which was attended by President 'Ali 'Abdallah Salih. The conference issued this statement: "The war being launched by the US and its allies against the brotherly Iraqi people is an unjust war and Muslims must support Iraq with their souls, money and blood, and with all possible means."[29] An even stronger reaction came from YRG officials who called for a Jihad against the US-led coalition saying that Iraq was confronting the "West's new crusaders."[30]

Although Yemen did not justify Iraq's invasion, and did condemn the annexation of Kuwait, so that its position could not actually be considered fully pro-Iraqi, its attitude toward the crisis was interpreted as supportive of Iraq both in the West and, even more so, in the Arab world.[31] Officially Yemen chose to place itself in the nonaligned camp, on the one hand, acknowledging that Iraq must pull out of Kuwait, but, on the other, criticizing the US for its desire to drive Iraq out of Kuwait, first by sanctions and later by force. The Yemeni view was that the Iraqi-Kuwaiti crisis was an internal Arab problem that must be solved by an inter-Arab solution.[32] Likewise, the issue of restoring the Al Sabah regime to Kuwait had to be decided by the Kuwaiti people and not by outside forces.[33] In adopting this approach, Yemen's policymakers ignored the direction of the mainstream Arab countries, led by Egypt, Syria and Saudi Arabia. They also misread the new world political map, failing to understand that in a world of a single superpower, there was no room for a nonaligned position. Once an overwhelming majority against Iraq was achieved, a neutral position and mediation attempts were perceived as acts opposing the majority. Yemen's attempt to play such a role was soon demonstrated to be unrealistic, and its political position cost the country and its people dearly, both economically and socially. The Saudis, like the Americans, took the view that countries that were not with them were against them, and translated their anger into political and economic punishment.

RELATIONS WITH THE ARAB WORLD AND IRAN
Facing the difficult task of improving relations with both the Arab world and the West during 1991, the Yemeni Government reassessed its foreign policy and adopted a more sophisticated approach. Once the results of the war became clear, the government was guided more by realpolitik than by previous loyalties. A major effort was made not to upset either the West or Yemen's Arab neighbors and to emphasize the political and economic benefits to them in restoring relations with Yemen.

Relations with Saudi Arabia
Yemen's relations with Saudi Arabia deteriorated as a result of Yemen's initial strong opposition to the presence of foreign armed forces in the Gulf and because of its neutralist position during the crisis. The Saudis cut off all aid to Yemen, expelled Yemenite workers, and withdrew the privileges that Yemenite workers had previously enjoyed there. The Yemeni Government tried to restore the links between the two countries during 1991. During the first half of the year, the Yemeni Government was concerned about Saudi Arabia's support for opposition elements within Yemen, and their relations were tense, characterized by mutual allegations of hostile activities leveled primarily in magazines and newspapers published in both countries. For example, a Yemenite newspaper reported in March that Saudi troops had occupied

the al-Baq'a border post in northwest Yemen, a claim that was emphatically denied by the Saudis and by the Yemeni Government.[34] While the truth of these allegations was difficult to establish, it was clear that Yemen's experiment in democracy, as well as its position on the Gulf crisis, were being carefully monitored by the Saudis, who were unlikely to tolerate instability at their backdoor.

With the goal to improve its economic situation by regaining financial support, efforts were made to improve relations with Riyadh. President Salih confirmed his government's intention to improve relations with Saudi Arabia in a statement in September 1991, declaring: "None of us can remove the other from the map of the region, so it is necessary to establish dialogue relations without interference in the internal affairs of each other."[35] Another effort to decrease hostility was the Yemeni Government's instruction to the country's government-sponsored newspapers on 19 November not to respond to Saudi media reports.[36] While both sides had a political interest in restoring relations, certain issues needed to be resolved, especially the border dispute.[37] The Yemeni Imam had ceded the three northern provinces of Jizan, Najran and 'Asir to the Saudi Kingdom in 1934, but no government since had been willing to ratify this agreement, and the current government viewed the issue as open to negotiation.

Notwithstanding such differences, the two states were prepared to move forward on the road of improved relations. By the end of 1991, it appeared likely that the Saudis would restore financial aid, if not directly then through charitable or international organizations. Meanwhile, Saudi investors increased their involvement in Yemen to the prewar level, mainly in the country's oil sector. The Saudi Nimr Petroleum Company was awarded an attractive Shabwa Block Four oil concession. Although Saudi investment was justifiable commercially, it aroused suspicion in Yemen as to the rationale behind it, i.e., that it was a Saudi attempt to gain more influence in Yemen, which might later be extended to such issues as Islam, democracy and pluralism.

Relations with Other States in the Region

Yemen's priority in dealing with the Arab world was normalizing relations with its neighbors and thus reentering the Arab political mainstream. It was particularly anxious to restore relations with Oman[38] (see chapter on Oman) in order to gain Oman's support as a regional ally. The Yemeni Government hoped that the Sultan of Oman would intercede in Riyadh on Yemen's behalf. In an effort to gain Oman's friendship, President Salih announced in December 1991 that an agreement on the long-standing border dispute with Oman was near. Any agreement on the border issue, however, was likely to evoke strong domestic opposition in Yemen, especially in the eastern provinces of the former PDRY, where such a potential move would be seen as a violation by the north-based regime of the unity treaty with the south.

The relations between the mainstream Arab states, such as Egypt and Syria, and Yemen, decreased markedly during 1991 both in volume and content. Effectively, Yemen was boycotted by the Arab states and an atmosphere of deep mistrust prevailed. Yemen's efforts to restore relations met with no response. Parallel to its efforts to reestablish relations with the mainstream Arab countries, Yemen sought alternative allies should its efforts in the Arab world fail. On 26 August, the deputy foreign minister of Iran, Husayn Shaykh al-Islam, arrived in San'a for talks. In

December, the speaker of the Iranian parliament, Mehdi Karubi, visited Yemen and met with President Salih and Vice President 'Ali Salim al-Bayd. Hosting the Iranian envoys in Yemen was a signal to Saudi Arabia that if its hostile attitude continued, Yemen could find another ally. The prospect of Yemen becoming an Iranian client, it was hoped, would prompt Saudi Arabia, Egypt and the Gulf states to reconsider their position toward Yemen.

RELATIONS WITH THE WEST

Yemen's main efforts in dealing with the West were devoted to creating a democratic image in an attempt to regain Western support and aid and end the isolation that developed when the war began. Western support was also needed domestically to counter strong opposition to democratic reform by the fundamentalist opposition (see above).

Yemen's efforts in the West seemed to have been productive mainly vis-à-vis France. During a four-day visit to Yemen at the end of October by French Foreign Minister Roland Dumas and Minister of Culture Jacques Lang, the French officials commended the country's efforts at democratization and expressed confidence in Yemeni success in this direction. San'a hoped that this visit would serve to improve Yemen's relations with other Western countries, which, for the most part, were reluctant to do so.

The relationship with the US proved difficult to improve. Soon after Yemen voted against the US position in the UN Security Council, the State Department slashed aid to Yemen (see above). In view of Yemen's position, and the anti-American demonstrations in San'a, the State Department on 10 January advised Americans to defer all travel to Yemen and ordered the departure of nonessential embassy personnel.[39]

With the outbreak of war, Yemeni leaders accused the US for causing it, since, had the US so desired, it could have found a peaceful solution to the conflict. Soon after the war ended, however, when the new world political balance became clear, the Yemeni Government attempted to approach the US in an effort to discuss restoring the previous level of US assistance, although it did not express contrition for its position. The government did articulate support and appreciation for the American commitment to solving the Arab-Israeli conflict, which, as Foreign Minister 'Abd al-Karim al-Iryani declared, could be accomplished only by the full implementation of Security Council Resolutions 242 and 338, a commitment which several previous US administrations had deliberately avoided making.[40]

These efforts seemed to have had some effect. In June President Bush sent a message to President Salih, commending Yemen's political pluralism and democratic approach. More important, there was an indication that the US had decided to resume its food aid program, although a definite date was not given.[41] Yet, while the US acknowledged Yemen's approaches, the State Department made it clear that any financial assistance would be dependent on Yemen's stance in the UN Security Council and on its progress domestically in the areas of human rights and political liberalization.

Attempting to gain credit with the US, Yemen voiced support for President Bush's peace initiative in the ME.[42] The US response was positive, but it was made clear that Yemen must try harder in order to gain US confidence and subsequently its financial aid. US Ambassador in San'a Arthur Hughes stated in an interview that perhaps there was more that Yemen could do besides expressing support for the US, and expressed the hope that Yemen would join the US peace talks.[43]

NOTES

For the place and frequency of publications cited here, and for the full name of the publication, news agency, radio station or monitoring service where an abbreviation is used, please see "List of Sources." Only in the case of more than one publication bearing the same name is the place of publication noted here.

1. *Al-Sharq al-Awsat,* 3 February 1991.
2. *Le Monde,* 10 July 1991.
3. *MEED,* 31 May 1991.
4. *Al-Thawra* (San'a), 20 February 1991.
5. R. San'a, 3 August — DR, 6 August 1991.
6. *MEED,* 26 July 1991.
7. Ibid., 27 September 1991.
8. *Al-Thawra* (San'a), 22 February 1991.
9. MENA, 29 October 1991, pp. 33–35.
10. *MEED,* 27 September 1991.
11. Ibid.
12. R. San'a, 21 May — DR, 22 May 1991.
13. Ibid.
14. R. Cairo (MENA), 12 May — DR, 15 May 1991.
15. *MEED,* 1 November 1991.
16. Ibid.
17. *Al-'Alam* (London), 16 March 1991.
18. R. Kuwait, 20 January 1991.
19. *Al-Akhbar,* 15 February — DR, 22 February 1991.
20. Ibid.
21. *Le Monde,* 10 July 1991.
22. R. Aden, 21 January — DR, 22 January 1991.
23. R. Aden, 14 January — DR, 15 January 1991.
24. WF, 14 January 1991.
25. R. Aden, 17 January — DR, 18 January 1991.
26. AFP, 26 January — DR, 28 January 1991.
27. R. Ankara, 31 January — DR, 1 February 1991.
28. R. Aden, 21 January — DR, 23 January 1991.
29. R. Aden, 30 January — DR, 31 January 1991.
30. AFP, 26 January — DR, 28 January 1991.
31. *Le Monde,* 20 February 1991.
32. R. Aden, 17 January — DR, 18 January 1991.
33. *ME,* March 1991, p. 25.
34. SPA, 15 April — DR, 15 April 1991.
35. R. Aden, 10 September — DR, 13 September 1991.
36. R. San'a, 17 November — DR, 22 November 1991.
37. Ibid.
38. R. San'a, 3 September — DR, 4 September 1991.
39. WF, 10 January 1991.
40. R. Aden, 14 May — DR, 18 May 1991.
41. R. San'a, 29 June — DR, 1 July 1991.
42. AFP, 5 October — DR, 7 October 1991.
43. WF, 30 July 1991.

INDEX